G000149532

HARRAP

SUPER-MINI
ITALIAN
DICTIONARY

English-Italian/Italian-English

HARRAP

SUPER-MINI
ITALIAN
DICTIONARY

English-Italian/Italian-English

HARRAP

This edition published in Great Britain 2001
by Chambers Harrap Publishers Ltd
7 Hopetoun Crescent, Edinburgh EH7 4AY

© Havas Éducation Référence 1996

ISBN 0 245 60696 3

Printed and bound in Great Britain by
Omnia Books Limited, Glasgow

Preface

This dictionary has been designed with beginners and travellers in mind.

With over 30,000 references and 40,000 translations, this new dictionary gives thorough coverage of general vocabulary plus extensive treatment of the language found on street signs and menus.

Clear sense markers are provided throughout, while special emphasis has been placed on basic words, with many examples of usage and a particularly user-friendly layout.

Easy to use and comprehensive, this handy book packs a lot of wordpower for users at school, at home and on the move. "Buona fortuna", and don't hesitate to send us your comments.

Prefazione

Questo dizionario è stato realizzato per rispondere alle esigenze di chi viaggia o comincia a studiare l'inglese.

Con più di 30 000 parole ed espressioni e oltre 40 000 traduzioni, questo nuovo dizionario comprende non solo la terminologia generale di base, ma anche molte espressioni che permettono di decifrare cartelli, segnali stradali e menu.

Le divisioni semantiche sono accuratamente indicate e la consultazione delle voci complesse di uso più frequente è facilitata dai numerosi esempi e dalla presentazione chiara ed efficace.

Completo e allo stesso tempo praticissimo, questo dizionario si rivelerà un indispensabile compagno di studio e di viaggio. "Good luck", e non esitate ad inviarci i vostri suggerimenti.

ABBREVIATIONS		**ABBREVIAZIONI**
abbreviation	*abbr*	abbreviazione
adjective	*adj*	aggettivo
adverb	*adv*	avverbio
adjective	*agg*	aggettivo
American English	*Am*	inglese americano
anatomy	*ANAT*	anatomia
article	*art*	articolo
auxiliary	*aus*	ausiliare
automobile, cars	*AUT(O)*	automobile
auxiliary	*aux*	ausiliare
adverb	*avv*	avverbio
British English	*Br*	inglese britannico
commerce, business	*COMM*	commercio
comparative	*compar*	comparativo
computers	*COMPUT*	informatica
conjunction	*conj/cong*	congiunzione
continuous	*cont*	forma progressiva
culinary, cooking	*CULIN*	cucina, culinaria
before	*dav*	davanti a
juridical, legal	*DIR*	diritto
exclamation	*excl/esclam*	esclamazione
feminine	*f*	femminile
informal	*fam*	familiare
figurative	*fig*	figurato
finance, financial	*FIN*	finanza
formal	*fml/form*	formale
inseparable	*fus*	non separabile
generally	*gen*	generalmente
geography	*GEOG*	geografia
gerund	*ger*	gerundio
grammar	*GRAMM*	grammatica
informal	*inf*	familiare
computers	*INFORM*	informatica
interrogative	*interr*	interrogativo

invariable	*inv*	invariabile
juridical, legal	*JUR*	diritto
masculine	*m*	maschile
mathematics	*MAT(H)*	matematica
medicine	*MED*	medicina
military	*MIL*	militare
music	*MUS*	musica
noun	*n*	sostantivo
nautical, maritime	*NAUT*	nautica
numeral	*num*	numerale
oneself	*o.s.*	
pejorative	*pej*	spregiativo
plural	*pl*	plurale
politics	*POL*	politica
past participle	*pp*	participio passato
preposition	*prep*	preposizione
pronoun	*pron*	pronome
past tense	*pt*	passato
	qc	qualcosa
	qn	qualcuno
registered trademark	®	marchio registrato
religion	*RELIG*	religione
noun	*s*	sostantivo
someone, somebody	*sb*	
school	*SCH/SCOL*	scuola
Scottish English	*Scot*	scozzese
separable	*sep*	separabile
singular	*sg*	singolare
subject	*sog*	soggetto
pejorative	*spreg*	spregiativo
something	*sthg*	
subject	*subj*	soggetto
superlative	*superl*	superlativo
technology	*TECH/TECNOL*	tecnica, tecnologia
verb	*v, vb*	verbo

intransitive verb	*vi*	verbo intransitivo
impersonal verb	*v impers*	verbo impersonale
vulgar	*volg*	volgare
reflexive verb	*vr*	verbo riflessivo
transitive verb	*vt*	verbo transitivo
vulgar	*vulg*	volgare
cultural equivalent	≃	equivalenza culturale

TRADEMARKS

Words considered to be trademarks have been designated in this dictionary by the symbol ®. However, neither the presence nor the absence of such designation should be regarded as affecting the legal status of any trademark.

MARCHI REGISTRATI

Le parole considerate marchi registrati sono contrassegnate in questo dizionario con il simbolo ®. In ogni caso, né la presenza né l'assenza di tale simbolo implica alcuna valutazione del reale stato giuridico di un marchio.

ENGLISH COMPOUNDS

A compound is a word or expression which has a single meaning but is made up of more than one word, e.g. **point of view, kiss of life, virtual reality** and **West Indies**. It is a feature of this dictionary that English compounds appear in the A–Z list in strict alphabetical order. The compound **blood test** will therefore come after **bloodshot** which itself follows **blood pressure**.

COMPOSTI INGLESI

In inglese si definiscono composti quelle espressioni che, pur essendo formate da più di una parola, costituiscono un'unica unità di significato, come ad es. **point of view, kiss of life, virtual reality** e **West Indies**. In questo dizionario i composti inglesi seguono l'ordine alfabetico generale. Il composto **blood test** figura perciò dopo **bloodshot** che, a sua volta, segue **blood pressure**.

Phonetic Transcription

English vowels

[ɪ]   pit, big, rid
[e]   pet, tend
[æ]   pat, bag, mad
[ʌ]   run, cut
[ɒ]   pot, log
[ʊ]   put, full
[ə]   mother, suppose
[i:] bean, weed
[ɑ:] barn, car, laugh
[ɔ:] born, lawn
[u:] loop, loose
[ɜ:] burn, learn, bird

English diphthongs

[eɪ] bay, late, great
[aɪ] buy, light, aisle
[ɔɪ] boy, foil
[əʊ] no, road, blow
[aʊ] now, shout, town
[ɪə] peer, fierce, idea
[eə] pair, bear, share
[ʊə] poor, sure, tour

Semi-vowels

you, spaniel   [j]
wet, why, twin   [w]

Consonants

pop, people   [p]
bottle, bib   [b]
train, tip   [t]
dog, did   [d]
come, kitchen   [k]
gag, great   [g]
chain, wretched   [tʃ]
jet, fridge   [dʒ]

Trascrizione Fonetica

Vocali italiane

[a]   pane, casa
[e]   verde, entrare
[ɛ]   letto, pezzo
[i]   vino, isola
[o]   monte, pozzo
[ɔ]   corpo, sciocco
[u]   una, cultura

Semivocali

ieri, viola
fuori, guasto

Consonanti

porta, sapore
barca, libro
torre, patata
dare, odore
cane, chiesa
gara, ghiro
cena, ciao
gente, gioco

fib, **ph**ysical	[f]	fine, afa
vine, livid	[v]	vero, o**vv**io
think, fifth	[θ]	
this, with	[ð]	
seal, peace	[s]	stella, casa
zip, his	[z]	sdraio, rosa
sheep, machine	[ʃ]	scimmia, ascia
usual, measure	[ʒ]	
how, perhaps	[h]	
metal, comb	[m]	mamma, amico
night, dinner	[n]	notte, anno
sung, parking	[ŋ]	
	[ɲ]	gnocchi, ogni
little, help	[l]	lana, pollo
	[ʎ]	gli, figlio
right, carry	[r]	re, dorato

The symbol ['] precedes a syllable carrying primary stress and the symbol [ˌ] precedes a syllable carrying secondary stress.

I simboli ['] e [ˌ] indicano rispettivamente un accento primario e uno secondario nella sillaba seguente.

The symbol [r] in English phonetics indicates that the final "r" is pronounced only when followed by a word beginning with a vowel. Note that it is nearly always pronounced in American English.

Il simbolo [r] nella trascrizione fonetica dell'inglese indica che la "r" in fine di parola viene pronunciata soltanto se seguita da una parola che comincia per vocale. Da notare che nell'inglese americano la "r" viene quasi sempre pronunciata.

The position of the tonic stress in Italian is indicated by a dot immediately beneath the accented vowel on Italian headwords (**camera, valigia**). No dot is given on those words which end in an accented vowel, as Italian spelling allows for a written accent in these cases (**città, perché**). Full phonetics have been provided for words of foreign origin which do not follow Italian pronunciation rules (**cracker** ['krɛker], **brioche** [bri'ɔʃ]).

L'accento nelle voci italiane è segnalato da un punto sotto la vocale accentata (**camera, valigia**), con l'eccezione delle parole con l'accento sull'ultima sillaba, per le quali l'ortografia italiana prevede l'accento grafico (**città, perché**). Le parole di origine straniera sono seguite dalla trascrizione fonetica nei casi in cui la pronuncia generalmente adottata non rispetta le regole fonetiche dell'italiano (**cracker** ['krɛker], **brioche** [bri'ɔʃ]).

ITALIAN VERBS

Key: *pr ind* = presente indicativo, *imperf* = imperfetto, *fut* = futuro, *cond* = condizionale, *pr cong* = presente congiuntivo, *imperat* = imperativo, *ger* = gerundio, *pp* = participio passato

AMARE: *pr ind* amo, ami, ama, amiamo, amate, amano, *imperf* amavo, amavi, amava, amavamo, amavate, amavano, *fut* amerò, amerai, amerà, ameremo, amerete, ameranno, *cond* amerei, ameresti, amerebbe, ameremmo, amereste, amerebbero, *pr cong* ami, ami, ami, amiamo, amiate, amino, *imperat* ama, ami, amate, *ger* amando, *pp* amato

andare: *pr ind* vado, vai, va, andiamo, andate, vanno, *fut* andrò, *cond* andrei, *pr cong* vada, vada, vada, andiamo, andiate, vadano, *imperat* va', vada, andate, *ger* andando, *pp* andato

aprire: *pr ind* apro, *pr cong* apra, *pp* aperto

avere: *pr ind* ho, hai, ha, abbiamo, avete, hanno, *imperf* avevo, *fut* avrò, *cond* avrei, *pr cong* abbia, *imperat* abbi, abbia, abbiate, *ger* avendo, *pp* avuto

bere: *pr ind* bevo, *imperf* bevevo, *fut* berrò, *cond* berrei, *pr cong* beva, *imperat* bevi, beva, bevete, *ger* bevendo, *pp* bevuto

cadere: *fut* cadrò

correre: *pp* corso

cuocere: *pr ind* cuocio, cuoci, cuoce, cuociamo, cuocete, cuociono, *pp* cotto

dare: *pr ind* do, dai, dà, diamo, date, danno, *fut* darò, *pr cong* dia, *imperat* da', dia, date

dire: *pr ind* dico, dici, dice, diciamo, dite, dicono, *imperf* dicevo, *fut* dirò, *pr cong* dica, dica, dica, diciamo, diciate, dicano, *imperat* di', dica, dite, *ger* dicendo, *pp* detto

dovere: *pr ind* devo, devi, deve, dobbiamo, dovete, devono, *fut* dovrò, *cond* dovrei, *pr cong* deva, deva, deva, dobbiamo, dobbiate, devano

essere: *pr ind* sono, sei, è, siamo, siete, sono, *imperf* ero, eri, era, eravamo, eravate, erano, *fut* sarò, *cond* sarei, *pr cong* sia, *imperat* sii, sia, siate, *ger* essendo, *pp* stato

fare: *pr ind* faccio, fai, fa, facciamo, fate, fanno, *imperf* facevo, *pr cong* faccia, *imperat* fai, faccia, fate, *ger* facendo, *pp* fatto

FINIRE: *pr ind* finisco, finisci, finisce, finiamo, finite, finiscono, *imperf* finivo, finivi, finiva, finivamo, finivate, finivano, *fut* finirò, finirai, finirà, finiremo, finirete, finiranno, *cond* finirei, finiresti, finirebbe, finiremmo, finireste, finirebbero, *pr cong* finisca, finisca, finisca, finiamo, finiate, finiscano, *imperat* finisci, finisca, finite, *ger* finendo, *pp* finito

giungere: *pp* giunto

leggere: *pp* letto

mettere: *pp* messo

morire: *pr ind* muoio, muori, muore, moriamo, morite, muoiono, *fut* morirò, *pr cong* muoia, *imperat* muori, muoia, morite, *pp* morto

muovere: *pp* mosso

nascere: *pp* nato

piacere: *pr ind* piaccio, piaci, piace, piacciamo, piacete, piacciono, *pr cong* piaccia, *pp* piaciuto

porre: *pr ind* pongo, poni, pone, poniamo, ponete, pongono, *imperf* ponevo, *fut* porrò, *cond* porrei, *pr cong* ponga, *imperat* poni, ponga, ponete, *ger* ponendo, *pp* posto

potere: *pr ind* posso, puoi, può, possiamo, potete, possono, *fut* potrò, *pr cong* possa

prendere: *pp* preso

ridurre: *pr ind* riduco, *imperf* riducevo, *fut* ridurrò, *pr cong* riduca, *ger* riducendo, *pp* ridotto

riempire: *pr ind* riempio, riempi, riempie, riempiamo, riempite, riempiono, *ger* riempiendo

rimanere: *pr ind* rimango, rimani, rimane, rimaniamo, rimanete,

rimangono, *fut* rimarrò, *pr cong* rimanga, *pp* rimasto
rispondere: *pp* risposto
salire: *pr ind* salgo, sali, sale, saliamo, salite, salgono, *pr cong* salga
sapere: *pr ind* so, sai, sa, sappiamo, sapete, sanno, *fut* saprò, *pr cong* sappia, *imperat* sappi, sappia, sappiate
scegliere: *pr ind* scelgo, scegli, sceglie, scegliamo, scegliete, scelgono, *pr cong* scelga, *imperat* scegli, scelga, scegliete, *pp* scelto
sciogliere: *pr ind* sciolgo, sciogli, scioglie, sciogliamo, sciogliete, sciolgono, *pr cong* sciolga, *imperat* sciogli, sciolga, sciogliete, *pp* sciolto
scrivere: *pp* scritto
sedere: *pr ind* siedo, siedi, siede, sediamo, sedete, siedono, *pr cong* sieda
SERVIRE: *pr ind* servo, servi, serve, serviamo, servite, servono, *imperf* servivo, servivi, serviva, servivamo, servivate, servivano, *fut* servirò, servirai, servirà, serviremo, servirete, serviranno, *cond* servirei, serviresti, servirebbe, serviremmo, servireste, servirebbero, *pr cong* serva, serva, serva, serviamo, serviate, servano, *imperat* servi, serva, servite, *ger* servendo, *pp* servito
spegnere: *pr ind* spengo, spegni, spegne, spegniamo, spegnete, spengono, *pr cong* spenga, *pp* spento
stare: *pr ind* sto, stai, sta, stiamo, state, stanno, *fut* starò, *pr cong* stia, *imperat* sta, stia, state, *pp* stato
tacere: *pr ind* taccio, taci, tace, tacciamo, tacete, tacciono, *pr cong* taccia, *pp* taciuto
TEMERE: *pr ind* temo, temi, teme, temiamo, temete, temono, *imperf* temevo, temevi, temeva, temevamo, temevate, temevano, *fut* temerò, temerai, temerà, temeremo, temerete, temeranno, *cond* temerei, temeresti, temerebbe, temeremmo, temereste, temerebbero, *pr cong* tema, tema, tema, temiamo, temiate, temano, *imperat* temi, tema, temete, *ger* temendo, *pp* temuto
tenere: *pr ind* tengo, tieni, tiene, teniamo, tenete, tengono, *fut* terrò, *pr cong* tenga
togliere: *pr ind* tolgo, togli, toglie, togliamo, togliete, tolgono, *pr cong* tolga, *imperat* togli, tolga, togliete, *pp* tolto
trarre: *pr ind* traggo, trai, trae, traiamo, traete, traggono, *fut* trarrò, *pr cong* tragga, *imperat* trai, tragga, traete, *ger* traendo, *pp* tratto
uscire: *pr ind* esco, esci, esce, usciamo, uscite, escono, *pr cong* esca
vedere: *fut* vedrò, *pp* visto
venire: *pr ind* vengo, vieni, viene, veniamo, venìte, vengono, *fut* verrò, *pr cong* venga, *pp* venuto
vivere: *pp* vissuto
volere: *pr ind* voglio, vuoi, vuole, vogliamo, volete, vogliono, *fut* vorrò, *cond* vorrei, *pr cong* voglia

VERBI IRREGOLARI INGLESI

Infinitive	Past Tense	Past Participle	Infinitive	Past Tense	Past Participle
arise	arose	arisen	creep	crept	crept
awake	awoke	awoken	cut	cut	cut
be	was/ were	been	deal	dealt	dealt
			dig	dug	dug
bear	bore	born(e)	do	did	done
beat	beat	beaten	draw	drew	drawn
begin	began	begun	dream	dreamed /dreamt	dreamed /dreamt
bend	bent	bent			
bet	bet /betted	bet /betted	drink	drank	drunk
			drive	drove	driven
bid	bid	bid	eat	ate	eaten
bind	bound	bound	fall	fell	fallen
bite	bit	bitten	feed	fed	fed
bleed	bled	bled	feel	felt	felt
blow	blew	blown	fight	fought	fought
break	broke	broken	find	found	found
breed	bred	bred	fling	flung	flung
bring	brought	brought	fly	flew	flown
build	built	built	forget	forgot	forgotten
burn	burnt /burned	burnt /burned	freeze	froze	frozen
			get	got	got (Am gotten)
burst	burst	burst			
buy	bought	bought	give	gave	given
can	could	–	go	went	gone
cast	cast	cast	grind	ground	ground
catch	caught	caught	grow	grew	grown
choose	chose	chosen	hang	hung	hung
come	came	come		/hanged	/hanged
cost	cost	cost	have	had	had

Infinitive	Past Tense	Past Participle	Infinitive	Past Tense	Past Participle
hear	heard	heard	pay	paid	paid
hide	hid	hidden	put	put	put
hit	hit	hit	quit	quit	quit
hold	held	held		/quitted	/quitted
hurt	hurt	hurt	read	read	read
keep	kept	kept	rid	rid	rid
kneel	knelt	knelt	ride	rode	ridden
	/kneeled	/kneeled	ring	rang	rung
know	knew	known	rise	rose	risen
lay	laid	laid	run	ran	run
lead	led	led	saw	sawed	sawn
lean	leant	leant	say	said	said
	/leaned	/leaned	see	saw	seen
leap	leapt	leapt	seek	sought	sought
	/leaped	/leaped	sell	sold	sold
learn	learnt	learnt	send	sent	sent
	/learned	/learned	set	set	set
leave	left	left	shake	shook	shaken
lend	lent	lent	shall	should	–
let	let	let	shed	shed	shed
lie	lay	lain	shine	shone	shone
light	lit	lit	shoot	shot	shot
	/lighted	/lighted	show	showed	shown
lose	lost	lost	shrink	shrank	shrunk
make	made	made	shut	shut	shut
may	might	–	sing	sang	sung
mean	meant	meant	sink	sank	sunk
meet	met	met	sit	sat	sat
mow	mowed	mown	sleep	slept	slept
		/mowed	slide	slid	slid

sling	slung	slung	strike	struck	struck
smell	smelt	smelt			/stricken
	/smelled	/smelled	swear	swore	sworn
sow	sowed	sown	sweep	swept	swept
		/sowed	swell	swelled	swollen
speak	spoke	spoken			/swelled
speed	sped	sped	swim	swam	swum
	/speeded	/speeded	swing	swung	swung
spell	spelt	spelt	take	took	taken
	/spelled	/spelled	teach	taught	taught
spend	spent	spent	tear	tore	torn
spill	spilt	spilt	tell	told	told
	/spilled	/spilled	think	thought	thought
spin	spun	spun	throw	threw	thrown
spit	spat	spat	tread	trod	trodden
split	split	split	wake	woke	woken
spoil	spoiled	spoiled		/waked	/waked
	/spoilt	/spoilt	wear	wore	worn
spread	spread	spread	weave	wove	woven
spring	sprang	sprung		/weaved	/weaved
stand	stood	stood	weep	wept	wept
steal	stole	stolen	win	won	won
stick	stuck	stuck	wind	wound	wound
sting	stung	stung	wring	wrung	wrung
stink	stank	stunk	write	wrote	written

ITALIANO-INGLESE
ITALIAN-ENGLISH

a (**ad** + *vocale*) *prep* 1. (*complemento di termine*) to; **dare qc a qn** to give sthg to sb, to give sb sthg; **chiedere qc a qn** to ask sb sthg. 2. (*stato in luogo*) at; **abito a Torino** I live in Turin; **stiamo a casa** let's stay (at) home; **la piscina è a due chilometri da qui** the swimming pool is two kilometres from here. 3. (*moto a luogo*) to; **andiamo a letto** let's go to bed; **torno a Roma** I'm going back to Rome; **mi porti allo stadio?** can you take me to the stadium?
4. (*temporale*) at; **c'è un volo alle 8.30** there's a flight at 8.30; **a domani!** see you tomorrow!; **al mattino** in the morning; **alla sera** in the evening.
5. (*modo, mezzo*): **alla milanese** in the Milanese style, the Milanese way; **riscaldamento a gas** gas heating; **a piedi** on foot; **vestire alla moda** to dress fashionably; **scrivere a matita** to write in pencil.
6. (*con prezzi*) at; **comprare qc a metà prezzo** to buy sthg half-price.
7. (*per caratteristica*): **camicia a maniche corte** short-sleeved shirt; **finestra a doppi vetri** double-glazed window.
8. (*per rapporto*) per, a; **50 chilometri all'ora** 50 kilometres per o an hour; **pagato a ore** paid by the hour.

A *abbr* = **autostrada**.

abbacchio *sm* spring lamb; ~ **alla romana** *lamb cooked slowly with white wine or vinegar, rosemary, anchovies and garlic*.

abbaglianti *smpl*: **accendere gli** ~ to put one's headlights on full beam (*Br*) o high beam (*Am*).

abbagliare *vt* (*accecare*) to dazzle.

abbaiare *vi* to bark.

abbandonare *vt* (*persona, luogo*) to abandon; (*ricerche*) to abandon, to give up.

abbandono *sm* (*di persona, luogo*) neglect; (*rinuncia*) abandonment.

abbassare *vt* to lower; (*volume, radio, tv*) to turn down □ **abbassarsi** *vr* (*persona*) to bend down; (*livello*) to drop; **abbassarsi a fare qc** to lower o.s. by doing sthg.

abbasso *esclam*: ~ **la scuola!** down with school!

abbastanza *avv* (*a sufficienza*)

enough; *(piuttosto)* rather, quite; **averne ~ di** to have had enough of.

abbattere *vt (muro)* to knock down; *(albero)* to cut down; *(cavallo)* to destroy; *(aereo)* to shoot down; *(sconfiggere)* to defeat □ **abbattersi** *vr* to lose heart.

abbattuto, -a *agg (depresso)* depressed.

abbazia *sf* abbey.

abbeverare *vt (animali)* to water □ **abbeverarsi** *vr* to drink.

abbia → **avere**.

abbiente *agg* well-off.

abbigliamento *sm* clothes *(pl)*; **~ donna** women's wear; **~ sportivo** sportswear; **~ uomo** menswear.

abbinare *vt:* **~ qc (a qc)** to link sthg (to sthg).

abboccare *vi* to bite.

abboccato, -a *agg* sweetish.

abbonamento *sm (a giornale)* subscription; *(a autobus, teatro)* season ticket; **fare l'~ (a qc)** *(a giornale)* to take out a subscription (to sthg); *(a autobus, teatro)* to buy a season ticket for sthg).

abbonarsi *vr:* **~ (a qc)** *(a autobus, teatro)* to buy a season ticket (for sthg); *(a giornale)* to subscribe (to sthg).

abbonato, -a *sm, f (a giornale)* subscriber; *(a autobus, teatro)* season ticket holder; *(a telefono)* subscriber; *(TV)* licence holder.

abbondante *agg* abundant.

abbondanza *sf* abundance.

abbordabile *agg (prezzo)* reasonable.

abbottonare *vt* to button up □ **abbottonarsi** *vr:* **abbottonarsi il cappotto** to button up one's coat.

abbottonatura *sf* buttons *(pl)*.

abbozzare *vt (disegno)* to sketch; **~ un sorriso** to smile faintly.

abbozzo *sm* sketch.

abbracciare *vt* to embrace, to hug; *(fede)* to embrace; *(professione)* to take up □ **abbracciarsi** *vr* to embrace, to hug one another.

abbraccio *sm* embrace, hug.

abbreviare *vt* to shorten.

abbreviazione *sf* abbreviation.

abbronzante *agg* suntan *(dav s)* ♦ *sm* suntan cream.

abbronzare *vt* to tan □ **abbronzarsi** *vr* to get a tan.

abbronzato, -a *agg* tanned.

abbronzatura *sf* suntan.

abbrustolire *vt (pane)* to toast; *(caffè)* to roast.

abdicare *vi* to abdicate.

abete *sm* fir tree.

abile *agg (bravo)* capable; *(mossa, manovra)* skilful; *(idoneo):* **~ (a qc)** fit (for sthg).

abilità *sf (bravura)* ability; *(astuzia)* cleverness.

abilmente *avv (con bravura)* skilfully; *(con astuzia)* cleverly.

abisso *sm* abyss.

abitacolo *sm (di auto)* inside; *(di aereo)* cockpit, cabin; *(di camion)* cab.

abitante *smf (di paese)* inhabitant; *(di casa)* occupant.

abitare *vi* to live ◆ *vt* to live in; **dove abita?** where do you live?; **abito a Roma** I live in Rome; **abito in Italia** I live in Italy.

abitato, -a *agg (casa)* occupied; *(paese)* inhabited ◆ *sm* built-up area.

abitazione *sf* house.

abito *sm (da donna)* dress; *(da uomo)* suit; **~ da sera** evening dress □ **abiti** *smpl* clothes.

abituale *agg* usual.

abitualmente *avv* usually.

abituare *vt* to accustom; **~ qn a fare qc** to accustom sb to doing sthg □ **abituarsi** *vr (adattarsi)*: **abituarsi a qc** to get used to sthg; **abituarsi a fare qc** to get used to doing sthg.

abitudine *sf* habit; **aver l'~ di fare qc** to be in the habit of doing sthg; **per ~** out of habit.

abolire *vt (tassa)* to abolish; *(legge)* to repeal; *(eliminare)* to eliminate.

aborigeno, -a *sm, f* aborigine.

abortire *vi (accidentalmente)* to miscarry; *(volontariamente)* to have an abortion.

aborto *sm (volontario)* abortion; **~ (spontaneo)** miscarriage.

abrogare *vt (legge)* to repeal.

Abruzzo *sm*: **l'~** the Abruzzo *(region of central Italy)*.

abside *sf* apse.

abusare : **abusare di** *v + prep (posizione, potere)* to take advantage of; *(persona)* to rape; **~ dell'alcool** to drink too much.

abusivo, -a *agg* unauthorized, unlawful.

abuso *sm (eccesso)* overindulgence; *(uso illecito)* abuse.

a.C. *(abbr di avanti Cristo)* BC.

accademia *sf* academy, school; **~ di belle arti** fine arts academy.

accadere *vi* to happen.

accaduto *sm*: **raccontare l'~** to describe what happened.

accalcarsi *vr* to crowd.

accampamento *sm* camp.

accampare *vt (truppe)* to encamp; *(richieste)* to make; *(diritti)* to assert □ **accamparsi** *vr (in tende)* to camp; *(fig: in alloggio)* to camp (out).

accanimento *sm (tenacia)* tenacity; *(odio)* fury.

accanito, -a *agg (odio)* fierce; *(lavoratore)* assiduous; **fumatore ~** chain smoker.

accanto *avv* nearby ◆ *agg inv* next door ◆ *prep*: **~ a** beside.

accaparrare *vt (fare incetta)* to buy up; *(voti, favore)* to secure, to gain; **accaparrarsi qc** to secure sthg for o.s.

accappatoio *sm* bathrobe.

accarezzare *vt (persona, animale)* to caress, to stroke; *(fig: idea)* to toy with.

accattone, -a *sm, f* beggar.

accavallare *vt (gambe)* to cross □ **accavallarsi** *vr (eventi)* to overlap.

accecare *vt (rendere cieco)* to blind; *(abbagliare)* to dazzle.

accedere *vi*: **~ a qc** to gain access to sthg.

accelerare *vi* to accelerate ◆ *vt* to speed up.

accelerato, -a *agg* quick ◆ *sm* stopping train.

acceleratore *sm* accelerator.

accendere *vt* (*fuoco, sigaretta*) to light; (*radio, luce, fornello, motore*) to turn on; (*speranza, odio*) to arouse; scusi, ha da ~? excuse me, have you got a light? □ **accendersi** *vr* (*prendere fuoco*) to catch fire; (*entrare in funzione*) to start up.

accendigas *sm inv* lighter for gas ring.

accendino *sm* (*cigarette*) lighter.

accennare *vt* (*menzionare*) to mention; (*indicare*) to point to; ~ un sorriso to half-smile □ **accennare a** *v + prep* (*menzionare*) to mention; (*alludere a*) to hint at; (*dare segno di*) to show signs of.

accensione *sf* ignition.

accentare *vt* (*parola, sillaba*) to stress.

accento *sm* accent; mettere l'~ su qc to stress sthg.

accentuare *vt* (*differenza, difetto, pregio*) to emphasize □ **accentuarsi** *vr* to become more marked.

accerchiare *vt* to encircle, to surround.

accertamento *sm* check.

accertare *vt* to check □ **accertarsi di** *vr + prep* to make sure of.

acceso, -a *pp* → **accendere** ◆ *agg* (*fuoco, sigaretta*) lighted; (*radio, luce, motore*) on; (*colore*) bright.

accessibile *agg* (*luogo*) accessible; (*prezzo*) affordable.

accesso *sm* (*entrata*) access; (MED) fit; (*fig: impeto*) outburst.

accessori *smpl* accessories.

accettare *vt* to accept; (*proposta*) to agree to; ~ di fare qc to agree to do sthg; 'si accettano carte di credito' 'credit cards welcome'.

accettazione *sf* (*locale*) reception; '~ bagagli' 'check-in'.

acchiappare *vt* to catch.

acciacco, -chi *sm* ailment.

acciaio *sm* steel; ~ inossidabile stainless steel.

accidentale *agg* accidental.

accidentalmente *avv* accidentally.

accidentato, -a *agg* uneven.

accidenti *esclam* (*con rabbia*) blast!, damn!; (*con stupore*) good heavens!

acciuffare *vt* to catch.

acciuga, -ghe *sf* anchovy; acciughe al limone *fresh anchovies marinated in lemon juice and dressed with oil.*

acclamare *vt* (*applaudire*) to cheer, to applaud; (*eleggere*) to acclaim.

accludere *vt* to enclose.

accogliente *agg* cosy.

accoglienza *sf* welcome.

accogliere *vt* to receive; (*dare il benvenuto*) to welcome.

accoltellare *vt* to knife.

accomodare *vt* to repair □ **accomodarsi** *vr* (*sedersi*) to sit down; (*venire avanti*) to come in; s'accomodi! (*si sieda*) take a seat!; (*venga avanti*) come in!

accompagnamento *sm* accompaniment.

accompagnare vt (persona) to go/come with, to accompany; (piatto, abito) to go with; (con musica) to accompany.

accompagnatore, -trice sm, f companion; ~ **turistico** tourist guide.

acconsentire vi: ~ **(a qc)** to agree (to sthg).

accontentare vt to satisfy □ **accontentarsi: accontentarsi di** vr + prep to be satisfied with.

acconto sm down payment; **dare un** ~ to pay a deposit; **in** ~ on account.

accorciare vt to shorten.

accordare vt (strumento) to tune; (concedere) to grant; (colori) to match □ **accordarsi** vr (mettersi d'accordo) to agree.

accordo sm (patto) agreement; (armonia) harmony; **d'~!** all right!; **andare d'~ con qn** to get on well with sb; **essere d'~ con** to agree with; **mettersi d'~ con qn** (trovare un accordo) to reach an agreement with sb; (per appuntamento) to make an arrangement with sb.

accorgersi : accorgersi di v + prep to notice.

accorrere vi (in aiuto) to rush up; (verso un luogo) to rush.

accorto, -a pp → **accorgersi** ♦ agg shrewd.

accostare vt (persona) to approach; (porta) to leave ajar; (avvicinare): ~ **qc a qc** to move sthg near sthg ♦ vi to pull in; (nave) to come alongside; (cambiare rotta) to change course; (in auto) to draw up.

accreditare vt (fatto, notizia) to confirm; (denaro) to credit.

accrescere vt to increase □ **accrescersi** vr to grow.

accucciarsi vr (cane) to lie down.

accudire vt (malato, bambino) to look after □ **accudire a** v + prep (casa, faccende) to attend to.

accumulare vt to accumulate; (denaro) to save; (accatastare) to pile up.

accurato, -a agg (lavoro) careful; (persona) thorough.

accusa sf (di una colpa) accusation; (DIR) charge.

accusare vt: ~ **qn (di qc)** (incolpare) to accuse sb of sthg; (DIR) to charge.

acerbo, -a agg unripe.

acero sm maple.

aceto sm vinegar.

acetone sm (per unghie) nail varnish remover.

ACI sm (abbr di Automobile Club d'Italia) = AA (Br), = AAA (Am).

acidità sf: ~ **di stomaco** heartburn.

acido, -a agg (sapore) sour; (commento, persona) sharp ♦ sm acid.

acino sm grape.

acne sf acne.

acqua sf water; **sott'~** underwater; ~ **corrente** running water; ~ **cotta** Tuscan soup made from stale bread, onions and tomatoes; ~ **dolce** fresh water; ~ **minerale (gassata/naturale)** (carbonated/still) mineral water; ~ **ossigenata** hydrogen peroxide; ~ **del rubinetto** tap water; ~ **salata** salt water; ~

tonica tonic water; **acque termali** hot springs; **~ in bocca!** keep it to yourself!; '**~ non potabile**' 'not drinking water'.

acquaforte (*pl* **acqueforti**) *sf* etching.

acquaio *sm* sink.

acquamarina (*pl* **acquemarine**) *sf* aquamarine.

acquaragia *sf* turpentine.

acquario *sm* aquarium □ **Acquario** *sm* Aquarius.

acquasanta *sf* holy water.

acquatico, -a, -ci, -che *agg* (*pianta, animale*) aquatic; (*SPORT*) water (*dav s*).

acquavite *sf* brandy.

acquazzone *sm* cloudburst.

acquedotto *sm* aqueduct.

acqueo *agg m* → **vapore**.

acquerello *sm* watercolour.

acquirente *smf* buyer.

acquisire *vt* (*ottenere*) to acquire.

acquistare *vt* (*comperare*) to buy; (*ottenere*) to acquire.

acquisto *sm* purchase; **fare acquisti** to shop.

acquolina *sf*: **far venire l'~ in bocca a qn** to make sb's mouth water.

acquoso, -a *agg* watery.

acrilico, -a, -ci, -che *agg & sm* acrylic.

acrobata, -i, -e *smf* acrobat.

acrobazia *sf* (*di acrobata*) acrobatic feat; (*di aereo*) stunt.

acropoli *sf inv* acropolis.

aculeo *sm* (*di vespa*) sting; (*di riccio*) spine; (*di pianta*) prickle.

acume *sm* acumen.

acustico, -a, -ci, -che *agg* acoustic.

acuto, -a *agg* (*voce, suono*) high-pitched; (*intenso*) intense; (*appuntito*) pointed; (*intelligente*) sharp; (*MAT*) acute.

ad → **a**.

adagio *avv* slowly; '**entrare/ uscire ~**' *sign warning drivers to enter or leave side roads etc slowly.*

adattamento *sm* (*adeguamento, di opera*) adaptation; (*modifica*) adjustment.

adattare *vt* to adapt □ **adattarsi** *vr*: **adattarsi (a qc)** (*adeguarsi*) to adapt (to sthg).

adatto, -a *agg*: **~ (a)** suitable (for); **~ a fare qc** suitable to do sthg.

addebitare *vt* to debit.

addestramento *sm* training.

addestrare *vt* to train.

addetto, -a *agg* (*persona*) responsible ♦ *sm, f* person responsible; **~ stampa** press attaché; **gli addetti ai lavori** (*fig*) the experts.

addio *esclam* goodbye!

addirittura *avv* (*perfino*) even; (*direttamente*) directly ♦ *esclam* really?

addirsi : **addirsi a** *vr + prep* to be suitable for.

additivo *sm* additive.

addizionale *agg* additional.

addizione *sf* addition.

addobbo *sm* decoration; **addobbi natalizi** Christmas decorations.

addolcire *vt* to sweeten.

addolorare vt to sadden □
addolorarsi vr to upset o.s.

addome sm abdomen.

addomesticare vt to house-train.

addormentare vt to send to sleep □ **addormentarsi** vr to fall asleep.

addossare vt (al muro) to lean; (attribuire) to lay.

addosso avv (sulla persona) on ◆ prep: ~ **a** (su) on; (contro) against; **mettersi qc** ~ to put sth on; **dare** ~ **a** (criticare) to attack; **eravamo uno** ~ **all'altro** we were right next to each other.

adeguare vt: ~ **qc a qc** to adjust sthg to sthg □ **adeguarsi** vr: **adeguarsi a qc** to adapt to sthg.

adeguato, -a agg adequate.

adempiere vt (compiere) to carry out; (esaudire) to grant.

adenoidi sfpl adenoids.

aderente agg (attillato) close-fitting; (adesivo) adhesive.

aderire vi: ~ **a qc** (attaccarsi) to stick to sthg; (partito) to join sthg; (proposta) to support sthg; (richiesta) to agree to sthg.

adesivo, -a agg adhesive ◆ sm (etichetta) sticky label.

adesso avv (ora) now; (tra poco) any moment now; (poco fa) just now.

adiacente agg adjacent.

adibire vt: ~ **qc a qc** to use sthg as sthg.

Adige sm: **l'~** the River Adige.

adirarsi vr to get angry.

adocchiare vt (scorgere) to

glimpse; (guardare) to eye.

adolescente smf adolescent.

adolescenza sf adolescence.

adoperare vt to use.

adorabile agg adorable.

adorare vt (persona, cosa) to adore; (divinità) to worship.

adottare vt (bambino) to adopt; (misure, decisione) to take.

adottivo, -a agg (figlio, patria) adopted; (genitori) adoptive.

adozione sf adoption.

adriatico, -a, -ci, -che agg Adriatic □ **Adriatico** sm: **l'Adriatico** the Adriatic (Sea).

adulterio sm adultery.

adulto, -a agg & sm, f (di età) adult.

aerare vt to air.

aereo, -a agg air (dav s) ◆ sm (aero)plane, aircraft; ~ **da turismo** light aircraft.

aerobica sf aerobics (sg).

aeronautica sf (aviazione) air-force.

aeroplano sm (aero)plane (Br), airplane (Am).

aeroporto sm airport.

aerosol sm aerosol.

A.F. (abbr di alta frequenza) HF.

afa sf closeness.

affabile agg affable.

affacciarsi vr (mostrarsi) to show o.s. □ **affacciarsi su** vr + prep to show o.s. at.

affamato, -a agg starving.

affannarsi vr (stancarsi) to tire o.s.; (agitarsi) to worry.

affanno sm (di respiro) breath-lessness; (ansia) worry.

affare *sm* business; *(faccenda)* business, affair; *(occasione)* bargain; *(fam: cosa)* thing; **è un ~!** it's a bargain!; **affari** business *(sg)*; **per affari** on business; **fare affari con** to do business with; **Affari Esteri** Foreign Affairs.

affascinante *agg* charming.

affascinare *vt* to charm, to fascinate.

affaticarsi *vr* to get tired.

affatto *avv* completely; **non ... ~** not ... at all; **niente ~** not at all.

affermare *vt* to affirm ▫ **affermarsi** *vr* to make a name for o.s.

affermativo, -a *agg* affirmative.

affermazione *sf (dichiarazione)* affirmation; *(successo)* success.

afferrare *vt (prendere)* to seize; *(capire)* to grasp ▫ **afferrarsi a** *vr + prep* to grasp at.

affettare *vt* to slice.

affettato, -a *agg (a fette)* sliced; *(artificioso)* affected ◆ *sm* sliced cold meat.

affetto, -a *sm (attaccamento)* affection ◆ *agg*: **essere ~ da** *(malattia)* to suffer from.

affettuoso, -a *agg* affectionate.

affezionarsi *vr*: **~ a** to become fond of.

affezionato, -a *agg* fond.

affidamento *sm (DIR)* custody; *(fiducia)*: **fare ~ su** to rely on.

affidare *vt* to entrust; **~ qn/qc a qn** to entrust sb/sthg to sb.

affiggere *vt (cartello, poster)* to stick up.

affilare *vt* to sharpen.

affilato, -a *agg (lama, punta)* sharp.

affinché *cong* in order that, so that.

affinità *sf inv* affinity.

affissione *sf*: **'divieto di ~'** 'post no bills'.

affisso, -a *pp* → **affiggere** ◆ *sm* poster.

affittare *vt (dare in affitto)* to let, to rent (out); *(prendere in affitto)* to rent; **'affittasi'** 'to let'.

affitto *sm* rent; **dare in ~** to let, to rent (out); **prendere in ~** to rent.

affliggere *vt* to torment ▫ **affliggersi** *vr* to torment o.s.

afflitto, -a *pp* → **affliggere** ◆ *agg* afflicted.

affluente *sm* tributary.

affluire *vi (fiume)* to flow; *(gente, merce)* to pour in.

affogare *vi & vt* to drown.

affogato *sm (gelato)* ice cream or 'semifreddo' with coffee, whisky or a liqueur poured over it.

affollato, -a *agg* crowded.

affondare *vi & vt* to sink.

affrancare *vt* to stamp.

affrancatura *sf* postage.

affresco, -schi *sm* fresco.

affrettare *vt* to hurry ▫ **affrettarsi** *vr* to hurry.

affrontare *vt (nemico)* to confront; *(spesa)* to meet; *(argomento)* to tackle.

affronto *sm* insult.

affumicato, -a *agg (cibo)* smoked; *(vetro)* tinted; *(annerito)* blackened.

afoso, -a *agg* close.

Africa *sf*: l'~ Africa.

africano, -a *agg & sm, f* African.

afta *sf* mouth ulcer.

agenda *sf* diary.

agente *sm* agent; ~ **di polizia** policeman (*f* policewoman); **gli agenti atmosferici** the elements.

agenzia *sf* (*impresa*) agency; (*succursale*) branch; ~ **di cambio** bureau de change; ~ **immobiliare** estate agent's (*Br*), real-estate agency (*Am*); ~ **di viaggi** travel agency.

agevolare *vt* (*facilitare*) to facilitate; (*aiutare*) to help.

agevolazione *sf*: ~ **di pagamento** easy (payment) terms (*pl*).

aggeggio *sm* thing.

aggettivo *sm* adjective.

agghiacciante *agg* terrible.

aggiornare *vt* (*persona, opera*) to bring up-to-date; (*seduta*) to postpone ❑ **aggiornarsi** *vr* to bring o.s. up-to-date.

aggiornato, -a *agg* up-to-date.

aggirare *vt* to get round ❑ **aggirarsi** *vr* to wander; **aggirarsi su** *vr + prep* to be about.

aggiudicare *vt* to award ❑ **aggiudicarsi** *vr* to gain.

aggiungere *vt* to add.

aggiunta *sf*: in ~ in addition.

aggiunto, -a *pp* → **aggiungere**.

aggiustare *vt* to mend ❑ **aggiustarsi** *vr* to come to an agreement.

agglomerato *sm*: ~ **urbano** built-up area.

aggrapparsi *vr* to cling on; ~ **a** to cling to.

aggravare *vt* to make worse ❑ **aggravarsi** *vr* to get worse.

aggredire *vt* to attack.

aggressione *sf* attack.

aggressivo, -a *agg* aggressive.

agguato *sm* ambush.

agiato, -a *agg* (*persona*) well-off; (*vita*) comfortable.

agile *agg* agile, nimble.

agio *sm*: essere a proprio ~ to feel at ease; mettersi a proprio ~ to make o.s. at home.

agire *vi* (*comportarsi*) to act; ~ **da** (*fare da*) to act as.

agitare *vt* to shake; (*mano*) to wave; (*coda*) to wag; (*turbare*) to upset; '~ **prima dell'uso**' 'shake before use' ❑ **agitarsi** *vr* (*turbarsi*) to get worked up; (*muoversi*) to writhe; (*mare*) to get rough; **agitarsi nel letto** to toss and turn in bed.

agitato, -a *agg* (*inquieto*) worried; (*mare*) rough.

agitazione *sf* (*inquietudine*) agitation; (*subbuglio*) turmoil.

agli = a + gli, → a.

aglio *sm* garlic.

agnello *sm* lamb; ~ **alla norcina** leg of lamb larded with ham, garlic, parsley and marjoram.

agnolotti *smpl* ravioli stuffed with pork, salami, Parmesan cheese and spinach.

ago (*pl* aghi) *sm* needle.

agonia *sf* agony.

agopuntura *sf* acupuncture.

agosto *sm* August, → **settembre**.

agricolo, -a *agg* agricultural.

agricoltore *sm (contadino)* farm worker; *(imprenditore)* farmer.

agricoltura *sf* agriculture.

agriturismo *sm* farm holidays *(pl)*.

 AGRITURISMO

A form of tourism popular in Italy, "agriturismo" offers people the opportunity to spend their summer holiday on traditional farms in the Italian countryside. This type of holiday is particularly popular with those who enjoy the outdoors lifestyle, good home cooking and healthy exercise in beautiful rural surroundings. As well as participating in a range of sports such as horseriding, walking, tennis and bowls, holidaymakers also have the opportunity to help on the farm.

---

agrodolce *sm*: in ~ in a sweet and sour sauce.

agrume *sm* citrus fruit.

aguzzare *vt* to sharpen; ~ **le orecchie** to prick up one's ears.

aguzzo, -a *agg* sharp.

ahi *esclam* ouch!

ai = a + i, → **a**.

Aia *sf*: l'~ The Hague.

AIDS *sm o sf* AIDS.

A.I.G. *(abbr di Associazione Italiana Alberghi per la Gioventù)* = YHA.

air-terminal ['ɜr 'tɛrmɪnal] *sm inv* air terminal.

aiuola *sf* flower bed.

aiutante *smf* assistant.

aiutare *vt* to help; ~ **qn (a fare qc)** to help sb (to do sthg).

aiuto *sm* help, assistance; *(assistente)* assistant; ~! help!; **chiedere ~** to ask for help; **essere di ~ a qn** to be of help to sb; **venire in ~ di qn** to come to sb's aid.

al = a + il, → **a**.

ala *(pl* **ali***)* *sf* wing; *(giocatore)* winger.

alano *sm* Great Dane.

alba *sf* dawn; **all'~** at dawn.

albanese *agg & smf* Albanian.

Albania *sf*: l'~ Albania.

albergatore, -trice *sm, f* hotelier.

albergo, -ghi *sm* hotel; ~ **diurno** *public toilets where people can also wash, have a haircut, get their clothes ironed etc.*; ~ **per la gioventù** youth hostel.

albero *sm* tree; *(di nave)* mast; *(di macchina)* shaft; ~ **genealogico** family tree; ~ **di Natale** Christmas tree.

albese *sf thin slices of raw beef served with oil, lemon and mushrooms or Parmesan cheese.*

albicocca, -che *sf* apricot.

albino, -a *agg & sm, f* albino.

album *sm inv* album; ~ **da disegno** sketch book.

albume *sm* egg white.

alcol = **alcool**.

alcolico, -a, -ci, -che *agg* alcoholic ◆ *sm* alcoholic drink.

alcolizzato, -a *sm, f* alcoholic.

alcool *sm* alcohol.

alcuno, -a *agg s:* non ... ~ *(nessuno)* no, not any ◻ **alcuni, -e** *agg pl* some, a few ♦ *pron pl* some; **alcuni di** some of, a few of.

aldilà *sm:* l'~ the next life.

alfabeto *sm* alphabet.

alfiere *sm (portabandiera)* standard bearer; *(negli scacchi)* bishop.

alga, -ghe *sf (di mare)* seaweed.

algebra *sf* algebra.

Algeria *sf:* l'~ Algeria.

aliante *sm* glider.

alibi *sm inv* alibi.

alice *sf* anchovy; **alici areganate** *anchovies cooked in oil, vinegar, garlic, parsley and oregano.*

alienazione *sf (pazzia)* insanity; *(DIR)* transfer.

alieno, -a *sm, f* alien.

alimentare *agg* food *(dav s)* ♦ *vt (nutrire)* to feed; *(fig: rafforzare)* to strengthen; *(rifornire)* to supply ◻ **alimentari** *smpl (cibi)* foodstuffs; **negozio di alimentari** grocer's.

alimentazione *sf (nutrimento)* nutrition; *(rifornimento)* supply.

alimento *sm* food ◻ **alimenti** *smpl* alimony *(sg).*

aliscafo *sm* hydrofoil.

alito *sm* breath.

all' = a + l', → a.

alla = a + la, → a.

allacciare *vt (scarpe)* to tie up; *(cintura, vestito)* to fasten; *(telefono, gas)* to connect ◻ **allacciarsi** *vr* to fasten.

allagare *vt* to flood ◻ **allagarsi** *vr* to flood.

allargare *vt (ampliare)* to widen; *(aprire)* to open ◻ **allargarsi** *vr* to

widen.

allarmare *vt* to alarm.

allarme *sm* alarm; ~ **d'incendio** fire alarm; **dare l'~** to give the alarm.

allattare *vt (al seno)* to breastfeed; *(artificialmente)* to bottlefeed.

alle = a + le, → a.

alleanza *sf* alliance.

allearsi *vr* to form an alliance.

allegare *vt* to enclose.

alleggerire *vt* to lighten.

allegria *sf* cheerfulness.

allegro, -a *agg (contento)* cheerful; *(colore)* bright; *(vivace)* lively ♦ *sm (MUS)* allegro.

allenamento *sm* training; **tenersi in** ~ to keep in training.

allenare *vt* to train ◻ **allenarsi** *vr* to train.

allenatore, -trice *sm, f* trainer, coach.

allentare *vt (vite, nodo)* to loosen; *(sorveglianza, disciplina)* to relax ◻ **allentarsi** *vr* to work loose.

allergia *sf* allergy.

allergico, -a, -ci, -che *agg* allergic; **essere** ~ **a qc** to be allergic to sthg.

allestire *vt (mostra, spettacolo)* to get ready.

allevamento *sm (attività)* breeding, rearing; *(animali)* stock.

allevare *vt (animale)* to breed; *(bambino)* to bring up.

allibratore *sm* bookmaker.

allievo, -a *sm, f* pupil, student.

alligatore *sm* alligator.

allineare .

allineare *vt* to align □ **allinear-si** *vr (mettersi in fila)* to line up.

allo = a + lo, → **a**.

allodola *sf* skylark.

alloggiare *vi* to stay.

alloggio *sm* accommodation.

allontanare *vt (mandare via)* to send away; *(pericolo)* to avert □ **allontanarsi** *vr* to go away.

allora *avv* then ♦ *cong (in tal caso)* then; *(ebbene)* well; **da ~** since then.

alloro *sm* laurel.

alluce *sm* big toe.

allucinante *agg (spaventoso)* terrifying; *(incredibile)* incredible.

allucinazione *sf* hallucination.

alludere : **alludere a** *v + prep* to allude to.

alluminio *sm* aluminium.

allungare *vt (accrescere)* to lengthen; *(gambe)* to stretch; *(diluire)* to water down □ **allungarsi** *vr (accrescersi)* to lengthen; *(distendersi)* to stretch out.

allusione *sf* allusion; **fare allusioni** to drop hints.

alluso *pp* → **alludere**.

alluvione *sf* flood.

almeno *avv* at least.

Alpi *sfpl*: **le ~** the Alps.

alpinismo *sm* climbing.

alpinista, -i, -e *smf* climber.

alpino, -a *agg* alpine.

alquanto *avv* somewhat.

alt *esclam* halt!

altalena *sf (con funi)* swing; *(su asse)* see-saw *(Br)*, teeter-totter *(Am)*.

altare *sm* altar.

alterare *vt* to affect □ **alterarsi** *vr (merce)* to be affected; *(irritarsi)* to get angry.

alternare *vt*: **~ qn/qc a** to alternate sb/sthg with □ **alternarsi** *vr* to alternate.

alternativa *sf* alternative.

alternato, -a *agg* alternate; *(corrente)* alternating.

alterno, -a *agg* alternate.

altezza *sf (statura, di cosa)* height; *(di acqua)* depth; *(altitudine)* altitude.

altezzoso, -a *agg* haughty.

altipiano = **altopiano**.

altitudine *sf* altitude.

alto, -a *agg* high; *(persona, edificio, albero)* tall; *(profondo)* deep; *(suono, voce)* loud ♦ *sm* top ♦ *avv* high; *(parlare)* loud; **è ~ due metri** he's two metres tall; **ad alta voce** out loud, aloud; **alta moda** haute couture; **dall'~ in basso** from top to bottom; **alti e bassi** ups and downs; **in ~** upwards.

altoparlante *sm* loudspeaker.

altopiano *(pl* altipiani*) sm* plateau.

altrettanto, -a *agg (tempo, latte)* as much; *(persone, libri)* as many ♦ *pron* the same ♦ *avv* equally; **auguri! - grazie, ~!** all the best! - thank you, the same to you!

altrimenti *avv (se no)* otherwise; *(diversamente)* differently.

altro, -a *agg* 1. *(diverso)* other; **ha un ~ modello?** have you got another O a different model?
2. *(supplementare)* other; **un ~**

caffè? another coffee?

3. *(rimanente)* other; **gli altri passeggeri sono pregati di restare al loro posto** would all remaining passengers please stay in their seats.

4. *(nel tempo)*: **l'~ giorno** the other day; **l'altr'anno** last year; **l'~ ieri** the day before yesterday; **domani l'~** the day after tomorrow.

5. *(in espressioni)*: **è tutt'~ che bello** it's far from being beautiful; **d'altra parte** on the other hand.

♦ *pron*: **l'~** the other (one); **un ~** another (one); **gli altri** *(il prossimo)* others, other people; **l'uno o l'~** one or the other; **se non ~** at least; **senz'~** of course; **tra l'~** among other things.

altroché *esclam* and how!

altronde : **d'altronde** *avv* on the other hand.

altrove *avv* elsewhere.

altrui *agg inv* other people's.

altruista, -i, -e *agg* altruistic.

altura *sf* high ground.

alunno, -a *sm, f* pupil.

alveare *sm* beehive.

alzare *vt (oggetto)* to lift; *(prezzi, volume, voce)* to raise □ **alzarsi** *vr (dal letto, dalla sedia)* to get up; *(aumentare)* to rise; *(vento)* to get up.

amaca, -che *sf* hammock.

amalgamare *vt* to combine □ **amalgamarsi** *vr* to combine.

amante *smf* lover ♦ *agg*: **~ di qc** fond of sthg.

amare *vt (persona)* to love; *(cosa)* to be fond of.

amareggiato, -a *agg* embit-

tered.

amarena *sf* sour black cherry.

amaretto *sm (biscotto)* macaroon; *(liquore)* a liqueur made with almonds.

amarezza *sf* bitterness.

amaro, -a *agg (sapore)* bitter; *(spiacevole)* nasty.

ambasciata *sf* embassy.

ambasciatore, -trice *sm, f* ambassador.

ambedue *agg inv & pron* both.

ambientare *vt (film)* to set □ **ambientarsi** *vr* to get used to a place.

ambiente *sm (natura)* environment; *(cerchia)* surroundings *(pl)*.

ambiguo, -a *agg (parola, testo)* ambiguous; *(comportamento, persona)* dubious.

ambizione *sf* ambition.

ambizioso, -a *agg* ambitious.

ambra *sf* amber.

ambulante *agg* itinerant.

ambulanza *sf* ambulance.

ambulatorio *sm* surgery.

America *sf*: **l'~** America; **l'~ latina** Latin America.

americano, -a *agg & sm, f* American.

amianto *sm* asbestos.

amichevole *agg* friendly.

amicizia *sf* friendship; **fare ~ (con qn)** to make friends (with sb).

amico, -a, -ci, -che *sm, f* friend; **~ del cuore** best friend.

amido *sm* starch.

ammaccare *vt* to dent.

ammaccatura *sf (su metallo)* dent; *(su gamba)* bruise.

ammaestrare *vt* to train.

ammainare *vt* to lower.

ammalarsi *vr* to fall ill.

ammalato, -a *agg* ill ♦ *sm, f* patient.

ammassare *vt* to amass, to pile up.

ammazzare *vt* to kill □ **ammazzarsi** *vr* to kill o.s.

ammenda *sf* fine.

ammesso, -a *pp* → **ammettere**.

ammettere *vt* (*riconoscere*) to admit; (*permettere*) to allow; (*a esame, scuola*) to accept; (*supporre*) to suppose, to assume.

amministrare *vt* to run, to manage.

amministratore *sm* (*di condominio*) manager; ~ **delegato** managing director.

ammirare *vt* to admire.

ammiratore, -trice *sm, f* admirer.

ammirazione *sf* admiration.

ammissione *sf* (*a esame*) admittance.

ammobiliato, -a *agg* furnished; **non** ~ unfurnished.

ammollo *sm* soaking; **lasciare qc in** ~ to leave sthg to soak.

ammoniaca *sf* ammonia.

ammonire *vt* (*rimproverare*) to warn; (*SPORT*) to book.

ammonizione *sf* (*rimprovero*) warning; (*SPORT*) booking.

ammontare : **ammontare a** *v + prep* to amount to.

ammorbidente *sm* fabric softener.

ammorbidire *vt* (*rendere morbido*) to soften.

ammortizzatore *sm* shock absorber.

ammucchiare *vt* to pile up.

ammuffito, -a *agg* mouldy.

ammutinamento *sm* mutiny.

amnistia *sf* amnesty.

amo *sm* bait.

amore *sm* love; **fare l'**~ (**con qn**) to make love (with sb); **amor proprio** self-esteem.

ampio, -a *agg* (*vasto*) wide; (*spazioso*) spacious; (*abbondante*) abundant.

ampliare *vt* to widen.

amplificatore *sm* amplifier.

amputare *vt* to amputate.

amuleto *sm* amulet.

anabbaglianti *smpl* dipped headlights (*Br*), dimmed headlights (*Am*).

anagrafe *sf* (*ufficio*) registry office (*Br*), office of vital statistics (*Am*).

analcolico, -a, -ci, -che *agg* non-alcoholic ♦ *sm* soft drink.

analfabeta, -i, -e *agg & smf* illiterate.

analisi *sf inv* (*studio*) analysis; (*MED*) test; ~ **del sangue** blood test.

analista, -i, -e *smf* analyst.

analizzare *vt* to analyse.

analogo, -a, -ghi, -ghe *agg* similar.

ananas *sm inv* pineapple.

anarchia *sf* anarchy.

ANAS *sf* (*abbr di Azienda Nazionale Autonoma delle Strade*) national road board.

anatomia *sf* anatomy.
anatomico, -a, -ci, -che *agg* (*sedile*) contoured.
anatra *sf* duck.
anca, -che *sf* hip.
anche *cong* (*pure*) too; (*persino*) even.
ancora[1] *sf* anchor.
ancora[2] *avv* (*tuttora*) still; (*persino*) even; (*di nuovo*) again; (*di più*) more, still; ~ **più bello** even more beautiful; ~ **un po'** a bit more; **una volta** once more; **non** ~ not yet.
andare *vi* 1. (*muoversi*) to go; **scusi, per** ~ **alla stazione?** could you tell me the way to the station, please?; ~ **a Napoli** to go to Naples; ~ **avanti/indietro** to go forwards/backwards; ~ **in vacanza** to go on holiday (*Br*), to go on vacation (*Am*).
2. (*strada*) to go.
3. (*indica uno stato*): **come va?** how are you?; ~ **bene/male** (*persona*) to be well/unwell; (*situazione*) to go well/badly.
4. (*piacere*): **il suo modo di fare non mi va** I don't like the way he behaves; **non mi va di mangiare** I don't feel like eating.
5. (*funzionare*) to work.
6. (*con participio passato*): **dove va messa la chiave?** where does the key go?; ~ **perso** (*essere smarrito*) to get lost.
7. (*in espressioni*): ~ **bene a qn** (*come misura*) to fit sb; **queste scarpe mi vanno bene** these shoes fit (me); **ti va bene andare al cinema?** do you feel like going to the cinema?; ~ **via** (*partire*) to leave; (*macchia*) to come out.
♦ *sm*: **a lungo** ~ in time.
❏ **andarsene** *vr* to go away.
andata *sf*: **all'**~ on the way there; ~ **e ritorno** return (ticket) (*Br*), round-trip ticket (*Am*).
andatura *sf* walk.
andirivieni *sm inv* coming and going.
anello *sm* (*da dito*) ring; (*di catena*) link; ~ **di fidanzamento** engagement ring.
anemia *sf* anaemia.
anestesia *sf* anaesthesia.
anestetico *sm* anaesthetic.
anfiteatro *sm* amphitheatre.
anfora *sf* amphora.
angelo *sm* angel.
angina *sf* tonsillitis; ~ **pectoris** angina.
anglicano, -a *agg* Anglican.
angolo *sm* corner; ~ **cottura** kitchen area; **all'**~ on the corner.
angora *sf*: **d'**~ angora (*dav s*).
angoscia *sf* anguish.
anguilla *sf* eel.
anguria *sf* watermelon.
anice *sm* aniseed.
anidride *sf*: ~ **carbonica** carbon dioxide.
anima *sf* soul.
animale *agg & sm* animal; ~ **domestico** pet.
animatore, -trice *sm, f*: ~ **turistico** entertainment organizer (*in holiday village*).
animo *sm* (*mente*) mind; (*cuore*) heart; (*coraggio*): **perdersi d'**~ to lose heart.
anitra = **anatra**.

annaffiare vt to water.

annaffiatoio sm watering can.

annata sf year; (di vino) vintage.

annegare vt & vi to drown ☐
annegarsi vr to drown o.s.

anniversario sm anniversary.

anno sm year; **buon ~!** Happy New Year!; **quanti anni hai?** how old are you?; **ho 21 anni** I'm 21; **un bambino di tre anni** a three-year-old; **~ accademico** academic year; **~ bisestile** leap year; **~ scolastico** school year.

annodare vt to tie.

annoiare vt to bore ☐ **annoiarsi** vr to get bored.

annotare vt (prendere nota) to note down; (commentare) to annotate.

annuale agg annual.

annuario sm yearbook.

annuire vi (con la testa) to nod.

annullare vt (partita, riunione, francobollo) to cancel; (matrimonio) to annul; (rendere vano) to destroy.

annunciare vt to announce; (indicare) to indicate.

annunciatore, -trice sm, f announcer.

Annunciazione sf: **l'~** the Annunciation.

annuncio sm announcement; **~ pubblicitario** advertisement; **annunci economici** classified ads.

annuo, -a agg annual, yearly.

annusare vt to smell.

annuvolamento sm clouding over.

ano sm anus.

anomalo, -a agg anomalous.

anonimo, -a agg anonymous.

anoressia sf anorexia.

anormale agg abnormal ◆ smf abnormal person.

ANSA sf (abbr di Agenzia Nazionale Stampa Associata) national press agency.

ansia sf anxiety.

ansimare vi to pant.

ansioso, -a agg (inquieto) anxious; (impaziente): **~ di fare qc** eager to do sthg.

anta sf (di finestra) shutter; (di armadio) door.

antagonista, -i, -e smf rival.

antartico, -a, -ci, -che agg Antarctic.

Antartide sf: **l'~** Antarctica.

anteguerra sm prewar period.

antenato, -a sm, f ancestor.

antenna sf aerial.

anteprima sf preview; **presentare qc in ~** to preview sthg.

anteriore agg (sedili, ruote) front (dav s); (nel tempo) previous.

antiabbaglianti = **anabbaglianti**.

antibiotico sm antibiotic.

anticamera sf anteroom.

antichità sf inv (passato) antiquity; (oggetto) antique.

anticipare vt (partenza) to bring forward; (denaro) to pay in advance.

anticipo sm (di denaro) advance; (di tempo): **il treno ha 10 minuti d'~** the train is 10 minutes early; **essere/arrivare in ~** to be/arrive early.

antico, -a, -chi, -che agg

(mobilio) antique; *(dell'antichità)* ancient.

anticoncezionale *agg & sm* contraceptive.

anticonformista, -i, -e *agg & smf* nonconformist.

anticorpo *sm* antibody.

antidoto *sm* antidote.

antifascista, -i, -e *agg & smf* antifascist.

antifurto *agg inv* antitheft *(dav s)* ◆ *sm* antitheft device.

antigelo *sm inv* antifreeze.

Antille *sfpl*: **le ~** the West Indies.

antimafia *agg inv* anti-Mafia.

antincendio *agg inv* fire *(dav s)*.

antinebbia *agg inv* fog *(dav s)* ◆ *sm inv* fog lamp.

antiorario *agg m → senso*.

antipasto *sm* hors d'œuvre; **~ di mare** mixed seafood hors d'œuvre; **~ a scelta** hors d'œuvres chosen from a buffet of grilled or baked vegetables, pickled foods, cold meats etc.

antipatia *sf* antipathy.

antipatico, -a, -ci, -che *agg* unpleasant.

antiquariato *sm (commercio)* antique trade; **oggetti d'~** antiques.

antiquario, -a *sm, f* antique dealer.

antiquato, -a *agg* old-fashioned.

antiruggine *agg inv* rustproof.

antirughe *agg inv* antiwrinkle *(dav s)*.

antisettico, -a, -ci, -che *agg & sm* antiseptic.

antitetanica *sf* antitetanus injection.

antivipera *sm inv* antiviper serum.

antologia *sf* anthology.

anulare *agg* ring *(dav s)* ◆ *sm* ring finger.

anzi *cong (al contrario)* on the contrary; *(o meglio)* or rather.

anziano, -a *agg (di età)* elderly; *(di carica)* senior ◆ *sm, f (vecchio)* senior citizen.

anziché *cong* rather than.

anzitutto *avv* first of all.

apatia *sf* apathy.

apatico, -a, -ci, -che *agg* apathetic.

ape *sf* bee.

aperitivo *sm* aperitif.

---

i APERITIVO

The tradition of taking an alcoholic or a non-alcoholic drink before lunch or dinner is common throughout Italy. Italians are especially fond of having an aperitif at some point during their Sunday stroll or "passeggiata". Although an aperitif is sometimes served at home, it is more usual to go out to a bar where, in addition to the usual range of drinks, there may be local or house specialities on offer. Drinks are generally accompanied by olives, crisps or other savoury snacks.

---

aperto, -a *pp → aprire* ◆ *agg* open ◆ *sm*: **all'~** in the open air.

apertura *sf* opening.

apice *sm* peak; **essere all'~ di qc**

to be at the height of sthg.

apicoltura *sf* beekeeping.

apnea *sf*: **in ~** *(subacqueo)* without breathing apparatus.

apolide *agg* stateless ◆ *smf* stateless person.

apostolo *sm* apostle.

apostrofo *sm* apostrophe.

appagare *vt* to satisfy.

appannare *vt (vetro)* to mist; *(fig: mente)* to dim ❑ **appannarsi** *vr (vetro)* to mist up; *(fig: vista, mente)* to grow dim.

apparato *sm (ANAT)* system; *(impianto)* apparatus.

apparecchiare *vt*: **~ la tavola** to lay the table.

apparecchio *sm (congegno)* device; *(aereo)* aircraft; *(per i denti)* brace; **~ acustico** hearing aid.

apparente *agg* apparent.

apparentemente *avv* apparently.

apparenza *sf*: **in** o **all'~** apparently.

apparire *vi (mostrarsi)* to appear; *(sembrare)* to seem.

appariscente *agg* striking.

apparso, -a *pp* → **apparire**.

appartamento *sm* flat *(Br)*, apartment *(Am)*.

appartenere : **appartenere a** *v + prep* to belong to.

appassionato, -a *agg* passionate ◆ *sm, f* fan; **essere ~ di qc** to be keen on sthe.

appello *sm (chiamata)* rollcall; *(DIR)* appeal; **fare ~ a** to appeal to; **fare l'~** to call the roll.

appena *avv (a fatica)* hardly; *(da*

poco) just; *(solo)* only, just ◆ *cong* as soon as; **non ~** as soon as.

appendere *vt* to hang up.

appendice *sf* appendix.

appendicite *sf* appendicitis.

Appennini *smpl*: **gli ~** the Apennines.

appeso, -a *pp* → **appendere**.

appetito *sm* appetite; **buon ~!** enjoy your meal!

appetitoso, -a *agg* appetizing.

appezzamento *sm* plot.

appiattire *vt* to flatten ❑ **appiattirsi** *vr (al suolo, contro il muro)* to flatten o.s.; *(diventare piatto)* to become flatter.

appiccare *vt*: **~ il fuoco a qc** to set fire to sthg.

appiccicare *vt* to stick ❑ **appiccicarsi** *vr*: **appiccicarsi (a)** to stick (to); *(fig: persona)* to cling (to).

appieno *avv* fully.

appigliarsi : **appigliarsi a** *vr + prep (afferrarsi)* to hold on to; *(fig: pretesto)* to cling to.

appiglio *sm (appoggio)* hold; *(fig: pretesto)* pretext.

appisolarsi *vr* to doze off.

applaudire *vt* to applaud.

applauso *sm* applause; **fare un ~** to give a round of applause.

applicare *vt* to apply ❑ **applicarsi** *vr* to apply o.s.

applicazione *sf (di cerotto, pomata)* application; *(attuazione)* enforcement.

appoggiare *vt (per terra, sul tavolo)* to put (down); *(sostenere)* to support; *(al muro)*: **~ qc a** o **contro**

qc to lean sthg against sthg ▫
appoggiarsi a *vr + prep* to lean against.

appoggiatesta *sm inv* head-rest.

apporre *vt (form)* to add.

appositamente *avv* on purpose; **~ per te** specially for you.

apposito, -a *agg* appropriate.

apposta *avv* deliberately; **fare qc ~** to do sthg on purpose.

apposto, -a *pp* → **apporre**.

apprendere *vt* to learn.

apprendista, -i, -e *smf* apprentice.

apprensivo, -a *agg* apprehensive.

appreso, -a *pp* → **apprendere**.

appretto *sm* starch.

apprezzamento *sm* appreciation.

apprezzare *vt* to appreciate.

approccio *sm* approach.

approdare *vi* to land; **non ~ a niente** to come to nothing.

approdo *sm (atto)* landing; *(luogo)* landing-place.

approfittare : approfittare di *v + prep* to take advantage of.

approfondire *vt (accentuare)* to deepen; *(studiare)* to study in depth.

appropriarsi : appropriarsi di *vr + prep* to appropriate.

approssimativo, -a *agg (calcolo)* approximate; *(conoscenza)* superficial.

approvare *vt (legge, proposta)* to pass; *(comportamento)* to approve of.

approvazione *sf* approval.

appuntamento *sm* appointment; *(amoroso)* date; **dare (un) ~ a qn** to arrange to meet sb; **prendere un ~ con** o **da qn** to make an appointment with sb.

appuntare *vt (matita)* to sharpen; *(fissare)* to pin; *(annotare)* to note.

appunto *sm (annotazione)* note; *(rimprovero)* reprimand ♦ *avv* exactly.

apribottiglie *sm inv* bottle opener.

aprile *sm* April, → **settembre**.

aprire *vt* to open; *(gas, acqua)* to turn on ♦ *vi* to open; **vai tu ad ~?** can you answer the door?; **'non ~ prima che il treno sia fermo'** 'do not open before the train has stopped' ❑ **aprirsi** *vr (porta)* to open; *(inchiesta)* to start up; *(confidarsi)*: **aprirsi con qc** to open one's heart to sb.

apriscatole *sm inv* can opener.

aquila *sf* eagle.

aquilone *sm* kite.

Arabia Saudita *sf*: **l'~** Saudi Arabia.

arabo, -a *agg & sm, f* Arab ♦ *sm (lingua)* Arabic.

arachide *sf* peanut.

aragosta *sf* lobster.

arancia, -ce *sf* orange.

aranciata *sf* orange juice.

arancini *smpl* rice balls *with a filling of tomatoes and mozzarella cheese (a Sicilian speciality)*.

arancio *sm* orange tree.

arancione *agg & sm* orange.

arare *vt* to plough.

aratro *sm* plough.

arazzo *sm* tapestry.

arbitrario, -a *agg* arbitrary.

arbitro *sm* referee.

arbusto *sm* shrub.

archeologia *sf* archaeology.

archeologico, -a, -ci, -che
agg archaeological.

architetto *sm* architect.

architettura *sf* architecture.

archivio *sm* (*luogo*) archives (*pl*);
(*raccolta*) files (*pl*); (*INFORM*) file.

arcipelago, -ghi *sm* archipelago.

arcivescovo *sm* archbishop.

arco, -chi *sm* (*volta*) arch; (*arma*)
bow; (*durata*): **nell'~ di due mesi** in
the space of two months.

arcobaleno *sm* rainbow.

ardere *vt & vi* to burn.

ardesia *sf* (*pietra*) slate.

ardire *vi* to dare ◆ *sm* daring.

ardore *sm* ardour.

area *sf* area; '**~ pedonale**' 'pedestrian precinct'; **~ di servizio** services (*pl*).

arena *sf* arena.

arenarsi *vr* to run aground.

argenteria *sf* silverware.

Argentina *sf*: **l'~** Argentina.

argentino, -a *agg & sm, f*
Argentinian.

argento *sm* silver; **d'~** silver.

argilla *sf* clay.

argine *sm* bank.

argomento *sm* (*tema*) subject;
(*ragionamento*) argument.

arguto, -a *agg* (*persona*) quick-
witted; (*discorso, battuta*) witty.

aria *sf* air; (*aspetto*) appearance;
ha l'~ familiare he looks familiar;
mandare all'~ qc to ruin sthg; **all'~
aperta** in the open air; **~ condizionata** air-conditioning; **darsi
delle arie** to fancy o.s.

arido, -a *agg* (*secco*) arid; (*fig*:
persona, cuore) cold.

ariete *sm* (*animale*) ram ❑
Ariete *sm* Aries.

aringa, -ghe *sf* herring.

arista *sf* saddle of pork.

aristocratico, -a, -ci, -che
agg aristocratic ◆ *sm, f* aristocrat.

aritmetica *sf* arithmetic.

Arlecchino *sm* Harlequin.

arma, -i *sf* (*strumento*) weapon;
(*di esercito*) division; **~ da fuoco**
firearm.

armadio *sm* cupboard; **~ a
muro** built-in cupboard.

armato, -a *agg* armed.

armatura *sf* armour.

armonia *sf* harmony.

arnese *sm* (*attrezzo*) tool; (*fam*:
oggetto) thing.

arnia *sf* beehive.

Arno *sm*: **l'~** the Arno.

aroma, -i *sm* (*odore*) aroma;
(*essenza*) flavouring ❑ **aromi** *mpl*
spices.

arpa *sf* harp.

arpione *sm* harpoon.

arrabbiarsi *vr* to get angry.

arrabbiato, -a *agg* angry;
all'arrabbiata → **penne**.

arrampicarsi *vr* to climb.

arrangiarsi *vr* to get by.

arredamento *sm* furnishings (*pl*).

arredare *vt* to furnish.

arrendersi *vr* to surrender.

arrestare *vt* (*catturare*) to arrest; (*emorragia, flusso*) to stop.

arresto *sm* (*cattura*) arrest; (*fermata*) stop; ~ **cardiaco** cardiac arrest.

arretrato, -a *agg* (*pagamento, giornale*) back (*dav s*); (*sottosviluppato*) backward; (*sorpassato*) old-fashioned ❑ **arretrati** *smpl* arrears.

arricchire *vt* to enrich ❑ **arricchirsi** *vr* to get rich.

arricciacapelli *sm inv* curling tongs (*pl*).

arricciare *vt* (*capelli, nastro*) to curl; ~ **il naso** to wrinkle one's nose.

arrivare *vi* to arrive; **arriverò a Firenze alle due** I'll get to Florence at two ❑ **arrivare a** *v + prep* (*grado, livello*) to reach; ~ **a fare qc** (*riuscire*) to manage to do sthg; (*giungere al punto di, osare*) to go so far as to do sthg.

arrivederci *esclam* goodbye!

arrivederla *esclam* goodbye!

arrivista, -i, -e *smf* social climber.

arrivo *sm* arrival; (*nello sport*) finishing line; **essere in ~** to be arriving; **'arrivi (nazionali/internazionali)'** '(domestic/international) arrivals'.

arrogante *agg* arrogant.

arrossire *vi* to blush.

arrostire *vt* to roast.

arrosto *sm* roast.

arrotolare *vt* to roll up.

arrotondare *vt* (*render tondo*) to round; (*numero*) to round off; (*stipendio*) to add to.

arrugginito, -a *agg* rusty.

arruolarsi *vr* to enlist.

arsenale *sm* (*di armi*) arsenal; (*cantiere*) dockyard.

arte *sf* art; (*abilità*) skill.

arteria *sf* artery.

artico, -a, -ci, -che *agg* Arctic.

articolazione *sf* joint.

articolo *sm* article; (*merce*) article, item; **articoli da regalo** gifts.

Artide *sf*: **l'~** the Arctic.

artificiale *agg* artificial.

artigianato *sm* craftsmanship; **di ~** handcrafted.

artigiano, -a *agg* craft (*dav s*) ◆ *sm, f* craftsman (*f* craftswoman).

artiglio *sm* claw.

artista, -i, -e *smf* artist.

artistico, -a, -ci, -che *agg* artistic.

arto *sm* limb.

artrite *sf* arthritis.

artrosi *sf* osteoarthritis.

ascella *sf* armpit.

ascendente *sm* (*influsso*) ascendancy; (*astrologico*) ascendant.

Ascensione *sf*: **l'~** the Ascension.

ascensore *sm* lift (*Br*), elevator (*Am*).

ascesso *sm* abscess.

ascia (*pl* **asce**) *sf* axe.

asciugacapelli *sm inv* hairdryer.

asciugamano *sm* towel.

asciugare *vt* to dry ☐ **asciugarsi** *vr* (*persona*) to dry o.s.; (*tinta, vestiti*) to dry.

asciutto, -a *agg* (*secco*) dry; (*magro*) thin.

ascoltare *vt* to listen to.

ascoltatore, -trice *sm, f* listener.

ascolto *sm*: **dare** ○ **prestare ~ a** to pay attention to; **essere in ~ to** be listening.

asfaltato, -a *agg* asphalt (*dav* s).

asfalto *sm* asphalt.

asfissia *sf* asphyxia.

asfissiare *vt & vi* to suffocate.

Asia *sf*: l'~ Asia.

asiatico, -a, -ci, -che *agg & sm, f* Asian.

asilo *sm* (*scuola*) nursery; **~ nido** crèche; **~ politico** political asylum.

asino *sm* donkey.

asma *sf* asthma.

asola *sf* buttonhole.

asparago *sm* asparagus.

aspettare *vt* to wait for; **mi aspetto una risposta** I expect an answer; **~ un bambino** to be expecting a child.

aspettativa *sf* (*previsione*) expectation; (*congedo*) leave.

aspetto *sm* (*apparenza*) appearance; (*punto di vista*) point of view; (*elemento*) aspect.

aspirapolvere *sm inv* vacuum cleaner.

aspirare *vt* (*inalare*) to breathe in; (*risucchiare*) to suck up ☐ **aspi-**

rare a *v + prep* to aspire to.

aspiratore *sm* extractor.

aspirina® *sf* aspirin.

aspro, -a *agg* (*sapore*) sour.

assaggiare *vt* to taste.

assai *avv* (*molto*) very; (*abbastanza*) enough.

assalire *vt* to attack.

assassinare *vt* to murder.

assassinio *sm* murder.

assassino, -a *sm, f* murderer.

asse *sf* board ◆ *sm* (*di auto*) axle; (*retta*) axis.

assedio *sm* siege.

assegnare *vt*: **~ qc (a qn)** (*casa, rendita*) to allocate sthg (to sb); (*incarico, compiti*) to assign sthg (to sb); (*premio*) to award sthg (to sb).

assegno *sm* (*bancario*) cheque; (*sussidio*) benefit; **~ a vuoto** bounced cheque; **~ circolare** bank draft; **~ di studio** study grant; **~ di viaggio** ○ **turistico** traveller's cheque; **contro ~** cash on delivery.

assemblea *sf* meeting.

assente *agg* (*da luogo*) absent; (*distratto*) vacant ◆ *smf* absentee.

assenza *sf* (*lontananza*) absence; (*mancanza*) lack.

assetato, -a *agg* thirsty.

assicurare *vt* (*auto, casa*) to insure; (*garantire*) to ensure; (*fissare*) to secure ☐ **assicurarsi** *vr* to insure o.s.; **assicurarsi di fare qc** to be sure to do sthg; **assicurarsi che** to make sure that.

assicurata *sf* registered letter.

assicurato, -a *agg* insured.

assicurazione *sf* (*contratto*) insurance; (*garanzia*) assurance; **~**

sulla vita life assurance.

assillare *vt (infastidire)* to pester; *(sog: pensiero)* to torment.

Assisi *sf* Assisi.

assistente *smf* assistant; **~ sociale** social worker; **~ di volo** steward (f stewardess).

assistenza *sf* aid.

assistere *vt* to assist; *(malato)* to care for ♦ *vi:* **~ (a qc)** *(a lezioni)* to attend (sthg); *(a scena)* to be present (at sthg).

assistito, -a *pp* → assistere.

asso *sm* ace.

associare *vt* to associate ❑

associarsi *vr:* **associarsi (a ○ con)** *(ditta)* to enter into a partnership (with); **associarsi a qc** *(club)* to join sthg.

associazione *sf* association.

assolto, -a *pp* → assolvere.

assolutamente *avv* absolutely.

assoluto, -a *agg* absolute.

assoluzione *sf (accusato)* acquittal; *(RELIG)* absolution.

assolvere *vt (accusato)* to acquit; *(RELIG)* to absolve; *(compito)* to carry out.

assomigliare : assomigliare a *v + prep* to resemble, to look like.

assonnato, -a *agg* sleepy.

assorbente *agg (tampone)* absorbent ♦ *sm:* **~ (igienico)** (sanitary) towel; **~ interno** tampon.

assorbire *vt* to absorb.

assordante *agg* deafening.

assortimento *sm* assortment.

assortito, -a *agg (vario)* assort-

ed; *(accordato)* matching.

assumere *vt (personale)* to take on; *(impegno)* to accept; *(atteggiamento)* to assume.

assunto, -a *pp* → assumere.

assurdità *sf inv* absurdity.

assurdo, -a *agg* absurd.

asta *sf (bastone)* pole; *(vendita)* auction.

astemio, -a *agg* teetotal.

astenersi : astenersi da *vr + prep* to abstain from.

asterisco, -schi *sm* asterisk.

astigmatico, -a, -ci, -che *agg* astigmatic.

astratto, -a *agg* abstract.

astrologia *sf* astrology.

astronauta, -i, -e *smf* astronaut.

astronomia *sf* astronomy.

astuccio *sm* case.

astuto, -a *agg (persona)* cunning; *(idea, azione)* shrewd.

astuzia *sf (furbizia)* shrewdness; *(stratagemma)* trick.

A.T. *abbr* = alta tensione.

ateo, -a *sm, f* atheist.

ATI *(abbr di Aerotrasporti Italiani)* Italian domestic airline.

atlante *sm (geografico)* atlas.

atlantico, -a, -ci, -che *agg* Atlantic.

Atlantico *sm:* **l'(Oceano) ~** the Atlantic (Ocean).

atleta, -i, -e *smf* athlete.

atletica *sf* athletics *(sg)*.

atletico, -a, -ci, -che *agg* athletic.

atmosfera *sf* atmosphere.

atmosferico, -a, -ci, -che
agg atmospheric.

atomico, -a, -ci, -che *agg*
atomic.

atomo *sm* atom.

atroce *agg* atrocious.

attaccante *sm* forward.

attaccapanni *sm inv* clothes
stand.

attaccare *vt (unire)* to attach;
(appendere) to hang up; *(assalire)* to
attack; *(trasmettere)* to give ❑
attaccarsi *vr* to stick.

attacco, -chi *sm* attack; *(presa)*
socket.

atteggiamento *sm* attitude.

attendere *vt* to wait for.

attentato *sm* attack.

attento, -a *agg (che presta attenzione)* attentive; *(prudente)* careful;
stai ~! *(non distrarti)* pay attention!;
(stai in guardia) be careful!; **'attenti
al cane'** 'beware of the dog';
'attenti al gradino' 'mind the step'.

attenzione *sf* attention; **~!** be
careful!; **fare ~** *(concentrarsi)* to pay
attention; *(essere prudente)* to be
careful.

atterraggio *sm* landing.

atterrare *vi* to land.

attesa *sf* wait; **essere in ~ di** to
be waiting for.

atteso, -a *pp* → **attendere**.

attestato *sm* certificate.

attico *sm* penthouse.

attillato, -a *agg* close-fitting.

attimo *sm* moment.

attirare *vt* to attract.

attitudine *sf* aptitude.

attività *sf inv* activity; *(occu-*

pazione) occupation; *(COMM)* assets
(pl).

attivo, -a *agg* active ♦ *sm*
assets *(pl)*.

atto *sm (azione, gesto)* act, deed;
(documento) document; *(di dramma)*
act; **mettere in ~** to put into
action.

attonito, -a *agg* astonished.

attorcigliare *vt* to twist.

attore, -trice *sm, f* actor *(f*
actress).

attorno *avv* around.

attracco, -chi *sm (manovra)*
docking; *(luogo)* mooring.

attraente *agg* attractive.

attrarre *vt (affascinare)* to
attract; *(richiamare)* to draw.

attrattiva *sf (richiamo)* attraction; *(qualità)* attractiveness.

attratto, -a *pp* → **attrarre**.

attraversamento *sm* crossing; **~ pedonale** pedestrian crossing.

attraversare *vt (strada, città)* to
cross; *(periodo)* to go through.

attraverso *prep (da parte a
parte)* across; *(per mezzo di)*
through.

attrazione *sf* attraction.

attrezzatura *sf* equipment.

attrezzo *sm* tool.

attribuire : **attribuire a** *v +
prep (opera)* to attribute to; **~ il
merito a qn** to give sb the credit.

attrice → **attore**.

attrito *sm* friction.

attuale *agg (presente)* present;
(moderno) topical.

attualità *sf inv* current events

(pl); **d'~** topical.

attualmente *avv* at present.

attuare *vt* to carry out.

attutire *vt (colpo, rumore)* to reduce.

audace *agg* bold.

audacia *sf* audacity.

audiovisivo, -a *agg* audio-visual.

auditorio *sm* auditorium.

audizione *sf* audition.

augurare *vt*: **~ qc a qn** to wish sb sthg; **augurarsi di fare qc** to hope to do sthg; **mi auguro che tutto vada bene** I hope that all goes well.

augurio *sm* wish; **auguri** greetings; **(tanti) auguri!** all the best!; *(per compleanno)* happy birthday!; **fare gli auguri a qn** to give sb one's best wishes.

aula *sf* classroom.

aumentare *vt & vi* to increase.

aumento *sm* increase.

aureola *sf* halo.

auricolare *sm* earphone.

aurora *sf* dawn.

ausiliare *agg & sm* auxiliary.

austero, -a *agg* austere.

Australia *sf*: **l'~** Australia.

australiano, -a *agg & sm, f* Australian.

Austria *sf*: **l'~** Austria.

austriaco, -a, -ci, -che *agg & sm, f* Austrian.

autenticare *vt* to authenticate.

autentico, -a, -ci, -che *agg (firma, quadro)* authentic; *(fatto)* true; **è un ~ cretino** he's a real cretin.

autista, -i, -e *smf* driver.

auto *sf inv* car.

autoabbronzante *agg* self-tanning ◆ *sm* fake tanning cream.

autoadesivo, -a *agg* self-adhesive ◆ *sm* sticker.

autoambulanza *sf* ambulance.

autobiografia *sf* autobiography.

autobus *sm inv* bus.

autocarro *sm* truck.

autocisterna *sf* tanker.

autocontrollo *sm* self-control.

autodidatta, -i, -e *smf* self-taught person.

autodromo *sm* racing track.

autogol *sm inv* own goal.

autografo *sm* autograph.

autogrill® *sm inv* motorway restaurant.

autolinea *sf* bus service.

automa, -i *sm* automaton.

automatico, -a, -ci, -che *agg* automatic.

automazione *sf* automation.

automezzo *sm* motor vehicle.

automobile *sf* car *(Br)*, automobile *(Am)*.

automobilismo *sm (sport)* motor racing; *(industria)* car industry *(Br)*, auto industry *(Am)*.

automobilista, -i, -e *smf* motorist.

autonoleggio *sm* car hire.

autonomia *sf (indipendenza)* autonomy; *(di veicolo)* range.

autonomo, -a *agg* independent, autonomous.

autopsia *sf* autopsy.

autoradio *sf inv* car radio.

autore, -trice *sm, f (di libro)* author; *(di quadro)* painter; **l'~ del delitto** the person who committed the crime.

autorevole *agg* authoritative.

autorimessa *sf* garage.

autorità *sf inv* authority.

autoritario, -a *agg* authoritarian.

autorizzare *vt* to authorize.

autorizzazione *sf* authorization.

autoscatto *sm* timer.

autoscontro *sm* Dodgem® car.

autoscuola *sf* driving school.

autoservizi *smpl* bus services.

autostop *sm* hitchhiking; **fare l'~** to hitchhike.

autostoppista, -i, -e *smf* hitchhiker.

autostrada *sf* motorway *(Br)*, freeway *(Am)*.

autostradale *agg* motorway *(Br) (dav s)*, freeway *(Am) (dav s)*.

autoveicolo *sm* motor vehicle.

autovettura *sf* motorcar.

autunno *sm* autumn *(Br)*, fall *(Am)*.

avambraccio *sm* forearm.

avanguardia *sf*: **d'~** avant-garde; **essere all'~** to be in the vanguard.

avanti *avv (stato in luogo)* in front; *(moto)* forward ◆ *prep*: **~ a** *(stato in luogo)* ahead of; *(moto)*

ahead of, in front of; **~!** *(invito a entrare)* come in!; *(esortazione)* come on!; **'avanti!'** *(al semaforo)* 'cross now', 'walk' *(Am)*; *(in banca)* 'enter'; **~ e indietro** backwards and forwards; **andare ~** to go on; **essere ~** *(nel lavoro, studio)* to be well ahead; **essere ~ negli anni** to be getting on (in years); **farsi ~** to come forward; **passare ~ a qn** to go in front of sb.

avanzare *vt (spostare avanti)* to move forward; *(proposta)* to put forward ◆ *vi (procedere)* to advance; *(restare)* to be left (over).

avanzo *sm (di cibo)* leftovers *(pl)*; *(di stoffa)* remnant.

avaria *sf (meccanico)* breakdown.

avariato, -a *agg (cibo)* off.

avaro, -a *agg* mean ◆ *sm, f* miser.

avena *sf* oats *(pl)*.

avere *vt* 1. *(possedere)* to have; **ha due fratelli** he's got two brothers; **non ho più soldi** I haven't got any money left.

2. *(come caratteristica)* to have; **~ occhi e capelli scuri** to have dark eyes and hair; **~ molta immaginazione** to have a lot of imagination.

3. *(età)*: **quanti anni hai?** how old are you?; **ho 18 anni** I'm 18 (years old).

4. *(portare addosso)* to have on, to wear; **ha un cappotto grigio** she's wearing a grey coat, she's got a grey coat on.

5. *(sentire)*: **~ caldo/freddo** to be hot/cold; **~ sonno** to be sleepy; **~ fame** to be hungry; **ho mal di testa** I've got a headache.

6. *(ottenere, ricevere)* to get.

7. *(in espressioni)*: **non ha niente a che fare** o **vedere con lui** that's got nothing to do with him; **non ne ho per molto** it won't take me long; ~ **da fare** to have things to do; **avercela con qn** to be angry with sb; **quanti ne abbiamo oggi?** what's the date today?

♦ *v aus* to have; **non ho finito** I haven't finished; **gli ho parlato ieri** I spoke to him yesterday.

❏ **averi** *smpl (beni)* wealth *(sg)*.

avi *smpl* ancestors.

aviazione *sf* aviation.

avido, -a *agg* greedy.

AVIS *sf (abbr di Associazione Volontari Italiani del Sangue)* blood donors' association.

avocado *sm inv* avocado.

avorio *sm* ivory.

avvallamento *sm* depression.

avvantaggiare *vt* to favour ❏ **avvantaggiarsi** *vr*: **avvantaggiarsi negli studi** to get ahead with one's studies; **avvantaggiarsi sui concorrenti** to get ahead of one's competitors; **avvantaggiarsi di** *vr* + *prep* to take advantage of.

avvelenamento *sm* poisoning.

avvelenare *vt* to poison; *(aria)* to pollute.

avvenente *agg* attractive.

avvenimento *sm* event.

avvenire *sm* future ♦ *vi* to happen.

avventarsi *vr*: ~ **su** o **contro** to rush at.

avventato, -a *agg* rash.

avventura *sf* adventure; *(amorosa)* affair.

avventurarsi *vr* to venture.

avventuroso, -a *agg* adventurous.

avvenuto, -a *pp* → **avvenire**.

avverarsi *vr* to come true.

avverbio *sm* adverb.

avversario, -a *agg* opposing ♦ *sm, f* opponent.

avvertenza *sf (avviso)* notice ❏ **avvertenze** *sfpl* instructions.

avvertimento *sm* warning.

avvertire *vt (avvisare)* to warn; *(dolore, fastidio)* to feel.

avviamento *sm (di motore)* starting; *(COMM)* goodwill.

avviare *vt (cominciare)* to start; *(indirizzare)* to introduce ❏ **avviarsi** *vr* to set off.

avvicinare *vt* to move closer ❏ **avvicinarsi** *vr*: **avvicinarsi (a)** to move close to (to).

avvilirsi *vr* to lose heart.

avvincente *agg* enthralling.

avvisare *vt (informare)* to inform; *(ammonire)* to warn.

avviso *sm (scritto)* notice; *(annuncio)* announcement; *(avvertimento)* warning; **a mio** ~ in my opinion.

avvistare *vt* to sight.

avvitare *vt (lampadina)* to screw in; *(con viti)* to screw.

avvizzire *vi* to wither.

avvocato *sm* lawyer.

avvolgere *vt (fascia)* to wrap round; *(tappeto)* to roll up; *(avviluppare)* to wrap up ❏ **avvolgersi** *vr (aggrovigliarsi)* to become tangled; *(avvilupparsi)* to wrap o.s. up.

avvolgibile *sm* roller blind.

avvolto, -a *pp* → **avvolgere**.

avvoltoio *sm* vulture.

azalea *sf* azalea.

azienda *sf* business, firm; ~ **agricola** farm.

azionare *vt* to operate.

azione *sf* action; *(COMM)* share.

azionista, -i, -e *smf* share-holder.

azoto *sm* nitrogen.

azzannare *vt* to sink one's teeth into.

azzardare *vt* to venture □ **azzardarsi** *vr*: **azzardarsi a fare qc** to dare to do sthg.

azzardo *sm* risk; **giocare d'~** to gamble.

azzeccare *vt* to get right.

azzuffarsi *vr* to scuffle.

azzurro, -a *agg & sm* blue □ **Azzurri** *smpl*: **gli Azzurri** the Italian national team.

babà *sm inv* rum baba.

babbo *sm (fam)* dad, daddy; **Babbo Natale** Father Christmas.

baby-sitter [bebi'sitter] *smf inv* babysitter.

bacca, -che *sf (frutto)* berry.

baccalà *sm inv* dried salt cod; ~ **alla fiorentina** dried salt cod cooked with garlic and tomato sauce; ~ **alla vicentina** dried salt cod poached in milk with onions, anchovies and parsley.

bacheca, -che *sf (pannello)* notice board; *(cassetta)* display case.

baciare *vt* to kiss □ **baciarsi** *vr* to kiss (each other).

bacinella *sf* bowl.

bacino *sm (in geografia, catino)* basin; *(ANAT)* pelvis.

bacio *sm* kiss; **baci di dama** *sweet pastries sandwiched together with chocolate cream.*

badare *vi*: ~ **a** *(prendersi cura di)* to look after; *(fare attenzione a)* to pay attention to; ~ **a o di fare qc** to take care to do sthg; **mio fratello non bada a spese** money's no object where my brother's concerned.

badia *sf* abbey.

baffi *smpl* moustache *(sg)*.

bagagliaio *sm (di macchina)* boot *(Br)*, trunk *(Am)*; *(di treno)* luggage van *(Br)*, baggage car *(Am)*.

bagaglio *sm* luggage, baggage; ~ **a mano** hand luggage; **ho un solo** ~ I have only one piece of luggage □ **bagagli** *smpl* luggage *(sg)*; **fare i bagagli** to pack.

bagliore *sm (di lampi)* flash; *(di fari)* glare.

bagna cauda *sf* oil, garlic and anchovy dip from Piedmont kept warm at the table and served with vegetables.

bagnare *vt* to wet; *(tovaglia, vestiti)* to get wet; *(annaffiare)* to water; *(sog: fiume)* to flow through; *(sog: mare)* to wash □ **bagnarsi** *vr* *(in mare)* to bathe; *(di pioggia,* *spruzzi*) to get wet.

bagnato, -a *agg* wet; **~ fradicio** soaked through.

bagnino, -a *sm, f* lifeguard.

bagno *sm (nella vasca)* bath; *(in piscina, mare)* swim; *(stanza)* bathroom; **fare il ~** *(nella vasca)* to have a bath; *(in mare)* to have a swim; **~ pubblico** public baths *(pl)* □ **bagni** *smpl (stabilimento)* bathing establishment.

bagnomaria *sm*: **cuocere a ~** to cook in a double saucepan.

bagnoschiuma *sm inv* bath foam.

baia *sf* bay.

baita *sf* chalet.

balaustra *sf* balustrade.

balbettare *vi* to stammer.

balcone *sm* balcony.

balena *sf* whale.

balla *sf (frottola)* fib; *(di merci)* bale.

ballare *vi & vt* to dance.

ballerina *sf (scarpa)* pump, → **ballerino**.

ballerino, -a *sm, f* dancer; *(classico)* ballet-dancer *(f* **ballerina**).

balletto *sm* ballet.

ballo *sm* dance; *(festa)* dance, ball; **essere in ~** to be at stake; **tirare in ~** *(coinvolgere)* to involve; *(menzionare)* to mention.

balneare *agg* bathing *(dav s)*.

balneazione *sf* bathing; **'divieto di balneazione'** 'no bathing'.

balsamo *sm (per capelli)* conditioner; *(pomata)* ointment.

Baltico *sm*: **il (Mar) ~** the Baltic

(Sea).

balzare *vi* to leap.

bambinaia *sf* nanny.

bambino, -a *sm, f* child; *(neonato)* baby.

bambola *sf* doll.

banale *agg* banal.

banana *sf* banana.

banca, -che *sf* bank; **~ dati** data bank.

bancarella *sf* stall.

bancario, -a *agg* bank *(dav s)* ♦ *sm, f* bank employee.

bancarotta *sf* bankruptcy.

banchina *sf (di porto)* quay; *(di stazione)* platform; **'~ non transitabile'** 'soft verges'.

banco, -chi *sm (di scuola)* desk; *(di negozio, bar)* counter; *(di mercato)* stall; *(banca)* bank; **~ di corallo** coral reef; **~ di nebbia** fog bank.

bancomat® *sm inv (sportello)* cash dispenser; *(tessera)* cash card; *(sistema)* automated banking.

bancone *sm* counter.

banconota *sf* bank note.

banda *sf (musicale)* band; *(striscia)* band, strip; *(di malviventi)* gang; *(di amici)* group.

bandiera *sf* flag.

bandito *sm* bandit.

bando *sm* announcement; **~ alle chiacchiere!** that's enough talking!

bar *sm inv* bar; **~-tabacchi** bar that also sells cigarettes and stamps.

 BAR

Italian bars are open throughout the day. You can have a coffee and a pastry for breakfast, a mid-morning snack, an aperitif or a toasted sandwich. You can eat standing at the counter, which is cheaper, but many bars also offer table service. Look out for the sign "munirsi dello scontrino", as this means you have to pay at the cash desk before being served at the counter.

bara sf coffin.

baracca, -che sf hut; (spreg: casa) dump; **mandare avanti la ~** (fam) to keep things going.

baraccone sm booth.

baratro sm barter.

barattolo sm jar; (di latta) can.

barba sf beard; **farsi la ~** to shave; **che ~!** what a bore!

barbaro, -a agg barbaric ♦ sm, f barbarian.

barbecue ['ba:bikju:] sm inv barbecue.

barbiere sm barber.

barbone, -a sm, f tramp.

barca, -che sf boat; **~ a remi** rowing boat (Br), rowboat (Am); **~ a vela** sailing boat (Br), sailboat (Am).

barcollare vi to stagger.

barella sf stretcher.

barista, -i, -e smf barman (f barmaid).

barman sm inv barman.

Barolo sm Barolo (full-bodied red wine from Piedmont).

barra sf rod, bar; (lineetta) stroke; (di barca) tiller.

barricare vt to barricade □ **barricarsi** vr: **barricarsi in/dietro** to barricade o.s. in/behind.

barriera sf barrier.

basare vt to base □ **basarsi su** vr + prep (persona) to base o.s. on.

base sf base; (fondamento) basis; a **~ di whisky** whisky-based; in **~ a qc** on the basis of sthg.

baseball ['beizbol] sm baseball.

basette sfpl sideboards.

basilica, -che sf basilica.

basilico sm basil.

basso, -a agg low; (persona) short; (acqua) shallow ♦ sm (fondo) bottom; (strumento, cantante) bass; in **~** at the bottom.

basta esclam that's enough!

bastare vi & v impers to be enough; **~ a qn** to be enough for sb; **basta che** so long as; **basta così!** that's enough!

bastone sm stick; **~ da passeggio** walking stick.

battaglia sf battle.

battello sm boat.

battere vt to beat; (testa) to hit; (ore) to strike; (zona) to scour ♦ vi (cuore) to beat; (sole, pioggia) to beat down; (urtare): **~ contro o in qc** to hit sthg; **si batteva i denti dal freddo** our teeth were chattering with the cold; **~ a macchina** to type; **~ le mani** to clap; **in un batter d'occhio** in the twinkling of an eye □ **battersi** vr to fight.

batteria sf (elettrica) battery; (strumento) drums (pl).

battesimo sm baptism.

battezzare vt to baptize.

battigia sf water's edge.

battistrada sm inv tread.

battito *sm* beat, beating; *(di orologio)* ticking; **~ cardiaco** heartbeat.

battuta *sf (spiritosaggine)* witty remark; *(teatrale)* cue; *(di tennis)* service.

baule *sm (da viaggio)* trunk; *(di auto)* boot *(Br)*, trunk *(Am)*.

bavaglino *sm* bib.

bavaglio *sm* gag.

bavarese *sf (dolce)* cold dessert made with eggs, milk and cream.

bavero *sm* collar.

bazzecola *sf (cosa poco importante)* trifle; *(cosa facile)*: **è una ~** it's no problem.

beato, -a *agg (felice)* happy; *(RELIG)* blessed; **~ te!** lucky you!

beauty-case [ˈbjuːti ˈkeɪs] *sm inv* beauty case.

beccare *vt* to peck; *(fam: sorprendere)* to catch; **beccarsi qc** *(fam) (raffreddore)* to catch sthg; *(ceffone)* to get sthg.

becco, -chi *sm* beak.

Befana *sf (festa)* Epiphany; *(personaggio)* legendary old woman who brings children their presents at the Epiphany.

BEFANA

According to legend, the "Befana" is a kindly old hag who delivers presents to children on the night before the Epiphany. Children leave out a stocking before going to bed, and the "Befana" comes down the chimney in the night, bringing sweets and other gifts to good boys and girls and lumps of coal to those who have been naughty.

beffa *sf* joke.

beffarsi : beffarsi di *vr + prep* to make fun of.

begli → **bello**.

bei → **bello**.

beige [bɛʒ] *agg inv & sm inv* beige.

bel → **bello**.

belga, -gi, -ghe *agg & smf* Belgian.

Belgio *sm*: **il ~** Belgium.

bella *sf (SPORT)* decider.

bellezza *sf* beauty; **che ~!** fantastic!

bello, -a *(dav sm* **bel** *(pl* **bei***) + consonante;* **bello** *(pl* **begli***) + s+consonante, gn, ps, z;* **bell'** *(pl* **begli***) + vocale) agg* 1. *(donna, cosa)* beautiful; *(uomo)* handsome; **farsi ~** to make o.s. beautiful; **le belle arti** fine arts.

2. *(piacevole)* pleasant, lovely.

3. *(tempo)* fine, beautiful; **la bella stagione** the summer months *(pl)*; **fa ~** it's lovely weather.

4. *(buono)* good.

5. *(lodevole)* good, kind.

6. *(grande)*: **un bel piatto di spaghetti** a nice big plate of spaghetti; **una bella dormita** a good sleep; **è una bella cifra** it's a considerable sum of money.

7. *(rafforzativo)*: **è bell'e (che) anda**to he's already gone; **è una bugia bell'e buona** it's an absolute lie; **alla bell'e meglio** somehow or other; **un bel niente** absolutely nothing.

◆ *sm* 1. *(bellezza)* beauty.

2. (punto culminante): **sul più ~** at that very moment; **il ~ è che ...** the best bit is that ...

belva sf wild beast.

belvedere sm inv scenic viewpoint.

benché cong although, though.

benda sf (fasciatura) bandage; (per occhi) blindfold.

bendare vt (ferita) to bandage; (occhi) to blindfold.

bene avv (compar & superl **meglio**)
1. (in modo soddisfacente) well; **avete mangiato ~?** did you enjoy your meal?
2. (nel modo giusto) well; **hai fatto ~** you did the right thing.
3. (in buona salute): **stare/sentirsi ~** to be/feel well.
4. (a proprio agio): **stare ~** to be o feel comfortable.
5. (esteticamente): **stare ~** to look good.
6. (rafforzativo): **è ben difficile** it's very difficult; **è ben più difficile del previsto** it's much more difficult than we thought; **lo credo** I can well believe it; **spero ~ che** I very much hope that.
7. (in espressioni): **è ~ che lo sappiate** it's as well that you know; **sarebbe ~ aspettare** it would be better to wait; **dire ~ di qn** to speak well of sb; **ti sta ~!** it serves you right!; **va ~** all right, OK.
◆ esclam **fine!, OK!**
◆ sm good; **è per il tuo ~** it's for your own good; **è un ~ per tutti** it is a good thing for everyone.
❑ **beni** smpl (proprietà) property (sg).

benedire vt to bless.

benedizione sf blessing.

beneducato, -a agg well-mannered.

beneficenza sf charity.

benessere sm wellbeing.

benestante agg well-to-do.

benevolo, -a agg benevolent.

beninteso avv certainly, of course.

benvenuto, -a agg & sm welcome; **benvenuti a Roma!** welcome to Rome!; **dare il ~ a qn** to welcome sb.

benzina sf petrol (Br), gas (Am); **fare ~** to get petrol (Br), to get gas (Am).

benzinaio, -a sm, f forecourt attendant.

bere vt to drink; **bevi qualcosa?** would you like something to drink?; **offrire da ~ a qn** to offer sb a drink.

bermuda smpl bermuda shorts.

bernoccolo sm bump.

bersaglio sm target.

besciamella sf béchamel sauce.

bestemmiare vi to curse, to swear.

bestia sf animal; **andare in ~** to fly into a rage.

bestiame sm livestock.

bevanda sf drink.

bevuto, -a pp → **bere**.

biancheria sf linen; **~ intima** underwear.

bianchetto sm correcting fluid.

bianco, -a, -chi, -che agg & sm white ◆ sm, f (persona) white man (*f* white woman); **riso in** ~ plain rice; **pesce in** ~ boiled fish; **in** ~ **e nero** black and white.

biasimare *vt* to blame.

bibbia *sf* bible.

biberon *sm inv* baby's bottle.

bibita *sf* drink.

biblioteca, -che *sf* library.

bicarbonato *sm*: ~ **(di sodio)** bicarbonate (of soda).

bicchiere *sm* glass.

bici *sf inv* (*fam*) bike.

bicicletta *sf* bicycle; **andare in** ~ to cycle.

bidè *sm inv* bidet.

bidone *sm* bin; (*fam*) (*imbroglio*) swindle; **fare un** ~ **a qn** (*fam*) (*imbrogliare*) to cheat sb; (*mancare a un appuntamento*) to stand sb up.

biennale *agg* (*ogni due anni*) two-yearly; (*per due anni*) two-year (*dav s*) □ **Biennale** *sf*: **la Biennale** the Venice Arts Festival.

 BIENNALE

Established in 1895, this international art festival takes place every two years in the gardens of the International Gallery of Modern Art in Venice. The selection of paintings and sculptures on view reflects the avant-garde emphasis of the festival, a trend which has become more pronounced in recent years and is not without its critics. Alongside the art festival there are festivals of music, theatre and architecture, as well as an annual film festival.

biforcarsi *vr* to fork.

BIGE *sm* reduced-price train ticket for people under 26.

bigiotteria *sf* costume jewellery; (*negozio*) costume jeweller's.

biglia = bilia.

bigliardo = biliardo.

bigliettaio, -a *sm, f* ticket inspector.

biglietteria *sf* ticket office; (*al teatro*) box office; ~ **automatica** ticket machine.

biglietto *sm* (*scontrino*) ticket; (*messaggio*) note; (*banconota*) (bank) note; **fare il** ~ to buy one's ticket; ~ **d'andata e ritorno** return (ticket); ~ **di (sola) andata** single (ticket); ~ **collettivo** party ticket; ~ **cumulativo** group ticket; ~ **gratuito** complimentary ticket; ~ **intero** full-price ticket; ~ **ridotto** reduced-price ticket; ~ **d'auguri** greetings card; ~ **da visita** visiting card.

bignè *sm inv* choux bun filled with custard or chocolate.

bigodino *sm* curler.

bigoli *smpl*: ~ **coi rovinazzi** large spaghetti from Veneto in a sauce made with chicken giblets.

bikini® *sm inv* bikini.

bilancia, -ce *sf* scales (*pl*) □ **Bilancia** *sf* Libra.

bilancio *sm* (COMM) balance sheet; ~ **preventivo** budget.

bilia *sf* (*di vetro*) marble; (*da biliardo*) billiard ball.

biliardo *sm* (*gioco*) billiards (*sg*); (*tavolo*) billiard table.

bilico : **in bilico** *avv* balanced.

bilingue *agg* bilingual.

bimbo, -a *sm, f* little boy (*f* little girl).

binario *sm* (*rotaie*) railway track; (*marciapiede*) platform; '**ai binari**' 'to the trains'.

binocolo *sm* binoculars (*pl*).

biologia *sf* biology.

biondo, -a *agg* blond (*f* blonde).

birichino, -a *agg* cheeky ♦ *sm, f* little rascal.

birillo *sm* skittle.

biro® *sf inv* Biro®.

birra *sf* beer; ~ **chiara** lager; ~ **scura** stout; ~ **alla spina** draught beer.

birreria *sf* pub.

bis *esclam* encore!

bisbigliare *vi & vt* to whisper.

biscotto *sm* biscuit.

bisessuale *agg* bisexual.

bisestile *agg* → **anno**.

bisnonno, -a *sm, f* great-grandfather (*f* great-grandmother).

bisognare *v impers*: **bisogna stare attenti** we/I must be careful; **bisogna che tu venga subito** you have to come at once.

bisogno *sm* need, necessity; **aver ~ di** to need.

bistecca, -che *sf* steak; ~ **al sangue** rare steak; ~ **alla fiorentina** *T-bone steak grilled or cooked over charcoal*.

bisticciare *vi* to bicker.

bitter *sm inv* bitters (*pl*).

bivio *sm* fork, junction.

bizza *sf* tantrum.

bizzarro, -a *agg* odd, ec-

centric.

bloccare *vt* to block; (*città*) to cut off; (*meccanismo*) to jam; (*prezzi*) to freeze ❑ **bloccarsi** *vr* (*ascensore*) to get stuck; (*porta*) to jam.

blocchetto *sm* (*quaderno*) notebook.

blocco, -chi *sm* block; (*quaderno*) notebook; (*di meccanismo*) blockage; (*di attività*) stoppage; ~ **stradale** roadblock; **in ~** en bloc.

blu *agg inv & sm inv* blue.

blue-jeans [blu'dʒins] *smpl* jeans.

blusa *sf* blouse.

boa *sm inv* (*serpente*) boa ♦ *sf* (*galleggiante*) buoy.

bobina *sf* (*di auto*) coil; (*di pellicola*) reel.

bocca, -che *sf* mouth; **in ~ al lupo!** good luck!

boccaccia, -ce *sf*: **fare le boccacce** to pull faces.

boccale *sm* jug.

boccia, -ce *sf* bowl.

bocciare *vt* (*studente*) to fail; (*proposta, progetto*) to reject.

boccone *sm* mouthful; **mangiare un ~** to have a bite to eat.

bocconi *avv* face downwards.

boicottare *vt* to boycott.

bolla *sf* bubble; (*vescica*) blister; (*COMM*) bill.

bollente *agg* boiling.

bolletta *sf* bill; (*ricevuta*) receipt.

bollettino *sm* bulletin; ~ **meteorologico** weather forecast.

bollire *vt & vi* to boil.

bollito, -a *agg* boiled ◆ *sm* beef, veal or chicken, served with a parsley sauce.

bollitore *sm* kettle.

bollo *sm (marchio)* stamp.

Bologna *sf* Bologna.

bolognese *agg* of/from Bologna; **alla ~** with meat and tomato sauce.

bomba *sf* bomb.

bombardare *vt* to bomb.

bombola *sf* cylinder.

bombolone *sm* doughnut.

bonaccia *sf* (dead) calm.

bonario, -a *agg* good-natured.

bonet *sm inv* chocolate-flavoured egg custard.

bontà *sf* goodness.

borbottare *vi* to grumble ◆ *vt* to mutter.

bordeaux [bor'do] *agg inv* maroon.

bordo *sm (orlo)* edge; *(guarnizione)* trim, border; *(di nave)* (ship's) side; **a ~ di** *(nave, aereo)* on board; *(auto)* in; *(moto)* on.

borghese *agg* middle-class; **in ~** in plain clothes.

borghesia *sf* middle classes *(pl)*.

borgo, -ghi *sm (paesino)* hamlet; *(quartiere)* district.

borotalco® *sm* talcum powder.

borraccia, -ce *sf* flask.

borsa *sf* bag; **~ dell'acqua calda** hot-water bottle; **~ del ghiaccio** ice bag; **~ della spesa** shopping bag; **~ di studio** grant □ **Borsa** *sf* Stock Exchange.

borsaiolo *sm* pickpocket.

borsellino *sm* purse.

borsetta *sf* handbag.

bosco, -schi *sm* wood.

botanico, -a, -ci, -che *agg* botanic ◆ *sm, f* botanist.

botta *sf* blow; *(rumore)* bang; **fare a botte** to come to blows.

botte *sf* barrel.

bottega, -ghe *sf* shop; *(laboratorio)* workshop.

bottegaio, -a *sm, f* shopkeeper.

bottiglia *sf* bottle.

bottiglione *sm* large bottle.

bottone *sm* button; **attaccare un ~ a qn** to buttonhole sb.

boutique [bu'tik] *sf inv* boutique.

box *sm inv (garage)* lock-up (garage); *(per bambini)* playpen; *(per animali)* pen.

boxe [bɔks] *sf* boxing.

boy-scout [bɔi'skaut] *sm inv* boy scout.

braccetto : **a braccetto** *avv* arm in arm.

bracciale *sm* bracelet.

braccialetto *sm* bracelet.

braccio *sm (arto: pl f* **braccia**) arm; *(di edificio: pl m* **bracci**) wing; *(di gru, fiume: pl m* **bracci**) arm; **~ di ferro** arm wrestling; **sotto ~** arm in arm.

bracciolo *sm* arm.

brace *sf* embers *(pl)*; **alla ~** charcoal-grilled.

braciola *sf* steak; *(con osso)* chop.

braille ['braj] *sm* braille.

branco, -chi *sm (di animali)* herd; *(spreg: di persone)* gang, bunch.

branda *sf* camp bed.

brasato *sm* braised beef.

Brasile *sm:* il ~ Brazil.

bravo, -a *agg* good; ~! well done!; ~ a fare qc good at doing sthg; ~ in qc good at sthg.

bresaola *sf* dried salt beef served thinly sliced.

bretelle *sfpl (per pantaloni)* braces; *(spalline)* straps.

breve *agg* short, brief; in ~ briefly; tra ~ shortly.

brevetto *sm (di invenzione)* patent; *(patente)* licence.

brezza *sf* breeze.

bricco, -chi *sm* jug.

briciola *sf* crumb.

briciolo *sm:* un ~ di qc a bit of sthg.

brillante *agg* brilliant; *(lucente)* bright ♦ *sm* diamond.

brillare *vi* to shine.

brillo, -a *agg* tipsy.

brindisi *sm inv* toast; fare un ~ a to toast.

brioche [bri'ɔʃ] *sf inv* round, sweet bread roll made with butter and eaten for breakfast.

britannico, -a, -ci, -che *agg* British.

brivido *sm* shiver, shudder.

brocca, -che *sf* jug.

brodo *sm* broth; pasta in ~ noodle soup; riso in ~ rice soup.

bronchite *sf* bronchitis.

brontolare *vi* to grumble; *(stomaco, tuono)* to rumble.

bronzo *sm* bronze.

bruciapelo : a bruciapelo *avv* point-blank.

bruciare *vt* to burn; *(distruggere)* to burn down ♦ *vi* to burn; *(produrre bruciore)* to sting ▫ **bruciarsi** *vr (persona)* to burn o.s.; *(oggetto)* to burn.

bruciato, -a *agg* burnt.

bruciatura *sf* burn.

bruno, -a *agg* dark.

bruschetta *sf* bread toasted with garlic and olive oil.

brusio *sm* buzz.

brutale *agg* brutal.

brutto, -a *agg (di aspetto)* ugly; *(tempo, giornata, strada)* bad; *(situazione, sorpresa, malattia)* nasty; *(rafforzativo)*: ~ imbroglione! you rotten cheat!; brutti ma buoni almond and hazelnut meringues.

Bruxelles [bru'ksɛl] *sf* Brussels.

buca, -che *sf* hole; ~ delle lettere letterbox.

bucare *vt* to make a hole o holes in; ~ una gomma to puncture a tyre ▫ **bucarsi** *vr (forarsi)* to have a puncture; *(pungersi)* to prick o.s.; *(fam: drogarsi)* to mainline.

bucatini *smpl:* ~ all'amatriciana dish from Lazio consisting of long, thin pasta tubes in a sauce of tomatoes, bacon, chillies and pecorino cheese.

bucato *sm* washing.

buccellato *sm* light, ring-shaped sponge cake from Sarzana and Lucca.

buccia, -ce *sf* skin.

buco, -chi *sm* hole.

budino *sm* type of egg custard

baked in a mould; ~ **di riso** egg custard made with rice, sultanas and sometimes rum.

bufera sf storm.

buffet [byˈfɛ] sm inv buffet.

buffo, -a agg funny.

bugia sf lie; (candeliere) candleholder.

bugiardo, -a agg lying ♦ sm, f liar.

buio, -a agg dark ♦ sm darkness; **far ~** to get dark.

Bulgaria sf: **la ~** Bulgaria.

bulgaro, -a agg Bulgarian.

bullone sm bolt.

buonanotte esclam good night!

buonasera esclam good evening!

buongiorno esclam (in mattinata) good morning!; (nel pomeriggio) good afternoon!

buongustaio, -a sm, f gourmet.

buono, -a agg (dav sm **buon** + consonante o vocale; **buono** + s + consonante, gn, ps, z) **1.** (di qualità) good.

2. (gradevole) good.

3. (generoso): ~ **(con)** good (to), kind (to).

4. (bravo, efficiente) good; **non essere ~ a nulla** to be no good at anything; **è ~ solo a criticare** all he can do is criticize.

5. (valido: biglietto, passaporto) valid.

6. (temperamento) good; **avere un buon carattere** to be good-natured; **essere di buon umore** to be in a good mood.

7. (occasione, momento) right.

8. (negli auguri): **buon appetito!** enjoy your meal!; **buon compleanno!** Happy Birthday!; **buona fortuna!** good luck!; **fate buon viaggio!** have a good journey!

9. (rafforzativo): **ci vuole un'ora buona** it takes a good hour.

10. (in espressioni): ~ **a sapersi** that's nice to know; **a buon mercato** cheap; **di buon'ora** early; **alla buona** (cena) simple; (vestirsi) simply; **farai i compiti, con le buone o con le cattive** like it or not, you'll do your homework.

♦ sm **1.** (aspetto positivo) good; **il ~ è che ...** the good thing is that ...

2. (tagliando) voucher; (invece di rimborso) credit note; ~ **sconto** voucher; ~ **del tesoro** treasury bill.

buonsenso sm common sense.

buonumore sm good humour.

burattino sm puppet.

burla sf prank, trick.

burocrazia sf bureaucracy.

burrasca, -sche sf storm.

burrida sf Sardinian dish made from dogfish cooked with garlic, vinegar, pine kernels and walnuts and served cold.

burro sm butter; ~ **di cacao** cocoa butter.

burrone sm ravine.

bus [bʌs] sm inv (abbr di autobus) bus.

bussare vi to knock.

bussola sf compass.

busta sf (per lettera) envelope; (di plastica, carta) bag; ~ **paga** pay packet.

busto sm bust; (indumento) corset.

butano sm butane.

buttafuori *sm inv* bouncer.

buttare *vt (gettare)* to throw; ~ **all'aria** qc to turn sthg upside down; ~ **fuori** qn to throw sb out; ~ **giù** *(abbattere)* to knock down; *(inghiottire)* to gulp down; ~ **(via)** *(gettare)* to throw away; *(sprecare)* to waste ❑ **buttarsi** *vr (gettarsi)* to jump; *(fig: tentare)* to have a go.

by-pass [bai'pas] *sm inv* bypass.

C

cabina *sf (di nave)* cabin; *(in spiaggia)* beach hut; *(in piscina)* cubicle; *(di camion)* cab; ~ **telefonica** telephone box.

cacao *sm* cocoa.

cacca *sf (fam)* poo.

caccia, -ce *sf (di animali)* hunting; *(inseguimento)* chase; ~ **al tesoro** treasure hunt.

cacciare *vt (animale)* to hunt; *(mandar via)* to get rid of; ~ **fuori** qc to throw sb out ❑ **cacciarsi** *vr*: **dove si sarà cacciato?** where has he got to?; **cacciarsi nei guai** to get into trouble.

cacciatora *sf → pollo.*

cacciavite *sm inv* screwdriver.

cacciucco, -chi *sm fish soup from Livorno, served with toast rubbed with garlic.*

cachemire ['kaʃmir] *sm* cashmere.

caciocavallo *sm hard pear-shaped cheese from southern Italy.*

cadavere *sm* corpse, dead body.

cadere *vi* to fall; *(capelli)* to fall out; *(abito)* to hang; **far** ~ to knock over.

caduta *sf* fall; **la** ~ **dei capelli** hair loss; **'~ massi'** 'beware falling rocks'.

caffè *sm inv* coffee; *(locale)* cafe; **prendere un** ~ to have a coffee; ~ **corretto** coffee with a dash of spirits; ~ **macchiato** coffee with a dash of milk.

 CAFFÈ

Drunk at any time of day, "caffè" (coffee) or "espresso", served in the traditional "tazzina" (little cup), is the typical Italian drink. In bars and restaurants, you can choose from a number of different versions: "normale" (normal), "ristretto" (concentrated), "lungo" (more diluted), "macchiato caldo" or "macchiato freddo" (with a drop of hot or cold milk), or "corretto" (with a drop of your chosen spirit). If you prefer coffee without caffeine, you can order a "hag®", a "decaffeinato" or, a recent addition, "caffè d'orzo" (made with barley).

caffeina *sf* caffeine.

caffellatte *sm inv* hot milk with coffee.

caffettiera *sf* coffeepot.

cagna *sf* bitch.

CAI *(abbr di Club Alpino Italiano)* Italian mountaineering association.

cala *sf* bay.

calabrone sm hornet.

calamaretti smpl squid (sg).

calamaro sm squid; **calamari ripieni** squid stuffed with anchovies, capers, breadcrumbs and parsley, and cooked in white wine.

calamita sf magnet.

calare vt to lower ◆ vi (prezzo, peso) to go down; (vento) to drop; (sole) to set.

calca, -che sf throng.

calcagno sm heel.

calce sf lime.

calciatore, -trice sm, f footballer.

calcio sm (pedata) kick; (sport) football (Br), soccer; (elemento chimico) calcium; (di arma) butt; **dare un ~ a** to kick; **prendere a calci** to kick.

calcolare vt to calculate; (prevedere) to reckon on, to take into account.

calcolatrice sf calculator.

calcolo sm (conteggio) calculation; (MED) stone; **fare i calcoli** to do one's calculations; **è andato tutto secondo i calcoli** everything went according to plan.

caldaia sf boiler.

caldo, -a agg warm; (a temperatura elevata) hot ◆ sm (calore) heat; **avere ~** to be hot; **è o fa ~** it's hot.

calendario sm calendar.

calma sf calm ◆ esclam calm down!

calmante sm tranquillizer.

calmare vt to calm; (dolore) to soothe ❑ **calmarsi** vr (persona) to

calm down; (mare) to become calm; (vento) to drop.

calmo, -a agg (tranquillo) peaceful, calm; (mare) calm.

calore sm warmth.

caloria sf (di cibo) calorie.

calorifero sm radiator.

caloroso, -a agg warm.

calpestare vt to tread on.

calunnia sf slander.

calvizie sf baldness.

calvo, -a agg bald.

calza sf (da donna) stocking; (da uomo) sock; **fare la ~** to knit.

calzagatto sm dish from Emilia Romagna consisting of polenta with beans, onions and bacon.

calzamaglia (pl **calzamaglie**) sf tights (pl) (Br), panty hose (pl) (Am).

calzante sm shoehorn.

calzare vt to put on ◆ vi to fit.

calzature sfpl footwear (sg).

calzettone sm knee(-length) sock.

calzino sm (short) sock.

calzolaio sm (riparatore) cobbler; (fabbricante) shoemaker.

calzoleria sf shoe shop.

calzoncini smpl shorts.

calzone sm (cibo) pasty made from pizza dough stuffed with cheese, tomato, ham and egg ❑ **calzoni** smpl trousers.

camaleonte sm chameleon.

cambiale sf bill.

cambiamento sm change.

cambiare vt & vi to change; ~ **le lire in sterline** to change lire into sterling; ~ **un biglietto da centomi-**

la to change a hundred thousand lire note ❏ **cambiarsi** *vr* to change (one's clothes).

cambio *sm (sostituzione)* change; *(di denaro)* exchange; *(di automobile)* gears *(pl)*; **dare il ~ a qn** to take over from sb; **fare a ~ (con qn)** to swap (with sb); **in ~ di qc** in exchange for sthg; **~ automatico** automatic gearbox.

camera *sf* room; **~ (da letto)** bedroom; **~ d'aria** inner tube; **~ con bagno** room with a bath; **~ blindata** vault; **Camera di Commercio** Chamber of Commerce; **Camera dei Deputati** = House of Commons *(Br)*, = House of Representatives *(Am)*; **~ con doccia** room with a shower; **~ doppia** double room; **~ a due letti** twin-bedded room; **~ matrimoniale** room with a double bed; **~ degli ospiti** guestroom, spare room; **~ singola** single room.

cameriere, -a *sm, f* waiter (*f* waitress).

camice *sm* white coat.

camicetta *sf* blouse.

camicia *sf (da uomo)* shirt; *(da donna)* blouse, shirt; **~ da notte** *(da donna)* nightdress; *(da uomo)* nightshirt.

caminetto *sm* fireplace, hearth.

camino *sm (focolare)* fireplace, hearth; *(comignolo)* chimney.

camion *sm inv* truck.

camioncino *sm* van.

cammello *sm* camel; *(tessuto)* camelhair.

cammeo *sm* cameo.

camminare *vi* to walk.

camminata *sf* walk.

cammino *sm* way; **mettersi in ~** to set off.

camomilla *sf* camomile.

camorra *sf* Camorra.

camoscio *sm* chamois; **giacca di ~ suede** jacket.

campagna *sf* country; *(propaganda, guerra)* campaign; **in ~** in the country; **andare in ~** to go to the country.

campana *sf* bell; **a ~** bell-shaped.

campanello *sm* bell; **suonare il ~** to ring the bell.

campanile *sm* bell-tower.

campare *vi* to get by.

campato, -a *agg:* **~ in aria** unfounded.

campeggiare *vi* to camp.

campeggiatore, -trice *sm, f* camper.

campeggio *sm (luogo)* campsite; *(attività)* camping.

camper *sm inv* camper van.

Campidoglio *sm:* **il ~** the Capitol.

camping *sm inv* campsite.

campionario *sm* (collection of) samples *(pl)*.

campionato *sm* championship.

campione, -essa *sm, f* champion ◆ *sm (esemplare)* sample.

campo *sm* field; *(accampamento)* camp; **~ da tennis** tennis court; **~ di golf** golf course; **~ profughi** refugee camp.

camposanto *(pl* campisanti)

sm cemetery.

Canada *sm*: il ~ Canada.

canadese *agg & smf* Canadian ♦ *sf (tenda)* ridge tent.

canaglia *sf* rogue.

canale *sm* channel; *(artificiale)* canal; ~ **navigabile** ship canal.

canapa *sf* hemp.

canarino *sm* canary.

canasta *sf* canasta.

cancellare *vt (con gomma)* to rub out; *(con penna)* to cross out; *(annullare)* to cancel.

cancelleria *sf (materiale)* stationery.

cancello *sm* gate.

cancerogeno, -a *agg* carcinogenic.

cancrena *sf (MED)* gangrene.

cancro *sm* cancer □ **Cancro** *sm* Cancer.

candeggina *sf* bleach.

candela *sf* candle; ~ **(di accensione)** spark plug.

candelabro *sm* candelabra.

candeliere *sm* candlestick.

candidato, -a *sm, f* candidate.

candido, -a *agg (bianco)* (pure) white; *(puro)* pure, innocent.

candito, -a *agg* candied ♦ *sm* candied fruit.

cane *sm* dog; ~ **da guardia** guard dog; ~ **guida** guide dog; ~ **lupo** Alsatian; ~ **poliziotto** police dog; **non c'era un** ~ there wasn't a soul there; **solo come un** ~ all alone; **tempo da cani** lousy weather; **una vita da cani** a dog's life; **'cani al guinzaglio'** 'dogs must be kept on a lead'.

canestro *sm* basket.

cangiante *agg* iridescent.

canguro *sm* kangaroo.

canicola *sf* heat.

canile *sm (cuccia)* kennel; *(allevamento)* kennels *(pl)*; ~ **municipale** dog pound.

canino *sm* canine.

canna *sf (pianta)* reed; *(di bicicletta)* crossbar; *(di fucile)* barrel; ~ **fumaria** chimney flue; ~ **da pesca** fishing rod; ~ **da zucchero** sugar cane.

cannariculi *smpl* thin curved *pastry covered in honey.*

cannella *sf (spezia)* cinnamon; *(rubinetto)* tap.

cannello *sm* blowlamp.

cannelloni *smpl* cannelloni *(sg).*

cannibale *smf* cannibal.

cannocchiale *sm* telescope.

cannolo *sm*: ~ **alla crema** *pastry tube filled with custard;* ~ **siciliano** *'cannolo' filled with sweetened ricotta cheese, candied fruit and chocolate.*

cannone *sm* gun.

cannuccia, -ce *sf* straw.

canoa *sf* canoe.

canone *sm (quota)* rent; *(regola)* rule.

canottaggio *sm* rowing.

canottiera *sf (biancheria)* vest *(Br),* undershirt *(Am); (per esterno)* sleeveless T-shirt.

canotto *sm* rubber dinghy; ~ **di salvataggio** lifeboat.

cantante *smf* singer.

cantare *vt & vi* to sing.

cantautore, -trice *sm, f* singer-songwriter.

cantiere sm (edile) building site; (navale) shipyard.

cantina sf (seminterrato) cellar; (per il vino) wine cellar; (negozio) wine shop.

canto sm (ARTE) singing; (canzone) song; (di uccello) chirping; d'altro ~ on the other hand.

cantonata sf: prendere una ~ to make a blunder.

cantone sm (in Svizzera) canton.

Canton Ticino sm: il ~ the canton of Ticino.

cantucci smpl wedge-shaped almond biscuits.

canzonare vt to tease.

canzone sf song.

caos sm chaos.

CAP abbr = **codice di avviamento postale**.

capace agg (esperto) able, capable; (ampio) capacious; essere ~ di fare qc to be able to do sthg; essere ~ di tutto to be capable of anything.

capacità sf inv (abilità) ability; (capienza) capacity.

capanna sf hut.

capannone sm (industriale) shed; (agricolo) barn.

caparbio, -a agg stubborn.

caparra sf deposit.

capello sm hair □ **capelli** smpl hair (sg); averne fin sopra i capelli to be fed up to the back teeth.

capezzolo sm nipple.

capillare sm capillary.

capire vt & vi to understand; non capisco I don't understand; scusi, non ho capito I'm sorry, I don't understand; si capisce! certainly! □ **capirsi** vr to understand each other.

capitale sf & sm capital ◆ agg (pena, peccato) capital; (fondamentale) fundamental.

capitaneria sf: ~ di porto port authorities (pl).

capitano sm captain.

capitare vi (accadere) to happen; (giungere) to turn up ◆ v impers to happen; ~ a qn to happen to sb; ~ a proposito to come at the right time.

capitello sm capital.

capitolino, -a agg Capitoline.

capitolo sm chapter.

capitombolo sm tumble.

capo sm (principale) boss; (testa, estremità) head; (di gruppo) leader; (di tribù) chief; ~ di vestiario item of clothing; andare a ~ to start a new paragraph; venire a ~ di qc to get through sthg; da ~ over again; da un ~ all'altro (di qc) from end to end (of sthg); in ~ a un mese within a month.

Capodanno sm New Year.

capofitto : a capofitto avv headfirst.

capolavoro sm masterpiece.

capolinea (pl **capilinea**) sm terminus.

capolino sm: fare ~ to peep in/out.

capoluogo, -ghi sm: ~ di provincia provincial capital, = county town (Br); ~ di regione regional capital.

capostazione (pl **capistazione**) smf station master.

capotavola (*mpl* **capitavola**, *fpl inv*) *smf* head of the table; **a ~ at** the head of the table.

capoufficio (*mpl* **capiufficio**, *fpl inv*) *smf* office manager (*f* manageress).

capoverso *sm* paragraph.

capovolgere *vt* (*barca, oggetto*) to overturn; (*fig: situazione*) to reverse ❑ **capovolgersi** *vr* (*barca*) to capsize; (*macchina*) to overturn; (*fig: situazione*) to be reversed.

capovolto, -a *pp* → **capovolgere**.

cappa *sf* (*di camino*) hood; (*mantello*) cape.

cappella *sf* chapel.

cappello *sm* hat; **~ di paglia** straw hat.

cappero *sm* caper.

cappone *sm* capon; **~ ripieno al forno** *capon stuffed with beef, Parmesan cheese and breadcrumbs.*

cappotto *sm* coat.

cappuccino *sm* cappuccino.

cappuccio *sm* hood; (*di penna*) cap.

capra *sf* goat.

Capri *sf* Capri.

capriccio *sm* tantrum; (*voglia*) whim; **fare i capricci** to be naughty.

capriccioso, -a *agg* naughty.

Capricorno *sm* Capricorn.

capriola *sf* somersault.

capriolo *sm* roe deer.

capro *sm*: **~ espiatorio** scapegoat.

capsula *sf* (*di farmaco*) capsule; (*di bottiglia*) cap.

carabiniere *sm* member of the Italian police force responsible for civil and military matters.

caraffa *sf* carafe, jug.

Caraibi *smpl*: **i ~** the Caribbean.

caramella *sf* sweet.

carato *sm* carat.

carattere *sm* character.

caratteristica, -che *sf* characteristic.

caratteristico, -a, -ci, -che *agg* characteristic.

caratterizzare *vt* to characterize.

carboidrato *sm* carbohydrate.

carbone *sm* coal.

carburante *sm* fuel.

carburatore *sm* carburettor.

carcerato, -a *sm, f* prisoner.

carcere (*pl f* **carceri**) *sm* prison.

carciofo *sm* artichoke; **carciofi alla romana** *sautéed or baked artichokes with parsley, mint and garlic.*

cardiaco, -a, -ci, -che *agg* cardiac, heart (*dav s*).

cardigan *sm inv* cardigan.

cardinale *agg* → **numero, punto** ◆ *sm* cardinal.

cardine *sm* hinge.

cardo *sm* thistle.

carenza *sf* lack, deficiency.

carestia *sf* famine.

carezza *sf* caress; (*a animale*) stroke.

carezzare *vt* to caress; (*animale*) to stroke.

carica, -che *sf* (*incarico*) position, office; (*elettrica, di arma*) charge; **in ~** in office.

caricare vt (mettere su) to load; (sveglia) to wind up; ~ qc di qc to load sthg with sthg; ~ qn di qc to weigh sb down with sthg.

carico, -a, -chi, -che agg (arma, macchina fotografica) loaded; (batteria) charged; (orologio) wound up ◆ sm load; ~ (di qc) weighed down (with sthg); **a ~ di** (spesa) charged to.

carie sf inv (dei denti) decay.

carino, -a agg (grazioso) pretty, lovely; (gentile) nice.

carnagione sf complexion.

carne sf meat; (ANAT) flesh; ~ di maiale/vitello pork/veal; ~ macinata O tritata mince.

carneficina sf massacre.

carnevale sm carnival.

---

i CARNEVALE

The period before Lent, from the Epiphany to Ash Wednesday, is carnival time in Italy. Most festivities take place during the last week of this period, Shrovetide. Both children and adults don masks, go to parties, play tricks on each other, and throw confetti ("coriandoli") and streamers. In some cities special organized events are held: Viareggio is particularly famous for its carnival procession, whilst in Venice the city gives itself over to open-air parties, theatre and concerts.

---

caro, -a agg expensive, dear; (amato) dear; **costare ~** to be expensive; **Caro Luca** Dear Luca.

carota sf carrot.

carovita sm high cost of living.

carpaccio sm thin slices of raw beef served with oil, lemon and shavings of Parmesan cheese.

carpire vt: ~ qc a qn (segreto) to get sthg out of sb.

carponi avv on all fours.

carrabile agg → **passo**.

carraio agg m → **passo**.

carreggiata sf carriageway.

carrello sm trolley.

carriera sf career; **far ~** to get on.

carro sm cart, wagon; ~ **armato** tank; ~ **attrezzi** breakdown truck (Br), tow truck (Am).

carrozza sf (cocchio) coach, carriage; (vagone) carriage (Br), car (Am); '~ letto' sleeping car; '~ ristorante' restaurant car.

carrozzeria sf bodywork.

carrozziere sm coachbuilder.

carrozzina sf pram (Br), baby carriage (Am).

carta sf paper; (tessera) card; **alla ~ à la carte;** ~ **d'argento** senior citizens' railcard; ~ **automobilistica** O **stradale** road map; ~ **da bollo** paper carrying a government duty stamp; ~ **di credito** credit card; ~ **geografica** map; ~ **d'identità** identity card; ~ **igienica** toilet paper; ~ **d'imbarco** boarding pass; ~ **da lettere** notepaper; ~ **da pacchi** brown paper, wrapping paper; ~ **da parati** wallpaper; ~ **stagnola** silver foil; ~ **verde** green card; ~ **dei vini** wine list; **carte da gioco** playing cards.

i CARTA D'IDENTITÀ

Every Italian citizen is issued with an identity card, an official document listing details such as place and date of birth, home address, profession, colour of eyes and hair, and marital status. It also contains a photograph of the bearer. By law Italians must show their identity card when asked to do so by the police, and when booking in at hotels. The card can be used instead of a passport for travel inside the European Union.

cartacarbone sf carbon paper.

cartaccia, -ce sf waste paper.

cartapesta sf papier-mâché.

cartella sf (di scolaro) schoolbag; (di professionista) briefcase; (per fogli) folder; (scheda) file; ~ **clinica** case history.

cartello sm (avviso) notice; (in dimostrazioni) placard; ~ **stradale** road sign.

cartellone sm (teatrale) playbill; ~ **(pubblicitario)** poster.

cartina sf: ~ **(geografica)** map.

cartoccio sm paper bag; **al** ~ in tin foil.

cartoleria sf stationer's.

cartolibreria sf stationer's and bookseller's.

cartolina sf (illustrata) (picture) postcard; ~ **postale** postcard.

cartone sm cardboard □ **cartoni animati** smpl cartoons.

casa sf (costruzione) house; (dimora) house, home; (ditta) firm; **andare a** ~ to go home; **essere a** ○ **in** ~ to be at home; **fatto in** ~ homemade; ~ **di cura** nursing home.

casalinga, -ghe sf housewife.

casalingo, -a, -ghi, -ghe agg homemade; (amante della casa) home-loving □ **casalinghi** smpl household articles.

cascare vi to fall down.

cascata sf waterfall.

cascina sf farmstead.

casco, -schi sm (protettivo) helmet; (per capelli) dryer; (di banane) bunch.

casella sf (riquadro) square; (scomparto) compartment; ~ **postale** post office box.

casello sm tollbooth.

caserma sf barracks (pl).

casino sm (fam: confusione) mess.

casinò sm inv casino.

caso sm chance; (eventualità) event; (poliziesco, medico) case; **fare** ~ **a** to pay attention to; **non è il** ~ **di offendersi** you shouldn't take offence; **a** ~ at random; **in** ~ **contrario** otherwise; **in ogni** ~ in any case; **nel** ~ **venisse** should he come; **per** ~ by chance; **in tutti i casi** at any rate; **'in** ~ **d'emergenza rompere il vetro'** 'in case of emergency break glass'.

casomai cong if by any chance.

cassa sf (contenitore) case, box; (di negozio) cash register; (di supermercato) checkout; (di banca) counter; (amplificatore) speaker; (di orologio) case; ~ **automatica prelievi** cash dispenser; ~ **continua** night safe; ~ **toracica** chest.

cassaforte (*pl* **casseforti**) *sf*
safe.

cassata *sf* ice cream dessert containing candied fruit, served in slices like a cake; ~ **siciliana** Sicilian dessert made with sponge, ricotta cheese, candied fruit and liqueur.

casseruola *sf* saucepan.

cassetta *sf* (*contenitore*) box; (*di musica, film*) tape; ~ **delle lettere** letterbox (*Br*), mailbox (*Am*); ~ **di sicurezza** strongbox.

cassetto *sm* drawer.

cassettone *sm* chest of drawers.

cassiere, -a *sm, f* (*di negozio*) cashier; (*di banca*) teller.

cassoela *sf* pork ribs with salami and savoy cabbage (a speciality of Lombardy).

cassonetto *sm* large dustbin on wheels.

castagna *sf* chestnut.

castagnaccio *sm* Tuscan cake made from chestnut flour, pine kernels and sometimes sultanas and rosemary.

castagno *sm* chestnut.

castano, -a *agg* chestnut.

castello *sm* castle.

castigo, -ghi *sm* punishment; **mettere qn in** ~ to punish sb.

castoro *sm* beaver.

castrare *vt* to castrate.

casual ['kaʒwal] *agg inv* casual.

casuale *agg* chance (*dav s*).

catacomba *sf* catacomb.

catalogare *vt* to catalogue.

catalogo, -ghi *sm* catalogue.

catamarano *sm* catamaran.

catarifrangente *sm* reflector.

catarro *sm* catarrh.

catasta *sf* stack.

catastrofe *sf* catastrophe.

categoria *sf* (*gruppo*) category; (*di albergo*) class.

catena *sf* chain; ~ **di montaggio** assembly line; **a** ~ chain (*dav s*); **catene (da neve)** (snow) chains.

catinella *sf* basin; **piovere a catinelle** to pour down.

catino *sm* basin.

catrame *sm* tar.

cattedra *sf* teacher's desk.

cattedrale *sf* cathedral.

cattiveria *sf* (*qualità*) wickedness; (*commento*) spiteful remark; (*atto*) spiteful act.

cattività *sf* captivity.

cattivo, -a *agg* bad; (*bambino*) naughty; (*sapore, odore*) bad, nasty; (*incapace*) poor.

cattolico, -a, -ci, -che *agg & sm, f* Catholic.

cattura *sf* capture.

catturare *vt* to capture.

caucciù *sm* rubber.

causa *sf* cause; (*DIR*) case; **a** o **per** ~ **di** because of.

causare *vt* to cause.

cautela *sf* caution, prudence.

cautelare *vt* to protect ❑
cautelarsi da *vr + prep* to take precautions against.

cauto, -a *agg* cautious, prudent.

cauzione *sf* security; (*DIR*) bail.

cava *sf* quarry.

cavalcare *vt* to ride.

cavalcavia *sm inv* flyover.

cavalcioni *avv*: **a ~ di** astride.

cavaliere *sm* (*chi cavalca*) rider; (*medioevale, titolo*) knight; (*in balli*) partner.

cavalleria *sf* (*MIL*) cavalry; (*cortesia*) chivalry.

cavallerizzo, -a *sm, f* (*istruttore*) riding instructor; (*di circo*) bareback rider.

cavalletta *sf* grasshopper.

cavalletto *sm* easel.

cavallo *sm* horse; (*di pantaloni*) crotch; (*negli scacchi*) knight; **andare a ~** to ride; **~ (vapore)** horsepower.

cavallone *sm* (*ondata*) breaker.

cavare *vt* to extract; **cavarsela** to manage, to cope.

cavatappi *sm inv* corkscrew.

cavatelli *smpl*: **~ alla foggiana** flat 'gnocchi' in a vegetable, cheese or meat sauce.

caverna *sf* cave.

cavia *sf* guinea pig; **fare da ~** to be a guinea pig.

caviale *sm* caviar.

caviglia *sf* ankle.

cavità *sf inv* (*buca*) hollow; (*ANAT*) chamber.

cavo, -a *agg* hollow ♦ *sm* cable; (*corda*) rope.

cavolfiore *sm* cauliflower.

cavolo *sm* cabbage; **che ~ vuole?** (*fam*) what the hell does he want?

cazzotto *sm* (*fam*) punch.

cc (*abbr di centimetro cubico*) cc.

c/c (*abbr di conto corrente*) a/c.

C.C. *abbr* = **Carabinieri**.

C.D. *sm inv* CD.

ce → **ci**.

cece *sm* chickpea.

Cecoslovacchia *sf*: **la ~** Czechoslovakia.

cedere *vt*: **~ qc (a qn)** to give sthg up (to sb) ♦ *vi* (*soffitto, pavimento*) to give way; **~ (a qc)** (*fig: persona*) to give in (to sthg), to yield (to sthg).

cedola *sf* coupon.

cedro *sm* lime.

CEE *sf* (*abbr di Comunità Economica Europea*) EEC.

ceffone *sm* slap.

celebrare *vt* to celebrate.

celebre *agg* famous.

celebrità *sf inv* fame.

celeste *agg & sm* sky-blue.

celibe *agg* single ♦ *sm* bachelor.

cella *sf* cell.

cellophane® ['tʃelofan] *sm* Cellophane®.

cellula *sf* cell; **~ fotoelettrica** photoelectric cell.

cellulare *sm* (*telefono*) mobile phone; (*furgone*) Black Maria.

cemento *sm* cement; **~ armato** reinforced concrete.

cena *sf* dinner.

cenare *vi* to have dinner.

cencio *sm* (*straccio*) rag □ **cenci** *smpl* (*CULIN*) Tuscan speciality of deep-fried sticks of dough sprinkled with sugar.

cenere *sf* ash.

cenno *sm* (*con la mano*) gesture; (*col capo*) nod; (*allusione*) hint; (*sintomo*) sign; **fare ~ a qn** to beckon to sb; **fare ~ di sì/no** to nod/shake one's head.

cenone *sm* New Year's Eve

dinner.

censimento *sm* census.

censura *sf (controllo)* censorship.

centenario, -a *agg (di età)* hundred-year-old; *(ogni cento anni)* centenary *(dav s)* ♦ *sm* centenary.

centerbe *sm inv type of liqueur made from herbs.*

centesimo, -a *num* hundredth, → **sesto**.

centigrado *agg m* → **grado**.

centimetro *sm* centimetre.

centinaio *(pl f* centinaia*) sm*: un ~ (di) a hundred.

cento *num* a o one hundred; ~ per ~ 100 per cent, → **sei**.

centomila *num* a o one hundred thousand, → **sei**.

centotredici *sm (numero telefonico)* ≃ 999 *(Br)*, ≃ 911 *(Am)*; *(polizia)* police *(pl)*.

centrale *agg (nel centro)* central; *(principale)* main ♦ *sf* head office; ~ **elettrica** electric power station.

centralinista, -i, -e *smf* operator.

centralino *sm* telephone exchange; *(di albergo, ditta)* switchboard.

centrare *vt* to hit the centre of.

centrifuga, -ghe *sf* spindryer.

centro *sm* centre; **fare** ~ *(colpire)* to hit the bull's eye; *(fig: risolvere)* to hit the nail on the head; ~ **abitato** built-up area; ~ **commerciale** shopping centre; ~ **storico** old town.

ceppo *sm (di albero)* stump; *(ciocco)* log.

cera *sf* wax.

ceramica *sf* pottery.

cerbiatto *sm* fawn.

cerca *sf*: **essere in** ~ **di qc** to be in search of sthg.

cercare *vt* to look for □ **cercare di** *v + prep*: ~ **di fare qc** to try to do sthg.

cerchio *sm* circle; **mettersi in** ~ **(intorno a)** to form a circle (around).

cereale *sm* cereal.

cerimonia *sf* ceremony.

cerino *sm* match.

cernia *sf* grouper.

cerniera *sf (di porte, finestre)* hinge; ~ **(lampo)** zip.

cerotto *sm* plaster.

certamente *avv* certainly.

certezza *sf* certainty; **sapere qc con** ~ to know sthg for sure.

certificato *sm* certificate; ~ **medico** medical certificate; ~ **di nascita** birth certificate.

certo, -a *agg* 1. *(convinto)* certain; **essere** ~ **di qc** to be certain of sthg; **sono** ~ **di aver prenotato** I'm positive I booked; **siete certi che sia lui?** are you sure it's him?

2. *(assicurato, evidente)* certain; **la vittoria è data per certa** victory is certain.

3. *(non specificato)* certain; **un** ~ **signor Rossi** a (certain) Mr Rossi; **c'è un** ~ **Paolo al telefono** there's someone called Paolo on the phone; **ho certe cose da fare** I have some things I need to do; **in certi casi** in some o certain cases.

4. *(qualche)*: **certi(-e)** some.

5. *(limitativo)* some; **avere un** ~

intuito to have some insight.
6. *(rafforzativo)* some; **ha certe idee!** he has some strange ideas!; **ha certi occhi azzurri!** he's got really blue eyes!; **avere una certa età** to be getting on.

◆ *avv*: **vieni anche tu? – ~!** are you coming too? – of course!; **di ~** certainly.

❑ **certi, -e** *pron (persone)* some (people); **certi dicono che ...** some people say that ...

certosa *sf* charterhouse.

cervello *sm* brain.

Cervino *sm*: **il ~** the Cervino.

cervo *sm* deer; **~ volante** stag beetle.

cesoie *sfpl* shears.

cespuglio *sm* bush.

cessare *vt* to stop.

cesso *sm* loo.

cesta *sf* basket.

cestino *sm (cesto)* basket; *(per cartacce)* wastepaper basket; **~ da viaggio** packed lunch.

cesto *sm* basket.

ceto *sm* class.

cetriolo *sm* cucumber.

champagne [ʃamˈpaɲ] *sm inv* champagne.

charter [ˈtʃarter] *sm inv* charter.

che *pron relativo* **1.** *(soggetto: persona)* who, that; **il dottore ~ mi ha visitato** the doctor who examined me.
2. *(complemento oggetto: persona)* whom, that; **la ragazza ~ hai conosciuto** the girl (whom o that) you met.
3. *(cosa, animale)* that, which; **la macchina ~ è in garage** the car

which o that is in the garage; **il treno ~ abbiamo perso** the train (which o that) we missed.
4. *(fam: in cui)*: **la sera ~ siamo usciti** the evening we went out.

◆ *pron interr & esclam* what; **~ ne pensi?** what do you think?; **~ ti succede?** what's the matter?; **non so ~ fare** I don't know what to do; **grazie! – non c'è di ~!** thank you! – don't mention it!; **ma ~ dici!** what are you saying!

◆ *agg interr* **1.** *(tra molti)* what; *(tra pochi)* which; **~ libro vuoi, questo o quello?** which book do you want, this one or that one?; **~ tipo è il tuo amico?** what's your friend like?
2. *(in esclamazioni)*: **~ strana idea!** what a strange idea!; **~ bello!** how lovely!

◆ *cong* **1.** *(introduce una subordinata)* that; **è difficile ~ venga** he's unlikely to come; **sai ~ non è vero** you know (that) it's not true; **sono così stanca ~ non mi reggo in piedi** I'm so tired (that) I can hardly stand up; **sono contenta ~ sia partito** I'm pleased (that) he left.
2. *(temporale)*: **è già un anno ~ è partito** it's already a year since he left; **è un po' ~ non lo vedo** I haven't seen him for a while.
3. *(comparativa)* than; **è più furbo ~ intelligente** he's cunning rather than intelligent; **è più bello ~ mai** he's more handsome than ever.
4. *(introduce alternativa)* whether; **~ tu venga o no, io ci vado** I'm going, whether you come or not.

check-in [tʃeˈkin] *sm inv* check-in.

chewing-gum [ˈtʃwingam] *sm* chewing-gum.

chi *pron relativo* 1. *(colui che)* the person who.

2. *(qualcuno che)*: **c'è ancora ~ crede alle sue storie** there are still people who believe his tales.

3. *(chiunque)* whoever, anyone who; **entra ~ vuole** anyone can come in.

◆ *pron interr* 1. *(soggetto)* who; **~ è?** who is it?; **~ è stato?** who was it?

2. *(complemento diretto)* who; **non so ~** I don't know who; **~ si vede!** look who's here!

3. *(complemento indiretto)* who, whom; **a ~ devo chiedere?** who should I ask?; **con ~ parti?** who are you leaving with?; **di ~ è questo ombrello?** whose umbrella is this?; **a ~ lo dici!** you're telling me!

chiacchierare *vi (conversare)* to chat; *(spettegolare)* to gossip.

chiacchiere *sfpl (pettegolezzi)* rumours, gossip *(sg)*; **fare due o quattro ~** to have a chat.

chiacchierone, -a *agg (loquace)* talkative; *(pettegolo)* gossipy.

chiamare *vt* to call □ **chiamarsi** *vr* to be called; **come ti chiami?** what's your name?; **mi chiamo …** my name is …

chiamata *sf* call.

Chianti *sm* Chianti.

chiarezza *sf* clarity.

chiarire *vt (mettere in chiaro)* to make clear; *(spiegare)* to clarify; *(problema)* to clear up □ **chiarirsi** *vr* to be cleared up.

chiaro, -a *agg* clear; *(colore)* light.

chiasso *sm* noise.

chiassoso, -a *agg* noisy.

chiave *sf* key; **chiudere a ~** to lock; **~ d'accensione** ignition key; **~ inglese** monkey wrench.

chiavetta *sf (dell'acqua, del gas)* tap; *(d'accensione)* key.

chic [sik] *agg inv* chic.

chicco, -chi *sm (di grano)* grain; *(di caffè)* bean; **~ d'uva** grape.

chiedere *vt (per sapere)* to ask; *(per avere)* to ask for; **~ qc a qn** to ask sb sthg □ **chiedere di** *v + prep (per notizie)* to ask after; *(al telefono)* to ask for.

chiesa *sf* church.

chiesto, -a *pp* → **chiedere**.

chiglia *sf* keel.

chilo *sm (chilogrammo)* kilo; **mezzo ~** di half a kilo of.

chilogrammo *sm* kilogram.

chilometro *sm* kilometre.

chimica *sf (disciplina)* chemistry, → **chimico**.

chimico, -a, -ci, -che *agg* chemical ◆ *sm, f* chemist.

chinarsi *vr* to bend.

chinotto *sm (bibita) a type of soft drink.*

chiocciola *sf* snail.

chiodo *sm* nail; **~ fisso** fixed idea; **chiodi di garofano** cloves.

chioma *sf (di albero)* foliage; *(capigliatura)* (head of) hair.

chiosco, -schi *sm* kiosk.

chiostro *sm* cloister.

chiromante *smf* fortune-teller.

chirurgia *sf* surgery; **~ estetica** plastic surgery.

chissà *avv* who knows?

chitarra *sf* guitar.

chiudere *vt* to close, to shut; *(acqua, gas)* to turn off; *(strada)* to close; *(definitivamente)* to close down, to shut down; *(concludere)* to end ♦ *vi* to close, to shut; *(definitivamente)* to close down, to shut down; **~ a chiave** to lock □ **chiudersi** *vr* to close, to shut; **chiudersi in casa** to lock o.s. in; **'si chiude da sé'** 'automatic door'.

chiunque *pron (indefinito)* anyone; *(relativo)* whoever; **~ sia** whoever it may be.

chiuso, -a *pp* → **chiudere** ♦ *agg* closed; *(persona)* reserved; **'~ per ferie'** 'closed for holidays'; **'~ per riposo settimanale'** 'weekly closing day'.

chiusura *sf (di negozio, ufficio, scuole)* closing; *(definitiva)* closure; *(termine)* end; *(dispositivo)* fastener.

ci *(diventa ce se precede lo, la, li, le, ne) pron personale* **1.** *(complemento oggetto)* us; **~ vedono** they can see us; **ascoltaci** listen to us.
2. *(complemento di termine)* (to) us; **~ può fare un favore?** can you do us a favour?; **non ce lo ha detto** he didn't tell us.
3. *(riflessivo)* ourselves; **~ laviamo** we wash ourselves.
4. *(reciproco)* each other; **~ vediamo stasera** see you tonight.
♦ *pron dimostrativo (a ciò, in ciò, su ciò)*: **~ penso io** I'll take care of it; **mettici un po' d'impegno!** put a bit of effort into it!; **quella sedia è vuota: posso appoggiarci la borsa?** that seat is empty: can I put my bag on it?; **~ puoi scommettere** you can bet on it.

♦ *avv* **1.** *(stato in luogo: qui)* here; *(stato in luogo: li)* there; **~ fermiamo una sola notte** we are staying (here/there) for just one night.
2. *(moto a luogo: qui)* here; *(moto a luogo: li)* there; **~ si può andare a piedi** you can walk there; **~ vengono spesso** they come here often.
3. *(moto per luogo)*: **~ passa l'autostrada** the motorway runs through it; **non ~ passa mai nessuno** nobody ever goes this/that way.
4. *(in espressioni)*: **c'è** there is; **~ sono** there are; **~ vuole un po' (di tempo)** it takes a bit of time; **io ~ sto** I agree; **non ~ sento/vedo** I can't hear/see.

ciabatta *sf (pantofola)* slipper; *(pane)* type of long, flat bread.

cialda *sf* wafer.

ciambella *sf (dolce)* ring-shaped cake; *(salvagente)* rubber ring; **~ di salvataggio** life buoy, life belt.

ciao *esclam (all'incontro)* hello!; *(di commiato)* bye!

ciascuno, -a *agg & pron* each; **~ di noi** each of us.

cibo *sm* food.

cicala *sf* cicada.

cicatrice *sf* scar.

cicca, -che *sf* cigarette end.

ciccione, -a *sm, f (fam)* fatty.

cicerone *sm* guide.

ciclabile *agg* → **pista**.

ciclamino *sm* cyclamen.

ciclismo *sm* cycling.

ciclista, -i, -e *smf* cyclist.

ciclo *sm* cycle.

ciclomotore *sm* moped.

ciclone *sm* cyclone.

cicogna *sf* stork.

cieco, -a, -chi, -che *agg* blind ◆ *sm, f* blind man (*f* woman).

cielo *sm* sky; (*paradiso*) heaven.

cifra *sf* (*numero*) figure; (*di denaro*) sum, figure.

ciglio *sm* (*di palpebra: pl f* **ciglia**) eyelash; (*di strada: pl m* **cigli**) edge.

cigno *sm* swan.

cigolare *vi* to squeak, to creak.

Cile *sm:* **il ~** Chile.

cilecca *sf:* **fare ~** to fail.

ciliegia, -gie o **-ge** *sf* cherry.

cilindro *sm* (*di motore*) cylinder; (*cappello*) top hat.

cima *sf* top; (*estremità*) end; **in ~** (**a qc**) at the top (of sthg); **da ~ a fondo** from top to bottom, from beginning to end; **~ alla genovese** *veal stuffed with bacon, sweetbreads, brains, mushrooms, peas and grated cheese, served cold in slices.*

cimice *sf* (*insetto*) bug; (*puntina*) drawing pin (*Br*), thumbtack (*Am*).

ciminiera *sf* chimney; (*di nave*) funnel.

cimitero *sm* cemetery.

Cina *sf:* **la ~** China.

cin cin *esclam* cheers!

Cinecittà *sf film studios in Rome.*

| *i* | CINECITTÀ |

Meaning "city of cinema", the name "Cinecittà" has been given to the film complex built in the suburbs of Rome in 1937. "Cinecittà" was most productive in the 1950s, when films like Fellini's *La dolce vita* were shot there, and it continues to be widely used by the Italian film industry.

cinema *sm inv* cinema.

cinepresa *sf* cine-camera.

cinese *agg, smf & sm* Chinese.

cingere *vt* to surround.

cinghia *sf* belt.

cinghiale *sm* wild boar.

cinguettare *vi* to chirp.

cinico, -a, -ci, -che *agg* cynical.

ciniglia *sf* chenille.

cinquanta *num* fifty, → **sei**.

cinquantesimo, -a *agg* fiftieth, → **sesto**.

cinquantina *sf* (*di età*): **essere sulla ~** to be about 50; **una ~ (di)** about 50.

cinque *num* five, → **sei**.

cinquecento *num* five hundred, → **sei** ❑ **Cinquecento** *sm:* **il Cinquecento** the sixteenth century.

cinto, -a *pp* → **cingere**.

cintura *sf* belt; (*punto vita*) waist; **~ di sicurezza** safety o seat belt; **'allacciare le cinture di sicurezza'** 'fasten your seat belts'.

ciò *pron* this, that; **~ che** what; **~ nonostante** nevertheless.

cioccolata *sf* chocolate; (*bevanda*) hot chocolate.

cioccolatino *sm* chocolate.

cioccolato *sm* chocolate.

cioè *avv* that is ◆ *cong* (*vale a dire*) that is; (*anzi*) or rather.

ciondolo *sm* pendant.

ciotola *sf* bowl.

ciottolo *sm* pebble.

cipolla *sf* onion.

cipresso *sm* cypress.

cipria *sf* face powder.

circa *avv & prep* about.

circo, -chi *sm* circus.

circolare *agg & sf* circular ◆ *vi* to circulate; *(veicoli)* to drive; *(persone)* to move along; *(notizia)* to go round.

circolazione *sf (di merce, moneta, giornali)* circulation; **mettere in** ~ *(notizia)* to spread; *(merce, moneta)* to put into circulation; ~ **sanguigna** circulation; ~ **stradale** traffic.

circolo *sm* circle.

circondare *vt* to surround.

circonferenza *sf* circumference.

circonvallazione *sf* ring road.

circoscrizione *sf* district.

circostante *agg* surrounding.

circostanza *sf* circumstance; **date le circostanze** in o under the circumstances.

circuito *sm* circuit.

ciste = cisti.

cisterna *sf* tank.

cisti *sf inv* cyst.

citare *vt (DIR)* to summon; *(menzionare)* to cite; *(opera, autore)* to quote.

citofono *sm* entry phone.

città *sf inv* town; *(importante)* city; ~ **universitaria** (university) campus ❏ **Città del Vaticano** *sf* Vatican City.

cittadinanza *sf* citizenship; *(abitanti)* citizens *(pl)*.

cittadino, -a *sm, f* citizen ◆ *agg* town, city *(dav s)*.

ciuco, -chi *sm* ass, donkey.

ciuffo *sm* tuft.

civetta *sf* owl; *(fig: donna)* flirt.

civico, -a, -ci, -che *agg* civic.

civile *agg* civil; *(civilizzato)* civilized ◆ *sm* civilian.

civiltà *sf inv* civilization.

clacson *sm inv* horn.

clamoroso, -a *agg* sensational.

clandestino, -a *agg (illegale)* illegal; *(segreto)* clandestine ◆ *sm, f* stowaway.

classe *sf* class; *(aula)* classroom; ~ **turistica** tourist class; **prima/seconda** ~ first/second class; **che fai?** what year are you in?

classico, -a, -ci, -che *agg (letteratura, arte, musica)* classical; *(moda, esempio)* classic.

classifica, -che *sf (sportiva)* league table; *(d'esame)* results *(pl)*; *(musicale)* charts *(pl)*.

classificare *vt (ordinare)* to classify; *(valutare)* to mark ❏ **classificarsi** *vr*: **classificarsi primo** to come first.

claudicante *agg (zoppicante)* limping.

clausola *sf (DIR)* clause.

clavicola *sf* clavicle.

claxon = clacson.

clero *sm* clergy.

cliente *smf (di negozio, bar)* customer; *(di professionista)* client.

clientela *sf (di negozio, bar)* clientele; *(di professionista)* clients *(pl)*.

clima, -i *sm* climate.

clinica, -che *sf* clinic.

cloro *sm* chlorine.

club [klab] *sm inv* club.

cm *(abbr di centimetro)* cm.

coagulare *vt (sangue)* to coagulate; *(latte)* to curdle □ **coagularsi** *vr (sangue)* to clot; *(latte)* to curdle.

coca *sf (fam: bibita)* Coke®.

Coca-Cola® *sf* Coca-Cola®.

cocaina *sf* cocaine.

coccinella *sf* ladybird.

coccio *sm (terracotta)* earthenware; *(frammento)* shard.

cocciuto, -a *agg* stubborn.

cocco, -chi *sm (albero)* coconut palm; *(frutto)* coconut.

coccodrillo *sm* crocodile.

coccolare *vt* to cuddle.

cocomero *sm* watermelon.

coda *sf (fila)* queue *(Br)*, line *(Am)*; *(di animale)* tail; **fare la ~** to queue *(Br)*, to stand in line *(Am)*; **mettersi in ~** to join the queue *(Br)* o line *(Am)*; **~ (di cavallo)** ponytail.

codardo, -a *agg* cowardly.

codesto, -a *agg & pron* this.

codice *sm* code; **~ (di avviamento) postale** postcode; **~ fiscale** tax code; **~ della strada** highway code.

coerente *agg* consistent.

coetaneo, -a *agg:* **siamo coetanei** we are the same age.

cofano *sm* bonnet *(Br)*, hood *(Am)*.

cogliere *vt* to pick; *(fig: occasione, momento)* to seize; **~ qn sul fatto** to catch sb redhanded.

cognac *sm inv* cognac.

cognato, -a *sm, f* brother-in-law *(f* sister-in-law).

cognome *sm* surname.

coi = con + i, → con.

coincidenza *sf (caso)* coincidence; *(aereo, treno)* connection.

coincidere *vi:* **~ (con qc)** *(oggetti)* to coincide (with sthg); *(versione dei fatti)* to agree (with sthg); *(date, eventi)* to clash (with sthg).

coinciso, -a *pp* → **coincidere**.

coinvolgere *vt:* **~ qn (in qc)** to involve sb (in sthg).

coinvolto, -a *pp* → **coinvolgere**.

col = con + il, → con.

colapasta = **scolapasta**.

colare *vt (filtrare)* to filter; *(pasta)* to drain ♦ *vi (liquido)* to drip; *(contenitore)* to leak; *(cera, burro)* to melt; **~ a picco** to sink.

colazione *sf (pranzo)* lunch; **(prima) ~** breakfast; **fare ~** *(al mattino)* to have breakfast.

colera *sm* cholera.

colica, -che *sf* colic.

colino *sm* colander.

colla *sf* glue.

collaborare *vi* to cooperate.

collaboratore, -trice *sm, f* collaborator.

collana *sf* necklace; *(serie)* series.

collant [kol'lan] *smpl* tights.

collare *sm* collar.

collasso *sm* collapse.

collaudo *sm* test.

colle *sm* hill.

collega, -ghi, -ghe *smf* colleague.

collegare *vt* to connect □ **collegarsi** *vr* to link up; **collegarsi con** *vr* + *prep (per telefono, radio, TV)* to link up with.

collegio *sm* boarding school.

collera *sf* anger; **essere in ~ (con qn)** to be angry (with sb).

colletta *sf* collection.

collettivo, -a *agg (comune)* common; *(di gruppo)* group *(dav s)*.

colletto *sm* collar.

collezionare *vt* to collect.

collezione *sf* collection; **fare la ~ di qc** to collect sthg.

collina *sf* hill.

collirio *sm* eyewash.

collisione *sf* impact.

collo *sm* neck; *(di abito)* collar, neck; *(pacco)* package.

collocamento *sm* employment.

collocare *vt (disporre)* to place.

colloquio *sm (conversazione)* talk; *(esame)* oral exam; **~ di lavoro** interview.

colmo, -a *agg* full ♦ *sm*: **è il ~!** it's the last straw!

colomba *sf* dove; *(dolce)* Easter cake.

Colombia *sf*: **la ~** Colombia.

colonia *sf* colony; *(per bambini)* summer camp; **(acqua di) ~** (eau de) cologne.

colonna *sf* column; **~ vertebrale** spine, spinal column.

colorante *sm (per alimenti)* food colouring; *(per tessuti)* dye.

colorare *vt* to colour.

colore *sm* colour; **di che ~?** what colour?; **di ~** coloured; **a colori** colour *(dav s)*.

coloro *pron mpl*: **~ che ...** those who ...

colosseo *sm*: **il Colosseo** the Colosseum.

i **IL COLOSSEO**

One of Rome's most visited monuments, the Colosseum was built between 75 and 80 AD. In its arena spectators watched gladiatorial contests, fights between men and animals, chariot races and simulated naval battles. Pillaged over the centuries, and attacked more recently by pollution, the amphitheatre nevertheless still retains some of its outer walls.

colpa *sf (responsabilità)* fault; *(reato)* offence; **dare la ~ (di qc) a qn/qc** to blame sb/sthg (for sthg); **per ~ di** through, owing to.

colpire *vt* to hit; *(impressionare, sog: malattia)* to strike.

colpo *sm* blow; *(sparo)* shot; *(alla porta)* knock; *(fam: infarto)* stroke; *(fam: rapina)* raid; **di ~** suddenly; **fare ~** to make a strong impression; **un ~ di fulmine** love at first sight; **~ di sole** sunstroke; **~ di stato** coup (d'état); **~ di telefono** phone call; **~ di testa** impulse; **~ di vento** gust of wind.

coltello *sm* knife.

coltivare *vt* to cultivate.

colto, -a *pp* → **cogliere** ♦ *agg* cultured.

coma *sm inv* coma.

comandante *sm (di nave)* captain; *(di esercito)* commanding officer.

comandare *vi* to be in command.

comando *sm* command; *(congegno)* control.

combaciare *vi* to fit together.

combattere *vt & vi* to fight.

combinare *vt (accordare)* to combine; *(organizzare)* to arrange; *(fam: fare)* to do.

combinazione *sf* combination; *(caso)* coincidence; **per ~** by chance.

combustibile *agg* combustibile ◆ *sm* fuel.

come *avv* 1. *(comparativo)* like; **ho dormito ~ un ghiro** I slept like a log; **~ me** like me; **~ sempre** as always; **~ se niente fosse** as if nothing had happened.
2. *(interrogativo)* how; **non so ~ fare** I don't know what to do; **~ sarebbe?** what do you mean?; **~ stai?** how are you?; **~ mai?** how come?
3. *(in qualità di)* as; **viaggiare ~ turista** to travel as a tourist.
4. *(in esclamazioni)* how; **~ mi dispiace!** I'm so sorry!
5. *(per esempio)* like; **mi piacciono i colori accesi ~ il rosso** I like bright colours like red.
◆ *cong* 1. *(nel modo in cui)* how; **mi ha spiegato ~ lo ha conosciuto** she told me how she met him; **fai ~ ti dico** do as I tell you; **~ vuole** as you like.
2. *(comparativa)* as; **non è caldo ~ pensavo** it's not as hot as I thought.
3. *(quanto)* how; **sai ~ mi piace il**

cioccolato you know how much I like chocolate.

cometa *sf* comet.

comfort *sm inv* comfort; **l'hotel dispone di tutti i ~** the hotel offers a wide range of amenities.

comico, -a, -ci, -che *agg* funny; *(genere)* comic ◆ *sm (attore)* comedian.

cominciare *vt & vi* to begin, to start; **~ a fare qc** to begin to do sthg, to begin doing sthg; **~ col fare qc** to begin by doing sthg.

comitiva *sf* group.

comizio *sm* meeting.

commedia *sf* play.

commemorare *vt* to commemorate.

commentare *vt* to comment on.

commento *sm* comment; *(a un testo, programma)* commentary.

commerciale *agg* commercial.

commerciante *smf (mercante)* trader; *(negoziante)* shopkeeper.

commerciare : commerciare in *v + prep* to deal in.

commercio *sm (vendita)* trade; **essere fuori ~** not to be for sale; **essere in ~** to be on the market.

commesso, -a *pp* → commettere ◆ *sm, f* shop assistant.

commestibile *agg* edible ▫ **commestibili** *smpl* foodstuffs.

commettere *vt (crimine)* to commit; *(errore)* to make.

commissario *sm (di polizia)* superintendent; *(d'esami)* member of an examining board; **~ tecnico** national coach.

commissione sf commission □
commissioni sfpl errands.

commosso, -a pp → **commuovere** ♦ agg moved.

commovente agg touching.

commozione sf (emozione)
emotion; ~ **cerebrale** concussion.

commuovere vt to move, to
touch □ **commuoversi** vr to be
moved, to be touched.

comò sm inv chest of drawers.

comodino sm bedside table.

comodità sf inv comfort.

comodo, -a agg comfortable;
(conveniente) convenient; (utile)
handy ♦ sm: fare ~ a qn to be
handy for sb; fare il proprio ~ to
do as one pleases; con ~ at one's
convenience.

compact disc ['kɔmpat 'disk]
sm inv compact disc.

compagnia sf company; (di
amici) group; fare ~ a qn to keep
sb company; ~ aerea airline; ~
d'assicurazione insurance company.

compagno, -a sm, f companion; (convivente) partner; ~ di scuola school friend; ~ di squadra team
mate.

comparire vi to appear.

compartimento sm (di locale,
spazio) section; (di treno) compartment.

compasso sm pair of compasses.

compatibile agg compatible;
un comportamento non ~ inexcusable behaviour.

compatire vt (aver compassione
di) to feel sorry for; (scusare)

make allowances for.

compatto, -a agg (ben unito)
compact; (folla) dense; (fig: solidale)
united.

compensare vt to compensate; ~ qn di qc to compensate sb
for sthg.

compenso sm (paga) payment;
(risarcimento) compensation; (ricompensa) recompense; in ~ on the
other hand.

comperare = comprare.

compere sfpl: far ~ to do the
shopping.

competente agg competent.

competere vi to compete □
competere a v + prep to be due
to.

competizione sf competition.

compiacere vt to please □
compiacersi vr: **compiacersi di** O
per qc to be delighted at sthg;
compiacersi con qn to congratulate
sb.

compiaciuto, -a pp → **compiacere**.

compiere vt (eseguire) to fulfil;
(concludere) to complete; **quando
compi gli anni?** when is your birthday?; **compie 15 anni a maggio** he'll
be 15 in May.

compilare vt to fill in.

compito sm (incarico) task;
(dovere) duty; (in classe) test □
compiti smpl homework (sg); **fare
i compiti** to do one's homework.

compleanno sm birthday;
buon ~! Happy Birthday!

complessivo, -a agg overall.

complesso, -a agg complex ♦
sm complex; (musicale) band.

group; **in** ○ **nel ~** on the whole.

completamente *avv* completely.

completare *vt* to complete.

completo, -a *agg* complete; *(pieno)* full ♦ *sm (vestiario)* suit; *(di oggetti)* set; **al ~** *(hotel, aereo)* fully booked; **c'era la famiglia al ~** the whole family was there.

complicare *vt* to complicate ❑

complicarsi *vr* to become complicated.

complicato, -a *agg* complicated.

complicazione *sf (difficoltà)* snag; *(di malattia)* complication.

complice *smf* accomplice.

complimentarsi *vr*: **~ con qn** to congratulate sb.

complimento *sm* compliment; **complimenti!** congratulations!; **non fare complimenti** don't stand on ceremony.

componente *smf (membro)* member ♦ *sf (aspetto)* element.

componibile *agg* fitted.

comporre *vt (musica, poesia)* to compose; *(parola)* to make up; *(numero di telefono)* to dial.

comportamento *sm* behaviour.

comportare *vt* to involve ❑

comportarsi *vr* to behave.

compositore, -trice *sm, f* composer.

composizione *sf* composition; **'~ principali treni'** *board showing the position of compartments, restaurant car etc making up main line trains.*

composto, -a *pp →* **comporre** ♦ *agg (persona, contegno)* composed; *(sostanza, parola)* compound ♦ *sm* compound; **~ da** composed of.

comprare *vt* to buy.

comprendere *vt (includere)* to include; *(capire)* to understand.

comprensione *sf* understanding.

comprensivo, -a *agg (tollerante)* understanding; *(inclusivo)* inclusive.

compreso, -a *pp →* **comprendere** ♦ *agg* inclusive; **~ nel prezzo** included in the price.

compressa *sf* tablet.

compromesso *sm* compromise.

compromettere *vt* to compromise.

computer [kom'pjuter] *sm inv* computer.

comunale *agg* municipal.

comune *agg* common; *(a più persone)* shared; *(ordinario)* ordinary ♦ *sm (edificio)* town hall; *(ente)* town council; *(area)* = borough; **avere qc in ~ (con qn)** to have sthg in common (with sb); **mettere qc in ~** to share sthg; **fuori del ~** out of the ordinary.

comunicare *vt* to communicate ♦ *vi (parlare, corrispondere)* to communicate; *(porta)*: **~ con** to lead to.

comunicazione *sf (atto)* communication; *(annuncio)* announcement; *(telefonica)* call; **dare la ~ a qn** to put a call through to sb.

comunione *sf (eucaristia)* Communion; **~ dei beni** *(DIR)* joint ownership of property.

comunismo *sm* communism.

comunista, -i, -e *agg & smf* communist.

comunità *sf inv* community; **la Comunità (Economica) Europea** the European (Economic) Community.

comunque *avv* anyway ♦ *cong* *(tuttavia)* however; *(in qualsiasi modo)* no matter how.

con *prep* with; **~ piacere!** with pleasure!; **viaggiare ~ il treno/la macchina** to travel by train/car.

concavo, -a *agg* concave.

concedere *vt (dare, accordare)* to grant; *(ammettere)* to concede; **~ a qn di fare qc** to allow sb to do sthg; **concedersi qc** to treat o.s. to sthg.

concentrare *vt* to concentrate; *(riassumere)* to condense ❑ **concentrarsi** *vr* to concentrate.

concentrato, -a *agg* concentrated, concentrating ♦ *sm* concentrate.

concentrazione *sf* concentration.

concepimento *sm* conception.

concepire *vt (figlio)* to conceive; *(idea)* to devise.

concerto *sm* concert.

concessionario *sm* agent.

concesso, -a *pp* → **concedere**.

concetto *sm* concept; *(opinione)* opinion.

conchiglia *sf* shell.

conciliare *vt (impegni, attività)* to reconcile; *(sonno)* to be conducive to; *(contravvenzione)* to settle on the spot.

concime *sm* fertilizer.

concludere *vt* to conclude ❑ **concludersi** *vr* to conclude.

conclusione *sf* conclusion; **in ~** in conclusion.

concluso, -a *pp* → **concludere**.

concordare *vt (stabilire)* to agree on; *(GRAMM)* to make agree ♦ *vi* to agree.

concorde *agg* in agreement.

concorrente *smf (in gara, affari)* competitor; *(ad un concorso)* contestant.

concorrenza *sf* competition.

concorso *sm* competition; *(esame)* competitive examination; **~ di bellezza** beauty contest.

concreto, -a *agg* concrete.

condanna *sf (sentenza)* sentence; *(pena)* conviction; *(disapprovazione)* condemnation.

condannare *vt (DIR)* to sentence; *(disapprovare)* to condemn.

condimento *sm (per insalata)* dressing; *(per carne)* seasoning.

condire *vt (insalata)* to dress; *(carne)* to season.

condividere *vt* to share.

condizionale *agg & sm* conditional ♦ *sf (DIR)* suspended sentence.

condizionatore *sm* air-conditioner.

condizione *sf* condition; **a ~ che** on condition that.

condoglianze *sfpl* condolences.

condominio *sm (edificio)* block of flats *(jointly owned)*; *(persone)* joint owners *(pl)*.

condotta *sf* conduct.

condotto, -a *pp* → **condurre** ◆ *sm* conduit; *(ANAT)* duct.

conducente *sm* driver; 'non parlare al ~' 'please do not speak to the driver whilst the vehicle is in motion'.

condurre *vt (affare, azienda)* to run; *(bambino, prigioniero)* to take; *(vita)* to lead; *(gas, acqua)* to carry.

conduttore, -trice *sm, f* driver ◆ *sm (di calore, elettricità)* conductor.

confarsi : **confarsi a** *vr + prep* to suit.

confederazione *sf* confederation.

conferenza *sf (riunione)* conference; *(discorso)* lecture; ~ **stampa** press conference.

conferire *vt (form)*: ~ **qc a qn** to confer sthg on sb.

conferma *sf* confirmation.

confermare *vt* to confirm.

confessare *vt* to confess □ **confessarsi** *vr (RELIG)* to confess; *(dichiararsi)*: **confessarsi colpevole** to plead guilty.

confessione *sf* confession.

confetto *sm (dolciume)* sugared almond; *(pastiglia)* pill.

confezionare *vt (merce)* to package; *(pacco)* to make up; *(vestiario)* to make.

confezione *sf (involucro)* packaging; *(di vestiario)* tailoring; ~ **regalo** gift pack.

confidare *vt*: ~ **qc a qn** to confide sthg to sb □ **confidare in** *v + prep* to have confidence in; **confidarsi** *vr*: **confidarsi con qn** to open one's heart to sb.

confidenziale *agg* confidential.

confinare : **confinare con** *v + prep* to border on; **confinarsi in** *vr + prep* to shut o.s. away in.

confine *sm (frontiera)* border; *(limite)* boundary.

confiscare *vt* to confiscate.

conflitto *sm (guerra)* conflict; *(contrasto)* clash.

confondere *vt* to confuse, to mix up; ~ **le idee a qn** to confuse sb □ **confondersi** *vr (mescolarsi)* to merge; *(sbagliarsi)* to get mixed up; *(turbarsi)* to become confused.

conformità *sf* conformity; **in ~ con** in accordance with.

confortare *vt* to comfort.

confortevole *agg* comfortable.

confrontare *vt* to compare.

confronto *sm* comparison; **in ~ (a)** in comparison (with); **nei miei confronti** towards me.

confusione *sf (caos)* confusion; *(disordine)* mess; *(chiasso)* racket, noise; **far ~** *(confondersi)* to get mixed up; *(far rumore)* to make a racket.

confuso, -a *pp* → **confondere** ◆ *agg* confused.

congedare *vt (lasciar andare)* to dismiss; *(MIL)* to demobilize □ **congedarsi** *vr (andar via)* to take one's leave; *(MIL)* to be demobilized.

congedo *sm* leave; *(MIL)* discharge.

congegno *sm* device.

congelare *vt* to freeze □ **congelarsi** *vr* to freeze; *(fig: persona, mani)* to be frozen.

congelato, -a *agg* frozen.

congelatore *sm* freezer.

congeniale *agg* congenial.

congenito, -a *agg* congenital.

congestione *sf* congestion.

congettura *sf* conjecture.

congiungere *vt* to join (together) □ **congiungersi** *vr (strade)* to meet.

congiuntivo *sm* subjunctive.

congiunto, -a *pp* → **congiungere** ◆ *sm, f* relative.

congiunzione *sf* conjunction.

congiura *sf* conspiracy.

congratularsi *vr:* ~ con qn per qc to congratulate sb on sthg.

congratulazioni *sfpl* congratulations.

congresso *sm* congress.

coniglio *sm* rabbit.

coniugato, -a *agg* married.

coniuge *smf* spouse.

connazionale *smf* fellow countryman · *(f* fellow countrywoman).

connettere *vt* to connect.

connotati *smpl* description *(sg)*.

cono *sm* cone; ~ **gelato** ice-cream cone.

conoscente *smf* acquaintance.

conoscenza *sf* knowledge; *(persona)* acquaintance; **perdere** ~

to lose consciousness.

conoscere *vt* to know; *(incontrare)* to meet.

conosciuto, -a *pp* → **conoscere** ◆ *agg* well-known.

conquista *sf (azione)* conquest; *(risultato, cosa ottenuta)* achievement.

conquistare *vt (impadronirsi di)* to conquer; *(ottenere)* to gain; *(persona)* to win over.

consanguineo, -a *sm, f* blood relation.

consapevole *agg:* ~ **di qc** aware of sthg.

conscio, -a, -sci, -sce *agg:* ~ **di qc** conscious of sthg.

consegna *sf (recapito)* delivery; *(custodia):* **dare qc in** ~ **a qn** to entrust sb with sthg.

consegnare *vt (recapitare)* to deliver; *(affidare)* to entrust.

conseguenza *sf* consequence; **di** ~ consequently.

conseguire *vt* to obtain ◆ *vi:* **ne consegue che …** it follows that …

consenso *sm* consent.

consentire *vt* to allow □ **consentire a** *v* + *prep* to agree to.

conserva *sf* preserve; ~ **di frutta** jam; ~ **di pomodoro** tomato sauce.

conservante *sm* preservative.

conservare *vt (tenere)* to keep; *(monumento, resti)* to preserve; '~ **in frigo'** 'keep refrigerated' □ **conservarsi** *vr (cibo)* to keep; *(monumento, resti)* to be preserved.

conservatore, -trice *sm, f* conservative.

considerare *vt* to consider □
considerarsi *vr* to consider o.s.

considerazione *sf*: **prendere in ~** to take into consideration.

considerevole *agg* considerable.

consigliare *vt (persona)* to advise; *(locale, metodo)* to recommend; **~ a qn di fare qc** to advise sb to do sthg □ **consigliarsi con** *vr + prep*: **consigliarsi con qn** to ask sb's advice.

consigliere *sm (funzionario)* adviser; *(politico)* councillor.

consiglio *sm (suggerimento)* piece of advice; *(riunione)* meeting; *(organo)* council; **dare un ~ a qn** to give sb some advice; **~ d'amministrazione** board; **il Consiglio dei Ministri =** the Cabinet.

consistere : consistere di *v + prep* to consist of; **consistere in** *v + prep* to consist in.

consistito, -a *pp* → **consistere**.

consolare *vt (confortare)* to console; *(sollevare)* to cheer up □ **consolarsi** *vr* to console o.s.

consolato *sm* consulate.

console *sm* consul.

consonante *sf* consonant.

constatare *vt* to notice.

consueto, -a *agg* usual.

consulente *smf* consultant.

consultare *vt* to consult □ **consultarsi** *vr* to confer; **consultarsi con** *vr + prep* to consult with.

consultorio *sm* advice bureau.

consumare *vt* to consume; *(logorare)* to wear out □ **con-**

sumarsi *vr* to wear out.

consumatore *sm* consumer.

consumazione *sf (bibita)* drink; *(spuntino)* snack; **la ~ al tavolo è più cara** it's more expensive to eat/drink sitting at a table; **'~ obbligatoria'** 'minimum charge'.

consumismo *sm* consumerism.

consumo *sm* consumption.

contabile *smf* accountant.

contabilità *sf inv (operazioni)* accountancy; *(libri)* accounts *(pl)*; *(ufficio)* accounts department.

contachilometri *sm inv =* mileometer.

contadino, -a *sm, f* farmer.

contagiare *vt* to infect.

contagocce *sm inv* dropper.

contante *agg* → **denaro** ♦ *sm* cash; **pagare in contanti** to pay in cash.

contare *vt & vi* to count; **avere i soldi contati** not to have a penny to spare □ **contare di** *v + prep*: **~ di fare qc** to intend to do sthg; **contare su** *vr + prep* to count on.

contatore *sm* meter.

contattare *vt* to contact.

contatto *sm* contact.

conte, -essa *sm, f* count *(f* countess).

contegno *sm* attitude.

contemporaneamente *avv* simultaneously.

contemporaneo, -a *agg* *(dello stesso tempo)* contemporaneous; *(attuale)* contemporary.

contendere *vt*: **~ qc a qn** to

compete with sb for sthg.

contenere *vt* to contain ❑ **contenersi** *vr* to contain o.s.

contenitore *sm* container.

contento, -a *agg* (*lieto*) happy, glad; (*soddisfatto*): ~ **(di)** pleased (with).

contenuto *sm* (*cosa racchiusa*) contents (*pl*); (*argomento*) content.

contestare *vt* to object to.

contestazione *sf* (*obiezione*) objection; (*protesta*) protest.

contesto *sm* context.

contiguo, -a *agg*: ~ **(a qc)** adjacent (to sthg).

continentale *agg* continental.

continente *sm* (*geografico*) continent; (*terraferma*) mainland.

contingente *sm* contingent.

continuamente *avv* (*senza interruzioni*) continuously; (*di frequente*) continually.

continuare *vt & vi* to continue ◆ *v impers*: **continua a piovere** it's still raining; ~ **a fare qc** to continue doing sthg.

continuazione *sf* continuation.

continuo, -a *agg* (*incessante*) continuous; (*serie, fila*) continual; **di** ~ continually.

conto *sm* (*calcolo*) calculation; (*di ristorante, albergo*) bill; (*bancario*) account; **mi porta il** ~, **per favore?** could you bring me the bill, please?; **fare** ~ **su** to rely on; **rendersi** ~ **di qc** to realize sthg; **tenere** ~ **di qc** to take account of sthg; ~ **corrente** current account; ~ **alla rovescia** countdown; **per** ~ **di qn** on behalf of sb; **fare i conti con qn**

(*fam*) to sort sb out; **in fin dei conti** all things considered.

contorno *sm* (*di pietanza*) vegetables (*pl*); (*linea*) outline.

contrabbando *sm* smuggling.

contrabbasso *sm* double bass.

contraccambiare *vt* to return.

contraccolpo *sm* rebound.

contraddire *vt* to contradict ❑ **contraddirsi** *vr* to contradict o.s.

contraddizione *sf* contradiction.

contraffare *vt* to falsify; (*firma*) to forge.

contrapporre *vt* to set against.

contrariamente *avv*: ~ **a** contrary to.

contrario, -a *agg* (*opposto*) opposite; (*sfavorevole*) unfavourable; ◆ *sm* opposite; **essere** ~ **a qc** to be against sthg; **avere qualcosa in** ~ to have an objection; **al** ~ on the contrary.

contrarre *vt* to contract ❑ **contrarsi** *vr* (*muscolo*) to contract.

contrassegno *sm* (*marchio*) mark; **spedire qc (in)** ~ to send sthg cash on delivery.

contrastare *vt* to hinder ◆ *vi*: ~ **(con)** to clash (with).

contrasto *sm* contrast; **essere in** ~ **con qc** (*opinione, esigenza*) to be in contrast with sthg.

contrattare *vt* to negotiate.

contrattempo *sm* hitch.

contratto, -a *pp* → **contrarre** ◆ *sm* contract.

contravvenzione *sf* fine.

contribuire : contribuire a *v* + *prep* to contribute to.

contributo *sm (partecipazione)* contribution; *(tassa)* levy.

contro *prep* against; ~ **di me** against me; **prendere qc** ~ **il mal di gola** to take sthg for one's sore throat.

controfigura *sf* stuntman (*f* stuntwoman).

controllare *vt* to control; *(verificare)* to check; '~ **il resto**' 'please check your change' ❑ **controllarsi** *vr* to control o.s.

controllo *sm (verifica)* check; *(sorveglianza)* supervision; *(dominio)* control; **perdere il** ~ to lose control; ~ **doganale** customs inspection; '~ **elettronico della velocità**' 'speed checks'; '~ **passaporti**' 'passport control'.

controllore *sm (di autobus, treni)* (ticket) inspector; ~ **di volo** air-traffic controller.

contromano *avv* in the wrong direction.

controproducente *agg* counterproductive.

controsenso *sm* contradiction in terms.

controvoglia *avv* reluctantly.

contusione *sf* bruise.

convalescenza *sf* convalescence.

convalidare *vt (biglietto)* to validate; *(dubbio, sospetto)* to confirm; '~ **all'inizio del viaggio**' 'stamp your ticket at the start of your journey'.

convegno *sm* conference.

convenevoli *smpl* civilities.

conveniente *agg* favourable; *(prezzo)* cheap; *(affare)* advantageous.

convenire *vi (riunirsi)* to gather; *(concordare)* to agree; *(tornare utile)* to be worthwhile ◆ *v impers (essere consigliabile)*: **conviene avvertirli** it is advisable to inform them; **ti conviene aspettare** you'd better wait.

convento *sm* convent.

convenuto *pp* → **convenire**.

convenzionale *agg* conventional.

convenzioni *sfpl* conventions.

conversazione *sf (chiacchierata)* conversation.

convertire *vt* to convert ❑ **convertirsi** *vr*: **convertirsi (a qc)** to convert (to sthg).

convincere *vt*: ~ **qn di qc** to convince sb of sthg; ~ **qn a fare qc** to persuade sb to do sthg.

convinto, -a *pp* → **convincere** ◆ *agg* convinced.

convivere *vi* to live together.

convocare *vt* to convene.

convoglio *sm* convoy.

convulsioni *sfpl* convulsions.

cooperativa *sf* cooperative.

coordinare *vt* to coordinate.

coperchio *sm* lid.

coperta *sf (da letto)* blanket; *(di nave)* deck.

copertina *sf* cover.

coperto, -a *pp* → **coprire** ◆ *agg (piscina, campo)* indoor *(dav s)*; *(persona)* wrapped up; *(cielo)* overcast ◆ *sm (a tavola)* place; *(al ri-*

storante) cover charge; **~ di qc** covered with sthg; **al ~** under cover.

copertone *sm (pneumatico)* tyre.

copia *sf* copy; **bella ~** final draft; **brutta ~** rough draft.

copiare *vt* to copy.

copione *sm* script.

coppa *sf (bicchiere)* goblet; *(di gelato)* tub; *(ciotola)* bowl; *(di regiseno, trofeo)* cup; **~ dell'olio** oil sump.

coppia *sf (paio)* pair; *(di sposi, amanti)* couple; **a coppie** in pairs.

copricostume *sm inv* beach robe.

coprifuoco, -chi *sm* curfew.

copriletto *sm inv* bedspread.

coprire *vt* to cover; **~ qn di qc** to cover sb with sthg; *(insulti)* to shower sb with sthg ▫ **coprirsi** *vr (con indumenti)* to cover o.s.; **coprirsi di qc** *(muffa, fango)* to be covered in sthg.

coraggio *sm (forza d'animo)* courage; *(faccia tosta)* cheek ◆ *esclam* cheer up!; *(forza)* come on!; **avere il ~ di fare qc** *(avere l'animo)* to have the nerve to do sthg; *(avere faccia tosta)* to have the cheek to do sthg.

coraggioso, -a *agg* courageous, brave.

corallo *sm* coral.

Corano *sm*: **il ~** the Koran.

corazzieri *smpl* the President's guard.

corda *sf (fune)* rope; *(spago, di strumento)* string; **tagliare la ~** *(fig)* to sneak off; **corde vocali** vocal cords.

cordiale *agg* warm.

cordone *sm* cord; *(di persone)* cordon; **~ ombelicale** umbilical cord.

coreografia *sf* choreography.

coriandolo *sm (spezia, pianta)* coriander ▫ **coriandoli** *smpl* confetti *(sg)*.

coricarsi *vr* to go to bed.

cornamusa *sf* bagpipes *(pl)*.

cornetta *sf* receiver.

cornetto *sm (pasta)* croissant; *(gelato)* cone.

cornice *sf* frame.

cornicione *sm* cornice.

corno *(pl f* **corna)** *sm* horn; **facciamo le corna!** *(fam)* ≈ touch wood!; **fare** ○ **mettere le corna a qn** *(fam)* to cheat on sb.

Cornovaglia *sf*: **la ~** Cornwall.

coro *sm* chorus; *(di chiesa)* choir.

corona *sf (reale)* crown; *(di fiori)* wreath.

corpo *sm* body; *(militare)* corps *(sg)*; **~ insegnante** teaching staff; **(a) ~ a ~** hand to hand.

corporatura *sf* build.

corporeo, -a *agg* bodily.

corredare *vt*: **~ qc di qc** to equip sthg with sthg.

corredo *sm (da sposa)* trousseau; *(attrezzatura)* kit.

correggere *vt* to correct.

corrente *agg (moneta)* valid; *(mese, anno)* current; *(comune)* everyday ◆ *sf (tendenza)* trend ◆ *sm*: **essere al ~ (di qc)** to be informed (about sthg); **mettere qn al ~ (di qc)** to inform sb (about sthg); **~ alternata** alternating current; **~ continua** direct current.

correntemente avv (speditamente) fluently; (comunemente) commonly.

correre vi to run; (affrettarsi) to rush ♦ vt to run; **~ dietro a qn** to run after sb.

corretto, -a pp → **correggere** ♦ agg (esatto) correct; (onesto) proper.

correzione sf correction; (di compiti) marking.

corridoio sm corridor.

corridore sm (atleta) runner; (pilota) racer.

corriera sf coach, bus.

corriere sm courier.

corrimano sm handrail.

corrispondente agg corresponding ♦ smf correspondent.

corrispondenza sf correspondence.

corrispondere vt to return ❑ **corrispondere a** v + prep to correspond to.

corrisposto, -a pp → **corrispondere**.

corrodere vt to corrode.

corrompere vt (comprare) to bribe; (traviare) to corrupt.

corroso, -a pp → **corrodere**.

corrotto, -a pp → **corrompere** ♦ agg (disonesto) corrupt.

corruzione sf (disonestà) corruption; (con denaro) bribery.

corsa sf (a piedi) running; (gara) race; (di mezzo pubblico) journey; **fare una ~** (correre) to run; (sbrigarsi) to dash; **di ~** in a rush; **corse dei cavalli** horse races.

corsia sf (di strada) lane; (di ospedale) ward; **~ preferenziale** bus and taxi lane; **~ di sorpasso** overtaking lane; **'~ chiusa'** 'lane closed'.

Corsica sf: **la ~** Corsica.

corso, -a pp → **correre** ♦ sm course; (strada) main street; **fare un ~ (di qc)** to take a course (in sthg); **~ accelerato** crash course; **~ d'acqua** watercourse; **corsi estivi** summer courses; **corsi serali** evening classes; **in ~** (denaro) in circulation; (riunione, lavori) in progress; **fuori ~** out of circulation.

corte sf (reale) court; **fare la ~ a qn** to court sb.

corteccia, -ce sf bark.

corteggiare vt to court.

corteo sm (manifestazione) demonstration; (processione) procession.

cortese agg polite.

cortesia sf (qualità) politeness; (atto) favour; **per ~** please.

cortile sm courtyard.

corto, -a agg short; **essere a ~ di qc** to be short of sthg.

cortocircuito sm short circuit.

corvo sm raven.

cosa sf thing; (faccenda) matter; **è una ~ da niente** it's nothing; **~?** what?; **~ c'è?** what's the matter?; **per prima ~** firstly.

coscia, -sce sf (di uomo) thigh; (di pollo, agnello) leg.

cosciente agg (sveglio) conscious; (consapevole) **~ di qc** aware o conscious of sthg.

coscienza sf conscience; **avere qc sulla ~** to have sthg on one's conscience.

coscio sm leg.

cosciotto sm leg.

così avv **1.** (in questo modo) like this/like that; **fai ~** do it this way; **~ ~** so-so; **per ~ dire** so to speak; **meglio ~** it's better like this; **proprio ~!** just like that!; **e ~ via** and so on.

2. (per descrivere misure) so; **una scatola larga ~ e lunga ~** a box so wide and so long.

3. (talmente) so; **è ancora ~ presto!** it's still so early!; **~ poco/tanto** so little/much; **una ragazza ~ bella** such a beautiful girl.

4. (conclusivo) so; **~, non hai ancora deciso** so you haven't decided yet.
◆ cong **1.** (perciò) so, therefore.

2. (a tal punto): **~ ... che** so ... (that); **sono ~ stanco che non sto in piedi** I'm so tired I can hardly stand up; **~ ... da** enough ... to; **è ~ sciocco da dire di no** he's silly enough to say no.

◆ agg inv: **non ho mai visto una macchina ~** I've never seen a car like that.

❑ **così che** cong: (affinché) so (that).

cosicché cong so that.

cosiddetto, -a agg so-called.

cosmetici smpl cosmetics.

coso sm (fam) thing.

cospargere vt: **~ qc di qc** to sprinkle sthg with sthg.

cosparso, -a pp → **cospargere**.

cospicuo, -a agg sizeable.

cospirare vi to conspire.

costa sf coast.

costante agg (stabile, durevole) constant; (persona) steadfast.

costare vi to cost; **quanto costa?** how much does it cost?; **~ caro** to be expensive.

costata sf chop.

costatare = **constatare**.

costeggiare vt (fiancheggiare) to go alongside; (navigare) to hug the coast of.

costellazione sf constellation.

costernato, -a agg dismayed.

costì avv there.

costiero, -a agg coastal.

costituire vt (formare) to constitute; (fondare) to set up ❑ **costituirsi** vr to give o.s. up.

costituzione sf constitution; (formazione) setting-up.

costo sm cost; **a tutti i costi** at all costs.

costola sf rib.

costoletta sf cutlet.

costoso, -a agg expensive.

costretto, -a pp → **costringere**.

costringere vt: **~ qn (a fare qc)** to force sb (to do sthg).

costruire vt (fabbricare) to build.

costruzione sf construction.

costume sm (uso) custom; (abito) costume; **~ da bagno** swimsuit.

cotechino sm pork sausage.

cotoletta sf chop; (di vitello) cutlet; **~ alla milanese** escalope of veal.

cotone

cotone *sm* cotton; ~ **idrofilo** cotton wool.

cotta *sf*: **prendersi una** ~ **per qn** *(fam)* to have a crush on sb.

cotto, -a *pp* → **cuocere** ♦ *agg* cooked; *(fam: innamorato)* head over heels in love; **ben** ~ well-done.

cottura *sf* cooking.

coupon [ku'pɔn] *sm inv* coupon.

cozza *sf* mussel.

C.P. *(abbr di casella postale)* P.O. Box.

cracker ['krɛker] *sm inv* cracker.

crampo *sm* cramp.

cranio *sm* skull.

cratere *sm* crater.

crauti *smpl sauerkraut flavoured with cumin and juniper, a speciality of Trento.*

cravatta *sf* tie.

creare *vt* to create.

creativo, -a *agg* creative.

creatore, -trice *sm, f* creator; **il Creatore** the Creator.

creatura *sf* creature.

credente *smf* believer.

credenza *sf (convinzione)* belief; *(mobile)* sideboard.

credere *vt* to believe; **credo di sì/no** I think/don't think so; **credo (che) sia vero** I think that's true; **credo di fare la cosa giusta** I think I'm doing the right thing □ **credere a** *v + prep* to believe; **non ci credo!** I don't believe it!; **credere in** *v + prep* to believe in; **credersi** *vr* to consider o.s.

credito *sm (COMM)* credit; *(fiducia)* trust.

crema *sf* cream; *(liquida)* custard; ~ **di asparagi** cream of asparagus soup; ~ **depilatoria** hair-removing cream; ~ **pasticcera** confectioner's custard; ~ **solare** suntan cream; **gelato alla** ~ vanilla ice-cream.

crematorio *sm* crematorium.

cremazione *sf* cremation.

crème caramel ['krɛm-'karamɛl] *sm inv* o *sf inv* crème caramel.

cremisi *agg inv* crimson.

cremoso, -a *agg* creamy.

crepaccio *sm* crevice.

crepapelle : a crepapelle *avv*: **ridere a** ~ to split one's sides laughing.

crepare *vi (fam: morire)* to snuff it; ~ **dal ridere** to die laughing.

crêpe [krɛp] *sf inv* pancake.

crepuscolo *sm (tramonto)* twilight.

crescere *vi* to grow; *(diventare adulto)* to grow up ♦ *vt* to bring up.

crescita *sf* growth.

cresima *sf* confirmation.

crespo, -a *agg* frizzy.

cresta *sf* crest.

creta *sf* clay.

cretino, -a *agg* idiot.

cric *sm inv (attrezzo)* jack.

criminale *agg & smf (criminoso)* criminal.

crimine *sm* crime.

criniera *sf* mane.

cripta *sf* crypt.

crisi *sf inv (fase difficile)* crisis; *(attacco)* fit; **in** ~ in a state of crisis.

cristallo *sm* crystal.

cristianesimo *sm* Christianity.

cristiano, -a *agg & sm, f* Christian.

Cristo *sm* Christ; **avanti ~ BC; dopo ~ AD.**

criterio *sm* (*regola*) criterion; (*buon senso*) common sense.

critica, -che *sf* (*biasimo*) criticism; (*i critici*) critics (*pl*), → **critico.**

criticare *vt* to criticize.

critico, -a, -ci, -che *agg* critical ◆ *sm, f* (*persona*) critic.

croccante *agg* crisp ◆ *sm* almond crunch.

crocchetta *sf* croquette.

croce *sf* cross; **la Croce Rossa** the Red Cross.

crocevia *sm inv* crossroads (*sg*).

crociera *sf* cruise.

crocifisso *sm* crucifix.

crollare *vi* (*edificio, ponte*) to collapse; (*fig: per stanchezza, dolore*) to break down.

crollo *sm* (*di edificio, ponte*) collapse; (*di prezzi*) slump.

cronaca, -che *sf* (*attualità*) news (*sg*); (*di partita*) commentary; **~ nera** crime news (*sg*).

cronico, -a, -ci, -che *agg* chronic.

cronista, -i, -e *smf* reporter.

cronologico, -a, -ci, -che *agg* chronological.

crosta *sf* (*di pane*) crust; (*di formaggio*) rind; (*di ferita*) scab.

crostacei *smpl* shellfish.

crostata *sf* fruit or jam tart with a pastry lattice topping.

crostino *sm* (*per minestra*) crouton; (*tartina*) canapé; **crostini di fegato** small pieces of toast spread with chicken liver pâté.

croupier [kru'pje] *sm inv* croupier.

cruciale *agg* crucial.

cruciverba *sm inv* crossword.

crudele *agg* cruel.

crudo, -a *agg* raw.

crusca *sf* bran.

cruscotto *sm* dashboard.

cubo *sm* cube.

cuccetta *sf* (*di treno*) couchette; (*di nave*) berth.

cucchiaiata *sf* spoonful.

cucchiaino *sm* teaspoon.

cucchiaio *sm* spoon.

cuccia, -ce *sf* dog's bed; **a ~!** down!

cucciolo *sm* cub; (*di cane*) puppy.

cucina *sf* (*stanza*) kitchen; (*attività, cibi*) cooking; (*elettrodomestico*) cooker; **~ casalinga** home cooking; **~ a gas** gas cooker.

cucinare *vt* to cook.

cucire *vt* to sew.

cucitura *sf* stitching.

cuculo *sm* cuckoo.

cuffia *sf* cap; (*per l'ascolto*) headphones (*pl*); '**è obbligatorio l'uso della ~**' 'swimming caps must be worn'.

cugino, -a *sm, f* cousin.

cui *pron relativo* 1. (*in complemento indiretto: persona*) who, whom; **l'amico a ~ ho prestato il libro** the friend I lent the book to, the friend to whom I lent the book; **l'amico di ~ ti ho parlato** the

friend I told you about; **la ragazza con ~ esco** the girl I'm going out with.
2. *(in complemento indiretto: cosa)* which; **il film a ~ mi riferisco** the film (which) I'm referring to; **l'appartamento in ~ vivo** the flat (which) I live in; **il motivo per ~ ti chiamo** the reason (that) I'm calling you.
3. *(tra articolo e sostantivo)*: **la città il ~ nome mi sfugge** the town whose name escapes me; **la persona alla ~ domanda rispondo** the person whose question I'm answering □ **per cui** *cong (perciò)* so; **sono stanco, per ~ vado a letto** I'm tired, so I'm going to bed.

culla *sf* cradle.

culmine *sm* peak.

culo *sm (volg)* arse *(Br)*, ass *(Am)*.

culto *sm* cult; *(adorazione)* worship.

cultura *sf* culture.

culturismo *sm* body-building.

cumulativo *agg m* → **biglietto**.

cumulo *sm (mucchio)* heap, pile.

cunetta *sf (avvallamento)* bump.

cuocere *vt & vi* to cook.

cuoco, -a, -chi, -che *sm, f* cook.

cuoio *sm* leather; **~ capelluto** scalp.

cuore *sm* heart; **avere a ~ qc** to care about sthg; **nel ~ della notte** in the middle of the night.

cupo, -a *agg (scuro)* dark; *(voce)* deep.

cupola *sf* dome.

cura *sf* care; *(trattamento, terapia)*

treatment; **avere ~ di** to take care of; **prendersi ~ di** to look after; **~ dimagrante** diet.

curare *vt (trattare)* to treat; *(guarire)* to cure.

curiosare *vi* to look around.

curiosità *sf inv* curiosity.

curioso, -a *agg (insolito)* curious; *(indiscreto)* inquisitive.

curva *sf* bend; **in ~** on a bend; **'~ pericolosa'** 'dangerous bend'.

curvare *vi (veicolo, autista)* to turn; *(strada)* to bend ◆ *vt* to bend.

curvo, -a *agg (linea)* curved; *(persona, spalle)* bent.

cuscino *sm (da divano)* cushion; *(guanciale)* pillow.

custode *smf* attendant; *(di scuola)* janitor.

custodia *sf (cura, controllo)* custody; *(astuccio)* case.

custodire *vt (assistere)* to look after; *(conservare)* to keep.

cute *sf* skin.

D

da *prep* 1. *(con verbo passivo)* by; **il viaggio è pagato dalla ditta** the trip is paid for by the company.
2. *(stato in luogo)* at; **abito ~ una zia** I'm living at an aunt's.
3. *(moto a luogo)* to; **andare dal medico/dal parrucchiere** to go to the doctor's/the hairdresser's.
4. *(moto per luogo)* through; **è entra-**

to **dall'ingresso principale** he came in through the main entrance; **il treno passa ~ Roma** the train goes via Rome.

5. *(indica l'origine, la provenienza)* from; **venire ~ Roma** to come from Rome; **ricevere una lettera ~ un amico** to get a letter from a friend.

6. *(indica tempo)* for; **aspetto ~ ore** I've been waiting for hours; **lavoro dalle 9 alle 5** I work from 9 to 5; **non lo vedo ~ ieri** I haven't seen him since yesterday; **comincerò ~ domani** I'll start from tomorrow.

7. *(indica condizione, funzione)* as; **~ grande voglio fare il pompiere** when I grow up I want to be a fireman; **fare ~ guida** to act as a guide.

8. *(indica la causa)* with; **tremare dal freddo** to shiver; **piangere dalla felicità** to cry for joy.

9. *(indica una caratteristica)* with; **una ragazza dagli occhi verdi** a girl with green eyes, a green-eyed girl; **una stanza ~ 200 000 lire a notte** a 200,000 lira a night room; **una bottiglia ~ un litro** a litre bottle.

10. *(indica il fine)*: **occhiali ~ sole** sunglasses; **qualcosa ~ mangiare** something to eat.

11. *(indica separazione)* from; **vedere ~ lontano/vicino** to see from a distance/close up; **essere lontano ~ casa** to be far from home; **la piscina è a 3 chilometri ~ qui** the swimming pool is 3 kilometres from here; **isolarsi ~ tutti** to cut o.s. off from everyone; **mettere qc ~ parte** to save sthg.

12. *(indica modo)* like; **trattare qn ~**

amico to treat sb like O as a friend; **puoi farlo ~ te** you can do it (for) yourself; **non è cosa ~ te!** it's not like you!

13. *(indica la conseguenza)*: **essere stanco ~ morire** to be dead tired.

daccapo *avv* from the beginning.

dado *sm (per gioco)* dice; *(estratto)* stock cube; *(per vite)* nut.

dagli = da + gli, → **da**.

dai[1] = da + i, → **da**.

dai[2] *esclam* go on!

daino *sm (animale)* deer.

dal = da + il, → **da**.

dall' = da + l', → **da**.

dalla = da + la, → **da**.

dalle = da + le, → **da**.

dallo = da + lo, → **da**.

daltonico, -a, -ci, -che *agg* colour-blind.

dama *sf (gioco)* draughts *(sg)*; *(nel ballo)* partner.

damigiana *sf* demijohn.

danaro = **denaro**.

dancing ['dɛnsin] *sm inv* dance hall.

danese *agg & sm* Danish ♦ *smf* Dane.

Danimarca *sf*: **la ~** Denmark.

danneggiare *vt (rovinare)* to damage; *(nuocere a)* to harm.

danno *sm (materiale)* damage; *(morale)* harm; **i danni** *(DIR)* damages.

dannoso, -a *agg* harmful.

danza *sf* dance.

dappertutto *avv* everywhere.

dappoco *agg inv (persona)* inept; *(questione)* insignificant.

dapprima *avv* at first.

dare *vt* to give; *(risultati)* to produce; *(film)*: **cosa danno all'Odeon?** what's on at the Odeon?; ~ **qc a qn** to give sth to sb, to give sb sthg; ~ **la mano a qn** to shake hands with sb; ~ **la nausea a qn** to make sb feel sick; ~ **la buonanotte a qn** to say goodnight to sb; ~ **da bere a qn** to give sb something to drink; ~ **una festa** to throw a party; ~ **del lei a qn** to address sb as 'lei'; ~ **del tu a qn** to address sb as 'tu'; ~ **qn per morto** to give sb up for dead; ~ **qc per scontato** to take sthg for granted; **darsi il cambio** to take it in turns; ~ **alla testa a qn** *(sog: alcool, successo)* to go to sb's head □ **dare su** *v* + *prep (finestra)* to look out onto; *(porta)* to lead to; **darsi a** *vr* + *prep (dedicarsi a)* to devote o.s. to; **darsi al bere** to take to drink.

data *sf* date; ~ **di nascita** date of birth.

dato, -a *pp* → **dare** ◆ *agg* particular ◆ *sm* datum; ~ **che** given that; **un** ~ **di fatto** a fact; **i dati** the data.

datore, -trice *sm, f.*: ~ **di lavoro** employer.

dattero *sm* date.

dattilografo, -a *sm, f* typist.

davanti *avv* in front; *(avanti)* ahead; *(nella parte anteriore)* at the front ◆ *agg inv* front *(dav s)* ◆ *sm* front ◆ *prep*: ~ **a** in front of; *(dirimpetto)* opposite.

davanzale *sm* windowsill.

davvero *avv* really.

d.C. *(abbr di dopo Cristo)* A.D.

dea *sf* goddess.

debito *sm* debt.

debole *agg* weak ◆ *sm*: **avere un** ~ **per** to have a weakness for.

debolezza *sf* weakness.

debuttare *vi* to make one's debut.

decaffeinato, -a *agg* decaffeinated.

decapitare *vt* to decapitate.

decappottabile *agg & sf* convertible.

deceduto, -a *agg* deceased.

decennio *sm* decade.

decente *agg* decent.

decesso *sm (form)* death.

decidere *vi* to decide on ◆ *vi* to decide; ~ **di fare qc** to decide to do sthg □ **decidersi** *vr*: **decidersi (a fare qc)** to make up one's mind (to do sthg).

decimale *agg* decimal.

decimo, -a *num* tenth, → **sesto**.

decina *sf* ten; *(circa dieci)* about ten; **decine di** dozens of.

decisione *sf* decision; **prendere una** ~ to make a decision.

deciso, -a *pp* → **decidere** ◆ *agg* decisive; ~ **a fare qc** determined to do sthg.

decollare *vi* to take off.

decollo *sm* takeoff.

decorare *vt* to decorate.

decotto *sm* decoction.

decreto *sm* decree.

dedica, -che *sf* dedication.

dedicare *vt*: ~ **qc a qn** *(poesia, canzone)* to dedicate sthg to sb; *(fig: consacrare)* to devote sthg to

❑ **dedicarsi a** *vr + prep* to devote o.s. to.

dedito, -a *agg*: ~ **a qc** *(studio)* devoted to sthg; *(droga, alcool)* addicted to sthg.

dedotto, -a *pp* → **dedurre**.

dedurre *vt (concludere)* to deduce; *(detrarre)* to deduct.

deduzione *sf* deduction.

deficiente *agg (spreg)* idiotic.

deficit *sm inv* deficit.

definire *vt* to define.

definitivo, -a *agg* definitive.

definizione *sf* definition.

deformare *vt* to deform; *(fig: travisare)* to distort ❑ **deformarsi** *vr* to become deformed.

defunto, -a *sm, f* deceased.

degenerare *vi* to degenerate.

degli = di + gli, → di.

degnarsi *vr*: ~ **di fare qc** to condescend to do sthg.

degno, -a *agg*: ~ **di** worthy of.

degradare *vt (peggiorare)* to degrade; *(MIL)* to demote.

degustazione *sf (assaggio)* tasting; *(negozio) specialist shop where beverages, especially wine or coffee, are tasted.*

dei = di + i, → di.

delegare *vt*: ~ **qn (a fare qc)** to delegate sb (to do sthg); ~ **qc a qn** to delegate sthg to sb.

delegazione *sf* delegation.

delfino *sm* dolphin.

delicatezza *sf (l'essere delicato)* delicacy; *(gentilezza)* consideration; *(atto gentile)* considerate act.

delicato, -a *agg* delicate; *(gentile)* considerate.

delineare *vt* to outline ❑ **delinearsi** *vr (essere visibile)* to be outlined; *(fig: presentarsi)* to take shape.

delinquente *smf* delinquent.

delirio *sm (MED)* delirium; *(esaltazione)* frenzy.

delitto *sm* crime.

delizioso, -a *agg (cibo)* delicious; *(gradevole)* delightful.

dell' = di + l', → di.

della = di + la, → di.

delle = di + le, → di.

dello = di + lo, → di.

delta *sm inv* delta.

deltaplano *sm* hang glider.

deludere *vt* to disappoint.

delusione *sf* disappointment.

deluso, -a *pp* → **deludere** ◆ *agg* disappointed.

democratico, -a, -ci, -che *agg* democratic.

democrazia *sf* democracy.

demolire *vt* to demolish.

demonio *sm* devil.

demoralizzare *vt* to demoralize ❑ **demoralizzarsi** *vr* to become demoralized.

denaro *sm* money; ~ **contante** cash.

denigrare *vt* to denigrate.

denominare *vt* to name.

denominazione *sf* name, denomination; ~ **d'origine controllata** *a mark guaranteeing that the product, especially wine, is of a good quality.*

densità *sf* density.

denso, -a *agg* thick.

dente *sm* tooth; ~ **da latte** milk

tooth; ~ **del giudizio** wisdom tooth; **al ~ al dente** *(cooked enough to be still firm when bitten)*; **mettere qc sotto i denti** to have a bite to eat; **armato fino ai denti** armed to the teeth.

dentiera *sf (denti finti)* dentures *(pl)*.

dentifricio *sm* toothpaste.

dentista, -i, -e *smf* dentist.

dentro *avv & prep* inside; **darci ~** *(fam)* to put one's back into it; **~ di sé** inwardly, inside; **qui/là ~** in here/there; **dal di ~** from the inside; **in ~** inwards.

denuncia, -ce o **-cie** *sf*: **fare la ~** to make a statement to the police; **~ dei redditi** income tax return.

denunciare *vt (sporgere denuncia contro)* to report; *(rendere noto)* to declare.

deodorante *sm (per il corpo)* deodorant; *(per ambiente)* air freshener.

deperibile *agg* perishable.

depilazione *sf* hair removal.

dépliant [depli'an] *sm inv* brochure.

deplorevole *agg* deplorable.

depositare *vt* to deposit; *(persona)* to leave ❑ **depositarsi** *vr* to settle.

deposito *sm* deposit; *(per autobus)* depot; *(per merci)* warehouse; *(di liquido)* sediment; **~ bagagli** left luggage office.

depravato, -a *sm, f* degenerate.

depressione *sf* depression.

depresso, -a *pp* → **deprimere**

◆ *agg* depressed.

deprimente *agg* depressing.

deprimere *vt* to depress ❑ **deprimersi** *vr* to become depressed.

deputato, -a *sm, f* ≈ Member of Parliament *(Br)*, ≈ Representative *(Am)*.

derattizzazione *sf* rodent control.

deriva *sf*: **andare alla ~** to drift.

derivare : **derivare da** *v + prep* to derive from.

dermatologo, -a, -gi o **-ghi, -ghe** *sm, f* dermatologist.

derubare *vt* to rob.

descritto, -a *pp* → **descrivere**.

descrivere *vt* to describe.

descrizione *sf* description.

deserto, -a *agg (disabitato)* deserted; *(senza vegetazione)* barren ◆ *sm* desert.

desiderare *vt* to want, to desire; *(sessualmente)* to desire; **desidera?** can I help you?; **~ fare qc** to wish to do sthg; **lasciare a ~** to leave much to be desired.

desiderio *sm* wish.

desideroso, -a *agg*: **~ di fare qc** eager to do sthg.

designare *vt* to designate.

desistere : **desistere da** *v + prep (form)* to give up.

desistito *pp* → **desistere**.

destinare *vt (assegnare, riservare)* to assign; *(indirizzare)* to address.

destinatario, -a *sm, f* addressee.

destinazione *sf* destination; arrivare a ~ to reach one's destination.

destino *sm* destiny, fate.

destra *sf (mano)* right hand; *(lato)* right; **la** ~ *(POL)* the right wing; **tenere la** ~ to keep to the right; **a** ~ *(stato in luogo)* on the right; *(moto a luogo)* right; **di** ~ *(dal lato destro)* right-hand.

destreggiarsi *vr (nel traffico)* to manoeuvre; *(fig: tra difficoltà)* to manage.

destro, -a *agg (opposto a sinistra)* right.

detenuto, -a *sm, f* prisoner.

detenzione *sf* detention.

detergente *agg* cleansing ♦ *sm (cosmetico)* cleansing cream; *(detersivo)* detergent.

deteriorare *vt* to impair ❑ **deteriorarsi** *vr* to deteriorate.

determinante *agg* decisive.

determinare *vt (stabilire)* to determine.

determinazione *sf* determination.

detersivo *sm* detergent.

detestare *vt* to detest.

detrarre *vt* to deduct.

detratto, -a *pp* → **detrarre**.

dettagliato, -a *agg* detailed.

dettaglio *sm* detail; **al** ~ *(COMM)* retail.

dettare *vt* to dictate; ~ **legge** to lay down the law.

dettato *sm* dictation.

detto, -a *pp* → **dire** ♦ *agg (soprannominato)* known as ♦ *sm* saying.

devastare *vt* to devastate.

deviare *vt* to divert ♦ *vi (di direzione)*: ~ **da qc** to turn off sthg.

deviazione *sf (del traffico)* detour; *(di fiume)* deviation.

devoto, -a *agg* devoted.

di *prep* 1. *(indica appartenenza)* of; **il libro** ~ **Marco** Marco's book; **la porta della camera** the bedroom door.

2. *(indica l'autore)* by; **un quadro** ~ **Giotto** a painting by Giotto.

3. *(partitivo)* of; **alcuni** ~ **noi** some of us.

4. *(nei paragoni)*: **sono più alto** ~ **te** I'm taller than you; **il migliore** ~ **tutti** the best of all.

5. *(indica argomento)* about, of; **un libro** ~ **storia** a history book; **parlare** ~ to talk about.

6. *(temporale)* in; **d'estate** in (the) summer; ~ **mattina** in the morning; ~ **notte** at/by night; ~ **sabato** on Saturdays.

7. *(indica provenienza)* from; ~ **dove sei?** where are you from?; **sono** ~ **Messina** I'm from Messina.

8. *(indica una caratteristica)*: **un bambino** ~ **due anni** a two-year-old child, a child of two; **una statua** ~ **marmo** a marble statue; **una torre** ~ **40 metri** a 40-metre tower; **un film** ~ **due ore** a two-hour film.

9. *(indica la causa)*: **urlare** ~ **dolore** to scream with pain; **sto morendo** ~ **fame!** I'm starving!; **soffrire** ~ **mal di testa** to suffer from headaches; **morire** ~ **vecchiaia** to die of old age.

10. *(indica contenuto)* of; **una bottiglia** ~ **vino** a bottle of wine.

11. *(seguito da infinito)*: **mi ha detto**

~ **non aspettare** he told me not to wait; **pensavo ~ uscire** I was thinking of going out; **capita ~ sbagliare** anyone can make a mistake; **mi sembra ~ conoscerlo** I think I know him.
12. *(in espressioni)*: **a causa ~** because of; **~ modo che** so as to; **dare del bugiardo a qn** to call sb a liar.
♦ *art* some; *(in negative)* any; **vorrei del pane** I'd like some bread; **ha degli spiccioli?** have you got any change?

diabete *sm* diabetes.

diabetico, -a, -ci, -che *agg* diabetic.

diaframma, -i *sm* diaphragm.

diagnosi *sf inv* diagnosis.

diagonale *agg & sf* diagonal.

diagramma, -i *sm* diagram.

dialetto *sm* dialect.

dialisi *sf* (MED) dialysis.

dialogo, -ghi *sm* dialogue.

diamante *sm* diamond.

diametro *sm* diameter.

diamine *esclam (certo)* absolutely!; **che ~ stai facendo?** what on earth are you doing?

diapositiva *sf* slide.

diario *sm* diary; *(a scuola)* homework book; *(calendario)* timetable.

diarrea *sf* diarrhoea.

diavolo *sm* devil; **che ~ vuole?** *(fam)* what the hell does he want?; **va al ~!** *(fam)* go to hell!

dibattito *sm* debate.

dica → **dire**.

dicembre *sm* December, → **settembre**.

diceria *sf* piece of gossip, rumour.

dichiarare *vt* to declare.

dichiarazione *sf* declaration.

diciannove *num* nineteen, → **sei**.

diciannovesimo, -a *num* nineteenth, → **sesto**.

diciassette *num* seventeen, → **sei**.

diciassettesimo, -a *num* seventeenth, → **sesto**.

diciottesimo, -a *num* eighteenth, → **sesto**.

diciotto *num* eighteen, → **sei**.

dieci *num* ten, → **sei**.

diecina = **decina**.

diesel ['dizel] *agg inv & sm inv* diesel.

dieta *sf* diet; **essere a ~** to be on a diet.

dietetico, -a, -ci, -che *agg* diet *(dav s)*.

dietro *avv (nella parte posteriore)* at/in the back; *(indietro)* behind ♦ *sm* back ♦ *prep*: **~ (a)** *(dopo)* after; *(di là da)* behind; **~ di me** behind me; **di ~** back *(dav s)*; **qui/lì ~** behind here/there; **~ pagamento** on payment.

difatti *cong* in fact.

difendere *vt* to defend ❑

difendersi *vr* to defend o.s.

difensore *sm* defender.

difesa *sf* defence.

difeso, -a *pp* → **difendere**.

difetto *sm* defect; *(morale)* fault; **~ di fabbricazione** manufacturing defect.

difettoso, -a *agg (meccanismo)*

faulty; *(vista, abito)* defective.

diffamare *vt (a parole)* to slander; *(per iscritto)* to libel.

differente *agg* different.

differenza *sf* difference; **non fa ~ it** doesn't make any difference; **a ~ di** unlike.

difficile *agg* difficult; **è ~ che esca** *(poco probabile)* it's unlikely that he'll go out.

difficoltà *sf inv* difficulty.

diffidare : diffidare di *v + prep* to mistrust.

diffidente *agg* mistrustful.

diffondere *vt* to spread □ **diffondersi** *vr* to spread.

diffusione *sf* diffusion.

diffuso, -a *pp* → **diffondere** ♦ *agg* widespread.

diga, -ghe *sf* dam.

digeribile *agg* digestible.

digerire *vt* to digest.

digestione *sf* digestion.

digestivo, -a *agg* digestive ♦ *sm* liqueur *drunk to aid digestion, after meals.*

digitale *agg* digital.

digitare *vt (INFORM)* to key in.

digiunare *vi* to fast.

digiuno, -a *sm* fasting ♦ *agg:* **essere ~** not to have eaten; **a ~ on** an empty stomach.

dignità *sf* dignity.

dilagante *agg (fenomeno)* rampant.

dilagare *vi* to be rampant.

dilaniare *vt* to tear to pieces.

dilapidare *vt* to squander.

dilatare *vt (pupille)* to dilate; *(gas, metallo, corpo)* to expand □

dilatarsi *vr (pupille)* to dilate; *(gas, metallo, corpo)* to expand.

dilazionare *vt* to defer.

dilemma, -i *sm* dilemma.

dilettante *smf* amateur.

diligente *agg* diligent.

diluire *vt (allungare)* to dilute; *(sciogliere)* to dissolve.

dilungarsi *vr:* **~ su** *(argomento)* to dwell upon; **~ in spiegazioni** to give a longwinded explanation.

diluvio *sm* downpour.

dimagrire *vi* to lose weight.

dimenare *vt (fianchi)* to swing; *(corpo)* to shake; *(coda)* to wag □ **dimenarsi** *vr* to fling o.s. about.

dimensione *sf* dimension.

dimenticanza *sf* oversight.

dimenticare *vt* to forget; *(lasciare)* to leave; **dimenticarsi qc** to leave sthg □ **dimenticarsi di** *vr + prep* to forget about; **dimenticarsi di fare qc** to forget to do sthg.

dimesso, -a *pp* → **dimettere** ♦ *agg* humble.

dimestichezza *sf* familiarity.

dimettere *vt* to discharge □ **dimettersi** *vr* to resign.

dimezzare *vt* to halve.

diminuire *vt* to reduce ♦ *vi* to decrease; *(prezzi)* to drop.

diminuzione *sf* fall; *(di prezzi)* drop.

dimissioni *sfpl* resignation *(sg)*; **dare le ~** to hand in one's resignation.

dimostrare *vt (manifestare)* to show; *(provare)* to prove; **dimostra meno di vent'anni** he doesn't look twenty □ **dimostrarsi** *vr* to

dimostrazione

prove to be.

dimostrazione *sf* (*d'affetto, simpatia*) show; (*di teoria*) proof; (*protesta, per prodotto*) demonstration.

dinamico, -a, -ci, -che *agg* dynamic.

dinamite *sf* dynamite.

dinamo *sf inv* dynamo.

dinanzi *prep*: ~ a (*davanti a*) in front of; (*alla presenza di*) before.

dinosauro *sm* dinosaur.

dintorni *smpl* outskirts; **nei ~ di** in the vicinity of.

dio (*pl* dei) *sm* god □ **Dio** *sm* God; **mio Dio!** my God!

diocesi *sf inv* diocese.

dipartimento *sm* department.

dipendente *agg* subordinate ♦ *smf* employee.

dipendenza *sf* (*subordinazione*) dependence; (*assuefazione*) addiction; **essere alle dipendenze di qn** to be employed by sb.

dipendere *vi*: ~ **da** to depend on; (*derivare*) to be due to; **dipende** it depends.

dipeso, -a *pp* → **dipendere**.

dipingere *vt* to paint.

dipinto, -a *pp* → **dipingere** ♦ *sm* painting.

diploma, -i *sm* diploma.

diplomarsi *vr* to obtain a diploma.

diplomatico, -a, -ci, -che *agg* diplomatic ♦ *sm* (*funzionario*) diplomat; (*pasta*) pastry made of layers of liqueur-soaked sponge, puff pastry and confectioner's custard, topped with icing sugar.

diplomazia *sf* diplomacy.

diradare *vt* to cut down on □

diradarsi *vr* (*nebbia, nubi*) to clear; (*vegetazione*) to thin out.

dire *vt* 1. (*pronunciare*) to say; ~ **di sì/no** to say yes/no.

2. (*esprimere, raccontare*) to say; ~ **qc a qn** to tell sb sthg; ~ **a qn che/perché** to tell sb that/why; ~ **la verità** to tell the truth; **dimmi tutto** tell me everything; **dica pure** (*in un negozio*) can I help you?

3. (*ordinare*): ~ **a qn di fare qc** to tell sb to do sthg.

4. (*sostenere*) to say; **dice che non è vero** he says it isn't true.

5. (*tradurre*): **come si dice 'scusi' in inglese?** what's the English for 'scusi'?

6. (*pensare*) to think; **che ne dite di ...?** how about ...?; **e ~ che ...!** to think that ...!

7. (*in espressioni*): **diciamo che ...** let's say that ...; **a ~ il vero ...** to tell the truth ...; **vuol ~ che ...** it means (that) ...; **non c'è che ~** there's no doubt about it; **il nome non mi dice niente** the name doesn't mean much to me; **dico davvero** o **sul serio!** I'm serious!; **a dir poco** at least; **a dir tanto** at most; **volevo ben ~!** I thought so! ♦ *v impers*: **si dice che ...** they say (that) ...; **si direbbe che ...** it seems (that) ...

direttamente *avv* (*per via diretta*) straight; (*senza intermediari*) directly.

direttissimo *sm* express train.

diretto, -a *pp* → **dirigere** ♦ *agg* direct ♦ *sm* (*treno*) through train; **essere ~ a** *(aereo, passeggero)* to be bound for; *(indirizzato)* to be intended for.

direttore, -trice *sm, f* manager (*f* manageress); *(di scuola elementare)* head (teacher) *(Br)*, principal *(Am)*; **~ d'orchestra** conductor.

direzione *sf* direction; *(di azienda)* management.

dirigente *smf* executive.

dirigere *vt (attenzione, sguardo)* to direct; *(scuola, azienda)* to run; *(orchestra)* to conduct □ **dirigersi** *vr* to head.

dirimpetto *avv* opposite.

diritto, -a *agg & avv* straight ♦ *sm* right; *(leggi)* law; *(di abito, stoffa)* right side; *(nel tennis)* forehand; *(nella maglia)* plain stitch; **andare ~** *(in linea retta)* to go straight on; **vai ~ a casa** go straight home; **sempre (a) ~** straight on; **avere ~ a qc** to be entitled to sthg.

dirittura *sf*: **~ d'arrivo** home straight.

diroccato, -a *agg* in ruins.

dirottare *vt* to hijack; *(traffico)* to divert.

dirotto, -a *agg*: **piovere a ~** to pour.

dirupo *sm* precipice.

disabitato, -a *agg* uninhabited.

disaccordo *sm* disagreement.

disadattato, -a *agg* maladjusted.

disagio *sm (scomodità)* discomfort; *(imbarazzo)* uneasiness; **essere a ~** to be ill at ease.

disapprovare *vt* to disap-

prove.

disarmare *vt* to disarm.

disarmo *sm* disarmament.

disastro *sm* disaster; *(danno)* damage.

disastroso, -a *agg* disastrous.

disattento, -a *agg* inattentive.

disavanzo *sm* deficit.

disavventura *sf* mishap.

discapito *sm*: **a ~ di** to the detriment of.

discarica, -che *sf* dump.

discendente *smf* descendant.

discepolo, -a *sm, f* disciple.

discesa *sf* slope; *(movimento)* descent; **in ~** downhill; **~ libera** downhill race; **'~ a mare'** 'this way down to the sea'.

dischetto *sm* diskette.

disciplina *sf (ubbidienza)* discipline; *(materia)* subject.

disciplinato, -a *agg* disciplined.

disc-jockey [disk 'dʒɔkei] *smf inv* disc jockey.

disco, -schi *sm (musicale)* record; *(per computer)* disk; **~ orario** parking disc; **~ volante** flying saucer.

discolpare *vt* to clear.

discorde *agg* conflicting.

discorrere : **discorrere di** *v + prep* to talk about.

discorso *pp* → **discorrere** ♦ *sm* speech; *(conversazione)* conversation, talk.

discoteca, -che *sf* disco.

discretamente *avv (abbastanza bene)* fairly well; *(con tatto)* discreetly.

discreto, -a *agg (persona)* discreet; *(abbastanza buono)* reasonably good.

discrezione *sf (tatto)* discretion; *(moderazione)* moderation.

discriminare *vt* to discriminate.

discussione *sf (dibattito)* discussion; *(litigio)* argument.

discusso, -a *pp →* discutere.

discutere *vt (parlare di)* to discuss; *(contestare)* to question ◆ *vi* to argue; ~ **di** ○ **su** *(dibattere)* to discuss.

disdetto, -a *pp →* disdire.

disdire *vt* to cancel.

disegnare *vt* to draw; *(progettare)* to design ◆ *vi* to draw.

disegno *sm* drawing; *(motivo)* design; *(progetto)* project; ~ **di legge** bill.

diseredare *vt* to disinherit.

disertare *vt & vi* to desert.

disertore *sm* deserter.

disfare *vt* to undo; *(valigia)* to unpack; *(maglia)* to unravel; *(sciogliere)* to melt.

disfatto, -a *pp →* disfare.

disgelo *sm* thaw.

disgrazia *sf (incidente)* accident.

disgraziato, -a *agg (persona)* wretched; *(viaggio)* ill-fated; *(anno)* unlucky ◆ *sm, f (sfortunato)* poor wretch; *(canaglia)* rogue.

disguido *sm* error.

disgustare *vt* to disgust.

disgusto *sm* disgust.

disgustoso, -a *agg* disgusting.

disidratare *vt* to dehydrate.

disinfestare *vt* to disinfest.

disinfettante *agg & sm* disinfectant.

disinfettare *vt* to disinfect.

disinibito, -a *agg* uninhibited.

disintegrare *vt* to cause to disintegrate.

disinteressarsi : disinteressarsi di *vr + prep* to take no interest in.

disinteresse *sm (indifferenza)* indifference; *(generosità)* unselfishness.

disintossicare *vt* to detoxify; ~ **l'organismo** to clear out one's system □ **disintossicarsi** *vr (da droga)* to be treated for drug addiction.

disintossicazione *sf (da droga)* treatment for drug addiction.

disinvolto, -a *agg* free and easy.

disinvoltura *sf* ease.

dislivello *sm (di quota)* difference in height; *(fig: differenza)* gap.

disoccupato, -a *agg* unemployed ◆ *sm, f* unemployed person.

disoccupazione *sf* unemployment.

disonesto, -a *agg* dishonest.

disopra *avv* above; *(al piano superiore)* upstairs ◆ *agg inv* above.

disordinato, -a *agg* untidy; *(vita)* disorderly.

disordine *sm (materiale)* untidiness; *(mentale)* confusion; **in** ~ in a mess.

disorganizzazione *sf* disorganization.

disorientato, -a *agg* disorientated.

disossare *vt* to bone.

disotto *avv* below; (*al piano inferiore*) downstairs ◆ *agg inv* below.

dispari *agg inv* odd.

disparte *avv*: **tenersi** o **starsene in ~** to keep to o.s.

dispendioso, -a *agg* expensive.

dispensa *sf* (*stanza*) larder; (*mobile*) sideboard; (*fascicolo*) instalment.

disperarsi *vr* to despair.

disperatamente *avv* desperately.

disperato, -a *agg* desperate.

disperazione *sf* desperation.

disperdere *vt* to disperse.

disperso, -a *pp* → **disperdere** ◆ *sm, f* missing person.

dispetto *sm* (*atto*) spiteful trick; (*stizza*) vexation; **fare un ~ a qn** to play a spiteful trick on sb; **fare qc per ~** to do sthg out of spite; **a ~ di** despite.

dispiacere *sm* (*dolore*) grief; (*rammarico*) regret ◆ *v impers*: **le dispiace se aspetto qui?** do you mind if I wait here?; **mi dispiace che sia andata così** I'm sorry it worked out that way; **mi dispiace di non potermi trattenere** I'm afraid I can't stop.

dispiaciuto, -a *pp* → **dispiacere** ◆ *agg* sorry.

disponibile *agg* available; (*persona*) willing to help.

disponibilità *sf* (*di posto, camere*) availability; (*di persona*) willingness to help; (*di denaro*) liquid assets (*pl*).

disporre *vt* to arrange □ **disporre di** *v + prep* (*poter usare*) to have at one's disposal; (*avere*) to have.

dispositivo *sm* device.

disposizione *sf* (*di mobili, oggetti*) arrangement; (*comando*) order; (*attitudine*) disposition; (*DIR*) provision; **essere a ~ di** to be at sb's disposal; **mettere qc a ~ di qn** to make sthg available to sb.

disposto, -a *pp* → **disporre** ◆ *agg*: **~ a fare qc** prepared to do sthg.

disprezzare *vt* to despise.

disprezzo *sm* contempt.

disputa *sf* argument.

dissanguare *vt* (*fig*: *persona*) to bleed white.

disseminare *vt* to spread.

dissenso *sm* (*disapprovazione*) dissent; (*contrasto*) disagreement.

dissenteria *sf* dysentery.

disservizio *sm* inefficiency.

dissestato, -a *agg* uneven.

dissidente *smf* dissident.

dissidio *sm* disagreement.

dissimulare *vt* to conceal.

dissoluto, -a *pp* → **dissolvere** ◆ *agg* dissolute.

dissolvere *vt* (*sciogliere*) to dissolve; (*nebbia, fumo*) to disperse.

dissuadere *vt*: **~ qn dal fare qc** to dissuade sb from doing sthg.

dissuaso, -a *pp* → **dissuadere**.

distaccare *vt* (*oggetti*) to

remove; *(dipendente)* to transfer; *(SPORT)* to outdistance □ **distaccarsi da** *vr + prep (fig: allontanarsi)* to withdraw from.

distacco, -chi *sm* separation; *(indifferenza)* detachment.

distante *agg & avv* far away; ~ **da** far from.

distanza *sf* distance; *(temporale):* **a ~ di due mesi** after two months; **tenere le distanze** to keep one's distance.

distanziare *vt (separare)* to space out; *(SPORT)* to outdistance.

distare *vi:* **quanto dista da qui?** how far is it from here?

distendere *vt (gamba, mano)* to stretch out; *(telo, coperta)* to spread; *(rilassare)* to relax □ **distendersi** *vr (sdraiarsi)* to lie down; *(rilassarsi)* to relax.

distesa *sf* expanse.

disteso, -a *pp →* **distendere**.

distillare *vt* to distil.

distilleria *sf* distillery.

distinguere *vt* to distinguish.

distintivo, -a *agg* distinctive ♦ *sm* badge.

distinto, -a *pp →* **distinguere** ♦ *agg (diverso)* different; *(immagine)* distinct; *(persona)* distinguished; **Distinti saluti** *(in lettera)* Yours faithfully.

distinzione *sf* distinction.

distogliere *vt:* ~ **qc da qn** to take sthg away from sb; ~ **qn da qc** to deter sb from sthg.

distolto, -a *pp →* **distogliere**.

distorsione *sf (MED)* sprain; *(di suono, immagine)* distortion.

distrarre *vt* to distract; *(divertire)* to amuse □ **distrarsi** *vr* to be distracted; *(divertirsi)* to amuse o.s.

distratto, -a *pp →* **distrarre** ♦ *agg (sbadato)* absent-minded; *(disattento)* inattentive.

distrazione *sf* distraction; *(svago)* amusement.

distretto *sm* district.

distribuire *vt (assegnare compiti)* to allocate; *(posta, giornali)* to distribute.

distributore *sm:* ~ **automatico** vending machine; ~ **(di benzina)** petrol pump *(Br)*, gasoline pump *(Am)*.

distribuzione *sf* distribution; *(ripartizione)* allocation.

distruggere *vt* to destroy.

distrutto, -a *pp →* **distruggere** ♦ *agg* shattered.

distruzione *sf* destruction.

disturbare *vt* to disturb; '**non ~ il conducente**' 'do not distract the driver' □ **disturbarsi** *vr* to bother.

disturbo *sm (fastidio)* bother; *(malessere)* disorder; *(di comunicazione)* interference.

disubbidiente *agg* disobedient.

disubbidire *vi:* ~ **(a qn)** to disobey (sb).

disumano, -a *agg* inhuman.

disuso *sm:* **in ~** obsolete.

ditale *sm* thimble.

dito *(pl f* **dita)** *sm* finger; *(misura)* drop; ~ **(del piede)** toe.

ditta *sf* company, firm.

dittatura *sf* dictatorship.

dittongo, -ghi *sm* diphthong.

diurno, -a *agg* daytime *(dav s)*.

diva → **divo**.

divampare *vi* to flare up.

divano *sm* sofa; ~ **letto** sofa-bed.

divaricare *vt* to open wide.

divenire *vi* to become.

diventare *vi* to become; ~ **rosso** *(persona)* to go red.

diversificare *vt* to diversify.

diversità *sf inv* diversity; *(l'esser diverso)* difference.

diversivo *sm* diversion.

diverso, -a *agg* different; ~ **da** different from □ **diversi, -e** *agg pl* various, several ♦ *pron pl* several; *(varie persone)* several (people).

divertente *agg* amusing.

divertimento *sm* amusement.

divertire *vt* to amuse □ **divertirsi** *vr* to enjoy o.s.

dividere *vt* to divide; *(spartire)* to share out; *(separare)* to separate; *(condividere)* to share □ **dividersi** *vr* *(ripartirsi)* to split up; *(coppia)* to separate.

divieto *sm* prohibition; '~ **di sosta**' 'no waiting'; '~ **di transito**' 'no thoroughfare'.

divinità *sf inv* divinity.

divino, -a *agg* divine.

divisa *sf* uniform.

divisione *sf* division.

diviso, -a *pp* → **dividere**.

divisorio, -a *agg* dividing.

divo, -a *sm, f* star.

divorare *vt* to devour.

divorziare *vi* to divorce.

divorziato, -a *agg* divorced ♦ *sm, f* divorced person.

divorzio *sm* divorce.

divulgare *vt* *(notizia)* to divulge; *(scienza, dottrina)* to popularize □ **divulgarsi** *vr* to spread.

dizionario *sm* dictionary.

D.J. [di:'dʒei] *smf* *(abbr di disc-jockey)* DJ.

D.N.A. *sm* DNA.

DOC *(abbr di Denominazione di Origine Controllata)* label guaranteeing the quality of an Italian wine.

doccia, -ce *sf* shower; **fare la** ~ to take o to have a shower.

docente *agg* teaching ♦ *smf* teacher; *(di università)* lecturer.

docile *agg* *(animale)* docile.

documentare *vt* to document □ **documentarsi** *vr* to gather information.

documentario *sm* documentary.

documento *sm* document □ **documenti** *smpl* documents.

dodicesimo, -a *num* twelfth, → **sesto**.

dodici *num* twelve, → **sei**.

dogana *sf* customs *(pl)*; **passare la** ~ to go through customs.

doganale *agg* customs *(dav s)*.

doganiere *sm* customs officer.

dolce *agg* sweet; *(persona, carattere)* gentle; *(suono, musica, voce)* soft ♦ *sm* *(torta)* cake; *(portata)* dessert.

dolcezza *sf* sweetness.

dolcificante *sm* sweetener.

dolciumi *smpl* confectionery *(sg)*.

dolere

dolere *vi* to hurt ▫ **dolersi di** *vr*
+ *prep (essere spiacente di)* to regret;
(lamentarsi di) to complain of.

dollaro *sm* dollar.

dolo *sm (DIR)* malice.

Dolomiti *sfpl*: **le ~** the
Dolomites.

dolore *sm (fisico)* pain; *(morale)*
sorrow.

doloroso, -a *agg (intervento)*
painful; *(situazione)* distressing.

domanda *sf (per sapere)* question; *(per ottenere)* request; *(COMM)*
demand; **fare una ~ a qn** to ask sb
a question; **fare ~** to apply.

domandare *vt (per sapere)* to
ask; *(per ottenere)* to ask for; **~ qc a
qn** to ask sb sthg ▫ **domandarsi**
vr to wonder.

domani *avv* tomorrow ◆ *sm
(giorno seguente)* tomorrow; **a ~!**
see you tomorrow!; **~ l'altro** the
day after tomorrow; **il ~** the
future; **~ mattina** tomorrow
morning; **~ sera** tomorrow
evening.

domare *vt (animale)* to tame;
(rivolta) to put down; *(incendio)* to
control.

domattina *avv* tomorrow
morning.

domenica, -che *sf* Sunday, →
sabato.

domestico, -a, -ci, -che
agg & sm, f domestic.

domicilio *sm* domicile; **a ~**
home *(dav s)*.

dominante *agg* dominant.

dominare *vt* to dominate;
(paese, popolo) to rule; *(situazione,
impulso)* to control ▫ **dominarsi** *vr*

to control o.s.

dominio *sm (potere)* power;
(controllo) control; *(territorio)* do-
minion; **essere di ~ pubblico** to be
common knowledge.

domino *sm* dominoes *(pl)*.

donare *vt* to give ◆ *vi*: **questo
colore ti dona** this colour suits
you; **~ il sangue** to give blood.

donatore, -trice *sm, f* giver;
(di sangue, organi) donor.

dondolare *vt* to rock ◆ *vi* to
sway ▫ **dondolarsi** *vr* to sway.

dondolo *sm* swing hammock;
cavallo/sedia a ~ rocking horse/
chair.

donna *sf* woman; *(nelle carte)*
queen; **~ di servizio** maid.

dono *sm* gift.

doping *sm* doping.

dopo *avv* afterwards; *(più tardi)*
later; *(nello spazio)* after ◆ *prep (di
tempo)* after; *(di luogo)* past, after ◆
agg inv after ◆ *cong*: **~ aver fatto qc**
after doing sthg; **il giorno ~** the
following day; **un giorno ~** a day
later; **a ~!** see you later!; **~ di me**
after me.

dopobarba *sm inv* aftershave.

dopodiché *avv* after which.

dopodomani *avv* the day after
tomorrow.

dopoguerra *sm* post-war period.

dopolavoro *sm workers' recreational club.*

dopopranzo *avv* in the early
afternoon.

doposcì *sm inv* après-ski.

doposcuola *sm inv* supervised

after-school activities.

dopotutto *avv* after all.

doppiaggio *sm* dubbing.

doppiare *vt* (*film*) to dub; (*SPORT*) to lap; (*NAUT*) to round.

doppiato, -a *agg* dubbed.

doppio, -a *agg & avv* double ◆ *sm* (*SPORT*) doubles; **ne ha il ~ di me** (*quantità*) he has twice as much as me; (*numero*) he has twice as many as me.

doppione *sm* duplicate.

doppiopetto *sm* double-breasted jacket.

dorato, -a *agg* (*di colore*) golden; (*ricoperto d'oro*) gilt.

dormiglione, -a *sm, f* sleepyhead.

dormire *vi* to sleep.

dormitorio *sm* dormitory.

dorso *sm* back; (*di libro*) spine.

dosaggio *sm* dosage.

dosare *vt* to measure out; (*MED*) to dose.

dose *sf* amount; (*MED*) dose.

dosso *sm* bump; **togliersi** o **levarsi qc di ~** to take sthg off.

dotare *vt*: ~ **qc di qc** to equip sthg with sthg.

dotato, -a *agg* gifted.

dote *sf* (*qualità*) gift; (*di sposa*) dowry.

Dott. (*abbr di dottore*) Dr.

dottorato *sm* doctorate.

dottore, -essa *sm, f* (*medico*) doctor; (*laureato*) graduate.

dottrina *sf* doctrine.

Dott.ssa (*abbr di dottoressa*) Dr.

dove *avv* where; **da ~ vieni?** where do you come from?; **di ~**

sei? where are you from?; **dov'è?** where is it?; ~ **vai?** where are you going?; **siediti ~ vuoi** sit wherever you like.

dovere *vt* 1. (*essere debitore di*): ~ **qc a qn** to owe sb sthg; **gli devo dei soldi/un favore** I owe him some money/a favour; **quanto le devo?** (*in negozio*) how much does it come to?

2. (*aver l'obbligo di*): ~ **fare qc** to have to do sthg; **comportarsi come si deve** to behave o.s. properly; **ora devo andare** I have to o must go now.

3. (*aver bisogno di*): ~ **fare qc** to have to do sthg; **devo dormire almeno otto ore** I need at least eight hours' sleep; **devi sapere che ...** you should know that ...

4. (*esprime un rimprovero*): **avreste dovuto pensarci prima** you should have thought of it earlier; **avrei dovuto saperlo** I should have known.

5. (*per suggerire*): **dovrebbe prendersi delle vacanze** he should o ought to take a holiday.

6. (*esprime probabilità*): **devono essere già le sette** it must be seven o'clock already; **il tempo dovrebbe rimettersi** the weather should improve.

7. (*esprime intenzione*): **dovevamo partire ieri, ma ...** we were due to leave yesterday, but ...

◆ *sm* duty; **avere dei doveri verso qn** to have a duty to sb.

dovunque *avv* (*in qualunque luogo*) wherever; (*dappertutto*) everywhere.

dovuto, -a *agg*: ~ **a** due to.

dozzina sf dozen; **una ~ di rose** a dozen roses.

drago, -ghi sm dragon.

dramma, -i sm drama.

drammatico, -a, -ci, -che agg dramatic.

drastico, -a, -ci, -che agg drastic.

drenare vt to drain.

dritto, -a agg & avv = diritto.

drizzare vt (raddrizzare) to straighten; **~ le orecchie** to prick up one's ears □ **drizzarsi** vr: **drizzarsi (in piedi)** to stand up.

droga, -ghe sf drug.

drogare vt to drug □ **drogarsi** vr to take drugs.

drogato, -a sm, f drug addict.

drogheria sf grocer's.

droghiere sm grocer.

dromedario sm dromedary.

dubbio, -a agg (incerto) doubtful; (equivoco) questionable ♦ sm doubt; **ho il ~ che menta** I suspect that he's lying; **essere in ~** to be in doubt; **mettere in ~ qc** to question sthg; **senza ~** without a doubt.

dubbioso, -a agg uncertain.

dubitare : **dubitare di** v + prep to doubt; (mettere in discussione) to question; **dubito che venga** I doubt whether he'll come.

duca, -chi sm duke.

duchessa sf duchess.

due num two, → **sei**.

duecento num two hundred, → **sei** □ **Duecento** sm: **il Duecento** the thirteenth century.

duemila num two thousand □ **il Duemila** sm the year two thou-

sand, → **sei**.

duepezzi sm inv (bikini) bikini; (abito) two-piece suit.

duna sf dune.

dunque cong (perciò) so; (allora) well ♦ sm: **venire al ~** to get to the point.

duomo sm cathedral.

duplex sm inv party line.

duplicato sm duplicate.

duplice agg double; **in ~ copia** in duplicate.

durante prep during.

durare vi to last ♦ vt: **~ fatica (a fare qc)** to tire o.s. out (doing sthg).

durata sf (periodo) duration.

durezza sf (di materiale) hardness; (insensibilità) severity.

duro, -a agg hard; (carne) tough; (ostinato) stubborn; (severo) harsh ♦ sm, f tough person; **tieni ~!** don't give in!

durone sm callus.

e (spesso **ed** + vocale) cong and; **~ io?** what about me?; **~ vacci!** well then, go!

è → **essere**.

E (abbr di est) E.

ebano sm ebony.

ebbene cong (allora) well.

ebbrezza sf (ubriachezza): **in**

stato di ~ drunk.

ebete *agg* idiotic.

ebollizione *sf* boiling.

ebraico, -a, -ci, -che *agg & sm* Hebrew.

ebreo, -a *agg* Jewish ◆ *sm, f* Jew.

Ebridi *sfpl:* **le (isole) ~** the Hébrides.

ecc. *(abbr di eccetera)* etc.

eccedenza *sf* excess.

eccedere *vt* to exceed □ **eccedere in** *v + prep:* **~ nel bere/mangiare** to drink/eat too much.

eccellente *agg* excellent.

eccellenza *sf* excellence; *(titolo)* Excellency.

eccellere *vi:* **~ (in qc)** to excel (at sthg).

eccelso *pp* → **eccellere.**

eccentrico, -a, -ci, -che *agg* eccentric.

eccessivo, -a *agg* excessive.

eccesso *sm* excess; **~ di velocità** speeding; **all'~** excessively; **bagaglio in ~** excess baggage.

eccetera *avv* etcetera.

eccetto *prep* except ◆ *cong:* **~ che** unless.

eccettuare *vt* to except.

eccezionale *agg* exceptional.

eccezione *sf* exception; **a ~ di** with the exception of; **d'~** exceptional; **senza ~** without exception.

eccidio *sm* massacre.

eccitante *agg* *(stimolante)* stimulating; *(provocante)* exciting.

eccitare *vt* *(curiosità)* to arouse □ **eccitarsi** *vr* to get excited; *(ses-*

sualmente) to become aroused.

eccitazione *sf* excitement.

ecclesiastico, -a, -ci, -che *agg* ecclesiastical ◆ *sm* ecclesiastic.

ecco *avv* here is; **~ lei** here you are; **~ fatto!** there, that's that!; **eccolo!** there he is!; **eccone uno!** there's one!

eccome *avv* you bet!

eclissi *sf inv* eclipse.

eco *(pl m* **echi)** *sf* echo.

ecologia *sf* ecology.

ecologico, -a, -ci, -che *agg* ecological.

economia *sf* economy; *(scienza)* economics *(sg);* **fare ~** to economize.

economico, -a, -ci, -che *agg (dell'economia)* economic; *(poco costoso)* economical.

ecosistema, -i *sm* ecosystem.

ECU *sm inv* ECU.

eczema *sm* eczema.

ed → **e.**

edera *sf* ivy.

edicola *sf* newsstand.

edificare *vt* to build.

edificio *sm* building.

edile *agg* building *(dav s).*

Edimburgo *sf* Edinburgh.

editore, -trice *agg* publishing *(dav s)* ◆ *sm* publisher.

editoria *sf* publishing (industry).

edizione *sf* edition; **~ speciale** special edition.

educare *vt (formare)* to educate; *(bambino)* to bring up.

educato, -a *agg* polite.

educazione *sf (maniere)* (good) manners *(pl)*; *(formazione)* training; ~ **fisica** physical education.

effervescente *agg* effervescent.

effettivamente *avv* in fact.

effettivo, -a *agg* actual, real.

effetto *sm* effect; **in effetti** in fact, actually.

effettuare *vt* to carry out.

efficace *agg* effective.

efficacia *sf* effectiveness.

efficiente *agg* efficient.

efficienza *sf* efficiency.

effimero, -a *agg (gioia, successo)* short-lived.

egemonia *sf (supremazia)* hegemony.

Egitto *sm*: l'~ Egypt.

egli *pron* he; ~ **stesso** he himself.

egocentrico, -a, -ci, -che *agg* egocentric.

egoismo *sm* selfishness.

egoista, -i, -e *agg* selfish.

egregio, -a, -gi, -gie *agg (nelle lettere)*: **Egregio Signore** Dear Sir.

eguagliare = **uguagliare.**

ehi *esclam* hey!

E.I. *abbr* = **Esercito Italiano.**

elaborare *vt (progetto, piano)* to work out; *(con computer)* to process.

elaborato, -a *agg* elaborate.

elaboratore *sm*: ~ **(elettronico)** computer.

elaborazione *sf*: ~ **dei dati** data processing.

elasticità *sf* elasticity; *(di mente)* flexibility.

elasticizzato, -a *agg* stretch *(dav s).*

elastico, -a, -ci, -che *agg* elastic; *(mente)* flexible ♦ *sm (gommino)* rubber band; *(da cucito)* elastic.

Elba *sf*: l'(isola d')~ Elba.

elefante *sm* elephant.

elegante *agg* elegant.

eleganza *sf* elegance.

eleggere *vt* to elect.

elementare *agg* elementary ❑

elementari *sfpl*: **le (scuole) elementari** primary school *(sg) (Br)*, grade school *(sg) (Am).*

elemento *sm (fattore)* element; *(di cucina)* unit; *(persona)* individual.

elemosina *sf* alms *(pl)*; **chiedere l'~** to beg.

elencare *vt* to list.

elenco, -chi *sm* list; ~ **telefonico** telephone directory.

eletto, -a *pp* → **eleggere.**

elettorale *agg* electoral.

elettore, -trice *sm, f* voter.

elettrauto *sm inv (officina)* workshop for electrical repairs on cars; *(persona)* car electrician.

elettricista, -i *sm* electrician.

elettricità *sf* electricity.

elettrico, -a, -ci, -che *agg* electric.

elettrodomestico, -ci *sm* electrical household appliance.

elettronico, -a, -ci, -che *agg* electronic.

elezione *sf* election.

elica, -che *sf* propeller.

elicottero *sm* helicopter.

eliminare *vt* to eliminate.

eliminatoria *sf* qualifying round.

ella *pron* she.

elmetto *sm* helmet.

elogio *sm* praise.

eloquente *agg* eloquent.

eludere *vt* to evade.

elusivo, -a *agg* elusive.

elvetico, -a, -ci, -che *agg* Swiss.

emaciato, -a *agg* emaciated.

emanare *vt* (luce) to send out; (calore) to give off; (legge) to issue.

emancipato, -a *agg* emancipated.

emarginato, -a *sm, f* social outcast.

ematoma, -i *sm* haematoma.

embrione *sm* embryo.

emergenza *sf* emergency.

emergere *vi* to emerge.

emerso, -a *pp* → **emergere**.

emicrania *sf* migraine.

emigrante *smf* emigrant.

emigrare *vi* (persona) to emigrate; (animale) to migrate.

Emilia Romagna *sf*: l'**~** Emilia Romagna (region in eastern central Italy).

emisfero *sm* hemisphere.

emittente *sf* broadcasting station.

emorragia *sf* hemorrhage.

emozionante *agg* thrilling.

emozione *sf* emotion.

emulsione *sf* emulsion.

enciclopedia *sf* encyclopedia.

ENEL *abbr* Italian national electric-ity company.

energia *sf* energy; **~ elettrica** electrical energy.

energico, -a, -ci, -che *agg* energetic.

enfasi *sf inv* emphasis.

enigma, -i *sm* enigma.

ennesimo, -a *agg* umpteenth.

enorme *agg* enormous.

enoteca, -che *sf* (negozio) vintage wine store; (bar) wine bar.

ente *sm* body, organization.

entrambi, -e *pron pl* both (of them) ◆ *agg pl*: **entrambe le città** both towns.

entrare *vi* to enter, to go in; **~ in qc** (trovar posto) to fit into sthg; (essere ammesso) to join sthg; **entra! come in!**; **questo non c'entra niente** that has nothing to do with it; **~ in una stanza** to enter a room; **~ in guerra** to go to war; **far ~ qn** to let sb in.

entrata *sf* entrance; '**~ libera**' (in museo) 'admission free'; (in negozio) 'browsers welcome' ❑ **entrate** *sfpl* (incasso) takings; (guadagno) income (sg).

entro *prep* (periodo) in, within; (scadenza) by.

entusiasmare *vt* to enthral ❑ **entusiasmarsi** *vr*: **entusiasmarsi (per)** to get excited (about).

entusiasmo *sm* enthusiasm.

entusiasta, -i, -e *agg* enthusiastic.

enunciare *vt* to enunciate.

Eolie *sfpl*: **le (isole) ~** the Aeolian Islands.

epatite *sf* hepatitis.

epidemia sf epidemic.

epidermide sf epidermis.

Epifania sf: l'~ the Epiphany.

epilessia sf epilepsy.

episodio sm episode.

epoca, -che sf (era, età) age; (tempo) time; **d'~** (mobile, costume) period (dav s).

eppure cong and yet, nevertheless.

equatore sm equator.

equazione sf equation.

equestre agg equestrian.

equilibrare vt to balance.

equilibrato, -a agg (proporzionato) balanced; (persona) well-balanced.

equilibrio sm (stabilità) balance; (posizione, stato) equilibrium; **perdere l'~** to lose one's balance.

equino, -a agg equine, horse (dav s).

equipaggiamento sm (di nave, aereo) fitting out; (sportivo) equipment.

equipaggio sm crew.

equitazione sf horse riding.

equivalente agg & sm equivalent.

equivalere : equivalere a v + prep to be equivalent to.

equivalso, -a pp → equivalere.

equivoco, -a, -ci, -che agg (ambiguo) equivocal; (poco onesto) dubious ♦ sm misunderstanding.

era sf age.

erba sf (prato) grass; (pianta) herb; **erbe aromatiche** herbs.

erbazzone sm spinach and Parmesan cheese tart topped with bacon and parsley (a speciality of Emilia Romagna).

erboristeria sf herbalist's.

erede smf heir (f heiress).

eredità sf inv inheritance; (biologica) heredity; **lasciare qc in ~ (a qn)** to bequeath sthg (to sb).

ereditare vt to inherit.

ereditario, -a agg hereditary.

eresia sf heresy.

eretico, -a, -ci, -che sm, f heretic.

eretto, -a pp → erigere ♦ agg erect.

ergastolo sm life imprisonment.

erigere vt to erect.

ernia sf hernia.

ero → essere.

eroe, eroina sm, f hero (f heroine).

erogare vt to supply.

eroico, -a, -ci, -che agg heroic.

eroina sf (droga) heroin, → eroe.

erosione sf erosion.

erotico, -a, -ci, -che agg erotic.

errare vi (vagare) to wander; (sbagliare) to be mistaken.

errore sm (di ortografia, calcolo) mistake; (colpa) error; **per ~** by mistake.

erta sf: **stare all'~** to be on the alert.

eruzione sf (di vulcano) eruption; (MED) rash.

esagerare vt & vi to exaggerate.

esagerato, -a *agg* excessive.

esalazione *sf* exhalation.

esaltare *vt (lodare)* to extol; *(entusiasmare)* to excite.

esame *sm* examination; **fare o dare un ~** to take an exam; **~ del sangue** blood test.

esaminare *vt (analizzare)* to examine; *(candidato)* to interview.

esattamente *avv & esclam* exactly.

esattezza *sf* accuracy.

esatto, -a *agg (giusto)* correct; *(preciso)* exact ♦ *esclam* exactly!

esattore *sm* collector.

esauriente *agg* exhaustive.

esaurimento *sm* exhaustion; **~ (nervoso)** nervous breakdown.

esaurire *vt* to exhaust ◻ **esaurirsi** *vr (merce)* to run out; *(persona)* to wear o.s. out.

esaurito, -a *agg (provviste, pozzo)* exhausted; *(merce)* sold out; *(persona)* worn out; **'tutto ~'** 'sold out'.

esausto, -a *agg* worn out.

esca *(pl* **esche)** *sf* bait.

escandescenza *sf*: **dare in escandescenze** to lose one's temper.

eschimese *smf* Eskimo.

esclamare *vi* to exclaim.

esclamazione *sf* exclamation.

escludere *vt* to exclude.

esclusiva *sf (di notizia)* scoop; *(DIR)* exclusive rights *(pl)*.

esclusivo, -a *agg* exclusive.

escluso, -a *pp →* **escludere**.

esco → **uscire**.

escogitare *vt* to come up with.

escursione *sf* excursion; **~ termica** temperature range.

esecutivo, -a *agg & sm* executive.

esecuzione *sf* execution; *(di concerto)* performance.

eseguire *vt* to carry out; *(in musica)* to perform.

esempio *sm* example; **ad o per ~** for example; **fare un ~** to give an example.

esentare *vt*: **~ qn/qc da qc** to exempt sb/sthg from sthg.

esente *agg*: **~ da** *(esonerato da)* exempt from; *(libero da)* free from.

esequie *sfpl* funeral rites.

esercitare *vt* to exercise; *(professione)* to practise ◻ **esercitarsi** *vr* to practise.

esercito *sm* army.

esercizio *sm* exercise; *(di professione)* practice; *(azienda, negozio)* business; **essere fuori ~** to be out of practice.

esibire *vt* to show ◻ **esibirsi** *vr* to perform.

esigente *agg* demanding.

esigenza *sf (bisogno)* requirement; *(pretesa)* demand.

esigere *vt (pretendere)* to demand; *(richiedere)* to require; *(riscuotere)* to collect.

esile *agg (sottile)* thin; *(persona)* slim.

esilio *sm* exile.

esistente *agg* existing.

esistenza *sf* existence.

esistere *vi* to exist.

esitare *vi* to hesitate.

esitazione sf hesitation.

esito sm outcome.

esorbitante agg exorbitant.

esordio sm debut.

esortare vt: ~ qn a fare qc to urge sb to do sthg.

esotico, -a, -ci, -che agg exotic.

espandere vt to expand ⬚

espandersi vr (ingrandirsi) to expand; (odori, liquidi) to spread.

espansione sf (allargamento) expansion; (di attività) growth.

espansivo, -a agg expansive.

espanso, -a pp → espandere.

espediente sm expedient.

espellere vt (da scuola) to expel; (MED) to excrete.

esperienza sf experience.

esperimento sm (prova) test; (scientifico) experiment.

esperto, -a agg (con esperienza) experienced; (bravo) skilful ◆ sm expert.

espiare vt to expiate.

esplicito, -a agg explicit.

esplodere vi to explode ◆ vt to fire.

esplorare vt to explore.

esploratore, -trice sm, f explorer.

esplosione sf explosion; (di gioia, ira) outburst.

esplosivo, -a agg & sm explosive.

esploso, -a pp → esplodere.

esporre vt (merce) to display; (opera d'arte) to show; (pellicola) to expose; (idea, fatto) to explain.

esportare vt to export.

esportazione sf (spedizione) exportation; (merce) exports (pl).

esposizione sf (di merce) display; (mostra) exhibition; (di pellicola) exposure; (resoconto) account.

esposto, -a pp → esporre ◆ sm petition ◆ agg: ~ a sud facing south.

espressione sf expression.

espressivo, -a agg expressive.

espresso, -a pp → esprimere ◆ sm (treno) express; (caffè) espresso; (lettera) express letter.

esprimere vt (pensiero, sentimento) to express ⬚ **esprimersi** vr (spiegarsi) to express o.s.; (parlare) to speak.

espulso, -a pp → espellere.

essenziale agg essential.

essere vi 1. (per descrivere) to be; **sono italiano** I'm Italian; **sei solo?** are you alone?; **siamo di Torino** we're from Turin; **Franco è (un) medico** Franco is a doctor.
2. (trovarsi) to be; **dove siete?** where are you?; **il museo è in centro** the museum is in the town centre; **sono a casa** I'm at home; **sono stato in Scozia tre volte** I've been to Scotland three times.
3. (esistere): **c'è** there is; **c'è un'altra possibilità** there's another possibility; **ci sono** there are; **ci sono vari alberghi** there are various hotels.
4. (con data, ora) to be; **oggi è martedì** today is Tuesday; **è l'una** it's one o'clock; **sono le due** it's two o'clock.
5. (con prezzo, peso): **quant'è? — (sono) 10 000 lire** how much is

it? – (that's) 10,000 lira; **sono due chili e mezzo** that's two and a half kilos.

6. *(indica appartenenza)*: ~ **di qn** to belong to sb; **questa macchina è di Paolo** this car is Paolo's.

7. *(indica bisogno, obbligo)*: **è da fare** it's still to be done; **la camera è da prenotare** the room is to be booked.

◆ *v impers* to be; **è tardi** it's late; **è vero che ...** it's true that ...; **oggi è freddo** it's cold today; **è meglio telefonare** it's better to phone.

◆ *v aus* **1.** *(in tempi passati)* to have, to be; **sono tornato ieri** I came back yesterday; **erano già usciti** they'd already gone out; **sono nata a Roma** I was born in Rome; **ti sei lavato?** did you wash yourself?

2. *(in passivi)* to be; **questo oggetto è fatto a mano** this object is handmade; **sono stato pagato ieri** I was paid yesterday.

◆ *sm (creatura)* being; ~ **umano** human being; **gli esseri viventi** the living.

essi, -e → **esso**.

esso, -a *pron* it □ **essi, -e** *pron pl* *(soggetto)* they; *(con preposizione)* them.

est *sm* east; **a** ~ **di Milano** east of Milan.

estate *sf* summer.

estendere *vt* to extend.

esteriore *agg (esterno)* external, outward; *(apparente)* superficial.

esterno, -a *agg* exterior; *(muro)* outer; *(pericolo)* external ◆ *sm* outside; **all'**~ on the outside.

estero, -a *agg* foreign ◆ *sm*: **l'**~ foreign countries *(pl)*; **all'**~

abroad.

esteso, -a *pp* → **estendere** ◆ *agg* extensive.

estetista, -i, -e *smf* beautician.

estinguere *vt (fuoco)* to extinguish; *(debito)* to settle □ **estinguersi** *vr (fuoco)* to go out; *(specie)* to become extinct.

estinto, -a *pp* → **estinguere**.

estintore *sm* (fire) extinguisher.

estivo, -a *agg* summer *(dav s)*.

estorcere *vt* to extort.

estraneo, -a *agg* unconnected ◆ *sm, f* stranger.

estrarre *vt* to extract; *(sorteggiare)* to draw.

estratto, -a *pp* → **estrarre** ◆ *sm (di sostanza)* essence; *(di libro)* extract; ~ **conto** bank statement.

estrazione *sf* extraction; ~ **a sorte** draw; ~ **sociale** social class.

estremità *sf inv* end ◆ *sfpl* extremities.

estremo, -a *agg (grande)* extreme; *(drastico)* drastic; *(ultimo)* final, last ◆ *sm (punto)* extreme; *(fig: limite)* limit □ **estremi** *smpl* details.

estroverso, -a *agg* extrovert.

estuario *sm* estuary.

esuberante *agg* exuberant.

età *sf inv* age; **abbiamo la stessa** ~ we are the same age; **la maggiore** ~ the legal age; **di mezza** ~ middle-aged; **la terza** ~ old age.

etere *sm* ether.

eternità *sf* eternity.

eterno, -a *agg* eternal.

eterogeneo, -a agg heterogeneous.

eterosessuale agg & smf heterosexual.

etica sf ethics.

etichetta sf (di prodotto) label; (cerimoniale) etiquette.

Etna sm: l'~ Mount Etna.

etrusco, -a, -schi, -sche agg Etruscan □ **Etruschi** smpl: **gli Etruschi** the Etruscans.

ettaro sm hectare.

etto sm = 100 grams.

ettogrammo sm hectogram.

eucaristia sf: l'~ the Eucharist.

euforia sf euphoria.

EUR sm residential area of Rome built on the site of the Rome Exhibition.

Europa sf: l'~ Europe.

europeo, -a agg & sm, f European.

eurovisione sf: **in ~** Eurovision (dav s).

eutanasia sf euthanasia.

evacuare vt to evacuate.

evacuazione sf evacuation.

evadere vt (tasse, fisco) to evade; (corrispondenza) to deal with ♦ vi: **~ (da qc)** to escape (from sthg).

evaporare vi to evaporate.

evasione sf escape; **~ fiscale** tax evasion; **d'~** escapist.

evasivo, -a agg evasive.

evaso, -a pp → evadere ♦ sm, f escapee.

evenienza sf: **in ogni ~** should the need arise.

evento sm event.

eventuale agg possible.

eventualità sf inv possibility.

eventualmente avv if necessary.

evidente agg (chiaro) clear; (ovvio) obvious.

evidenza sf evidence; **mettere in ~** to highlight.

evitare vt to avoid; **~ di fare qc** to avoid doing sthg; **~ qc a qn** to spare sb sthg.

evocare vt (ricordare) to recall; (spiriti) to evoke.

evoluto, -a agg (tecnica, paese) advanced; (persona) broadminded.

evoluzione sf (biologica) evolution; (progresso) progress.

evviva esclam hurrah!

ex prep: l'~ **presidente** the former president; **la sua ~ moglie** his ex-wife.

extra agg inv & sm inv extra.

extracomunitario, -a agg from outside the EU ♦ sm, f immigrant from a non-EU country.

extraconiugale agg extramarital.

extraterrestre smf alien.

F

fa¹ → fare.

fa² avv: **un anno ~** a year ago; **tempo ~** some time ago.

fabbisogno sm needs (pl).

fabbrica, -che sf factory.

fabbricare vt (costruire) to build; (produrre) to make.

faccenda *sf (questione)* affair, matter ❑ **faccende** *sfpl*: **faccende (domestiche)** housework *(sg)*.

facchino *sm* porter.

faccia, -ce *sf* face; **di ~ a** opposite; **~ a ~** face to face; **che ~ tosta!** what a nerve!

facciata *sf (di edificio)* facade; *(di pagina)* side.

faccio → **fare**.

facile *agg* easy; **è ~ che il treno sia in ritardo** the train is likely to be late.

facilità *sf (caratteristica)* easiness; *(attitudine)* ease.

facilitare *vt* to make easier.

facoltà *sf inv* faculty; *(potere)* power.

facoltativo, -a *agg* optional.

facsimile *sm inv* facsimile.

fagiano *sm* pheasant.

fagiolino *sm* French bean *(Br)*, string bean *(Am)*.

fagiolo *sm* bean; **fagioli all'uccelletto** white beans cooked with tomatoes and pepper *(a Tuscan speciality)*.

fagotto *sm* bundle; *(strumento)* bassoon; **far ~** to pack one's bags and leave.

fai da te *sm inv* do-it-yourself.

falange *sf* finger bone.

falciare *vt* to mow.

falda *sf (di cappello)* brim; *(d'acqua)* water table; *(di monte)* slope.

falegname *sm* carpenter.

falla *sf* leak.

fallimento *sm* failure; *(DIR)* bankruptcy.

fallire *vi (DIR)* to go bankrupt; *(non riuscire)*: **~ (in qc)** to fail (in sthg) ◆ *vt* to miss.

fallo *sm* foul.

falò *sm inv* bonfire.

falsificare *vt* to forge.

falso, -a *agg* false; *(gioiello)* fake; *(banconota, quadro)* forged ◆ *sm* forgery.

fama *sf* fame; *(reputazione)* reputation.

fame *sf* hunger; **aver ~** to be hungry.

famiglia *sf* family.

familiare *agg (della famiglia)* family *(dav s)*; *(noto)* familiar; *(atmosfera)* friendly; *(informale)* informal ❑ **familiari** *smpl* relations.

famoso, -a *agg* famous.

fanale *sm* light.

fanatico, -a, -ci, -che *agg* fanatical.

fango, -ghi *sm* mud.

fanno → **fare**.

fannullone, -a *sm, f* loafer.

fantascienza *sf* science fiction.

fantasia *sf (immaginazione)* imagination ◆ *agg inv* patterned.

fantasma, -i *sm* ghost.

fantastico, -a, -ci, -che *agg* fantastic; *(immaginario)* fantasy *(dav s)*.

fantino *sm* jockey.

fantoccio *sm* puppet.

farabutto *sm* crook.

faraglione *sm* stack.

faraona *sf* guinea fowl.

farcito, -a *agg (pollo)* stuffed; *(torta)* filled.

fard *sm inv* blusher.

fare *vt* 1. *(fabbricare, preparare)* to

make; ~ **progetti** to make plans; ~ **da mangiare** to cook.

2. *(attuare)* to make; ~ **un viaggio** to go on a trip; ~ **un sogno** to dream.

3. *(essere occupato in)* to do; **cosa fai stasera?** what are you doing tonight?; **fa il meccanico** he's a mechanic; ~ **l'università** to go to university; **faccio tennis** I play tennis.

4. *(percorrere)* to do; **che percorso facciamo per rientrare?** which route shall we take to go back?

5. *(suscitare)* to make; **mi fa pena** I feel sorry for him; **farsi male** to hurt o.s.; ~ **paura** to be frightening; ~ **chiasso** to be noisy.

6. *(atteggiarsi a)* to play, to act; ~ **lo scemo** to behave like an idiot.

7. *(indica il risultato)*: **2 più 2 fa 4** 2 and 2 makes 4; **quanto fa?** what's the total?

8. *(credere)*: **ti facevo più furbo** I thought you were smarter than that.

9. *(acquisire)*: **farsi degli amici** to make friends; **farsi la macchina nuova** *(fam)* to get a new car.

10. *(con infinito)* to make; **far credere qc a qn** to make sb believe sthg; **far vedere qc a qn** to show sb sthg; **far costruire qc** to have sthg built.

11. *(in espressioni)*: **non ~ caso a** not to pay attention to; **non fa niente** *(non importa)* it doesn't matter; **farcela** to manage; **non ce la faccio più** I can't go on; **far bene/male (a qn)** to be good/bad (for sb).

♦ *vi* 1. *(agire)* to do; **come si fa a uscire?** how do you get out?; **fai**

come ti pare do as you like; **non fa che ripetere le stesse cose** all he does is repeat the same things; **darsi da ~** to get busy.

2. *(fam: dire)* to say.

♦ *v impers* to be; **fa bello/brutto** it's lovely/awful weather; **fa caldo/freddo** it's hot/cold.

❑ **farsi** *vr (diventare)*: **farsi grande** to grow up; **farsi furbo** *(fam)* to get smart; **farsi vivo** to get in touch; **farsi avanti/indietro** *(spostarsi)* to move forward/back.

farfalla *sf* butterfly; **cravatta a ~** bow tie.

farina *sf* flour; ~ **gialla** maize flour.

farinata *sf type of bread similar to a very thin 'focaccia' but made from chickpea flour (a speciality of Liguria).*

faringite *sf* pharyngitis.

farmacia *sf (negozio)* chemist's *(Br)*, drugstore *(Am)*; *(scienza)* pharmacy; **'farmacie di turno'** 'duty chemists'.

farmacista, -i, -e *smf* pharmacist.

farmaco, -ci *sm* medicine.

faro *sm (per navi)* lighthouse; *(di veicoli)* headlight; *(per aerei)* beacon.

farsa *sf* farce.

farsumagru *sm inv beef roll stuffed with mince, pecorino cheese, sausage and boiled eggs, cooked in Marsala and tomato puree (a Sicilian speciality).*

fascia, -sce *sf (striscia)* strip, band; *(medica)* bandage; *(di territorio)* strip; *(di popolazione)* band; ~ **elastica** elastic bandage; ~ **oraria**

time band.

fasciare vt to bandage.

fasciatura sf bandage.

fascicolo sm (di rivista) issue; (di documenti) file.

fascino sm charm.

fascio sm (d'erba, di fibri) bunch; (di legna) bundle; (di luce) beam.

fascismo sm Fascism.

fascista, -i, -e agg & smf Fascist.

fase sf phase; (di motore) stroke.

fast food [fast'fud] sm inv fast-food restaurant.

fastidio sm bother, trouble; **dare ~ a qn** to annoy sb; **le dà ~ se fumo?** do you mind if I smoke?

fastidioso, -a agg inconvenient.

fastoso, -a agg sumptuous.

fasullo, -a agg (falso) fake.

fata sf fairy.

fatale agg (mortale) fatal; (inevitabile) inevitable; (sguardo) irresistible.

fatalità sf inv (inevitabilità) inevitability; (destino) fate; (disgrazia) misfortune.

fatica sf hard work; (stanchezza) fatigue; **fare ~ a fare qc** to have difficulty doing sthg; **a ~** hardly.

faticoso, -a agg (stancante) exhausting; (difficile) hard.

fatidico, -a, -ci, -che agg fateful.

fato sm fate.

fatto, -a pp → fare ◆ sm (cosa concreta) fact; (avvenimento) event ◆ agg: **~ a mano** hand-made; **~ in casa** home-made; **il ~ è che ...** the

fact is that ...; **cogliere qn sul ~** to catch sb in the act; **in ~ di vini ...** when it comes to wine ...; **sono fatti miei** that's my business.

fattoria sf farm.

fattorino sm (per consegne) delivery man; (d'albergo) messenger.

fattura sf invoice; (magia) spell.

fauna sf fauna.

favola sf fairy tale; (cosa bella) dream.

favoloso, -a agg fabulous.

favore sm favour; **per ~** please.

favorevole agg favourable; (voto) in favour.

favorire vt (promuovere) to promote; (aiutare) to favour; **vuoi ~?** would you like some?

favorito, -a agg favourite.

fazzoletto sm (da naso) handkerchief; (per la testa) headscarf.

febbraio sm February, → settembre.

febbre sf fever; **avere la ~** to have a temperature.

feci sfpl excrement (sg).

fecondazione sf fertilization.

fede sf faith; (anello) wedding ring; **aver ~ in** to have faith in; **essere in buona/cattiva ~** to act in good/bad faith.

fedele agg faithful; (cliente) loyal; (preciso) accurate ◆ smf believer.

fedeltà sf (lealtà) faithfulness, loyalty; (precisione) accuracy.

federa sf pillowcase.

federazione sf federation.

fegato sm liver; (fig: coraggio) guts (pl); **~ alla veneziana** thinly *sliced calves' liver and onions.*

felice agg happy.

felicità sf happiness.

felicitarsi vr: ~ **con qn per qc** to congratulate sb on sthg.

felino, -a agg & sm feline.

felpa sf (maglia) sweatshirt; (tessuto) plush.

femmina sf (animale) female; (figlia, ragazza) girl.

femminile agg female; (rivista, modi) women's (dav s); (GRAMM) feminine ◆ sm feminine.

femminismo sm feminism.

fenomenale agg phenomenal.

fenomeno sm phenomenon.

feriale agg working (dav s).

ferie sfpl holidays (Br), vacation (sg) (Am); **andare in** ~ to go on holiday (Br), to go on vacation (Am); **essere in** ~ to be on holiday (Br), to be on vacation (Am).

ferire vt (colpire) to injure; (addolorare) to hurt ❑ **ferirsi** vr to injure o.s.

ferita sf wound.

ferito, -a agg injured ◆ sm, f injured person.

fermaglio sm clip.

fermare vt to stop; (bottone) to fasten; (sospetto) to detain ◆ vi to stop ❑ **fermarsi** vr to stop; (sostare) to stay; **fermarsi a fare qc** to stop to do sthg.

fermata sf stop; ~ **dell'autobus** bus stop; '~ **prenotata**' 'bus stopping'; '~ **a richiesta**' 'request stop'.

fermento sm ferment.

fermo, -a agg (persona) still; (veicolo) stationary; (mano, voce) steady; (orologio) stopped; (saldo) firm; **stare** ~ to keep still.

fermo posta avv & sm inv poste restante (Br), general delivery (Am).

feroce agg (animale) ferocious; (dolore) terrible.

ferragosto sm (giorno) Italian public holiday which falls on 15 August; (periodo) August holidays (pl).

---

i FERRAGOSTO

August 15, the feast of the Assumption, is a national holiday in Italy and marks the peak of the holiday season. The Italian name, "Ferragosto", comes from the Latin "feriae augustae", meaning "August holidays". Cities become ghost towns, as families and groups of friends flock to the coast, the mountains and the lakes, and most factories and businesses close down.

---

ferramenta sf ironmonger's (Br), hardware store (Am).

ferro sm iron; **toccare** ~ to touch wood; ~ **battuto** wrought iron; ~ **da calza** knitting needle; ~ **da stiro** iron; **carne ai ferri** grilled meat.

ferrovia sf railway (Br), railroad (Am); **Ferrovie dello Stato** Italian railway system, = British Rail (Br), = Amtrak (Am).

ferroviario, -a agg railway (Br) (dav s), railroad (Am) (dav s).

fertile agg fertile.

fervido, -a agg fervent, ardent.

fesso, -a agg (fam) stupid.

fessura *sf* crack; *(per gettone, moneta)* slot.

festa *sf (religiosa)* feast; *(giorno festivo)* holiday; *(ricevimento)* party; *(ricorrenza)*: **la ~ della mamma** Mother's Day; **far ~ to** have a holiday; **far ~ a qn** to give sb a warm welcome; **buone feste!** *(a Natale)* Merry Christmas!

 FESTA DELLE DONNE

Since the 1970s, March 8 has been celebrated as National Women's Day in Italy. Meetings, debates and conferences on women's issues are held, and there is now a tradition of presenting women with the gift of a bunch of mimosa.

festeggiare *vt (ricorrenza)* to celebrate; *(persona)* to throw a party for.

festival *sm inv* festival.

 FESTIVAL DI SPOLETO

Also known as the "Festival dei Due Mondi" (Festival of the Two Worlds), the Festival of Spoleto has been held every June and July since 1958. It hosts top-class performances of opera, theatre, music and ballet, attracting internationally renowned artists and a cosmopolitan audience.

festivo, -a *agg* festive; **giorno ~** holiday; **orario ~** *timetable for Sundays and public holidays.*

festone *sm* festoon.

festoso, -a *agg* merry.

feto *sm* foetus.

fetta *sf* slice.

fettuccine *sfpl ribbons of egg pasta.*

fettunta *sf toast flavoured with garlic and olive oil (a Tuscan speciality).*

FF.SS. *abbr* = BR *(Br)*, = Amtrak *(Am)*.

fiaba *sf* fairy tale.

fiaccola *sf* torch.

fiamma *sf* flame; **dare alle fiamme** to set on fire.

fiammifero *sm* match.

fiancheggiare *vt* to border.

fianco, -chi *sm (di persona)* hip; *(di edificio, collina)* side; **di ~ a** next to.

fiasco, -schi *sm* flask; **fare ~** to flop.

fiato *sm (respiro)* breath; *(resistenza)* stamina; **avere il ~ grosso** to be out of breath.

fibbia *sf* buckle.

fibra *sf* fibre.

ficcanaso *(pl m* **ficcanasi**, *pl f inv) smf* busybody.

ficcare *vt* to put □ **ficcarsi** *vr:* **dove ti eri ficcato?** where did you get to?

fico, -chi *sm* fig; **~ d'India** prickly pear.

fidanzamento *sm* engagement.

fidanzarsi *vr* to get engaged.

fidanzato, -a *agg* engaged ♦ *sm, f* fiancé *(f* fiancée).

fidarsi *vr:* **~ di** to trust.

fidato, -a *agg* trustworthy.

fiducia *sf* confidence.

fiducioso, -a *agg* confident.

fieno *sm* hay.

fiera *sf* fair.

fiero, -a *agg* proud.

fifa *sf* (*fam*) fright.

figlio, -a *sm, f* son (*f* daughter), child; ~ **unico** only child.

figura *sf* figure; (*illustrazione*) illustration, picture; (*di posti*) **fare bella/brutta ~** to create a good/bad impression.

figurare *vi* to appear ♦ *vt*: **figurarsi qc** to imagine sthg □ **figurarsi** *vr*: **figurati!** of course not!

figurina *sf* picture card.

fila *sf* (*coda*) queue (*Br*), line (*Am*); (*di macchine*) line; (*di posti*) row; (*serie*) series; **fare la ~** to queue (*Br*), to stand in line (*Am*); **di ~** in succession.

filare *vt* (*lana*) to spin ♦ *vi* (*ragno, baco*) to spin; (*formaggio*) to go stringy; (*discorso*) to be coherent; (*fam: andarsene*) to split; **fila!** off you go!; ~ **diritto** to toe the line.

filastrocca, -che *sf* nursery rhyme.

filatelia *sf* philately, stamp-collecting.

filatelli *smpl* *thin strips of egg pasta served with a sauce made from pork, tomatoes, chillis and pecorino cheese (a speciality of Calabria).*

filatieddi = **filatelli**.

filetto *sm* fillet; ~ **al pepe verde** fillet steak with green peppercorns.

film *sm inv* film (*Br*), movie (*Am*).

filò *sm* thread; (*cavo*) wire; (*di lama, rasoio*) edge; (*di pane*) stick; ~ **d'erba** blade of grass; ~ **spinato** barbed wire; **fil di ferro** wire; **per ~ e per segno** word for word.

filobus *sm inv* trolleybus.

filosofia *sf* philosophy.

filtrare *vt & vi* to filter.

filtro *sm* (*apparecchio*) filter; (*di sigarette*) filter tip.

fin → **fino**.

finale *agg & sf* final ♦ *sm* end, ending.

finalmente *avv* at (long) last.

finanza *sf* finance; (*di frontiera*) = Customs and Excise □ **finanze** *sfpl* finances.

finanziere *sm* (*banchiere*) financier; (*di frontiera*) customs officer; (*per tasse*) = Inland Revenue officer (*Br*), = Internal Revenue officer (*Am*).

finché *cong* (*per tutto il tempo*) as long as; (*fino a quando*) until.

fine *agg* (*sottile*) thin; (*polvere*) fine; (*elegante*) refined; (*vista, udito*) keen, sharp ♦ *sf* (*conclusione*) end ♦ *sm* (*scopo*) aim; **lieto ~** happy ending; ~ **settimana** weekend; **alla ~** in the end.

finestra *sf* window.

finestrino *sm* window.

fingere *vt* (*simulare*) to feign; ~ **di fare qc** to pretend to do sthg □ **fingersi** *vr*: **fingersi malato** to pretend to be ill.

finimondo *sm* pandemonium.

finire *vt* to finish ♦ *vi* to finish; (*avere esito*) to end; (*cacciarsi*) to get to; ~ **col fare qc** to end up doing sthg; ~ **di fare qc** to finish doing sthg.

finlandese *agg & sm* Finnish ◆ *smf* Finn.

Finlandia *sf*: **la ~** Finland.

fino, -a *agg (sottile)* thin; *(oro, argento)* pure; *(udito, vista)* keen, sharp ◆ *avv* even ◆ *prep*: **~ a** *(di tempo)* until; *(di luogo)* as far as; **~ da** *(luogo)* as far as; **fin da domani** from tomorrow; **fin da ieri** since yesterday; **~ qui/lì** as far as here/there.

finocchio *sm* fennel.

finora *avv* so far.

finta *sf (finzione)* pretence; *(nel pugilato)* feint; *(nel calcio)* dummy; **fare ~ di fare qc** to pretend to do sthg.

finto, -a *pp* → **fingere** ◆ *agg* false.

fiocco, -chi *sm (di nastro)* bow; *(di neve)* flake; **coi fiocchi** *(ottimo)* excellent, first-rate.

fiocina *sf* harpoon.

fioco, -a, -chi, -che *agg (voce)* faint; *(luce)* dim.

fioraio, -a *sm, f* florist.

fiore *sm* flower; **a fior d'acqua** on the surface of the water; **a fiori** *(stoffa)* with a floral pattern; **fiori di zucca ripieni** *fried courgette flowers stuffed with breadcrumbs, parsley and anchovies* ❏ **fiori** *smpl (nelle carte)* clubs.

fiorentino, -a *agg & sm, f* Florentine.

fiorire *vi (albero)* to blossom; *(fiore)* to bloom.

Firenze *sf* Florence.

firma *sf (sottoscrizione)* signature; *(marca)* designer brand.

firmare *vt* to sign.

fiscale *agg* tax *(dav s)*.

fischiare *vi* to whistle ◆ *vt* to whistle; *(disapprovare)* to boo.

fischio *sm* whistle.

fisco *sm* = Inland Revenue *(Br)*, = Internal Revenue *(Am)*.

fisica *sf (materia)* physics *(sg)*, → **fisico**.

fisico, -a, -ci, -che *agg* physical ◆ *sm (corpo)* physique ◆ *sm, f* physicist.

fisionomia *sf* face.

fissare *vt (guardare)* to stare at; *(rendere fisso)* to fix; *(appuntamento)* to arrange; *(camera, volo)* to book ❏

fissarsi *vr*: **fissarsi di fare qc** to set one's heart on doing sthg.

fisso, -a *agg (fissato)* fixed; *(impiego)* permanent; *(reddito)* regular ◆ *avv*: **guardare ~** to stare.

fitta *sf* sharp pain.

fitto, -a *agg* thick ◆ *sm (affitto)* rent.

fiume *sm* river.

fiutare *vt (sog: cane)* to smell; *(fig: accorgersi di)* to get wind of.

flacone *sm* bottle.

flagrante *agg*: **cogliere qc in ~** to catch sb in the act.

flash [fleʃ] *sm inv* flash.

flessibile *agg* flexible.

flessione *sf (sulle gambe)* knee-bend; *(a terra)* sit-up; *(calo)* dip.

flesso, -a *pp* → **flettere**.

flettere *vt* to bend.

flipper *sm inv* pinball machine.

F.lli *abbr* Bros.

flora *sf* flora.

flotta *sf* fleet.

fluido

fluido, -a *agg & sm* fluid.

fluire *vi* to flow.

flusso *sm* flow; *(in fisica)* flux.

fluttuare *vi (ondeggiare)* to rise and fall; *(FIN)* to fluctuate.

F.M. *(abbr di Modulazione di frequenza)* FM.

focaccia, -ce *sf (dolce)* bun; *(pane)* type of flat salted bread made with olive oil; ~ **alla valdostana** 'focaccia' filled with fontina cheese.

foce *sf* mouth.

focolare *sm* hearth.

fodera *sf (interna)* lining; *(esterna)* cover.

foglia *sf* leaf.

foglio *sm (di carta, di metallo)* sheet; *(documento)* document; *(banconota)* note; ~ **rosa** provisional driving licence; ~ **di via** expulsion order.

fogna *sf* sewer.

fognature *sfpl* sewers.

föhn [fɔn] = **fon**.

folclore *sm* folklore.

folcloristico, -a, -ci, -che *agg* folk *(dav s)*.

folgorare *vt (sog: fulmine)* to strike; *(sog: alta tensione)* to electrocute.

folla *sf* crowd.

folle *agg (pazzo)* mad; *(TECNOL)* idle; **in** ~ *(di auto)* in neutral.

follia *sf (pazzia)* madness; *(atto)* act of madness.

folto, -a *agg* thick.

fon *sm inv* hairdryer.

fondale *sm* bottom (of the sea).

fondamentale *agg* fundamental, basic.

fondamento *sm* foundation □ **fondamenta** *sfpl* foundations.

fondare *vt* to found; *(basare)*: ~ **qc su qc** to base sthg on sthg □ **fondarsi su** *vr + prep* to be based on.

fondazione *sf* foundation.

fondere *vt* to melt; *(aziende)* to merge ♦ *vi* to melt □ **fondersi** *vr* to melt.

fondo, -a *agg (profondo)* deep ♦ *sm* bottom; *(di strada)* surface; *(di liquido)* dregs *(pl)*; *(sfondo)* background; *(SPORT)* long distance race; *(proprietà)* property; **andare a** ~ *(affondare)* to sink; **conoscere a** ~ to know very well; **in** ~ *(fig: tutto sommato)* after all; **andare fino in** ~ **a qc** *(approfondire)* to get to the bottom of sthg; **in** ~ **(a qc)** at the bottom (of sthg); *(stanza)* at the back (of sthg); *(libro, mese)* at the end (of sthg) □ **fondi** *smpl (denaro)* funds.

fonduta *sf* fondue.

fonetica *sf* phonetics *(sg)*.

fontana *sf* fountain.

fonte *sf (sorgente)* spring; *(origine)* source ♦ *sm*: ~ **battesimale** font.

fontina *sf* a hard cheese made from cow's milk (a speciality of the Valle d'Aosta).

foraggio *sm* fodder.

forare *vt (praticare un foro in)* to pierce; *(gomma)* to puncture; *(biglietto)* to punch; *(pallone)* to burst.

forbici *sfpl* scissors.

forca, -che *sf (attrezzo)* pitchfork; *(patibolo)* gallows *(pl)*.

forchetta *sf* fork.

forcina *sf* hairpin.

foresta *sf* forest.

forestiero, -a *agg* foreign ◆ *sm, f* foreigner.

forfora *sf* dandruff.

forma *sf* shape; *(tipo)* form; *(stampo)* mould; **essere in ~** to be fit; **a ~ di** in the shape of □ **forme** *sfpl (del corpo)* figure *(sg)*.

formaggino *sm* processed cheese.

formaggio *sm* cheese.

---

i FORMAGGIO

Cheese is a mainstay of the Italian diet, whether used as a filling for a roll, eaten as part of a main course, or served as a course in its own right. The cheese course in Italy comes after the main course and before fruit or dessert. Between 250 and 300 varieties of cheese may be found: soft ones, like "mozzarella", "ricotta", "robiola", "gorgonzola" and "bel paese"; and hard ones, like "caciocavallo", "provolone", "grana", "parmigiano" and "pecorino". These last three are grated onto pasta dishes and sprinkled on top of soups.

---

formale *agg* formal.

formalità *sf inv* formality.

formare *vt* to form; *(comporre)* to make up; *(persona)* to train □ **formarsi** *vr* to form.

formato *sm* size.

formazione *sf* formation; *(istruzione)* education; **~ professionale** professional training.

formica®¹ *sf* Formica®.

formica², -che *sf* ant.

formicolio *sm (intorpidimento)* pins and needles *(pl)*.

formidabile *agg* fantastic, amazing.

formula *sf (chimica)* formula; *(frase rituale)* set phrase; **~ uno** formula one.

fornaio, -a *sm, f* baker.

fornello *sm (di elettrodomestico)* ring; **~ elettrico** hotplate.

fornire *vt*: **~ qc a qn** to supply sb with sthg; **~ qn/qc di qc** to supply sb/sthg with sthg.

fornitore, -trice *sm, f* supplier.

forno *sm* oven; **~ a legna** wood-burning stove; **~ a microonde** microwave (oven).

foro *sm (buco)* hole; *(romano)* forum.

forse *avv* perhaps, maybe; *(circa)* about.

forte *agg* strong; *(suono)* loud; *(luce, colore)* bright ◆ *avv (vigorosamente)* hard; *(ad alta voce)* loudly; *(velocemente)* fast ◆ *sm (fortezza)* fort; *(specialità)* strong point.

fortezza *sf* fortress.

fortuito, -a *agg* chance *(dav s)*, fortuitous.

fortuna *sf* luck; *(patrimonio)* fortune; **buona ~!** good luck!; **portare ~** to bring luck; **per ~** luckily, fortunately.

fortunatamente *avv* luckily, fortunately.

fortunato, -a *agg (persona)* lucky; *(evento)* successful.

forviare = **fuorviare**.

forza *sf* strength; *(in fisica, violenza)* force; **a ~ di** by dint of; **per ~**

(naturalmente) of course; *(contro la volontà)* against one's will; **le forze armate** the armed forces.

forzare *vt (porta, finestra)* to force open; *(obbligare):* ~ **qn a fare qc** to force sb to do sthg.

foschia *sf* haze.

fossa *sf (buca)* pit, hole; *(tomba)* grave.

fossato *sm* ditch; *(di castello)* moat.

fossile *sm* fossil.

fosso *sm* ditch.

foto *sf inv* photo.

fotocopia *sf* photocopy.

fotocopiare *vt* to photocopy.

fotogenico, -a, -ci, -che *agg* photogenic.

fotografare *vt* to photograph.

fotografia *sf (ARTE)* photography; *(immagine)* photograph; ~ **a colori** colour photograph; ~ **in bianco e nero** black and white photograph.

fotografo, -a *sm, f* photographer.

fototessera *sf* passport-size photograph.

fra = **tra**.

fracassare *vt* to smash.

fracasso *sm* crash.

fradicio, -a, -ci, -ce *agg* soaked.

fragile *agg* fragile; *(persona)* delicate.

fragola *sf* strawberry.

fragore *sm* loud noise.

fraintendere *vt* to misunderstand.

frammento *sm* fragment.

frana *sf* landslide; *(fig: persona):* **essere una** ~ to be useless.

francese *agg & sm* French ♦ *smf (abitante)* Frenchman *(f* Frenchwoman); **i francesi** the French.

Francia *sf:* **la** ~ France.

franco, -a, -chi, -che *agg (sincero)* frank; *(COMM)* free ♦ *sm* franc; **farla franca** to get away with it.

francobollo *sm* stamp.

frangia, -ge *sf* fringe.

frantumare *vt* to smash ❑ **frantumarsi** *vr* to smash.

frantumi *smpl:* **andare in** ~ to smash; *(sogno)* to be shattered.

frappé *sm inv* (milk) shake.

frase *sf (GRAMM)* sentence; *(espressione)* expression.

frastuono *sm* din.

frate *sm (monaco)* friar; *(pasta)* ring doughnut.

fratellastro *sm* stepbrother.

fratello *sm* brother.

frattempo *sm:* **nel** ~ in the meantime, meanwhile.

frattura *sf* fracture.

frazione *sf (parte)* fraction; *(di comune)* village.

freccia, -ce *sf* arrow; ~ **di direzione** indicator; **mettere la** ~ to put the indicator on.

freddo, -a *agg & sm* cold; **aver** ~ to be cold; **è o fa** ~ it's cold.

freddoloso, -a *agg:* **essere** ~ to feel the cold.

freezer ['fridzer] *sm inv* freezer.

fregare *vt (strofinare)* to rub; *(fam: imbrogliare)* to trick; ~ **qc a qn** *(fam: rubare)* to nick sthg from sb;

fregarsene (di qc) *(volg)* not to give a damn (about sthg).

frenare *vi* to brake ◆ *vt (rabbia, entusiasmo)* to curb; *(lacrime)* to hold back; *(avanzata, progresso)* to hold up.

frenata *sf* braking; **fare una ~** to brake.

frenetico, -a, -ci, -che *agg* hectic.

freno *sm (di veicolo)* brake; *(per cavallo)* bit; **~ a mano** handbrake.

frequentare *vt (corso, scuola)* to attend; *(locale)* to go to; *(persona)* to mix with.

frequente *agg* frequent.

fresco, -a, -schi, -sche *agg* fresh; *(temperatura)* cool; *(notizie)* recent ◆ *sm (temperatura)* cool; **è o fa ~** it's cool; **mettere al ~** to put in a cool place; **stare ~** to be way out.

fretta *sf (urgenza)* hurry; *(rapidità)* haste; **avere ~** to be in a hurry; **in ~ e furia** in a hurry.

fricassea *sf stewed meat and vegetables in an egg and lemon sauce.*

friggere *vt* to fry ◆ *vi* to sizzle.

frigo *sm inv* fridge.

frigobar *sm inv* minibar.

frigorifero *sm* refrigerator.

frittata *sf* omelette.

frittella *sf* fritter; **frittelle di mele** apple fritters.

fritto, -a *pp* → **friggere** ◆ *agg* fried ◆ *sm:* **~ misto** mixed deep-fried fish and seafood.

frittura *sf:* **~ di pesce** deep-fried fish and seafood.

frivolo, -a *agg* frivolous.

frizione *sf (di auto)* clutch; *(massaggio)* massage.

frizzante *agg* fizzy; *(vino)* sparkling.

frode *sf* fraud.

frontale *agg* frontal; *(scontro)* head-on.

fronte *sf* forehead ◆ *sm* front; **di ~** opposite; **di ~ a** *(faccia a faccia)* opposite; *(in una fila)* in front of; *(in confronto a)* compared with.

frontiera *sf* frontier.

frottola *sf (bugia)* lie.

frugare *vi & vt* to search.

frullare *vt* to whisk.

frullato *sm* milk shake.

frullatore *sm* blender, liquidizer.

frullino *sm* whisker.

frusta *sf (per animali)* whip.

frustino *sm (riding)* crop.

frutta *sf* fruit; **~ secca** dried fruit and nuts.

fruttivendolo *sm (negozio)* greengrocer's.

frutto *sm* fruit; *(profitto)* profit; **frutti di mare** seafood *(sg)*.

F.S. = **FF.SS.**

fucile *sm* rifle.

fuga, -ghe *sf* escape; **~ di gas** gas leak.

fuggire *vi (allontanarsi)* to escape; *(rifugiarsi)* to run away.

fulmine *sm* bolt of lightning.

fumare *vt* to smoke ◆ *vi* to smoke; *(emettere vapore)* to steam; **'vietato ~'** 'no smoking'.

fumatore, -trice *sm, f* smoker; **fumatori o non fumatori?** smoking or non-smoking?

fumetti *smpl (vignette)* cartoon strip *(sg); (giornalino)* comics.

fumo *sm* smoke; *(vapore)* steam.

fune *sf* rope.

funebre *agg* funeral *(dav s); (lugubre)* funereal.

funerale *sm* funeral.

fungo, -ghi *sm* mushroom; *(MED)* fungus; ~ **mangereccio** edible mushroom.

funicolare *sf* funicular railway.

funivia *sf* cable way.

funzionamento *sm* functioning.

funzionare *vi* to work ❏ **funzionare da** *v + prep* to act as.

funzione *sf* function; *(compito)* duty; *(religiosa)* service; **essere in ~** to be working; **in ~ di** *(secondo)* according to.

fuoco, -chi *sm* fire; *(fornello)* ring; *(in ottica)* focus; **al ~!** fire!; **dar ~ a qc** to set fire to sthg; **fare ~** to fire; **prender ~** to catch fire; **fuochi d'artificio** fireworks.

fuorché *cong* except.

fuori *avv* out, outside; *(fuori di casa)* out; *(all'aperto)* outdoors, outside ◆ *prep*: ~ **(di)** out of, outside; **far ~ qn** *(fam)* to kill sb; **essere ~ di sé** to be beside oneself; **lasciare ~** to leave out; **tirare ~** to get out; ~ **luogo** uncalled for; ~ **mano** out of the way; **andare ~ strada** to leave the road; '~ **servizio**' 'out of order'.

fuoribordo *sm inv* outboard.

fuorilegge *smf inv* outlaw.

fuoristrada *sm inv* Jeep® ◆ *agg inv*: **moto ~** trail bike.

fuorviare *vt* to mislead.

furbo, -a *agg* clever, smart; *(spreg)* cunning.

furgone *sm* van.

furia *sf (ira)* fury; *(impeto)* violence; **a ~ di fare qc** by (means of) doing sthg; **andare su tutte le furie** to get into a towering rage.

furioso, -a *agg* furious.

furore *sm* fury; **far ~** to be all the rage.

furto *sm* theft; ~ **con scasso** burglary.

fusa *sfpl*: **fare le ~** to purr.

fusione *sf (di cera, metallo)* melting; *(unione)* fusion.

fuso, -a *pp* → **fondere** ◆ *sm*: ~ **orario** time zone.

fustino *sm* tub.

fusto *sm (di pianta)* stem; *(contenitore)* drum; *(fam: ragazzo)* hunk.

futile *agg* futile.

futuro, -a *agg & sm* future.

G

gabbia *sf* cage.

gabbiano *sm* seagull.

gabinetto *sm (bagno)* toilet; *(ministero)* cabinet; *(di dentista)* surgery.

gaffe [gaf] *sf inv* blunder.

gala *sf (sfarzo)* pomp; *(festa)* gala.

galassia *sf* galaxy.

galateo *sm* etiquette.

galera *sf* prison.

galla *sf*: **stare a ~** to float; **venire a ~** (*fig*) to come out.

galleggiante *agg* floating ♦ *sm* (*boa*) buoy; (*per la pesca*) float.

galleria *sf* (*traforo*) tunnel; (*museo*) gallery; (*di teatro*) circle; (*di cinema*) balcony; (*strada coperta*) arcade.

galletta *sf* cracker.

gallina *sf* hen.

gallo *sm* cock.

gamba *sf* leg; **essere in ~** to be smart.

gamberetto *sm* shrimp.

gambero *sm* prawn.

gamberoni *smpl*: **~ alla griglia** grilled crayfish.

gambo *sm* stem.

gancio *sm* hook.

gangheri *smpl*: **essere fuori dai ~** to fly off the handle.

gara *sf* (*nello sport*) race; (*concorso*) competitive bidding; **fare a ~** to compete.

garage [ga'raʒ] *sm inv* garage.

garantire *vt* to guarantee.

garanzia *sf* (*di merce*) guarantee; (*di debito*) guarantee, security.

gareggiare *vi* to compete.

gargarismo *sm*: **fare i gargarismi** to gargle.

garza *sf* gauze.

garzone *sm* boy.

gas *sm inv* gas; **dare ~** to step on the gas; **~ lacrimogeno** tear gas.

gasato, -a = **gassato**.

gasolio *sm* diesel (oil).

gassato, -a *agg* (*bevanda*) fizzy.

gassosa *sf* fizzy drink.

gastronomia *sf* gastronomy; (*negozio*) delicatessen.

gastronomico, -a, -ci, -che *agg* gastronomic.

gattino, -a *sm, f* kitten.

gatto, -a *sm, f* cat; **~ delle nevi** snow cat; **eravamo in quattro gatti** there were only a few of us.

gazzetta *sf* gazette.

G.d.F. *abbr* = **Guardia di Finanza**.

gel *sm inv* gel.

gelare *vi, vt & v impers* to freeze.

gelateria *sf* ice-cream shop (*Br*), ice-cream parlour (*Am*).

gelatina *sf* gelatine; **~ di frutta** fruit jelly.

gelato, -a *agg* frozen ♦ *sm* ice cream.

---

i GELATO

Although ice cream is associated with the summer months, it is eaten in Italy all year round and at any time of day. "Gelaterie", or ice-cream shops, specialize in the production and sale of a seemingly endless variety of flavours, ranging from traditional fruit, chocolate and coffee to the more exotic. "Gelato artigianale" means that the ice cream has been made on the premises.

---

gelido, -a *agg* freezing, icy.

gelo *sm* (*freddo*) intense cold; (*ghiaccio*) ice.

gelosia *sf* jealousy.

geloso, -a *agg* jealous.

gemello, -a *agg* twin □ **gemel-**

li *smpl (di camicia)* cuff links;
Gemelli *smpl* Gemini *(sg).*

gemere *vi* to moan.

gemma *sf (pietra)* gem; *(di pianta)* bud.

generale *agg & sm* general; **in ~** in general.

generalità *sfpl* particulars.

generalmente *avv* generally.

generare *vt (produrre)* to generate, to produce.

generatore *sm* generator.

generazione *sf* generation.

genere *sm (tipo)* kind, type; *(di arte)* genre; *(GRAMM)* gender; *(di animali, vegetali)* genus; **il ~ umano** mankind; **in ~** generally ▫ **generi** *smpl*: **generi alimentari** foodstuffs.

generico, -a, -ci, -che *agg (generale)* generic; *(vago)* vague; **medico ~** general practitioner.

genero *sm* son-in-law.

generoso, -a *agg* generous.

gengiva *sf* gum.

geniale *agg* brilliant.

genio *sm* genius; **andare a ~ a qn** to be liked by sb.

genitali *smpl* genitals.

genitore *sm* parent; **i nostri genitori** our parents.

gennaio *sm* January, → **settembre.**

Genova *sf* Genoa.

gente *sf* people *(pl).*

gentile *agg* kind, nice; **Gentile Signore** Dear Sir; **Gentile Signor G. Paoli** Mr G. Paoli.

gentilezza *sf* kindness; **per ~** please.

gentiluomo *(pl* **gentiluomini)**

sm gentleman.

genuino, -a *agg* genuine.

geografia *sf* geography.

geologia *sf* geology.

geometria *sf* geometry.

geranio *sm* geranium.

gerarchia *sf* hierarchy.

gergo, -ghi *sm (di giovani)* slang; *(specialistico)* jargon.

Germania *sf*: **la ~** Germany.

germe *sm* germ.

gerundio *sm* gerund.

gesso *sm* chalk; *(per frattura)* plaster.

gestione *sf* management.

gestire *vt* to run.

gesto *sm* gesture.

gestore *sm* manager.

Gesù *sm* Jesus.

gettare *vt (lanciare)* to throw; *(buttar via)* to throw away; *(grido)* to utter; *(acqua)* to spout; *(scultura)* to cast; **'non ~ alcun oggetto dal finestrino'** 'do not throw objects out of the window' ▫ **gettarsi** *vr*: **gettarsi da/in** to throw o.s. from/into; **gettarsi in** *(fiume)* to flow into.

getto *sm (d'acqua, gas)* jet; *(vapore)* puff; **di ~** *(scrivere)* in one go.

gettone *sm* token; **~ telefonico** telephone token.

ghiacciaio *sm* glacier.

ghiacciato, -a *agg* frozen; *(freddo)* ice-cold.

ghiaccio *sm* ice.

ghiacciolo *sm (gelato)* ice lolly *(Br),* Popsicle® *(Am); (di fontana)* icicle.

ghiaia sf gravel.

ghiandola sf gland.

ghiotto, -a agg (persona) greedy; (cibo) appetizing.

già avv already; (precedentemente) already, before ♦ esclam of course!, yes!; di ~? already?

giacca, -che sf jacket; ~ a vento windcheater.

giacché cong as, since.

giaccone sm heavy jacket.

giacere vi to lie.

giallo, -a agg (colore) yellow; (carnagione) sallow ♦ sm (colore) yellow; (romanzo) detective story; film ~ thriller; ~ dell'uovo yolk.

gianduiotto sm hazelnut chocolate.

Giappone sm: il ~ Japan.

giapponese agg, smf & sm Japanese.

giardinaggio sm gardening.

giardiniera sf (verdure) starter of mixed pickled vegetables, → giardiniere.

giardiniere, -a sm, f gardener.

giardino sm garden; ~ botanico botanical gardens (pl); ~ d'infanzia nursery, kindergarten; ~ pubblico park; ~ zoologico zoo.

gigante agg (enorme) gigantic ♦ sm giant.

gigantesco, -a, -schi, -sche agg gigantic.

gilè sm inv waistcoat.

gin [dʒin] sm inv gin.

ginecologo, -a, -gi, -ghe sm, f gynaecologist.

ginestra sf broom.

Ginevra sf Geneva.

ginnastica sf gymnastics (sg); fare ~ to do exercises.

ginocchio (pl m ginocchi o pl f ginocchia) sm knee; stare in ~ to be on one's knees, to kneel.

giocare vi to play; (scommettere) to gamble ♦ vt to play; (scommettere) to gamble; (ingannare) to take in; sai ~ a tennis? can you play tennis? giocarsi il posto to lose one's job.

giocatore, -trice sm, f player; ~ d'azzardo gambler.

giocattolo sm toy.

gioco, -chi sm game; (divertimento) play; mettere in ~ qc to risk sthg; ~ d'azzardo game of chance; ~ di parole pun; per ~ as a joke.

giocoliere sm juggler.

gioia sf joy; (gioiello) jewel; darsi alla pazza ~ to live it up.

gioielleria sf jeweller's shop.

gioiello sm jewel, piece of jewellery.

giornalaio, -a sm, f newsagent (Br), newsdealer (Am).

giornale sm (quotidiano) newspaper; (rivista) magazine; ~ radio news bulletin.

giornaliero, -a agg daily.

giornalista, -i, -e smf journalist.

giornata sf day; oggi è una bella ~ it's lovely today; ~ lavorativa working day; vivere alla ~ to live for the day.

giorno sm (ventiquattro ore) day; (opposto alla notte) day, daytime; (periodo di luce) daylight; a giorni alterni on alternate days; l'altro ~ the other day; ~ feriale working day; **~ festivo** holiday; **~ libero** day off; **al ~** by the day, per day; **di ~** by day, during the day.

giostra *sf* merry-go-round.

giovane *agg* young; **da ~** as a young man/woman; **i giovani** young people.

giovanile *agg* youthful.

giovanotto *sm* young man.

giovare : **giovare a** *v + prep* to be good for □ **giovarsi di** *vr + prep* to make use of.

giovedì *sm inv* Thursday; **~ grasso** *last Thursday of Carnival, before Lent,* → **sabato**.

gioventù *sf (età)* youth; *(giovani)* young people *(pl)*.

giovinezza *sf* youth.

giradischi *sm inv* record player.

giraffa *sf* giraffe.

giramento *sm*: **~ di testa** dizziness.

girare *vt* to turn; *(visitare)* to go round; *(filmare)* to shoot; *(assegno, cambiale)* to endorse ♦ *vi* to turn; *(velocemente)* to spin; *(terra)* to revolve; *(andare in giro)* to go around □ **girarsi** *vr* to turn around.

girarrosto *sm* spit.

girasole *sm* sunflower.

girata *sf (passeggiata)* stroll; *(in macchina)* drive; *(FIN)* endorsement.

girello *sm (di carne)* topside; *(per bambini)* baby-walker.

girevole *agg* turning, revolving.

giro *sm (viaggio)* tour; *(rotazione)* turn; *(di amici, colleghi)* circle; *(di pista)* lap; **fare un ~** *(a piedi)* to go for a walk; *(in macchina)* to go for a

drive; *(in bicicletta)* to go for a ride; **fare il ~ di** *(città, negozi)* to go round; **~ d'affari** turnover; **~ di parole** circumlocution; **~ di prova** test drive; **in ~** around; **nel ~ di un anno** in the space of a year; **prendere in ~ qn** to tease sb, to pull sb's leg; **essere su di giri** to be excited.

girotondo *sm* ring-a-ring-o'-roses.

gita *sf* trip; **andare in ~ a Roma** to go on a trip to Rome.

giù *avv* down; *(al piano di sotto)* downstairs; **in ~** down, downwards; **~ di lì** thereabouts; **~ per le scale** down the stairs; **essere ~** *(fig: essere depresso)* to be low.

giubbotto *sm* jacket.

giudicare *vt (valutare)* to judge; *(reputare)* to consider; *(DIR)* to find ♦ *vi* to judge.

giudice *sm* judge; *(nello sport)* umpire.

giudizio *sm* judgment; *(opinione)* opinion; *(a scuola)* report; **a mio ~** in my opinion.

giugno *sm* June, → **settembre**.

giungere *vi*: **~ a/in** to reach.

giungla *sf* jungle.

giunta *sf* committee; **per ~** in addition.

giunto, -a *pp* → **giungere**.

giuramento *sm* oath.

giurare *vt* to swear ♦ *vi* to take an oath.

giuria *sf (di gare, concorsi)* judges *(pl)*; *(di tribunale)* jury.

giustificare *vt* to justify.

giustificazione *sf (scusa)* excuse; *(SCOL)* note (of absence).

giustizia *sf* justice.

giusto, -a *agg (equo)* fair, just; *(vero, adeguato)* right; *(esatto)* correct ♦ *avv (esattamente)* correctly; *(proprio)* just; **cercavo ~ te!** you're just the person I was looking for!

gli *art mpl (dav s + consonante, gn, ps, z, vocale e h)* the, → **il** ♦ *pron (a lui)* (to) him; *(a esso)* (to) it; *(a loro)* (to) them; **glielo hai detto?** have you told him/her?; **gliene devo due** I owe him/her two (of them).

gliela → **gli**.

gliele → **gli**.

glieli → **gli**.

glielo → **gli**.

gliene → **gli**.

globale *agg* global.

globo *sm* globe.

globulo *sm*: **~ rosso/bianco** red/white corpuscle.

gloria *sf* glory.

gnocchi *smpl* gnocchi *(small dumplings made from potatoes and flour or from semolina)*.

goal [gɔl] *sm inv* goal.

gobba *sf (su schiena)* hump; *(rigonfiamento)* bump.

gobbo, -a *agg* hunchbacked; *(curvo)* round-shouldered ♦ *sm* hunchback.

goccia, -ce *sf* drop.

gocciolare *vi & vt* to drip.

godere *vt*: **godersi qc** to enjoy sthg □ **godere di** *v + prep (avere)* to enjoy; **~ di una riduzione** to benefit from a reduction.

goffo, -a *agg* clumsy.

gola *sf* throat; *(golosità)* greed; *(di monte)* gorge.

golf *sm inv (maglia)* sweater, jumper; *(sport)* golf.

golfo *sm* gulf.

goloso, -a *agg* greedy.

gomito *sm* elbow.

gomma *sf* rubber; *(per cancellare)* rubber *(Br)*, eraser *(Am)*; *(pneumatico)* tyre; **bucare** ○ **forare una ~** to have a puncture; **~ a terra** flat tyre; **~ (da masticare)** chewing gum.

gommapiuma® *sf* foam rubber.

gommone *sm* rubber dinghy.

gondola *sf* gondola.

gondoliere *sm* gondolier.

gonfiare *vt (pallone, gomme)* to inflate; *(dilatare, ingrossare)* to swell; *(notizia, impresa)* to exaggerate □ **gonfiarsi** *vr* to swell; *(fiume)* to rise.

gonfio, -a *agg (piede, occhi)* swollen; *(stomaco)* bloated.

gonna *sf* skirt; **~ a pieghe** pleated skirt; **~ pantalone** culottes *(pl)*.

gorgogliare *vi* to gurgle.

gorgonzola *sm* Gorgonzola *(a strong green-veined cheese made from cow's milk)*.

gorilla *sm inv (animale)* gorilla; *(guardia del corpo)* bodyguard.

goulash ['gulaʃ] *sm* goulash.

governante *sf (per bambini)* governess; *(di casa)* housekeeper.

governare *vt* to govern; *(animale)* to look after.

governatore *sm* governor.

governo *sm* government.

gracile *agg* delicate.

gradazione *sf (di colori)* scale;

(sfumatura) shade; ~ **alcolica** alcoholic strength.

gradevole *agg* pleasant.

gradinata *sf (scalinata)* (flight of) steps; *(in stadi, teatri)* tiers *(pl)*.

gradino *sm* step.

gradire *vt (regalo)* to like, to appreciate; *(desiderare)* to like; **gradisce un caffè?** would you like a coffee?

grado *sm* degree; *(sociale)* level; *(MIL)* rank; **quanti gradi ha questo vino?** how strong is this wine?; **essere in ~ di fare qc** to be able to do sthg; ~ **centigrado** centigrade.

graduale *agg* gradual.

graduatoria *sf* (ranked) list.

graffetta *sf (fermaglio)* clip; *(di pinzatrice)* staple.

graffiare *vt* to scratch.

graffio *sm* scratch.

grafica *sf* graphics *(pl)*.

grafico, -a, -ci, -che *agg (rappresentazione, arti)* graphic ♦ *sm, f (pubblicitario)* designer ♦ *sm* graph.

grammatica, -che *sf (disciplina)* grammar; *(libro)* grammar book.

grammo *sm* gram.

grana *sf (fam) (seccatura)* trouble; *(soldi)* cash ♦ *sm inv* a hard cheese similar to Parmesan.

granaio *sm* granary, barn.

Gran Bretagna *sf*: **la ~** Great Britain.

granché *pron*: **non ne so (un) ~** I don't know much about it; **non è (un) ~** it's nothing special.

granchio *sm* crab; **prendere un**

~ *(fig)* to blunder.

grande *(a volte* **gran)** *agg (ger* big; *(albero)* tall; *(rumore)* loud *(scrittore, affetto, capacità)* great ♦ *sn (adulto)* grown-up, adult; ~ **magaz zino** department store; **cosa fara da ~?** what will you do when yo grow up?; **fare le cose in ~** to d things on a grand scale; **è un gran bugiardo** he's such a liar; **fa u gran caldo** it's very hot.

grandezza *sf (dimensioni)* size *(eccellenza)* greatness.

grandinare *v impers* to hail.

grandine *sf* hail.

granello *sm (di sale, sabbia, pol vere)* grain.

granita *sf* granita *(crushed ic with syrup, fruit juice or coffee poure over)*.

grano *sm* wheat.

granturco *sm* maize.

grappa *sf (acquavite)* grapp *(spirit distilled from grape marc)*.

grappolo *sm* bunch.

grasso, -a *agg (persona)* fat *(cibo)* fatty; *(pelle, capelli)* greasy ♦ *sm* fat; *(unto)* grease.

grassoccio, -a, -ci, -ce *ag* plump.

grata *sf* grating.

gratis *avv* free.

gratitudine *sf* gratitude.

grato, -a *agg* grateful.

grattacielo *sm* skyscraper.

grattare *vt* to scratch; *(formag gio)* to grate; *(fam: rubare)* to pinch **grattarsi il naso/la gamba** t scratch one's nose/leg ❑ **grattars** *vr* to scratch o.s.

rattugia sf grater.

rattugiare vt to grate.

ratuito, -a agg free.

rave agg (malattia, ferita) serius; (danno, perdite) serious, great; responsabilità) heavy; (sacrificio) reat; (voce, suono) deep; (contegno) olemn.

ravemente avv seriously.

ravidanza sf pregnancy.

ravità sf (in fisica) gravity; (setà) seriousness.

razia sf grace; (DIR) pardon.

razie esclam thank you!; ~ ante o mille! thank you so much!; dei fiori o per i fiori thank you or the flowers; ~ a thanks to.

razioso, -a agg pretty, charmng.

Grecia sf: la ~ Greece.

reco, -a, -ci, -che agg & m, f Greek.

regge (pl f greggi) sm flock.

reggio, -a, -gi, -ge agg raw, nrefined; (tessuto) unbleached; diamante) rough, uncut ◆ sm rude oil.

rembiule sm (da cucina) apron; er bambini) smock.

rezzo = greggio.

ridare vi to shout; (di dolore) to ell, to cry out ◆ vt to shout.

rido (pl f grida) sm (di persona) hout, cry; di ~ famous.

rigio, -a, -gi, -gie agg & sm rey.

riglia sf grill; alla ~ grilled.

rigliata sf mixed grill (of meat r fish).

rill sm = griglia.

grilletto sm trigger.

grillo sm cricket.

grinta sf determination.

grinzoso, -a agg (tessuto) creased; (pelle) wrinkled.

grissini smpl bread-sticks.

grolla sf wooden goblet or bowl, typical of the Valle d'Aosta.

grondare vi to stream □ **grondare di** v + prep to drip with.

groppa sf rump.

groppo sm tangle; avere un ~ alla gola to have a lump in one's throat.

grossista, -i, -e smf wholesaler.

grosso, -a agg big, large; (spesso) thick; (importante) important; (grave) great ◆ sm majority; dirla grossa to tell a whopping lie; questa volta l'hai fatta grossa! you've really done it this time!; sbagliarsi di ~ to make a big mistake; mare ~ rough sea; pezzo ~ big shot; sale ~ coarse salt.

grossolano, -a agg (persona) coarse; (lavoro) crude; (errore) gross.

grossomodo avv roughly, approximately.

grotta sf cave.

grottesco, -a, -schi, -sche agg grotesque.

groviera sm o sf Gruyère cheese.

groviglio sm tangle.

gru sf inv (macchina) crane.

gruccia, -ce sf (stampella) crutch; (per abiti) coat hanger.

grugnire vi to grunt.

grumo sm (di sangue) clot; (di farina) lump.

gruppo sm group; ~ **sanguigno** blood group.

gruviera = **groviera**.

guadagnare vt (soldi) to earn; (ottenere) to gain; **guadagnarsi da vivere** to earn one's living.

guadagno sm (denaro) earnings (pl); (tornaconto) profit.

guado sm ford.

guai esclam: ~ **a te!** you'll be for it!

guaio sm (pasticcio) trouble; (inconveniente) problem; **essere nei guai** to be in trouble; **mettere qn nei guai** to get sb into trouble.

guancia, -ce sf cheek.

guanciale sm pillow.

guanto sm glove.

guardaboschi sm inv forest ranger.

guardacoste sm inv (persona) coastguard; (nave) (coastguard's) patrol boat.

guardalinee sm inv linesman.

guardamacchine sm inv car park attendant.

guardare vt (osservare) to look at, to watch; (televisione, film) to watch; (bambini, borsa) to look after ♦ vi (edificio) to look, to face; (badare): **non ~ a spese** to spare no expense; **guarda!** look! □ **guardarsi** vr to look at o.s.; **guardarsi da** vr + prep to look at o.s.; **guardarsi dal fare qc** to be careful not to do sthg.

guardaroba sm inv wardrobe; (di locale) cloakroom.

guardia sf guard; (attivi) watch, guard duty; **fare la ~ a** guard; **mettere qn in ~ contro** to warn sb about sthg; ~ **del cor** bodyguard; **Guardia di Finan** military body responsible for custo and fiscal matters; ~ **forestale** fore ranger; ~ **medica** first-aid statio **di ~** on duty.

guardiano sm caretaker; ~ **no** **turno** night watchman.

guardrail [gar'drɛil] sm inv cras barrier.

guarire vi to recover; (ferita) heal ♦ vt to cure; (ferita) to heal.

guarnizione sf (ornamen trim; (contorno) accompanimen garnish; (per recipienti) seal; (di au gasket.

guastafeste smf inv spoilspor

guastare vt to spoil □ **guasta si** vr (meccanismo) to break dow (cibo) to go bad; (tempo) to chang for the worse.

guasto, -a agg (radio) broke (ascensore, telefono) out of orde (cibo) bad ♦ sm breakdown; **un ~** **motore** engine trouble.

guerra sf war; **essere in ~** to at war; ~ **mondiale** World War.

guerriglia sf guerrilla warfare

gufo sm owl.

guglia sf spire.

guida sf guide; (di veicolo) dri ing; ~ **a destra** right-hand drive; **a sinistra** left-hand drive.

guidare vt (veicolo) to driv (accompagnare) to guide; **sai ~?** ca you drive?

guidatore, -trice sm, f drive

guinzaglio sm lead.

guscio *sm (di lumaca)* shell.

gustare *vt (cibo)* to taste; *(godersi)* to enjoy.

gusto *sm* taste; **al ~ di banana** banana-flavoured; **mangiare di ~** to enjoy one's food; **ridere di ~** to laugh heartily; **ci ha preso ~** he's come to like it.

gustoso, -a *agg* tasty.

H

ha → avere.

habitat *sm inv* habitat.

hai → avere.

hall [ol] *sf inv* hall, foyer.

hamburger [am'burger] *sm inv* hamburger.

handicap ['endikap] *sm inv* handicap.

handicappato, -a *agg* handicapped ♦ *sm, f* handicapped person, disabled person.

hanno → avere.

henné *sm inv* henna.

hg *(abbr di ettogrammo)* hg.

hi-fi [ai'fai] *sm inv* hi-fi.

hippy *agg inv & smf inv* hippy.

ho → avere.

hobby *sm inv* hobby.

hockey *sm* hockey *(Br)*, field hockey *(Am)*; **~ su ghiaccio** ice hockey.

hostess *sf inv (di volo)* airhostess.

hotel *sm inv* hotel.

I

i *art mpl* the, → **il**.

iceberg ['aizberg] *sm inv* iceberg.

Iddio *sm* God.

idea *sf* idea; *(opinione, impressione)* impression; *(progetto):* **avere ~ di fare qc** to think of doing sthg; **neanche per ~!** don't even think about it!; **non avere la più pallida ~ di qc** not to have the slightest idea about sthg; **non ne ho ~** I've no idea; **cambiare ~** to change one's mind.

ideale *agg & sm* ideal.

ideare *vt (metodo, sistema)* to devise; *(viaggio)* to plan.

idem *avv (fam: lo stesso)* the same.

identico, -a, -ci, -che *agg* identical.

identità *sf inv* identity.

ideologia, -gie *sf* ideology.

idiota, -i, -e *agg* idiotic, stupid ♦ *smf* idiot.

idolo *sm* idol.

idoneo, -a *agg (adatto):* **~ a** suitable for; *(MIL)* fit for.

idrante *sm* hydrant.

idratante *agg* moisturizing.

idratare *vt* to moisturize.

idraulico, -a, -ci, -che *agg* hydraulic ♦ *sm* plumber; **impianto ~** plumbing.

idrofilo *agg m* → **cotone**.

idrogeno *sm* hydrogen.

idroscalo *sm* seaplane base.

idrosolubile *agg* soluble (in water).

iella *sf (fam)* bad luck.

ieri *avv* yesterday; ~ **mattina** yesterday morning; ~ **notte** last night; **l'altro ~, ~ l'altro** the day before yesterday; **la posta di ~** yesterday's mail.

igiene *sf* hygiene.

igienico, -a, -ci, -che *agg* hygienic.

ignorante *agg* ignorant.

ignorare *vt (non sapere)* not to know; *(trascurare)* to ignore.

ignoto, -a *agg* unknown.

il *(mpl* i; *dav sm* lo *(pl* gli) *+ s+consonante, gn, ps, z; f* la, *fpl* le; *dav sm o sf* l' *+ vocale e* h) *art* 1. *(gen)* the. 2. *(con nome comune)* the; ~ **lago** the lake; **la finestra** the window; **lo studente** the student; **l'isola** the island. 3. *(con nome astratto):* ~ **tempo** time; **la vita** life. 4. *(con titolo):* ~ **Signor Pollini** Mr Pollini; **la regina Elisabetta** Queen Elizabeth. 5. *(con nomi geografici):* ~ **Po** the Po; **le Dolomiti** the Dolomites. 6. *(indica possesso):* **si è rotto ~ naso** he broke his nose; **ha i capelli biondi** she has fair hair. 7. *(indica il tempo):* ~ **sabato** *(tutti i sabati)* on Saturdays; *(quel sabato)* on Saturday; **la sera** in the evening; **è ~ 29 dicembre** it's the 29th of December; **dopo le tre** after three o'clock. 8. *(ciascuno):* **5 000 lire l'uno** 5,000 lira each.

illazione *sf* inference.

illecito, -a *agg* illicit.

illegale *agg* illegal.

illegittimo, -a *agg* illegitimate.

illeso, -a *agg* unhurt.

illimitato, -a *agg (spazio, tempo)* unlimited; *(fiducia)* absolute.

illudere *vt* to deceive ▫ **illudersi** *vr* to deceive o.s.

illuminare *vt* to light up, to illuminate.

illuminazione *sf* lighting; *(fig: intuizione)* enlightenment.

illusione *sf (falsa apparenza)* illusion; *(falsa speranza)* delusion.

illusionista, -i, -e *smf* conjurer.

illuso, -a *pp →* **illudere** ◆ *sm, f:* **essere un ~** to be fooling o.s.

illustrare *vt* to illustrate.

illustrazione *sf* illustration, picture.

imballaggio *sm* packaging.

imballare *vt* to pack (up).

imbalsamare *vt* to embalm.

imbarazzante *agg* embarrassing.

imbarazzare *vt* to embarrass.

imbarazzato, -a *agg* embarrassed.

imbarcadero *sm* landing stage.

imbarcare *vt (passeggero)* to board; *(merce)* to load ▫ **imbarcarsi** *vr* to board.

imbarcazione *sf* boat; **imbarcazioni da diporto** pleasure boats.

imbarco, -chi *sm (salita a bordo)* boarding; *(carico)* loading;

(luogo) point of departure.

imbattersi : imbattersi in *vr* + *prep* to run into.

imbecille *agg* stupid, idiotic ◆ *smf* imbecile, idiot.

imbellire *vt* to embellish ◆ *vi* to become more beautiful.

imbiancare *vt* to whitewash ◆ *vi (diventare bianco)* to turn white.

imbianchino *sm* decorator.

imboccare *vt (bambino)* to feed; *(strada)* to turn into.

imboccatura *sf (di condotto)* mouth; *(di strada)* entrance; *(di strumento musicale)* mouthpiece.

imbocco, -chi *sm* entrance.

imbottigliare *vt (liquido)* to bottle; *(nave)* to blockade; è rimasto imbottigliato he got stuck in a traffic jam.

imbottire *vt (cuscino)* to stuff; *(giacca)* to pad.

imbottito, -a *agg* stuffed; *(indumento)* padded, quilted; panino ~ filled roll.

imbranato, -a *agg (fam)* clumsy.

imbrattare *vt* to dirty.

imbrogliare *vt (ingannare)* to deceive; *(ingarbugliare)* to entangle.

imbroglio *sm* swindle.

imbroglione, -a *sm, f* swindler.

imbronciato, -a *agg* sulky.

imbucare *vt* to post *(Br)*, to mail *(Am)*.

imburrare *vt* to butter.

imbuto *sm* funnel.

imitare *vt* to imitate.

imitazione *sf* imitation.

immacolato, -a *agg (bianco)* pure white; *(puro)* immaculate, pure.

immaginare *vt (rappresentarsi)* to imagine; *(supporre)* to suppose; si immagini! don't mention it!; ~ di fare qc to imagine doing sthg.

immaginazione *sf* imagination.

immagine *sf* image.

immatricolare *vt (auto)* to register; *(studente)* to enrol.

immaturo, -a *agg* immature.

immedesimarsi : immedesimarsi in *vr* + *prep* to identify with.

immediatamente *avv* immediately.

immediato, -a *agg* immediate.

immenso, -a *agg* immense, enormous.

immergere *vt* to immerse ❏ **immergersi** *vr* to dive; **immergersi in** *vr* + *prep (dedicarsi a)* to immerse o.s. in.

immersione *sf* dive.

immerso, -a *pp* → **immergere**.

immesso, -a *pp* → **immettere**.

immettere *vt* to introduce.

immigrante *smf* immigrant.

immigrato, -a *sm, f* immigrant.

imminente *agg* imminent.

immobile *agg* immobile ◆ *sm* property *(Br)*, real estate *(Am)*.

immobiliare *agg* property *(dav*

s) (Br), real estate (dav s) (Am).

immodesto, -a agg immodest.

immondizia sf rubbish.

immorale agg immoral.

immortale agg immortal.

immunità sf immunity.

immunizzare vt to immunize.

impacchettare vt to wrap.

impacciato, -a agg (goffo) awkward; (imbarazzato) embarrassed.

impacco, -chi sm compress.

impadronirsi : impadronirsi di vr + prep (città, beni) to take possession of; (lingua) to master.

impalcatura sf scaffolding.

impallidire vi to go pale.

impalpabile agg impalpable.

impappinarsi vr to stumble.

imparare vt to learn; ~ **a fare qc** to learn to do sthg.

imparziale agg impartial, unbiased.

impassibile agg impassive.

impastare vt (pane) to knead; (mescolare) to mix.

impasto sm (di farina) dough; (amalgama) mixture.

impatto sm impact.

impaurire vt to frighten □ **impaurirsi** vr to get frightened.

impaziente agg impatient; **essere ~ di fare qc** to be impatient to do sthg.

impazzire vi to go mad.

impedimento sm obstacle.

impedire vt (ostacolare) to obstruct; (vietare): ~ **a qn di fare qc** to prevent sb from doing sthg.

impegnare vt (occupare) to keep busy; (dare in pegno) to pawn □ **impegnarsi** vr to commit o.s.; **impegnarsi a fare qc** to undertake to do sthg; **impegnarsi in qc** to commit o.s. to sthg.

impegnativo, -a agg (lavoro) demanding, exacting; (promessa) binding.

impegnato, -a agg (occupato) busy; (militante) committed.

impegno sm commitment; (incombenza) engagement, appointment.

impellente agg pressing, urgent.

impenetrabile agg impenetrable.

impennarsi vr (cavallo) to rear (up); (moto) to do a wheelie; (aereo) to climb.

impennata sf (di cavallo) rearing; (di moto) wheelie; (di aereo) climb.

impensabile agg unthinkable, inconceivable.

impepata sf: ~ **di cozze** mussels cooked with lots of pepper or chilli (a speciality of Naples).

imperativo sm imperative.

imperatore, -trice sm, f emperor (f empress).

imperfezione sf imperfection.

impermeabile agg waterproof ♦ sm raincoat.

impero sm empire.

impersonale agg impersonal.

impersonare vt to play.

impertinente agg impertinent.

imperturbabile *agg* imperturbable.

imperversare *vi (calamità)* to rage; *(fam: moda)* to be all the rage.

impervio, -a *agg* passable with difficulty.

impeto *sm (forza)* force; *(slancio)* surge.

impianto *sm (installazione)* installation; *(elettrico, del gas, antifurto)* system; *(macchinario)* plant; ~ **di riscaldamento** heating system; ~ **sportivo** sports complex; impianti di risalita ski lifts.

impiccare *vt* to hang □ **impiccarsi** *vr* to hang o.s.

impiccione, -a *sm, f* busybody.

impiegare *vt (tempo)* to take; *(utilizzare)* to use; *(assumere)* to employ □ **impiegarsi** *vr* to get a job.

impiegato, -a *sm, f* employee; ~ **di banca** bank clerk.

impiego, -ghi *sm (lavoro)* work, employment; *(uso)* use.

impigliare *vt* to entangle □ **impigliarsi** *vr*: **impigliarsi in qc** to get entangled in sthg.

impigrire *vt* to make lazy ♦ *vi* to become lazy □ **impigrirsi** *vr* to become lazy.

implacabile *agg* implacable, relentless.

implicare *vt (comportare)* to imply, to entail; *(coinvolgere)* to involve.

implicato, -a *agg*: **essere ~ in qc** to be implicated in sthg.

implicazione *sf* implication.

implicito, -a *agg* implicit.

implorare *vt* to implore.

impolverare *vt* to cover with dust □ **impolverarsi** *vr* to get dusty.

imponente *agg* imposing.

impopolare *agg* unpopular.

imporre *vt (volontà, silenzio)* to impose; *(costringere)*: ~ **a qn di fare qc** to make sb do sthg □ **imporsi** *vr (farsi ubbidire)* to impose o.s., to assert o.s.; *(avere successo)* to be successful; **imporsi di fare qc** to make o.s. do sthg.

importante *agg* important.

importanza *sf* importance; **avere ~** to be important, to matter; **dare ~ a qc** to give weight to sthg.

importare *vt* to import ♦ *vi* to matter, to be important ♦ *v impers* to matter; **non importa!** it doesn't matter!; **non mi importa** I don't care.

importato, -a *agg* imported.

importazione *sf* importation; *(prodotto)* import.

importo *sm* amount.

importunare *vt* to bother.

impossessarsi : **impossessarsi di** *vr + prep* to take possession of.

impossibile *agg* impossible ♦ *sm*: **fare l'~** to do all one can.

imposta, -a *pp* → **imporre** ♦ *sf (tassa)* tax, duty; *(di finestra)* shutter.

impostare *vt (lettera)* to post (Br), to mail (Am); *(lavoro)* to plan; *(domanda)* to formulate.

imposto, -a *pp* → **imporre**.

impostore, -a *sm, f* impostor.

impotente *agg* powerless; *(MED)* impotent.

impraticabile *agg* impassable.

imprecare *vi* to curse.

imprecazione *sf* curse.

impregnare *vt*: ~ **qc (di qc)** *(inzuppare)* to soak sthg (with sthg); *(di fumo, odore)* to impregnate sthg (with sthg).

imprenditore, -trice *sm, f* *(industriale)* entrepreneur; *(appaltatore)* contractor.

impreparato, -a *agg* unprepared.

impresa *sf* *(azione)* undertaking; *(ditta)* business.

impresario, -a *sm, f* *(teatrale)* impresario; ~ **edile** building constructor.

impressionante *agg* impressive.

impressionare *vt* *(turbare)* to disturb; *(colpire)* to impress ❏ **impressionarsi** *vr* to get upset.

impressione *sf* impression; *(sensazione)* impression, feeling; **ho l'~ di conoscerlo** I have the impression o feeling I know him; **fare ~** *(colpire)* to impress; *(turbare)* to upset; **fare buona/cattiva ~** to make a good/bad impression.

impresso, -a *pp* → **imprimere**.

imprestare *vt*: ~ **qc a qn** to lend sthg to sb.

imprevisto, -a *agg* unexpected ◆ *sm* unexpected event; **salvo imprevisti** circumstances permitting.

imprigionare *vt* *(incarcerare)* to imprison; *(tenere chiuso)* to confine.

imprimere *vt* to print; *(movimento)* to transmit.

improbabile *agg* improbable, unlikely.

impronta *sf* *(di piede, mano, zampa)* print; ~ **digitale** fingerprint.

improvvisamente *avv* suddenly, unexpectedly.

improvvisare *vt* to improvise ❏ **improvvisarsi** *vr*: **si è improvvisato cuoco** he acted as cook.

improvvisata *sf* surprise.

improvviso, -a *agg* *(inatteso)* sudden, unexpected; *(istantaneo)* sudden; **all'~** suddenly.

imprudente *agg* *(persona)* unwise, imprudent; *(azione)* rash.

imprudenza *sf* rash action.

impudente *agg* impudent.

impugnare *vt* *(stringere)* to grasp; *(DIR)* to contest.

impugnatura *sf* handle.

impulsivo, -a *agg* impulsive.

impulso *sm* impulse; **d'~** on impulse.

impuntarsi *vr* *(bambino)* to stop dead; *(cavallo)* to jib; *(ostinarsi)* to dig one's heels in.

imputare *vt*: ~ **qc a qn** to attribute sthg to sb; ~ **qn di qc** to accuse sb of sthg.

imputato, -a *sm, f* defendant.

in *prep* 1. *(stato in luogo)* in; **abitare ~ campagna** to live in the country; **essere ~ casa** to be at home; **l'ho lasciato ~ macchina/nella borsa** I left it in the car/in the bag; **vivo ~ Italia** I live in Italy; **avere qc ~**

mente to have sthg in mind.

2. *(moto a luogo)* to; **andare ~ Italia** to go to Italy; **andare ~ montagna** to go to the mountains; **mettersi qc ~ testa** to get sthg into one's head; **entrare ~ macchina** to get into the car; **entrare nella stanza** to go into the room.

3. *(indica un momento)* in; **~ primavera** in spring; **nel 1995** in 1995.

4. *(indica durata)* in; **l'ho fatto ~ cinque minuti** I did it in five minutes; **~ giornata** within the day.

5. *(indica modo)*: **parlare ~ italiano** to speak in Italian; **~ silenzio** in silence; **sono ancora in pigiama** I'm still in my pyjamas; **quant'è ~ lire?** how much is that in lira?; **~ vacanza** on holiday *(Br)*, on vacation *(Am)*.

6. *(indica mezzo)* by; **pagare ~ contanti** to pay cash; **viàggiare ~ macchina** to travel by car.

7. *(indica materia)* made of; **statua ~ bronzo** bronze statue.

8. *(indica fine)*: **ha speso un capitale in libri** he spent a fortune on books; **dare ~ omaggio** to give as a free gift; **~ onore di** in honour of.

9. *(con valore distributivo)*: **siamo partiti ~ tre** three of us left; **~ tutto sono 10 000 lire** it's 10,000 lira in total.

inàbile *agg*: **~ (a qc)** unfit (for sthg).

inaccessìbile *agg (luogo)* inaccessible; *(persona)* unapproachable.

inaccettàbile *agg* unacceptable.

inadatto, -a *agg* unsuitable.

inadeguato, -a *agg (insuffi-*

ciente) inadequate; *(non idoneo)* unsuitable.

inagìbile *agg* unfit for use.

inalare *vt* to inhale.

inalberarsi *vr* to get angry.

inalterato, -a *agg* unchanged.

inamidare *vt* to starch.

inammissìbile *agg* inadmissible.

inappetenza *sf* lack of appetite.

inappuntàbile *agg (persona)* faultless, irreproachable; *(lavoro, vestito)* impeccable.

inarcare *vt (schiena)* to arch; **~ le sopracciglia** to raise one's eyebrows □ **inarcarsi** *vr* to arch.

inaridire *vt* to dry (up) □ **inaridirsi** *vr* to dry up.

inaspettato, -a *agg* unexpected.

inasprire *vt* to make worse □ **inasprirsi** *vr* to become bitter.

inattendìbile *agg* unbelievable, unreliable.

inatteso, -a *agg* unexpected.

inattività *sf* inactivity.

inattuàbile *agg* impractical, unfeasible.

inaudito, -a *agg* unheard-of, unprecedented.

inaugurare *vt (luogo, mostra)* to open; *(monumento)* to unveil.

inavvertenza *sf* carelessness.

inavvertitamente *avv* inadvertently.

incagliarsi *vr (nave)* to run aground; *(fig: trattative)* to break down.

incalcolàbile *agg* incalculable.

incallito, -a agg (mani, piedi) calloused; (fig: fumatore, giocatore) inveterate.

incalzare vt (inseguire) to pursue; (fig: premere) to press ◆ vi to be imminent.

incamminarsi vr to set out.

incantevole agg enchanting.

incanto sm (incantesimo) enchantment; (asta) auction; **come per ~** as if by magic.

incapace agg incapable.

incapacità sf (inettitudine) incapacity; (DIR) incompetence.

incappare : incappare in v + prep to run into.

incaricare vt to entrust; **~ qn di qc** to entrust sb with sthg; **~ qn di fare qc** to ask sb to do sthg □ **incaricarsi di** vr + prep to undertake to.

incaricato, -a agg: **~ di qc** entrusted with sthg ◆ sm, f representative.

incarico, -chi sm task.

incarnare vt to embody.

incarnirsi vr to become ingrown.

incartare vt to wrap up; **me lo può ~?** can you wrap it up for me?

incassare vt (denaro) to receive; (assegno) to cash; (colpo, offesa) to take; (mobile) to build in.

incasso sm takings (pl).

incastrare vt (connettere) to join; (fam: intrappolare) to catch □ **incastrarsi** vr (rimanere bloccato) to get stuck; (combaciare) to fit together.

incastro sm joint; **a ~** interlocking.

incatenare vt (legare) to chain.

incauto, -a agg imprudent, rash.

incavato, -a agg hollow; (occhi) sunken.

incavo sm hollow.

incavolarsi vr (fam) to lose one's temper.

incendiare vt (dare fuoco a) to set fire to □ **incendiarsi** vr to catch fire.

incendio sm fire.

incenerire vt to incinerate.

incenso sm incense.

incensurato, -a agg: **essere ~** to have no previous convictions.

incentivo sm incentive.

inceppare vt to block, to obstruct □ **incepparsi** vr to jam.

incerata sf (tela) oilcloth; (giaccone) oilskin.

incertezza sf uncertainty.

incerto, -a agg uncertain; (tempo) variable.

incetta sf: **fare ~ di qc** to buy sthg up.

inchiesta sf enquiry.

inchinarsi vr (uomo) to bow; (donna) to curtsy.

inchino sm (di uomo) bow; (di donna) curtsy.

inchiodare vt to nail.

inchiostro sm ink.

inciampare vi to trip; **~ in qc** to trip over sthg.

incidente sm accident; **~ stradale** road accident.

incidere vt (intagliare) to engrave; (canzone) to record; (ascesso) to lance □ **incidere su** v +

prep to affect.

incinta *agg f* pregnant.

incirca *avv:* all'~ approximately, about.

incisione *sf (taglio)* cut; *(in arte)* engraving; *(di disco, canzone)* recording; *(MED)* incision.

incisivo, -a *agg* incisive ♦ *sm* incisor.

inciso, -a *pp* → incidere ♦ *sm:* per ~ incidentally.

incitare *vt* to incite.

incivile *agg (non civilizzato)* uncivilized; *(maleducato)* rude.

inclinazione *sf* inclination.

includere *vt (accludere)* to enclose; *(comprendere)* to include.

incluso, -a *pp* → includere ♦ *agg (accluso)* enclosed; *(compreso)* included; ~ nel prezzo included in the price.

incognito *sm:* in ~ incognito.

incollare *vt (sovrapporre)* to stick; *(unire)* to stick, to glue ☐ **incollarsi** *vr (stare vicino):* incollarsi a qn to stick close to sb.

incolpare *vt:* ~ qn (di qc) to blame sb (for sthg).

incolume *agg* unhurt.

incominciare *vt & vi* to begin, to start; ~ a fare qc to begin to do sthg o doing sthg, to start to do sthg o doing sthg.

incompatibile *agg* incompatible.

incompetente *agg* incompetent.

incompiuto, -a *agg* unfinished, incomplete.

incompleto, -a *agg* incomplete.

incomprensibile *agg* incomprehensible.

inconcepibile *agg* inconceivable.

inconcludente *agg (persona)* ineffectual; *(discorsi)* inconclusive.

incondizionato, -a *agg* unconditional.

inconfondibile *agg* unmistakable.

inconsapevole *agg* unaware.

inconscio, -a, -sci, -sce *agg* unconscious.

incontaminato, -a *agg* uncontaminated.

incontentabile *agg* impossible to please.

incontinenza *sf* incontinence.

incontrare *vt* to meet; *(difficoltà, favore)* to meet with ☐ **incontrarsi** *vr* to meet.

incontrario : all'incontrario *avv (fam) (alla rovescia)* back to front; *(all'indietro)* backwards.

incontro *sm* meeting; *(casuale)* encounter; *(sportivo)* match ♦ *avv* towards; andare/venire ~ a qn *(avanzare verso)* to go/to come towards sb; *(incontrare)* to go/to come to meet sb; *(fig: con compromesso)* to meet sb halfway; andare ~ a qc *(spese)* to incur; *(difficoltà)* to encounter.

inconveniente *sm* setback, problem.

incoraggiare *vt* to encourage.

incosciente *agg (privo di coscienza)* unconscious; *(irresponsabile)* irresponsible.

incredibile *agg* incredible.

incrementare *vt* to increase.

incremento *sm* increase.

incrociare *vt* to cross; *(persona, veicolo)* to pass; ~ **le gambe/braccia** to cross one's legs/arms; ~ **le dita** to cross one's fingers ◻ **incrociarsi** *vr (strade, linee)* to cross; *(persone, veicoli)* to pass each other.

incrocio *sm (crocevia)* crossroads *(sg)*; *(combinazione)* cross-breed.

incubatrice *sf* incubator.

incubo *sm* nightmare.

incurabile *agg* incurable.

incurante *agg*: ~ **di** careless of, indifferent to.

incuriosire *vt* to make curious ◻ **incuriosirsi** *vr* to become curious.

incustodito, -a *agg* unattended.

indaco *sm* indigo.

indaffarato, -a *agg* busy.

indagine *sf (di polizia)* investigation; *(studio)* research.

indebolire *vt* to weaken ◻ **indebolirsi** *vr* to weaken, to become weak.

indecente *agg* indecent.

indecifrabile *agg* indecipherable.

indeciso, -a *agg* uncertain.

indefinito, -a *agg* indefinite.

indegno, -a *agg* disgraceful.

indelebile *agg* indelible.

indenne *agg* unhurt.

indennità *sf inv (rimborso)* payment; *(risarcimento)* compensation.

indescrivibile *agg* indescribable.

indeterminativo, -a *ag* indefinite.

indeterminato, -a *agg* inde terminate, vague.

India *sf*: l'~ India.

indiano, -a *agg & sm, f* Indian.

indicare *vt (mostrare)* to show *(col dito)* to point to; *(suggerire)* t recommend.

indicatore *sm (TECNOL)* gauge ~ **della benzina** petrol gauge; ~ **d direzione** indicator; ~ **di velocit** speedometer.

indicazione *sf (segnalazione* indication; *(informazione)* piece o information; *(prescrizione)* direc tion.

indice *sm (dito)* index finger; *(a libro)* index; *(lancetta)* needle *(indizio)* rating.

indietro *avv* back; *(moto a luogo* backwards; **essere** ~ *(col lavoro)* t be behind; *(orologio)* to be slow; **rimandare** ~ to send back; **tornar** ~ to go back; **all'**~ backwards.

indifeso, -a *agg* defenceless.

indifferente *agg (insensibile* indifferent; *(irrilevante)* insignifi cant; **mi è** ~ it's all the same t me.

indigeno, -a *sm, f* native.

indigente *agg* destitute.

indigestione *sf* indigestion.

indigesto, -a *agg* indigestible.

indimenticabile *agg* unfor gettable.

indipendente *agg* independ ent.

indipendenza *sf* independ ence.

indire *vt (concorso)* to announce; *(elezioni)* to call.

indiretto, -a *agg* indirect.

indirizzare *vt (lettera, discorso)* to address; *(mandare)* to refer.

indirizzo *sm* address; **scuola a ~ tecnico** = technical college.

indisciplinato, -a *agg* undisciplined.

indiscreto, -a *agg* indiscreet.

indiscrezione *sf (invadenza)* indiscretion; *(notizia)* unconfirmed report.

indiscusso, -a *agg* undisputed.

indiscutibile *agg* unquestionable.

indispensabile *agg* indispensable.

indispettire *vt* to annoy □ **indispettirsi** *vr* to become annoyed.

indisponente *agg* annoying.

indistruttibile *agg* indestructible.

individuale *agg* individual.

individuare *vt* to identify.

individuo *sm* individual.

indiziato, -a *agg* suspected ♦ *sm, f* suspect.

indizio *sm (segno)* sign; *(per polizia)* clue; *(DIR)* piece of evidence.

indole *sf* nature.

indolenzito, -a *agg* aching, stiff.

indolore *agg* painless.

indomani *sm:* **l'~** the next day.

indossare *vt (mettere addosso)* to put on; *(avere addosso)* to wear.

indossatore, -trice *sm, f* model.

indotto, -a *pp* → **indurre**.

indovinare *vt* to guess; *(prevedere)* to predict; *(azzeccare)* to get right.

indovinello *sm* riddle.

indovino, -a *sm, f* fortuneteller.

indubbiamente *avv* undoubtedly.

indugiare *vi (temporeggiare)* to take one's time.

indugio *sm* delay; **senza ~** without delay.

indulgente *agg* indulgent.

indumento *sm* garment; **indumenti** *(abiti)* clothes.

indurire *vt* to harden □ **indurirsi** *vr* to harden.

indurre *vt:* **~ qn a fare qc** to induce sb to do sthg.

industria *sf* industry; *(stabilimento)* industrial plant.

industriale *agg* industrial ♦ *sm* industrialist.

inebetito, -a *agg* stunned.

inebriante *agg* intoxicating.

ineccepibile *agg* unexceptionable.

inedito, -a *agg* unpublished.

inefficiente *agg* inefficient.

ineluttabile *agg* inescapable.

inerente *agg:* **~ a** concerning.

inerme *agg* unarmed, defenceless.

inerzia *sf* inactivity.

inesatto, -a *agg* inaccurate.

inesauribile *agg* inexhaustible.

inesistente *agg* nonexistent.

inesperienza sf inexperience.

inesperto, -a agg inexperienced.

inestimabile agg inestimable.

inevaso, -a agg outstanding.

inevitabile agg inevitable.

inevitabilmente avv inevitably.

in extremis avv in extremis.

infallibile agg infallible.

infantile agg (di, per bambini) child (dav s); (immaturo) infantile.

infanzia sf (periodo) childhood; (bambini) children (pl); **prima ~** infancy.

infarinare vt (di farina) to cover with flour; (cospargere) to sprinkle.

infarto sm heart attack.

infastidire vt to annoy □ **infastidirsi** vr to get annoyed.

infatti cong in fact.

infatuarsi : infatuarsi di vr + prep to become infatuated with.

infatuazione sf infatuation.

infedele agg unfaithful.

infedeltà sf inv infidelity.

infelice agg unhappy; (sfavorevole) unsuccessful; (mal riuscito) poor; (inopportuno) unfortunate.

infelicità sf unhappiness.

inferiore agg (sottostante) lower; (per qualità) inferior ◆ smf inferior; **~ a** (minore) below; (peggiore) inferior to.

infermeria sf infirmary; (di scuola) sickbay.

infermiere, -a sm, f nurse.

infermo, -a agg infirm.

infernale agg (fam: terribile) terrible; (diabolico) diabolical.

inferno sm hell.

inferriata sf grating.

infestare vt to infest.

infettare vt to infect □ **infettarsi** vr to become infected.

infettivo, -a agg infectious; **malattie infettive** infectious diseases.

infezione sf infection.

infiammabile agg flammable.

infiammare vt (incendiare) to set alight; (MED) to inflame □ **infiammarsi** vr (incendiarsi) to catch fire; (MED) to become inflamed.

infiammazione sf inflammation.

infilare vt (introdurre) to insert; (ago) to thread; (anello, vestito) to slip on □ **infilarsi in** vr + prep to slip into.

infine avv (alla fine) finally; (insomma) in short.

infinità sf infinity; **un'~ di** countless.

infinito, -a agg (illimitato) infinite; (enorme, innumerevole) countless ◆ sm (spazio, tempo) infinite; (GRAMM) infinitive.

infischiarsi : infischiarsene di vr + prep not to care about.

inflazione sf inflation.

inflessibile agg inflexible.

infliggere vt to inflict.

inflitto, -a pp → **infliggere**.

influente agg influential.

influenza sf influence; (malattia) flu; **avere ~ su** to have an influence on; **avere l'~** to have flu.

influenzare vt to influence.

influire : influire su v + prep to

have an effect on.

influsso sm influence.

infondato, -a agg unfounded.

infondere vt to instil.

inforcare vt (fieno) to fork up; (bicicletta, moto) to get onto; (occhiali) to put on.

informale agg informal.

informare vt: ~ qn (di qc) to inform sb (of sthg) □ **informarsi** vr: **informarsi di** o **su** to find out about.

informatica sf information technology.

informativo, -a agg informative.

informatore sm informer.

informazione sf piece of information; **chiedere informazioni (a qn)** to ask (sb) for information; 'informazioni' 'information'.

informicolirsi vr: **mi si è informicolita una gamba** I've got pins and needles in my leg.

infortunio sm accident.

infossarsi vr (terreno) to sink; (guance) to become hollow.

infradito sm inv o sf inv flip-flop.

infrangere vt to break □ **infrangersi** vr to break.

infrangibile agg unbreakable.

infranto, -a pp → infrangere ◆ agg broken.

infrazione sf infringement.

infreddolito, -a agg chilled.

infuori avv: **all'~** outwards; **all'~ di** apart from.

infusione sf infusion.

infuso, -a pp → infondere ◆ sm herb tea.

ingannare vt (imbrogliare) to deceive; (tempo) to while away □ **ingannarsi** vr to be mistaken.

inganno sm deception.

ingarbugliare vt to tangle; (situazione, conti) to muddle □ **ingarbugliarsi** vr to become tangled; (situazione) to become muddled; (impappinarsi) to falter.

ingegnere sm engineer.

ingegneria sf engineering.

ingegno sm (intelligenza) intelligence; (creatività) ingenuity.

ingegnoso, -a agg ingenious.

ingelosire vt to make jealous □ **ingelosirsi** vr to become jealous.

ingente agg huge.

ingenuo, -a agg naive.

ingerire vt to ingest.

ingessare vt to put in plaster.

Inghilterra sf: **l'~** England.

inghiottire vt to swallow; (sopportare) to put up with.

ingiallire vi to yellow.

ingigantire vt (foto) to enlarge; (fig: problema) to exaggerate.

inginocchiarsi vr to kneel down.

ingiù avv: (all')~ downwards.

ingiustizia sf (qualità) injustice; (atto) unjust act.

ingiusto, -a agg unfair.

inglese agg English ◆ smf Englishman (f Englishwoman) ◆ sm (lingua) English.

ingoiare vt (inghiottire) to swallow; (fig: sopportare) to put up with.

ingolfare vt to flood □ **ingolfarsi** vr to flood.

ingombrante *agg* cumbersome.

ingombrare *vt (passaggio, strada)* to obstruct; *(tavolo, stanza)* to clutter up.

ingombro, -a *agg* obstructed ♦ *sm*: **essere d'~** to be in the way.

ingordo, -a *agg* greedy.

ingorgo, -ghi *sm* traffic jam.

ingranaggio *sm (meccanismo)* gear; *(fig: operazioni, attività)* machinery.

ingranare *vt* to engage ♦ *vi (ingranaggio)* to engage; *(fam: prendere avvio)* to get going.

ingrandimento *sm* enlargement; *(ottico)* magnification.

ingrandire *vt* to enlarge; *(con microscopio, lente)* to magnify □ **ingrandirsi** *vr (di misura)* to get bigger; *(d'importanza)* to become more important.

ingrassare *vi* to put on weight ♦ *vt (animali)* to fatten up; *(motore)* to grease.

ingrediente *sm* ingredient.

ingresso *sm (porta)* entrance; *(stanza)* hall; *(permesso di entrare)* admission; **'~ gratuito'** 'admission free'; **'~ libero'** 'admission free'.

ingrossare *vt (gambe, fegato)* to cause to swell □ **ingrossarsi** *vr (gambe, fegato)* to swell.

ingrosso *avv*: **all'~** *(vendita)* wholesale; *(grossomodo)* about, roughly.

inguine *sm* groin.

inibire *vt* to inhibit.

iniettare *vt* to inject.

iniezione *sf* injection.

inimicare *vt*: **inimicarsi qn** to make an enemy of sb.

inimitabile *agg* inimitable.

ininterrottamente *avv* nonstop.

ininterrotto, -a *agg* continuous, unbroken.

iniziale *agg & sf* initial.

inizialmente *avv* initially.

iniziare *vt & vi* to begin, to start; **~ qn a qc** to introduce sb to sthg; **~ a fare qc** to begin O start to do sthg.

iniziativa *sf* initiative; **prendere l'~** to take the initiative.

inizio *sm* start, beginning; **all'~** at the start, at the beginning; **dare ~ a qc** to start O begin sthg; **avere ~** to start, to begin.

innaffiare = **annaffiare**.

innalzare *vt* to erect.

innamorarsi *vr*: **~ (di qn)** to fall in love (with sb).

innamorato, -a *agg*: **~ (di qn)** in love (with sb).

innanzi *avv* in front ♦ *prep (davanti a)* in front of; *(prima di)* before.

innanzitutto *avv* first of all.

innato, -a *agg* innate.

innervosire *vt* to make nervous □ **innervosirsi** *vr* to get nervous.

innescare *vt (bomba)* to prime; *(fig: fenomeno, meccanismo)* to trigger.

innestare *vt (pianta)* to graft; *(meccanismo, marcia)* to engage.

inno *sm* hymn; **~ nazionale** national anthem.

innocente *agg* innocent.

innocuo, -a *agg* harmless.

innovazione *sf* innovation.

innumerevole *agg* countless.

inodore *agg* odourless.

inoffensivo, -a *agg* inoffensive.

inoltrare *vt* to forward ◻ **inoltrarsi** *vr* to advance.

inoltrato, -a *agg* late.

inoltre *avv* besides.

inondazione *sf* flood.

inopportuno, -a *agg* inappropriate.

inorridire *vt* to horrify ◆ *vi* to be horrified.

inosservato, -a *agg*: **passare ~** to go unnoticed.

inquadrare *vt* (*personaggio, avvenimento*) to place; (*con telecamera*): **~ qn/qc** to get sb/sthg in the shot.

inquadratura *sf* shot.

inqualificabile *agg* contemptible.

inquietante *agg* disturbing.

inquilino, -a *sm, f* tenant.

inquinamento *sm* pollution.

inquinare *vt* (*contaminare*) to pollute; (*fig: prove*) to corrupt.

inquinato, -a *agg* polluted.

insabbiare *vt* to shelve ◻ **insabbiarsi** *vr* (*nave*) to run aground; (*pratica, progetto*) to be shelved.

insaccato *sm* sausage.

insalata *sf* (*di verdure*) salad; (*lattuga*) lettuce; **~ mista** mixed salad; **~ di mare** seafood salad; **~ di riso** rice salad; **~ russa** Russian salad (*cold diced cooked vegetables mixed with mayonnaise*).

insalatiera *sf* salad bowl.

insaponare *vt* to soap ◻ **insaponarsi** *vr* to soap o.s.

insapore *agg* tasteless.

insaporire *vt* to flavour.

insaputa *sf*: **all'~ di qn** without sb's knowledge.

inscenare *vt* to stage.

insegna *sf* sign.

insegnamento *sm* teaching.

insegnante *smf* teacher.

insegnare *vt & vi* to teach; **~ qc a qn** to teach sb sthg; **~ a qn a fare qc** to teach sb to do sthg.

inseguire *vt* to pursue.

insenatura *sf* inlet, creek.

insensato, -a *agg* (*persona*) foolish; (*discorso, idea*) senseless.

insensibile *agg* insensitive.

inseparabile *agg* inseparable.

inserire *vt* (*introdurre*) to insert; (*includere*) to put in ◻ **inserirsi** *vr*: **inserirsi in qc** (*entrare a far parte di*) to become part of sthg.

inserto *sm* insert.

inserviente *smf* attendant.

inserzione *sf* advertisement.

insetticida, -i *sm* insecticide.

insetto *sm* insect.

insicurezza *sf* insecurity.

insicuro, -a *agg* insecure.

insidia *sf* hidden danger.

insieme *avv* together ◆ *sm* (*totalità*) whole; (*MAT*) set ◆ *prep*: **~ a** o **con** with; **mettere ~** (*raccogliere*) to put together; **tutto ~** all together; **tutti ~** all together; **nell'~** taken as a whole.

insignificante *agg* insignificant.

insinuare *vt* to insinuate.

insinuazione *sf* insinuation.

insipido, -a *agg* insipid.

insistente *agg* (persona, richieste) insistent; (pioggia, dolore) persistent.

insistere *vi* to insist; ~ **a** o **col fare qc** to persist in doing sthg.

insoddisfacente *agg* unsatisfactory.

insoddisfatto, -a *agg*: ~ **di** dissatisfied with.

insolazione *sf* sunstroke.

insolente *agg* insolent.

insolito, -a *agg* unusual.

insoluto, -a *agg* (non risolto) unsolved; (non pagato) outstanding.

insomma *avv* well ♦ *esclam* for Heaven's sake!

insonne *agg* (persona) unable to sleep; (notte) sleepless.

insonnia *sf* insomnia.

insonnolito, -a *agg* sleepy.

insopportabile *agg* unbearable.

insorgere *vi* (popolo) to rise up; (difficoltà) to arise.

insospettire *vt* to arouse suspicions in □ **insospettirsi** *vr* to become suspicious.

insozzare *vt* to dirty.

insperato, -a *agg* unhoped-for.

inspiegabile *agg* inexplicable.

inspirare *vt* to breathe in.

installare *vt* to install.

instaurare *vt* to establish.

insù *avv*: (all')~ upwards.

insuccesso *sm* failure.

insudiciare *vt* to dirty □ **insudiciarsi** *vr* to get dirty.

insufficiente *agg* insufficient.

insulina *sf* insulin.

insultare *vt* to insult.

insulto *sm* insult.

intaccare *vt* to attack; (fare tacche in) to cut into; (risparmi) to break into.

intanto *avv* (nel frattempo) meanwhile.

intarsio *sm* inlay.

intasare *vt* to block □ **intasarsi** *vr* to become blocked.

intatto, -a *agg* (intero) intact; (mai toccato) untouched.

integrale *agg* (totale) complete; (pane, farina) wholemeal.

integrare *vt* to integrate □ **integrarsi** *vr* to integrate.

integrità *sf* integrity.

integro, -a *agg* (intero) intact; (onesto) honest.

intelaiatura *sf* framework.

intelletto *sm* intellect.

intellettuale *agg & smf* intellectual.

intelligente *agg* intelligent.

intelligenza *sf* intelligence.

intemperie *sfpl* bad weather (sg).

intendere *vt* (capire) to understand; (udire) to hear; (avere intenzione di): ~ **fare qc** to intend to do sthg; **non intende ragioni** he won't listen to reason; **intendersela con qn** to have an affair with sb □ **intendersi di** *vr + prep* to know about.

intenditore, -trice *sm, f*
expert.

intensificare *vt* to intensify ❑
intensificarsi *vr* to intensify.

intensità *sf* intensity.

intensivo, -a *agg* intensive.

intenso, -a *agg* intense.

intento, -a *sm* intention ◆ *agg*:
~ (a fare qc) intent (on doing
sthg).

intenzione *sf* intention; **aver ~
di fare qc** to intend to do sthg.

interamente *avv* completely.

intercalare *sm* catchphrase ◆
vt to insert.

intercettare *vt* to intercept.

intercity [inter'siti] *sm inv* fast
train connecting major Italian cities.

interdetto, -a *agg* taken
aback.

interessamento *sm (interesse)*
interest; *(intervento)* intervention.

interessante *agg* interesting;
in stato ~ *(incinta)* expecting.

interessare *vt (destare l'interesse
di)* to interest; *(riguardare)* to concern ◆ *vi*: ~ **a qn** to interest sb; **ciò
non mi interessa** I'm not interested
in it ❑ **interessarsi a** *vr + prep* to
be interested in; **interessarsi di**
vr + prep (per informazioni) to find
out about; *(per lavoro, hobby)* to be
interested in.

interessato, -a *agg (parte-
cipe)* interested; *(calcolatore)* self-
interested.

interesse *sm* interest; *(tornaconto)* self-interest ❑ **interessi** *smpl*
interests.

interferire *vi* to interfere.

interiezione *sf* interjection.

interiora *sfpl* entrails.

interiore *agg (lato, parte)* interi-
or.

interlocutore, -trice *sm, f*
interlocutor.

intermezzo *sm* interval.

interminabile *agg* endless.

intermittente *agg* intermit-
tent.

internazionale *agg* international.

interno, -a *agg (di dentro)* interior, internal; *(nazionale)* domestic
◆ *sm* interior; *(telefono)* extension;
(in indirizzo): ~ **20** flat 20; **all'~**
inside ❑ **interni** *smpl*: **ministero
degli Interni** = Home Office *(Br)*,
Department of the Interior *(Am)*.

intero, -a *agg* whole; *(prezzo)*
full; *(latte)* full-cream; **per ~** in full.

interpretare *vt* to interpret;
(recitare) to perform.

interprete *smf (traduttore)*
interpreter; *(attore, musicista)* performer.

interrogare *vt (studente)* to
examine; *(sospetto)* to question.

interrogativo, -a *agg (sguardo)* enquiring; *(GRAMM)* interrogative ◆ *sm* question.

interrogazione *sf* oral examination.

interrompere *vt* to interrupt;
(linea telefonica, strada) to cut off ❑
interrompersi *vr* to stop.

interrotto, -a *pp* → **interrompere** ◆ *agg* cut off.

interruttore *sm* switch.

intersecare vt to intersect.

interurbana sf long-distance call.

interurbano, -a agg (trasporti) intercity; (chiamata) long-distance.

intervallo sm interval.

intervenire vi to intervene; (partecipare) to take part; (MED) to operate.

intervento sm (intromissione) intervention; (partecipazione) participation; (discorso) speech; (MED) operation.

intervenuto, -a pp → intervenire.

intervista sf interview.

intesa sf (tra persone) understanding; (tra stati) agreement.

inteso, -a pp → intendere ◆ agg: **resta ~ che** it is understood that; **siamo intesi?** are we agreed?

intestare vt (lettera) to address; **~ qc a qn** (casa, auto) to register sthg in sb's name; (assegno) to make sthg out to sb.

intestino sm intestine.

intimare vt to order.

intimidire vt to intimidate.

intimità sf (spazio privato) privacy; (familiarità) intimacy.

intimo, -a agg intimate; (cerimonia, parti) private; (interiore) innermost; (igiene) personal ◆ sm (persona) close friend.

intimorire vt to frighten.

intingolo sm sauce.

intitolare vt (libro, film) to entitle; (via, piazza): **~ a** to name after □ **intitolarsi** vr to be entitled.

intollerabile agg unbearable.

intollerante agg intolerant.

intolleranza sf intolerance.

intonaco, -ci o **-chi** sm plaster.

intonare vt (canto) to intone; (vestiti): **~ qc a qc** to match sthg with sthg □ **intonarsi** vr to go together.

intontire vt to stun.

intorno avv around, round ◆ prep: **~ a** around.

intossicare vt to poison.

intossicato, -a agg poisoned.

intossicazione sf poisoning.

intraducibile agg untranslatable.

intralciare vt to hamper.

intramontabile agg timeless.

intramuscolare agg → iniezione.

intransigente agg intransigent.

intransitivo, -a agg intransitive.

intraprendente agg enterprising.

intraprendere vt to undertake.

intrapreso, -a pp → intraprendere.

intrattabile agg (persona) intractable; (prezzo) non-negotiable.

intrattenere vt (persona) to entertain; (relazioni, rapporti) to maintain □ **intrattenersi** vr: **intrattenersi su qc** to dwell on sthg.

intrecciare vt (capelli) to plait, to braid; (nastri) to intertwine □ **intrecciarsi** vr (fili) to intertwine.

intrigante *agg* scheming.

intrigo, -ghi *sm (macchinazione)* intrigue.

introdurre *vt* to introduce; *(moneta)* to insert; 'vietato ~ cani' 'dogs not allowed' □ **introdursi** *vr (uso, tecnica)* to be introduced; *(entrare)* to enter.

introduzione *sf* introduction.

introito *sm (incasso)* income.

intromettersi *vr (immischiarsi)* to interfere; *(interporsi)* to intervene.

introvabile *agg* not to be found.

introverso, -a *agg* introverted.

intruso, -a *sm, f* intruder.

intuire *vt (cogliere)* to grasp; *(accorgersi)* to realize.

intuito *sm* intuition.

intuizione *sf* intuition.

inumidire *vt* to dampen □ **inumidirsi** *vr* to become damp.

inutile *agg* useless; *(superfluo)* pointless.

inutilmente *avv* in vain.

invadente *agg* intrusive.

invadere *vt* to invade.

invaghirsi : invaghirsi di *vr + prep* to take a fancy to.

invalido, -a *agg* disabled ◆ *sm, f* disabled person.

invano *avv* in vain.

invasione *sf* invasion.

invasore *sm* invader.

invecchiare *vi (persona)* to grow old; *(vino)* to age ◆ *vt (vino, formaggio)* to age; *(persona)* to make look older.

invece *avv* but ◆ *prep*: ~ **di** instead of.

inveire *vi*: ~ **(contro)** to rail (against).

inventare *vt* to invent; **si è inventato tutto** he made it all up.

inventario *sm (registrazione)* stocktaking; *(lista)* inventory.

inventore, -trice *sm, f* inventor.

invenzione *sf* invention.

invernale *agg* winter *(dav s)*.

inverno *sm* winter; **in** o **d'~** in (the) winter.

inverosimile *agg* unbelievable.

inversione *sf (di ordine, tendenza)* inversion; *(di marcia)* U-turn.

inverso, -a *agg & sm* opposite; **fare qc all'~** to do sthg the wrong way round.

invertire *vt (ordine)* to invert; ~ **la marcia** to do a U-turn.

investimento *sm* investment.

investire *vt (denaro)* to invest; *(persona, animale)* to knock down.

inviare *vt* to send.

inviato, -a *sm, f (incaricato)* envoy; *(giornalista)* correspondent.

invidia *sf* envy.

invidiare *vt* to envy; ~ **qc a qn** to envy sb sthg.

invidioso, -a *agg* envious.

invincibile *agg (imbattibile)* invincible.

invio *sm (spedizione)* dispatching; *(merci)* consignment.

inviperito, -a *agg* furious.

invischiarsi : invischiarsi in *vr + prep* to get involved in.

invisibile *agg* invisible.

invitare *vt* to invite; ~ **qn a fare qc** *(proporre di)* to invite sb to do sthg; *(sollecitare)* to request sb to do sthg.

invitato, -a *sm, f* guest.

invito *sm* invitation.

invocare *vt (Dio)* to invoke; *(chiedere)* to beg for; *(legge, diritto)* to cite.

invogliare *vt* to tempt.

involontario, -a *agg* involuntary.

involtino *sm* thin slice of meat, rolled up and sometimes stuffed; ~ **primavera** spring roll.

involucro *sm* covering.

inzaccherare *vt* to splash with mud.

inzuppare *vt* to soak; *(biscotto)* to dip.

io *pron* I; **sono** ~ it's me; ~ **stesso** I myself.

iodio *sm* iodine.

iogurt = yogurt.

Ionio *sm*: **lo** ~, **il mar** ~ the Ionian (Sea).

ipertensione *sf* hypertension.

ipnosi *sf* hypnosis.

ipnotizzare *vt* to hypnotize.

ipocrisia *sf* hypocrisy.

ipocrita, -i, -e *agg* hypocritical ♦ *smf* hypocrite.

ipoteca, -che *sf* mortgage.

ipotesi *sf inv* hypothesis.

ippica *sf* horse racing.

ippico, -a, -ci, -che *agg* horse *(dav s)*.

ippodromo *sm* racecourse.

ippopotamo *sm* hippo-potamus.

Iran *sm*: **l'**~ Iran.

Iraq *sm*: **l'**~ Iraq.

iride *sf (di occhio)* iris; *(arcobaleno)* rainbow.

iris *sf inv* iris.

Irlanda *sf*: **l'**~ Ireland; **l'**~ **del Nord** Northern Ireland.

irlandese *agg* Irish ♦ *sm* Irishman *(f* Irishwoman).

ironia *sf* irony.

ironico, -a, -ci, -che *agg* ironic.

irradiare *vt* to light up ♦ *vi* to radiate.

irraggiungibile *agg* unreachable.

irragionevole *agg* unreasonable.

irrazionale *agg* irrational.

irreale *agg* unreal.

irrecuperabile *agg (oggetto)* irretrievable; *(fig: persona)* irredeemable.

irregolare *agg* irregular; *(discontinuo)* uneven.

irregolarità *sf inv* irregularity; *(discontinuità)* unevenness.

irremovibile *agg* inflexible.

irreparabile *agg* irreparable.

irrequieto, -a *agg* restless.

irresponsabile *agg* irresponsible.

irreversibile *agg* irreversible.

irriducibile *agg* unyielding.

irrigare *vt* to irrigate.

irrigidirsi *vr* to stiffen.

irrilevante *agg* insignificant.

irrisorio, -a *agg* ridiculous.

irritàbile *agg* irritable.

irritante *agg* irritating.

irritare *vt* to irritate ▫ **irritarsi** *vr* to become irritated.

irrompere : **irrompere in** *v + prep* to burst into.

irrotto, -a *pp* → **irrompere**.

irruènte *agg* impetuous.

irruzione *sf* raid.

iscritto, -a *pp* → **iscrivere** ♦ *agg*: **essere ~ a qc** *(ad un circolo, partito)* to be a member of sthg; *(all'università)* to be enrolled in sthg; *(ad un esame)* to be entered for sthg; **per ~** in writing.

iscrivere *vt*: **~ qn (a qc)** *(scuola)* to register sb (at sthg), to enrol sb (at sthg); *(corso)* to register sb (for sthg), to enrol sb (for sthg) ▫ **iscriversi** *vr*: **iscriversi (a)** *(circolo, partito)* to become a member (of); *(university)* to enrol (in); *(esame)* to enter.

iscrizione *sf (a università)* enrolment; *(a esame)* entry; *(a partito)* membership; *(funeraria)* inscription.

Islanda *sf*: **l'~** Iceland.

islandese *agg* Icelandic ♦ *smf* Icelander.

isola *sf* island; **~ pedonale** pedestrian precinct.

isolamento *sm (solitudine)* isolation; *(elettrico, termico)* insulation; *(acustico)* soundproofing.

isolante *agg* insulating ♦ *sm* insulator.

isolare *vt (tenere lontano)* to isolate; *(da freddo, corrente elettrica)* to insulate; *(da rumore)* to soundproof ▫ **isolarsi** *vr* to cut o.s. off.

isolato, -a *agg* isolated ♦ *sm* block.

ispettore *sm* inspector.

ispezionare *vt* to inspect.

ispezione *sf* inspection.

ispirare *vt* to inspire ▫ **ispirarsi a** *vr + prep* to draw one's inspiration from.

Israele *sm* Israel.

issare *vt* to hoist.

istantanea *sf* snapshot.

istantaneo, -a *agg* instantaneous, instant.

istante *sm* instant; **all'~** instantly, at once.

istèrico, -a, -ci, -che *agg* hysterical.

istigare *vt*: **~ qn a fare qc** to incite sb to do sthg.

istinto *sm* instinct.

istituire *vt* to institute.

istituto *sm (organismo)* institute; *(universitario)* department; **~ di bellezza** beauty salon.

istituzione *sf* institution; **le istituzioni** *(le autorità)* the Establishment.

istmo *sm* (GEOG) isthmus.

istrice *sm (animale)* porcupine.

istruire *vt (insegnare a)* to teach; *(informare)* to instruct.

istruito, -a *agg* educated.

istruttore, -trice *sm, f* instructor.

istruzione *sf (insegnamento)* education; *(cultura)* learning ▫ **istruzioni** *sfpl*: **istruzioni (per l'uso)** instructions (for use).

Italia *sf*: **l'~** Italy.

italiano, -a *agg & sm, f* Italian.

itinerario *sm (percorso)* route; *(descrizione)* itinerary; **~ turistico** *(percorso)* tourist route.

Iugoslavia *sf:* **la ~** Yugoslavia.

IVA *sf (abbr di imposta sul valore aggiunto)* VAT.

J

jazz [dʒets] *sm* jazz.

jeans [dʒins] *smpl* jeans ♦ *sm (tessuto)* denim.

jeep® [dʒip] *sf inv* Jeep®.

jolly ['dʒɔlli] *sm inv* joker.

Jonio = **Ionio**.

jota *sf bean soup with onions and turnips marinated in wine (a speciality of Friuli).*

Jugoslavia = **Iugoslavia**.

juke-box [dʒu'bɔks] *sm inv* juke-box.

K

karaoke *sm inv (gioco)* karaoke; *(locale)* karaoke bar.

karatè *sm* karate.

Kenia *sm:* **il ~** Kenya.

kg *(abbr di chilogrammo)* kg.

killer *smf inv* killer.

kitsch [kitʃ] *agg inv* kitsch.

kiwi ['kiwi] *sm inv* kiwi fruit.

km *(abbr di chilometro)* km.

k.o. *avv:* **mettere qn ~** to knock sb out.

koala *sm inv* koala.

K-way® [ki'wei] *sm inv* cagoule.

L

l' → **la, lo**.

la (**l'** *dav vocale e h) art f* the, → **il** ♦ *pron (persona)* her; *(animale, cosa)* it; *(forma di cortesia)* you.

là *avv* there; **di ~** *(nella stanza accanto)* in there; *(moto da luogo)* from there; *(nei paraggi)* over there; **al di ~ di** beyond.

labbro *(pl f* **labbra)** *sm (ANAT)* lip.

labirinto *sm (di strade, corridoi)* labyrinth; *(giardino)* maze.

laboratorio *sm (scientifico)* laboratory; *(artigianale)* workshop; **~ linguistico** language laboratory.

lacca, -che *sf (per capelli)* lacquer, hair spray; *(vernice)* lacquer.

laccio *sm* lace.

lacerare *vt* to tear, to rip ❑ **lacerarsi** *vr* to tear.

lacero, -a *agg* torn.

lacrima *sf* tear; **in lacrime** in tears.

lacrimogeno *agg m* → **gas**.

lacuna *sf* gap.

ladro, -a *sm, f* thief.

laggiù avv (in basso) down there; (lontano) over there.

lagnarsi vr (piagnucolare) to moan, to groan; (protestare): ~ (di) to complain (about).

lago, -ghi sm lake.

I LAGHI

The most famous of the many Italian lakes are undoubtedly those in northern Italy: Lake Garda (the largest), Lake Maggiore and Lake Como. Millions of Italian and foreign tourists alike visit them every year, attracted by their scenic splendour and pleasant climate, the grand villas and lush gardens lining their shores, and the many varieties of wild flower to be found in the area. In summer the lakes attract swimmers, sunbathers and watersports enthusiasts looking for an alternative to the coastal resorts.

laguna sf lagoon.

laico, -a, -ci, -che agg lay (dav s).

lama sf blade.

lamentarsi vr (emettere lamenti) to groan, to moan; ~ (di) (dimostrarsi insoddisfatto) to complain (about).

lamentela sf complaint, complaining (sg).

lametta sf razor blade.

lamiera sf sheet metal.

lampada sf lamp; **fare la ~** to use a sunlamp; **~ da tavolo** table lamp.

lampadario sm chandelier.

lampadina sf light bulb; **~ ta-**

scabile torch (Br), flashlight (Am).

lampeggiare vi to flash.

lampeggiatore sm (freccia) indicator; (di ambulanza) flashing light.

lampione sm streetlight.

lampo sm (fulmine) flash of lightning; (bagliore) flash ♦ sf inv (cerniera) zip (Br), zipper (Am).

lampone sm raspberry.

lana sf wool; **pura ~ vergine** pure new wool.

lancetta sf hand.

lancia, -ce sf (arma) lance; (imbarcazione) launch.

lanciare vt (pietra, palla) to throw; (missile) to launch; (grido) to give; (insulto) to hurl; (fig: appello, moda, prodotto) to launch ❑ **lanciarsi** vr to throw o.s.; **lanciarsi in qc** (mare) to throw o.s. into sthg; (impresa) to embark on sthg.

lancinante agg piercing, shooting.

lancio sm (tiro) throw; (di prodotti, missile) launch.

languido, -a agg languid.

languore sm (di stomaco) hunger pangs (pl).

lapide sf (funeraria) tombstone; (commemorativa) plaque.

lapis sm inv pencil.

lapsus sm inv slip.

lardo sm lard, bacon fat.

larghezza sf (dimensione) width, breadth; (abbondanza) generosity.

largo, -a, -ghi, -ghe agg wide, broad; (indumento) loose; (percentuale, parte) large ♦ sm width; (piazza) square; (alto mare):

andare al ~ to take to the open sea; **è ~ 10 metri** it's 10 metres wide; **stare ○ tenersi alla larga (da)** to keep one's distance (from); **farsi ~** to push one's way.

larva *sf (insetto)* larva.

lasagne *sfpl* lasagne *(sg)*.

lasciare *vt* to leave; *(cessare di tenere)* to let go of; **posso ~ i bagagli in camera?** can I leave the luggage in the room?; **~ la porta aperta** to leave the door open; **~ qn in pace** to leave sb in peace; **lasciar detto a qn che ...** to leave sb word that ...; **~ a desiderare** to leave a lot to be desired; **prendere o ~** take it or leave it; **~ la presa** to let go ♦ *vb aus:* **lasciami vedere** let me see; **lascia che faccia come vuole** let him do as he wants; **lascia perdere!** forget it!; **lasciar credere qc a qn** to let sb believe sthg; **lascialo stare!** leave him alone! ❏ **lasciarsi** *vr (separarsi)* to leave each other; **lasciarsi andare** to let o.s. go; **lasciarsi convincere** to allow o.s. to be persuaded.

laser *sm inv & agg inv* laser.

lassativo *sm* laxative.

lassù *avv* up there.

lastra *sf (di ghiaccio, vetro)* sheet; *(di pietra)* slab; *(radiografia)* plate.

laterale *agg* lateral, side *(dav s)*.

latino, -a *agg & sm* Latin.

latino-americano, -a *agg* Latin-American.

latitudine *sf* latitude.

lato *sm* side; **a ~ (di qc)** beside (sthg); **da un ~ ... dall'altro ...** on the one hand ... on the other hand ...

latta *sf* tin.

lattaio, -a *sm, f* milkman (f milkwoman).

lattante *smf* baby.

latte *sm* milk; **~ detergente** cleansing milk; **~ intero** full cream milk; **~ magro ○ scremato** skimmed milk; **~ in polvere** powdered milk; **~ di soia** soya milk.

latteria *sf* dairy.

latticini *smpl* dairy products.

lattina *sf* can.

lattuga, -ghe *sf* lettuce.

laurea *sf* degree.

laurearsi *vr* to graduate; **~ in qc** to graduate in sthg.

laureato, -a *agg & sm, f* graduate; **è ~ in legge** he has a law degree.

lava *sf* lava.

lavaggio *sm* washing; **~ automatico** *(per auto)* car wash.

lavagna *sf* blackboard.

lavanda *sf* lavender; **fare una ~ gastrica a qn** to pump sb's stomach.

lavanderia *sf* laundry; **~ automatica** launderette; **~ a secco** dry cleaner's.

lavandino *sm* sink.

lavapiatti *sf inv* dishwasher.

lavare *vt* to wash; **~ a secco qc** to dry-clean sthg; **lavarsi le mani** to wash one's hands; **lavarsi i denti** to clean one's teeth ❏ **lavarsi** *vr* to wash o.s.

lavasecco *sm inv o sf inv* dry cleaner's.

lavastoviglie *sf inv* dishwasher.

lavatrice *sf* washing machine.

lavorare *vi & vt* to work; ~ a **maglia** to knit.

lavorativo, -a *agg* working *(dav s)*.

lavorato, -a *agg (mobile, tessuto)* elaborate; *(terreno)* cultivated.

lavoratore, -trice *sm, f* worker.

lavorazione *sf (di legno)* carving; *(di cotone)* manufacture.

lavoro *sm* work; *(occupazione)* work, job; '**lavori in corso**' 'men at work'; **lavori stradali** road works.

le *art fpl* the, → **il** ◆ *pron (complemento oggetto)* them; *(a lei)* (to) her; *(forma di cortesia)* (to) you.

leader ['lider] *smf inv* leader.

leale *agg* loyal.

lecca lecca *sm inv* lollipop.

leccare *vt* to lick.

lecito, -a *agg* permitted.

lega, -ghe *sf (associazione)* league; *(alleanza politica)* alliance; *(di metalli)* alloy.

legale *agg* legal ◆ *smf (avvocato)* lawyer.

legalizzare *vt* to legalize.

legame *sm (sentimentale)* tie; *(nesso)* link.

legare *vt (con catena, laccio)* to tie (up); *(sog: sentimento, interesse)* to bind.

legge *sf* law.

leggenda *sf (favola)* legend; *(didascalia)* key.

leggendario, -a *agg* legendary.

leggere *vt & vi* to read.

leggerezza *sf (di materiale, corpo)* lightness; *(fig: sconsideratezza)* thoughtlessness.

leggero, -a *agg* light; *(caffè, tè)* weak; *(di poca importanza)* slight.

legittimo, -a *agg* legitimate; **legittima difesa** self-defence.

legna *sf* firewood.

legname *sm* wood.

legno *sm (materia)* wood; *(pezzo)* piece of wood, stick.

legumi *smpl* pulses.

lei *pron (soggetto)* she; *(complemento oggetto, con preposizione)* her; *(forma di cortesia)* you; **è ~** it's her; **io sto bene, e ~?** I'm fine, and you?; ~ **stessa** she herself/you yourself.

lentamente *avv* slowly.

lente *sf* lens; ~ **di ingrandimento** magnifying glass; **lenti a contatto** contact lenses.

lentezza *sf* slowness.

lenticchie *sfpl* lentils.

lento, -a *agg* slow; *(allentato)* loose ◆ *sm* slow dance.

lenza *sf* fishing line.

lenzuolo *(pl f* **lenzuola)** *sm* sheet.

leone *sm* lion ❑ **Leone** *sm* Leo.

leopardo *sm* leopard.

lepre *sf* hare; ~ **in salmì** marinated hare in a sauce made from its offal.

lesbica, -che *sf* lesbian.

lesione *sf* lesion.

lesso, -a *agg* boiled ◆ *sm* boiled beef.

letale *agg* lethal.

letame *sm* manure.

lettera *sf* letter; **alla ~** literally ❑ **lettere** *sfpl (facoltà)* = arts.

letteratura *sf* literature.

lettino *sm (del medico)* couch; *(per bambini)* cot.

letto, -a *pp* → **leggere** ◆ *sm* bed; **andare a ~** to go to bed; **~ matrimoniale** O **a due piazze** double bed; **~ a una piazza** single bed; **letti a castello** bunk beds; **letti gemelli** twin beds.

lettore, -trice *sm, f (di libro, giornale)* reader; *(di università)* foreign language assistant ◆ *sm:* **~ di compact** CD player.

lettura *sf* reading.

leva *sf* lever; *(militare)* conscription; **fare ~ su qc** *(fig)* to play on sthg; **~ del cambio** gear lever *(Br)*, gear shift *(Am)*.

levante *sm* east.

levare *vt (togliere)* to remove; *(alzare)* to raise O **levarsi** *vr (vento)* to get up, to rise.

levata *sf* collection.

levatoio *agg m* → **ponte**.

levigare *vt* to smooth.

lezione *sf* lesson; *(all'università)* lecture.

lezioso, -a *agg* affected.

lezzo *sm* stink.

li *pron mpl* them.

lì *avv* there; **essere ~ (~) per fare qc** to be on the point of doing sthg; **da ~ in poi** *(tempo)* from then on; *(spazio)* from that point onwards.

Libano *sm:* **il ~** Lebanon.

libeccio *sm* southwest wind.

libellula *sf* dragonfly.

liberale *agg* liberal.

liberamente *avv* freely.

liberare *vt (prigioniero)* to free, to release; *(camera, posto)* to vacate O **liberarsi** *vr (annullare un impegno)* to free o.s.; **liberarsi di** to get rid of.

libero, -a *agg* free; **essere ~ di fare qc** to be free to do sthg; **~ professionista** self-employed professional; **'libero'** *(su taxi)* 'for hire'; *(in toilette)* 'vacant'.

libertà *sf inv* freedom; *(permesso)* liberty; **mettere in ~ qn** to free sb.

Libia *sf:* **la ~** Libya.

libreria *sf (negozio)* bookshop; *(mobile)* bookcase.

libretto *sm (MUS)* libretto; **~ degli assegni** cheque book; **~ di circolazione** log book; **~ di risparmio** savings book; **~ universitario** university report card.

libro *sm* book; **~ giallo** thriller.

licenza *sf (autorizzazione)* licence; *(militare)* leave; **~ media** school-leaving certificate.

licenziamento *sm* dismissal.

licenziare *vt* to dismiss O **licenziarsi** *vr* to resign.

liceo *sm* secondary school *(Br)*, high school *(Am)*.

lido *sm* beach; **il Lido di Venezia** the Venice Lido.

lieto, -a *agg (contento):* **~ di conoscerla!** pleased to meet you!; **molto ~!** pleased to meet you!

lievitare *vi* to rise.

lievito *sm* yeast; **~ di birra** brewer's yeast.

Liguria *sf:* **la ~** Liguria.

lillà *agg inv & sm inv* lilac.

lima *sf* file.

limetta *sf*: ~ **per unghie** nail file.
limitare *vt* to limit, to restrict ❑
limitarsi *vr*: **limitarsi a fare qc** to limit o.s. to do sthg; **limitarsi nel bere** to restrict one's drinking.
limitato, -a *agg* limited.
limite *sm* (*confine*) border; (*punto estremo*) limit; ~ **di velocità** speed limit; **entro certi limiti** within certain limits; **al** ~ if the worst comes to the worst.
limitrofo, -a *agg* neighbouring.
limonata *sf* lemonade.
limone *sm* lemon.
limpido, -a *agg* clear.
linea *sf* line; (*itinerario*) route; **mantenere la** ~ to look after one's figure; **avere qualche** ~ **di febbre** to have a slight temperature; **linee urbane** local buses; **in** ~ **d'aria** as the crow flies; **in** ~ **di massima** as a general rule; **a grandi linee** in broad outline; **è caduta la** ~ we have been cut off.
lineare *agg* linear.
lineetta *sf* dash.
lingua *sf* (ANAT & CULIN) tongue; (*linguaggio*) language; ~ **madre** mother tongue; ~ **straniera** foreign language.
linguaggio *sm* language; ~ **dei segni** sign language.
linguetta *sf* tongue.
linguistico, -a, -ci, -che *agg* linguistic.
lino *sm* linen.
linoleum *sm* linoleum.
liofilizzato, -a *agg* freeze-dried.

liquefare *vt* to melt ❑ **liquefarsi** *vr* to melt.
liquefatto, -a *pp* → **liquefare**.
liquidare *vt* (*società, beni*) to liquidate; (*merce*) to sell off; (*sbarazzarsi di*) to get rid of; (*fig: questione, problema*) to solve.
liquidazione *sf* (*di merci*) selling off, clearance; (*indennità*) severance pay.
liquido, -a *agg* liquid ♦ *sm* liquid; (*denaro*) cash.
liquirizia *sf* liquorice.
liquore *sm* liqueur.
lira *sf* lira; **non avere una** ~ not to have a penny (*Br*), not to have a dime (*Am*).
lirica *sf* opera.
lirico, -a, -ci, -che *agg* (*musica*) lyric.
lisca, -sche *sf* fishbone.
liscio, -a, -sci, -sce *agg* (*pietra, pelle*) smooth; (*capelli*) straight; (*whisky*) neat ♦ *sm* (*ballo*) ballroom dance; **andar** ~ to go smoothly.
lista *sf* list; **essere in** ~ **d'attesa** to be on a waiting list; ~ **dei vini** wine list.
listino *sm*: ~ **(dei) prezzi** price list: ~ **dei cambi** exchange rate.
Lit *abbr* = **lira**.
lite *sf* quarrel.
litigare *vi* to quarrel.
litigio *sm* quarrel.
litorale *sm* coast.
litoraneo, -a *agg* coastal.
litro *sm* litre.
livello *sm* (*altezza, piano*) level; ~

del mare sea level.

livido, -a agg (per percosse) black and blue ◆ sm bruise; ~ **per il freddo** blue with cold.

lo art the, → **il** ◆ pron (persona) him; (animale, cosa) it; ~ **so** I know.

locale agg local ◆ sm (stanza) room; (luogo pubblico) premises (pl); ~ **notturno** night club.

località sf inv locality.

locanda sf inn.

locandina sf theatre poster.

locomotiva sf locomotive.

lodare vt to praise.

lode sf (elogio) praise; **laurearsi con 110 e ~** to graduate with first-class honours (Br), to graduate summa cum laude (Am).

loggia, -ge sf loggia.

loggione sm: **il ~** the gods (pl).

logica sf logic.

logico, -a, -ci, -che agg logical.

logorare vt to wear out □ **logorarsi** vr to wear out.

logorio sm wear and tear.

Lombardia sf: **la ~** Lombardy.

lombardo, -a agg Lombard.

lombata sf loin.

lombrico, -chi sm earthworm.

Londra sf London.

longitudine sf longitude.

lontananza sf (distanza) distance; (di persona) absence; **in ~** in the distance.

lontano, -a agg (luogo) distant, faraway; (nel tempo) far off; (assente) absent; (parente) distant ◆ avv far; **è ~?** is it far?; **è ~ 3**

chilometri it's 3 kilometres from here; ~ **da** far (away) from; **da ~** from far away; **più ~** farther.

loquace agg talkative.

lordo, -a agg gross.

loro pron (soggetto) they; (complemento oggetto, con preposizione) them; (form: complemento di termine) (to) them; ~ **stessi** they themselves □ **il loro** (f **la loro**, mpl **i loro**, fpl **le loro**) agg their ◆ pron theirs.

losco, -a, -schi, -sche agg suspicious, shady.

lotta sf struggle, fight.

lottare vi to fight.

lotteria sf lottery.

lotto sm (gioco) lottery; (di terreno) lot.

lozione sf lotion.

L.P. sm inv LP.

lubrificante sm lubricant.

lucchetto sm padlock.

luccicare vi to sparkle.

lucciola sf glow-worm, firefly.

luce sf light; (elettricità) electricity; **dare alla ~** to give birth to; **mettere in ~ qc** to highlight sthg; ~ **del sole** sunlight; **luci d'arresto** brake lights; **luci di direzione** indicators; **luci di posizione** parking lights; **film a luci rosse** porno film.

lucernario sm skylight.

lucertola sf lizard.

lucidare vt to polish.

lucidatrice sf floor polisher.

lucido, -a agg (pavimento, tessuto) shiny; (fig: mente, persona) lucid ◆ sm (da proiettore) acetate; ~ **da scarpe** shoe polish.

lucro *sm* profit.

luganega, -ghe *sf type of sausage (a speciality of Veneto and Lombardy).*

luglio *sm* July, → **settembre**.

lugubre *agg* gloomy.

lui *pron (soggetto)* he; *(complemento oggetto, con preposizione)* him; **è ~** it's him; **~ stesso** he himself.

lumaca, -che *sf* snail.

lume *sm* lamp; **a ~ di candela** by candlelight.

luminaria *sf* illuminations *(pl)*.

luminoso, -a *agg* luminous, bright.

luna *sf* moon; **~ di miele** honeymoon; **~ park** funfair; **~ piena** full moon.

lunario *sm*: **sbarcare il ~** to make ends meet.

lunedì *sm inv* Monday, → **sabato**.

lunghezza *sf* length; **~ d'onda** wavelength.

lungo, -a, -ghi, -ghe *agg* long; *(caffè)* weak; **è ~ 3 metri** it's 3 metres long; **saperla lunga** to know what's what; **a ~** for a long time; **di gran lunga** by far; **in ~ e in largo** far and wide; **andare per le lunghe** to drag on.

lungofiume *sm* embankment.

lungolago, -ghi *sm road around a lake.*

lungomare *sm* promenade.

lunotto *sm* rear window.

luogo, -ghi *sm* place; *(di delitto, incidente)* scene; **aver ~** to take place; **dare ~ a qc** to give rise to sthg; **~ comune** commonplace; **~**

di culto place of worship; **~ di nascita** place of birth; **del ~** local; **in primo ~** in the first place.

lupini *smpl* lupins.

lupo *sm* wolf.

lurido, -a *agg* filthy.

lusinga, -ghe *sf* flattery.

lusingare *vt* to flatter.

lussare *vt* to dislocate.

Lussemburgo *sm*: **il ~** Luxembourg.

lusso *sm* luxury; **di ~** de luxe, luxury.

lussuoso, -a *agg* luxurious.

lussureggiante *agg* luxuriant.

lussuria *sf* lust.

lustrare *vt* to polish.

lustrino *sm* sequin.

lustro, -a *agg* shiny.

lutto *sm* mourning; **essere in ~** to be in mourning.

ma *cong* but.

macabro, -a *agg* macabre.

macché *esclam* of course not!

maccheroni *smpl* macaroni *(sg)*; **~ alla chitarra** *flat ribbons of egg pasta in a sauce of either tomatoes and chillis, or lamb (a speciality of Abruzzo).*

macchia *sf (chiazza)* spot, stain; *(di colore)* spot; *(bosco)* scrub.

macchiare *vt* to stain, to mark

❑ **macchiarsi** vr (persona) to get stains o marks on one's clothes; (abiti, tappeto) to become stained o marked.

macchiato, -a agg stained.

macchina sf (automobile) car; (apparecchio) machine; **andare in ~** to go by car, to drive; **~ fotografica** camera; **~ da scrivere** typewriter.

macchinario sm machinery.

macchinetta sf (caffettiera) percolator; **~ mangiasoldi** slot machine.

macchinista, -i sm (di treno) driver; (di nave) engineer.

macedonia sf fruit salad.

macellaio, -a sm, f butcher.

macelleria sf butcher's.

macerie sfpl rubble (sg).

macigno sm rock, boulder.

macinacaffè sm inv coffee grinder.

macinapepe sm inv pepper grinder.

macinare vt (grano) to mill, to grind; (caffè, pepe) to grind; (carne) to mince (Br), to grind (Am).

macinato, -a agg minced (Br), ground (Am) ◆ sm mince (Br), ground beef (Am).

macrobiotico, -a, -ci, -che agg macrobiotic.

Madonna sf Madonna.

madre sf mother.

madrelingua agg inv mother tongue (dav s) ◆ sf mother tongue.

madreperla sf mother-of-pearl.

madrina sf godmother.

maestrale sm northwest wind.

maestro, -a sm, f teacher ◆ sm (MUS) maestro; (artigiano, artista) master; **~ di tennis** tennis coach.

mafia sf Mafia.

mafioso, -a agg of the Mafia, Mafia (dav s) ◆ sm, f member of the Mafia.

magari esclam if only! ◆ avv maybe.

magazzino sm warehouse.

maggio sm May; **il primo ~** May Day, → **settembre**.

IL PRIMO MAGGIO

Since the end of the Second World War, May 1 has been celebrated all over Italy as a workers' festival. It is a national holiday and is the occasion of trade union meetings and marches in the cities.

maggioranza sf majority; **nella ~ dei casi** in the majority of cases.

maggiore agg (comparativo: più grande, più numeroso) larger, bigger; (di quantità) greater; (più importante) major, more important; (più vecchio) elder, older; (superlativo: più grande, più numeroso) largest, biggest; (di quantità) greatest (più importante) most important; (più vecchio) eldest, oldest ◆ sm (MIL) major; **andare per la ~** to be very popular; **la ~ età** the age of majority; **la maggior parte (di)** the majority (of).

maggiorenne agg of age ◆ smf person who has come of age.

maggiormente avv much more.

magia sf magic.

magico, -a, -ci, -che *agg*
magic.

magistratura *sf* magistracy.

maglia *sf* (*indumento*) sweater,
jersey; (*di sportivo, tessuto*) jersey;
(*di catena*) link; **lavorare a ~** to knit.

maglieria *sf* knitwear.

maglietta *sf* T-shirt; (*canottiera*)
vest (*Br*), undershirt (*Am*).

maglione *sm* sweater, jumper.

magnate *sm* magnate.

magnetico, -a, -ci, -che
agg magnetic.

magnifico, -a, -ci, -che *agg*
magnificent.

mago, -a, -ghi, -ghe *sm, f*
(*stregone*) sorcerer (*f* sorceress);
(*illusionista*) magician.

magro, -a *agg* (*persona*) thin;
(*formaggio, yogurt*) low-fat; (*carne*)
lean; (*fig: scarso*) meagre.

mai *avv* never; (*qualche volta*):
l'hai ~ visto? have you ever seen
him?; **non ... ~** never; **~ più** never
again.

maiale *sm* (*animale*) pig; (*carne*)
pork; **~ alle mele** pork with brandy-
flavoured apple sauce.

maiolica *sf* majolica.

maionese *sf* mayonnaise.

mais *sm* maize.

maiuscola *sf* capital letter.

maiuscolo, -a *agg* capital.

mal = male.

malafede *sf* bad faith.

malaga *sm*: **gelato al ~** rum and
raisin ice cream.

malandato, -a *agg* (*persona*) in
poor shape; (*oggetto*) shabby.

malanno *sm* ailment.

malapena : **a malapena** *avv*
hardly, scarcely.

malato, -a *agg* ill, sick ♦ *sm, f*
sick person, patient; **essere ~ di
cuore** to have a bad heart.

malattia *sf* illness, disease;
essere in ~ to be on sick leave.

malavita *sf* underworld.

malconcio, -a, -ci, -ce *agg*
in a sorry state.

maldestro, -a *agg* (*poco abile*)
inept; (*impacciato, goffo*) clumsy.

maldicenza *sf* malicious gossip.

male *sm* (*ingiustizia*) evil; (*dolore*)
pain; (*malattia*) complaint ♦ *avv*
badly; **ti fa ~?** does it hurt?; **mi
fanno ~ i piedi** my feet hurt; **fare
del ~ a qn** to hurt sb; **non c'è ~!**
not bad!; **mal d'aereo** airsickness;
mal d'auto carsickness; **mal di gola**
sore throat; **mal di mare** seasick-
ness; **mal di stomaco** stomachache; **mal di testa** headache;
andare a ~ to go off; **restarci** o
rimanerci ~ to be disappointed;
sentirsi ~ to feel ill; **di ~ in peggio**
from bad to worse.

maledetto, -a *pp* → maledire
♦ *agg* damned.

maledire *vt* to curse.

maledizione *sf* curse.

maleducato, -a *agg* rude.

maleducazione *sf* rudeness.

maleodorante *agg* smelly.

malessere *sm* (*fisico*) ailment;
(*mentale*) uneasiness.

malfamato, -a *agg* notorious.

malfattore, -trice *sm, f*
wrongdoer.

malfermo, -a *agg* unsteady.

malformazione *sf* malformation, deformity.

malgrado *prep* in spite of ◆ *cong* although; **mio ~** against my will.

malignità *sf inv* (*d'animo*) malice; (*insinuazione*) spiteful remark.

maligno, -a *agg* (*persona, commento*) malicious; (*MED*) malignant.

malinconia *sf* melancholy.

malinconico, -a, -ci, -che *agg* gloomy.

malincuore : a malincuore *avv* reluctantly.

malintenzionato, -a *agg* ill-intentioned.

malinteso *sm* misunderstanding.

malizia *sf* cunning, malice.

malizioso, -a *agg* malicious.

malleabile *agg* malleable.

malmenare *vt* to beat up.

malnutrizione *sf* malnutrition.

malore *sm*: **ho avuto un ~** I suddenly felt ill.

malridotto, -a *agg* in a bad state.

malsano, -a *agg* unhealthy.

Malta *sf* Malta.

maltagliati *smpl* soup pasta, cut into irregular shapes.

maltempo *sm* bad weather.

malto *sm* malt.

maltrattare *vt* to ill-treat.

malumore *sm* bad temper; **essere di ~** to be in a bad mood.

malvagio, -a, -gi, -gie *agg* wicked.

malvolentieri *avv* unwillingly.

mamma *sf* mum (*Br*), mom (*Am*); **~ mia!** my goodness!

mammella *sf* (*di donna*) breast; (*di animale*) udder.

mammifero *sm* mammal.

manager ['mɛnadʒər] *smf inv* manager (*f* manageress).

manata *sf* slap.

mancanza *sf* (*scarsità, assenza*) lack; (*colpa*) fault; **sentire la ~ di qn** to miss sb; **in ~ di** for lack of.

mancare *vi* (*non esserci*) to be missing; (*essere lontano*) to be away; (*form: morire*) to pass away ◆ *vt* (*colpo, bersaglio*) to miss; **è mancata la luce per due ore** the electricity was off for two hours; **mi manchi molto** I miss you a lot; **manca il latte** there's no milk; **mi manca il tempo** I haven't got the time; **mi mancano mille lire** I still need a thousand lire; **ci è mancato poco che cadesse** it nearly fell; **manca un quarto alle quattro** it's quarter to four ❑ **mancare a** *v* + *prep* (*promessa*) to fail to keep; **mancare di** *v* + *prep* to lack.

mancia, -ce *sf* tip; **dare la ~ (a qn)** to tip (sb).

manciata *sf* handful.

mancino, -a *agg* left-handed.

manco *avv* (*fam*) not even; **~ per sogno** o **per idea** I wouldn't dream of it.

mandarancio *sm* clementine.

mandare *vt* to send; (*grido*) to give; **~ a chiamare qn** to send for sb; **~ via qn** to send sb away; **~ avanti qn** to send sb on ahead;

avanti qc to provide for sthg; **~ giù** to swallow.

mandarino *sm* mandarin (orange), tangerine.

mandata *sf (di chiave)* turn; **chiudere a doppia ~** to double-lock.

mandato *sm (DIR)* warrant; **~ d'arresto** arrest warrant.

mandibola *sf* jaw.

mandolino *sm* mandolin.

mandorla *sf* almond.

maneggiare *vt (strumenti, attrezzi)* to handle; *(denaro)* to manage, to deal with.

maneggio *sm* riding school.

manetta *sf* handle □ **manette** *sfpl* handcuffs.

mangereccio *agg m* → **fungo**.

mangiare *vt (cibo)* to eat; *(fig: patrimonio)* to squander; *(negli scacchi)* to take ♦ *vi* to eat; **far da ~** to do the cooking; **mangiarsi le parole** to mumble.

mangiasoldi *agg inv* → **macchinetta**.

mangime *sm* fodder.

mangione, -a *sm, f* glutton.

mania *sf (fissazione)* obsession; **avere la ~ di fare qc** to have a habit of doing sthg.

maniaco, -a, -ci, -che *agg* manic ♦ *sm, f* maniac.

manica, -che *sf* sleeve; **a maniche corte** o **a mezze maniche** short-sleeved □ **Manica** *sf*: **la Manica, il Canale della Manica** the (English) Channel.

manicaretto *sm* delicacy.

manichino *sm (di negozio)* dummy; *(per artisti)* model.

manico, -ci *sm* handle.

manicomio *sm (ospedale)* mental hospital; *(fig: confusione)* madhouse.

manicure *sf inv (persona)* manicurist; *(trattamento)* manicure.

maniera *sf* way; **in ~ che** so that; **in ~ da fare qc** so as to do sthg; **in tutte le maniere** at all costs.

manifestare *vt* to show ♦ *vi* to demonstrate □ **manifestarsi** *vr* to appear.

manifestazione *sf (corteo)* demonstration; *(di sentimento)* show; *(di malattia)* symptom; *(spettacolo)* event.

manifesto *sm (cartellone)* poster.

maniglia *sf (di porta)* handle; *(di autobus)* strap.

manipolare *vt (con le mani)* to handle; *(fig: alterare)* to manipulate.

mano, -i *sf* hand; *(di vernice)* coat; **dare una ~ a qn** to give sb a hand; **darsi la ~** to shake hands; **fatto a ~** handmade; **di seconda ~** second-hand; **man ~** gradually; **andare contro ~** to drive on the wrong side of the road; **essere alla ~** to be easygoing; **fare man bassa** to take everything; **fuori ~** out of the way; **stare con le mani in ~** to twiddle one's thumbs.

manodopera *sf (lavoratori)* workforce; *(costo)* labour.

manomesso, -a *pp* → **manomettere**.

manomettere *vt (serratura)* to

force.

manopola sf knob, control.

manovale sm labourer.

manovella sf handle.

manovra sf manoeuvre.

manovrare vt (congegno) to operate; (fig: persona) to manipulate ◆ vi (MIL) to manoeuvre; (fig: tramare) to plot.

manrovescio sm slap.

mansarda sf attic.

mansione sf task, job.

mantella sf cape.

mantello sm (di animale) coat; (indumento) cloak.

mantenere vt to keep; (sostentare) to support ❑ **mantenersi** vr (pagarsi da vivere) to support o.s.; (conservarsi) to stay, to keep.

mantenimento sm maintenance.

manuale agg & sm manual.

manubrio sm (di bicicletta, moto) handlebars (pl); (di congegno) handle.

manutenzione sf maintenance.

manzo sm (carne) beef.

mappa sf map.

mappamondo sm (globo) globe; (su carta) map of the world.

maraschino sm maraschino (cherry liqueur).

maratona sf marathon.

marca, -che sf (di prodotto) brand; (scontrino) ticket; ~ **da bollo** revenue stamp; **prodotto di ~** quality product.

marcare vt to mark; (goal) to score.

marchio sm mark; (di bestiame) brand; ~ **di fabbrica** trademark; ~ **registrato** registered trademark.

marcia, -ce sf march; (di auto) gear; (SPORT) walking; **fare ~ indietro** to reverse; **mettersi in ~** to start off.

marciapiede sm pavement (Br), sidewalk (Am); (di stazione) platform.

marciare vi to march.

marcio, -a, -ci, -ce agg rotten.

marcire vi (cibo) to rot; (ferita) to fester.

marco, -chi sm mark.

mare sm sea; **andare al ~** to go to the seaside; **il Mare del Nord** the North Sea.

marea sf tide; **alta ~** high tide; **bassa ~** low tide.

mareggiata sf stormy sea.

maresciallo sm ≃ warrant officer.

margarina sf margarine.

margherita sf daisy.

margine sm (di pagina) margin; (di strada, bosco) edge.

marina sf navy.

marinaio sm sailor.

marinare vt to marinate; ~ **la scuola** to play truant.

marinaro, -a agg (popoli, tradizioni) seafaring; **alla marinara** cooked with seafood.

marinata sf marinade.

marino, -a agg sea (dav s).

marionetta sf marionette.

marito sm husband.

maritozzo sm type of sweet

*bread containing sultanas, pine ker-
nels and candied peel (a speciality of
Lazio).*

marittimo, -a *agg (clima)*
maritime; *(scalo)* coastal; **località
marittima** seaside resort.

marmellata *sf* jam; *(di arance)*
marmalade.

marmitta *sf (di auto, moto)*
silencer; *(pentola)* large cooking
pot.

marmo *sm* marble.

marocchino, -a *agg & sm, f*
Moroccan.

Marocco *sm:* il ~ Morocco.

marrone *agg inv* brown ♦ *sm
(colore)* brown; *(frutto)* chestnut.

marron glacé [mar'ron gla'se]
sm inv marron glacé *(crystallized
chestnut).*

marsala *sm inv* Marsala *(sweet
fortified wine).*

marsupio *sm (borsello)* bum bag
(Br), fanny pack (Am); *(di animale)*
pouch.

martedì *sm inv* Tuesday, →
sabato.

martellare *vt* to hammer ♦ *vi*
to throb.

martello *sm* hammer.

martini® *sm inv (vermut)* Martini; *(cocktail)* Martini cocktail.

martire *smf* martyr.

marzapane *sm* marzipan.

marziale *agg* martial.

marziano, -a *sm, f* Martian.

marzo *sm* March, → **settembre.**

mascalzone *sm* scoundrel.

mascara *sm inv* mascara.

mascarpone *sm* mascarpone
(type of cream cheese).

mascella *sf* jaw.

maschera *sf* mask; *(costume)*
fancy dress; *(di bellezza)* face pack;
(di cinema, teatro) usher (f usherette).

mascherare *vt (volto)* to mask;
(emozioni) to conceal □ **mascherarsi** *vr:* **mascherarsi (da)** to
dress up (as).

maschile *agg (GRAMM)* masculine; *(sesso, anatomia)* male; *(abiti)*
men's *(dav s)*; *(per ragazzi)* boy's
(dav s).

maschio, -a *agg* male ♦ *sm
(animale, individuo)* male; *(ragazzo,
figlio, neonato)* boy; **figlio ~** son.

mascolino, -a *agg* masculine.

mascotte [ma'skɔt] *sf inv* mas-
cot.

masochista, -i, -e *smf*
masochist.

massa *sf* mass; **una ~ di** *(errori,
gente)* loads of; *(mattoni, legna)* a
pile of; **la ~** the masses *(pl)*; **di ~**
mass *(dav s)*; **in ~** en masse.

massacro *sm* massacre.

massaggiare *vt* to massage.

massaggiatore, -trice *sm, f*
masseur (f masseuse).

massaggio *sm* massage.

massaia *sf* housewife.

massiccio, -a, -ci, -ce *agg
(corporatura)* stout, big; *(edificio)*
solid; **oro ~** solid gold ♦ *sm* mas-
sif.

massima *sf (detto)* maxim; *(temperatura)* maximum temperature;
in linea di ~ generally speaking.

massimo, -a *agg & sm* maximum; **al ~** at most.

mass media *smpl* mass media.

masso *sm* rock.

masticare *vt* to chew.

mastice *sm* putty.

mastino *sm* mastiff.

matassa *sf* skein.

matematica *sf* mathematics (*sg*).

matematico, -a, -ci, -che *agg* mathematical; (*sicuro*) certain.

materassino *sm* air bed; (*da ginnastica*) mat.

materasso *sm* mattress.

materia *sf* (*in fisica*) matter; (*materiale*) material; (*disciplina, argomento*) subject; **materie prime** raw materials.

materiale *agg* material ◆ *sm* material; (*attrezzatura*) equipment; **beni ~** worldly goods; **~ sintetico** man-made material.

maternità *sf inv* (*condizione*) motherhood; (*di ospedale*) maternity ward; **essere in ~** to be on maternity leave.

materno, -a *agg* maternal; (*paese, lingua*) mother (*dav s*).

matita *sf* pencil.

matrigna *sf* stepmother.

matrimoniale *agg* matrimonial.

matrimonio *sm* marriage; (*cerimonia*) wedding.

mattatoio *sm* slaughterhouse.

mattina *sf* morning; **di ~** in the morning.

mattinata *sf* morning.

mattiniero, -a *agg*: **essere ~** to be an early riser.

mattino *sm* morning.

matto, -a *agg* mad ◆ *sm*, *f* madman (*f* madwoman); **andare ~ per** to be crazy about.

mattone *sm* brick.

mattonella *sf* tile.

maturare *vi & vt* (*frutta, grano*) to ripen; (*persona*) to mature.

maturità *sf* (*diploma, esame*) = A levels (*pl*) (*Br*), = SATs (*pl*) (*Am*).

---

i MATURITÀ

The "maturità" examination is sat by students aged 18 to 19 in the final year of "scuola superiore". Depending on the type of school, the "maturità" is classed as either classical, scientific, technical or artistic, and a pass allows the student to go on to university. The exam consists of two written and two oral parts: the same written paper in Italian is sat at all schools. The final mark out of 60 covers all subjects, and is based on both the exam results and on continuous assessment over the previous three years.

---

maturo, -a *agg* (*frutto*) ripe; (*persona*) mature.

mazza *sf* (*bastone*) club; (*da baseball, cricket*) bat; **~ da golf** golf club.

mazzo *sm* (*di fiori, chiavi*) bunch; (*di carte*) pack.

me *pron* me, → **mi**.

MEC *abbr* = Mercato Comune Europeo.

meccanica *sf* (*scienza*) mechanics (*sg*), → **meccanico**.

meccanico, -a, -ci, -che *agg*

mechanical ◆ *sm* mechanic.

meccanismo *sm* mechanism.

mèche [mɛʃ] *sfpl* streaks.

medaglia *sf* medal.

medaglione *sm* (*gioiello*) locket; ~ **di vitello** veal medallion.

medesimo, -a *agg* same.

media *sf* (*valore intermedio*) average; (*di voti*) average mark (*Br*), average grade (*Am*); **in** ~ on average; **le** (**scuole**) **medie** = secondary school (*sg*) (*Br*), junior high school (*sg*) (*Am*).

mediante *prep* by means of.

mediatore, -trice *sm, f* mediator; (*COMM*) middleman.

medicare *vt* to dress.

medicina *sf* medicine.

medicinale *agg* medicine, drug.

medico, -a, -ci, -che *agg* medical ◆ *sm* doctor; ~ **di guardia** doctor on call.

medievale *agg* medieval.

medio, -a *agg* average; (*di mezzo*) middle ◆ *sm*: (*dito*) ~ middle finger.

mediocre *agg* mediocre.

medioevale = medievale.

medioevo *sm* Middle Ages (*pl*).

meditare *vt* to plan ◆ *vi* to meditate.

mediterraneo, -a *agg* Mediterranean ❑ **Mediterraneo** *sm*: **il** (**mar**) **Mediterraneo** the Mediterranean (Sea).

medusa *sf* jellyfish.

megafono *sm* megaphone.

meglio *avv* 1. (*comparativo*) better; **mi sento** ~ **di ieri** I feel better than I did yesterday; **andare** ~ to

get better; **così va** ~ that's better; **per** ~ **dire** or rather.
2. (*superlativo*) best; **è la cosa che mi riesce** ~ it's the thing I do best; **le persone** ~ **vestite** the best-dressed people.
◆ *agg inv* 1. (*migliore*) better; **la tua macchina è** ~ **della mia** your car is better than mine.
2. (*in costruzioni impersonali*) better; **è** ~ **rimanere qui** it would be better to stay here; **è** ~ **che te lo dica** I'd better tell you.
◆ *sm*: **fare del proprio** ~ to do one's best; **agire per il** ~ to do the right thing.
◆ *sf*: **avere la** ~ **su qn** to get the better of sb.

mela *sf* apple.

melagrana *sf* pomegranate.

melanzana *sf* aubergine (*Br*), eggplant (*Am*); **melanzane alla parmigiana** fried aubergine slices covered in tomato and Parmesan cheese.

melenso, -a *agg* dull.

melma *sf* mud.

melo *sm* apple tree.

melodia *sf* melody.

melodramma, -i *sm* melodrama.

melone *sm* melon.

membro, -i *sm* (*di club, associazione*) member.

memorabile *agg* memorable.

memoria *sf* memory; **sapere qc a** ~ to know sthg by heart.

mendicante *smf* beggar.

meno *avv* 1. (*in comparativi*) less; ~ **di** less than; ~ **vecchio** (**di**) younger (than); **camminate** ~ **in fretta** don't walk so fast; **ne voglio**

(di) ~ I want less; ~ **lo vedo meglio sto** the less I see him, the better I feel.

2. *(in superlativi)* least; **la camera ~ cara** the cheapest room; **il ~ interessante** the least interesting; **fare il ~ possibile** to do as little as possible; **la macchina che costa ~ (di tutte)** the least expensive car (of all); **è Luca che mi preoccupa** ~ Luca worries me the least.

3. *(no)*: **non so se accettare o** ~ I don't know whether to accept or not.

4. *(nelle ore)*: **le nove** ~ **un quarto** a quarter to nine *(Br)*, a quarter of nine *(Am)*.

5. *(nelle sottrazioni, nelle temperature)* minus.

6. *(in espressioni)*: **non essere da** ~ **(di qn)** to be just as good (as sb); **fare a** ~ **di** to do without; ~ **male (che) c'eri tu!** thank goodness you were there!; **venir** ~ **a** *(promessa)* to break; *(impegno)* not to fulfil; **non poteva fare a** ~ **di urlare** he couldn't help screaming.

♦ *prep* except (for); **c'erano tutti** ~ **(che) lei** they were all there except (for) her; **pensa a tutto** ~ **che a divertirsi** enjoying himself is the last thing on his mind.

♦ *agg inv* less; **oggi c'è** ~ **gente** there are fewer people today.

❏ **a meno che** *cong* unless; **vengo a** ~ **che non piova** I'm coming unless it rains.

menopausa *sf* menopause.

mensa *sf* canteen.

mensile *agg & sm* monthly.

mensola *sf* shelf.

menta *sf* mint; *(bibita)* peppermint cordial.

mentale *agg* mental.

mentalmente *avv* mentally.

mente *sf* mind; **avere in** ~ **di qc** to be thinking of doing sthg; **imparare/sapere qc a** ~, to learn/know sthg by heart; **sfuggire o passare di** ~ **a qn** to slip sb's mind; **tenere a** ~ **qc** to bear sthg in mind.

mentire *vi* to lie.

mento *sm* chin.

mentre *cong (temporale)* while; *(avversativa)* while, whereas.

menu *sm inv* menu.

menzionare *vt* to mention.

menzogna *sf* lie.

meraviglia *sf (stupore)* amazement; *(cosa, persona)* marvel; **a** ~ perfectly.

meravigliare *vt* to amaze ❏ **meravigliarsi di** *vr + prep* to be amazed at.

meraviglioso, -a *agg* wonderful.

mercante *sm* trader.

mercantile *agg* merchant *(dav s)* ♦ *sm (nave)* merchant ship.

mercanzia *sf* goods *(pl)*, merchandise.

mercatino *sm* local market.

mercato *sm* market; ~ **dei cambi** foreign exchange market; ~ **nero** black market; **a buon** ~ cheap; **Mercato Comune Europeo** Common Market.

MERCATO

Almost every Italian town has an indoor or outdoor market selling food, flowers and plants. Once or twice a week there will also be a general market with stalls selling clothes, shoes and household items among other things. Prices are generally lower than in shops, and shoppers and stallholders often haggle.

merce *sf* goods *(pl)*, merchandise.

merceria *sf* haberdasher's *(Br)*, notions store *(Am)*.

mercoledì *sm inv* Wednesday, → **sabato**.

mercurio *sm* mercury.

merda *sf & esclam (volg)* shit.

merenda *sf* afternoon snack.

meridionale *agg* southern ♦ *smf* southerner.

Meridione *sm*: **il ~** the South of Italy.

meringa, -ghe *sf* meringue.

meritare *vt* to deserve ♦ *vi* to be good; **meritarsi qc** to deserve sthg.

merito *sm (qualità)* merit; *(riconoscimento)* credit; **per ~ di qn** thanks to sb; **finire a pari ~** to tie.

merlo *sm (uccello)* blackbird; *(di mura)* battlement.

merluzzo *sm* cod.

meschino, -a *agg (spregevole)* mean.

mescolare *vt (mischiare)* to mix; *(insalata)* to toss; *(caffè)* to stir; *(mettere in disordine)* to mix up ❏ **mescolarsi** *vr (confondersi)* to mingle.

mese *sm* month.

messa *sf* mass.

messaggio *sm* message.

Messico *sm*: **il ~** Mexico.

messinscena *sf (teatrale)* production; *(finzione)* act.

messo, -a *pp* → **mettere**.

mestiere *sm (professione)* job; *(artigianale)* craft; *(manuale)* trade.

mestolo *sm* ladle.

mestruazioni *sfpl* period *(sg)*.

meta *sf (destinazione)* destination; *(scopo)* aim, goal.

metà *sf inv (parte)* half; *(punto di mezzo)* middle; **dividere qc a ~** to divide sthg in half; **essere a ~ strada** to be halfway; **fare a ~ (con qn)** to go halves (with sb).

metabolismo *sm* metabolism.

metafora *sf* metaphor.

metallico, -a, -ci, -che *agg (di metallo)* metal *(dav s)*; *(rumore, voce)* metallic.

metallo *sm* metal.

metano *sm* methane.

meteorologico, -a, -ci, -che *agg* meteorological, weather *(dav s)*.

meticoloso, -a *agg* meticulous.

metodico, -a, -ci, -che *agg* methodical.

metodo *sm* method.

metrico, -a, -ci, -che *agg* metric.

metro *sm (unità di misura)* metre; *(nastro)* tape measure; *(a stecche)* rule; **~ cubo** cubic metre; **~ quadrato** square metre.

metronotte *sm inv* night security guard.

metropoli *sf inv* metropolis.

metropolitana *sf* under-ground (Br), subway (Am).

mettere *vt* 1. *(collocare)* to put; ~ **un annuncio** to place an advert; ~ **i piatti in tavola** to set the table; ~ **qn alla prova** to put sb to the test; ~ **i libri in ordine** to tidy (up) the books; ~ **l'antenna dritta** to put the aerial straight.

2. *(indossare)*: **mettersi qc** to put sthg on; **mettersi una sciarpa** to put a scarf on, to wear a scarf; **cosa mi metto oggi?** what shall I wear today?

3. *(tempo)*: **metterci: ci si mette un'ora per andare** it takes an hour to get there.

4. *(dedicare)*: ~ **attenzione in qc** to do sthg with care; **mettercela tutta** to do one's best.

5. *(far funzionare)* to put on; ~ **gli abbaglianti** to put one's headlights on full beam.

6. *(suscitare)*: ~ **appetito a qn** to make sb hungry; ~ **paura a qn** to scare sb.

7. *(supporre)*: **mettiamo che non venga** let's suppose he doesn't come.

8. *(in espressioni)*: ~ **avanti/indietro l'orologio** to put the clock for-ward/back; ~ **in chiaro qc** to clear sthg up; ~ **in dubbio qc** to cast doubt on sthg; **mettersi in testa di fare qc** to get it into one's head to do sthg; ~ **insieme** to put together. ❑ **mettersi** *vr* 1. *(porsi)*: **mettiti a sedere qui** sit here; **mettersi a tavola** to sit down to eat; **mettersi nei guai** to get into trouble.

2. *(vestirsi)*: **mettersi in pigiama** to put one's pyjamas on.

3. *(cominciare)*: **mettersi a fare qc** to start doing sthg; **s'è messo a gri-dare** he started screaming; **metter-si in viaggio** to set off.

4. *(in espressioni)*: **mettersi d'accor-do** to agree; **mettersi bene/male** to turn out well/badly; **mettersi con qn** *(in società)* to go into partner-ship with sb; *(in coppia)* to go out with sb.

mezza *sf*: **la ~** *(mezzogiorno e mezzo)* half-past twelve.

mezzaluna *(pl* **mezzelune)** *sf (parte di luna)* half moon; *(coltello)* chopping blade; *(islamica)* cres-cent.

mezzanino *sm* mezzanine floor.

mezzanotte *sf* midnight.

mezzo, -a *agg* half ◆ *sm (metà)* half; *(parte centrale)* middle; *(stru-mento, procedimento)* means; *(veicolo)* vehicle ◆ *avv*: ~ **pieno** half-full; ~ **chilo** half a kilo; ~ **litro** half a litre; **mezza pensione** half board; **abiti di mezza stagione** spring/autumn clothes; **a mezze maniche** short-sleeved; **di mezza età** middle-aged; **quello di ~** the one in the middle, the middle one; **per ~ di** by means of; **le cinque e mezza** ○ ~ half-past five; **non vuole andarci di ~** he doesn't want to get involved; **fare a ~ (con qn)** to share (with sb); **levarsi** ○ **togliersi di ~** to get out of the way; **mezzi di comunicazione (di massa)** (mass) media; **mezzi pubblici** public trans-port *(sg)*; **mezzi di trasporto** means of transport ❑ **mezzi** *smpl (eco-*

nomici) means.

mezzogiorno *sm (ora)* midday, noon ◻ **Mezzogiorno** *sm*: il **Mezzogiorno** Southern Italy.

 MEZZOGIORNO

The south of Italy, including Sicily and Sardinia, is called "il Mezzogiorno". This area is less industrial than the rest of the country, but is rich in art and culture and is blessed with spectacular scenery.

mezzora *sf* half an hour.

mi *(diventa* **me** *se precede* lo, la, li, le, ne) *pron (complemento oggetto)* me; *(complemento di termine)* (to) me; *(riflessivo)* myself; **me li dai?** will you give them to me?

miagolare *vi* to miaow.

mica *avv (fam):* **non ci avrai ~ creduto?** you didn't believe it, did you?; **non sono ~ scemo!** I'm not stupid, am I!; **~ male** not bad (at all).

miccia, -ce *sf* fuse.

micidiale *agg (mortale)* deadly; *(dannoso)* murderous; *(insopportabile)* unbearable.

micosi *sf inv (MED)* fungus.

microfono *sm* microphone.

microscopio *sm* microscope.

midolla *sf (mollica)* crumb.

midollo *(pl f* **midolla)** *sm* marrow.

mie → **mio**.

miei → **mio**.

miele *sm* honey.

migliaio *(pl f* **migliaia)** *sm* thousand; **un ~ (di persone)** about a thousand (people); **a migliaia** by the thousand.

miglio *sm (unità di misura: pl f* **miglia)** mile; *(pianta)* millet.

miglioramento *sm* improvement.

migliorare *vt* to improve ◆ *vi (tempo, situazione)* to improve; *(malato)* to get better.

migliore *agg (comparativo)* better; **il/la ~** *(superlativo)* the best.

mignoio *sm* little finger *(Br)*, pinkie *(Am)*; *(del piede)* little toe.

mila *pl →* **mille.**

milanese *agg* Milanese ◆ *smf* person from Milan.

Milano *sf* Milan.

miliardo *sm* thousand million *(Br)*, billion *(Am)*.

milione *sm* million.

militare *agg* military ◆ *sm* serviceman; **fare il ~** to do one's military service.

mille *(pl* **mila)** *num* a 0 one thousand, → **sei.**

millefoglie *sm inv* millefeuille *(Br)*, napoleon *(Am)*.

millennio *sm* millennium.

millepiedi *sm inv* millipede.

millesimo, -a *num* thousandth, → **sesto.**

millimetro *sm* millimetre.

milza *sf* spleen.

mimare *vt* to mime.

mimetizzare *vt* to camouflage ◻ **mimetizzarsi** *vr (animali, piante)* to camouflage o.s.

mimo *sm* mime.

mimosa *sf* mimosa.

min. *(abbr di minimo, di minu-*

to) min.

mina *sf (esplosiva)* mine; *(di matita)* lead.

minaccia, -ce *sf* threat.

minacciare *vt* to threaten; **~ di fare qc** to threaten to do sthg.

minaccioso, -a *agg* threatening, menacing.

minatore *sm* miner.

minerale *agg & sm* mineral.

minestra *sf* soup; **~ in brodo** noodle broth; **~ di verdure** vegetable soup.

minestrone *sm* minestrone.

miniatura *sf* miniature.

miniera *sf* mine.

minigolf *sm* minigolf.

minigonna *sf* miniskirt.

minima *sf* minimum temperature.

minimizzare *vt* to minimize.

minimo, -a *agg (il più piccolo)* slightest, least; *(il più basso)* lowest; *(molto piccolo)* very small, slight ♦ *sm (parte più piccola)* minimum; *(di motore)* idling speed; **come ~** at the very least.

ministero *sm (settore amministrativo)* ministry.

ministro *sm* minister; **~ degli Esteri** Foreign Secretary *(Br)*, Secretary of State *(Am)*.

minoranza *sf* minority; **essere in ~** to be in a minority.

minore *agg (comparativo: di età)* younger; *(di grandezza)* smaller; *(di importanza)* minor; *(numero)* lower; *(grado)* lesser; *(superlativo: di età)* youngest; *(di grandezza)* smallest; *(di importanza)* least important; *(di*

numero) lowest ♦ *smf (minorenne)* minor.

minorenne *smf* minor.

minuscola *sf* small letter.

minuscolo, -a *agg (scrittura)* small; *(molto piccolo)* tiny.

minuto, -a *agg (persona, corpo)* small; *(piccolo)* tiny, minute; *(fine)* fine ♦ *sm (unità)* minute.

mio *(f* mia, *mpl* miei, *fpl* mie) *agg*: **il ~ (la mia)** my ♦ *pron*: **il ~ (la mia)** mine; **~ padre** my father; **un ~ amico** a friend of mine; **questa bici è mia** this bike is mine.

miope *agg* short-sighted.

mira *sf* aim; **prendere la ~** to take aim; **prendere di ~ qc** *(fig)* to pick on sb.

miracolo *sm* miracle.

miraggio *sm* mirage.

mirare *vi*: **~ a** to aim at.

miriade *sf* multitude; **una ~ di** a multitude of.

mirtillo *sm* blueberry.

miscela *sf (miscuglio)* mixture; *(di caffè)* blend; *(benzina)* petrol and oil mixture.

mischia *sf* brawl; *(nel rugby)* scrum.

mischiare *vt* to mix; **~ le carte** to shuffle the cards ❏ **mischiarsi** *vr* to mix.

miseria *sf (extreme)* poverty; *(quantità insufficiente)*: **è costato una ~** it cost next to nothing; **porca ~!** *(volg: accidenti)* damn!, bloody hell!

misericordia *sf* mercy.

misero, -a *agg (povero)* poor, poverty-stricken; *(infelice)* wretched, miserable; *(insufficiente)* miserable.

missile *sm* missile.

missionario, -a *sm, f* missionary.

missione *sf* mission.

misterioso, -a *agg* mysterious.

mistero *sm* mystery.

misto, -a *agg* mixed ♦ *sm* mixture; **insalata mista** mixed salad; ~ **lana** woollen blend; ~ **cotone** cotton blend.

misura *sf* (unità, provvedimento) measure; (dimensione) measurement; (taglia) size; (moderazione) moderation; **prendere le misure di qc** to measure sthg; **su ~** made-to-measure.

misurare *vt* to measure; (abito) to try on; (vista) to test ♦ *vi* to measure ◻ **misurarsi con** *vr + prep* to compete with.

misurino *sm* measure.

mite *agg* mild.

mito *sm* myth.

mitra *sm inv* submachine gun.

mitragliatrice *sf* machine gun.

mittente *smf* sender.

mobile *agg* movable ♦ *sm* piece of furniture; **mobili** (mobilia) furniture (sg).

mobilia *sf* furniture.

mobilitare *vt* to mobilize.

moca *sf inv* coffee machine.

mocassino *sm* mocassin.

moda *sf* fashion; **essere** o **andare di ~** to be in fashion; **passare di ~** to go out of fashion; **alla ~** fashionable; **di ~** fashionable.

modellare *vt* to model.

modellino *sm* model.

modello, -a *sm, f* model ♦ *sm* model; (per sarta) pattern; (modulo) form.

moderare *vt* to moderate.

moderato, -a *agg* moderate.

moderno, -a *agg* modern.

modestia *sf* modesty.

modesto, -a *agg* modest.

modico, -a, -ci, -che *agg* low.

modifica, -che *sf* alteration.

modo *sm* way; (opportunità) chance; (GRAMM: verbale) mood; **a ~ mio** in my way; **in ~ da fare qc** so as to do sthg; **~ di dire** expression; **di ~ che** so that; **in nessun ~** in no way; **in ogni ~** anyway; **in qualche ~** in some way; **in tutti i modi** in every way.

modulazione *sf*: ~ **di frequenza** frequency modulation.

modulo *sm* form.

moglie, -gli *sf* wife.

mole *sf* (dimensione) massive shape; (quantità): **una ~ di lavoro** masses of work.

molestare *vt* to annoy.

molesto, -a *agg* annoying.

molla *sf* (meccanica) spring ◻ **molle** *sfpl* (per camino, ghiaccio) tongs.

mollare *vt* (allentare) to slacken; (lasciar andare) to let go; (fam: fidanzato) to ditch ♦ *vi* (desistere) to give in; ~ **un ceffone a qn** (fam: dare uno schiaffo) to slap sb.

molle *agg* (morbido) soft; (fig: persona) weak.

molletta sf (per capelli) hair grip; (per panni) clothes peg.

mollica, -che sf crumb.

molo sm (di porto) jetty.

molteplice agg (complesso) complex □ **molteplici** agg pl (numerosi) numerous, various.

moltiplicare vt to multiply.

moltiplicazione sf (MAT) multiplication; (accrescimento) increase.

moltitudine sf multitude.

molto, -a agg 1. (in grande quantità) a lot of, much; **non ho ~ tempo** I don't have (very) much time; **hai molta fame?** are you very hungry?

2. (di numero elevato): **molti(-e)** a lot of, many; **ci sono molti turisti** there are a lot of tourists.

♦ pron a lot, much; **molti** (molta gente) many (people); **molti di noi** many of us.

♦ avv 1. (con verbi) a lot, (very) much; **mi piace ~** I like it a lot o very much.

2. (con aggettivi, avverbi) very; (con participio passato) much; **è ~ simpatica** she's very nice; **è ~ meglio così** it's much better like this; **è ~ presto/tardi** it's very early/late; **~ volentieri!** certainly!.

momentaneamente avv at the moment.

momentaneo, -a agg momentary.

momento sm moment; (circostanza) time; **all'ultimo ~** at the last moment; **da un ~ all'altro** (tra poco) (at) any moment; **dal ~ che** since; **per il ~** for the time being; a

momenti (tra poco) soon; (quasi) nearly.

monaca, -che sf nun.

monaco, -ci sm monk.

monarchia sf monarchy.

monastero sm (di monaci) monastery; (di monache) convent.

mondano, -a agg (di società) society (dav s); (terreno) earthly.

mondiale agg world (dav s).

mondo sm world.

moneta sf (di metallo) coin; (valuta) currency; **~ spicciola** change.

monetario, -a agg monetary.

monolocale sm studio flat (Br), studio apartment (Am).

monopattino sm scooter.

monopolio sm monopoly.

monosci sm inv monoski.

monotono, -a agg (ripetitivo) monotonous; (noioso) dull.

montacarichi sm inv goods lift.

montagna sf mountain; (zona) the mountains (pl); **andare in ~** to go to the mountains; **montagne russe** roller coaster (sg).

montanaro, -a sm, f mountain dweller.

montano, -a agg mountain (dav s).

montare vi (salire) to go up; (cavalcare) to ride ♦ vt (congegno) to assemble; (cavallo, pietra preziosa) to mount; (panna) to whip; (albumi) to whisk; (fecondare) to cover; **~ in macchina** to get into a car; **~ in treno** to get on a train; **montarsi la testa** to become bigheaded.

montatura sf (di occhiali)

frames (pl); (di gioiello) setting.

monte sm mountain; **andare a ~** to come to nothing; **mandare a ~ qc** to upset sthg; **~ premi** prize money; **il Monte Bianco** Mont Blanc.

montone sm (animale) ram; (carne) mutton; (giaccone) sheepskin jacket.

montuoso, -a agg mountainous.

monumento sm monument.

mora sf (commestibile) blackberry; (del gelso) mulberry; (DIR) default.

morale agg moral ♦ sf morals (pl); (insegnamento) moral ♦ sm morale; **essere giù di ~** to be feeling down.

morbido, -a agg soft.

morbillo sm measles (sg).

morbo sm disease.

morboso, -a agg morbid.

mordere vt to bite.

morfina sf morphine.

moribondo, -a agg dying.

morire vi to die; (estinguersi) to die out; **~ di fame** to die of hunger; **~ di noia** to die of boredom; **~ dal ridere** to kill o.s. laughing; **bello da ~** stunning.

mormorare vi (bisbigliare) to whisper; (sparlare) to gossip ♦ vt to murmur.

moro, -a agg dark.

morso, -a pp → **mordere** ♦ sm bite; (di briglia) bit.

mortadella sf Mortadella (large pork sausage served cold in thin slices).

mortale agg mortal; (letale) deadly ♦ sm mortal.

mortalità sf mortality.

morte sf death; **avercela a ~ con qn** to have it in for sb.

mortificare vt to mortify.

morto, -a pp → **morire** ♦ agg dead ♦ sm, f dead man (f dead woman); **fare il ~** (nell'acqua) to float on one's back.

mosaico, -ci sm mosaic.

mosca, -sche sf fly; **~ cieca** blind man's buff.

Mosca sf Moscow.

moscato sm muscatel (sweet wine).

moscerino sm gnat.

moschettone sm spring clip.

moscone sm (insetto) bluebottle; (imbarcazione) pedalo.

mossa sf movement; (negli scacchi) move.

mosso, -a pp → **muovere** ♦ agg (mare) rough; (capelli) wavy; (fotografia) blurred.

mostarda sf mustard.

mostra sf exhibition; **mettersi in ~** to draw attention to o.s.; **in ~** on show; **la Mostra del cinema di Venezia** Venice Film Festival.

---

[i] LA MOSTRA DEL CINEMA DI VENEZIA

The Venice Film Festival, or the "Mostra internazionale d'arte cinematografica di Venezia", has been held every year since 1938 during the last week in August and the first week in September. Film fans flock to the Palazzo del Cinema in Lido di Venezia to see the celebrities, to watch important new films and retrospectives, and to attend premières. The festival concludes with the awarding of prizes, including the prestigious "Leone d'oro" (golden lion).

mostrare *vt* to show □ **mostrarsi** *vr* to look; **mostrarsi in pubblico** to appear in public.

mostro *sm* monster.

mostruoso, -a *agg (orrendo)* monstrous; *(feroce)* ferocious; *(smisurato)* incredible.

motel *sm inv* motel.

motivo *sm (causa)* reason; *(di stoffa)* pattern; *(musicale)* tune; **per quale ~?** for what reason?; **senza ~** without a reason.

moto *sm (in fisica)* motion; *(movimento)* movement; *(esercizio fisico)* exercise ◆ *sf inv* motorbike; **mettere in ~** *(AUTO)* to start.

motocicletta *sf* motorcycle.

motocross *sm* motocross.

motore *sm* motor, engine; **a ~** motor *(dav s)*.

motorino *sm* moped; **~ d'avviamento** starter.

motoscafo *sm* motorboat.

motto *sm* maxim.

mousse [mus] *sf inv* mousse.

movimentare *vt* to liven up.

movimento *sm (attività)* activity.

mozzafiato *agg inv* breathtaking.

mozzare *vt* to cut off; **~ il fiato a qn** to take sb's breath away.

mozzarella *sf* mozzarella *(a round fresh cheese from Naples made from cow's or buffalo's milk)*; **~ in carrozza** mozzarella sandwiched between two slices of bread, then dipped in egg and fried.

mozzicone *sm* stub.

mozzo, -a *agg* cut off ◆ *sm* ship's boy.

mucca, -che *sf* cow.

mucchio *sm (cumulo)* heap; **un ~ di** *(fig: grande quantità)* loads of.

muffa *sf* mould.

muffole *sfpl* mittens.

mugolare *vi* to whine.

mulattiera *sf* mule track.

mulatto, -a *agg & sm, f* mulatto.

mulinello *sm (vortice)* whirl; *(da pesca)* reel.

mulino *sm* mill; **~ a vento** windmill.

mulo *sm* mule.

multa *sf* fine.

multare *vt* to fine.

multiplo, -a *agg & sm* multiple.

multiproprietà *sf inv* timeshare.

mungere *vt* to milk.

municipale *agg* municipal.

municipio *sm* town hall.

munire *vt:* **~ qn/qc di qc** to equip sb/sthg with sthg □ **munirsi di** *vr + prep* to equip o.s. with.

muovere *vt* to move; *(critica, accusa)* to make □ **muoversi** *vr* to move; *(fam: sbrigarsi)* to hurry up, to get a move on.

mura *sfpl* walls.

murare *vt* to wall up.

muratore *sm* bricklayer.

murena sf moray eel.

muro sm wall.

muscolare agg muscular, muscle (dav s).

muscolo sm muscle; **muscoli** (forza) brawn (sg).

muscoloso, -a agg muscular.

museo sm museum.

museruola sf muzzle.

musica sf music; ~ **classica** classical music; ~ **leggera** light music.

musicale agg musical.

musicista, -i, -e smf musician.

muso sm (di animale) muzzle; (fam & spreg: di persona) mug; (di auto) front end; (aereo) nose; **tenere il** ~ to sulk.

muta sf (da sub) wet suit; (di cani) pack.

mutamento sm change.

mutande sfpl pants.

mutandine sfpl knickers.

mutare vt & vi to change.

mutazione sf change; (genetica) mutation.

mutilato, -a sm, f person who has lost a limb; ~ **di guerra** disabled ex-serviceman (Br), disabled war veteran (Am).

muto, -a agg dumb; (silenzioso) silent; (cinema, consonante) silent.

mutua sf = National Health Service.

mutuo, -a agg mutual ◆ sm loan; (per casa) mortgage.

N

N (abbr di nord) N.

nafta sf (olio combustibile) fuel oil; (gasolio) diesel oil.

naftalina sf mothballs (pl).

nailon® sm nylon.

nanna sf (fam): **andare a** ~ to go to beddy-byes.

nano, -a agg & sm, f dwarf.

napoletana sf a type of coffee percolator.

napoletano, -a agg & sm, f Neapolitan.

Napoli sf Naples.

narice sf nostril.

narrare vt to tell.

narrativa sf fiction.

nasale agg nasal.

nascere vi to be born; (pianta) to come up; (sole) to rise; (fiume) to have its source; (dente) to come through; (attività, impresa) to start up; **sono nata il 31 luglio del 1965** I was born on the 31st of July 1965 ❑ **nascere da** v + prep to arise from.

nascita sf (di bambino, animale) birth; (di attività, movimento) start; **data di** ~ date of birth; **luogo di** ~ place of birth.

nascondere vt to hide; (dissimulare) to hide, to conceal ❑ **nascondersi** vr to hide.

nascondino sm hide and seek.

nascosto, -a pp → **nascon-**

dere ◆ *agg* hidden; **di ~** secretly.

naso *sm* nose; **ficcare il ~ in qc** to poke one's nose into sthg.

nastro *sm* ribbon; **~ adesivo** adhesive tape; **~ trasportatore** conveyor belt.

Natale *sm* Christmas.

---

i **NATALE**

Italian Christmas celebrations begin on Christmas Eve with a dinner at which special regional dishes are served. The rest of the evening is normally spent playing "tombola" (line bingo) or cards, and in some families the gifts which were placed under the Christmas tree or by the "presepe" (crib) are exchanged now rather than on the 25th. Churchgoers then attend midnight mass. Christmas Day itself is usually spent with the family. Lunch is traditionally rounded off with a "panettone", a domed cake containing raisins and candied fruit.

---

natalità *sf* birth rate.

natante *sm* craft.

nato, -a *pp* → **nascere** ◆ *agg* (*fig: per natura*) born; **nata Mattei** (*da nubile*) née Mattei.

NATO *sf* NATO.

natura *sf* nature; **~ morta** still life.

naturale *agg* natural.

naturalmente *avv* naturally; (*certamente sì*) naturally, of course.

naufragare *vi* (*nave*) to be wrecked; (*persona*) to be shipwrecked.

naufragio *sm* shipwreck.

naufrago, -a, -ghi, -ghe *sm, f* shipwrecked person.

nausea *sf* nausea.

nauseante *agg* nauseating.

nauseare *vt* to make sick.

nautico, -a, -ci, -che *agg* nautical.

navale *agg* naval.

navata *sf* nave.

nave *sf* ship; **~ passeggeri** passenger ship; **~ traghetto** ferry.

navetta *sf* shuttle; **~ (spaziale)** space shuttle.

navigabile *agg* navigable.

navigare *vi* (*nave*) to sail; (*persona*) to navigate.

navigazione *sf* navigation.

naviglio *sm* (*nave*) vessel; (*canale*) canal.

nazionale *agg* national ◆ *sf* (*squadra*) national team.

nazionalità *sf inv* nationality.

nazione *sf* nation.

ne *pron* 1. (*di lui*) of/about him; (*di lei*) of/about her; (*di loro*) of/about them; **~ apprezzo l'onestà** I value his honesty.

2. (*di un insieme*) of it, of them; **hai dei panini? – ~ vorrei due** have you got any rolls? – I'd like two (of them).

3. (*di ciò*) about it; **non parliamone più** let's not talk about it any more; **non ~ ho idea** I've no idea.

4. (*da ciò*): **~ deriva che ...** it follows that ...

◆ *avv* (*di là*) from there; **~ veniamo proprio ora** we've just come from there.

né *cong*: **né ... né** neither ... nor; **~ l'uno ~ l'altro sono italiani** neithe of them are Italian; **non si è fatto ~ sentire ~ vedere** I haven't heard from him or seen him; **non voglio ~ il primo ~ il secondo** I don't want either the first one or the second.

neanche *cong & avv* not even; **non ... ~** not even ...; **~ io lo conosco** I don't know him either; **non ho mangiato – ~ io** I haven't eaten – neither have I o I haven't either; **~ per sogno** o **per idea!** not on your life!

nebbia *sf* fog.

nebulizzatore *sm* spray.

necessariamente *avv* necessarily.

necessario, -a *agg* necessary ◆ *sm* necessities (*pl*); **è ~** it must be done; **~ per toeletta** toiletries (*pl*).

necessità *sf inv* (*bisogno*) necessity.

necessitare : **necessitare di** *v + prep* to need, to require.

necrologio *sm* (*annuncio*) obituary.

negare *vt* to deny; (*rifiutare*): **~ qc (a qn)** to refuse (sb) sthg; **~ di aver fatto qc** to deny having done sthg.

negativo, -a *agg & sm* negative.

negato, -a *agg*: **essere ~ per qc** to be hopeless at sthg.

negli = in + gli, → in.

negligente *agg* negligent.

negoziante *smf* shopkeeper.

negozio *sm* shop; **~ di giocattoli** toy shop.

negro, -a *agg & sm, f* black.

nei = in + i, → in.

nel = in + il, → in.

nell' = in + l', → in.

nella = in + la, → in.

nelle = in + le, → in.

nello = in + lo, → in.

nemico, -a, -ci, -che *agg* (*esercito, stato*) enemy (*dav s*); (*ostile*) hostile ◆ *sm, f* enemy.

nemmeno = **neanche**.

neo *sm* mole.

neofascismo *sm* neofascism.

neon *sm* neon.

neonato, -a *sm, f* newborn baby.

neozelandese *agg* New Zealand (*dav s*) ◆ *smf* New Zealander.

neppure = **neanche**.

nero, -a *agg* (*colore*) black; (*scuro*) dark; (*pane*) wholemeal ◆ *sm* black.

nervo *sm* nerve; **dare ai** o **sui nervi a qc** to get on sb's nerves.

nervosismo *sm* nervousness.

nervoso, -a *agg* nervous ◆ *sm*: **avere il ~** to be on edge.

nespola *sf* medlar.

nessuno, -a *agg* no ◆ *pron* (*non una persona*) nobody, no one; (*non una cosa*) none; (*qualcuno*): **c'è ~?** is anybody in?; **nessuna città è bella quanto Roma** there's no city more beautiful than Rome; **non c'è nessun posto libero** there aren't any free seats; **da nessuna parte** nowhere; **~ lo sa** nobody knows; **non ho visto ~** I didn't see anybody; **~ di noi** none of us; **~ dei due** neither of them; **non me ne piace ~** I don't like any of them.

nettezza *sf*: ~ urbana refuse department.

netto, -a *agg (preciso)* clear; *(deciso)* definite; *(peso, stipendio)* net.

netturbino *sm* dustman.

neutrale *agg* neutral.

neutralizzare *vt* to neutralize.

neutro, -a *agg* neutral; essere ~ *(imparziale)* to be neutral ♦ *sm (in linguistica)* neuter.

neve *sf* snow.

nevicare *v impers* to snow; **nevica** it's snowing.

nevicata *sf* snowfall.

nevischio *sm* sleet.

nevralgia *sf* neuralgia.

nevrotico, -a, -ci, -che *agg* neurotic.

nicchia *sf* niche.

nicotina *sf* nicotine.

nido *sm* nest.

niente *pron* 1. *(nessuna cosa)* nothing; non ... ~ nothing; non faccio ~ la domenica I do nothing on Sundays, I don't do anything on Sundays; ~ di ~ nothing at all; grazie! – di ~! thank you – not at all.
2. *(qualcosa)* anything; le serve ~? do you need anything?; non per ~, ma ... not that it matters, but ...
3. *(poco)* da ~ *(cosa)* not important; *(persona)* worthless.
♦ *agg inv (fam: nessuno)*: non ha ~ buon senso he has no common sense; ~ paura! never fear!
♦ *avv*: non ... ~ not ... at all; non me ne importa ~ I couldn't care less; questo non c'entra ~ this

doesn't come into it at all; non fa ~ it doesn't matter; ti piace? – per ~! do you like it? – not at all!
♦ *sm*: basta un ~ per farlo contento the slightest thing makes him happy; un bel ~ nothing at all.

nientemeno *avv* no less, actually ♦ *esclam* you don't say!

night(-club) ['nait(-'klʌb)] *sm inv* nightclub.

Nilo *sm*: il ~ the Nile.

ninnananna *sf* lullaby.

ninnolo *sm* knick-knack.

nipote *smf (di zii)* nephew *(f* niece); *(di nonni)* grandson *(f* granddaughter).

nitido, -a *agg* well-defined.

nitrire *vi* to neigh.

no *avv* no; c'eri anche tu, ~? you were there too, weren't you?; lo sai, ~, com'è fatto you know, don't you, what he's like?; lo vuoi o ~? do you want it or not?; ~ di certo certainly not; perché ~? why not?

nobile *agg & smf* noble.

nobiltà *sf (aristocrazia)* nobility; *(di animo, azione)* nobleness.

nocciola *sf* hazelnut ♦ *agg inv* hazel.

nocciolina *sf*: ~ (americana) peanut.

nocciolo[1] *sm (di frutto)* stone.

nocciolo[2] *sm (albero)* hazel.

noce *sf & sm* walnut; ~ di cocco coconut; ~ moscata nutmeg.

nocivo, -a *agg* harmful.

nodo *sm* knot; avere un ~ alla gola to have a lump in one's throat.

noi *pron (soggetto)* we; *(complemento oggetto, con preposizione)* us; **da ~** *(nel nostro paese)* in our country; **~ stessi** we ourselves.

noia *sf (tedio)* boredom; *(fastidio)* nuisance; **gli è venuto a ~** he's tired of it; **dar ~ a qn** to annoy sb; **avere delle noie con** to have trouble with.

noioso, -a *agg (monotono)* boring; *(fastidioso)* annoying.

noleggiare *vt (prendere a nolo)* to hire; *(dare a nolo)* to hire out.

noleggio *sm* hire *(Br)*, rental; **prendere qc a ~** to hire sthg.

nolo = **noleggio**.

nome *sm* name; *(GRAMM)* noun; **conoscere qn di ~** to know sb by name; **a ~ di qn** on behalf of sb; **~ di battesimo** Christian name; **~ da ragazza** maiden name.

nominare *vt (menzionare)* to mention; *(eleggere)* to appoint.

non *avv* not, → **affatto, ancora** ecc.

nonché *cong (e anche)* as well as; *(tanto meno)* let alone.

noncurante *agg*: **~ (di)** indifferent (to).

nondimeno *cong* nevertheless, however.

nonno, -a *sm, f* grandfather (*f* grandmother).

nonnulla *sm inv*: **un ~** a trifle.

nono, -a *num* ninth, → **sesto**.

nonostante *prep* in spite of ♦ *cong* although.

non vedente *smf* blind person.

nord *sm* north ♦ *agg inv* north, northern; **a ~ (di)** north (of); **nel ~** in the north.

nordest *sm* northeast.

nordico, -a, -ci, -che *agg* Nordic.

nordovest *sm* northwest.

norma *sf* rule; **di ~** as a rule; **a ~ di legge** according to the law.

normale *agg* normal.

normalità *sf* normality.

normanno, -a *agg* Norman.

norvegese *agg, smf & sm* Norwegian.

Norvegia *sf*: **la ~** Norway.

nostalgia *sf* nostalgia; **avere ~ di casa** o **di paese** to be homesick.

nostro, -a *agg*: **il ~ (la nostra)** our ♦ *pron*: **il ~ (la nostra)** ours; **~ padre** our father; **un ~ amico** a friend of ours; **questa casa è nostra** it's our house.

nota *sf* note; *(conto)* bill; *(elenco)* list; **prendere ~ (di qc)** to make a note (of sthg).

notaio *sm* notary public.

notare *vt (osservare, accorgersi di)* to notice; *(annotare)* to note down; **farsi ~** to get o.s. noticed.

notevole *agg (differenza, prezzo)* considerable; *(persona)* remarkable.

notificare *vt (form)* to notify.

notizia *sf (informazione)* news *(sg)*, piece of news; **le ultime notizie** the latest news; **avere notizie di qn** to hear from sb.

notiziario *sm* news *(sg)*.

noto, -a *agg* well-known; **rendere ~ qc a qn** to make sthg known to sb.

nottambulo, -a *sm, f* night bird.

notte sf night; **di ~** at night; **una ~ in bianco** a sleepless night.

notturno, -a agg night (dav s); **animale ~** nocturnal animal.

novanta num ninety, → **sei**.

novantesimo, -a num ninetieth, → **sesto**.

nove num nine, → **sei**.

novecento num nine hundred, → **sei** □ **Novecento** sm: **il Novecento** the twentieth century.

novella sf short story.

novembre sm November, → **settembre**.

novità sf inv (cosa nuova) something new; (fatto, notizia recente) (piece of) news (sg); **le ~ musicali** the latest releases.

nozione sf notion, idea; **nozioni** (di matematica, francese) rudiments.

nozze sfpl wedding (sg); **~ d'oro** golden wedding.

nube sf cloud.

nubifragio sm rainstorm.

nubile agg single.

nuca, -che sf nape of the neck.

nucleare agg nuclear.

nucleo sm (di cellula, atomo) nucleus; (di persone) group; (di soldati, polizia) squad; **~ familiare** family unit.

nudismo sm nudism.

nudista, -i, -e smf nudist.

nudo, -a agg (persona) naked; (parete) bare; **mettere a ~ qc** to lay sthg bare ◆ sm (ARTE) nude.

nugolo sm: **un ~ di** a host of.

nulla = niente.

nullità sf inv (di ragionamento, documento) nullity; (persona) nobody.

nullo, -a agg (non valido) (null and) void; (SPORT) drawn.

numerale agg & sm numeral.

numerare vt to number.

numero sm (MAT: quantità) number; (segno, cifra) numeral; (di scarpe) size; (di rivista) issue; **~ civico** house number; **~ chiuso** selective entry system; **~ di conto** account number; **~ di targa** numberplate; **~ di telefono** telephone number; **~ verde** ≃ freefone number (Br), ≃ toll-free number (Am); **dare i numeri** (fig) to be off one's head.

numeroso, -a agg (molteplice) numerous; (grande) large.

numismatica sf numismatics (sg).

nuocere : **nuocere a** v + prep to harm.

nuora sf daughter-in-law.

nuotare vi to swim.

nuoto sm swimming.

nuovamente avv again.

Nuova Zelanda sf: **la ~** New Zealand.

nuovo, -a agg new; **di ~** again; **~ di zecca** brand-new.

nuraghe, -ghi sm prehistoric stone monument in Sardinia.

nutriente agg nutritious.

nutrimento sm nourishment.

nutrire vt (con cibo) to feed; (fig: sentimento) to feel □ **nutrirsi di** vr + prep to feed on.

nuvola sf cloud; **cascare dalle nuvole** to be flabbergasted.

nuvoloso, -a agg cloudy.

O

O *cong* or; ~ ... ~ either ... or.

O *(abbr di ovest)* W.

oasi *sf inv* oasis.

obbediente = ubbidiente.

obbedire = ubbidire.

obbligare *vt*: ~ qn a fare qc to force sb to do sthg.

obbligato, -a *agg (percorso, passaggio)* fixed; *(costretto)*: ~ a fare qc obliged to do sthg.

obbligatorio, -a *agg* compulsory.

obbligo, -ghi *sm* obligation; avere l'~ di fare qc to be obliged to do sthg.

obelisco, -schi *sm* obelisk.

obeso, -a *agg* obese.

obiettare *vt* to object.

obiettivo, -a *agg* objective ◆ *sm (fotografico)* lens; *(bersaglio, scopo)* objective.

obiettore *sm* objector; ~ di coscienza conscientious objector.

obiezione *sf* objection.

obitorio *sm* mortuary.

obliquo, -a *agg* slanting.

obliterare *vt* to stamp.

oblò *sm inv* porthole.

obsoleto, -a *agg* obsolete.

oca *(pl* oche*) sf* goose.

occasione *sf (momento favorevole)* opportunity; *(affare)* bargain; *(causa, circostanza)* occasion; avere ~ di fare qc to have the chance to do sthg; cogliere l'~ per fare qc to take the opportunity to do sthg; d'~ second-hand.

occhiaie *sfpl* bags, rings.

occhiali *smpl*: ~ (da vista) glasses; ~ da sole sunglasses.

occhiata *sf*: dare un'~ a to have a look at.

occhiello *sm* buttonhole.

occhio *sm* eye; a ~ nudo with the naked eye; tenere O non perdere d'~ qn/qc to keep an eye on sb/sthg; a ~ e croce roughly; costare un ~ della testa to cost a fortune; saltare O balzare all'~ to be obvious; a quattr'occhi in private; sognare a occhi aperti to daydream.

occhiolino *sm*: fare l'~ (a qn) to wink (at sb).

occidentale *agg (zona)* west, western; *(cultura, società)* Western.

occidente *sm* west ❑ Occidente *sm*: l'Occidente the West.

occorrente *sm* everything necessary.

occorrenza *sf*: all'~ if need be.

occorrere *vi* to be necessary; occorre aspettare you/we have to wait; mi occorre tempo I need time.

occorso, -a *pp* → occorrere.

occulto, -a *agg* occult.

occupare *vt (ingombrare)* to take up; *(paese, università)* to occupy; *(impegnare)* to keep busy ❑ occuparsi di *vr* + *prep (prendersi cura di)* to take care of, to look after; *(impicciarsi in)* to interfere in; *(interessarsi di)*: si occupa di politica he's in politics; occupati dei fatti tuoi!

mind your own business!

occupato, -a *agg (sedia, posto)* taken; *(telefono, bagno)* engaged; *(impegnato)* busy.

occupazione *sf (impiego)* occupation; *(in economia)* employment.

Oceania *sf:* l'~ Oceania.

oceano *sm* ocean.

oculista, -i, -e *smf* eye specialist.

odiare *vt* to hate.

odio *sm* hatred.

odioso, -a *agg* hateful, odious.

odorare *vt* to smell ❑ **odorare di** *v + prep* to smell of.

odorato *sm (sense of)* smell.

odore *sm* smell ❑ **odori** *(da cucina) smpl* herbs.

offendere *vt* to offend ❑ **offendersi** *vr* to take offence.

offensivo, -a *agg* offensive.

offerto, -a *pp* → **offrire** ♦ *sf (proposta)* offer; *(donazione)* donation; *(FIN)* supply; ~ **speciale** special offer.

offesa *sf* offence.

offeso, -a *pp* → **offendere** ♦ *agg* offended.

officina *sf (di fabbrica)* workshop; *(per auto)* garage.

offrire *vt* to offer; *(cena, caffè)* to pay for; ~ **da bere a qn** to buy sb a drink ❑ **offrirsi di** *vr + prep:* **offrirsi di fare qc** to offer to do sthg.

offuscare *vt (luce)* to darken; *(vista, mente, memoria)* to dim ❑ **offuscarsi** *vr (vista)* to dim.

oggettivo, -a *agg* objective.

oggetto *sm* object; *(ufficio)*

oggetti smarriti lost property (office) *(Br)*, lost-and-found office *(Am)*.

oggi *avv* today; *(attualmente)* nowadays; ~ **pomeriggio** this afternoon; **il giornale di** ~ today's newspaper; **dall'**~ **al domani** from one day to the next.

oggigiorno *avv* nowadays.

ogni *agg inv (tutti)* every, each; *(distributivo)* every; **gente di** ~ **tipo** all sorts of people; ~ **giorno/ mese/anno** every day/month/year; ~ **tre giorni** every three days; **in** ~ **caso** in any case; **ad** ~ **modo** anyway; ~ **tanto** every so often; ~ **volta che** whenever.

Ognissanti *sm* All Saints' Day.

ognuno, -a *pron* everyone, everybody; ~ **di voi** each of you.

Olanda *sf:* l'~ Holland.

olandese *agg & sm* Dutch ♦ *smf* Dutchman (f Dutchwoman); **gli olandesi** the Dutch.

oleoso, -a *agg* oily.

olfatto *sm* sense of smell.

oliare *vt* to oil.

oliera *sf* oil and vinegar cruet.

olimpiadi *sfpl:* **le** ~ the Olympic Games.

olio *sm* oil; ~ **(extra-vergine) d'oliva** (extra-virgin) olive oil; ~ **di semi** vegetable oil; **sott'**~ in oil.

oliva *sf* olive; **olive farcite all'anconetana** olives stuffed with meat and vegetables, then covered in breadcrumbs and fried.

olivastro, -a *agg (carnagione)* sallow.

olivo *sm* olive tree.

olmo *sm* elm.

oltraggio *sm* (DIR) offence.

oltralpe : **d'oltralpe** *agg* on the other side of the Alps.

oltranza : **a oltranza** *avv* to the (bitter) end.

oltre *prep* (*di là da*) beyond; (*più di*) over, more than; (*in aggiunta a*) as well as, besides ♦ *avv* (*più in là*) further; ~ **a** (*all'infuori di*) apart from; (*in aggiunta a*) as well as; **non ~ le cinque** no later than five o'clock.

oltrepassare *vt* to go beyond.

omaggio *sm* (*tributo*) homage; (*regalo*) gift; **in ~** (*con prodotto*) free.

ombelico, -chi *sm* navel.

ombra *sf* (*zona*) shade; (*figura*) shadow; **all'~** in the shade.

ombrello *sm* umbrella.

ombrellone *sm* beach umbrella.

ombretto *sm* eye shadow.

omeopatia *sf* homeopathy.

omesso, -a *pp →* omettere.

omettere *vt* to omit; ~ **di fare qc** to omit to do sthg.

omicidio *sm* murder.

omissione *sf* omission.

omogeneizzato *sm* baby food.

omogeneo, -a *agg* (*uniforme*) homogeneous; (*armonico*) harmonious.

omonimo, -a *sm, f* (*persona*) namesake.

omosessuale *smf* homosexual.

On. (*abbr di onorevole*) Hon.

onda *sf* wave; **andare in ~** to go on the air; **mandare in ~ qc** to broadcast sthg; **onde lunghe/medie/corte** long/medium/short wave (*sg*); **'onde pericolose'** sign warning swimmers to take care.

ondata *sf* wave; **a ondate** in waves.

ondulato, -a *agg* (*terreno*) undulating; (*capelli*) wavy; (*lamiera, carta*) corrugated.

onere *sm* (*form*) burden; **oneri fiscali** (DIR) taxes.

onestà *sf* honesty.

onesto, -a *agg* honest.

onnipotente *agg* omnipotent.

onomastico *sm* name day.

---

i ONOMASTICO

A long with their birthdays, Italians also celebrate their "onomastico", or name day, albeit in a minor way. This is the day when the saint after whom they are named is honoured. Relatives and friends send cards, small gifts or simply their best wishes.

---

onorare *vt* (*celebrare*) to honour; (*fare onore a*) to do credit to.

onorario, -a *agg* (*cittadinanza, console*) honorary ♦ *sm* fee.

onore *sm* honour; **fare ~ a qc** (*pranzo*) to do justice to sthg; (*scuola, famiglia*) to be a credit to sthg; **in ~ di** in honour of; **fare gli onori di casa** to be the host (*f* hostess); **farsi ~** to distinguish o.s.

onorevole (*parlamentare*) Honourable ♦ *smf* = Member of Parliament (*Br*), = Congressman (*f* Congresswoman) (*Am*).

ONU *(abbr di Organizzazione delle Nazioni Unite)* UN.

opaco, -a, -chi, -che *agg (vetro)* opaque; *(colore, metallo)* dull.

opera *sf* work; *(in musica)* opera; **è tutta ~ sua!** it's all his doing!; **mettersi all'~** to get down to work; **~ d'arte** work of art; **opere pubbliche** public works.

operaio, -a *agg* working-class ♦ *sm, f* worker.

operare *vt (realizzare)* to carry out; *(MED)* to operate on ♦ *vi (agire)* to act ❏ **operarsi** *vr (compiersi)* to take place; *(subire un'operazione)* to have an operation.

operatore, -trice *sm, f (di televisione, cinema)* cameraman *(f* camerawoman); **~ turistico** tour operator.

operazione *sf* operation; *(FIN)* transaction.

opinione *sf* opinion; **l'~ pubblica** public opinion.

opporre *vt (argomenti, ragioni)* to put forward; **~ resistenza** to put up some resistance; **~ un rifiuto** to refuse ❏ **opporsi** *vr:* **opporsi (a)** to oppose.

opportunità *sf inv* opportunity.

opportuno, -a *agg* opportune.

opposizione *sf* opposition.

opposto, -a *pp* → **opporre** ♦ *agg (lato, senso)* opposite; *(idee)* opposing ♦ *sm* opposite.

oppressione *sf* oppression.

oppresso, -a *pp* → **opprimere.**

opprimente *agg* oppressive.

opprimere *vt (popolo).* to oppress; *(angosciare)* to weigh down.

oppure *cong (o invece)* or; *(se no)* or else, otherwise.

optare : optare per *v + prep* to opt for.

opuscolo *sm* brochure.

ora *sf* hour; *(momento)* time ♦ *avv* now; **a che ~ parte il treno?** what time does the train leave?; **è ~ di partire** it's time to leave; **che ~ è?, che ore sono?** what's the time?; **e ~?** now what?; **~ come ~** right now; **~ legale** summertime; **~ locale** local time; **~ di punta** rush hour; **50 km all'~** 50 km an hour; **di buon'~** early; **d'~ in poi** o **in avanti** from now on; **fare le ore piccole** to stay up till the small hours.

orale *agg & sm* oral.

oramai → **ormai.**

orario, -a *agg (segnale)* time *(dav s)*; *(velocità)* per hour; *(tariffa)* hourly ♦ *sm (di lavoro, visite)* hours *(pl)*; *(tabella)* timetable; **fuori ~** after hours; **in ~** on time; **~ di arrivo** arrival time; **~ di partenza** departure time; **~ di apertura** opening hours *(pl)*; **~ di chiusura** closing time; **~ d'ufficio** office hours *(pl)*.

orata *sf* sea bream.

orbita *sf (di satellite)* orbit; *(di occhio)* eye socket.

orchestra *sf* orchestra.

ordigno *sm* device.

ordinare *vt (al ristorante, bar)* to order; *(disporre in ordine)* to put in order; *(comandare):* **~ a qn di fare**

qc to order sb to do sthg.

ordinario, -a *agg (normale)*
ordinary; *(mediocre, scadente)* poor.

ordinato, -a *agg* tidy.

ordinazione *sf* order.

ordine *sm* order; **essere in ~**
(stanza) to be tidy; *(documenti)* to
be in order; **mettere in ~ qc** *(stanza)* to tidy sthg; *(documenti)* to put
sthg in order; **~ pubblico** public
order.

orecchiabile *agg* catchy.

orecchiette *sfpl* tiny ear-shaped
pasta from Puglia.

orecchino *sm* earring.

orecchio *(pl f* **orecchie)** *sm* ear;
avere ~ to have a good ear (for
music).

orecchioni *smpl* mumps *(sg).*

oreficeria *sf (negozio)* jeweller's.

orfano, -a *agg & sm, f* orphan.

organico, -a, -ci, -che *agg*
organic ♦ *sm* staff.

organismo *sm (essere vivente)*
organism; *(ente)* body.

organizzare *vt* to organize ❑
organizzarsi *vr* to organize o.s.

organizzato, -a *agg* organized.

organizzatore, -trice *sm, f*
organizer.

organizzazione *sf* organization.

organo *sm* organ.

orgasmo *sm* orgasm.

orgoglio *sm* pride.

orgoglioso, -a *agg* proud.

orientale *agg (paese, prodotto)*
eastern; *(persona)* oriental ♦ *smf*

Oriental.

orientamento *sm (posizione)*
orientation; *(fig: indirizzo)* leanings
(pl); **perdere l'~** to lose one's bear-
ings; **~ professionale** careers guidance.

orientare *vt (carta)* to orientate
❑ **orientarsi** *vr* to find one's bear-
ings.

oriente *sm* east ❑ **Oriente** *sm:*
l'Oriente the East.

origano *sm* oregano.

originale *agg* original; *(stravagante)* eccentric ♦ *sm* original.

originario, -a *agg (iniziale)*
original; *(paese, lingua)* native.

origine *sf* origin; *(causa)* origin,
cause; **avere ~ da qc** to originate
from sthg; **dare ~ a qc** to cause
sthg; **di ~ italiana** of Italian origin.

origliare *vi* to eavesdrop.

orina = **urina.**

oriundo, -a *sm, f:* **essere ~ italiano** to be of Italian extraction.

orizzontale *agg* horizontal.

orizzonte *sm* horizon.

orlo *sm (di fosso)* edge; *(di bicchiere)* rim; *(di gonna, pantaloni)*
hem.

orma *sf* footprint.

ormai *avv (a questo punto)* by
now; *(a quel punto)* by then; *(quasi)*
almost; **~ è tardi** it's too late now.

ormeggiare *vt & vi* to moor.

ormeggio *sm* mooring.

ormone *sm* hormone.

ornamento *sm* ornament.

ornare *vt* to decorate.

oro *sm* gold; **d'~** gold.

orologio *sm* clock; *(da polso)*

watch.

oroscopo sm horoscope.

orrendo, -a agg (spaventoso, atroce) horrendous; (brutto) horrible, awful.

orribile agg horrible.

orrore sm horror.

orsacchiotto sm teddy bear.

orso sm bear.

ortaggio sm vegetable.

ortica, -che sf nettle.

orticaria sf hives (pl).

orto sm vegetable garden.

ortodosso, -a agg orthodox.

ortografia sf spelling.

orzaiolo sm stye.

orzo sm barley.

osare vt: ~ (fare qc) to dare (to do sthg).

osceno, -a agg obscene.

oscillare vi (dondolare) to swing; (fig: variare) to vary.

oscillazione sf (di pendolo) swing; (di prezzi) fluctuation; (di temperatura) variation.

oscurità sf darkness.

oscuro, -a agg dark ♦ sm: essere all'~ di qc to be in the dark about sthg.

ospedale sm hospital.

ospitale agg (persona) hospitable; (paese) friendly.

ospitalità sf hospitality; mi ha dato ~ per una notte he put me up for a night.

ospitare vt to put up.

ospite smf (chi ospita) host (f hostess); (ospitato) guest.

ospizio sm old people's home.

ossa pl → osso.

osseo, -a agg bone (dav s).

osservare vt (guardare) to observe, to watch; (rilevare) to notice; (rispettare, mantenere) to observe; far ~ qc a qn to point sthg out to sb.

osservatorio sm observatory.

osservazione sf (esame) observation; (commento) observation, remark; (rimprovero) criticism.

ossessionare vt to obsess.

ossessione sf obsession.

ossia cong that is.

ossidare vt to oxidize ❏ ossidarsi vr to oxidize.

ossido sm oxide; ~ di carbonio carbon monoxide.

ossigenare vt to oxygenate; (capelli) to bleach.

ossigeno sm oxygen.

osso sm (umano: pl f ossa) bone; (di carne: pl m ossi) bone.

ossobuco (pl ossibuchi) sm veal knuckle cooked on the bone in tomatoes and white wine (a speciality of Milan).

ostacolare vt to obstruct.

ostacolo sm obstacle; (in atletica) hurdle; (in equitazione) fence.

ostaggio sm hostage.

ostello sm: ~ (della gioventù) (youth) hostel.

ostentare vt to flaunt.

osteria sf inn.

ostetrica, -che sf midwife.

ostia sf (RELIG) host.

ostile agg hostile.

ostilità sf hostility ♦ sfpl (MIL) hostilities.

ostinarsi *vr*: ~ **a fare qc** to persist in doing sthg.

ostinato, -a *agg* obstinate.

ostinazione *sf* persistence.

ostrica, -che *sf* oyster.

ostruire *vt* to obstruct, to block.

ottanta *num* eighty, → **sei**.

ottantesimo, -a *num* eightieth, → **sesto**.

ottantina *sf*: **una ~ (di)** about eighty; **essere sull'~** to be in one's eighties.

ottavo, -a *num* eighth, → **sesto**.

ottenere *vt* to get.

ottico, -a, -ci, -che *agg* (*nervo*) optic; (*strumento*) optical ◆ *sm* optician.

ottimale *agg* optimum.

ottimismo *sm* optimism.

ottimista, -i, -e *smf* optimist.

ottimo, -a *agg* excellent, very good.

otto *num* eight, → **sei** ◆ *sm*: ~ **volante** roller coaster.

ottobre *sm* October, → **settembre**.

ottocento *num* eight hundred, → **sei** ▫ **Ottocento** *sm*: **l'Ottocento** the nineteenth century.

ottone *sm* brass.

otturare *vt* to fill.

otturazione *sf* filling.

ottuso, -a *agg* obtuse.

ovale *agg* oval.

ovatta *sf* cotton wool.

overdose *sf inv* overdose.

ovest *sm & agg inv* west; **a ~ (di qc)** west (of sthg).

ovile *sm* sheepfold.

ovino, -a *agg* sheep (*dav s*).

ovovia *sf* ski lift (*with oval cabins*).

ovunque = **dovunque**.

ovvero *cong* or, in other words.

ovviare *vi*: ~ **a qc** to avoid sthg.

ovvio, -a *agg* obvious.

ozio *sm* idleness.

ozono *sm* ozone.

P

pacato, -a *agg* calm.

pacca, -che *sf* pat.

pacchetto *sm* (*di sigarette, caramelle*) packet; (*pacco*) parcel.

pacchiano, -a *agg* garish.

pacco, -chi *sm* parcel.

pace *sf* peace; **in ~** in peace; **fare (la) ~** to make it up.

pacemaker [pei'smæker] *sm inv* pacemaker.

pacifico, -a, -ci, -che *agg* peaceful ▫ **Pacifico** *sm*: **il Pacifico** the Pacific.

pacifista, -i, -e *agg & smf* pacifist.

padella *sf* (*da cucina*) frying pan; (*per malati*) bedpan.

padiglione *sm* (*di ospedale, fiera*) pavilion; (*di giardino*) marquee.

Padova *sf* Padua.

padre *sm* father.

padrino *sm* godfather.

padrone, -a *sm, f* owner; **essere ~ di fare qc** to be free to do sthg; **~ di casa** landlord (*f* landlady).

paesaggio *sm* landscape; (*panorama*) scenery.

paese *sm* (*nazione*) country; (*villaggio*) village; **~ di provenienza** country of origin; **mandare qn a quel ~** (*volg*) to tell sb to get lost ❑ **Paesi Bassi** *smpl*: **i Paesi Bassi** the Netherlands.

paffuto, -a *agg* plump, chubby.

paga, -ghe *sf* pay.

pagamento *sm* payment; **'~ pedaggio'** 'toll to be paid here'.

pagano, -a *agg & sm, f* pagan.

pagare *vt* to pay; (*offrire*) to buy; **quanto l'hai pagato?** how much did you pay for it?; **~ con assegno** to pay by cheque; **~ con carta di credito** to pay by credit card; **~ in contanti** to pay cash.

pagella *sf* (school) report.

pagina *sf* page.

paglia *sf* straw.

pagliaccio *sm* clown.

pagnotta *sf* round loaf.

paio (*pl f* **paia**) *sm* pair; **un ~ di** (*alcuni*) a couple of; **un ~ di scarpe** a pair of shoes.

Pakistan *sm*: **il ~** Pakistan.

pala *sf* (*vanga*) shovel; (*di mulino, elica*) blade.

palato *sm* palate.

palazzo *sm* (*signorile*) palace; (*edificio*) building; (*condominio*) block of flats (*Br*), apartment building (*Am*); **~ di giustizia** law courts (*pl*); **~ dello sport** indoor stadium.

palco, -chi *sm* (*palcoscenico*) stage; (*pedana*) stand; (*a teatro*) box.

palcoscenico, -ci *sm* stage.

Palermo *sf* Palermo.

Palestina *sf*: **la ~** Palestine.

palestra *sf* gymnasium.

paletta *sf* (*giocattolo, per giardiniere*) spade; (*per lo sporco*) dustpan; (*di polizia, capostazione*) signalling disc.

paletto *sm* stake.

palio *sm*: **mettere qc in ~** to offer sthg as a prize ❑ **Palio** *sm*: **il Palio (di Siena)** the Palio (*traditional horse race held in the centre of Siena*).

IL PALIO DI SIENA

Siena's famous horse race attracts thousands of visitors to Tuscany on July 2 and August 16 every year. Representatives of Siena's 17 "contrade" (districts) parade in Renaissance costumes, and 10 districts enter a horse and rider in the race which follows. The race is very rough, and the walls of the Piazza del Campo are padded to protect the contestants. The winner is awarded a "palio" (painted banner), and is paraded through the town.

---

palla *sf* ball; **che palle!** (*volg*) what a drag!

pallacanestro *sf* basketball.

pallanuoto *sf* water polo.

pallavolo *sf* volleyball.

pallido, -a *agg* pale.

palloncino *sm* balloon.

pallone sm (palla) ball; (da calcio) football; ~ **aerostatico** hot air balloon.

pallottola sf bullet.

palma sf palm tree.

palmo sm palm.

palo sm (di legno) post; (di telefono) pole; ~ **della luce** lamppost.

palombaro sm (deep sea) diver.

palpebra sf eyelid.

palude sf marsh, swamp.

panca, -che sf bench.

pancarrè sm sliced bread.

pancetta sf bacon.

panchina sf (di parco) bench; (di giardino) garden seat.

pancia, -ce sf (fam) belly.

panciotto sm waistcoat.

panda sm inv panda.

pandoro sm conical sponge cake eaten at Christmas.

pane sm bread; (pagnotta) loaf; (di burro) block; ~ **a** o **in cassetta** sliced bread; ~ **integrale** wholemeal bread; ~ **tostato** toast; **pan dolce** Christmas cake with candied fruit (a speciality of Genoa); **pan di Spagna** sponge cake.

 i PANE

A staple of the Mediterranean diet, bread is eaten with all Italian meals and waiters bring it automatically to the restaurant table. The main varieties are "pane bianco" (white bread), which is either "comune" (plain) or "speciale" (made with oil), and "pane integrale" (wholemeal bread). It is sold in loaves or sticks or as rolls, and its shapes and names differ from region to region and city to city.

---

panetteria sf bakery.

panettone sm traditional dome-shaped Christmas cake containing raisins and candied fruit.

panforte sm very rich round, flat cake made with almonds, hazelnuts, candied fruits and spices (a speciality of Siena).

pangrattato sm breadcrumbs (pl).

panico sm panic.

panificio sm baker's.

panino sm roll; ~ **imbottito** o **ripieno** filled roll; ~ **al prosciutto** ham roll.

paninoteca, -che sf sandwich bar.

panna sf: ~ **(montata)** whipped cream; ~ **cotta** cold dessert made from cream and sugar, eaten with chocolate or fruit sauce; ~ **da cucina** cream.

panne : **in panne** agg inv: **ho l'auto in** ~ my car has broken down.

pannello sm panel.

panno sm cloth; **mettersi nei panni di qn** to put o.s. in sb's shoes.

pannocchia sf cob.

pannolino sm nappy (Br), diaper (Am).

panorama, -i sm panorama.

panoramico, -a, -ci, -che agg panoramic.

panpepato sm = gingerbread.

pantaloni *smpl* trousers *(Br)*, pants *(Am)*.

pantera *sf* panther.

pantofole *sfpl* slippers.

panzanella *sf* Tuscan salad of tomatoes, anchovies, tuna, onion and herbs, whose special ingredient is moistened bread.

panzerotti *smpl* large ravioli stuffed with cheese and tomato, and fried in oil.

paonazzo, -a *agg* purple.

papà *sm inv (fam)* daddy, dad.

papavero *sm* poppy.

papera *sf (errore):* **fare una ~ to** make a slip of the tongue, → **papero.**

papero, -a *sm, f* gosling.

papillon [papi'jon] *sm inv* bow tie.

pappa *sf (fam)* baby food.

pappagallo *sm (animale)* parrot; *(per malati)* bedpan.

pappardelle *sfpl* large noodles; **~ alla lepre** 'pappardelle' served with hare sauce.

paprica *sf* paprika.

para *sf* crepe rubber.

parabola *sf (MAT)* parabola; *(RELIG)* parable.

parabrezza *sm inv* windscreen.

paracadute *sm inv* parachute.

paracarro *sm* post.

paradiso *sm (RELIG)* paradise, heaven.

paradossale *agg* paradoxical.

paradosso *sm* paradox.

parafango, -ghi *sm* mudguard.

parafulmine *sm* lightning conductor.

paraggi *smpl:* **nei ~** in the neighbourhood.

paragonare *vt:* **~ con** to compare with.

paragone *sm* comparison.

paragrafo *sm* paragraph.

paralisi *sf inv* paralysis.

paralizzare *vt* to paralyse.

parallela *sf* parallel □ **parallele** *sfpl (attrezzo)* parallel bars.

parallelo, -a *agg & sm* parallel.

paralume *sm* lampshade.

parapetto *sm* parapet.

parare *vt (colpi)* to parry; *(occhi)* to shield; *(nel calcio)* to save.

parassita, -i *sm* parasite.

parata *sf (militare)* parade; *(nel calcio)* save.

paraurti *sm inv* bumper.

paravento *sm* screen.

parcella *sf* fee.

parcheggiare *vt* to park.

parcheggio *sm (area)* car park *(Br)*, parking lot *(Am)*; *(manovra)* parking; **~ a pagamento** car park where drivers must pay to park; **~ riservato** private car park.

parchimetro *sm* parking meter.

parco, -chi *sm* park; **~ giochi** o **dei divertimenti** swing park.

---

i **PARCHI NAZIONALI**

F ive Italian national parks have been created by the government to protect the environment and preserve the balance of nature in these designated areas. They are areas of great natural beauty, and are well equipped to welcome visitors. In the Alps the Parco del Gran Paradiso shelters the ibex, and the Parco dello Stelvio the chamois. In the central Apennines are the Parco Nazionale d'Abruzzo and the Parco del Circeo, and in the south is the Parco Nazionale della Calabria.

parecchio, -a *agg* quite a lot of ◆ *pron* quite a lot ◆ *avv (con agg)* quite; *(con verbo)* quite a lot; **è ~ (tempo)** che aspetto I've been waiting for quite a while.

pareggiare *vt (capelli, orlo)* to make even; *(terreno)* to level; *(bilancio, conti)* to balance ◆ *vi* to draw.

pareggio *sm (in partite)* draw; *(del bilancio)* balance.

parente *smf* relative.

parentela *sf (vincolo)* relationship; *(famiglia)* relatives *(pl)*.

parentesi *sf inv (segno)* bracket; *(commento)* digression; **tra ~ in** brackets.

pareo *sm* pareo.

parere *sm (opinione)* opinion ◆ *vi (sembrare)* to seem; *(apparire)* to look ◆ *v impers*: **pare che** it seems that; **che te ne pare?** what do you think?; **fate come vi pare** do as you like; **mi pare di no** I don't think so; **mi pare di sì** I think so; **mi pare (che) vada bene** it seems (to be) all right; **pare (che) sia vero** it seems (to be) true.

parete *sf (di stanza)* wall; *(di montagna)* face.

pari *agg inv (in partite, giochi,* *superficie)* level; *(numero)* even ◆ *sm inv* equal; **alla ~ *(ragazza)*** au pair; **ora siamo ~** now we're even; **essere ~ a *(uguale)*** to be the same as, to be equal to; **essere alla ~** to be even; **mettersi in ~ con qc** to catch up with sthg; **~ ~** word for word.

Parigi *sf* Paris.

parlamentare *agg* parliamentary ◆ *smf* = Member of Parliament *(Br)*, = Congressman (f Congresswoman) *(Am)*.

parlamento *sm* parliament.

parlantina *sf (fam)*: **avere una buona ~** to have the gift of the gab.

parlare *vi* to talk, to speak ◆ *vt (lingua)* to speak; **~ (a qn) di** to talk o to speak (to sb) about; **parla italiano?** do you speak Italian?

Parma *sf* Parma.

parmigiano *sm* Parmesan (cheese).

parola *sf* word; **prendere la ~** to (begin to) speak; **rivolgere la ~ a qn** to talk to sb; **rimangiarsi la ~** to go back on one's word; **~ d'onore** word of honour; **~ d'ordine** password; **parole crociate** crossword (puzzle) *(sg)*; **è una ~!** it's not easy!

parolaccia, -ce *sf* swearword.

parrocchia *sf (chiesa)* parish church; *(zona)* parish.

parroco, -ci *sm* parish priest.

parrucca, -che *sf* wig.

parrucchiere, -a *sm, f (per signora)* hairdresser.

parso, -a *pp* → **parere**.

parte *sf (di stanza)* part; *(lato)* side; *(direzione)* way; *(quota)* share; *(DIR)* party; **fare ~ di qc** to be part of sthg; **mettere da ~ qc** *(risparmiare)* to put sthg aside; **prendere ~ a qc** to take part in sthg; **stare dalla ~ di** to be on the side of; **la maggior ~ di** most of; **la maggior ~ degli italiani** most Italians; **a ~ questo** apart from that; **a ~** *(spese, pacco)* separate; *(pagare, incartare)* separately; **da ~ di qn** from; *(ringraziare)* on sb's behalf; **d'altra ~** on the other hand; **dall'altra ~** the other way; **da nessuna ~** nowhere; **da ogni ~** everywhere; **da qualche ~** somewhere; **da questa ~** this way; **in ~** partly.

partecipare : partecipare a *v + prep* *(intervenire)* to take part in; *(spese)* to contribute to; *(gioia, dolore)* to share in.

partenza *sf* departure; *(nello sport)* start; **essere in ~ (per Roma)** to be about to leave (for Rome); **'partenze nazionali/internazionali'** 'domestic/international departures'.

participio *sm* participle.

particolare *agg* particular; *(caratteristico)* distinctive ◆ *sm* detail; **niente di ~** nothing special; **in ~** in particular.

particolareggiato, -a *agg* detailed.

partigiano, -a *sm, f* partisan.

partire *vi* *(persona)* to leave; *(treno, aereo)* to depart; *(nello sport)* to start; *(colpo)* to go off; **~ da** from; **parto da Milano alle cinque** I leave Milan at five.

partita *sf* *(competizione)* match; *(a carte, a tennis)* game; *(di merce)* consignment; **~ IVA** VAT registra-

tion number.

partito *sm* party.

parto *sm* birth.

partorire *vt* to give birth to.

parziale *agg* *(limitato)* partial; *(ingiusto)* biased.

pascolo *sm* pasture.

Pasqua *sf* Easter.

pasquale *agg* Easter *(dav s)*.

Pasquetta *sf* Easter Monday.

 PASQUETTA

In Italy, Easter still retains its religious significance. Holy Week culminates in a Mass celebrated by the Pope from the balcony of St Peter's, and on Easter Sunday families have a special lunch and exchange Easter eggs. In many regions Easter Monday, a national holiday, is called "Pasquetta". It is traditionally celebrated with a picnic in the country or by the sea.

---

passabile *agg* passable.

passaggio *sm* *(transito)* passage; *(varco)* thoroughfare; *(in macchina)* lift; *(cambiamento)* change; **essere di ~** to be passing through; **~ a livello** level crossing *(Br)*, grade crossing *(Am)*; **~ pedonale** pedestrian crossing.

passamontagna *sm inv* balaclava.

passante *smf* *(persona)* passerby ◆ *sm* *(per cintura)* loop.

passaporto *sm* passport.

passare *vi* to go by; *(da un'apertura)* to go through; *(fare una visita)* to call in; *(cessare)* to go away;

(proposta) to be passed ♦ *vt (attraversare)* to cross; *(trascorrere)* to spend; *(cera, vernice)* to apply; *(esame)* to pass; *(oltrepassare)* to go beyond; *(verdure)* to puree; *(porgere)* to pass; **mi è passato di mente!** it slipped my mind!; **ti passo Matteo** *(al telefono)* here's Matteo; **il treno passa da Firenze** the train goes via Florence; **~ l'aspirapolvere** to vacuum; **qc a qn** to pass O to give sb sthg; **~ avanti a qn** to push in front of sb; **~ da** O **per scemo** to be taken for a fool; **~ sopra qc** *(fig: tollerare)* to overlook; **passarsela bene** to get on well; **come te la passi?** how are you getting on?

passatempo *sm* pastime.

passato, -a *agg (trascorso)* over ♦ *sm* past; **~ di verdure** thin vegetable soup.

passaverdura *sm inv* vegetable mill.

passeggero, -a *agg* passing ♦ *sm, f* passenger.

passeggiare *vi* to walk.

passeggiata *sf (camminata)* walk; *(strada)* promenade; **fare una ~** to take a walk.

PASSEGGIATA

The Italian custom of taking a stroll with friends or family has survived many changes in fashion and still brings different generations together. Courting couples, families and teenagers alike meet up on Sunday morning or in the late afternoon and stroll slowly round the main square or the park, or along the main street or the promenade. They may stop to say hello to friends and acquaintances, to have an aperitif or to buy cakes and pastries for dessert.

passeggino *sm* pushchair.

passeggio *sm*: **andare a ~** to go for a walk.

passerella *sf (passaggio)* footbridge; *(di aereo, nave)* gangway; *(di sfilata)* catwalk.

passerotto *sm* sparrow.

passione *sf* passion.

passivo, -a *agg* passive ♦ *sm (GRAMM)* passive; *(COMM)* liabilities *(pl)*.

passo *sm (movimento)* step; *(andatura)* pace; *(rumore)* footstep; *(valico)* pass; **allungare il ~** to quicken one's pace; **fare il primo ~** *(fig)* to make the first move; **a d'uomo** dead slow; **'~ carraio** O **carrabile'** 'keep clear'; **fare due quattro passi** to go for a short walk; **a due passi** a stone's throw away; **di questo ~** at this rate.

pasta *sf* pasta; *(impasto)* dough; *(pasticcino)* pastry; *(di colla)* paste; **in brodo** soup with pasta in it; **~ frolla** shortcrust pastry; **~ sfoglia** puff pastry.

PASTA

Most Italians eat pasta at least once a day, and an infinite variety of types can be found: "spaghetti", "bucatini" and "tagliatelle" are just a few examples of "pasta lunga" (long pasta); "penne", "rigatoni" and "fusilli" are common types of "pasta corta" (short pasta). The basic dough is just flour and water, but it can be varied by using a different type of flour and by adding different ingredients and flavourings. "Pasta integrale" is wholemeal pasta, "pasta all'uovo" is enriched with egg, and "pasta verde" is flavoured with spinach. The tradition of making one's own pasta ("pasta fatta in casa") still survives in many families.

---

pastasciutta *sf* pasta.

pastella *sf* batter.

pasticca, -che = pastiglia.

pasticceria *sf* = cake shop.

pasticcino *sm* pastry.

pasticcio *sm (vivanda)* pie; *(disordine)* mess; *(guaio)* trouble; **essere nei pasticci** to be in trouble.

pasticcione, -a *sm, f* bungler.

pastiera *sf Neapolitan Easter tart with a filling of ricotta cheese and candied fruit*.

pastiglia *sf* pastille.

pastizzada *sf horse meat or beef and vegetables marinated in wine, generally served with polenta (a speciality of Veneto)*.

pasto *sm* meal.

pastore *sm (di greggi)* shepherd; *(sacerdote)* minister; ~ **tedesco** German shepherd, Alsatian *(Br)*.

pastorizzato, -a *agg* pasteurized.

patata *sf* potato; **patate fritte** chips *(Br)*, French fries *(Am)*.

patatine *sfpl* crisps *(Br)*, chips *(Am)*.

pâté *sm inv* pâté.

patente *sf* licence; ~ **(di guida)** driving licence *(Br)*, driver's license *(Am)*.

paternità *sf* paternity.

paterno, -a *agg* paternal.

patetico, -a, -ci, -che *agg* pathetic.

patire *vt & vi* to suffer.

patria *sf* homeland.

patrigno *sm* stepfather.

patrimonio *sm (beni)* property; *(culturale, spirituale)* heritage.

patrono *sm* patron saint.

pattinaggio *sm* skating; ~ **su ghiaccio** ice skating.

pattinare *vi* to skate; ~ **su ghiaccio** to ice-skate.

pattini *smpl*: ~ **a rotelle** roller skates; ~ **da ghiaccio** ice skates.

pattino *sm pedalo with oars*.

patto *sm (accordo)* pact; **a ~ che** on condition that.

pattuglia *sf* patrol.

pattumiera *sf* dustbin.

paura *sf* fear; **avere ~ (di)** to be afraid (of); **avere ~ di fare qc** to be afraid of doing sthg; **fare ~ a qn** to frighten sb; **per ~ di fare qc** for fear of doing sthg; **per ~ che** for fear that.

pauroso, -a *agg (spaventoso)* frightening; *(timoroso)* fearful.

pausa *sf (intervallo)* break; *(MUS)* pause; **fare una ~** to take a break.

pavimento *sm* floor.

pavone *sm* peacock.

paziente *agg & smf* patient.

pazienza *sf* patience; **perdere la ~** to lose one's patience; **~!** never mind!

pazzamente *avv* madly.

pazzesco, -a, -schi, -sche *agg* crazy.

pazzia *sf* madness; *(azione)* crazy thing.

pazzo, -a *agg (malato)* mad ◆ *sm, f* madman *(f* madwoman); **andare ~ per qc** to be crazy about sthg; **essere ~ di qn** to be crazy about sb; **darsi alla pazza gioia** to live it up.

peccare *vi* to sin; **~ di qc** to be guilty of sthg.

peccato *sm* sin; **è un ~ che ...** it's a pity that ...; **(che) ~!** what a pity!

peccatore, -trice *sm, f* sinner.

pecora *sf* sheep.

pecorino *sm* a cheese made from ewe's milk.

pedaggio *sm* toll.

pedalare *vi* to pedal.

pedale *sm* pedal; **a pedali** pedal *(dav s)*.

pedana *sf (poggiapiedi)* footboard; *(in atletica)* springboard; *(nella scherma)* piste.

pedata *sf (impronta)* footmark; *(calcio)* kick.

pediatra, -i, -e *smf* pediatrician.

pedicure *sm* pedicure.

pedina *sf* piece.

pedonale *agg* pedestrian *(dav s)*.

pedone *sm* pedestrian; *(negli scacchi)* pawn.

peggio *avv & agg inv* worse ◆ *smf*: **il/la ~** the worst; **~ per te!** so

much the worse for you!; **temere il ~** to fear the worst; **alla ~** if the worst comes to the worst; **~ che mai** worse than ever.

peggioramento *sm* deterioration.

peggiorare *vt & vi* to worsen.

peggiore *agg (comparativo)* worse; *(superlativo)* worst ◆ *smf*: **il/la ~** the worst.

pelare *vt* to peel.

pelato, -a *agg* bald □ **pelati** *smpl* peeled tomatoes.

pelle *sf* skin; *(conciata)* leather; **avere la ~ d'oca** to have goose pimples.

pellegrinaggio *sm* pilgrimage.

pelletteria *sf (prodotti)* leather goods *(pl)*; *(negozio)* leather goods shop.

pelliccia, -ce *sf (di animale)* fur; *(indumento)* fur coat.

pellicola *sf* film; **~ a colori** colour film.

pelo *sm (del corpo, di tessuto)* hair; *(di animale)* fur; **ce l'ho fatta per un ~** I made it by the skin of my teeth; **c'è mancato un ~ che lo investissero** they narrowly missed hitting him.

peloso, -a *agg* hairy.

peltro *sm* pewter.

peluche [pe'luʃ] *sm inv (tessuto)* plush; *(pupazzo)* cuddly toy.

pena *sf (condanna)* sentence; *(cruccio)* anxiety; *(pietà)* pity; *(RELIG)* torment; **mi fanno ~** I feel sorry for them; **(non) vale la ~ di andarci** it's (not) worth going; **~ di morte** death penalty; **a mala ~** hardly.

penalità *sf inv* penalty.

pendente *agg (appeso)* hanging; *(conto)* pending ♦ *sm (ciondolo)* pendant; *(orecchino)* drop earring.

pendenza *sf (inclinazione)* slope; *(di conto)* outstanding account.

pendere *vi (essere appeso)* to hang; *(essere inclinato)* to slope.

pendici *sfpl* slopes.

pendio *sm* slope.

pendola *sf* pendulum clock.

pendolare *smf* commuter.

pene *sm* penis.

penetrare *vi*: ~ **in** qc *(entrare in)* to enter sthg; *(sog: chiodo, liquido)* to penetrate sthg.

penicillina *sf* penicillin.

penisola *sf* peninsula.

penitenza *sf (religiosa)* penitence; *(nei giochi)* forfeit.

penitenziario *sm* prison.

penna *sf* pen; *(di uccello)* feather; **~ a sfera** ballpoint pen; **~ stilografica** fountain pen; ❏ **penne** *sfpl* pasta quills; **penne all'arrabbiata** *'penne' in a spicy sauce of tomatoes and chillies.*

pennarello *sm* felt-tip pen.

pennello *sm (da pittore)* brush; *(per vernici, tinte)* paintbrush; **~ da barba** shaving brush; **a ~** like a glove.

penombra *sf* half-light.

penoso, -a *agg* painful.

pensare *vi* to think ♦ *vt (immaginare)* to think; *(escogitare)* to think up; **cosa ne pensi?** what do you think (of it)?; **~ a** *(riflettere su, ricordare)* to think about; *(occuparsi di)* to see to; **pensa a un numero**

think of a number; **~ di fare** qc to be thinking of doing sthg; **penso di no** I don't think so; **penso di sì** I think so; **pensarci su** to think it over.

pensiero *sm* thought; *(preoccupazione)* worry; **stare in ~ per** qn to be worried about sb.

pensile *agg* hanging ♦ *sm* wall cupboard.

pensilina *sf (di stazione)* platform roof; *(per autobus)* bus shelter.

pensionante *smf* lodger.

pensionato, -a *sm, f (persona)* pensioner ♦ *sm (per studenti)* hostel.

pensione *sf (somma)* pension; *(albergo)* boardinghouse; *(vitto e alloggio)* board and lodging; **andare in ~** to retire; **essere in ~** to be retired; **~ completa** full board; **mezza ~** half board.

Pentecoste *sf* Whitsun.

pentirsi *vr*: **~ di** qc to regret sthg; **~ di aver fatto** qc to regret doing sthg.

pentola *sf* pot; **~ a pressione** pressure cooker.

penultimo, -a *agg* penultimate.

pepare *vt* to pepper.

pepato, -a *agg* peppery.

pepe *sm* pepper.

peperonata *sf stewed sliced peppers, tomatoes and onions.*

peperoncino *sm* chilli pepper; **~ rosso** red chilli pepper.

peperone *sm (capsicum)* pepper.

per *prep* 1. *(indica lo scopo, la desti-*

nazione) for; **è ~ te** it's for you; **fare qc ~ i soldi** to do sthg for money; **equipaggiarsi ~ la montagna** to kit o.s. out for the mountains; **~ fare qc** (in order) to do sthg; **sono venuto ~ vederti** I've come to see you; **è abbastanza grande ~ capire certe cose** he's old enough to understand these things.

2. *(attraverso)* through; **ti ho cercato ~ tutta la città** I've been looking for you all over town.

3. *(moto a luogo)* for, to; **il treno ~ Genova** the Genoa train; **partire ~ Napoli** to leave for Naples.

4. *(indica una durata, una scadenza)* for; **~ tutta la vita** for one's whole life; **sarò di ritorno ~ le cinque** I'll be back by five; **l'ho vista ~ Pasqua** I saw her at Easter; **fare qc ~ tempo** to do sthg in time; **~ sempre** forever.

5. *(indica il mezzo, il modo)* by; **gli ho parlato ~ telefono** I talked to him over the phone; **viaggiare ~ mare** to travel by sea; **fare qc ~ scherzo** to do sthg for a joke; **~ caso** by chance.

6. *(indica la causa)* for; **piangere ~ la rabbia** to cry with rage; **viaggiare ~ lavoro** to travel on business; **~ aver fatto qc** for doing sthg.

7. *(con valore distributivo)* per; **entrare uno ~ volta** to go in one at a time; **uno ~ uno** one by one.

8. *(come)* as; **tenere qc ~ certo** to take sthg for granted.

9. *(indica il prezzo)*: **lo ha venduto ~un milione** he sold it for a million lira.

10. *(MAT)*: **2 ~ 3 fa 6** 2 times 3 makes 6.

11. *(indica la conseguenza)*: **è troppo bello ~ essere vero** it's too good to be true.

12. *(indica limitazione)* for; **~ me, vi sbagliate** as far as I'm concerned, you are wrong; **~ questa volta** this time.

pera *sf* pear.

peraltro *avv* what is more.

perbene *agg inv* decent ◆ *avv* properly.

percentuale *sf* percentage.

percepire *vt* *(sentire)* to perceive; *(ricevere)* to receive.

perché *avv* why; **~ corri?** why are you running?; **~ non ci andiamo?** why don't we go?; **spiegami ~ lo hai fatto** tell me why you did it; **~ no?** why not?; **chissà ~** who knows why; **ecco ~** that's why.

◆ *cong* **1.** *(per il fatto che)* because; **vado ~ ho fretta** I'm going because I'm in a hurry; **~ sì/no!** (just) because!

2. *(affinché)* so that; **telefona ~ non stiano in pensiero** phone so that (they) don't worry.

3. *(cosicché)*: **è troppo complicato ~ si possa capire** it's too complicated for anyone to understand.

◆ *sm inv (ragione)* reason; **senza un ~** for no reason.

perciò *cong* therefore.

percorrere *vt (regione)* to travel over; *(distanza)* to cover.

percorso, -a *pp* → **percorrere** ◆ *sm* journey.

percosse *sfpl* blows.

percosso, -a *pp* → **percuotere**.

percuotere vt (form) to beat.

perdere vt to lose; (treno, lezione, film) to miss; (tempo, denaro) to waste; (liquido, gas) to leak; ~ **sangue** to lose blood; **lasciare** ~ not to bother; **non avere nulla da** ~ to have nothing to lose; ~ **la testa** to lose one's head □ **perdersi** vr to get lost.

perdita sf loss; (di acqua, gas) leak; **una** ~ **di tempo** a waste of time; **a** ~ **d'occhio** as far as the eye can see.

perdonare vt to forgive.

perdono sm (di colpa, peccato) pardon; (scusa) forgiveness.

perdutamente avv desperately.

perfettamente avv perfectly.

perfetto, -a agg perfect.

perfezionare vt to perfect.

perfezione sf perfection; **alla** ~ perfectly.

perfido, -a agg treacherous.

perfino avv even.

perforare vt to pierce.

pergola sf pergola.

pericolante agg unsafe.

pericolo sm danger; **essere fuori** ~ to be out of danger; **essere in** ~ to be in danger; **'**~ **(di morte)'** 'danger of death'.

pericoloso, -a agg dangerous.

periferia sf outskirts (pl).

perimetro sm perimeter.

periodico, -a, -ci, -che agg periodic ♦ sm periodical.

periodo sm period.

perito sm (esperto) expert; ~ **chimico** qualified chemist.

perla sf pearl.

perlustrare vt to patrol.

permaloso, -a agg touchy.

permanente agg permanent ♦ sf perm; **'permanente'** 'at all times'.

permanenza sf continued stay.

permesso, -a pp → **permettere** ♦ sm (autorizzazione) permission; (congedo) leave; (documento) permit; **(è)** ~? (per entrare) may I come in?; ~! (per passare) excuse me!; ~ **di soggiorno** residence permit.

permettere vt to allow; ~ **a qn di fare qc** to allow sb to do sthg; **potersi** ~ **qc** (spesa, acquisto) to be able to afford sthg; **permettersi di fare qc** (prendersi la libertà) to take the liberty of doing sthg; **potersi** ~ **di fare qc** (finanziariamente) to be able to afford to do sthg.

perno sm hinge.

pernottamento sm overnight stay.

però cong (ma) but; (tuttavia) however.

perpendicolare agg perpendicular.

perplesso, -a agg puzzled.

perquisire vt to search.

perquisizione sf search.

perseguitare vt to persecute.

perseverare vi to persevere.

persiana sf shutter.

persiano, -a agg Persian ♦ sm (pelliccia) Persian lamb.

persino = **perfino**.

persistente agg persistent.

perso, -a *pp* → **perdere**.

persona *sf* person; **c'è una ~ che ti aspetta** there's somebody waiting for you; **conoscere qn di ~** to know sb personally; **in ~** in person.

personaggio *sm (di libro, film)* character; *(pubblico, politico)* figure.

personale *agg* personal ♦ *sm (dipendenti)* personnel, staff; *(fisico)* build.

personalità *sf inv* personality.

personalmente *avv* personally.

persuadere *vt* to persuade; **~ qn a fare qc** to persuade sb to do sthg; **~ qn di qc** to convince sb of sthg.

persuaso, -a *pp* → **persuadere**.

pertanto *cong (perciò)* therefore.

perturbare *vt* to upset.

perturbazione *sf* disturbance.

Perugia *sf* Perugia.

pesante *agg* heavy; *(fig: persona, film)* boring; *(scherzo)* in bad taste.

pesare *vt* to weigh ♦ *vi* to weigh; *(essere pesante)* to be heavy; *(essere spiacevole)* to be hard □ **pesarsi** *vr* to weigh o.s.

pesca, -sche *sf (frutto)* peach; *(attività)* fishing; **pesche ripiene** *peaches stuffed with macaroons and baked in white wine;* **andare a ~** to go fishing; **~ di beneficenza** lucky dip; **~ subacquea** underwater fishing.

pescare *vt (pesce)* to catch; *(carta)* to draw; *(trovare)* to find

out; **mi piace ~** I like fishing.

pescatore *sm* fisherman.

pesce *sm* fish; **~ d'aprile!** April Fool! □ **Pesci** *smpl* Pisces *(sg)*.

 PESCE D'APRILE

April 1 is the occasion for tricks and practical jokes in Italy, as it is in Britain, but in Italy it is named after the paper fish which children secretly attach to the backs of their friends and of passers-by. Recently, newspapers have joined in the fun by publishing fake news stories to catch out the unwary.

pescheria *sf* fishmonger's.

pescivendolo, -a *sm, f* fishmonger.

peso *sm* weight; **lancio del ~** shotput; **~ lordo** gross weight; **~ netto** net weight; **essere di ~ a qn** to be a burden on sb.

pessimismo *sm* pessimism.

pessimista, -i, -e *smf* pessimist.

pessimo, -a *agg* dreadful.

pestare *vt (calpestare)* to tread on; *(uva, aglio)* to crush; *(picchiare)* to beat up.

pesto, -a *agg:* **buio ~** pitch-black; **occhio ~** black eye ♦ *sm:* **~ (alla genovese)** pesto *(sauce made from basil, pine kernels, garlic, olive oil and cheese; a speciality of Genoa)*.

petalo *sm* petal.

petardo *sm* firecracker.

petroliera *sf* oil tanker.

petrolio *sm* oil.

pettegolezzi *smpl* gossip *(sg)*.

pettinare *vt* to comb □ **pettinarsi** *vr* to comb one's hair.

pettine *sm* comb.

petto *sm (torace)* chest; *(seno)* breast; **~ di pollo** chicken breast; **a doppio ~** double-breasted.

pezzo *sm* piece; *(di spazio, tempo)* bit; **è un bel ~ che ti cerco** I've been looking for you for quite a while; **andare in (mille) pezzi** to be smashed (to smithereens); **cadere a pezzi** to fall to pieces; **~ di ricambio** spare part; **~ grosso** *(fig)* big shot.

piacere *sm* pleasure; *(favore)* favour ♦ *vi*: **mi piace** I like it; **mi piacciono i tulipani** I like tulips; **mi ha fatto molto ~ vederla** I was delighted to see her; **per ~** please; **~ (di conoscerla)!** pleased to meet you!; **~ mio!** the pleasure is mine!

piacevole *agg* pleasant.

piaga, -ghe *sf (lesione)* sore; *(fig: flagello)* plague.

pianerottolo *sm* landing.

pianeta, -i *sm* planet.

piangere *vi* to cry, to weep.

pianista, -i, -e *smf* pianist.

piano, -a *agg (piatto)* flat; *(MAT)* plane ♦ *avv (lentamente)* slowly; *(a bassa voce)* softly ♦ *sm (di edificio)* floor, storey; *(GEOG & MAT)* plane; *(livello)* level; *(programma, disegno)* plan; *(pianoforte)* piano; **andarci ~** to act with caution; **piano piano** *(poco a poco)* little by little; *(lentamente)* very slowly; **abitano al primo ~** they live on the first floor *(Br)*, they live on the second floor *(Am)*; **il ~ di sopra/di sotto** the floor above/below; **in primo ~** in the foreground.

piano-bar *sm inv* bar with music provided by pianist.

pianoforte *sm* piano.

pianoterra = **pianterreno**.

pianta *sf* plant; *(di piede)* sole; *(di città)* map; *(di casa)* plan; **~ grassa** succulent.

piantare *vt (semi)* to plant; *(conficcare)* to knock in; *(fam: abbandonare)* to leave; **piantala!** stop it!

pianterreno *sm* ground floor *(Br)*, first floor *(Am)*; **al ~** on the ground floor *(Br)*, on the first floor *(Am)*.

pianto *pp* → **piangere** ♦ *sm* crying, weeping.

pianura *sf* plain; **la ~ padana** the Paduan Plain.

piastrella *sf* tile.

piattaforma *sf (superficie piana)* platform; *(galleggiante)* rig.

piattino *sm* saucer.

piatto, -a *agg (piano)* flat; *(monotono)* dreary ♦ *sm (recipiente)* plate, dish; *(vivanda)* dish; *(portata)* course; **~ freddo** cold dish; **~ del giorno** today's special; **~ tipico** typical dish; **primo ~** first course; **secondo ~** second course; **lavare i piatti** to wash the dishes; **piatti pronti** ready meals.

piazza *sf* square; **fare ~ pulita di** to make a clean sweep of.

piazzale *sm* large square.

piazzare *vt (collocare)* to place; *(vendere)* to sell □ **piazzarsi** *vr (in gara)* to be placed.

piccante *agg* spicy.

picchetto sm (di tenda) peg; (di scioperanti, soldati) picket.

picchiare vt (dar botte) to beat (up); (testa, pugni) to bang ♦ vi (alla porta, sul tavolo) to thump; (sole) to beat down; ~ **contro il muro** (urtare) to hit the wall ◻ **picchiarsi** vr to fight.

piccino, -a agg small.

piccione sm pigeon.

picco, -chi sm (vetta) peak; **a** ~ vertically; **colare a** ~ to sink.

piccolo, -a agg small; (breve) short; (di poco conto) slight.

piccozza sf ice-axe.

picnic [pik'nik] sm inv picnic.

pidocchio sm louse.

piede sm foot; (di mobile) leg; **andare a piedi** to go on foot; **essere a piedi** to be on foot; **in piedi** standing; **prendere** ~ to gain ground.

piedistallo sm pedestal.

piega, -ghe sf fold; (di gonna) pleat; (di pantaloni, grinza) crease; **prendere una brutta** ~ to take a turn for the worse.

piegare vt to bend; (foglio, tovaglia) to fold; (letto, sedia) to fold up ◻ **piegarsi** vr (curvarsi) to bend; (letto, sedia) to fold up; **piegarsi a** vr + prep to give in to.

pieghevole agg (flessibile) pliable; (sedia, tavolo) folding.

Piemonte sm: **il** ~ Piedmont.

piena sf flood.

pieno, -a agg full ♦ sm (di carburante) full tank; (culmine) peak; ~ **di** full of; ~ **di sé** full of oneself; **a stomaco** ~ on a full stomach; **in** ~ **inverno** in the middle of winter; **il**

~, **per favore** fill her up, please.

pietà sf (compassione) pity; **avere** ~ **di qn** to take pity on sb; **come attore fa** ~ as an actor he's useless.

pietanza sf dish, course.

pietoso, -a agg (che sente pietà) compassionate; (che ispira pietà) pitiful.

pietra sf stone; ~ **dura** semi-precious stone; ~ **preziosa** precious stone.

pigiama, -i sm pyjamas (pl).

pigiare vt to press.

pigliare vt (prendere) to take; (afferrare) to grab.

pigna sf pine cone.

pignolo, -a agg fussy, meticulous.

pignorare vt (DIR) to distrain.

pigrizia sf laziness.

pigro, -a agg lazy.

pila sf (cumulo) pile; (batteria) battery.

pilastro sm pillar.

pillola sf pill.

pilone sm pylon; (di ponte) pier.

pilota, -i, -e smf (di aereo, nave) pilot; (di auto) driver.

pinacoteca, -che sf art gallery.

pineta sf pinewood.

ping-pong sm table tennis.

pinguino sm (animale) penguin; (gelato) chocolate-coated ice cream on a stick.

pinna sf (di pesce) fin; (per nuotare) flipper.

pino sm (albero) pine tree; (legno) pine.

pinoccate *sfpl*: ~ **alla perugina** *almond and pine kernel sweets*.

pinolo *sm* pine kernel.

pinzare *vt (con graffette)* to staple; *(sog: granchio)* to nip.

pinze *sfpl (utensile)* pliers.

pinzette *sfpl* tweezers.

pinzimonio *sm* dip of seasoned oil.

pioggia, -ge *sf* rain.

piolo *sm* rung.

piombare *vi (giungere)* to arrive unexpectedly; *(fig: nella disperazione)* to plunge; *(gettarsi)*: ~ **su** to fall upon.

piombino *sm (per pacchi)* lead seal; *(da pesca)* sinker.

piombo *sm* lead; **senza** ~ unleaded.

piovere *v impers* to rain ♦ *vi (pietre, proiettili, insulti)* to rain down; *(proteste)* to pour in; **piove** it's raining.

piovigginare *v impers* to drizzle.

piovoso, -a *agg* rainy.

pipa *sf* pipe.

pipì *sf (fam)*: **fare (la)** ~ to have a wee.

pipistrello *sm* bat.

pirata, -i *agg & sm* pirate; ~ **della strada** road hog.

Pirenei *smpl*: **i** ~ the Pyrenees.

pirofila *sf* Pyrex® dish.

piromane *smf* pyromaniac.

piroscafo *sm* steamer.

Pisa *sf* Pisa.

pisarei *smpl*: ~ **e fasò piacentini** *'gnocchi' in a sauce of beans, tomatoes and other vegetables.*

pisciare *vi (volg)* to piss.

piscina *sf* swimming pool.

pisello *sm* pea.

pisolino *sm*: **fare un** ~ to take a nap.

pista *sf (traccia)* trail; *(per corse)* track; *(da sci)* run; *(di aeroporto)* runway; ~ **da ballo** dance floor; ~ **ciclabile** cycle lane.

pistacchio *sm* pistachio.

pistola *sf* pistol, gun.

pitta *sf tart made with a yeasted dough and filled with tomatoes, anchovies, tuna and capers or ricotta cheese and boiled eggs.*

pittore, -trice *sm, f* painter.

pittoresco, -a, -schi, -sche *agg* picturesque.

pittura *sf* painting; '~ **fresca**' 'wet paint'.

pitturare *vt* to paint.

più *avv* 1. *(in comparativi)*: ~ **(di)** more (than); **ho fatto** ~ **tardi del solito** I was later than usual; ~ **triste che mai** sadder than ever; ~ **poco** ~ **di** just over; **di** ~ *(in maggior quantità)* more; **l'ho pagato di** ~ I paid more for it.

2. *(in superlativi)*: **la** ~ **bella città** the most beautiful city; **la collina** ~ **alta** the highest hill; **il** ~ **grande** the biggest; **il** ~ **velocemente possibile** as quickly as possible.

3. *(oltre)* any more; **non parlo** ~ I'm not saying any more; **mai** ~ never again.

4. *(in espressioni)*: ~ **o meno** more or less; **per di** ~ what's more; **tre di** o **in** ~ three more; ~ **ci pensi, peggio è** the more you think about it, the worse it seems.

◆ *prep* **1.** *(con l'aggiunta di)* plus; **siamo in sei ~ gli ospiti** there are six of us plus guests.
2. *(MAT)*: **3 ~ 3 fa 6** 3 plus 3 makes 6.
◆ *agg inv* **1.** *(in quantità, numero maggiore)* more; **ho ~ lavoro del solito** I've got more work than usual; **ho fatto ~ punti di te** I got more points than you; **~ siamo, meglio è** the more of us there are, the better.
2. *(diversi)* several; **l'ho ripetuto ~ volte** I repeated it several times.
◆ *sm inv* **1.** *(la maggior parte)* most; **il ~ delle volte** more often than not; **parlare del ~ e del meno** to talk about this and that.
2. *(la maggioranza)*: **i ~** the majority.

piuma *sf* feather.

piumino. *sm* *(trapunta)* duvet; *(giaccone)* quilted jacket.

piumone® *sm* *(trapunta)* duvet.

piuttosto *avv* rather; **~ che** rather than.

pizza *sf* pizza; **~ capricciosa** *pizza with cheese, tomato, artichokes and capers*; **~ margherita** *pizza with cheese and tomato*; **~ napoletana** *pizza with cheese, tomato, anchovies and capers*; **~ quattro stagioni** *pizza with a different topping on each quarter.*

PIZZA

Originally from Naples, pizza is now internationally popular. In Italy it can be bought at the bar or the baker's, either "al taglio" (cut into rectangles) or as "pizzette" (small pizzas), as well as at pizzerias, which Italians generally go to in the evening. Besides the traditional "margherita" (just cheese and tomato) and "napoletana" (cheese, tomato, anchovies and capers), many other varieties can be found. Pizzas with a mixture of vegetables, with mushrooms, with cold meats, and with different cheeses are particularly popular.

pizzaiola *sf*: **alla ~** *in a tomato, garlic and oregano sauce.*

pizzeria *sf* pizzeria, pizza restaurant.

pizzetta *sf small pizza eaten as a snack.*

pizzicagnolo, -a *sm, f* delicatessen owner.

pizzicare *vt (con le dita)* to pinch; *(pungere)* to sting ◆ *vi (prudere)* to itch; *(cibo)* to be spicy.

pizzicheria *sf* delicatessen.

pizzico, -chi *sm* dash; **un ~ di sale** a pinch of salt.

pizzicotto *sm* pinch.

pizzo *sm (merletto)* lace; *(barba)* goatee.

placare *vt (ira)* to pacify; *(fame, sete)* to satisfy ❑ **placarsi** *vr (vento)* to die down; *(mare)* to become calmer.

placca, -che *sf (targa)* plate; *(dentaria)* plaque.

placcare *vt (rivestire)* to plate; **placcato d'oro** gold-plated.

plagiare *vt (libro, canzone)* to plagiarize; *(persona)* to coerce.

plagio *sm (imitazione)* plagiarism; *(di persona)* coercion.

plancia, -ce *sf* bridge.

planetario, -a *agg* planetary
♦ *sm* planetarium.

plasmare *vt* to mould.

plastica, -che *sf (sostanza)*
plastic; *(MED)* plastic surgery.

plastico, -a, -ci, -che *agg*
plastic ♦ *sm (modello)* model;
(esplosivo) plastic explosive.

plastilina® *sf* Plasticine®.

piatano *sm* plane tree.

piatea *sf (settore)* stalls *(pl); (pub-blico)* audience.

plausibile *agg* plausible.

plico, -chi *sm* parcel.

plurale *agg & sm* plural.

pneumatico, -ci *sm* tyre.

po' = poco.

Po *sm*: il ~ the Po.

poco, -a, -chi, -che *agg* 1. *(in
piccola quantità)* little, not much; **ha
poca fantasia** he doesn't have
much imagination; **a ~ prezzo**
cheap.
2. *(in piccolo numero)*: **pochi** few,
not many; **in poche parole** in few
words.
♦ *sm* little.
♦ *pron* 1. *(una piccola quantità)* (a)
little; *(un piccolo numero)* few, not
many; **pochi** *(non molta gente)*
few (people); **pochi di noi** few of
us.
2. *(in espressioni)*: **aver ~ da fare** to
have little to do; **ci vuole ~ a
capire che ...** it doesn't take much
to understand that ...; **siamo tor-nati da ~** we've just got back; **è
una cosa da ~** it's nothing; **per ~**
nearly; **tra ~** soon, shortly; **(a) ~ a
poco** little by little.
♦ *avv* 1. *(con verbo)* little, not

much; **mangia ~** he doesn't eat
much.
2. *(con aggettivo, avverbio)* not very;
~ lontano da qui not very far from
here; **è ~ simpatica** she's not very
nice; **sta poco bene** he's not very
well.
3. *(indica tempo)*: **durare ~** not to
last long; **~ dopo/prima** shortly
afterwards/before ❑ **un po'** *avv* a
bit, a little; **restiamo ancora un po'**
we'll stay a bit longer; **un po' di** a
bit of, a little; **compra un po' di
pane** buy some bread.

podere *sm* farm.

poderoso, -a *agg* powerful.

podio *sm* podium.

poesia *sf (ARTE)* poetry; *(compo-nimento)* poem.

poeta, -essa, -i, -esse *sm, f*
poet.

poetico, -a, -ci, -che *agg*
poetic.

poggiare *vt* to rest ♦ *vi*: **~ su qc**
to rest on sthg.

poggiatesta *sm inv* headrest.

poi *avv* then; *(dopo)* later.

poiché *cong* as, since.

polare *agg* polar.

polaroid® *sf inv* Polaroid®.

polemica, -che *sf* controversy.

polemico, -a, -ci, -che *agg*
(persona, tono) argumentative; *(di-scorso)* controversial.

polenta *sf* polenta *(type of
savoury porridge made with maize
flour)*; **~ concia valdostana** *'polenta'
cooked with soft cheeses and served
with Parmesan cheese*; **~ e osei**
*'polenta' served with small birds
wrapped in pork loin and flavoured*

with sage (a speciality of Lombardy);
~ pasticciata alla veneta *'polenta'
baked in a meat, tomato and sausage
sauce.*

poliambulatorio *sm* ≈
health centre.

poliestere *sm* polyester.

polistirolo *sm* polystyrene.

politica, -che *sf (scienza)* politics *(sg)*; *(linea di condotta)* policy, →
politico.

politico, -a, -ci, -che *agg*
political ♦ *sm, f* politician.

polizia *sf* police; **~ stradale** traffic police.

poliziesco, -a, -schi, -sche
agg police *(dav s)*; *(romanzo, film)*
detective *(dav s)*.

poliziotto, -a *sm, f* policeman
(f policewoman*)*.

polizza *sf* policy; **~ di assicurazione** insurance policy.

pollaio *sm* hen house.

pollame *sm* poultry.

pollice *sm* thumb; *(unità di
misura)* inch.

polline *sm* pollen.

pollo *sm* chicken; **~ arrosto** roast
chicken; **~ alla cacciatora** *chicken in
a sauce of mushrooms, tomatoes,
olives, herbs and wine;* **~ alla diavola**
*chicken cut open and flattened out,
marinated in lemon juice.*

polmone *sm* lung.

polmonite *sf* pneumonia.

polo *sm* pole ♦ *sf inv* polo shirt; **il
~ Nord/Sud** the North/South Pole.

Polonia *sf*: **la ~** Poland.

polpaccio *sm* calf.

polpastrello *sm* fingertip.

polpetta *sf* meatball.

polpettone *sm* meat loaf.

polpo *sm* octopus.

polsino *sm* cuff.

polso *sm* wrist; *(MED)* pulse.

poltiglia *sf* paste.

poltrona *sf* armchair; *(di teatro)*
seat in the stalls.

poltrone, -a *sm, f* lazy person.

polvere *sf* dust; **latte in ~** powdered milk; **sapone in ~** soap powder.

polveroso, -a *agg* dusty.

pomata *sf* ointment.

pomeridiano, -a *agg* afternoon *(dav s)*.

pomeriggio *sm* afternoon; **di ~**
in the afternoon.

pomice *sf* pumice.

pomo *sm* knob; **~ d'Adamo**
Adam's apple.

pomodoro *sm* tomato; **pomodori ripieni** *tomatoes stuffed with
breadcrumbs, parsley, garlic and egg.*

pompa *sf* pump; *(sfarzo)* pomp;
pompe funebri undertaker's *(sg)*.

pompare *vt* to pump.

Pompei *n* Pompei.

 POMPEI

One of the world's most famous
archaeological sites, the ancient town of Pompei, not far from
Naples, was totally buried in 79 AD
when Mount Vesuvius erupted.
Today it is open to the public, and
offers a unique insight into the
ancient Roman way of life.

---

pompelmo *sm* grapefruit.

pompiere *sm* fireman.

pomposo, -a *agg (sfarzoso)* full of pomp; *(ostentato)* pompous.

ponderare *vt & vi* to ponder.

ponente *sm* west.

ponte *sm* bridge; *(di nave)* deck; *(impalcatura)* scaffolding; ~ **levatoio** drawbridge; **fare il** ~ *to have the day off between a national holiday and a weekend;* **il Ponte Vecchio** the Ponte Vecchio.

 IL PONTE VECCHIO

O ne of Italy's most picturesque bridges, the Ponte Vecchio has come to be the symbol of Florence. Built in 1345 and so the oldest bridge in the city (hence its name), it stands at the narrowest point of the Arno and is connected to the Uffizi Gallery and the Pitti Palace by an arcade. The Ponte Vecchio is famous for the goldsmiths and silversmiths which line it on both sides.

---

pontefice *sm* pontiff.

pony *sm inv* pony; ~ **express** express courier service.

popcorn *sm* popcorn.

popolare *agg* popular; *(popolano)* working-class *(dav s)* ♦ *vt* to populate.

popolarità *sf* popularity.

popolazione *sf* population.

popolo *sm* people *(pl)*.

popone *sm* melon.

poppa *sf (NAUT)* stern.

poppare *vt* to suck (from the breast).

porcellana *sf* porcelain.

porcellino *sm (maialino)* piglet; ~ **d'India** guinea pig.

porcino *sm* cep *(edible brown mushroom with nutty flavour)*.

porco, -ci *sm (animale)* pig; *(carne)* pork.

porcospino *sm* porcupine.

porgere *vt (tendere)* to hold out; *(dare)* to give; **porgo distinti saluti** *(in lettera)* yours sincerely.

pornografico, -a, -ci, -che *agg* pornographic.

poro *sm* pore.

porpora *agg inv* crimson.

porre *vt* to put; *(condizioni, limiti)* to set; *(riporre)* to place; *(supporre)*: **poniamo che ...** let us suppose that ...; ~ **una domanda** to ask a question; ~ **fine a qc** to put an end to sthg.

porro *sm (verdura)* leek; *(MED)* wart.

porta *sf* door; *(di città)* gate; *(nel calcio)* goal.

portabagagli *sm inv (bagagliaio)* boot *(Br)*, trunk *(Am)*; *(sul tetto)* roof rack.

portacenere *sm inv* ashtray.

portachiavi *sm inv* key ring.

portacipria *sm inv* compact.

portaerei *sf inv* aircraft carrier.

portafinestra *(pl* **portefinestre)** *sf* French window.

portafoglio *sm (per denaro)* wallet; *(FIN & POL)* portfolio.

portafortuna *sm inv* lucky charm.

portagioie *sm inv* jewel box.

portalettere = **postino**.

portamento *sm* bearing.

portamonete *sm inv* purse.

portapacchi *sm inv* luggage rack.

portare *vt (trasportare)* to carry; *(condurre, prendere)* to take; *(abiti, occhiali)* to wear; *(barba, capelli lunghi)* to have; *(fig: spingere)* to drive; ~ **qc a qn** *(consegnare)* to take sthg to sb; **portar via** to take; ~ **avanti** to carry on; ~ **fortuna** to bring luck.

portasapone *sm inv* soap dish.

portasigarette *sm inv* cigarette case.

portata *sf (piatto)* course; *(di veicolo)* capacity; *(di fiume)* flow; *(importanza)* importance; **essere a ~ di mano** to be within reach; **alla ~ di tutti** within everybody's grasp.

portatile *agg* portable; ~ **di handicap** disabled.

portatore, -trice *sm, f (di assegno)* bearer.

portatovagliolo *sm* napkin ring.

portauovo *sm inv* eggcup.

portico *sm* portico.

portiera *sf* door.

portiere, -a *sm, f (portinaio)* concierge, caretaker; *(di albergo)* porter; *(nel calcio)* goalkeeper.

portineria *sf (di palazzo)* caretaker's lodge; *(di albergo)* reception.

porto, -a *pp* → **porgere** ◆ *sm* port; ~ **d'armi** licence to carry firearms.

Portogallo *sm*: **il ~** Portugal.

portoghese *agg, sm & sf* Portuguese.

portone *sm* main entrance.

porzione *sf* portion; *(di cibo)* helping.

posa *sf* pose; **mettersi in ~** to pose.

posacenere *sm inv* ashtray.

posare *vt* to put down ◆ *vi* to pose ❑ **posarsi** *vr (uccello)* to perch.

posate *sfpl* cutlery *(sg)*.

positivo, -a *agg* positive.

posizione *sf* position.

posologia *sf* dosage.

possedere *vt (cose)* to own, to possess; *(qualità)* to have, to possess.

possessivo, -a *agg* possessive.

possesso *sm* possession, ownership; **essere in ~ di qc** to be in possession of sthg.

possibile *agg* possible ◆ *sm*: **fare (tutto) il ~ (per fare qc)** to do everything possible (to do sthg); **ma non è ~!** it can't be true!; **il più presto ~** as soon as possible; **se ~** if possible; **il più ~** *(quantità)* as much as possible; *(numero)* as many as possible.

possibilità *sf inv (eventualità)* possibility; *(occasione)* chance; *(capacità)*: **avere la ~ di fare qc** to be able to do sthg.

posta *sf (negozio)* post office; *(lettere, servizio)* post, mail; **per ~** by post O mail; ~ **aerea** air mail.

postale *agg* postal, post *(dav s)*.

posteggiare *vt* to park.

posteggiatore, -trice *sm, f*

car park attendant *(Br)*, parking lot attendant *(Am)*.

posteggio *sm* car park *(Br)*, parking lot *(Am)*; **~ a pagamento** *car park where drivers must pay to park*.

poster *sm inv* poster.

posteriore *agg (nello spazio)* rear, back; *(nel tempo)* later.

posticipare *vt* to postpone.

postino, -a *sm, f* postman *(f postwoman)*.

posto, -a *pp* → **porre** ◆ *sm* place; *(spazio)* room; *(per persona)* place, seat; *(impiego)* job; **mettere a ~** to tidy (up); **~ di blocco** roadblock; **~ letto** bed; **~ di polizia** police station; **al ~ di** in (the) place of.

potabile *agg* → **acqua**.

potare *vt* to prune.

potente *agg* powerful.

potere *vi* 1. *(essere in grado di)* can, to be able; **non ci posso andare** I can't go, I'm not able to go; **puoi farmi un favore?** can you do me a favour?; **non posso farci niente** I can't do anything about it. 2. *(avere il permesso di)* can, to be able; **non potete parcheggiare qui** you can't park here; **posso entrare?** can o may I come in? 3. *(esprime eventualità)*: **può far freddo** it can get cold; **possono aver perso il treno** they might o could have missed the train; **potrei sbagliarmi** I could be wrong; **può darsi** perhaps; **può darsi che sia partito** he may o might have left. 4. *(esprime suggerimento)*: **puoi provare** you can try.

5. *(in espressioni)*: **non ne posso più!** *(sono stufo)* I can't take any more!; *(sono stanco)* I'm exhausted!; **a più non posso** *(correre)* really fast; *(lavorare)* really hard; **si può fare** it can be done. ◆ *sm* 1. *(comando)* power; **essere al ~** to be in power. 2. *(facoltà)* power, ability.

povero, -a *agg* poor ◆ *sm, f* poor man *(f woman)*; **i poveri** the poor; **~ di qc** lacking in sthg.

pozza *sf* pool.

pozzanghera *sf* puddle.

pozzo *sm* well; **~ petrolifero** oil well.

pranzare *vi* to have lunch.

pranzo *sm (di mezzogiorno)* lunch; *(banchetto)* dinner.

prassi *sf* usual procedure.

pratica, -che *sf* practice; *(esperienza)* practical experience; *(documenti)* paperwork; **mettere in ~ qc** to put sthg into practice; **in ~** in practice.

praticamente *avv (quasi)* practically; *(concretamente)* in a practical way.

pratico, -a, -ci, -che *agg* practical.

prato *sm (distesa d'erba)* meadow; *(di giardino)* lawn.

preavviso *sm* notice.

precario, -a *agg* precarious.

precauzione *sf* precaution.

precedente *agg* preceding, previous ◆ *sm* precedent; **senza precedenti** unprecedented; **precedenti penali** criminal record *(sg)*.

precedenza *sf (in auto)* right of way; *(priorità)* priority; **dare la ~**

premio

(a) *(in auto)* to give way (to).

precedere *vt (nello spazio)* to be ahead of; *(nel tempo)* to precede.

precipitare *vi (cadere)* to fall; *(fig: situazione)* to come to a head ❑ **precipitarsi** *vr* to rush.

precipitazione *sf (atmosferica)* precipitation; *(fretta)* haste.

precipizio *sm* precipice.

precisare *vt* to specify.

precisione *sf (esattezza)* precision; *(accuratezza)* accuracy.

preciso, -a *agg* precise; **sono le due precise** it's exactly two o'clock.

precoce *agg (bambino)* precocious; *(vecchiaia)* premature.

preda *sf* prey; **essere in ~ a qc** to be prey to sthg.

predetto, -a *pp →* **predire**.

predica, -che *sf (RELIG)* sermon; *(fam: ramanzina)* telling-off.

predire *vt* to foretell.

predisporre *vt* to prepare; **~ qn/qc a qc** to predispose sb/sthg to sthg.

predisposizione *sf* tendency.

predominare *vi* to predominate.

prefabbricato, -a *agg* prefabricated.

preferenza *sf* preference.

preferire *vt* to prefer; **~ qn/qc a** to prefer sb/sthg to.

preferito, -a *agg* favourite.

prefiggersi *vr:* **~ uno scopo** to set o.s. a goal.

prefisso, -a *pp →* **prefiggersi** ♦ *sm* code.

pregare *vi* to pray ♦ *vt (Dio)* to pray to; **~ qn di fare qc** *(supplicare)* to beg sb to do sthg; *(chiedere a)* to ask sb to do sthg; **i passeggeri sono gentilmente pregati di non fumare** passengers are kindly requested not to smoke.

preghiera *sf* prayer.

pregiato, -a *agg* precious.

pregio *sm (qualità)* good quality; *(valore)* value.

pregiudicare *vt* to prejudice.

pregiudicato, -a *sm, f* previous offender.

pregiudizio *sm* prejudice.

prego *esclam (risposta a ringraziamento)* don't mention it!; *(invito a sedersi)* take a seat!; *(invito ad entrare prima)* after you!

preistorico, -a, -ci, -che *agg* prehistoric.

prelavaggio *sm* prewash.

prelevare *vt (soldi)* to withdraw; *(campione, sangue)* to take.

prelievo *sm (in banca)* withdrawal; *(MED)* sample.

preliminare *agg & sm* preliminary.

pre-maman *agg inv* maternity *(dav s)*.

prematuro, -a *agg* premature.

premere *vt* to press ♦ *vi:* **~ su** to press on ❑ **premere a** *v + prep:* **~ a qn** to matter to sb.

premiare *vt (dare un premio)* to give a prize to; *(merito, onestà)* to reward.

premiazione *sf* prize-giving.

premio *sm (vincita)* prize; *(ricompensa)* reward; **~ (di assicurazione)** (insurance) premium.

premunirsi *vr:* ~ **contro qc** to protect o.s. against sthg.

premuroso, -a *agg* thoughtful.

prendere *vt* 1. *(afferrare)* to take.

2. *(portare con sé)* to take; **prendi l'ombrello** take the umbrella.

3. *(mezzi di trasporto, strada)* to take; ~ **il treno** to take the train; **prenda la prima a destra** take the first on the right.

4. *(mangiare, bere)* to have; **andiamo a** ~ **un caffè** let's go for a coffee; ~ **qualcosa da bere** to have something to drink; **che cosa prendete?** *(da bere)* what would you like to drink?

5. *(lezioni, voto, stipendio)* to get; ~ **qc in affitto** to rent sthg.

6. *(interpretare)* to take; **prenderla bene/male** to take it well/badly.

7. *(catturare, sorprendere)* to catch; **quanti pesci hai preso?** how many fish have you caught?; ~ **qn con le mani nel sacco** to catch sb redhanded.

8. *(malattia, stato fisico)*: ~ **freddo** to catch cold; ~ **il sole** to sunbathe; **prendersi un raffreddore** to catch a cold.

9. *(sottrarre)*: ~ **qc a qn** to take sthg (away) from sb.

10. *(scambiare)*: ~ **qn per** to take sb for.

11. *(in espressioni)*: **andare a** ~ *(persona)* to meet; *(cosa)* to go to get; **prendersi cura di** to look after; ~ **fuoco** to catch fire; ~ **un impegno** to take on a commitment; ~ **le misure di** *(oggetto, persona)* to measure; **che ti prende?** what's the

matter with you?; **prendersela** *(offendersi)* to get annoyed; *(preoccupare)* to worry; **prendersela con qn** *(arrabbiarsi)* to get angry with sb.

◆ *vi* 1. *(colla, cemento)* to set; *(fuoco)* to catch.

2. *(cominciare)*: ~ **a fare qc** to start doing sthg.

prendisole *sm inv* sundress.

prenotare *vt* to book; **ho prenotato una camera** I've booked a room.

prenotazione *sf* booking.

preoccupare *vt* to worry ❏ **preoccuparsi** *vr:* **preoccuparsi (per)** to worry (about); **preoccuparsi di** *vr + prep (occuparsi di)* to think about.

preoccupato, -a *agg* worried.

preoccupazione *sf* worry.

preparare *vt* to prepare; *(documenti, cose)* to get ready; *(esame, concorso)* to prepare for; *(da mangiare)* to cook ❏ **prepararsi** *vr (vestirsi)* to get ready; ~ **a fare qc** to get ready to do sthg.

preparativi *smpl* preparations.

preposizione *sf* preposition.

prepotente *agg* domineering ◆ *smf* bully.

presa *sf (il prendere)* grip; *(nello sport, appiglio)* hold; *(di acqua, gas)* supply point; *(di sale, pepe)* pinch; *(di colla, cemento)* setting; *(di città)* capture; *(per spina)*: ~ **(di corrente)** socket; **far** ~ to set; **far** ~ **su qn** to captivate sb; ~ **d'aria** air intake; **essere alle prese con** to be up against.

presbite *agg* longsighted.

prescìndere : prescindere da *v + prep* to leave aside; **a ~ da** apart from.

prescritto, -a *pp* → prescrivere.

prescrivere *vt* to prescribe.

presentare *vt* to present; *(domanda, dimissioni)* to submit; *(persona)*: **~ qn a qn** to introduce sb to sb; **le presento mia moglie** this is my wife ☐ **presentarsi** *vr (farsi conoscere)* to introduce o.s.; *(recarsi)* to present o.s.; *(capitare)* to arise; *(mostrarsi)* to look.

presentatore, -trice *sm, f* presenter.

presentazione *sf* presentation; **fare le presentazioni** to make the introductions.

presente *agg* present ♦ *smf*: **i presenti** those present; **tener ~ che** to bear in mind that; **aver ~** to remember.

presentimento *sm* presentiment.

presenza *sf* presence; **in ~ di tutti** in front of everybody.

presepe = presepio.

presepio *sm* Nativity scene, crib.

preservativo *sm* condom.

preside *smf* headteacher *(Br)*, principal *(Am)*.

presidente *smf* president; **~ del Consiglio** Prime Minister; **il ~ della Repubblica** the Italian President.

preso, -a *pp* → prendere.

pressappoco *avv* more or less.

pressare *vt* to press.

pressione *sf* pressure; **far ~ su qn** to put pressure on sb; **essere sotto ~** to be under pressure.

presso *prep (sulle lettere)* c/o; *(vicino a)* near; *(alle dipendenze di)* for, with; **~ qn** *(a casa di)* at sb's home ☐ **pressi** *smpl*: **nei pressi di Siena** in the vicinity of Siena.

prestare *vt* to lend; **~ qc (a qn)** *(denaro, oggetti)* to lend (sb) sthg, to lend sthg (to sb); **~ aiuto a qn** to lend sb a hand; **~ attenzione a** to pay attention to ☐ **prestarsi a** *vr + prep*: **prestarsi a fare qc** to offer to do sthg.

prestazione *sf* performance ☐ **prestazioni** *sfpl* services.

prestigiatore, -trice *sm, f* conjurer.

prestito *sm* loan; **dare in ~ qc (a qn)** to lend sthg (to sb); **prendere qc in ~ (da qn)** to borrow sthg (from sb).

presto *avv (fra poco)* soon; *(in fretta)* quickly; *(nella giornata, nel tempo)* early; **fai ~!** hurry up!; **a ~!** see you soon!; **al più ~** as soon as possible.

presumere *vt* to presume.

presunto, -a *pp* → presumere.

presuntuoso, -a *agg* conceited.

prete *sm* priest.

pretendere *vt* to claim; *(a torto)* to pretend; **pretende che tutti lo ascoltino** he expects everyone to listen to him; **pretende di essere il migliore** he thinks he's the best.

preteso, -a *pp* → pretendere.

pretesto sm (scusa) excuse, pretext; (occasione) opportunity.

prevalente agg prevalent.

prevalere vi to prevail.

prevedere vt to foresee □ **prevedere di** v + prep to expect.

prevenire vt (anticipare) to forestall; (evitare) to prevent.

preventivo, -a agg preventive ♦ sm estimate.

prevenzione sf prevention.

previdenza sf foresight; ~ **sociale** social security (Br), welfare (Am).

previo, -a agg: ~ **pagamento** upon payment.

previsione sf (valutazione) prediction; (aspettativa) expectation; **in ~ di** in anticipation of; **previsioni del tempo** o **meteorologiche** weather forecast.

previsto, -a pp → prevedere ♦ agg expected ♦ sm: **più/meno del** ~ more/less than expected.

prezioso, -a agg precious, valuable.

prezzemolo sm parsley.

prezzo sm price; ~ **comprensivo del servizio** price including service charge; **a buon** ~ cheap.

prigione sf prison.

prigioniero, -a agg (rinchiuso) imprisoned; (catturato) captive ♦ sm, f prisoner.

prima avv (in precedenza) before; (più presto) earlier; (per prima cosa, nello spazio) first; (un tempo) once ♦ sf (di teatro) first night; (marcia) first gear; (in treno, aereo) first class ♦ cong before ♦ prep: ~ **di** before; **fai ~ di qua** it's quicker this way; ~ **che arrivi** before he arrives; ~ **di fare qc** before doing sthg; ~ **o poi** sooner or later; ~ **d'ora** before now; ~ **di tutto** first of all; **l'anno** ~ the year before.

primario, -a agg primary ♦ sm (MED) chief physician.

primato sm (supremazia) primacy; (SPORT) record.

primavera sf spring.

primitivo, -a agg (uomo, civiltà) primitive; (originario) original.

primo, -a agg first; (nel tempo) early ♦ sm (portata) first course; (giorno) first; **il** ~ **(di) marzo** the first of March; **di prima qualità** first-class; **ai primi d'ottobre** in early October; **sulle prime** at first, in the beginning.

primogenito, -a agg & sm, f firstborn.

principale agg main, principal ♦ smf manager, boss.

principe sm prince.

principessa sf princess.

principiante smf beginner.

principio sm (inizio, origine) beginning; (concetto, norma) principle; **in** o **al** ~ at first; **per** ~ on principle.

priorità sf inv (precedenza) priority.

privare vt: ~ **qn di qc** to deprive sb of sthg □ **privarsi di** vr + prep: **privarsi di qc** to go without sthg.

privato, -a agg private ♦ sm, f (cittadino) private citizen ♦ sm: **in** ~ in private.

privilegiare vt to favour.

privo, -a agg: ~ **di qc** without sthg, lacking in sthg.

pro *sm inv*: **a che ~?** for what purpose?; **i ~ e i contro** the pros and cons.

probabile *agg* probable; **è ~ che piova** it will probably rain.

probabilità *sf inv* probability.

probabilmente *avv* probably.

problema, -i *sm* problem.

proboscide *sf* trunk.

procedere *vi (avanzare, progredire)* to proceed; *(agire)* to behave.

procedimento *sm* procedure.

processare *vt* to try.

processione *sf* procession.

processo *sm (DIR)* trial; *(operazione, metodo)* process.

procinto *sm*: **essere in ~ di fare qc** to be about to do sthg.

proclamare *vt* to proclaim.

procurare *vt*: **~ qc a qn** to obtain sthg for sb, to get sthg for sb; **procurarsi qc** to get sthg.

prodotto, -a *pp* → **produrre** ♦ *sm* product.

produrre *vt* to produce; *(provocare)* to cause.

produttore, -trice *sm, f* producer.

produzione *sf* production.

Prof. *(abbr di professore)* Prof.

profano, -a *agg* profane ♦ *sm* layman.

professionale *agg* professional.

professione *sf* profession.

professionista, -i, -e *smf* *(avvocato, medico)* professional person; *(non dilettante)* professional.

professore, -essa *sm, f*

teacher; *(all'università)* professor.

profilo *sm* profile; **di ~** in profile.

profiterole [profite'rɔl] *sm inv* profiteroles *(pl)*.

profitto *sm* profit; **trarre ~ da qc** to take advantage of sthg.

profondità *sf inv* depth.

profondo, -a *agg* deep.

Prof.ssa *(abbr di professoressa)* Prof.

profugo, -a, -ghi, -ghe *sm, f* refugee.

profumare *vt* to perfume ♦ *vi* to smell good; **~ di** to smell of.

profumato, -a *agg* scented.

profumeria *sf* perfumery.

profumo *sm (odore)* scent, fragrance; *(cosmetico)* perfume.

progettare *vt* to plan.

progetto *sm* plan.

programma, -i *sm* programme; *(per vacanze, serata)* plan; *(SCOL)* syllabus; *(INFORM)* program.

programmare *vt (pianificare)* to plan; *(INFORM)* to program.

progredire *vi (avanzare)* to advance; *(migliorare)* to progress.

progressivo, -a *agg* progressive.

progresso *sm* progress; **fare progressi** to make progress.

proibire *vt* to forbid; **~ a qn di fare qc** to forbid sb to do sthg; **è proibito fumare** smoking is prohibited.

proiettare *vt (film)* to show; *(luce, ombra)* to cast.

proiettile *sm* bullet.

proiezione *sf (di film)* projection, showing.

proletariato *sm* proletariat.

prolunga, -ghe *sf* extension.

prolungare *vt* to prolong ❑ **prolungarsi** *vr* to go on.

promessa *sf* promise; **mantenere una ~** to keep a promise.

promesso, -a *pp* → **promettere.**

promettere *vt*: **~ qc (a qn)** to promise (sb) sthg; **~ (a qn) di fare qc** to promise (sb) to do sthg; **promette bene!** that's a good start!

promontorio *sm* promontory.

promosso, -a *pp* → **promuovere.**

promotore, -trice *sm, f* promoter.

promozione *sf* promotion; *(SCOL)*: **avere la ~** to go up a class.

promulgare *vt* to promulgate.

promuovere *vt (SCOL)* to pass; *(impiegato, iniziativa)* to promote.

pronome *sm* pronoun.

pronto, -a *agg* ready ◆ *esclam* hello! *(on the phone)*; **essere ~ a fare qc** to be ready to do sthg; **~ soccorso** first aid; **~, chi parla?** hello, who's speaking?

pronuncia, -ce *sf* pronunciation.

pronunciare *vt (parola, lettera)* to pronounce; *(dire)* to say ❑ **pronunciarsi** *vr (parola, lettera)* to be pronounced; *(dichiararsi)* to declare o.s.

pronunzia = **pronuncia.**

proporre *vt*: **~ qc (a qn)** to propose sthg (to sb); **~ di fare qc** to suggest doing sthg ❑ **proporsi di**

vr + prep: **proporsi di fare qc** to decide to do sthg.

proporzionato, -a *agg* well proportioned.

proporzione *sf (MAT)* ratio; **in ~ a** in proportion to.

proposito *sm (progetto)* intention; **fare qc di ~** to do sthg on purpose; **a ~, ...** by the way, ...; **capitare a ~** *(avvenimento)* to happen at the right time.

proposta *sf* proposal.

proposto, -a *pp* → **proporre.**

proprietà *sf inv* property; **'~ privata'** 'private property'.

proprietario, -a *sm, f* owner.

proprio, -a *agg (possessivo)* own; *(senso)* literal, exact; *(tipico)* characteristic ◆ *avv (veramente)* really; *(precisamente)* just; *(affatto)*: **non ne ho ~ idea** I really have no idea; **~ così** that's just it; **non ~** not exactly; **mettersi in ~** to set up on one's own.

prora *sf (di nave)* prow; *(di aereo)* nose.

prosa *sf* prose.

prosciutto *sm* ham; **~ cotto** (cooked) ham; **~ crudo** Parma ham.

proseguire *vt* to carry on with, to continue ◆ *vi* to carry on, to continue.

prospettiva *sf (di disegno, punto di vista)* perspective; *(possibilità)* prospect.

prossimità *sf*: **in ~ di qc** near sthg.

prossimo, -a *agg* next ◆ *sm* neighbour.

prostituta *sf* prostitute.

protagonista, -i, -e *smf* protagonist.

proteggere *vt*: ~ qn/qc (da) to protect sb/sthg (from).

protesta *sf* protest.

protestante *agg & smf* Protestant.

protestare *vi & vt* to protest.

protetto, -a *pp* → proteggere.

protezione *sf* protection.

prototipo *sm* prototype.

prova *sf* (*dimostrazione, conferma*) proof; (*esperimento*) test, trial; (*DIR*) proof, evidence; (*di spettacolo*) rehearsal; (*esame*) exam; **dar ~ di abilità** to prove to be skilful; **mettere qn alla ~** to put sb to the test; **fino a ~ contraria** until (it's) proved otherwise; **in ~** on trial; **fare le prove** to rehearse.

provare *vt* (*cibo*) to try; (*vestito*) to try on; (*sentire*) to feel, to experience; (*dimostrare*) to show; (*tentare*): **~ a fare qc** to try to do sthg; **provarsi qc** to try sthg on ❑ **provarsi a** *vr + prep*: **provarsi a fare qc** to try to do sthg.

provenienza *sf* origin; **in ~ da** (*treno, aereo*) from.

provenire : **provenire da** *v + prep* to come from; **proveniente da** (*treno, aereo*) from.

provenuto, -a *pp* → provenire.

proverbio *sm* proverb.

provetta *sf* test tube.

provincia, -ce o **-cie** *sf* (*ente*) province; (*opposta a grandi città*) provinces (*pl*).

provinciale *agg* provincial ◆ *sf* main road.

provino *sm* (*audizione*) audition; (*fotografico*) screen test.

provocante *agg* provocative.

provocare *vt* (*causare*) to cause; (*sfidare*) to provoke.

provocazione *sf* provocation.

provolone *sm* a hard cheese made from cow's milk.

provvedere *vi* (*prendere provvedimenti*) to take measures; (*occuparsi di*): **~ (a qc)** to provide (for sthg).

provvedimento *sm* measure.

provvisorio, -a *agg* temporary, provisional.

provviste *sfpl* supplies.

prua *sf* prow.

prudente *agg* cautious, prudent.

prudenza *sf* caution, prudence; 'prudenza' 'caution'.

prudere *vi* to itch; **mi prude una gamba** my leg is itchy.

prugna *sf* plum; **~ secca** prune.

pruno *sm* prickle, thorn.

prurito *sm* itch.

P.S. (*abbr di postscriptum*) PS ◆ *abbr* = Pubblica Sicurezza.

pseudonimo *sm* pseudonym.

psicanalisi *sf* psychoanalysis.

psiche *sf* psyche.

psichiatra, -i, -e *smf* psychiatrist.

psicologia *sf* psychology.

psicologo, -a, -gi, -ghe *sm, f* psychologist.

P.T. (*abbr di poste e telecomunicazioni*) PO.

P.T.P. (*abbr di posto telefonico pub-*

blico) payphone.

pubblicare *vt* to publish.

pubblicazione *sf* publication ❏ **pubblicazioni** *sfpl*: ~ **(matrimoniali)** (marriage) banns.

pubblicità *sf inv* (annuncio) advertisement; (divulgazione) publicity; (attività) advertising.

pubblico, -a, -ci, -che *agg* public; (statale) state (dav s) ◆ *sm* (utenti) public; (spettatori) audience; **in ~** in public; **la Pubblica Sicurezza** the police.

pube *sm* pubis.

pudore *sm* modesty.

pugilato *sm* boxing.

pugile *sm* boxer.

Puglia *sf*: **la ~** Apulia.

pugnalare *vt* to stab.

pugno *sm* (mano) fist; (colpo) punch; (quantità) handful.

pulce *sf* flea.

Pulcinella *sm* Punch.

pulcino *sm* chick.

puledro, -a *sm, f* colt (*f* filly).

pulire *vt* to clean; **pulirsi il viso/le scarpe** to clean one's face/shoes.

pulita *sf*: **dare una ~** to clean up.

pulito, -a *agg* clean; (coscienza) clear.

pulizia *sf* (stato) cleanliness; (atto) cleaning; **fare le pulizie** to do the cleaning.

pullman *sm inv* coach.

pullover *sm inv* pullover.

pulmino *sm* minibus.

pulsante *sm* button.

pulsare *vi* to beat.

puma *sm inv* puma.

pungere *vt* to sting.

pungiglione *sm* sting.

punire *vt* to punish.

punizione *sf* (castigo) punishment; (nel calcio) free kick.

punta *sf* (di matita, spillo, coltello) point; (di continente, dita) tip; **in ~ dei piedi** (camminare) on tiptoe.

puntare *vt* (arma) to aim; (scommettere) to bet; **~ i piedi** to dig one's heels in.

puntata *sf* (episodio) episode; (scommessa) bet; **teleromanzo a puntate** serial.

punteggiatura *sf* punctuation.

punteggio *sm* score.

puntina *sf*: **~ (da disegno)** drawing pin.

puntino *sm* dot; **fare qc a ~** to do sthg properly; **puntini di sospensione** suspension points.

punto, -a *pp* → **pungere** ◆ *sm* point; (segno grafico) full stop (Br), period (Am); (MED, di cucito) stitch; **~ esclamativo** exclamation mark; **~ interrogativo** question mark; **~ di riferimento** point of reference, landmark; **~ di ritrovo** meeting point; **~ vendita** point of sale; **e virgola** semi-colon; **~ di vista** point of view; **due punti** colon; **punti cardinali** points of the compass; **essere sul ~ di fare qc** to be about to do sthg; **essere a buon ~** to be at a good point; **fare il ~ della situazione** to take stock; **mettere a ~ qc** to adjust sthg; **di ~ in bianco** all of a sudden; **a tal ~ che** to such an extent that; **le tre in ~** three o'clock sharp.

puntuale agg punctual.

puntualità sf punctuality.

puntura sf (di insetto) sting; (di spillo) prick; (fam: iniezione) injection.

punzecchiare vt (pungere) to prick; (fig: infastidire) to tease.

pupazzo sm puppet.

pupilla sf pupil.

purché cong provided that.

pure avv (anche) also, too ♦ cong even if; **pur di fare qc** just to do sthg; **faccia ~!** please do!, go ahead!

purè sm (di patate) mashed potatoes with milk, butter and Parmesan cheese.

purezza sf purity.

purga, -ghe sf laxative.

purgatorio sm Purgatory.

puro, -a agg pure; (verità) simple.

purosangue agg inv thoroughbred.

purtroppo avv unfortunately.

pustola sf pimple.

putiferio sm row.

putrefare vi to putrefy, to rot.

putrefatto, -a pp → putrefare ♦ agg rotten.

putrido, -a agg putrid.

puttana sf (volg) whore.

puzza sf = puzzo.

puzzare vi to stink.

puzzo sm stink.

puzzola sf polecat.

puzzolente agg stinking.

Q

qua avv here; **al di ~ di** on this side of; **di ~ e di là** here and there; **per di ~** this way.

quaderno sm exercise book.

quadrante sm (di orologio) face; (di bussola) quarter.

quadrare vi (bilancia) to balance; (coincidere) to correspond; **non mi quadra** (fam) there's something not quite right about it.

quadrato, -a agg & sm square; **2 al ~** 2 squared.

quadretto sm: **a quadretti** (tessuto) checked; (foglio) squared.

quadrifoglio sm four-leaf clover.

quadrimestre sm (SCOL) term; (periodo) period of four months.

quadro sm (pittura) painting; (fig: situazione) picture; (TECNOL) board, panel; (in azienda) executive ❑ **quadri** smpl (nelle carte) diamonds.

quadruplo, -a agg & sm quadruple.

quaggiù avv down here.

quaglia sf quail.

qualche agg 1. (alcuni) a few, some; **restiamo solo ~ giorno** we are only staying a few days; **~ volta** a few times; **c'è ~ novità?** is there any news?
2. (indeterminato) some; **l'ho letto in ~ articolo** I read it in some article; **hai ~ libro da prestarmi?** have

you any books to lend me?; **in ~ modo** somehow; **da ~ parte** somewhere.

3. *(un certo)* some; **ci siamo frequentati per ~ tempo** we've been seeing each other for some time; **~ cosa** = qualcosa.

qualcheduno, -a = qualcuno.

qualcosa *pron* something; *(nelle interrogative)* anything; **~ di nuovo** something new; **~ da bere** something to drink; **qualcos'altro** something else.

qualcuno, -a *pron (uno)* someone, somebody; *(nelle interrogative)* anyone, anybody; *(alcuni)* some; *(alcuni: nelle interrogative)* any; **qualcun altro** *(persona)* someone else; **~ di voi** some of you; *(nelle interrogative)* any of you.

quale *agg interr* 1. *(persona)* which; **qual è il tuo scrittore preferito?** who is your favourite writer?; **da ~ dentista sei stato?** which dentist have you been to?

2. *(cosa)* which, what; **non so ~ libro scegliere** I don't know which book to choose; **in ~ albergo hai prenotato?** which hotel have you booked?

◆ *agg relativo* such as, like; **alcuni animali quali il cane** some animals such as the dog.

◆ *pron interr* which (one); **~ vuole di questi cappelli?** which of these hats do you want?; **non so ~ scegliere** I don't know which (one) to choose.

◆ *pron relativo* 1. *(soggetto)*: **il/la ~** *(persona)* who; *(cosa)* which, that; **suo fratello, il ~ è un mio amico** his brother, who is a friend of mine.

2. *(con preposizioni: persona)* who(m); *(cosa)* which, that; **l'albergo nel ~ alloggio** the hotel (that) I'm staying in; **la persona con la ~ parlavo** the person (whom) I was talking to; **l'uomo del ~ conosco il figlio** the man whose son I know.

3. *(in qualità di)* as; **vengo ~ accompagnatore** I'm coming as a tour guide.

qualifica, -che *sf* qualification.

qualificare *vt* to describe, to define ❑ **qualificarsi** *vr* to qualify.

qualificativo, -a *agg* qualifying.

qualità *sf inv* quality; *(varietà)* type; **in ~ di** in one's capacity as.

qualsiasi = qualunque.

qualunque *agg (quale che)* whatever; **~ cosa** anything; **~ cosa succeda** whatever happens; **~ persona** anyone; **prendine uno ~** take whichever you want.

quando *avv & cong* when; **da ~ sono qui** from when I got here; **da ~ sei qui?** how long have you been here?; **da ~ in qua** since when; **di ~ sono queste foto?** when were these photos taken?

quantità *sf inv* quantity, amount; **una ~ di** a lot o lots of.

quanto, -a *agg interr* 1. *(quantità)* how much; *(numero)* how many; **~ tempo ci vuole?** how long does it take?; **quanti anni hai?** how old are you?

2. *(in frasi esclamative)* what; **quanta fatica sprecata!** what a waste of energy!

♦ *agg relativo* (*quantità*) as much as; (*numero*) as many as; **puoi restare quanti giorni vuoi** you can stay for as many days as you like.
♦ *pron interr* (*quantità*) how much; (*numero*) how many; **prima di comprare il pane guarda ~ ce n'è** before buying the bread see how much there is; **quanti ne vuoi?** how many do you want?; **quanti ne abbiamo oggi?** what's the date today?
♦ *pron relativo* (*quello che: quantità*) as much as; (*numero*) as many as; **dammene ~ ti pare** give me as much as you want; **per ~ ne so as** far as I know.
♦ *avv* 1. (*interrogativo: quantità*) how much; (*numero*) how many; **quant'è?** how much is it? **~ ti fermi?** how long are you staying?; **~ è alta questa montagna?** how high is this mountain?; **~ mi dispiace!** I'm so sorry!; **~ costa/costano?** how much is it/are they?
2. (*relativo*) as much as; **mi sforzo ~ posso** I try as hard as I can; **~ prima** as soon as possible.
3. (*in espressioni*): **in ~** (*perché*) as; **per ~** however.

quaranta *num* forty, → **sei**.

quarantena *sf* quarantine.

quarantesimo, -a *num* fortieth, → **sesto**.

quarantina *sf*: **una ~** (**di**) about forty; **essere sulla ~** to be in one's forties.

quaresima *sf* (RELIG): **la ~** Lent.

quarta *sf* (*marcia*) fourth gear.

quartetto *sm* quartet.

quartiere *sm* area, district; **quartier generale** headquarters (*pl*).

quarto, -a *num* fourth ♦ *sm* (*parte*) quarter; **un ~ d'ora** a quarter of an hour; **le tre e un ~** quarter past three (*Br*), quarter after three (*Am*); **le tre meno un ~** quarter to three (*Br*), quarter of three (*Am*); **un ~ di vino** a quarter litre of wine, → **sesto**.

quarzo *sm* quartz.

quasi *avv* nearly ♦ *cong* as if; **~ mai** hardly ever; **~ sempre** almost always; **~ ~ vengo anch'io** I might just come too.

quassù *avv* up here.

quattordicesimo, -a *num* fourteenth, → **sesto**.

quattordici *num* fourteen, → **sei**.

quattrini *smpl* (*fam*) money (*sg*).

quattro *num* four; **farsi in ~** (**per fare qc**) to go out of one's way (to do sthg); **eravamo ~ gatti** (*fam*) there were only a few of us there; **in ~ e quattr'otto** in less than no time, → **sei**.

quattrocento *num* four hundred, → **sei** ▢ **Quattrocento** *sm*: **il Quattrocento** the fifteenth century.

quei → **quello**.

quegli → **quello**.

quello, -a (*dav sm* **quel** (*pl* **quei**) + *consonante;* **quello** (*pl* **quegli**) + *s+consonante, gn, ps, x, z;* **quell'** (*pl* **quegli**) + *vocale*) *agg* 1. (*indica lontananza*) that, those (*pl*); **quella casa** that house; **quegli alberi** those trees; **quei bambini** those children.
2. (*per sottolineare*): **spegni quella tv!**

switch that TV off!

3. *(per cosa, persona già nota)* that, those *(pl)*; **non mi piace quella gente** I don't like those people.

♦ *pron* 1. *(indica lontananza)* that (one), those (ones) *(pl)*; **quella è la mia macchina** that one's my car; **prendo ~ in offerta** I'll take the one on special offer; **~ lì** that one (there).

2. *(con pronome relativo)*: **faccio ~ che posso** I'll do what I can; **quelli che potevano si sono fermati** those who could, stopped.

quercia, -ce *sf* oak.

querelare *vt* to bring a legal action against.

quesito *sm* query.

questionario *sm* questionnaire.

questione *sf* question; **è ~ di giorni** it's a matter of days; **in ~** in question.

questo, -a *agg* 1. *(indica prossimità)* this, these *(pl)*; **questa finestra è aperta** this window is open; **partiamo ~ giovedì** we're leaving this Thursday.

2. *(simile)* such; **non uscire con questa pioggia** don't go out in rain like this.

3. *(il seguente/precedente)* this, these *(pl)*; **~ è il mio consiglio** this is my advice.

♦ *pron* 1. *(indica prossimità)* this (one), these (ones) *(pl)*; **~ è Franco** this is Franco; **~ qui** o **qua** this one (here).

2. *(per riassumere)* that; **~ è tutto** that's all; **questa è bella!** that's rich!

questura *sf (organo)* police headquarters *(pl)*.

qui *avv* here; **da ~ in avanti** from now on; **di** o **da ~** from here; **di ~ a un anno** in a year's time; **di ~ a poco** in a little while.

quiete *sf* quiet.

quindi *cong* so, therefore.

quindicesimo, -a *num* fifteenth, → **sesto**.

quindici *num* fifteen; **~ giorni** a fortnight, → **sei**.

quindicina *sf* about fifteen; **una ~ di giorni** about a fortnight.

quinta *sf (marcia)* fifth gear □ **quinte** *sfpl (di teatro)* wings.

quintale *sm* = 100 kilograms.

quinto, -a *num* fifth, → **sesto**.

quintuplo *sm*: **il ~ del prezzo normale** five times the normal price.

Quirinale *nm*: **il ~** *official residence of the President of Italy.*

---

i IL QUIRINALE

The "Palazzo del Quirinale" has been the official residence of the president of the Italian republic since 1947. It overlooks the square of the same name in Rome and is guarded by armed policemen in full dress uniform. It is here that the president receives foreign heads of state on official business.

---

quota *sf (altitudine)* altitude; *(di denaro, bene)* share; **perdere ~** to lose height; **prendere ~** to climb; **~ d'iscrizione** *(a circolo)* membership fee.

quotato, -a *agg* valued.

quotidianamente *avv* daily.

quotidiano, -a *agg* daily ◆ *sm* daily (newspaper).

quoziente *sm* quotient; **~ d'intelligenza** IQ.

R

rabarbaro *sm* rhubarb.

rabbia *sf (collera)* anger, rage; *(malattia)* rabies; **far ~ a qn** to drive sb mad.

rabbino *sm* rabbi.

rabbioso, -a *agg* angry; *(MED)* rabid.

rabbonire *vt* to calm down ▫ **rabbonirsi** *vr* to calm down.

rabbrividire *vi (di freddo)* to shiver; *(di paura)* to shudder.

raccapezzarsi *vr:* **non mi ci raccapezzo** I can't make it out.

raccapricciante *agg* horrifying.

raccattapalle *smf inv* ball-boy (*f* ball-girl).

raccattare *vt* to pick up.

racchetta *sf (da tennis)* racket; *(da ping-pong)* bat *(Br)*, paddle *(Am)*; *(da sci)* ski pole.

raccogliere *vt (da terra)* to pick up; *(frutti, fiori)* to pick; *(mettere insieme)* to collect; *(voti)* to win ▫ **raccogliersi** *vr (radunarsi)* to meet, to gather; *(in meditazione,*

preghiera) to gather one's thoughts.

raccolta *sf* collection; *(agricola)* harvest; **fare la ~ di qc** to collect sthg.

raccolto, -a *pp →* **raccogliere** ◆ *sm* harvest, crop.

raccomandare *vt* to recommend; *(affidare)* to entrust; **~ a qn di fare qc** to urge sb to do sthg ▫ **raccomandarsi** *vr:* **raccomandarsi a** to appeal to; **mi raccomando, non fare tardi!** don't be late now, will you!

raccomandata *sf* registered letter.

raccomandato, -a *agg (lettera)* registered; *(candidato)* recommended.

raccomandazione *sf (consiglio)* recommendation.

raccontare *vt* to tell.

racconto *sm (esposizione)* account; *(romanzo)* short story.

raccordo *sm* connection, link; *(di autostrada)* slip road *(Br)*, entrance/exit ramp *(Am)*; **~ anulare** ring road *(Br)*, beltway *(Am)*.

racimolare *vt* to scrape together.

rada *sf* harbour.

radar *sm inv* radar.

raddoppiare *vt (rendere doppio)* to double; *(aumentare)* to redouble ◆ *vi* to double.

radente *agg (tiro, volo)* very low.

radere *vt* to shave; **~ qc al suolo** to raze sthg to the ground ▫ **radersi** *vr* to shave.

radiare *vt* to strike off.

radiatore *sm* radiator.

radiazione *sf* radiation.

radicale *agg* radical.

radicalmente *avv* radically, completely.

radicchio *sm* chicory.

radice *sf* root; ~ **quadrata** square root.

radio *sf inv* radio; *(stazione)* radio station; **alla** ~ on the radio.

radioamatore, -trice *sm, f* radio ham.

radioascoltatore, -trice *sm, f* listener.

radioattivo, -a *agg* radioactive.

radiocomandato, -a *agg* remote-controlled.

radiografia *sf* X-ray.

radioso, -a *agg* bright.

radiotaxi *sm inv* minicab.

rado, -a *agg* sparse; **di** ~ rarely.

radunare *vt (persone)* to gather; *(cose)* to assemble □ **radunarsi** *vr* to gather.

raduno *sm* meeting.

rafano *sm* radish.

raffermo, -a *agg* stale.

raffica, -che *sf (di vento)* gust; *(di mitra)* burst.

raffigurare *vt* to portray.

raffinato, -a *agg* refined; *(stile)* sophisticated.

raffineria *sf* refinery.

rafforzare *vt* to strengthen.

raffreddare *vt* to cool; *(fig: rapporti, interesse)* to cool, to dampen □ **raffreddarsi** *vr (bevanda, cibo)* to get cold; *(fig: persona, amicizia)* to cool down; *(ammalarsi)* to catch a cold.

raffreddato, -a *agg:* **essere** ~ to have a cold.

raffreddore *sm* cold.

rafia *sf* raffia.

ragazza *sf (giovane donna)* girl; *(fidanzata)* girlfriend; ~ **madre** single mother.

ragazzata *sf* childish trick.

ragazzo *sm (giovane)* boy; *(fidanzato)* boyfriend.

raggiante *agg* radiant, beaming.

raggio *sm (di sole, infrarosso)* ray; *(area)* range; *(MAT)* radius; *(di ruota)* spoke.

raggirare *vt* to trick, to cheat.

raggiungere *vt (persona)* to catch up; *(luogo)* to reach; *(fig: fine)* to achieve.

raggiunto, -a *pp* → **raggiungere**.

raggomitolarsi *vr* to curl up.

raggranellare *vt* to scrape together.

raggrinzire *vt & vi* to shrivel up □ **raggrinzirsi** *vr* to shrivel.

raggruppare *vt (mettere insieme)* to assemble; *(a gruppi)* to group together □ **raggrupparsi** *vr* to assemble.

ragguagli *smpl:* **dare** ~ to give details.

ragionamento *sm (riflessione)* reasoning; *(discorso)* argument.

ragionare *vi* to reason □ **ragionare di** *v + prep (parlare di)* to argue about.

ragione *sf* reason; **avere** ~ to be right; **dare** ~ **a qn** to side with sb.

a maggior ~ even more so.

ragioneria sf (materia) account-ancy; (scuola) commercial school; (reparto) accounts (pl).

ragionevole agg reasonable.

ragioniere, -a sm, f accountant.

ragliare vi to bray.

ragnatela sf cobweb, spider's web.

ragno sm spider.

ragù sm inv sauce of minced beef, tomatoes and onions.

RAI sf Italian broadcasting corporation.

rallegramenti smpl congratulations.

rallentare vt to slow down.

rally ['rɛlli] sm inv rally.

ramaiolo sm ladle.

ramanzina sf telling-off.

rame sm copper.

ramino sm rummy.

rammaricarsi : rammaricarsi di vr + prep to regret.

rammendare vt (stoffa) to mend; (lana) to darn.

rammentare vt to remember; ~ qc a qn to remind sb of sthg ▫ **rammentarsi di** vr + prep to remember.

rammollito, -a agg soft.

ramo sm branch.

ramoscello sm twig.

rampa sf flight (of stairs); ~ di lancio launch pad.

rampicante agg climbing.

rampone sm (fiocina) harpoon; (in alpinismo) crampon.

rana sf frog.

rancido, -a agg rancid.

rancore sm rancour.

randagio, -a, -gi, -gie o **-ge** agg stray.

randello sm club.

rango, -ghi sm rank.

rannicchiarsi vr to huddle up.

rannuvolarsi vr to cloud over.

ranocchio sm frog.

rantolo sm death rattle.

rapa sf turnip.

rapace agg predatory ◆ sm bird of prey.

rapare vt to crop.

rapida sf rapids (pl).

rapidamente avv rapidly, fast.

rapidità sf rapidity.

rapido, -a agg (svelto) fast; (breve) quick, rapid ◆ sm express (train).

rapimento sm kidnapping.

rapina sf robbery; ~ a mano armata armed robbery.

rapinare vt to rob.

rapinatore, -trice sm, f robber.

rapire vt to kidnap.

rapitore, -trice sm, f kidnapper.

rapporto sm (resoconto) report; (tra persone) relationship; (connessione) connection, relation; (MAT) ratio; **rapporti sessuali** sexual intercourse (sg).

rapprendersi vr to curdle.

rappresentante smf representative.

rappresentare vt to represent; (raffigurare) to depict; (mettere in scena) to stage, to perform.

rappresentazione *sf (spettacolo)* performance; *(raffigurazione)* representation.

rappreso, -a *pp* → **rapprendersi**.

raramente *avv* rarely.

rarità *sf inv (scarsità)* rarity; *(oggetto)* rare thing.

raro, -a *agg* rare.

rasare *vt* to shave □ **rasarsi** *vr* to shave.

rasato, -a *agg* shaven.

raschiare *vt* to scrape.

rasentare *vt (sfiorare)* to graze; *(muro)* to hug, to keep close to; *(fig: avvicinarsi a)* to border on.

rasente *prep* close to.

raso, -a *pp* → **radere** ♦ *agg (cucchiaio)* level; ~ **terra** close to the ground.

rasoio *sm* razor; ~ **elettrico** electric razor.

rassegna *sf* review; *(cinematografica, teatrale)* season; **passare in** ~ *(MIL)* to review.

rassegnare *vt:* ~ **le dimissioni** to hand in one's resignation □ **rassegnarsi** *vr* to resign o.s.

rasserenarsi *vr* to clear up.

rassettare *vt (stanza, capelli)* to tidy (up); *(vestito)* to mend.

rassicurare *vt* to reassure.

rassodare *vt (terreno)* to harden; *(muscoli)* to tone.

rassomigliare : rassomigliare a *v + prep* to resemble.

rastrellare *vt (foglie)* to rake; *(fig: zona)* to comb.

rastrello *sm* rake.

rata *sf* instalment; **pagare qc a rate** to pay for sthg in instalments.

rateale *agg* by o in instalments.

ratificare *vt (DIR)* to ratify.

ratto *sm* rat.

rattoppare *vt* to patch.

rattrappire *vt* to numb □ **rattrappirsi** *vr* to go numb.

rattristare *vt* to make sad □ **rattristarsi** *vr* to become sad.

rauco, -a, -chi, -che *agg* raucous.

ravanello *sm* radish.

ravioli *smpl* ravioli.

ravvicinare *vt (avvicinare)* to bring closer; *(rappacificare)* to reconcile □ **ravvicinarsi** *vr* to be reconciled.

ravvivare *vt* to brighten up.

razionale *agg* rational.

razionalità *sf* rationality.

razionare *vt* to ration.

razione *sf* ration.

razza *sf (di persone)* race; *(di animali)* breed; *(pesce)* ray; **che ~ di domanda è questa?** *(fam)* what sort of question is that?

razzia *sf* raid.

razziale *agg* racial.

razzismo *sm* racism.

razzista, -i, -e *agg & smf* racist.

razzo *sm* rocket.

razzolare *vi* to scratch about.

re *sm inv* king.

reagire *vi:* ~ **(a qc)** to react (to sthg).

reale *agg (vero)* real; *(di re)* royal.

realista, -i, -e *smf* realist.

realizzare *vt (progetto)* to carry

out; *(sogno)* to fulfil; *(film)* to produce; *(rendersi conto di)* to realize; *(COMM)* to realize ☐ **realizzarsi** *vr (persona)* to be fulfilled; *(progetto)* to be carried out; *(sogno)* to come true.

realizzazione *sf (attuazione)* carrying-out.

realmente *avv* really.

realtà *sf inv* reality; **in ~** in reality.

reato *sm* offence, crime.

reattore *sm (aereo)* jet; *(motore)* jet engine; *(in fisica)* reactor.

reazionario, -a *agg* reactionary.

reazione *sf* reaction.

rebus *sm inv* game in which pictures represent the syllables of words.

recapitare *vt* to deliver.

recapito *sm (luogo)* address; *(consegna)* delivery; **~ telefonico** (tele)phone number.

recare *vt*: **~ disturbo a qn** to disturb sb ☐ **recarsi** *vr* to go.

recensione *sf* review.

recente *agg* recent; **di ~** recently.

recentemente *avv* recently.

recessione *sf* recession.

recidere *vt* to cut off.

recintare *vt* to fence in.

recinto *sm (spazio)* enclosure; *(recinzione)* fence.

recipiente *sm* container.

reciproco, -a, -ci, -che *agg* reciprocal.

reciso, -a *pp* → recidere.

recita *sf* play.

recitare *vt (poesia)* to recite;

(ruolo) to play ◆ *vi* to act.

reclamare *vi* to complain ◆ *vt* to claim.

réclame [re'klam] *sf inv* advertising.

reclamo *sm (protesta)* complaint.

reclinabile *agg* reclining.

reclusione *sf (DIR)* imprisonment.

reclutare *vt* to recruit.

record *sm inv* record.

recuperare *vt (riprendere)* to recover, to get back; *(svantaggio, tempo)* to make up; *(rottami)* to salvage.

redatto, -a *pp* → redigere.

redattore, -trice *sm, f* editor.

redazione *sf (stesura)* writing; *(ufficio)* editorial department; *(personale)* editorial staff.

redditizio, -a *agg* profitable.

reddito *sm* income.

redigere *vt (articolo, lettera)* to write; *(documento, contratto)* to draw up.

redini *sfpl* reins.

referendum *sm inv* referendum.

referenze *sfpl* references.

referto *sm* medical report.

refettorio *sm* refectory, dining hall.

refrigerare *vt* to refrigerate.

refurtiva *sf* stolen goods *(pl)*.

regalare *vt (dono)* to give (as a present); *(dare gratis)* to give away.

regalo *sm (dono)* present, gift.

regata *sf* regatta.

reggere *vt (tenere)* to hold; *(sostenere)* to bear, to support; *(sopportare)* to bear; *(governare)* to govern; *(GRAMM)* to take, to be followed by ♦ *vi (durare)* to last; *(essere logico)* to stand up, to hold good; *(resistere):* ~ **a qc** to withstand sthg ◻ **reggersi** *vr:* **non mi reggo in piedi** I can't stand up.

reggia, -ge *sf* palace.

reggicalze *sm inv* suspender belt.

reggimento *sm* regiment.

reggipetto = **reggiseno**.

reggiseno *sm* bra.

regia *sf (di film)* direction; *(di dramma)* production.

regime *sm (politico)* regime; *(alimentare)* diet.

regina *sf* queen.

regionale *agg* regional.

regione *sf* region.

---

i | REGIONE

For administrative purposes Italy is divided up into 20 regions. Each region is made up of different provinces ("province"), and each province is made up of municipalities known as "comuni". Five of the regions have a special statute granting them a greater degree of autonomy than the others: they are Valle d'Aosta, Friuli-Venezia Giulia, Trentino-Alto Adige, Sicily and Sardinia.

---

regista, -i, -e *smf* director.

registrare *vt* to register; *(su cassetta)* to record; *(COMM)* to enter.

registratore *sm* tape recorder; ~ **di cassa** cash register.

registrazione *sf (di nascita, morte)* registration; *(di musica, programma)* recording; *(COMM)* entry.

registro *sm* register; ~ **di classe** attendance register.

regnare *vi* to reign.

regno *sm* kingdom; *(fig: ambito)* realm ◻ **Regno Unito** *sm:* **il Regno Unito** the United Kingdom.

regola *sf* rule; **essere in** ~ to be (all) in order; **fare qc a** ~ **d'arte** to do sthg perfectly.

regolabile *agg* adjustable.

regolamento *sm* regulations *(pl)*.

regolare *agg* regular ♦ *vt* to regulate; *(apparecchio, macchina)* to adjust; *(questione, conto)* to settle ◻ **regolarsi** *vr (comportarsi)* to behave; *(moderarsi)* to control o.s.; **regolarsi nel bere/mangiare** to watch what one drinks/eats.

regolarmente *avv* regularly.

regolo *sm* ruler; ~ **calcolatore** slide rule.

regredire *vi* to regress.

reintegrare *vt* to reinstate.

relativamente *avv* relatively, comparatively; ~ **a** in relation to, as regards.

relativo, -a *agg* relative; ~ **a** relating to.

relax *sm* relaxation.

relazione *sf* relationship; *(amorosa)* affair; *(resoconto)* report.

relegare *vt* to relegate.

religione *sf* religion.

religioso, -a *agg* religious ♦

sm, f monk (*f* nun).

reliquia *sf* relic.

relitto *sm* wreck, piece of wreckage.

remare *vi* to row.

remo *sm* oar.

rendere *vt (restituire)* to give back, to return; *(far diventare)* to make; *(produrre)* to yield ♦ *vi (persona, azienda)* to do well; *(lavoro)* to pay well; **~ possibile qc** to make sthg possible; **~ l'idea** *(persona)* to make o.s. clear ❏ **rendersi** *vr (diventare)* to become; **rendersi utile** to make o.s. useful.

rendiconto *sm (relazione)* report; *(COMM)* statement of accounts.

rendimento *sm (efficienza)* efficiency; *(di scolaro, macchina)* performance.

rendita *sf* unearned income; **vivere di ~** *(fig: studente)* to get by on one's past performance.

rene *sm* kidney.

renitente *agg* reluctant; **è ~ ai consigli** he won't listen to advice; **essere ~ alla leva** *to fail to report for military service.*

renna *sf* reindeer.

Reno *sm*: **il ~ the** Rhine.

reparto *sm (di negozio)* department; *(d'ospedale)* ward; *(MIL)* unit.

repentaglio *sm*: **mettere a ~ qc** to put sthg at risk.

reperibile *agg (merce, persona)* available; *(al lavoro)* on call.

reperto *sm (resto)* find; *(resoconto)* report.

repertorio *sm (teatrale)* repertoire; *(elenco)* index.

replica, -che *sf (in televisione)* repeat; *(a teatro)* repeat performance.

replicare *vt* to reply.

repressione *sf* repression.

represso, -a *pp* → **reprimere.**

reprimere *vt* to repress ❏ **reprimersi** *vr* to restrain o.s.

repubblica, -che *sf* republic.

repubblicano, -a *agg* republican.

repulsione *sf* repulsion.

reputare *vt* to consider.

reputazione *sf* reputation.

requisire *vt* to requisition.

requisito *sm* requisite.

resa *sf (l'arrendersi)* surrender; *(restituzione)* return; *(rendimento)* yield; **~ dei conti** *(fig)* day of reckoning.

residence ['rɛzidɛns] *sm inv* residential hotel.

residente *agg* resident.

residenza *sf* residence.

residenziale *agg* residential.

residuo, -a *agg* residual, remaining ♦ *sm (avanzo)* remainder; *(scoria)* waste.

resina *sf* resin.

resistente *agg (robusto)* strong; *(durevole)* durable; **~ al calore** heatproof, heat-resistant.

resistenza *sf* resistance; *(di materiale)* strength; *(a fatica, dolore)* endurance; **~ (elettrica)** (electrical) resistance.

resistere *vi (tener duro)* to hold out ❏ **resistere a** *v + prep (opporsi)* to resist; *(sopportare)* to withstand.

resistito, -a *pp* → **resistere.**

reso, -a *pp* → rendere.

resoconto *sm* account.

respingere *vt* to reject; *(attacco, aggressore)* to repel; *(SCOL)* to fail.

respinto, -a *pp* → respingere.

respirare *vi & vt* to breathe.

respiratore *sm* *(per immersione)* aqualung; *(MED)* respirator.

respirazione *sf* breathing; **~ artificiale** artificial respiration.

respiro *sm* *(respirazione)* breathing; *(movimento)* breath; **tirare un ~ di sollievo** to heave a sigh of relief.

responsabile *agg* responsible ♦ *smf* *(in azienda, negozio)* person in charge; *(colpevole)* culprit; **essere ~ di qc** *(incaricato di)* to be in charge of sthg; *(colpevole di)* to be responsible for sthg.

responsabilità *sf inv* responsibility; *(colpa)* responsibility, liability.

ressa *sf* crowd.

restare *vi* to stay, to remain; *(avanzare)* to be left, to remain; *(trovarsi)* to be; **~ a piedi** to remain standing; **mi restano pochi giorni** I only have a few days left.

restaurare *vt* to restore.

restauro *sm* restoration.

restituire *vt* to give back, to return.

resto *sm* rest, remainder; *(di denaro)* change; *(MAT)* remainder; **del ~** moreover, besides ❑ **resti** *smpl* *(ruderi)* ruins; *(di cibo)* leftovers; *(di persona, animale)* remains.

restringere *vt* *(dimensioni)* to reduce; *(tessuto)* to shrink; *(limitare)* to limit, to restrict ❑ **restringersi**

vr *(strada)* to (become) narrow; *(stoffa)* to shrink; *(per numero, estensione)* to reduce.

resurrezione *sf* resurrection.

resuscitare = risuscitare.

rete *sf* net; *(recinzione)* wire fence; *(radiotelevisiva, stradale)* network; *(del letto)* bedsprings *(pl)*; *(nel calcio: punto)* goal.

reticente *agg* reticent.

reticolato *sm* *(intreccio di linee)* network; *(recinzione)* fencing, wire netting.

retina *sf* *(ANAT)* retina.

retino *sm* net.

retorico, -a, -ci, -che *agg* *(spreg)* pompous.

retribuire *vt* to remunerate, to pay.

retribuzione *sf* remuneration, pay.

retro *sm inv* back; **sul ~** at the back; **vedi ~** see over.

retrocedere *vi* to recede; *(SPORT)* to be relegated.

retrocesso, -a *pp* → retrocedere.

retrogrado, -a *agg* retrograde.

retromarcia *sf* reverse.

retroscena *sm inv* *(antefatti)* background.

retrospettivo, -a *agg* retrospective.

retrovisore *sm* rear-view mirror.

retta *sf* *(linea)* straight line; *(di pensionato)* charge; **dar ~ a** to pay attention to.

rettangolare *agg* rectangular.

rettangolo *sm* rectangle.

rettificare *vt (form)* to rectify.

rettile *sm* reptile.

rettilineo, -a *agg & sm* straight.

retto, -a *pp → reggere ♦ agg (diritto)* straight; *(persona, comportamento)* honest; **angolo ~** right angle.

rettore *sm* rector.

reumatismi *smpl* rheumatism *(sg)*.

reversibile *agg* reversible.

revisionare *vt (apparecchio, macchina)* to service, to overhaul; *(testo)* to revise.

revisione *sf (di apparecchio)* service; *(di conti)* audit(ing); *(di scritto)* revision.

revocare *vt* to revoke.

revolver *sm inv* revolver.

riabilitare *vt* to rehabilitate.

riacquistare *vt* to regain.

riaggiustare *vt* to readjust.

rialzare *vt* to raise □ **rialzarsi** *vr* to get up.

rialzo *sm* rise.

rianimazione *sf (reparto)* intensive care.

riaperto, -a *pp → riaprire.*

riapertura *sf* reopening; **~ delle scuole** beginning of the school term.

riaprire *vt & vi* to reopen □ **riaprirsi** *vr* to reopen.

riarmo *sm* rearming.

riassetto *sm* reorganization.

riassumere *vt (ricapitolare)* to summarize; *(impiegato)* to re-employ; *(riprendere)* to resume.

riassunto, -a *pp → riassumere ♦ sm* summary.

riattaccare *vt (attaccare di nuovo)* to re-attach; *(bottone)* to sew back on; *(ricominciare)* to start again; *(al telefono)* to hang up.

riavere *vt (avere di nuovo)* to have again; *(avere indietro)* to get back; *(riacquistare)* to regain, to recover □ **riaversi da** *vr + prep* to recover from.

ribadire *vt* to confirm.

ribaltabile *agg* folding.

ribaltare *vt* to overturn.

ribassare *vt* to lower ♦ *vi* to fall.

ribasso *sm* fall, reduction.

ribattere *vt (palla)* to return ♦ *vi (replicare)* to answer back.

ribellarsi *vr* to rebel; **~ a qn** to rebel against sb.

ribelle *agg* rebellious.

ribellione *sf* rebellion.

ribes *sm inv*: **~ nero** blackcurrant; **~ rosso** redcurrant.

ribollire *vi (fig)* to seethe.

ribrezzo *sm* horror; **far ~ a qn** to revolt sb.

ricadere *vi (cadere di nuovo)* to fall again; *(in errore, vizio)* to relapse; *(capelli, vestiti)* to hang down □ **ricadere su** *v + prep* to fall on.

ricalcare *vt* to trace.

ricamare *vt* to embroider.

ricambiare *vt (sentimento, favore)* to return; *(cambiare di nuovo)* to change again.

ricambio *sm (sostituzione)* exchange, replacement; **in ~** in return ❏ **ricambi** *smpl* spare parts.

ricamo *sm* embroidery.

ricapitolare *vt* to summarize.

ricaricare *vt (macchina fotografica, arma)* to reload; *(batteria)* to recharge; *(orologio)* to wind up.

ricattare *vt* to blackmail.

ricatto *sm* blackmail.

ricavare *vt (estrarre)* to extract; *(ottenere)* to obtain.

ricavato *sm (guadagno)* proceeds *(pl)*.

ricchezza *sf* wealth ❏ **ricchezze** *sfpl* wealth *(sg)*; ~ **naturali** natural resources.

ricciarelli *smpl diamond-shaped sweets made from marzipan (a speciality of Siena)*.

riccio, -a, -ci, -ce *agg* curly ♦ *sm (di capelli)* curl; *(animale)* hedgehog; ~ **di mare** sea urchin.

ricciolo *sm* curl.

ricciuto, -a *agg* curly.

ricco, -a, -chi, -che *agg* rich, wealthy; ~ **di qc** rich in sthg.

ricerca, -che *sf* research; *(di persona, di cosa)* search; **essere alla** ~ **di** to be in search of.

ricercare *vt (cercare di nuovo)* to look for (again); *(ladro)* to look for, to search for.

ricercatezza *sf* refinement.

ricercato, -a *agg (elegante)* refined; *(apprezzato)* in demand, sought-after; **essere** ~ **dalla polizia** to be wanted by the police.

ricercatore, -trice *sm, f* researcher.

ricetta *sf* recipe; ~ **medica** prescription.

ricettazione *sf* receiving (stolen goods).

ricevere *vt (lettera, regalo)* to receive, to get; *(schiaffo, palla)* to get; *(accogliere)* to welcome; *(ospite)* to entertain; *(cliente, paziente)* to receive.

ricevimento *sm* reception.

ricevitore *sm* receiver.

ricevuta *sf* receipt; **mi può fare una ~?** may I have a receipt?

ricezione *sf* reception.

richiamare *vt (ritelefonare, per far tornare)* to call back; *(attirare)* to attract; *(rimproverare)* to reprimand; ~ **alla mente qc a qn** to remind sb of sthg.

richiamo *sm (per far tornare)* call; *(attrazione)* appeal, attraction; *(di vaccinazione)* booster.

richiedere *vt (ridomandare)* to ask again; *(aiuto, spiegazioni)* to ask for; *(necessitare di)* to require; **gli ho richiesto le chiavi** *(indietro)* I asked him for my keys back.

richiesta *sf (domanda)* request; *(esigenza)* demand; **a** ~ on request.

richiesto, -a *pp* = **richiedere** ♦ *agg* in demand, sought-after.

richiudere *vt* to close again.

riciclare *vt* to recycle.

ricollegare *vt (centri isolati)* to reconnect; *(fatti, discorsi)* to connect, to relate ❏ **ricollegarsi** *vr*: **ricollegarsi a** *(riferirsi)* to refer to; *(fatto)* to be connected with.

ricominciare *vt & vi* to begin again, to start again; ~ **a fare qc** to begin again, to resume doing sthg.

ricompensa *sf* reward.

ricompensare *vt* to reward.

ricomporre *vt* to reconstruct ❑ **ricomporsi** *vr* to regain one's composure.

ricomposto, -a *pp* → **ricomporre**.

riconciliare *vt* to reconcile ❑ **riconciliarsi** *vr* to be reconciled.

ricondotto, -a *pp* → **ricondurre**.

ricondurre *vt* (*in luogo*) to take back, to bring back.

riconferma *sf* (*conferma ulteriore*) reconfirmation; (*dimostrazione*) proof.

riconfermare *vt* to reconfirm.

riconoscente *agg* grateful.

riconoscere *vt* to recognize; (*ammettere*) to admit.

riconquistare *vt* (*territorio*) to reconquer; (*stima, rispetto*) to regain.

riconsegnare *vt* to give back.

ricoperto, -a *pp* → **ricoprire**.

ricopiare *vt* to copy.

ricoprire *vt* (*poltrona, dolce*) to cover; (*carica*) to hold; ~ **qn/qc di qc** to cover sb/sthg with sthg.

ricordare *vt* to remember, to recall; ~ **qc a qn** to remind sb of sthg; **non mi ricordo l'indirizzo** I don't remember the address ❑ **ricordarsi di** *vr + prep* to remember; **ricordarsi di aver fatto qc** to remember doing o having done sthg; **ricordarsi di fare qc** to remember to do sthg.

ricordo *sm* (*memoria*) memory; (*oggetto*) souvenir.

ricorrente *agg* recurrent.

ricorrenza *sf* anniversary.

ricorrere *vi* (*ripetersi*) to recur ❑ **ricorrere a** *v + prep* (*rivolgersi a*) to turn to; (*utilizzare*) to resort to.

ricorso, -a *pp* → **ricorrere** ◆ *sm* (*DIR*) appeal; **far ~ a qc** (*utilizzare*) to resort to sthg.

ricostruire *vt* (*edificio*) to rebuild; (*fatto*) to reconstruct.

ricotta *sf* ricotta (*soft cheese made from milk whey*).

ricoverare *vt*: ~ **qn in ospedale** to admit sb to hospital.

ricreare *vt* (*creare di nuovo*) to recreate.

ricreazione *sf* (*a scuola*) break.

ricredersi *vr* to change one's mind.

ricucire *vt* to mend.

ricuperare = **recuperare**.

ridacchiare *vi* to snigger.

ridare *vt* (*dare di nuovo*) to give again; (*restituire*) to give back.

ridere *vi* to laugh; **morire dal ~** to die laughing ❑ **ridere di** *v + prep* to laugh at.

ridetto, -a *pp* → **ridire**.

ridicolo, -a *agg* ridiculous.

ridimensionare *vt*: ~ **un problema** to get a problem into perspective.

ridire *vt* (*ripetere*) to repeat; **avere qualcosa da ~** to find fault.

ridondante *agg* redundant.

ridosso *sm*: **a ~** (*di qc*) behind (sthg).

ridotto, -a *pp* → **ridurre** ◆ *agg* (*prezzo*) reduced; (*formato*) smaller; ~ **male** in a bad state.

ridurre *vt* to reduce ❑ **ridursi** *vr* (*diminuire*) to shrink; **ridursi a** *vr*

+ *prep* to be reduced to.

riduzione *sf* reduction.

rielaborare *vt* to redesign.

riempire *vt* to fill; *(modulo)* to fill in; ~ **di** to fill with ❑ **riempirsi di** *vr* + *prep (stadio, cinema)* to fill with; *(fam: mangiare)* to stuff o.s. with.

rientrare *vi (entrare di nuovo)* to go/come back in; *(a casa, in patria)* to return; *(essere compreso)* to be included; *(avere una rientranza)* to curve inwards.

riepilogo, -ghi *sm* summary.

rievocare *vt (ricordare)* to recall; *(far ricordare)* to commemorate.

rifare *vt (fare di nuovo)* to do again; *(ricostruire)* to rebuild; ~ **il letto** to make the bed ❑ **rifarsi di** *vr* + *prep (perdita)* to recover; **rifarsi di qc su qn** to get one's own back on sb for sth.

rifatto, -a *pp* → **rifare**.

riferimento *sm* reference; **fare ~ a** to refer to.

riferire *vt*: ~ **qc (a qn)** to report sth (to sb) ❑ **riferirsi a** *vr* + *prep* to refer to.

rifilare *vt*: ~ **qc a qn** *(fam: merce)* to palm sth off on sb; *(fam: compito)* to saddle sb with sth.

rifiniture *sfpl* finishing touches.

rifiorire *vi* to flower again.

rifiutare *vt* to refuse; ~ **di fare qc** to refuse to do sth.

rifiuto *sm* refusal ❑ **rifiuti** *smpl (spazzatura)* rubbish *(sg)* (Br), trash *(sg)* (Am).

riflessione *sf* reflection.

riflessivo, -a *agg* reflexive.

riflesso, -a *pp* → **riflettere** ◆ *sm (luce)* reflection; *(conseguenza)* repercussion; *(MED)* reflex.

riflettere *vt & vi* to reflect; ~ **su** to reflect on, to think about ❑ **riflettersi** *vr* to be reflected; **riflettersi su** *vr* + *prep (influire)* to influence, to have repercussions on.

riflettore *sm (di teatro)* spotlight; *(di stadio)* floodlight.

riflusso *sm (flusso contrario)* flow; *(di marea)* ebb.

riforma *sf* reform.

riformare *vt* to reform; *(MIL)* to invalid out.

rifornimento *sm*: **fare ~ di qc** to stock up with sth ❑ **rifornimenti** *smpl* supplies.

rifornire *vt*: ~ **qn/qc di** to supply sb/sth with ❑ **rifornirsi di** *vr* + *prep* to stock up with.

rifrangere *vt* to refract.

rifratto, -a *pp* → **rifrangere**.

rifugiarsi *vr* to take refuge.

rifugiato, -a *sm, f* refugee.

rifugio *sm (riparo)* shelter, refuge; ~ **alpino** mountain hut.

riga, -ghe *sf* line; *(di capelli)* parting; *(righello)* ruler; **mettersi in ~** to get into line; **a righe** *(tessuto)* striped; *(foglio)* lined.

rigare *vt* to scratch ◆ *vi*: ~ **diritto** to toe the line.

rigattiere *sm* junk dealer.

rigettare *vt (gettare indietro)* to throw back; *(respingere)* to reject; *(fam: vomitare)* to throw up.

rigetto *sm (MED)* rejection.

rigidità *sf (di oggetto)* rigidity; *(del corpo)* stiffness; *(di clima)* harshness; *(di regolamento, persona)* strictness.

rigido, -a *agg (non elastico)* rigid; *(membra)* stiff; *(clima)* harsh; *(severo)* strict.

rigirare *vt (voltare)* to turn (round); **~ il discorso** to change the subject □ **rigirarsi** *vr (voltarsi)* to turn round; *(nel letto)* to turn over.

rigo, -ghi *sm* line.

rigoglioso, -a *agg* luxuriant.

rigore *sm* rigour; *(SPORT)* penalty; **essere di ~** to be compulsory.

rigoroso, -a *agg* rigorous.

rigovernare *vt* to wash up.

riguardare *vt (guardare di nuovo)* to look at again; *(controllare)* to check; *(concernere)* to concern □ **riguardarsi** *vr* to look after o.s.; **riguardati!** look after yourself!, take care!; **questo non ti riguarda** this has nothing to do with you.

riguardo *sm (attenzione)* care; *(stima)* regard, respect; **~ a** with regard to.

rilanciare *vt* to relaunch.

rilancio *sm* relaunch; *(economico)* recovery.

rilasciare *vt (intervista)* to give; *(ostaggio)* to release; *(documento, diploma)* to issue.

rilassare *vt* to relax □ **rilassarsi** *vr* to relax.

rilegare *vt* to bind.

rilento *avv*: **a ~** slowly.

rilevante *agg* relevant.

rilevare *vt (notare)* to notice; *(mettere in evidenza)* to point out;

(dati) to collect; *(COMM)* to take over.

rilievo *sm* relief; **mettere in ~ qc** to emphasize sthg.

riluttante *agg* reluctant.

rima *sf* rhyme.

rimandare *vt (mandare di nuovo)* to send again; *(mandare indietro)* to send back; *(riunione, esame)* to postpone; **~ qn a qc** *(in testo)* to refer sb to sthg; **~ qn in italiano** *(SCOL)* to make sb resit their Italian exam.

rimando *sm* cross-reference.

rimanente *agg* remaining ♦ *sm* remainder.

rimanenza *sf* remainder.

rimanere *vi (in luogo)* to stay, to remain; *(nel tempo)* to last, to remain; *(avanzare)* to be left; *(essere)* to be; **mi sono rimaste diecimila lire** I have ten thousand lire left; **siamo rimasti in due** there are (only) two of us left; **sono rimasto solo** I was left on my own; **~ indietro** *(di luogo)* to be left behind; *(nel lavoro)* to fall behind.

rimarginare *vt* to heal □ **rimarginarsi** *vr* to heal.

rimasto, -a *pp* → **rimanere**.

rimasuglio *sm* scrap.

rimbalzare *vi (palla)* to bounce; *(proiettile)* to ricochet.

rimbalzo *sm (di palla)* bounce; *(di proiettile)* ricochet.

rimbambito, -a *agg* daft.

rimboccare *vt (lenzuola, coperta)* to tuck in; *(maniche, pantaloni)* to turn up; **rimboccarsi le maniche** to roll up one's sleeves.

rimbombare *vi* to rumble.

rimborsare *vt* to reimburse, to refund.

rimborso *sm* refund; **~ spese** refund of expenses.

rimediare *vt (fam: procurarsi)* to find ♦ *vi*: **~ a qc** *(sbaglio, danno)* to make amends for sthg.

rimedio *sm* remedy; **porre ~ a qc** to remedy sthg.

rimescolare *vt (liquido)* to mix well; *(carte)* to shuffle.

rimessa *sf (per veicoli)* garage; *(per aerei)* hangar; *(nel calcio)* throw-in.

rimesso, -a *pp* → **rimettere**.

rimettere *vt (mettere di nuovo)* to put back; *(indossare di nuovo)* to put back on; *(perdonare)* to forgive, to pardon; *(vomitare)* to vomit; **~ a posto** to tidy up; **rimetterci (qc)** to lose (sthg) ❑ **rimettersi** *vr (guarire)* to get better, to recover; *(tempo)* to clear up; **rimettersi a fare qc** to start doing sthg again.

rimmel® *sm inv* mascara.

rimodernare *vt* to modernize.

rimontare *vt* to reassemble ♦ *vi* to catch up.

rimorchiare *vt (veicolo)* to tow; *(fam: ragazza)* to pick up.

rimorchiatore *sm* tug.

rimorchio *sm (operazione)* towing; *(di veicolo)* trailer.

rimorso *sm* remorse.

rimosso, -a *pp* → **rimuovere**.

rimozione *sf (spostamento)* removal; *(da carica, impiego)* dismissal; '**~ forzata** ○ **coatta**' 'towaway zone'.

rimpatriare *vt* to repatriate ♦ *vi* to go home.

rimpiangere *vt*: **~ di aver fatto qc** to regret doing sthg.

rimpianto, -a *pp* → **rimpiangere** ♦ *sm* regret.

rimpiattino *sm* hide-and-seek.

rimpiazzare *vt* to replace.

rimpicciolire *vt* to make smaller ♦ *vi* to become smaller.

rimpinzarsi : rimpinzarsi di *vr + prep* to stuff o.s. with.

rimproverare *vt* to scold.

rimprovero *sm* scolding.

rimuginare *vt* to brood over ♦ *vi*: **~ (su qc)** to ponder (sthg).

rimuovere *vt (spostare)* to remove; *(da carica)* to dismiss.

Rinascimento *sm*: **il ~** the Renaissance.

rinascita *sf (di foglie, capelli)* regrowth; *(economica, sociale)* revival.

rincalzare *vt (lenzuola)* to tuck in; *(muro, scala)* to prop up.

rincarare *vi* to increase in price.

rincasare *vi* to return home.

rinchiudere *vt* to confine ❑ **rinchiudersi in** *vr + prep* to shut o.s. up in.

rinchiuso, -a *pp* → **rinchiudere**.

rincorrere *vt* to chase.

rincorsa *sf* run-up.

rincorso, -a *pp* → **rincorrere**.

rincrescere *vi*: **mi rincresce che tu parta** I'm sorry you're leaving; **mi rincresce di non poterti aiutare** I'm sorry I can't help you.

rinculo *sm* recoil.

rinfacciare *vt*: ~ qc a qn (*colpa, difetto*) to reproach sb with O for sthg; (*favore*) to throw sthg in sb's face.

rinforzare *vt* (*muscoli, capelli*) to strengthen; (*rendere più solido*) to reinforce.

rinforzo *sm* reinforcement.

rinfrescante *agg* refreshing.

rinfrescare *vt* (*atmosfera*) to cool ◆ *v impers*: è **rinfrescato** it's got cooler; ~ **la memoria a** qn to refresh sb's memory ▫ **rinfrescarsi** *vr* (*ristorarsi*) to refresh o.s.; (*lavarsi*) to freshen up.

rinfresco, -schi *sm* reception.

rinfusa : **alla rinfusa** *avv* higgledy-piggledy.

ringhiare *vi* to snarl.

ringhiera *sf* (*di balcone*) railings (*pl*); (*di scala*) banisters (*pl*).

ringiovanire *vt*: ~ qn to make sb look younger ◆ *vi* to look young again, to be rejuvenated.

ringraziamento *sm* thanks (*pl*).

ringraziare *vt* to thank; ~ qn **di** qc to thank sb for sthg.

rinnegare *vt* (*persona*) to disown; (*fede*) to renounce.

rinnovamento *sm* (*cambiamento*) updating; (*di impianti, locale*) renovation.

rinnovare *vt* to renew; (*locale*) to renovate.

rinnovo *sm* (*di contratto, guardaroba*) renewal; (*di casa*) renovation.

rinoceronte *sm* rhinoceros.

rinomato, -a *agg* famous.

rinsaldare *vt* to strengthen.

rintocco, -chi *sm* (*di campana*) toll; (*di orologio*) chime.

rintracciare *vt* to track down.

rintronare *vt* to deafen ◆ *vi* to boom.

rinuncia, -ce *sf* renunciation.

rinunciare : **rinunciare a** *v + prep* (*rifiutare*) to renounce; (*privarsi di*) to give up; ~ **a fare** qc to give up doing sthg.

rinunzia = rinuncia.

rinunziare = renunciare.

rinvenire *vt* (*trovare*) to find; (*scoprire*) to find out ◆ *vi* to come round/to, to revive.

rinvenuto, -a *pp* → rinvenire.

rinviare *vt* to return; ~ qc (**a**) (*posporre*) to postpone sthg (until).

rinvio *sm* (*di lettera, palla*) return; (*di appuntamento, riunione*) postponement; (*a pagina, capitolo*) cross-reference.

rione *sm* quarter.

riordinare *vt* (*mettere in ordine*) to tidy up; (*cambiare ordine*) to reorganize.

riorganizzare *vt* to reorganize.

riparare *vt* (*aggiustare*) to repair; (*proteggere*) to protect; (*rimediare*) to make up for ▫ **ripararsi** *vr* to shelter; **ripararsi da** qc to shelter/protect o.s. from sthg.

riparazione *sf* repair.

riparo *sm* (*protezione*) protection; (*rifugio*) shelter.

ripartire *vt* (*eredità, guadagno*) to share out; (*compiti, responsabilità*) to allocate ◆ *vi* to leave again.

ripassare *vt* to go over ◆ *vi* to go/come back.

ripensare : **ripensare a** *v + prep (riflettere su)* to think over; *(cambiare idea)* to change one's mind about; *(ricordare)* to recall.

ripercosso, -a *pp →* **ripercuotersi**.

ripercuotersi : **ripercuotersi su** *vr + prep* to influence.

ripercussione *sf* repercussion.

ripescare *vt (dall'acqua)* to fish out; *(ritrovare)* to find.

ripetere *vt* to repeat ❏ **ripetersi** *vr (persona)* to repeat o.s.; *(avvenimento)* to happen again.

ripetitivo, -a *agg* repetitive.

ripetizione *sf (replica)* repetition ❏ **ripetizioni** *sfpl* private lessons.

ripiano *sm* shelf.

ripicca, -che *sf*: **per ~** out of spite.

ripido, -a *agg* steep.

ripiegare *vt (lenzuola)* to fold (up); *(piegare di nuovo)* to refold ◆ *vi (indietreggiare)* to retreat ❏ **ripiegare su** *v + prep (rassegnarsi a)* to make do with.

ripiego, -ghi *sm* expedient; **per ~** as a makeshift.

ripieno, -a *agg*: **~ (di qc)** *(casa, cassetto)* full (of sthg); *(panino)* filled (with sthg); *(tacchino)* stuffed (with sthg) ◆ *sm (di panino)* filling.

riporre *vt (mettere al suo posto)* to put back; *(mettere via)* to put away; **~ la propria fiducia in qn** to place one's trust in sb.

riportare *vt (restituire, ricondurre)* to take/bring back; *(riferire)*

to report, to tell; *(ottenere)* to obtain.

riposare *vi (rilassarsi)* to rest; *(dormire)* to sleep ◆ *vt* to rest ❏ **riposarsi** *vr (rilassarsi)* to rest; *(dormire)* to sleep.

riposo *sm* rest; *(sonno)* sleep; **a ~** retired.

ripostiglio *sm* store room.

riposto, -a *pp →* **riporre**.

riprendere *vt (prendere di nuovo)* to take again; *(ritirare)* to take back; *(ricominciare)* to resume; *(rimproverare)* to reproach; *(filmare)* to shoot, to film ◆ *vi*: **~ a fare qc** to start doing sthg again ❏ **riprendersi da** *vr + prep* to recover from.

ripresa *sf (di attività)* resumption; *(da malattia)* recovery; *(di motore)* acceleration; *(cinematografica)* shot; **a più riprese** several times.

ripreso, -a *pp →* **riprendere**.

riprodotto, -a *pp →* **riprodurre**.

riprodurre *vt* to reproduce ❏ **riprodursi** *vr* to reproduce.

riproduzione *sf* reproduction.

riprova *sf* confirmation.

riprovevole *agg* reprehensible.

ripugnante *agg* disgusting.

ripugnare *vi*: **~ a qn** *(disgustare qn)* to repel o disgust sb.

ripulire *vt (pulire)* to clean up; *(rubare)* to clean out.

riquadro *sm* square; *(di parete, soffitto)* panel.

risalire *vt* to go back up.

risalire a *v + prep* to go back to.

risaltare *vi* to stand out.

risalto *sm* prominence; **mettere in ~ qc** to make sthg stand out.

risaputo, -a *agg*: **è ~ che ...** it is common knowledge that ...

risarcimento *sm* compensation.

risarcire *vt*: **~ qn (di qc)** to compensate sb (for sthg).

risata *sf* laugh.

riscaldamento *sm* heating; **~ centrale** central heating.

riscaldare *vt* (*stanza*) to heat; (*mani*) to warm; (*cibo*) to heat up □ **riscaldarsi** *vr* (*persona*) to warm up; (*diventare caldo*) to get warmer.

riscatto *sm* ransom.

rischiarare *vt* to light up □ **rischiararsi** *vr* to clear.

rischiare *vt* to risk ♦ *vi*: **rischio di arrivare in ritardo** I'm likely to be late; **ha rischiato di essere investito** he nearly got run over.

rischio *sm* risk; **correre il ~ di fare qc** to run the risk of doing sthg.

rischioso, -a *agg* risky.

risciacquare *vt* to rinse.

riscontrare *vt* to find.

riscontro *sm* (*conferma*) confirmation.

riscosso, -a *pp* → riscuotere.

riscuotere *vt* (*somma*) to collect; (*stipendio, pensione*) to receive; (*assegno*) to cash; (*successo, consenso*) to win, to earn.

risentire : **risentire di** *v + prep* to be affected by □ **risentirsi** *vr*: **risentirsi di** ○ **per qc** to take offence at sthg.

riserva *sf* (*provvista, giocatore*) reserve; (*di caccia, pesca*) preserve; (*restrizione*) reservation; **essere in ~** (*AUTO*) to be low on petrol (*Br*) o gas (*Am*); **di ~** in reserve.

riservare *vt* to save; (*prenotare*) to book, to reserve.

riservato, -a *agg* (*posto, carattere*) reserved; (*informazione, lettera*) confidential.

risi e bisi *smpl* rice and pea soup (*a speciality of Veneto*).

risiedere *vi* to reside.

riso *pp* → ridere ♦ *sm* (*cereale*) rice; (*il ridere: pl* f **risa**) laughter.

risolto, -a *pp* → risolvere.

risoluto, -a *agg* (*deciso*) determined.

risoluzione *sf* (*decisione*) resolution.

risolvere *vt* (*problema, caso*) to solve; (*questione*) to resolve □ **risolversi** *vr* (*problema*) to resolve itself; **risolversi a** *vr + prep*: **risolversi a fare qc** to make up one's mind to do sthg; **risolversi in** *vr + prep* (*andare a finire*) to turn out.

risonanza *sf* resonance; **avere grande ~** (*fatto, notizia*) to arouse a great deal of interest.

risorgere *vi* (*risuscitare*) to revive; (*problema*) to recur.

risorsa *sf* resort □ **risorse** *sfpl* resources.

risorto, -a *pp* → risorgere.

risotto *sm* risotto; **~ alla boscaiola** risotto with tomatoes, mushrooms and parsley; **~ di mare** seafood risotto; **~ alla milanese** risotto with saffron and lots of

Parmesan cheese; ~ **ai tartufi** *risotto with truffles.*

risparmiare *vi* to save ♦ *vt* (*non consumare*) to save; (*non uccidere*) to spare; (*evitare*): ~ **qc a qn** to spare sb sthg.

risparmio *sm* (*somma*) savings (*pl*); (*di tempo, soldi, fatica*) saving.

rispecchiare *vt* to reflect.

rispettabile *agg* respectable.

rispettare *vt* to respect; **farsi ~** to command respect.

rispettivamente *avv* respectively.

rispettivo, -a *agg* respective.

rispetto *sm* respect; **mancare di ~ (a qn)** to be disrespectful (to sb); **~ a** (*a paragone di*) compared to; (*in relazione a*) as for.

rispettoso, -a *agg* respectful.

risplendere *vi* to shine.

rispondere *vi* to answer, to reply; (*freni*) to respond ❑ **rispondere a** *v + prep* (*corrispondere*) to meet; **~ a qn** to answer sb; **rispondere di** *v + prep* to be responsible for.

risposta *sf* answer; (*azione*) response; **in ~ a qc** in reply to sthg.

risposto *pp* → **rispondere**.

rissa *sf* brawl.

ristabilire *vt* to restore ❑ **ristabilirsi** *vr* to recover.

ristagnare *vi* (*acqua*) to become stagnant; (*fig: industria*) to stagnate.

ristampa *sf* (*opera*) reprint.

ristorante *sm* restaurant.

ristoro *sm* refreshment.

ristretto, -a *pp* → **restringere** ♦ *agg* (*numero*) limited; (*brodo*) thick; (*uso*) restricted.

ristrutturare *vt* (*azienda*) to reorganize; (*casa*) to alter.

risucchiare *vt* to suck in.

risultare *vi* to turn out to be; **mi risulta che ...** I understand that ...; **non mi risulta** not as far as I know ❑ **risultare da** *v + prep* to result from.

risultato *sm* result.

risuolare *vt* to resole.

risuscitare *vt* to resuscitate.

risvegliare *vt* (*dal sonno*) to wake up; (*memoria, appetito*) to awaken.

risvolto *sm* (*di pantaloni*) turn-up (*Br*), cuff (*Am*); (*di giacca*) lapel; (*fig: conseguenza*) implication.

ritagliare *vt* to cut out.

ritaglio *sm* (*di giornale*) cutting; (*di stoffa*) scrap; **nei ritagli di tempo** in one's spare time.

ritardare *vi* to be late ♦ *vt* (*rimandare*) to delay; (*rallentare*) to slow down.

ritardatario, -a *sm, f* latecomer.

ritardo *sm* (*di treno, pagamento*) delay; **in ~** late.

ritenere *vt* (*giudicare*) to believe; (*somma*) to deduct.

ritentare *vt* to try again.

ritirare *vt* to withdraw; (*pacco, da lavanderia*) to collect; (*insulto, promessa*) to take back ❑ **ritirarsi** *vr* (*da attività*) to retire; (*restringersi*) to shrink.

ritirata *sf* retreat.

ritiro sm (di pacco) collection; (di patente, passaporto) confiscation; (sportivo, spirituale) retreat; (da attività) retirement.

ritmo sm (MUS) rhythm; (di pulsazioni) beat; (di vita, lavoro) pace.

rito sm rite.

ritornare vi (andare, venire di nuovo) to return, to go/come back; (ricomparire) to recur; (ridiventare): ~ **pulito** to be clean again.

ritornello sm chorus.

ritorno sm return; **essere di ~** to be back.

ritrarre vt (ritirare) to withdraw; (rappresentare) to portray.

ritratto, -a pp → **ritrarre** ◆ sm portrait.

ritrovare vt (cosa persa) to find; (riacquistare) to regain □ **ritrovarsi** vr (incontrarsi) to meet; (in situazione) to find o.s.

ritrovo sm meeting place.

ritto, -a agg upright.

riunione sf (incontro) meeting; (riconciliazione) reconciliation.

riunire vt to bring together □ **riunirsi** vr to meet.

riuscire vi (avere esito) to turn out; (aver successo) to succeed; ~ **a fare qc** to manage to do sthg; ~ **in qc** to succeed in sthg.

riva sf (di fiume) bank; (di lago, mare) shore.

rivale agg & smf rival.

rivalutare vt to revalue.

rivedere vt (vedere di nuovo) to see again; (riesaminare) to review; (ripassare) to revise □ **rivedersi** vr to meet again.

rivelare vt to reveal.

rivendicare vt (diritto, bene) to claim; (attentato) to claim responsibility for.

rivendita sf (negozio) dealer.

rivenditore, -trice sm, f retailer; ~ **autorizzato** authorized dealer.

riversare vt (fig: affetto) to lavish; (colpa) to heap □ **riversarsi** vr to pour.

rivestimento sm covering.

rivestire vt (poltrona) to cover; (carica) to hold; (ruolo) to play □ **rivestirsi** vr to get dressed again.

riviera sf coast.

---

i | **LA RIVIERA ADRIATICA**

The bathing resorts which line the winding Adriatic coast are collectively known as "la Riviera Adriatica". Tourists from the rest of Italy and from abroad flock to famous resorts like Jesolo near Venice and Rimini on the Romagna coast. Renowned for its beautiful beaches and its first-rate amenities, Rimini is the quintessential Italian seaside town, teeming with life 24 hours a day.

---

rivincita sf (di partita) return match; (rivalsa) revenge.

rivisto, -a pp → **rivedere** ◆ sf (giornale) magazine.

rivolgere vt (parola) to address; (attenzione, occhiata) to direct □ **rivolgersi a** vr + prep to go and speak to.

rivoltante agg revolting.

rivoltare vt (rigirare) to turn over; (disgustare) to disgust ◻ **rivoltarsi** vr to rebel.

rivoltella sf revolver.

rivolto, -a pp → **rivolgere** ◆ sf revolt.

rivoluzionario, -a agg & sm, f revolutionary.

rivoluzione sf revolution.

rizzare vt to stand on end ◻ **rizzarsi** vr to stand up.

roastbeef ['rɔzbif] sm inv joint of beef braised or grilled, then served sliced.

roba sf (cose) stuff, things (pl); ~ da mangiare things to eat; ~ da matti! (well I) never!

robiola sf a type of soft rindless cheese.

robot sm inv (automa) robot; (da cucina) food processor.

robusto, -a agg robust, sturdy.

rocca, -che sf fortress.

roccaforte sf stronghold.

rocchetto sm reel, spool.

roccia, -ce sf rock.

roccioso, -a agg rocky.

roco, -a, -chi, -che agg hoarse.

rodaggio sm running-in.

rodere vt to gnaw ◻ **rodersi di** vr + prep to be consumed with.

rogna sf (malattia) scabies; (fam: guaio) nuisance.

rognone sm kidney; **rognoni alla romana** kidneys fried with garlic, parsley and white wine.

Roma sf Rome.

Romania sf: **la ~** Romania.

romanico, -a, -ci, -che agg Romanesque.

romano, -a agg & sm, f Roman.

romanticismo sm romanticism.

romantico, -a, -ci, -che agg romantic.

romanzo sm (libro) novel.

rombo sm (rumore) roar; (pesce) turbot; **a rombi** (disegno) diamond-patterned.

rompere vt to break; (fidanzamento) to break off; (strappare) to tear ◆ vi (coppia) to break up; **rompersi una gamba** to break one's leg; **smetti di ~!** (fam) lay off! ◻ **rompersi** vr to break.

rompicapo sm puzzle.

rompiscatole smf inv (fam) pest, pain in the neck.

rondine sf swallow.

ronzare vi to buzz.

ronzio sm (di insetti) buzzing; (rumore) drone.

rosa agg inv (di colore) pink; (sentimentale) sentimental ◆ sf rose ◆ sm (colore) pink.

rosé sm inv rosé.

rosicchiare vt to gnaw, to nibble.

rosmarino sm rosemary.

roso, -a pp → **rodere**.

rosolare vt to brown.

rosolia sf German measles (sg).

rosone sm (di soffitti) ceiling rose; (vetrata) rose window.

rospo sm toad.

rossetto sm lipstick.

rosso, -a agg & sm red; ~ **d'uovo** egg yolk.

rosticceria sf shop selling cooked

food such as roast chicken, lasagna etc.

rosticciana *sf* grilled or fried pork.

rotaie *sfpl* rails.

rotazione *sf* rotation.

rotella *sf* cog.

rotolare *vi (palla, valanga)* to roll ❑ **rotolarsi** *vr* to roll.

rotolo *sm* roll; **andare a rotoli** to go to rack and ruin.

rotonda *sf* circular terrace.

rotondo, -a *agg* round.

rotta *sf* route.

rottame *sm* scrap.

rotto, -a *pp →* **rompere ◆** *agg (spezzato, guasto)* broken; *(strappato)* torn.

rottura *sf (azione)* breaking; *(interruzione)* breaking-off; *(fam: seccatura)* nuisance.

roulette [ru'lɛt] *sf* roulette.

roulotte [ru'lɔt] *sf inv* caravan.

routine [ru'tin] *sf inv* routine.

rovente *agg* red-hot.

rovescia *sf:* **alla ~** upside down; *(sottosopra)* inside out.

rovesciare *vt (liquido)* to spill; *(tavolo, sedia)* to overturn; *(situazione)* to turn upside down ❑ **rovesciarsi** *vr (versarsi)* to spill; *(capovolgersi)* to overturn; *(barca)* to capsize.

rovescio *sm (di vestito, stoffa)* wrong side; *(pioggia)* downpour; *(nel tennis)* backhand; **al ~** *(con l'interno all'esterno)* inside out; *(con il davanti didietro)* back to front.

rovina *sf* ruin; **andare in ~** to collapse ❑ **rovine** *sfpl* ruins.

rovinare *vt* to ruin ❑ **rovinarsi**

vr (cosa) to be ruined; *(persona)* to be ruined.

rovo *sm* bramble bush.

rozzo, -a *agg* rough.

ruba *sf:* **andare a ~** to sell like hot cakes.

rubare *vt* to steal ◆ *vi:* **hanno rubato in casa mia** my house has been burgled; **~ qc a qn** to steal sthg from sb.

rubinetto *sm* tap.

rubino *sm* ruby.

rubrica, -che *sf (di indirizzi)* address book; *(di giornale)* column.

ruderi *smpl* ruins.

rudimentale *agg* rudimentary, basic.

ruffiano, -a *sm, f* creep.

ruga, -ghe *sf* wrinkle.

rugby ['rɛgbi] *sm* rugby.

ruggine *sf* rust.

ruggire *vi* to roar.

rugiada *sf* dew.

rullino *sm* roll of film; **un ~ da 24** a 24-exposure film.

rullo *sm (rotolo, arnese)* roller; *(di tamburo)* roll.

rum *sm inv* rum.

rumore *sm* noise.

rumoroso, -a *agg* noisy.

ruolo *sm* role.

ruota *sf* wheel; **~ di scorta** spare wheel.

ruotare *vi & vt* to rotate.

rupe *sf* cliff.

ruscello *sm* stream.

ruspa *sf* excavator.

Russia *sf:* **la ~** Russia.

russo, -a *agg, sm & sf* Russian.

rustico, -a, -ci, -che *agg* rustic.

ruttare *vi* to belch.

ruvido, -a *agg* rough.

ruzzolare *vi* to tumble down.

ruzzolone *sm* tumble.

S

sabato *sm* Saturday; **torniamo ~** we'll be back on Saturday; **oggi è ~** it's Saturday today; **~ 6 maggio** Saturday 6 May; **~ pomeriggio** Saturday afternoon; **~ prossimo** next Saturday; **~ scorso** last Saturday; **di ~** on Saturdays; **a ~!** see you Saturday!

sabbia *sf* sand.

sabotare *vt* to sabotage.

sacca, -che *sf (borsa)* bag.

saccarina *sf* saccharin.

saccente *agg* conceited.

saccheggiare *vt (case, villaggi)* to loot; *(fig: con acquisti)* to buy up.

sacchetto *sm* bag.

sacco, -chi *sm (di carta, nylon®)* bag; *(di iuta)* sack; **un ~ di** a lot of; **~ a pelo** sleeping bag.

sacerdote *sm* priest.

sacrificare *vt* to sacrifice □ **sacrificarsi** *vr* to make sacrifices.

sacrificio *sm* sacrifice.

sacro, -a *agg* sacred.

sadico, -a, -ci, -che *agg* sadistic ◆ *sm, f* sadist.

safari *sm inv* safari.

saggezza *sf* wisdom.

saggio, -a, -gi, -ge *agg* wise ◆ *sm (persona)* wise man, sage; *(campione)* sample; *(libro, ricerca)* essay.

Sagittario *sm* Sagittarius.

sagoma *sf (profilo, forma)* outline; *(fam: persona)* character.

sagra *sf* festival, feast.

---

i SAGRA

A "sagra" is a local festival held in celebration of the agricultural produce typical of a particular town or village (wine, truffles, cherries and so on). As well as sampling and buying the local produce, you can eat and drink in the open air and sometimes dance to the music of the local brass band.

---

sai → **sapere**.

saint-honoré [sɛtɔnɔ're] *sm inv* dessert consisting of a puff pastry base topped with cream and surrounded by choux buns.

sala *sf (salotto)* living room; *(di palazzo)* hall; **~ d'aspetto** o **d'attesa** waiting room; **~ da gioco** gaming room; **~ operatoria** operating theatre; **~ da pranzo** dining room.

salame *sm* salami.

salare *vt* to salt.

salario *sm* wage.

salatini *smpl* salted crackers.

salato, -a *agg (con sale)* salted; *(con troppo sale)* salty; *(fam: caro)* expensive.

saldare *vt (metalli)* to weld; *(de-*

bito, conto) to settle.

saldo, -a *agg (resistente, stabile)* firm ◆ *sm* balance ❑ **saldi** *mpl* sales.

sale *sm* salt; **~ grosso** cooking salt.

salice *sm* willow; **~ piangente** weeping willow.

saliente *agg* salient.

saliera *sf* saltcellar *(Br)*, salt shaker *(Am)*.

salire *vt (scale)* to go up ◆ *vi* to go up; *(aereo)* to climb; **~ in** o **su** *(treno, moto)* to get onto; *(auto)* to get into; **~ su** *(tetto, podio)* to climb onto; **~ a bordo** to board.

salita *sf* climb; **in ~** uphill.

saliva *sf* saliva.

salmì *sm* → **lepre**.

salmone *sm* salmon.

salone *sm (sala)* sitting room; *(mostra)* show.

salotto *sm* lounge.

salpare *vi (partire)* to set sail ◆ *vt:* **~ l'ancora** to weigh anchor.

salsa *sf* sauce; **~ di pomodoro** tomato sauce.

salsiccia, -ce *sf* sausage.

saltare *vt (scavalcare)* to jump (over); *(omettere)* to skip ◆ *vi* to jump; **fare ~ qc** to blow sthg up; **~ fuori (da qc)** to jump out (from sthg); **~ giù da qc** to jump down from sthg; **~ su (qc)** to jump on (sthg).

saltimbocca *sm inv* thin slices of veal rolled up with ham and sage.

salto *sm (balzo)* jump; *(visita):* **fare un ~ in città** to pop into town; **~ in alto/lungo** high/long

jump; **~ con l'asta** pole vault.

salumeria *sf* delicatessen.

salumi *smpl* cold meats and salami.

salutare *vt (incontrandosi)* to greet, to say hello to; *(andando via)* to say goodbye to ❑ **salutarsi** *vr (incontrandosi)* to say hello; *(andando via)* to say goodbye; **salutamelo!** say hello to him from me!

salute *sf* health; **bere alla ~ di qn** to drink to sb's health.

saluto *sm (incontrandosi)* greeting; *(andando via)* goodbye; *(col capo)* nod; *(con la mano)* wave.

salvadanaio *sm* moneybox.

salvagente *sm (giubbotto)* life jacket; *(ciambella)* life buoy; *(spartitraffico)* traffic island.

salvaguardare *vt* to safeguard.

salvare *vt (vita, persona)* to survive; *(onore)* to protect ❑ **salvarsi** *vr* to save o.s.

salvataggio *sm* rescue.

salvavita® *sm inv* fuse box.

salve *esclam (fam)* hello!

salvezza *sf* safety.

salvia *sf* sage.

salvietta *sf* wet wipe.

salvo, -a *agg* safe ◆ *prep* except for; **essere in ~** to be safe; **~ imprevisti** barring accidents.

san → **santo**.

sandali *smpl* sandals.

sangue *sm* blood; **a ~ freddo** in cold blood.

sanguinare *vi* to bleed.

sanità *sf* health service.

sanitario, -a *agg (sistema,*

servizio) health *(dav s)*; *(condizioni)*
sanitary ❑ **sanitari** *smpl* bathroom fittings.
San Marino *sf* San Marino.

i SAN MARINO

In central northern Italy, not far
from the Adriatic coast, sits San
Marino, one of the world's smallest
countries. Although it is only 60
kilometres square, it is a fully independent sovereign state, and has its
own currency and stamps.

sano, -a *agg* healthy; ~ e salvo
safe and sound; ~ come un pesce
as fit as a fiddle.
San Silvestro *sf*: la notte di ~
New Year's Eve.

i SAN SILVESTRO

New Year's Eve is known as "San
Silvestro" in Italy. People either
spend the evening at home, with
family and friends, or go out to a
"veglione" (dance) which lasts until
the small hours of New Year's Day.
A "cenone" (big dinner) is eaten, and
on the stroke of midnight bottles of
"spumante" (sparkling wine) are
uncorked and everyone wishes each
other "buon anno" (Happy New
Year). Firecrackers are let off and in
some areas the tradition of throwing
old objects out of the window still
survives.

santo, -a *agg* holy ♦ *sm, f* saint;
Santo Stefano = Boxing Day; **tutto
il ~ giorno** all day long.

i SANTO

Every village, town and city in
Italy has its own patron saint,
honoured once a year with a festival
combining religious processions and
ceremonies with other more secular
events. The streets are decorated
with illuminations and there is often
a funfair and sweet stalls. Schools
and businesses are closed for the
day.

santuario *sm* sanctuary.
sanzione *sf* sanction.
sapere *vt* to know; **mi sa che
non viene** I don't think he's coming; ~ **fare qc** to know how to do
sthg; **sai sciare?** can you ski?; **far ~
qc a qn** to let sb know sthg ❑
sapere di *v + prep* to taste of.
sapone *sm* soap; ~ **da bucato** =
household soap.
saponetta *sf* bar of soap.
sapore *sm* taste, flavour.
saporito, -a *agg* tasty.
saracinesca, -sche *sf* shutter.
sarcastico, -a, -ci, -che *agg*
sarcastic.
sarde *sfpl*: ~ **e beccaficu** *fried sar-
dines stuffed with breadcrumbs,
pecorino cheese and tomatoes.*
Sardegna *sf*: la ~ Sardinia.
sardina *sf* sardine.
sardo, -a *agg & sm, f* Sardinian.
sarto, -a *sm, f* dressmaker; *(per
azienda)* tailor.
sartù *sm inv*: ~ **di riso** *rice mould
filled with liver, mushrooms, peas,
meatballs, mozzarella cheese and*

boiled eggs (a speciality of Naples).

sasso *sm* stone.

sassofono *sm* saxophone.

satellite *sm (naturale, artificiale)* satellite; *(TV)* satellite TV.

satira *sf* satire.

sauna *sf* sauna.

savoiardi *smpl* sponge fingers.

saziare *vt* to satisfy.

sazietà *sf:* **mangiare a ~** to eat one's fill.

sazio, -a *agg* full.

sbadato, -a *agg* careless.

sbadigliare *vi* to yawn.

sbadiglio *sm* yawn.

sbafo *sm:* **a ~** at somebody else's expense.

sbagliare *vt* to get wrong ♦ *vi (fare un errore)* to make a mistake; *(avere torto)* to be wrong; **~ mira** to miss one's aim; **~ strada** to take the wrong road; **ho sbagliato a contare** I counted wrong ❑

sbagliarsi *vr (fare un errore)* to make a mistake; *(avere torto)* to be wrong; **sbagliarsi di grosso** to be completely wrong.

sbagliato, -a *agg* wrong.

sbaglio *sm* mistake; **fare uno ~** to make a mistake; **fare qc per ~** to do sthg by mistake.

sballottare *vt* to toss about.

sbalzare *vt* to throw.

sbalzo *sm (di temperatura)* sudden change.

sbandare *vi* to skid.

sbandata *sf* skid; **prendersi una ~ per qn** to fall for sb.

sbandierare *vt (sventolare)* to wave; *(ostentare)* to show off.

sbando *sm:* **allo ~** adrift.

sbaraglio *sm:* **andare allo ~** to risk everything.

sbarazzare *vt* to clear up ❑

sbarazzarsi di *vr + prep* to get rid of.

sbarazzino, -a *agg* cheeky.

sbarcare *vt (merce)* to unload; *(passeggeri)* to disembark ♦ *vi (da nave)* to disembark.

sbarco *sm (di merci)* unloading; *(di passeggeri)* disembarkation.

sbarra *sf (spranga)* bar; *(segno grafico)* stroke; *(di passaggio a livello)* barrier.

sbarrare *vt (porta, finestra)* to bar; *(passaggio)* to block; **~ gli occhi** to open one's eyes wide.

sbarrato, -a *agg (strada)* blocked; *(porta)* barred; *(casella)* crossed; *(parola)* crossed out; *(occhi)* wide open.

sbatacchiare *vt* to bang, to slam.

sbattere *vt* to beat; *(porta)* to bang, to slam ♦ *vi* to bang; **~ contro (muro)** to bang against, to knock against; **~ fuori qn** to throw sb out ❑ **sbattersene** *vr (fam)* not to give a damn.

sbattuto, -a *agg* downcast.

sbavare *vi* to dribble.

sbellicarsi *vr:* **~ dal ridere** to split one's sides laughing.

sbiadire *vt* to fade ❑ **sbiadirsi** *vr* to fade.

sbiadito, -a *agg* faded.

sbiancare *vi* to grow pale ♦ *vt* to bleach.

sbieco, -a, -chi, -che *agg:* **di ~** *(obliquamente)* at an angle.

sbigottire vt to dismay □ **sbigottirsi** vr to be dismayed.

sbigottito, -a agg dismayed, aghast.

sbilanciare vt to unbalance □ **sbilanciarsi** vr (perdere l'equilibrio) to lose one's balance; (fig: compromettersi) to compromise o.s.

sbirciare vt (con curiosità) to eye; (di sfuggita) to peep at.

sbizzarrirsi vr to satisfy one's whims.

sbloccare vt to unblock; ~ **la situazione** to get things moving □ **sbloccarsi** vr (meccanismo) to become unblocked; (situazione) to return to normal.

sboccare : sboccare in v + prep (fiume) to flow into; (strada) to lead into; (concludersi con) to end in.

sboccato, -a agg foulmouthed.

sbocciare vi to bloom.

sbocco, -chi sm (di strada) end; (di fiume) mouth; (fig: esito) way out.

sbornia sf (fam): prendersi una ~ to get plastered.

sborsare vt (pagare) to pay out.

sbottare vi (in risata) to burst out; (di rabbia) to explode.

sbottonare vt to unbutton; sbottonarsi la giacca to undo one's jacket □ **sbottonarsi** vr (fam: confidarsi) to open up.

sbracciarsi vr to wave one's arms about.

sbracciato, -a agg (vestito) sleeveless; (persona) with bare arms.

sbraitare vi to shout.

sbranare vt to tear to pieces.

sbriciolare vt to crumble □ sbriciolarsi vr (pane, muro) to crumble.

sbrigare vt (faccenda) to deal with □ **sbrigarsi** vr to hurry; sbrigarsi a fare qc to hurry up and do sthg.

sbrodolare vt to stain.

sbronza sf (fam): prendersi una ~ to get plastered.

sbronzo, -a agg (fam) plastered.

sbucare vi (uscire) to come out; (saltar fuori) to spring out.

sbucciare vt to peel; sbucciarsi un ginocchio to graze one's knee.

sbuffare vi (per fastidio, noia) to snort; (per caldo) to pant.

scabroso, -a agg indecent.

scacchi smpl chess (sg); a ~ (tessuto) checked.

scacciare vt (persona, animale) to drive away; (preoccupazioni) to dispel.

scadente agg (prodotto) poorquality; (qualità) poor.

scadenza sf (di cibo) sell-by date; (di documento, contratto) expiry date; (di medicinali) "use-by" date; (per iscrizione, consegna) deadline.

scadere vi to expire; (cibo) to pass its sell-by date.

scaffale sm shelf.

scafo sm hull.

scaglia sf (frammento) flake, chip; (di pesce) scale.

scagliare vt to throw □ scagliarsi contro vr + prep (assalire) to hurl o.s. against; (fig:

scapestrato

insultare) to hurl abuse at.

scaglione *sm* echelon; **a scaglioni** in groups.

scala *sf (gradini)* stairs *(pl)*, staircase; *(a pioli)* ladder; *(di valori)* scale; **su larga ~** on a large scale; **~ mobile** escalator; **le scale** the stairs.

scalare *vt (mura, montagna)* to climb; *(somma)* to knock off; *(capelli)* to layer.

scalata *sf* climb.

scalatore, -trice *sm, f* climber.

scalcinato, -a *agg (fig: casa)* shabby.

scaldabagno *sm* water heater.

scaldare *vt* to heat □ **scaldarsi** *vr (al fuoco, al sole)* to warm o.s.; *(fig: accalorarsi)* to get excited.

scaleo *sm* stepladder.

scalfire *vt* to scratch.

scalinata *sf* flight of steps.

scalino *sm* step.

scalmanarsi *vr* to get worked up.

scalo *sm* call; **fare ~ a** *(in aereo)* to make a stopover at; *(in nave)* to call at; **~ merci** goods yard *(Br)*, freight yard *(Am)*.

scaloppina *sf* escalope.

scalpore *sm (risonanza)* stir; **fare** □ **destare ~** to cause a stir.

scaltro, -a *agg* shrewd.

scalzo, -a *agg* barefooted.

scambiare *vt* to exchange, to swap; **~ qn/qc per** *(confondere)* to mistake sb/sthg for; **scambiarsi qc** to exchange sthg.

scambio *sm (di regali, opinioni)* exchange; *(confusione)* mistake;

(COMM) trade; **fare a ~ con qn** to swap with sb.

scampagnata *sf* trip to the country.

scampare *vt* to escape; **scamparla (bella)** to have a narrow escape □ **scampare a** *v + prep* to escape.

scampo *sm*: **non c'è (via di) ~** there is no way out; **trovare ~ in qc** to find safety in sthg □ **scampi** *smpl* scampi *(sg)*.

scampolo *sm* remnant.

scandalizzare *vt* to make a spectacle of o.s. □ **scandalizzarsi** *vr* to be scandalized.

scandalo *sm* scandal; **dare ~ to** make a spectacle of o.s.; **fare ~** to cause a scandal.

scandaloso, -a *agg* scandalous.

Scandinavia *sf*: **la ~** Scandinavia.

scandire *vt* to articulate.

scannare *vt (animale)* to butcher; *(persona)* to cut the throat of.

scansafatiche *smf inv* idler, waster.

scansare *vt (spostare)* to shift; *(colpo)* to ward off; *(difficoltà, fatica)* to avoid; *(persona)* to shun □ **scansarsi** *vr* to step aside.

scanso *sm*: **a ~ di equivoci** (in order) to avoid any misunderstandings.

scantinato *sm* basement.

scanzonato, -a *agg* easygoing.

scapaccione *sm* slap.

scapestrato, -a *agg* dissolute.

scapito *sm*: **a ~ di** to the detriment of.

scapolo *sm* bachelor.

scappamento *sm* → **tubo.**

scappare *vi (fuggire)* to escape; *(da casa)* to run away; *(andare)* to rush; **mi è scappato detto** I let it slip; **mi è scappato di mano** it slipped out of my hands; **mi è scappato di mente** it slipped my mind; **mi è scappato da ridere** I couldn't help laughing; **lasciarsi ~ l'occasione** to miss an opportunity.

scappatella *sf* casual affair.

scappatoia *sf* way out.

scarabocchiare *vt* to scrawl ◆ *vi* to scribble.

scarafaggio *sm* cockroach.

scaramanzia *sf*: **per ~** for luck.

scaraventare *vt* to hurl ☐ **scaraventarsi** *vr* to fling o.s.

scarcerare *vt* to release.

scarica, -che *sf (di pugni)* hail; *(di pistola)* volley; **~ elettrica** electrical discharge.

scaricare *vt (merci, camion, arma)* to unload; *(passeggeri)* to let off; *(batteria)* to run down; *(fig: colpa)* to shift ☐ **scaricarsi** *vr (batteria)* to go flat; *(fig: rilassarsi)* to unwind.

scarico, -a, -chi, -che *agg (camion, arma)* unloaded; *(batteria)* flat ◆ *sm (di merci)* unloading; *(di scarica)* dump; **'divieto di ~'** 'no dumping'.

scarlatto, -a *agg* scarlet.

scarpa *sf* shoe; **che numero di scarpe porta?** what size shoe do you take?; **scarpe da ginnastica** plimsolls *(Br)*, sneakers *(Am)*.

scarpata *sf* slope.

scarponi *smpl* boots; **~ da sci** ski boots.

scarseggiare *vi* to be scarce ☐ **scarseggiare di** *v + prep* to be short of.

scarsità *sf inv* scarcity, shortage.

scarso, -a *agg* scarce; **un chilo ~** just under a kilo.

scartare *vt (regalo)* to unwrap; *(eliminare)* to reject; *(nelle carte)* to discard.

scarto *sm (scelta)* discarding; *(cosa scartata)* reject; *(differenza)* gap, difference.

scassinare *vt* to break open.

scasso *sm* → **furto.**

scatenare *vt* to provoke, to stir up ☐ **scatenarsi** *vr (temporale)* to break; *(persona)* to go wild.

scatenato, -a *agg (persona, ballo)* wild.

scatola *sf* box; *(di latta)* tin, can; **in ~** *(cibo)* tinned, canned; **rompere le scatole a qn** *(fam)* to get up sb's nose.

scattante *agg* agile.

scattare *vt (foto)* to take ◆ *vi (balzare)* to jump; *(molla, congegno)* to be released; *(allarme)* to go off; *(manifestare ira)* to fly into a rage; **far ~** *(molla, congegno)* to release; *(allarme)* to set off.

scatto *sm (di congegno)* release; *(rumore)* click; *(di foto)* shot; *(balzo)* fit; **di ~** suddenly.

scaturire : **scaturire da** *v + prep (sgorgare)* to gush from; *(fig: derivare)* to come from.

scavalcare *vt (muro, ostacolo)* to climb over; *(fig: concorrenti)* to overtake.

scavare vt (fossa, terreno) to dig; (render cavo) to hollow out.

scavo sm excavation.

scegliere vt to choose.

scelta sf choice; (raccolta) selection; **non avere ~** to have no choice; **'frutta o formaggio a ~'** 'choice of fruit or cheese'.

scelto, -a pp → **scegliere** ◆ agg (gruppo) select; (frutta) choice.

scemo, -a agg (fam) stupid, silly.

scena sf scene.

scenata sf row, scene.

scendere vi (venir giù) to go/come down; (da treno) to get off; (diminuire) to go down ◆ vt to go/come down; **~ dal treno** to get off the train; **~ dalla macchina** to get out of the car.

sceneggiato sm serial.

sceneggiatura sf screenplay.

scervellarsi vr to rack one's brains.

sceso, -a pp → **scendere**.

scettico, -a, -ci, -che agg sceptical.

scheda sf (cartoncino) card; (modulo) form; **~ magnetica** magnetic card.

schedare vt (libro) to catalogue; **è stato schedato dalla polizia** he has a police record.

schedario sm (raccolta) file; (mobile) filing cabinet.

schedina sf = pools coupon.

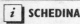

The coupon you fill in to play "totocalcio" (the football pools) is called a "schedina"; it can be bought at tobacconists and bars. Players must predict the results of 13 games, marking the coupon with 1 for a home win, 2 for an away win, and X for a draw. Winners receive prizes ranging from a few thousand to several billion lire.

---

scheggia, -ge sf splinter.

scheletro sm skeleton.

schema, -i sm plan.

scherma sf fencing.

schermo sm screen.

scherno sm derision.

scherzare vi to joke.

scherzo sm (battuta, gesto) joke; (brutto tiro) trick; **è uno ~** (cosa facile) it's child's play; **fare qc per ~** to do sthg for a laugh.

scherzoso, -a agg playful.

schiaccianoci sm inv nutcrackers (pl).

schiacciare vt (comprimere) to crush; (noce) to crack; (pulsante) to press; (fig: avversario) to overwhelm; (SPORT) to smash ❑

schiacciarsi vr to get squashed.

schiacciata sf (focaccia) type of flat salted bread made with olive oil; (SPORT) smash.

schiacciato, -a agg (appiattito) flat; (deformato) squashed.

schiaffo sm slap.

schiamazzi smpl screams.

schiantare vt to break ❑

schiantarsi vr to break up.

schianto sm (rumore) crash; **è uno ~!** (fam) she's/it's a knockout!

schiarire vt to lighten ❑

schiarirsi vr (cielo) to clear up; (co-

lore) to become lighter; **schiarirsi la voce** to clear one's throat.

schiavitù *sf* slavery.

schiavo, -a *sm, f* slave ◆ *agg:* ~ **di** a slave to.

schiena *sf* back.

schienale *sm* back.

schiera *sf* group.

schierare *vt (esercito, squadra)* to draw up; *(libri, oggetti)* to line up □

schierarsi *vr (mettersi in fila)* to line up; **schierarsi con/contro qn** to side with/oppose sb.

schietto, -a *agg (persona)* frank; *(vino)* not watered-down.

schifezza *sf:* **essere una ~** *(cibo)* to be disgusting; *(film)* to be awful.

schifo *sm* disgust; **mi fa ~** it makes me sick; **fare ~** *(cibo, insetto)* to be disgusting; *(film)* to be awful.

schifoso, -a *agg (disgustoso)* disgusting; *(pessimo, brutto)* awful.

schioccare *vt (dita)* to snap; *(lingua)* to click.

schiuma *sf (marina)* foam; *(di sapone)* lather; **~ da barba** shaving foam.

schivare *vt* to dodge, to avoid.

schivo, -a *agg* reserved, shy.

schizzare *vt* to splash ◆ *vi (acqua, getto)* to spurt; *(fig: saltar via)* to dart away.

schizzo *sm (spruzzo)* stain, splash; *(disegno)* sketch.

sci *sm inv (attrezzo)* ski; *(attività)* skiing; **~ d'acqua** water skiing; **~ da fondo** cross-country skiing.

scia *sf (di nave)* wake; *(di profumo, fumo)* trail.

sciacquare *vt* to rinse; **sciac-**

quarsi la bocca to rinse out one's mouth.

sciacquone *sm* flush; **tirare lo ~** to flush the toilet.

sciagura *sf* disaster.

sciagurato, -a *agg (sfortunato)* unlucky; *(cattivo)* wicked.

scialacquare *vt* to squander.

scialbo, -a *agg (colore)* pale; *(sapore)* bland; *(persona)* dull.

scialle *sm* shawl.

scialuppa *sf* sloop; **~ di salvataggio** lifeboat.

sciame *sm* swarm.

sciangai *sm (gioco)* pick-up-sticks.

sciare *vi* to ski.

sciarpa *sf* scarf.

sciatore, -trice *sm, f* skier.

sciatto, -a *agg* untidy.

scientifico, -a, -ci, -che *agg* scientific.

scienza *sf (studio della realtà)* science; *(sapere)* knowledge □ **scienze** *sfpl* science *(sg)*.

scienziato, -a *sm, f* scientist.

scimmia *sf* monkey.

scimmiottare *vt* to ape.

scindere *vt (dividere)* to divide.

scintilla *sf* spark.

scintillare *vi* to sparkle.

scioccare *vt* to shock.

sciocchezza *sf (cosa stupida)* silly thing; *(cosa poco importante)* trifle.

sciocco, -a, -chi, -che *agg* silly.

sciogliere *vt (nodo)* to untie; *(capelli)* to loosen; *(animale)* to let loose; *(ghiaccio, burro)* to melt;

(pastiglia, società) to dissolve; *(mistero)* to solve; *(assemblea)* to close ❑ **sciogliersi** *vr (nodo)* to come untied; *(neve, burro)* to melt.

scioglilingua *sm inv* tongue twister.

sciolto, -a *pp* → **sciogliere** ♦ *agg (disinvolto)* easy; *(agile)* agile.

sciopero *sm* strike; **essere in ~** to be on strike.

sciovia *sf* ski lift.

scippare *vt:* ~ **qn** to snatch sb's bag.

scippo *sm* bagsnatching.

sciroppo *sm (medicina)* cough mixture; *(di frutta)* syrup.

scissione *sf (separazione)* split.

scisso, -a *pp* → **scindere**.

sciupare *vt (vestito, libro)* to spoil, to ruin ❑ **sciuparsi** *vr (rovinarsi)* to get spoiled; *(deperire)* to become run down.

scivolare *vi (scorrere)* to glide; *(perdere l'equilibrio)* to slip, to slide.

scivolo *sm (gioco)* slide.

scivoloso, -a *agg* slippery.

scoccare *vt (freccia)* to shoot ♦ *vi (ore)* to strike.

scocciare *vt (fam)* to annoy ❑ **scocciarsi** *vr (fam)* to be annoyed.

scodella *sf* bowl.

scodinzolare *vi* to wag its tail.

scogliera *sf* rocks *(pl)*.

scoglio *sm (roccia)* rock; *(fig)* stumbling block.

scoiattolo *sm* squirrel.

scolapasta *sm inv* colander.

scolapiatti *sm inv* draining rack.

scolare *vt* to drain.

scolaro, -a *sm, f* schoolboy (f schoolgirl).

scolastico, -a, -ci, -che *agg* school *(dav s)*.

scollare *vt (staccare)* to unstick ❑ **scollarsi** *vr* to come unstuck.

scollato, -a *agg (abito)* low-cut.

scollatura *sf* neckline.

scolorire *vt* to fade ❑ **scolorirsi** *vr* to fade.

scolpire *vt* to sculpt; *(legno)* to carve; *(iscrizione)* to engrave.

scombussolare *vt* to upset.

scommessa *sf* bet.

scommesso, -a *pp* → **scommettere**.

scommettere *vt* to bet.

scomodare *vt* to bother ❑ **scomodarsi** *vr* to put o.s. out; **scomodarsi a fare qc** to go to the bother of doing sthg.

scomodo, -a *agg (poltrona)* uncomfortable; *(orario)* inconvenient.

scompagnato, -a *agg (calzini)* odd.

scomparire *vi (sparire)* to disappear.

scomparso, -a *pp* → **scomparire**.

scompartimento *sm (di treno)* compartment.

scomparto *sm* compartment.

scompigliare *vt (capelli)* to ruffle, to mess up.

scompiglio *sm* confusion.

scomporre *vt (mobile, armadio)* to take to pieces ❑ **scomporsi** *vr (perdere il controllo)* to lose one's composure.

scomposto, -a pp → **scomporre**.

sconcertare vt to disconcert.

sconcio, -a, -ci, -ce agg (osceno) obscene.

sconfiggere vt to defeat.

sconfinare vi (uscire dai confini) to cross the border; (fig): ~ **da** to stray from.

sconfinato, -a agg boundless.

sconfitta sf defeat.

sconfitto, -a pp → **sconfiggere**.

sconforto sm dejection.

scongelare vt to defrost.

scongiurare vt (supplicare) to implore; (pericolo, minaccia) to ward off.

sconnesso, -a agg (ragionamento) incoherent.

sconosciuto, -a agg unknown ♦ sm, f stranger.

sconsiderato, -a agg thoughtless.

sconsigliare vt to advise against; ~ **qc a qn** to advise sb against sthg; ~ **a qn di fare qc** to advise sb against doing sthg.

scontare vt (detrarre) to deduct; (pena) to serve; (colpa, errore) to pay for.

scontato, -a agg (prezzo) discounted; (previsto) taken for granted; **dare qc per ~** to take sthg for granted.

scontento, -a agg: ~ **(di)** dissatisfied (with).

sconto sm discount; **fare uno ~** to give a discount.

scontrarsi vr (urtarsi) to collide; (combattere, discordare) to clash.

scontrino sm receipt; **'munirsi dello scontrino alla cassa'** 'pay at the till and obtain a receipt'.

scontro sm (urto) collision; (combattimento, fig) clash.

scontroso, -a agg surly.

sconveniente agg (indecente) improper.

sconvolgente agg disturbing.

sconvolgere vt (persona) to disturb, to shake; (ordine, piani) to upset.

sconvolto, -a pp → **sconvolgere**.

scopa sf (arnese) broom.

scoperta sf discovery.

scoperto, -a pp → **scoprire** ♦ agg uncovered; (capo, braccia) bare.

scopo sm purpose, aim; **allo ~ di fare qc** in order to do sthg; **a che ~?** for what purpose?

scoppiare vi (spaccarsi) to burst; (esplodere) to explode; ~ **dal caldo** (fam) to be boiling (hot); ~ **a piangere** to burst into tears; ~ **a ridere** to burst out laughing.

scoppio sm (rumore, di pneumatico) bang; (esplosione) explosion; (di risa) burst; (di guerra) outbreak; **a ~ ritardato** delayed-action.

scoprire vt to discover; (liberare da copertura) to uncover □ **scoprirsi** vr (svestirsi) to dress less warmly; (rivelarsi) to give o.s. away.

scoraggiare vt to discourage □ **scoraggiarsi** vr to become discouraged.

scorbutico, -a, -ci, -che agg (scontroso) cantankerous.

scrivania

scorciatoia sf short cut; **prendere una ~** to take a short cut.

scordare vt to forget ◻ **scordarsi di** vr + prep to forget; **scordarsi di fare qc** to forget to do sthg.

scorgere vt to see, to make out.

scorpacciata sf: **fare una ~ (di qc)** to stuff o.s. (with sthg).

scorpione sm scorpion ◻ **Scorpione** sm Scorpio.

scorrazzare vi to run around.

scorrere vi (liquido, fiume, traffico) to flow; (fune) to run; (tempo) to pass ◆ vt (giornale, libro) to glance through.

scorretto, -a agg (errato) incorrect; (sleale) unfair.

scorrevole agg (porta) sliding; (traffico, stile) flowing.

scorrimento sm (di traffico) flow.

scorsa sf: **dare una ~ a qc** to glance through sthg.

scorso, -a pp → scorrere ◆ agg last.

scorta sf: **fare ~ di qc** to stock up with sthg; **di ~** spare.

scortare vt to escort.

scortese agg impolite.

scorticare vt (pelle) to graze; (animale) to skin.

scorto, -a pp → scorgere.

scorza sf (di albero) bark; (di frutto) peel.

scorzanera sf type of bitter-tasting root vegetable.

scosceso, -a agg steep.

scossa sf (movimento) jolt; (elettrica) shock.

scosso, -a pp → scuotere ◆ agg shaken.

scossone sm jolt.

scostare vt to move aside ◻ **scostarsi** vr to move aside.

scotch®¹ [skɔtʃ] sm inv (nastro adesivo) = Sellotape® (Br), Scotch® tape (Am).

scotch² [skɔtʃ] sm inv (whisky) Scotch.

scottadito : **a scottadito** avv piping hot.

scottare vt (ustionare) to burn; (cuocere) to scald ◆ vi (bevanda, pietanza) to be too hot ◻ **scottarsi** vr to burn o.s.

scottatura sf burn.

scotto, -a agg overcooked.

scout ['skaut] smf inv scout.

scovare vt (negozio, ristorante) to discover.

Scozia sf: **la ~** Scotland.

scozzese agg Scottish ◆ smf Scotsman (f Scotswoman); **gli scozzesi** the Scots.

screditare vt to discredit.

screpolare vt to crack ◻ **screpolarsi** vr to crack.

screziato, -a agg streaked.

screzio sm disagreement.

scricchiolare vi to creak.

scricchiolio sm creaking.

scriminatura sf parting.

scritta sf inscription.

scritto, -a pp → scrivere ◆ agg written ◆ sm (opera) work; (cosa scritta) letter.

scrittore, -trice sm, f writer.

scrittura sf writing.

scrivania sf writing desk.

scrivere vt & vi to write; ~ **a qn** to write to sb □ **scriversi** vr (parola): **come si scrive 'cuore'?** how do you write O spell 'cuore'?

scroccare vt (fam) to scrounge.

scrollare vt (agitare) to shake; (spalle) to shrug; **scrollarsi qc di dosso** to shake sthg off.

scrosciare vt (pioggia) to pelt down; (applausi) to thunder.

scroscio sm (d'acqua) pelting; (d'applausi) thunder.

scrostare vt (intonaco) to strip off □ **scrostarsi** vr (pareti, tegame) to peel.

scrupolo sm (timore) scruple; (diligenza) conscientiousness; **senza scrupoli** unscrupulous.

scrupoloso, -a agg (persona) scrupulous; (resoconto, lavoro) meticulous.

scrutare vt to scrutinize; (orizzonte) to search.

scucire vt (cucitura) to unpick □ **scucirsi** vr to come unstitched.

scuderia sf stable.

scudetto sm (SPORT) championship shield.

scudo sm shield.

sculacciare vt to spank.

scultore, -trice sm, f sculptor.

scultura sf sculpture.

scuola sf school; **andare a ~ to** go to school; **~ elementare** = primary school (Br), grade school (Am)(for children aged from 6 to 11); **~ guida** driving school; **~ materna** nursery school (for children aged from 3 to 5); **~ media** first three years of secondary school for children aged

from 11 to 14; **~ dell'obbligo** compulsory education; **scuole tecniche** schools which prepare their students for practical professions; **scuole serali** evening classes.

scuotere vt to shake; (spalle) to shrug □ **scuotersi** vr to shake o.s.

scurire vt to darken ◆ vi to grow dark □ **scurirsi** vr to grow dark.

scuro, -a agg dark ◆ sm (buio) darkness.

scusa sf excuse; **chiedere ~ (a qn)** to apologize (to sb).

scusare vt (perdonare) to forgive; (giustificare) to excuse □ **scusarsi** vr to apologize; **(mi) scusi, dov'è la stazione?** excuse me, where is the station?; **scusi!** sorry!

sdebitarsi vr: ~ **con qn di qc** to repay sb for sthg.

sdentato, -a agg toothless.

sdolcinato, -a agg oversentimental.

sdraia sf deckchair.

sdraiarsi vr to lie down.

sdraio sm: **(sedia a) ~** deckchair.

sdrammatizzare vt to play down.

sdrucciolare vi to slip.

se cong 1. (nel caso in cui) if; **rimani ~ vuoi** stay if you want; **~ è possibile** if it's possible; **~ fossi in te** if I were you; **~ non sbaglio ...** if I'm not wrong ...
2. (dato che) if; **~ lo dici, sarà vero** if you say so, it must be true.
3. (con frasi dubitative & interrogative indirette) whether, if; **vedi ~ puoi venire** see whether O if you can come; **chiedile ~ le piace** ask her if

she likes it.

4. *(esprime un suggerimento)*: **e ~ andassimo al cinema?** how about going to the cinema?

5. *(esprime un augurio)* if; **~ solo potessi!** if only I could!

6. *(in espressioni)*: **anche ~** even if; **~ mai** if ever; **neanche ~** even if; **~ non altro** if nothing else; **~ no** otherwise.

◆ *pron* → **si**.

sé *pron (per cosa)* itself; *(per persona)* himself/herself/themselves; **tenere qc per ~** to keep sthg for oneself; **pensa solo a se stesso** he only thinks of himself.

sebbene *cong* although.

sec. *(abbr di secolo)* c.

secca, -che *sf (di mare, fiume)* shallows *(pl)*.

seccare *vt* to dry; *(prosciugare)* to dry up; *(infastidire)* to annoy ☐ **seccarsi** *vr* to dry; *(prosciugarsi)* to dry up; *(infastidirsi)* to get annoyed.

seccato, -a *agg (infastidito)* annoyed.

seccatore, -trice *sm, f* nuisance.

seccatura *sf (fastidio)* nuisance.

secchiello *sm (contenitore)* bucket.

secchio *sm* bucket.

secchione, -a *sm, f (fam)* swot.

secco, -a, -chi, -che *agg* dry; *(funghi, prugne)* dried; *(brusco)* curt ◆ *sm*: **essere a ~ di qc** *(fig: non avere)* to be without sthg; **tirare in ~ una barca** to beach a boat; **lavare a ~** to dry-clean.

secolare *agg (vecchio di secoli)* age-old.

secolo *sm* century; *(periodo lungo)*: **non lo vedo da secoli** I haven't seen him for ages.

seconda *sf (marcia)* second gear; **viaggiare in ~** to travel second-class; **a ~ di** according to.

secondario, -a *agg* secondary; **scuola secondaria** secondary school.

secondo, -a *num* second ◆ *agg (altro)* second ◆ *sm (tempo)* second; *(portata)* main course ◆ *prep* according to; **~ me** in my opinion; **di seconda mano** second-hand, → **sesto**.

sedano *sm* celery.

sedativo *sm* sedative.

sede *sf (di organizzazione)* headquarters *(pl)*; *(di azienda)* head office.

sedentario, -a *agg* sedentary.

sedere *sm (parte del corpo)* bottom ◆ *vi*: **mettersi a ~** to sit down ☐ **sedersi** *vr* to sit down.

sedia *sf* chair.

sedicesimo, -a *num* sixteenth, → **sesto**.

sedici *num* sixteen, → **sei**.

sedile *sm (di veicolo)* seat.

sedotto, -a *pp* → **sedurre**.

seducente *agg* seductive.

sedurre *vt (uomo, donna)* to seduce; *(sog: idea, proposta)* to appeal to.

seduta *sf* session.

sega, -ghe *sf* saw.

segale *sf* rye.

segare *vt* to saw.

seggio *sm* seat; **~ elettorale**

polling station.

seggiola *sf* chair.

seggiolino *sm (sedia pieghevole)* folding chair.

seggiolone *sm (per bambini)* high chair.

seggiovia *sf* chair lift.

segnalare *vt (comunicare)* to point out; *(indicare)* to indicate.

segnalazione *sf (indicazione)* indication; *(raccomandazione)* recommendation.

segnale *sm (indicazione)* signal; *(stradale)* sign; ~ **acustico** sound signal; ~ **d'allarme** alarm; ~ **orario** time signal.

segnaletica *sf (stradale)* road signs *(pl)*.

segnalibro *sm* bookmark.

segnaposto *sm* place card.

segnare *vt (mettere un segno)* to mark; *(indicare)* to indicate; *(SPORT)* to score; **segnarsi qc** to make a note of sthg.

segno *sm* sign; *(lettera, numero)* symbol; *(contrassegno, traccia)* mark; **fare ~ a qn di fare qc** to signal sb to do sthg; **fare ~ di no** to shake one's head; **fare ~ di sì** to nod one's head; **perdere il ~** to lose one's place; **cogliere** o **colpire nel ~** *(fig)* to hit the mark.

segretario, -a *sm, f* secretary.

segreteria *sf (di azienda, scuola)* secretary's office; *(di partito)* position of Secretary □ **segreteria telefonica** *sf* answering machine.

segreto, -a *agg & sm* secret.

seguente *agg* following, next.

seguire *vt* to follow ◆ *vi* to follow; *(continuare)*: **segue a pag. 70**

continued on page 70.

seguito *sm (proseguimento)* continuation; *(risultato)* result; *(scorta)* retinue; *(favore)* following; **in ~ a** following; **di ~** at a stretch, on end; **in ~** subsequently.

sei[1] → **essere**.

sei[2] *agg num* six; **ha ~ anni** he/she is six (years old); **sono le ~** it's six o'clock; **il ~ gennaio** the sixth of January; **pagina ~** page six; **il ~ di picche** the six of spades; **erano in ~** there were six of them.

seicento *num* six hundred, → **sei** □ **Seicento** *sm*: **il Seicento** the seventeenth century.

selciato *sm* cobbles *(pl)*, cobbled surface.

selettivo, -a *agg* selective.

selezionare *vt* to select.

selezione *sf* selection.

self-service ['sɛl 'sɛrvis] *agg inv* & *sm inv* self-service.

sella *sf* saddle.

selvaggina *sf* game.

selvaggio, -a, -gi, -ge *agg* wild; *(tribù)* savage; *(delitto)* brutal ◆ *sm, f* savage.

selvatico, -a, -ci, -che *agg* wild.

semaforo *sm (apparecchio)* traffic lights *(pl)*.

sembrare *vi* to seem ◆ *v impers*: **sembra che** it seems that; **mi sembra di conoscerlo** I think I know him; **sembra stia per piovere** it looks like it's going to rain.

seme *sm* seed; *(nocciolo)* stone; *(di carte da gioco)* suit.

semestre *sm* six-month period; *(SCOL)* semester.

semifinale *sf* semifinal.

semifreddo *sm* dessert similar to ice cream.

seminare *vt* to sow.

seminario *sm* seminar; *(RELIG)* seminary.

seminterrato *sm* basement.

semmai *cong* if (ever) ◆ *avv* if anything.

semolino *sm* semolina.

semplice *agg* simple; *(filo, consonante)* single; **è una ~ proposta** it's just a suggestion.

semplicemente *avv* simply.

semplicità *sf* simplicity.

semplificare *vt* to simplify.

sempre *avv* always; *(ancora)* still; **va ~ meglio/peggio** things are getting better and better/worse and worse; **~ che ci riesca** provided he manages it; **da ~** always; **di ~ usual; per ~** forever.

senape *sf* mustard.

senato *sm* senate.

senatore, -trice *sm, f* senator.

sennò *avv (altrimenti)* otherwise.

seno *sm (petto)* breast.

sensazionale *agg* sensational.

sensazione *sf* sensation, feeling; **fare ~** to cause a sensation.

sensibile *agg* sensitive; *(notevole)* noticeable; **~ a** *(caldo, freddo)* sensitive to; *(complimenti)* susceptible to.

sensibilità *sf* sensitivity.

senso *sm (facoltà, coscienza)* sense; *(sentimento, impressione)* feeling; *(significato)* meaning, sense; *(direzione)* direction; **non avere ~ to**

make no sense; **a ~ unico** one-way; **in ~ orario** clockwise; **perdere i sensi** to lose consciousness.

sentenza *sf (di processo)* sentence; *(massima)* maxim.

sentiero *sm* path.

sentimentale *agg* sentimental.

sentimento *sm* feeling.

sentire *vt (udire)* to hear; *(percepire, con il tatto)* to feel; *(odore)* to smell; *(sapore)* to taste; **senti!** listen! ❏ **sentirsi** *vr (bene, stanco, allegro)* to feel; **sentirsi di fare qc** to feel like doing sthg; **sentirsi bene/male** to feel well/ill; *(telefonarsi)*: **ci sentiamo domani** speak to you tomorrow.

senza *prep & cong* without; **~ di me** without me; **senz'altro** certainly, of course; **~ dubbio** undoubtedly; **~ che tu te ne accorga** without you noticing it.

senzatetto *smf inv* homeless person.

separare *vt* to separate ❏ **separarsi** *vr (coniugi)* to separate; *(gruppo)* to split up; **separarsi da** *vr + prep (coniuge)* to separate from.

separato, -a *agg (disgiunto)* separate; *(coniuge)* separated.

separazione *sf* separation.

sepolto, -a *pp* → **seppellire**.

seppellire *vt* to bury.

seppia *sf* cuttlefish.

sequenza *sf* sequence.

sequestrare *vt (DIR)* to sequestrate; *(persona)* to kidnap.

sequestro *sm (DIR)* sequestration; *(rapimento)* kidnapping.

sera *sf* evening; **di ~** in the evening.

serale *agg* evening *(dav s)*.

serata *sf* evening; *(ricevimento)* party.

serbare *vt* to put aside, to keep; **~ rancore a qn** to bear sb a grudge.

serbatoio *sm (di veicolo)* tank.

serbo *sm:* **avere qc in ~** to have sthg in store; **tenere qc in ~** to put sthg aside.

serenata *sf* serenade.

sereno, -a *agg (tempo, cielo)* clear; *(persona)* calm ◆ *sm (bel tempo)* fine weather.

serie *sf inv (successione)* series *(inv)*; *(insieme)* set; *(SPORT)* division; **produzione in ~** mass production.

serietà *sf* seriousness; *(coscienziosità)* reliability.

serio, -a *agg* serious; *(coscienzioso)* reliable ◆ *sm:* **sul ~** *(davvero)* seriously; **prendere qn/qc sul ~** to take sb/sthg seriously.

serpente *sm* snake; *(pelle)* snakeskin.

serra *sf (per piante)* greenhouse.

serranda *sf* rolling shutter.

serrare *vt (chiudere)* to close; *(stringere)* to shut tightly.

serratura *sf* lock.

servire *vt* to serve ◆ *vi (in tennis, pallavolo)* to serve; *(essere utile)* to be of use; **~ a fare qc** to be used for doing sthg; **~ a qn** to be of use to sb; **mi serve un martello** I need a hammer; **~ da** to be used as ▫ **servirsi** *vr (prendere da mangiare/bere)* to help o.s.; **servirsi da** to shop at; **servirsi di** *vr + prep (utilizzare)* to use.

servitù *sf (condizione)* slavery; *(personale)* domestic staff.

servizio *sm* service; *(di piatti, bicchieri)* set; *(giornalistico)* report; **essere di ~** to be on duty; '**~ compreso**' 'service included'; **~ militare** military service ▫ **servizi** *smpl (di abitazione)* kitchen and bathroom.

sessanta *num* sixty, → **sei**.

sessantesimo, -a *num* sixtieth, → **sesto**.

sessantina *sf:* **una ~ (di)** about sixty; **essere sulla ~** to be in one's sixties.

sesso *sm* sex.

sessuale *agg* sexual.

sesto, -a *agg num & pron num* sixth ◆ *sm (frazione)* sixth; **rimettersi in ~** to recover.

seta *sf* silk.

setacciare *vt (separare)* to sieve.

sete *sf* thirst; **avere ~** to be thirsty.

settanta *num* seventy, → **sei**.

settantesimo, -a *num* seventieth, → **sesto**.

settantina *sf:* **una ~ (di)** about seventy; **essere sulla ~** to be in one's seventies.

sette *num* seven, → **sei**.

settecento *num* seven hundred, → **sei** ▫ **Settecento** *sm:* **il Settecento** the eighteenth century.

settembre *sm* September; **a** o **in ~** in September; **lo scorso ~** last September; **il prossimo ~** next September; **all'inizio di ~** at the beginning of September; **alla fine di ~** at the end of September; **il**

due ~ the second of September.

settentrionale *agg* northern.

settentrione *sm* north.

setter *sm inv* setter.

settimana *sf* week.

settimanale *agg* weekly ◆ *sm* weekly publication.

settimo, -a *num* seventh, → **sesto**.

settore *sm* sector.

severamente *avv*: '**è ~ vietato attraversare i binari**' 'crossing the track is strictly forbidden'.

severo, -a *agg* strict, severe.

sevizie *sfpl* torture *(sg)*.

sexy *agg inv* sexy.

sezione *sf* section; *(MED)* dissection.

sfaccendato, -a *agg* lazy.

sfacchinata *sf* hard work.

sfacciato, -a *agg (persona)* cheeky.

sfacelo *sm (rovina)* ruin.

sfamare *vt* to feed □ **sfamarsi** *vr* to satisfy one's hunger.

sfare *vt* to undo.

sfarzo *sm* pomp, magnificence.

sfasciare *vt (sbendare)* to unbandage; *(rompere)* to smash □ **sfasciarsi** *vr (rompersi)* to fall to pieces.

sfaticato, -a *agg* lazy.

sfatto, -a *pp* → **sfare**.

sfavorevole *agg* unfavourable.

sfera *sf* sphere.

sferrare *vt (attacco)* to launch; ~ **un colpo contro qn** to lash out at sb.

sfibrare *vt* to exhaust.

sfida *sf* challenge.

sfidare *vt* to challenge; *(pericolo, morte)* to defy; ~ **qn a fare qc** to challenge sb to do sthg.

sfiducia *sf* distrust.

sfigurare *vt* to disfigure ◆ *vi* to make a bad impression.

sfilare *vt (togliere)* to take off ◆ *vi (marciare)* to parade; **sfilarsi le scarpe** to slip off one's shoes □ **sfilarsi** *vr (calze)* to ladder.

sfilata *sf (corteo)* march; *(di moda)* fashion show.

sfinire *vt* to exhaust.

sfiorare *vt* to skim (over).

sfiorire *vi* to wither.

sfitto, -a *agg* vacant.

sfizioso, -a *agg* enticing.

sfocato, -a = **sfuocato**.

sfociare : **sfociare in** *v + prep (fiume)* to flow into.

sfoderare *vt (giacca)* to remove the lining from; *(spada)* to draw; *(fig)* to show off.

sfoderato, -a *agg* unlined.

sfogare *vt* to give vent to □ **sfogarsi** *vr (aprirsi)* to pour out one's feelings; **sfogarsi su qn** *(scaricare la collera)* to vent one's anger on sb.

sfoggiare *vt* to show off.

sfogliare *vt (giornale)* to leaf through.

sfogliatelle *sfpl* puff pastries filled with spiced ricotta cheese and candied fruit.

sfogo, -ghi *sm (passaggio)* outlet; *(di sentimenti)* outburst; *(eruzione cutanea)* rash; **dare ~ a qc** to give vent to sthg.

sfoltire *vt* to thin.

sfondare *vt (contenitore)* to break the bottom of; *(porta)* to break down ❑ **sfondarsi** *vr (contenitore)* to burst at the bottom.

sfondo *sm* background.

sformato *sm savoury pudding made with vegetables and cheese or sometimes with meat, baked in a mould and then turned out.*

sfornare *vt (pane, dolci)* to take out of the oven.

sfortuna *sf* misfortune; **portare ~** to bring bad luck.

sfortunatamente *avv* unfortunately.

sfortunato, -a *agg* unlucky.

sforzare *vt* to force; *(occhi, voce, motore)* to strain ❑ **sforzarsi** *vr* to make an effort.

sforzo *sm* effort; **fare uno ~** to make an effort.

sfottere *vt (fam)* to tease.

sfratto *sm* eviction.

sfrecciare *vi (scappare)* to shoot past.

sfregare *vt (strofinare)* to rub.

sfregio *sm (taglio)* gash.

sfrenato, -a *agg* unrestrained.

sfrontato, -a *agg* impudent.

sfruttamento *sm* exploitation.

sfruttare *vt* to exploit.

sfuggire *vi (scappare)* to escape ❑ **sfuggire a** *v + prep (sottrarsi a)* to escape from; **~ di mano a qn** to slip out of sb's hands; **~ di mente a qn** to slip sb's mind; **non gli sfugge nulla** he misses nothing.

sfuggita : di sfuggita *avv* in passing.

sfumare *vt (colore)* to shade off; *(capelli)* to taper ♦ *vi (colore)* to shade off; *(svanire)* to vanish.

sfumato, -a *agg (colore)* soft.

sfumatura *sf (tonalità)* shade; *(fig: piccola differenza)* touch, hint; *(di capelli)* tapering.

sfuocato, -a *agg* blurred, out of focus.

sfuriata *sf (sfogo violento)* outburst of anger; *(rimprovero)* telling off.

sgabello *sm* stool.

sgabuzzino *sm* storage room.

sgambetto *sm*: **fare lo ~ a qn** to trip sb up.

sganciare *vt (vestito, allacciatura)* to unfasten; *(rimorchio, vagone)* to uncouple; *(bombe)* to drop; *(fam: soldi)* to fork out ❑ **sganciarsi** *vr (staccarsi)* to come undone.

sgarbato, -a *agg* impolite.

sghignazzare *vi* to laugh scornfully.

sgobbare *vi (fam)* to slog.

sgocciolare *vt (bottiglia)* to drain ♦ *vi* to drip.

sgolarsi *vr* to make o.s. hoarse.

sgomb(e)rare *vt (strada, soffitta)* to clear.

sgombero, -a = sgombro.

sgombro, -a *agg* clear ♦ *sm (evacuazione)* evacuation; *(pesce)* mackerel.

sgomentare *vt* to dismay ❑ **sgomentarsi** *vr* to be dismayed.

sgominare *vt* to rout.

sgonfiare *vt* to deflate ❑ **sgonfiarsi** *vr (canotto)* to deflate; *(caviglia)* to go down.

sgorbio *sm (scarabocchio)* scribble; *(fig: persona)* fright.

sgradevole *agg* unpleasant.

sgradito, -a *agg* unwelcome.

sgranare *vt (fagioli)* to shell.

sgranchirsi *vr*: ~ **le gambe** to stretch one's legs.

sgranocchiare *vt* to munch.

sgraziato, -a *agg* graceless.

sgretolare *vt (frantumare)* to cause to crumble ❑ **sgretolarsi** *vr* to crumble.

sgridare *vt* to scold.

sguaiato, -a *agg* coarse.

sgualcire *vt* to crumple ❑ **sgualcirsi** *vr* to become crumpled.

sguardo *sm (occhiata)* look; *(espressione)* expression.

sguinzagliare *vt (cane)* to take off the lead.

sgusciare *vt (fagioli)* to shell ♦ *vi (sfuggire)* to slip away.

shampoo ['ʃampo] *sm inv* shampoo.

shock [ʃɔk] *sm inv* shock.

si *(diventa se quando precede lo, la, li, le, ne)* *pron* **1.** *(riflessivo: persona)* himself (f herself), themselves (pl); *(impersonale)* oneself; *(cosa, animale)* itself, themselves (pl); **lavarsi** to wash (oneself); ~ **stanno preparando** they are getting ready. **2.** *(con verbo transitivo)*: **lavarsi i denti** to brush one's teeth; ~ **è comprato un vestito** he bought himself a suit. **3.** *(reciproco)* each other, one another; ~ **sono conosciuti a Roma** they met in Rome. **4.** *(impersonale)*: ~ **può sempre**

provare one o you can always try; ~ **dice che ...** they say that ..., it is said that ...; ~ **vede che è stanco** one o you can see he's tired; '~ **prega di non fumare** 'please do not smoke'; **non ~ sa mai** you never know. **5.** *(passivo)*: **questi prodotti ~ trovano dappertutto** these products are found everywhere.

sì *avv & sm inv* yes; **dire di ~** to say yes; **uno ~ e uno no** every other one.

sia[1] → **essere**.

sia[2] *cong*: ~ **... che**, ~ **... ~** both ... and; ~ **... che** ~ **che** whether ... or; ~ **che tu venga**, ~ **che tu non venga** whether you come or not.

siamo → **essere**.

sicché *cong (e quindi)* and so.

siccità *sf inv* drought.

siccome *cong* as, since.

Sicilia *sf*: **la ~** Sicily.

siciliano, -a *agg & sm, f* Sicilian.

sicura *sf (di auto)* safety lock; *(di arma)* safety catch.

sicurezza *sf (mancanza di pericolo)* safety, security; *(certezza)* certainty; **di ~** safety *(dav s)*, security *(dav s)*.

sicuro, -a *agg* safe; *(amico, informazione)* reliable; *(fiducioso)* confident; *(certo)* certain ♦ *avv* certainly; **di ~** certainly; **andare sul ~** to play safe; **essere ~ di sè** to be sure of o.s.; **al ~** in a safe place.

Siena *sf* Siena.

siepe *sf* hedge.

sieropositivo, -a *agg* HIV-positive.

siete → essere.

Sig. *(abbr di signor)* Mr.

Sig.a *(abbr di signora)* Ms.

sigaretta *sf* cigarette.

sigaro *sm* cigar.

Sigg. *abbr* Messrs.

sigla *sf (abbreviazione)* acronym; *(musicale)* signature tune; ~ **automobilistica** two-letter abbreviation of province on a vehicle's number plate.

Sig.na *(abbr di signorina)* Miss.

significare *vt* to mean; **che cosa significa?** what does it mean?

significativo, -a *agg (discorso)* significant; *(sguardo)* meaningful.

significato *sm* meaning.

signor *sm* → signore.

signora *sf (donna)* lady; *(moglie)* wife; **buon giorno ~** good morning (Madam); *(in una lettera)* **Dear Madam; la ~ Poli** Mrs Poli; **signore e signori** ladies and gentlemen.

signore *sm (uomo)* gentleman; **buon giorno ~** good morning (Sir); **il ~ desidera?** what can I do for you, sir?; **Gentile Signore** *(in una lettera)* Dear Sir; **i Signori Rossi** *(màrito e moglie)* Mr and Mrs Rossi; **il Signor Martini** Mr Martini.

signorina *sf (ragazza)* young lady; **buon giorno ~** good morning (Madam); **la ~ Logi** Miss Logi.

Sig.ra *abbr* Mrs.

silenzio *sm* silence; **fare ~** to be quiet.

silenzioso, -a *agg* quiet, silent.

sillaba *sf* syllable.

simbolico, -a, -ci, -che *agg* symbolic.

simbolo *sm* symbol.

simile *agg (analogo)* similar; *(tale)*: **una persona ~** such a person; **~ a** similar to.

simmetrico, -a, -ci, -che *agg* symmetric(al).

simpatia *sf (inclinazione)* liking; *(qualità)* pleasantness.

simpatico, -a, -ci, -che *agg* nice.

simulare *vt (fingere)* to feign; *(imitare)* to simulate.

simultaneo, -a *agg* simultaneous.

sin = sino.

sinagoga, -ghe *sf* synagogue.

sincero, -a *agg (persona)* sincere; *(dolore, gioia)* genuine, heartfelt.

sindacalista, -i, -e *smf* trade unionist.

sindacato *sm (di lavoratori)* trade union.

sindaco, -ci *sm* mayor.

sinfonia *sf* symphony.

singhiozzo *sm* hiccups *(pl)* ❑ **singhiozzi** *smpl* sobs; **a singhiozzi** *(fig)* by fits and starts.

singolare *agg (originale)* unusual; *(GRAMM)* singular ◆ *sm (GRAMM)* singular.

singolo, -a *agg* single.

sinistra *sf*: **la ~** the left; *(POL)* the left (wing); **scrivere con la ~** to write with one's left hand; **a ~** left; **a ~ di** to the left of.

sinistro, -a *agg* left; *(minaccioso)* sinister ◆ *sm* accident.

sino = fino.

sinonimo *sm* synonym.

sintesi *sf inv (riassunto)* summary.

sintetico, -a, -ci, -che *agg (artificiale)* synthetic; *(succinto)* brief.

sintetizzare *vt (riassumere)* to summarize.

sintomo *sm* symptom.

sintonizzare *vt* to tune in □ **sintonizzarsi su** *vr + prep* to tune in to.

sipario *sm* curtain.

sirena *sf (apparecchio)* siren; *(nella mitologia)* mermaid.

siringa, -ghe *sf (per iniezioni)* syringe; *(da cucina)* = piping bag.

sistema, -i *sm* system.

sistemare *vt (ordinare)* to tidy up; *(risolvere)* to sort out, to settle; *(alloggiare)* to find accommodation (Br) o accommodations (Am) for; *(procurare un lavoro a)* to find a job for; *(maritare)* to marry off □ **sistemarsi** *vr (risolversi)* to be settled; *(trovare alloggio)* to find accommodation (Br) o accommodations (Am); *(trovare lavoro)* to find work; *(sposarsi)* to marry.

sistematico, -a, -ci, -che *agg* systematic.

sistemazione *sf (disposizione)* arrangement; *(alloggio)* accommodation (Br), accommodations (Am); *(lavoro)* employment.

situare *vt* to situate, to locate.

situazione *sf* situation.

skate-board ['skeit 'bɔrd] *sm inv* skateboard.

ski-lift [ski'lift] *sm inv* ski lift.

ski-pass [ski'pas] *sm inv* ski pass.

slacciare *vt* to undo.

slanciato, -a *agg* slender.

slancio *sm (balzo)* dash; *(fig)* burst.

slavina *sf* snowslide.

slavo, -a *agg* Slavonic, Slav.

sleale *agg (persona)* disloyal; *(azione)* treacherous.

slegare *vt* to untie.

slip *sm inv* briefs *(pl)*.

slitta *sf* sledge.

slittare *vi* to slide; *(automobile)* to skid.

slogan *sm inv* slogan.

slogare *vt* to dislocate.

slogatura *sf* dislocation.

smacchiatore *sm* stain remover.

smagliante *agg* dazzling.

smagliare *vt (collant, calze)* to ladder.

smagliatura *sf (di calze)* ladder; *(della pelle)* stretch mark.

smaltire *vt (merce)* to sell off; *(rifiuti)* to discharge; *(cibo)* to digest; ~ **la sbornia** to get over one's hangover.

smalto *sm (per metalli, di denti)* enamel; *(per ceramica)* glaze; *(per unghie)* nail varnish.

smania *sf (agitazione)* restlessness; *(desiderio)* craving; **aver la ~ di qc** to have a craving for sthg.

smarrire *vt* to lose □ **smarrirsi** *vr* to get lost.

smarrito, -a *agg* lost; *(sbigottito)* bewildered.

smascherare *vt* to unmask.

smemorato, -a *agg* absent-minded.

smentire vt (notizia) to deny; (testimonianza) to refute.

smentita sf (di notizia) denial.

smeraldo sm emerald.

smesso, -a pp → smettere.

smettere vt to stop; (abito) to stop wearing; **smettere di fare qc** to stop doing sthg; **smettila!** stop it!

smidollato, -a agg spineless.

sminuire vt to belittle.

sminuzzare vt to crumble.

smistamento sm (di posta, pacchi) sorting; (di treni) shunting.

smistare vt (posta) to sort; (treni) to shunt.

smisurato, -a agg enormous, huge.

smodato, -a agg excessive.

smog sm inv smog.

smoking sm inv dinner jacket (Br), tuxedo (Am).

smontabile agg that can be dismantled.

smontare vt (macchina, libreria) to take to pieces; (fig: far perdere l'entusiasmo a) to discourage ◆ vi (da cavallo) to dismount; (da turno di lavoro) to finish (work).

smorfia sf grimace.

smorfioso, -a agg simpering.

smorzare vt (suoni) to muffle; (colore) to tone down; (entusiasmo) to dampen.

smosso, -a pp → smuovere.

smottamento sm landslide.

smunto, -a agg pinched.

smuovere vt (spostare) to shift; (da proposito, intenzione) to deter.

smussare vt (spigolo) to round off.

snack-bar sm inv snack bar.

snaturato, -a agg inhuman.

snello, -a agg slim, slender.

snervante agg exhausting.

snidare vt to flush out.

snobismo sm snobbery.

snodare vt (slegare) to untie; (arti) to loosen up ❑ **snodarsi** vr (slegarsi) to come loose.

sobbalzare vi (balzare) to jolt; (trasalire) to jump.

sobborgo, -ghi sm suburb.

sobrio, -a agg sober.

socchiudere vt (porta) to leave ajar; (occhi) to half-close.

socchiuso, -a pp → socchiudere.

soccorrere vt to help.

soccorso, -a pp → soccorrere ◆ sm help, aid; **~ stradale** breakdown service.

sociale agg social.

socialista, -i, -e agg socialist.

socializzare vi to socialize.

società sf inv (gruppo umano) society; (associazione) association, club; (COMM) company; **~ per azioni** limited company (Br), incorporated company (Am).

socievole agg sociable.

socio, -a, -ci, cie sm, f (di circolo) member; (COMM) partner.

soda®[1] sf soda.

soda[2] sf (bevanda) soda water.

soddisfacente agg satisfactory.

soddisfare vt to satisfy.

soddisfatto, -a agg satisfied; **essere ~ di** (contento) to be satisfied with.

soddisfazione *sf* satisfaction.

sodo, -a *agg* hard, firm.

sofà *sm inv* sofa.

sofferente *agg* suffering.

sofferto, -a *pp* → **soffrire**.

soffiare *vi* to blow ◆ *vt* to blow; **~ qn/qc a qn** to pinch sb/sthg from sb; **soffiarsi il naso** to blow one's nose.

soffiata *sf (fam)* tip-off.

soffice *agg* soft.

soffio *sm (di fiato, vento)* breath; **~ al cuore** heart murmur.

soffitta *sf* attic.

soffitto *sm* ceiling.

soffocante *agg* suffocating, stifling.

soffocare *vt* to suffocate ◆ *vi* to suffocate.

soffriggere *vt & vi* to fry lightly.

soffrire *vt (patire)* to suffer; *(sopportare)* to bear ◆ *vi* to suffer □ **soffrire di** *v + prep* to suffer from.

soffritto *sm* lightly fried onions and herbs.

sofisticato, -a *agg* sophisticated.

software ['sɔftwɛr] *sm* software.

soggetto, -a *agg*: **essere ~ a** to be subject to ◆ *sm* subject.

soggezione *sf (sottomissione)* subjection; *(imbarazzo)* uneasiness; **dare ~ a qn** to make sb ill at ease.

soggiorno *sm (permanenza)* stay; *(stanza)* living room.

soglia *sf* threshold.

sogliola *sf* sole.

sognare *vt* to dream of o about

◆ *vi* to dream; **~ ad occhi aperti** to daydream.

sogno *sm* dream; **fare un brutto ~** to have a bad dream.

soia *sf* soya.

solaio *sm* attic.

solamente *avv* only, just.

solare *agg* solar, sun *(dav s)*.

solarium *sm inv* solarium.

solco, -chi *sm (in terreno)* furrow; *(incisione)* groove; *(scia)* wake.

soldato *sm* soldier; **~ semplice** private.

soldo *sm*: **non avere un ~** to be penniless □ **soldi** *smpl (denaro)* money *(sg)*.

sole *sm* sun; **prendere il ~** to sunbathe.

soleggiato, -a *agg* sunny.

solenne *agg* solemn.

solere *v impers*: **come si suol dire** as they say.

soletta *sf (suola)* insole.

solfo = **zolfo**.

solidale *agg*: **essere ~ con qn** to be in agreement with sb.

solidarietà *sf* solidarity.

solido, -a *agg & sm* solid.

solista, -i, -e *smf* soloist.

solitario, -a *agg (persona)* lonely, solitary; *(luogo)* lonely ◆ *sm (di carte)* patience *(Br)*, solitaire *(Am)*; *(brillante)* solitaire.

solito, -a *agg* usual; **essere ~ fare qc** to be in the habit of doing sthg; **(come) al ~** as usual; **di ~** usually.

solitudine *sf* solitude.

sollecitare *vt (risposta, pagamento)* to press for.

solleone sm (caldo) summer heat; (periodo) dog days (pl).

solletico sm tickling; **soffrire il ~** to be ticklish.

sollevamento sm lifting; **~ pesi** (SPORT) weight lifting.

sollevare vt (tirare su) to lift, to raise; (problema, questione) to raise; (fare insorgere) to stir up ❏ **sollevarsi** vr (da terra) to get up; (insorgere) to rise up.

sollevato, -a agg (confortato) relieved.

sollievo sm relief.

solo, -a agg (senza compagnia) alone; (isolato) lonely; (unico) only ♦ avv (soltanto) only, just; **c'è un ~ posto a sedere** there's only one seat; **da ~** by oneself; **ho ~ 5 000 lire** I only have 5,000 lire; **non ~ ... ma anche** not only ... but also; **a ~** (MUS) solo.

soltanto avv only.

solubile agg soluble; **caffè ~** instant coffee.

soluzione sf solution.

Somalia sf: **la ~** Somalia.

somaro, -a sm, f (asino) donkey, ass; (fig: a scuola) dunce.

somiglianza sf resemblance.

somigliare : **somigliare a** v + prep (nell'aspetto) to look like; (nel modo di essere) to be like ❏ **somigliarsi** vr to be alike.

somma sf sum.

sommare vt (MAT) to add up.

sommario, -a agg brief ♦ sm (di libro) index.

sommergere vt to submerge; **~ di** (fig) to overwhelm with.

sommergibile sm submarine.

sommerso, -a pp → **sommergere** ♦ agg (isola, città) underwater.

somministrare vt to administer.

sommità sf inv (cima) summit.

sommo, -a agg highest; (eccellente) outstanding, excellent; **per sommi capi** in short, in brief.

sommossa sf uprising.

sommozzatore, -trice sm, f (deep-sea) diver.

sonda sf (spaziale, MED) probe.

sondaggio sm (indagine) survey.

sondare vt (fondo marino) to sound; (intenzioni, opinioni) to sound out.

sonnambulo, -a agg: **essere ~** to sleepwalk.

sonnellino sm nap.

sonnifero sm sleeping pill.

sonno sm sleep; **avere ~** to be sleepy; **prendere ~** to fall asleep.

sono → **essere**.

sonoro, -a agg (onde, di film) sound (dav s); (voce, risata, schiaffo) ringing ♦ sm (di film) soundtrack.

sontuoso, -a agg sumptuous.

soppiatto : **di soppiatto** avv secretly.

sopportare vt (peso) to support, to bear; (umiliazione, dolore) to bear; (tollerare) to put up with.

soppresso, -a pp → **sopprimere**.

sopprimere vt (legge) to abolish; (servizio, treno) to withdraw, to do away with; (parola) to delete.

sopra prep (su) on; (al di sopra di)

above; (al di là di) over; (riguardo a) about, on ♦ avv (in alto) above; (in lettera, scritto): **come precisato ~** as detailed above; **al di ~ di** above; **di ~** upstairs.

soprabito sm overcoat.

sopracciglio (pl f **sopracciglia**) sm eyebrow.

sopraffare vt to overcome.

sopraffatto, -a pp → **sopraffare**.

sopraggiungere vi (giungere all'improvviso) to arrive (unexpectedly); (accadere) to occur (unexpectedly).

sopraggiunto, -a pp → **sopraggiungere**.

sopralluogo, -ghi sm (di polizia) on-the-spot investigation; (visita) inspection.

soprammobile sm ornament.

soprannaturale agg supernatural.

soprannome sm nickname.

soprano sm soprano.

soprassalto : **di soprassalto** avv with a start.

soprattutto avv above all, especially.

sopravvalutare vt to overestimate.

sopravvento sm: **avere il ~ su** to have the upper hand over.

sopravvissuto, -a pp → **sopravvivere** ♦ sm, f survivor.

sopravvivere vi to survive ❑ **sopravvivere a** v + prep to survive.

soprelevata sf elevated section.

soprintendente smf (a attività, lavoro) superintendent, supervisor.

soprintendenza sf (attività) supervision; (ufficio) superintendency.

sopruso sm abuse of power.

soqquadro sm: **mettere qc a ~** to turn sthg upside down.

sorbetto sm sorbet.

sorbire vt to sip; **sorbirsi qn/qc** (fig) to put up with sb/sthg.

sorcio sm mouse.

sordido, -a agg sordid, squalid.

sordina sf: **in ~** softly.

sordo, -a agg (non udente) deaf; (rumore, tonfo) muffled, dull ♦ sm, f deaf person.

sordomuto, -a agg deaf and dumb ♦ sm, f deaf and dumb person.

sorella sf sister.

sorellastra sf stepsister.

sorgente sf (d'acqua) spring; (di fiume, elettricità, calore) source.

sorgere vi to rise; (sospetto, dubbio) to arise.

sorpassare vt (AUTO) to overtake; (superare) to exceed.

sorpassato, -a agg old-fashioned.

sorpasso sm (di veicolo) overtaking; **fare un ~** to overtake.

sorprendere vt (cogliere) to catch; (stupire) to surprise ❑ **sorprendersi di** vr + prep to be surprised at.

sorpresa sf surprise; **fare una ~ a qn** to give sb a surprise; **di ~** by surprise.

sorpreso, -a *pp* → **sorprendere**.

sorreggere *vt* to support.

sorretto, -a *pp* → **sorreggere**.

sorridente *agg* smiling.

sorridere *vi* to smile.

sorriso, -a *pp* → **sorridere** ♦ *sm* smile.

sorsata *sf* gulp.

sorso *sm* (*sorsata*) gulp; (*piccola quantità*) sip.

sorta *sf* kind, sort.

sorte *sf* fate; **tirare a ~** to draw lots.

sorteggio *sm* draw.

sortilegio *sm* spell.

sorveglianza *sf* supervision; (*POLIZIA*) surveillance.

sorvegliare *vt* to watch.

sorvolare *vt* (*territorio*) to fly over ♦ *vi*: **~ su** (*territorio*) to fly over; (*fig*) to pass over.

S.O.S. *sm* SOS; **lanciare un ~** to send out an SOS.

sosia *smf inv* double.

sospendere *vt* (*attaccare*) to hang; (*attività, pagamenti, funzionario*) to suspend.

sospensione *sf* suspension.

sospeso, -a *pp* → **sospendere** ♦ *agg* (*interrotto*) suspended; **lasciare qc in ~** to leave sthg unfinished; **tenere qn in ~** to keep sb in suspense.

sospettare *vt* to suspect ♦ *vi*: **~ di qn** (*avere sospetti su*) to suspect sb; (*diffidare di*) to be suspicious of sb.

sospetto, -a *agg* suspicious ♦

sm, f suspect ♦ *sm* suspicion.

sospirare *vi* to sigh; **farsi ~** to keep sb waiting.

sospiro *sm* sigh; **tirare un ~ di sollievo** to heave a sigh of relief.

sosta *sf* (*in luogo*) stop; (*pausa*) break; **fare ~ a/in** to make a stop at/in; **'divieto di ~'** 'no waiting'; **senza ~** nonstop; **'~ consentita solo per carico e scarico'** 'no waiting except for loading and unloading'.

sostantivo *sm* noun.

sostanza *sf* substance.

sostanzioso, -a *agg* (*cibo*) nourishing; (*notevole*) substantial.

sostare *vi* (*fermarsi*) to stop.

sostegno *sm* support.

sostenere *vt* to support; **~ che** to maintain (that); **~ gli esami** to sit exams ❑ **sostenersi** *vr* (*tenersi dritto*) to hold o.s. up.

sostenitore, -trice *sm, f* supporter.

sostentamento *sm* maintenance.

sostenuto, -a *agg* (*tono, stile*) elevated; (*ritmo, passo*) sustained.

sostituire *vt* (*rimpiazzare*) to replace; (*prendere il posto di*) to take over from; **~ qn/qc con** to substitute sb/sthg with; **~ qn/qc a** to substitute sb/sthg for.

sostituto, -a *sm, f* substitute.

sostituzione *sf* substitution.

sottaceti *smpl* pickles.

sottana *sf* (*gonna*) skirt; (*di prete*) cassock.

sotterfugio *sm* subterfuge.

sotterraneo, -a *agg* under-

sovietico

ground; *(fig)* clandestine, secret ◆ *sm* cellar.

sottigliezza *sf (di spessore)* thinness; *(fig)* subtlety; *(dettaglio)* quibble.

sottile *agg (non spesso)* thin; *(capelli)* fine; *(slanciato)* slim; *(vista, odorato, ingegno)* sharp, keen; **non andare per il ~** not to mince matters.

sottintendere *vt* to imply.

sottinteso, -a *pp* → **sottintendere** ◆ *sm* allusion.

sotto *prep* under; *(più in basso di)* below ◆ *avv (in posizione inferiore)* underneath; *(più in basso, in scritto)* below; **al di ~ di** under, below; **sott'olio** in oil; **di ~** *(al piano inferiore)* downstairs.

sottobanco *avv (comprare)* under the counter.

sottobicchiere *sm* coaster.

sottobosco *sm* undergrowth.

sottobraccio *avv (prendere)* by the arm; *(camminare)* arm in arm.

sottofondo *sm (MUS)* background music.

sottolineare *vt* to underline; *(dare risalto a)* to emphasize.

sottolio → **sotto**.

sottomarino, -a *agg* underwater *(dav s)* ◆ *sm* submarine.

sottomesso, -a *pp* → **sottomettere** ◆ *agg* submissive.

sottomettere *vt (al proprio dominio)* to subdue ⊔ **sottomettersi** *vr + prep* to submit to.

sottopassaggio *sm (per auto)* underpass; *(per pedoni, in stazione)* subway, underpass; **'servirsi del ~'** 'please use the subway'.

sottoporre *vt:* **~ qn a qc** to subject sb to sthg; **~ qc a qn** to submit sthg to sb ⊔ **sottoporsi a** *vr + prep (subire)* to undergo.

sottoposto, -a *pp* → **sottoporre**.

sottoscala *sm inv* cupboard under the stairs.

sottoscritto, -a *pp* → **sottoscrivere** ◆ *sm, f* undersigned.

sottoscrivere *vt* to sign ⊔ **sottoscrivere a** *v + prep* to subscribe to.

sottosopra *avv* upside down.

sottostante *agg* lower.

sottosuolo *sm (di terreno)* subsoil; *(locale)* basement.

sottosviluppato, -a *agg* underdeveloped.

sottoterra *avv* underground.

sottotitoli *smpl* subtitles.

sottovalutare *vt* to underestimate.

sottoveste *sf* underskirt.

sottovoce *avv* in a low voice.

sottovuoto *avv* vacuum-packed.

sottrarre *vt (MAT)* to subtract; *(fondi)* to take away, to remove; **~ qc a qn** *(rubare)* to steal sthg from sb ⊔ **sottrarsi a** *vr + prep* to escape, to avoid.

sottratto, -a *pp* → **sottrarre**.

sottrazione *sf (MAT)* subtraction; *(furto)* removal.

souvenir [suve'nir] *sm inv* souvenir.

sovietico, -a, -ci, -che *agg* soviet.

sovraccaricare vt to over-load.

sovrano, -a agg & sm, f sovereign.

sovrapporre vt to put on top of.

sovrapposto, -a pp → sovrapporre.

sovrastare vt (valle, paese) to overhang.

sovrumano, -a agg superhuman.

sovvenzionare vt to subsidize.

sovversivo, -a agg subversive.

sozzo, -a agg filthy.

S.p.A. (abbr di società per azioni) ≃ Ltd (Br), ≃ Inc. (Am).

spaccare vt to break, to split ❏ **spaccarsi** vr to break, to split.

spaccatura sf split.

spacciare vt (droga) to push ❏ **spacciarsi per** vr + prep to pass o.s. off as.

spacciatore, -trice sm, f (di droga) pusher.

spacco, -chi sm split; (di gonna) slit.

spaccone, -a sm, f boaster.

spada sf sword.

spaesato, -a agg disorientated.

spaghetteria sf restaurant specializing in pasta dishes.

spaghetti smpl spaghetti (sg); ~ aglio, olio e peperoncino spaghetti with garlic, chilli and olive oil; ~ alla carbonara spaghetti in an egg, bacon and cheese sauce; ~ pomodoro e basilico spaghetti in a fresh tomato and basil sauce; ~ alla puttanesca spaghetti in a sauce of tomatoes, anchovies, olives and capers; ~ alle vongole spaghetti in a clam sauce.

Spagna sf: la ~ Spain.

spagnolo, -a agg Spanish ◆ sm, f Spaniard ◆ sm (lingua) Spanish.

spago, -ghi sm string.

spaiato, -a agg odd.

spalancare vt to open wide.

spalla sf shoulder; **voltare le spalle a qn** to turn one's back on sb; **di spalle** from behind.

spalliera sf (di letto) head; (SPORT) wall bars (pl).

spallina sf (di reggiseno, sottoveste) strap; (imbottitura) shoulder pad.

spalmare vt to spread.

spalti smpl (di stadio) terraces.

spandere vt (versare) to pour; (spargere) to spread ❏ **spandersi** vr to spread.

spappolare vt to pulp ❏ **spappolarsi** vr to get mushy.

sparare vi to fire ◆ vt (colpo, fucilata) to fire.

sparecchiare vi to clear the table ◆ vt: ~ la tavola to clear the table.

spareggio sm (SPORT) play-off.

spargere vt (sparpagliare) to scatter; (versare) to spill; (divulgare) to spread ❏ **spargersi** vr (sparpagliarsi) to scatter; (divulgarsi) to spread.

sparire vi to disappear.

sparlare : sparlare di v + prep to run down.

sparo sm shot.

sparpagliare vt to scatter ❏

sparpagliarsi vr to scatter.

sparso, -a pp → **spargere** ♦ agg scattered.

spartire vt (dividere) to share out.

spartitraffico sm inv central reservation (Br), median strip (Am).

spasmo sm spasm.

spassarsela vr to have a good time.

spasso sm (film, scena) amusement, fun; (persona) laugh, scream; (passeggiata): **andare a ~** to go for a walk; **essere a ~** (fig) to be out of work.

spauracchio sm scarecrow.

spaventapasseri sm inv scarecrow.

spaventare vt to frighten ❑ **spaventarsi** vr to become frightened.

spavento sm (paura) fear, fright; **far ~ a qn** to give sb a fright.

spaventoso, -a agg frightening.

spazientirsi vr to lose one's patience.

spazio sm space.

spazioso, -a agg spacious.

spazzaneve sm inv snowplough.

spazzare vt (pavimento) to sweep; (sporco, foglie) to sweep up.

spazzatura sf (rifiuti) rubbish.

spazzino, -a sm, f road sweeper.

spazzola sf (per capelli) hairbrush; (per abiti) clothes brush; **~ da scarpe** shoe brush.

spazzolare vt to brush.

spazzolino sm: **~ (da denti)** toothbrush.

spazzolone sm scrubbing brush.

specchiarsi vr to look at o.s. (in a mirror).

specchietto sm (da borsetta) pocket mirror; (prospetto) scheme, table; **~ (retrovisore)** rear-view mirror.

specchio sm mirror.

speciale agg special.

specialista, -i, -e sm, f specialist.

specialità sf inv speciality; **~ della casa** speciality of the house.

specialmente avv especially.

specie sf inv (di piante, animali) species (inv); (sorta) kind ♦ avv especially; **una ~ di** a kind of.

specificare vt to specify.

specifico, -a, -ci, -che agg specific.

speculare vi to speculate.

speculazione sf speculation.

spedire vt to send.

spedizione sf (di lettera, merci) sending; (viaggio) expedition.

spegnere vt (fuoco, sigaretta) to put out; (luce, TV, gas) to turn off.

spellare vt (coniglio) to skin ❑ **spellarsi** vr to peel.

spendere vt & vi to spend.

spensierato, -a agg carefree.

spento, -a pp → **spegnere** ♦ agg (colore) dull; (sguardo) lifeless.

speranza sf hope.

sperare vt to hope for; **spero che venga** I hope he'll come; **spero**

di sì I hope so; ~ **di fare qc** to hope to do sthg □ **sperare in** v + prep to trust in.

sperduto, -a agg (luogo) out-of-the-way; (persona) lost.

spericolato, -a agg fearless.

sperimentale agg experimental.

sperimentare vt (sottoporre a esperimento, fig) to test; (fare esperienza di) to experience.

sperma, -i sm sperm.

sperperare vt to squander.

spesa sf (somma) expense; (acquisti) shopping; **fare la ~** to do the shopping; **fare spese** (acquisti) to go shopping □ **spese** sfpl (uscite) expenses; **spese postali** postage (sg); **spese di viaggio** travel expenses; **a spese di** at the expense of.

spesso, -a agg thick ♦ avv often.

spessore sm thickness.

Spett. abbr = **spettabile**.

spettabile agg (nelle lettere): ~ **ditta** Messrs ... & Co.

spettacolo sm (rappresentazione) show; (vista) sight.

spettare : **spettare a** v + prep to be up to; **spetta a te dirglielo** it's up to you to tell him.

spettatore, -trice sm, f (di spettacolo) member of the audience; (di avvenimento) onlooker.

spettinare vt: ~ **qn** to ruffle sb's hair □ **spettinarsi** vr to get one's hair messed up.

spettro sm (fantasma) spectre.

spezia sf spice.

spezzare vt (rompere) to break; (viaggio, giornata) to break (up) □ **spezzarsi** vr to break.

spezzatino sm stew.

spezzato, -a agg (diviso) broken ♦ sm (vestito) jacket and trousers.

spezzettare vt to break into small pieces.

spia sf (di polizia) informer; (agente) spy; (luminosa) warning light; (indizio) indication, sign; **fare la ~** to be a sneak.

spiacente agg: **essere ~ (di fare qc)** to be sorry (for doing sthg).

spiacevole agg unpleasant.

spiaggia, -ge sf beach; ~ **privata** private beach.

spianare vt (terreno) to level; (pasta) to roll out; ~ **il terreno** (fig) to prepare the ground.

spiare vt to spy on.

spiazzo sm open space.

spiccare vi (risaltare) to stand out ♦ vt: ~ **un balzo** to jump; ~ **il volo** to fly off.

spiccato, -a agg marked, strong.

spicchio sm (d'arancia) segment; (di mela, pera) slice; ~ **d'aglio** clove of garlic.

spicciarsi vr to hurry up.

spicciolo, -a agg: **moneta spicciola** small change □ **spiccioli** smpl small change.

spiedino sm (pietanza) kebab.

spiedo sm spit; **allo ~** spit-roasted.

spiegare vt (far capire) to explain; (vele) to unfurl; (lenzuola) to unfold; **~ qc a qn** to explain sthg to sb □ **spiegarsi** *vr (farsi capire)* to make o.s. clear; *(diventare chiaro)* to become clear; **spieghiamoci!** let's get things straight!

spiegazione *sf* explanation.

spietato, -a *agg* ruthless.

spiga, -ghe *sf (di grano)* ear.

spigolo *sm (di mobile, muro)* corner.

spilla *sf* brooch; **~ da balia** safety pin.

spillare *vt (soldi)*: **~ qc a qn** to tap sb for sthg.

spillo *sm (da sarto)* pin.

spilorcio, -a, -ci, -ce *agg* mean, stingy.

spina *sf (di pianta)* thorn; *(di riccio)* spine; *(lisca)* bone; *(elettrica)* plug; **birra alla ~** draught beer; **~ dorsale** backbone.

spinaci *smpl* spinach *(sg)*.

spinello *sm (fam: sigaretta)* joint.

spingere *vt & vi* to push; **~ qn a fare qc** to press sb to do sthg □ **spingersi** *vr* to push on.

spinoso, -a *agg* prickly, thorny.

spinta *sf (pressione, urto)* push; *(incoraggiamento)* incentive, spur; *(raccomandazione)*: **dare una ~ a qn** to pull strings for sb.

spinto, -a *pp →* **spingere ♦** *agg (scabroso)* risqué.

spintone *sm* push, shove.

spionaggio *sm* espionage.

spioncino *sm* peephole, spy hole.

spiraglio *sm (fessura)* chink; *(di luce)* gleam, glimmer.

spirale *sf* spiral; *(anticoncezionale)* coil.

spirito *sm (intelletto)* mind; *(fantasma, disposizione d'animo, RELIG)* spirit; *(vivacità d'ingegno)* wit; *(senso dell'umorismo)* humour; *(alcol)*: **ciliegie sotto ~** cherries preserved in alcohol.

spiritoso, -a *agg* witty.

spirituale *agg* spiritual.

splendente *agg* shining.

splendere *vi* to shine.

splendido, -a *agg (bellissimo)* magnificent.

splendore *sm* splendour; *(luce)* brilliance.

spogliare *vt (svestire)* to undress; **~ qn di qc** *(derubare, privare)* to strip sb of sthg □ **spogliarsi** *vr* to undress.

spogliarello *sm* striptease.

spogliatoio *sm (di palestra, piscina)* changing room; *(di abitazione)* dressing room.

spoglio *sm (di schede elettorali)* counting.

spola *sf (bobina)* spool; **fare la ~ (tra)** to go to and fro (between).

spolpare *vt* to strip the flesh off.

spolverare *vt & vi* to dust.

sponda *sf (di fiume)* bank; *(di lago)* shore; *(di letto)* edge; *(di biliardo)* cushion.

sponsorizzare *vt* sponsor.

spontaneo, -a *agg* spontaneous; *(non artificioso)* natural.

spopolare *vt* to depopulate ♦ *vi* to draw the crowds □ **spopolarsi** *vr* to become depopulated.

sporadico, -a, -ci, -che *agg*

sporadic.

sporcare vt to dirty; **sporcarsi le mani** to get one's hands dirty ❑ **sporcarsi** vr to get dirty.

sporcizia sf (l'esser sporco) dirtiness; (cosa sporca) dirt.

sporco, -a, -chi, -che agg dirty ◆ sm dirt.

sporgente agg protruding; (occhi) bulging.

sporgere vt to put out ◆ vi to stick out ❑ **sporgersi** vr to lean out.

sport sm inv sport.

sporta sf shopping bag.

sportello sm (di mobile, treno) door; (di banca, posta) window, counter; **~ automatico** cash dispenser.

sportivo, -a agg (programma, campo) sports (dav s); (persona) sporty; (abbigliamento) casual; (comportamento, spirito) sporting ◆ sm, f sportsman (f sportswoman).

sporto, -a pp → sporgere.

sposare vt to marry ❑ **sposarsi** vr to get married; **sposarsi con** vr + prep to marry.

sposato, -a agg married.

sposo, -a sm, f bridegroom (f bride); **gli sposi** the newlyweds.

spossante agg exhausting.

spostare vt to move; (cambiare) to change ❑ **spostarsi** vr to move.

spot sm inv (faretto) spotlight; (pubblicità) advert.

spranga, -ghe sf bar.

spray sm inv spray.

sprecare vt to waste.

spreco, -chi sm waste.

spregiudicato, -a agg (senza scrupoli) unscrupulous.

spremere vt (arancia, limone) to squeeze.

spremiagrumi sm inv lemon squeezer.

spremuta sf fresh fruit juice; **~ di arancia** freshly-squeezed orange juice.

sprezzante agg scornful.

sprigionare vt to emit ❑ **sprigionarsi** vr to emanate.

sprizzare vi to spurt.

sprofondare vi (crollare) to collapse; (affondare) to sink.

sproporzionato, -a agg out of all proportion.

sproposito sm blunder; (somma esagerata): **costa uno ~** it costs a fortune; **parlare a ~** to talk out of turn.

sprovveduto, -a agg inexperienced.

sprovvisto, -a agg: **~ di** lacking in; **cogliere qn alla sprovvista** to catch sb unawares.

spruzzare vt (profumo) to spray; (acqua) to sprinkle; (persona) to splash.

spruzzatore sm spray.

spruzzo sm spray.

spugna sf (da bagno) sponge; (tessuto) towelling.

spuma sf (schiuma) foam, froth.

spumante sm sparkling wine.

---

i **SPUMANTE**

The sparkling wine called "spumante" can be drunk as an

aperitif or as a dessert wine, and comes in sweet, dry or muscat versions, the latter being named after the grape variety. This Italian answer to champagne gets its name from the fact that it releases lots of bubbles, or foam ("spuma"), when uncorked. No birthday or wedding is complete without "spumante", and it is also traditional to open a bottle at midnight on New Year's Eve.

---

spumone sm (dolce) a foamy dessert made from whisked egg white, milk and sugar.

spuntare vi (apparire) to appear ♦ vt (tagliare la punta di) to break the point of; **spuntarsi i capelli** to trim one's hair; **spuntarla** (fig) to make it.

spuntino sm snack.

spunto sm (punto di partenza) starting point.

sputare vt to spit out ♦ vi to spit.

sputo sm spit.

squadra sf (di operai, SPORT) squad, team; (strumento) set square.

squadrare vt (scrutare) to look at closely; (foglio, blocco) to square.

squagliare vt to melt; **squagliarsela** (fam) to clear off ❑ **squagliarsi** vr to melt.

squalificare vt to disqualify.

squallido, -a agg wretched, miserable.

squallore sm wretchedness, misery.

squalo sm shark.

squama sf scale.

squamarsi vr to flake off.

squarciagola : a squarciagola avv at the top of one's voice.

squarciare vt to rip.

squartare vt to quarter.

squattrinato, -a agg penniless.

squilibrato, -a agg unbalanced.

squilibrio sm (fisico) disequilibrium; (psichico) derangement; (disparità) imbalance.

squillo sm (di telefono, campanello) ring; (di tromba) blare.

squisito, -a agg (cibo) delicious; (raffinato) exquisite; (persona) delightful.

sradicare vt (albero) to uproot.

srotolare vt to unroll.

stabile agg stable; (lavoro, occupazione) steady ♦ sm (edificio) building.

stabilimento sm (complesso) factory, plant; **~ balneare** bathing establishment.

---

i | **STABILIMENTI BALNEARI**

Many Italian seaside resorts have their "stabilimenti balneari", bathing clubs on the beach which provide a bar, showers and changing huts, and hire out beach umbrellas, deckchairs and pedalos. Some even organize volleyball tournaments, treasure hunts and dances.

---

stabilire vt to establish; (fissare) to fix; **~ che** (decidere) to decide (that) ❑ **stabilirsi** vr to settle.

stabilità *sf* stability.

staccare *vt (separare)* to detach, to separate; *(SPORT)* to leave behind ♦ *vi (risaltare)* to stand out; *(fam: finire il lavoro)* to knock off □ **staccarsi** *vr (bottone, cerotto)* to come off; **staccarsi da** *(venir via da)* to come off; *(fig: allontanarsi)* to move away from.

staccionata *sf (recinzione)* fence; *(SPORT)* hurdle.

stadio *sm (SPORT)* stadium; *(fase)* stage.

staffa *sf (di sella, pantaloni)* stirrup; **perdere le staffe** *(fig)* to fly off the handle.

staffetta *sf (SPORT)* relay race.

stagionale *agg* seasonal ♦ *smf* seasonal worker.

stagionato, -a *agg* seasoned.

stagione *sf* season; **alta/bassa ~** high/low season; **vestiti di mezza ~** clothes for spring and autumn.

stagno, -a *agg (a tenuta d'acqua)* watertight; *(a tenuta d'aria)* airtight ♦ *sm (laghetto)* pond; *(metallo)* tin.

stagnola *sf* tinfoil.

stalla *sf (per cavalli)* stable; *(per bovini)* cowshed.

stamattina *avv* this morning.

stambecco, -chi *sm* ibex.

stampa *sf (tecnica)* printing; *(con stampante, opera)* print; *(giornalisti)*: **la ~** the press; **'stampe'** 'printed matter'.

stampante *sf (INFORM)* printer.

stampare *vt* to print; *(pubblicare)* to publish; *(nella memoria)* to impress.

stampatello *sm* block letters *(pl)*.

stampella *sf* crutch.

stampo *sm* mould; *(fig: sorta)* type.

stancare *vt (affaticare)* to tire; *(stufare)* to bore □ **stancarsi** *vr* to get tired; **stancarsi di** *(stufarsi di)* to grow tired of.

stanchezza *sf* tiredness.

stanco, -a, -chi, -che *agg* tired; *(stufo)* **~ di** fed up with; **~ morto** dead tired.

stanghetta *sf (di occhiali)* leg.

stanotte *avv* tonight; *(nella notte appena passata)* last night.

stante *agg*: **a sé ~** separate, independent.

stantio, -a *agg (cibo)* stale.

stanza *sf (camera)* room; **~ da bagno** bathroom; **~ da letto** bedroom.

stanziare *vt* to allocate.

stare *vi (rimanere)* to stay; *(abitare)* to live; *(con gerundio)*: **sto leggendo** I'm reading; **come sta?** how are you?; **ti sta bene!** (it) serves you right!; **ci stai?** is that OK with you?; **sta a voi decidere** it's up to you to decide; **queste scarpe mi stanno strette** these shoes are tight; **~ per fare qc** to be about to do sthg; **~ bene/male** to be well/not very well; **~ a guardare** to watch; **~ in piedi** to stand (up); **~ seduto** to sit, to be sitting; **~ simpatico a qn** to like sb; **~ zitto** to shut up; **starci** to fit.

starnutire *vi* to sneeze.

starnuto *sm* sneeze.

stasera *avv* this evening, tonight.

statale *agg* state *(dav s)*, government *(dav s)* ◆ *smf* civil servant ◆ *sf* main road.

statistica, -che *sf (disciplina)* statistics *(pl)*; *(dati)* statistic.

stato *pp* → **essere, stare** ◆ *sm (condizione)* state, condition; *(nazione)* state; **essere in ~ interessante** to be pregnant; **~ d'animo** state of mind; **~ civile** marital status; **gli Stati Uniti (d'America)** the United States (of America).

statua *sf* statue.

statunitense *agg* United States *(dav s)*, of the United States.

statura *sf (fisica)* height.

statuto *sm* statute.

stazionario, -a *agg (immutato)* unchanged.

stazione *sf* station; **~ degli autobus** bus station; **~ balneare** seaside resort; **~ centrale** central station; **~ ferroviaria** railway station *(Br)*, railroad station *(Am)*; **~ di polizia** police station; **~ sciistica** ski resort; **~ di servizio** petrol station *(Br)*, gas station *(Am)*; **~ termale** spa.

stecca, -che *sf (asticella)* stick; *(di sigarette)* carton; *(da biliardo)* cue.

steccato *sm* fence.

stella *sf* star; **stelle filanti** shooting stars; **albergo a tre stelle** three-star hotel.

stellato, -a *agg* starry.

stelo *sm (di fiore)* stem.

stemma, -i *sm* coat of arms.

stendere *vt (allungare)* to stretch (out); *(panni, vele)* to spread (out); *(bucato)* to hang out ❑ **stendersi** *vr (sdraiarsi)* to lie down.

stenografare *vt* to take down in shorthand.

stentare *vi*: **~ a fare qc** to find it hard to do sthg.

stento *sm*: **a ~** with difficulty ❑ **stenti** *smpl (privazioni)* hardship *(sg)*.

sterco, -chi *sm* dung.

stereo *sm inv* stereo.

stereotipo *sm* stereotype.

sterile *agg (uomo, donna)* sterile.

sterilizzare *vt* to sterilize.

sterlina *sf* pound (sterling).

sterminare *vt* to exterminate.

sterminato, -a *agg* immense.

sterminio *sm* extermination.

sterzare *vi* to steer.

sterzo *sm* steering.

steso, -a *pp* → **stendere**.

stesso, -a *agg* same; *(in persona, proprio)*: **il presidente ~** the president himself ○ in person ◆ *pron*: **lo ~/la stessa** the same (one); **io ~** I myself; **lei stessa** she herself; **lo faccio per me ~** I'm doing it for myself; **fare qc lo ~** to do sthg just the same; **fa ○ è lo ~** it doesn't matter; **per me è lo ~** it's all the same to me.

stesura *sf (atto)* drafting; *(documento)* draft.

stile *sm* style; **~ libero** freestyle.

stilista, -i, -e *smf* designer.

stilografica, -che *sf* fountain pen.

stima *sf (valutazione)* valuation; *(apprezzamento)* esteem; **fare la ~ di qc** to estimate the value of sthg; **avere ~ di qn** to have a high opinion of sb.

stimare *vt* (*valutare*) to value; (*ritenere*) to consider; (*apprezzare*) to respect.

stimolare *vt* to stimulate; ~ **qn a fare qc** to spur sb on to do sthg.

stimolo *sm* stimulus.

stingere *vi* to fade □ **stingersi** *vr* to fade.

stinto, -a *pp* → **stingere**.

stipendio *sm* salary.

stipite *sm* (*di porta, finestra*) jamb.

stipulare *vt* to draw up.

stirare *vt* (*con il ferro*) to iron.

stiro *sm* → **asse, ferro**.

stirpe *sf* stock, birth.

stitichezza *sf* constipation.

stivale *sm* boot.

stivaletto *sm* ankle boot.

stizza *sf* anger.

stizzirsi *vr* to get irritated.

stoccafisso *sm* wind-dried cod, stockfish.

stoffa *sf* material, fabric; **avere la ~ di** to have the makings of.

stola *sf* stole.

stolto, -a *agg* stupid.

stomaco, -chi o **-ci** *sm* stomach.

stonato, -a *agg* (MUS) off key.

stop *sm inv* (AUTO: *segnale*) stop sign; (AUTO: *luce*) brake light (*Br*), stoplight ◆ *esclam* stop!; '**stop con segnale rosso**' 'stop when light is on red'.

storcere *vt* to twist; ~ **il naso** to turn up one's nose; **storcersi una caviglia** to twist one's ankle □ **storcersi** *vr* to twist.

stordire *vt* to stun.

stordito, -a *agg* stunned.

storia *sf* (*avvenimenti umani, materia, opera*) history; (*vicenda, invenzione*) story; (*faccenda*) business (*no pl*); (*scusa*) excuse.

storico, -a, -ci, -che *agg* historic(al) ◆ *sm, f* historian.

stormo *sm* (*di uccelli*) flock.

storpiare *vt* (*rendere storpio*) to cripple; (*parola*) to mangle; (*concetto*) to twist.

storta *sf*: **prendere una ~ al piede** to sprain one's foot.

storto, -a *pp* → **storcere** ◆ *agg* (*chiodo*) twisted, bent; (*gambe, quadro*) crooked; **andare ~** to go wrong.

stoviglie *sfpl* dishes.

strabico, -a, -ci, -che *agg* (*persona*) squint-eyed; (*occhi*) squint.

straccadenti *smpl* type of very hard biscuit.

stracchino *sm* a creamy cow's milk cheese from Lombardy.

stracciare *vt* (*vestito, foglio*) to tear.

stracciatella *sf* (*gelato*) chocolate-chip ice cream; (*minestra*) broth enriched with eggs, semolina and Parmesan cheese.

straccio *sm* rag; (*per pulizie*) duster, cloth.

straccione, -a *sm, f* ragamuffin.

strada *sf* road; (*urbana*) street; (*percorso*) way; ~ **facendo** on the way; **tagliare la ~ a qn** to cut across sb; ~ **panoramica** scenic route; ~ **senza uscita** dead end; '~ **deformata**' 'uneven road surface';

'**~ privata**' 'private road'; '**~ transitabile con catene**' 'road negotiable with chains'.

stradale *agg* road *(dav s)* ◆ *sf* traffic police.

strafalcione *sm (sproposito)* howler.

straforo : **di straforo** *avv* on the sly.

strafottente *agg* arrogant.

strage *sf* massacre.

stralunato, -a *agg (occhi)* rolling; *(persona)* dazed.

stramazzare *vi* to fall heavily.

strangolare *vt* to strangle.

straniero, -a *agg* foreign ◆ *sm, f* foreigner.

strano, -a *agg* strange.

straordinario, -a *agg* extraordinary; *(treno)* special ◆ *sm (lavoro)* overtime.

strapazzare *vt* to ill-treat ❑ **strapazzarsi** *vr* to tire o.s. out.

strappo *sm (in tessuto, MED)* tear; *(fam: passaggio)* lift *(Br)*, ride *(Am)*; **fare uno ~ alla regola** to make an exception to the rule.

straripare *vi* to overflow.

strascico, -chi *sm (di abito)* train; *(fig: conseguenza)* aftereffect.

strascinati *smpl* squares of pasta in a tomato and minced meat sauce (a speciality of Calabria).

stratagemma, -i *sm* stratagem.

strategia *sf* strategy.

strato *sm (di polvere, di crema)* layer; *(di vernice, smalto)* coat.

stravagante *agg* eccentric.

stravedere : **stravedere per** *v*

+ *prep* to be crazy about.

stravisto *pp* → **stravedere**.

stravolgere *vt* to distort.

stravolto, -a *pp* → **stravolgere**.

strazio *sm*: **essere uno ~** *(libro, film)* to be awful; *(persona)* to be a pain.

strega, -ghe *sf* witch.

stregone *sm (mago)* sorcerer; *(di tribù)* witchdoctor.

stremare *vt* to exhaust.

stremo *sm*: **essere allo ~ delle forze** to be at the end of one's tether.

strepitoso, -a *agg* resounding.

stress *sm* stress.

stressante *agg* stressful.

stretta *sf* grip; **~ di mano** handshake; **mettere alle strette qn** to put sb in a tight corner.

strettamente *avv (serratamente)* tightly; *(rigorosamente)* strictly.

stretto, -a *pp* → **stringere** ◆ *agg (strada, stanza)* narrow; *(vestito, scarpe)* tight; *(rigoroso, preciso)* strict ◆ *sm* strait; **parenti stretti** close family (sg).

strettoia *sf* bottleneck.

striato, -a *agg* streaked.

stridere *vi (freni)* to creak; *(cicale, grilli)* to chirr; *(colori)* to clash.

strillare *vi & vt* to scream.

strillo *sm* scream.

striminzito, -a *agg (vestito)* shabby; *(persona)* skinny.

stringa, -ghe *sf* lace.

stringato, -a agg concise.

stringere vt (vite, nodo) to tighten; (denti, pugno) to clench; (labbra) to press; (tenere stretto) to grip; (abito) to take in; (patto, accordo) to conclude ♦ vi to be tight; ~ qn tra le braccia to hug sb; ~ la mano a qn to shake hands with sb; ~ i tempi to get a move on; il tempo stringe time is short ☐ **stringersi** vr to squeeze up.

striscia, -sce sf (nastro) strip; (riga) stripe; **strisce (pedonali)** zebra crossing (sg).

strisciare vi (serpente) to slither; (passare rasente) to scrape ♦ vt (macchina) to scrape; (piedi) to drag.

striscione sm banner.

stritolare vt to crush.

strizzare vt to wring out; ~ l'occhio to wink.

strofinaccio sm cloth.

strofinare vt to rub.

stroncare vt to break off; (rivolta) to put down; (libro, film) to pan.

stropicciare vt (braccio, occhi) to rub; (vestito) to crease.

strozzapreti smpl 'gnocchi' either in a meat sauce, or made with eggs and spinach and served with butter and cheese.

strozzare vt (strangolare) to strangle; (sog: cibo) to choke ☐ **strozzarsi** vr to choke.

strudel sm inv apple strudel.

strumento sm (musicale, di precisione) instrument; (di fabbro, meccanico) tool.

strusciare vt to rub ☐ **strusciarsi** vr to rub o.s.

strutto sm lard.

struttura sf structure.

struzzo sm ostrich.

stuccare vt (buco) to plaster; (vetro) to putty.

stucco, -chi sm (malta) plaster; (decorazione) stucco; **rimanere di ~** to be dumbfounded.

studente, -essa sm, f student; (di liceo) pupil.

studentesco, -a, -schi, -sche agg student (dav s).

studentessa → **studente**.

studiare vt & vi to study.

studio sm (attività) studying; (ricerca, stanza) study; (di professionista) office; (di televisione, radio) studio; ~ **medico** surgery (Br), office (Am); **gli studi** (scuola, università) studies.

studioso, -a agg studious ♦ sm, f scholar.

stufa sf stove; ~ **elettrica** heater.

stufare vt (seccare): **mi hai stufato con le tue chiacchiere!** I'm sick and tired of you talking! ☐ **stufarsi** vr: **stufarsi (di)** (fam) to get fed up (with). .

stufato sm stew.

stufo, -a agg (fam): **essere ~ (di)** to be fed up (with).

stuoia sf straw mat.

stupefacente agg amazing ♦ sm drug.

stupendo, -a agg marvellous.

stupidaggine sf stupid thing.

stupido, -a agg stupid.

stupire vt to amaze ☐ **stupirsi di** vr + prep to be amazed by.

stupore sm astonishment.

stupro *sm* rape.

sturare *vt* to unblock.

stuzzicadenti *sm inv* tooth-pick.

stuzzicare *vt (irritare)* to tease; ~ l'appetito to whet one's appetite.

su *prep* **1.** *(stato in luogo)* on; **le chiavi sono sul tavolo** the keys are on the desk; **a 2 000 metri sul livello del mare** at 2,000 metres above sea level; **una casa sul mare** a house by the sea.
2. *(moto a luogo)* on, onto; **venite sulla terrazza** come onto the terrace.
3. *(argomento)* about, on; **un libro sulla vita di Napoleone** a book about Napoleon's life.
4. *(tempo)* around; **vengo sul tardo pomeriggio** I'll come in the late afternoon; **sul momento** at that moment; **sul presto** fairly early.
5. *(prezzo e misura)* about; **costerà sulle 200 000 lire** it will cost about 200,000 lira; **peserà sui tre chili** he weighs about three kilos; **un uomo sulla quarantina** a man about forty years old.
6. *(modo)*: **facciamo dolci solo ~ ordinazione** we only make cakes to order; **~ appuntamento** by appointment; **vestito ~ misura** made-to-measure suit; **parlare sul serio** to be serious; **nove volte ~ dieci** nine times out of ten.
♦ *avv* **1.** *(in alto)* up; *(al piano di sopra)* upstairs; **in ~** *(verso l'alto)* up(wards); *(in poi)* onwards; **dai 18 anni in ~** from the age of 18 onwards.
2. *(per esortare)* come on; **~, sbri-**gatevi! come on, hurry up!; **~ con la vita!** cheer up!

sub *smf inv* diver.

subacqueo, -a *agg* underwater ♦ *sm, f* diver.

subbuglio *sm* turmoil; **essere in ~** to be in a turmoil.

subdolo, -a *agg* sly.

subentrare *vi*: ~ a qn to take sb's place.

subire *vt (ingiustizia, conseguenze)* to suffer; *(operazione)* to undergo; **~ un torto** to be wronged.

subissare *vt*: ~ qn di qc to shower sb with sthg.

subito *avv (immediatamente)* straightaway, immediately, at once; **torno ~** I'll be right back.

sublime *agg* sublime.

subordinato, -a *agg*: ~ a *(dipendente da)* dependent on.

suburbano, -a *agg* suburban.

succedere *vi (accadere)* to happen; ~ a qn *(subentrare)* to succeed sb; **che cos'è successo?** what happened? ❑ **succedersi** *vr* to follow one another.

successivamente *avv* afterwards.

successivo, -a *agg* following.

successo, -a *pp* → succedere ♦ *sm* success; **di ~** successful.

successore *sm* successor.

succhiare *vt* to suck.

succhiotto *sm* dummy.

succinto, -a *agg (conciso)* succinct; *(abito)* scanty.

succo, -chi *sm* juice; ~ **di frutta** fruit juice; ~ **di pomodoro** tomato juice.

sud *sm* south ◆ *agg inv* south; **a ~ (di qc)** south (of sthg); **nel ~** in the south.

Sudafrica *sm*: **il ~** South Africa.

Sudamerica *sm*: **il ~** South America.

sudare *vi* to sweat.

suddetto, -a *agg* above-mentioned.

suddividere *vt* to subdivide.

sudest *sm* southeast.

sudicio, -a, -ci, -ce o **-cie** *agg* dirty.

sudore *sm* sweat.

sudovest *sm* southwest.

sue → **suo**.

sufficiente *agg* (*che basta*) enough, sufficient; (*tono, atteggiamento*) arrogant ◆ *sm* (*SCOL*) pass.

sufficienza *sf*: **a ~** enough.

suffragio *sm* (*voto*) vote; **~ universale** universal suffrage.

suggerimento *sm* suggestion.

suggerire *vt* (*consigliare*) to suggest; (*risposta*) to tell.

suggestionare *vt* to influence.

suggestivo, -a *agg* evocative.

sughero *sm* cork.

sugli = **su** + **gli**, → **su**.

sugo, -ghi *sm* (*condimento*) sauce; (*di arrosto*) juices (*pl*); (*succo*) juice; **~ di pomodoro** tomato sauce.

sui = **su** + **i**, → **su**.

suicidarsi *vr* to commit suicide.

suicidio *sm* suicide.

suino, -a *agg* pork (*dav s*) ◆ *sm* pig.

sul = **su** + **il**, → **su**.

sull' = **su** + **l'**, → **su**.

sulla = **su** + **la**, → **su**.

sulle = **su** + **le**, → **su**.

sullo = **su** + **lo**, → **su**.

suo (*f* **sua**, *mpl* **suoi**, *fpl* **sue**) *agg* (*di lui*) his; (*di lei*) her; (*di esso, essa*) its; (*forma di cortesia*) your; (*proprio*) one's ◆ *pron* (*di lui*) his; (*di lei*) hers; (*di esso, essa*) its; (*forma di cortesia*) yours; (*proprio*) one's; **i suoi** (*di lui*) his family; (*di lei*) her family.

suocero, -a *sm, f* father-in-law (*f* mother-in-law) ❑ **suoceri** *smpl* in-laws.

suoi → **suo**.

suola *sf* sole.

suolo *sm* (*terra*) ground; (*terreno*) soil.

suonare *vt* (*strumento*) to play; (*campanello*) to ring; (*clacson*) to sound; (*allarme*) to set off; (*ore*) to strike ◆ *vi* (*musicista*) to play; (*telefono, campana*) to ring; (*allarme, sveglia*) to go off; (*fig: parole*) to sound.

suono *sm* sound.

suora *sf* nun.

super *sf inv* four-star (petrol) (*Br*), premium (*Am*).

superare *vt* (*confine, traguardo, fiume*) to cross; (*limite*) to exceed; (*veicolo*) to overtake; (*esame, concorso, prova*) to pass; (*ostacolo*) to overcome; (*essere migliore di*) to beat; **ha superato la trentina** he is over 30.

superbo, -a *agg* (*arrogante*) haughty; (*grandioso*) superb.

superficiale *agg* superficial.

superficie, -ci *sf* surface; (*MAT*) area.

superfluo, -a *agg* superfluous.

superiore *sm, f* superior ♦ *agg* *(di sopra)* upper; *(quantità, numero)* larger, greater; *(prezzo)* higher; *(qualità)* superior; **di età ~ ai 26 anni** above 26.

superlativo *sm* superlative.

supermercato *sm* supermarket.

superstrada *sf* = (toll-free) motorway *(Br)*, = (toll-free) expressway *(Am)*.

suppergiù *avv* more or less.

supplementare *agg* extra.

supplemento *sm* supplement; *(di prezzo)* extra charge; **~ rapido** additional charge for fast train.

supplente *smf (SCOL)* supply teacher.

supporre *vt* to suppose.

supposta *sf* suppository.

supposto, -a *pp* → **supporre**.

surriscaldare *vt* to overheat.

suscitare *vt* to arouse.

susina *sf* plum.

susseguire *vt* to follow □ **susseguirsi** *vr* to follow one another.

sussidio *sm* subsidy.

sussulto *sm (sobbalzo)* start.

sussurrare *vt* to whisper.

svagarsi *vr (divertirsi)* to enjoy o.s.; *(distrarsi)* to take one's mind off things.

svago, -ghi *sm (divertimento)* fun; *(passatempo)* pastime.

svaligiare *vt* to burgle.

svalutare *vt* to devalue.

svanire *vi* to disappear, to vanish.

svantaggio *sm (aspetto negativo)* disadvantage; **essere in ~** *(SPORT)* to be behind.

svariato, -a *agg (vario)* varied; *(numeroso)* various.

svedese *agg & sm* Swedish ♦ *smf* Swede.

sveglia *sf (orologio)* alarm clock; **la ~ è alle sei** we have to get up at six.

svegliare *vt* to wake (up) □ **svegliarsi** *vr* to wake up.

sveglio, -a *agg (desto)* awake; *(intelligente)* smart.

svelare *vt* to reveal.

svelto, -a *agg* quick; **alla svelta** quickly.

svendita *sf* sale.

svenire *vi* to faint.

sventare *vt* to foil.

sventolare *vt* to wave ♦ *vi* to flutter.

sventura *sf (sfortuna)* bad luck, misfortune; *(disgrazia)* disaster.

svenuto, -a *pp* → **svenire**.

svestire *vt* to undress □ **svestirsi** *vr* to get undressed.

Svezia *sf*: **la ~** Sweden.

sviare *vt* to distract; **~ il discorso** to change the subject.

svignarsela *vr (fam)* to sneak off.

sviluppare *vt* to develop □ **svilupparsi** *vr (ragazzo)* to grow; *(industria, attività)* to expand, to grow; *(incendio, infezione)* to spread.

sviluppo *sm* development; **età dello ~** puberty.

svincolo *sm (stradale)* motorway junction.

svitare *vt* to unscrew.

Svizzera *sf*: la ~ Switzerland.

svizzero, -a *agg & sm, f* Swiss.

svogliato, -a *agg* listless.

svolgere *vt (attività, lavoro)* to carry out; *(srotolare)* to unroll, to unwind; *(tema)* to write □ **svolgersi** *vr (fatto, film)* to take place; *(srotolarsi)* to unwind.

svolta *sf* turn; *(mutamento)* turning point.

svoltare *vi* to turn; ~ **a sinistra** to turn left.

svolto, -a *pp* → svolgere.

svuotare *vt* to empty.

T

tabaccaio, -a *sm, f* tobacconist.

tabaccheria *sf* tobacconist's.

tabacco, -chi *sm* tobacco.

tabella *sf (cartellone)* board; *(prospetto)* table; ~ **oraria** timetable.

tabellone *sm (con orari)* timetable (board); *(per affissioni)* billboard.

tabù *sm inv* taboo.

tacca, -che *sf* notch.

taccagno, -a *agg* mean.

tacchino *sm* turkey.

tacciare *vt*: ~ **qn di qc** to accuse sb of sthg.

tacco, -chi *sm* heel; **tacchi a spillo** stilettos.

taccuino *sm* notebook.

tacere *vi* to be quiet ♦ *vt* to keep quiet about.

taciturno, -a *agg* taciturn.

tafano *sm* horsefly.

tafferuglio *sm* brawl.

taglia *sf (misura)* size; *(corporatura)* build; ~ **unica** one size.

tagliacarte *sm inv* paper knife.

taglialegna *sm inv* woodcutter.

tagliando *sm* coupon.

tagliare *vt* to cut; *(affettare)* to slice; *(carne)* to carve; *(legna)* to chop; *(recidere)* to cut off; *(ritagliare)* to cut out; *(intersecare)* to cut across; *(vino)* to mix; ~ **corto** to cut short; ~ **la strada a qn** to cut in front of sb; **tagliarsi i capelli** to have one's hair cut □ **tagliarsi** *vr* to cut o.s.

tagliatelle *sfpl* tagliatelle *(sg)*.

tagliaunghie *sm inv* nail clippers *(pl)*.

tagliente *agg* sharp.

tagliere *sm* chopping board.

taglio *sm* cut; *(di stoffa)* length; *(parte tagliente)* edge; ~ **cesareo** (MED) caesarean section; **banconote di piccolo/grosso** ~ small/large denomination bank notes.

tagliuzzare *vt* to cut into small pieces.

tailleur [ta'jœr] *sm inv* suit *(for women)*.

Taiwan *sm*: **il** ~ Taiwan.

talco *sm* talcum powder.

tale *agg dimostrativo* **1.** *(di questo*

tipo) such; **non ammetto tali atteggiamenti** I won't allow such behaviour.

2. *(così grande)*: **mi hai fatto una ~ paura!** you gave me such a fright!; **è un ~ disordinato!** he's so untidy!; **fa un ~ freddo!** it's so cold!; **è di una gentilezza ~ che non si può dirgli di no** he's so nice (that) you can't say no to him; **fa un rumore ~ da farti venire il mal di testa** it makes so much noise (that) it gives you a headache.

3. *(in paragoni)*: **~ ... ~** like ... like; **~ madre ~ figlia** like mother like daughter; **~ quale** just like; **è ~ quale lo ricordavo** he's just like I remembered.

♦ *agg indefinito (non precisato)*: **ti cerca un tal signor Marchi** someone called Mr Marchi is looking for you; **il giorno ~ all'ora ~** on such and such a day at such and such a time.

♦ *pron indefinito (persona non precisata)*: **un ~ mi ha chiesto di te** some man asked me about you; **quel ~** that person.

taleggio *sm* a type of soft cheese from Lombardy.

talento *sm* talent.

talloncino *sm* counterfoil.

tallone *sm* heel.

talmente *avv* so.

talora *avv* sometimes.

talpa *sf* mole.

talvolta *avv* sometimes.

tamburellare *vi* to drum.

tamburello *sm (strumento)* tambourine; *(gioco)* ball game played with a round bat.

tamburo *sm* drum.

Tamigi *sm*: **il ~** the Thames.

tamponamento *sm* collision; **~ a catena** pileup.

tamponare *vt (AUTO)* to bump into; *(ferita)* to plug.

tampone *sm (MED)* wad; *(assorbente interno)* tampon.

tana *sf* den.

tandem *sm inv* tandem.

tanfo *sm* stench.

tanga *sm inv* tanga.

tangente *sf (MAT)* tangent; *(quota)* share.

tangenziale *sf* bypass.

tango, -ghi *sm* tango.

tanica, -che *sf (recipiente)* (jerry) can.

tantino : **un tantino** *avv* a little, a bit.

tanto, -a *agg* **1.** *(in grande quantità)* a lot of, much; *(così tanto)* such a lot of, so much; **abbiamo ancora ~ tempo** we've still got a lot of time; **lo conosco da ~ tempo** I've known him for a long time.

2. *(in numero elevato)*: **tanti(-e)** a lot of, many; *(così tanti)* such a lot of, so many; **ho tanti amici** I've got a lot of O many friends; **tanti auguri!** all the best!; *(di compleanno)* happy birthday!

3. *(in paragoni)*: **~ ... quanto** *(quantità)* as much ... as; *(numero)* as many ... as; **non ho tanta immaginazione quanta ne hai tu** I haven't got as much imagination as you; **ha tanti fratelli quante sorelle** he's got as many brothers as sisters.

♦ *pron* **1.** *(una grande quantità)* a lot, much; *(così tanto)* such a lot, so much; **mi piace il cioccolato e ne mangio** ~ I like chocolate and eat a lot of it; **c'è ~ da fare** there's a lot o plenty to do.

2. *(un grande numero)*: **tanti(-e)** many, a lot; *(così tanti)* so many, such a lot; **è una ragazza come tante** she's just an ordinary girl; **l'hanno visto in tanti** many people saw it.

3. *(una quantità indeterminata)*: **di questi soldi tanti sono per la casa, tanti per le tue spese** so much of this money is for the house and so much for your expenses; **pago un ~ al mese** I pay so much per month.

4. *(in paragoni)*: **~ quanto** as much as; **tanti quanti** as many as.

5. *(in espressioni)*: **~ vale che tu stia a casa** you may as well stay at home; **di ~ in ~** from time to time.
◆ *avv* **1.** *(molto)* very; **ti ringrazio ~** thank you very much; **non ~** *(poco)* not much; **~ meglio!** so much the better!

2. *(così)* so; **è ~ sciocco da crederci** he's silly enough to believe it; **è ~ grasso che non ci passa** he's so fat that he can't get through; **non pensavo piovesse ~** I didn't think it rained so much.

3. *(in paragoni)*: **~ ... quanto** as ... as; **non studia ~ quanto potrebbe** he doesn't study as much as he could.

4. *(soltanto)*: **~ per divertirsi/parlare** just for enjoyment/for the sake of talking; **~ per cambiare** just for a change; **una volta ~** for once.
◆ *cong* after all.

tappa *sf (fermata)* stop; *(parte di*

tragitto, nel ciclismo) stage.

tappare *vt (buco, falla)* to plug; *(bottiglia)* to cork; **tapparsi le orecchie** to turn a deaf ear.

tapparella *sf* store.

tappeto *sm (da pavimento)* carpet; *(più piccolo)* rug; **mandare qn al ~** *(SPORT)* to floor sb.

tappezzare *vt (pareti)* to paper; *(poltrona)* to cover.

tappezzeria *sf (tessuto)* soft furnishings *(pl)*; *(carta da parati)* wallpaper.

tappo *sm (di plastica, metallo)* top; *(di sughero)* cork; *(fam: spreg: persona bassa)* shorty.

taralli *smpl* ring-shaped biscuits flavoured with aniseed and pepper (a speciality of southern Italy).

tarantella *sf* tarantella *(a folk dance from the South of Italy)*.

tarantola *sf* tarantula.

tarchiato, -a *agg* stocky.

tardare *vi (arrivare tardi)* to be late ◆ *vt (ritardare)* to delay; **~ a fare qc** to be late in doing sthg.

tardi *avv* late; **fare ~** to be late; **più ~** later; **al più ~** at the latest; **sul ~** late in the day.

targa, -ghe *sf (di auto)* number-plate; *(con indicazione)* plate.

targhetta *sf (su campanello)* nameplate; *(piccola targa)* tag.

tariffa *sf (di) rate; *(di trasporti)* fare; **~ ridotta** reduced fare; **~ unica** flat rate.

tarlo *sm* woodworm.

tarma *sf* moth.

tarocchi *smpl* tarot cards.

tartagliare *vi* to stammer, to

stutter.

tartaro sm tartar.

tartaruga, -ghe sf (di terra) tortoise; (di mare) turtle; (materiale) tortoiseshell.

tartina sf canapé.

tartufo sm (fungo) truffle; (gelato) type of chocolate ice cream.

tasca, -sche sf (di giacca, pantaloni) pocket.

tascabile agg pocket (dav s) ♦ sm paperback.

taschino sm breast pocket.

tassa sf (imposta) tax; (per servizio) fee; ~ **di iscrizione** membership fee.

tassametro sm taximeter.

tassare vt to tax.

tassativo, -a agg peremptory.

tassello sm plug.

tassì = taxi.

tassista, -i, -e smf taxi driver.

tasso sm (indice) rate; (percentuale) percentage; (animale) badger; ~ **di cambio** exchange rate.

tastare vt (polso) to take; ~ **il terreno** (fig) to see how the land lies.

tastiera sf keyboard.

tasto sm (di pianoforte, computer) key; (di TV, radio) button.

tastoni avv: **procedere (a)** ~ to feel one's way.

tattico, -a, -ci, -che agg tactical.

tatto sm (senso) touch; (fig: accortezza) tact.

tatuaggio sm tattoo.

tatuare vt to tattoo.

tavola sf (MAT: mobile) table; (asse) plank; **mettersi** O **andare a** ~ to sit down to eat; ~ **calda** snack bar.

tavoletta sf bar.

tavolino sm (da salotto) small table; (di bar) table; (scrivania) writing desk.

tavolo sm table.

taxi sm inv taxi.

tazza sf cup; (del water) toilet bowl; **una** ~ **di caffè** a cup of coffee.

tazzina sf coffee cup.

T.C.I. (abbr di Touring Club Italiano) = AA, = RAC.

te pron you, → **ti**.

tè sm inv tea.

teatrale agg theatrical.

teatrino sm puppet theatre.

teatro sm theatre; ~ **tenda** marquee used for public performances.

tecnica, -che sf technique; (tecnologia) technology, → **tecnico**.

tecnico, -a, -ci, -che agg technical ♦ sm, f technician.

tecnologia sf technology.

tecnologico, -a, -ci, -che agg technological.

tedesco, -a, -schi, -sche agg, sm & sf German.

tegame sm pan.

teglia sf baking tin.

tegola sf tile.

teiera sf teapot.

tel. (abbr di telefono) tel.

tela sf (tessuto) cloth; (quadro) canvas; ~ **cerata** oilcloth.

telaio sm (per tessere) loom; (di macchina) chassis; (di finestra, letto) frame.

telecamera *sf* television camera.

telecomando *sm* remote control.

telecronaca, -che *sf* television report.

teleferica, -che *sf* cableway.

telefilm *sm inv* TV film *(Br)*, TV movie *(Am)*.

telefonare *vi & vt* to (tele)phone; ~ **a qn** to (tele)phone sb.

telefonata *sf* (tele)phone call; ~ **a carico (del destinatario)** reverse charge call.

telefonico, -a, -ci, -che *agg* (tele)phone *(dav s)*.

telefonino *sm* mobile phone.

telefonista, -i, -e *smf* switchboard operator.

telefono *sm* telephone; ~ **cellulare** mobile phone; ~ **a gettoni** payphone; ~ **pubblico** public phone; *(cabina)* call box; ~ **a scatti** metered phone; ~ **a scheda (magnetica)** cardphone; **al** ~ on the phone; **per** ~ by phone.

telegiornale *sm* television news *(sg)*.

telegrafare *vt & vi* to cable, to telegraph.

telegramma, -i *sm* telegram.

teleobiettivo *sm* telephoto lens.

Telepass® *sm inv* motorway toll card.

teleromanzo *sm* serial.

teleschermo *sm* television screen.

telescopio *sm* telescope.

teleselezione *sf* direct dialling.

televisione *sf* television; **alla** ~ on television.

televisivo, -a *agg* television *(dav s)*.

televisore *sm* television (set); ~ **in bianco e nero** black-and-white television; ~ **a colori** colour television.

telex *sm inv* telex.

telo *sm* cloth.

tema, -i *sm (argomento, soggetto)* topic, subject; *(SCOL)* essay; *(MUS)* theme.

temere *vt* to fear, to be afraid of ♦ *vi* to be afraid; **temo che non venga** I'm afraid he won't come; **temo di no** I'm afraid not; **temo di sì** I'm afraid so; **temo di non farcela** I'm afraid I can't make it ❑ **temere per** *v + prep* to fear for.

tempera *sf* tempera.

temperamatite *sm inv* pencil sharpener.

temperamento *sm (carattere)* temperament; *(carattere forte)* strong character.

temperato, -a *agg (clima, stagione)* temperate.

temperatura *sf* temperature.

temperino *sm (coltello)* penknife; *(temperamatite)* pencil sharpener.

tempesta *sf* storm; ~ **di neve** blizzard.

tempestare *vt:* ~ **qn di domande** to bombard sb with questions.

tempestivo, -a *agg* timely.

tempestoso, -a *agg* stormy.

tempia sf temple (ANAT).

tempio sm temple (building).

tempo sm (cronologico, ritmo) time; (meteorologico) weather; (GRAMM) tense; (di partita) half; (di film) part; **quanto ~ ci vuole?** how long does it take?; **avere il ~ di o per fare qc** to have the time to do sthg; **fare qc per ~** to do sthg in time; **perdere ~** to waste time; **~ di cottura** cooking time; **~ libero** free time; **~ fa** some time ago; **in ~** in time; **allo stesso ~** at the same time.

temporale agg (GRAMM) of time ◆ sm (thunder)storm.

temporaneo, -a agg temporary.

temporeggiare vi to play for time.

tenace agg (persona, carattere) tenacious.

tenacia sf tenacity.

tenaglie sfpl pliers.

tenda sf (di finestra) curtain; (da campeggio) tent; **~ canadese** ridge tent.

tendenza sf tendency.

tendere vt (elastico, muscoli) to stretch; (corda) to tighten; (mano) to hold out ❏ **tendere a** v + prep: **~ a qc** (propendere per) to be inclined to sthg; (essere simile a) to verge on sthg; **~ a fare qc** to tend to do sthg.

tendine sm tendon.

tenebre sfpl darkness (sg).

tenente sm lieutenant.

tenere vt 1. (reggere) to hold; **~ qc in mano** to hold sthg (in one's hand); **~ qn per mano** to hold sb by the hand.

2. (mantenere) to keep; **~ la finestra aperta** to keep the window open; **~ le mani in tasca** to keep one's hands in one's pockets; **~ qc a mente** to remember sthg; **~ il posto a qn** to keep a seat for sb; **~ qn occupato** to keep sb busy; **tenga pure il resto** keep the change.

3. (promessa, segreto) to keep.

4. (conferenza, riunione) to hold; **~ un discorso** to make a speech.

5. (non allontanarsi da): **~ la destra/sinistra** to keep right/left; **~ la strada** to hold the road.

6. (in espressioni): **tieni!** (dando qc) here!; **la lana tiene caldo** wool is warm; **~ compagnia a qn** to keep sb company; **~ conto di qc** to take sthg into account; **~ d'occhio qn** to keep an eye on sb.

◆ vi (corda, diga) to hold; **questa colla non tiene** this glue isn't sticking; **~ duro** to hold out!

❏ **tenere a** v + prep (dare importanza a) to care about; **~ a fare qc** to be keen to do sthg; **tenere per** v + prep (fare il tifo per) to support; **per che squadra tieni?** which team do you support?; **tenersi** vr 1. (reggersi): **tenersi (a)** to hold on (to); **tieni forte!** hold on!

2. (restare): **tieni pronto** be ready; **tenersi in disparte** to stand apart; **tenersi a disposizione di qn** to be at sb's disposal; **tenersi a distanza** to keep one's distance.

3. (aver luogo) to be held.

tenerezza sf tenderness.

tenero, -a agg (cibo) tender; (materia) soft.

tenia *sf* tapeworm.

tennis *sm* tennis; ~ **da tavolo** table tennis.

tennista, -i, -e *smf* tennis player.

tenore *sm* (*tono*) tone; (*MUS*) tenor; ~ **di vita** standard of living.

tensione *sf* tension; **alta** ~ high voltage.

tentacolo *sm* tentacle.

tentare *vt* (*sperimentare*) to try; (*allettare*) to tempt; ~ **di fare qc** to try o to attempt to do sthg.

tentativo *sm* attempt.

tentazione *sf* temptation.

tentennare *vi* (*oscillare*) to wobble; (*esitare*) to hesitate.

tentoni *avv*: **andare (a)** ~ to feel one's way.

tenuta *sf* (*abbigliamento*) clothes (*pl*); (*di liquidi, gas*) capacity; (*podere*) estate; **a** ~ **d'aria** airtight; ~ **di strada** roadholding.

teoria *sf* theory; **in** ~ in theory.

teoricamente *avv* theoretically.

teorico, -a, -ci, -che *agg* theoretical.

tepore *sm* warmth.

teppista, -i, -e *smf* hooligan.

tequila [te'kila] *sf inv* tequila.

terapeutico, -a, -ci, -che *agg* therapeutic.

terapia *sf* therapy.

tergicristallo *sm* windscreen wiper.

tergiversare *vi* to avoid the issue.

tergo *sm*: **a** ~ overleaf.

terital® *sm* Terylene®.

termale *agg* thermal.

terme *sfpl* (*stabilimento*) spa (*sg*); (*nell'antica Roma*) baths.

termico, -a, -ci, -che *agg* (*di temperatura*) thermal.

terminal *sm inv* (air) terminal.

terminale *agg* final ◆ *sm* terminal.

terminare *vt* to finish ◆ *vi* to end.

termine *sm* (*fine*) end; (*scadenza*) deadline; (*parola*) term; **portare a** ~ **condurre a** ~ **qc** to bring sthg to a conclusion; **a breve/lungo** ~ short-/long-term; **senza mezzi termini** without beating about the bush ❑ **termini** *smpl* terms.

termite *sf* termite.

termometro *sm* thermometer.

termos = **thermos**.

termosifone *sm* radiator.

termostato *sm* thermostat.

terra *sf* (*pianeta*) Earth; (*terraferma, territorio*) land; (*suolo*) ground; (*sostanza*) soil; ~ **battuta** (*SPORT*) clay; **a** o **per** ~ (*sedere*) on the ground; (*cadere*) to the ground; **essere a** ~ to feel low; **essere** ~ ~ to be down to earth.

terracotta *sf* terracotta.

terraferma *sf* dry land.

terrapieno *sm* embankment.

terrazza *sf* terrace.

terrazzo *sm* (*balcone*) balcony; (*di terreno*) terrace.

terremoto *sm* earthquake.

terreno, -a *agg* (*vita*) earthly; (*beni*) worldly ◆ *sm* (*suolo*) land; (*appezzamento*) plot of land.

terreo, -a *agg* wan.

terrestre *agg (del pianeta)* of the Earth; *(di terraferma)* land *(dav s)*.

terribile *agg* terrible; *(irrequieto)* wild.

terrificante *agg* terrifying.

terrina *sf* tureen.

territoriale *agg* territorial.

territorio *sm (nazionale, straniero)* territory; *(montuoso, desertico)* region.

terrore *sm* terror.

terrorismo *sm* terrorism.

terrorista, -i, -e *smf* terrorist.

terrorizzare *vt* to terrorize.

terso, -a *agg* clear.

terza *sf (marcia)* third gear.

terzetto *sm* trio.

terzino *sm* fullback.

terzo, -a *num* third; **la terza età** old age ◻ **terzi** *smpl (altri)* others, → **sesto**.

terzultimo, -a *sm, f* third from last.

tesa *sf* brim.

teschio *sm* skull.

tesi *sf inv* theory; ~ **(di laurea)** thesis.

teso, -a *pp* → **tendere** ◆ *agg (corda)* taut; *(faccia, situazione)* tense; *(rapporti)* strained.

tesoreria *sf* treasury.

tesoro *sm (oggetti preziosi, denaro)* treasure; *(naturale)* resources *(pl)*; *(fam: appellativo)* darling; **ministro del Tesoro** Chancellor of the Exchequer *(Br)*, Secretary of the Treasury *(Am)*.

tessera *sf* membership card; ~ **magnetica** magnetic card.

tessere *vt* to weave.

tessile *agg* textile *(dav s)*.

tessitura *sf* weaving.

tessuto *sm (stoffa)* material; *(muscolare, osseo)* tissue.

test *sm inv* test; ~ **di gravidanza** pregnancy test.

testa *sf* head; **di** ~ *(vagone)* front; **mettersi in** ~ **di fare qc** to set one's mind on doing sthg; **dalla** ~ **ai piedi** from head to foot; **essere in** ~ **(a qc)** to be in the lead (in sthg); **fare qc di** ~ **propria** to do sthg off one's own bat; **montarsi la** ~ to become bigheaded; **perdere la** ~ to lose one's head; **dare alla** ~ **a qn** to go to sb's head; **essere fuori di** ~ to be out of one's mind; **fare a** ~ **o croce** to toss up; **a** ~ each.

testamento *sm* will.

testardo, -a *agg* stubborn.

testaroli *smpl* broad pasta in a 'pesto' sauce *(a speciality of La Spezia)*.

teste *smf* witness.

testicolo *sm* testicle.

testimone *smf* witness.

testimoniare *vt (il vero, falso)* to testify; *(provare)* to prove ◆ *vi* to testify.

testina *sf* head.

testo *sm* text.

testone, -a *sm, f* stubborn person.

testuggine *sf* tortoise.

tetano *sm* tetanus.

tetro, -a *agg* gloomy.

tettarella *sf* teat.

tette *sfpl (fam)* boobs.

tetto *sm* roof; **i senza ~** the homeless.

tettoia *sf* canopy.

Tevere *sm*: **il ~** the Tiber.

TG *sm inv* TV news *(sg)*.

thermos *sm inv* Thermos flask®.

thriller *sm inv* thriller.

ti *(diventa te se precede lo, la, li, le, ne) pron (complemento oggetto)* you; *(complemento di termine)* (to) you; *(riflessivo)* yourself; **te lo do** I'll give them to you.

tibia *sf* tibia.

tic *sm inv (nervoso)* tic; *(rumore)* tick.

ticchettio *sm* ticking.

ticket *sm inv (MED)* prescription charge.

tiepido, -a *agg* lukewarm.

tifare: **tifare per** *v + prep* to support.

tifo *sm (SPORT)*: **fare il ~ per** to be a fan of.

tifone *sm* typhoon.

tifoso, -a *sm, f* supporter, fan.

tiglio *sm* lime.

tigrato, -a *agg* striped.

tigre *sm o f* tiger.

tilt *sm*: **andare in ~** to stop functioning.

timballo *sm* pie.

timbrare *vt* to stamp.

timbro *sm (arnese, marchio)* stamp; *(di voce)* timbre.

timer ['taimer] *sm inv* timer.

timidezza *sf* shyness.

timido, -a *agg (persona, sguardo)* shy, timid; *(tentativo, accenno)* bashful.

timo *sm* thyme.

timone *sm* rudder.

timore *sm* fear.

timpano *sm* eardrum.

tinello *sm* small dining room.

tingere *vt* to dye; **tingersi i capelli** to dye one's hair.

tinozza *sf* tub.

tinta *sf (materiale)* paint; *(colore)* colour; **farsi la ~** *(dal parrucchiere)* to have one's hair dyed; **in ~ unita** in one colour.

tintarella *sf (fam)* suntan.

tintinnare *vi* to tinkle.

tinto, -a *pp →* **tingere** ♦ *agg* dyed.

tintoria *sf* dry cleaner's.

tintura *sf*: **~ di iodio** iodine.

tipa *sf (fam) (donna)* woman; *(ragazza)* girl.

tipico, -a, -ci, -che *agg* typical.

tipo *sm (specie)* type, kind; *(modello)* type; *(fam: individuo)* bloke (Br), guy (Am).

tipografia *sf (stabilimento)* printing works *(sg)*.

tipografo, -a *sm, f* printer.

TIR *sm inv (abbr di Transports Internationaux Routiers)* HGV.

tiramisù *sm inv* dessert made from sponge soaked in coffee and covered with sweetened cream cheese and cocoa.

tiranno, -a *sm, f* tyrant.

tirare *vt* to pull; *(lanciare)* to throw; *(riga, tende)* to draw; *(sparare)* to fire ♦ *vi* to be tight; **tira vento** it's windy; **~ calci contro qc**

to kick sthg; ~ **diritto** to go straight on; ~ **fuori** to pull out; ~ **a indovinare** to guess; ~ **a sorte** to draw lots; ~ **su** to lift; **tirarsi indietro** *(rinunciare)* to draw back; **'tirare'** *(su porta)* 'pull'.

tiratore *sm* shot.

tiratura *sf (di giornale)* circulation.

tirchio, -a *agg (fam)* mean.

tiro *sm (d'arma)* shooting; *(SPORT)* shot; *(traino)* draught; ~ **con l'arco** archery; **giocare un brutto ~ a qn** to play a nasty trick on sb.

tirocinio *sm* apprenticeship.

tiroide *sf* thyroid.

tirrenico, -a, -ci, -che *agg* Tyrrhenian.

Tirreno *sm*: **il (mar) ~** the Tyrrhenian Sea.

tisana *sf* herb tea.

titolare *smf* owner.

titolo *sm* title; ~ **di studio** academic qualification; **titoli di credito** instruments of credit.

titubante *agg* hesitant.

tivù *sf inv (fam)* TV, telly *(Br)*.

tizio, -a *sm, f* person.

tizzone *sm* ember.

toast [tɔst] *sm inv* toasted sandwich.

toccare *vt* to touch; *(tastare)* to feel; *(argomento)* to touch on; *(riguardare)* to concern ♦ *vi* to touch the bottom; **'vietato ~'** 'do not touch' ❑ **toccare a** *v + prep (spettare)* to be up to; *(capitare)* to happen to; **a chi tocca?** whose turn is it?; **mi tocca ricomprarlo** I have to buy it back.

tocco, -chi *sm* touch.

toga, -ghe *sf (di magistrato)* robe.

togliere *vt (rimuovere)* to take off; *(privare di)* to take away; *(liberare)* to get out; ~ **qc a qn** to take sthg (away) from sb; **ciò non toglie che ...** this doesn't mean that ...; **togliersi gli occhiali** to take one's glasses off; ~ **l'appetito a qn** to put sb off his food.

toilette [twa'lɛt] *sf inv* toilet.

tollerabile *agg* tolerable.

tollerante *agg* tolerant.

tollerare *vt* to tolerate.

tolto, -a *pp* → **togliere**.

tomba *sf* grave.

tombino *sm* manhole.

tombola *sf* ≃ bingo.

tonaca, -che *sf* habit.

tonalità *sf inv (di colore)* shade; *(MUS)* key.

tondo, -a *agg (circolare)* round.

tonfo *sm (rumore)* thud; *(caduta)* fall.

tonico, -a, -ci, -che *agg & sm* tonic.

tonificare *vt* to tone up.

tonnellata *sf* ton.

tonno *sm* tuna fish; ~ **in scatola** tinned tuna fish.

tono *sm* tone; **essere giù di ~** to be under the weather.

tonsille *sfpl* tonsils.

tonto, -a *agg* stupid; **fare il finto ~** to pretend not to understand.

top *sm inv* top.

topaia *sf* dump.

topazio *sm* topaz.

topless *sm inv*: **essere in** ~ to be topless.

topo *sm* mouse.

toppa *sf (di stoffa)* patch; *(di serratura)* keyhole.

torace, -ci *sm* thorax, chest.

torbido, -a *agg* cloudy.

torcere *vt (panni)* to wring; *(piegare)* to twist □ **torcersi** *vr* to double up.

torchio *sm* press.

torcia, -ce *sf* torch.

torcicollo *sm* stiff neck.

torero *sm* bullfighter.

Torino *sf* Turin.

tormenta *sf* blizzard.

tormentare *vt (procurare fastidio)* to annoy □ **tormentarsi** *vr* to fret.

tormento *sm (angoscia)* torment; *(fastidio)* nuisance.

tornaconto *sm* advantage.

tornante *sm* hairpin bend.

tornare *vi* to go/come back; *(ridiventare)* to become again; *(riuscire giusto)* to be correct; ~ **utile** to come in handy; ~ **a casa** to go/come home.

torneo *sm* tournament.

toro *sm* bull □ **Toro** *sm* Taurus.

torre *sf (edificio)* tower; *(negli scacchi)* rook; ~ **di controllo** control tower; **la** ~ **di Pisa** the Leaning Tower of Pisa.

The famous bell tower of Pisa cathedral, known as the "Torre Pendente" (Leaning Tower), stands in the magnificent Campo dei Miracoli. The building dates back to the late XIIth century but is now closed to the public. A total of 294 steps lead up the spiral staircase to the bell chamber above. It was from here that Galileo conducted his famous experiments regarding the laws of gravity.

---

torrefazione *sf (negozio) shop where coffee is roasted and sold.*

torrente *sm* torrent.

torrido, -a *agg* torrid.

torrione *sm* keep.

torrone *sm* nougat.

torsione *sf* twisting.

torso *sm* torso; **a** ~ **nudo** barechested.

torsolo *sm* core.

torta *sf (dolce)* cake; ~ **gelato** icecream gâteau; ~ **di mele** apple tart; ~ **pasqualina** *puff-pastry tart filled with spinach, ricotta cheese, Parmesan cheese and eggs (a speciality of Genoa);* ~ **salata** flan.

tortellini *smpl* tortellini; ~ **all'emiliana** *'tortellini' filled with pork, ham, Parmesan cheese and spices, generally served in broth.*

tortiera *sf* cake tin.

tortino *sm* pie.

torto, -a *pp* → **torcere** ♦ *sm (ingiustizia)* wrong; *(colpa)*: **avere** ~ to be wrong; **a** ~ wrongly.

tortora *sf* turtledove.

tortuoso, -a *agg* winding.

tortura *sf* torture.

torturare *vt* to torture.

tosaerba *sm inv o sf inv* lawnmower.

tosare *vt (pecora)* to shear; *(siepe)* to clip.

Toscana *sf:* **la ~** Tuscany.

toscano, -a *agg* Tuscan.

tosse *sf* cough.

tossico, -a, -ci, -che *agg* toxic.

tossicomane *smf* drug addict.

tossire *vi* to cough.

tosta *agg* f → **faccia**.

tostapane *sm inv* toaster.

tostare *vt* to toast.

tot *agg inv & pron inv (quantità)* so much; *(numero)* so many *(pl)*.

totale *agg & sm* total; **in ~** in total.

totalità *sf:* **la ~ di** all of.

totalizzare *vt* to score.

totano *sm* squid.

totip *sm betting game based on horse racing similar to the pools.*

totocalcio *sm* pools *(pl)*.

toupet [tu'pe] *sm inv* toupee.

tournée [tur'ne] *sf inv* tour.

tovaglia *sf* tablecloth.

tovagliolo *sm* napkin.

tozzo, -a *agg* squat ◆ *sm:* **un ~ di pane** a crust of bread.

tra *prep (in mezzo a due)* between; *(in mezzo a molti)* among(st); *(di tempo, distanza)* in; **tenere qn ~ le braccia** to hold sb in one's arms; **quale preferisci ~ questi?** which one of these do you like best?; **detto ~ (di) noi** between me and you; **~ sé e sé** to oneself.

traballare *vi* to stagger.

trabiccolo *sm (fam)* car.

traboccare *vi* to overflow.

trabocchetto *sm* trap.

tracannare *vt* to gulp down.

traccia, -ce *sf (segno)* mark; *(indizio)* trace.

tracciare *vt (solco)* to trace; *(disegnare)* to draw.

tracciato *sm (percorso)* route; *(grafico)* graph.

trachea *sf* windpipe.

tracolla *sf* shoulder bag; **a ~** over one's shoulder.

tradimento *sm (slealtà)* treachery; *(adulterio)* infidelity; **a ~** by surprise.

tradire *vt* to betray; *(coniuge)* to be unfaithful to ❑ **tradirsi** *vr* to give o.s. away.

traditore, -trice *sm, f* traitor.

tradizionale *agg* traditional.

tradizione *sf* tradition.

tradotto, -a *pp* → **tradurre**.

tradurre *vt* to translate.

traduttore, -trice *sm, f* translator.

traduzione *sf* translation.

trafelato, -a *agg* breathless.

trafficare *vt* to deal in ◆ *vi* to busy o.s.

traffico, -ci *sm (di veicoli)* traffic; *(di droga, armi)* dealing.

trafiggere *vt* to pierce.

trafiletto *sm* short article.

trafitto, -a *pp* → **trafiggere**.

traforo *sm* tunnel.

tragedia *sf* tragedy.

traghetto *sm* ferry.

tragico, -a, -ci, -che *agg* tragic.

tragitto *sm* journey.

traguardo *sm* finishing line.

traiettoria *sf* trajectory.

trainare *vt (tirare)* to tow.

traino *sm (operazione)* pulling; *(di auto)* towing.

tralasciare *vt* to leave out.

traliccio *sm (per elettricità)* pylon.

tram *sm inv* tram.

trama *sf* plot.

tramandare *vt* to pass on.

trambusto *sm* turmoil.

tramezzino *sm* sandwich.

tramite *prep* through.

tramontana *sf* north wind.

tramonto *sm* sunset.

tramortire *vt* to stun.

trampolino *sm (per tuffi)* springboard, divingboard; *(sci)* ski jump.

tramutare *vt*: ~ qn/qc in to change sb/sthg into ▫ **tramutarsi in** *vr + prep* to turn into.

trancio *sm* slice.

tranello *sm* trap.

trangugiare *vt* to gulp down.

tranne *prep* except (for); ~ **che** unless.

tranquillante *sm* tranquillizer.

tranquillità *sf (stato d'animo)* calm; *(di luogo)* peacefulness; *(sicurezza)* peace of mind.

tranquillizzare *vt* to reassure ▫ **tranquillizzarsi** *vr* to calm down.

tranquillo, -a *agg* quiet; *(non preoccupato)* calm; **stai** ~ don't worry.

transalpino, -a *agg* trans-alpine.

transatlantico, -a, -ci, -che *agg* transatlantic ♦ *sm* ocean liner.

transatto *pp* → **transigere**.

transazione *sf* transaction.

transenna *sf* barrier.

transigere *vi*: **in fatto di puntualità non transige** she won't stand for people being late.

transistor *sm inv* transistor.

transitabile *agg* passable.

transitare *vi* to pass.

transitivo, -a *agg (GRAMM)* transitive.

transito *sm* transit; **'divieto di** ~' 'no entry'.

transizione *sf* transition.

trapano *sm* drill.

trapassare *vt* to pierce.

trapelare *vi* to leak out.

trapezio *sm (di circo)* trapeze.

trapezista, -i, -e *smf* trapeze artist.

trapiantare *vt* to transplant.

trapianto *sm* transplant.

trappola *sf* trap.

trapunta *sf* quilt.

trarre *vt*: ~ **in inganno** qn to deceive sb; ~ **origine da** qc to come from sthg; ~ **in salvo** qn to rescue sb; ~ **vantaggio da** qc to benefit from sthg.

trasalire *vi* to jump.

trasandato, -a *agg* shabby.

trasbordare *vt* to transfer ♦ *vi* to change ship/plane/train.

trascinare *vt* to drag ▫ **trascinarsi** *vr (strisciare)* to drag o.s. along; *(nel tempo)* to drag on.

trascorrere *vt* to spend ♦ *vi* to pass.

trascorso, -a *pp* → **trascorrere**.

trascritto, -a *pp* → **trascrivere**.

trascrivere *vt* to transcribe.

trascurabile *agg* negligible.

trascurare *vt* (*lavoro, persona*) to neglect; (*dettagli*) to disregard.

trascurato, -a *agg* neglected.

trasferibile *agg* (*biglietto*) transferable ♦ *sm* transfer.

trasferimento *sm* transfer.

trasferire *vt* (*impiegato*) to transfer; (*negozio, sede*) to move ▢ **trasferirsi** *vr* to move.

trasferta *sf* (*viaggio*) transfer; (*indennità*) travelling expenses (*pl*); (*SPORT*) away game.

trasformare *vt* to transform; **~ qc in qc** to turn sthg into sthg; (*edificio, stanza*) to convert sthg into sthg ▢ **trasformarsi** *vr* to change completely; **trasformarsi in** to turn into.

trasformatore *sm* transformer.

trasformazione *sf* transformation.

trasfusione *sf* transfusion.

trasgredire *vt* to disobey.

traslocare *vi* to move.

trasloco, -chi *sm* (*di mobili*) removal; (*trasferimento*) move.

trasmesso, -a *pp* → **trasmettere**.

trasmettere *vt* (*RADIO, TV*) to broadcast; (*malattia*) to pass on; (*far pervenire*) to send.

trasmissione *sf* (*programma*) programme; (*TECNOL*) transmission.

trasparente *agg* (*acqua*) transparent; (*vestito*) see-through.

trasparenza *sf* transparency.

traspirazione *sf* perspiration.

trasportare *vt* to transport.

trasporto *sm* transport.

trastullarsi *vr* (*divertirsi*) to amuse o.s.; (*perdere tempo*) to waste time.

trasversale *agg* (*obliquo*) cross (*dav s*); (*via*) side (*dav s*).

trattamento *sm* treatment.

trattare *vt* (*persona*) to treat; (*argomento*) to discuss; (*negoziare*) to negotiate; (*commerciare*) to deal in ▢ **trattare di** *v* + *prep* to deal with; **trattarsi** *vr*: **di cosa si tratta?** what is it about?

trattative *sfpl* negotiations.

trattato *sm* (*patto*) treaty; (*testo*) treatise.

trattenere *vt* (*far rimanere*) to detain; (*lacrime, risa*) to hold back; (*somma*) to deduct; **~ qn dal fare qc** to stop sb doing sthg ▢ **trattenersi** *vr* to stay; **quanto si trattiene?** how long are you staying?; **trattenersi dal fare qc** to stop o.s. doing sthg.

trattenuta *sf* deduction.

trattino *sm* (*tra parole*) hyphen; (*per discorso diretto*) dash.

tratto, -a *pp* → **trarre** ♦ *sm* (*di penna*) stroke; (*di strada, mare*) stretch; **ad un ~, d'un ~** suddenly ▢ **tratti** *smpl* features.

trattore *sm* tractor.

trattoria *sf* restaurant specializing in local cuisine.

 TRATTORIA

In the past the term "trattoria" was used to describe an inexpensive family-run restaurant, but today "trattorie" can be very expensive. They serve traditional Italian food typical of the region in rustic-looking but often upmarket surroundings.

---

trauma, -i *sm (shock)* shock; *(MED)* trauma.

travagliato, -a *agg* troubled.

travaglio *sm* labour.

travasare *vt* to decant.

trave *sf* beam.

traveggole *sfpl*: avere le ~ to be seeing things.

traveller's cheque ['traveler 'tʃɛk] *sm inv* traveller's cheque.

traversa *sf (via)* side street; *(SPORT)* crossbar.

traversare *vt* to cross.

traversata *sf (marittima)* crossing; *(aerea)* flight.

traverso, -a *agg* side *(dav s)* ◆ *avv*: di ~ crosswise.

travestimento *sm* disguise.

travestire *vt* to dress up □ **travestirsi da** *vr + prep* to dress up as.

travisare *vt* to misinterpret.

travolgere *vt* to sweep away.

travolto, -a *pp* → travolgere.

tre *num* three, → sei.

treccia, -ce *sf* plait.

trecento *num* three hundred, → sei □ **Trecento** *sm*: il ~ the fourteenth century.

tredicesima *sf* Christmas bonus.

tredicesimo, -a *num* thirteenth, → sesto.

tredici *num* thirteen, → sei.

tregua *sf (armistizio)* truce; *(sosta)* rest.

trekking *sm* trekking.

tremare *vi*: ~ **(di)** *(paura)* to shake o tremble (with); *(freddo)* to shiver o tremble (with).

tremarella *sf (fam)* shivers *(pl)*.

tremendo, -a *agg* terrible, awful.

trementina *sf* turpentine.

tremila *num* three thousand, → sei.

Tremiti *sfpl*: le (isole) ~ the Tremiti Islands.

tremito *sm* shudder.

trenino *sm* toy train.

treno *sm* train; ~ **diretto** fast train; ~ **espresso** express train; ~ **intercity** Intercity train®; ~ **interregionale** long-distance train; ~ **merci** goods train *(Br)*, freight train *(Am)*; ~ **regionale** local train; 'treni in arrivo' 'arrivals'; 'treni in partenza' 'departures'.

trenta *num* thirty, → sei.

trentesimo, -a *num* thirtieth, → sesto.

trentina *sf*: una ~ **(di)** about thirty; essere sulla ~ to be in one's thirties.

Trentino *sm*: il ~-Alto Adige Trentino-Alto Adige.

tresca, -sche *sf* intrigue.

triangolare *agg* triangular.

triangolo *sm* triangle.

tribolare *vi* to suffer.

tribù *sf inv* tribe.

tribuna *sf* stand.

tribunale *sm* court.

tributo *sm* tax.

tricheco, -chi *sm* walrus.

triciclo *sm* tricycle.

tricolore *agg* three-coloured.

tridimensionale *agg* three-dimensional.

triennio *sm* three-year period.

Trieste *sf* Trieste.

trifoglio *sm* clover.

trifolato, -a *agg* (*verdura, carne*) *cooked in oil, garlic and parsley.*

triglia *sf* red mullet.

trimestre *sm* (*tre mesi*) quarter; (*SCOL*) term.

trincea *sf* trench.

trinciapollo *sm inv* poultry shears (*pl*).

trio *sm* trio.

trionfale *agg* triumphal.

trionfare *vi* (*vincere*) to triumph.

trionfo *sm* triumph.

triplicare *vt* to triple.

triplice *agg* triple.

triplo, -a *agg* triple ♦ *sm*: **il ~** three times as much.

trippa *sf* tripe.

triste *agg* sad; (*luogo*) gloomy.

tristezza *sf* (*afflizione*) sadness; (*squallore*) dreariness.

tritacarne *sm inv* mincer (*Br*), grinder (*Am*).

tritaghiaccio *sm inv* ice crusher.

tritare *vt* to chop; (*carne*) to mince (*Br*), to grind (*Am*).

trito, -a *agg* chopped ♦ *sm* chopped ingredients (*pl*); **~ e ritrito** (*fig*) trite.

triturare *vt* to mince (*Br*), to grind (*Am*).

trivellare *vt* to drill.

triviale *agg* crude.

trofeo *sm* trophy.

tromba *sf* trumpet; **~ d'aria** whirlwind; **~ delle scale** stairwell.

trombone *sm* trombone.

troncare *vt* to cut off.

tronco, -chi *sm* trunk.

trono *sm* throne.

tropicale *agg* tropical.

tropico *sm* tropic; **i tropici** the tropics.

troppo, -a *agg* 1. (*in quantità eccessiva*) too much; **c'è troppa acqua** there's too much water.
2. (*in numero eccessivo*): **troppi(-e)** too many; **ho mangiato troppi biscotti** I've eaten too many biscuits.
♦ *pron* 1. (*una quantità eccessiva*) too much; **ho poco tempo libero, tu ~** I have little free time, you have too much.
2. (*un numero eccessivo*): **troppi(-e)** too many; **non voglio altri problemi, ne ho fin troppi** I don't want any more problems, I've got too many already; **lo sanno in troppi** too many people know.
♦ *avv* 1. (*in misura eccessiva*) too; **sei ~ stanco** you are too tired; **parla ~**

velocemente he speaks too quickly; **spendo** ~ I spend too much; **ho bevuto un bicchiere di** ~ I've had one drink too many; **essere di** ~ to be in the way.

2. *(molto):* **non mi sento** ~ **bene** I'm not feeling too good.

trota sf trout.

trottare vi to trot.

trotto sm trot.

trottola sf spinning top.

troupe [trup] sf inv troupe.

trovare vt to find; *(per caso)* to come across; **andare a** ~ **qn** to go and see sb ❑ **trovarsi** vr *(essere, stare)* to be; *(incontrarsi)* to meet.

trovata sf good idea.

truccare vt *(attore)* to make up; *(motore)* to soup up; *(risultato, partita)* to fix ❑ **truccarsi** vr to make o.s. up.

trucco, -chi sm *(artificio, inganno)* trick; *(cosmetico)* make-up; *(operazione)* making-up.

truce agg fierce.

trucidare vt to slaughter.

truciolo sm shaving.

truffa sf fraud.

truffare vt to swindle.

truffatore, -trice sm, f swindler.

truppa sf troop.

tu pron you ❖ sm: **a** ~ **per** ~ face to face; ~ **stesso** you yourself; **se lo dici** ~! if you say so!

tubare vi to coo.

tubatura sf piping, pipes *(pl)*.

tubercolosi sf tuberculosis.

tubero sm tuber.

tubetto sm tube.

tubo sm pipe; ~ **di scappamento** exhaust (pipe).

tue → **tuo.**

tuffarsi vr *(in acqua)* to dive.

tuffo sm dive.

tulipano sm tulip.

tumbada sf baked egg custard with crushed macaroons.

tumore sm tumour.

tunica, -che sf tunic.

Tunisia sf: **la** ~ Tunisia.

tunnel sm inv tunnel.

tuo *(f* **tua,** *mpl* **tuoi,** *fpl* **tue)** agg: **il** ~ **(la tua)** your ◆ pron: **il** ~ **(la tua)** yours; ~ **padre** your father; **un** ~ **amico** a friend of yours; **questi soldi sono tuoi** this is your money.

tuoi → **tuo.**

tuonare v impers: **tuona** it's thundering.

tuono sm *(di lampo)* thunder.

tuorlo sm: ~ **(d'uovo)** yolk.

turacciolo sm *(di sughero)* cork; *(di plastica)* top.

turare vt *(buco)* to plug; *(orecchie, naso)* to block ❑ **turarsi** vr: ~ **il naso** to hold one's nose.

turbamento sm *(sconcerto)* anxiety.

turbante sm *(copricapo)* turban.

turbare vt *(sconcertare)* to trouble.

turbolento, -a agg *(persona)* boisterous.

turchese agg & sm turquoise.

Turchia sf: **la** ~ Turkey.

turismo sm tourism.

turista, -i, -e smf tourist.

turistico, -a, -ci, -che agg

tourist *(dav s)*.

turno *sm (di lavoro)* shift; *(di gioco)* turn; **è il tuo ~** it's your turn; **fare a ~ (a fare qc)** to take turns (to do sthg); **essere di ~** to be on duty.

tuta *sf (da lavoro)* overalls *(pl)*; *(sportiva)* tracksuit.

tutela *sf* protection.

tutelare *vt* to protect ❑ **tutelarsi** *vr* to protect o.s.

tutina *sf* romper suit.

tuttavia *cong* yet, nevertheless.

tutto, -a *agg* **1.** *(la totalità di)* all (of), the whole (of); **~ il vino** all the wine; **~ il giorno** all day, the whole day; **in tutta Europa** all over Europe; **tutti i presenti** everyone present; **tutte le piante** all the plants; **tutti e cinque** all five of us/you/them; **tutti e due** both of us/you/them; **tutta una pizza** a whole pizza.

2. *(ogni)* **tutti(-e)** every; **telefona tutti i giorni** he phones every day; **in tutti i casi** in every case; **tutte le volte che** every time (that).

3. *(esclusivamente)* all; **è tutta colpa tua** it's all your fault; **è ~ casa e chiesa** he's a family man and a regular churchgoer.

4. *(molto)* very; **è tutta contenta** she's very happy; **sei ~ sporco** you're all dirty.

◆ *pron* **1.** *(la totalità)* all; **bevilo ~** drink all of it; **li ho visti tutti** I've seen all of them; **in ~** *(nel complesso)* in all; **in ~ fanno 300 000 lire** that's 300,000 lira in all.

2. *(la totalità della gente)*: **tutti** everyone, all; **verremo tutti** *(quan-*

ti)* we will all come, everybody will come; **tutti voi** all of you.

3. *(ogni cosa)* everything; **mi ha raccontato ~** he told me everything; **non è ~** that's not everything; **vende di ~** it sells all sorts of things; **mangio un po' di ~** I eat a bit of everything; **in ~ e per ~** completely; **~ compreso** all in; **~ esaurito** sold out; **~ sommato** all things considered.

4. *(qualunque cosa)* anything; **è capace di ~** he's capable of anything.

◆ *avv (interamente)* completely; **tutt'altro** anything but; **~ il contrario** quite the opposite; **del ~** completely; **tutt'al più** at the most.

◆ *sm*: **il ~** the lot; **il ~ per ~** everything.

tuttora *avv* still.

tutù *sm inv* tutu.

T.V. *sf inv* TV.

tweed [twid] *sm* tweed.

U

ubbidiente *agg* obedient.

ubbidire *vi* to obey.

ubriacare *vt*: **~ qn** to get sb drunk ❑ **ubriacarsi** *vr* to get drunk.

ubriaco, -a, -chi, -che *agg & sm, f* drunk.

uccello *sm* bird.

uccidere *vt* to kill □ **uccidersi**
vr to kill o.s.

udienza *sf (colloquio)* audience;
(DIR) hearing.

udire *vt* to hear.

udito *sm* hearing.

uffa *esclam* tut!

ufficiale *agg* official ♦ *sm (MIL)*
officer; *(funzionario)*: ~ **giudiziario**
clerk of the court.

ufficialmente *avv* officially.

ufficio *sm* office; ~ **cambi**
bureau de change; ~ **di colloca-**
mento employment office; ~ **infor-**
mazioni information bureau; ~
oggetti smarriti lost property
office *(Br)*, lost-and-found office
(Am); ~ **postale** post office; ~ **turis-**
tico tourist office.

Uffizi *mpl*: **gli** ~ the Uffizi *(art*
gallery in Florence).

---

i **GLI UFFIZI**

Situated by the Arno river in
Florence, the Galleria degli Uffizi
is one of the world's most important
museums. It is called the "Uffizi"
because it was originally built in the
XVIth century to house government
offices. Although it specializes in
masterpieces from the Italian
Renaissance, the U-shaped gallery
also contains countless works of art
from other periods and by non-
Italian artists.

Ufo *sm inv* UFO.

uggioso, -a *agg* dull.

uguaglianza *sf* equality.

uguagliare *vt* to equal.

uguale *agg (identico)* the same;
(pari) equal ♦ *avv*: **costano** ~ they
cost the same; **essere** ~ **a** *(identico)*
to be the same as; *(pari)* to be
equal to; *(MAT)* to equal.

ugualmente *avv (in modo*
uguale) equally; *(lo stesso)* all the
same.

ulcera *sf* ulcer.

uliva = oliva.

ulivo = olivo.

ulteriore *agg* further.

ultimare *vt* to finish.

ultimatum *sm inv* ultimatum.

ultimo, -a *agg* last; *(più recente)*
latest ♦ *sm, f* last (one); **da** ~ in the
end; **fino all'**~ till the end; **per** ~
last; **l'**~ **piano** the top floor.

ultravioletto, -a *agg* ultraviolet.

umanità *sf* humanity.

umano, -a *agg* human; *(benevo-*
lo) humane.

umidità *sf (di clima)* humidity;
(di stanza, muro) dampness.

umido, -a *agg (bagnato)* damp;
(clima) humid ♦ *sm*: **in** ~ stewed.

umile *agg* humble.

umiliante *agg* humiliating.

umiliare *vt* to humiliate □
umiliarsi *vr* to humble o.s.

umiliazione *sf* humiliation.

umore *sm* mood; **essere di**
buon/cattivo ~ to be in a good/bad
mood.

umorismo *sm* humour.

umoristico, -a, -ci, -che
agg humorous.

un → uno.

un' → uno.

unanime *agg* unanimous.

unanimità *sf* unanimity; **all'~** unanimously.

uncinetto *sm* crochet hook.

undicesimo, -a *num* eleventh, → **sesto**.

undici *num* eleven, → **sei**.

ungere *vt* (*padella, teglia*) to grease; (*macchiare*) to get greasy □ **ungersi** *vr* (*macchiarsi*) to get covered in grease; **ungersi di crema solare** to put suntan lotion on.

Ungheria *sf*: **l'~** Hungary.

unghia *sf* nail.

unicamente *avv* only.

unico, -a, -ci, -che *agg* (*singolo*) only; (*incomparabile*) unique.

unifamiliare *agg* one-family (*dav s*).

uniformare *vt* (*adeguare*) to adapt; (*superficie*) to level □ **uniformarsi a** *vr + prep* to comply with.

uniforme *agg & sf* uniform.

unione *sf* union; **l'Unione Sovietica** the Soviet Union.

unire *vt* (*mettere insieme*) to join; (*persone*) to unite; (*collegare*) to link; (*mescolare*) to combine □ **unirsi** *vr* (*associarsi*) to join together; (*strade*) to meet.

unità *sf inv* unit; (*unione*) unity; **~ di misura** unit of measurement.

unito, -a *agg* (*amici, parenti*) close; (*da uno scopo*) united; (*oggetti*) joined.

universale *agg* universal.

università *sf inv* university.

universitario, -a *agg* university (*dav s*).

universo *sm* universe.

uno, -a (*dav sm* **un** + *consonante* O *vocale*, **uno** + *s+consonante, gn, ps, x, z; dav sf* **un'** + *vocale*, **una** + *consonante*) *art indeterminativo* a, an; **~ studente** a student; **una donna** a woman; **un albero** a tree; **un'arancia** an orange; **un giorno ci andrò** one day I'll go; **ho avuto una fortuna!** it was such a stroke of luck!
◆ *pron* **1.** (*uno qualunque*) one; **me ne dai ~?** can you give me one (of them)?; **~ dei miei libri/dei migliori** one of my books/of the best; **l'un l'altro** each other, one another; **sanno tutto l'~ dell'altro** they know everything about each other; **l'~ o l'altro** either (of you/them/us); **né l'~ né l'altro** neither (of you/them/us); **l'~ e l'altro** both (of you/them/us).
2. (*un tale*) someone, somebody; **sta parlando con una** he's talking to some woman.
3. (*uso impersonale*) one, you; **se si può** if one O you can.
◆ *num* one, → **sei**.

unto, -a *pp* → **ungere** ◆ *sm* grease.

untuoso, -a *agg* greasy.

uomo (*pl* **uomini**) *sm* man; **d'affari** businessman; **da ~** men's.

uovo (*pl f* **uova**) *sm* egg; **~ in camicia** poached egg; **~ alla coque** boiled egg; **~ di Pasqua** Easter egg; **~ sodo** hard-boiled egg; **~ al tegamino** fried egg; **uova strapazzate** scrambled eggs.

uragano *sm* hurricane.

urbano, -a *agg* urban.

urgente *agg* urgent.

urgenza *sf (necessità)* urgency; *(MED)* emergency; **essere operato d'~** to have emergency surgery.

urgere *vi* to be needed urgently.

urina *sf* urine.

urlare *vi (persona)* to scream; *(animale)* to howl ♦ *vt* to yell.

urlo *sm (di persona: pl f* **urla)** scream; *(di animale: pl m* **urli)** howl.

urna *sf:* **andare alle urne** to go to the polls.

urrà *esclam* hurrah!

URSS *sf:* **l'(ex) ~** the former USSR.

urtare *vt (scontrare)* to bump into; *(irritare)* to annoy ♦ *vi:* **~ contro** o **in qc** to bump into sthg ❑ **urtarsi** *vr (scontrarsi)* to collide; *(irritarsi)* to get annoyed.

urto *sm* crash.

USA *smpl:* **gli ~** the USA *(sg)*.

usanza *sf* custom.

usare *vt* to use; **~ fare qc** to be in the habit of doing sthg; **qui usa così** it's the custom here.

usato, -a *agg (consumato)* worn; *(di seconda mano)* used ♦ *sm* second-hand goods *(pl)*.

usciere, -a *sm, f* usher.

uscio *sm* door.

uscire *vi* to go out; *(libro, numero)* to come out; **~ di strada** to go off the road.

uscita *sf (porta)* exit, way out; *(al cinema, ristorante)* evening out; *(di autostrada)* junction; *(di libro)* publication; *(di film)* release; *(COMM)* expenditure; **ci vediamo all'~ da scuola** I'll meet you after school; **~ di sicurezza** o **emergenza** emergency exit.

usignolo *sm* nightingale.

uso *sm (impiego)* use; *(abitudine)* custom; **fuori ~** out of use; **'per ~ esterno'** 'for external use'.

USSL *(abbr di Unità Socio-Sanitaria Locale)* local health and social centre.

ustionare *vt* to burn; **ustionarsi un braccio** to burn one's arm.

ustione *sf* burn.

usuale *agg* common.

usufruire: usufruire di *v + prep* to make use of.

usuraio, -a *sm, f* moneylender.

utensile *sm* tool; **utensili da cucina** kitchen utensils.

utente *smf* user.

utero *sm* uterus.

utile *agg* useful ♦ *sm (COMM)* profit; **rendersi ~** to be helpful; **posso esserle ~?** can I help you?

utilità *sf* usefulness; **essere di grande ~** to be of great use.

utilitaria *sf* economy car.

utilizzare *vt* to use, to make use of.

uva *sf* grapes *(pl)*.

uvetta *sf* raisins *(pl)*.

va → **andare**.

vacanza *sf* holiday *(Br)*, vacation *(Am)*; **andare/essere in ~** to go/be on holiday *(Br)*, to go/be on vacation *(Am)*.

vacca, -che *sf* cow.

vaccinare *vt* to vaccinate.

vaccinazione *sf* vaccination.

vacillare *vi (barcollare)* to sway; *(fig: memoria, coraggio)* to be failing.

vado → **andare**.

vagabondo, -a *sm, f (senza dimora fissa)* tramp; *(fannullone)* loafer.

vagare *vi* to wander.

vagina *sf* vagina.

vagito *sm* wailing.

vaglia *sm inv* money order; ~ **postale** postal order.

vagliare *vt (valutare)* to weigh up.

vago, -a, -ghi, -ghe *agg* vague.

vagone *sm* carriage *(Br)*, car *(Am)*; ~ **letto** sleeper; ~ **ristorante** restaurant car.

vai → **andare**.

valanga, -ghe *sf* avalanche.

Val d'Aosta = **Valle d'Aosta**.

valere *vi (biglietto)* to be valid; *(regola)* to apply; *(avere valore)* to be worth ♦ *vt (avere un valore di)* to be worth; *(equivalere a)* to be equal to; ~ **la pena di fare qc** to be worth doing sthg; **far** ~ **qc** to assert sthg; **vale a dire** that is to say ❏ **valersi di** *vr + prep* to take advantage of.

valevole *agg* valid.

valico, -chi *sm* pass.

validità *sf* validity.

valido, -a *agg (valevole)* valid; *(efficace)* effective; *(abile)* capable.

valigia, -gie ○ **-ge** *sf* suitcase; **fare le valigie** to pack.

vallata *sf* valley.

valle *sf* valley ❏ **Valle d'Aosta**

sf: **la Valle d'Aosta** Valle d'Aosta.

valore *sm* value; *(validità)* validity; *(talento)* merit ❏ **valori** *smpl (gioielli)* valuables; *(ideali)* values.

valorizzare *vt* to bring out.

valoroso, -a *agg* courageous.

valso, -a *pp* → **valere**.

valuta *sf* currency.

valutare *vt (quadro, persona)* to value; *(valore, peso)* to estimate.

valutazione *sf (di un bene)* valuation; *(calcolo sommario)* estimate; *(SCOL)* assessment.

valvola *sf (in meccanica)* valve; *(in elettrotecnica)* fuse.

vampata *sf* blaze.

vampiro *sm* vampire.

vandalismo *sm* vandalism.

vandalo, -a *sm, f* vandal.

vanga, -ghe *sf* spade.

vangelo *sm* gospel.

vanificare *vt* to nullify.

vaniglia *sf* vanilla.

vanità *sf* vanity.

vanitoso, -a *agg* vain.

vanno → **andare**.

vano, -a *agg* vain ♦ *sm (stanza)* room; *(apertura)* opening.

vantaggio *sm* advantage; *(in competizioni)* lead; **trarre** ~ **da qc** to benefit from sthg; **essere in** ~ to be in the lead.

vantaggioso, -a *agg* favourable.

vantarsi *vr* to boast; ~ **di fare qc** to boast about doing sthg.

vanvera *sf*: **parlare a** ~ to talk nonsense.

vapore *sm*: ~ **(acqueo)** steam; **cuocere a** ~ to steam.

vaporetto *sm* steamer.

vaporizzatore *sm* spray.

vaporoso, -a *agg (abito)* floaty.

varare *vt (legge)* to pass; *(nave)* to launch.

varcare *vt* to cross.

varco, -chi *sm* passage.

variabile *agg* variable.

variante *sf* variation.

variare *vt* to vary ♦ *vi (modificarsi)* to vary; *(essere diverso)* to fluctuate.

variazione *sf* variation.

varice *sf* varicose vein.

varicella *sf* chickenpox.

variegato, -a *agg* variegated.

varietà *sf inv* variety ♦ *sm inv* variety show.

vario, -a *agg (svariato)* varied; *(numeroso, diverso)* various.

variopinto, -a *agg* multi-coloured.

vasca, -sche *sf (contenitore)* tank; *(di fontana)* basin; *(nel nuoto)* length; *~ (da bagno)* bath.

vaschetta *sf* basin.

vasellame *sm* crockery.

vasetto *sm (di yogurt)* pot; *(di marmellata)* jar.

vaso *sm* vase; *(per piante)* pot.

vassoio *sm* tray.

vasto, -a *agg (superficie)* vast.

Vaticano *sm: il ~ the* Vatican.

---

i ❘ IL VATICANO

The Vatican City, situated on the right bank of the Tiber in Rome, is the Pope's official residence. The Basilica of Saint Peter, one of the most magnificent Catholic churches in the world, stands here. The Vatican is an independent country, with its own currency and stamps, and the Pope is the head of state. The vast number of works of art concentrated here make it one of Italy's most important cultural centres.

---

ve → **vi**.

vecchiaia *sf* old age.

vecchio, -a *agg* old; *(sorpassato)* old-fashioned ♦ *sm, f* old man (*f* old woman).

vece *sf*: **fare le veci di qn** to take sb's place.

vedere *vt & vi* to see; **vedrò di fare qualcosa** I'll see what I can do; **questo non ha niente a che ~ con me** this has nothing to do with me; **non la posso ~** *(fig)* I can't stand her; **non vedo l'ora di arrivare** I can't wait to get there; **farsi ~ da uno specialista** to see a specialist; **da qui si vede il mare** you can see the sea from there ❑ **vedersi** *vr (guardarsi)* to see o.s.; *(incontrarsi)* to meet; **ci vediamo!** see you!

vedovo, -a *sm, f* widower (*f* widow).

veduta *sf* view.

vegetale *agg* vegetable *(dav s)* ♦ *sm* plant.

vegetariano, -a *agg* vegetarian.

vegetazione *sf* vegetation.

veglia *sf* wakefulness.

veglione *sm* ball.

veicolo *sm* vehicle; '**veicoli lenti**'

'slow lane'.

vela sf (tela) sail; (sport) sailing.

velare vt to veil.

veleno sm poison.

velenoso, -a agg (sostanza) poisonous.

velina sf tissue paper.

vellutato, -a agg velvety.

velluto sm velvet; ~ **a coste** cord.

velo sm (indumento) veil.

veloce agg fast.

velocemente avv quickly.

velocità sf speed; '~ **max 15 kmh**' = 'maximum speed 10 mph'.

vena sf vein; **non essere in ~ di qc** not to be in the mood for sthg.

vendemmia sf grape harvest.

vendemmiare vi to harvest the grapes.

vendere vt to sell; '**vendesi**' 'for sale'.

vendetta sf revenge.

vendicare vt to avenge ❑ **vendicarsi** vr to avenge o.s.; **vendicarsi di** to take one's revenge for; **vendicarsi su qn** to take one's revenge on sb.

vendita sf sale; **essere in ~** to be on sale; '**in ~ qui**' 'on sale here'.

venditore, -trice sm, f seller; ~ **ambulante** pedlar.

venerdì sm inv Friday, → **sabato**.

Venezia sf Venice.

veneziana sf venetian blind, → **veneziano**.

veneziano, -a agg & sm, f Venetian.

venire vi to come; **mi viene da piangere** I feel like crying; **quanto vengono le mele?** how much are the apples?; ~ **bene/male** to turn out well/badly; ~ **giù** to come down; ~ **via** (persona) to leave; (macchia) to come out; (etichetta) to come off; ~ **a sapere qc** to learn sthg.

ventata sf gust.

ventesimo, -a num twentieth, → **sesto**.

venti num twenty, → **sei**.

ventilare vt to ventilate.

ventilatore sm ventilator.

ventina sf: **una ~ (di)** about twenty; **essere sulla ~** to be in one's twenties.

vento sm wind; '**forte ~ laterale**' 'strong side wind'.

ventosa sf (di gomma) suction pad.

ventoso, -a agg windy.

ventre sm stomach.

venturo, -a agg next.

venuto, -a → **venire**.

veramente avv really.

veranda sf veranda.

verbale sm minutes (pl).

verbo sm verb.

verde agg green ♦ sm (colore) green; (vegetazione) greenery.

verdetto sm verdict.

verdura sf vegetables (pl).

verduraio, -a sm, f greengrocer.

vergine agg virgin; (cassetta) blank ❑ **Vergine** sf Virgo.

vergogna sf (pentimento, scandalo) shame; (timidezza) shyness;

(imbarazzo) embarrassment.

vergognarsi vr: ~ **(di)** *(per disonore)* to be ashamed (of); *(per timidezza)* to be embarrassed (about).

vergognoso, -a agg *(scandaloso)* shameful; *(timido)* shy.

verifica, -che sf check.

verificare vt to check □ **verificarsi** vr to happen.

verità sf truth; **dire la ~** to tell the truth.

verme sm worm.

vermicelli smpl vermicelli *(sg)*.

vermut sm inv vermouth.

vernice sf *(sostanza)* paint; *(pelle)* patent leather; **'~ fresca'** 'wet paint'.

verniciare vt to paint.

vero, -a agg *(reale)* true; *(autentico)* real, genuine ♦ sm truth.

verosimile agg likely, probable.

verruca, -che sf wart.

versamento sm deposit.

versante sm slopes *(pl)*.

versare vt *(in recipiente)* to pour; *(rovesciare)* to spill; *(pagare)* to pay; *(depositare)* to deposit □ **versarsi** vr to spill.

versatile agg versatile.

versione sf version; *(traduzione)* translation.

verso sm *(di poesia)* line; *(di animale)* cry; *(direzione)* direction ♦ prep *(in direzione di, nei confronti di)* towards; *(in prossimità di)* near; *(di tempo, età)* around, about; **non c'è ~ di convincerlo** there's no way of convincing him; **fare il ~ a qn** to

mimic sb.

vertebra sf vertebra.

verticale agg & sf vertical.

vertice sm peak; *(MAT)* vertex.

vertigine sf dizziness; **soffrire di vertigini** to be afraid of heights.

vescovo sm bishop.

vespa sf wasp.

vestaglia sf dressing gown.

veste sf: **in ~ di** as.

vestiario sm wardrobe, clothes *(pl)*.

vestire vt & vi to dress □ **vestirsi** vr to get dressed.

vestito sm *(da uomo)* suit; *(da donna)* dress □ **vestiti** smpl *(indumenti)* clothes.

Vesuvio sm: **il ~** Vesuvius.

veterinario, -a sm, f vet(erinary surgeon) *(Br)*, veterinarian *(Am)*.

vetrata sf *(di casa)* glass door/window; *(di chiesa)* stained glass window.

vetrina sf *(di negozio)* shop window.

vetro sm *(materiale)* glass; *(frammento)* piece of glass; *(di finestra)* windowpane; *(di auto)* window.

vetta sf top.

vettovaglie sfpl supplies.

vettura sf *(automobile)* car; *(di treno)* carriage *(Br)*, car *(Am)*.

vezzeggiativo sm term of endearment.

vezzo sm habit.

vi *(diventa* **ve** *se precede lo, la, li, le, ne)* pron *(complemento oggetto)* you; *(complemento di termine)* (to) you; *(riflessivo)* yourselves; *(reciproco)* each other ◆ *avv* = **ci**; **ve li do** I'll give them to you.

via *sf* way; *(strada)* street, road ◆ *avv* away ◆ *prep* via ◆ *esclam (per scacciare)* go away!; *(in gara, gioco)* go! ◆ *sm inv*: **dare il ~** (SPORT) to give the starting signal; **dare il ~ a qc** *(progetto)* to give the green light to sthg; **~ aerea** *(posta)* by airmail; **~ mare** by sea; **~ terra** overland; **in ~ eccezionale** as an exception; **per ~ di** *(a causa di)* because of; **in ~ di guarigione** on the road to recovery; **una ~ di mezzo** a middle course; **e così ~** and so on.

viabilità *sf* practicability.

Viacard® *sf inv credit card for motorway tolls.*

viaggiare *vi* to travel.

viaggiatore, -trice *sm, f* passenger.

viaggio *sm* travel; *(tragitto)* journey; *(gita)* trip; **buon ~!** have a good trip!; **essere in ~** to be away; **fare un ~** to go on a trip; **~ d'affari** business trip; **~ di nozze** honeymoon; **~ organizzato** package tour.

viale *sm (corso)* avenue; *(in un parco)* path.

viavai *sm* coming and going.

vibrare *vi* to vibrate.

vibrazione *sf* vibration.

vice *smf inv* deputy.

vicenda *sf* event ▫ **a vicenda** *avv* in turn.

viceversa *avv* vice versa.

vicinanza *sf* proximity; **nelle vicinanze (di qc)** in the vicinity (of sthg).

vicinato *sm (zona)* neighbour-

hood; *(vicini)* neighbours *(pl)*.

vicino, -a *agg (nello spazio)* near, nearby; *(nel tempo)* close at hand ◆ *sm, f* neighbour ◆ *avv* nearby ◆ *prep*: **~ a** *(accanto a)* next to; *(nei pressi di)* near; **~ di casa** neighbour; **da ~** close up.

vicolo *sm* alley; **~ cieco** blind alley.

video *sm inv (musicale)* video; *(schermo)* screen.

videocassetta *sf* video(cassette).

videocitofono *sm entryphone with closed circuit TV.*

videogame ['videogeim] = **videogioco**.

videogioco, -chi *sm* video game.

videoregistratore *sm* video(recorder) *(Br)*, VCR *(Am)*.

Videotel® *sm* = Viewdata®.

vietare *vt* to forbid; **~ a qn di fare qc** to forbid sb to do sthg; **~ qc a qn** to forbid sthg to sb.

vietato, -a *agg* forbidden; **'~ l'accesso'** 'no entry'; **'~ l'accesso ai mezzi non autorizzati'** 'no entry for unauthorized vehicles'; **'è ~ fare il bagno nelle ore notturne'** 'no swimming at night'; **'~ fumare'** 'no smoking'; **'~ ai minori'** 'adults only'.

Vietnam *sm*: **il ~** Vietnam.

vigilare *vt* to watch over.

vigile *agg* watchful ◆ *smf*: **~ (urbano)** *local police officer who deals mainly with traffic offences*; **i vigili del fuoco** the fire brigade.

vigilia *sf* eve; **~ di Natale** Christmas Eve.

vigliacco, -a, -chi, -che agg cowardly ♦ sm, f coward.

vigna sf vines (pl).

vigore sm vigour; **in ~** (DIR) in force.

vile agg cowardly.

villa sf villa.

villaggio sm village; **~ turistico** holiday village.

villano, -a agg rude ♦ sm, f boor.

villeggiatura sf holiday (Br), vacation (Am).

villetta sf cottage.

vimini smpl wicker (sg).

vinavil® sm glue.

vincere vt (gioco, partita, battaglia) to win; (avversario) to beat ♦ vi to win.

vincita sf (vittoria) win; (premio) winnings (pl).

vincitore, -trice sm, f winner.

vincolo sm (legame) tie; (obbligo) obligation.

vino sm wine; **~ bianco** white wine; **~ rosso** red wine.

---

i VINO

Wines are produced in every Italian region, and their names reflect either the area where they are produced (like "Chianti") or the grape varieties they are made from ("moscato"). "Vino da tavola" on a label indicates an inexpensive table wine, while DOC ("denominazione d'origine controllata"), DOCG ("denominazione d'origine controllata e garantita"), and VQPRD

("vino di qualità prodotto in regioni delimitate") all indicate that the wine is of superior quality.

vinto, -a pp → **vincere** ♦ agg (partita) won; (concorrente) beaten; **darla vinta a qn** to let sb have their way; **non darsi per ~** not to give up.

viola agg inv & sm inv purple ♦ sf (fiore) violet.

violare vt to violate.

violentare vt to rape.

violento, -a agg violent.

violenza sf violence.

violino sm violin.

viottolo sm track.

vipera sf viper.

virare vi (NAUT) to come about; (aereo) to turn.

virgola sf (GRAMM) comma; (MAT) point.

virgolette sfpl quotation marks.

virile agg manly.

virtù sf inv virtue.

virus sm inv virus.

viscere sfpl entrails.

viscido, -a agg slimy.

viscosa sf viscose.

visibile agg (che si vede) visible; (chiaro) evident.

visibilità sf visibility.

visiera sf peak.

visionare vt to examine.

visione sf (vista) sight; (modo di vedere) view; (apparizione) vision; **prendere ~ di qc** to look over sthg; **prima ~** TV premiere.

visita sf (di amico) visit; (di medico)

examination; **fare ~ a** qn to pay sb a visit; **~ medica** medical examination.

visitare vt to visit; *(sog: medico)* to examine.

viso sm face.

vispo, -a agg lively.

vissuto, -a pp → vivere.

vista sf *(facoltà)* (eye)sight; *(possibilità di vedere)* sight; *(panorama)* view; **conoscere** qn **di ~** to know sb by sight; **a prima ~** at first sight.

visto, -a pp → vedere ♦ sm visa.

vistoso, -a agg gaudy.

vita sf life; *(ANAT)* waist.

vitale agg vital.

vitamina sf vitamin.

vite sf *(pianta)* vine; *(utensile)* screw.

vitello sm *(animale)* calf; *(carne)* veal; *(pelle)* calfskin; **~ tonnato** boiled veal served cold with tuna mayonnaise.

vittima sf victim.

vitto sm food; **~ e alloggio** board and lodging.

vittoria sf victory.

viva esclam: **~ le vacanze!** hurray for the holidays!

vivace agg *(persona)* lively; *(colore)* bright.

vivacità sf vivacity.

vivaio sm *(di piante)* nursery; *(di pesci)* hatchery.

vivanda sf food.

vivente agg → essere.

vivere vi to live ♦ vt *(vita)* to live; *(passare)* to live through.

viveri smpl food *(sg)*.

vivo, -a agg *(vivente)* alive, living; *(persona)* lively; *(colore)* bright; **dal ~** from life; **farsi ~ (con** qn**)** to get in touch (with sb).

viziare vt to spoil.

viziato, -a agg *(bambino)* spoilt; *(aria)* stale.

vizio sm *(cattiva abitudine)* bad habit; *(morale)* vice; *(difetto)* defect.

V.le *(abbr di viale)* Ave.

vocabolario sm *(dizionario)* dictionary; *(lessico)* vocabulary.

vocabolo sm word.

vocale agg vocal ♦ sf vowel.

vocazione sf *(inclinazione)* natural bent.

voce sf *(suono)* voice; *(diceria)* rumour; *(di elenco)* entry; **a bassa/alta ~** in a low/loud voice; **sotto ~** in a whisper.

voga sf: **essere in ~** to be in fashion.

vogatore, -trice sm, f oarsman *(f* oarswoman*)* ♦ sm rowing machine.

voglia sf *(desiderio)* desire; *(sulla pelle)* birthmark; **avere ~ di fare** qc to feel like doing sthg; **avere ~ di** qc to feel like sthg; **levarsi la ~ di** qc to satisfy one's desire for sthg; **contro ~** unwillingly.

voi pron you; **~ stessi** you yourselves.

volano sm shuttlecock.

volante agg flying ♦ sm *(di veicolo)* steering wheel ♦ sf *(polizia)* flying squad.

volantino sm leaflet.

volare vi to fly.

volatile *sm* bird.

vol-au-vent [volo'van] *sm inv* vol-au-vent.

volenteroso, -a *agg* willing.

volentieri *avv* (*con piacere*) willingly; (*come risposta*) with pleasure.

volere *vt* 1. (*desiderare, esigere*) to want; **cosa vuoi?** what do you want?; **voglio delle spiegazioni** I want some explanations; **~ fare qc** to want to do sthg; **voglio che tu venga** I want you to come; **cosa volete fare stasera?** what do you want to do tonight?; **ti vogliono al telefono** you're wanted on the phone; **come vuoi** as you like; **vorrei un cappuccino** I'd like a cappuccino; **vorrei andare** I'd like to go; **senza volerlo** unintentionally; **se si vuole accomodare?** if you would care to take a seat?

2. (*consentire a*): **se tua madre vuole, ti porto al cinema** if your mother agrees, I'll take you to the cinema; **vogliamo andare?** shall we go?

3. (*soldi*): **quanto vuole per questo orologio?** how much do you want for this watch?

4. (*credere*) to think; **la leggenda vuole che ...** legend has it that ...

5. (*decidersi a*): **la macchina non vuole partire** the car won't start.

6. (*necessitare di*) **volerci** (*coraggio, materiale*) to need; (*tempo*) to take; **ci vuole pazienza** you must be patient; **ci vogliono ancora dieci minuti per finire** it'll take another ten minutes to finish.

7. (*in espressioni*): **voler bene a qn** (*affetto*) to be fond of sb; (*amare*) to love sb; **voler dire** to mean; **volerne a qn** to have a grudge against sb.

◆ *sm* will, wish; **contro il ~ di qn** against sb's wishes.

volgare *agg* vulgar.

volgere *vt* to turn; **il tempo volge al bello** the weather's getting better; **~ al termine** to draw to an end.

volo *sm* flight; **~ charter** charter flight; **~ di linea** scheduled flight; **capire qc al ~** to understand sthg straightaway.

volontà *sf inv* will; **buona ~** goodwill; **a ~** as much as one likes.

volontario, -a *agg* voluntary ◆ *sm, f* volunteer.

volpe *sf* fox.

volt *sm inv* volt.

volta *sf* (*circostanza*) time; (*di edificio*) vault; **a sua ~** in his/her turn; **di ~ in ~** from time to time; **una ~** once; **due volte** twice; **tre volte** three times; **una ~ che** once; **una ~ tanto** just for once; **uno per O alla ~** one at a time; **a volte** sometimes.

voltafaccia *sm inv* about-turn.

voltare *vt & vi* to turn; **~ l'angolo** to turn the corner; **~ pagina** to turn over a new leaf ❑ **voltarsi** *vr* to turn.

voltastomaco *sm* nausea; **dare il ~ a qn** to make sb feel sick.

volto, -a *pp* → **volgere** ◆ *sm* face.

volubile *agg* fickle.

volume *sm* volume.

voluminoso, -a *agg* voluminous, bulky.

vomitare *vt & vi* to vomit, to throw up.

vomito *sm* vomit.

vongola *sf* clam.

vorace *agg (animale)* voracious; *(persona)* greedy.

voragine *sf* abyss.

vortice *sm* whirl.

vostro, -a *agg*: **il ~ (la vostra)** your ♦ *pron*: **il ~ (la vostra)** yours; **~ padre** your father; **un ~ amico** a friend of yours; **sono vostri questi bagagli?** is this your luggage?

votare *vt* to vote on ♦ *vi* to vote.

votazione *sf (procedimento)* vote; *(SCOL)* marks *(pl)*.

voto *sm (DIR)* vote; *(SCOL)* marks *(pl)*.

vulcanico, -a, -ci, -che *agg* volcanic.

vulcano *sm* volcano.

vulnerabile *agg* vulnerable.

vuotare *vt* to empty □ **vuotarsi** *vr* to empty.

vuoto, -a *agg* empty; *(pagina)* blank ♦ *sm (spazio vuoto)* empty space; *(bottiglia)* empty (bottle); *(in fisica)* vacuum; **andare a ~** to fail; **parlare a ~** to waste one's breath.

wafer ['vafer] *sm inv* wafer.

Walkman® *sm inv* Walkman®, personal stereo.

water (closet) ['vater ('kloz)] *sm inv* toilet.

watt [vat] *sm inv* watt.

wc *(abbr di water closet)* WC.

week-end [wi'kɛnd] *sm inv* weekend.

western ['wɛstern] *agg inv*: **film ~** western.

whisky ['wiski] *sm inv* whisky.

windsurf ['windsɔrf] *sm inv (tavola)* windsurf board; *(sport)* windsurfing.

würstel ['vurstel] *sm inv* frankfurter.

xenofobia *sf* xenophobia.

xilofono *sm* xylophone.

yacht [jɔt] *sm inv* yacht.

yoga *sm* yoga.

yogurt *sm inv* yoghurt.

Z

zabaione *sm cream dessert made from egg yolks whipped with sugar and Marsala.*

zafferano *sm* saffron.

zaino *sm* rucksack.

zampa *sf* paw; **a quattro zampe** on all fours.

zampillo *sm* spurt.

zampirone *sm* mosquito repellent.

zampone *sm boiled pig's trotter stuffed with minced meat and spices.*

zanna *sf (di elefante)* tusk; *(di car-*

nivori) fang.

zanzara *sf* mosquito.

zanzariera *sf* mosquito net.

zappa *sf* hoe.

zappare *vt* to hoe.

zattera *sf* raft.

zavorra *sf* ballast.

zazzera *sf* fringe.

zebra *sf* zebra □ **zebre** *sfpl (fam)* zebra crossing *(sg) (Br)*, crosswalk *(sg) (Am)*.

zecca, -che *sf (insetto)* tick; *(officina di monete)* mint.

zelante *agg* zealous.

zelo *sm* zeal.

zenzero *sm* ginger.

zeppo, -a *agg* crammed.

zeppole *sfpl* type of ring doughnut eaten at carnival time in the south of Italy.

zerbino *sm* doormat.

zero *sm* zero; *(SPORT)* nil; **sotto ~** subzero.

zigomo *sm* cheekbone.

zigzag *sm inv* zigzag.

zimbello *sm* laughingstock.

zingaro, -a *sm, f* gipsy.

zio, -a *sm, f* uncle *(f* aunt).

zip *sm inv* zip.

zitella *sf (spreg)* spinster.

zitto, -a *agg* silent; **state zitti!** be quiet!

zoccolo *sm (calzatura)* clog; *(di cavallo)* hoof.

zodiaco *sm* zodiac.

zolfo *sm* sulphur.

zolla *sf* clod.

zolletta *sf* lump.

zona *sf* area; ~ **blu** o **verde** *zone where traffic is restricted;* ~ **disco** parking meter zone; ~ **industriale** industrial estate; '~ **militare**' 'army property'; ~ **pedonale** pedestrian precinct *(Br)*, pedestrian zone *(Am)*.

zonzo : **a zonzo** *avv*: **andare a ~** to wander about.

zoo *sm inv* zoo.

zoom [dzum] *sm inv* zoom.

zoppicare *vi* to limp.

zoppo, -a *agg* lame.

zucca, -che *sf* pumpkin.

zuccherato, -a *agg* sweetened.

zuccheriera *sf* sugar bowl.

zucchero *sm* sugar; ~ **filato** candyfloss; ~ **vanigliato** vanilla sugar; ~ **a velo** icing sugar *(Br)*, confectioner's sugar *(Am)*.

zuccheroso, -a *agg* sugary.

zucchina *sf* courgette; **zucchine ripiene** *courgettes stuffed with minced meat, breadcrumbs, eggs and spices.*

zucchino = **zucchina**.

zuccone, -a *sm, f (sciocco)* blockhead; *(testardo)* stubborn person.

zuccotto *sm* ice-cream sponge.

zuffa *sf* brawl.

zuppa *sf* soup; ~ **inglese** = trifle *(Br)*, dessert made from sponge soaked in liqueur, with custard and chocolate.

zuppiera *sf* tureen.

zuppo, -a *agg*: ~ **(di)** soaked (with).

Zurigo *sf* Zurich.

a [*stressed* eɪ, *unstressed* ə] (**an** *before vowel or silent 'h'*) *indefinite article* **1.** un/uno (una/un'); **a restaurant** un ristorante; **a brush** uno spazzolino; **a chair** una sedia; **an island** un'isola; **a friend** un amico (un'amica); **to be a doctor** essere medico, fare il medico.

2. (*instead of the number one*) un/uno (una/un'); **a month ago** un mese fa; **a hundred and twenty pounds** centoventi sterline; **a thousand** mille; **four and a half** quattro e mezzo.

3. (*in prices, ratios*) a; **£2 a kilo** 2 sterline al chilo; **three times a week** tre volte alla settimana.

AA *n* (*Br: abbr of Automobile Association*) ≃ ACI *m*.

aback [ə'bæk] *adv*: **to be taken ~** restare sbalordito(-a).

abandon [ə'bændən] *vt* abbandonare.

abattoir ['æbətwɑːʳ] *n* mattatoio *m*.

abbey ['æbɪ] *n* abbazia *f*.

abbreviation [ə,briːvɪ'eɪʃn] *n* abbreviazione *f*.

abdomen ['æbdəmən] *n* addome *m*.

abide [ə'baɪd] *vt*: **I can't ~ him** non lo sopporto ❑ **abide by** *vt fus* rispettare.

ability [ə'bɪlətɪ] *n* capacità *f inv*.

able ['eɪbl] *adj* capace; **to be ~ to do sthg** essere capace di fare qc, poter fare qc.

abnormal [æb'nɔːml] *adj* anormale.

aboard [ə'bɔːd] *adv* a bordo ◆ *prep* a bordo di, su.

abolish [ə'bɒlɪʃ] *vt* abolire.

aborigine [,æbə'rɪdʒənɪ] *n* aborigeno *m* (-a *f*).

abort [ə'bɔːt] *vt* (*call off*) sospendere.

abortion [ə'bɔːʃn] *n* aborto *m*; **to have an ~** abortire.

about [ə'baʊt] *adv* **1.** (*approximately*) circa, più o meno; **~ 50 people** una cinquantina di persone; **~ a thousand** un migliaio; **at ~ six o'clock** verso le sei.

2. (*referring to place*) qua e là; **to walk ~** camminare.

3. (*on the point of*): **to be ~ to do sthg** stare per fare qc.

◆ *prep* **1.** (*concerning*) su, a proposito di; **a book ~ Scotland** un libro sulla Scozia; **what's it ~?** di che cosa si tratta?; **I'll talk to you ~ it** te ne parlerò; **what ~ a coffee?** cosa ne diresti di un caffè?

2. (*referring to place*) per, in giro per;

there are lots of hotels ~ the town ci sono molti alberghi nella città.

above [ə'bʌv] *prep* sopra ◆ *adv* *(higher)* (di) sopra; *(more)* oltre; ~ **all** soprattutto.

abroad [ə'brɔːd] *adv* all'estero.

abrupt [ə'brʌpt] *adj* *(sudden)* improvviso(-a).

abscess ['æbses] *n* ascesso *m*.

absence ['æbsəns] *n* assenza *f*.

absent ['æbsənt] *adj* assente.

absent-minded [-'maɪndɪd] *adj* distratto(-a).

absolute ['æbsəluːt] *adj* assoluto(-a).

absolutely [*adv* 'æbsəluːtlı, *excl* ˌæbsə'luːtlı] *adv* *(completely)* assolutamente ◆ *excl* assolutamente!

absorb [əb'sɔːb] *vt* assorbire.

absorbed [əb'sɔːbd] *adj*: **to be ~ in sthg** essere assorto(-a) in qc.

absorbent [əb'sɔːbənt] *adj* assorbente.

abstain [əb'steɪn] *vi*: **to ~ (from)** astenersi (da).

absurd [əb'sɜːd] *adj* assurdo(-a).

ABTA ['æbtə] *n* associazione delle agenzie di viaggio britanniche.

abuse [*n* ə'bjuːs, *vb* ə'bjuːz] *n* *(insults)* insulti *mpl*; *(wrong use)* abuso *m*; *(maltreatment)* maltrattamento *m* ◆ *vt* *(insult)* insultare; *(use wrongly)* abusare di; *(maltreat)* maltrattare.

abusive [ə'bjuːsɪv] *adj* offensivo(-a).

AC *(abbr of alternating current)* c.a.

academic [ˌækə'demɪk] *adj* *(educational)* accademico(-a) ◆ *n* professore *m* universitario (professoressa *f* universitaria).

academy [ə'kædəmɪ] *n* acca-

demia *f*.

accelerate [ək'seləreɪt] *vi* accelerare.

accelerator [ək'seləreɪtəʳ] *n* acceleratore *m*.

accent ['æksent] *n* accento *m*.

accept [ək'sept] *vt* accettare.

acceptable [ək'septəbl] *adj* accettabile.

access ['ækses] *n* accesso *m*.

accessible [ək'sesəbl] *adj* *(place)* accessibile.

accessories [ək'sesərɪz] *npl* accessori *mpl*.

access road *n* strada *f* d'accesso.

accident ['æksɪdənt] *n* incidente *m*; **by ~** per caso.

accidental [ˌæksɪ'dentl] *adj* accidentale.

accident insurance *n* assicurazione *f* contro gli infortuni.

accident-prone *adj* soggetto(-a) a frequenti infortuni.

acclimatize [ə'klaɪmətaɪz] *vi* acclimatarsi.

accommodate [ə'kɒmədeɪt] *vt* alloggiare.

accommodation [əˌkɒmə'deɪʃn] *n* alloggio *m*.

accommodations [əˌkɒmə'deɪʃnz] *npl* *(Am)* = **accommodation**.

accompany [ə'kʌmpənɪ] *vt* accompagnare.

accomplish [ə'kʌmplɪʃ] *vt* realizzare.

accord [ə'kɔːd] *n*: **of one's own ~** di propria iniziativa.

accordance [ə'kɔːdəns] *n*: **in ~ with** in conformità a.

according [ə'kɔːdɪŋ]: **according**

to *prep* secondo.

accordion [əˈkɔːdɪən] *n* fisarmonica *f*.

account [əˈkaʊnt] *n* (*at bank, shop*) conto *m*; (*report*) resoconto *m*; **to take into ~** tener conto di; **on no ~** in nessun caso; **on ~ of** a causa di ❑ **account for** *vt fus* (*explain*) spiegare; (*constitute*) rappresentare.

accountant [əˈkaʊntənt] *n* ragioniere *m* (-a *f*).

account number *n* numero *m* di conto.

accumulate [əˈkjuːmjʊleɪt] *vt* accumulare.

accurate [ˈækjʊrət] *adj* preciso(-a).

accuse [əˈkjuːz] *vt*: **to ~ sb of sthg** accusare qn di qc.

accused [əˈkjuːzd] *n*: **the ~** l'imputato *m* (-a *f*).

ace [eɪs] *n* (*card*) asso *m*.

ache [eɪk] *n* dolore *m* ❤ *vi*: **my head ~s** mi fa male la testa.

achieve [əˈtʃiːv] *vt* ottenere.

acid [ˈæsɪd] *adj* acido(-a) ❤ *n* acido *m*.

acid rain *n* pioggia *f* acida.

acknowledge [əkˈnɒlɪdʒ] *vt* (*accept*) riconoscere; (*letter*) accusare ricevuta di.

acne [ˈækni] *n* acne *f*.

acorn [ˈeɪkɔːn] *n* ghianda *f*.

acoustic [əˈkuːstɪk] *adj* acustico(-a).

acquaintance [əˈkweɪntəns] *n* (*person*) conoscente *mf*.

acquire [əˈkwaɪər] *vt* acquisire.

acre [ˈeɪkər] *n* = 4 046,9 m², acro *m*.

acrobat [ˈækrəbæt] *n* acrobata *mf*.

across [əˈkrɒs] *prep* (*to, on other side of*) dall'altra parte di; (*from one side to the other of*) attraverso, da una parte all'altra di ❤ *adv* (*to other side*) dall'altra parte; **to walk ~ sthg** attraversare qc (a piedi); **to drive ~ sthg** attraversare qc (in macchina); **10 miles ~** largo 10 miglia; **~ from** di fronte a.

acrylic [əˈkrɪlɪk] *n* acrilico *m*.

act [ækt] *vi* agire; (*behave*) comportarsi; (*in play, film*) recitare ❤ *n* atto *m*; (*POL*) legge *f*; (*performance*) numero *m*; **to ~ as** (*serve as*) fare da.

action [ˈækʃn] *n* azione *f*; **to take ~** agire; **to put sthg into ~** mettere in pratica qc; **out of ~** (*machine*) fuori uso; (*person*) fuori combattimento.

active [ˈæktɪv] *adj* (*busy*) attivo(-a).

activity [ækˈtɪvətɪ] *n* attività *f inv*.

activity holiday *n* vacanza organizzata per ragazzi con attività ricreative di vario genere.

act of God *n* causa *f* di forza maggiore.

actor [ˈæktər] *n* attore *m*.

actress [ˈæktrɪs] *n* attrice *f*.

actual [ˈæktʃʊəl] *adj* (*real*) effettivo(-a), reale; (*itself*) in sé.

actually [ˈæktʃʊəlɪ] *adv* (*really*) veramente; (*in fact*) in effetti.

acupuncture [ˈækjʊpʌŋktʃər] *n* agopuntura *f*.

acute [əˈkjuːt] *adj* acuto(-a).

ad [æd] *n* (*inf*) (*for product*) pubblicità *f inv*; (*for job*) annuncio *m*.

AD (*abbr of Anno Domini*) d.C.

adapt [ə'dæpt] vt adattare ◆ vi
adattarsi.

adapter [ə'dæptə'] n (for foreign
plug) adattatore m; (for several
plugs) presa f multipla.

add [æd] vt (put, say in addition)
aggiungere; (numbers, prices) sommare ❑ **add up** vt sep sommare;
add up to vt fus (total) ammontare
a.

adder ['ædə'] n vipera f.

addict ['ædɪkt] n tossicodipendente mf.

addicted [ə'dɪktɪd] adj: **to be ~
to** sthg essere assuefatto(-a) a qc.

addiction [ə'dɪkʃn] n dipendenza f.

addition [ə'dɪʃn] n (added thing)
aggiunta f; (in maths) addizione f;
in ~ inoltre; **in ~ to** oltre a.

additional [ə'dɪʃənl] adj supplementare.

additive ['ædɪtɪv] n additivo m.

address [ə'dres] n (on letter) indirizzo m ◆ vt (speak to) rivolgersi a;
(letter) indirizzare.

address book n rubrica f.

addressee [,ædre'si:] n destinatario m (-a f).

adequate ['ædɪkwət] adj ade-
guato(-a).

adhere [əd'hɪə'] vi: **to ~ to** (stick
to) aderire a; (obey) rispettare.

adhesive [əd'hi:sɪv] adj adesi-
vo(-a) ◆ n adesivo m.

adjacent [ə'dʒeɪsənt] adj adiacente.

adjective ['ædʒɪktɪv] n aggettivo
m.

adjoining [ə'dʒɔɪnɪŋ] adj conti-
guo(-a).

adjust [ə'dʒʌst] vt aggiustare ◆

vi: **to ~ to** adattarsi a.

adjustable [ə'dʒʌstəbl] adj
regolabile.

adjustment [ə'dʒʌstmənt] n (of
machine) regolazione f; (of plan)
modifica f.

administration
[əd,mɪnɪ'streɪʃn] n amministrazione
f.

administrator [əd'mɪnɪstreɪtə']
n amministratore m (-trice f).

admiral ['ædmərəl] n ammira-
glio m.

admire [əd'maɪə'] vt ammirare.

admission [əd'mɪʃn] n (permission to enter, entrance cost) ingresso
m.

admission charge n ingresso
m.

admit [əd'mɪt] vt (confess)
ammettere; (allow to enter) far
entrare; **to ~ to** sthg ammettere qc; **'~s one'** (on ticket) 'valido per
una sola persona'.

adolescent [,ædə'lesnt] n adolescente mf.

adopt [ə'dɒpt] vt adottare.

adopted [ə'dɒptɪd] adj adotti-
vo(-a).

adorable [ə'dɔ:rəbl] adj adorabile.

adore [ə'dɔ:r] vt adorare.

Adriatic [eɪdrɪ'ætɪk] n: **the ~
(Sea)** l'Adriatico m, il mar
Adriatico.

adult ['ædʌlt] n adulto m (-a f) ◆
adj (entertainment, films) per adulti;
(animal) adulto(-a).

adult education n = educazione f permanente.

adultery [ə'dʌltərɪ] n adulterio
m.

advance [əd'vɑːns] n (money) anticipo m; (movement) avanzamento m ♦ adj (payment) anticipato(-a) ♦ vt anticipare ♦ vi (move forward) avanzare; (improve) fare progressi; ~ **warning** preavviso m.

advance booking n prenotazione f anticipata.

advanced [əd'vɑːnst] adj (student) di livello avanzato; (level) avanzato(-a).

advantage [əd'vɑːntɪdʒ] n vantaggio m; **to take ~ of** approfittare di.

adventure [əd'ventʃəʳ] n avventura f.

adventurous [əd'ventʃərəs] adj avventuroso(-a).

adverb ['ædvɜːb] n avverbio m.

adverse ['ædvɜːs] adj avverso(-a).

advert ['ædvɜːt] = **advertisement**.

advertise ['ædvətaɪz] vt (product, event) fare pubblicità a.

advertisement [əd'vɜːtɪsmənt] n (for product) pubblicità f inv; (for job) annuncio m.

advice [əd'vaɪs] n consigli mpl; **a piece of ~** un consiglio; **to ask for sb's ~** chiedere consiglio a qn.

advisable [əd'vaɪzəbl] adj consigliabile.

advise [əd'vaɪz] vt consigliare; **to ~ sb to do sthg** consigliare a qn di fare qc; **to ~ sb against doing sthg** sconsigliare a qn di fare qc.

advocate [n 'ædvəkət, vb 'ædvəkeɪt] n (JUR) avvocato m (difensore) ♦ vt sostenere.

aerial ['eərɪəl] n antenna f.

aerobics [eə'rəʊbɪks] n aerobica f.

aerodynamic [ˌeərəʊdaɪ'næmɪk] adj aerodinamico(-a).

aeroplane ['eərəpleɪn] n aeroplano m.

aerosol ['eərəsɒl] n aerosol m.

affair [ə'feəʳ] n (event) affare m; (love affair) relazione f.

affect [ə'fekt] vt (influence) incidere su.

affection [ə'fekʃn] n affetto m.

affectionate [ə'fekʃnət] adj affettuoso(-a).

affluent ['æfluənt] adj ricco(-a).

afford [ə'fɔːd] vt: **to be able to ~ sthg** potersi permettere qc; **I can't ~ it** non me lo posso permettere; **I can't ~ the time** non ho tempo; **to be able to ~ sthg** potersi permettere qc.

affordable [ə'fɔːdəbl] adj accessibile.

afloat [ə'fləʊt] adj a galla.

afraid [ə'freɪd] adj spaventato(-a); **to be ~ of** aver paura di; **I'm ~ so/not** temo di sì/di no.

Africa ['æfrɪkə] n l'Africa f.

African ['æfrɪkən] adj africano(-a) ♦ n africano m (-a f).

after ['ɑːftəʳ] prep & adv dopo ♦ conj dopo che; **he arrived ~ me** arrivò dopo di me; **a quarter ~ ten** (Am) le dieci e un quarto; **to be ~ sb/sthg** (in search of) cercare qn/qc; **~ all** dopo tutto □ **afters** npl dessert m.

aftercare ['ɑːftəkeəʳ] n assistenza f postospedaliera.

aftereffects ['ɑːftərɪˌfekts] npl conseguenze fpl; (of illness) postumi mpl.

afternoon [ˌɑːftə'nuːn] n pomeriggio m; **good ~!** buon giorno! (il pomeriggio).

afternoon tea n spuntino

pomeridiano a base di tramezzini, dolci, tè o caffè.

aftershave ['ɑːftəʃeɪv] *n* dopobarba *m.*

aftersun ['ɑːftəsʌn] *n* doposole *m.*

afterwards ['ɑːftəwədz] *adv* dopo.

again [ə'gen] *adv* ancora, di nuovo; ~ **and** ~ più volte; **never ...** ~ **non ...** mai più.

against [ə'genst] *prep* contro; **to lean** ~ **sthg** appoggiarsi a qc; ~ **the law** contro la legge.

age [eɪdʒ] *n* età *f*; **under** ~ minorenne; **I haven't seen him for** ~**s** (*inf*) non lo vedo da secoli.

aged [eɪdʒd] *adj*: ~ **eight** di otto anni.

age group *n* fascia *f* d'età.

age limit *n* limite *m* d'età.

agency ['eɪdʒənsɪ] *n* agenzia *f.*

agenda [ə'dʒendə] *n* ordine *m* del giorno.

agent ['eɪdʒənt] *n* agente *mf.*

aggression [ə'greʃn] *n* aggressività *f*; **act of** ~ aggressione *f.*

aggressive [ə'gresɪv] *adj* aggressivo(-a).

agile [*Br* 'ædʒaɪl, *Am* 'ædʒəl] *adj* agile.

agility [ə'dʒɪlətɪ] *n* agilità *f.*

agitated ['ædʒɪteɪtɪd] *adj* agitato(-a).

ago [ə'gəʊ] *adv*: **a month** ~ un mese fa; **how long** ~? quanto tempo fa?

agonizing ['ægənaɪzɪŋ] *adj* (*pain*) atroce; (*decision*) straziante.

agony ['ægənɪ] *n* (*physical*) dolore *m* atroce; (*mental*) agonia *f.*

agree [ə'griː] *vi* (*be in agreement*) essere d'accordo; (*consent*) acconsentire; (*correspond*) concordare; **it doesn't** ~ **with me** (*food*) mi fa male; **to** ~ **to sthg** accettare qc; **to** ~ **to do sthg** accettare di fare qc ❑ **agree on** *vt fus* (*time, price*) concordare, mettersi d'accordo su.

agreed [ə'griːd] *adj* stabilito(-a); **to be** ~ (*person*) essere d'accordo.

agreement [ə'griːmənt] *n* accordo *m*; **in** ~ **with** d'accordo con.

agriculture ['ægrɪkʌltʃər] *n* agricoltura *f.*

ahead [ə'hed] *adv* (*in front*) davanti; (*forwards*) avanti; **the months** ~ i prossimi mesi; **to be** ~ (*winning*) condurre; ~ **of** (*in front of*) davanti a; (*in better position than*) in vantaggio su; (*in time*) in anticipo su.

aid [eɪd] *n* aiuto *m* ◆ *vt* aiutare; **in** ~ **of** a favore di; **with the** ~ **of** con l'aiuto di.

AIDS [eɪdz] *n* AIDS *m.*

ailment ['eɪlmənt] *n* (*fml*) acciacco *m.*

aim [eɪm] *n* (*purpose*) scopo *m* ◆ *vt* (*gun, camera, hose*) puntare ◆ *vi*: **to** ~ (**at**) mirare (a); **to** ~ **to do sthg** avere l'intenzione di fare qc.

air [eər] *n* aria *f* ◆ *vt* (*room*) arieggiare ◆ *adj* aereo(-a); (*travel*) in aereo; **by** ~ (*travel*) in aereo; (*send*) via aerea.

airbed ['eəbed] *n* materassino *m.*

airborne ['eəbɔːn] *adj* in volo.

air-conditioned [-kən'dɪʃnd] *adj* con aria condizionata.

air-conditioning [-kən'dɪʃnɪŋ] *n* aria *f* condizionata.

aircraft ['eəkrɑːft] (*pl inv*) *n* aeromobile *m.*

aircraft carrier [-ˌkærɪər] *n*

portaerei *f inv.*

airfield ['eəfi:ld] *n* campo *m* d'aviazione.

airforce ['eəfɔ:s] *n* aeronautica *f* militare.

air freshener [-ˌfreʃnəʳ] *n* deodorante *m* per ambienti.

airhostess ['eəˌhəʊstɪs] *n* hostess *f inv.*

airing cupboard ['eərɪŋ-] *n* sgabuzzino della caldaia dove viene riposta la biancheria ad asciugare.

airletter ['eəˌletəʳ] *n* aerogramma *m*.

airline ['eəlaɪn] *n* compagnia *f* aerea.

airliner ['eəˌlaɪnəʳ] *n* aereo *m* di linea.

airmail ['eəmeɪl] *n* posta *f* aerea; **by ~** per via aerea.

airplane ['eəpleɪn] *n (Am)* aeroplano *m*.

airport ['eəpɔ:t] *n* aeroporto *m*.

air raid *n* incursione *f* aerea.

airsick ['eəsɪk] *adj*: **to be ~** soffrire di mal d'aria.

air steward *n* assistente *m* di volo.

air stewardess *n* assistente *f* di volo.

air traffic control *n (people)* controllori *mpl* di volo.

airy ['eərɪ] *adj* arioso(-a).

aisle [aɪl] *n (in church)* navata *f*; *(in plane, cinema)* corridoio *m*; *(in supermarket)* corsia *f*.

aisle seat *n* posto *m* corridoio.

ajar [ə'dʒɑ:ʳ] *adj* socchiuso(-a).

alarm [ə'lɑ:m] *n* allarme *m* ◆ *vt* allarmare.

alarm clock *n* sveglia *f*.

alarmed [ə'lɑ:md] *adj (door, car)* dotato(-a) di allarme.

alarming [ə'lɑ:mɪŋ] *adj* allarmante.

Albert Hall ['ælbət-] *n*: **the ~** l'Albert Hall *f (sala concerti di Londra)*.

---

album ['ælbəm] *n* album *m inv.*

alcohol ['ælkəhɒl] *n* alcool *m*.

alcohol-free *adj* analcolico(-a).

alcoholic [ˌælkə'hɒlɪk] *adj* alcolico(-a) ◆ *n* alcolizzato *m* (-a *f*).

alcoholism ['ælkəhɒlɪzm] *n* alcolismo *m*.

alcove ['ælkəʊv] *n* rientranza *f*.

ale [eɪl] *n* birra *f*.

alert [ə'lɜ:t] *adj* vigile ◆ *vt* allertare.

A levels *npl* ≈ esami *mpl* di maturità.

---

ne sulla base della votazione finale, che risulta pertanto estremamente importante.

algebra ['ældʒɪbrə] *n* algebra *f*.

alias ['eɪlɪəs] *adv* alias.

alibi ['ælɪbaɪ] *n* alibi *m inv*.

alien ['eɪlɪən] *n (foreigner)* straniero *m (-a f)*; *(from outer space)* alieno *m (-a f)*.

alight [ə'laɪt] *adj* in fiamme ◆ *vi (fml: from train, bus)*: **to ~ (from)** scendere (da).

align [ə'laɪn] *vt* allineare.

alike [ə'laɪk] *adj* simile ◆ *adv* allo stesso modo; **to look ~** assomigliarsi.

alive [ə'laɪv] *adj (living)* vivo(-a).

all [ɔːl] *adj* tutto(-a); **~ the food** tutto il cibo; **~ the money** tutti i soldi; **~ the houses** tutte le case; **~ trains stop at Tonbridge** tutti i treni fermano a Tonbridge; **~ the time** sempre; **~ day** tutto il giorno.
◆ *adv* 1. *(completely)* completamente, interamente; **~ alone** tutto solo (tutta sola).
2. *(in scores)*: **it's two ~** sono due pari.
3. *(in phrases)*: **~ but empty** quasi vuoto; **~ over** *(finished)* finito.
◆ *pron* 1. *(the whole amount)* tutto(-a); **~ of the work** tutto il lavoro; **is that ~?** *(in shop)* basta così?
2. *(everybody, everything)* tutti(-e); **~ of the girls/rooms** tutte le ragazze/camere; **~ of us went** ci siamo andati tutti.
3. *(with superlative)*: **the best of ~** il migliore di tutti.
4. *(in phrases)*: **in ~** *(in total)* in tutto; *(in summary)* nel complesso;

can I help you at ~? posso esserle di aiuto?

Allah ['ælə] *n* Allah *m*.

allege [ə'ledʒ] *vt* asserire.

allergic [ə'lɜːdʒɪk] *adj*: **to be ~ to** essere allergico(-a) a.

allergy ['ælədʒɪ] *n* allergia *f*.

alleviate [ə'liːvɪeɪt] *vt* alleviare.

alley ['ælɪ] *n (narrow street)* vicolo *m*.

alligator ['ælɪɡeɪtə'] *n* alligatore *m*.

all-in *adj (Br: inclusive)* tutto compreso *(inv)*.

all-night *adj (bar, petrol station)* aperto(-a) tutta la notte.

allocate ['æləkeɪt] *vt (money, task)* assegnare.

allotment [ə'lɒtmənt] *n (Br: vegetables)* piccolo lotto di terra preso in affitto per coltivarvi ortaggi.

allow [ə'laʊ] *vt (permit)* permettere; *(time, money)* calcolare; **to ~ sb to do sthg** permettere a qn di fare qc; **to be ~ed to do sthg** avere il permesso di fare qc, poter fare qc ❑ **allow for** *vt fus* tener conto di.

allowance [ə'laʊəns] *n (state benefit)* assegno *m*; *(for expenses)* indennità *f inv*; *(Am: pocket money)* paghetta *f*.

all right *adv (satisfactorily)* bene; *(yes, okay)* va bene ◆ *adj*: **is everything ~?** va tutto bene?; **is it ~ if I smoke?** Le dispiace se fumo?; **are you ~?** ti senti bene?; **how was the film? – it was ~** com'era il film? – niente di speciale; **how are you? – I'm ~** come stai? – non c'è male.

ally ['ælaɪ] *n* alleato *m (-a f)*.

almond ['ɑːmənd] *n* mandorla *f*.

almost ['ɔːlməʊst] *adv* quasi.

alone [ə'ləʊn] *adj* solo(-a) ◆ *adv*

da solo(-a); **to leave sb ~** lasciare qn in pace; **to leave sthg ~** lasciar stare qc.

along [əˈlɒŋ] *prep* lungo ◆ *adv*: **to walk ~** camminare; **to bring sthg ~** portare qc; **all ~** sempre; **~ with** insieme a.

alongside [ə,lɒŋˈsaɪd] *prep* accanto a ◆ *adv*: **to come ~** accostare.

aloof [əˈluːf] *adj* distaccato(-a).

aloud [əˈlaʊd] *adv* a voce alta.

alphabet [ˈælfəbet] *n* alfabeto *m*.

Alps [ælps] *npl*: **the ~** le Alpi.

already [ɔːlˈredɪ] *adv* già.

also [ˈɔːlsəʊ] *adv* anche.

altar [ˈɔːltəʳ] *n* altare *m*.

alter [ˈɔːltəʳ] *vt* cambiare.

alteration [,ɔːltəˈreɪʃn] *n* modifica *f*.

alternate [*Br* ɔːlˈtɜːnət, *Am* ˈɔːltərnət] *adj* alterni(-e).

alternating current [ˈɔːltə-neɪtɪŋ-] *n* corrente *f* alternata.

alternative [ɔːlˈtɜːnətɪv] *adj* alternativo(-a) ◆ *n* alternativa *f*.

alternatively [ɔːlˈtɜːnətɪvlɪ] *adv* in alternativa.

alternator [ˈɔːltəneɪtəʳ] *n* alternatore *m*.

although [ɔːlˈðəʊ] *conj* sebbene, benché.

altitude [ˈæltɪtjuːd] *n* altitudine *f*.

altogether [,ɔːltəˈgeðəʳ] *adv* (*completely*) del tutto; (*in total*) in tutto.

aluminium [,æljʊˈmɪnɪəm] *n* (*Br*) alluminio *m*.

aluminum [əˈluːmɪnəm] (*Am*) = **aluminium.**

always [ˈɔːlweɪz] *adv* sempre.

am [æm] → **be.**

a.m. (*abbr of ante meridiem*): **at two ~** alle due di notte; **at ten ~** alle dieci di mattina.

amateur [ˈæmətəʳ] *n* dilettante *mf*.

amazed [əˈmeɪzd] *adj* stupito(-a).

amazing [əˈmeɪzɪŋ] *adj* incredibile.

Amazon [ˈæməzn] *n* (*river*): **the ~** il Rio delle Amazzoni.

ambassador [æmˈbæsədəʳ] *n* ambasciatore *m* (-trice *f*).

amber [ˈæmbəʳ] *adj* (*traffic lights*) giallo(-a); (*jewellery*) d'ambra.

ambiguous [æmˈbɪgjʊəs] *adj* ambiguo(-a).

ambition [æmˈbɪʃn] *n* ambizione *f*.

ambitious [æmˈbɪʃəs] *adj* ambizioso(-a).

ambulance [ˈæmbjʊləns] *n* ambulanza *f*.

ambush [ˈæmbʊʃ] *n* imboscata *f*.

amenities [əˈmiːnətɪz] *npl* (*in hotel*) comfort *m inv*; (*in town*) strutture *fpl* (*sportive, ricreative ecc.*).

America [əˈmerɪkə] *n* l'America *f*.

American [əˈmerɪkən] *adj* americano(-a) ◆ *n* (*person*) americano *m* (-a *f*).

amiable [ˈeɪmɪəbl] *adj* amabile.

ammunition [,æmjʊˈnɪʃn] *n* munizioni *fpl*.

amnesia [æmˈniːzɪə] *n* amnesia *f*.

among(st) [əˈmʌŋ(st)] *prep* tra, fra.

amount [əˈmaʊnt] *n* (*quantity*) quantità *f inv*; (*sum*) somma *f* ❑

amount to *vt fus (total)* ammontare a.

amp [æmp] *n* ampere *m inv*; **a 13-~ plug** una spina con fusibile da 13 ampere.

ample ['æmpl] *adj* più che sufficiente.

amplifier ['æmplɪfaɪə'] *n* amplificatore *m*.

amputate ['æmpjʊteɪt] *vt* amputare.

Amtrak ['æmtræk] *n compagnia ferroviaria statunitense.*

amuse [ə'mju:z] *vt* divertire.

amusement arcade [ə'mju:z-mənt-] *n* sala *f* giochi.

amusement park *n* luna park *m inv.*

amusements [ə'mju:zmənts] *npl* giostre e giochi al luna park.

amusing [ə'mju:zɪŋ] *adj* divertente.

an [*stressed* æn, *unstressed* ən] → **a**.

anaemic [ə'ni:mɪk] *adj (Br: person)* anemico(-a).

anaesthetic [ˌænɪs'θetɪk] *n (Br)* anestetico *m*.

analgesic [ˌænæl'dʒi:sɪk] *n* analgesico *m*.

analyse ['ænəlaɪz] *vt* analizzare.

analyst ['ænəlɪst] *n* analista *mf*.

analyze ['ænəlaɪz] *(Am)* = **analyse**.

anarchy ['ænəkɪ] *n* anarchia *f*.

anatomy [ə'nætəmɪ] *n (science)* anatomia *f*; *(of animal)* struttura *f*; *(of person)* corpo *m*.

ancestor ['ænsestə'] *n* antenato *m* (-a *f*).

anchor ['æŋkə'] *n* àncora *f*.

anchovy ['æntʃəvɪ] *n* acciuga *f*.

ancient ['eɪnʃənt] *adj (customs, monument)* antico(-a).

and [*strong form* ænd, *weak form* ənd, ən] *conj* e, ed *(before vowel)*; **more ~ more** sempre più; **~ you? e tu?; a hundred ~ one** centouno; **to try ~ do sthg** cercare di fare qc; **to go ~ see** andare a vedere.

Andes ['ændi:z] *npl*: **the ~** le Ande.

anecdote ['ænɪkdəʊt] *n* aneddoto *m*.

anemic [ə'ni:mɪk] *(Am)* = **anaemic**.

anesthetic [ˌænɪs'θetɪk] *(Am)* = **anaesthetic**.

angel ['eɪndʒl] *n* angelo *m*.

anger ['æŋgə'] *n* rabbia *f*.

angina [æn'dʒaɪnə] *n* àngina *f* pectoris.

angle ['æŋgl] *n* angolo *m*; **at an ~** storto(-a).

angler ['æŋglə'] *n* pescatore *m* (-trice *f*).

angling ['æŋglɪŋ] *n* pesca *f*.

angry ['æŋgrɪ] *adj (person)* arrabbiato(-a); *(words)* pieno(-a) di rabbia; **to get ~ (with sb)** arrabbiarsi (con qn).

animal ['ænɪml] *n* animale *m*.

aniseed ['ænɪsi:d] *n* semi *mpl* d'anice.

ankle ['æŋkl] *n* caviglia *f*.

annex ['æneks] *n (building)* edificio *m* annesso.

annihilate [ə'naɪəleɪt] *vt* annientare.

anniversary [ˌænɪ'vɜːsərɪ] *n* anniversario *m*.

announce [ə'naʊns] *vt* annunciare.

announcement [ə'naʊnsmənt] *n* annuncio *m*.

announcer [ə'naʊnsə^r] *n* annunciatore *m* (-trice *f*).

annoy [ə'nɔɪ] *vt* dare fastidio a.

annoyed [ə'nɔɪd] *adj* seccato(-a); **to get ~ (with sb)** arrabbiarsi (con qn).

annoying [ə'nɔɪɪŋ] *adj* seccante, irritante.

annual ['ænjʊəl] *adj* annuale.

anonymous [ə'nɒnɪməs] *adj* anonimo(-a).

anorak ['ænəræk] *n* giacca *f* a vento.

another [ə'nʌðə^r] *adj* un altro (un'altra) ◆ *pron* un'altro (un'altra *f*); **can I have ~ (one)?** posso prenderne un altro?; **in ~ two weeks** fra altre due settimane; **one ~** l'un l'altro (l'un l'altra); **to help one ~** aiutarsi (l'un l'altro); **to talk to one ~** parlarsi; **one after ~** uno dopo l'altro (una dopo l'altra).

answer ['ɑːnsə^r] *n* risposta *f* ◆ *vt* rispondere a ◆ *vi* rispondere; **to ~ the door** andare ad aprire (la porta); **to ~ the phone** rispondere al telefono ❑ **answer back** *vi* rispondere male.

answering machine ['ɑːnsə-rɪŋ-] = **answerphone**.

answerphone ['ɑːnsəfəʊn] *n* segreteria *f* telefonica.

ant [ænt] *n* formica *f*.

Antarctic [æn'tɑːktɪk] *n*: **the ~** l'Antartide *f*.

antenna [æn'tenə] *n* (*Am*: *aerial*) antenna *f*.

anthem ['ænθəm] *n* inno *m*.

antibiotics [ˌæntɪbaɪ'ɒtɪks] *npl* antibiotici *mpl*.

anticipate [æn'tɪsɪpeɪt] *vt* (*expect*) aspettarsi; (*guess correctly*) prevedere.

anticlimax [ˌæntɪ'klaɪmæks] *n* delusione *f*.

anticlockwise [ˌæntɪ'klɒkwaɪz] *adv* (*Br*) in senso antiorario.

antidote ['æntɪdəʊt] *n* antidoto *m*.

antifreeze ['æntɪfriːz] *n* antigelo *m*.

antihistamine [ˌæntɪ'hɪstəmɪn] *n* antistaminico *m*.

antiperspirant [ˌæntɪ'pɜːspə-rənt] *n* deodorante *m* (ad azione antitraspirante).

antiquarian bookshop [ˌæntɪ'kweərɪən-] *n* libreria *f* antiquaria.

antique [æn'tiːk] *n* pezzo *m* d'antiquariato.

antique shop *n* negozio *m* d'antiquariato.

antiseptic [ˌæntɪ'septɪk] *n* antisettico *m*.

antisocial [ˌæntɪ'səʊʃl] *adj* (*person*) asociale; (*behaviour*) incivile.

antlers ['æntləz] *npl* palchi *mpl*.

anxiety [æŋ'zaɪətɪ] *n* ansia *f*.

anxious ['æŋkʃəs] *adj* (*worried*) preoccupato(-a); (*eager*) ansioso(-a).

any ['enɪ] *adj* **1.** (*in questions*): **have you got ~ money?** hai (dei) soldi?; **have you got ~ postcards?** ha delle cartoline?; **is there ~ coffee left?** c'è ancora del caffè?

2. (*in negatives*): **I haven't got ~ money** non ho soldi; **I haven't got ~ Italian stamps** non ho nessun francobollo italiano; **we don't have ~ rooms** non abbiamo camere libere.

3. (*no matter which*) qualunque, qualsiasi; **take ~ one you like** pren-

di quello che preferisci.
♦ *pron* 1. *(in questions)* ne; **I'm looking for a hotel – are there ~ nearby?** sto cercando un albergo – ce ne sono da queste parti?
2. *(in negatives)* ne; **I don't want ~ (of them)** non ne voglio.
3. *(no matter which one)*: **you can sit at ~ of the tables** potete sedere a qualsiasi tavolo.
♦ *adv* 1. *(in questions)*: **is that ~ better?** così va un po' meglio?; **is there ~ more ice cream?** c'è ancora un po' di gelato?; **~ other questions?** altre domande?
2. *(in negatives)*: **he's not ~ better** non c'è nessun miglioramento; **we can't wait ~ longer** non possiamo più aspettare.

anybody ['enɪˌbɒdɪ] = **anyone**.

anyhow ['enɪhaʊ] *adv* comunque; *(carelessly)* alla rinfusa.

anyone ['enɪwʌn] *pron (someone)* qualcuno; *(any person)* chiunque; **is ~ there?** c'è nessuno?; **there wasn't ~ in** non c'era nessuno.

anything ['enɪθɪŋ] *pron (something)* qualcosa; *(no matter what)* qualunque cosa, qualsiasi cosa; **have you ~ bigger?** ha niente di più grande?; **I don't want ~ to eat** non voglio mangiare niente.

anyway ['enɪweɪ] *adv* comunque.

anywhere ['enɪweər] *adv (in questions)* da qualche parte; *(with negative)* da nessuna parte; *(any place)* dovunque, da qualunque parte OR qualsiasi parte; **did you go ~ else?** siete andati da qualche altra parte?; **~ you like** dove vuoi.

apart [ə'pɑːt] *adv (separated)*: **the towns are 5 miles ~** le due città distano 8 km l'una dall'altra; **we live ~** non viviamo insieme; **to**

come ~ andare in pezzi; **~ from** *(except for)* a parte; *(as well as)* oltre a.

apartheid [ə'pɑːtheɪt] *n* apartheid *f*.

apartment [ə'pɑːtmənt] *n (Am)* appartamento *m*.

apathetic [æpə'θetɪk] *adj* apatico(-a).

ape [eɪp] *n* scimmia *f*.

aperitif [əˌperə'tiːf] *n* aperitivo *m*.

aperture ['æpətʃər] *n (of camera)* apertura *f*.

APEX ['eɪpeks] *n (plane ticket)* biglietto *m* APEX; *(Br: train ticket)* biglietto ferroviario con data prefissata e dal prezzo ridotto comprato due settimane prima della partenza.

apiece [ə'piːs] *adv (for each item)* l'uno (l'una); *(to, for each person)* ciascuno(-a).

apologetic [əˌpɒlə'dʒetɪk] *adj*: **to be ~** scusarsi.

apologize [ə'pɒlədʒaɪz] *vi*: **to ~ (to sb for sthg)** scusarsi (con qn per qc).

apology [ə'pɒlədʒɪ] *n* scuse *fpl*.

apostrophe [ə'pɒstrəfɪ] *n* apostrofo *m*.

appal [ə'pɔːl] *vt (Br)* sconvolgere.

appall [ə'pɔːl] *(Am)* = **appal**.

appalling [ə'pɔːlɪŋ] *adj* spaventoso(-a).

apparatus [æpə'reɪtəs] *n (device)* apparecchio *m*; *(in gym)* attrezzatura *f*.

apparently [ə'pærəntlɪ] *adv (it seems)* a quanto pare; *(evidently)* evidentemente.

appeal [ə'piːl] *n (JUR)* appello *m*; *(fundraising campaign)* raccolta *f* di fondi ◆ *vi (JUR)* fare appello; **to ~ to sb for help** chiedere aiuto a qn; **it doesn't ~ to me** non mi attira.

appear [ə'pɪəʳ] *vi* apparire; *(seem)* sembrare; *(before court)* comparire; **it ~s that** sembra che.

appearance [ə'pɪərəns] *n (arrival)* comparsa *f*; *(look)* aspetto *m*.

appendices [ə'pendɪsi:z] *pl* → **appendix**.

appendicitis [ə,pendɪ'saɪtɪs] *n* appendicite *f*.

appendix [ə'pendɪks] *(pl -dices) n* appendice *f*.

appetite [æpɪtaɪt] *n* appetito *m*.

appetizer ['æpɪtaɪzəʳ] *n* stuzzichino *m*.

appetizing ['æpɪtaɪzɪŋ] *adj* appetitoso(-a).

applaud [ə'plɔ:d] *vt & vi* applaudire.

applause [ə'plɔ:z] *n* applauso *m*.

apple ['æpl] *n* mela *f*.

apple charlotte [-'ʃɑ:lət] *n* dolce di pane o pan di Spagna, ripieno di mele e pane sbriciolato e cotto in forno.

apple crumble *n* mele cotte ricoperte da uno strato di pasta frolla sbriciolata.

apple juice *n* succo *m* di mela.

apple pie *n* torta *f* di mele ricoperta di pasta.

apple sauce *n* mele *fpl* grattugiate.

apple tart *n* crostata *f* di mele.

apple turnover [-'tɜ:n,əʊvəʳ] *n* sfogliatella *f* di mele.

appliance [ə'plaɪəns] *n* apparecchio *m*; **electrical/domestic ~** elettrodomestico *m*.

applicable [ə'plɪkəbl] *adj*: **to be**

~ (to) essere applicabile (a); **if ~** se pertinente.

applicant ['æplɪkənt] *n* candidato *m* (-a *f*).

application [,æplɪ'keɪʃn] *n (for job, membership)* domanda *f*.

application form *n* modulo *m* di domanda.

apply [ə'plaɪ] *vt (lotion, paint)* dare; *(brakes)* azionare ◆ *vi*: **to ~ (to sb for sthg)** *(make request)* fare domanda (per qc presso qn); **to ~ (to sb)** *(be applicable)* essere valido (per qn); **to ~ for a job** fare domanda di lavoro.

appointment [ə'pɔɪntmənt] *n (with doctor, hairdresser, businessman)* appuntamento *m*; **to have/make an ~ (with)** avere/prendere un appuntamento (con); **by ~** per OR su appuntamento.

appreciable [ə'pri:ʃəbl] *adj* apprezzabile.

appreciate [ə'pri:ʃɪeɪt] *vt* apprezzare; *(understand)* rendersi conto di.

apprehensive [,æprɪ'hensɪv] *adj* preoccupato(-a).

apprentice [ə'prentɪs] *n* apprendista *mf*.

apprenticeship [ə'prentɪʃɪp] *n* apprendistato *m*.

approach [ə'prəʊtʃ] *n (road)* accesso *m*; *(to problem, situation)* approccio *m* ◆ *vt (come nearer to)* avvicinare; *(problem, situation)* affrontare ◆ *vi* avvicinarsi.

appropriate [ə'prəʊprɪət] *adj* adatto(-a).

approval [ə'pru:vl] *n* approvazione *f*.

approve [ə'pru:v] *vi*: **to ~ (of sb/sthg)** approvare (qn/qc).

approximate [əˈprɒksɪmət] *adj* approssimativo(-a).

approximately [əˈprɒksɪmətlɪ] *adv* circa.

Apr. *(abbr of April)* apr.

apricot [ˈeɪprɪkɒt] *n* albicocca *f*.

April [ˈeɪprəl] *n* aprile *m*, → September.

April Fools' Day *n* il primo aprile, giorno in cui si fanno i 'pesci d'aprile'.

---

i APRIL FOOLS' DAY

Come in Italia, anche in Gran Bretagna il primo aprile è occasione di scherzi e burle di ogni genere. A differenza dell'Italia, però, non è consentito fare scherzi dopo mezzogiorno e non esiste la tradizione del pesce di carta.

---

apron [ˈeɪprən] *n* grembiule *m* (da cucina).

apt [æpt] *adj (appropriate)* appropriato(-a); **to be ~ to do sthg** avere tendenza a fare qc.

aquarium [əˈkweərɪəm] *(pl -ria [-rɪə])* *n* acquario *m*.

Aquarius [əˈkweərɪəs] *n* Acquario *m*.

aqueduct [ˈækwɪdʌkt] *n* acquedotto *m*.

Arab [ˈærəb] *adj* arabo(-a) ♦ *n (person)* arabo *m* (-a *f*).

Arabic [ˈærəbɪk] *adj* arabo(-a) ♦ *n (language)* arabo *m*.

arbitrary [ˈɑːbɪtrərɪ] *adj* arbitrario(-a).

arc [ɑːk] *n* arco *m*.

arcade [ɑːˈkeɪd] *n (for shopping)* galleria *f*; *(of video games)* sala *f* giochi.

arch [ɑːtʃ] *n* arco *m*.

archaeology [ˌɑːkɪˈɒlədʒɪ] *n* archeologia *f*.

archbishop [ˌɑːtʃˈbɪʃəp] *n* arcivescovo *m*.

archery [ˈɑːtʃərɪ] *n* tiro *m* con l'arco.

archipelago [ˌɑːkɪˈpeləgəʊ] *n* arcipelago *m*.

architect [ˈɑːkɪtekt] *n* architetto *mf*.

architecture [ˈɑːkɪtektʃəʳ] *n* architettura *f*.

archives [ˈɑːkaɪvz] *npl* archivi *mpl*.

Arctic [ˈɑːktɪk] *n*: **the ~** l'Artide *f*.

are [*weak form* əʳ, *strong form* ɑːʳ] → be.

area [ˈeərɪə] *n (region)* zona *f*; *(space, zone)* area *f*; *(surface size)* superficie *f*; **dining ~** zona pranzo.

area code *n (Am)* prefisso *m*.

arena [əˈriːnə] *n (at circus)* pista *f*; *(sports ground)* campo *m*.

aren't = are not.

Argentina [ˌɑːdʒənˈtiːnə] *n* l'Argentina *f*.

argue [ˈɑːgjuː] *vi (quarrel)*: **to ~ (with sb about sthg)** litigare (con qn per qc) ♦ *vt*: **to ~ (that)** ... sostenere (che) ...

argument [ˈɑːgjʊmənt] *n (quarrel)* discussione *f*; *(reason)* argomento *m*.

arid [ˈærɪd] *adj* arido(-a).

Aries [ˈeəriːz] *n* Ariete *m*.

arise [əˈraɪz] *(pt arose, pp arisen [əˈrɪzn])* *vi (problem, opportunity)* presentarsi; **to ~ from** derivare da.

aristocracy [ˌærɪˈstɒkrəsɪ] *n* aristocrazia *f*.

arithmetic [əˈrɪθmətɪk] n aritmetica f.

arm [ɑ:m] n (of person) braccio m; (of chair) bracciolo m; (of garment) manica f.

armbands [ˈɑ:mbændz] npl (for swimming) braccioli mpl.

armchair [ˈɑ:mtʃeəʳ] n poltrona f.

armed [ɑ:md] adj armato(-a).

armed forces npl: **the ~** le forze armate.

armor (Am) = **armour**.

armour [ˈɑ:məʳ] n (Br) armatura f.

armpit [ˈɑ:mpɪt] n ascella f.

arms [ɑ:mz] npl (weapons) armi fpl.

army [ˈɑ:mɪ] n esercito m.

A road n (Br) strada f statale.

aroma [əˈrəʊmə] n aroma m.

aromatic [ˌærəˈmætɪk] adj aromatico(-a).

arose [əˈrəʊz] pt → **arise**.

around [əˈraʊnd] adv in giro ♦ prep (surrounding) intorno a; (to the other side of) dall'altra parte di; (near) vicino a; (all over) per; (approximately) circa; **~ here** (in the area) da queste parti; **~ the corner** dietro l'angolo; **to turn ~** girarsi; **to look ~** (turn head) guardarsi intorno; (in shop, city) dare un'occhiata in giro; **at ~ two o'clock** verso le due; **is Paul ~?** c'è Paul?

arouse [əˈraʊz] vt destare.

arrange [əˈreɪndʒ] vt (flowers, books) sistemare; (meeting, event) organizzare; **to ~ to do sthg (with sb)** mettersi d'accordo (con qn) per fare qc.

arrangement [əˈreɪndʒmənt] n (agreement) accordo m; (layout) disposizione f; **by ~** su richiesta; **to make ~s (to do sthg)** fare il necessario (per fare qc).

arrest [əˈrest] n arresto m ♦ vt arrestare; **under ~** in arresto.

arrival [əˈraɪvl] n arrivo m; **on ~** all'arrivo; **new ~** (person) nuovo arrivato m (nuova arrivata f).

arrive [əˈraɪv] vi arrivare; **to ~ at** (place) arrivare in/a.

arrogant [ˈærəgənt] adj arrogante.

arrow [ˈærəʊ] n freccia f.

arson [ˈɑ:sn] n incendio m doloso.

art [ɑ:t] n arte f ❑ **arts** npl (humanities) discipline fpl umanistiche; **the ~s** (fine arts) l'arte f.

artefact [ˈɑ:tɪfækt] n manufatto m.

artery [ˈɑ:tərɪ] n arteria f.

art gallery n galleria f d'arte.

arthritis [ɑ:ˈθraɪtɪs] n artrite f.

artichoke [ˈɑ:tɪtʃəʊk] n carciofo m.

article [ˈɑ:tɪkl] n articolo m.

articulate [ɑ:ˈtɪkjʊlət] adj chiaro(-a).

artificial [ˌɑ:tɪˈfɪʃl] adj artificiale.

artist [ˈɑ:tɪst] n artista mf.

artistic [ɑ:ˈtɪstɪk] adj (design) artistico(-a); (person) dotato(-a) di senso artistico.

arts centre n centro m artistico.

as [unstressed əz, stressed æz] adv (in comparisons): **~ ... ~** (così) ... come; **~ white ~ snow** bianco come la neve; **he's ~ tall ~ I am** è alto quanto me; **~ many ~ tanti** ...

quanti (tante ... quante); ~ **much** ~ tanto ... quanto (tanta ... quanta); **twice ~ big** due volte più grande.

♦ *conj* **1.** *(referring to time)* mentre, nel momento in cui; ~ **the plane was coming in to land** nel momento in cui l'aereo si preparava ad atterrare.

2. *(referring to manner)* come; ~ **expected ...** come previsto ...; **do ~ you like** fa' come vuoi.

3. *(introducing a statement)* come; ~ **you know ...** come sai ...

4. *(because)* poiché, dato che.

5. *(in phrases):* ~ **for** quanto a; ~ **from** (a partire) da; ~ **if** come se; **it looks ~ if it will rain** sembra che stia per piovere.

♦ *prep (referring to function, job)* come; **to work ~ a teacher** fare l'insegnante.

asap *(abbr of as soon as possible)* il più presto possibile.

ascent [ə'sent] *n (climb)* scalata *f.*

ascribe [ə'skraɪb] *vt:* **to ~ sthg to** attribuire qc a.

ash [æʃ] *n (from cigarette, fire)* cenere *f*; *(tree)* frassino *m.*

ashore [ə'ʃɔːʳ] *adv* a riva.

ashtray ['æʃtreɪ] *n* portacenere *m inv.*

Asia [Br 'eɪʒə, Am 'eɪʒə] *n* l'Asia *f.*

Asian [Br 'eɪʃn, Am 'eɪʒn] *adj* asiatico(-a) ♦ *n* asiatico *m* (-a *f*).

aside [ə'saɪd] *adv (to one side)* di lato; **to move ~** spostarsi.

ask [ɑːsk] *vt (person)* chiedere a; *(request)* chiedere; *(invite)* invitare ♦ *vi:* **to ~ about sthg** chiedere informazioni su qc; **to ~ sb sthg** chiedere qc a qn; **to ~ sb about sthg** chiedere a qn di qc; **to ~ sb to**

do sthg chiedere a qn di fare qc; **to ~ sb for sthg** chiedere qc a qn; **to ~ a question** fare una domanda; **can I ~ you about this translation?** posso farti qualche domanda su questa traduzione? ❑ **ask for** *vt fus (ask to talk to)* chiedere di; *(request)* chiedere.

asleep [ə'sliːp] *adj* addormentato(-a); **to be ~** dormire; **to fall ~** addormentarsi.

asparagus [ə'spærəgəs] *n* asparagi *mpl.*

asparagus tips *npl* punte *fpl* d'asparagi.

aspect ['æspekt] *n* aspetto *m.*

aspirin ['æsprɪn] *n* aspirina® *f.*

ass [æs] *n (animal)* asino *m.*

assassinate [ə'sæsɪneɪt] *vt* assassinare.

assault [ə'sɔːlt] *n* aggressione *f* ♦ *vt* aggredire.

assemble [ə'sembl] *vt (bookcase, model)* montare ♦ *vi* riunirsi.

assembly [ə'semblɪ] *n (at school)* riunione quotidiana di alunni e professori.

assembly hall *n (at school)* locale di una scuola dove alunni e professori si riuniscono ogni giorno prima delle lezioni.

assembly point *n* punto di raduno in caso di emergenza.

assert [ə'sɜːt] *vt (fact, innocence)* sostenere; *(authority)* far valere; **to ~ o.s.** farsi valere.

assess [ə'ses] *vt (person, situation, effect)* valutare; *(value, damage, cost)* stimare.

assessment [ə'sesmənt] *n (of person, situation, effect)* valutazione *f*; *(of value, damage, cost)* stima *f.*

asset ['æset] *n (valuable person,*

thing) punto *m* di forza.

assign [ə'saɪn] *vt*: **to ~ sthg to sb** (*give*) assegnare qc a qn; **to ~ sb to do sthg** (*designate*) incaricare qn di fare qc.

assignment [ə'saɪnmənt] *n* (*task*) incarico *m*; (*SCH*) ricerca *f*.

assist [ə'sɪst] *vt* aiutare.

assistance [ə'sɪstəns] *n* aiuto *m*; **to be of ~ (to sb)** essere d'aiuto (a qn).

assistant [ə'sɪstənt] *n* assistente *mf*.

associate [*n* ə'səʊʃɪət, *vb* ə'səʊʃɪeɪt] *n* (*partner*) socio *m* (-a *f*); (*colleague*) collega *mf* ◆ *vt*: **to ~ sb/sthg with** associare qn/qc a; **to be ~d with** venire associato a.

association [ə,səʊsɪ'eɪʃn] *n* associazione *f*.

assorted [ə'sɔːtɪd] *adj* assortito(-a).

assortment [ə'sɔːtmənt] *n* assortimento *m*.

assume [ə'sjuːm] *vt* (*suppose*) supporre; (*control*) assumere; (*responsibility*) assumersi.

assurance [ə'ʃʊərəns] *n* (*promise*) promessa *f*; (*insurance*) assicurazione *f*.

assure [ə'ʃʊər] *vt* assicurare; **to ~ sb (that)** ... assicurare a qn che ...

asterisk ['æstərɪsk] *n* asterisco *m*.

asthma ['æsmə] *n* asma *f*.

asthmatic [æs'mætɪk] *adj* asmatico(-a).

astonished [ə'stɒnɪʃt] *adj* stupito(-a).

astonishing [ə'stɒnɪʃɪŋ] *adj* incredibile.

astound [ə'staʊnd] *vt* sbalordire.

astray [ə'streɪ] *adv*: **to go ~** smarrirsi.

astrology [ə'strɒlədʒɪ] *n* astrologia *f*.

astronomy [ə'strɒnəmɪ] *n* astronomia *f*.

asylum [ə'saɪləm] *n* (*mental hospital*) manicomio *m*.

at [*unstressed* ət, *stressed* æt] *prep* **1.** (*indicating place, position*) a; **~ school** a scuola; **~ the hotel** in OR all'albergo; **~ home** a casa; **~ my mother's** da mia madre.
2. (*indicating direction*): **to throw sthg ~** tirare qc contro; **to look ~ sb/sthg** guardare qn/qc; **to smile ~ sb** sorridere a qn.
3. (*indicating time*) a; **~ nine o'clock** alle nove; **~ night** di notte.
4. (*indicating rate, level, speed*) a; **it works out ~ £5 each** viene 5 sterline a testa; **~ 60 km/h** a 60km/h.
5. (*indicating activity*): **she's ~ lunch** sta pranzando; **to be good/bad ~ sthg** essere/non essere bravo in qc.
6. (*indicating cause*): **shocked ~ sthg** scioccato da qc; **angry ~ sb** arrabbiato con qn; **delighted ~ sthg** contentissimo di qc.

ate [*Br* et, *Am* eɪt] *pt* → **eat**.

atheist ['eɪθɪɪst] *n* ateo *m* (-a *f*).

athlete ['æθliːt] *n* atleta *mf*.

athletics [æθ'letɪks] *n* atletica *f*.

Atlantic [ət'læntɪk] *n*: **the ~ (Ocean)** l'Atlantico *m*, l'Oceano *m* Atlantico.

atlas ['ætləs] *n* atlante *m*.

atmosphere ['ætməsfɪər] *n* atmosfera *f*; (*air in room*) aria *f*.

atom ['ætəm] *n* atomo *m*.

A to Z *n* (*map*) stradario *m*.

atrocious [əˈtrəʊʃəs] *adj (very bad)* orrendo(-a).

attach [əˈtætʃ] *vt* attaccare; **to ~ sthg to sthg** attaccare qc a qc.

attachment [əˈtætʃmənt] *n (device)* accessorio *m*.

attack [əˈtæk] *n* attacco *m* ♦ *vt* aggredire.

attacker [əˈtækəʳ] *n* aggressore *m*.

attain [əˈteɪn] *vt (fml)* conseguire.

attempt [əˈtempt] *n* tentativo *m* ♦ *vt* tentare; **to ~ to do sthg** tentare di fare qc.

attend [əˈtend] *vt (meeting)* partecipare a; *(school)* frequentare; *(mass)* ascoltare ❏ **attend to** *vt fus (deal with)* occuparsi di.

attendance [əˈtendəns] *n (people at concert, match)* affluenza *f; (at school)* frequenza *f*.

attendant [əˈtendənt] *n (at public toilets, cloakroom)* addetto *m* (-a *f); (at museum)* custode *mf*.

attention [əˈtenʃn] *n* attenzione *f;* **to pay ~ (to)** fare attenzione (a).

attic [ˈætɪk] *n* soffitta *f*.

attitude [ˈætɪtjuːd] *n* atteggiamento *m*.

attorney [əˈtɜːnɪ] *n (Am)* avvocato *m*.

attract [əˈtrækt] *vt* attirare.

attraction [əˈtrækʃn] *n (liking)* attrazione *f; (attractive feature)* attrattiva *f*.

attractive [əˈtræktɪv] *adj* attraente.

attribute [əˈtrɪbjuːt] *vt:* **to ~ sthg to** attribuire qc a.

aubergine [ˈəʊbəʒiːn] *n (Br)* melanzana *f*.

auburn [ˈɔːbən] *adj* castano ramato *(inv)*.

auction [ˈɔːkʃn] *n* asta *f*.

audience [ˈɔːdɪəns] *n (of play, concert, film)* pubblico *m; (of TV)* telespettatori *mpl; (of radio)* ascoltatori *mpl*.

audio [ˈɔːdɪəʊ] *adj* audio *(inv)*.

audio-visual [-ˈvɪʒʊəl] *adj* audiovisivo(-a).

auditorium [ˌɔːdɪˈtɔːrɪəm] *n* sala *f*.

Aug. *(abbr of August)* ago.

August [ˈɔːgəst] *n* agosto *m*, → **September**.

aunt [ɑːnt] *n* zia *f*.

au pair [ˌəʊˈpeəʳ] *n* ragazza *f* alla pari.

aural [ˈɔːrəl] *adj* uditivo(-a).

Australia [ɒˈstreɪlɪə] *n* l'Australia *f*.

Australian [ɒˈstreɪlɪən] *adj* australiano(-a) ♦ *n* australiano *m* (-a *f*).

Austria [ˈɒstrɪə] *n* l'Austria *f*.

Austrian [ˈɒstrɪən] *adj* austriaco(-a) ♦ *n* austriaco *m* (-a *f*).

authentic [ɔːˈθentɪk] *adj* autentico(-a).

author [ˈɔːθəʳ] *n (of book, article)* autore *m* (-trice *f); (by profession)* scrittore *m* (-trice *f*).

authority [ɔːˈθɒrɪtɪ] *n* autorità *f inv;* **the authorities** le autorità.

authorization [ˌɔːθəraɪˈzeɪʃn] *n* autorizzazione *f*.

authorize [ˈɔːθəraɪz] *vt* autorizzare; **to ~ sb to do sthg** autorizzare qn a fare qc.

autobiography [ˌɔːtəbaɪˈɒgrəfɪ] *n* autobiografia *f*.

autograph [ˈɔːtəgrɑːf] *n* autografo m.

automatic [ˌɔːtəˈmætɪk] adj automatico(-a) ◆ n (car) automobile f con cambio automatico.

automatically [ˌɔːtəˈmætɪklɪ] adv automaticamente.

automobile [ˈɔːtəməbiːl] n (Am) automobile f.

autumn [ˈɔːtəm] n autunno m; **in (the)** ~ in autunno.

auxiliary (verb) [ɔːgˈzɪljən-] n ausiliare m.

available [əˈveɪləbl] adj disponibile.

avalanche [ˈævəlɑːnʃ] n valanga f.

Ave. (abbr of avenue) V.le.

avenue [ˈævənjuː] n viale m.

average [ˈævərɪdʒ] adj medio(-a); (not very good) mediocre ◆ n media f; **on** ~ in media.

aversion [əˈvɜːʃn] n avversione f.

aviation [ˌeɪvɪˈeɪʃn] n aviazione f.

avid [ˈævɪd] adj avido(-a).

avocado [ˌævəˈkɑːdəʊ] (pl -s OR -es) n: ~ **(pear)** avocado m inv.

avoid [əˈvɔɪd] vt evitare; **to** ~ **doing sthg** evitare di fare qc.

await [əˈweɪt] vt attendere.

awake [əˈweɪk] (pt awoke, pp awoken) adj sveglio(-a) ◆ vi svegliarsi.

award [əˈwɔːd] n premio m ◆ vt: **to** ~ **sb sthg** (prize) assegnare qc a qn; (damages, compensation) accordare qc a qn.

aware [əˈweəʳ] adj consapevole; **to be** ~ **of** rendersi conto di.

away [əˈweɪ] adv via; (look, turn) da un'altra parte; **to drive** ~ allontanarsi; **to walk** ~ allontanarsi; **to**

go ~ **on holiday** partire per le vacanze; **to put sthg** ~ mettere via qc, mettere a posto qc; **to take sthg** ~ **(from sb)** portare via qc (a qn), prendere qc (a qn); **far** ~ molto lontano; **it's 10 miles** ~ **(from here)** è a 10 miglia (da qui); **the festival is two weeks** ~ mancano due settimane al festival.

awesome [ˈɔːsəm] adj (impressive) imponente; (inf: excellent) fantastico(-a).

awful [ˈɔːfəl] adj orribile; **I feel** ~ sto malissimo; **an** ~ **lot of** un mucchio di.

awfully [ˈɔːflɪ] adv (very) molto, terribilmente.

awkward [ˈɔːkwəd] adj (movement) sgraziato(-a); (position) goffo(-a); (shape, size) poco funzionale; (situation, question) imbarazzante; (task, time) difficile.

awning [ˈɔːnɪŋ] n tenda f.

awoke [əˈwəʊk] pt → **awake**.

awoken [əˈwəʊkən] pp → **awake**.

axe [æks] n scure f.

axle [ˈæksl] n asse m.

B

BA (abbr of Bachelor of Arts) (degree) laurea f in materie umanistiche; (person) laureato m (-a f) in materie umanistiche.

babble [ˈbæbl] vi balbettare.

baby [ˈbeɪbɪ] n bambino m (-a f); **to have a** ~ avere un bambino; ~

sweetcorn piccole spighe di mais.
baby carriage n (Am) carrozzina f.
baby food n alimenti mpl per l'infanzia.
baby-sit vi fare da baby-sitter.
baby wipe n salvietta f umidificata (per bambini).
back [bæk] adv indietro ◆ n (of person) schiena f; (of chair) schienale m; (of car, book, bank note) retro m; (of room) fondo m; (of hand) dorso m ◆ adj (seat, wheels) posteriore ◆ vi (car, driver) fare retromarcia ◆ vt (support) appoggiare; **to put sthg ~** rimettere qc (a posto); **to arrive ~** ritornare; **to give sthg ~** restituire OR dare indietro qc; **to write ~ to sb** rispondere a qn; **at the ~ of** sul retro di, dietro; **in ~ of** (Am) sul retro di, dietro; **~ to front** davanti di dietro ❏ **back up** vt sep (support) appoggiare ◆ vi (car, driver) fare retromarcia.
backache ['bækeɪk] n mal m di schiena.
backbone ['bækbəʊn] n spina f dorsale.
back door n porta f posteriore.
backfire [ˌbæk'faɪəʳ] vi (car) fare un'autoaccensione.
background ['bækgraʊnd] n sfondo m; (of person) background m inv.
backlog ['bæklɒg] n cumulo m; **a ~ of work** del lavoro arretrato.
backpack ['bækpæk] n zaino m.
backpacker ['bækpækəʳ] n persona che viaggia con zaino e sacco a pelo.
back seat n sedile m posteriore.
backside [ˌbæk'saɪd] n (inf) sedere m.
back street n viuzza f.
backstroke ['bækstrəʊk] n dorso m (nel nuoto).
backwards ['bækwədz] adv (look) indietro; (fall, move) all'indietro; (wrong way round) al contrario.
bacon ['beɪkən] n pancetta f, bacon m; **~ and eggs** uova fpl e pancetta.
bacteria [bæk'tɪərɪə] npl batteri mpl.
bad [bæd] (compar **worse**, superl **worst**) adj cattivo(-a); (harmful) dannoso(-a); (accident, wound) brutto(-a); (eyesight, heart) debole; (arm, leg) malandato(-a); **drinking is ~ for you** bere ti fa male; **to go ~** (milk, yoghurt) andare a male; **not ~** (film, food, journey) niente male; **how are you? — not ~** come stai? — non c'è male.
badge [bædʒ] n distintivo m.
badger ['bædʒəʳ] n tasso m.
badly ['bædlɪ] (compar **worse**, superl **worst**) adv male; (injured) gravemente; (affected) profondamente; (very much) tanto.
badly paid [-peɪd] adj mal pagato(-a).
badminton ['bædmɪntən] n badminton m.
bad-tempered [-'tempəd] adj irascibile.
bag [bæg] n sacchetto m; (handbag) borsa f; (piece of luggage) borsone m; **a ~ of crisps** un sacchetto di patatine.
bagel ['beɪgəl] n panino a forma di ciambella.
baggage ['bægɪdʒ] n bagagli mpl.
baggage allowance n franchigia f bagaglio.

baggage reclaim *n* ritiro *m* bagagli.

baggy ['bægı] *adj* largo(-a).

bagpipes ['bægpaɪps] *npl* cornamusa *f*.

bail [beɪl] *n* cauzione *f*.

bait [beɪt] *n* esca *f*.

bake [beɪk] *vt* cuocere (al forno) ♦ *n*: **vegetable ~** verdure *fpl* al forno.

baked [beɪkt] *adj* cotto(-a) al forno.

baked Alaska [-ə'læskə] *n* meringata *f*.

baked beans *npl* fagioli *mpl* al sugo di pomodoro.

baked potato *n* patata *f* cotta al forno con la buccia.

baker ['beɪkər] *n* fornaio *m* (-a *f*); **~'s** *(shop)* panificio *m*, panetteria *f*.

Bakewell tart ['beɪkwel-] *n* torta con una base di pasta frolla, uno strato di marmellata e uno di pan di Spagna alle mandorle, ricoperta da una glassa dal caratteristico aspetto a onde.

balance ['bæləns] *n* (of person) equilibrio *m*; (of bank account, remainder) saldo *m* ♦ *vt* (object) tenere in equilibrio.

balcony ['bælkənı] *n* balcone *m*.

bald [bɔːld] *adj* calvo(-a).

bale [beɪl] *n* balla *f*.

ball [bɔːl] *n* (SPORT) palla *f*; (in football, rugby) pallone *m*; (in golf, table tennis) pallina *f*; (of wool, string) gomitolo *m*; (dance) ballo *m*; **on the ~** (fig) in gamba.

ballad ['bæləd] *n* ballata *f*.

ballerina [,bælə'riːnə] *n* ballerina *f*.

ballet ['bæleɪ] *n* balletto *m*.

ballet dancer *n* ballerino *m* classico (ballerina classica *f*).

balloon [bə'luːn] *n* (at party etc) palloncino *m*.

ballot ['bælət] *n* (vote) votazione *f* a scrutinio segreto.

ballpoint pen ['bɔːlpɔɪnt-] *n* penna *f* a sfera.

ballroom ['bɔːlrʊm] *n* sala *f* da ballo.

ballroom dancing *n* ballo *m* liscio.

bamboo [bæm'buː] *n* bambù *m*.

bamboo shoots *npl* germogli *mpl* di bambù.

ban [bæn] *n* divieto *m* ♦ *vt* vietare; **to ~ sb from doing sthg** vietare a qn di fare qc.

banana [bə'nɑːnə] *n* banana *f*.

banana split *n* banana split *f* inv.

band [bænd] *n* (musical group) banda *f*; (for rock, jazz) complesso *m*, gruppo *m*; (strip of paper, rubber) striscia *f*.

bandage ['bændɪdʒ] *n* benda *f* ♦ *vt* fasciare.

B and B *abbr* = **bed and breakfast.**

bandstand ['bændstænd] *n* palco *m* dell'orchestra.

bang [bæŋ] *n* (of gun, explosion) scoppio *m* ♦ *vt* sbattere.

banger ['bæŋər] *n* (Br: inf: sausage) salsiccia *f*; **~s and mash** salsicce e purè di patate.

bangle ['bæŋgl] *n* braccialetto *m*.

bangs [bæŋz] *npl* (Am) frangia *f*.

banister ['bænɪstər] *n* ringhiera *f*.

banjo ['bændʒəʊ] (pl **-s** OR **-es**) *n* banjo *m* inv.

bank [bæŋk] *n (for money)* banca *f; (of river, lake)* riva *f; (slope)* scarpata *f.*

bank account *n* conto *m* bancario.

bank book *n* libretto *m* di banca.

bank charges *npl* commissioni *fpl* bancarie.

bank clerk *n* impiegato *m* (-a *f*) di banca.

bank draft *n* assegno *m* circolare.

banker ['bæŋkə'] *n* banchiere *m.*

banker's card *n* carta *f* assegni.

bank holiday *n (Br)* giorno *m* festivo.

bank manager *n* direttore *m* (-trice *f*) di banca.

bank note *n* banconota *f.*

bankrupt ['bæŋkrʌpt] *adj* fallito(-a).

bank statement *n* estratto *m* conto.

banner ['bænə'] *n* striscione *m.*

bannister ['bænɪstə'] = **banister**.

banquet ['bæŋkwɪt] *n (formal dinner)* banchetto *m; (at Indian restaurant etc)* menu per più persone.

bap [bæp] *n (Br)* panino *m.*

baptize [*Br* bæp'taɪz, *Am* 'bæptaɪz] *vt* battezzare.

bar [bɑ:'] *n (pub, in hotel)* bar *m inv; (counter in pub)* banco *m; (of metal, wood)* sbarra *f; (of chocolate)* tavoletta *f* ♦ *vt (obstruct)* sbarrare; **a ~ of soap** una saponetta.

barbecue ['bɑ:bɪkju:] *n* barbecue *m inv* ♦ *vt* arrostire alla griglia.

barbecue sauce *n* salsa picante usata per condire carne o pesce alla griglia.

barbed wire [bɑ:bd-] *n* filo *m* spinato.

barber ['bɑ:bə'] *n* barbiere *m;* **~'s** *(shop)* barbiere *m.*

bar code *n* codice *m* a barre.

bare [beə'] *adj (feet, arms)* nudo(-a); *(head)* scoperto(-a); *(room, cupboard)* vuoto(-a); **the ~ minimum** il minimo indispensabile.

barefoot [,beə'fut] *adv* a piedi nudi.

barely ['beəlɪ] *adv (hardly)* appena; *(with difficulty)* a malapena.

bargain ['bɑ:gɪn] *n (agreement)* accordo *m; (cheap buy)* occasione *f* ♦ *vi (haggle)* contrattare sul prezzo ❑ **bargain for** *vt fus* aspettarsi.

bargain basement *n* reparto *m* occasioni.

barge [bɑ:dʒ] *n* chiatta *f* ❑ **barge in** *vi* fare irruzione; **to ~ in on sb** interrompere qn.

bark [bɑ:k] *n (of tree)* corteccia *f* ♦ *vi* abbaiare.

barley ['bɑ:lɪ] *n* orzo *m.*

barmaid ['bɑ:meɪd] *n* barista *f.*

barman ['bɑ:mən] *(pl* **-men** [-mən]) *n* barista *m.*

bar meal *n* pasto leggero servito in un bar o un pub.

barn [bɑ:n] *n* granaio *m.*

barometer [bə'rɒmɪtə'] *n* barometro *m.*

baron ['bærən] *n* barone *m.*

baroque [bə'rɒk] *adj* barocco(-a).

barracks ['bærəks] *npl* caserma *f.*

barrage ['bærɑ:ʒ] *n (of questions)*

raffica f; *(of criticism)* ondata f.

barrel ['bærəl] n *(of beer, wine, oil)* barile m; *(of gun)* canna f.

barren ['bærən] adj *(land, soil)* sterile.

barricade [ˌbærɪ'keɪd] n barricata f.

barrier ['bærɪər] n barriera f.

barrister ['bærɪstər] n *(Br)* avvocato m.

bartender ['bɑːtendər] n *(Am)* barista m.

barter ['bɑːtər] vi barattare.

base [beɪs] n base f ♦ vt: to ~ sthg on basare qc su; I'm ~d in London ho base a Londra.

baseball ['beɪsbɔːl] n baseball m.

baseball cap n cappellino m da baseball.

basement ['beɪsmənt] n seminterrato m.

bases ['beɪsiːz] pl → basis.

bash [bæʃ] vt *(inf)* sbattere.

basic ['beɪsɪk] adj *(fundamental)* fondamentale; *(accommodation, meal)* semplice ▫ **basics** npl: the ~s i rudimenti.

basically ['beɪsɪklɪ] adv *(in conversation)* in sostanza; *(fundamentally)* fondamentalmente.

basil ['bæzl] n basilico m.

basin ['beɪsn] n *(washbasin)* lavabo m; *(bowl)* terrina f.

basis ['beɪsɪs] *(pl -ses)* n base f; on a weekly ~ settimanalmente; on the ~ of sulla base di.

basket ['bɑːskɪt] n cesto m.

basketball ['bɑːskɪtbɔːl] n *(game)* pallacanestro f.

basmati rice [bəz'mætɪ-] n tipo di riso aromatico utilizzato nella cucina indiana.

bass¹ [beɪs] n *(singer)* basso m ♦ adj: ~ guitar basso m.

bass² [bæs] n *(freshwater fish)* pesce m persico; *(sea fish)* spigola f, branzino m.

bassoon [bə'suːn] n fagotto m.

bastard ['bɑːstəd] n *(vulg)* stronzo m (-a f).

bat [bæt] n *(in cricket, baseball)* mazza f; *(in table tennis)* racchetta f; *(animal)* pipistrello m.

batch [bætʃ] n *(of goods)* lotto m; *(of people)* scaglione m.

bath [bɑːθ] n bagno m; *(tub)* vasca f *(da bagno)* ♦ vt fare il bagno a; to have a ~ fare il bagno □ **baths** npl *(Br: public swimming pool)* piscina f.

bathe [beɪð] vi fare il bagno.

bathing ['beɪðɪŋ] n *(Br)* balneazione f.

bathrobe ['bɑːθrəʊb] n *(for bathroom, swimming pool)* accappatoio m; *(dressing gown)* vestaglia f.

bathroom ['bɑːθrʊm] n bagno m.

bathroom cabinet n armadietto m del bagno.

bathtub ['bɑːθtʌb] n vasca f da bagno.

baton ['bætən] n *(of conductor)* bacchetta f; *(truncheon)* manganello m.

batter ['bætər] n *(CULIN)* pastella f ♦ vt picchiare.

battered ['bætəd] adj *(CULIN)* ricoperto di pastella e fritto.

battery ['bætərɪ] n *(for radio)* pila f; *(for car)* batteria f.

battery charger [-ˌtʃɑːdʒər] n caricabatteria m inv.

battle ['bætl] n battaglia f.

battlefield ['bætlfiːld] n campo

m di battaglia.

battlements [ˈbætlmənts] *npl* parapetto *m*.

battleship [ˈbætlʃɪp] *n* corazzata *f*.

bay [beɪ] *n* (on coast) baia *f*; (for parking) posto *m* macchina.

bay leaf *n* foglia *f* d'alloro.

bay window *n* bow-window *m inv*.

B & B *abbr* = bed and breakfast.

BC (abbr of before Christ) a.C.

be [biː] (*pt* was, were, *pp* been) *vi*
1. (exist) essere; **there is** c'è; **there are** ci sono; **are there any shops near here?** ci sono dei negozi qui vicino?

2. (referring to location) essere; **the hotel is near the airport** l'albergo è OR si trova vicino all'aeroporto.

3. (referring to movement): **has the postman been?** è venuto il postino?; **have you ever been to Ireland?** sei mai stato in Irlanda?; **I'll ~ there in ten minutes** sarò lì tra dieci minuti.

4. (occur) essere; **my birthday is in November** il mio compleanno è in novembre.

5. (identifying, describing) essere; **he's a doctor** è medico; **I'm Italian** sono italiano; **I'm hot/cold** ho caldo/freddo.

6. (referring to health) stare; **how are you?** come sta?; **I'm fine** sto bene; **she's ill** è malata.

7. (referring to age): **how old are you?** quanti anni hai?; **I'm 14 (years old)** ho 14 anni.

8. (referring to cost) costare; **how much is it?** (item) quanto costa?; (meal, shopping) quant'è?; **it's £10**

(item) costa 10 sterline; (meal, shopping) sono 10 sterline.

9. (referring to time, dates) essere; **what time is it?** che ore sono?; **it's ten o'clock** sono le dieci; **it's the 9th of April** è il 9 aprile.

10. (referring to measurement) essere; **it's 2 m wide/long** è largo/lungo 2 m; **I'm 6 feet tall** sono alto 1 metro e 80; **I'm 8 stone** peso 50 chili.

11. (referring to weather) fare; **it's hot/cold** fa caldo/freddo; **it's sunny** c'è il sole; **it's windy** c'è vento; **it's going to be nice today** oggi farà bello.

♦ *aux vb* 1. (forming continuous tense): **I'm learning Italian** sto imparando l'italiano; **what are you reading?** cosa stai leggendo?, cosa leggi?; **he's arriving tomorrow** arriva domani, arriverà domani; **we've been visiting the museum** abbiamo visitato il museo.

2. (forming passive) essere; **the flight was delayed** il volo è stato ritardato.

3. (with infinitive to express order): **all rooms are to ~ vacated by 10 a.m.** tutte le camere devono essere lasciate libere per le 10.

4. (with infinitive to express future tense): **the race is to start at noon** la corsa è prevista per mezzogiorno.

5. (in tag questions): **it's cold, isn't it?** fa freddo, (non è) vero?

beach [biːtʃ] *n* spiaggia *f*.

bead [biːd] *n* (of glass, wood etc) grano *m*.

beak [biːk] *n* becco *m*.

beaker [ˈbiːkəʳ] *n* bicchiere *m*.

beam [biːm] *n* (of light) raggio *m*; (of wood, concrete) trave *f* ♦ *vi* (smile) sorridere.

bean [bi:n] n fagiolo m; (of coffee) chicco m.

bean curd [-kɜːd] n tofu m.

beansprouts ['bi:nsprauts] npl germogli mpl di soia.

bear [beəʳ] (pt bore, pp borne) n (animal) orso m ◆ vt (support) reggere; (endure) sopportare; **to ~ left/right** tenersi sulla sinistra/destra.

bearable ['beərəbl] adj sopportabile.

beard [bɪəd] n barba f.

bearer ['beərəʳ] n (of cheque) portatore m; (of passport) titolare mf.

bearing ['beərɪŋ] n (relevance) attinenza f; **to get one's ~s** orizzontarsi.

beast [bi:st] n bestia f.

beat [bi:t] (pt beat, pp beaten [bi:tn]) n (of heart, pulse) battito m; (MUS) tempo m ◆ vt battere; (eggs, cream) sbattere ❑ **beat down** vi (sun, rain) battere ◆ vt sep: **I ~ him down to £20** gli ho fatto abbassare il prezzo a 20 sterline; **beat up** vt sep pestare.

beautiful ['bju:tɪful] adj bello(-a).

beauty ['bju:tɪ] n bellezza f.

beauty parlour n istituto m di bellezza.

beauty spot n (place) bellezza f naturale.

beaver ['bi:vəʳ] n castoro m.

became [bɪˈkeɪm] pt → become.

because [bɪˈkɒz] conj perché; **~ of** a causa di.

beckon ['bekən] vi: **to ~ (to)** fare cenno (a).

become [bɪˈkʌm] (pt **became**, pp

become) vi diventare; **what became of him?** cosa ne è stato di lui?

bed [bed] n letto m; (of sea) fondo m; (CULIN) strato m; **in ~** a letto; **to get out of ~** alzarsi; **to go to ~** andare a letto; **to go to ~ with sb** andare a letto con qn; **to make the ~** fare il letto.

bed and breakfast n (Br) = pensione f.

---

i BED AND BREAKFAST

I "B & B", anche detti "guest houses", sono delle abitazioni private che hanno una o più camere riservate ad ospiti paganti. Si trovano in tutte le città e principali località turistiche e sono di solito meno care degli alberghi. Nel prezzo della camera è inclusa la tipica colazione all'inglese, a base di uova e pancetta, salsicce, pane tostato, tè o caffè.

---

bedclothes ['bedkləʊðz] npl lenzuola fpl e coperte fpl.

bedding ['bedɪŋ] n biancheria f da letto.

bed linen n lenzuola fpl (e federe fpl).

bedroom ['bedrom] n camera f da letto.

bedside table ['bedsaɪd-] n comodino m.

bedsit ['bed,sɪt] n (Br) camera f ammobiliata.

bedspread ['bedspred] n copriletto m inv.

bedtime ['bedtaɪm] n ora f di andare a letto.

bee [bi:] n ape f.

beech [bi:tʃ] n faggio m.

beef [bi:f] n manzo m; ~ Wellington pasticcio m di manzo.

beefburger ['bi:f,bɜ:gəʳ] n hamburger m inv.

beehive ['bi:haɪv] n alveare m.

been [bi:n] pp → be.

beer [bɪəʳ] n birra f.

BEER

La birra è di granlunga la bevanda alcolica più diffusa in Gran Bretagna. Qui, le birre si dividono in due categorie principali: "bitter" e "lager". La "bitter", conosciuta in Scozia come "heavy", è birra scura e ha un sapore amarognolo, mentre la "lager" è la birra chiara diffusa anche nel resto d'Europa. La "real ale" è un particolare tipo di birra scura, prodotto da piccole birrerie con metodi tradizionali e generalmente è più cara. Negli Stati Uniti la birra è prevalentemente birra chiara.

beer garden n giardino per i clienti di un pub.

beer mat n sottobicchiere m.

beetle ['bi:tl] n scarabeo m.

beetroot ['bi:tru:t] n barbabietola f.

before [bɪ'fɔ:ʳ] adv prima ◆ prep prima di; (fml: in front of) davanti a ◆ conj: ~ it gets too late prima che sia troppo tardi; I've been there ~ ci sono già stato; ~ doing sthg prima di fare qc; ~ you leave prima di partire; the day ~ il giorno prima; the week ~ last due settimane fa.

beforehand [bɪ'fɔ:hænd] adv in anticipo.

befriend [bɪ'frend] vt trattare da amico.

beg [beg] vi elemosinare ◆ vt: to ~ sb to do sthg supplicare qn di fare qc; to ~ for sthg elemosinare qc.

began [bɪ'gæn] pt → begin.

beggar ['begəʳ] n mendicante mf.

begin [bɪ'gɪn] (pt began, pp begun) vt & vi cominciare, iniziare; to ~ doing OR to do sthg cominciare a fare qc; to ~ by doing sthg cominciare col fare qc; to ~ with (at the start) all'inizio; (firstly) per prima cosa.

beginner [bɪ'gɪnəʳ] n principiante mf.

beginning [bɪ'gɪnɪŋ] n inizio m.

begun [bɪ'gʌn] pp → begin.

behalf [bɪ'hɑ:f] n: on ~ of a nome di.

behave [bɪ'heɪv] vi comportarsi; to ~ (o.s.) (be good) comportarsi bene.

behavior [bɪ'heɪvjəʳ] (Am) = behaviour.

behaviour [bɪ'heɪvjəʳ] n comportamento m.

behind [bɪ'haɪnd] adv (at the back) dietro; (late) indietro ◆ prep (at the back of) dietro ◆ n (inf) didietro m; to leave sthg ~ dimenticare qc; to stay ~ restare indietro; we're all ~ you (supporting) siamo tutti con te.

beige [beɪʒ] adj beige (inv).

being ['bi:ɪŋ] n essere m; to come into ~ nascere.

belated [bɪ'leɪtɪd] adj tardivo(-a).

belch [beltʃ] vi ruttare.

Belgian ['beldʒən] adj belga ◆ n belga mf.

Belgian waffle n (Am) cialda

dalla caratteristica superficie a quadretti che si mangia con sciroppo d'acero, panna o frutta.

Belgium ['beldʒəm] n il Belgio.

belief [bɪ'liːf] n (faith) fede f; (opinion) convinzione f.

believe [bɪ'liːv] vt credere ♦ vi: to ~ in (God) credere in; to ~ in doing sthg credere che sia giusto fare qc.

believer [bɪ'liːvəʳ] n credente mf.

bell [bel] n (of church) campana f; (of phone) suoneria f; (of door) campanello m.

bellboy ['belbɔɪ] n fattorino m d'albergo.

bellow ['beləʊ] vi muggire.

belly ['belɪ] n (inf) pancia f.

belly button n (inf) ombelico m.

belong [bɪ'lɒŋ] vi (be in right place) essere al suo posto; to ~ to (property) appartenere a; (to club, party) far parte di; where does this ~? dove sta questo?

belongings [bɪ'lɒŋɪŋz] npl effetti mpl personali.

below [bɪ'ləʊ] adv sotto; (downstairs) di sotto; (in text) qui sotto ♦ prep sotto.

belt [belt] n (for clothes) cintura f; (TECH) cinghia f.

beltway ['beltweɪ] n (Am) raccordo m anulare. •

bench [bentʃ] n panchina f.

bend [bend] (pt & pp bent) n (in road) curva f; (in river) ansa f; (in pipe) gomito m ♦ vt piegare ♦ vi (road, river, pipe) fare una curva ❑ **bend down** vi abbassarsi; **bend over** vi chinarsi.

beneath [bɪ'niːθ] adv & prep sotto.

beneficial [ˌbenɪ'fɪʃl] adj benefico(-a).

benefit ['benɪfɪt] n (advantage) beneficio m; (money) indennità f inv ♦ vt giovare a ♦ vi: to ~ (from) beneficiare (di); for the ~ of per.

benign [bɪ'naɪn] adj (MED) benigno(-a).

bent [bent] pt & pp → bend.

bereaved [bɪ'riːvd] adj (family) del defunto.

beret ['bereɪ] n basco m.

Bermuda shorts [bə'mjuːdə] npl bermuda mpl.

berry ['berɪ] n bacca f.

berserk [bə'zɜːk] adj: to go ~ andare su tutte le furie.

berth [bɜːθ] n (for ship) ormeggio m; (in ship, train) cuccetta f.

beside [bɪ'saɪd] prep (next to) accanto a; that's ~ the point questo non c'entra.

besides [bɪ'saɪdz] adv inoltre ♦ prep oltre a.

best [best] adj migliore ♦ adv meglio ♦ n: the ~ il migliore (la migliore); a pint of ~ (beer) ≈ un boccale di birra scura; I like this one ~ questo mi piace più di tutti; she played ~ ha giocato meglio di tutti; the ~ thing to do is ... la miglior cosa da fare è ...; to make the ~ of sthg accontentarsi di qc; to do one's ~ fare del proprio meglio; '~ before ...' 'da consumarsi preferibilmente entro ...'; at ~ per bene che vada; all the ~! auguri!

best man n testimone m (di nozze).

best-seller [ˌ'seləʳ] n (book) best seller m inv.

bet [bet] (pt & pp bet) n scommessa f ♦ vt scommettere ♦ vi: **to ~ (on)** scommettere (su); **I ~ (that) you can't do it** scommetto che non sei capace di farlo.

betray [bɪ'treɪ] vt tradire.

better ['betər] adj migliore ♦ adv meglio; **she's ~ at tennis than me** è più brava di me a tennis; **are you ~ now?** stai meglio adesso?; **you had ~ ...** faresti meglio a ...; **to get ~** migliorare.

betting ['betɪŋ] n scommesse fpl.

betting shop n (Br) = sala f scommesse.

between [bɪ'twiːn] prep tra, fra ♦ adv (in time) nel frattempo; **in ~** (in space) in mezzo; (in time) nel frattempo.

beverage ['bevərɪdʒ] n (fml) bevanda f.

beware [bɪ'weər] vi: **to ~ of** stare attento a; **'~ of the dog'** 'attenti al cane'.

bewildered [bɪ'wɪldəd] adj sconcertato(-a).

beyond [bɪ'jɒnd] prep oltre ♦ adv più avanti; **~ doubt** senza dubbio; **~ reach** irraggiungibile.

biased ['baɪəst] adj di parte.

bib [bɪb] n (for baby) bavaglino m.

bible ['baɪbl] n bibbia f.

biceps ['baɪseps] n bicipite m.

bicycle ['baɪsɪkl] n bicicletta f.

bicycle path n pista f ciclabile.

bicycle pump n pompa f per la bicicletta.

bid [bɪd] (pt & pp **bid**) n (at auction) offerta f; (attempt) tentativo m ♦ vt (money) fare un'offerta di ♦ vi: **to ~ (for)** fare un'offerta (per).

bidet ['biːdeɪ] n bidè m inv.

big [bɪg] adj grande; (problem, mistake, risk) grosso(-a); **my ~ brother** mio fratello maggiore; **how ~ is it?** quanto è grande?

bike [baɪk] n (inf) (bicycle) bici f inv; (motorcycle) moto f inv.

biking ['baɪkɪŋ] n: **to go ~** (on bicycle) andare in bicicletta; (on motorcycle) andare in moto.

bikini [bɪ'kiːnɪ] n bikini® m inv.

bikini bottom n pezzo m di sotto del bikini®.

bikini top n pezzo m di sopra del bikini®.

bilingual [baɪ'lɪŋgwəl] adj bilingue.

bill [bɪl] n (for meal, hotel room) conto m; (for electricity etc) bolletta f; (Am: bank note) banconota f; (at cinema, theatre) programma m; (POL) proposta f di legge; **can I have the ~, please?** il conto, per favore.

billboard ['bɪlbɔːd] n tabellone m.

billfold ['bɪlfəuld] n (Am) portafoglio m.

billiards ['bɪljədz] n biliardo m.

billion ['bɪljən] n (thousand million) miliardo m; (Br: million million) mille miliardi.

bin [bɪn] n (rubbish bin) pattumiera f; (wastepaper bin) cestino m; (for flour) barattolo m; (on plane) armadietto m in alto; **bread ~** portapane m inv.

bind [baɪnd] (pt & pp **bound**) vt (tie up) legare.

binding ['baɪndɪŋ] n (of book) rilegatura f; (for ski) attacco m.

bingo ['bɪŋgəu] n = tombola f.

i BINGO

Questo gioco, simile alla tombola, è molto popolare in Gran Bretagna. I giocatori comprano delle cartelle con dei numeri, da contrassegnare man mano che vengono estratti. Vince chi completa per primo una fila di numeri o l'intera cartella. Si gioca in grandi sale, spesso ex cinema ristrutturati, e si vincono premi, talvolta in denaro.

binoculars [bɪˈnɒkjuləz] *npl* binocolo *m*.

biodegradable [ˌbaɪəʊdɪˈgreɪdəbl] *adj* biodegradabile.

biography [baɪˈɒgrəfɪ] *n* biografia *f*.

biological [ˌbaɪəˈlɒdʒɪkl] *adj* biologico(-a).

biology [baɪˈɒlədʒɪ] *n* biologia *f*.

birch [bɜːtʃ] *n* betulla *f*.

bird [bɜːd] *n* uccello *m*; (Br: inf: woman) pollastrella *f*.

bird-watching [-ˌwɒtʃɪŋ] *n* osservazione *f* degli uccelli.

Biro® [ˈbaɪərəʊ] (pl -s) *n* biro® *f inv*.

birth [bɜːθ] *n* nascita *f*; by ~ di nascita; to give ~ to dare alla luce, partorire.

birth certificate *n* certificato *m* di nascita.

birth control *n* controllo *m* delle nascite.

birthday [ˈbɜːθdeɪ] *n* compleanno *m*; happy ~! buon compleanno!

birthday card *n* biglietto *m* d'auguri di compleanno.

birthday party *n* festa *f* di compleanno.

birthplace [ˈbɜːθpleɪs] *n* luogo *m* di nascita.

biscuit [ˈbɪskɪt] *n* (Br) biscotto *m*; (Am: scone) focaccina di pasta non lievitata da mangiare con burro e marmellata o insieme a piatti salati.

bishop [ˈbɪʃəp] *n* (RELIG) vescovo *m*; (in chess) alfiere *m*.

bistro [ˈbiːstrəʊ] (pl -s) *n* ristorantino *m*.

bit [bɪt] *pt* → bite ♦ *n* (piece) pezzetto *m*; (of drill) punta *f*; (of bridle) morso *m*; (amount): a ~ un po'; a ~ of money un po' di soldi; to do a ~ of reading leggere un po'; not a ~ per niente; ~ by ~ a poco a poco.

bitch [bɪtʃ] *n* (vulg: woman) stronza *f*; (dog) cagna *f*.

bite [baɪt] (pt bit, pp bitten) *n* morso *m*; (from insect) puntura *f* ♦ *vt* mordere; (subj: insect) pungere; to have a ~ to eat mangiare un boccone.

bitter [ˈbɪtəʳ] *adj* (taste, food) amaro(-a); (weather, wind) pungente; (person) amareggiato(-a); (argument, conflict) aspro(-a) ♦ *n* (Br: beer) tipo di birra amarognola.

bitter lemon *n* limonata *f* amara.

bizarre [bɪˈzɑːʳ] *adj* bizzarro(-a).

black [blæk] *adj* nero(-a) ♦ *n* (colour) nero *m*; (person) negro *m* (-a *f*) ❑ **black out** *vi* perdere conoscenza.

black and white *adj* in bianco e nero.

blackberry [ˈblækbrɪ] *n* mora *f*.

blackbird [ˈblækbɜːd] *n* merlo *m*.

blackboard [ˈblækbɔːd] *n* lavagna *f*.

black cherry n ciliegia f nera.

blackcurrant [,blæk'kʌrənt] n ribes m inv nero.

black eye n occhio m nero.

Black Forest gâteau n torta f di cioccolato e panna.

black ice n strato m di ghiaccio invisibile.

blackmail ['blækmeɪl] n ricatto m ◆ vt ricattare.

blackout ['blækaʊt] n (power cut) black-out m inv.

black pepper n pepe m nero.

black pudding n (Br) sanguinaccio m.

blacksmith ['blæksmɪθ] n fabbro m.

bladder ['blædə^r] n vescica f.

blade [bleɪd] n (of knife, saw) lama f; (of propeller, oar) pala f; (of grass) filo m.

blame [bleɪm] n colpa f ◆ vt incolpare; **to ~ sthg for sthg** incolpare qn di qc; **to ~ sthg on sb** dare a qn la colpa di qc.

bland [blænd] adj (food) insipido(-a).

blank [blæŋk] adj (space, cassette) vuoto(-a); (page) bianco(-a); (expression) assente ◆ n (empty space) spazio m (in) bianco.

blank cheque n assegno m in bianco.

blanket ['blæŋkɪt] n coperta f.

blast [blɑːst] n (explosion) esplosione f; (of wind) raffica f; (of air) folata f ◆ excl (inf) maledizione!; **at full ~** a tutto volume.

blaze [bleɪz] n (fire) incendio m ◆ vi (fire) ardere; (sun, light) risplendere.

blazer ['bleɪzə^r] n blazer m inv.

bleach [bliːtʃ] n candeggina f ◆ vt (clothes) candeggiare; (hair) decolorare.

bleak [bliːk] adj triste.

bleed [bliːd] (pt & pp bled [bled]) vi sanguinare.

blend [blend] n (of coffee, whisky) miscela f ◆ vt mescolare.

blender ['blendə^r] n frullatore m.

bless [bles] vt benedire; **~ you!** (said after sneeze) salute!

blessing ['blesɪŋ] n benedizione f.

blew [bluː] pt → **blow**.

blind [blaɪnd] adj cieco(-a) ◆ n (for window) tendina f avvolgibile ◆ npl: **the ~** i non vedenti.

blind corner n svolta f senza visibilità.

blindfold ['blaɪndfəʊld] n benda f ◆ vt bendare.

blind spot n (AUT) punto m senza visibilità.

blink [blɪŋk] vi battere le palpebre.

blinkers ['blɪŋkəz] npl (Br) paraocchi mpl.

bliss [blɪs] n estasi f.

blister ['blɪstə^r] n vescica f.

blizzard ['blɪzəd] n bufera f di neve.

bloated ['bləʊtɪd] adj (after eating) strapieno(-a).

blob [blɒb] n (of paint) chiazza f.

block [blɒk] n (of stone, wood, ice) blocco m; (building) palazzo m; (Am: in town, city) isolato m ◆ vt (obstruct) bloccare; **to have a ~ed (up) nose** avere il naso chiuso ❑ **block up** vt sep ostruire.

blockage ['blɒkɪdʒ] n ostruzione f.

block capitals *npl* stampatello *m* maiuscolo.

block of flats *n* condominio *m*.

bloke [bləʊk] *n (Br: inf)* tipo *m*, tizio *m*.

blond [blɒnd] *adj* biondo(-a) ◆ *n* biondo *m*.

blonde [blɒnd] *adj* biondo(-a) ◆ *n* bionda *f*.

blood [blʌd] *n* sangue *m*.

blood donor *n* donatore *m* (-trice *f*) di sangue.

blood group *n* gruppo *m* sanguigno.

blood poisoning *n* setticemia *f*.

blood pressure *n* pressione *f* sanguigna; **to have high ~** avere la pressione alta; **to have low ~** avere la pressione bassa.

bloodshot ['blʌdʃɒt] *adj* arrossato(-a).

blood test *n* analisi *f inv* del sangue.

blood transfusion *n* trasfusione *f* di sangue.

bloody ['blʌdɪ] *adj (hands, handkerchief)* insanguinato(-a); *(Br: vulg: damn)* maledetto(-a) ◆ *adv (Br: vulg)* veramente.

bloody mary [-'meərɪ] *n* Bloody Mary *m inv*.

bloom [blu:m] *n* fiore *m* ◆ *vi* fiorire; **in ~** in fiore.

blossom ['blɒsəm] *n* fiori *mpl*.

blot [blɒt] *n* macchia *f*.

blotch [blɒtʃ] *n* chiazza *f*.

blotting paper ['blɒtɪŋ-] *n* carta *f* assorbente.

blouse [blaʊz] *n* camicetta *f*.

blow [bləʊ] *(pt* blew, *pp* blown) *vt*

(subj: wind) soffiare; *(whistle, trumpet)* suonare; *(bubbles)* fare ◆ *vi* soffiare; *(fuse)* saltare ◆ *n* colpo *m*; **to ~ one's nose** soffiarsi il naso ▫ **blow up** *vt sep (cause to explode)* far saltare in aria; *(inflate)* gonfiare ◆ *vi (explode)* saltare in aria.

blow-dry *n* piega *f* föhn ◆ *vt* fonare.

blown [bləʊn] *pp* → blow.

BLT *n* panino imbottito con pancetta, lattuga e pomodoro.

blue [blu:] *adj* azzurro(-a); *(film)* spinto(-a) ◆ *n* azzurro *m* ▫ **blues** *n (MUS)* blues *m*.

bluebell ['blu:bel] *n* campanula *f*.

blueberry ['blu:bərɪ] *n* mirtillo *m*.

bluebottle ['blu:ˌbɒtl] *n* moscone *m*.

blue cheese *n* formaggio con muffa di stagionatura.

bluff [blʌf] *n (cliff)* promontorio *m* ◆ *vi* bleffare.

blunder ['blʌndə*r*] *n* cantonata *f*.

blunt [blʌnt] *adj (pencil)* spuntato(-a); *(knife)* non affilato(-a); *(fig: person)* brusco(-a).

blurred [blɜːd] *adj (photo)* sfocato(-a); *(vision)* offuscato(-a).

blush [blʌʃ] *vi* arrossire.

blusher ['blʌʃə*r*] *n* fard *m inv*.

blustery ['blʌstərɪ] *adj* burrascoso(-a).

board [bɔ:d] *n (plank)* tavola *f*; *(notice board, for games)* tabellone *m*; *(for chess)* scacchiera *f*; *(blackboard)* lavagna *f*; *(of company)* consiglio *m* d'amministrazione ◆ *vt (plane, ship)* imbarcarsi su; *(bus)* salire su; **~ and lodging** vitto e alloggio; **full ~** pensione *f* completa; **half ~** mezza pensione; **on ~** *adv* a bordo ◆ *prep* su.

board game *n* gioco *m* di società.

boarding ['bɔːdɪŋ] *n* imbarco *m*.

boarding card *n* carta *f* d'imbarco.

boardinghouse ['bɔːdɪŋhaʊs, *pl* -hauzɪz] *n* pensione *f*.

boarding school *n* collegio *m*.

board of directors *n* consiglio *m* d'amministrazione.

boast [bəʊst] *vi*: **to ~ (about sthg)** vantarsi (di qc).

boat [bəʊt] *n* (small) barca *f*; (large) nave *f*; **by ~** in barca.

bob [bɒb] *n* (hairstyle) carré *m inv*.

bobby pin ['bɒbɪ-] *n* (Am) forcina *f*.

bodice ['bɒdɪs] *n* corpino *m*.

body ['bɒdɪ] *n* corpo *m*; (of car) carrozzeria *f*; (organization) organismo *m*.

bodyguard ['bɒdɪgɑːd] *n* (person) guardia *f* del corpo.

bodywork ['bɒdɪwɜːk] *n* carrozzeria *f*.

bog [bɒg] *n* pantano *m*.

bogus ['bəʊgəs] *adj* falso(-a).

boil [bɔɪl] *vt* (water) bollire, far bollire; (kettle) mettere a bollire; (food) lessare ◆ *vi* bollire ◆ *n* (on skin) foruncolo *m*.

boiled egg [bɔɪld-] *n* uovo *m* alla coque.

boiled potatoes [bɔɪld-] *npl* patate *fpl* lesse.

boiler ['bɔɪləʳ] *n* caldaia *f*.

boiling (hot) ['bɔɪlɪŋ-] *adj* (inf) (water) bollente; **I'm ~** sto morendo di caldo; **it's ~** si scoppia dal caldo.

bold [bəʊld] *adj* (brave) audace.

bollard ['bɒlɑːd] *n* (Br: on road) colonnina *f* spartitraffico.

bolt [bəʊlt] *n* (on door, window) chiavistello *m*; (screw) bullone *m* ◆ *vt* (door, window) sprangare.

bomb [bɒm] *n* bomba *f* ◆ *vt* bombardare.

bombard [bɒm'bɑːd] *vt* bombardare.

bomb scare *n* allarme causato dalla presunta presenza di una bomba.

bomb shelter *n* rifugio *m* antiaereo.

bond [bɒnd] *n* (tie, connection) legame *m*.

bone [bəʊn] *n* (of person, animal) osso *m*; (of fish) lisca *f*.

boned [bəʊnd] *adj* (chicken) disossato(-a); (fish) senza lische.

boneless ['bəʊnləs] *adj* (chicken, pork) disossato(-a).

bonfire ['bɒn,faɪəʳ] *n* falò *m inv*.

bonnet ['bɒnɪt] *n* (Br: of car) cofano *m*.

bonus ['bəʊnəs] (pl -es) *n* (extra money) gratifica *f*; (additional advantage) extra *m inv*.

bony ['bəʊnɪ] *adj* (fish) pieno(-a) di spine; (chicken) pieno di ossi.

boo [buː] *vi* fischiare.

boogie ['buːgɪ] *vi* (inf) ballare.

book [bʊk] *n* libro *m*; (for writing in) quaderno *m*; (of tickets, stamps) blocchetto *m*; (of matches) pacchetto *m* ◆ *vt* (reserve) prenotare ❑

book in *vi* (at hotel) registrarsi.

bookable ['bʊkəbl] *adj* (seats, flight) prenotabile.

bookcase ['bʊkkeɪs] *n* libreria *f*.

booking ['bʊkɪŋ] n (reservation) prenotazione f.

booking office n (at theatre) botteghino m; (at station) ufficio m prenotazioni.

bookkeeping ['bʊk,ki:pɪŋ] n contabilità f.

booklet ['bʊklɪt] n opuscolo m.

bookmaker's ['bʊk,meɪkəz] n = sala f scommesse.

bookmark ['bʊkmɑ:k] n segnalibro m.

bookshelf ['bʊkʃelf] (pl -shelves [-ʃelvz]) n scaffale m.

bookshop ['bʊkʃɒp] n libreria f.

bookstall ['bʊkstɔ:l] n bancarella f di libri.

bookstore ['bʊkstɔ:ʳ] = bookshop.

book token n buono m libri.

boom [bu:m] n (sudden growth) boom m inv ◆ vi (voice, guns) tuonare.

boost [bu:st] vt (profits, production) incrementare; (confidence) aumentare; (spirits) sollevare.

booster ['bu:stəʳ] n (injection) richiamo m.

boot [bu:t] n (shoe) stivale m; (for walking) scarpone m; (for football) scarpetta f; (Br: of car) bagagliaio m.

booth [bu:ð] n (for telephone) cabina f; (at fairground) baraccone m.

booze [bu:z] n (inf) alcool m ◆ vi (inf) sbevazzare.

bop [bɒp] n (inf: dance): **to have a ~** ballare.

border ['bɔ:dəʳ] n (of country) frontiera f; (edge) orlo m; **the Borders** zona di confine fra Inghilterra

e Scozia.

bore [bɔ:ʳ] pt → **bear** ◆ n (inf) noia f ◆ vt (person) annoiare; (hole) praticare.

bored [bɔ:d] adj annoiato(-a).

boredom ['bɔ:dəm] n noia f.

boring ['bɔ:rɪŋ] adj noioso(-a).

born [bɔ:n] adj: **to be ~** nascere.

borne [bɔ:n] pp → **bear**.

borough ['bʌrə] n = comune m.

borrow ['bɒrəʊ] vt: **to ~ sthg (from sb)** prendere in prestito qc (da qn).

bosom ['bʊzəm] n seno m.

boss [bɒs] n capo m ◻ **boss around** vt sep dare ordini a.

bossy ['bɒsɪ] adj autoritario(-a).

botanical garden [bə'tænɪkl-] n giardino m botanico.

both [bəʊθ] adj & pron tutti(-e) e due, entrambi(-e) ◆ adv: **~ ... and** sia ... sia, sia ... che; **it is ~ stupid and dangerous** è stupido e pericoloso insieme; **~ of them** entrambi, tutti e due; **~ of us** entrambi, tutti e due.

bother ['bɒðəʳ] vt (worry) preoccupare; (annoy, pester) disturbare ◆ vi preoccuparsi ◆ n (trouble) fatica f; **I can't be ~ed** non ne ho voglia; **don't ~, I'll go!** non ti scomodare, vado io!; **it's no ~!** non c'è problema!

bottle ['bɒtl] n bottiglia f; (for baby) biberon m inv.

bottle bank n campana f per la raccolta del vetro.

bottled ['bɒtld] adj imbottigliato(-a); **~ beer** birra in bottiglia; **~ water** acqua minerale.

bottle opener [-,əʊpnəʳ] n apribottiglie m inv.

bottom ['bɒtəm] *adj (lowest, last)* ultimo(-a); *(worst)* più basso(-a) ♦ *n* fondo *m*; *(of hill)* piedi *mpl*; *(buttocks)* sedere *m*; **the ~ shelf** l'ultimo scaffale in basso; **~ gear** prima *f*.

bought [bɔːt] *pt & pp* → **buy**.

boulder ['bəuldə^r] *n* masso *m*.

bounce [bauns] *vi (rebound)* rimbalzare; *(jump)* saltare; *(cheque)* essere scoperto.

bouncer ['baunsə^r] *n (inf)* buttafuori *m inv*.

bouncy ['baunsɪ] *adj (person)* pimpante.

bound [baund] *pt & pp* → **bind** ♦ *vi* saltellare ♦ *adj*: **it's ~ to rain** pioverà di sicuro; **to be ~ for** essere diretto(-a) a; **it's out of ~s** l'accesso è vietato.

boundary ['baundrɪ] *n* confine *m*.

bouquet [bu'keɪ] *n* bouquet *m inv*; *(big bunch of flowers)* mazzo *m* di fiori.

bourbon ['bɜːbən] *n* bourbon *m inv*.

bout [baut] *n (of illness)* attacco *m*; *(of activity)* periodo *m*.

boutique [buːˈtiːk] *n* boutique *f inv*.

bow[1] [bau] *n (of head)* inchino *m*; *(of ship)* prua *f* ♦ *vi* inchinarsi.

bow[2] [bəu] *n (knot)* fiocco *m*; *(weapon)* arco *m*; *(MUS)* archetto *m*.

bowels ['bauəlz] *npl (ANAT)* intestino *m*.

bowl [bəul] *n* ciotola *f*; *(for washing)* bacinella *f*; *(of toilet)* tazza *f*; **fruit ~** fruttiera *f*; **salad ~** insalatiera *f*; **sugar ~** zuccheriera *f* ❑ **bowls** *npl* bocce *fpl*.

bowling alley ['bəulɪŋ-] *n (building)* bowling *m inv*.

bowling green ['bəulɪŋ-] *n* campo *m* di bocce.

bow tie [ˌbəu-] *n* farfalla *f*.

box [bɒks] *n* scatola *f*; *(on form)* casella *f*; *(in theatre)* palco *m* ♦ *vi* fare del pugilato; **a ~ of chocolates** una scatola di cioccolatini; **jewellery ~** portagioie *m inv*; **tool ~** cassetta *f* degli attrezzi.

boxer ['bɒksə^r] *n (fighter)* pugile *m*.

boxer shorts *npl* boxer *mpl*.

boxing ['bɒksɪŋ] *n* pugilato *m*.

Boxing Day *n* Santo Stefano *m*.

---

i | **BOXING DAY**

Giorno festivo in tutta la Gran Bretagna, il 26 dicembre era in passato il giorno in cui i garzoni di bottega e i servitori ricevevano in dono somme extra di denaro dette "Christmas boxes". Oggi la tradizione sopravvive sotto forma di mance elargite ai lattai, agli spazzini e ai ragazzi che consegnano i giornali.

---

boxing gloves *npl* guantoni *mpl*.

boxing ring *n* ring *m inv*.

box office *n* botteghino *m*.

boy [bɔɪ] *n* ragazzo *m*; *(son)* figlio *m* ♦ *excl (inf)*: **(oh) ~!** accidenti!

boycott ['bɔɪkɒt] *vt* boicottare.

boyfriend ['bɔɪfrend] *n* ragazzo *m*.

boy scout *n* boy-scout *m inv*.

BR *abbr* = **British Rail**.

bra [brɑː] *n* reggiseno *m*.

brace [breɪs] *n (for teeth)* apparecchio *m* (per i denti) ❑ **braces**

Br) bretelle *fpl.*

bracelet ['breɪslɪt] *n* braccialetto
n.

bracken ['brækn] *n* felce *f.*

bracket ['brækɪt] *n (written symbol)* parentesi *f inv; (support)* reggi-
mensola *m inv.*

brag [bræg] *vi* vantarsi.

braid [breɪd] *n (hairstyle)* treccia *f;
on clothes)* passamano *m.*

brain [breɪn] *n* cervello *m.*

brainy ['breɪnɪ] *adj (inf)* sve-
glio(-a).

braised [breɪzd] *adj* brasato(-a).

brake [breɪk] *n* freno *m* ◆ *vi* frenare.

brake block *n* freno *m.*

brake fluid *n* fluido *m* dei
reni.

brake light *n* stop *m inv.*

brake pad *n* pastiglia *f (del
freno).*

brake pedal *n (pedale m del)
reno m.*

bran [bræn] *n* crusca *f.*

branch [brɑːntʃ] *n* ramo *m; (of
bank, company)* filiale *f* ◻ **branch
off** *vi* diramarsi.

branch line *n* diramazione *f.*

brand [brænd] *n* marca *f* ◆ *vt:* **to
- sb (as)** bollare qn (come).

brand-new *adj* nuovo(-a) di
ecca.

brandy ['brændɪ] *n* brandy *m inv.*

brash [bræʃ] *adj (pej)* sfronta-
o(-a).

brass [brɑːs] *n* ottone *m.*

brass band *n* fanfara *f.*

brasserie ['bræsərɪ] *n* ≈ tratto-
a *f.*

brassiere [Br 'bræsɪəʳ, Am brə'zɪr]
reggiseno *m.*

brat [bræt] *n (inf)* discolo *m* (-a
f).

brave [breɪv] *adj* coraggioso(-a).

bravery ['breɪvərɪ] *n* coraggio *m.*

bravo [,brɑː'vəʊ] *excl* bravo(-a)!

brawl [brɔːl] *n* rissa *f.*

Brazil [brə'zɪl] *n* il Brasile.

brazil nut *n* noce *f* del Brasile.

breach [briːtʃ] *vt (contract)* rompere; *(confidence)* tradire.

bread [bred] *n* pane *m; ~ and
butter* pane *m* imburrato.

bread bin *n (Br)* portapane *m
inv.*

breadboard ['bredbɔːd] *n*
tagliere *m (per il pane).*

bread box *(Am)* = **bread bin.**

breadcrumbs ['bredkrʌmz] *npl*
pangrattato *m.*

breaded ['bredɪd] *adj* impana-
to(-a).

bread knife *n* coltello *m* da
pane.

bread roll *n* panino *m.*

breadth [bretθ] *n* larghezza *f,*
ampiezza *f.*

break [breɪk] *(pt* broke, *pp* broken) *n (interruption)* interruzione *f;
(rest, pause)* pausa *f; (SCH)* ricreazione *f* ◆ *vt* rompere; *(law, rule)*
infrangere; *(promise, contract)* non
rispettare; *(a record)* battere ◆ *vi*
rompersi; *(dawn)* spuntare; *(voice)*
cambiare; **without a ~** senza
sosta; **a lucky ~** un colpo di fortuna; **to ~ one's leg** rompersi la
gamba; **to ~ the news to sb** dare
una notizia a qn; **to ~ one's journey** fare una sosta ◻ **break down**
vi (car, machine) guastarsi ◆ *vt sep
(door, barrier)* abbattere; **break in**
vi (enter by force) fare irruzione;

break off vt (detach) staccare; (holiday) interrompere ◆ vi (stop suddenly) interrompersi; **break out** vi (fire, war, panic) scoppiare; **he broke out in a rash** gli è venuto uno sfogo; **break up** vi (with spouse, partner) lasciarsi; (meeting, marriage, school) finire.

breakage ['breɪkɪdʒ] n danni mpl.

breakdown ['breɪkdaʊn] n (of car) guasto m; (in communications, negotiation) interruzione f; (mental) esaurimento m nervoso.

breakdown truck n carro m attrezzi.

breakfast ['brekfəst] n colazione f; to have ~ fare colazione; to have sthg for ~ mangiare qc a colazione.

breakfast cereal n cereali mpl.

break-in n scasso m.

breakwater ['breɪk,wɔ:tər] n frangiflutti m inv.

breast [brest] n (of woman) seno m; (of chicken, duck) petto m.

breastbone ['brestbəʊn] n sterno m.

breast-feed vt allattare (al seno).

breaststroke ['breststrəʊk] n nuoto m a rana.

breath [breθ] n (of person) alito m; (air inhaled) respiro m; out of ~ senza fiato; to go for a ~ of fresh air andare a prendere una boccata d'aria.

Breathalyser® ['breθəlaɪzər] (Br) etilometro m.

Breathalyzer® ['breθəlaɪzər] (Am) = **Breathalyser®**.

breathe [bri:ð] vi respirare ❑

breathe in vi inspirare; **breathe out** vi espirare.

breathtaking ['breθ,teɪkɪŋ] adj mozzafiato (inv).

breed [bri:d] (pt & pp **bred** [bred]) n (of animal) razza f; (of plant) varietà f inv ◆ vt (animals) allevare ◆ vi riprodursi.

breeze [bri:z] n brezza f.

breezy ['bri:zɪ] adj (weather, day) ventilato(-a).

brew [bru:] vt (tea) fare ◆ vi: the tea/coffee is ~ed il tè/caffè è pronto.

brewery ['brʊərɪ] n fabbrica f di birra.

bribe [braɪb] n bustarella f, tangente f ◆ vt corrompere.

bric-a-brac ['brɪkəbræk] n ciarpame, frusaglie fpl.

brick [brɪk] n mattone m.

bricklayer ['brɪk,leɪər] n muratore m.

brickwork ['brɪkwɜ:k] n muratura f di mattoni.

bride [braɪd] n sposa f.

bridegroom ['braɪdɡrʊm] n sposo m.

bridesmaid ['braɪdzmeɪd] n damigella f d'onore.

bridge [brɪdʒ] n ponte m; (card game) bridge m.

bridle ['braɪdl] n briglia f.

bridle path n sentiero m (per cavalli).

brief [bri:f] adj breve ◆ vt mettere al corrente; **in ~** in breve.

briefs npl mutande fpl.

briefcase ['bri:fkeɪs] n (hard) ventiquattr'ore f inv; (soft) cartella f.

briefly ['bri:flɪ] adv brevemente.

brigade [brɪ'geɪd] *n* brigata *f*.

bright [braɪt] *adj (light, sun)* vivido(-a); *(weather, room, idea)* luminoso(-a); *(clever)* sveglio(-a); *(lively, cheerful, in colour)* vivace.

brilliant ['brɪljənt] *adj* brillante; *(inf: wonderful)* stupendo(-a).

brim [brɪm] *n (of hat)* tesa *f*; **it's full to the ~** è pieno fino all'orlo.

brine [braɪn] *n* salamoia *f*.

bring [brɪŋ] *(pt & pp* **brought)** *vt* portare ❑ **bring along** *vt sep* portare; **bring back** *vt sep* riportare; **bring in** *vt sep (introduce)* introdurre; *(earn)* rendere; **bring out** *vt sep (new product)* far uscire; **bring up** *vt sep (child)* allevare; *(subject)* sollevare; *(food)* vomitare.

brink [brɪŋk] *n*: **on the ~ of sthg** sull'orlo di qc; **on the ~ of doing sthg** sul punto di fare qc.

brisk [brɪsk] *adj (quick)* rapido (-a); *(efficient)* energico(-a); *(wind)* pungente.

bristle ['brɪsl] *n (of brush)* setola *f*; *(on chin)* pelo *m* ispido.

Britain ['brɪtn] *n* la Gran Bretagna.

British ['brɪtɪʃ] *adj* britannico(-a) ♦ *npl*: **the ~** i Britannici.

British Rail *n* = le Ferrovie dello Stato.

British Telecom [-'telɪkɒm] *n* = la Telecom Italia.

Briton ['brɪtn] *n* britannico *m* (-a *f*).

brittle ['brɪtl] *adj* friabile.

broad [brɔːd] *adj* ampio(-a); *(accent)* marcato(-a).

B road *n (Br)* = strada *f* provinciale.

broad bean *n* fava *f*.

broadcast ['brɔːdkɑːst] *(pt & pp* broadcast) *n* trasmissione *f* ♦ *vt* trasmettere.

broadly ['brɔːdlɪ] *adv (in general)* grossomodo; **~ speaking** in linea di massima.

broccoli ['brɒkəlɪ] *n* broccoli *mpl*.

brochure ['brəʊʃər] *n* opuscolo *m*.

broiled [brɔɪld] *adj (Am)* alla griglia.

broke [brəʊk] *pt* → **break** ♦ *adj (inf)* al verde.

broken ['brəʊkn] *pp* → **break** ♦ *adj* rotto(-a); *(English, Italian)* stentato(-a).

bronchitis [brɒŋ'kaɪtɪs] *n* bronchite *f*.

bronze [brɒnz] *n* bronzo *m*.

brooch [brəʊtʃ] *n* spilla *f*.

brook [brʊk] *n* ruscello *m*.

broom [bruːm] *n* scopa *f*.

broomstick ['bruːmstɪk] *n* manico *m* di scopa.

broth [brɒθ] *n* brodo *m*.

brother ['brʌðər] *n* fratello *m*.

brother-in-law *n* cognato *m*.

brought [brɔːt] *pt & pp* → **bring**.

brow [braʊ] *n (forehead)* fronte *f*; *(eyebrow)* sopracciglio *m*.

brown [braʊn] *adj (tanned)* abbronzato(-a); *(eyes, hair)* castano(-a) ♦ *n* marrone *m*.

brown bread *n* pane *m* integrale.

brownie ['braʊnɪ] *n (CULIN)* biscotto con noci e cioccolato.

Brownie ['braʊnɪ] *n* giovane esploratrice *f*, coccinella *f*.

brown rice *n* riso *m* integrale.

brown sauce n (Br) salsa piccante, usata con la carne e i salumi.

brown sugar n zucchero m di canna.

browse [brauz] vi (in shop) dare un'occhiata; **to ~ through** (book, paper) sfogliare.

browser ['brauzə*] n: **'~s welcome'** 'entrata libera'.

bruise [bru:z] n livido m.

brunch [brʌntʃ] n brunch m inv.

brunette [bru:'net] n bruna f.

brush [brʌʃ] n (for hair) spazzola f; (for teeth) spazzolino m; (for painting) pennello m ♦ vt spazzolare; (clean, tidy) spazzare; (move with hand) scostare; **to ~ one's hair** spazzolarsi i capelli; **to ~ one's teeth** lavarsi i denti.

Brussels ['brʌslz] n Bruxelles f.

brussels sprouts npl cavoletti mpl di Bruxelles.

brutal ['bru:tl] adj brutale.

BSc n (abbr of Bachelor of Science) (titolare di una) laurea in discipline scientifiche.

BT abbr = British Telecom.

bubble ['bʌbl] n bolla f.

bubble bath n bagnoschiuma m inv.

bubble gum n gomma f da masticare (con cui si può fare le bolle).

bubbly ['bʌbli] n (inf) spumante m.

buck [bʌk] n (Am: inf: dollar) dollaro m; (male animal) maschio m.

bucket ['bʌkit] n secchio m.

Buckingham Palace ['bʌkiŋəm-] n il Palazzo di Buckingham (residenza della famiglia reale britannica).

buckle ['bʌkl] n fibbia f ♦ vt (fasten) allacciare ♦ vi (warp) piegarsi.

buck's fizz [,bʌks'fiz] n bibita a base di champagne e succo d'arancia.

bud [bʌd] n germoglio m ♦ vi germogliare.

Buddhist ['budist] n buddista mf.

buddy ['bʌdi] n (inf) amico m.

budge [bʌdʒ] vi spostarsi.

budgerigar ['bʌdʒərigɑ:*] n pappagallino m.

budget ['bʌdʒit] adj (holiday, travel) a basso prezzo ♦ n bilancio m preventivo; **the Budget** (Br) la Legge finanziaria ❑ **budget for** vt fus: **to ~ for sthg** preventivare la spesa di qc.

budgie ['bʌdʒi] n (inf) pappagallino m.

buff [bʌf] n (inf) patito m (-a f).

buffalo ['bʌfələu] (pl -s OR -es) n bufalo m.

buffalo wings npl (Am) ali fp di pollo fritte.

buffer ['bʌfə*] n (on train) respingente m.

buffet [Br 'bufei, Am bə'fei] n buffet m inv.

buffet car n vagone m ristorante.

bug [bʌg] n (insect) insetto m; (inf: mild illness) virus m inv ◆ vt (inf: annoy) dare fastidio a.

buggy ['bʌgɪ] n (pushchair) passeggino m; (Am: pram) carrozzina f.

bugle ['bju:gl] n tromba f.

build [bɪld] (pt & pp built) n corporatura f ◆ vt costruire ❑ **build up** vt sep aumentare ◆ vi accumularsi.

builder ['bɪldər] n costruttore m (-trice f).

building ['bɪldɪŋ] n edificio m.

building site n cantiere m edile.

building society n (Br) = istituto m di credito edilizio.

built [bɪlt] pt & pp → build.

built-in adj incorporato(-a).

built-up area n agglomerato m urbano.

bulb [bʌlb] n (for lamp) lampadina f; (of plant) bulbo m.

Bulgaria [bʌl'geərɪə] n la Bulgaria.

bulge [bʌldʒ] vi essere rigonfio(-a).

bulk [bʌlk] n: **the ~ of** la maggior parte di; **in ~** all'ingrosso.

bulky ['bʌlkɪ] adj ingombrante.

bull [bʊl] n toro m.

bulldog ['bʊldɒg] n bulldog m inv.

bulldozer ['bʊldəʊzər] n bulldozer m inv.

bullet ['bʊlɪt] n proiettile m, pallottola f.

bulletin ['bʊlɪtɪn] n (on radio, TV) notiziario m; (publication) bollettino m.

bullfight ['bʊlfaɪt] n corrida f.

bull's-eye n centro m (del bersaglio).

bully ['bʊlɪ] n prepotente mf ◆ vt fare il prepotente con.

bum [bʌm] n (inf: bottom) sedere m; (Am: inf: tramp) barbone m (-a f).

bum bag n (Br) marsupio m.

bumblebee ['bʌmblbiː] n bombo m.

bump [bʌmp] n (on knee, leg) rigonfiamento m; (on head) bernoccolo m; (on road) cunetta f; (sound) tonfo m; (minor accident) scontro m leggero ◆ vt (head, leg) sbattere ❑ **bump into** vt fus (hit) sbattere contro; (meet) imbattersi in.

bumper ['bʌmpər] n (on car) paraurti m inv; (Am: on train) respingente m.

bumpy ['bʌmpɪ] adj (road) dissestato(-a); **the flight was ~** c'è stata un po' di turbolenza durante il volo.

bun [bʌn] n (cake) focaccia f; (bread roll) panino m; (hairstyle) crocchia f.

bunch [bʌntʃ] n (of people) gruppo m; (of flowers, keys) mazzo m; (of grapes) grappolo m; (of bananas) casco m.

bundle ['bʌndl] n fascio m.

bung [bʌŋ] n tappo m.

bungalow ['bʌŋgələʊ] n casa a un solo piano.

bunion ['bʌnjən] n rigonfiamento m dell'alluce.

bunk [bʌŋk] n (bed) cuccetta f.

bunk bed n letto m a castello.

bunker ['bʌŋkər] n bunker m inv; (for coal) carbonaia f.

bunny ['bʌnɪ] *n* coniglietto *m*.

buoy [*Br* bɔɪ, *Am* 'buːɪ] *n* boa *f*.

buoyant ['bɔɪənt] *adj* galleggiante.

BUPA ['buːpə] *n compagnia d'assicurazione britannica per assistenza medica privata.*

burden ['bɜːdn] *n (load)* carico *m*; *(responsibility)* peso *m*.

bureaucracy [bjʊə'rɒkrəsɪ] *n* burocrazia *f*.

bureau de change [ˌbjʊərəʊdə'ʃɒndʒ] *n* agenzia *f* di cambio.

burger ['bɜːgə*ʳ*] *n* hamburger *m inv*; *(made with nuts, vegetables etc)* hamburger vegetariano.

burglar ['bɜːglə*ʳ*] *n* scassinatore *m* (-trice *f*).

burglar alarm *n* allarme *n* antifurto.

burglarize ['bɜːgləraɪz] *(Am)* = **burgle**.

burglary ['bɜːglərɪ] *n* furto *m* con scasso.

burgle ['bɜːgl] *vt* scassinare.

burial ['berɪəl] *n* sepoltura *f*.

burn [bɜːn] *(pt & pp* burnt OR burned) *n* bruciatura *f* ◆ *vt & vi* bruciare ❏ **burn down** *vt sep* incendiare ◆ *vi:* **the building was ~ed down** l'edificio è stato interamente distrutto dalle fiamme.

burning (hot) ['bɜːnɪŋ-] *adj* rovente.

Burns' Night [bɜːnz-] *n festa celebrata in onore del poeta scozzese Robert Burns il 25 gennaio.*

---

i | **BURNS' NIGHT**

Il 25 gennaio gli scozzesi commemorano la nascita del poeta Robert Burns (1759–96). La tradizione vuole che in occasione di questa ricorrenza si allestiscano le cosiddette "Burns' Suppers", cene a base di piatti tradizionali scozzesi, come l'haggis, accompagnate da whisky. Durante queste cene i commensali recitano a turno versi delle poesie di Burns.

---

burnt [bɜːnt] *pt & pp* → burn.

burp [bɜːp] *vi (inf)* ruttare.

burrow ['bʌrəʊ] *n* tana *f*.

burst [bɜːst] *(pt & pp* burst) *n* scoppio *m* ◆ *vt* far scoppiare ◆ *vi* scoppiare; **he ~ into the room** irruppe nella stanza; **to ~ into tears** scoppiare in lacrime; **to ~ open** *(door)* spalancarsi.

bury ['berɪ] *vt* seppellire.

bus [bʌs] *n* autobus *m inv*; **by ~ in** autobus.

bus conductor [-ˌkən'dʌktə*ʳ*] *n* bigliettaio *m* (-a *f*).

bus driver *n* conducente *mf*.

bush [bʊʃ] *n* cespuglio *m*.

business ['bɪznɪs] *n* affari *mpl*; *(shop, firm)* impresa *f*; *(affair)* faccenda *f*; **mind your own ~!** fatti gli affari tuoi!; **'~ as usual'** 'aperto (regolarmente)'.

business card *n* biglietto *f* da visita.

business class *n* business class *f inv*.

business hours *npl* orario *m* di apertura.

businessman ['bɪznɪsmæn] (pl -men [-men]) n uomo m d'affari.

business studies npl = amministrazione f aziendale.

businesswoman ['bɪznɪs,wumən] (pl -women [-wɪmɪn]) n donna f d'affari.

busker ['bʌskər] n (Br) musicista mf ambulante.

bus lane n corsia f preferenziale (per autobus).

bus pass n abbonamento m all'autobus.

bus shelter n pensilina f.

bus station n stazione f degli autobus.

bus stop n fermata f dell'autobus.

bust [bʌst] n (of woman) seno m ◆ adj: **to go ~** (inf) fallire.

bustle ['bʌsl] n (activity) trambusto m.

bus tour n gita f in autobus.

busy ['bɪzɪ] adj occupato(-a); (day, schedule) pieno(-a); (street, office) affollato(-a); **to be ~ doing sthg** essere occupato a fare qc.

busy signal n (Am) segnale m di occupato.

but [bʌt] conj ma, però ◆ prep tranne; **the last ~ one** il penultimo (la penultima); **~ for** a parte.

butcher ['butʃər] n macellaio m (-a f); **~'s** (shop) macelleria f.

butt [bʌt] n (of rifle) calcio m; (of cigarette, cigar) mozzicone m.

butter ['bʌtər] n burro m ◆ vt imburrare.

butter bean n fagiolo m bianco.

buttercup ['bʌtəkʌp] n ranunculo m.

butterfly ['bʌtəflaɪ] n farfalla f.

butterscotch ['bʌtəskɒtʃ] n caramella dura di zucchero e burro.

buttocks ['bʌtəks] npl natiche fpl.

button ['bʌtn] n bottone m; (Am: badge) distintivo m.

buttonhole ['bʌtnhəʊl] n (hole) occhiello m.

button mushroom n champignon m inv.

buttress ['bʌtrɪs] n contrafforte m.

buy [baɪ] (pt & pp bought) vt comprare ◆ n: **a good ~** un buon acquisto; **to ~ sthg for sb, to ~ sb sthg** comprare qc per qn, comprare qc a qn.

buzz [bʌz] vi ronzare ◆ n (inf: phone call): **to give sb a ~** dare un colpo di telefono a qn.

buzzer ['bʌzər] n cicalino m.

by [baɪ] prep 1. (expressing cause, agent) da; **he was hit ~ a car** è stato investito da un'automobile; **funded ~ the government** finanziato dal governo; **a book ~ Joyce** un libro di Joyce. 2. (expressing method, means): **~ car/train/plane** in macchina/treno/aereo; **~ post/phone** per posta/telefono; **to pay ~ credit card** pagare con la carta di credito; **to win ~ cheating** vincere con l'imbroglio. 3. (near to, beside) vicino a, accanto a; **~ the sea** (holiday) al mare; (town) sul mare. 4. (past) davanti a; **a car went ~ the house** un'automobile è passata davanti alla casa. 5. (via) da; **go out ~ the door on the left** uscite dalla porta sulla sinistra.

6. *(with time)*: **be there ~ nine** trovati lì per le nove; **~ day/night** di giorno/notte; **~ now** ormai.

7. *(expressing quantity)* a; **sold ~ the dozen/thousand** venduti a dozzine/migliaia; **prices fell ~ 20%** i prezzi sono diminuiti del 20%; **we charge ~ the hour** facciamo pagare a ore.

8. *(expressing meaning)*: **what do you mean ~ that?** cosa intendi dire con questo?

9. *(in sums, measurements)* per; **two metres ~ five** due metri per cinque.

10. *(according to)* per, secondo; **~ law** per legge; **it's fine ~ me** per me va bene.

11. *(expressing gradual process)*: **bit ~ bit** (a) poco a poco; **one ~ one** uno per uno; **year ~ year** di anno in anno.

12. *(in phrases)*: **~ mistake** per errore; **~ oneself** *(alone)* (da) solo; *(unaided)* da solo; **he's a lawyer ~ profession** è avvocato di professione.

◆ *adv (past)*: **to go ~** passare.

bye(-bye) [baɪ(baɪ)] *excl (inf)* ciao!

bypass ['baɪpɑːs] *n (road)* circonvallazione *f*.

C

C *(abbr of Celsius, centigrade)* C.

cab [kæb] *n (taxi)* taxi *m inv*; *(of lorry)* cabina *f*.

cabaret ['kæbəreɪ] *n* spettacolo

m di cabaret.

cabbage ['kæbɪdʒ] *n* cavolo *m*.

cabin ['kæbɪn] *n* cabina *f*; *(wooden house)* capanna *f*.

cabin crew *n* personale *m* di bordo.

cabinet ['kæbɪnɪt] *n (cupboard)* armadietto *m*; *(POL)* consiglio *m* di gabinetto.

cable ['keɪbl] *n* cavo *m*.

cable car *n* funivia *f*.

cable television *n* televisione *f* via cavo.

cactus ['kæktəs] *(pl* -tuses OR -ti [-taɪ]) *n* cactus *m inv*.

Caesar salad [ˌsiːzə-] *n* insalata di lattuga, acciughe, olive, crostini e parmigiano.

cafe ['kæfeɪ] *n* caffè *m*.

cafeteria [ˌkæfɪ'tɪərɪə] *n* ristorante *m* self-service.

cafetière [kæf'tjeəʳ] *n* tipo di caffettiera con pressa che separa la polvere dal caffè ottenuto.

caffeine ['kæfiːn] *n* caffeina *f*.

cage [keɪdʒ] *n* gabbia *f*.

cagoule [kə'guːl] *n (Br)* K-way® *m inv*.

Cajun ['keɪdʒən] *adj tipico della popolazione di origine francese della Louisiana.*

| i | CAJUN |

Coloni di origine francese, i "Cajuns" si stabilirono inizialmente nella Nuova Scozia da dove, nel diciottesimo secolo, furono deportati in Louisiana. Lì svilupparono una lingua ed una cultura proprie ed oggi sono conosciuti per la loro cucina, caratterizzata dall'uso

di spezie piccanti, e per la loro musica folkloristica, in cui predominano
il violino e la fisarmonica.

cake [keɪk] n (large) torta f; (small)
pasta f; (of soap) pezzo m.

calculate [ˈkælkjʊleɪt] vt calcolare.

calculator [ˈkælkjʊleɪtəʳ] n calcolatrice f.

calendar [ˈkælɪndəʳ] n calendario m.

calf [kɑːf] (pl **calves**) n (of cow)
vitello m; (part of leg) polpaccio m.

call [kɔːl] n (visit) visita f; (phone
call) telefonata f; (of bird) richiamo
m; (at airport) chiamata f; (at hotel)
sveglia f ◆ vt chiamare; (meeting)
convocare; (elections, strike) indire
◆ vi (visit) passare; (phone) chiamare; on ~ (nurse, doctor) reperibile; to
pay sb a ~ fare una visita a qn; to
be ~ed chiamarsi; what is he ~ed?
come si chiama?; to ~ sb a liar
dare del bugiardo a qn; to ~ sb's
name chiamare qn; this train ~s at
.. questo treno ferma a ...; who's
~ing? chi parla? ❑ **call back** vt sep
richiamare ◆ vi (phone again)
richiamare; (visit again) ripassare;
call for vt fus (come to fetch) passare
a prendere; (demand) chiedere;
(require) richiedere; **call on** vt fus
(visit) fare visita a; to ~ on sb to do
sthg chiedere a qn di fare qc; **call**
out vt sep (name, winner) annunciare;
(doctor, fire brigade) chiamare ◆
vi gridare; **call up** vt sep (MIL) chiamare alle armi; (telephone) chiamare.

call box n cabina f telefonica.

caller [ˈkɔːləʳ] n (visitor) visitatore
m (-trice f); (on phone) persona che
chiama.

calm [kɑːm] adj calmo(-a) ◆ vt
calmare ❑ **calm down** vt sep calmare ◆ vi calmarsi.

Calor gas® [ˈkælə-] n butano m.

calorie [ˈkælərɪ] n caloria f.

calves [kɑːvz] pl → **calf**.

camcorder [ˈkæm,kɔːdəʳ] n
videocamera f.

came [keɪm] pt → **come**.

camel [ˈkæml] n cammello m.

camembert [ˈkæməmbeəʳ] n
camembert m inv.

camera [ˈkæmərə] n (for photo-
graphs) macchina f fotografica; (for
filming) macchina da presa.

cameraman [ˈkæmərəmæn] (pl
-**men** [-men]) n cameraman m inv.

camera shop n fotografo m.

camisole [ˈkæmɪsəʊl] n canottiera f.

camp [kæmp] n (for holidaymakers) campeggio m, camping m
inv; (for soldiers, prisoners) campo m
◆ vi accamparsi.

campaign [kæmˈpeɪn] n campagna f ◆ vi: to ~ (for/against) fare
una campagna (per/contro).

camp bed n branda f.

camper [ˈkæmpəʳ] n (person)
campeggiatore m (-trice f); (van)
camper m inv.

camping [ˈkæmpɪŋ] n: to go ~
andare in campeggio.

camping stove n fornello m
da campeggio.

campsite [ˈkæmpsaɪt] n campeggio m, camping m inv.

campus [ˈkæmpəs] (pl -**es**) n
campus m inv.

can¹ [kæn] n (of food) scatola f; (of
drink) lattina f; (of paint) barattolo
m; (of oil) latta f.

can² [weak form kən, strong form

kæn] (*pt & conditional* **could**) *aux vb*
1. *(be able to)* potere; ~ **you help me?** puoi aiutarmi?; **I ~ see you** ti vedo.
2. *(know how to)* sapere; ~ **you drive?** sai guidare?; **I ~ speak Italian** parlo (l')italiano.
3. *(be allowed to)* potere; **you can't smoke here** è proibito fumare qui.
4. *(in polite requests)* potere; ~ **you tell me the time?** mi può dire l'ora?, mi sa dire l'ora?; ~ **I speak to the manager?** posso parlare al direttore?
5. *(expressing occasional occurrence)*: **it ~ get cold at night** può fare freddo la notte.
6. *(expressing possibility)* potere; **they could be lost** si potrebbero essere persi.

Canada ['kænədə] *n* il Canada.

Canadian [kə'neɪdɪən] *adj* canadese ♦ *n* canadese *mf*.

canal [kə'næl] *n* canale *m*.

canapé ['kænəpeɪ] *n* tartina *f*.

cancel ['kænsl] *vt* annullare.

cancellation [,kænsə'leɪʃn] *n* annullamento *m*.

cancer ['kænsə^r] *n* cancro *m*.

Cancer ['kænsə^r] *n* Cancro *m*.

candidate ['kændɪdət] *n* candidato *m* (-a *f*).

candle ['kændl] *n* candela *f*.

candlelit dinner ['kændllɪt-] *n* cena *f* a lume di candela.

candy ['kændɪ] *n* (Am) (confectionery) dolciumi *mpl*; (sweet) caramella *f*.

candyfloss ['kændɪflɒs] *n* (Br) zucchero *m* filato.

cane [keɪn] *n* (for walking) bastone *m*; (for punishment) bacchetta *f*; (for furniture, baskets) vimini *mpl*.

canister ['kænɪstə^r] *n* (for tea) barattolo *m*; (for gas) bombola *f*.

cannabis ['kænəbɪs] *n* cannabis *f*.

canned [kænd] *adj* (food) in scatola; (drink) in lattina.

cannon ['kænən] *n* cannone *m*.

cannot ['kænɒt] = **can not**.

canoe [kə'nu:] *n* canoa *f*.

canoeing [kə'nu:ɪŋ] *n* canottaggio *m*.

canopy ['kænəpɪ] *n* (over bed etc) baldacchino *m*.

can't [kɑ:nt] = **cannot**.

cantaloup(e) ['kæntəlu:p] *n* melone *m* (cantalupo).

canteen [kæn'ti:n] *n* mensa *f*.

canvas ['kænvəs] *n* (for tent, bag) tela *f*.

cap [kæp] *n* (hat) berretto *m*; (of pen, bottle) tappo *m*; (contraceptive) diaframma *m*.

capable ['keɪpəbl] *adj* (competent) capace; **to be ~ of doing sthg** essere capace di fare qc.

capacity [kə'pæsɪtɪ] *n* (ability) capacità *f inv*; (of stadium, theatre) capienza *f*.

cape [keɪp] *n* (of land) capo *m*; (cloak) cappa *f*.

capers ['keɪpəz] *npl* capperi *mpl*.

capital ['kæpɪtl] *n* (of country) capitale *f*; (money) capitale *m*; (letter) maiuscola *f*.

capital punishment *n* pena *f* capitale.

cappuccino [,kæpʊ'tʃi:nəʊ] (*pl* **-s**) *n* cappuccino *m*.

Capricorn *n* Capricorno *m*.

capsicum ['kæpsɪkəm] *n* peperone *m*.

capsize [kæp'saɪz] *vi* rovesciarsi

capsule ['kæpsju:l] *n (for medicine)* capsula *f*.

captain ['kæptɪn] *n* capitano *m*.

caption ['kæpʃn] *n* didascalia *f*.

capture ['kæptʃər] *vt (person, animal)* catturare; *(town, castle)* conquistare.

car [kɑːr] *n (motorcar)* automobile *f*, macchina *f*; *(railway wagon)* vagone *m*.

carafe [kə'ræf] *n* caraffa *f*.

caramel ['kærəmel] *n (sweet)* caramella *f* mou®; *(burnt sugar)* caramello *m*.

carat ['kærət] *n* carato *m*; **24-~ gold** oro a 24 carati.

caravan ['kærəvæn] *n (Br)* roulotte *f inv*.

caravanning ['kærəvænɪŋ] *n (Br)*: **to go ~** andare in vacanza in roulotte.

caravan site *n (Br)* campeggio *m* per roulotte.

carbohydrate [ˌkɑːbəʊ'haɪdreɪt] *n (in foods)* carboidrato *m*.

carbon ['kɑːbən] *n* carbone *m*.

carbon copy *n* copia *f* fatta con carta carbone.

carbon dioxide [-daɪ'ɒksaɪd] *n* anidride *f* carbonica.

carbon monoxide [-mɒ'nɒksaɪd] *n* monossido *m* di carbonio.

car boot sale *n (Br)* mercatino di oggetti usati esposti nei bagagliai aperti delle automobili dei venditori.

carburetor [ˌkɑːbə'retər] *(Am)* = **carburettor**.

carburettor [ˌkɑːbə'retər] *n (Br)* carburatore *m*.

car crash *n* incidente *m* automobilistico.

card [kɑːd] *n (for filing, notes)* scheda *f*; *(for greetings)* biglietto *m*; *(showing membership)* tessera *f*; *(of businessperson)* biglietto da visita; *(postcard)* cartolina *f*; *(playing card)* carta *f*; *(cardboard)* cartoncino *m*; **~s** *(game)* carte *fpl*.

cardboard ['kɑːdbɔːd] *n* cartone *m*.

car deck *n* ponte *m* auto.

cardiac arrest [ˌkɑːdɪæk-] *n* arresto *m* cardiaco.

cardigan ['kɑːdɪgən] *n* cardigan *m inv*.

care [keər] *n* cura *f* ◆ *vi*: **I don't ~** non me ne importa; **to take ~ of** *(look after)* prendersi cura di; *(deal with)* occuparsi di; **would you ~ to ...?** *(fml)* se vuole ...?; **to take ~ to do sthg** stare attento a fare qc; **take ~!** *(goodbye)* stammi bene!; **with ~** con cura; **to ~ about** *(think important)* avere a cuore; *(person)* voler bene a.

career [kə'rɪər] *n* carriera *f*.

carefree ['keəfriː] *adj* spensierato(-a).

careful ['keəful] *adj (cautious)* attento(-a); *(driver)* prudente; *(thorough)* accurato(-a); **be ~!** attento(-a)!

carefully ['keəflɪ] *adv (cautiously)* con cautela; *(thoroughly)* attentamente.

careless ['keələs] *adj (inattentive)* sbadato(-a); *(unconcerned)* spensierato(-a).

caretaker ['keəˌteɪkər] *n (Br)* custode *mf*.

car ferry *n* traghetto *m*.

cargo ['kɑːgəʊ] *(pl* **-es** OR **-s)** *n* carico *m*.

car hire *n (Br)* autonoleggio *m*.

Caribbean [*Br* ˌkærɪ'biːən, *Am* kə'rɪbɪən] *n*: **the ~** (*area*) i Caraibi.

caring ['keərɪŋ] *adj* premuroso(-a).

carnation [kɑː'neɪʃn] *n* garofano *m*.

carnival ['kɑːnɪvl] *n* carnevale *m*.

carousel [ˌkærə'sel] *n* (*for luggage*) nastro *m* trasportatore; (*Am: merry-go-round*) giostra *f*.

carp [kɑːp] *n* carpa *f*.

car park *n* (*Br*) parcheggio *m*.

carpenter ['kɑːpəntə^r] *n* falegname *m*.

carpentry ['kɑːpəntrɪ] *n* falegnameria *f*.

carpet ['kɑːpɪt] *n* (*rug*) tappeto *m*; (*wall-to-wall*) moquette *f inv*.

car rental *n* (*Am*) autonoleggio *m*.

carriage ['kærɪdʒ] *n* carrozza *f*.

carriageway ['kærɪdʒweɪ] *n* (*Br*) carreggiata *f*.

carrier (bag) ['kærɪə^r-] *n* sacchetto *m*.

carrot ['kærət] *n* carota *f*.

carrot cake *n* torta *f* di carote.

carry ['kærɪ] *vt* portare; (*disease*) essere portatore di ♦ *vi* (*voice, sound*) arrivare ❑ **carry on** *vi* continuare ♦ *vt fus* (*continue*) continuare; (*conduct*) compiere; **to ~ on doing sthg** continuare a fare qc; **carry out** *vt sep* (*work, repairs, investigation*) effettuare; (*plan*) portare a compimento; (*order*) eseguire; (*promise*) adempiere.

carrycot ['kærɪkɒt] *n* (*Br*) culla *f* portatile.

carryout ['kærɪaʊt] *n* (*Am & Scot: meal*) cibo *m* da asporto.

carsick ['kɑːˌsɪk] *adj*: **to be ~** soffrire il mal d'auto.

cart [kɑːt] *n* (*for transport*) carro *m*; (*inf: video game cartridge*) cartuccia *f*; (*Am: in supermarket*) carrello *m*.

carton ['kɑːtn] *n* (*of milk, juice*) cartone *m*; (*box*) scatola *f*.

cartoon [kɑː'tuːn] *n* (*drawing*) vignetta *f*; (*comic strip*) fumetto *m*; (*film*) cartone *m* animato.

cartridge ['kɑːtrɪdʒ] *n* cartuccia *f*.

carve [kɑːv] *vt* (*wood, stone*) intagliare; (*meat*) tagliare.

carvery ['kɑːvərɪ] *n* ristorante dove si mangia carne arrosto, tagliata appositamente al banco per il cliente.

car wash *n* autolavaggio *m*.

case [keɪs] *n* (*Br: suitcase*) valigia *f*; (*container*) custodia *f*; (*instance, patient*) caso *m*; (*JUR: trial*) causa *f*; **in any ~** in ogni caso; **in ~ it rains** nel caso che piova; **in ~ of** in caso di; **(just) in ~** in caso di necessità; **in that ~** allora.

cash [kæʃ] *n* (*coins, notes*) contanti *mpl*; (*money in general*) soldi *mpl* ♦ *vt*: **to ~ a cheque** incassare un assegno; **to pay ~** pagare in contanti.

cash desk *n* cassa *f*.

cash dispenser [-ˌdɪ'spensə^r] *n* cassa *f* automatica.

cashew (nut) ['kæʃuː-] *n* noce *f* di acagiù.

cashier [kæ'ʃɪə^r] *n* cassiere *m* (-a *f*).

cashmere [kæʃ'mɪə^r] *n* cachemire *m*.

cashpoint ['kæʃpɔɪnt] *n* (*Br*) cassa *f* automatica.

cash register *n* registratore *m* di cassa.

casino [kə'siːnəʊ] (pl -s) n casinò m inv.

cask [kɑːsk] n barile m.

cask-conditioned [-ˌkən'dɪʃnd] adj fermentato(-a) in barili.

casserole ['kæsərəʊl] n (stew) stufato m; ~ (dish) casseruola f.

cassette [kæ'set] n cassetta f.

cassette recorder n registratore m (a cassette).

cast [kɑːst] (pt & pp cast) n (actors) cast m inv; (for broken bone) ingessatura f ◆ vt (shadow, light, look) gettare; **to ~ doubt on** mettere in dubbio; **to ~ one's vote** votare ❑ **cast off** vi (boat, ship) salpare.

caster ['kɑːstə'] n rotella f.

caster sugar n (Br) zucchero m semolato.

castle ['kɑːsl] n (building) castello m; (in chess) torre f.

casual ['kæʒʊəl] adj (relaxed) disinvolto(-a); (offhand) noncurante; (clothes) casual (inv); ~ **work** lavoro occasionale.

casualty ['kæʒjʊəltɪ] n (injured person) ferito m (-a f); (dead person) morto m (-a f); ~ **(ward)** pronto soccorso m.

cat [kæt] n gatto m.

catalog ['kætəlɒg] (Am) = **catalogue**.

catalogue ['kætəlɒg] n catalogo m.

catapult ['kætəpʌlt] n fionda f.

cataract ['kætərækt] n (in eye) cateratta f.

catarrh [kə'tɑː'] n catarro m.

catastrophe [kə'tæstrəfɪ] n catastrofe f.

catch [kætʃ] (pt & pp caught) vt prendere; (surprise, hear) cogliere;

(attention) attirare ◆ vi (become hooked) impigliarsi ◆ n (of window, door) fermo m; (snag) intoppo m ❑ **catch up** vt sep raggiungere ◆ vi: **to ~ up (with sthg)** (sleep, work) recuperare (qc); **to ~ up with sb** raggiungere qn.

catching ['kætʃɪŋ] adj (inf) contagioso(-a).

category ['kætəgərɪ] n categoria f.

cater ['keɪtə']: **cater for** vt fus (Br) (needs) provvedere a; (anticipate) tenere conto di; (tastes) soddisfare.

caterpillar ['kætəpɪlə'] n bruco m.

cathedral [kə'θiːdrəl] n cattedrale f, duomo m.

Catholic ['kæθlɪk] adj cattolico(-a) ◆ n cattolico m (-a f).

Catseyes® ['kætsaɪz] npl (Br) catarifrangenti mpl.

cattle ['kætl] npl bestiame m.

cattle grid n griglia metallica posta sul suolo stradale per impedire il passaggio di pecore, mucche etc.

caught [kɔːt] pt & pp → **catch**.

cauliflower ['kɒlɪˌflaʊə'] n cavolfiore m.

cauliflower cheese n cavolfiore gratinato con besciamella.

cause [kɔːz] n causa f; (justification) ragione f ◆ vt causare; **to ~ sb to make a mistake** far fare un errore a qn.

causeway ['kɔːzweɪ] n strada f rialzata.

caustic soda [ˌkɔːstɪk-] n soda f caustica.

caution ['kɔːʃn] n (care) cautela f; (warning) avvertimento m.

cautious ['kɔːʃəs] *adj* cauto(-a).

cave [keɪv] *n* grotta *f* □ **cave in** *vi* crollare.

caviar(e) ['kævɪɑːʳ] *n* caviale *m*.

cavity ['kævətɪ] *n* (*in tooth*) carie *f inv*.

CD *n* (*abbr of compact disc*) CD *m inv*.

CDI *n* (*abbr of compact disc interactive*) CDI *m inv*.

CD player *n* lettore *m* di compact disc.

CDW *n* (*abbr of collision damage waiver*) franchigia *f*.

cease [siːs] *vt & vi* (*fml*) cessare.

ceasefire ['siːsˌfaɪəʳ] *n* cessate il fuoco *m inv*.

ceilidh ['keɪlɪ] *n* festa scozzese o irlandese con danze folcloristiche.

---

i CEILIDH

Il "ceilidh" è una tradizionale forma di intrattenimento scozzese o irlandese con musica, canti e balli. In passato i "ceilidh" erano serate organizzate da un numero ristretto di parenti e amici, mentre i "ceilidh" moderni sono spesso grandi feste danzanti aperte al pubblico.

---

ceiling ['siːlɪŋ] *n* soffitto *m*.

celebrate ['selɪbreɪt] *vt* (*win, birthday*) festeggiare; (*Mass*) celebrare ◆ *vi* festeggiare.

celebration [ˌselɪ'breɪʃn] *n* (*event*) festa *f* □ **celebrations** *npl* (*festivities*) festeggiamenti *mpl*.

celebrity [sɪ'lebrɪtɪ] *n* (*person*) celebrità *f inv*.

celeriac [sɪ'lerɪæk] *n* sedano *m*

rapa.

celery ['selərɪ] *n* sedano *m*.

cell [sel] *n* (*of plant, body*) cellula *f*; (*in prison*) cella *f*.

cellar ['seləʳ] *n* cantina *f*.

cello ['tʃeləʊ] (*pl* -s) *n* violoncello *m*.

Cellophane® ['seləfeɪn] *n* cellophane® *m*.

Celsius ['selsɪəs] *adj* Celsius (*inv*).

cement [sɪ'ment] *n* cemento *m*.

cement mixer *n* betoniera *f*.

cemetery ['semɪtrɪ] *n* cimitero *m*.

cent [sent] *n* (*Am*) cent *m inv*.

center ['sentəʳ] (*Am*) = **centre**.

centigrade ['sentɪgreɪd] *adj* centigrado(-a).

centimetre ['sentɪˌmiːtəʳ] *n* centimetro *m*.

centipede ['sentɪpiːd] *n* centopiedi *m inv*.

central ['sentrəl] *adj* centrale.

central heating *n* riscaldamento *m* autonomo.

central locking [-'lɒkɪŋ] *n* chiusura *f* delle porte centralizzata.

central reservation *n* (*Br*) zona *f* spartitraffico.

centre ['sentəʳ] *n* (*Br*) centro *m* ◆ *adj* (*Br*) centrale; **the ~ of attention** il centro dell'attenzione.

century ['sentʃʊrɪ] *n* secolo *m*.

ceramic [sɪ'ræmɪk] *adj* di ceramica □ **ceramics** *npl* oggetti *mpl* di ceramica.

cereal ['sɪərɪəl] *n* (*breakfast food*) cereali *mpl*.

ceremony ['serɪmənɪ] *n* cerimonia *f*.

certain ['sɜːtn] *adj* certo(-a),

she's ~ to be late farà tardi di sicuro; **to be ~ of sthg** essere certo di qc; **to make ~ (that)** assicurarsi che.

certainly ['sɜːtnlɪ] *adv* certamente, certo.

certificate [sə'tɪfɪkət] *n* certificato *m*.

certify ['sɜːtɪfaɪ] *vt (declare true)* attestare.

chain [tʃeɪn] *n* catena *f*; *(of islands)* arcipelago *m* ◆ *vt*: **to ~ sthg to sthg** incatenare qc a qc.

chain store *n* negozio che fa parte di una catena.

chair [tʃeər] *n* sedia *f*.

chair lift *n* seggiovia *f*.

chairman ['tʃeəmən] *(pl -men* [-mən]) *n* presidente *m*.

chairperson ['tʃeə,pɜːsn] *(pl -s)* *n* presidente *m* (-essa *f*).

chairwoman ['tʃeə,wʊmən] *(pl -women* [-,wɪmɪn]) *n* presidentessa *f*.

chalet ['ʃæleɪ] *n* chalet *m inv*; *(at holiday camp)* bungalow *m inv*.

chalk [tʃɔːk] *n* gesso *m*; **a piece of ~** un gesso.

chalkboard ['tʃɔːkbɔːd] *n (Am)* lavagna *f*.

challenge ['tʃælɪndʒ] *n* sfida *f* ◆ *vt (question)* mettere in discussione; **to ~ sb (to sthg)** sfidare qn (a qc).

chamber ['tʃeɪmbər] *n (room)* sala *f*.

chambermaid ['tʃeɪmbəmeɪd] *n* cameriera *f* (d'albergo).

champagne [,ʃæm'peɪn] *n* champagne *m inv*.

champion ['tʃæmpjən] *n* campione *m* (-essa *f*).

championship ['tʃæmpjənʃɪp] *n* campionato *m*.

chance [tʃɑːns] *n (luck)* caso *m*; *(possibility)* probabilità *f inv*; *(opportunity)* possibilità *f inv*, occasione *f* ◆ *vt*: **to ~ it** *(inf)* provarci; **to take a ~** rischiare; **by ~** per caso; **I came on the off ~ you'd be here** sono venuto per vedere se per caso ci fossi.

Chancellor of the Exchequer [,tʃɑːnsələrəvðəɪks'tʃekər] *n (Br)* = ministro *m* del Tesoro.

chandelier [,ʃændə'lɪər] *n* lampadario *m*.

change [tʃeɪndʒ] *n (alteration)* cambiamento *m*; *(money received back)* resto *m*; *(coins)* spiccioli *mpl* ◆ *vt* cambiare ◆ *vi* cambiare; *(change clothes)* cambiarsi; **a ~ of clothes** vestiti *mpl* di ricambio; **do you have ~ for a pound?** mi può cambiare una sterlina?; **for a ~** per cambiare; **to get ~d** cambiarsi; **to ~ money** cambiare i soldi; **to ~ a nappy** cambiare un pannolino; **to ~ a wheel** cambiare una ruota; **to ~ trains/planes** cambiare treno/aereo; **all ~!** *(on train)* per tutte le altre stazioni si cambia!

changeable ['tʃeɪndʒəbl] *adj (weather)* variabile.

change machine *n* distributore automatico di monete.

changing room ['tʃeɪndʒɪŋ-] *n (for sport)* spogliatoio *m*; *(in shop)* camerino *m*.

channel ['tʃænl] *n* canale *m*; **the (English) Channel** la Manica.

Channel Islands *npl*: **the ~** le Isole della Manica.

Channel Tunnel *n*: **the ~** il

tunnel sotto la Manica.

 CHANNEL TUNNEL

Chiamato anche Eurotunnel, il "Channel Tunnel" è il collegamento ferroviario costruito sotto la Manica tra Cheriton, vicino a Folkestone, e Coquelles, nei pressi di Calais. Inaugurato nel 1994, consente il trasporto di automezzi su un treno chiamato "Le Shuttle". Treni passeggeri piuttosto frequenti collegano direttamente Londra a Parigi e ad altre capitali europee.

---

chant [tʃɑ:nt] vt (RELIG) cantare; (words, slogan) scandire.

chaos ['keɪɒs] n caos m.

chaotic [keɪ'ɒtɪk] adj caotico(-a).

chap [tʃæp] n (Br: inf) tipo m.

chapatti [tʃə'pætɪ] n pane m azzimo indiano.

chapel ['tʃæpl] n cappella f.

chapped [tʃæpt] adj screpolato(-a).

chapter ['tʃæptə'] n capitolo m.

character ['kærəktə'] n carattere m; (in film, book, play) personaggio m; (inf: person, individual) tipo m.

characteristic [ˌkærəktə'rɪstɪk] adj caratteristico(-a) ♦ n caratteristica f.

charcoal ['tʃɑ:kəʊl] n (for barbecue) carbone m di legna.

charge [tʃɑ:dʒ] n (price) spesa f; (JUR) accusa f ♦ vt (customer) far pagare; (money) chiedere; (JUR) accusare; (battery) ricaricare ♦ vi (ask money) far pagare; (rush) precipitarsi; **to be in ~ (of)** essere re-

sponsabile (di); **to take ~ (of)** assumere la responsabilità (di); **free of ~** gratis; **extra ~** supplemento m; **there is no ~ for service** il servizio è gratuito.

char-grilled ['tʃɑ:grɪld] adj alla brace.

charity ['tʃærətɪ] n (organization) ente m di beneficenza; **to give to ~** dare soldi in beneficenza.

charity shop n negozio che vende articoli vari, il cui ricavato è destinato ad un ente di beneficenza.

charm [tʃɑ:m] n (attractiveness) fascino m ♦ vt affascinare.

charming ['tʃɑ:mɪŋ] adj affascinante.

chart [tʃɑ:t] n (diagram) grafico m; (map) carta f; **the ~s** l'hit-parade f inv.

chartered accountant [ˌtʃɑ:təd-] n esperto m (-a f) contabile.

charter flight ['tʃɑ:tə-] n volo m charter.

chase [tʃeɪs] n inseguimento m ♦ vt inseguire.

chat [tʃæt] n chiacchierata f ♦ vi chiacchierare; **to have a ~ (with)** fare quattro chiacchiere (con) ❑

chat up vt sep (Br: inf) agganciare.

château ['ʃætəʊ] n castello m.

chat show n (Br) talk show m inv.

chatty ['tʃætɪ] adj (person) chiacchierone(-a); (letter) pieno di pettegolezzi.

chauffeur ['ʃəʊfə'] n autista m.

cheap [tʃi:p] adj a buon mercato; (pej: low-quality) dozzinale.

cheap day return n biglietto di andata e ritorno a prezzo ridotto, valido per un solo giorno e soggetto a *restrizioni di orario.*

cheaply [ˈtʃiːplɪ] *adv* a basso prezzo.

cheat [tʃiːt] *n* imbroglione *m* (-a *f*) ♦ *vi* imbrogliare ♦ *vt*: **to ~ sb out of sthg** sottrarre qc a qn con l'inganno.

check [tʃek] *n* (*inspection*) controllo *m*; (*Am: bill*) conto *m*; (*Am: tick*) segno *m*; (*Am*) = **cheque** ♦ *vt* controllare; (*Am: tick*) spuntare ♦ *vi* verificare; **to ~ for sthg** controllare qc; **to ~ on sthg** controllare qc ❑ **check in** *vt sep* (*luggage*) far passare al check-in ♦ *vi* (*at hotel*) farsi registrare; (*at airport*) fare il check-in; **check off** *vt sep* spuntare; **check out** *vi* saldare il conto e andarsene; **check up** *vi*: **to ~ up (on)** fare delle indagini (su).

checked [tʃekt] *adj* a quadri.

checkers [ˈtʃekəz] *n* (*Am*) dama *f*.

check-in desk *n* banco *m* dell'accettazione bagagli OR del check-in.

checkout [ˈtʃekaʊt] *n* cassa *f*.

checkpoint [ˈtʃekpɔɪnt] *n* posto *m* di blocco.

checkroom [ˈtʃekrʊm] *n* (*Am*) deposito *m* bagagli.

checkup [ˈtʃekʌp] *n* check-up *m inv.*

cheddar (cheese) [ˈtʃedəʳ-] *n* tipo di formaggio semi-stagionato.

cheek [tʃiːk] *n* guancia *f*; **what a ~!** che faccia tosta!

cheeky [ˈtʃiːkɪ] *adj* sfacciato(-a).

cheer [tʃɪəʳ] *n* acclamazione *f* ♦ *vi* acclamare.

cheerful [ˈtʃɪəfʊl] *adj* allegro(-a); (*colour*) vivace.

cheerio [ˌtʃɪərɪˈəʊ] *excl* (*Br: inf*)

ciao!

cheers [tʃɪəz] *excl* (*when drinking*) cincin!; (*Br: inf: thank you*) grazie!

cheese [tʃiːz] *n* formaggio *m.*

cheeseboard [ˈtʃiːzbɔːd] *n* (*cheese and biscuits*) piatto *m* di formaggi.

cheeseburger [ˈtʃiːzbɜːgəʳ] *n* cheeseburger *m inv* (*panino con hamburger e formaggio fuso*).

cheesecake [ˈtʃiːzkeɪk] *n dolce a base di biscotti, formaggio fresco e panna.*

chef [ʃef] *n* chef *m inv.*

chef's special *n* specialità *f inv* della casa.

chemical [ˈkemɪkl] *adj* chimico(-a) ♦ *n* sostanza *f* chimica.

chemist [ˈkemɪst] *n* (*Br: pharmacist*) farmacista *mf*; (*scientist*) chimico *m* (-a *f*); **~'s** (*Br: shop*) farmacia *f.*

chemistry [ˈkemɪstrɪ] *n* chimica *f.*

cheque [tʃek] *n* (*Br*) assegno *m*; **to pay by ~** pagare con un assegno.

chequebook [ˈtʃekbʊk] *n* libretto *m* degli assegni.

cheque card *n* carta *f* assegni.

cherry [ˈtʃerɪ] *n* ciliegia *f.*

chess [tʃes] *n* scacchi *mpl.*

chest [tʃest] *n* (*of body*) torace *m*; (*box*) cassa *f.*

chestnut [ˈtʃesnʌt] *n* castagna *f* ♦ *adj* (*colour*) castano(-a).

chest of drawers *n* cassettone *m.*

chew [tʃuː] *vt* masticare ♦ *n* (*sweet*) caramella *f* (morbida).

chewing gum [ˈtʃuːɪŋ-] *n* gomma *f* da masticare.

chic [ʃiːk] *adj* alla moda, chic (inv).

chicken ['tʃɪkɪn] *n (bird)* gallina *f; (meat)* pollo *m*.

chicken breast *n* petto *m* di pollo.

chicken Kiev [-'kiːev] *n* filetto di pollo farcito con burro all'aglio, impanato e fritto.

chicken pox [-pɒks] *n* varicella *f*.

chickpea ['tʃɪkpiː] *n* cece *m*.

chicory ['tʃɪkən] *n* cicoria *f*.

chief [tʃiːf] *adj (highest-ranking)* capo *(inv); (main)* principale ◆ *n* capo *m*.

chiefly ['tʃiːflɪ] *adv (mainly)* principalmente; *(especially)* soprattutto.

child [tʃaɪld] *(pl* **children)** *n (young boy, girl)* bambino *m* (-a *f); (son, daughter)* figlio *m* (-a *f*).

child abuse *n* maltrattamento *m* di minori.

child benefit *n (Br)* = assegno *m* di famiglia.

childhood ['tʃaɪldhʊd] *n* infanzia *f*.

childish ['tʃaɪldɪʃ] *adj (pej)* infantile.

childminder ['tʃaɪld,maɪndə'] *n (Br)* bambinaia *f*.

children ['tʃɪldrən] *pl* → **child**.

childrenswear ['tʃɪldrənzweə'] *n* abbigliamento *m* per bambini.

child seat *n (in car)* seggiolino *m* per bambini.

Chile ['tʃɪlɪ] *n* il Cile.

chill [tʃɪl] *n (illness)* infreddatura *f* ◆ *vt* raffreddare; **there's a ~ in the air** l'aria è fredda.

chilled [tʃɪld] *adj* freddo(-a); **'serve ~'** 'servire fresco'.

chilli ['tʃɪlɪ] *(pl* **-ies)** *n (vegetable)* peperoncino *m* piccante; *(dish)* = **chilli con carne**.

chilli con carne ['tʃɪlɪkɒn-'kɑːnɪ] *n* piatto messicano a base di carne e fagioli rossi cotti in spezie e salsa piccante.

chilly ['tʃɪlɪ] *adj* freddo(-a).

chimney ['tʃɪmnɪ] *n* camino *m*.

chimneypot ['tʃɪmnɪpɒt] *n* comignolo *m*.

chimpanzee [,tʃɪmpən'ziː] *n* scimpanzé *m inv*.

chin [tʃɪn] *n* mento *m*.

china ['tʃaɪnə] *n (material)* porcellana *f*.

China ['tʃaɪnə] *n* la Cina.

Chinese [,tʃaɪ'niːz] *adj* cinese ◆ *n (language)* cinese *m* ◆ *npl*: **the ~** i cinesi; **a ~ restaurant** un ristorante cinese.

chip [tʃɪp] *n (small piece)* scheggia *f; (mark)* scheggiatura *f; (counter)* fiche *f inv; (COMPUT)* chip *m inv* ◆ *vt* scheggiare ❑ **chips** *npl (Br: French fries)* patate *fpl* fritte; *(Am: crisps)* patatine *fpl*.

chiropodist [kɪ'rɒpədɪst] *n* callista *mf*.

chisel ['tʃɪzl] *n* cesello *m*.

chives [tʃaɪvz] *npl* erba *f* cipollina.

chlorine ['klɔːriːn] *n* cloro *m*.

choc-ice ['tʃɒkaɪs] *n (Br)* blocco di gelato ricoperto di cioccolato.

chocolate ['tʃɒkələt] *n (food)* cioccolato *m*, cioccolata *f; (sweet)* cioccolatino *m; (drink)* cioccolata ◆ *adj* al cioccolato.

chocolate biscuit *n* biscotto *m* al cioccolato.

choice [tʃɔɪs] *n* scelta *f* ◆ *adj*

(meat, ingredients) di prima qualità; **the dressing of your ~** il condimento di vostra scelta.

choir ['kwaɪəʳ] *n* coro *m*.

choke [tʃəʊk] *n (AUT)* (valvola *f* dell')aria *f inv* ♦ *vt* soffocare ♦ *vi (on fishbone etc)* strozzarsi; *(to death)* soffocare.

cholera ['kɒlərə] *n* colera *m*.

choose [tʃuːz] *(pt* chose, *pp* chosen) *vt & vi* scegliere; **to ~ to do sthg** scegliere di fare qc.

chop [tʃɒp] *n (of meat)* braciola *f* ♦ *vt* tagliare ◻ **chop down** *vt sep* abbattere; **chop up** *vt sep* tagliare a pezzetti.

chopper ['tʃɒpəʳ] *n (inf: helicopter)* elicottero *m*.

chopping board ['tʃɒpɪŋ-] *n* tagliere *m*.

choppy ['tʃɒpɪ] *adj* increspato(-a).

chopsticks ['tʃɒpstɪks] *npl* bastoncini *mpl* cinesi.

chop suey [,tʃɒp'suːɪ] *n piatto cinese a base di riso, striscioline di maiale o pollo, verdura e germogli di soia.*

chord [kɔːd] *n* accordo *m*.

chore [tʃɔːʳ] *n* faccenda *f*.

chorus ['kɔːrəs] *n (part of song)* ritornello *m*; *(group of singers, dancers)* coro *m*.

chose [tʃəʊz] *pt* → choose.

chosen ['tʃəʊzn] *pp* → choose.

choux pastry [ʃuː-] *n* pasta *f* per bignè.

chowder ['tʃaʊdəʳ] *n zuppa di pesce o frutti di mare.*

chow mein [,tʃaʊ'meɪn] *n piatto cinese di tagliolini fritti con verdure, carne o frutti di mare.*

Christ [kraɪst] *n* Cristo *m*.

christen ['krɪsn] *vt (baby)* battezzare.

Christian ['krɪstʃən] *adj* cristiano(-a) ♦ *n* cristiano *m* (-a *f*).

Christian name *n* nome *m* di battesimo.

Christmas ['krɪsməs] *n* Natale *m*; **Happy ~!** Buon Natale!

Christmas card *n* biglietto *m* d'auguri di Natale.

Christmas carol [-'kærəl] *n* canto *m* di Natale.

Christmas Day *n* il giorno di Natale.

Christmas Eve *n* la vigilia di Natale.

Christmas pudding *n dolce tradizionale natalizio a base di uva passa e frutta candita.*

Christmas tree *n* albero *m* di Natale.

chrome [krəʊm] *n* cromo *m*.

chuck [tʃʌk] *vt (inf) (throw)* buttare; *(boyfriend, girlfriend)* mollare ◻ **chuck away** *vt sep* buttare via.

chunk [tʃʌŋk] *n* pezzo *m*.

church [tʃɜːtʃ] *n* chiesa *f*; **to go to ~** andare in chiesa.

churchyard ['tʃɜːtʃjɑːd] *n* cimitero *m*.

chute [ʃuːt] *n* scivolo *m*.

chutney ['tʃʌtnɪ] *n salsa piccante agrodolce a base di frutta e spezie.*

cider ['saɪdəʳ] *n* sidro *m*.

cigar [sɪ'gɑːʳ] *n* sigaro *m*.

cigarette [,sɪgə'ret] *n* sigaretta *f*.

cigarette lighter *n* accendino *m*.

cinema ['sɪnəmə] *n* cinema *m inv*.

cinnamon ['sɪnəmən] *n* cannella *f*.

circle ['sɜ:kl] n (shape, ring) cerchio m; (in theatre) galleria f ◆ vt (draw circle around) cerchiare; (move round) girare intorno a ◆ vi (plane) girare in circolo.

circuit ['sɜ:kɪt] n (track) circuito m; (lap) giro m.

circular ['sɜ:kjʊlə'] adj circolare ◆ n circolare f.

circulation [,sɜ:kjʊ'leɪʃn] n (of blood) circolazione f; (of newspaper, magazine) tiratura f.

circumstances ['sɜ:kəmstənsɪz] npl circostanze fpl; **in** OR **under the ~** date le circostanze.

circus ['sɜ:kəs] n circo m.

cistern ['sɪstən] n (of toilet) serbatoio m dell'acqua.

citizen ['sɪtɪzn] n cittadino m (-a f).

city ['sɪtɪ] n città f inv; **the City** la City (il centro finanziario di Londra).

city centre n centro m (della) città.

city hall n (Am) municipio m.

civilian [sɪ'vɪljən] n civile m.

civilized ['sɪvɪlaɪzd] adj (society) civilizzato(-a); (person, evening) cortese.

civil rights [,sɪvl-] npl diritti mpl civili.

civil servant [,sɪvl-] n impiegato m (-a f) statale.

civil service [,sɪvl-] n amministrazione f pubblica.

civil war [,sɪvl-] n guerra f civile.

cl (abbr of centilitre) cl.

claim [kleɪm] n (assertion) affermazione f; (demand) richiesta f, domanda f; (for insurance) domanda di indennizzo ◆ vt (allege) affer-

mare, sostenere; (demand) richiedere; (credit, responsibility) rivendicare ◆ vi (on insurance) richiedere l'indennizzo.

claimant ['kleɪmənt] n (of benefit) richiedente mf.

claim form n modulo m per il rimborso.

clam [klæm] n vongola f.

clamp [klæmp] n (for car) ganascia f (bloccaruota) ◆ vt (car) bloccare con ganasce.

clap [klæp] vi applaudire.

claret ['klærət] n vino rosso di Bordeaux.

clarinet [,klærə'net] n clarinetto m.

clash [klæʃ] n (noise) rumore m metallico; (confrontation) scontro m ◆ vi (colours) stonare; (event, date) coincidere.

clasp [klɑ:sp] n (fastener) fermaglio m ◆ vt stringere.

class [klɑ:s] n classe f; (teaching period) lezione f ◆ vt: **to ~ sb/sthg (as)** classificare qn/qc (come).

classic ['klæsɪk] adj classico(-a) ◆ n classico m.

classical ['klæsɪkl] adj classico(-a).

classical music n musica f classica.

classification [,klæsɪfɪ'keɪʃn] n classificazione f.

classified ads [,klæsɪfaɪd-] npl piccoli annunci mpl.

classroom ['klɑ:srʊm] n aula f.

claustrophobic [,klɔ:strə'fəʊbɪk] adj (person) claustrofobo(-a); (place, situation) claustrofobico(-a).

claw [klɔ:] n (of bird, cat, dog) artiglio m; (of crab, lobster) pinza f.

clay [kleɪ] n argilla f.

clean [kliːn] vt pulire ◆ adj pulito(-a); **to ~ one's teeth** lavarsi i denti; **I have a ~ driving licence** non sono mai stato multato per infrazioni gravi.

cleaner ['kliːnər] n (person) addetto m (-a f) alle pulizie; (substance) detergente m.

cleanse [klenz] vt pulire.

cleanser ['klenzər] n detergente m.

clear [klɪər] adj chiaro(-a); (transparent) trasparente; (unobstructed) libero(-a); (view) sgombro(-a); (day, sky) sereno(-a) ◆ vt (road, path) sgombrare; (pond) ripulire; (jump over) saltare; (declare not guilty) scagionare; (authorize) autorizzare; (cheque) autorizzare l'accreditamento di ◆ vi (weather) schiarirsi; (fog) levarsi; **to be ~ (about sthg)** avere capito esattamente (qc); **to be ~ of sthg** (not touching) essere staccato da qc; **to ~ one's throat** schiarirsi la voce; **to ~ the table** sparecchiare ❑ **clear up** vt sep (room, toys) mettere a posto; (problem, confusion) chiarire ◆ vi (weather) schiarirsi; (tidy up) mettere a posto.

clearance ['klɪərəns] n (authorization) autorizzazione f; (free distance) distanza f; (for takeoff) autorizzazione f (al decollo).

clearance sale n liquidazione f totale della merce.

clearing ['klɪərɪŋ] n radura f.

clearly ['klɪəlɪ] adv chiaramente.

clearway ['klɪəweɪ] n (Br) strada f con divieto di fermata.

clementine ['kleməntaɪn] n mandarancio m.

clerk [Br klɑːk, Am klɜːrk] n (in office) impiegato m (-a f); (Am: in shop) commesso m (-a f).

clever ['klevər] adj (person) intelligente; (idea, device) ingegnoso(-a).

click [klɪk] n scatto m ◆ vi (make sound) schioccare.

client ['klaɪənt] n cliente mf.

cliff [klɪf] n (by the sea) scoglio m; (inland) rupe f.

climate ['klaɪmɪt] n clima m.

climax ['klaɪmæks] n culmine m.

climb [klaɪm] vt salire su; (tree) arrampicarsi su; (mountain) scalare ◆ vi salire; (plane) prendere quota ❑ **climb down** vt fus scendere da ◆ vi scendere; **climb up** vt fus salire su.

climber ['klaɪmər] n (person) scalatore m (-trice f).

climbing ['klaɪmɪŋ] n alpinismo m; **to go ~** fare alpinismo.

climbing frame n (Br) castello m (gioco per bambini).

clingfilm ['klɪŋfɪlm] n (Br) pellicola f (per alimenti).

clinic ['klɪnɪk] n clinica f.

clip [klɪp] n (fastener) fermaglio m; (for paper) graffetta f; (of film, programme) sequenza f ◆ vt (fasten) fermare insieme; (cut) tagliare; (tickets) forare.

cloak [kləʊk] n mantello m.

cloakroom ['kləʊkrʊm] n (for coats) guardaroba m inv; (Br: toilet) toilettes fpl.

clock [klɒk] n orologio m; (mileometer) contachilometri m inv; **round the ~** 24 ore su 24.

clockwise ['klɒkwaɪz] adv in senso orario.

clog [klɒg] n zoccolo m ◆ vt intasare.

close¹ [kləʊs] *adj* vicino(-a); *(relation, contact, resemblance)* stretto(-a); *(friend)* intimo(-a); *(examination)* attento(-a); *(race, contest)* combattuto(-a) ♦ *adv* vicino; **~ by** vicino; **~ to** *(near)* vicino a; *(on the verge of)* sull'orlo di.

close² [kləʊz] *vt* chiudere ♦ *vi* *(door, jar, eyes)* chiudersi; *(shop, office)* chiudere; *(deadline, offer, meeting)* finire ❏ **close down** *vt sep & vi* chiudere (definitivamente).

closed [kləʊzd] *adj* chiuso(-a).

closely ['kləʊslɪ] *adv* *(related, involved)* strettamente; *(follow, examine)* da vicino, attentamente.

closet ['klɒzɪt] *n* (Am) armadio *m*.

close-up ['kləʊs-] *n* primo piano *m*.

closing time ['kləʊzɪŋ-] *n* orario *m* di chiusura.

clot [klɒt] *n (of blood)* grumo *m*.

cloth [klɒθ] *n (fabric)* stoffa *f*, tessuto *m*; *(piece of cloth)* strofinaccio *m*, panno *m*.

clothes [kləʊðz] *npl* vestiti *mpl*, abiti *mpl*.

clothesline ['kləʊðzlaɪn] *n* filo *m* della biancheria.

clothes peg *n (Br)* molletta *f*.

clothespin ['kləʊðzpɪn] *(Am)* = **clothes peg**.

clothes shop *n* negozio *m* di abbigliamento.

clothing ['kləʊðɪŋ] *n* abbigliamento *m*.

clotted cream [,klɒtɪd-] *n* panna molto densa tipica della Cornovaglia.

cloud [klaʊd] *n* nuvola *f*.

cloudy ['klaʊdɪ] *adj (sky, day)* nuvoloso(-a); *(liquid)* torbido(-a).

clove [kləʊv] *n (of garlic)* spicchio *m* ❏ **cloves** *npl (spice)* chiodi *mpl* di garofano.

clown [klaʊn] *n* pagliaccio *m*.

club [klʌb] *n (organization)* club *m inv*, circolo *m*; *(nightclub)* locale *m* notturno; *(stick)* mazza *f* ❏ **clubs** *npl (in cards)* fiori *mpl*.

clubbing ['klʌbɪŋ] *n*: **to go ~** *(inf)* andare in discoteca.

club class *n* club class *f inv*.

club sandwich *n (Am) sandwich a due o più strati.*

club soda *n (Am)* acqua *f* di seltz.

clue [kluː] *n (information)* indizio *m*; *(in crossword)* definizione *f*; **I haven't got a ~** non ho la minima idea.

clumsy ['klʌmzɪ] *adj (person)* goffo(-a).

clutch [klʌtʃ] *n* frizione *f* ♦ *vt* tenere stretto, afferrare.

cm *(abbr of centimetre)* cm.

c/o *(abbr of care of)* c/o.

Co. *(abbr of company)* C.ia.

coach [kəʊtʃ] *n (bus)* pullman *m inv*, autobus *m inv*; *(of train)* carrozza *f*; *(SPORT)* allenatore *m* (-trice *f*).

coach party *n (Br)* gruppo *m* in viaggio organizzato in pullman.

coach station *n* stazione *f* dei pullman.

coach trip *n (Br)* escursione *f* in pullman.

coal [kəʊl] *n* carbone *m*.

coal mine *n* miniera *f* di carbone.

coarse [kɔːs] *adj (rough)* ruvido(-a); *(vulgar)* rozzo(-a).

coast [kəʊst] *n* costa *f*.

coaster ['kəʊstə'] n (for glass) sottobicchiere m.

coastguard ['kəʊstgɑːd] n guardia f costiera.

coastline ['kəʊstlaɪn] n costa f.

coat [kəʊt] n cappotto m; (of animal) pelo m ♦ vt: **to ~ sthg (with)** ricoprire qc (con OR di).

coat hanger n gruccia f (per abiti).

coating ['kəʊtɪŋ] n rivestimento m.

cobbled street ['kɒbld-] n strada f in acciottolato.

cobbles ['kɒblz] npl ciottoli mpl.

cobweb ['kɒbweb] n ragnatela f.

Coca-Cola® [,kəʊkə'kəʊlə] n Coca-Cola® f.

cocaine [kəʊ'keɪn] n cocaina f.

cock [kɒk] n (male chicken) gallo m.

cock-a-leekie [,kɒkə'liːkɪ] n zuppa f di porri e pollo.

cockerel ['kɒkrəl] n galletto m.

cockles ['kɒklz] npl cardii mpl.

cockpit ['kɒkpɪt] n cabina f di pilotaggio.

cockroach ['kɒkrəʊtʃ] n scarafaggio m.

cocktail ['kɒkteɪl] n cocktail m inv.

cocktail party n cocktail m inv.

cock-up n (Br: vulg) casino m.

cocoa ['kəʊkəʊ] n (drink) cacao m.

coconut ['kəʊkənʌt] n noce f di cocco.

cod [kɒd] (pl inv) n merluzzo m.

code [kəʊd] n codice m; (dialling code) prefisso m.

cod-liver oil n olio m di fegato di merluzzo.

coeducational [,kəʊedjuː'keɪʃənl] adj misto(-a).

coffee ['kɒfɪ] n caffè m inv; **black/white ~** caffè nero/macchiato; **ground/instant ~** caffè macinato/istantaneo.

coffee bar n (Br) caffè m inv.

coffee break n pausa f per il caffè.

coffeepot ['kɒfɪpɒt] n caffettiera f.

coffee shop n (cafe) caffè m inv, bar m inv; (in store etc) caffetteria f.

coffee table n tavolino m (basso).

coffin ['kɒfɪn] n bara f.

cog(wheel) ['kɒg(wiːl)] n ingranaggio m.

coil [kɔɪl] n (of rope) rotolo m; (Br: contraceptive) spirale f ♦ vt avvolgere, arrotolare.

coin [kɔɪn] n moneta f.

coinbox ['kɔɪnbɒks] n (Br) telefono m a monete.

coincide [,kəʊɪn'saɪd] vi: **to ~ (with)** coincidere (con).

coincidence [kəʊ'ɪnsɪdəns] n coincidenza f.

Coke® [kəʊk] n coca® f.

colander ['kʌləndə'] n colino m.

cold [kəʊld] adj freddo(-a) ♦ n (illness) raffreddore m; (low temperature) freddo m; **I'm ~** ho freddo; **it's ~** fa freddo; **to get ~** (food, drink) raffreddarsi; (person) avere freddo; (weather) venire freddo; **to catch ~** prendere freddo; **to catch a ~** prendere il raffreddore.

cold cuts (Am) = **cold meats**.

cold meats npl affettati mpl.

coleslaw ['kəʊlslɔː] n insalata di

cavolo, carote, cipolle e maionese.

colic ['kɒlɪk] *n* colica *f.*

collaborate [kə'læbəreɪt] *vi* collaborare.

collapse [kə'læps] *vi (building, tent)* crollare; *(person)* avere un collasso.

collar ['kɒlə'] *n (of shirt, coat)* colletto *m*; *(of dog, cat)* collare *m.*

collarbone ['kɒləbəʊn] *n* clavicola *f.*

colleague ['kɒliːg] *n* collega *mf.*

collect [kə'lekt] *vt* raccogliere; *(as a hobby)* collezionare; *(go and get)* andare a prendere ◆ *vi (dust, leaves, crowd)* raccogliersi ◆ *adv (Am):* **to call ~** fare una telefonata a carico del destinatario.

collection [kə'lekʃn] *n (of stamps, coins etc)* collezione *f*, raccolta *f*; *(of stories, poems)* raccolta; *(of money)* colletta *f*; *(of mail)* levata *f.*

collector [kə'lektə'] *n (as a hobby)* collezionista *m.*

college ['kɒlɪdʒ] *n (school)* istituto *m* superiore; *(Br: of university)* tipo di organizzazione indipendente di studenti e professori in cui si dividono certe università; *(Am: university)* università *f inv.*

collide [kə'laɪd] *vi:* **to ~ (with)** scontrarsi (con).

collision [kə'lɪʒn] *n* collisione *f.*

cologne [kə'ləʊn] *n* (acqua *f* di) colonia *f.*

colon ['kəʊlən] *n (GRAMM)* due punti *mpl.*

colonel ['kɜːnl] *n* colonnello *m.*

colony ['kɒlənɪ] *n* colonia *f.*

color ['kʌlə'] *(Am)* = **colour.**

colour ['kʌlə'] *n* colore *m* ◆ *adj*

(photograph, film) a colori ◆ *vt (hair)* tingere; *(food)* colorare ❑ **colour in** *vt sep* colorare.

colour-blind *adj* daltonico(-a).

colourful ['kʌləfʊl] *adj* vivace.

colouring ['kʌlərɪŋ] *n (of food)* colorante *m*; *(complexion)* colorito *m.*

colouring book *n* album *m inv* da colorare.

colour supplement *n* supplemento *m* a colori.

colour television *n* televisione *f* a colori.

column ['kɒləm] *n* colonna *f*; *(newspaper article)* rubrica *f.*

coma ['kəʊmə] *n* coma *m inv.*

comb [kəʊm] *n* pettine *m* ◆ *vt:* **to ~ one's hair** pettinarsi.

combination [,kɒmbɪ'neɪʃn] *n* combinazione *f.*

combine [kəm'baɪn] *vt:* **to ~ sthg (with)** combinare qc (con).

combine harvester ['kɒmbaɪn-'hɑːvɪstə'] *n* mietitrebbia *f.*

come [kʌm] *(pt* came, *pp* come) *vi* 1. *(move)* venire; **we came by taxi** siamo venuti in taxi; **~ and see!** vieni a vedere!; **~ here!** vieni qui!

2. *(arrive)* arrivare; **they still haven't ~** non sono ancora arrivati; **to ~ home** tornare a casa; **'coming soon'** 'prossimamente'.

3. *(in order):* **to ~ first** *(in sequence)* venire per primo; *(in competition)* arrivare primo; **to ~ last** *(in sequence)* venire per ultimo; *(in competition)* arrivare ultimo.

4. *(reach):* **to ~ up/down** to arrivare a.

5. *(become):* **to ~ undone** slacciarsi; **to ~ true** realizzarsi.

6. *(be sold):* **they ~ in packs of six** si

vendono in confezioni da sei.

❏ **come across** vt fus (person) imbattersi in; (thing) trovare (per caso); **come along** vi (progress) procedere; (arrive) arrivare; ~ **along!** (as encouragement) forza!; (hurry up) sbrigati!; **come apart** vi cadere a pezzi; **come back** vi tornare; **come down** vi (price) calare; **come down with** vt fus (illness) buscarsi; **come from** vt fus venire da; **come in** vi (enter) entrare; (arrive) arrivare; (tide) salire; ~ **in!** avanti!; **come off** vi (become detached) staccarsi, venir via; (succeed) riuscire; **come on** vi (project) procedere; (student) fare progressi; ~ **on!** (as encouragement) forza!; (hurry up) sbrigati!; **come out** vi uscire; (photo) venire, riuscire; (stain) scomparire; (sun, moon) apparire; **come over** vi (visit) venire; **come round** vi (visit) venire; (regain consciousness) riprendere conoscenza; **come to** vt fus (subj: bill): **it ~s to £10** viene 10 sterline; **come up** vi (go upstairs) salire; (be mentioned) essere sollevato(-a); (happen, arise) presentarsi; (sun, moon) sorgere; **come up with** vt fus (idea) proporre.

comedian [kə'miːdjən] n comico m (-a f).

comedy ['kɒmədɪ] n commedia f; (humour) humour m.

comfort ['kʌmfət] n (ease) benessere m; (luxury) comfort m inv, comodità f inv; (consolation) conforto m ♦ vt confortare, consolare.

comfortable ['kʌmftəbl] adj comodo(-a); (after operation) in condizioni stazionarie; (financially) agiato(-a); **I don't feel ~ here** non

mi sento a mio agio qui.

comic ['kɒmɪk] adj comico(-a) ♦ n (person) comico m (-a f); (magazine) giornalino m.

comical ['kɒmɪkl] adj comico(-a).

comic strip n fumetto m.

comma ['kɒmə] n virgola f.

command [kə'mɑːnd] n (order) comando m, ordine m; (mastery) padronanza f ♦ vt (order) ordinare a; (be in charge of) comandare.

commander [kə'mɑːndər] n comandante m.

commemorate [kə'meməreɪt] vt commemorare.

commence [kə'mens] vi (fml) cominciare.

comment ['kɒment] n commento m ♦ vi commentare.

commentary ['kɒməntrɪ] n (on TV) telecronaca f; (on radio) radiocronaca f.

commentator ['kɒmənteɪtər] n (on TV) telecronista mf; (on radio) radiocronista mf.

commerce ['kɒmɜːs] n commercio m.

commercial [kə'mɜːʃl] adj commerciale ♦ n pubblicità f inv.

commercial break n intervallo m pubblicitario.

commission [kə'mɪʃn] n commissione f.

commit [kə'mɪt] vt (crime, sin) commettere; **to ~ o.s. (to doing sthg)** impegnarsi (a fare qc); **to ~ suicide** suicidarsi.

committee [kə'mɪtɪ] n comitato m.

commodity [kə'mɒdətɪ] n merce f, articolo m.

common ['kɒmən] *adj* comune; *(pej: vulgar)* volgare ◆ *n (Br: land)* prato *m* pubblico; **in ~** *(shared)* in comune.

commonly ['kɒmənlɪ] *adv (generally)* comunemente.

Common Market *n* Mercato *m* comune.

common room *n (for teachers)* sala *f* professori; *(for students)* sala di ritrovo.

common sense *n* buon senso *m*.

Commonwealth ['kɒmənwelθ] *n*: **the ~** il Commonwealth.

communal ['kɒmjʊnl] *adj (bathroom, kitchen)* in comune.

communicate [kə'mju:nɪkeɪt] *vi*: **to ~ (with)** comunicare (con).

communication [kə,mju:nɪ'keɪʃn] *n* comunicazione *f*.

communication cord *n (Br)* freno *m* di emergenza.

communist ['kɒmjʊnɪst] *n* comunista *mf*.

community [kə'mju:nətɪ] *n* comunità *f inv*.

community centre *n* centro *m* sociale.

commute [kə'mju:t] *vi* fare il pendolare.

commuter [kə'mju:təʳ] *n* pendolare *mf*.

compact [*adj* kəm'pækt, *n* 'kɒmpækt] *adj* compatto(-a) ◆ *n (for make-up)* portacipria *m inv*; *(Am: car)* utilitaria *f*.

compact disc [,kɒmpækt-] *n* compact disc *m inv*.

compact disc player *n* lettore *m* di compact disc.

company ['kʌmpənɪ] *n (business)*

società *f inv*, compagnia *f*; *(companionship, guests)* compagnia; **to keep sb ~** fare OR tenere compagnia a qn.

company car *n* auto *f* della ditta.

comparatively [kəm'pærətɪvlɪ] *adv* relativamente.

compare [kəm'peəʳ] *vt*: **to ~ sthg (with)** confrontare qc (con); **~d with** paragonato a.

comparison [kəm'pærɪsn] *n* confronto *m*, paragone *m*; **in ~ with** in confronto a.

compartment [kəm'pɑ:tmənt] *n (of train)* scompartimento *m*; *(section)* compartimento *m*.

compass ['kʌmpəs] *n (magnetic)* bussola *f*; **(a pair of) ~es** un compasso.

compatible [kəm'pætəbl] *adj* compatibile.

compensate ['kɒmpenseɪt] *vt* risarcire ◆ *vi*: **to ~ (for sthg)** compensare (qc); **to ~ sb for sthg** compensare qn di OR per qc.

compensation [,kɒmpen'seɪʃn] *n (money)* risarcimento *m*.

compete [kəm'pi:t] *vi (take part)* gareggiare, concorrere; **to ~ with sb for sthg** competere con qn per qc.

competent ['kɒmpɪtənt] *adj* competente.

competition [,kɒmpɪ'tɪʃn] *n (race, contest)* gara *f*, competizione *f*; *(rivalry)* concorrenza *f*; **the ~** *(rivals)* la concorrenza.

competitive [kəm'petətɪv] *adj (price)* competitivo(-a); *(person)* che ha spirito di competizione.

competitor [kəm'petɪtəʳ] *n* concorrente *mf*.

complain [kəm'pleɪn] *vi*: to ~ **(about)** lamentarsi (di).

complaint [kəm'pleɪnt] *n (statement)* lamentela *f*, reclamo *m*; *(illness)* malattia *f*.

complement ['kɒmplɪ,ment] *vt* completare.

complete [kəm'pli:t] *adj* completo(-a) ♦ *vt* completare; *(a form)* riempire; ~ **with** completo di.

completely [kəm'pli:tlɪ] *adv* completamente.

complex ['kɒmpleks] *adj* complesso(-a) ♦ *n* complesso *m*.

complexion [kəm'plekʃn] *n (of skin)* carnagione *f*.

complicated ['kɒmplɪkeɪtɪd] *adj* complicato(-a).

compliment [*n* 'kɒmplɪmənt, *vb* 'kɒmplɪment] *n* complimento *m* ♦ *vt* fare i complimenti a.

complimentary [,kɒmplɪ'mentərɪ] *adj (seat, ticket)* (in) omaggio *(inv)*; *(words, person)* lusinghiero(-a).

compose [kəm'pəʊz] *vt* comporre; **to be ~d of** essere composto da OR di.

composed [kəm'pəʊzd] *adj* composto(-a), calmo(-a).

composer [kəm'pəʊzəʳ] *n* compositore *m* (-trice *f*).

composition [,kɒmpə'zɪʃn] *n (essay)* composizione *f*.

compound ['kɒmpaʊnd] *n (substance)* composto *m*; *(word)* parola *f* composta.

comprehensive [,kɒmprɪ'hensɪv] *adj* esauriente, completo(-a).

comprehensive (school) *n* *(Br)* scuola secondaria ad ammissione non selettiva.

compressed air [kəm'prest-] *n* aria *f* compressa.

comprise [kəm'praɪz] *vt* comprendere.

compromise ['kɒmprəmaɪz] *n* compromesso *m*.

compulsory [kəm'pʌlsərɪ] *adj* obbligatorio(-a).

computer [kəm'pju:təʳ] *n* computer *m inv*.

computer game *n* gioco *m* su computer.

computerized [kəm'pju:təraɪzd] *adj* computerizzato(-a).

computer operator *n* operatore *m* (-trice *f*) di computer.

computer programmer [-'prəʊgræməʳ] *n* programmatore *m* (-trice *f*).

computing [kəm'pju:tɪŋ] *n* informatica *f*.

con [kɒn] *n (inf: trick)* truffa *f*; **all mod ~s** tutti i comfort.

conceal [kən'si:l] *vt* nascondere.

conceited [kən'si:tɪd] *adj (pej)* presuntuoso(-a).

concentrate ['kɒnsəntreɪt] *vi* concentrarsi ♦ *vt*: **to be ~d** *(in one place)* essere concentrato; **to ~ on** sthg concentrarsi su qc.

concentrated ['kɒnsəntreɪtɪd] *adj (juice, soup, baby food)* concentrato(-a).

concentration [,kɒnsən'treɪʃn] *n* concentrazione *f*.

concern [kən'sɜ:n] *n (worry)* preoccupazione *f*; *(matter of interest)* affare *m*; *(COMM)* azienda *f* ♦ *vt (be about)* trattare di; *(worry)* preoccupare; *(involve)* riguardare; **to be ~ed about** essere preoccupato per; **to be ~ed with** riguardare; **to ~ o.s. with** sthg preoccuparsi di qc;

as far as I'm ~ed per quanto mi riguarda.

concerned [kən'sɜːnd] *adj (worried)* preoccupato(-a).

concerning [kən'sɜːnɪŋ] *prép* riguardo a, circa.

concert ['kɒnsət] *n* concerto *m*.

concession [kən'seʃn] *n (reduced price)* riduzione *f*.

concise [kən'saɪs] *adj* conciso(-a).

conclude [kən'kluːd] *vt* concludere ♦ *vi (fml: end)* concludersi.

conclusion [kən'kluːʒn] *n* conclusione *f*.

concrete ['kɒŋkriːt] *adj (building, path)* di cemento; *(idea, plan)* concreto(-a) ♦ *n* calcestruzzo *m*, cemento *m* armato.

concussion [kən'kʌʃn] *n* commozione *f* cerebrale.

condensation [ˌkɒnden'seɪʃn] *n* condensazione *f*.

condensed milk [kən'denst-] *n* latte *m* condensato.

condition [kən'dɪʃn] *n* condizione *f*; *(illness)* malattia *f*; **to be out of ~** non essere in forma; **on ~ that** a condizione che (+ *subjunctive)*.

conditioner [kən'dɪʃnər] *n (for hair)* balsamo *m*; *(for clothes)* ammorbidente *m*.

condo ['kɒndəʊ] *(Am: inf)* = **condominium.**

condom ['kɒndəm] *n* preservativo *m*.

condominium [ˌkɒndə'mɪnɪəm] *n (Am) (block of flats)* condominio *m*; *(flat)* appartamento *m* in un condominio.

conduct [*vb* kən'dʌkt, *n* 'kɒndʌkt]

vt (investigation, business) dirigere, condurre; *(MUS)* dirigere ♦ *n (fml: behaviour)* condotta *f*; **to ~ o.s.** *(fml)* comportarsi.

conductor [kən'dʌktər] *n (MUS)* direttore *m (-trice f)* d'orchestra; *(on bus)* bigliettaio *m (-a f)*; *(Am: on train)* capotreno *mf*.

cone [kəʊn] *n* cono *m*; *(on roads)* cono spartitraffico.

confectioner's [kən'fekʃnəz] *n (shop)* negozio *m* di dolciumi.

confectionery [kən'fekʃnərɪ] *n* dolciumi *mpl*.

conference ['kɒnfərəns] *n* conferenza *f*.

confess [kən'fes] *vi*: **to ~ (to sthg)** confessare (qc).

confession [kən'feʃn] *n* confessione *f*.

confidence ['kɒnfɪdəns] *n (self-assurance)* sicurezza *f* di sé; *(trust)* fiducia *f*; **to have ~ in** avere fiducia in.

confident ['kɒnfɪdənt] *adj (self-assured)* sicuro(-a) di sé; *(certain)* sicuro.

confined [kən'faɪnd] *adj* ristretto(-a).

confirm [kən'fɜːm] *vt* confermare.

confirmation [ˌkɒnfə'meɪʃn] *n* conferma *f*; *(RELIG)* cresima *f*.

conflict [*n* 'kɒnflɪkt, *vb* kən'flɪkt] *n* conflitto *m* ♦ *vi*: **to ~ (with)** essere in conflitto (con).

conform [kən'fɔːm] *vi*: **to ~ (to)** conformarsi (a).

confuse [kən'fjuːz] *vt* confondere; **to ~ sthg with sthg** confondere qc con qc.

confused [kən'fjuːzd] *adj* confuso(-a).

confusing [kən'fju:zɪŋ] *adj* (*explanation, plot*) confuso(-a).

confusion [kən'fju:ʒn] *n* confusione *f*.

congested [kən'dʒestɪd] *adj* (*street*) congestionato(-a).

congestion [kən'dʒestʃn] *n* (*traffic*) congestione *f*.

congratulate [kən'grætʃʊleɪt] *vt*: **to ~ sb (on sthg)** congratularsi con qn (per qc o di qc).

congratulations [kən,grætʃʊ'leɪʃənz] *excl* congratulazioni!

congregate ['kɒŋgrɪgeɪt] *vi* riunirsi.

Congress ['kɒŋgres] *n* (*Am*) il Congresso.

conifer ['kɒnɪfər] *n* conifera *f*.

conjunction [kən'dʒʌŋkʃn] *n* (*GRAMM*) congiunzione *f*.

conjurer ['kʌndʒərər] *n* prestigiatore *m* (-trice *f*).

connect [kə'nekt] *vt* collegare, connettere; (*telephone, machine*) collegare; (*caller on phone*) dare la linea a ♦ *vi*: **to ~ with** (*train, plane*) avere la coincidenza con; **to ~ sthg with sthg** (*associate*) collegare qc con o a qc.

connecting flight [kə'nektɪŋ-] *n* volo *m* di coincidenza.

connection [kə'nekʃn] *n* (*link*) collegamento *m*; (*train, plane*) coincidenza *f*; **it's a bad ~** (*on phone*) la linea è disturbata; **a loose ~** (*in machine*) un contatto difettoso; **in ~ with** riguardo a, a proposito di.

conquer ['kɒŋkər] *vt* (*country*) conquistare.

conscience ['kɒnʃəns] *n* coscienza *f*.

conscientious [,kɒnʃɪ'enʃəs] *adj* coscienzioso(-a).

conscious ['kɒnʃəs] *adj* (*awake*) cosciente; (*deliberate*) consapevole; **to be ~ of** (*aware*) essere consapevole di.

consent [kən'sent] *n* consenso *m*.

consequence ['kɒnsɪkwəns] *n* (*result*) conseguenza *f*.

consequently ['kɒnsɪkwəntlɪ] *adv* di conseguenza.

conservation [,kɒnsə'veɪʃn] *n* tutela *f* dell'ambiente.

conservative [kən'sɜ:vətɪv] *adj* conservatore(-trice) □ **Conservative** *adj* conservatore(-trice) ♦ *n* conservatore *m* (-trice *f*).

conservatory [kən'sɜ:vətrɪ] *n* veranda *f* vetrata.

consider [kən'sɪdər] *vt* considerare; **to ~ doing sthg** pensare di fare qc.

considerable [kən'sɪdrəbl] *adj* considerevole.

consideration [kən,sɪdə'reɪʃn] *n* considerazione *f*; **to take sthg into ~** prendere qc in considerazione.

considering [kən'sɪdərɪŋ] *prep* considerando.

consist [kən'sɪst] : **consist in** *vt fus* consistere in; **to ~ in doing sthg** consistere nel fare qc □ **consist of** *vt fus* essere composto di o da.

consistent [kən'sɪstənt] *adj* (*coherent*) coerente; (*worker, performance*) costante.

consolation [,kɒnsə'leɪʃn] *n* consolazione *f*.

console ['kɒnsəʊl] *n* console *f* *inv*.

consonant ['kɒnsənənt] *n* consonante *f*.

conspicuous [kən'spɪkjʊəs] *adj*

cospicuo(-a).

constable ['kʌnstəbl] *n* *(Br)* agente *m* di polizia.

constant ['kɒnstənt] *adj* *(unchanging)* costante; *(continuous)* continuo(-a).

constantly ['kɒnstəntlɪ] *adv* *(all the time)* continuamente.

constipated ['kɒnstɪpeɪtɪd] *adj* stitico(-a).

constitution [,kɒnstɪ'tjuːʃn] *n* costituzione *f*.

construct [kən'strʌkt] *vt* costruire.

construction [kən'strʌkʃn] *n* costruzione *f*; **under ~** in costruzione.

consul ['kɒnsəl] *n* console *m*.

consulate ['kɒnsjʊlət] *n* consolato *m*.

consult [kən'sʌlt] *vt* consultare.

consultant [kən'sʌltənt] *n* *(Br: doctor)* specialista *mf*.

consume [kən'sjuːm] *vt* consumare.

consumer [kən'sjuːməʳ] *n* consumatore *m* (-trice *f*).

contact ['kɒntækt] *n* *(communication)* contatto *m*; *(person)* conoscenza *f* ◆ *vt* mettersi in contatto con; **in ~ with** *(in communication with)* in contatto con; *(touching)* a contatto con.

contact lens *n* lente *f* a contatto.

contagious [kən'teɪdʒəs] *adj* contagioso(-a).

contain [kən'teɪn] *vt* contenere.

container [kən'teɪnəʳ] *n* *(box etc)* contenitore *m*, recipiente *m*.

contaminate [kən'tæmɪneɪt] *vt* contaminare.

contemporary [kən'tempərərɪ] *adj* contemporaneo(-a) ◆ *n* contemporaneo *m* (-a *f*).

contend [kən'tend] **: contend with** *vt fus* affrontare.

content [*adj* kən'tent, *n* 'kɒntent] *adj* contento(-a) ◆ *n* *(of vitamins, fibre etc)* contenuto *m* ❏ **contents** *npl* *(things inside)* contenuto *m*; *(at beginning of book)* indice *m*.

contest [*n* 'kɒntest, *vb* kən'test] *n* *(competition)* gara *f*, concorso *m*; *(struggle)* lotta *f* ◆ *vt* *(election, seat)* candidarsi per; *(decision, will)* contestare.

context ['kɒntekst] *n* contesto *m*.

continent ['kɒntɪnənt] *n* continente *m*; **the Continent** *(Br)* l'Europa *f* continentale.

continental [,kɒntɪ'nentl] *adj* *(Br: European)* (dell'Europa) continentale.

continental breakfast *n* colazione *f* continentale.

continental quilt *n* *(Br)* piumone® *m*.

continual [kən'tɪnjʊəl] *adj* continuo(-a).

continually [kən'tɪnjʊəlɪ] *adv* continuamente, di continuo.

continue [kən'tɪnjuː] *vt & vi* continuare; **to ~ doing sthg** continuare a fare qc; **to ~ with sthg** continuare con qc.

continuous [kən'tɪnjʊəs] *adj* continuo(-a).

continuously [kən'tɪnjʊəslɪ] *adv* continuamente, senza interruzione.

contraception [,kɒntrə'sepʃn] *n* contraccezione *f*.

contraceptive [,kɒntrə'septɪv] *n* contraccettivo *m*.

contract [n 'kɒntrækt, vb kən'trækt] n contratto m ◆ vt (fml: illness) contrarre.

contradict [,kɒntrə'dɪkt] vt contraddire.

contraflow ['kɒntrəfləʊ] n (Br) sistema che permette il traffico nei due sensi su una stessa carreggiata dell'autostrada per lavori in corso o per un incidente.

contrary ['kɒntrərɪ] n: **on the ~** al contrario.

contrast [n 'kɒntrɑːst, vb kən-'trɑːst] n contrasto m ◆ vt mettere in contrasto; **in ~ to** contrariamente a.

contribute [kən'trɪbjuːt] vt (help, money) dare (come contributo) ◆ vi: **to ~** contribuire a.

contribution [,kɒntrɪ'bjuːʃn] n contributo m.

control [kən'trəʊl] n controllo m; (operating device) comando m ◆ vt controllare; (machine) regolare; **to be in ~** avere la situazione sotto controllo; **to get out of ~** (situation) sfuggire di mano; **to go out of ~** (car, plane) non rispondere ai comandi; **under ~** sotto controllo □ **controls** npl comandi mpl.

control tower n torre f di controllo.

controversial [,kɒntrə'vɜːʃl] adj controverso(-a); (person) polemico(-a).

convenience [kən'viːnjəns] n comodità f inv; **at your ~** quando Le è più comodo.

convenient [kən'viːnjənt] adj comodo(-a); **would tomorrow be ~?** domani andrebbe bene?

convent ['kɒnvənt] n convento m.

conventional [kən'venʃənl] adj convenzionale.

conversation [,kɒnvə'seɪʃn] n conversazione f.

conversion [kən'vɜːʃn] n (change) trasformazione f; (of currency) conversione f; (to building) ristrutturazione f.

convert [kən'vɜːt] vt (change) trasformare; (currency, person) convertire; **to ~ sthg into** trasformare qc in.

converted [kən'vɜːtɪd] adj (barn, loft) ristrutturato(-a).

convertible [kən'vɜːtəbl] n cabriolet m inv.

convey [kən'veɪ] vt (fml: transport) trasportare; (idea, impression) dare.

convict [n 'kɒnvɪkt, vb kən'vɪkt] n carcerato m (-a f) ◆ vt: **to ~ sb (of)** giudicare qn colpevole (di).

convince [kən'vɪns] vt: **to ~ sb (of sthg)** convincere qn (di qc); **to ~ sb to do sthg** convincere qn a fare qc.

convoy ['kɒnvɔɪ] n convoglio m.

cook [kʊk] n cuoco m (-a f) ◆ vt (meal) cucinare; (food) cuocere ◆ vi (person) cucinare; (food) cuocere.

cookbook ['kʊk,bʊk] = **cookery book.**

cooker ['kʊkəʳ] n cucina f (elettrodomestico).

cookery ['kʊkərɪ] n cucina f.

cookery book n libro m di cucina.

cookie ['kʊkɪ] n (Am) biscotto m.

cooking ['kʊkɪŋ] n cucina f.

cooking apple n mela f da cuocere.

cooking oil n olio m per cucinare.

cool [ku:l] *adj (temperature)* fresco(-a); *(calm)* calmo(-a); *(unfriendly)* freddo(-a); *(inf: great)* fantastico (-a) ◆ *vt* raffreddare ❏ **cool down** *vi (become colder)* raffreddarsi; *(become calmer)* calmarsi.

cooperate [kəʊˈɒpəreɪt] *vi* collaborare, cooperare.

cooperation [kəʊˌɒpəˈreɪʃn] *n* collaborazione *f*.

cooperative [kəʊˈɒpərətɪv] *adj (helpful)* disposto(-a) a collaborare.

coordinates [kəʊˈɔːdɪnəts] *npl (clothes)* coordinati *mpl*.

cope [kəʊp] *vi*: **to ~ with** far fronte a; **I can't ~!** non ce la faccio!

copilot [ˈkəʊˌpaɪlət] *n* secondo pilota *m*.

copper [ˈkɒpə^r] *n (metal)* rame *m*; *(Br: inf: coin)* moneta in rame da uno o due penny.

copy [ˈkɒpɪ] *n* copia *f* ◆ *vt* copiare.

cord(uroy) [ˈkɔːd(ərɔɪ)] *n* velluto *m* a coste.

core [kɔː^r] *n (of fruit)* torsolo *m*.

coriander [ˌkɒrɪˈændə^r] *n* coriandolo *m (spezia)*.

cork [kɔːk] *n (in bottle)* tappo *m* (di sughero).

corkscrew [ˈkɔːkskruː] *n* cavatappi *m inv*.

corn [kɔːn] *n (Br: crop)* cereali *mpl*; *(Am: maize)* granturco *m*; *(on foot)* callo *m*.

corned beef [ˌkɔːnd-] *n* carne *f* di manzo in scatola.

corner [ˈkɔːnə^r] *n* angolo *m*; *(bend in road)* curva *f*; *(in football)* calcio *m* d'angolo; **it's just around the ~** è qui dietro l'angolo.

corner shop *n (Br)* negozietto *m (di alimentari e prodotti per la casa)*.

cornet [ˈkɔːnɪt] *n (Br: ice-cream cone)* cornetto *m*.

cornflakes [ˈkɔːnfleɪks] *npl* corn-flakes *mpl*.

corn-on-the-cob *n* pannocchia *f* bollita.

Cornwall [ˈkɔːnwɔːl] *n* la Cornovaglia.

corporal [ˈkɔːpərəl] *n* caporale *m*.

corpse [kɔːps] *n* cadavere *m*.

correct [kəˈrekt] *adj* giusto(-a) ◆ *vt* correggere.

correction [kəˈrekʃn] *n* correzione *f*.

correspond [ˌkɒrɪˈspɒnd] *vi*: **to ~ (to)** *(match)* corrispondere (a); **to ~ (with)** *(exchange letters)* essere in corrispondenza (con).

corresponding [ˌkɒrɪˈspɒndɪŋ] *adj* corrispondente.

corridor [ˈkɒrɪdɔː^r] *n* corridoio *m*.

corrugated iron [ˈkɒrəgeɪtɪd-] *n* lamiera *f* ondulata.

corrupt [kəˈrʌpt] *adj* corrotto(-a).

cosmetics [kɒzˈmetɪks] *npl* cosmetici *mpl*.

cost [kɒst] *(pt & pp* cost*)* *n* costo *m*; *(fig: loss)* prezzo *m* ◆ *vt* costare; **how much does it ~?** quanto costa?

costly [ˈkɒstlɪ] *adj (expensive)* costoso(-a).

costume [ˈkɒstjuːm] *n* costume *m*.

cosy [ˈkəʊzɪ] *adj (Br: room, house)* accogliente.

cot [kɒt] *n (Br: for baby)* lettino *m* (per bambini); *(Am: camp bed)* brandina f.

cottage ['kɒtɪdʒ] n cottage m inv.

cottage cheese n formaggio m magro in fiocchi.

cottage pie n (Br) pasticcio a base di carne macinata e purè di patate.

cotton ['kɒtn] adj di cotone ♦ n cotone m.

cotton candy n (Am) zucchero m filato.

cotton wool n cotone m idrofilo.

couch [kaʊtʃ] n divano m; (at doctor's) lettino m.

couchette [kuːˈʃet] n cuccetta f.

cough [kɒf] n tosse f ♦ vi tossire; to have a ~ avere la tosse.

cough mixture n sciroppo m per la tosse.

could [kʊd] pt → can.

couldn't ['kʊdnt] = could not.

could've ['kʊdəv] = could have.

council ['kaʊnsl] n (Br: of town) comune m; (Br: of county) = regione f; (organization) consiglio m.

council house n (Br) casa f popolare.

councillor ['kaʊnsələr] n (Br: of town, county) consigliere m (-a f).

council tax n (Br) = tassa f comunale.

count [kaʊnt] vt & vi contare ♦ n (nobleman) conte m ❑ **count on** vt fus contare su.

counter ['kaʊntər] n (in shop) banco m; (in bank) sportello m; (in board game) fiche f inv.

counterclockwise [ˌkaʊntəˈklɒkwaɪz] adv (Am) in senso antiorario.

counterfoil ['kaʊntəfɔɪl] n matrice f.

countess ['kaʊntɪs] n contessa f.

country ['kʌntrɪ] n paese m; (countryside) campagna f ♦ adj di campagna.

country and western n (musica f) country m.

country house n villa f di campagna.

country road n strada f di campagna.

countryside ['kʌntrɪsaɪd] n campagna f.

county ['kaʊntɪ] n contea f.

couple ['kʌpl] n coppia f; a ~ (of) un paio (di).

coupon ['kuːpɒn] n (for discount etc) buono m; (for orders, enquiries) tagliando m.

courage ['kʌrɪdʒ] n coraggio m.

courgette [kɔːˈʒet] n (Br) zucchino m.

courier ['kʊrɪər] n (for holidaymakers) accompagnatore m (-trice f); (for delivering letters) corriere m.

course [kɔːs] n corso m; (of meal) portata f; (of treatment, injections) ciclo m; (of ship, plane) rotta f; (for golf) campo m; **of ~** (certainly) certo; (evidently) naturalmente; **of ~ not** certo che no; **in the ~ of** nel corso di, durante.

court [kɔːt] n (JUR: building, room) tribunale m; (SPORT) campo m; (of king, queen) corte f.

courtesy coach ['kɜːtɪsɪ-] n pullman m inv gratuito (di hotel, aeroporto, ecc.).

court shoes npl scarpe fpl décolleté.

courtyard ['kɔːtjɑːd] n cortile m.

cousin ['kʌzn] n cugino m (-a f).

cover ['kʌvə'] n (covering) fodera f; (lid) coperchio m; (of book, magazine) copertina f; (blanket) coperta f; (insurance) copertura f ♦ vt coprire; (apply to) comprendere; (discuss) trattare; (report) fare un servizio su; **to be ~ed in** essere ricoperto di OR da; **to ~ sthg with sthg** coprire qc con qc; **to take ~** mettersi al riparo ❑ **cover up** vt sep (put cover on) coprire; (facts, truth) nascondere.

cover charge n coperto m.

cover note n (Br) polizza f di assicurazione provvisoria.

cow [kaʊ] n vacca f.

coward ['kaʊəd] n vigliacco m (-a f).

cowboy ['kaʊbɔɪ] n cow-boy m inv.

crab [kræb] n granchio m.

crack [kræk] n (in cup, glass) incrinatura f, crepa f; (gap) fessura f ♦ vt (cup, glass, wood) incrinare; (nut) schiacciare; (egg) rompere; (whip) schioccare ♦ vi (cup, glass, wood) incrinarsi; **to ~ a joke** (inf) fare una battuta.

cracker ['krækə'] n (biscuit) cracker m inv; (for Christmas) tubo di cartone rivestito di carta da regalo che quando viene aperto produce uno scoppio e rilascia una sorpresa. Tipico delle feste natalizie.

cradle ['kreɪdl] n culla f.

craft [krɑ:ft] n (skill) arte f; (trade) artigianato m; (boat: pl inv) imbarcazione f.

craftsman ['krɑ:ftsmən] (pl -men [-mən]) n artigiano m.

cram [kræm] vt: **to ~ sthg into** stipare qc in; **to be crammed with** essere stipato di.

cramp [kræmp] n crampo m; **stomach ~s** crampi allo stomaco.

cranberry ['krænbəri] n mirtillo m.

cranberry sauce n salsa f di mirtilli.

crane [kreɪn] n (machine) gru f inv.

crap [kræp] adj (vulg) di merda ♦ n (vulg) merda f.

crash [kræʃ] n (accident) incidente m; (noise) schianto m ♦ vt (car) sfasciare ♦ vi (car, train) schiantarsi; (plane) precipitare ❑ **crash into** vt fus schiantarsi contro.

crash helmet n casco m.

crash landing n atterraggio m di fortuna.

crate [kreɪt] n cassa f.

crawl [krɔ:l] vi (baby) andare carponi; (person) strisciare; (insect) muoversi lentamente; (traffic) andare a passo d'uomo ♦ n (swimming stroke) stile m libero.

crawler lane ['krɔ:lə'-] n (Br) corsia f per veicoli lenti.

crayfish ['kreɪfɪʃ] (pl inv) n gambero m di fiume.

crayon ['kreɪɒn] n matita f colorata.

craze [kreɪz] n mania f.

crazy ['kreɪzɪ] adj matto(-a), pazzo(-a); **to be ~ about** andare matto per.

crazy golf n minigolf m.

cream [kri:m] n crema f; (fresh) panna f ♦ adj (in colour) color crema (inv).

cream cake n (Br) torta f alla panna.

cream cheese n formaggio m cremoso.

cream sherry n sherry m inv dolce.

cream tea n (Br) merenda a base di tè e 'scones', serviti con marmellata e panna.

creamy ['kri:mɪ] adj (food) alla panna; (texture) cremoso(-a).

crease [kri:s] n grinza f.

creased [kri:st] adj sgualcito(-a).

create [kri:'eɪt] vt creare.

creative [kri:'eɪtɪv] adj creativo(-a).

creature ['kri:tʃə'] n creatura f.

crèche [kreʃ] n (Br) nursery f inv.

credit ['kredɪt] n (praise) merito m; (money) credito m; (part of school, university course) sezione completata di un corso di studio; **to be in ~** essere in attivo ❑ **credits** npl (of film) titoli mpl.

credit card n carta f di credito; **to pay by ~** pagare con la carta di credito; **'all major ~s accepted'** 'si accettano tutte le maggiori carte di credito'.

creek [kri:k] n (inlet) insenatura f; (Am: river) ruscello m.

creep [kri:p] (pt & pp **crept**) vi (crawl) strisciare; (walk) muoversi furtivamente ♦ n (inf: groveller) leccapiedi mf inv.

cremate [krɪ'meɪt] vt cremare.

crematorium [,kremə'tɔ:rɪəm] n crematorio m.

crepe [kreɪp] n (thin pancake) crêpe f inv.

crept [krept] pt & pp → **creep**.

cress [kres] n crescione m.

crest [krest] n cresta f; (emblem) stemma m.

crew [kru:] n (of ship, plane) equipaggio m.

crew neck n girocollo m.

crib [krɪb] n (Am: cot) lettino m (per bambini).

cricket ['krɪkɪt] n (game) cricket m; (insect) grillo m.

crime [kraɪm] n crimine m.

criminal ['krɪmɪnl] adj criminale ♦ n criminale mf.

cripple ['krɪpl] n storpio m (-a f) ♦ vt (subj: disease, accident) storpiare.

crisis ['kraɪsɪs] (pl **crises** ['kraɪsi:z]) n crisi f inv.

crisp [krɪsp] adj (bacon, pastry) croccante; (fruit, vegetable) sodo(-a) ❑ **crisps** npl (Br) patatine fpl.

crispy ['krɪspɪ] adj croccante.

critic ['krɪtɪk] n critico m (-a f).

critical ['krɪtɪkl] adj critico(-a).

criticize ['krɪtɪsaɪz] vt criticare.

crockery ['krɒkərɪ] n stoviglie fpl.

crocodile ['krɒkədaɪl] n coccodrillo m.

crocus ['krəʊkəs] (pl **-es**) n croco m.

crooked ['krʊkɪd] adj (bent, twisted) storto(-a).

crop [krɒp] n (kind of plant) coltivazione f; (harvest) raccolto m ❑ **crop up** vi saltare fuori.

cross [krɒs] adj arrabbiato(-a) ♦ n croce f; (mixture) incrocio m ♦ vt (road, river, ocean) attraversare; (arms, legs) incrociare; (Br: cheque) sbarrare ♦ vi (intersect) incrociarsi ❑ **cross out** vt sep sbarrare; **cross over** vt fus (road) attraversare.

crossbar ['krɒsbɑ:'] n (of goal) traversa f; (of bicycle) canna f.

cross-Channel ferry n traghetto m di servizio sulla Manica.

cross-country (running) n
corsa f campestre.

crossing ['krɒsɪŋ] n (on road)
attraversamento m; (sea journey)
traversata f.

crossroads ['krɒsrəʊdz] (pl inv)
n incrocio m.

crosswalk ['krɒswɔːk] n (Am)
passaggio m pedonale.

crossword (puzzle) ['krɒs-wɜːd-] n cruciverba m inv.

crotch [krɒtʃ] n (of person) infor-
catura f.

crouton ['kruːtɒn] n crostino m.

crow [krəʊ] n cornacchia f.

crowbar ['krəʊbɑːʳ] n piede m di
porco.

crowd [kraʊd] n folla f; (at match)
spettatori mpl.

crowded ['kraʊdɪd] adj affolla-
to(-a).

crown [kraʊn] n (of king, queen, on
tooth) corona f; (of head) sommità f
inv.

Crown Jewels npl: the ~ i
gioielli della Corona.

---

[i] CROWN JEWELS

Indossati dal sovrano in occasione
di cerimonie importanti, i gioielli
della Corona britannica sono esposti
nella Torre di Londra. I gioielli
dell'antica corona di Scozia sono
invece esposti al castello di Edimburgo.

crucial ['kruːʃl] adj cruciale.

crude [kruːd] adj (drawing)
abbozzato(-a); (estimate) approssi-
mativo(-a); (rude) rozzo(-a).

cruel [krʊəl] adj crudele.

cruelty ['krʊəltɪ] n crudeltà f.

cruet (set) ['kruːɪt-] n ampol-
liera f.

cruise [kruːz] n crociera f ◆ vi
(car, plane, ship) andare a velocità
di crociera.

cruiser ['kruːzəʳ] n (pleasure boat)
cabinato m.

crumb [krʌm] n briciola f.

crumble ['krʌmbl] n frutta cotta
ricoperta da uno strato di pasta frolla
sbriciolata ◆ vi (building, cliff) sgretolarsi; (pastry, cake, cheese) sbriciolarsi.

crumpet ['krʌmpɪt] n tipo di
focaccina da mangiarsi calda con
burro, marmellata, ecc.

crunchy ['krʌntʃɪ] adj croccante.

crush [krʌʃ] n (drink) spremuta f
◆ vt schiacciare; (ice) frantumare.

crust [krʌst] n crosta f.

crusty ['krʌstɪ] adj croccante.

crutch [krʌtʃ] n (stick) stampella
f; (between legs) = crotch.

cry [kraɪ] n urlo m, grido m; (of
bird) verso m ◆ vi (weep) piangere;
(shout) urlare, gridare □ **cry out** vi
urlare, gridare.

crystal ['krɪstl] n (in jewellery etc)
cristallo m; (glass) cristallo m.

cub [kʌb] n (animal) cucciolo m.

Cub [kʌb] n lupetto m.

cube [kjuːb] n cubo m; (of sugar,
ice) cubetto m.

cubicle ['kjuːbɪkl] n cabina f.

Cub Scout = Cub.

cuckoo ['kʊkuː] n cuculo m.

cucumber ['kjuːkʌmbəʳ] n cetriolo m.

cuddle ['kʌdl] n coccola f.

cuddly toy ['kʌdlɪ-] n pupazzo

m di peluche.

cue [kju:] *n* (*in snooker, pool*) stecca *f*.

cuff [kʌf] *n* (*of sleeve*) polsino *m*; (*Am: of trousers*) risvolto *m*.

cuff links *npl* gemelli *mpl*.

cuisine [kwɪ'zi:n] *n* cucina *f*.

cul-de-sac ['kʌldəsæk] *n* vicolo *m* cieco.

cult [kʌlt] *n* (*RELIG*) culto *m* ◆ *adj* di culto.

cultivate ['kʌltɪveɪt] *vt* (*grow*) coltivare.

cultivated ['kʌltɪveɪtɪd] *adj* (*person*) raffinato(-a).

cultural ['kʌltʃərəl] *adj* culturale.

culture ['kʌltʃəʳ] *n* cultura *f*.

cumbersome ['kʌmbəsəm] *adj* ingombrante.

cumin ['kju:mɪn] *n* cumino *m*.

cunning ['kʌnɪŋ] *adj* furbo(-a).

cup [kʌp] *n* tazza *f*; (*trophy, competition, of bra*) coppa *f*.

cupboard ['kʌbəd] *n* (*for food, dishes*) credenza *f*; (*for clothes*) armadio *m*.

curator [ˌkjʊə'reɪtəʳ] *n* conservatore *m* (*di museo*).

curb [kɜ:b] (*Am*) = **kerb**.

curd cheese [kɜ:d-] *n* cagliata *f*.

cure [kjʊəʳ] *n* (*for illness*) cura *f* ◆ *vt* (*illness, person*) curare; (*food*) trattare.

curious ['kjʊərɪəs] *adj* curioso(-a).

curl [kɜ:l] *n* (*of hair*) riccio *m* ◆ *vt* (*hair*) arricciare.

curler ['kɜ:ləʳ] *n* bigodino *m*.

curly ['kɜ:lɪ] *adj* riccio(-a).

currant ['kʌrənt] *n* uvetta *f*.

currency ['kʌrənsɪ] *n* (*money*) moneta *f*.

current ['kʌrənt] *adj* attuale ◆ *n* corrente *f*.

current account *n* (*Br*) conto *m* corrente.

current affairs *npl* attualità *f*.

currently ['kʌrəntlɪ] *adv* attualmente.

curriculum [kə'nkjələm] *n* curricolo *m*.

curriculum vitae [-'vi:taɪ] *n* (*Br*) curriculum vitae *m inv*.

curried ['kʌrɪd] *adj* al curry.

curry ['kʌrɪ] *n* piatto *m* al curry.

curse [kɜ:s] *vi* bestemmiare.

cursor ['kɜ:səʳ] *n* cursore *m*.

curtain ['kɜ:tn] *n* (*in house*) tenda *f*; (*in theatre*) sipario *m*.

curve [kɜ:v] *n* curva *f* ◆ *vi* curvare.

curved [kɜ:vd] *adj* curvo(-a).

cushion ['kʊʃn] *n* (*for sitting on*) cuscino *m*.

custard ['kʌstəd] *n* crema *f* gialla.

custom ['kʌstəm] *n* (*tradition*) usanza *f*; **'thank you for your ~'** 'arrivederci e grazie'.

customary ['kʌstəmrɪ] *adj* abituale.

customer ['kʌstəməʳ] *n* (*of shop*) cliente *mf*.

customer services *n* (*department*) servizio *m* clienti.

customs ['kʌstəmz] *n* dogana *f*; **to go through ~** passare la dogana.

customs duty *n* dazio *m* doganale.

customs officer *n* doganiere *m*.

cut [kʌt] (*pt & pp* **cut**) *n* taglio *m*; (*in taxes*) riduzione *f* ◆ *vt & vi* tagliare; **~ and blow-dry** taglio e piega föhn; **to ~ o.s.** tagliarsi; **to ~ one's finger** tagliarsi un dito; **to have one's hair ~** tagliarsi i capelli; **to ~ the grass** tagliare l'erba; **to ~ sthg open** aprire qc ◻ **cut back** *vi:* **to ~ back on sthg** ridurre qc; **cut down** *vt sep (tree)* tagliare; **cut down on** *vt fus* ridurre; **cut off** *vt sep (supply)* sospendere; **I've been ~ off** *(on phone)* è caduta la linea; **to be ~ off** *(isolated)* rimanere isolato; **cut out** *vt sep (newspaper article, photo)* ritagliare ◆ *vi (engine)* spegnersi; **to ~ out** smoking smettere di fumare; **~ it out!** *(inf)* dacci un taglio!; **cut up** *vt sep* tagliare a pezzetti.

cute [kju:t] *adj* carino(-a).

cut-glass *adj* in vetro intagliato.

cutlery ['kʌtləri] *n* posate *fpl*.

cutlet ['kʌtlɪt] *n (of meat)* costoletta *f; (of nuts, vegetables)* crocchetta *f*.

cut-price *adj* a prezzo scontato.

cutting ['kʌtɪŋ] *n (from newspaper)* ritaglio *m*.

CV *n (Br: abbr of curriculum vitae)* curriculum *m inv*.

cwt *abbr* = **hundredweight**.

cycle ['saɪkl] *n (bicycle)* bicicletta *f; (series)* ciclo *m* ◆ *vi* andare in bicicletta.

cycle hire *n* noleggio *m* biciclette.

cycle lane *n* pista *f* ciclabile.

cycle path *n* pista *f* ciclabile.

cycling ['saɪklɪŋ] *n* ciclismo *m;* **to go ~** andare in bicicletta.

cycling shorts *npl* pantaloncini *mpl* da ciclista.

cyclist ['saɪklɪst] *n* ciclista *mf*.

cylinder ['sɪlɪndər] *n (of gas)* bombola *f; (in engine)* cilindro *m*.

cynical ['sɪnɪkl] *adj* cinico(-a).

Czech [tʃek] *adj* ceco(-a) ◆ *n (person)* ceco *m* (-a *f*); *(language)* ceco *m*.

Czechoslovakia [,tʃekəslə-'vækɪə] *n* la Cecoslovacchia.

Czech Republic *n:* **the ~** la Repubblica Ceca.

D

dab [dæb] *vt (wound)* tamponare.

dad [dæd] *n (inf)* papà *m inv*, babbo *m*.

daddy ['dædɪ] *n (inf)* papà *m inv*, babbo *m*.

daddy longlegs [-'lɒŋlegz] *(pl inv)* *n* tipula *f*.

daffodil ['dæfədɪl] *n* giunchiglia *f*.

daft [dɑ:ft] *adj (Br: inf)* stupido(-a).

daily ['deɪlɪ] *adj* quotidiano(-a) ◆ *adv.* quotidianamente ◆ *n:* **a ~ (newspaper)** un quotidiano.

dairy ['deərɪ] *n (on farm)* caseificio *m; (shop)* latteria *f*.

dairy product *n* latticino *m*.

daisy ['deɪzɪ] *n* margherita *f*.

dam [dæm] *n* diga *f*.

damage ['dæmɪdʒ] *n* danno *m* ◆ *vt* danneggiare; *(back, leg)* lesionare.

damn [dæm] *excl (inf)* accidenti! ◆ *adj (inf)* maledetto(-a); **I don't**

give a ~ non me ne importa un accidente.

damp [dæmp] *adj* umido(-a) ◆ *n* umidità *f*.

damson ['dæmzn] *n* susina *f* damaschina.

dance [dɑ:ns] *n* danza *f*; *(social event)* ballo *m* ◆ *vi* ballare; **to have a ~** ballare.

dance floor *n (in club)* pista *f* da ballo.

dancer ['dɑ:nsə'] *n* ballerino *m* (-a *f*).

dancing ['dɑ:nsɪŋ] *n* danza *f*; **to go ~** andare a ballare.

dandelion ['dændɪlaɪən] *n* dente *m* di leone.

dandruff ['dændrʌf] *n* forfora *f*.

Dane [deɪn] *n* danese *mf*.

danger ['deɪndʒə'] *n* pericolo *m*; **in ~** in pericolo.

dangerous ['deɪndʒərəs] *adj* pericoloso(-a).

Danish ['deɪnɪʃ] *adj* danese ◆ *n (language)* danese *m*.

Danish pastry *n* sfoglia *f* alla frutta.

dare [deə'] *vt*: **to ~ to do sthg** osare fare qc; **to ~ sb to do sthg** sfidare qn a fare qc; **how ~ you!** come ti permetti!

daring ['deərɪŋ] *adj* audace.

dark [dɑ:k] *adj (room, night)* buio(-a); *(colour, skin)* scuro(-a); *(person)* bruno(-a) ◆ *n*: **after ~** col buio; **the ~** il buio.

dark chocolate *n* cioccolata *f* fondente.

dark glasses *npl* occhiali *mpl* scuri.

darkness ['dɑ:knɪs] *n* oscurità *f*.

darling ['dɑ:lɪŋ] *n (term of affec-*

tion) caro *m* (-a *f*).

dart [dɑ:t] *n* freccia *f* ❏ **darts** *n (game)* freccette *fpl*.

dartboard ['dɑ:tbɔ:d] *n* bersaglio *m* per freccette.

dash [dæʃ] *n (of liquid)* goccio *m*; *(in writing)* trattino *m* ◆ *vi* precipitarsi.

dashboard ['dæʃbɔ:d] *n* cruscotto *m*.

data ['deɪtə] *n* dati *mpl*.

database ['deɪtəbeɪs] *n* data base *m inv*.

date [deɪt] *n (day)* data *f*; *(meeting)* appuntamento *m*; *(Am: person)* ragazzo *m* (-a *f*); *(fruit)* dattero *m* ◆ *vt (cheque, letter)* datare; *(person)* uscire con ◆ *vi (become unfashionable)* passare di moda; **what's the ~?** quanti ne abbiamo oggi?; **to have a ~ with sb** avere (un) appuntamento con qn.

date of birth *n* data *f* di nascita.

daughter ['dɔ:tə'] *n* figlia *f*.

daughter-in-law *n* nuora *f*.

dawn [dɔ:n] *n* alba *f*.

day [deɪ] *n (of week)* giorno *m*; *(period, working day)* giornata *f*; **what ~ is it today?** che giorno è oggi?; **what a lovely ~!** che bella giornata!; **to have a ~ off** avere un giorno libero; **to have a ~ out** trascorrere una giornata fuori; **by ~** *(travel)* di giorno; **the ~ after tomorrow** dopodomani; **the ~ before** il giorno prima; **the ~ before yesterday** l'altro ieri, ieri l'altro; **the following ~** il giorno dopo; **have a nice ~!** buona giornata!

daylight ['deɪlaɪt] *n (light)* luce *f* (del giorno); *(dawn)* alba *f*.

day return *n (Br: railway ticket)*

biglietto di andata e ritorno valido per un giorno.

dayshift ['deɪʃɪft] *n* turno *m* di giorno.

daytime ['deɪtaɪm] *n* giorno *m*.

day-to-day *adj (everyday)* quotidiano(-a).

day trip *n* gita *f (di un giorno)*.

dazzle ['dæzl] *vt* abbagliare.

DC *(abbr of direct current)* c.c.

dead [ded] *adj* morto(-a); *(battery)* scarico(-a) ♦ *adv* proprio; **the line has gone ~** è caduta la linea; **~ on time** in perfetto orario; **it's ~ ahead** è proprio a diritto; **'~ slow'** 'a passo d'uomo'.

dead end *n (street)* strada *f* senza uscita.

deadline ['dedlaɪn] *n* termine *m* ultimo, scadenza *f*.

deaf [def] *adj* sordo(-a) ♦ *npl:* **the ~ i** non udenti.

deal [diːl] *(pt & pp dealt)* *n (agreement)* accordo *m* ♦ *vt (cards)* dare; **a good/bad ~** un buon/cattivo affare; **a great ~ of** una gran quantità di; **it's a ~!** affare fatto! ❑ **deal in** *vt fus* commerciare in; **deal with** *vt fus (handle)* affrontare; *(be about)* trattare di.

dealer ['diːlə^r] *n (COMM)* commerciante *mf*; *(in drugs)* spacciatore *m* (-trice *f*).

dealt [delt] *pt & pp* → **deal**.

dear [dɪə^r] *adj* caro(-a) ♦ *n:* **my ~** mio caro (mia cara); **Dear Sir** Gentile Signore; **Dear Madam** Gentile Signora; **Dear John** Caro John; **oh ~!** oh Dio!

death [deθ] *n* morte *f*.

debate [dɪ'beɪt] *n* dibattito *m* ♦ *vt (wonder)* riflettere su.

debit ['debɪt] *n* debito *m* ♦ *vt (account)* addebitare su.

debt [det] *n (money owed)* debito *m*; **to be in ~** essere indebitato.

Dec. *(abbr of December)* dic.

decaff ['diːkæf] *n (inf)* caffè *m inv* decaffeinato.

decaffeinated [dɪ'kæfɪneɪtɪd] *adj* decaffeinato(-a).

decanter [dɪ'kæntə^r] *n* bottiglia *f* da liquore.

decay [dɪ'keɪ] *n (of wood)* disfacimento *m*; *(of building)* rovina *f*; *(of tooth)* carie *f* ♦ *vi (rot)* putrefarsi.

deceive [dɪ'siːv] *vt* ingannare.

decelerate [ˌdiː'seləreɪt] *vi* decelerare.

December [dɪ'sembə^r] *n* dicembre *m*, → **September**.

decent ['diːsnt] *adj (adequate, respectable)* decente; *(kind)* carino(-a); *(people)* perbene *inv*.

decide [dɪ'saɪd] *vt & vi* decidere; **to ~ to do sthg** decidere di fare qc ❑ **decide on** *vt fus* scegliere.

decimal ['desɪml] *adj* decimale.

decimal point *n* = virgola *f*.

decision [dɪ'sɪʒn] *n* decisione *f*; **to make a ~** prendere una decisione.

decisive [dɪ'saɪsɪv] *adj (person)* deciso(-a); *(event, factor)* decisivo(-a).

deck [dek] *n (level of ship)* ponte *m*; *(exposed part of ship)* coperta *f*; *(of bus)* piano *m*; *(of cards)* mazzo *m*.

deckchair ['dektʃeə^r] *n* sedia *f* a sdraio.

declare [dɪ'kleə^r] *vt* dichiarare; **to ~ (that)** dichiarare che; **'goods to ~'** 'articoli da dichiarare'; **'noth-**

ing to ~' 'nulla da dichiarare'.

decline [dɪ'klaɪn] n calo m; (of country) declino m ◆ vi (get worse) peggiorare; (refuse) declinare.

decorate ['dekəreɪt] vt (with wallpaper) tappezzare; (with paint) pitturare; (make attractive) decorare.

decoration [,dekə'reɪʃn] n (decorative object) decorazione f.

decorator ['dekəreɪtər] n imbianchino m.

decrease [n 'di:kri:s, vb di:'kri:s] n diminuzione f ◆ vi diminuire.

dedicated ['dedɪkeɪtɪd] adj (committed) devoto(-a).

deduce [dɪ'dju:s] vt dedurre.

deduct [dɪ'dʌkt] vt dedurre.

deduction [dɪ'dʌkʃn] n deduzione f.

deep [di:p] adj profondo(-a); (colour) intenso(-a) ◆ adv in profondità; **the pool is 2 metres ~** la piscina è profonda 2 metri.

deep end n (of swimming pool) parte dove l'acqua è più alta.

deep freeze n congelatore m.

deep-fried [-'fraɪd] adj fritto(-a).

deep-pan adj: ~ pizza pizza a pasta alta e soffice.

deer [dɪər] (pl inv) n cervo m.

defeat [dɪ'fi:t] n sconfitta f ◆ vt (team, army, government) sconfiggere.

defect ['di:fekt] n difetto m.

defective [dɪ'fektɪv] adj difettoso(-a).

defence [dɪ'fens] n difesa f.

defend [dɪ'fend] vt difendere.

defense [dɪ'fens] (Am) = defence.

deficiency [dɪ'fɪʃnsɪ] n (lack)

carenza f.

deficit ['defɪsɪt] n deficit m inv.

define [dɪ'faɪn] vt definire.

definite ['defɪnɪt] adj (clear) preciso(-a); (certain) sicuro(-a); (improvement) deciso(-a).

definite article n articolo m determinativo.

definitely ['defɪnɪtlɪ] adv (certainly) senz'altro.

definition [defɪ'nɪʃn] n (of word) definizione f.

deflate [dɪ'fleɪt] vt (tyre) sgonfiare.

deflect [dɪ'flekt] vt (ball) deviare.

defogger [,di:'fɒgər] n (Am) deumidificatore m.

deformed [dɪ'fɔ:md] adj deformato(-a).

defrost [,di:'frɒst] vt (food) scongelare; (fridge) sbrinare; (Am: demist) disappannare.

degree [dɪ'gri:] n (unit of measurement, amount) grado m; (qualification) = laurea f; **to have a ~ in sthg** avere una laurea in qc.

dehydrated [,di:haɪ'dreɪtɪd] adj (food) liofilizzato(-a); (person) disidratato(-a).

de-ice [,di:'aɪs] vt togliere il ghiaccio da.

de-icer [,di:'aɪsər] n antighiaccio m.

dejected [dɪ'dʒektɪd] adj sconsolato(-a).

delay [dɪ'leɪ] n ritardo m ◆ vt (flight, departure) ritardare; (person) trattenere ◆ vi indugiare; **without ~** senza indugio.

delayed [dɪ'leɪd] adj (train, flight) in ritardo.

delegate [n 'delɪgət, vb 'delɪgeɪt] n

delegato m (-a f) ◆ vt (person) delegare.

delete [dɪˈliːt] vt cancellare.

deli [ˈdelɪ] n (inf: abbr of delicatessen) negozio m di specialità gastronomiche.

deliberate [dɪˈlɪbərət] adj (intentional) intenzionale.

deliberately [dɪˈlɪbərətlɪ] adv (intentionally) deliberatamente.

delicacy [ˈdelɪkəsɪ] n (food) leccornia f.

delicate [ˈdelɪkət] adj delicato(-a).

delicatessen [ˌdelɪkəˈtesn] n negozio m di specialità gastronomiche.

delicious [dɪˈlɪʃəs] adj squisito(-a).

delight [dɪˈlaɪt] n (feeling) gioia f ◆ vt deliziare; **to take (a) ~ in doing sthg** provare piacere a fare qc.

delighted [dɪˈlaɪtɪd] adj felicissimo(-a).

delightful [dɪˈlaɪtfʊl] adj delizioso(-a).

deliver [dɪˈlɪvəʳ] vt (goods, letters, newspaper) consegnare; (speech, lecture) tenere; (baby) far nascere.

delivery [dɪˈlɪvərɪ] n (of goods, letters) consegna f; (birth) parto m.

delude [dɪˈluːd] vt illudere.

de luxe [dəˈlʌks] adj di lusso.

demand [dɪˈmɑːnd] n (request) richiesta f; (claim) rivendicazione f; (COMM) domanda f; (requirement) esigenza f ◆ vt (request forcefully) pretendere; (require) richiedere; **to ~ to do sthg** esigere di fare qc; **in ~** richiesto.

demanding [dɪˈmɑːndɪŋ] adj esi-

gente.

demerara sugar [deməˈreərə] n zucchero m di canna.

demist [ˌdiːˈmɪst] vt (Br) disappannare.

demister [ˌdiːˈmɪstəʳ] n (Br) deumidificatore m.

democracy [dɪˈmɒkrəsɪ] n democrazia f.

Democrat [ˈdeməkræt] n (Am) democratico m (-a f).

democratic [deməˈkrætɪk] adj democratico(-a).

demolish [dɪˈmɒlɪʃ] vt (building) demolire.

demonstrate [ˈdemənstreɪt] vt (prove) dimostrare; (machine, appliance) mostrare il funzionamento di ◆ vi dimostrare.

demonstration [demənˈstreɪʃn] n dimostrazione f.

denial [dɪˈnaɪəl] n (refusal) rifiuto m; (statement) smentita f.

denim [ˈdenɪm] n denim m ❑ **denims** npl jeans mpl.

denim jacket n giubbotto m di jeans.

Denmark [ˈdenmɑːk] n la Danimarca.

dense [dens] adj (crowd, forest) fitto(-a); (smoke) denso(-a).

dent [dent] n ammaccatura f.

dental [ˈdentl] adj dentale.

dental floss [-flɒs] n filo m interdentale.

dental surgeon n dentista mf.

dental surgery n (place) studio m dentistico.

dentist [ˈdentɪst] n dentista mf; **to go to the ~'s** andare dal dentista.

dentures [ˈdentʃəz] npl dentiera f.

deny [dɪ'naɪ] *vt* negare.

deodorant [diː'əʊdərənt] *n* deodorante *m*.

depart [dɪ'pɑːt] *vi* partire.

department [dɪ'pɑːtmənt] *n* (of business, shop) reparto *m*; (of government) ministero *m*; (of school, university) dipartimento *m*.

department store *n* grandi magazzini *mpl*.

departure [dɪ'pɑːtʃəʳ] *n* partenza *f*; '~s' (at airport) 'partenze'.

departure lounge *n* sala *f* partenze.

depend [dɪ'pend] *vi*: it ~s dipende □ **depend on** *vt fus* dipendere da; ~ing on a seconda di.

dependable [dɪ'pendəbl] *adj* affidabile.

deplorable [dɪ'plɔːrəbl] *adj* deplorevole.

deport [dɪ'pɔːt] *vt* espellere.

deposit [dɪ'pɒzɪt] *n* deposito *m* ♦ *vt* depositare.

deposit account *n* (Br) conto *m* vincolato.

depot ['diːpəʊ] *n* (Am: for buses, trains) stazione *f*.

depressed [dɪ'prest] *adj* depresso(-a).

depressing [dɪ'presɪŋ] *adj* deprimente.

depression [dɪ'preʃn] *n* depressione *f*.

deprive [dɪ'praɪv] *vt*: to ~ sb of sthg privare qn di qc.

depth [depθ] *n* (distance down) profondità *f inv*; **out of one's ~** (when swimming) dove non si tocca; (fig: unable to cope) non all'altezza; **~ of field** (in photography) profondità di campo.

deputy ['depjʊtɪ] *adj* vice (inv).

derailleur [də'reɪljəʳ] *n* deragliatore *m*.

derailment [dɪ'reɪlmənt] *n* deragliamento *m*.

derelict ['derəlɪkt] *adj* abbandonato(-a).

derv [dɜːv] *n* (Br) benzina *f* diesel.

descend [dɪ'send] *vt & vi* scendere.

descendant [dɪ'sendənt] *n* discendente *mf*.

descent [dɪ'sent] *n* discesa *f*.

describe [dɪ'skraɪb] *vt* descrivere.

description [dɪ'skrɪpʃn] *n* descrizione *f*.

desert [*n* 'dezət, *vb* dɪ'zɜːt] *n* deserto *m* ♦ *vt* abbandonare.

deserted [dɪ'zɜːtɪd] *adj* deserto(-a).

deserve [dɪ'zɜːv] *vt* meritare.

design [dɪ'zaɪn] *n* (pattern) disegno *m*; (art) design *m*; (of machine, building) progetto *m* ♦ *vt* (dress) disegnare; (machine, building) progettare; **to be ~ed for** essere concepito per.

designer [dɪ'zaɪnəʳ] *n* (of clothes) stilista *mf*; (of building) architetto *m*; (of product) designer *mf inv* ♦ *adj* (clothes, sunglasses) firmato(-a).

desirable [dɪ'zaɪərəbl] *adj* desiderabile.

desire [dɪ'zaɪəʳ] *n* desiderio *m* ♦ *vt* desiderare; **it leaves a lot to be ~d** lascia molto a desiderare.

desk [desk] *n* (in home, office) scrivania *f*; (at airport, station, of pupil) banco *m*; (at hotel) portineria *f*.

desktop publishing ['desk-ˌtɒp-] n desktop publishing m.

despair [dɪ'speəʳ] n disperazione f.

despatch [dɪ'spætʃ] = dispatch.

desperate ['despərət] adj disperato(-a); **to be ~ for sthg** avere un disperato bisogno di qc.

despicable [dɪ'spɪkəbl] adj spregevole.

despise [dɪ'spaɪz] vt disprezzare.

despite [dɪ'spaɪt] prep nonostante.

dessert [dɪ'zɜ:t] n dessert m inv.

dessertspoon [dɪ'zɜ:tspu:n] n cucchiaino m.

destination [ˌdestɪ'neɪʃn] n destinazione f.

destroy [dɪ'strɔɪ] vt distruggere.

destruction [dɪ'strʌkʃn] n distruzione f.

detach [dɪ'tætʃ] vt staccare.

detached house [dɪ'tætʃt-] n villetta f unifamiliare.

detail ['di:teɪl] n dettaglio m; **in ~** dettagliatamente ❑ **details** npl (facts) informazioni fpl.

detailed ['di:teɪld] adj dettagliato(-a).

detect [dɪ'tekt] vt (sense) avvertire; (find) scoprire.

detective [dɪ'tektɪv] n detective mf inv; **a ~ story** un racconto poliziesco.

detention [dɪ'tenʃn] n (SCH) punizione che consiste nel trattenere un alunno a scuola oltre l'orario scolastico.

detergent [dɪ'tɜ:dʒənt] n detersivo m.

deteriorate [dɪ'tɪərɪəreɪt] vi deteriorarsi.

determination [dɪˌtɜ:mɪ'neɪʃn] n determinazione f.

determine [dɪ'tɜ:mɪn] vt (control) determinare; (find out) accertare.

determined [dɪ'tɜ:mɪnd] adj risoluto(-a); **to be ~ to do sthg** essere determinato a fare qc.

deterrent [dɪ'terənt] n deterrente m.

detest [dɪ'test] vt detestare.

detour ['di:ˌtʊəʳ] n deviazione f.

detrain [ˌdi:'treɪn] vi (fml) scendere dal treno.

deuce [dju:s] n (in tennis) parità f.

devastate ['devəsteɪt] vt devastare.

develop [dɪ'veləp] vt sviluppare; (machine, method) perfezionare; (illness, habit) contrarre ◆ vi (evolve) svilupparsi.

developing country [dɪ'veləpɪŋ-] n paese m in via di sviluppo.

development [dɪ'veləpmənt] n sviluppo m; **a housing ~** un complesso residenziale.

device [dɪ'vaɪs] n congegno m.

devil ['devl] n diavolo m; **what the ~ ...?** (inf) che diavolo ...?

devise [dɪ'vaɪz] vt escogitare.

devoted [dɪ'vəʊtɪd] adj (person) affezionato(-a).

dew [dju:] n rugiada f.

diabetes [ˌdaɪə'bi:ti:z] n diabete m.

diabetic [ˌdaɪə'betɪk] adj (person) diabetico(-a); (chocolate) per diabetici ◆ n diabetico m (-a f).

diagnosis [ˌdaɪəg'nəʊsɪs] (pl -oses [-əʊsi:z]) n diagnosi f inv.

diagonal [daɪ'ægənl] adj diagonale.

diagram ['daɪəgræm] n diagramma m.

dial ['daɪəl] n (of telephone) disco m combinatore; (of clock) quadrante m; (of radio) scala f ◆ vt (number) comporre.

dialling code ['daɪəlɪŋ-] n (Br) prefisso m telefonico.

dialling tone ['daɪəlɪŋ-] n (Br) segnale m di libero.

dial tone (Am) = **dialling tone**.

diameter [daɪ'æmɪtə'] n diametro m.

diamond ['daɪəmənd] n (gem) diamante m ◻ **diamonds** npl (in cards) quadri mpl.

diaper ['daɪpə'] n (Am) pannolino m.

diarrhoea [,daɪə'rɪə] n diarrea f.

diary ['daɪərɪ] n (for appointments) agenda f; (journal) diario m.

dice [daɪs] (pl inv) n dado m.

diced [daɪst] adj a dadini.

dictate [dɪk'teɪt] vt dettare.

dictation [dɪk'teɪʃn] n dettato m.

dictator [dɪk'teɪtə'] n dittatore m (-trice f).

dictionary ['dɪkʃənrɪ] n dizionario m.

did [dɪd] pt → do.

die [daɪ] (pt & pp died, cont dying ['daɪɪŋ]) vi morire; **to be dying for sthg** (inf) morire dalla voglia di qc; **to be dying to do sthg** (inf) morire dalla voglia di fare qc ◻ **die away** vi spegnersi; **die out** vi scomparire.

diesel ['diːzl] n (fuel) gasolio m; (car) diesel m inv.

diet ['daɪət] n (for slimming, health) dieta f; (food eaten) alimentazione f ◆ vi essere a dieta ◆ adj dietetico(-a).

diet Coke® n coca f light®.

differ ['dɪfə'] vi: **to ~ (from)** (disagree) non essere d'accordo (con); (be dissimilar) essere diverso (da).

difference ['dɪfrəns] n differenza f; **it makes no ~** è lo stesso; **a ~ of opinion** una divergenza di opinioni.

different ['dɪfrənt] adj diverso(-a); **to be ~ (from)** essere diverso (da); **a ~ route** un'altra strada.

differently ['dɪfrəntlɪ] adv in modo diverso.

difficult ['dɪfɪkəlt] adj difficile.

difficulty ['dɪfɪkəltɪ] n difficoltà f inv.

dig [dɪg] (pt & pp dug) vt & vi scavare ◻ **dig out** vt sep (rescue) estrarre; (find) scovare; **dig up** vt sep (from ground) dissotterrare.

digest [dɪ'dʒest] vt digerire.

digestion [dɪ'dʒestʃn] n digestione f.

digestive (biscuit) [dɪ'dʒestɪv-] n (Br) biscotto di frumento con farina integrale.

digit ['dɪdʒɪt] n (figure) cifra f; (finger, toe) dito m.

digital ['dɪdʒɪtl] adj digitale.

dill [dɪl] n aneto m.

dilute [daɪ'luːt] vt (liquid) diluire.

dim [dɪm] adj (light) debole; (room) buio(-a); (inf: stupid) ottuso(-a) ◆ vt (light) abbassare.

dime [daɪm] n (Am) moneta f da dieci centesimi di dollaro.

dimensions [dɪ'menʃnz] npl dimensioni fpl.

din [dɪn] n baccano m.

dine [daɪn] vi cenare ◻ **dine out**

vi cenare fuori.

diner ['daɪnəʳ] *n (Am: restaurant)* ≃ tavola *f* calda; *(person)* cliente *mf*.

 DINER

Piccoli ristoranti senza grandi pretese, i "diners" sono situati principalmente lungo autostrade e strade statali, ma si trovano anche in città. Servono pasti leggeri e sono frequentati soprattutto da camionisti e automobilisti di passaggio. A volte hanno il caratteristico aspetto di vecchi vagoni ferroviari.

---

dinghy ['dɪŋgɪ] *n (with sail, oars)* barca *f; (for racing)* dinghy *m inv; (made of rubber)* canotto *m*.

dingy ['dɪndʒɪ] *adj (clothes)* sporco(-a); *(town, hotel)* squallido(-a).

dining car ['daɪnɪŋ-] *n* carrozza *f* ristorante.

dining hall ['daɪnɪŋ-] *n* refettorio *m*.

dining room ['daɪnɪŋ-] *n* sala *f* da pranzo.

dinner ['dɪnəʳ] *n (at lunchtime)* pranzo *m; (in evening)* cena *f;* **to have ~** *(at lunchtime)* pranzare; *(in evening)* cenare.

dinner jacket *n* giacca *f* dello smoking.

dinner party *n* cena *f*.

dinner set *n* servizio *m* da tavola.

dinner suit *n* smoking *m inv*.

dinnertime ['dɪnətaɪm] *n (at lunchtime)* ora *f* di pranzo; *(in evening)* ora di cena.

dinosaur ['daɪnəsɔːʳ] *n* dino-

sauro *m*.

dip [dɪp] *n (in road, land)* avvallamento *m; (food)* salsetta cremosa in cui intingere patatine o verdure crude ◆ *vt (into liquid)* immergere ◆ *vi (road, land)* digradare; **to have a ~** *(swim)* fare una nuotatina; **to one's headlights** *(Br)* spegnere gli abbaglianti.

diploma [dɪ'pləʊmə] *n* diploma *m*.

dipstick ['dɪpstɪk] *n* asta *f* di livello.

direct [dɪ'rekt] *adj* diretto(-a) ◆ *adv (go)* direttamente; *(travel)* senza fermarsi ◆ *vt:* **can you ~ me to the railway station?** mi può indicare la strada per la stazione?

direct current *n* corrente *f* continua.

direction [dɪ'rekʃn] *n (of movement)* direzione *f;* **to ask for ~s** chiedere indicazioni ❏ **directions** *npl (instructions)* istruzioni *fpl*.

directly [dɪ'rektlɪ] *adv (exactly)* proprio; *(soon)* subito.

director [dɪ'rektəʳ] *n (of company)* amministratore *m* (-trice *f*); *(of film, play, TV programme)* regista *mf; (organizer)* direttore *m* (-trice *f*).

directory [dɪ'rektərɪ] *n* elenco *m*.

directory enquiries *n (Br)* informazioni *fpl* elenco abbonati.

dirt [dɜːt] *n* sporcizia *f; (earth)* terra *f*.

dirty ['dɜːtɪ] *adj* sporco(-a).

disability [ˌdɪsə'bɪlətɪ] *n* handicap *m inv; (through old age, illness)* invalidità *f inv*.

disabled [dɪs'eɪbld] *adj* disabile ◆ *npl:* **the ~** i portatori di handicap; **'~ toilet'** 'toilette per portatori di handicap'.

disadvantage [ˌdɪsəd'vɑːntɪdʒ] *n* svantaggio *m*.

disagree [ˌdɪsə'griː] *vi* non essere d'accordo; **to ~ with sb (about)** non essere d'accordo con qn (su); **those mussels ~d with me** quelle cozze mi hanno fatto male.

disagreement [ˌdɪsə'griːmənt] *n* (argument) discussione *f*; (dissimilarity) disaccordo *m*.

disappear [ˌdɪsə'pɪər] *vi* sparire.

disappearance [ˌdɪsə'pɪərəns] *n* scomparsa *f*.

disappoint [ˌdɪsə'pɔɪnt] *vt* deludere.

disappointed [ˌdɪsə'pɔɪntɪd] *adj* deluso(-a).

disappointing [ˌdɪsə'pɔɪntɪŋ] *adj* deludente.

disappointment [ˌdɪsə'pɔɪntmənt] *n* delusione *f*.

disapprove [ˌdɪsə'pruːv] *vi*: **to ~ of** disapprovare.

disarmament [dɪs'ɑːməmənt] *n* disarmo *m*.

disaster [dɪ'zɑːstər] *n* disastro *m*.

disastrous [dɪ'zɑːstrəs] *adj* disastroso(-a).

disc [dɪsk] *n* (Br) disco *m*; (Br: CD) compact disc *m inv*; **I slipped a ~** mi è venuta l'ernia al disco.

discard [dɪ'skɑːd] *vt* scartare.

discharge [dɪs'tʃɑːdʒ] *vt* (prisoner) rilasciare; (patient) dimettere; (soldier) congedare; (smoke, gas) emettere; (liquid) scaricare.

discipline ['dɪsɪplɪn] *n* disciplina *f*.

disc jockey *n* disc-jockey *mf inv*.

disco ['dɪskəu] (*pl* -s) *n* (place) di-scoteca *f*; (event) festa *f*.

discoloured [dɪs'kʌləd] *adj* scolorito(-a).

discomfort [dɪs'kʌmfət] *n* fastidio *m*.

disconnect [ˌdɪskə'nekt] *vt* staccare; (gas supply) chiudere; (pipe) scollegare.

discontinued [ˌdɪskən'tɪnjuːd] *adj* (product) di fine serie.

discotheque ['dɪskəutek] *n* (place) discoteca *f*; (event) festa *f*.

discount ['dɪskaunt] *n* sconto *m*.

discover [dɪ'skʌvər] *vt* scoprire.

discovery [dɪ'skʌvərɪ] *n* scoperta *f*.

discreet [dɪ'skriːt] *adj* discreto(-a).

discrepancy [dɪ'skrepənsɪ] *n* discrepanza *f*.

discriminate [dɪ'skrɪmɪneɪt] *vi*: **to ~ against sb** discriminare contro qn.

discrimination [dɪˌskrɪmɪ'neɪʃn] *n* (unfair treatment) discriminazione *f*.

discuss [dɪ'skʌs] *vt* discutere.

discussion [dɪ'skʌʃn] *n* discussione *f*.

disease [dɪ'ziːz] *n* malattia *f*.

disembark [ˌdɪsɪm'bɑːk] *vi* sbarcare.

disgrace [dɪs'greɪs] *n* (shame) vergogna *f*; **it's a ~!** è una vergogna!

disgraceful [dɪs'greɪsful] *adj* vergognoso(-a).

disguise [dɪs'gaɪz] *n* travestimento *m* ♦ *vt* travestire; **in ~** travestito.

disgust [dɪs'gʌst] *n* disgusto *m* ♦ *vt* disgustare.

disgusting [dɪs'gʌstɪŋ] *adj* disgustoso(-a).

dish [dɪʃ] *n* piatto *m*; **to do the ~es** fare i piatti; **'~ of the day'** 'piatto del giorno' ❑ **dish up** *vt sep* servire.

dishcloth ['dɪʃklɒθ] *n* strofinaccio *m*.

disheveled [dɪˈʃevəld] *(Am)* = **dishevelled**.

dishevelled [dɪˈʃevəld] *adj (Br: hair)* arruffato(-a); *(appearance)* trasandato(-a).

dishonest [dɪsˈɒnɪst] *adj* disonesto(-a).

dish towel *n (Am)* strofinaccio *m*.

dishwasher ['dɪʃˌwɒʃəʳ] *n (machine)* lavastoviglie *f inv*.

disinfectant [ˌdɪsɪnˈfektənt] *n* disinfettante *m*.

disintegrate [dɪsˈɪntɪɡreɪt] *vi* disintegrarsi.

disk [dɪsk] *n (Am)* = **disc**; *(COMPUT)* dischetto *m*.

disk drive *n* drive *m inv*.

dislike [dɪsˈlaɪk] *n (poor opinion)* antipatia *f* ♦ *vt*: **I ~ them** non mi piacciono; **to take a ~ to** prendere in antipatia.

dislocate ['dɪsləkeɪt] *vt*: **to ~ one's shoulder** slogarsi la spalla.

dismal ['dɪzml] *adj (weather, place)* deprimente; *(terrible)* pessimo(-a).

dismantle [dɪsˈmæntl] *vt* smontare.

dismay [dɪsˈmeɪ] *n* sgomento *m*.

dismiss [dɪsˈmɪs] *vt (not consider)* ignorare; *(from job)* licenziare; *(from classroom)* congedare.

disobedient [ˌdɪsəˈbiːdjənt] *adj* disubbidiente.

disobey [ˌdɪsəˈbeɪ] *vt* disubbidire.

disorder [dɪsˈɔːdəʳ] *n (confusion)* disordine *m*; *(illness)* disturbo *m*.

disorganized [dɪsˈɔːɡənaɪzd] *adj* disorganizzato(-a).

dispatch [dɪˈspætʃ] *vt* inviare.

dispense [dɪˈspens]: **dispense with** *vt fus* fare a meno di.

dispenser [dɪˈspensəʳ] *n (device)* distributore *m*.

dispensing chemist [dɪˈspensɪŋ-] *n (Br: shop)* farmacia *f*.

disperse [dɪˈspɜːs] *vt* disperdere ♦ *vi* disperdersi.

display [dɪˈspleɪ] *n (of goods)* esposizione *f*; *(public event)* spettacolo *m*; *(readout)* schermo *m* ♦ *vt (goods, information)* esporre; *(feeling, quality)* manifestare; **on ~** in mostra.

displeased [dɪsˈpliːzd] *adj* contrariato(-a).

disposable [dɪˈspəʊzəbl] *adj* usa e getta *(inv)*.

dispute [dɪˈspjuːt] *n (argument)* controversia *f*; *(industrial)* vertenza *f* ♦ *vt* mettere in discussione.

disqualify [ˌdɪsˈkwɒlɪfaɪ] *vt* squalificare; **he is disqualified from driving** *(Br)* gli hanno ritirato la patente.

disregard [ˌdɪsrɪˈɡɑːd] *vt* ignorare.

disrupt [dɪsˈrʌpt] *vt* disturbare.

disruption [dɪsˈrʌpʃn] *n* disordine *m*.

dissatisfied [ˌdɪsˈsætɪsfaɪd] *adj* insoddisfatto(-a).

dissolve [dɪˈzɒlv] *vt* sciogliere ♦ *vi* sciogliersi.

dissuade [dɪˈsweɪd] *vt*: **to ~ sb from doing sthg** dissuadere qn dal fare qc.

distance ['dɪstəns] n distanza f; **from a ~** da lontano; **in the ~** in lontananza.

distant ['dɪstənt] adj distante; (in time) lontano(-a).

distilled water [dɪ'stɪld-] n acqua f distillata.

distillery [dɪ'stɪlərɪ] n distilleria f.

distinct [dɪ'stɪŋkt] adj (separate) distinto(-a); (noticeable) chiaro(-a).

distinction [dɪ'stɪŋkʃn] n (difference) distinzione f; (mark in exam) lode f.

distinctive [dɪ'stɪŋktɪv] adj inconfondibile.

distinguish [dɪ'stɪŋgwɪʃ] vt (perceive) distinguere; **to ~ sthg from sthg** distinguere qc da qc.

distorted [dɪ'stɔːtɪd] adj distorto(-a).

distract [dɪ'strækt] vt distrarre.

distraction [dɪ'strækʃn] n distrazione f.

distress [dɪ'stres] n (pain) sofferenza f; (anxiety) angoscia f.

distressing [dɪ'stresɪŋ] adj doloroso(-a).

distribute [dɪ'strɪbjuːt] vt distribuire.

distributor [dɪ'strɪbjutər] n (COMM) distributore m; (AUT) spinterogeno m.

district ['dɪstrɪkt] n regione f; (of town) quartiere m.

district attorney n (Am) ≃ procuratore m della Repubblica.

disturb [dɪ'stɜːb] vt (interrupt) disturbare; (worry) turbare; (move) muovere; **'do not ~'** 'non disturbare'.

disturbance [dɪ'stɜːbəns] n (violence) disordini mpl.

ditch [dɪtʃ] n fossato m.

ditto ['dɪtəʊ] adv idem.

divan [dɪ'væn] n divano m.

dive [daɪv] (pt Am **-d** OR **dove**, pt Br **-d**) n (of swimmer) tuffo m ◆ vi tuffarsi; (under sea) immergersi.

diver ['daɪvər] n (from divingboard, rock) tuffatore m (-trice f); (under sea) sommozzatore m (-trice f).

diversion [daɪ'vɜːʃn] n (of traffic) deviazione f; (amusement) diversivo m.

divert [daɪ'vɜːt] vt (traffic, river) deviare; (attention) distrarre.

divide [dɪ'vaɪd] vt dividere ❑ **divide up** vt sep dividere.

diving ['daɪvɪŋ] n (from divingboard, rock) tuffi mpl; (under sea) immersioni fpl; **to go ~** fare sub.

divingboard ['daɪvɪŋbɔːd] n trampolino m.

division [dɪ'vɪʒn] n divisione f; (in football league) serie f.

divorce [dɪ'vɔːs] n divorzio m ◆ vt divorziare da.

divorced [dɪ'vɔːst] adj divorziato(-a).

DIY n (abbr of do-it-yourself) il fai da te.

dizzy ['dɪzɪ] adj: **I feel ~** mi gira la testa.

DJ n (abbr of disc jockey) discjockey mf inv.

do [duː] (pt **did**, pp **done**, pl **dos**) aux vb 1. (in negatives): **don't ~ that!** non farlo!; **she didn't listen** non ha ascoltato.
2. (in questions): **~ you like it?** ti piace?; **how ~ you do it?** come si fa?

3. *(referring to previous verb)*: **I eat more than you ~** io mangio più di te; **you made a mistake – no I didn't!** ti sei sbagliato – non è vero!; **so – I** anch'io.

4. *(in question tags)* vero?, non è vero?; **so, you like Scotland, ~ you?** e così ti piace la Scozia, non è vero?

5. *(for emphasis)*: **I ~ like this bedroom** questa camera mi piace proprio; **~ come in!** si accomodi!

♦ *vt* 1. *(perform)* fare; **to ~ one's homework** fare i compiti; **what is she doing?** cosa sta facendo?; **what can I ~ for you?** in cosa posso esserle utile?

2. *(attend to)*: **to ~ one's hair** pettinarsi; **to ~ one's make-up** truccarsi; **to ~ one's teeth** lavarsi i denti.

3. *(cause)* fare; **to ~ damage** danneggiare; **to ~ sb good** fare bene a qn.

4. *(have as job)*: **what do you ~?** che lavoro fai?

5. *(provide, offer)* fare; **we ~ pizzas for under £4** facciamo pizze a meno di 4 sterline.

6. *(study)* fare.

7. *(subj: vehicle)* fare; **the car was doing 50 mph** la macchina andava a 80 all'ora.

8. *(inf: visit)* fare; **we're doing Scotland next week** la settimana prossima facciamo la Scozia.

♦ *vi* 1. *(behave, act)* fare; **~ as I say** fai come ti dico.

2. *(progress, get on)* andare; **to ~ badly** andare male; **to ~ well** andare bene.

3. *(be sufficient)* bastare; **will £5 ~?** bastano 5 sterline?

4. *(in phrases)*: **how do you ~?** piacere!; **what has that got to ~ with**

it? e questo che c'entra?

♦ *n (party)* festa *f*; **the ~s and don'ts** le cose da fare e da non fare.

❑ **do out of** *vt sep (inf)*: **to ~ sb out of sthg** fregare qc a qn; **do up** *vt sep (fasten)* allacciare; *(decorate)* rinnovare; *(wrap up)* impacchettare; **do with** *vt fus (need)*: **I could ~ with a drink** mi ci vuole proprio un bicchierino; **do without** *vt fus* fare a meno di.

dock [dɒk] *n (for ships)* molo *m*; *(JUR)* banco *m* degli imputati ♦ *vi* attraccare.

doctor ['dɒktə'] *n* dottore *m* (-essa *f*); **to go to the ~'s** andare dal dottore.

document ['dɒkjumənt] *n* documento *m*.

documentary [,dɒkju'mentəri] *n* documentario *m*.

Dodgems® ['dɒdʒəmz] *npl (Br)* autoscontri *mpl*.

dodgy ['dɒdʒi] *adj (Br: inf: plan)* rischioso(-a); *(car)* poco sicuro(-a).

does [*weak form* dəz, *strong form* dʌz] → **do**.

doesn't ['dʌznt] = **does not**.

dog [dɒg] *n* cane *m*.

dog food *n* cibo *m* per cani.

doggy bag ['dɒgi] *n* sacchetto per portar via gli avanzi di un pasto consumato al ristorante.

do-it-yourself *n* il fai da te.

dole [dəʊl] *n*: **to be on the ~** *(Br)* prendere il sussidio di disoccupazione.

doll [dɒl] *n* bambola *f*.

dollar ['dɒlə'] *n* dollaro *m*.

Dolomites ['dɒləmaɪts] *npl*: **the ~** le Dolomiti.

dolphin ['dɒlfɪn] n delfino m.

dome [dəʊm] n cupola f.

domestic [də'mestɪk] adj (of house, family) domestico(-a); (of country) nazionale, interno(-a).

domestic appliance n elettrodomestico m.

domestic flight n volo m nazionale.

domestic science n economia f domestica.

dominate ['dɒmɪneɪt] vt dominare.

dominoes ['dɒmɪnəʊz] n domino m.

donate [də'neɪt] vt donare.

donation [də'neɪʃn] n donazione f.

done [dʌn] pp → do ◆ adj (finished) finito(-a); (cooked) cotto(-a).

donkey ['dɒŋkɪ] n asino m.

don't [dəʊnt] = do not.

door [dɔː'] n (of building) porta f; (of vehicle, cupboard) sportello m.

doorbell ['dɔːbel] n campanello m.

doorknob ['dɔːnɒb] n pomello m.

doorman ['dɔːmən] (pl -men) n portiere m.

doormat ['dɔːmæt] n zerbino m.

doormen ['dɔːmən] pl → doorman.

doorstep ['dɔːstep] n gradino m della porta; (Br: inf: piece of bread) grossa fetta f di pane.

doorway ['dɔːweɪ] n porta f.

dope [dəʊp] n (inf: any illegal drug) roba f; (marijuana) erba f.

dormitory ['dɔːmɪtrɪ] n dormitorio m.

Dormobile® ['dɔːmə,biːl] n cam-

per m inv.

dosage ['dəʊsɪdʒ] n dosaggio m.

dose [dəʊs] n (amount) dose f; (of illness) attacco m.

dot [dɒt] n punto m; **on the ~** (fig) in punto.

dotted line ['dɒtɪd-] n linea f punteggiata.

double ['dʌbl] adj doppio(-a) ◆ adv (twice) due volte ◆ n (twice the amount) doppio m; (alcohol) dose f doppia ◆ vt & vi raddoppiare; **~ three, two, eight** trentatrè, ventotto; **a ~ whisky** un doppio whisky; **to bend sthg ~** piegare qc in due ❑ **doubles** n (in tennis) doppio m.

double bed n letto m matrimoniale.

double-breasted [-'brestɪd] adj a doppio petto.

double cream n (Br) panna molto densa ad alto contenuto di grassi.

double-decker (bus) [-'dekə'-] n autobus m inv a due piani.

double doors npl porte fpl a due battenti.

double-glazing [-'gleɪzɪŋ] n doppi vetri mpl.

double room n camera f per due.

doubt [daʊt] n dubbio m ◆ vt dubitare di; **I ~ it** ne dubito; **I ~ she'll be there** dubito che ci sarà; **in ~** in dubbio; **no ~** (almost certainly) senza dubbio.

doubtful ['daʊtfʊl] adj (uncertain) incerto(-a); **it's ~ that ... is** improbabile che ... (+ subjunctive).

dough [dəʊ] n pasta f, impasto m (per pane, dolci).

doughnut ['dəʊnʌt] n bombolone m.

dove[1] [dʌv] n (bird) colomba f.

dove[2] [dəʊv] pt (Am) → **dive**.

Dover ['dəʊvə^r] n Dover.

Dover sole n sogliola f di Dover.

down [daʊn] adv 1. (towards the bottom) giù; ~ **here** quaggiù; ~ **there** laggiù; **to fall** ~ cadere.
2. (along): **I'm going ~ to the shops** vado ai negozi.
3. (downstairs): **I'll come ~ later** scenderò più tardi.
4. (southwards): **we're going ~ to London** andiamo a Londra.
5. (in writing): **to write sthg ~** scrivere qc.
◆ prep 1. (towards the bottom of): **they ran ~ the hill** corsero giù per la collina.
2. (along) lungo; **I was walking ~ the street** camminavo lungo la strada.
◆ adj (inf: depressed) giù (inv).
◆ n (feathers) piumino m.
❑ **downs** npl (Br) colline fpl.

downhill [,daʊn'hɪl] adv in discesa.

Downing Street ['daʊnɪŋ-] n Downing Street f (strada di Londra dove si trova la residenza del primo ministro).

i **DOWNING STREET**

Questa strada di Londra è divenuta famosa in quanto ospita al numero 10 la residenza ufficiale del primo ministro e al numero 11 quella del Cancelliere dello Scacchiere (ministro delle Finanze). L'espressione "Downing Street" designa, per estensione, il primo ministro stesso e i suoi collaboratori.

downpour ['daʊnpɔ:^r] n acquazzone m.

downstairs [,daʊn'steəz] adj di sotto ◆ adv al piano di sotto; **to go** ~ scendere giù.

downtown [,daʊn'taʊn] adj (hotel) del centro; (train) per il centro ◆ adv in centro; ~ **New York** il centro di New York.

down under adv (Br: inf: in Australia) in Australia.

downwards ['daʊnwədz] adv verso il basso.

doz. abbr = **dozen**.

doze [dəʊz] vi fare un pisolino.

dozen ['dʌzn] n dozzina f; **a** ~ **eggs** una dozzina di uova.

Dr (abbr of doctor) Dott. m (Dott.ssa f)

drab [dræb] adj grigio(-a).

draft [drɑːft] n (early version) bozza f; (money order) tratta f; (Am) = **draught**.

drag [dræg] vt (pull along) trascinare ◆ vi (along ground) strascicare; **what a ~!** (inf) che seccatura! ❑ **drag on** vi trascinarsi.

dragonfly ['drægnflaɪ] n libellula f.

drain [dreɪn] n (sewer) fogna f; (grating in street) tombino m ◆ vt (tank, radiator) svuotare ◆ vi (vegetables, washing-up) scolare.

draining board ['dreɪnɪŋ-] n scolatoio m.

drainpipe ['dreɪnpaɪp] n tubo m di scarico.

drama ['drɑːmə] n (play, exciting event) dramma m; (art) teatro m; (excitement) emozioni fpl.

dramatic [drə'mætɪk] adj (impressive) sensazionale.

drank [dræŋk] pt → **drink**.

drapes [dreɪps] npl (Am) tende fpl.

drastic ['dræstɪk] adj drastico(-a); (improvement) netto(-a).

drastically ['dræstɪklɪ] adv sensibilmente.

draught [drɑːft] n (Br: of air) corrente f d'aria.

draught beer n birra f alla spina.

draughts [drɑːfts] n (Br) dama f.

draughty ['drɑːftɪ] adj pieno(-a) di correnti d'aria.

draw [drɔː] (pt drew, pp drawn) vt (with pen, pencil) disegnare; (line) tracciare; (pull) tirare; (attract) attirare; (conclusion) trarre ♦ vi (with pen, pencil) disegnare; (SPORT) pareggiare ♦ n (SPORT: result) pareggio m; (lottery) estrazione f; to ~ the curtains tirare le tende ❑ **draw out** vt sep (money) prelevare; **draw up** vt sep (list, plan) stendere ♦ vi (car, bus) accostarsi.

drawback ['drɔːbæk] n inconveniente m.

drawer [drɔːr] n cassetto m.

drawing ['drɔːɪŋ] n disegno m.

drawing pin n (Br) puntina f da disegno.

drawing room n salotto m.

drawn [drɔːn] pp → **draw**.

dreadful ['dredful] adj terribile.

dream [driːm] n sogno m ♦ vt sognare ♦ vi: to ~ (of) sognare (di); a ~ house una casa di sogno.

dress [dres] n vestito m; (clothes) abbigliamento m ♦ vt vestire;

(wound) fasciare; (salad) condire ♦ vi (get dressed) vestirsi; (in particular way) vestire; to be ~ed in essere vestito di; to get ~ed vestirsi ❑ **dress up** vi mettersi in ghingheri.

dress circle n prima galleria f.

dresser ['dresər] n (Br: for crockery) credenza f; (Am: chest of drawers) comò m inv.

dressing ['dresɪŋ] n (for salad) condimento m; (for wound) fasciatura f.

dressing gown n vestaglia f.

dressing room n camerino m.

dressing table n toilette f inv.

dressmaker ['dres,meɪkər] n sarta f.

dress rehearsal n prova f generale.

drew [druː] pt → **draw**.

dribble ['drɪbl] vi (liquid) gocciolare; (baby) sbavare.

drier ['draɪər] = **dryer**.

drift [drɪft] n (of snow) cumulo m ♦ vi (in wind) essere spinto dal vento; (in water) essere spinto dalla corrente.

drill [drɪl] n trapano m ♦ vt (hole) fare.

drink [drɪŋk] (pt drank, pp drunk) n bevanda f; (alcoholic) bicchierino m ♦ vt & vi bere; would you like a ~? vuoi qualcosa da bere?; to have a ~ (alcoholic) bere un bicchierino.

drinkable ['drɪŋkəbl] adj (safe to drink) potabile; (wine) bevibile.

drinking water ['drɪŋkɪŋ-] n acqua f potabile.

drip [drɪp] n (drop) goccia f; (MED) flebo f inv ♦ vi gocciolare.

drip-dry adj che non si stira.

dripping (wet) ['drɪpɪŋ-] *adj* fradicio(-a).

drive [draɪv] (*pt* drove, *pp* driven ['drɪvn]) *n* (*journey*) viaggio *m* (in macchina); (*in front of house*) viale *m* d'accesso ◆ *vi* (*drive car*) guidare; (*travel in car*) andare in macchina ◆ *vt* (*car, bus, train*) guidare; (*take in car*) portare (in macchina); (*operate, power*): **it's driven by electricity** funziona a elettricità; **it's two hours' ~ from here** è a due ore di macchina da qui; **to go for a ~** andare a fare un giro in macchina; **to ~ sb to do sthg** spingere qn a fare qc; **to ~ sb mad** far diventare matto qn; **can you ~ me to the station?** mi accompagni alla stazione?

drivel ['drɪvl] *n* scemenze *fpl*.

driven *pp* → drive.

driver ['draɪvə^r] *n* (*of car, bus*) conducente *mf*; (*of train*) macchinista *mf*; (*of taxi*) tassista *mf*.

driver's license (*Am*) = driving licence.

driveshaft ['draɪvʃɑːft] *n* albero *m* motore.

driveway ['draɪvweɪ] *n* vialetto *m* d'accesso.

driving lesson ['draɪvɪŋ-] *n* lezione *f* di guida.

driving licence ['draɪvɪŋ-] *n* (*Br*) patente *f* di guida.

driving test ['draɪvɪŋ-] *n* esame *m* di guida.

drizzle ['drɪzl] *n* pioggerellina *f*.

drop [drɒp] *n* (*drip*) goccia *f*; (*small amount*) goccio *m*; (*distance down*) salto *m*; (*decrease*) calo *m*; (*in wages*) riduzione *f* ◆ *vt* lasciar cadere; (*reduce*) ridurre; (*from vehicle*) far scendere; (*omit*) saltare ◆ *vi* (*fall*) cadere; (*decrease*) diminuire;

to ~ a hint that far capire che; **to ~ sb a line** scrivere due righe a qn □ **drop in** *vi* (*inf*) fare un salto; **drop off** *vt sep* (*from vehicle*) far scendere ◆ *vi* (*fall asleep*) addormentarsi; (*fall off*) staccarsi; **drop out** *vi* (*of college, race*) ritirarsi.

drought [draut] *n* siccità *f inv*.

drove [drəuv] *pt* → drive.

drown [draun] *vi* annegare.

drug [drʌg] *n* (*MED*) farmaco *m*; (*stimulant*) droga *f* ◆ *vt* drogare.

drug addict *n* tossicodipendente *mf*.

druggist ['drʌgɪst] *n* (*Am*) farmacista *mf*.

drum [drʌm] *n* (*MUS*) tamburo *m*; (*container*) fusto *m* □ **drums** *npl* batteria *f*.

drummer ['drʌmə^r] *n* batterista *mf*.

drumstick ['drʌmstɪk] *n* (*of chicken*) coscia *f* (di pollo).

drunk [drʌŋk] *pp* → drink ◆ *adj* ubriaco(-a) ◆ *n* ubriaco *m* (-a *f*); **to get ~** ubriacarsi.

dry [draɪ] *adj* secco(-a); (*weather, day*) asciutto(-a) ◆ *vt* asciugare ◆ *vi* asciugarsi; **to ~ o.s.** asciugarsi; **to ~ one's hair** asciugarsi i capelli □ **dry up** *vi* (*become dry*) seccarsi; (*dry the dishes*) asciugare i piatti.

dry-clean *vt* pulire a secco.

dry cleaner's *n* lavanderia *f* (a secco).

dryer ['draɪə^r] *n* (*for clothes*) asciugabiancheria *m inv*; (*for hair*) asciugacapelli *m inv*.

dry-roasted peanuts [-'rəustɪd-] *npl* arachidi *fpl* tostate.

DSS *n* (*Br*) ministero britannico per la previdenza sociale.

DTP n (abbr of desktop publishing) desktop publishing m.

dual carriageway ['dju:əl-] n (Br) strada f a doppia carreggiata.

dubbed [dʌbd] adj (film) doppiato(-a).

dubious ['dju:bjəs] adj (suspect) dubbio(-a).

duchess ['dʌtʃɪs] n duchessa f.

duck [dʌk] n anatra f ◆ vi abbassarsi.

due [dju:] adj (expected) atteso(-a); (owed) dovuto(-a); **to be ~** (bill, rent) scadere; **in ~ course** a tempo debito; **~ to** a causa di.

duet [dju:'et] n duetto m.

duffel bag ['dʌfl-] n sacca f da viaggio.

duffel coat ['dʌfl-] n montgomery m inv.

dug [dʌg] pt & pp → dig.

duke [dju:k] n duca m.

dull [dʌl] adj (boring) noioso(-a); (not bright) spento(-a); (weather) coperto(-a); (pain) sordo(-a).

dumb [dʌm] adj (inf: stupid) stupido(-a); (unable to speak) muto(-a).

dummy ['dʌmɪ] n (Br: for baby) ciuccio m; (for clothes) manichino m.

dump [dʌmp] n (for rubbish) discarica f; (inf: place) porcile m ◆ vt (drop carelessly) gettare; (get rid of) scaricare.

dumpling ['dʌmplɪŋ] n gnocco di pasta cotto al vapore e servito insieme agli stufati.

dune [dju:n] n duna f.

dungarees [,dʌŋgə'ri:z] npl (for work) tuta f; (Br: fashion item) salopette f inv.

dungeon ['dʌndʒən] n segreta f.

duplicate ['dju:plɪkət] n duplicato m.

during ['djʊərɪŋ] prep durante.

dusk [dʌsk] n crepuscolo m.

dust [dʌst] n polvere f ◆ vt spolverare.

dustbin ['dʌstbɪn] n (Br) pattumiera f.

dustcart ['dʌstkɑ:t] n (Br) camion m inv delle immondizie.

duster ['dʌstər] n straccio m (per spolverare).

dustman ['dʌstmən] (pl -men [-mən]) n (Br) netturbino m.

dustpan ['dʌstpæn] n paletta f (per la spazzatura).

dusty ['dʌstɪ] adj polveroso(-a).

Dutch [dʌtʃ] adj olandese ◆ n (language) olandese m ◆ npl: **the ~** gli olandesi.

Dutchman ['dʌtʃmən] (pl -men [-mən]) n olandese m.

Dutchwoman ['dʌtʃ,wumən] (pl -women [-,wɪmɪn]) n olandese f.

duty ['dju:tɪ] n (moral obligation) dovere m; (tax) dazio m, tassa f; **to be on ~** essere in OR di servizio; **to be off ~** essere fuori servizio, essere libero ❑ **duties** npl (job) mansioni fpl.

duty chemist's n farmacia f di turno.

duty-free adj esente da dazio ◆ n duty free m inv.

duty-free shop n duty free shop m inv.

duvet ['du:veɪ] n piumone® m.

dwarf [dwɔ:f] (pl **dwarves** [dwɔ:vz]) n nano m (-a f).

dwelling ['dwelɪŋ] n (fml) abitazione f.

dye [daɪ] n tinta f ◆ vt tingere.

dynamite ['daɪnəmaɪt] n dinamite f.

dynamo ['daɪnəməʊ] (pl -s) n (on bike) dinamo f inv.

dyslexic [dɪs'leksɪk] adj dislessico(-a).

E (abbr of east) E.

E111 n E111 m.

each [iːtʃ] adj ogni (inv), ciascuno(-a) ♦ pron ciascuno m (-a f), ognuno m (-a f); ~ one ognuno; ~ of them ognuno di loro; one ~ uno ciascuno; one of ~ uno di ognuno; they know ~ other si conoscono.

eager ['iːgəʳ] adj (pupil, expression) entusiasta; to be ~ to do sthg essere impaziente di fare qc.

eagle ['iːgl] n (bird) aquila f.

ear [ɪəʳ] n orecchio m; (of corn) spiga f.

earache ['ɪəreɪk] n: to have ~ avere mal m d'orecchi.

earl [ɜːl] n conte m.

early ['ɜːlɪ] adj (childhood) primo(-a); (train) di buon'ora; (before usual or arranged time) anticipato(-a), precoce ♦ adv presto; in the ~ morning di primo mattino; in the ~ 20th century all'inizio del XX secolo; at the earliest al più presto; ~ on presto; to have an ~ night andare a letto presto.

earn [ɜːn] vt (money) guadagnare; (praise, success) guadagnarsi; to ~ a living guadagnarsi da vivere.

earnings ['ɜːnɪŋz] npl guadagni mpl.

earphones ['ɪəfəʊnz] npl cuffie fpl.

earplugs ['ɪəplʌgz] npl tappi mpl per le orecchie.

earrings ['ɪərɪŋz] npl orecchini mpl.

earth [ɜːθ] n terra f ♦ vt (Br: appliance) mettere a terra; how on ~ ...? come diavolo ...?

earthenware ['ɜːθnweəʳ] adj di terracotta.

earthquake ['ɜːθkweɪk] n terremoto m.

ease [iːz] n (lack of difficulty) facilità f ♦ vt (pain, problem) alleviare; at ~ a proprio agio; with ~ con facilità ❑ **ease off** vi (pain, rain) attenuarsi.

easily ['iːzɪlɪ] adv facilmente; (by far) senza dubbio.

east [iːst] n est m ♦ adj dell'est ♦ adv a est; in the ~ of England nell'Inghilterra orientale; the East (Asia) l'Oriente m.

eastbound ['iːstbaʊnd] adj diretto(-a) a est.

Easter ['iːstəʳ] n Pasqua f.

eastern ['iːstən] adj orientale, dell'est ❑ **Eastern** adj (Asian) orientale.

Eastern Europe n l'Europa f dell'Est.

eastwards ['iːstwədz] adv verso est.

easy ['iːzɪ] adj facile; (without problems) tranquillo(-a); to take it ~ prendersela con calma.

easygoing [ˌiːzɪ'gəʊɪŋ] adj rilassato(-a).

eat [iːt] (pt ate, pp eaten ['iːtn]) vt

& *vi* mangiare ❏ **eat out** *vi* mangiare fuori.

eating apple ['iːtɪŋ-] *n* mela *f* (da mangiare cruda).

ebony ['ebənɪ] *n* ebano *m*.

EC *n (abbr of European Community)* CE *f*.

eccentric [ɪk'sentrɪk] *adj* eccentrico(-a).

echo ['ekəʊ] *(pl* -es) *n* eco *f* ♦ *vi* fare eco.

ecology [ɪ'kɒlədʒɪ] *n* ecologia *f*.

economic [ˌiːkə'nɒmɪk] *adj* economico(-a) ❏ **economics** *n* economia *f*.

economical [ˌiːkə'nɒmɪkl] *adj (car, system)* economico(-a); *(person)* parsimonioso(-a).

economize [ɪ'kɒnəmaɪz] *vi* economizzare, risparmiare.

economy [ɪ'kɒnəmɪ] *n* economia *f*.

economy class *n* classe *f* economica.

economy size *adj* in confezione economica.

ecstasy ['ekstəsɪ] *n* estasi *f inv*.

ECU ['ekjuː] *n* ECU *m inv*.

eczema ['eksɪmə] *n* eczema *m*.

edge [edʒ] *n* bordo *m*; *(of knife)* taglio *m*.

edible ['edɪbl] *adj* commestibile.

Edinburgh ['edɪnbrə] *n* Edimburgo *f*.

Edinburgh Festival *n*: the ~ il festival di Edimburgo.

---

i **EDINBURGH FESTIVAL**

La capitale scozzese ospita ogni anno, nel mese di agosto, un fe-stival internazionale di musica, teatro e danza di altissima qualità. Parallelamente alle rappresentazioni più classiche del programma ufficiale, la sezione "Fringe" del festival propone centinaia di produzioni indipendenti, messe in scena in piccoli locali sparsi un po' in tutta la città.

edition [ɪ'dɪʃn] *n* edizione *f*; *(of TV programme)* puntata *f*.

editor ['edɪtər] *n (of newspaper, magazine)* direttore *m* (-trice *f*); *(of book)* curatore *m* (-trice *f*); *(of film, TV programme)* tecnico *m* (-a *f*) del montaggio.

editorial [ˌedɪ'tɔːrɪəl] *n* editoriale *m*.

educate ['edʒʊkeɪt] *vt* istruire.

education [ˌedʒʊ'keɪʃn] *n* istruzione *f*.

EEC *n* C.E.E. *f*.

eel [iːl] *n* anguilla *f*.

effect [ɪ'fekt] *n* effetto *m*; **to put sthg into ~** mettere qc in atto; **to take ~** *(drug)* fare effetto; *(law)* entrare in vigore.

effective [ɪ'fektɪv] *adj (successful)* efficace; *(law, system)* effettivo(-a).

effectively [ɪ'fektɪvlɪ] *adv (successfully)* efficacemente; *(in fact)* effettivamente.

efficient [ɪ'fɪʃənt] *adj* efficiente.

effort ['efət] *n* sforzo *m*; **to make an ~ to do sthg** fare uno sforzo per fare qc; **it's not worth the ~** non ne vale la pena.

e.g. *adv* ad es.

egg [eg] *n* uovo *m*.

egg cup *n* portauovo *m inv*.

egg mayonnaise *n* uova *fpl* sode in maionese.

eggplant ['eɡplɑːnt] n (Am) melanzana f.

egg white n albume m.

egg yolk n tuorlo m.

Egypt ['iːdʒɪpt] n l'Egitto m.

eiderdown ['aɪdədaʊn] n piumone® m.

eight [eɪt] num otto, → **six**.

eighteen [,eɪ'tiːn] num diciotto, → **six**.

eighteenth [,eɪ'tiːnθ] num diciottesimo(-a), → **sixth**.

eighth [eɪtθ] num ottavo(-a), → **sixth**.

eightieth ['eɪtɪɪθ] num ottantesimo(-a), → **sixth**.

eighty ['eɪtɪ] num ottanta, → **six**.

Eire ['eərə] n la Repubblica d'Irlanda.

Eisteddfod [aɪ'stedfəd] n festival culturale gallese.

---

i EISTEDDFOD

Questo festival si tiene ogni anno in Galles, nel mese di agosto, per celebrare la lingua e la cultura della regione. Nel corso della manifestazione, le cui origini risalgono al dodicesimo secolo, si svolgono gare di musica, poesia e teatro.

---

either adj: ~ **book will do** va bene sia l'uno che l'altro libro ◆ pron: **I'll take** ~ **(of them)** prendo o l'uno(-a) o l'altro(-a); **I don't like** ~ **(of them)** non mi piace né l'uno(-a) né l'altro(-a). ◆ adv: **I can't** ~ non posso neanch'io; ~ ... **or** o ... o; **on** ~ **side** su entrambi i lati.

eject [ɪ'dʒekt] vt (cassette) espellere.

elaborate [ɪ'læbrət] adj (needlework, design) elaborato(-a).

elastic [ɪ'læstɪk] n elastico m.

elastic band n (Br) elastico m.

elbow ['elbəʊ] n (of person) gomito m.

elder ['eldəʳ] adj più vecchio(-a), maggiore.

elderly ['eldəlɪ] adj anziano(-a) ◆ npl: **the** ~ gli anziani.

eldest ['eldɪst] adj: **the** ~ **son/daughter** il figlio/la figlia maggiore.

elect [ɪ'lekt] vt eleggere; **to** ~ **to do sthg** (fml: choose) scegliere di fare qc.

election [ɪ'lekʃn] n elezione f.

electric [ɪ'lektrɪk] adj elettrico(-a).

electrical goods [ɪ'lektrɪkl-] npl apparecchi mpl elettrici.

electric blanket n coperta f elettrica.

electric drill n trapano m elettrico.

electric fence n recinto m elettrificato.

electrician [,ɪlek'trɪʃn] n elettricista mf.

electricity [,ɪlek'trɪsətɪ] n elettricità f.

electric shock n scossa f elettrica.

electrocute [ɪ'lektrəkjuːt] vt fulminare.

electronic [,ɪlek'trɒnɪk] adj elettronico(-a).

elegant ['elɪɡənt] adj elegante.

element ['elɪmənt] n elemento m; (of fire, kettle) resistenza f; **the**

~s *(weather)* gli elementi.

elementary [‚elɪ'mentərɪ] *adj* elementare.

elephant ['elɪfənt] *n* elefante *m*.

elevator ['elɪveɪtə'] *n (Am)* ascensore *m*.

eleven [ɪ'levn] *num* undici, → **six**.

eleventh [ɪ'levnθ] *num* undicesimo(-a), → **sixth**.

eligible ['elɪdʒəbl] *adj* che ha i requisiti.

eliminate [ɪ'lɪmɪneɪt] *vt* eliminare.

Elizabethan [ɪ‚lɪzə'biːθn] *adj* elisabettiano(-a) *(seconda metà del XVI sec.)*.

elm [elm] *n* olmo *m*.

else [els] *adv*: **I don't want anything ~** non voglio nient'altro; **anything ~?** altro?; **everyone ~** tutti gli altri; **nobody ~** nessun altro; **nothing ~** nient'altro; **somebody ~** qualcun altro; **something ~** qualcos'altro; **somewhere ~** da qualche altra parte; **what ~?** che altro?; **who ~?** chi altri?; **or ~** altrimenti.

elsewhere [els'weə'] *adv* altrove.

embankment [ɪm'bæŋkmənt] *n (next to river)* argine *m*; *(next to road, railway)* terrapieno *m*.

embark [ɪm'bɑːk] *vi (board ship)* imbarcarsi.

embarkation card [‚embɑː-keɪʃn-] *n* carta *f* d'imbarco.

embarrass [ɪm'bærəs] *vt* imbarazzare.

embarrassed [ɪm'bærəst] *adj* imbarazzato(-a).

embarrassing [ɪm'bærəsɪŋ] *adj* imbarazzante.

embarrassment [ɪm'bærəs-mənt] *n* imbarazzo *m*.

embassy ['embəsɪ] *n* ambasciata *f*.

emblem ['embləm] *n* emblema *m*.

embrace [ɪm'breɪs] *vt* abbracciare.

embroidered [ɪm'brɔɪdəd] *adj* ricamato(-a).

embroidery [ɪm'brɔɪdərɪ] *n* ricamo *m*.

emerald ['emərəld] *n* smeraldo *m*.

emerge [ɪ'mɜːdʒ] *vi* emergere.

emergency [ɪ'mɜːdʒənsɪ] *n* emergenza *f* ♦ *adj* di emergenza; **in an ~** in caso di emergenza.

emergency exit *n* uscita *f* di sicurezza.

emergency landing *n* atterraggio *m* di emergenza.

emergency services *npl* servizi *mpl* di pronto intervento.

emigrate ['emɪgreɪt] *vi* emigrare.

emit [ɪ'mɪt] *vt* emettere.

emotion [ɪ'məʊʃn] *n* emozione *f*.

emotional [ɪ'məʊʃənl] *adj* emotivo(-a).

emphasis ['emfəsɪs] *(pl* **-ases** [-əsiːz]*)* *n* enfasi *f*; **to put the ~ on sthg** dare importanza a qc.

emphasize ['emfəsaɪz] *vt* sottolineare.

empire ['empaɪə'] *n* impero *m*.

employ [ɪm'plɔɪ] *vt* impiegare.

employed [ɪm'plɔɪd] *adj* impiegato(-a).

employee [ɪm'plɔɪiː] *n* dipendente *mf*.

employer [ɪm'plɔɪə'] *n* datore *m* (-trice *f*) di lavoro.

employment [ɪm'plɔɪmənt] n impiego m.

employment agency n agenzia f di collocamento.

empty ['emptɪ] adj vuoto(-a); (threat, promise) vano(-a) ◆ vt vuotare.

EMU n (abbr of Economic Monetary Union) unione f economica e monetaria.

emulsion (paint) [ɪ'mʌlʃn-] n pittura f a emulsione.

enable [ɪ'neɪbl] vt: to ~ sb to do sthg permettere a qn di fare qc.

enamel [ɪ'næml] n smalto m.

enclose [ɪn'kləʊz] vt (surround) cingere, circondare; (with letter) allegare.

enclosed [ɪn'kləʊzd] adj (space) contenuto(-a), limitato(-a).

encounter [ɪn'kaʊntər] vt incontrare.

encourage [ɪn'kʌrɪdʒ] vt incoraggiare; to ~ sb to do sthg incoraggiare qn a fare qc.

encouragement [ɪn'kʌrɪdʒmənt] n incoraggiamento m.

encyclopedia [ɪn,saɪklə'piːdjə] n enciclopedia f.

end [end] n fine f; (purpose) fine m ◆ vt (story, evening, holiday) finire; (war, practice) finire, mettere fine a ◆ vi finire; to come to an ~ finire, giungere alla fine; to put an ~ to sthg mettere fine a qc; for days on ~ per giorni e giorni; in the ~ alla fine; to make ~s meet sbarcare il lunario ❑ end up vi finire; to ~ up doing sthg finire con il fare qc.

endangered species [ɪn'deɪndʒəd-] n specie f inv in via d'estinzione.

ending ['endɪŋ] n (of story, film, book) fine f; (GRAMM) desinenza f.

endive ['endaɪv] n (curly) indivia f (riccia); (chicory) cicoria f.

endless ['endlɪs] adj interminabile, senza fine.

endorsement [ɪn'dɔːsmənt] n (of driving licence) infrazione registrata sulla patente.

endurance [ɪn'djʊərəns] n resistenza f, sopportazione f.

endure [ɪn'djʊər] vt sopportare.

enemy ['enɪmɪ] n nemico m (-a f).

energy ['enədʒɪ] n energia f.

enforce [ɪn'fɔːs] vt (law) applicare, far rispettare.

engaged [ɪn'geɪdʒd] adj (to be married) fidanzato(-a); (Br: phone) occupato(-a); (toilet) occupato(-a); to get ~ fidanzarsi.

engaged tone n (Br) segnale m di occupato.

engagement [ɪn'geɪdʒmənt] n (to marry) fidanzamento m; (appointment) appuntamento m.

engagement ring n anello m di fidanzamento.

engine ['endʒɪn] n (of vehicle) motore m; (of train) locomotiva f.

engineer [,endʒɪ'nɪər] n (of roads, machinery) ingegnere m; (to do repairs) tecnico m (-a f).

engineering [,endʒɪ'nɪərɪŋ] n ingegneria f.

engineering works npl (on railway line) lavori mpl in corso.

England ['ɪŋglənd] n l'Inghilterra f.

English ['ɪŋglɪʃ] adj inglese ◆ n (language) inglese m ◆ npl: the ~ gli inglesi.

English breakfast n colazione f all'inglese.

English Channel n: the ~ la Manica.

Englishman ['ɪŋglɪʃmən] (pl -men [-mən]) n inglese m.

Englishwoman ['ɪŋglɪʃˌwʊmən] (pl -women [-ˌwɪmɪn]) n inglese f.

engrave [ɪn'greɪv] vt incidere.

engraving [ɪn'greɪvɪŋ] n incisione f.

enjoy [ɪn'dʒɔɪ] vt godersi; **to ~ doing sthg** divertirsi a fare qc; **I ~ swimming** mi piace nuotare; **to ~ o.s.** divertirsi; **~ your meal!** buon appetito!

enjoyable [ɪn'dʒɔɪəbl] adj piacevole.

enjoyment [ɪn'dʒɔɪmənt] n piacere m.

enlargement [ɪn'lɑːdʒmənt] n (of photo) ingrandimento m.

enormous [ɪ'nɔːməs] adj enorme.

enough [ɪ'nʌf] adj abbastanza (inv), sufficiente ◆ pron & adv abbastanza; **~ time** abbastanza tempo; **is that ~?** è abbastanza?, basta?; **it's not big ~** non è abbastanza grande; **to have had ~ (of)** averne abbastanza (di).

enquire [ɪn'kwaɪər] vi informarsi.

enquiry [ɪn'kwaɪərɪ] n (question) domanda f; (investigation) indagine f, inchiesta f; **'Enquiries'** 'Informazioni'.

enquiry desk n banco m informazioni.

enrol [ɪn'rəʊl] vi (Br) iscriversi.

enroll [ɪn'rəʊl] (Am) = **enrol**.

en suite bathroom [ɒn'swiːt] n bagno m privato.

ensure [ɪn'ʃʊər] vt garantire, assicurare.

entail [ɪn'teɪl] vt comportare.

enter ['entər] vt entrare in; (college, competition) iscriversi a; (on form) scrivere ◆ vi entrare; (in competition) iscriversi.

enterprise ['entəpraɪz] n (company) impresa f; (plan) iniziativa f.

entertain [ˌentə'teɪn] vt (amuse) divertire.

entertainer [ˌentə'teɪnər] n intrattenitore m (-trice f).

entertaining [ˌentə'teɪnɪŋ] adj divertente.

entertainment [ˌentə'teɪnmənt] n (amusement) divertimento m; (show) spettacolo m.

enthusiasm [ɪn'θjuːzɪæzm] n entusiasmo m.

enthusiast [ɪn'θjuːzɪæst] n appassionato m (-a f).

enthusiastic [ɪnˌθjuːzɪ'æstɪk] adj entusiasta.

entire [ɪn'taɪər] adj intero(-a).

entirely [ɪn'taɪəlɪ] adv completamente.

entitle [ɪn'taɪtl] vt: **to ~ sb to sthg** dare a qn diritto a qc; **to ~ sb to do sthg** dare diritto a qn di fare qc.

entrance ['entrəns] n entrata f, ingresso m.

entrance fee n biglietto m d'ingresso.

entry ['entrɪ] n (door, gate, admission) entrata f, ingresso m; (in dictionary) voce f; (piece in competition) cosa f presentata; **'no ~'** (sign on door) 'ingresso vietato'; (road sign) 'divieto d'accesso'.

envelope ['envələʊp] n busta f.

envious ['envɪəs] *adj* invidio-so(-a).

environment [ɪn'vaɪərənmənt] *n* ambiente *m*; **the ~** l'ambiente (naturale).

environmental [ɪn,vaɪərən'mentl] *adj* ambientale.

environmentally friendly [ɪn,vaɪərən'mentlɪ-] *adj* che rispetta l'ambiente, ecologico(-a).

envy ['envɪ] *vt* invidiare.

epic ['epɪk] *n* epopea *f*.

epidemic [,epɪ'demɪk] *n* epide-mia *f*.

epileptic [,epɪ'leptɪk] *adj* epiletti-co(-a).

episode ['epɪsəud] *n* episodio *m*.

equal ['i:kwəl] *adj* (*of same amount*) uguale; (*with equal rights*) uguale, pari (*inv*) ♦ *vt* (*number*) fare; **to be ~ to** (*number*) essere uguale a.

equality [ɪ'kwɒlətɪ] *n* uguaglian-za *f*.

equalize ['i:kwəlaɪz] *vi* pareggia-re.

equally ['i:kwəlɪ] *adv* (*bad, good, matched*) ugualmente; (*pay, treat, share*) equamente; (*at the same time*) allo stesso modo.

equation [ɪ'kweɪʒn] *n* equazio-ne *f*.

equator [ɪ'kweɪtər] *n*: **the ~** l'equatore *m*.

equip [ɪ'kwɪp] *vt*: **to ~ sb/sthg with** fornire qn/qc di.

equipment [ɪ'kwɪpmənt] *n* attrezzatura *f*.

equipped [ɪ'kwɪpt] *adj*: **to be ~ with** essere fornito(-a) di.

equivalent [ɪ'kwɪvələnt] *adj* equivalente ♦ *n* equivalente *m*.

erase [ɪ'reɪz] *vt* (*letter, word*) can-cellare.

eraser [ɪ'reɪzər] *n* gomma *f*.'

erect [ɪ'rekt] *adj* (*person, posture*) eretto(-a) ♦ *vt* (*tent*) montare; (*monument*) erigere.

ERM *n* meccanismo *m* di cambio (dello SME).

erotic [ɪ'rɒtɪk] *adj* erotico(-a).

errand ['erənd] *n* commissione *f*.

erratic [ɪ'rætɪk] *adj* irregolare, incostante.

error ['erər] *n* errore *m*.

escalator ['eskəleɪtər] *n* scala *f* mobile.

escalope ['eskələp] *n* cotoletta *f* alla milanese.

escape [ɪ'skeɪp] *n* fuga *f* ♦ *vi*: **to ~ (from)** (*from prison*) evadere (da); (*from danger*) fuggire (da); (*leak*) fuoriuscire (da).

escort [*n* 'eskɔ:t, *vb* ɪ'skɔ:t] *n* (*guard*) scorta *f* ♦ *vt* accompagna-re.

espadrilles ['espə,drɪlz] *npl* espadrilles *fpl*.

especially [ɪ'speʃəlɪ] *adv* (*in par-ticular*) specialmente, soprattutto; (*on purpose*) apposta; (*very*) particol-armente.

esplanade [,esplə'neɪd] *n* pas-seggiata *f* (a mare).

essay ['eseɪ] *n* (*at school, university*) composizione *f*, tema *m*.

essential [ɪ'senʃl] *adj* (*indispen-sable*) essenziale ❑ **essentials** *npl*: **the ~s** l'essenziale *m*; **the bare ~s** il minimo indispensabile.

essentially [ɪ'senʃəlɪ] *adv* essen-zialmente.

establish [ɪ'stæblɪʃ] *vt* (*set up, create*) fondare; (*fact, truth*) stabi-

evidence

lire.

establishment [ɪˈstæblɪʃmənt] *n (business)* azienda *f*.

estate [ɪˈsteɪt] *n (land in country)* proprietà *f inv*; *(for housing)* complesso *m* residenziale; *(Br: car)* = **estate car**.

estate agent *n (Br)* agente *mf* immobiliare.

estate car *n (Br)* station wagon *f inv*.

estimate [*n* ˈestɪmət, *vb* ˈestɪmeɪt] *n (guess)* stima *f*; *(from builder, plumber)* preventivo *m* ◆ *vt* stimare, valutare.

estuary [ˈestjʊərɪ] *n* estuario *m*.

ethnic minority [ˈeθnɪk-] *n* minoranza *f* etnica.

EU *n (abbr of European Union)* U.E.

Eurocheque [ˈjʊərəʊtʃek] *n* eurochèque *m inv*.

Europe [ˈjʊərəp] *n* l'Europa *f*.

European [ˌjʊərəˈpɪən] *adj* europeo(-a) ◆ *n* europeo *m* (-a *f*).

European Community *n* Comunità *f* Europea.

evacuate [ɪˈvækjʊeɪt] *vt* evacuare.

evade [ɪˈveɪd] *vt (person, issue)* evitare; *(responsibility)* sottrarsi a.

evaporated milk [ɪˈvæpəreɪtɪd-] *n* latte *m* concentrato.

eve [iːv] *n*: **on the ~ of** alla vigilia di.

even [ˈiːvn] *adj (uniform, equal)* regolare, uniforme; *(level, flat)* liscio(-a), piano(-a); *(contest)* pari, alla pari; *(number)* pari *(inv)* ◆ *adv* perfino, anche; **to break ~** fare pari; **not ~** nemmeno; **~ so** ciò nonostante; **~ though** anche se.

evening [ˈiːvnɪŋ] *n* sera *f*; *(event, period)* serata *f*; **good ~!** buona sera!; **in the ~** di OR la sera.

evening classes *npl* corsi *mpl* serali.

evening dress *n (formal clothes)* abito *m* da sera; *(woman's garment)* vestito *m* da sera.

evening meal *n* cena *f*.

event [ɪˈvent] *n (occurrence)* evento *m*, avvenimento *m*; *(SPORT)* prova *f*; **in the ~ of** *(fml)* in caso di.

eventual [ɪˈventʃʊəl] *adj* finale.

eventually [ɪˈventʃʊəlɪ] *adv* alla fine.

ever [ˈevər] *adv* mai; **it's the worst ~** è il peggiore che sia mai esistito; **he was ~ so angry** era veramente arrabbiato; **for ~** *(eternally)* per sempre; **we've been waiting for ~** aspettiamo da tantissimo; **hardly ~** quasi mai ❏ **ever since** *adv* fin da allora ◆ *prep* da ... in poi ◆ *conj* fin da quando.

every [ˈevrɪ] *adj* ogni *(inv)*; **~ day** ogni giorno, tutti i giorni; **~ other day** ogni due giorni; **one in ~ ten** uno su dieci; **we make ~ effort ...** facciamo ogni sforzo ...; **~ so often** ogni tanto.

everybody [ˈevrɪˌbɒdɪ] = **everyone**.

everyday [ˈevrɪdeɪ] *adj* di ogni giorno, quotidiano(-a).

everyone [ˈevrɪwʌn] *pron* ognuno *m* (-a *f*), tutti *mpl* (-e *fpl*).

everyplace [ˈevrɪˌpleɪs] *(Am)* = **everywhere**.

everything [ˈevrɪθɪŋ] *pron* tutto, ogni cosa.

everywhere [ˈevrɪweər] *adv* dappertutto; *(wherever)* dovunque.

evidence [ˈevɪdəns] *n (proof)*

prova f; (legal statement) testimonianza f.

evident ['evidənt] adj evidente.

evidently ['evidəntli] adv evidentemente.

evil ['i:vl] adj cattivo(-a), malvagio(-a) ◆ n male m.

ex [eks] n (inf: wife, husband, partner) ex mf.

exact [ig'zækt] adj esatto(-a); '~ fare ready please' 'si prega di munirsi dell'esatta somma per il biglietto'.

exactly [ig'zæktli] adv & excl esattamente.

exaggerate [ig'zædʒəreit] vt & vi esagerare.

exaggeration [ig,zædʒə'reiʃn] n esagerazione f.

exam [ig'zæm] n esame m; to take an ~ fare un esame.

examination [ig,zæmi'neiʃn] n esame m; (MED) visita f.

examine [ig'zæmin] vt esaminare; (MED) visitare.

example [ig'za:mpl] n esempio m; for ~ per esempio.

exceed [ik'si:d] vt (be greater than) superare; (go beyond) oltrepassare.

excellent ['eksələnt] adj eccellente.

except [ik'sept] prep & conj eccetto, tranne; ~ for a parte, all'infuori di; '~ for access' 'escluso residenti'; '~ for loading' 'escluso (per le operazioni di) carico'.

exception [ik'sepʃn] n (thing excepted) eccezione f.

exceptional [ik'sepʃnəl] adj eccezionale.

excerpt ['eksɜ:pt] n estratto m.

excess [ik'ses, before nouns 'ekses]

adj in eccesso ◆ n eccesso m.

excess baggage n bagaglio m in eccedenza.

excess fare n (Br) supplemento m.

excessive [ik'sesiv] adj eccessivo(-a).

exchange [iks'tʃeindʒ] n (of telephones) centralino m; (of students) scambio m ◆ vt scambiare; to ~ sthg for sthg scambiare qc con qc; we're here on an ~ siamo qui con uno scambio.

exchange rate n tasso m di cambio.

excited [ik'saitid] adj eccitato(-a).

excitement [ik'saitmənt] n eccitazione f; (exciting thing) cosa f eccitante.

exciting [ik'saitiŋ] adj eccitante, emozionante.

exclamation mark [,eksklə'meiʃn-] n (Br) punto m esclamativo.

exclamation point [,eksklə'meiʃn-] (Am) = **exclamation mark**.

exclude [ik'sklu:d] vt escludere.

excluding [ik'sklu:diŋ] prep escluso(-a).

exclusive [ik'sklu:siv] adj esclusivo(-a) ◆ n esclusiva f; ~ of escluso(-a).

excursion [ik'skɜ:ʃn] n escursione f.

excuse [n ik'skju:s, vb ik'skju:z] n scusa f ◆ vt (forgive) scusare; (let off) dispensare; ~ me! mi scusi!

ex-directory adj (Br) fuori elenco.

execute ['eksikju:t] vt (kill) giu

stiziare.

executive [ɪgˈzekjʊtɪv] *adj (room)* per dirigenti ♦ *n (person)* dirigente *mf.*

exempt [ɪgˈzempt] *adj:* ~ **(from)** esente (da).

exemption [ɪgˈzempʃn] *n* esenzione *f.*

exercise [ˈeksəsaɪz] *n* esercizio *m* ♦ *vi* fare esercizio OR del moto; **to do** ~**s** fare degli esercizi.

exercise book *n* quaderno *m.*

exert [ɪgˈzɜːt] *vt* esercitare.

exhaust [ɪgˈzɔːst] *vt* esaurire ♦ *n:* ~ **(pipe)** tubo *m* di scappamento.

exhausted [ɪgˈzɔːstɪd] *adj* esausto(-a).

exhibit [ɪgˈzɪbɪt] *n (in museum, gallery)* oggetto *m* esposto ♦ *vt (in exhibition)* esporre.

exhibition [ˌeksɪˈbɪʃn] *n (of art)* esposizione *f*, mostra *f.*

exist [ɪgˈzɪst] *vi* esistere.

existence [ɪgˈzɪstəns] *n* esistenza *f;* **to be in** ~ esistere.

existing [ɪgˈzɪstɪŋ] *adj* esistente.

exit [ˈeksɪt] *n* uscita *f* ♦ *vi* uscire.

exotic [ɪgˈzɒtɪk] *adj* esotico(-a).

expand [ɪkˈspænd] *vi (in size)* espandersi; *(in number)* aumentare.

expect [ɪkˈspekt] *vt (believe likely)* aspettarsi, prevedere; *(await)* aspettare; **to** ~ **to do sthg** prevedere di fare qc; **to** ~ **sb to do sthg** *(require)* aspettarsi che qn faccia qc; **to be** ~**ing** *(be pregnant)* aspettare un bambino.

expedition [ˌekspɪˈdɪʃn] *n* spedizione *f; (short outing)* gita *f.*

expel [ɪkˈspel] *vt (from school)* espellere.

expense [ɪkˈspens] *n* spesa *f,* costo *m;* **at the** ~ **of** *(fig)* a spese di ❏ **expenses** *npl (of business trip)* spese *fpl.*

expensive [ɪkˈspensɪv] *adj* costoso(-a), caro(-a).

experience [ɪkˈspɪərɪəns] *n* esperienza *f* ♦ *vt* provare.

experienced [ɪkˈspɪərɪənst] *adj* esperto(-a).

experiment [ɪkˈsperɪmənt] *n* esperimento *m* ♦ *vi* fare esperimenti.

expert [ˈekspɜːt] *adj (advice)* esperto(-a); *(treatment)* apposito(-a) ♦ *n* esperto *m* (-a *f*).

expire [ɪkˈspaɪəʳ] *vi* scadere.

expiry date [ɪkˈspaɪərɪ-] *n* data *f* di scadenza.

explain [ɪkˈspleɪn] *vt* spiegare.

explanation [ˌekspləˈneɪʃn] *n* spiegazione *f.*

explode [ɪkˈspləʊd] *vi (bomb)* esplodere.

exploit [ɪkˈsplɔɪt] *vt (person)* sfruttare.

explore [ɪkˈsplɔːʳ] *vt (place)* esplorare.

explosion [ɪkˈspləʊʒn] *n (of bomb etc)* esplosione *f.*

explosive [ɪkˈspləʊsɪv] *n* esplosivo *m.*

export [*n* ˈekspɔːt, *vb* ɪkˈspɔːt] *n (of goods)* esportazione *f; (goods themselves)* merce *f* d'esportazione ♦ *vt* esportare.

exposed [ɪkˈspəʊzd] *adj (place)* non riparato(-a).

exposure [ɪkˈspəʊʒəʳ] *n (photograph)* foto *f inv;* (MED) assideramento *m; (to heat, radiation)* esposizione *f.*

express [ɪkˈspres] *adj (letter, deliv-*

ery, train) espresso(-a) ◆ n (train) espresso m ◆ vt esprimere ◆ adv per espresso.

expression [ɪk'spreʃn] n espressione f.

expresso [ɪk'spresəʊ] (pl -s) n espresso m.

expressway [ɪk'spresweɪ] n (Am) autostrada f (urbana).

extend [ɪk'stend] vt prolungare; (hand) offrire ◆ vi estendersi.

extension [ɪk'stenʃn] n (of building) sala f annessa; (for phone at work) interno m; (for phone in private house) apparecchio m supplementare; (for permit, essay) proroga f.

extension lead n prolunga f.

extensive [ɪk'stensɪv] adj (area) esteso(-a), ampio(-a); (damage) grave; (selection) ampio.

extent [ɪk'stent] n (of damage, knowledge) estensione f; **to a certain** ~ fino ad un certo punto; **to what** ~ …? fino a che punto …?

exterior [ɪk'stɪərɪər] adj esterno(-a) ◆ n (of car, building) esterno m.

external [ɪk'stɜːnl] adj esterno(-a).

extinct [ɪk'stɪŋkt] adj estinto(-a).

extinction [ɪk'stɪŋkʃn] n estinzione f.

extinguish [ɪk'stɪŋgwɪʃ] vt (fire, cigarette) spegnere.

extinguisher [ɪk'stɪŋgwɪʃər] n estintore m.

extortionate [ɪk'stɔːʃnət] adj esorbitante.

extra ['ekstrə] adj (additional) extra (inv), supplementare; (spare) altro(-a), in più ◆ n extra m inv ◆ adv (especially) eccezionalmente;

(more) di più; ~ **charge** supplemento m; ~ **large** extra-large (inv) □ **extras** npl (in price) spese fpl supplementari.

extract [n 'ekstrækt, vb ɪk'strækt] n (of yeast, malt etc) estratto m; (from book, opera) brano m ◆ vt (tooth) estrarre.

extractor fan [ɪk'stræktə-] n (Br) aspiratore m.

extraordinary [ɪk'strɔːdnrɪ] adj straordinario(-a).

extravagant [ɪk'strævəgənt] adj dispendioso(-a).

extreme [ɪk'striːm] adj estremo(-a) ◆ n estremo m.

extremely [ɪk'striːmlɪ] adv estremamente.

extrovert ['ekstrəvɜːt] n estroverso m (-a f).

eye [aɪ] n occhio m; (of needle) cruna f ◆ vt osservare attentamente; **to keep an** ~ **on** tenere d'occhio.

eyebrow ['aɪbraʊ] n sopracciglio m.

eye drops npl collirio m, gocce fpl per gli occhi.

eyeglasses ['aɪglɑːsɪz] npl (Am) occhiali mpl.

eyelash ['aɪlæʃ] n ciglio m.

eyelid ['aɪlɪd] n palpebra f.

eyeliner ['aɪˌlaɪnər] n eye-liner m inv.

eye shadow n ombretto m.

eyesight ['aɪsaɪt] n vista f.

eye test n esame m oculistico.

eyewitness [ˌaɪ'wɪtnɪs] n testimone mf oculare.

F

F (abbr of Fahrenheit) F.

fabric ['fæbrɪk] n (cloth) stoffa f, tessuto m.

fabulous ['fæbjʊləs] adj favoloso(-a).

facade [fə'sɑːd] n facciata f.

face [feɪs] n faccia f; (of cliff, mountain) parete f; (of clock, watch) quadrante m ◆ vt essere di fronte a; (accept, cope with) affrontare; **to be ~d with** avere di fronte □ **face up to** vt fus affrontare.

facecloth ['feɪsklɒθ] n (Br) panno m di spugna.

facial ['feɪʃl] n trattamento m del viso.

facilitate [fə'sɪlɪteɪt] vt (fml) facilitare.

facilities [fə'sɪlɪtɪːz] npl attrezzature fpl.

facsimile [fæk'sɪmɪlɪ] n facsimile m inv.

fact [fækt] n fatto m; **in ~** in effetti.

factor ['fæktər] n fattore m; **~ ten suntan lotion** crema f abbronzante a fattore di protezione dieci.

factory ['fæktərɪ] n fabbrica f.

faculty ['fæklti] n facoltà f inv.

FA Cup n = coppa f Italia (di calcio).

fade [feɪd] vi (light, sound) affievolirsi; (flower) appassire; (jeans, wallpaper) sbiadire, sbiadirsi.

faded ['feɪdɪd] adj (jeans) sbiadito(-a).

fag [fæg] n (Br: inf: cigarette) siga-

retta f.

Fahrenheit ['færənhaɪt] adj Fahrenheit (inv).

fail [feɪl] vt (exam) non superare ◆ vi fallire; (in exam) essere bocciato; (engine) guastarsi; **to ~ to do sthg** (not do) non fare qc.

failing ['feɪlɪŋ] n difetto m ◆ prep: **~ that** se no.

failure ['feɪljər] n fallimento m; (unsuccessful person) fallito m (-a f); (act of neglecting) mancanza f.

faint [feɪnt] vi svenire ◆ adj debole; (outline) indistinto(-a); **I haven't the ~est idea** non ho la più pallida idea.

fair [feər] adj (just) giusto(-a), equo(-a); (quite large, quite good) discreto(-a); (hair, person) biondo(-a); (skin) chiaro(-a); (weather) bello(-a) ◆ n (funfair) luna park m inv; (trade fair) fiera f; **~ enough!** mi sembra giusto!

fairground ['feəɡraʊnd] n luna park m inv.

fair-haired [-'heəd] adj biondo(-a).

fairly ['feəlɪ] adv (quite) abbastanza.

fairy ['feərɪ] n fata f.

fairy tale n fiaba f.

faith [feɪθ] n fede f.

faithfully ['feɪθfʊlɪ] adv: **Yours ~** Distinti saluti.

fake [feɪk] n (painting etc) falso m ◆ vt (signature, painting) falsificare.

fall [fɔːl] (pt fell, pp fallen ['fɔːln]) vi cadere; (number, pound, night) scendere ◆ n caduta f; (decrease) abbassamento m; (Am: autumn) autunno m; **to ~ asleep** addormentarsi; **to ~ ill** ammalarsi; **to ~ in love** innamorarsi □ **falls** npl (water-

fall) cascate *fpl*; **fall behind** *vi (with work, rent)* rimanere indietro; **fall down** *vi (lose balance)* cadere; **fall off** *vi* cadere; **fall out** *vi (hair, teeth)* cadere; *(argue)* litigare; **fall over** *vi* cadere per terra; **fall through** *vi* fallire.

false [fɔːls] *adj* falso(-a).

false alarm *n* falso allarme *m*.

false teeth *npl* dentiera *f*.

fame [feɪm] *n* fama *f*.

familiar [fəˈmɪljəʳ] *adj (known)* familiare; *(informal)* (troppo) confidenziale; **to be ~ with** *(know)* conoscere.

family [ˈfæmlɪ] *n* famiglia *f* ♦ *adj (size)* familiare, da famiglia; *(film, holiday)* per famiglie.

family planning clinic [-ˈplænɪŋ-] *n* = consultorio *m* familiare.

family room *n (at hotel)* camera *f* familiare; *(at pub, airport)* sala *f* per famiglie con bambini.

famine [ˈfæmɪn] *n* carestia *f*.

famished [ˈfæmɪʃt] *adj (inf)* molto affamato(-a).

famous [ˈfeɪməs] *adj* famoso(-a).

fan [fæn] *n (held in hand)* ventaglio *m*; *(electric)* ventilatore *m*; *(enthusiast)* ammiratore *m* (-trice *f*); *(supporter)* tifoso *m* (-a *f*).

fan belt *n* cinghia *f* del ventilatore.

fancy [ˈfænsɪ] *vt (inf: feel like)* avere voglia di ♦ *adj (elaborate)* ricercato(-a); **I ~ her** *(inf)* mi piace; **~ (that)!** pensa un po'!

fancy dress *n* costume *m* (per maschera).

fan heater *n* stufa *f* elettrica con ventilatore.

fanlight [ˈfænlaɪt] *n (Br)* lunetta *f*.

fantastic [fænˈtæstɪk] *adj* fantastico(-a).

fantasy [ˈfæntəsɪ] *n (imagined thing)* fantasia *f*.

far [fɑːʳ] *(compar* **further** OR **farther,** *superl* **furthest** OR **farthest)** *adv* lontano; *(in degree)* molto, assai ♦ *adj* **at the ~ end (of)** in fondo (a); **how ~ is it (to London)?** quanto è lontano (da Londra)?; **as ~ as** *(place)* fino a; **as ~ as I'm concerned** per quanto mi riguarda; **as ~ as I know** per quel che ne so; **~ better** assai migliore; **by ~** di gran lunga; **so ~** *(until now)* finora; **to go too ~** *(behave unacceptably)* oltrepassare i limiti.

farce [fɑːs] *n (ridiculous situation)* farsa *f*.

fare [feəʳ] *n (on bus, train etc)* tariffa *f*; *(fml: food)* cibo *m* ♦ *vi* passarsela.

Far East *n*: **the ~** l'Estremo Oriente *m*.

fare stage *n (Br)* fermata di autobus dove il prezzo del biglietto cambia.

farm [fɑːm] *n* fattoria *f*.

farmer [ˈfɑːməʳ] *n* agricoltore *m*.

farmhouse [ˈfɑːmhaʊs, *pl* -haʊzɪz] *n* casa *f* colonica.

farming [ˈfɑːmɪŋ] *n* agricoltura *f*; *(of animals)* allevamento *m*.

farmland [ˈfɑːmlænd] *n* terreno *m* coltivabile.

farmyard [ˈfɑːmjɑːd] *n* aia *f*.

farther [ˈfɑːðəʳ] → **far**.

farthest [ˈfɑːðəst] → **far**.

fascinating [ˈfæsɪneɪtɪŋ] *adj* affascinante.

fascination [ˌfæsɪˈneɪʃn] *n* fascino m.

fashion ['fæʃn] n moda f; (manner) modo m, maniera f; **to be in ~** essere di moda; **to be out of ~** essere fuori moda.

fashionable ['fæʃnəbl] adj di moda, alla moda.

fashion show n sfilata f di moda.

fast [fɑ:st] adv (quickly) velocemente, rapidamente; (securely) saldamente ♦ adj veloce, rapido(-a); **to be ~** (clock) andare avanti; **~ asleep** profondamente addormentato; **a ~ train** un treno diretto.

fasten ['fɑ:sn] vt (belt) allacciare; (coat) abbottonare; (two things) fissare.

fastener ['fɑ:snər] n chiusura f, fermaglio m.

fast food n: **~ outlet** fast food m inv.

fat [fæt] adj grasso (-a) ♦ n grasso m.

fatal ['feɪtl] adj (accident, disease) mortale.

father ['fɑ:ðər] n padre m.

Father Christmas n (Br) Babbo m Natale.

father-in-law n suocero m.

fattening ['fætnɪŋ] adj che fa ingrassare.

fatty ['fæti] adj grasso (-a).

faucet ['fɔ:sɪt] n (Am) rubinetto m.

fault ['fɔ:lt] n (responsibility) colpa f; (flaw) difetto m; (in machine) guasto m; **it's your ~** è colpa tua.

faulty ['fɔ:lti] adj difettoso (-a).

favor ['feɪvər] (Am) = **favour**.

favour ['feɪvər] n (Br: kind act) favore m ♦ vt (prefer) preferire; **to**

be in ~ of essere in favore di; **to do sb a ~** fare un favore a qn.

favourable ['feɪvrəbl] adj favorevole.

favourite ['feɪvrɪt] adj favorito(-a) ♦ n favorito m (-a f).

fawn [fɔ:n] adj fulvo chiaro (inv).

fax [fæks] n fax m inv ♦ vt (document) inviare per fax, faxare; (person) inviare un fax a.

fear [fɪər] n paura f ♦ vt (be afraid of) avere paura di, temere; **for ~ of** per paura di.

feast [fi:st] n (meal) banchetto m.

feather ['feðər] n penna f, piuma f.

feature ['fi:tʃər] n (characteristic) caratteristica f; (in newspaper, on radio, TV) servizio m (speciale) ♦ vt (subj: film) avere come protagonista; **~s** (of face) lineamenti mpl.

feature film n lungometraggio m.

Feb. (abbr of February) feb.

February ['februəri] n febbraio m, → **September**.

fed [fed] pp → **feed**.

fed up adj stufo(-a); **to be ~ with** essere stufo di.

fee [fi:] n pagamento m; (of doctor, lawyer) onorario m.

feeble ['fi:bəl] adj debole.

feed [fi:d] (pt & pp **fed**) vt (person, animal) dare da mangiare a; (baby) allattare; (insert) immettere.

feel [fi:l] (pt & pp **felt**) vt (touch) tastare, toccare; (experience) sentire; (think) credere, pensare ♦ vi sentirsi; (seem) essere ♦ n (of material): **I like the ~ of it** è piacevole al tatto; **to ~ cold/hungry** avere freddo/fame; **to ~ like** (fancy) avere voglia di; **to ~ up to doing sthg** sentirsela di fare qc.

feeling ['fi:lɪŋ] *n* (*emotion*) sentimento *m*; (*sensation*) sensazione *f*; (*belief*) opinione *f*; **to hurt sb's ~s** ferire i sentimenti di qn.

feet [fi:t] → **foot**.

fell [fel] *pt* → **fall** ◆ *vt* (*tree*) abbattere.

fellow ['felǝʊ] *n* (*man*) tipo *m*, individuo *m* ◆ *adj*: **my ~ students** i miei compagni di classe.

felt [felt] *pt & pp* → **feel** ◆ *n* feltro *m*.

felt-tip pen *n* pennarello *m*.

female ['fi:meɪl] *adj* femminile; (*child, animal*) femmina ◆ *n* (*animal*) femmina *f*.

feminine ['femɪnɪn] *adj* femminile.

feminist ['femɪnɪst] *n* femminista *mf*.

fence [fens] *n* recinto *m*.

fencing ['fensɪŋ] *n* (*SPORT*) scherma *f*.

fend [fend] *vi*: **to ~ for o.s.** provvedere a se stesso.

fender ['fendǝʳ] *n* (*for fireplace*) parafuoco *m*; (*Am: on car*) parafango *m*.

fennel ['fenl] *n* finocchio *m*.

fern [fɜ:n] *n* felce *f*.

ferocious [fǝ'rǝʊʃǝs] *adj* feroce.

ferry ['feri] *n* traghetto *m*.

fertile ['fɜ:taɪl] *adj* (*land*) fertile.

fertilizer ['fɜ:tɪlaɪzǝʳ] *n* fertilizzante *m*.

festival ['festɪvl] *n* (*of music, arts etc*) festival *m inv*; (*holiday*) festa *f*.

feta cheese ['fetǝ] *n* formaggio *bianco di latte di pecora di origine greca.*

fetch [fetʃ] *vt* andare a prendere; (*be sold for*) essere venduto per.

fete [feɪt] *n* festa *f* all'aperto (*a scopo di beneficenza*).

 FETE

Vengono così chiamate le feste all'aperto organizzate, soprattutto nei mesi estivi, per raccogliere soldi da destinare ad opere di beneficenza o al finanziamento di iniziative e progetti per il quartiere. Comprendono gare, forme varie di intrattenimento e la vendita di prodotti fatti in casa.

---

fever ['fi:vǝʳ] *n* (*MED*) febbre *f*; **to have a ~** avere la febbre.

feverish ['fi:vǝrɪʃ] *adj* (*having a fever*) febbricitante.

few [fju:] *adj* pochi(-e); ◆ *pron* pochi *mpl* (-e *fpl*) ❑ **a few** *adj* qualche (*inv*) ◆ *pron* alcuni *mpl* (-e *fpl*); **quite a ~** parecchi.

fewer ['fju:ǝʳ] *adj & pron* meno (*inv*).

fiancé [fɪ'ɒnseɪ] *n* fidanzato *m*.

fiancée [fɪ'ɒnseɪ] *n* fidanzata *f*.

fib [fɪb] *n* (*inf*) (piccola) bugia *f*.

fiber ['faɪbǝʳ] (*Am*) = **fibre**.

fibre ['faɪbǝʳ] *n* fibra *f*.

fibreglass ['faɪbǝglɑ:s] *n* fibra *f* di vetro.

fickle ['fɪkl] *adj* incostante, volubile.

fiction ['fɪkʃn] *n* narrativa *f*.

fiddle ['fɪdl] *n* (*violin*) violino *m* ◆ *vi*: **to ~ with sthg** giocherellare con qc.

fidget ['fɪdʒɪt] *vi* agitarsi.

field [fiːld] n campo m.

field glasses npl binocolo m.

fierce [fɪəs] adj feroce; (storm, heat) violento(-a).

fifteen [fɪfˈtiːn] num quindici, → **six**.

fifteenth [ˌfɪfˈtiːnθ] num quindicesimo(-a), → **sixth**.

fifth [fɪfθ] num quinto(-a), → **sixth**.

fiftieth [ˈfɪftɪəθ] num cinquantesimo(-a), → **sixth**.

fifty [ˈfɪftɪ] num cinquanta, → **six**.

fig [fɪg] n fico m.

fight [faɪt] (pt & pp fought) n rissa f; (argument) lite f; (struggle) lotta f ◆ vt combattere; (person) azzuffarsi con ◆ vi (physically) combattere; (quarrel) litigare; (struggle) lottare; **to have a ~ with sb** fare a pugni con qn ❑ **fight back** vi difendersi; **fight off** vt sep (attacker) respingere; (illness) vincere.

fighting [ˈfaɪtɪŋ] n combattimento m.

figure [Br ˈfɪgəʳ, Am ˈfɪgjər] n figura f; (number, statistic) cifra f ❑ **figure out** vt sep riuscire a capire.

file [faɪl] n (folder) cartella f; (box) schedario m; (information on person) scheda f; (COMPUT) file m inv; (tool) lima f ◆ vt (complaint, petition) presentare; (nails) limare; **in single ~** in fila indiana.

filing cabinet [ˈfaɪlɪŋ-] n schedario m.

fill [fɪl] vt riempire; (role) ricoprire; (tooth) otturare ❑ **fill in** vt sep (form) riempire; **fill out = fill in**; **fill up** vt sep riempire; **~ her up!** (with petrol) il pieno, per favore!

filled roll [ˈfɪld-] n panino m imbottito.

fillet [ˈfɪlɪt] n filetto m.

fillet steak n bistecca f di filetto.

filling [ˈfɪlɪŋ] n (of cake, sandwich) ripieno m; (in tooth) otturazione f ◆ adj: **it's very ~** sazia molto.

filling station n stazione f di servizio.

film [fɪlm] n (at cinema) film m inv; (for camera) pellicola f ◆ vt filmare.

film star n divo m (-a f) del cinema.

filter [ˈfɪltəʳ] n filtro m.

filthy [ˈfɪlθɪ] adj sudicio(-a).

fin [fɪn] n pinna f.

final [ˈfaɪnl] adj ultimo(-a); (decision) definitivo(-a) ◆ n finale f.

finalist [ˈfaɪnəlɪst] n finalista mf.

finally [ˈfaɪnəlɪ] adv (at last) finalmente; (lastly) infine.

finance [n ˈfaɪnæns, vb faɪˈnæns] n (money) finanziamento m; (profession) finanza f ◆ vt finanziare ❑ **finances** npl finanze fpl.

financial [fɪˈnænʃl] adj finanziario(-a).

find [faɪnd] (pt & pp found) vt trovare; (find out) scoprire ◆ n scoperta f; **to ~ the time to do sthg** trovare il tempo di fare qc ❑ **find out** vt sep (fact, truth) scoprire ◆ vi: **to ~ out (about sthg)** (learn) scoprire (qc); (get information) informarsi (su qc).

fine [faɪn] adv (thinly) finemente; (well) bene ◆ n multa f ◆ vt multare ◆ adj (good) buono(-a); (weather, day) bello(-a); (thin) sottile; **it's ~** (satisfactory) va bene; **I'm ~** (in health) sto bene.

fine art n belle arti fpl.

finger ['fɪŋgə^r] n dito m.

fingernail ['fɪŋgəneɪl] n unghia f.

fingertip ['fɪŋgətɪp] n polpastrello m.

finish ['fɪnɪʃ] n fine f; (on furniture) finitura f ◆ vt & vi finire; **to ~ doing sthg** finire di fare qc ❑ **finish off** vt sep finire; **finish up** vi finire; **to ~ up doing sthg** finire a fare qc.

Finland ['fɪnlənd] n la Finlandia.

Finn [fɪn] n finlandese mf.

Finnan haddock ['fɪnən-] n (Scot) eglefino m affumicato (tipico della Scozia).

Finnish ['fɪnɪʃ] adj finlandese ◆ n (language) finlandese m.

fir [fɜ:^{r}] n abete m.

fire ['faɪə^r] n fuoco m; (uncontrolled) incendio m; (device) stufa f ◆ vt (from job) licenziare; **to ~ a gun** sparare; **on ~** in fiamme; **to catch ~** prendere fuoco; **to make a ~** accendere un fuoco.

fire alarm n allarme m antincendio.

fire brigade n (Br) vigili mpl del fuoco.

fire department (Am) = **fire brigade**.

fire engine n autopompa f.

fire escape n scala f antincendio.

fire exit n uscita f di sicurezza.

fire extinguisher n estintore m.

fire hazard n: **it's a ~** rappresenta un pericolo di incendio.

fireman ['faɪəmən] (pl -men [-mən]) n vigile m del fuoco.

fireplace ['faɪəpleɪs] n caminetto m.

fire regulations npl norme fpl antincendio.

fire station n caserma f dei vigili del fuoco.

firewood ['faɪəwʊd] n legna f da ardere.

firework display ['faɪəwɜːk-] n fuochi mpl d'artificio.

fireworks ['faɪəwɜːks] npl (rockets) fuochi mpl d'artificio.

firm [fɜːm] adj (fruit) sodo(-a); (mattress) duro(-a); (structure) solido(-a); (grip) saldo(-a); (decision, belief) fermo(-a) ◆ n ditta f.

first [fɜːst] adj primo(-a) ◆ adv prima; (for the first time) per la prima volta ◆ n (event) novità f inv ◆ pron: **the ~** il primo (la prima); ~ **(gear)** prima f; ~ **thing (in the morning)** per prima cosa; **for the ~ time** per la prima volta; **the ~ of January** il primo gennaio; **at ~** dapprima; ~ **of all** prima di tutto.

first aid n pronto soccorso m.

first-aid kit n cassetta f del pronto soccorso.

first class n (mail) posta celere, di solito consegnata entro uno o due giorni; (on train, plane, ship) prima classe f.

first-class adj (stamp) per consegna celere; (ticket) di prima (classe); (very good) di prima qualità.

first floor n (Br: floor above ground floor) primo piano m; (Am: ground floor) pianterreno m.

firstly ['fɜːstlɪ] adv in primo luogo.

First World War n: **the ~** la prima guerra mondiale.

fish [fɪʃ] (pl inv) n pesce m ◆ vi pescare.

fish and chips n pesce m e patate fritti.

FISH AND CHIPS

È il piatto da asporto inglese per eccellenza. Il pesce viene fritto in una pastella a base di farina, latte e uova e viene servito, insieme a patate fritte, avvolto in carta da pacchi prima e quindi in carta di giornale. Spesso è consumato direttamente per strada. I negozi di "fish and chips", molto diffusi in tutta la Gran Bretagna, vendono anche altri cibi fritti, come ad esempio salsicce, pollo, salsicce di sanguinaccio, e spesso anche tortine di carne.

---

fishcake ['fɪʃkeɪk] n crocchetta f di pesce.

fisherman ['fɪʃəmən] (pl -men [-mən]) n pescatore m.

fish farm n vivaio m.

fish fingers npl (Br) bastoncini mpl di pesce.

fishing ['fɪʃɪŋ] n pesca f; **to go ~** andare a pesca.

fishing boat n barca f da pesca.

fishing rod n canna f da pesca.

fishmonger's ['fɪʃˌmʌŋgəz] n (shop) pescheria f.

fish sticks (Am) = **fish fingers**.

fish supper n (Scot) pesce m e patate fritte.

fist [fɪst] n pugno m.

fit [fɪt] adj (healthy) in forma ◆ vt (be right size for) andare (bene) a; (kitchen, bath) installare; (a lock) mettere; (insert) inserire ◆ vi (be right size) andare bene ◆ n (of coughing, anger) attacco m; (epileptic) crisi f inv epilettica; **they're a good ~** (clothes, shoes) sono della misura giusta; **to**

be ~ for sthg (suitable) essere adatto(-a) a qc; **~ to eat** buono(-a) da mangiare; **it doesn't ~** (object) non c'entra; **it doesn't ~ me** (jacket, skirt) non mi sta OR va; **to get ~** rimettersi in forma; **to keep ~** tenersi in forma ❑ **fit in** vt sep (find time to do) trovare il tempo per ◆ vi (belong) inserirsi.

fitness ['fɪtnɪs] n (health) forma f.

fitted carpet [ˌfɪtəd-] n moquette f inv.

fitted sheet [ˌfɪtəd-] n lenzuolo m con gli angoli.

fitting room ['fɪtɪŋ-] n camerino m.

five [faɪv] num cinque, → **six**.

fiver ['faɪvər] n (Br: inf) cinque sterline fpl; (note) banconota f da cinque sterline.

fix [fɪks] vt (attach, decide on) fissare; (mend) riparare; (drink, food) preparare; (arrange) organizzare ❑ **fix up** vt sep: **to ~ sb up with sthg** procurare qc a qn.

fixture ['fɪkstʃər] n (SPORT) incontro m; **~s and fittings** installazioni fpl.

fizzy ['fɪzɪ] adj frizzante.

flag [flæg] n bandiera f.

flake [fleɪk] n (of snow) fiocco m ◆ vi sfaldarsi.

flame [fleɪm] n fiamma f.

flammable ['flæməbl] adj infiammabile.

flan [flæn] n flan m inv.

flannel ['flænl] n (material) flanella f; (Br: for washing face) panno m di spugna ❑ **flannels** npl pantaloni mpl di flanella.

flap [flæp] n (of envelope) linguetta f; (of pocket) risvolto m ◆ vt (wings) battere.

flapjack ['flæpdʒæk] n (Br) biscotto m di avena.

flare [fleəʳ] n (signal) razzo m.

flared [fleəd] adj (trousers) a zampa d'elefante; (skirt) scampanato(-a).

flash [flæʃ] n (of light) lampo m; (for camera) flash m inv ◆ vi (light) lampeggiare; **a ~ of lightning** un lampo; **to ~ one's headlights** lampeggiare.

flashlight ['flæʃlaɪt] n torcia f elettrica.

flask [flɑːsk] n (Thermos) thermos® m inv; (hip flask) borraccia f.

flat [flæt] adj piatto(-a); (battery) scarico(-a); (drink) sgasato(-a); (rate, fee) unico(-a) ◆ adv (level) in piano ◆ n (Br: apartment) appartamento m; **a ~ (tyre)** una gomma a terra; **~ out** a più non posso.

flatter ['flætəʳ] vt adulare.

flavor ['fleɪvər] (Am) = flavour.

flavour ['fleɪvəʳ] n (Br: taste) sapore m; (of ice cream) gusto m.

flavoured ['fleɪvəd] adj: **lemon-~** al gusto di limone.

flavouring ['fleɪvərɪŋ] n aroma m.

flaw [flɔː] n difetto m.

flea [fliː] n pulce f.

flea market n mercato m delle pulci.

fleece [fliːs] n (downy material) vello m.

fleet [fliːt] n (of ships) flotta f.

Flemish ['flemɪʃ] adj fiammingo(-a) ◆ n (language) fiammingo m.

flesh [fleʃ] n (of person, animal) carne f; (of fruit, vegetable) polpa f.

flew [fluː] pt → fly.

flex [fleks] n cavetto m.

flexible ['fleksəbl] adj flessibile.

flick [flɪk] vt (a switch) premere; (with finger) colpire con il dito ◻ **flick through** vt fus sfogliare.

flies [flaɪz] npl (of trousers) patta f.

flight [flaɪt] n volo m; **a ~ (of stairs)** una rampa (di scale).

flight attendant n assistente mf di volo.

flimsy ['flɪmzɪ] adj (object) poco consistente; (clothes) leggero(-a).

fling [flɪŋ] (pt & pp flung) vt lanciare.

flint [flɪnt] n (of lighter) pietrina f.

flip-flop [flɪp-] n (Br: shoe) infradito m inv or f inv.

flipper ['flɪpəʳ] n (Br: of swimmer) pinna f.

flirt [flɜːt] vi: **to ~ (with sb)** flirtare (con qn).

float [fləʊt] n (for swimming) tavoletta f; (for fishing) galleggiante m; (in procession) carro m; (drink) bevanda con del gelato aggiunto ◆ vi galleggiare.

flock [flɒk] n (of birds) stormo m; (of sheep) gregge m ◆ vi (people) accalcarsi.

flood [flʌd] n alluvione f ◆ vt inondare ◆ vi straripare.

floodlight ['flʌdlaɪt] n riflettore m.

floor [flɔːʳ] n (of room) pavimento m; (storey) piano m; (of nightclub) pista f.

floorboard ['flɔːbɔːd] n asse f del pavimento.

floor show n varietà m inv.

flop [flɒp] n (inf) fiasco m.

floppy disk ['flɒpɪ-] n floppy disk m inv.

floral ['flɔːrəl] adj (pattern) floreale.

Florence ['flɒrəns] n Firenze f.

Florida Keys ['flɒrɪdə-] npl: the ~ l'arcipelago m Keys.

FLORIDA KEYS

Gruppo di piccole isole che si estende per oltre 150 chilometri al largo della costa meridionale della Florida, le "Florida Keys" comprendono le famose località di Key West e Key Largo. Una rete di strade e ponti, la "Overseas Highway", collega le isole fra di loro.

---

florist's ['flɒrɪsts] n (shop) fioraio m.

flour ['flaʊər] n farina f.

flow [fləʊ] n (of river, blood) flusso m ♦ vi (river, blood) scorrere.

flower ['flaʊər] n fiore m.

flowerbed ['flaʊəbed] n aiuola f.

flowerpot ['flaʊəpɒt] n vaso m da fiori.

flown [fləʊn] pp → fly.

fl oz abbr = fluid ounce.

flu [fluː] n influenza f.

fluent ['fluːənt] adj: to be ~ in Italian, to speak ~ Italian parlare italiano correntemente.

fluff [flʌf] n (on clothes) pelucchi mpl.

fluid ounce ['fluːɪd-] n = 0,03 l.

flume [fluːm] n canale m.

flung [flʌŋ] pp → fling.

flunk [flʌŋk] vt (Am: inf: exam) essere bocciato(-a) a.

fluorescent [flʊə'resənt] adj fluorescente.

flush [flʌʃ] vi (toilet) funzionare ♦

vt: to ~ the toilet tirare lo sciacquone.

flute [fluːt] n flauto m traverso.

fly [flaɪ] (pt flew, pp flown) n (insect) mosca f; (of trousers) patta f ♦ vt (plane, helicopter) pilotare; (airline) viaggiare con; (transport) trasportare in aereo ♦ vi volare; (passenger) andare in aereo; (pilot a plane) pilotare un aereo; (flag) sventolare.

fly-drive n fly and drive m inv.

flying ['flaɪɪŋ] n: I'm frightened of ~ ho paura di volare.

flyover ['flaɪ,əʊvər] n (Br) cavalcavia m inv.

flypaper ['flaɪ,peɪpər] n carta f moschicida.

flysheet ['flaɪʃiːt] n telo m protettivo.

FM n FM f.

foal [fəʊl] n puledro m.

foam [fəʊm] n (bubbles) schiuma f; (foam rubber) gommapiuma® f.

focus ['fəʊkəs] n (of camera) fuoco m ♦ vi (with camera, binoculars) mettere a fuoco; **in** ~ a fuoco; **out of** ~ sfocato.

fog [fɒg] n nebbia f.

fogbound ['fɒgbaʊnd] adj bloccato(-a) dalla nebbia.

foggy ['fɒgɪ] adj nebbioso(-a).

fog lamp n antinebbia m inv.

foil [fɔɪl] n (thin metal) carta f di alluminio.

fold [fəʊld] n (in paper, material) piega f ♦ vt piegare; (wrap) avvolgere; to ~ one's arms incrociare le braccia □ **fold up** vi (chair, bed, bicycle) piegarsi.

folder ['fəʊldər] n cartella f.

foliage ['fəʊlɪdʒ] n fogliame m.

folk [fəuk] npl (people) gente f ◆ n:
~ (music) folk m ❑ folks npl (inf:
relatives): my ~s i miei.

follow ['fɒləu] vt seguire; (in
order, time) seguire a ◆ vi seguire;
~ed by (in time) seguito da; as ~s
come segue ❑ **follow on** vi (come
later) seguire.

following ['fɒləuıŋ] adj (next)
successivo(-a); (mentioned below)
seguente ◆ prep dopo.

follow on call n chiamata f
successiva.

fond [fɒnd] adj: to be ~ of amare.

fondue ['fɒndu:] n fonduta f.

food [fu:d] n cibo m.

food poisoning [-.pɔıznıŋ] n
avvelenamento m da cibo.

food processor [-.prəusesər] n
tritatutto-frullatore m inv elettrico.

foodstuffs ['fu:dstʌfs] npl generi
mpl alimentari.

fool [fu:l] n (idiot) stupido m (-a
f); (pudding) mousse f inv di frutta
◆ vt ingannare.

foolish ['fu:lıʃ] adj stupido(-a).

foot [fut] (pl feet) n (of person)
piede m; (of animal) zampa f; (measurement) = 30,48 cm, piede; (of hill,
cliff, bed) piedi mpl; (of wardrobe, tripod, stairs) base f; by ~ a piedi; on
~ a piedi.

football ['futbɔ:l] n (Br: soccer)
calcio m; (Am: American football)
football m americano; (ball) pallone m.

footballer ['futbɔ:lər] n (Br) calciatore m (-trice f).

football pitch n (Br) campo m
di calcio.

footbridge ['futbrıdʒ] n sovrap-
passaggio m.

footpath ['futpɑ:θ, pl -pɑ:ðz] n
sentiero m.

footprint ['futprınt] n orma f.

footstep ['futstep] n passo m.

footwear ['futweər] n calzature
fpl.

for [fɔ:r] prep 1. (expressing intention, purpose, reason) per; this book
is ~ you questo libro è per te; what
did you do that ~? perché l'hai
fatto?; what's it ~? a cosa serve?; a
town famous ~ its wine una città
famosa per il suo vino; ~ this reason per questo motivo; to go ~ a
walk andare a fare una passeggiata; '~ sale' 'vendesi'.
2. (during) I've lived here ~ ten
years abito qui da dieci anni, sono
dieci anni che abito qui; we talked
~ hours abbiamo chiacchierato
per ore.
3. (by, before) per; be there ~ eight
p.m. trovati lì per le otto di sera;
I'll do it ~ tomorrow lo farò per
domani.
4. (on the occasion of) per; I got
socks ~ Christmas ho avuto dei
calzini per Natale; what's ~ dinner? cosa c'è per cena?
5. (on behalf of) per; to do sthg ~
sb fare qc per qn.
6. (with time and space) per; there's
no room ~ your suitcase non c'è
posto per la tua valigia; have you
got time ~ a coffee? hai tempo per
un caffè?; it's time ~ dinner è ora
di cena.
7. (expressing distance) per; 'road
works ~ 20 miles' 'lavori in corso
per 32 chilometri'.
8. (expressing destination) per; a
ticket ~ Edinburgh un biglietto per
Edimburgo; this train is ~ London
only questo treno ferma solo a

Londra.

9. (expressing price): **I bought it ~ £5** l'ho comprato per 5 sterline, l'ho pagato 5 sterline.

10. (expressing meaning) per; **what's the Italian ~ 'boy'?** come si dice 'boy' in italiano?

11. (with regard to) per; **it's warm ~ November** fa caldo per essere novembre; **it's easy ~ you** è facile per te; **it's too far ~ us to walk** è troppo lontano per andarci a piedi.

forbid [fə'bɪd] (pt **-bade** [-'beɪd], pp **-bidden**) vt proibire, vietare; **to ~ sb to do sthg** proibire OR vietare a qn di fare qc.

forbidden [fə'bɪdn] adj proibito(-a).

force [fɔːs] n forza f ♦ vt forzare; **to ~ sb to do sthg** costringere qn a fare qc; **to ~ one's way through** farsi strada con la forza; **the ~s** le forze armate.

ford [fɔːd] n guado m.

forecast ['fɔːkɑːst] n previsione f.

forecourt ['fɔːkɔːt] n spiazzo m.

forefinger ['fɔːˌfɪŋgəʳ] n indice m.

foreground ['fɔːgraʊnd] n primo piano m.

forehead ['fɔːhed] n fronte f.

foreign ['fɒrən] adj straniero(-a); (travel) all'estero.

foreign currency n valuta f estera.

foreigner ['fɒrənəʳ] n straniero m (-a f).

foreign exchange n cambio m.

Foreign Secretary n (Br) ministro m degli Esteri.

foreman ['fɔːmən] (pl **-men** [-mən]) n (of workers) capo operaio m.

forename ['fɔːneɪm] n (fml) nome m (di battesimo).

foresee [fɔː'siː] (pt **-saw** [-'sɔː], pp **-seen** [-'siːn]) vt prevedere.

forest ['fɒrɪst] n foresta f.

forever [fə'revəʳ] adv (eternally) per sempre; (continually) in continuazione.

forgave [fə'geɪv] pt → **forgive**.

forge [fɔːdʒ] vt (copy) falsificare.

forgery ['fɔːdʒərɪ] n (copy) falso m.

forget [fə'get] (pt **-got**, pp **-gotten**) vt dimenticare; (give up) lasciar perdere ♦ vi dimenticarsi; **to ~ about sthg** dimenticarsi di qc; **to ~ how to do sthg** dimenticare come si fa qc; **to ~ to do sthg** dimenticare di fare qc; **~ it!** lascia perdere!

forgetful [fə'getfʊl] adj smemorato(-a).

forgive [fə'gɪv] (pt **-gave**, pp **-given** [-'gɪvn]) vt perdonare.

forgot [fə'gɒt] pt → **forget**.

forgotten [fə'gɒtn] pp → **forget**.

fork [fɔːk] n (for eating with) forchetta f; (for gardening) forca f; (of road, path) bivio m ❑ **forks** npl (of bike, motorbike) forcelle fpl.

form [fɔːm] n (type, shape) forma f; (piece of paper) modulo m; (SCH) classe f ♦ vt formare; (constitute) costituire; (produce) creare ♦ vi formarsi; **off ~** giù di forma; **on ~** in forma; **to ~ part of** fare parte di.

formal ['fɔːml] adj formale.

formality [fɔː'mælətɪ] n formalità f inv; **it's just a ~** è solo una formalità.

format ['fɔ:mæt] n formato m.

former ['fɔ:mə^r] adj (previous) precedente; (first) primo(-a) ♦ pron: the ~ il primo; the ~ President l'ex Presidente.

formerly ['fɔ:məlɪ] adv precedentemente.

formula ['fɔ:mjʊlə] (pl -as OR -ae [i:]) n formula f.

fort [fɔ:t] n forte m.

forthcoming [fɔ:θ'kʌmɪŋ] adj (future) prossimo(-a).

fortieth ['fɔ:tɪθ] num quarantesimo(-a), → sixth.

fortnight ['fɔ:tnaɪt] n (Br) quindici giorni mpl.

fortunate ['fɔ:tʃnət] adj fortunato(-a).

fortunately ['fɔ:tʃnətlɪ] adv fortunatamente.

fortune ['fɔ:tʃu:n] n fortuna f; it costs a ~ (inf) costa una fortuna.

forty ['fɔ:tɪ] num quaranta, → six.

forward ['fɔ:wəd] adv (move, lean) in avanti ♦ n (SPORT) attaccante mf ♦ vt spedire; to look ~ to doing sthg non vedere l'ora di fare qc.

forwarding address ['fɔ:wədɪŋ-] n recapito m nuovo.

fought [fɔ:t] pp → fight.

foul [faul] adj (unpleasant) disgustoso(-a) ♦ n fallo m.

found [faund] pp → find ♦ vt fondare.

foundation (cream) [faun'deɪʃn-] n fondotinta m inv.

foundations [faun'deɪʃnz] npl fondamenta fpl.

fountain ['fauntɪn] n fontana f.

fountain pen n penna f stilografica.

four [fɔ:^r] num quattro, → six.

four-star (petrol) n super f inv.

fourteen [fɔ:'ti:n] num quattordici, → six.

fourteenth [fɔ:'ti:nθ] num quattordicesimo(-a), → sixth.

fourth [fɔ:θ] num quarto(-a), → sixth.

four-wheel drive n (car) veicolo m a quattro ruote motrici.

fowl [faul] (pl inv) n volatile m.

fox [fɒks] n volpe f.

foyer ['fɔɪeɪ] n (of hotel) hall f inv; (of theatre) foyer m inv.

fraction ['frækʃn] n frazione f.

fracture ['fræktʃə^r] n frattura f ♦ vt fratturare.

fragile ['frædʒaɪl] adj fragile.

fragment ['frægmənt] n frammento m.

fragrance ['freɪgrəns] n profumo m.

frail [freɪl] adj debole.

frame [freɪm] n (of window, tent, bicycle) telaio m; (of picture, photo) cornice f; (of glasses) montatura f ♦ vt (photo, picture) incorniciare.

France [frɑ:ns] n la Francia.

frank [fræŋk] adj franco(-a).

frankfurter ['fræŋkfɜ:tə^r] n würstel m inv.

frankly ['fræŋklɪ] adv francamente.

frantic ['fræntɪk] adj frenetico(-a).

fraud [frɔ:d] n (crime) frode f.

freak [fri:k] adj strano(-a) ♦ n (inf: fanatic) fanatico m (-a f).

freckles ['freklz] npl lentiggini fpl.

free [fri:] *adj* libero(-a); *(costing nothing)* gratuito(-a) ♦ *vt (prisoner)* liberare ♦ *adv* gratis; **for ~** gratis; **~ of charge** gratis; **to be ~ to do sthg** essere libero di fare qc.

freedom ['fri:dəm] *n* libertà *f*.

freefone ['fri:fəʊn] *n (Br)* = numero *m* verde.

free gift *n* omaggio *m*.

free house *n (Br)* pub *m inv (che può vendere qualsiasi birra, non appartenendo a nessuna ditta).*

free kick *n* calcio *m* di punizione.

freelance ['fri:lɑ:ns] *adj* freelance *(inv).*

freely ['fri:lɪ] *adv* liberamente; *(available)* facilmente.

free period *n (SCH)* ora *f* di buco.

freepost ['fri:pəʊst] *n* affrancatura *f* a carico del destinatario.

free-range *adj (chicken)* ruspante; *(eggs)* di galline ruspanti.

free time *n* tempo *m* libero.

freeway ['fri:weɪ] *n (Am)* superstrada *f*.

freeze [fri:z] *(pt* froze, *pp* frozen) *vt* congelare ♦ *vi* gelare ♦ *v impers:* **it's freezing** fa un freddo polare.

freezer ['fri:zə] *n (deep freeze)* congelatore *m*; *(part of fridge)* freezer *m inv*.

freezing ['fri:zɪŋ] *adj* gelato(-a); *(temperatures)* sotto zero.

freezing point *n* temperatura *f* di congelamento.

freight [freɪt] *n (goods)* carico *m*.

French [frentʃ] *adj* francese ♦ *n (language)* francese *m* ♦ *npl:* **the ~** i francesi.

French bean *n* fagiolino *m*.

French bread *n* baguette *f inv*.

French dressing *n (in UK)* condimento per insalata a base di olio e aceto; *(in US)* condimento per insalata a base di maionese e ketchup.

French fries *npl* patatine *fpl* fritte.

Frenchman ['frentʃmən] *(pl* -men [-mən]) *n* francese *m*.

French toast *n (fried bread)* fetta di pane passata nell'uovo e fritta.

French windows *npl* portafinestra *f*.

Frenchwoman ['frentʃˌwʊmən] *(pl* -women [-ˌwɪmɪn]) *n* francese *f*.

frequency ['fri:kwənsɪ] *n* frequenza *f*.

frequent ['fri:kwənt] *adj* frequente.

frequently ['fri:kwəntlɪ] *adv* frequentemente.

fresh [freʃ] *adj* fresco(-a); *(water)* dolce; *(new)* nuovo(-a); **to get some ~ air** prendere un po' d'aria fresca.

fresh cream *n* panna *f* fresca.

freshen ['freʃn]: **freshen up** *vi* rinfrescarsi.

freshly ['freʃlɪ] *adv* appena.

fresh orange (juice) *n* spremuta *f* d'arancia.

Fri. *(abbr of Friday)* ven.

Friday ['fraɪdɪ] *n* venerdì *m inv*, → **Saturday.**

fridge [frɪdʒ] *n* frigorifero *m*.

fried egg [fraɪd-] *n* uovo *m* al tegame.

fried rice [fraɪd-] *n* piatto cinese a base di riso fritto.

friend [frend] *n* amico *m* (-a *f*); **to be ~s with sb** essere amico di qn; **to make ~s with sb** fare amicizia con qn.

friendly ['frɛndlɪ] *adj* cordiale; **to be ~ with** sb essere amico di qn.

friendship ['frɛndʃɪp] *n* amicizia f.

fries [fraɪz] = **French fries**.

fright [fraɪt] *n* spavento *m*, paura f; **to give** sb a ~ fare paura a qn.

frighten ['fraɪtn] *vt* spaventare, far paura a.

frightened ['fraɪtnd] *adj (scared)* spaventato(-a); **to be ~ (that)** ... *(worried)* avere paura che ...; **to be ~ of** avere paura di.

frightening ['fraɪtnɪŋ] *adj* spaventoso(-a).

frightful ['fraɪtful] *adj (very bad, unpleasant)* terribile.

frilly ['frɪlɪ] *adj* arricciato(-a).

fringe [frɪndʒ] *n* frangia f.

frisk [frɪsk] *vt* perquisire.

fritter ['frɪtəʳ] *n* frittella f.

fro [frəʊ] *adv* → **to**.

frog [frɒg] *n* rana f.

from [frɒm] *prep* **1.** *(expressing origin, source)* da; **I'm ~ England** sono inglese; **I bought it ~ a supermarket** l'ho comprato al supermercato; **the train ~ Manchester** il treno (proveniente) da Manchester.

2. *(expressing removal, deduction)* da; **away ~ home** lontano da casa; **to take** sthg (away) ~ sb prendere qc a qn; **10% will be deducted ~ the total** dal totale verrà dedotto il 10%.

3. *(expressing distance)* da; **5 miles ~ London** a 5 miglia da Londra; **it's not far ~ here** non è lontano (da qui).

4. *(expressing position)* da; **~ here you can see the valley** da qui si vede la valle.

5. *(expressing starting time)* da; **open ~ nine to five** aperto dalle nove alle cinque; **~ next year** dall'anno prossimo.

6. *(expressing change)* da; **the price has gone up ~ £1 to £2** il prezzo è salito da 1 a 2 sterline.

7. *(expressing range)* da; **tickets are ~ £10** i biglietti vanno dalle 10 sterline in su.

8. *(as a result of)*: **I'm tired ~ walking all day** sono stanco per aver camminato tutto il giorno.

9. *(expressing protection)* da; **sheltered ~ the wind** al riparo dal vento.

10. *(in comparisons)*: **different ~** diverso da.

fromage frais [,frɒmɑːʒ'freɪ] *n* formaggio fresco cremoso.

front [frʌnt] *adj* anteriore ♦ *n* parte f anteriore; *(of weather)* fronte *m*; *(by the sea)* lungomare *m*; **in ~** *(further forward)* avanti; *(in the lead)* d'avanti; **in ~ of** davanti a.

front door *n* porta f principale.

frontier [frʌn'tɪəʳ] *n* frontiera f.

front page *n* prima pagina f.

front seat *n* sedile *m* anteriore.

frost [frɒst] *n* gelo *m*.

frosty ['frɒstɪ] *adj (morning, weather)* gelato(-a).

froth [frɒθ] *n* spuma f.

frown [fraʊn] *n* fronte f aggrottata ♦ *vi* aggrottare la fronte.

froze [frəʊz] *pt* → **freeze**.

frozen ['frəʊzn] *pp* → **freeze** ♦ *adj* gelato(-a); *(food)* congelato(-a).

fruit [fruːt] *n (food)* frutta f; *(variety, single fruit)* frutto *m*; **a piece of ~** un frutto; **~s of the forest** frutti di bosco.

fruit cake n torta con frutta secca.

fruiterer ['fru:tərəʳ] n (Br) fruttivendolo m (-a f).

fruit juice n succo m di frutta.

fruit machine n (Br) slotmachine f inv.

fruit salad n macedonia f.

frustrating [frʌ'streitiŋ] adj frustrante.

frustration [frʌ'streiʃn] n frustrazione f.

fry [frai] vt soffriggere; (deep-fry) friggere.

frying pan ['fraiiŋ-] n padella f.

ft abbr = **foot, feet.**

fudge [fʌdʒ] n dolciume gommoso fatto con burro, latte e zucchero.

fuel ['fjuəl] n (for engine) carburante m; (for heating) combustibile m.

fuel pump n pompa f del carburante.

fulfil [fol'fil] vt (Br) (promise) mantenere; (duty, role, need) adempiere; (conditions, request) soddisfare; (instructions) eseguire.

fulfill [fol'fil] (Am) = **fulfil.**

full [fol] adj pieno(-a); (extent, fare) intero(-a); (name) completo(-a) ♦ adv (directly) in pieno; **I'm ~ (up)** sono pieno; **at ~ speed** a tutta velocità; **in ~** per esteso.

full board n pensione f completa.

full-cream milk n latte m intero.

full-length adj (skirt, dress) lungo(-a).

full moon n luna f piena.

full stop n punto m.

full-time adj & adv a tempo pieno.

fully ['foli] adv (completely) completamente.

fully-licensed adj autorizzato a vendere alcolici.

fumble ['fʌmbl] vi (search clumsily) rovistare.

fun [fʌn] n divertimento m; **it's good ~** è divertente; **for ~** per divertimento; **to have ~** divertirsi; **to make ~ of** prendere in giro.

function ['fʌŋkʃn] n (role) funzione f; (formal event) ricevimento m ♦ vi funzionare.

fund [fʌnd] n (of money) fondo m ♦ vt finanziare ❑ **funds** npl fondi mpl.

fundamental [,fʌndə'mentl] adj fondamentale.

funeral ['fju:nərəl] n funerale m.

funfair ['fʌnfeəʳ] n luna park m inv.

funky ['fʌŋki] adj (inf: music) funky (inv).

funnel ['fʌnl] n (for pouring) imbuto m; (on ship) fumaiolo m.

funny ['fʌni] adj (amusing) divertente; (strange) strano(-a); **to feel ~** (ill) sentirsi strano.

fur [fɜ:ʳ] n pelliccia f.

fur coat n pelliccia f.

furious ['fjuəriəs] adj (angry) furioso(-a).

furnished ['fɜ:niʃt] adj ammobiliato(-a).

furnishings ['fɜ:niʃiŋz] npl arredamento m.

furniture ['fɜ:nitʃəʳ] n mobilia f; **a piece of ~** un mobile.

furry ['fɜ:ri] adj peloso(-a).

further ['fɜ:ðəʳ] → **far** ♦ adv (in distance) più lontano; (more) di più ♦ adj (additional) ulteriore; **until ~**

notice fino a nuovo avviso.

furthermore [ˌfɜːðəˈmɔːʳ] adv
inoltre.

furthest [ˈfɜːðɪst] → **far** ◆ adj
(most distant) il più lontano (la più
lontana) ◆ adv (in distance) il più
lontano (possibile).

fuse [fjuːz] n (of plug) fusibile m;
(on bomb) detonatore m ◆ vi (plug,
device) saltare.

fuse box n scatola f dei fusibili.

fuss [fʌs] n (agitation) confusione
f; (complaints) storie fpl.

fussy [ˈfʌsɪ] adj (person) difficile.

future [ˈfjuːtʃəʳ] n futuro m ◆ adj
futuro(-a); **in ~** in futuro.

G

g (abbr of gram) g.

gable [ˈgeɪbl] n timpano m.

gadget [ˈgædʒɪt] n aggeggio m.

Gaelic [ˈgeɪlɪk] n gaelico m.

gag [gæg] n (inf: joke) gag f inv.

gain [geɪn] n (improvement) avanzamento m; (profit) guadagno m ◆
vt guadagnare; (weight) aumentare
di; (confidence, speed, popularity)
acquistare; (achieve) ottenere;
(subj: clock, watch) andare avanti di
◆ vi (get benefit): **to ~ from sthg**
trarre vantaggio da qc.

gale [geɪl] n burrasca f.

gallery [ˈgælərɪ] n galleria f.

gallon [ˈgælən] n (Br) = 4,546 l,
gallone m; (Am) = 3,791 l, gallone.

gallop [ˈgæləp] vi galoppare.

gamble [ˈgæmbl] n azzardo m ◆
vi (bet money) giocare d'azzardo.

gambling [ˈgæmblɪŋ] n gioco m
d'azzardo.

game [geɪm] n (gen, in tennis)
gioco m; (of football, squash, cards)
partita f; (wild animals, meat) cac-
ciagione f ❑ **games** n (SCH) =
attività fpl sportive ◆ npl (sporting
event) gare fpl.

gammon [ˈgæmən] n coscia di
maiale da cuocere.

gang [gæŋ] n (of criminals) banda
f; (of friends) gruppo m.

gangster [ˈgæŋstəʳ] n gangster m
inv.

gangway [ˈgæŋweɪ] n (for ship)
passerella f; (Br: in bus, aeroplane,
theatre) corridoio m.

gaol [dʒeɪl] (Br) = **jail**.

gap [gæp] n (space) buco m; (of
time) intervallo m; (difference) diva-
rio m.

garage [ˈgærɑːʒ, ˈgærɪdʒ] n (for
keeping car) garage m inv; (Br: for
petrol) stazione f di servizio; (for
repairs) autofficina f; (Br: for selling
cars) concessionaria f.

garbage [ˈgɑːbɪdʒ] n (Am: refuse)
spazzatura f.

garbage can n (Am) pattumiera f.

garbage truck n (Am) camion
m inv della nettezza urbana.

garden [ˈgɑːdn] n giardino m ◆ vi
fare giardinaggio ❑ **gardens** npl
(public park) giardini mpl pubblici.

garden centre n vivaio m.

gardener [ˈgɑːdnəʳ] n giardiniere m (-a f).

gardening [ˈgɑːdnɪŋ] n giardinaggio m.

garden peas *npl* piselli *mpl*.

garlic ['gɑ:lɪk] *n* aglio *m*.

garlic bread *n* ≃ bruschetta *f*.

garlic butter *n* burro *m* all'aglio.

garment ['gɑ:mənt] *n* indumento *m*.

garnish ['gɑ:nɪʃ] *n* guarnizione *f* ◆ *vt* guarnire.

gas [gæs] *n* gas *m inv*; *(Am: petrol)* benzina *f*.

gas cooker *n (Br)* cucina *f* a gas.

gas cylinder *n* bombola *f* del gas.

gas fire *n (Br)* stufa *f* a gas.

gasket ['gæskɪt] *n* guarnizione *f*.

gas mask *n* maschera *f* antigas.

gasoline ['gæsəli:n] *n (Am)* benzina *f*.

gasp [gɑ:sp] *vi (in shock)* rimanere senza fiato.

gas pedal *n (Am)* acceleratore *m*.

gas station *n (Am)* stazione *f* di servizio.

gas stove *(Br)* = **gas cooker**.

gas tank *n (Am)* serbatoio *m* della benzina.

gasworks ['gæswɜ:ks] *(pl inv)* *n* officina *f* del gas.

gate [geɪt] *n (to garden, field)* cancello *m*; *(at airport)* uscita *f*.

gâteau ['gætəʊ] *(pl -x* [-z]) *n (Br)* torta *f*.

gateway ['geɪtweɪ] *n (entrance)* entrata *f*.

gather ['gæðər] *vt (collect)* raccogliere; *(speed)* acquistare; *(understand)* dedurre ◆ *vi (come together)* riunirsi.

gaudy ['gɔ:dɪ] *adj* vistoso(-a).

gauge [geɪdʒ] *n (for measuring)* indicatore *m*; *(of railway track)* scartamento *m* ◆ *vt (calculate)* misurare.

gauze [gɔ:z] *n* garza *f*.

gave [geɪv] *pt* → **give**.

gay [geɪ] *adj (homosexual)* gay *(inv)*.

gaze [geɪz] *vi*: **to ~ at** fissare.

GB *(abbr of Great Britain)* GB.

GCSE *n* esami sostenuti a conclusione della scuola dell'obbligo.

---

i **GCSE**

Con questa abbreviazione si fa riferimento agli esami sostenuti dagli studenti inglesi, gallesi e irlandesi fra i 15 e i 16 anni d'età, a conclusione della scuola dell'obbligo. I "GCSEs" furono introdotti nel 1986 al posto degli "O levels", dai quali si differenziano in quanto la votazione finale dipende non solo dai risultati dell'esame ma anche dal profitto riportato durante il corso di studi in quella specifica disciplina. Gli studenti che intendono sostenere gli "A levels" devono superare i "GCSEs" in almeno cinque materie.

gear [gɪər] *n (wheel)* ingranaggio *m*; *(speed)* marcia *f*; *(belongings)* roba *f*; *(equipment, clothes)* attrezzatura *f*; **in ~** con la marcia inserita.

gearbox ['gɪəbɒks] *n* cambio *m*.

gear lever *n* leva *f* del cambio.

gear shift *(Am)* = **gear lever**.

gear stick *(Br)* = **gear lever**.

geese [gi:s] *pl* → **goose**.

gel [dʒel] *n* gel *m inv*.

gelatine [,dʒelə'ti:n] *n* gelatina *f*.

gem [dʒem] n gemma f.

Gemini ['dʒemɪnaɪ] n Gemelli mpl.

gender ['dʒendəʳ] n genere m.

general ['dʒenərəl] adj generale; (idea, statement) generico(-a) ♦ n generale m; in ~ in generale; (usually) in genere.

general anaesthetic n anestesia f totale.

general election n elezioni fpl politiche.

generally ['dʒenərəlɪ] adv generalmente.

general practitioner [-præk'tɪʃənəʳ] n medico m generico.

general store n drogheria f.

generate ['dʒenəreɪt] vt generare.

generation [,dʒenə'reɪʃn] n generazione f.

generator ['dʒenəreɪtəʳ] n generatore m.

generosity [,dʒenə'rɒsətɪ] n generosità f.

generous ['dʒenərəs] adj generoso(-a).

genitals ['dʒenɪtlz] npl genitali mpl.

genius ['dʒiːnjəs] n genio m.

gentle ['dʒentl] adj (careful) delicato(-a); (kind) gentile; (movement, breeze) leggero(-a).

gentleman ['dʒentlmən] (pl -men [-mən]) n signore m; (with good manners) gentiluomo m; 'gentlemen' (men's toilets) 'uomini'.

gently ['dʒentlɪ] adv (carefully) delicatamente.

gents [dʒents] n (Br) toilette f inv degli uomini.

genuine ['dʒenjuɪn] adj (authentic)

autentico(-a); (sincere) sincero(-a).

geographical [dʒɪə'græfɪkl] adj geografico(-a).

geography [dʒɪ'ɒgrəfɪ] n geografia f.

geology [dʒɪ'ɒlədʒɪ] n geologia f.

geometry [dʒɪ'ɒmətrɪ] n geometria f.

Georgian ['dʒɔːdʒən] adj (architecture etc) georgiano(-a) (del periodo dei re Giorgio I–IV, 1714–1830).

geranium [dʒɪ'reɪnjəm] n geranio m.

German ['dʒɜːmən] adj tedesco(-a) ♦ n (person) tedesco m (-a f); (language) tedesco m.

German measles n rosolia f.

Germany ['dʒɜːmənɪ] n la Germania.

germs [dʒɜːmz] npl germi mpl.

gesture ['dʒestʃəʳ] n (movement) gesto m.

get [get] (pt & pp **got**, Am pp **gotten**) vt 1. (obtain) ottenere; (job, house) trovare; **I got some crisps from the shop** ho comprato delle patatine al negozio; **she got a job** ha trovato lavoro.

2. (receive) ricevere; **I got a book for Christmas** mi hanno regalato un libro per Natale; **you ~ a lot of rain here in winter** qui piove molto in inverno.

3. (means of transport) prendere; **let's ~ a taxi** prendiamo un taxi.

4. (fetch) andare a prendere; **could you ~ me the manager?** (in shop) mi può chiamare il direttore?; (on phone) mi può passare il direttore?

5. (illness) avere, prendere; **I've got a headache** ho mal di testa.

6. (cause to become, do): **to ~ sthg done** (do) fare qc; (have done) far

fare qc; **to ~ sb to do sthg** far fare qc a qn; **I can't ~ it open** non riesco ad aprirlo; **can I ~ my car repaired here?** posso far riparare qui la mia macchina?

7. *(move):* **to ~ sthg in/out** far entrare/uscire qc; **I can't ~ it through the door** non riesco a farlo passare dalla porta.

8. *(understand)* capire; **to ~ a joke** capire una barzelletta.

9. *(time, chance)* avere, trovare; **we didn't ~ the chance to see every-thing** non siamo riusciti a vedere tutto.

10. *(answer):* **I'll ~ it!** *(phone)* rispondo io!; *(door)* vado io!, → **have.**

♦ *vi* 1. *(become)* diventare; **it's get-ting late** si sta facendo tardi; **to ~ bored** annoiarsi; **to ~ ready** prepararsi; **to ~ lost** perdersi; **~ lost!** *(inf)* vattene!

2. *(arrive)* arrivare; **when does the train ~ here?** a che ora arriva il treno?

3. *(go):* **to ~ to/from** andare a/da.

4. *(manage):* **to ~ to do sthg** riuscire a fare qc.

♦ *aux vb:* **to ~ delayed** essere trattenuto; **to ~ killed** essere ucciso.

❑ **get back** *vi (return)* ritornare; **get in** *vi (arrive)* arrivare; *(enter)* entrare; **get into** *vt fus (enter)* entrare in; **to ~ into the car** salire in macchina; **to ~ into bed** mettersi a letto; **to ~ into trouble** mettersi nei guai; **get off** *vi (leave train, bus)* scendere; *(depart)* partire; **get on** *vi (enter train, bus)* salire; *(in rela-tionship)* andare d'accordo; **how are you getting on?** come va la vita?; **get out** *vi (of car, bus, train)* scendere; **get through** *vi (on phone)*

ottenere la comunicazione; **get up** *vi* alzarsi.

get-together *n (inf)* riunione *f*.

ghastly ['gɑ:stlɪ] *adj (inf)* terribi-le.

gherkin ['gɜ:kɪn] *n* cetriolino *m*.

ghetto blaster ['getəʊˌblɑ:stəʳ] *n (inf)* stereo *m* portatile.

ghost [gəʊst] *n* fantasma *m*.

giant ['dʒaɪənt] *adj* gigantesco(-a) ♦ *n (in stories)* gigante *m*.

giblets ['dʒɪblɪts] *npl* rigaglie *fpl*.

giddy ['gɪdɪ] *adj (dizzy):* **I feel ~** mi gira la testa.

gift [gɪft] *n* regalo *m*; *(talent)* talen-to *m*.

gifted ['gɪftɪd] *adj* dotato(-a).

gift shop *n* negozio *m* di artico-li da regalo.

gift voucher *n (Br)* buono *m* acquisto.

gig [gɪg] *n (inf: concert)* concerto *m*.

gigantic [dʒaɪ'gæntɪk] *adj* gigan-tesco(-a).

giggle ['gɪgl] *vi* ridacchiare.

gill [dʒɪl] *n (measurement)* = 0,142 l.

gimmick ['gɪmɪk] *n* trovata *f*.

gin [dʒɪn] *n* gin *m inv*; **~ and tonic** gin tonic.

ginger ['dʒɪndʒəʳ] *n* zenzero *m* ♦ *adj (colour)* rosso(-a).

ginger ale *n* bibita analcolica gas-sata allo zenzero.

ginger beer *n* bibita analcolica allo zenzero.

gingerbread ['dʒɪndʒəbred] *n* torta o biscotto allo zenzero.

gipsy ['dʒɪpsɪ] *n* zingaro *m* (-a *f*).

giraffe [dʒɪ'rɑ:f] *n* giraffa *f*.

girdle ['gɜ:dl] *n* panciera *f*.

girl [gɜ:l] *n (child)* bambina *f*;

(young woman) ragazza f; *(daughter)* femmina f.

girlfriend ['gɜːlfrend] n *(of boy, man)* ragazza f; *(of girl, woman)* amica f.

girl guide n *(Br)* giovane f esploratrice.

girl scout *(Am)* = **girl guide**.

giro ['dʒaɪrəʊ] n *(system)* giroconto m.

give [gɪv] *(pt* **gave**, *pp* **given** ['gɪvn]) vt dare; *(a smile, speech)* fare; *(attention)* prestare; *(time)* dedicare; **to ~ sb sthg** dare qc a qn; *(as present)* regalare qc a qn; **to ~ sthg a push** dare una spinta a qc; **to ~ sb a kiss** dare un bacio a qn; **it took an hour, ~ or take a few minutes** c'è voluta un'ora, minuto più minuto meno; **'~ way'** 'dare la precedenza' ❑ **give away** vt sep *(get rid of)* dare via; *(reveal)* rivelare; **give back** vt sep restituire; **give in** vi arrendersi; **give off** vt fus emettere; **give out** vt sep *(distribute)* distribuire; **give up** vt sep *(cigarettes, chocolate)* rinunciare a; *(seat)* cedere ◆ vi *(admit defeat)* arrendersi; **to ~ up smoking** smettere di fumare.

glacier ['glæsjəʳ] n ghiacciaio m.

glad [glæd] adj contento(-a); **to be ~ to do sthg** essere contento di fare qc.

gladly ['glædlɪ] adv *(willingly)* volentieri.

glamorous ['glæmərəs] adj affascinante.

glance [glɑːns] n sguardo m ◆ vi: **to ~ (at)** dare uno sguardo (a).

gland [glænd] n ghiandola f.

glandular fever ['glændjʊlə-] n mononucleosi f.

glare [gleəʳ] vi *(person)* lanciare sguardi truci; *(sun, light)* abbagliare.

glass [glɑːs] n *(material)* vetro m; *(container, glassful)* bicchiere m ◆ adj di vetro ❑ **glasses** npl occhiali mpl.

glassware ['glɑːsweəʳ] n oggetti mpl in vetro.

glen [glen] n *(Scot)* valle f.

glider ['glaɪdəʳ] n aliante m.

glimpse [glɪmps] vt intravedere.

glitter ['glɪtəʳ] vi luccicare.

global warming [.gləʊbl'wɔːmɪŋ] n effetto m serra.

globe [gləʊb] n globo m; **the ~** *(Earth)* il globo.

gloomy ['gluːmɪ] adj cupo(-a).

glorious ['glɔːrəs] adj *(weather, sight)* magnifico(-a); *(victory, history)* glorioso(-a).

glory ['glɔːrɪ] n gloria f.

gloss [glɒs] n *(shine)* lucido m; ~ *(paint)* vernice f lucida.

glossary ['glɒsərɪ] n glossario m.

glossy ['glɒsɪ] adj *(magazine)* patinato(-a); *(photo)* lucido(-a).

glove [glʌv] n guanto m.

glove compartment n vano m portaoggetti.

glow [gləʊ] n barlume m ◆ vi brillare.

glucose ['gluːkəʊs] n glucosio m.

glue [gluː] n colla f ◆ vt incollare.

gnat [næt] n pappataci m inv.

gnaw [nɔː] vt rosicchiare.

go [gəʊ] *(pt* **went**, *pp* **gone**, *pl* **goes**) vi 1. *(move, travel, attend)* andare; **to ~ home** andare a casa; **to ~ to Italy** andare in Italia; **to ~ by bus** andare con l'autobus; **to ~ to school** andare a scuola; **to ~ for**

a **walk** andare a fare una passeggiata; **to ~ and do sthg** andare a fare qc; **to ~ shopping** andare a fare spesa.

2. *(leave)* andarsene; *(bus, train)* partire; **it's time to ~** è ora d'andare; **~ away!** vattene!

3. *(become)* diventare; **she went pale** è impallidita; **the milk has gone sour** il latte è inacidito.

4. *(expressing future tense)*: **to be going to do sthg** stare per fare qc; *(intend to do)* avere intenzione di fare qc; **I'm going to be sick** sto per vomitare; **I'm going to phone them tonight** ho intenzione di chiamarli stasera.

5. *(function)* funzionare; **the car won't ~** la macchina non parte.

6. *(stop working)* rompersi; **the fuse has gone** è saltato il fusibile.

7. *(time)* passare.

8. *(progress)* andare; **to ~ well** andar bene.

9. *(bell, alarm)* suonare.

10. *(match, be appropriate)*: **to ~ (with)** andare (con).

11. *(be sold)* essere venduto(-a); **'everything must ~'** 'svendita totale'.

12. *(fit)* entrare.

13. *(lead)* andare, portare; **where does this path ~?** dove porta questo sentiero?

14. *(belong)* andare.

15. *(in phrases)*: **to let ~ of sthg** *(drop)* lasciare (andare) qc; **to ~** *(Am: to take away)* da asportare; **there are only three weeks to ~** mancano solo tre settimane.

◆ *n* **1.** *(turn)* turno *m*; **it's your ~** tocca a te.

2. *(attempt)* prova *f*, tentativo *m*; **to have a ~ at sthg** provare qc; **'50p a**

~' *(in game)* '50 pence a partita'.

❑ **go ahead** *vi (take place)* aver luogo; **~ ahead!** fai pure!; **go back** *vi (return)* ritornare; **go down** *vi (decrease)* abbassarsi, scendere; *(sun)* tramontare; *(tyre)* sgonfiarsi; **go down with** *vt fus (inf: illness)* prendere; **go in** *vi (enter)* entrare; **go off** *vi (alarm, bell)* suonare; *(go bad)* andare a male; *(lights, heating)* spegnersi; **go on** *vi (happen)* succedere; *(lights, heating)* accendersi; *(continue)* continuare; **to ~ on doing sthg** continuare a fare qc; **go out** *vi (leave house)* uscire; *(light, fire, cigarette)* spegnersi; *(have relationship)*: **to ~ out (with sb)** stare insieme (a qn); **to ~ out for a meal** andare a mangiare fuori; **go over** *vt fus (check)* controllare; **go round** *vi (revolve)* girare; *(be enough)* bastare per tutti; **go through** *vt fus (experience)* passare; *(spend)* spendere; *(search)* esaminare; **go up** *vi (increase)* aumentare; **go without** *vt fus* fare a meno di.

goal [gəʊl] *n (posts)* porta *f*; *(point scored)* goal *m inv*; *(aim)* scopo *m*.

goalkeeper ['gəʊl,ki:pə^r] *n* portiere *m*.

goalpost ['gəʊlpəʊst] *n* palo *m*.

goat [gəʊt] *n* capra *f*.

gob [gɒb] *n (Br: inf: mouth)* bocca *f*.

god [gɒd] *n* dio *m* ❑ **God** *n* Dio *m*.

goddaughter ['gɒd,dɔ:tə^r] *n* figlioccia *f*.

godfather ['gɒd,fɑ:ðə^r] *n* padrino *m*.

godmother ['gɒd,mʌðə^r] *n* madrina *f*.

gods [gɒdz] *npl*: **the ~** *(Br: inf: in*

theatre) il loggione.

godson ['gɒdsʌn] *n* figlioccio *m*.

goes [gəʊz] → **go**.

goggles ['gɒglz] *npl (for swimming)* occhialini *mpl*; *(for skiing)* occhiali *mpl* da neve.

going ['gəʊɪŋ] *adj (available)* disponibile; **the ~ rate** la tariffa corrente.

go-kart [-kɑːt] *n* go-kart *m inv*.

gold [gəʊld] *n* oro *m* ♦ *adj* d'oro.

goldfish ['gəʊldfɪʃ] *(pl inv) n* pesce *m* rosso.

gold-plated [-'pleɪtɪd] *adj* placcato(-a) d'oro.

golf [gɒlf] *n* golf *m*.

golf ball *n* pallina *f* da golf.

golf club *n (place)* circolo *m* del golf; *(piece of equipment)* mazza *f* da golf.

golf course *n* campo *m* di golf.

golfer ['gɒlfəʳ] *n* golfista *mf*.

gone [gɒn] *pp* → **go** ♦ *prep (Br: past)*: **it's ~ ten** sono le dieci passate.

good [gʊd] *(compar* **better,** *superl* **best)** *adj* buono(-a); *(enjoyable)* bello(-a); *(skilled, well-behaved)* bravo(-a); *(kind)* gentile **• n** bene *m*; **the weather's ~** fa bel tempo; **to have a ~ time** divertirsi; **to be ~ at sthg** saper fare qc bene; **a ~ ten minutes** dieci minuti buoni; **in ~ time** in anticipo; **to make ~ sthg** compensare qc; **for ~** per sempre; **for the ~ of** per il bene di; **to do sb ~** far bene a qn; **it's no ~** *(there's no point)* è inutile; **~ afternoon!** buon giorno!; **~ evening!** buona sera!; **~ morning!** buon giorno!; **~ night!** buona notte! ❑ **goods** *npl* merce *f*.

goodbye [gʊd'baɪ] *excl* arrivederci!

Good Friday *n* Venerdì *m* Santo.

good-looking [-'lʊkɪŋ] *adj* attraente.

goods train [gʊdz-] *n* treno *m* merci.

goose [guːs] *(pl* **geese)** *n* oca *f*.

gooseberry ['gʊzbərɪ] *n* uva *f* spina.

gorge [gɔːdʒ] *n* gola *f*.

gorgeous ['gɔːdʒəs] *adj* stupendo(-a).

gorilla [gə'rɪlə] *n* gorilla *m inv*.

gossip ['gɒsɪp] *n (about someone)* pettegolezzi *mpl* ♦ *vi (about someone)* fare pettegolezzi; *(chat)* chiacchierare; **to have a ~** chiacchierare.

gossip column *n* cronaca *f* rosa.

got [gɒt] *pt & pp* → **get**.

gotten ['gɒtn] *pp (Am)* → **get**.

goujons ['guːdʒɒnz] *npl (of fish)* frittelle *fpl*.

goulash ['guːlæʃ] *n* gulasch *m inv*.

gourmet ['gʊəmeɪ] *n* buongustaio *m (-a f)* ♦ *adj* per intenditori.

govern ['gʌvən] *vt (country, city)* governare.

government ['gʌvnmənt] *n* governo *m*.

gown [gaʊn] *n (dress)* abito *m* lungo.

GP *abbr* = **general practitioner**.

grab [græb] *vt (take hold of)* afferrare.

graceful ['greɪsfʊl] *adj (elegant)* aggraziato(-a).

grade [greɪd] *n (quality)* categoria *f*; *(in exam)* voto *m*; *(Am: year at school)* classe *f*.

gradient ['greɪdjənt] n pendenza f.

gradual ['grædʒʊəl] adj graduale.

gradually ['grædʒʊəlɪ] adv gradualmente.

graduate [n 'grædʒʊət, vb 'grædʒʊeɪt] n (from university) laureato m (-a f); (Am: from high school) diplomato m (-a f) ♦ vi (from university) laurearsi; (Am: from high school) diplomarsi.

graduation [ˌgrædʒʊ'eɪʃn] n (ceremony at university) consegna f delle lauree; (Am: ceremony at school) consegna dei diplomi.

graffiti [grə'fiːtɪ] n graffiti mpl.

grain [greɪn] n (seed) chicco m; (crop) cereali mpl; (of sand, salt) granello m.

gram [græm] n grammo m.

grammar ['græmər] n grammatica f.

grammar school n (in UK) scuola secondaria più selettiva e tradizionale delle altre.

gramme [græm] = **gram**.

gramophone ['græməfəʊn] n grammofono m.

gran [græn] n (Br: inf) nonna f.

grand [grænd] adj (impressive) grandioso(-a) ♦ n (inf) (£1,000) mille sterline fpl; ($1,000) mille dollari mpl.

grandad ['grændæd] n (inf) nonno m.

grandchild ['græntʃaɪld] n (pl -children [-ˌtʃɪldrən]) n nipote mf.

granddaughter ['grænˌdɔːtər] n nipote f.

grandfather ['grændˌfɑːðər] n nonno m.

grandma ['grænmɑː] n (inf)

nonna f.

grandmother ['grænˌmʌðər] n nonna f.

grandpa ['grænpɑː] n (inf) nonno m.

grandparents ['grænˌpeərənts] npl nonni mpl.

grandson ['grænsʌn] n nipote m.

granite ['grænɪt] n granito m.

granny ['grænɪ] n (inf) nonna f.

grant [grɑːnt] n (POL) sovvenzione f; (for university) borsa f di studio ♦ vt (fml: give) concedere; **to take sthg for ~ed** dare qc per scontato; **to take sb for ~ed** pensare di poter sempre contare su qn.

grapefruit ['greɪpfruːt] n pompelmo m.

grapefruit juice n succo m di pompelmo.

grapes [greɪps] npl uva f.

graph [grɑːf] n grafico m.

graph paper n carta f millimetrata.

grasp [grɑːsp] vt afferrare.

grass [grɑːs] n (plant) erba f; (lawn) prato m; **'keep off the ~'** 'non calpestare il prato'.

grasshopper ['grɑːsˌhɒpər] n cavalletta f.

grate [greɪt] n grata f.

grated ['greɪtɪd] adj grattugiato(-a).

grateful ['greɪtfʊl] adj (person) grato(-a).

grater ['greɪtər] n grattugia f.

gratitude ['grætɪtjuːd] n gratitudine f.

gratuity [grə'tjuːɪtɪ] n (fml) mancia f.

grave¹ [greɪv] adj (mistake, news, concern) grave ♦ n tomba f.

grave² [grɑːv] *adj* (*accent*) grave.

gravel ['grævl] *n* ghiaia *f*.

graveyard ['greɪvjɑːd] *n* cimitero *m*.

gravity ['grævətɪ] *n* gravità *f*.

gravy ['greɪvɪ] *n* salsa ottenuta dal sugo di carne arrosto e resa più densa con della farina.

gray [greɪ] (*Am*) = **grey**.

graze [greɪz] *vt* (*injure*) scorticare, escoriare.

grease [griːs] *n* (*for machine*) olio *m*, lubrificante *m*; (*animal fat*) grasso *m*.

greaseproof paper ['griːspruːf-] *n* (*Br*) carta *f* oleata.

greasy ['griːsɪ] *adj* (*food, skin, hair*) grasso(-a); (*tools, clothes*) unto(-a).

great [greɪt] *adj* grande; (*very good*) eccellente, fantastico(-a); (that's) ~! fantastico!

Great Britain *n* la Gran Bretagna.

ⓘ GREAT BRITAIN

La Gran Bretagna è un'isola che comprende l'Inghilterra, la Scozia e il Galles. Non va confusa con il Regno Unito, che include l'Irlanda del Nord, o con le Isole Britanniche, di cui fanno parte anche la Repubblica d'Irlanda, l'Isola di Man, le Orcadi, le Shetlands e le Isole della Manica.

---

great-grandfather *n* bisnonno *m*.

great-grandmother *n* bisnonna *f*.

greatly ['greɪtlɪ] *adv* molto.

Greece [griːs] *n* la Grecia.

greed [griːd] *n* avidità *f*.

greedy ['griːdɪ] *adj* avido(-a).

Greek [griːk] *adj* greco(-a) ♦ *n* (*person*) greco *m* (-a *f*); (*language*) greco *m*.

Greek salad *n* insalata *f* greca (a base di pomodori, cetriolo, formaggio greco e olive nere).

green [griːn] *adj* verde; (*environmentalist*) ambientalista; (*inf: inexperienced*) inesperto(-a) ♦ *n* (*colour*) verde *m*; (*in village*) prato *m* pubblico; (*on golf course*) green *m inv* ❑ **greens** *npl* (*vegetables*) verdura *f*.

green beans *npl* fagiolini *mpl*.

green card *n* (*Br: for car*) carta *f* verde; (*Am: work permit*) permesso *m* di soggiorno.

green channel *n* uscita di porto o aeroporto riservata ai passeggeri che non hanno niente da dichiarare.

greengage ['griːngeɪdʒ] *n* susina *f* Regina Claudia.

greengrocer's ['griːngrəʊsəz] *n* (*shop*) negozio *m* di frutta e verdura.

greenhouse ['griːnhaʊs, *pl* -haʊzɪz] *n* serra *f*.

greenhouse effect *n* effetto *m* serra.

green light *n* (*go-ahead*): **to give sb the ~** dare il via libera a qn.

green pepper *n* peperone *m* verde.

Greens [griːnz] *npl*: **the ~** i Verdi.

green salad *n* insalata *f* verde.

greet [griːt] *vt* (*say hello to*) salutare.

greeting ['griːtɪŋ] *n* saluto *m*.

grenade [grə'neɪd] *n* granata *f*.

grew [gruː] *pt* → **grow**.

grey [greɪ] *adj* grigio(-a) ◆ *n* grigio *m*; **to go ~** diventar grigio.

greyhound ['greɪhaʊnd] *n* levriero *m*.

grid [grɪd] *n* (*grating*) grata *f*; (*on map etc*) reticolato *m*.

grief [gri:f] *n* dolore *m*; **to come to ~** (*plan*) naufragare; (*person*) finire male.

grieve [gri:v] *vi* affliggersi.

grill [grɪl] *n* (*on cooker*) grill *m inv*; (*for open fire*) griglia *f*; (*part of restaurant*) area di un ristorante dove si cucina alla griglia ◆ *vt* cuocere ai ferri OR alla griglia.

grille [grɪl] *n* (AUT) griglia *f*.

grilled [grɪld] *adj* alla griglia, ai ferri.

grim [grɪm] *adj* (*expression*) severo(-a); (*place*) lugubre; (*news*) triste.

grimace ['grɪməs] *n* smorfia *f*.

grimy ['graɪmɪ] *adj* sudicio(-a).

grin [grɪn] *n* (gran) sorriso *m* ◆ *vi* fare un gran sorriso.

grind [graɪnd] (*pt & pp* **ground**) *vt* (*pepper, coffee*) macinare.

grip [grɪp] *n* (*hold*) presa *f*; (*of tyres*) tenuta *f* di strada; (*handle*) impugnatura *f*; (*bag*) borsa *f* da viaggio ◆ *vt* (*hold*) afferrare.

gristle ['grɪsl] *n* cartilagine *f*.

groan [grəʊn] *n* lamento *m* ◆ *vi* lamentarsi.

groceries ['grəʊsərɪz] *npl* generi *mpl* alimentari.

grocer's ['grəʊsəz] *n* (*shop*) drogheria *f*.

grocery ['grəʊsərɪ] *n* (*shop*) drogheria *f*.

groin [grɔɪn] *n* inguine *m*.

groove [gru:v] *n* solco *m*.

grope [grəʊp] *vi* andare a tastoni; **to ~ for sthg** cercare qc a tastoni.

gross [grəʊs] *adj* (*weight, income*) lordo(-a).

grossly ['grəʊslɪ] *adv* (*extremely*) estremamente.

grotty ['grɒtɪ] *adj* (Br: *inf*) squallido(-a).

ground [graʊnd] *pt & pp* → **grind** ◆ *n* (*surface of earth*) terra *f*; (*soil*) terreno *m*; (SPORT) campo *m* ◆ *adj* (*coffee*) macinato(-a) ◆ *vt* (Am: *electrical connection*) mettere a terra; **to be ~ed** (*plane*) essere trattenuto a terra; **on the ~** a OR per terra ☐ **grounds** *npl* (*of building*) terreni *mpl*; (*of coffee*) fondi *mpl*; (*reason*) motivo *m*, ragione *f*.

ground floor *n* pianterreno *m*.

groundsheet ['graʊndʃi:t] *n* telo *m* impermeabile.

group [gru:p] *n* gruppo *m*.

grouse [graʊs] (*pl inv*) *n* (*bird*) gallo *m* cedrone.

grovel ['grɒvl] *vi* (*be humble*) umiliarsi.

grow [grəʊ] (*pt* **grew**, *pp* **grown**) *vi* (*person, animal, plant*) crescere; (*fears, traffic*) aumentare; (*company, city*) espandersi; (*become*) diventare ◆ *vt* (*plant, crop*) coltivare; (*beard*) farsi crescere; **to ~ old** invecchiare ☐ **grow up** *vi* crescere, diventare grande.

growl [graʊl] *vi* (*dog*) ringhiare.

grown [grəʊn] *pp* → **grow**.

grown-up *adj* adulto(-a) ◆ *n* adulto *m* (-a *f*).

growth [grəʊθ] *n* (*increase*) crescita *f*; (MED) tumore *m*.

grub [grʌb] *n* (*inf: food*) cibo *m*.

grubby ['grʌbɪ] *adj* (*inf*) sporco(-a).

grudge [grʌdʒ] n rancore m ◆ vt: **to ~ sb sthg** invidiare qc a qn.

grueling ['gruəlɪŋ] (Am) = **gruelling**.

gruelling ['gruəlɪŋ] adj (Br) estenuante.

gruesome ['gru:səm] adj raccapricciante.

grumble ['grʌmbl] vi (complain) lagnarsi.

grumpy ['grʌmpɪ] adj (inf) scorbutico(-a).

grunt [grʌnt] vi grugnire.

guarantee [ˌgærən'ti:] n garanzia f ◆ vt garantire.

guard [gɑ:d] n (of prisoner etc) guardia f; (Br: on train) capotreno mf; (protective cover) schermo m di protezione ◆ vt (watch over) sorvegliare; **to be on one's ~** stare in guardia.

guess [ges] n supposizione f ◆ vt & vi indovinare; **I ~ (so)** penso di sì; **have a ~!** indovina!

guest [gest] n (in home) ospite mf; (in hotel) cliente mf.

guesthouse ['gesthaus, pl -hauzɪz] n pensione f.

guestroom ['gestrum] n camera f degli ospiti.

guidance ['gaɪdəns] n guida f, direzione f.

guide [gaɪd] n guida f ◆ vt guidare □ **Guide** n (Br) giovane esploratrice f.

guidebook ['gaɪdbuk] n guida f.

guide dog n cane m guida.

guided tour ['gaɪdɪd-] n visita f guidata.

guidelines ['gaɪdlaɪnz] npl direttive fpl.

guilt [gɪlt] n colpa f.

guilty ['gɪltɪ] adj colpevole; **to feel ~** sentirsi in colpa.

guinea pig ['gɪnɪ-] n cavia f.

guitar [gɪ'tɑ:ʳ] n chitarra f.

guitarist [gɪ'tɑ:rɪst] n chitarrista mf.

gulf [gʌlf] n (of sea) golfo m.

Gulf War n: **the ~** la guerra del Golfo.

gull [gʌl] n gabbiano m.

gullible ['gʌləbl] adj credulone(-a).

gulp [gʌlp] n (of drink) sorso m.

gum [gʌm] n gomma f da masticare; (adhesive) colla f □ **gums** npl gengive fpl.

gun [gʌn] n (pistol) pistola f; (rifle) fucile m; (cannon) cannone m.

gunfire ['gʌnfaɪəʳ] n sparatoria f.

gunshot ['gʌnʃɒt] n sparo m.

gust [gʌst] n (of wind) raffica f.

gut [gʌt] n (inf: stomach) stomaco m □ **guts** npl (inf) (intestines) budella fpl; (courage): **to have ~s** avere fegato.

gutter ['gʌtəʳ] n (beside road) cunetta f; (of house) grondaia f.

guy [gaɪ] n (inf: man) tipo m □ **guys** npl (Am: inf: people) gente f.

Guy Fawkes Night [-'fɔ:ks-] n festa che si celebra il 5 novembre per ricordare il fallimento della Congiura delle polveri.

---

i | **GUY FAWKES NIGHT**

Chiamata anche "Bonfire Night" (la notte dei falò), questa festa viene celebrata il 5 novembre di ogni anno con falò e fuochi artificiali, e segna l'anniversario della scoperta della Congiura delle polveri, complotto di ispirazione cattolica il cui obiettivo era l'uccisione di re Giacomo I e la distruzione del Parlamento britannico (1605). Per l'occasione i bambini realizzano dei pupazzi raffiguranti Guy Fawkes, uno dei cospiratori, con i quali girano per le strade chiedendo soldi ai passanti. La sera, poi, i pupazzi vengono messi in cima ai falò e bruciati.

guy rope n cavo m.

gym [dʒɪm] n palestra f, (school lesson) ginnastica f.

gymnast ['dʒɪmnæst] n ginnasta mf.

gymnastics [dʒɪm'næstɪks] n ginnastica f.

gym shoes npl scarpe fpl da ginnastica.

gynaecologist [ˌgaɪnə'kɒlədʒɪst] n ginecologo m (-a f).

gypsy ['dʒɪpsɪ] = gipsy.

H

H (abbr of hospital) H ◆ abbr = hot.

habit ['hæbɪt] n (custom) abitudine f.

hacksaw ['hæksɔː] n seghetto m.

had [hæd] pt & pp → have.

haddock ['hædək] (pl inv) n eglefino m (pesce simile al merluzzo).

hadn't ['hædnt] = had not.

haggis ['hægɪs] n piatto tipico scozzese a base di avena e frattaglie di pecora.

haggle ['hægl] vi mercanteggiare.

hail [heɪl] n grandine f ◆ v impers grandinare.

hailstone ['heɪlstəun] n chicco m di grandine.

hair [heəʳ] n (on head) capelli mpl; (on animal) pelo m; (on human skin) peli mpl; (individual hair on head) capello m; (individual hair on skin) pelo m; to have one's ~ cut tagliarsi i capelli.

hairband ['heəbænd] n cerchietto m per capelli.

hairbrush ['heəbrʌʃ] n spazzola f per capelli.

hairclip ['heəklɪp] n fermaglio m per capelli.

haircut ['heəkʌt] n (style) taglio m di capelli; to have a ~ farsi tagliare i capelli.

hairdo ['heəduː] (pl -s) n acconciatura f, pettinatura f.

hairdresser ['heəˌdresəʳ] n parrucchiere m (-a f); ~'s (salon) negozio m di parrucchiere; to go to the ~'s andare dal parrucchiere.

hairdryer ['heəˌdraɪəʳ] n asciugacapelli m inv, föhn m inv.

hair gel n gel m inv per capelli, gommina f.

hairgrip ['heəgrɪp] n (Br) molletta f (per capelli).

hairnet ['heənet] n retina f (per capelli).

hairpin bend ['heəpɪn-] n tornante m.

hair remover [-rɪˌmuːvəʳ] n crema f depilatoria.

hair rollers [-'rəʊləz] npl bigodini mpl.

hair slide n fermacapelli m inv.

hairspray ['heəspreɪ] n lacca f per capelli.

hairstyle ['heəstaɪl] n acconciatura f, pettinatura f.

hairy ['heərɪ] adj (person, chest,
legs) peloso(-a).

half [Br hɑːf, Am hæf] (pl **halves**) n
metà f inv; (of match) tempo m; (half
pint) mezza pinta f; (child's ticket)
biglietto m ridotto ♦ adj mezzo(-a)
♦ adv: ~ **cooked** cotto a metà; ~
full mezzo pieno; **I'm** ~ **Scottish**
per metà sono scozzese; **a day and
a** ~ un giorno e mezzo; **four and a**
~ quattro e mezzo; ~ **past seven**
sette e mezza; ~ **as big as** la metà
di; **an hour and a** ~ un'ora e
mezza; ~ **an hour** mezz'ora; ~ **a
dozen** mezza dozzina; ~ **price** a
metà prezzo.

half board n mezza pensione
f.

half-day n mezza giornata f.

half fare n mezza tariffa f.

half portion n mezza porzione f.

half-price adj a metà prezzo.

half term n (Br) vacanza a metà
trimestre.

half time n intervallo m.

halfway [hɑːfˈweɪ] adv (in space) a
metà strada; (in time) a metà.

halibut ['hælɪbət] (pl inv) n halibut m inv.

hall [hɔːl] n (of house) ingresso m;
(large room, building) sala f, salone
m; (country house) maniero m.

hallmark ['hɔːlmɑːk] n (on silver,
gold) marchio m.

hallo [həˈləʊ] = **hello**.

hall of residence n casa f
dello studente.

Halloween [ˌhæləʊˈiːn] n vigilia f
d'Ognissanti.

Il 31 ottobre, la vigilia di
Ognissanti, è, secondo la tradizione popolare, la notte dei fantasmi e delle streghe. In questa occasione i bambini giocano a "trick or
treat", gioco che consiste nel recarsi
mascherati a casa dei vicini minac-
ciandoli di far loro uno scherzo
("trick") se questi non regalano loro
soldi, caramelle o frutta (il "treat").
Altra tradizione associata alla cele-
brazione di Halloween sia in Gran
Bretagna che negli Stati Uniti sono le
lanterne di zucca, ottenute svuotan-
do e intagliando un viso in grandi
zucche gialle, all'interno delle quali
vengono poste delle candele.

---

halt [hɔːlt] vi fermarsi ♦ n: **to
come to a** ~ fermarsi.

halve [Br hɑːv, Am hæv] vt dimezzare.

halves [Br hɑːvz, Am hævz] pl →
half.

ham [hæm] n (meat) prosciutto m
(cotto).

hamburger ['hæmbɜːgəʳ] n
(beefburger) hamburger m inv; (Am:
mince) carne f macinata.

hamlet ['hæmlɪt] n paesino m.

hammer ['hæməʳ] n martello m
♦ vt (nail) piantare.

hammock ['hæmək] n amaca f.

hamper ['hæmpəʳ] n cesta f.

hamster ['hæmstəʳ] n criceto m.

hamstring ['hæmstrɪŋ] n tendine m del ginocchio.

hand [hænd] n mano f; (of clock,
watch, dial) lancetta f; **to give sb a**
~ dare una mano a qn; **to get out**

of ~ sfuggire di mano; **by ~ a mano; in ~** *(time)* a disposizione; **on the one ~** da una parte; **on the other ~** d'altra parte ◻ **hand in** vt sep consegnare; **hand out** vt sep distribuire; **hand over** vt sep *(give)* consegnare.

handbag ['hændbæg] n borsetta f.

handbasin ['hændbeisn] n lava-bo m.

handbook ['hændbuk] n ma-nuale m.

handbrake ['hændbreik] n freno a mano.

hand cream n crema f per le mani.

handcuffs ['hændkʌfs] npl ma-nette fpl.

handful ['hændful] n *(amount)* manciata f.

handicap ['hændikæp] n handi-cap m inv.

handicapped ['hændikæpt] adj handicappato(-a) ◆ npl: **the ~** i portatori di handicap.

handkerchief ['hæŋkətʃif] *(pl* **-chiefs** OR **-chieves** [-tʃi:vz]) n faz-zoletto m.

handle ['hændl] n *(of door, window)* maniglia f; *(of knife, pan, suit-case)* manico m ◆ vt *(touch)* toccare; *(deal with)* occuparsi di; **'~ with care'** 'fragile'.

handlebars ['hændlbɑːz] npl manubrio m.

hand luggage n bagaglio m a mano.

handmade [,hænd'meid] adj fatto(-a) a mano.

handout ['hændaut] n *(leaflet)* volantino m.

handrail ['hændreil] n corri-

mano m.

handset ['hændset] n ricevitore m; **'please replace the ~'** 'si prega di riporre il ricevitore'.

handshake ['hændʃeik] n stretta f di mano.

handsome ['hænsəm] adj *(man)* bello(-a).

handstand ['hændstænd] n ver-ticale f.

handwriting ['hænd,raitiŋ] n calligrafia f.

handy ['hændi] adj *(useful)* utile; *(convenient)* comodo(-a); *(good with one's hands)* abile; *(near)* vicino(-a), a portata di mano; **to come in ~** *(inf)* tornare utile.

hang [hæŋ] *(pt & pp* **hung)** vt appendere; *(execute: pt & pp* **hanged)** impiccare ◆ vi *(be suspend-ed)* penzolare, pèndere ◆ n: **to get the ~ of sthg** fare la mano a qc ◻ **hang about** vi *(Br: inf)* ciondola-re; **hang around** *(inf)* = **hang about; hang down** vi penzolare; **hang on** vi *(inf: wait)* aspettare; **hang out** vt sep *(washing)* stendere ◆ vi *(inf)* stare; **hang up** vi *(on phone)* riagganciare.

hangar ['hæŋəʳ] n hangar m inv.

hanger ['hæŋəʳ] n gruccia f, stampella f.

hang gliding n deltaplano m.

hangover ['hæŋ,əuvəʳ] n postu-mi mpl di sbornia.

hankie ['hæŋki] n *(inf)* fazzolet-to m.

happen ['hæpən] vi succedere, accadere; **I ~ed to catch sight of him** mi è capitato di vederlo.

happily ['hæpili] adv *(luckily)* for-tunatamente.

happiness ['hæpinis] n felicità f.

happy ['hæpɪ] *adj* felice; **to be ~ about sthg** essere contento(-a) di qc; **to be ~ to do sthg** *(willing)* fare qc volentieri; **to be ~ with sthg** essere soddisfatto di qc; **Happy Birthday!** buon compleanno!; **Happy Christmas!** buon Natale!; **Happy New Year!** buon anno!

happy hour *n (inf)* momento della giornata, di solito nel tardo pomeriggio, in cui, nei bar, le bevande vengono vendute a prezzo ridotto.

harassment ['hærəsmənt] *n* molestie *fpl*.

harbor ['hɑːbər] *(Am)* = **harbour**.

harbour ['hɑːbər] *n (Br)* porto *m*.

hard [hɑːd] *adj* duro(-a); *(difficult)* difficile; *(strenuous)* faticoso(-a); *(forceful)* forte; *(winter, frost)* rigido(-a); *(drugs)* pesante ◆ *adv (work)* duro; *(listen)* attentamente; *(hit)* con forza; *(rain)* a dirotto.

hardback ['hɑːdbæk] *n* edizione *f* rilegata.

hardboard ['hɑːdbɔːd] *n* pannello *m* di legno compresso.

hard-boiled egg [-bɔɪld-] *n* uovo *m* sodo.

hard disk *n* hard disk *m inv*, disco *m* rigido.

hardly ['hɑːdlɪ] *adv* a malapena, appena; **~ ever** quasi mai.

hardship ['hɑːdʃɪp] *n (difficult conditions)* privazioni *fpl*; *(difficult circumstance)* avversità *fpl*.

hard shoulder *n (Br)* corsia *f* d'emergenza.

hard up *adj (inf)* in bolletta.

hardware ['hɑːdweər] *n (tools, equipment)* ferramenta *fpl*; *(COMPUT)* hardware *m*.

hardwearing [,hɑːd'weərɪŋ] *adj*

(Br) resistente.

hardworking [,hɑːd'wɜːkɪŋ] *adj* instancabile.

hare [heər] *n* lepre *f*.

harm [hɑːm] *n (injury)* male *m*; *(damage)* danno *m* ◆ *vt (injure)* far male a; *(damage)* danneggiare.

harmful ['hɑːmful] *adj* nocivo(-a).

harmless ['hɑːmlɪs] *adj* innocuo(-a).

harmonica [hɑː'mɒnɪkə] *n* armonica *f*.

harmony ['hɑːmənɪ] *n* armonia *f*.

harness ['hɑːnɪs] *n (for horse)* finimenti *mpl*; *(for child)* briglie *fpl*.

harp [hɑːp] *n* arpa *f*.

harsh [hɑːʃ] *adj (weather)* rigido(-a); *(conditions)* duro(-a); *(cruel)* severo(-a); *(sound)* sgradevole.

harvest ['hɑːvɪst] *n (of corn, fruit)* raccolto *m*; *(of grapes)* vendemmia *f*.

has [weak form həz, strong form hæz] → **have**.

hash browns [hæʃ-] *npl (Am)* frittelle *fpl* di patate.

hasn't ['hæznt] = **has not**.

hassle ['hæsl] *n (inf: problem)* seccatura *f*.

hastily ['heɪstɪlɪ] *adv (rashly)* precipitosamente.

hasty ['heɪstɪ] *adj (hurried)* affrettato(-a); *(rash)* precipitoso(-a).

hat [hæt] *n* cappello *m*.

hatch [hætʃ] *n (for food)* passavivande *m inv* ◆ *vi (egg)* schiudersi.

hatchback ['hætʃ,bæk] *n (car)* tre OR cinque porte *f inv*.

hatchet ['hætʃɪt] *n* accetta *f*.

hate [heɪt] *n* odio *m* ◆ *vt* odiare

detestare; **to ~ doing sthg** detestare fare qc.

hatred ['heɪtrɪd] *n* odio *m*.

haul [hɔ:l] *vt* trascinare ♦ *n*: **a long ~** un percorso lungo e faticoso.

haunted ['hɔ:ntɪd] *adj (house)* abitato(-a) da fantasmi.

have [hæv] (*pt & pp* **had**) *aux vb* 1. *(to form perfect tenses: gen)* avere; *(with many intransitive verbs)* essere; **I ~ finished** ho finito; **~ you been there? — no, I haven't** ci sei stato? – no; **the train had already gone** il treno era già partito.

2. *(must)*: **to ~ (got) to do sthg** dover fare qc; **do you ~ to pay?** si deve pagare?

♦ *vt* 1. *(possess)*: **to ~ (got)** avere; **do you ~ OR ~ you got a double room?** avete una camera doppia?; **she has (got) brown hair** ha i capelli castani.

2. *(experience)* avere; **to ~ a cold** avere il raffreddore; **we had a great time** ci siamo divertiti un mondo.

3. *(replacing other verbs)*: **to ~ breakfast** fare colazione; **to ~ dinner** cenare; **to ~ lunch** pranzare; **to ~ a drink** bere qualcosa; **to ~ a shower** fare una doccia; **to ~ a swim** fare una nuotata; **to ~ a walk** fare una passeggiata.

4. *(cause to be)*: **to ~ sthg done** far fare qc; **to ~ one's hair cut** farsi tagliare i capelli.

5. *(be treated in a certain way)*: **I've had my wallet stolen** mi hanno rubato il portafoglio.

haversack ['hævəsæk] *n* zaino *m*.

havoc ['hævək] *n* caos *m*.

hawk [hɔ:k] *n* falco *m*.

hawker ['hɔ:kə^r] *n* venditore *m*

(-trice *f*) ambulante.

hay [heɪ] *n* fieno *m*.

hay fever *n* raffreddore *m* da fieno.

haystack ['heɪˌstæk] *n* pagliaio *m*.

hazard ['hæzəd] *n* rischio *m*, pericolo *m*.

hazardous ['hæzədəs] *adj* rischioso(-a), pericoloso(-a).

hazard warning lights *npl* *(Br)* luci *fpl* di emergenza.

haze [heɪz] *n* foschia *f*.

hazel ['heɪzl] *adj* nocciola *(inv)*.

hazelnut ['heɪzlˌnʌt] *n* nocciola *f*.

hazy ['heɪzɪ] *adj (misty)* offuscato(-a).

he [hi:] *pron* lui, egli; **~'s tall** è alto.

head [hed] *n (of body)* testa *f*, capo *m*; *(of queue, page, bed)* cima *f*; *(of company, department, table)* capo *m*; *(head teacher of primary or lower secondary school)* direttore *m* (-trice *f*) di scuola; *(head teacher of upper secondary school)* preside *mf*; *(of beer)* schiuma *f* ♦ *vt (list)* essere in testa a; *(organization)* dirigere, essere a capo di ♦ *vi* dirigersi; **£10 a ~** 10 sterline a testa; **~s or tails?** testa o croce? ❑ **head for** *vt fus* dirigersi verso OR a.

headache ['hedeɪk] *n (pain)* mal *m* di testa; **to have a ~** avere mal di testa.

heading ['hedɪŋ] *n* intestazione *f*.

headlamp ['hedlæmp] *(Br)* = **headlight**.

headlight ['hedlaɪt] *n* fanale *m* anteriore.

headline ['hedlaɪn] n (in news-paper) titolo m; (on TV, radio) notizie fpl principali.

headmaster [,hed'mɑːstəʳ] n (of primary or lower secondary school) direttore m di scuola; (of upper secondary school) preside m.

headmistress [,hed'mɪstrɪs] n (of primary or lower secondary school) direttrice f di scuola; (of upper secondary school) preside f.

head of state n capo m di Stato.

headphones ['hedfəʊnz] npl cuffie fpl.

headquarters [,hed'kwɔːtəz] npl (of company, bank) sede f centrale; (of police, army) quartiere m generale.

headrest ['hedrest] n poggiatesta m inv.

headroom ['hedrʊm] n (under bridge) altezza f massima.

headscarf ['hedskɑːf] (pl -scarves [-skɑːvz]) n foulard m inv.

head start n vantaggio m.

head teacher n (of primary or lower secondary school) direttore m (-trice f) di scuola; (of upper secondary school) preside mf.

head waiter n capocameriere m.

heal [hiːl] vt curare ♦ vi guarire.

health [helθ] n salute f; to be in good ~ essere in buona salute; to be in poor ~ essere in cattive condizioni di salute; your (very) good ~! alla tua salute!

health centre n centro m sanitario.

health food n cibo m naturale.

health food shop n negozio m di prodotti naturali.

health insurance n assicurazione f contro le malattie.

healthy ['helθɪ] adj sano(-a).

heap [hiːp] n mucchio m; ~s of (inf) un mucchio di.

hear [hɪəʳ] (pt & pp heard [hɜːd]) vt sentire; (case, evidence) esaminare ♦ vi sentire; to ~ about sthg sapere OR sentire di qc; to ~ from sb ricevere notizie da qn; to have heard of aver sentito parlare di.

hearing ['hɪərɪŋ] n (sense) udito m; (at court) udienza f; to be hard of ~ esser duro d'orecchi.

hearing aid n apparecchio m acustico.

heart [hɑːt] n cuore m; to know sthg (off) by ~ sapere qc a memoria; to lose ~ scoraggiarsi ◻ **hearts** npl (in cards) cuori mpl.

heart attack n infarto m.

heartbeat ['hɑːtbiːt] n (rhythm) battito m cardiaco.

heartburn ['hɑːtbɜːn] n bruciore m di stomaco.

heart condition n: to have a ~ avere un disturbo cardiaco.

hearth [hɑːθ] n focolare m.

hearty ['hɑːtɪ] adj (meal) abbondante, sostanzioso(-a).

heat [hiːt] n (warmth) calore m; (warm weather) caldo m; (of oven) temperatura f ◻ **heat up** vt sep riscaldare.

heater ['hiːtəʳ] n (for room) stufa f; (radiator) radiatore m; (in car) riscaldamento m; (for water) scaldabagno m.

heath [hiːθ] n brughiera f.

heather ['heðəʳ] n erica f.

heating ['hiːtɪŋ] n riscaldamento m.

heat wave n ondata f di caldo.

heave [hi:v] vt (push) spingere (con forza); (pull) tirare (con forza); (lift) sollevare (con forza).

Heaven [hevn] n paradiso m.

heavily ['hevɪlɪ] adv (smoke, drink) molto; (rain) a dirotto.

heavy ['hevɪ] adj pesante; (rain, traffic) intenso(-a); (fighting) violento(-a); (losses, defeat) grave; **how is it?** quanto pesa?; **to be a ~ smoker** essere un fumatore accanito.

heavy cream n (Am) panna molto densa ad alto contenuto di grassi.

heavy goods vehicle n (Br) veicolo m per trasporti pesanti.

heavy industry n industria f pesante.

heavy metal n heavy metal m.

heckle ['hekl] vt interrompere di continuo.

hectic ['hektɪk] adj frenetico(-a).

hedge [hedʒ] n siepe f.

hedgehog ['hedʒhɒg] n riccio m.

heel [hi:l] n (of person) calcagno m; (of shoe) tacco m.

hefty ['heftɪ] adj (person) robusto(-a); (fine) salato(-a).

height [haɪt] n altezza f; (peak period) apice m; **what ~ is it?** quanto è alto?

heir [eər] n erede m.

heiress ['eərɪs] n erede f.

held [held] pt & pp = **hold**.

helicopter ['helɪkɒptər] n elicottero m.

he'll [hi:l] = **he will**, = **he shall**.

Hell [hel] n inferno m.

hello [hə'ləʊ] excl (as greeting) ciao!; (more formal) buongiorno!;

(on phone) pronto!; (to attract attention) ehi!

helmet ['helmɪt] n casco m.

help [help] n aiuto m ◆ vt aiutare; (contribute to) contribuire a ◆ vi aiutare, essere d'aiuto ◆ excl aiuto!; **I can't ~ it** non ci posso fare niente; **to ~ sb (to) do sthg** aiutare qn a fare qc; **to ~ o.s. (to sthg)** servirsi (di qc); **can I ~ you?** (in shop) desidera? ❑ **help out** vi aiutare, dare una mano.

helper ['helpər] n (assistant) aiutante mf; (Am: cleaner) uomo m (donna f) delle pulizie.

helpful ['helpful] adj (person) di grande aiuto; (useful) utile.

helping ['helpɪŋ] n porzione f.

helpless ['helplɪs] adj impotente; (child) indifeso(-a).

hem [hem] n orlo m.

hemophiliac [,hi:mə'fɪliæk] n emofiliaco m (-a f).

hemorrhage ['hemərɪdʒ] n emorragia f.

hen [hen] n gallina f.

hepatitis [,hepə'taɪtɪs] n epatite f.

her [hɜːr] adj il suo (la sua), i suoi (le sue) (pl) ◆ pron (direct) la; (indirect) le; (after prep, stressed) lei; **~ brother** suo fratello; **I know ~** la conosco; **it's ~** è lei; **send it to ~** mandaglielo, mandalo a lei; **tell ~** diglielo; **tell ~ that ...** dille che ...; **he's worse than ~** lui è peggio di lei.

herb [hɜːb] n erba f.

herbal tea ['hɜːbl-] n tè m inv d'erbe.

herd [hɜːd] n (of cattle) mandria f.

here [hɪər] adv qui, qua; **~'s your book** eccoti il libro; **~ you are**

eccoti (qui OR qua).

heritage ['hɛrɪtɪdʒ] n eredità f, patrimonio m.

heritage centre n centro informazioni in luoghi di interesse storico.

hernia ['hɜ:njə] n ernia f.

hero ['hɪərəʊ] (pl -es) n eroe m.

heroin ['herəʊɪn] n eroina f (droga).

heroine ['herəʊɪn] n eroina f.

heron ['herən] n airone m.

herring ['herɪŋ] n aringa f.

hers [hɜ:z] pron il suo (la sua), i suoi (le sue) (pl); a friend of ~ un suo amico.

herself [hɜ:'self] pron (reflexive) si; (after prep) se stessa, sé; she did it ~ l'ha fatto da sola.

hesitant ['hezɪtənt] adj esitante.

hesitate ['hezɪteɪt] vi esitare.

hesitation [,hezɪ'teɪʃn] n esitazione f.

heterosexual [,hetərəʊ'seksʊəl] adj eterosessuale ♦ n eterosessuale mf.

hey [heɪ] excl (inf) ehi!

HGV abbr = heavy goods vehicle.

hi [haɪ] excl (inf) ciao!

hiccup ['hɪkʌp] n: to have (the) ~s avere il singhiozzo.

hide [haɪd] (pt hid [hɪd], pp hidden ['hɪdn]) vt nascondere ♦ vi nascondersi ♦ n (of animal) pelle f.

hideous ['hɪdɪəs] adj raccapricciante.

hi-fi ['haɪfaɪ] n hi-fi m inv.

high [haɪ] adj alto(-a); (price, speed, temperature) alto, elevato(-a); (wind) forte; (sound, voice) acuto (-a), alto; (inf: from drugs) fatto(-a) ♦ n (weather front) anticiclone m ♦

adv alto, in alto; how ~ is it? quanto è alto?; it's 10 metres ~ è alto 10 metri.

high chair n seggiolone m.

high-class adj di lusso.

Higher ['haɪəʳ] n (Scot) esame sostenuto alla fine di studi secondari.

higher education n istruzione f universitaria.

high heels npl tacchi mpl alti.

high jump n salto m in alto.

Highland Games ['haɪlənd-] npl: the ~ gare sportive disputate all'aperto nelle Highlands scozzesi.

---

i HIGHLAND GAMES

L'origine di queste manifestazioni sportive e musicali che hanno luogo in Scozia durante l'estate risale alle riunioni fra i diversi clan delle Highlands. I giochi odierni comprendono gare di corsa, di salto in lungo e di salto in alto, accanto a gare di danze tradizionali e di cornamusa. Un'altra competizione tipica di questa manifestazione è quella del lancio del tronco ("tossing the caber"), prova di forza che consiste nel lanciare un lungo tronco d'abete il più lontano possibile.

Highlands ['haɪləndz] npl: the ~ le Highlands fpl (regione montuosa nel nord della Scozia).

highlight ['haɪlaɪt] n (best part) clou m inv ♦ vt (emphasize) evidenziare □ highlights npl (of football match etc) sintesi f inv; (in hair) colpi mpl di sole.

highly ['haɪlɪ] adv (extremely) molto; (very well) molto bene; to think ~ of sb avere grande stima di qn.

high-pitched [-'pɪtʃt] *adj* acuto (-a).

high-rise *adj* con tanti piani.

high school *n* (in UK) = scuola *f* secondaria inferiore e superiore; (in US) = scuola secondaria superiore.

high season *n* alta stagione *f*.

high-speed train *n* treno *m* ad alta velocità.

high street *n* (Br) strada *f* principale.

high tide *n* alta marea *f*.

highway ['haɪweɪ] *n* (Am: between towns) superstrada *f*; (Br: any main road) strada *f* principale.

Highway Code *n* (Br) codice *m* stradale.

hijack ['haɪdʒæk] *vt* dirottare.

hijacker ['haɪdʒækə'] *n* dirottatore *m* (-trice *f*).

hike [haɪk] *n* lunga camminata *f* ♦ *vi* fare una lunga camminata.

hiking ['haɪkɪŋ] *n*: **to go ~** andare a fare lunghe camminate.

hilarious [hɪ'leərɪəs] *adj* spassoso(-a).

hill [hɪl] *n* collina *f*, colle *m*.

hillwalking ['hɪlwɔːkɪŋ] *n*: **to go ~** fare lunghe camminate.

hilly ['hɪlɪ] *adj* collinoso(-a).

him [hɪm] *pron* (direct) lo; (indirect) gli; (after prep, stressed) lui; **I know ~** lo conosco; **it's ~** è lui; **send it to ~** mandaglielo, mandalo a lui; **tell ~** diglielo; **tell ~ that** ... digli che ...; **she's worse than ~** lei è peggio di lui.

himself [hɪm'self] *pron* (reflexive) si; (after prep) se stesso, sé; **he did it ~** l'ha fatto da solo.

hinder ['hɪndə'] *vt* ostacolare.

Hindu ['hɪnduː] (pl -s) *adj* indù (inv) ♦ *n* (person) indù *mf inv*.

hinge [hɪndʒ] *n* cardine *m*.

hint [hɪnt] *n* (indirect suggestion) accenno *m*, allusione *f*; (piece of advice) consiglio *m*; (slight amount) accenno, punta *f* ♦ *vi*: **to ~ at sthg** alludere a qc.

hip [hɪp] *n* fianco *m*.

hippopotamus [,hɪpə'pɒtəməs] *n* ippopotamo *m*.

hippy ['hɪpɪ] *n* hippy *mf inv*.

hire ['haɪə'] *vt* (car, bicycle, television) noleggiare; **'for ~'** (boats) 'a noleggio'; (taxi) 'libero' ❑ **hire out** *vt sep* (car, bicycle, television) dare a noleggio.

hire car *n* (Br) vettura *f* a noleggio.

hire purchase *n* (Br) acquisto *m* rateale.

his [hɪz] *adj* il suo (la sua), i suoi (le sue) (pl) ♦ *pron* il suo (la sua), i suoi (le sue) (pl); **~ brother** suo fratello; **a friend of ~** un suo amico.

historical [hɪ'stɒrɪkəl] *adj* storico(-a).

history ['hɪstərɪ] *n* storia *f*; (record) passato *m*.

hit [hɪt] (pt & pp hit) *vt* colpire; (bang) sbattere, picchiare ♦ *n* (record, play, film) successo *m*.

hit-and-run *adj*: **~ accident** incidente in cui l'automobilista colpevole non si ferma a prestare soccorso.

hitch [hɪtʃ] *n* (problem) contrattempo *m* ♦ *vt*: **to ~ a lift** farsi dare un passaggio ♦ *vi* fare l'autostop.

hitchhike ['hɪtʃhaɪk] *vi* fare l'autostop.

hitchhiker ['hɪtʃhaɪkə'] *n* autostoppista *mf*.

hive [haɪv] *n (of bees)* alveare *m*.

HIV-positive *adj* sieropositivo(-a).

hoarding ['hɔːdɪŋ] *n (Br: for adverts)* tabellone *m* per pubblicità.

hoarse [hɔːs] *adj* rauco(-a).

hoax [həʊks] *n* burla *f*.

hob [hɒb] *n* piano *m* di cottura.

hobby ['hɒbɪ] *n* hobby *m inv*, passatempo *m*.

hock [hɒk] *n (wine)* vino *m* bianco del Reno.

hockey ['hɒkɪ] *n (on grass)* hockey *m* su prato; *(Am: ice hockey)* hockey su ghiaccio.

hoe [həʊ] *n* zappa *f*.

Hogmanay ['hɒgmэneɪ] *n (Scot)* l'ultimo *m* dell'anno.

hold [həʊld] *(pt & pp held)* vt tenere; *(contain)* contenere; *(possess)* avere, possedere ◆ *vi (weather)* mantenersi; *(luck, offer)* permanere; *(on telephone)* restare in linea ◆ *n (grip)* presa *f; (of ship)* stiva *f; (of aircraft)* bagagliaio *m;* **to ~ sb prisoner** tenere prigioniero qn; **~ the line, please** resti in linea, per favore ❏ **hold back** *vt sep (restrain)* trattenere; *(keep secret)* tenere segreto; **hold on** *vi (wait)* aspettare, attendere; *(on telephone)* restare in linea; **to ~ on to sthg** *(grip)* tenersi (stretto) a qc; **hold out** *vt sep (hand)* porgere, tendere; **hold up** *vt sep (delay)* bloccare.

holdall ['həʊldɔːl] *n (Br)* borsone *m* da viaggio.

holder ['həʊldэr] *n (of passport, licence)* titolare *mf*, proprietario *m* (-a *f*); *(container)* contenitore *m*.

holdup ['həʊldʌp] *n (delay)* ritardo *m*.

hole [həʊl] *n (in sock, wall)* buco *m; (in ground, golf)* buca *f*.

holiday ['hɒlɪdeɪ] *n (Br: period of time)* vacanze *fpl; (time off work)* ferie *fpl; (public holiday)* festa *f* ◆ *vi (Br)* trascorrere le vacanze; **to be on ~** essere in vacanza; **to go on ~** andare in vacanza.

holidaymaker ['hɒlɪdɪˌmeɪkэr] *n (Br)* villeggiante *mf*.

holiday pay *n (Br)* retribuzione *f* delle ferie.

Holland ['hɒlэnd] *n* l'Olanda *f*.

hollow ['hɒləʊ] *adj* cavo(-a).

holly ['hɒlɪ] *n* agrifoglio *m*.

Hollywood ['hɒlɪwʊd] *n* Hollywood *f*.

---

i HOLLYWOOD

Quartiere di Los Angeles, Hollywood è, fin dal 1911, il cuore dell'industria cinematografica americana. Ha avuto il suo momento di maggior fulgore negli anni quaranta e cinquanta, quando gli immensi studi della Twentieth Century Fox, della Paramount e della Warner Brothers producevano centinaia di film all'anno, e resta tuttora una delle più grandi attrazioni turistiche d'America.

---

holy ['həʊlɪ] *adj* sacro(-a).

home [həʊm] *n* casa *f; (own country)* patria *f; (for old people)* istituto *m*, ricovero *m* ◆ *adv* a casa ◆ *adj (not foreign)* interno(-a), nazionale; *(cooking)* casereccio(-a); **at ~** *(in one's house)* a casa; **to make o.s. at ~** fare come se si fosse a casa propria; **to go ~** andare a casa; **to leave ~** *(for good)* andarsene di casa; ~ **address** indirizzo *m* di casa; ~ **number** numero *m* (telefonico) di casa.

home economics *n* economia *f* domestica.

home help *n* (*Br*) collaboratore *m* domestico (collaboratrice domestica *f*).

homeless ['həumlıs] *npl*: **the ~** i senzatetto.

homemade [,həum'meıd] *adj* (*food*) casereccio(-a).

homeopathic [,həumıəu'pæθık] *adj* omeopatico(-a).

Home Secretary *n* (*Br*) ministro *m* degli Interni.

homesick ['həumsık] *adj*: **to be ~** avere nostalgia di casa.

homework ['həumwɜːk] *n* compiti *mpl* a casa.

homosexual [,hɒmə'sekʃʋəl] *adj* omosessuale ◆ *n* omosessuale *mf*.

honest ['ɒnɪst] *adj* (*trustworthy*) onesto(-a); (*frank*) sincero(-a), franco(-a).

honestly ['ɒnɪstlɪ] *adv* (*truthfully*) onestamente; (*frankly*) sinceramente, francamente.

honey ['hʌnɪ] *n* miele *m*.

honeymoon ['hʌnɪmuːn] *n* luna *f* di miele, viaggio *m* di nozze.

honor ['ɒnər] (*Am*) = **honour.**

honour ['ɒnər] *n* (*Br*) onore *m*.

honourable ['ɒnrəbl] *adj* onorevole.

hood [hʊd] *n* (*of jacket, coat*) cappuccio *m*; (*on convertible car*) capote *f inv*; (*Am: car bonnet*) cofano *m*.

hoof [huːf] *n* zoccolo *m*.

hook [hʊk] *n* gancio *m*; (*for fishing*) amo *m*; **off the ~** (*telephone*) staccato.

hooligan ['huːlɪgən] *n* teppista *mf*, hooligan *mf inv*.

hoop [huːp] *n* cerchio *m*.

hoot [huːt] *vi* (*driver*) suonare il clacson.

Hoover® ['huːvər] *n* (*Br*) aspirapolvere *m inv*.

hop [hɒp] *vi* (*person*) saltellare su una gamba.

hope [həup] *n* speranza *f* ◆ *vt* sperare; **to ~ for sthg** sperare in qc; **to ~ to do sthg** sperare di fare qc; **I ~ so** spero di sì.

hopeful ['həupful] *adj* (*optimistic*) fiducioso(-a).

hopefully ['həupfəlɪ] *adv* (*with luck*) se tutto va bene.

hopeless ['həuplɪs] *adj* (*without any hope*) disperato(-a); **he's ~!** (*inf*) è un disastro!

hops [hɒps] *npl* luppolo *m*.

horizon [hə'raɪzn] *n* orizzonte *m*.

horizontal [,hɒrɪ'zɒntl] *adj* orizzontale.

horn [hɔːn] *n* (*of car*) clacson *m inv*; (*on animal*) corno *m*.

horoscope ['hɒrəskəup] *n* oroscopo *m*.

horrible ['hɒrəbl] *adj* orribile.

horrid ['hɒrɪd] *adj* (*very bad*) orrendo(-a); (*unkind*) odioso(-a); (*food, drink*) pessimo(-a).

horrific [hɒ'rɪfɪk] *adj* orripilante, terrificante.

hors d'oeuvre [ɔː'dɜːvrə] *n* antipasto *m*.

horse [hɔːs] *n* cavallo *m*.

horseback ['hɔːsbæk] *n*: **on ~** a cavallo.

horse chestnut *n* ippocastano *m*.

horse-drawn carriage n carrozza f a cavalli.

horsepower ['hɔːs,pauər] n cavallo m vapore.

horse racing n ippica f.

horseradish (sauce) ['hɔːs-,rædɪʃ] n salsa f di rafano.

horse riding n equitazione f.

horseshoe ['hɔːsʃuː] n ferro m di cavallo.

hose [həuz] n (hosepipe) tubo m per annaffiare.

hosepipe ['həuzpaɪp] n tubo m per annaffiare.

hosiery ['həuzɪərɪ] n calzetteria f.

hospitable [hɒ'spɪtəbl] adj ospitale.

hospital ['hɒspɪtl] n ospedale m; in ~ all'ospedale.

hospitality [,hɒspɪ'tælətɪ] n ospitalità f.

host [həust] n (of party, event) ospite m; (of show, TV programme) conduttore m (-trice f).

hostage ['hɒstɪdʒ] n ostaggio m.

hostel ['hɒstl] n (youth hostel) ostello m.

hostess ['həustes] n (on aeroplane) hostess f inv; (of party, event) ospite f.

hostile [Br 'hɒstaɪl, Am 'hɒstl] adj ostile.

hostility [hɒ'stɪlətɪ] n ostilità f.

hot [hɒt] adj caldo(-a); (spicy) piccante; **to be ~** (person) aver caldo; **it's ~** fa caldo.

hot chocolate n cioccolata f calda.

hot-cross bun n panino dolce con uvetta e spezie tipico del periodo pasquale.

hot dog n hot dog m inv (panino imbottito con würstel e senape).

hotel [həu'tel] n hotel m inv, albergo m.

hot line n telefono m rosso.

hotplate ['hɒtpleɪt] n piastra f.

hotpot ['hɒtpɒt] n spezzatino di carne con patate.

hot-water bottle n borsa f dell'acqua calda.

hour ['auər] n ora f; **I've been waiting for ~s** è un secolo che aspetto.

hourly ['auəlɪ] adj (per hour) orario(-a); (every hour) ogni ora ♦ adv (per hour) a ore; (every hour) ogni ora.

house [n haus, pl 'hauzız, vb hauz] n casa f; (SCH) uno dei gruppi in cui sono divisi gli alunni di una scuola media o superiore in occasione di competizioni sportive ecc. ♦ vt (person) alloggiare.

household ['haushəuld] n famiglia f.

housekeeping ['haus,kiːpɪŋ] n amministrazione f della casa.

House of Commons n (Br) Camera f dei Comuni.

House of Lords n (Br) Camera f dei Lord.

Houses of Parliament npl (Br: building) palazzo m del Parlamento.

ⓘ **HOUSES OF PARLIAMENT**

Il parlamento britannico comprende la Camera dei Comuni (House of Commons) e la Camera dei Lord (House of Lords). Ha sede a Londra, nel Palazzo di Westminster, sulla riva del Tamigi. Gli edifici attuali risalgono alla metà del diciannovesimo secolo, quando vennero costruiti sulle macerie del palazzo originario, distrutto da un incendio nel 1834.

housewife ['hauswaif] (*pl* **-wives** [-waivz]) *n* casalinga *f*.

house wine *n* vino *m* della casa.

housewives *pl* → housewife.

housework ['hausw3:k] *n* lavori *mpl* di casa.

housing ['hauzin] *n* alloggi *mpl*.

housing estate *n* (*Br*) complesso *m* residenziale.

housing project (*Am*) = housing estate.

hovercraft ['hɒvəkrɑ:ft] *n* hovercraft *m inv*.

hoverport ['hɒvəpɔ:t] *n* porto *m* per hovercraft.

how [hau] *adv* 1. (*asking about way or manner*) come; ~ **do you get there?** come ci si arriva?; ~ **does it work?** come funziona?; **tell me** ~ **to do it** dimmi come devo fare.
2. (*asking about health, quality*) come; ~ **are you?** come stai?; ~ **are you doing?** come va?; ~ **are things?** come vanno le cose?; ~ **do you do** piacere!; ~ **is your room?** com'è la tua camera?
3. (*asking about degree, amount*): ~ **tall is he?** quanto è alto?; ~ **far is it?** quanto dista?; ~ **long will it take?** quanto tempo ci vorrà?; ~ **many?** quanti(-e)?; ~ **much?** quanto(-a)?; ~ **much is it?** quant'è?; ~ **old are you?** quanti anni hai?
4. (*in phrases*): ~ **about some coffee?** cosa ne diresti di un caffè?; ~ **lovely!** che bello!

however [hau'evər] *adv* (*nevertheless*) tuttavia; ~ **difficult it is** per quanto sia difficile.

howl [haul] *vi* ululare.

HP *abbr* = hire purchase.

HQ *n* (*abbr of headquarters*) Q.G. *m*.

hub airport [hʌb-] *n* aeroporto *m* principale.

hubcap ['hʌbkæp] *n* coprimozzo *m*.

hug [hʌg] *vt* abbracciare ◆ *n*: **to give sb a** ~ abbracciare qn.

huge [hju:dʒ] *adj* enorme.

hull [hʌl] *n* scafo *m*.

hum [hʌm] *vi* (*bee, machine*) ronzare; (*person*) canterellare.

human ['hju:mən] *adj* umano(-a) ◆ *n*: ~ **(being)** essere *m* umano.

humanities [hju:'mænətiz] *npl* materie *fpl* umanistiche.

human rights *npl* diritti *mpl* dell'uomo.

humble ['hʌmbl] *adj* umile.

humid ['hju:mid] *adj* umido(-a).

humidity [hju:'midəti] *n* umidità *f*.

humiliating [hju:'milieitin] *adj* umiliante.

humiliation [hju:,mili'eiʃn] *n* umiliazione *f*.

hummus ['huməs] *n* salsetta cremosa a base di ceci, aglio e pasta di sesamo.

humor ['hju:mər] (*Am*) = humour.

humorous ['hju:mərəs] *adj* (*story*) umoristico(-a); (*person*) spiritoso(-a).

humour ['hju:mər] *n* umorismo *m*; **sense of** ~ senso *m* dell'umorismo.

hump [hʌmp] n (bump) dosso m; (of camel) gobba f.

humpbacked bridge ['hʌmpbækt-] n ponte m a schiena d'asino.

hunch [hʌntʃ] n impressione f.

hundred ['hʌndrəd] num cento; a ~ cento, → **six**.

hundredth ['hʌndrətθ] num centesimo(-a), → **sixth**.

hundredweight ['hʌndrədweɪt] n (in UK) = 50,8 kg; (in US) = 45,4 kg.

hung [hʌŋ] pt & pp → **hang**.

Hungarian [hʌŋ'geərɪən] adj ungherese ♦ n (person) ungherese mf; (language) ungherese m.

Hungary ['hʌŋgərɪ] n l'Ungheria f.

hunger ['hʌŋgər] n fame f.

hungry ['hʌŋgrɪ] adj affamato(-a); **to be ~** avere fame.

hunt [hʌnt] n (Br: for foxes) caccia f ♦ vt & vi cacciare; **to ~ (for sb/sthg)** (search) cercare (qn/qc).

hunting ['hʌntɪŋ] n caccia f.

hurdle ['hɜːdl] n (SPORT) ostacolo m.

hurl [hɜːl] vt (throw) scaraventare, scagliare.

hurricane ['hʌrɪkən] n uragano m.

hurry ['hʌrɪ] vt (person) mettere fretta a ♦ vi affrettarsi, sbrigarsi □ n: **to be in a ~** avere fretta; **to do sthg in a ~** fare qc in fretta □ **hurry up** vi sbrigarsi.

hurt [hɜːt] (pt & pp **hurt**) vt (injure) fare male a; (emotionally) ferire ♦ vi far male; **my arm ~s** mi fa male il braccio; **I ~ my arm** mi sono fatto male al braccio; **to ~ o.s.** farsi male.

husband ['hʌzbənd] n marito m.

hustle ['hʌsl] n: **~ and bustle** attività f febbrile.

hut [hʌt] n capanna f.

hyacinth ['haɪəsɪnθ] n giacinto m.

hydrofoil ['haɪdrəfɔɪl] n aliscafo m.

hygiene ['haɪdʒiːn] n igiene f.

hygienic [haɪ'dʒiːnɪk] adj igienico(-a).

hymn [hɪm] n inno m.

hypermarket ['haɪpəˌmɑːkɪt] n ipermercato m.

hyphen ['haɪfn] n trattino m.

hypocrite ['hɪpəkrɪt] n ipocrita mf.

hypodermic needle [ˌhaɪpə-'dɜːmɪk-] n ago m ipodermico.

hysterical [hɪs'terɪkl] adj (person) isterico(-a); (inf: very funny) esilarante.

I [aɪ] pron io; **I'm tall** sono alto.

ice [aɪs] n ghiaccio m; (ice cream) gelato m.

iceberg ['aɪsbɜːg] n iceberg m inv.

iceberg lettuce n lattuga f iceberg.

icebox ['aɪsbɒks] n (Am: fridge) frigorifero m.

ice-cold adj ghiacciato(-a).

ice cream n gelato m.

ice cube n cubetto m di ghiaccio.

ice hockey n hockey m su ghiaccio.

Iceland ['aɪslənd] n l'Islanda f.

ice lolly n (Br) ghiacciolo m.

ice rink n pista f di pattinaggio su ghiaccio.

ice skates npl pattini mpl da ghiaccio.

ice-skating n pattinaggio m su ghiaccio; **to go ~** andare a pattinare sul ghiaccio.

icicle ['aɪsɪkl] n ghiacciolo m.

icing ['aɪsɪŋ] n glassa f.

icing sugar n zucchero m a velo.

icy ['aɪsɪ] adj (covered with ice) ghiacciato(-a); (very cold) gelido(-a), gelato(-a).

I'd [aɪd] = **I would, I had.**

ID n (abbr of identification) documento m (d'identità).

ID card n carta f d'identità.

IDD code n prefisso m (teleselettivo) internazionale.

idea [aɪ'dɪə] n idea f; **I've no ~** non ne ho idea.

ideal [aɪ'dɪəl] adj ideale ◆ n ideale m.

ideally [aɪ'dɪəlɪ] adv idealmente; (suited) perfettamente.

identical [aɪ'dentɪkl] adj identico(-a).

identification [aɪ,dentɪfɪ'keɪʃn] n (document) documento m d'identità.

identify [aɪ'dentɪfaɪ] vt identificare.

identity [aɪ'dentətɪ] n identità f inv.

idiom ['ɪdɪəm] n (phrase) espressione f idiomatica.

idiot ['ɪdɪət] n idiota mf.

idle ['aɪdl] adj (lazy) ozioso(-a); (not working) inattivo(-a); (unemployed) disoccupato(-a) ◆ vi (engine) girare al minimo.

idol ['aɪdl] n (person) idolo m.

idyllic [ɪ'dɪlɪk] adj idilliaco(-a).

i.e. (abbr of id est) cioè.

if [ɪf] conj se; **~ I were you** se fossi in te; **~ not** (otherwise) se no.

ignition [ɪg'nɪʃn] n (AUT) accensione f.

ignorant ['ɪgnərənt] adj ignorante.

ignore [ɪg'nɔːr] vt ignorare.

ill [ɪl] adj (in health) malato(-a); (bad) cattivo(-a).

I'll [aɪl] = **I will, I shall.**

illegal [ɪ'liːgl] adj illegale.

illegible [ɪ'ledʒəbl] adj illeggibile.

illegitimate [,ɪlɪ'dʒɪtɪmət] adj illegittimo(-a).

illiterate [ɪ'lɪtərət] adj analfabeta.

illness ['ɪlnɪs] n malattia f.

illuminate [ɪ'luːmɪneɪt] vt illuminare.

illusion [ɪ'luːʒn] n illusione f.

illustration [,ɪlə'streɪʃn] n illustrazione f.

I'm [aɪm] = **I am.**

image ['ɪmɪdʒ] n immagine f.

imaginary [ɪ'mædʒɪnrɪ] adj immaginario(-a).

imagination [ɪ,mædʒɪ'neɪʃn] n immaginazione f.

imagine [ɪ'mædʒɪn] vt immaginare.

imitate ['ɪmɪteɪt] vt imitare.

imitation [,ɪmɪ'teɪʃn] n imitazione f ◆ adj finto(-a).

immaculate [ɪˈmækjʊlət] *adj (very clean)* immacolato(-a), lindo(-a); *(perfect)* impeccabile.

immature [ˌɪməˈtjʊəʳ] *adj* immaturo(-a).

immediate [ɪˈmiːdjət] *adj (without delay)* immediato(-a).

immediately [ɪˈmiːdjətlɪ] *adv (at once)* immediatamente, subito ♦ *conj (Br)* non appena.

immense [ɪˈmens] *adj* immenso(-a).

immersion heater [ɪˈmɜːʃn-] *n* scaldabagno *m inv* elettrico.

immigrant [ˈɪmɪgrənt] *n* immigrato *m (-a f)*.

immigration [ˌɪmɪˈgreɪʃn] *n (to country)* immigrazione *f; (section of airport, port)* dogana *f*.

imminent [ˈɪmɪnənt] *adj* imminente.

immune [ɪˈmjuːn] *adj*: **to be ~ to** *(MED)* essere immune da.

immunity [ɪˈmjuːnətɪ] *n (MED)* immunità *f*.

immunize [ˈɪmjuːnaɪz] *vt* immunizzare.

impact [ˈɪmpækt] *n* impatto *m*.

impair [ɪmˈpeəʳ] *vt* danneggiare.

impatient [ɪmˈpeɪʃnt] *adj* impaziente; **to be ~ to do sthg** essere impaziente di fare qc.

imperative [ɪmˈperətɪv] *n (GRAMM)* imperativo *m*.

imperfect [ɪmˈpɜːfɪkt] *n (GRAMM)* imperfetto *m*.

impersonate [ɪmˈpɜːsəneɪt] *vt (for amusement)* imitare. '

impertinent [ɪmˈpɜːtɪnənt] *adj* impertinente.

implement [*n* ˈɪmplɪmənt, *vb* ˈɪmplɪment] *n* attrezzo *m*; *(for* *cooking)* utensile *m* ♦ *vt* mettere in atto, realizzare.

implication [ˌɪmplɪˈkeɪʃn] *n (consequence)* implicazione *f*.

imply [ɪmˈplaɪ] *vt (suggest)* lasciar intendere, sottintendere.

impolite [ˌɪmpəˈlaɪt] *adj* scortese.

import [*n* ˈɪmpɔːt, *vb* ɪmˈpɔːt] *n* merce *f* d'importazione ♦ *vt* importare.

importance [ɪmˈpɔːtns] *n* importanza *f*.

important [ɪmˈpɔːtnt] *adj* importante.

impose [ɪmˈpəʊz] *vt* imporre ♦ *vi* approfittare; **to ~ sthg on** imporre qc a.

impossible [ɪmˈpɒsəbl] *adj* impossibile.

impractical [ɪmˈpræktɪkl] *adj* non pratico(-a).

impress [ɪmˈpres] *vt* fare una buona impressione a.

impression [ɪmˈpreʃn] *n* impressione *f*.

impressive [ɪmˈpresɪv] *adj* impressionante.

improbable [ɪmˈprɒbəbl] *adj (event)* improbabile; *(story, excuse)* inverosimile.

improper [ɪmˈprɒpəʳ] *adj (incorrect, illegal)* scorretto(-a); *(rude)* sconveniente.

improve [ɪmˈpruːv] *vt & vi* migliorare □ **improve on** *vt fus* migliorare.

improvement [ɪmˈpruːvmənt] *n (in weather, health)* miglioramento *m; (to home)* miglioria *f*.

improvise [ˈɪmprəvaɪz] *vi* improvvisare.

impulse ['ɪmpʌls] n impulso m; on ~ d'impulso.

impulsive [ɪm'pʌlsɪv] adj impulsivo(-a).

in [ɪn] prep 1. (expressing place, position) in; ~ **a box** in una scatola; ~ **the bedroom** in camera da letto; ~ **the street** per strada; ~ **Scotland** in Scozia; ~ **Sheffield** a Sheffield; ~ **the United States** negli Stati Uniti; ~ **here/there** qui/là dentro; ~ **the sun** al sole; ~ **the rain** sotto la pioggia; ~ **the middle** al centro; **an article** ~ **the paper** un articolo sul giornale.

2. (participating in) in; **who's** ~ **the play?** chi recita nella commedia?

3. (expressing arrangement) in; ~ **a row** in fila; **they come** ~ **packs of three** vengono venduti in pacchetti da tre.

4. (with time): ~ **April** in aprile; ~ **the afternoon** di OR nel pomeriggio; **at ten o'clock** ~ **the morning** alle dieci del mattino; ~ **1994** nel 1994; **it'll be ready** ~ **an hour** sarà pronto fra un'ora; **they're arriving** ~ **two weeks** arriveranno fra due settimane.

5. (expressing means): **to write** ~ **ink** scrivere a penna; ~ **writing** per iscritto; **they were talking** ~ **English** parlavano in inglese.

6. (wearing): **the man** ~ **the blue jacket** l'uomo con la giacca blu; **dressed** ~ **white** vestito di bianco.

7. (expressing state): ~ **a bad mood** di pessimo umore; **to be** ~ **a hurry** essere di fretta; **to cry** ~ **pain** gridare di dolore; **to be** ~ **pain** soffrire; ~ **ruins** in rovina.

8. (with regard to): **a rise** ~ **prices** un aumento dei prezzi; **to be 50 metres** ~ **length** essere lungo 50

metri.

9. (with numbers, ratios): **one** ~ **ten** uno su dieci; ~ **dozens** a dozzine.

10. (expressing age): **she's** ~ **her thirties** è sulla trentina.

11. (with colours): **it comes** ~ **green or blue** è disponibile in verde o in blu.

12. (with superlatives) di; **the best** ~ **the world** il migliore del mondo.
♦ adv 1. (inside) dentro; **you can go** ~ **now** ora può entrare; **come** ~**!** avanti!

2. (at home, work): **she's not** ~ non c'è; **to stay** ~ stare a casa.

3. (train, bus, plane): **the train's not** ~ **yet** il treno non è ancora arrivato.

4. (tide): **the tide is** ~ c'è alta marea.
♦ adj (inf: fashionable) alla moda.

inability [,ɪnə'bɪlətɪ] n: ~ **(to do sthg)** incapacità f (di fare qc).

inaccessible [,ɪnək'sesəbl] adj inaccessibile.

inaccurate [ɪn'ækjurət] adj inesatto(-a), impreciso(-a).

inadequate [ɪn'ædɪkwət] adj inadeguato(-a).

inappropriate [ɪnə'prəuprɪət] adj non adatto(-a).

inauguration [ɪ,nɔːgju'reɪʃn] n inaugurazione f; (of president etc) insediamento m in carica.

incapable [ɪn'keɪpəbl] adj: **to be** ~ **of doing sthg** essere incapace di fare qc.

incense ['ɪnsens] n incenso m.

incentive [ɪn'sentɪv] n incentivo m.

inch [ɪntʃ] n = 2,5 cm, pollice m.

incident ['ɪnsɪdənt] n episodio m, caso m.

incidentally [ˌɪnsɪ'dentəlɪ] *adv* a proposito.

incline ['ɪnklaɪn] *n* pendio *m*.

inclined [ɪn'klaɪnd] *adj (sloping)* inclinato(-a); **to be ~ to do sthg** essere propenso(-a) a fare qc.

include [ɪn'kluːd] *vt* includere, comprendere.

included [ɪn'kluːdɪd] *adj (in price)* compreso(-a); **to be ~ in sthg** essere compreso in qc.

including [ɪn'kluːdɪŋ] *prep* compreso(-a).

inclusive [ɪn'kluːsɪv] *adj*: **from the 8th to the 16th ~** dall'8 al 16 compreso; **~ of VAT** IVA compresa.

income ['ɪŋkʌm] *n* reddito *m*.

income support *n (Br)* = sussidio *m* di indigenza.

income tax *n* imposta *f* sul reddito.

incoming ['ɪn,kʌmɪŋ] *adj* in arrivo.

incompetent [ɪn'kɒmpɪtənt] *adj* incompetente.

incomplete [ˌɪnkəm'pliːt] *adj* incompleto(-a).

inconsiderate [ˌɪnkən'sɪdərət] *adj* sconsiderato(-a).

inconsistent [ˌɪnkən'sɪstənt] *adj* incoerente.

incontinent [ɪn'kɒntɪnənt] *adj* incontinente.

inconvenient [ˌɪnkən'viːnjənt] *adj* scomodo(-a).

incorporate [ɪn'kɔːpəreɪt] *vt* incorporare.

incorrect [ˌɪnkə'rekt] *adj (answer, number)* sbagliato(-a); *(information)* inesatto(-a).

increase [*n* 'ɪnkriːs, *vb* ɪn'kriːs] *n* aumento *m* ♦ *vt & vi* aumentare;

an ~ in sthg un aumento di qc.

increasingly [ɪn'kriːsɪŋlɪ] *adv* sempre più.

incredible [ɪn'kredəbl] *adj* incredibile.

incredibly [ɪn'kredəblɪ] *adv (very)* incredibilmente.

incur [ɪn'kɜːr] *vt* incorrere in.

indecisive [ˌɪndɪ'saɪsɪv] *adj* indeciso(-a).

indeed [ɪn'diːd] *adv (for emphasis)* davvero; *(certainly)* certamente.

indefinite [ɪn'defɪnɪt] *adj (time, number)* indefinito(-a), indeterminato(-a); *(answer, opinion)* vago(-a).

indefinitely [ɪn'defɪnətlɪ] *adv (closed, delayed)* indefinitamente.

independence [ˌɪndɪ'pendəns] *n* indipendenza *f*.

independent [ˌɪndɪ'pendənt] *adj* indipendente.

independently [ˌɪndɪ'pendəntlɪ] *adv* indipendentemente.

independent school *n (Br)* scuola *f* privata.

index ['ɪndeks] *n (of book)* indice *m*; *(in library)* catalogo *m*.

index finger *n* dito *m* indice.

India ['ɪndjə] *n* l'India *f*.

Indian ['ɪndjən] *adj* indiano(-a) ♦ *n* indiano *m* (-a *f*); **an ~ restaurant** un ristorante indiano.

Indian Ocean *n*: **the ~** l'oceano *m* Indiano.

indicate ['ɪndɪkeɪt] *vi (AUT)* mettere la freccia ♦ *vt* indicare.

indicator ['ɪndɪkeɪtər] *n (AUT)* indicatore *m* di direzione, freccia *f*.

indifferent [ɪn'dɪfrənt] *adj (uninterested)* indifferente; *(not very good)* mediocre.

indigestion [ˌɪndɪ'dʒestʃn] *n*

indigestione f.

indigo ['ɪndɪgəʊ] *adj* indaco *(inv)*.

indirect [,ɪndɪ'rekt] *adj* non diretto(-a).

individual [,ɪndɪ'vɪdʒʊəl] *adj* individuale ♦ *n* individuo *m*.

individually [,ɪndɪ'vɪdʒʊəlɪ] *adv* individualmente.

Indonesia [,ɪndə'ni:zjə] *n* l'Indonesia f.

indoor ['ɪndɔːʳ] *adj (swimming pool)* coperto(-a); *(sports)* praticato(-a) al coperto.

indoors [,ɪn'dɔːz] *adv* dentro.

indulge [ɪn'dʌldʒ] *vi*: **to ~ in** sthg concedersi qc.

industrial [ɪn'dʌstrɪəl] *adj* industriale.

industrial estate *n (Br)* zona f industriale.

industry ['ɪndəstrɪ] *n* industria f.

inedible [ɪn'edɪbl] *adj (unpleasant)* immangiabile; *(unsafe)* non commestibile.

inefficient [,ɪnɪ'fɪʃnt] *adj* inefficiente.

inequality [,ɪnɪ'kwɒlətɪ] *n* disuguaglianza f.

inevitable [ɪn'evɪtəbl] *adj* inevitabile.

inevitably [ɪn'evɪtəblɪ] *adv* inevitabilmente.

inexpensive [,ɪnɪk'spensɪv] *adj* poco costoso(-a).

infamous ['ɪnfəməs] *adj* infame.

infant ['ɪnfənt] *n* bambino *m* (-a f).

infant school *n (Br)* scuola f elementare *(per bambini da 5 a 7 anni)*.

infatuated [ɪn'fætjʊeɪtɪd] *adj*: **to be ~ with** essere infatuato(-a) di.

infected [ɪn'fektɪd] *adj* infetto(-a).

infectious [ɪn'fekʃəs] *adj* contagioso(-a).

inferior [ɪn'fɪərɪəʳ] *adj (person)* inferiore; *(goods, quality)* scadente.

infinite ['ɪnfɪnət] *adj* infinito(-a).

infinitely ['ɪnfɪnətlɪ] *adv* infinitamente.

infinitive [ɪn'fɪnɪtɪv] *n* infinito *m*.

infinity [ɪn'fɪnətɪ] *n (in space, MATH)* infinito *m*.

infirmary [ɪn'fɜːmərɪ] *n* ospedale *m*.

inflamed [ɪn'fleɪmd] *adj (MED)* infiammato(-a).

inflammation [,ɪnflə'meɪʃn] *n (MED)* infiammazione f.

inflatable [ɪn'fleɪtəbl] *adj* gonfiabile.

inflate [ɪn'fleɪt] *vt* gonfiare.

inflation [ɪn'fleɪʃn] *n (of prices)* inflazione f.

inflict [ɪn'flɪkt] *vt* infliggere.

in-flight *adj* durante il volo.

influence ['ɪnflʊəns] *vt* influenzare ♦ *n*: **~ (on)** influenza f(su).

inform [ɪn'fɔːm] *vt* informare.

informal [ɪn'fɔːml] *adj (occasion, dress)* informale.

information [,ɪnfə'meɪʃn] *n* informazioni *fpl*; **a piece of ~** un'informazione.

information desk *n* banco *m* informazioni.

information office *n* ufficio *m* informazioni.

informative [ɪn'fɔːmətɪv] *adj* istruttivo(-a).

infuriating [ɪn'fjʊərieɪtɪŋ] *adj* molto irritante.

ingenious [ɪn'dʒiːnjəs] *adj* ingegnoso(-a).

ingredient [ɪnˈɡriːdjənt] n ingrediente m.

inhabit [ɪnˈhæbɪt] vt abitare.

inhabitant [ɪnˈhæbɪtənt] n abitante mf.

inhale [ɪnˈheɪl] vi aspirare.

inhaler [ɪnˈheɪləʳ] n inalatore m.

inherit [ɪnˈherɪt] vt ereditare.

inhibition [ˌɪnhɪˈbɪʃn] n inibizione f.

initial [ɪˈnɪʃl] adj iniziale ◆ vt siglare ❑ **initials** npl iniziali fpl.

initially [ɪˈnɪʃəlɪ] adv inizialmente.

initiative [ɪˈnɪʃətɪv] n iniziativa f.

injection [ɪnˈdʒekʃn] n iniezione f.

injure [ˈɪndʒəʳ] vt (physically) ferire; **to ~ o.s.** ferirsi; **to ~ one's arm** ferirsi al braccio.

injured [ˈɪndʒəd] adj (physically) ferito(-a).

injury [ˈɪndʒərɪ] n (physical) ferita f.

ink [ɪŋk] n inchiostro m.

inland [adj ˈɪnlənd, adv ɪnˈlænd] adj interno(-a) ◆ adv nell'interno.

Inland Revenue n (Br) = Fisco m.

inn [ɪn] n locanda f.

inner [ˈɪnəʳ] adj interno(-a), interiore.

inner city n quartieri vicino al centro di una città, generalmente sinonimo di problemi sociali.

inner tube n camera f d'aria.

innocence [ˈɪnəsəns] n innocenza f.

innocent [ˈɪnəsənt] adj innocente(-a).

inoculate [ɪˈnɒkjʊleɪt] vt: **to ~ sb (against sthg)** vaccinare qn (contro qc).

inoculation [ɪˌnɒkjʊˈleɪʃn] n vaccinazione f.

input [ˈɪnpʊt] (pt & pp input OR -ted) vt (COMPUT) immettere.

inquire [ɪnˈkwaɪəʳ] = enquire.

inquiry [ɪnˈkwaɪərɪ] = enquiry.

insane [ɪnˈseɪn] adj pazzo(-a), matto(-a).

insect [ˈɪnsekt] n insetto m.

insect repellent [-rəˈpelənt] n insettifugo m.

insensitive [ɪnˈsensətɪv] adj insensibile.

insert [ɪnˈsɜːt] vt inserire, introdurre.

inside [ɪnˈsaɪd] prep dentro, all'interno di ◆ adv dentro ◆ adj (internal) interno(-a) ◆ n: **the ~** (interior) l'interno m; (AUT: in UK) la sinistra; (AUT: in Europe, US) la destra; **~ out** (clothes) a rovescio.

inside lane n (AUT: in UK) corsia f di sinistra; (in Europe, US) corsia f di destra.

inside leg n interno m gamba.

insight [ˈɪnsaɪt] n (glimpse) idea f.

insignificant [ˌɪnsɪɡˈnɪfɪkənt] adj insignificante.

insinuate [ɪnˈsɪnjʊeɪt] vt insinuare.

insist [ɪnˈsɪst] vi insistere; **to ~ on doing sthg** insistere nel fare qc.

insole [ˈɪnsəʊl] n soletta f.

insolent [ˈɪnsələnt] adj insolente.

insomnia [ɪnˈsɒmnɪə] n insonnia f.

inspect [ɪnˈspekt] vt (object) ispezionare; (ticket, passport) controllare.

inspection [ɪnˈspekʃn] *n (of object)* ispezione *f*; *(of ticket, passport)* controllo *m*.

inspector [ɪnˈspektəʳ] *n (on bus, train)* controllore *m*; *(in police force)* ispettore *m* (-trice *f*).

inspiration [ˌɪnspəˈreɪʃn] *n* ispirazione *f*.

instal [ɪnˈstɔːl] *(Am)* = install.

install [ɪnˈstɔːl] *vt (Br)* installare.

installment [ɪnˈstɔːlmənt] *(Am)* = instalment.

instalment [ɪnˈstɔːlmənt] *n (payment)* rata *f*; *(episode)* puntata *f*, parte *f*.

instance [ˈɪnstəns] *n (example, case)* esempio *m*, caso *m*; **for ~** per OR ad esempio.

instant [ˈɪnstənt] *adj (results, success)* immediato(-a); *(coffee)* solubile ◆ *n (moment)* istante *m*.

instant coffee *n* caffè *m inv* solubile.

instead [ɪnˈsted] *adv* invece; **~ of** invece di.

instep [ˈɪnstep] *n* collo *m* del piede.

instinct [ˈɪnstɪŋkt] *n* istinto *m*.

institute [ˈɪnstɪtjuːt] *n* istituto *m*.

institution [ˌɪnstɪˈtjuːʃn] *n* istituzione *f*.

instructions [ɪnˈstrʌkʃnz] *npl* istruzioni *fpl*.

instructor [ɪnˈstrʌktəʳ] *n* istruttore *m* (-trice *f*).

instrument [ˈɪnstrumənt] *n* strumento *m*.

insufficient [ˌɪnsəˈfɪʃnt] *adj* insufficiente.

insulating tape [ˈɪnsjuleɪtɪŋ-] *n* nastro *m* isolante.

insulation [ˌɪnsjuˈleɪʃn] *n (material)* isolante *m*.

insulin [ˈɪnsjulɪn] *n* insulina *f*.

insult [*n* ˈɪnsʌlt, *vb* ɪnˈsʌlt] *n* insulto *m* ◆ *vt* insultare.

insurance [ɪnˈʃuərəns] *n* assicurazione *f*.

insurance certificate *n* certificato *m* di assicurazione.

insurance company *n* compagnia *f* di assicurazione.

insurance policy *n* polizza *f* di assicurazione.

insure [ɪnˈʃuəʳ] *vt* assicurare.

insured [ɪnˈʃuəd] *adj*: **to be ~** essere assicurato(-a).

intact [ɪnˈtækt] *adj* intatto(-a).

intellectual [ˌɪntəˈlektjuəl] *adj* intellettuale ◆ *n* intellettuale *mf*.

intelligence [ɪnˈtelɪdʒəns] *n (cleverness)* intelligenza *f*.

intelligent [ɪnˈtelɪdʒənt] *adj* intelligente.

intend [ɪnˈtend] *vt (mean)*: **to ~ to do sthg** avere intenzione di fare qc; **you weren't ~ed to know** non dovevi saperlo.

intense [ɪnˈtens] *adj* intenso(-a).

intensity [ɪnˈtensəti] *n* intensità *f*.

intensive [ɪnˈtensɪv] *adj* intensivo(-a).

intensive care *n* terapia *f* intensiva.

intent [ɪnˈtent] *adj*: **to be ~ on doing sthg** essere deciso(-a) a fare qc.

intention [ɪnˈtenʃn] *n* intenzione *f*.

intentional [ɪnˈtenʃənl] *adj* intenzionale.

intentionally [ɪnˈtenʃənəlɪ] *adv* intenzionalmente, apposta.

interchange ['ɪntətʃeɪndʒ] n (on motorway) svincolo m.

intercity® [ˌɪntə'sɪtɪ] n (Br) intercity m inv.

intercom ['ɪntəkɒm] n interfono m.

interest ['ɪntrəst] n interesse m ◆ vt interessare; **to take an ~ in sthg** interessarsi di OR a qc.

interested ['ɪntrəstɪd] adj interessato(-a); **to be ~ in sthg** interessarsi di qc.

interesting ['ɪntrəstɪŋ] adj interessante.

interest rate n tasso m d'interesse.

interfere [ˌɪntə'fɪəʳ] vi (meddle) immischiarsi; **to ~ with sthg** (damage) interferire con qc.

interference [ˌɪntə'fɪərəns] n (on TV, radio) interferenza f.

interior [ɪn'tɪərɪəʳ] adj interno(-a) ◆ n interno m.

intermediate [ˌɪntə'mi:djət] adj intermedio(-a).

intermission [ˌɪntə'mɪʃn] n (at cinema, theatre) intervallo m.

internal [ɪn'tɜ:nl] adj interno(-a).

internal flight n volo m interno.

international [ˌɪntə'næʃənl] adj internazionale.

international flight n volo m internazionale.

interpret [ɪn'tɜ:prɪt] vi fare da interprete.

interpreter [ɪn'tɜ:prɪtəʳ] n interprete mf.

interrogate [ɪn'terəgeɪt] vt interrogare.

interrupt [ˌɪntə'rʌpt] vt interrompere.

intersection [ˌɪntə'sekʃn] n (of roads) incrocio m.

interval ['ɪntəvl] n intervallo m.

intervene [ˌɪntə'vi:n] vi (person, event) intervenire.

interview ['ɪntəvju:] n (on TV, in magazine) intervista f; (for job) colloquio m ◆ vt (on TV, in magazine) intervistare; (for job) fare un colloquio a.

interviewer ['ɪntəvju:əʳ] n (on TV, in magazine) intervistatore m (-trice f).

intestine [ɪn'testɪn] n intestino m.

intimate ['ɪntɪmət] adj intimo(-a).

intimidate [ɪn'tɪmɪdeɪt] vt intimidire.

into ['ɪntʊ] prep (inside) in, dentro; (against) contro, in; (concerning) su; **4 ~ 20 goes 5 (times)** il 4 nel 20 ci sta 5 volte; **to translate ~ Italian** tradurre in italiano; **to change ~ sthg** trasformarsi in qc; **to be ~ sthg** (inf: like) essere appassionato di qc.

intolerable [ɪn'tɒlrəbl] adj intollerabile.

intransitive [ɪn'trænzətɪv] adj intransitivo(-a).

intricate ['ɪntrɪkət] adj intricato(-a).

intriguing [ɪn'tri:gɪŋ] adj affascinante.

introduce [ˌɪntrə'dju:s] vt presentare; **I'd like to ~ you to Fred** ti presento Fred.

introduction [ˌɪntrə'dʌkʃn] n (to book, programme) introduzione f; (to person) presentazione f.

introverted ['ɪntrəvɜ:tɪd] adj introverso(-a).

intruder [ɪn'truːdəʳ] *n* intruso *m* (-a *f*).

intuition [ˌɪntjuː'ɪʃn] *n (feeling)* intuizione *f*; *(faculty)* intuito *m*.

invade [ɪn'veɪd] *vt* invadere.

invalid [*adj* ɪn'vælɪd, *n* 'ɪnvəlɪd] *adj (ticket, cheque)* non valido(-a) ◆ *adj* invalido *m* (-a *f*).

invaluable [ɪn'væljʊəbl] *adj* inestimabile.

invariably [ɪn'veərɪəblɪ] *adv* sempre, invariabilmente.

invasion [ɪn'veɪʒn] *n* invasione *f*.

invent [ɪn'vent] *vt* inventare.

invention [ɪn'venʃn] *n* invenzione *f*.

inventory [ˈɪnventrɪ] *n* inventario *m*.

inverted commas [ɪn'vɜːtɪd-] *npl* virgolette *fpl*.

invest [ɪn'vest] *vt* investire ◆ *vi*: to ~ in sthg investire in qc.

investigate [ɪn'vestɪgeɪt] *vt* indagare.

investigation [ɪnˌvestɪ'geɪʃn] *n* indagine *f*.

investment [ɪn'vestmənt] *n* investimento *m*.

invisible [ɪn'vɪzɪbl] *adj* invisibile.

invitation [ˌɪnvɪ'teɪʃn] *n* invito *m*.

invite [ɪn'vaɪt] *vt* invitare; to ~ sb to do sthg *(ask)* invitare qn a fare qc; to ~ sb round invitare qn.

invoice ['ɪnvɔɪs] *n* fattura *f*.

involve [ɪn'vɒlv] *vt (entail)* richiedere, comportare; what does it ~? che cosa comporta?; to be ~d in sthg essere coinvolto in qc.

involved [ɪn'vɒlvd] *adj (entailed)* richiesto(-a), necessario(-a).

inwards ['ɪnwədz] *adv* verso l'interno.

IOU *n* pagherò *m inv*.

IQ *n* Q.I. *m*.

Iran [ɪ'rɑːn] *n* l'Iran *m*.

Iraq [ɪ'rɑːk] *n* l'Iraq *m*.

Ireland ['aɪələnd] *n* l'Irlanda *f*.

iris ['aɪərɪs] *(pl -es)* *n (flower)* giaggiolo *m*, iris *f inv*.

Irish ['aɪrɪʃ] *adj* irlandese ◆ *n (language)* irlandese *m* ◆ *npl*: the ~ gli irlandesi.

Irish coffee *n* Irish coffee *m inv* *(caffè con whisky e panna)*.

Irishman ['aɪrɪʃmən] *(pl -men* [-mən]*)* *n* irlandese *m*.

Irish stew *n* spezzatino di agnello con patate e cipolle.

Irishwoman ['aɪrɪʃˌwʊmən] *(pl -women* [-ˌwɪmɪn]*)* *n* irlandese *f*.

iron ['aɪən] *n (metal)* ferro *m*; *(for clothes)* ferro da stiro; *(golf club)* mazza *f* da golf ◆ *vt* stirare.

ironic [aɪ'rɒnɪk] *adj* ironico(-a).

ironing board ['aɪənɪŋ-] *n* asse *f* da stiro.

ironmonger's ['aɪənˌmʌŋgəz] *n (Br)* ferramenta *f*.

irrelevant [ɪ'reləvənt] *adj* non pertinente, irrilevante.

irresistible [ˌɪrɪ'zɪstəbl] *adj* irresistibile.

irrespective [ˌɪrɪ'spektɪv]: irrespective of *prep* a prescindere da.

irresponsible [ˌɪrɪ'spɒnsəbl] *adj* irresponsabile.

irrigation [ˌɪrɪ'geɪʃn] *n* irrigazione *f*.

irritable ['ɪrɪtəbl] *adj* irritabile.

irritate ['ɪrɪteɪt] *vt* irritare.

irritating ['ɪrɪteɪtɪŋ] *adj* irritante.

IRS *n (Am)* = Fisco *m*.

is [ɪz] → be.

Islam ['ɪzlɑːm] n (religion) islamismo m.

island ['aɪlənd] n isola f.

isle [aɪl] n isola f.

isolated ['aɪsəleɪtɪd] adj isolato(-a).

Israel ['ɪzreɪəl] n Israele m.

issue ['ɪʃuː] n (problem, subject) questione f, problema m; (of newspaper, magazine) numero m ♦ vt (statement, passport, document) rilasciare; (stamps, bank notes) emettere.

it [ɪt] pron 1. (referring to specific thing: subject, after prep) esso(-a); (direct object) lo (la); (indirect object) gli (le); ~'s big è grande; she hit ~ l'ha colpito; give ~ to me dammelo; tell me about ~ parlamene; we went to ~ ci siamo andati. 2. (nonspecific): ~'s nice here si sta bene qui; ~'s me sono io; who is ~? chi è? 3. (used impersonally): ~'s hot fa caldo; ~'s six o'clock sono le sei; ~'s Sunday è domenica.

Italian [ɪ'tæljən] adj italiano(-a) ♦ n (person) italiano m (-a f); (language) italiano m; an ~ restaurant un ristorante italiano.

Italian Riviera n: the ~ la Riviera Ligure.

Italy ['ɪtəlɪ] n l'Italia f.

itch [ɪtʃ] vi (arm, leg) prudere; (person) avere prurito.

item ['aɪtəm] n (object) articolo m; (on agenda) punto m; news ~ notizia f.

itemized bill ['aɪtəmaɪzd-] n bolletta f con lettura dettagliata.

its [ɪts] adj il suo (la sua), i suoi (le sue) (pl).

it's [ɪts] = it is, it has.

itself [ɪt'self] pron (reflexive) si; (after prep), se stesso(-a) sé; the house ~ is fine la casa in sé va bene.

I've [aɪv] = I have.

ivory ['aɪvərɪ] n avorio m.

ivy ['aɪvɪ] n edera f.

J

jab [dʒæb] n (Br: inf: injection) puntura f.

jack [dʒæk] n (for car) cric m inv; (playing card) fante m.

jacket ['dʒækɪt] n (garment) giacca f; (of book) sopraccoperta f; (Am: of record) copertina f; (of potato) buccia f.

jacket potato n patata cotta al forno con la buccia.

jack-knife vi piegarsi su se stesso (camion).

Jacuzzi® [dʒə'kuːzɪ] n vasca f con idromassaggio.

jade [dʒeɪd] n giada f.

jail [dʒeɪl] n prigione f.

jam [dʒæm] n (food) marmellata f; (of traffic) ingorgo m; (inf: difficult situation) pasticcio m ♦ vt (pack tightly) stipare ♦ vi (get stuck) bloccarsi; the roads are jammed le strade sono intasate.

jam-packed [-'pækt] adj (inf) stipato(-a).

Jan. [dʒæn] (abbr of January) gen.

janitor ['dʒænɪtə^r] n (Am & Scot) bidello m (-a f).

January ['dʒænjʊərɪ] n gennaio m, → **September**.

Japan [dʒə'pæn] n il Giappone.

Japanese [,dʒæpə'ni:z] adj giapponese ♦ n (language) giapponese m ♦ npl: **the** ~ i giapponesi.

jar [dʒɑ:^r] n barattolo m, vasetto m.

javelin ['dʒævlɪn] n giavellotto m.

jaw [dʒɔ:] n mascella f.

jazz [dʒæz] n jazz m.

jealous ['dʒeləs] adj geloso(-a).

jeans [dʒi:nz] npl jeans mpl.

jeep® [dʒi:p] n jeep® f inv.

Jello® ['dʒeləʊ] n (Am) gelatina f.

jelly ['dʒelɪ] n (dessert) gelatina f; (Am: jam) marmellata f.

jellyfish ['dʒelɪfɪʃ] (pl inv) n medusa f.

jeopardize ['dʒepədaɪz] vt mettere a repentaglio.

jerk [dʒɜ:k] n (movement) strattone m, scossa f; (inf: idiot) imbecille mf.

jersey ['dʒɜ:zɪ] (pl -s) n (garment) maglia f.

jet [dʒet] n (aircraft) aviogetto m; (of liquid, gas) getto m; (outlet) ugello m.

jetfoil ['dʒetfɔɪl] n aliscafo m.

jet lag n jetleg m.

jet-ski n acqua-scooter m inv.

jetty ['dʒetɪ] n molo m.

Jew [dʒu:] n ebreo m (-a f).

jewel ['dʒu:əl] n gioiello m ❑ **jewels** npl (jewellery) gioielli mpl.

jeweler's ['dʒu:ələz] (Am) = **jeweller's**.

jeweller's ['dʒu:ələz] n (Br) gioielleria f.

jewellery ['dʒu:əlrɪ] n (Br) gioielli mpl.

jewelry ['dʒu:əlrɪ] (Am) = **jewellery**.

Jewish ['dʒu:ɪʃ] adj ebreo(-a).

jigsaw (puzzle) ['dʒɪgsɔ:-] n puzzle m inv.

jingle ['dʒɪŋgl] n (of advert) motivo m musicale di pubblicità.

job [dʒɒb] n lavoro m; **to lose one's** ~ perdere il lavoro.

job centre n (Br) ufficio m di collocamento.

jockey ['dʒɒkɪ] (pl -s) n fantino m (-a f).

jog [dʒɒg] vt (bump) urtare lievemente ♦ vi fare footing ♦ n: **to go for a** ~ andare a fare del footing.

jogging ['dʒɒgɪŋ] n footing m; **to go** ~ fare del footing.

join [dʒɔɪn] vt (club, organization) iscriversi a; (fasten together) unire; (other people, celebrations) unirsi a; (road, river) congiungersi con; (connect) collegare; **to** ~ **a queue** mettersi in fila ❑ **join in** vt fus prendere parte a ♦ vi partecipare.

joint [dʒɔɪnt] adj comune ♦ n (of body) articolazione f; (Br: of meat) taglio m di carne per arrosto; (in structure) giuntura f.

joke [dʒəʊk] n scherzo m; (story) barzelletta f ♦ vi scherzare.

joker ['dʒəʊkə^r] n (playing card) jolly m inv, matta f.

jolly ['dʒɒlɪ] adj (cheerful) allegro(-a) ♦ adv (Br: inf: very) molto.

jolt [dʒəʊlt] n scossa f, sobbalzo m.

jot [dʒɒt]: **jot down** vt sep annotare in fretta.

journal ['dʒɜːnl] *n (professional magazine)* rivista *f; (diary)* diario *m.*

journalist ['dʒɜːnəlıst] *n* giornalista *mf.*

journey ['dʒɜːnı] *(pl -s) n* viaggio *m.*

joy [dʒɔı] *n* gioia *f.*

joypad ['dʒɔıpæd] *n (of video game)* comandi *mpl.*

joyrider ['dʒɔıraıdə'] *n* chi ruba un'auto per farci un giro e poi l'abbandona.

joystick ['dʒɔıstık] *n (of video game)* joystick *m inv.*

judge [dʒʌdʒ] *n* giudice *mf* ◆ *vt* giudicare.

judg(e)ment ['dʒʌdʒmənt] *n* giudizio *m.*

judo ['dʒuːdəʊ] *n* judo *m.*

jug [dʒʌg] *n* brocca *f*, caraffa *f.*

juggernaut ['dʒʌgənɔːt] *n (Br)* grosso autotreno *m*, bestione *m.*

juggle ['dʒʌgl] *vi* fare giochi di destrezza *(con palle, birilli, ecc.).*

juice [dʒuːs] *n* succo *m; (from meat)* sugo *m.*

juicy ['dʒuːsı] *adj (food)* succoso(-a).

jukebox ['dʒuːkbɒks] *n* juke-box *m inv.*

Jul. *(abbr of July)* lug.

July [dʒuː'laı] *n* luglio *m*, → September.

jumble sale ['dʒʌmbl-] *n (Br)* vendita *f* di cose usate *(a scopo di beneficenza).*

---

i JUMBLE SALE

L e "jumble sales" sono delle vendite dell'usato che si tengono solitamente in sale parrocchiali o municipali. Libri, vestiti e casalinghi usati vengono venduti a prezzi bassissimi per raccogliere soldi, di solito per beneficenza.

---

jumbo ['dʒʌmbəʊ] *adj (inf: big)* gigante.

jumbo jet *n* jumbo-jet *m inv.*

jump [dʒʌmp] *n* salto *m*, balzo *m* ◆ *vi* saltare, balzare; *(with fright)* sussultare; *(increase)* salire ◆ *vt (Am):* **to ~ the train/bus** viaggiare sul treno/sull'autobus senza pagare; **to ~ the queue** *(Br)* saltare la fila.

jumper ['dʒʌmpə'] *n (Br: pullover)* maglione *m*, pullover *m inv; (Am: dress)* scamiciato *m.*

jump leads *npl* cavi *mpl* per batteria.

Jun. *(abbr of June)* giu.

junction ['dʒʌŋkʃn] *n (of roads)* incrocio *m; (of railway lines)* nodo *m* ferroviario; *(on motorways)* uscita *f.*

June [dʒuːn] *n* giugno *m*, → September.

jungle ['dʒʌŋgl] *n* giungla *f.*

junior ['dʒuːnjə'] *adj (of lower rank)* di grado inferiore, subalterno(-a); *(Am: after name)* junior ◆ *n (younger person):* **to be sb's ~** essere più giovane di qn.

junior school *n (Br)* scuola *f* elementare *(per bambini da 7 a 11 anni).*

junk [dʒʌŋk] *n (inf: unwanted things)* cianfrusaglie *fpl.*

junk food *n (inf)* porcherie *fpl.*

junkie ['dʒʌŋkı] *n (inf)* drogato *m (-a f).*

junk shop *n* negozio *m* di rigattiere.

jury ['dʒʊərɪ] n giuria f.

just [dʒʌst] adv (recently, slightly) appena; (in the next moment) giusto; (exactly) proprio; (only) solo ◆ adj giusto(-a); **to be ~ about to do sthg** stare per fare qc; **to have ~ done sthg** avere appena fatto qc; **~ about** (almost) praticamente, quasi; (only) ~ per un pelo; **I've (only) ~ arrived** sono arrivato (appena) adesso; **I'm ~ coming** vengo (subito); **~ a minute!** (solo) un minuto!

justice ['dʒʌstɪs] n giustizia f.

justify ['dʒʌstɪfaɪ] vt giustificare.

jut [dʒʌt]: **jut out** vi sporgersi.

juvenile ['dʒuːvənaɪl] adj (young) giovanile; (childish) puerile; (crime) minorile.

K

kangaroo [ˌkæŋɡəˈruː] n canguro m.

karate [kəˈrɑːtɪ] n karate m.

kebab [kɪˈbæb] n: (shish) ~ spiedino m di carne; (doner) ~ pane azzimo imbottito con carne di agnello, insalata e salsa piccante.

keel [kiːl] n chiglia f.

keen [kiːn] adj (enthusiastic) entusiasta; (eyesight, hearing) acuto(-a); **to be ~ on sthg** essere appassionato(-a) di qc; **to be ~ to do sthg** avere voglia di fare qc.

keep [kiːp] (pt & pp kept) vt tenere; (promise) mantenere; (appointment) rispettare; (delay) trattenere ◆ vi (food) mantenersi; (remain) restare; **to ~ (on) doing sthg** (continuously) continuare a fare qc; (repeatedly) fare qc di continuo; **to ~ sb from doing sthg** impedire a qn di fare qc; **'~ back!'** state indietro!; **'~ in lane!'** 'restare in corsia'; **'~ left'** 'tenere la sinistra'; **'~ off the grass!'** 'vietato calpestare l'erba'; **'~ out!'** 'vietato l'accesso'; **'~ your distance!'** 'mantenere la distanza (di sicurezza)'; **to ~ clear (of)** stare lontano (da) ❑ **keep up** vt sep mantenere, continuare ◆ vi: **to ~ up (with)** tenersi al passo (con).

keep-fit n (Br) ginnastica f.

kennel ['kenl] n canile m.

kept [kept] pt & pp → keep.

kerb [kɜːb] n (Br) orlo m del marciapiede.

kerosene ['kerəsiːn] n (Am) cherosene m.

ketchup ['ketʃəp] n ketchup m.

kettle ['ketl] n bollitore m; **to put the ~ on** mettere l'acqua a bollire.

key [kiː] n chiave f; (of piano, typewriter) tasto m; (of map) leggenda f ◆ adj chiave (inv).

keyboard ['kiːbɔːd] n tastiera f.

keyhole ['kiːhəʊl] n buco m della serratura.

keypad ['kiːpæd] n tastiera f.

key ring n portachiavi m inv.

kg (abbr of kilogram) kg.

kick [kɪk] n (of foot) calcio m ◆ vt dare calci a, prendere a calci.

kickoff ['kɪkɒf] n calcio m d'inizio.

kid [kɪd] n (inf) (child) bimbo m (-a f), bambino m (-a f); (young person) ragazzo m (-a f) ◆ vi (joke) scherzare.

kidnap [ˈkɪdnæp] vt rapire.

kidnaper [ˈkɪdnæpər] (Am) = **kidnapper**.

kidnapper [ˈkɪdnæpəʳ] n (Br) rapitore m (-trice f).

kidney [ˈkɪdnɪ] (pl -s) n (organ) rene m; (food) rognone m.

kidney bean n fagiolo m comune.

kill [kɪl] vt (person) uccidere, ammazzare; (time) ammazzare; **my feet are ~ing me!** i piedi mi fanno un male!

killer [ˈkɪləʳ] n assassino m (-a f).

kilo [ˈkiːləʊ] (pl -s) n chilo m.

kilogram n [ˈkɪləgræm] n chilogrammo m.

kilometre [ˈkɪləˌmiːtəʳ] n chilometro m.

kilt [kɪlt] n kilt m inv.

kind [kaɪnd] adj gentile, buono(-a) ♦ n (sort, type) genere m, tipo m; **~ of** (Am: inf) un po'.

kindergarten [ˈkɪndəˌgɑːtn] n asilo m infantile.

kindly [ˈkaɪndlɪ] adv: **would you ~ ...?** potrebbe ..., per favore?

kindness [ˈkaɪndnɪs] n gentilezza f, cortesia f.

king [kɪŋ] n re m inv.

kingfisher [ˈkɪŋˌfɪʃəʳ] n martin m inv pescatore.

king prawn n gambero m.

king-size bed n letto largo 160 cm.

kiosk [ˈkiːɒsk] n (for newspapers etc) chiosco m, edicola f; (Br: phone box) cabina f (telefonica).

kipper [ˈkɪpəʳ] n aringa f affumicata.

kiss [kɪs] n bacio m ♦ vt baciare.

kiss of life n respirazione f bocca a bocca.

kit [kɪt] n (set) attrezzatura f; (clothes) completo m; (for assembly) scatola f di montaggio.

kitchen [ˈkɪtʃɪn] n cucina f.

kitchen unit n mobile m componibile (da cucina).

kite [kaɪt] n (toy) aquilone m.

kitten [ˈkɪtn] n gattino m (-a f).

kitty [ˈkɪtɪ] n (of money) cassa f comune.

kiwi fruit [ˈkiːwiː-] n kiwi m inv.

Kleenex® [ˈkliːneks] n fazzoletto m di carta.

km (abbr of kilometre) km.

km/h (abbr of kilometres per hour) km/h.

knack [næk] n: **to have the ~ of doing sthg** avere l'abilità di fare qc.

knackered [ˈnækəd] adj (Br: inf) stanco morto (stanca morta).

knapsack [ˈnæpsæk] n zaino m.

knee [niː] n ginocchio m.

kneecap [ˈniːkæp] n rotula f.

kneel [niːl] (pt & pp **knelt** [nelt]) vi inginocchiarsi.

knew [njuː] pt → **know**.

knickers [ˈnɪkəz] npl (Br: underwear) mutandine fpl.

knife [naɪf] (pl **knives**) n coltello m.

knight [naɪt] n (in history) cavaliere m; (in chess) cavallo m.

knit [nɪt] vt fare a maglia.

knitted [ˈnɪtɪd] adj fatto(-a) a maglia.

knitting [ˈnɪtɪŋ] n lavoro m a maglia.

knitting needle n ferro m (da calza).

knitwear ['nɪtweəʳ] *n* maglieria *f*.

knives [naɪvz] *pl* → knife.

knob [nɒb] *n* (on door etc) pomello *m*; (on machine) manopola *f*.

knock [nɒk] *n* (at door) colpo *m* ◆ *vt* (head, elbow) battere; (chair, table) battere contro ◆ *vi* (at door etc) bussare ❑ **knock down** *vt sep* (pedestrian) investire; (building) demolire; (price) ribassare; **knock out** *vt sep* (make unconscious) tramortire; (of competition) eliminare; **knock over** *vt sep* (glass, vase) rovesciare; (pedestrian) investire.

knocker ['nɒkəʳ] *n* (on door) battente *m*.

knot [nɒt] *n* nodo *m*.

know [nəʊ] (*pt* knew, *pp* known) *vt* sapere; (person, place) conoscere; **to get to ~ sb** imparare a conoscere qc; **to ~ about sthg** (understand) saperne di qc; (have heard) sapere di qc; **to ~ how to do sthg** saper fare qc; **to ~ of** sapere di; **to be ~n as** essere noto come; **to let sb ~ sthg** far sapere qc a qn; **you ~** (for emphasis) sai.

knowledge ['nɒlɪdʒ] *n* conoscenza *f*; **to my ~** che io sappia.

known [nəʊn] *pp* → know.

knuckle ['nʌkl] *n* (of hand) nocca *f*; (of pork) garretto *m*.

Koran [kɒ'rɑ:n] *n*: **the ~** il Corano.

l (abbr of litre) l.

L (abbr of learner) = P.

lab [læb] *n* (inf) laboratorio *m*.

label ['leɪbl] *n* cartellino *m*, etichetta *f*.

labor ['leɪbər] (Am) = labour.

laboratory [Br lə'bɒrətrɪ, Am 'læbrə,tɔːrɪ] *n* laboratorio *m*.

labour ['leɪbəʳ] *n* (work) lavoro *m*; **to be in ~** (MED) avere le doglie.

labourer ['leɪbərəʳ] *n* manovale *m*.

Labour Party *n* (Br) partito *m* laburista.

labour-saving *adj* che fa risparmiare fatica.

lace [leɪs] *n* (material) merletto *m*; (for shoe) laccio *m*.

lace-ups *npl* scarpe *fpl* con i lacci.

lack [læk] *n* carenza *f* ◆ *vt* non avere ◆ *vi*: **to be ~ing** mancare.

lacquer ['lækəʳ] *n* (for hair) lacca *f*; (paint) vernice *f*.

lad [læd] *n* (inf) ragazzo *m*.

ladder ['lædəʳ] *n* (for climbing) scala *f*; (Br: in tights) smagliatura *f*.

ladies ['leɪdɪz] *n* (Br: toilet) toilette *f inv* per signore.

ladies room (Am) = ladies.

ladieswear ['leɪdɪz,weəʳ] *n* abbigliamento *m* da donna.

ladle ['leɪdl] *n* mestolo *m*.

lady ['leɪdɪ] *n* signora *f*.

ladybird ['leɪdɪbɜːd] *n* coccinella *f*.

ladybug n (Am) = **ladybird**.

lag [læg] vi (trade) ristagnare; **to ~ behind** (move more slowly) restare indietro.

lager ['lɑ:gəʳ] n birra f (chiara).

lagoon [lə'gu:n] n laguna f.

laid [leɪd] pt & pp → **lay**.

lain [leɪn] pp → **lie**.

lake [leɪk] n lago m.

Lake District n: **the ~** la regione dei laghi (nel nordovest dell'Inghilterra).

lamb [læm] n agnello m.

lamb chop n braciola f OR costoletta f d'agnello.

lame [leɪm] adj zoppo(-a).

lamp [læmp] n lampada f; (bicycle lamp) fanale m; (in street) lampione m.

lamppost ['læmppəʊst] n lampione m.

lampshade ['læmpʃeɪd] n paralume m.

land [lænd] n terra f ◆ vi (plane) atterrare; (passengers) sbarcare; (fall) cadere.

landing ['lændɪŋ] n (of plane) atterraggio m; (on stairs) pianerottolo m.

landlady ['lænd,leɪdɪ] n (of house) padrona f di casa; (of pub) proprietaria f.

landlord ['lændlɔ:d] n (of house) padrone m di casa; (of pub) proprietario m.

landmark ['lændmɑ:k] n punto m di riferimento.

landscape ['lændskeɪp] n paesaggio m.

landslide ['lændslaɪd] n (of earth, rocks) frana f.

lane [leɪn] n (narrow road) stradi-

na f; (on road, motorway) corsia f; **'get in ~'** 'disporsi su più file'.

language ['læŋgwɪdʒ] n (of a people, country) lingua f; (system, words) linguaggio m.

lap [læp] n (of person) grembo m; (of race) giro m.

lapel [lə'pel] n risvolto m.

lapse [læps] vi (passport, membership) scadere.

lard [lɑ:d] n strutto m.

larder ['lɑ:dəʳ] n dispensa f.

large [lɑ:dʒ] adj grande; (person, dog, sum) grosso(-a).

largely ['lɑ:dʒlɪ] adv in gran parte.

large-scale adj su vasta scala.

lark [lɑ:k] n allodola f.

laryngitis [,lærɪn'dʒaɪtɪs] n laringite f.

lasagne [lə'zænjə] n lasagne fpl.

laser ['leɪzəʳ] n laser m inv.

lass [læs] n (inf) ragazza f.

last [lɑ:st] adj ultimo(-a); (week, year, month) scorso(-a) ◆ adv (most recently) l'ultima volta; (after everything else) per ultimo ◆ vi (continue) durare ◆ pron: **the ~** to come l'ultimo ad arrivare; **the ~** but one il penultimo (la penultima); **the day before ~** l'altro ieri; **~ year** l'anno scorso; **the ~ year** l'ultimo anno; **at ~** finalmente; **to arrive ~** arrivare (per) ultimo; **it won't ~ till tomorrow** (food) non va fino a domani.

lastly ['lɑ:stlɪ] adv infine.

last-minute adj dell'ultimo momento.

latch [lætʃ] n serratura f a scatto; **the door is on the ~** la porta non è chiusa a chiave.

late [leɪt] *adj (not on time)* in ritardo; *(after usual time)* tardi *(inv)*; *(dead)* defunto(-a); *(morning, afternoon)* tardo(-a) ♦ *adv (not on time)* in ritardo; *(after usual time)* tardi; in ~ June, ~ in June verso la fine di giugno; **the train is running two hours** ~ il treno viaggia con due ore di ritardo.

lately ['leɪtlɪ] *adv* ultimamente.

late-night *adj* aperto(-a) fino a tardi; ~ **opening** apertura prolungata *(di negozi)*.

later ['leɪtə^r] *adj (train)* successivo(-a) ♦ *adv:* ~ **(on)** più tardi; **at a** ~ **date** in futuro.

latest ['leɪtɪst] *adj:* **the** ~ **fashion** l'ultima moda; **the** ~ l'ultimo(-a); **at the** ~ al più tardi.

lather ['lɑːðə^r] *n* schiuma f.

Latin ['lætɪn] *n* latino m.

Latin America *n* l'America f Latina.

Latin American *adj* latino-americano(-a) ♦ *n* latino-americano m (-a f).

latitude ['lætɪtjuːd] *n (distance from Equator)* latitudine f.

latter ['lætə^r] *n:* **the** ~ quest'ultimo(-a).

laugh [lɑːf] *n* risata f ♦ *vi* ridere; **to have a** ~ *(Br: inf)* farsi due risate □ **laugh at** *vt fus (mock)* ridere di.

laughter ['lɑːftə^r] *n* riso m.

launch [lɔːntʃ] *vt (boat)* varare; *(new product)* lanciare.

laund(e)rette [lɔːn'dret] *n* lavanderia f *(automatica)*.

laundry ['lɔːndrɪ] *n (washing)* bucato m; *(place)* lavanderia f.

lavatory ['lævətrɪ] *n* gabinetto m.

lavender ['lævəndə^r] *n* lavanda f.

lavish ['lævɪʃ] *adj (meal, decoration)* sontuoso(-a).

law [lɔː] *n* legge f; **to be against the** ~ essere contro la legge.

lawn [lɔːn] *n* prato m.

lawnmower ['lɔːn,məʊə^r] *n* tagliaerba m inv.

lawyer ['lɔːjə^r] *n (in court)* avvocato m; *(solicitor)* notaio m.

laxative ['læksətɪv] *n* lassativo m.

lay [leɪ] *(pt & pp* laid*) pt → lie* ♦ *vt (place)* poggiare; *(egg)* fare; **to** ~ **the table** apparecchiare la tavola □ **lay off** *vt sep (worker)* licenziare; **lay on** *vt sep (food, transport)* fornire; *(entertainment)* organizzare; **lay out** *vt sep (display)* disporre.

lay-by *(pl* lay-bys*) n* piazzola f sosta.

layer ['leɪə^r] *n* strato m.

layman ['leɪmən] *(pl* -men [-mən]*) n* profano m (-a f).

layout ['leɪaʊt] *n (of building)* struttura f; *(of streets)* tracciato m.

lazy ['leɪzɪ] *adj* pigro(-a).

lb *abbr* = **pound**.

lead[1] [liːd] *(pt & pp* led*) vt (take)* condurre; *(team, party, march)* guidare; *(procession)* aprire ♦ *vi (be winning)* condurre ♦ *n (for dog)* guinzaglio m; *(cable)* cavo m; **to** ~ **sb to do sthg** indurre qn a fare qc; **to** ~ **to** portare a; **to** ~ **the way** fare strada; **to be in the** ~ essere in testa.

lead[2] [led] *n* piombo m; *(for pencil)* mina f ♦ *adj* di piombo.

leaded petrol ['ledɪd-] *n* benzina f con piombo.

leader ['liːdə^r] *n (of group)* capo

m; *(of union, party)* leader *mf inv*; *(in race)* chi è in testa.

leadership ['liːdəʃɪp] *n (position)* direzione *f*.

lead-free [led-] *adj* senza piombo.

leading ['liːdɪŋ] *adj (most important)* principale.

lead singer [liːd-] *n* cantante *mf* (solista).

leaf [liːf] *(pl leaves) n (of tree)* foglia *f*.

leaflet ['liːflɪt] *n* dépliant *m inv*.

league [liːg] *n (SPORT)* campionato *m*; *(association)* lega *f*.

leak [liːk] *n (hole)* buco *m*; *(of gas, water)* perdita *f* ◆ *vi (tank)* perdere; *(roof)* gocciolare.

lean [liːn] *(pt & pp leant [lent] OR -ed) adj (meat)* magro(-a); *(person, animal)* asciutto(-a) ◆ *vi (bend)* piegarsi; *(building)* pendere ◆ *vt*: **to ~ sthg against sthg** appoggiare qc a qc; **to ~ on** appoggiarsi a □ **lean forward** *vi* sporgersi (in avanti); **lean over** *vi* sporgersi.

leap [liːp] *(pt & pp leapt [lept] OR -ed) vi (jump)* balzare.

leap year *n* anno *m* bisestile.

learn [lɜːn] *(pt & pp learnt OR -ed) vt* imparare; **to ~ (how) to do sthg** imparare a fare qc; **to ~ about sthg** *(hear about)* venire a sapere di qc; *(study)* studiare qc.

learner (driver) ['lɜːnə^r-] *n* guidatore *m* (-trice *f*) principiante.

learnt [lɜːnt] *pt & pp → learn.*

lease [liːs] *n* contratto *m* d'affitto ◆ *vt* affittare; **to ~ sthg from sb** affittare qc da qn; **to ~ sthg to sb** affittare qc a qn.

leash [liːʃ] *n* guinzaglio *m*.

least [liːst] *adv* meno (di tutti) ◆ *adj* meno ... di tutti ◆ *pron*: **(the) ~** meno di tutti; **at ~** almeno; **the ~ he could do** il minimo che potesse fare.

leather ['leðə^r] *n* cuoio *m*, pelle *f* □ **leathers** *npl (of motorcyclist)* tuta *f* in pelle da motociclista.

leave [liːv] *(pt & pp left)* vt lasciare; *(school)* finire ◆ *vi (go away)* andarsene; *(train, bus)* partire ◆ *n (time off work)* permesso *m*; **to ~ a message** lasciare un messaggio, → **left** □ **leave behind** *vt sep (not take away)* lasciare; **leave out** *vt sep* tralasciare.

leaves [liːvz] *pl → leaf.*

Lebanon ['lebənən] *n* il Libano.

lecture ['lektʃə^r] *n (at university)* lezione *f*; *(at conference)* conferenza *f*.

lecturer ['lektʃərə^r] *n* docente *mf* (universitario).

lecture theatre *n* aula *f (ad anfiteatro).*

led [led] *pt & pp → lead¹.*

ledge [ledʒ] *n (of window)* davanzale *m*.

leek [liːk] *n* porro *m*.

left [left] *pt & pp → leave* ◆ *adj (not right)* sinistro(-a) ◆ *adv* a sinistra ◆ *n* sinistra *f*; **on the ~** a sinistra; **there are none ~** sono finiti.

left-hand *adj (side)* sinistro(-a); *(lane)* di sinistra.

left-hand drive *n* guida *f* a sinistra.

left-handed [-'hændɪd] *adj (person)* mancino(-a); *(implement)* per mancini.

left-luggage locker *n (Br)* armadietto *m* per deposito bagagli.

left-luggage office n (Br) deposito m bagagli.

left-wing adj di sinistra.

leg [leg] n gamba f; (of animal) zampa f; ~ **of lamb** coscia f d'agnello.

legal ['li:gl] adj legale.

legal aid n assistenza f legale gratuita.

legalize ['li:gəlaɪz] vt legalizzare.

legal system n sistema f legale.

legend ['ledʒənd] n leggenda f.

leggings ['legɪŋz] npl fuseaux mpl, pantacollant mpl.

legible ['ledʒɪbl] adj leggibile.

legislation [,ledʒɪs'leɪʃn] n legislazione f.

legitimate [lɪ'dʒɪtɪmət] adj legittimo(-a).

leisure [Br 'leʒə', Am 'li:ʒər] n tempo m libero.

leisure centre n centro m sportivo.

leisure pool n piscina f.

lemon ['lemən] n limone m.

lemonade [,lemə'neɪd] n limonata f.

lemon curd [-kɜːd] n (Br) sorta di marmellata a base di succo e scorza di limone, uova, burro e zucchero.

lemon juice n succo m di limone.

lemon meringue pie n dolce composto da una base di pasta frolla e uno strato di crema al limone rivestito di meringa.

lemon sole n limanda f (varietà di sogliola).

lemon tea n tè m al limone.

lend [lend] (pt & pp lent) vt prestare; **to ~ sb sthg** prestare

qc a qn.

length [leŋθ] n (in distance) lunghezza f; (in time) durata f; (of swimming pool) vasca f.

lengthen ['leŋθən] vt allungare.

lens [lenz] n lente f.

lent [lent] pt & pp → **lend**.

Lent [lent] n la Quaresima.

lentils ['lentlz] npl lenticchie fpl.

Leo (pl -s) n Leone m.

leopard ['lepəd] n leopardo m.

leopard-skin adj a pelle di leopardo.

leotard ['li:əta:d] n calzamaglia f.

leper ['lepə'] n lebbroso m (-a f).

lesbian ['lezbɪən] adj lesbico(-a) ♦ n lesbica f.

less [les] adj, adv & pron meno; ~ **than 20** meno di 20.

lesson ['lesn] n (class) lezione f.

let [let] (pt & pp let) vt (allow) lasciare; (rent out) affittare; **to ~ sb do sthg** lasciar fare qc a qn; **to ~ go of sthg** mollare qc; **to ~ sb have sthg** (give) dare qc a qn; **to ~ sb know sthg** far sapere qc a qn; **~'s go!** andiamo!; **'to ~'** 'affittasi' ❑ **let in** vt sep (allow to enter) far entrare; **let off** vt sep (excuse): **to ~ sb off doing sthg** dispensare qn dal fare qc; **can you ~ me off at the station?** mi fa scendere alla stazione?; **let out** vt sep (allow to go out) far uscire.

letdown ['letdaʊn] n (inf) delusione f.

lethargic [lə'θɑ:dʒɪk] adj apatico(-a).

letter ['letə'] n lettera f.

letterbox ['letəbɒks] n (Br) buca f delle lettere.

lettuce ['letɪs] n lattuga f.

leuk(a)emia [lu:'ki:mɪə] n leucemia f.

level ['levl] adj (flat) piano(-a); (horizontal) orizzontale ◆ n livello m; (storey) piano m; **to be ~ with** essere allo stesso livello di.

level crossing n (Br) passaggio m a livello.

lever [Br 'li:vər, Am 'levər] n leva f.

liability [ˌlaɪə'bɪlətɪ] n (responsibility) responsabilità f.

liable ['laɪəbl] adj: **to be ~ to do sthg** avere la tendenza a fare qc; **to be ~ for sthg** rispondere di qc.

liaise [lɪ'eɪz] vi: **to ~ with** mantenere i contatti con.

liar ['laɪər] n bugiardo m (-a f).

liberal ['lɪbərəl] adj (tolerant) liberale; (generous) generoso(-a).

Liberal Democrat Party n Partito m Liberaldemocratico.

liberate ['lɪbəreɪt] vt liberare.

liberty ['lɪbətɪ] n libertà f inv.

Libra n Bilancia f.

librarian [laɪ'breərɪən] n bibliotecario m (-a f).

library ['laɪbrərɪ] n biblioteca f.

Libya ['lɪbɪə] n la Libia.

lice [laɪs] npl pidocchi mpl.

licence ['laɪsəns] n (Br: official document) licenza f ◆ vt (Am) = **license; driving ~** patente f (di guida); **TV ~** abbonamento m alla televisione.

license ['laɪsəns] vt (Br) autorizzare ◆ n (Am) = **licence**.

licensed ['laɪsənst] adj (restaurant, bar) munito di licenza per la vendita di alcolici.

licensing hours ['laɪsənsɪŋ-] npl (Br) orario in cui è consentita la vendita di alcolici.

lick [lɪk] vt leccare.

lid [lɪd] n (cover) coperchio m.

lie [laɪ] (pt lay, pp lain, cont lying) n bugia f ◆ vi (tell lie: pt & pp lied) mentire; (lie horizontal) essere disteso; (lie down) sdraiarsi; (be situated) trovarsi; **to tell ~s** dire bugie; **to ~ about sthg** mentire su qc ❑ **lie down** vi sdraiarsi.

lieutenant [Br lef'tenənt, Am lu:'tenənt] n tenente m.

life [laɪf] (pl lives) n vita f.

life assurance n assicurazione f sulla vita.

life belt n salvagente m.

lifeboat ['laɪfbəʊt] n scialuppa f di salvataggio.

lifeguard ['laɪfgɑːd] n bagnino m (-a f).

life jacket n giubbotto m di salvataggio.

lifelike ['laɪflaɪk] adj fedele.

life preserver [-prɪ'zɜːvər] n (Am) (life belt) salvagente m; (life jacket) giubbotto m di salvataggio.

life-size adj a grandezza naturale.

lifespan ['laɪfspæn] n vita f.

lifestyle ['laɪfstaɪl] n stile m di vita.

lift [lɪft] n (Br: elevator) ascensore m ◆ vt (raise) sollevare, alzare ◆ vi (fog) alzarsi; **to give sb a ~** dare un passaggio a qn ❑ **lift up** vt sep sollevare, alzare.

light [laɪt] (pt & pp lit OR -ed) adj leggero(-a); (not dark) chiaro(-a); (traffic) scorrevole ◆ n luce f; (of car, bike) faro m ◆ vt (fire, cigarette) accendere; (room, stage) illuminare; **have you got a ~?** hai da accende-

link

re?; **to set ~ to** sthg dar fuoco a qc □ **lights** *npl* (*traffic lights*) semaforo *m*; **light up** *vt sep* (*house, road*) illuminare ◆ *vi* (*inf: light a cigarette*) accendersi una sigaretta.

light bulb *n* lampadina *f*.

lighter ['laɪtə^r] *n* accendino *m*.

light-hearted [-'ha:tɪd] *adj* gioviale.

lighthouse ['laɪthaʊs, *pl* -haʊzɪz] *n* faro *m*.

lighting ['laɪtɪŋ] *n* illuminazione *f*.

light meter *n* contatore *m* della luce.

lightning ['laɪtnɪŋ] *n* lampi *mpl*, fulmini *mpl*.

lightweight ['laɪtweɪt] *adj* (*clothes, object*) leggero(-a).

like [laɪk] *prep* come; (*typical of*) tipico di ◆ *vt* (*want*) volere; **I ~ it** mi piace; **I ~ them** mi piacciono; **I ~ going out** mi piace uscire; **I'd ~ to sit down** vorrei sedermi; **I'd ~ a drink** vorrei bere qualcosa; **what's it ~?** com'è?; **to look ~ sb** assomigliare a qn; **do it ~ this** fallo così; **it's not ~ him** non è da lui.

likelihood ['laɪklɪhʊd] *n* probabilità *f*.

likely ['laɪklɪ] *adj* probabile.

likeness ['laɪknɪs] *n* somiglianza *f*.

likewise ['laɪkwaɪz] *adv* allo stesso modo; **to do ~** fare lo stesso.

lilac ['laɪlək] *adj* lilla (*inv*).

Lilo® ['laɪləʊ] (*pl* -s) *n* (*Br*) materassino *m* (pneumatico).

lily ['lɪlɪ] *n* giglio *m*.

lily of the valley *n* mughetto *m*.

limb [lɪm] *n* arto *m*.

lime [laɪm] *n* (*fruit*) limetta *f*; ~ (*juice*) succo *m* di limetta.

limestone ['laɪmstəʊn] *n* calcare *m*.

limit ['lɪmɪt] *n* limite *m* ◆ *vt* limitare; **the city ~s** i confini della città.

limited ['lɪmɪtɪd] *adj* (*restricted*) limitato(-a); (*in company name*) a responsabilità limitata.

limp [lɪmp] *adj* floscio(-a) ◆ *vi* zoppicare.

line [laɪn] *n* linea *f*; (*row*) fila *f*; (*Am: queue*) coda *f*, fila; (*of words on page*) riga *f*; (*of poem, song*) verso *m*; (*for fishing*) lenza *f*; (*rope, washing line*) corda *f*; (*of business, work*) settore *m*, ramo *m* ◆ *vt* (*coat, drawers*) foderare; **in ~** (*aligned*) allineato; **it's a bad ~** la linea è disturbata; **the ~ is engaged** la linea è occupata; **to drop sb a ~** (*inf*) mandare due righe a qn; **to stand in ~** (*Am*) stare in fila □ **line up** *vt sep* (*arrange*) organizzare ◆ *vi* allinearsi.

lined [laɪnd] *adj* (*paper*) rigato(-a), a righe.

linen ['lɪnɪn] *n* (*cloth*) lino *m*; (*tablecloths, sheets*) biancheria *f*.

liner ['laɪnə^r] *n* (*ship*) nave *f* di linea.

linesman ['laɪnzmən] (*pl* -men [-mən]) *n* guardalinee *m inv*.

linger ['lɪŋɡə^r] *vi* (*in place*) attardarsi.

lingerie ['lænʒərɪ] *n* biancheria *f* intima (*femminile*).

lining ['laɪnɪŋ] *n* (*of coat, jacket*) fodera *f*; (*of brake*) guarnizione *f*.

link [lɪŋk] *n* (*connection*) collegamento *m*; (*between countries, companies*) relazione *f* ◆ *vt* (*connect*) collegare; **rail ~** collegamento ferroviario; **road ~** collegamento stradale.

lino ['laɪnəʊ] n (Br) linoleum m.

lion ['laɪən] n leone m.

lioness ['laɪənes] n leonessa f.

lip [lɪp] n (of person) labbro m.

lip salve [-sælv] n burro m di cacao.

lipstick ['lɪpstɪk] n rossetto m.

liqueur [lɪ'kjʊəʳ] n liquore m (dolce).

liquid ['lɪkwɪd] n liquido m.

liquor ['lɪkər] n (Am) superalcolico m.

liquorice ['lɪkərɪs] n liquirizia f.

lisp [lɪsp] n difetto f di pronuncia (relativo alla lettera s).

list [lɪst] n lista f, elenco m ♦ vt elencare.

listen ['lɪsn] vi: **to ~ (to)** ascoltare.

listener ['lɪsnəʳ] n (on radio) ascoltatore m (-trice f).

lit [lɪt] pt & pp → **light**.

liter ['liːtər] n (Am) = **litre**.

literally ['lɪtərəlɪ] adv letteralmente.

literary ['lɪtərərɪ] adj letterario(-a).

literature ['lɪtrətʃəʳ] n letteratura f; (printed information) materiale m illustrativo.

litre ['liːtəʳ] n (Br) litro m.

litter ['lɪtəʳ] n (rubbish) rifiuti mpl.

litterbin ['lɪtəbɪn] n (Br) cestino m dei rifiuti.

little ['lɪtl] adj piccolo(-a); (not much) poco(-a) ♦ pron & adv poco; **as ~ as possible** il meno possibile; **~ by ~** poco a poco ▫ **a little** pron & adv un po' ♦ adj un po' di.

little finger n mignolo m.

live¹ [lɪv] vi vivere; (have home) vivere, abitare; **to ~ with sb** vivere con qn ▫ **live together** vi vivere insieme.

live² [laɪv] adj (alive) vivo(-a); (programme, performance) dal vivo; (wire) sotto tensione ♦ adv in diretta.

lively ['laɪvlɪ] adj (person) vivace; (place, atmosphere) animato(-a).

liver ['lɪvəʳ] n fegato m.

lives [laɪvz] pl → **life**.

living ['lɪvɪŋ] adj vivente ♦ n: **to earn a ~** guadagnarsi da vivere; **what do you do for a ~?** che lavoro fa?

living room n soggiorno m.

lizard ['lɪzəd] n lucertola f.

load [ləʊd] n (thing carried) carico m ♦ vt caricare; **~s of** (inf) un sacco di.

loaf [ləʊf] (pl loaves) n: **a ~ (of bread)** una pagnotta.

loan [ləʊn] n prestito m ♦ vt prestare.

loathe [ləʊð] vt detestare.

loaves [ləʊvz] pl → **loaf**.

lobby ['lɒbɪ] n (hall) atrio m.

lobster ['lɒbstəʳ] n aragosta f.

local ['ləʊkl] adj locale; (train) regionale ♦ n (inf: local person) abitante mf del posto; (Br: pub) bar m vicino; (Am: train) regionale m; (Am: bus) autobus m inv.

local anaesthetic n anestesia f locale.

local call n chiamata f urbana.

local government n amministrazione f locale.

locate [Br ləʊˈkeɪt, Am ˈləʊkeɪt] vt (find) localizzare; **to be ~d** essere situato.

location [ləʊˈkeɪʃn] *n (place)* posizione *f*.

loch [lɒk] *n (Scot)* lago *m*.

lock [lɒk] *n (on door, drawer)* serratura *f*; *(for bike)* lucchetto *m*; *(on canal)* chiusa *f* ◆ *vt (door, drawer, car)* chiudere a chiave; *(keep safely)* chiudere ◆ *vi (become stuck)* bloccarsi ❑ **lock in** *vt sep* chiudere dentro; **lock out** *vt sep* chiudere fuori; **lock up** *vt sep (imprison)* mettere dentro ◆ *vi* chiudere porte e finestre.

locker [ˈlɒkəʳ] *n* armadietto *m*.

locker room *n (Am)* spogliatoio *m*.

locket [ˈlɒkɪt] *n* medaglione *m*.

locomotive [ˌləʊkəˈməʊtɪv] *n* locomotiva *f*.

locum [ˈləʊkəm] *n (doctor)* medico *m* sostituto.

locust [ˈləʊkəst] *n* locusta *f*.

lodge [lɒdʒ] *n (for skiers)* rifugio *m*; *(for hunters)* casino *m* di caccia ◆ *vi (stay)* alloggiare; *(get stuck)* conficcarsi.

lodger [ˈlɒdʒəʳ] *n* pensionante *mf*.

lodgings [ˈlɒdʒɪŋz] *npl* camera *f* ammobiliata.

loft [lɒft] *n* soffitta *f*.

log [lɒg] *n (piece of wood)* ceppo *m*.

logic [ˈlɒdʒɪk] *n* logica *f*.

logical [ˈlɒdʒɪkl] *adj* logico(-a).

logo [ˈləʊgəʊ] *(pl -s) n* logo *m inv*.

loin [lɔɪn] *n* lombata *f*.

loiter [ˈlɔɪtəʳ] *vi (remain)* attardarsi; *(walk around)* bighellonare.

lollipop [ˈlɒlɪpɒp] *n* lecca lecca *m inv*.

lolly [ˈlɒlɪ] *n (inf: lollipop)* lecca lecca *m inv*; *(Br: ice lolly)* ghiac-

ciolo *m*.

Lombardy *n* la Lombardia.

London [ˈlʌndən] *n* Londra *f*.

Londoner [ˈlʌndənəʳ] *n* londinese *mf*.

lonely [ˈləʊnlɪ] *adj (person)* solo(-a); *(place)* isolato(-a).

long [lɒŋ] *adj* lungo(-a) ◆ *adv* molto; **it's 2 metres ~** è lungo 2 metri; **it's two hours ~** dura due ore; **how ~ is it?** *(in length)* quanto è lungo?; *(in time)* quanto dura?; **a ~ time** molto tempo; **all day ~** tutto il giorno; **as ~ as** *(provided that)* purché; **for ~** per molto tempo; **no ~er** non più; **so ~!** *(inf)* ciao! ❑ **long for** *vt fus* desiderare ardentemente.

long-distance *adj (phone call)* interurbano(-a).

long drink *n* long drink *m inv*.

long-haul *adj* su lunga distanza.

longitude [ˈlɒndʒɪtjuːd] *n* longitudine *f*.

long jump *n* salto *m* in lungo.

long-life *adj (milk, fruit juice)* a lunga conservazione; *(battery)* a lunga durata.

longsighted [ˌlɒŋˈsaɪtɪd] *adj* presbite.

long-term *adj* a lungo termine.

long wave *n* onde *fpl* lunghe.

longwearing [ˌlɒŋˈweərɪŋ] *adj (Am)* resistente.

loo [luː] *(pl -s) n (Br: inf)* gabinetto *m*.

look [lʊk] *n (glance)* sguardo *m*, occhiata *f*; *(appearance)* aspetto *m* ◆ *vi* guardare; *(seem)* sembrare; **you don't ~ well** non hai una gran bella cera; **to ~ onto** *(building*

164

room) dare su; **to have a ~** dare un'occhiata; **(good) ~s** bellezza *f*; **I'm just ~ing** *(in shop)* sto solo guardando; **~ out!** attento! ❏ **look after** *vt fus* occuparsi di; **look at** *vt fus (observe)* guardare; *(examine)* vedere; **look for** *vt fus* cercare; **look forward to** *vt fus* non veder l'ora di; **look out for** *vt fus* cercare; **look round** *vt fus (city, museum)* visitare; *(shop)* fare un giro da ◆ *vi* girarsi; **look up** *vt sep (in dictionary, phone book)* cercare.

loony ['lu:nɪ] *n (inf)* pazzo *m* (-a *f*).

loop [lu:p] *n* cappio *m*.

loose [lu:s] *adj (not fixed firmly)* allentato(-a); *(sweets, sheets of paper)* sciolto(-a); *(clothes)* largo(-a); **to let sb/sthg ~** lasciar libero qn/qc.

loosen ['lu:sn] *vt* allentare.

lop-sided ['-saɪdɪd] *adj* storto(-a).

lord [lɔ:d] *n* lord *m inv*.

lorry ['lɒrɪ] *n (Br)* camion *m inv*.

lorry driver *n (Br)* camionista *mf*.

lose [lu:z] *(pt & pp* lost) *vt & vi* perdere; **to ~ weight** dimagrire.

loser ['lu:zəʳ] *n (in contest)* perdente *mf*.

loss [lɒs] *n* perdita *f*.

lost [lɒst] *pt & pp →* lose ◆ *adj (person)* perso(-a); **to get ~** *(lose way)* perdersi.

lost-and-found office *n (Am)* ufficio *m* oggetti smarriti.

lost property office *n (Br)* ufficio *m* oggetti smarriti.

lot [lɒt] *n (group of people)* gruppo *m*; *(at auction)* lotto *m*; *(Am: car park)* parcheggio *m*; **a ~** *(large*

amount) molto(-a), molti(-e) *(pl)*; *(to a great extent, often)* molto; **a ~ of time** molto tempo; **a ~ of problems** molti problemi; **~s (of)** molto(-a), molti(-e) *(pl)*, un sacco (di); **the ~** *(everything)* tutto quanto (tutta quanta).

lotion ['ləʊʃn] *n* lozione *f*.

lottery ['lɒtərɪ] *n* lotteria *f*.

loud [laʊd] *adj (music, noise)* forte; *(voice)* alto(-a); *(colour, clothes)* sgargiante.

loudspeaker [,laʊd'spi:kəʳ] *n* altoparlante *m*.

lounge [laʊndʒ] *n (in house)* salotto *m*, soggiorno *m*; *(at airport)* sala *f* partenze.

lounge bar *n (Br)* sala di un pub più confortevole e più cara del 'public bar' *m*.

lousy ['laʊzɪ] *adj (inf: poor-quality)* schifoso(-a).

lout [laʊt] *n* teppista *mf*.

love [lʌv] *n* amore *m*; *(in tennis)* zero *m* ◆ *vt* amare; **I ~ reading** mi piace molto leggere; **I'd ~ a coffee** mi andrebbe un caffè; **I'd ~ to help** vorrei tanto aiutare; **to be in ~ (with)** essere innamorato (di); **(with) ~ from** *(in letter)* con affetto.

love affair *n* relazione *f*.

lovely ['lʌvlɪ] *adj (very beautiful)* bello(-a); *(very nice)* delizioso(-a).

lover ['lʌvəʳ] *n (sexual partner)* amante *mf*; *(enthusiast)* appassionato *m* (-a *f*).

loving ['lʌvɪŋ] *adj* affettuoso(-a).

low [ləʊ] *adj* basso(-a); *(quantity)* piccolo(-a); *(supply)* scarso(-a); *(standard, quality, opinion)* scadente; *(depressed)* depresso(-a) ◆ *n (area of low pressure)* area *f* di bassa pressione; **we're ~ on petrol** abbiamo

luxury

poca benzina.

low-alcohol *adj* a basso contenuto alcolico.

low-calorie *adj* ipocalorico(-a).

low-cut *adj* scollato(-a).

lower ['ləuər] *adj* inferiore ♦ *vt* abbassare.

lower sixth *n* (Br) primo anno di studi superiori per studenti di 17 anni che prepareranno gli 'A levels'.

low-fat *adj* magro(-a).

low tide *n* bassa marea *f*.

loyal ['lɔɪəl] *adj* fedele.

loyalty ['lɔɪəltɪ] *n* fedeltà *f*.

lozenge ['lɒzɪndʒ] *n* (sweet) pasticca *f*, pastiglia *f*.

LP *n* LP *m inv*.

L-plate *n* (Br) targa indicante che chi guida la vettura non ha ancora preso la patente.

Ltd (abbr of limited) ≃ Srl.

lubricate ['lu:brɪkeɪt] *vt* lubrificare.

luck [lʌk] *n* fortuna *f*; **bad ~** sfortuna *f*; **good ~!** buona fortuna!; **with ~** con un po' di fortuna.

luckily ['lʌkɪlɪ] *adv* fortunatamente.

lucky ['lʌkɪ] *adj* fortunato(-a); **to be ~** essere fortunato.

ludicrous ['lu:dɪkrəs] *adj* ridicolo(-a).

lug [lʌg] *vt* (inf) trascinare.

luggage ['lʌgɪdʒ] *n* bagagli *mpl*.

luggage compartment *n* bagagliaio *m*.

luggage locker *n* armadietto *m* per deposito bagagli.

luggage rack *n* (on train) portabagagli *m*.

lukewarm ['lu:kwɔ:m] *adj* tiepido(-a).

lull [lʌl] *n* pausa *f*.

lullaby ['lʌləbaɪ] *n* ninnananna *f*.

lumbago [lʌm'beɪgəu] *n* lombaggine *f*.

lumber ['lʌmbər] *n* (Am: timber) legname *m*.

luminous ['lu:mɪnəs] *adj* fosforescente.

lump [lʌmp] *n* (of coal, mud, butter) pezzo *m*; (of sugar) zolletta *f*; (on body) nodulo *m*.

lump sum *n* compenso *m* forfettario.

lumpy ['lʌmpɪ] *adj* (sauce) grumoso(-a); (mattress) pieno(-a) di bozzi.

lunatic ['lu:nətɪk] *n* pazzo *m* (-a *f*).

lunch [lʌntʃ] *n* pranzo *m*; **to have ~** pranzare.

luncheon ['lʌntʃən] *n* (fml) pranzo *m*.

luncheon meat *n* ≃ carne di maiale *f* in scatola.

lunch hour *n* pausa *f* pranzo.

lunchtime ['lʌntʃtaɪm] *n* ora *f* di pranzo.

lung [lʌŋ] *n* polmone *m*.

lunge [lʌndʒ] *vi*: **to ~ at** gettarsi su.

lurch [lɜ:tʃ] *vi* barcollare.

lure [ljuər] *vt* attirare.

lurk [lɜ:k] *vi* (person) stare in agguato.

lush [lʌʃ] *adj* (grass, field) rigoglioso(-a).

lust [lʌst] *n* (sexual desire) libidine *f*.

Luxembourg ['lʌksəmbɜ:g] *n* il Lussemburgo.

luxurious [lʌg'ʒuərɪəs] *adj* di lusso.

luxury ['lʌkʃərɪ] *adj* di lusso ♦ *n*

lusso m.

lying ['laɪɪŋ] cont → **lie**.

lyrics ['lɪrɪks] npl parole fpl.

m (abbr of metre) m ♦ abbr = **mile**.

M (Br: abbr of motorway) A; (abbr of medium) M.

MA n (abbr of Master of Arts) (titolare di) master in materie umanistiche.

mac [mæk] n (Br: inf: coat) impermeabile m.

macaroni [,mækə'rəʊnɪ] n maccheroni mpl.

macaroni cheese n maccheroni mpl gratinati.

machine [mə'ʃi:n] n macchina f.

machinegun [mə'ʃi:ngʌn] n mitragliatrice f.

machinery [mə'ʃi:nərɪ] n macchine fpl.

machine-washable adj lavabile in lavatrice.

mackerel ['mækrəl] (pl inv) n sgombro m.

mackintosh ['mækɪntɒʃ] n (Br) impermeabile m.

mad [mæd] adj pazzo(-a), matto(-a); (angry) arrabbiato(-a); (uncontrolled) furioso(-a); **to be ~ about** (inf: like a lot) andare pazzo per; **like ~** come un matto.

Madam ['mædəm] n (form of address) signora f.

made [meɪd] pt & pp → **make**.

madeira [mə'dɪərə] n madera m.

made-to-measure adj fatto (-a) su misura.

madness ['mædnɪs] n pazzia f.

magazine [,mægə'zi:n] n (journal) rivista f.

maggot ['mægət] n verme m.

magic ['mædʒɪk] n magia f.

magician [mə'dʒɪʃn] n (conjurer) mago m (-a f).

magistrate ['mædʒɪstreɪt] n magistrato m.

magnet ['mægnɪt] n calamita f.

magnetic [mæg'netɪk] adj magnetico(-a).

magnificent [mæg'nɪfɪsənt] adj magnifico(-a).

magnifying glass ['mægnɪfaɪŋ-] n lente f d'ingrandimento.

mahogany [mə'hɒgənɪ] n mogano m.

maid [meɪd] n cameriera f.

maiden name ['meɪdn-] n nome m da nubile.

mail [meɪl] n posta f ♦ vt (Am) spedire.

mailbox ['meɪlbɒks] n (Am) cassetta f delle lettere.

mailman ['meɪlmən] (pl -men [-mən]) n (Am) postino m.

mail order n vendita f per corrispondenza.

main [meɪn] adj principale.

main course n portata f principale.

main deck n ponte m principale, coperta f.

mainland ['meɪnlənd] n: **the ~** il continente.

main line n linea f principale.

mainly ['meɪnlɪ] *adv* principalmente.

main road *n* strada *f* principale.

mains [meɪnz] *npl:* **the ~** le condutture.

main street *n* (*Am*) corso *m*.

maintain [meɪn'teɪn] *vt* (*keep*) mantenere; (*in good condition*) provvedere alla manutenzione di.

maintenance ['meɪntənəns] *n* (*of car, machine*) manutenzione *f*; (*money*) alimenti *mpl*.

maisonette [,meɪzə'net] *n* (*Br*) appartamento *m* (su due piani).

maize [meɪz] *n* granturco *m*, mais *m*.

major ['meɪdʒər] *adj* (*important*) importante; (*most important*) principale ♦ *n* (*MIL*) maggiore *m* ♦ *vi* (*Am*): **to ~ in** laurearsi in.

majority [mə'dʒɒrətɪ] *n* maggioranza *f*.

major road *n* strada *f* principale.

make [meɪk] (*pt & pp* made) *vt* 1. (*produce, manufacture*) fare; **to be made of** essere (fatto) di; **to ~ lunch/supper** preparare il pranzo/la cena; **made in Japan** fabbricato in Giappone.

2. (*perform, do*) fare; (*decision*) prendere; **to ~ a mistake** fare un errore; **to ~ a phone call** fare una telefonata.

3. (*cause to be*) rendere; **to ~ sthg better** migliorare qc; **to ~ sb happy** rendere felice qn.

4. (*cause to do, force*) fare; **to ~ sb do sthg** far fare qc a qn, costringere qn a fare qc; **it made her laugh** l'ha fatta ridere.

5. (*amount to, total*) fare; **that ~s £5** fanno 5 sterline.

6. (*calculate*): **I ~ it £4** mi viene 4 sterline; **I ~ it seven o'clock** io faccio le sette.

7. (*earn*) fare; **to ~ a loss** registrare una perdita.

8. (*inf: arrive in time for*): **I don't think we'll ~ the 10 o'clock train** non credo che ce la faremo per il treno delle 10.

9. (*friend, enemy*) farsi.

10. (*have qualities for*): **this would ~ a lovely bedroom** sarebbe una camera (da letto) molto carina.

11. (*bed*) fare, rifare.

12. (*in phrases*): **to ~ do (with)** arrangiarsi (con); **to ~ good** (*damage*) risarcire; **to ~ it** (*arrive on time, be able to go*) farcela.

♦ *n* (*of product*) marca *f*.

❑ **make out** *vt sep* (*cheque, receipt*) fare; (*form*) compilare; (*see, hear*) distinguere, capire; **make up** *vt sep* (*invent*) inventare; (*comprise*) costituire, comporre; (*difference*) coprire; **make up for** *vt fus* compensare.

makeshift ['meɪkʃɪft] *adj* di fortuna.

make-up *n* (*cosmetics*) trucco *m*.

malaria [mə'leərɪə] *n* malaria *f*.

Malaysia [mə'leɪzɪə] *n* la Malesia.

male [meɪl] *adj* maschile; (*child, animal*) maschio ♦ *n* (*animal*) maschio *m*.

malfunction [mæl'fʌŋkʃn] *vi* (*fml*) funzionare male.

malignant [mə'lɪgnənt] *adj* (*tumour*) maligno(-a).

mall [mɔːl] *n* (*shopping centre*) centro *m* commerciale.

 MALL

L unga distesa di verde nel cuore di Washington DC, il Mall si estende dal Campidoglio al Lincoln Memorial. Lungo di esso si trovano i musei della Smithsonian Institution, gallerie d'arte, la Casa Bianca, il Washington Memorial e il Jefferson Memorial. Il muro ("the Wall"), sul quale sono incisi i nomi dei soldati morti o dispersi nella guerra del Vietnam, si trova all'estremità occidentale del Mall.

Nel Regno Unito il Mall è il nome del lungo viale alberato nel centro di Londra, che porta da Buckingham Palace a Trafalgar Square.

mallet ['mælɪt] *n* maglio *m*.

malt [mɔ:lt] *n* malto *m*.

maltreat [,mæl'tri:t] *vt* maltrattare.

malt whisky *n* whisky *m inv* di malto.

mammal ['mæml] *n* mammifero *m*.

man [mæn] (*pl* **men**) *n* uomo *m* ◆ *vt* (*office*) dotare di personale; (*phones*) rispondere a.

manage ['mænɪdʒ] *vt* (*company, business*) dirigere; (*suitcase*) farcela a portare; (*job*) riuscire a fare; (*food*) farcela a mangiare ◆ *vi* (*cope*) farcela; **can you ~ Friday?** venerdì ti andrebbe bene?; **to ~ to do sthg** riuscire a fare qc.

management ['mænɪdʒmənt] *n* direzione *f*.

manager ['mænɪdʒə*] *n* (*of business, bank, shop*) direttore *m*; (*of sports team*) allenatore *m*.

manageress [,mænɪdʒə'res] *n* (*of business, bank, shop*) direttrice *f*.

managing director ['mænɪdʒ-ɪŋ-] *n* amministratore *m* delegato.

mandarin ['mændərɪn] *n* mandarino *m*.

mane [meɪn] *n* criniera *f*.

maneuver [mə'nu:vər] (*Am*) = **manoeuvre**.

mangetout [,mɒnʒ'tu:] *n* pisello *m* mangiatutto.

mangle ['mæŋgl] *vt* (*body*) straziare.

mango ['mæŋgəʊ] (*pl* **-es** OR **-s**) *n* mango *m*.

Manhattan [mæn'hætən] *n* Manhattan *f*.

 MANHATTAN

Q uartiere centrale di New York, è diviso in tre zone principali: Downtown, Midtown e Upper Manhattan. Vi si trovano alcuni fra i grattacieli più famosi del mondo, quali l'Empire State Building e il Chrysler Building, e luoghi celebri quali Central Park, la Quinta Strada (Fifth Avenue), Broadway e il Greenwich Village.

manhole ['mænhəʊl] *n* pozzo *m* d'ispezione.

maniac ['meɪnɪæk] *n* (*inf*) pazzo *m* (*-a f*).

manicure ['mænɪkjʊə*] *n* manicure *f inv*.

manifold ['mænɪfəʊld] *n* (*AUT*) collettore *m*.

manipulate [mə'nɪpjʊlaɪt] *vt* (*person*) manipolare; (*machine, controls*) manovrare.

mankind [ˌmænˈkaɪnd] n l'umanità f.

manly [ˈmænlɪ] adj virile.

man-made adj artificiale.

manner [ˈmænəʳ] n (way) modo m □ **manners** npl maniere fpl.

manoeuvre [məˈnuːvəʳ] n (Br) manovra f ◆ vt (Br) manovrare.

manor [ˈmænəʳ] n grande casa f di campagna.

mansion [ˈmænʃn] n casa f signorile.

manslaughter [ˈmænˌslɔːtəʳ] n omicidio m colposo.

mantelpiece [ˈmæntlpiːs] n mensola f del caminetto.

manual [ˈmænjʊəl] adj manuale ◆ n manuale m.

manufacture [ˌmænjʊˈfæktʃəʳ] n fabbricazione f ◆ vt (produce) fabbricare.

manufacturer [ˌmænjʊˈfæktʃərəʳ] n fabbricante m.

manure [məˈnjʊəʳ] n concime m.

many [ˈmenɪ] (compar **more**, superl **most**) adj molti(-e) ◆ pron molti mpl (-e fpl); **how ~?** quanti(-e)?; **so ~** così tanti(-e); **too ~** troppi(-e); **take as ~ as you like** prendine quanti ne vuoi; **twice as ~ as** il doppio di.

map [mæp] n (of country) carta f geografica; (of town) pianta f.

Mar. (abbr of March) mar.

marathon [ˈmærəθn] n maratona f.

marble [ˈmɑːbl] n (stone) marmo m; (glass ball) bilia f, pallina f (di vetro).

march [mɑːtʃ] n (demonstration) marcia f ◆ vi (walk quickly) avanzare con passo deciso.

March [mɑːtʃ] n marzo m, →

September.

mare [meəʳ] n giumenta f.

margarine [ˌmɑːdʒəˈriːn] n margarina f.

margin [ˈmɑːdʒɪn] n margine m.

marina [məˈriːnə] n porto m turistico.

marinated [ˈmærɪneɪtɪd] adj marinato(-a).

marital status [ˈmærɪtl-] n stato m civile.

mark [mɑːk] n (spot) macchia f; (cut, symbol) segno m; (SCH) voto m; (of gas oven) numero corrispondente a una certa temperatura ◆ vt (blemish) macchiare; (put symbol on) segnare; (correct) correggere; (show position of) indicare.

marker pen [ˈmɑːkə-] n (grosso) pennarello m.

market [ˈmɑːkɪt] n mercato m.

marketing [ˈmɑːkɪtɪŋ] n marketing m.

marketplace [ˈmɑːkɪtpleɪs] n (place) piazza f del mercato.

markings [ˈmɑːkɪŋz] npl (on road) segnaletica f orizzontale.

marmalade [ˈmɑːməleɪd] n marmellata f di agrumi.

marquee [mɑːˈkiː] n padiglione m.

marriage [ˈmærɪdʒ] n matrimonio m.

married [ˈmærɪd] adj sposato(-a); **to get ~** sposarsi.

marrow [ˈmærəʊ] n (vegetable) zucca f.

marry [ˈmærɪ] vt sposare ◆ vi sposarsi.

marsh [mɑːʃ] n palude f.

martial arts [ˌmɑːʃl-] npl arti fpl marziali.

marvellous [ˈmɑːvələs] adj (Br)

meraviglioso(-a).

marvelous ['mɑːvələs] *(Am)* = **marvellous**.

marzipan ['mɑːzɪpæn] *n* marzapane *m*.

mascara [mæs'kɑːrə] *n* mascara *m inv*.

masculine ['mæskjʊlɪn] *adj* maschile; *(woman)* mascolino(-a).

mashed potatoes [mæʃt-] *npl* purè *m inv* di patate.

mask [mɑːsk] *n* maschera *f*.

masonry ['meɪsnrɪ] *n* muratura *f*.

mass [mæs] *n (large amount)* massa *f*; *(RELIG)* messa *f*; **~es (of)** *(inf: lots)* un sacco (di).

massacre ['mæsəkər] *n* massacro *m*.

massage [*Br* 'mæsɑːʒ, *Am* mə'sɑːʒ] *n* massaggio *m* ◆ *vt* massaggiare.

masseur [mæ'sɜːr] *n* massaggiatore *m*.

masseuse [mæ'sɜːz] *n* massaggiatrice *f*.

massive ['mæsɪv] *adj* enorme.

mast [mɑːst] *n (on boat)* albero *m*.

master ['mɑːstər] *n (at school)* insegnante *m*; *(of servant, dog)* padrone *m* ◆ *vt (learn)* imparare a fondo.

masterpiece ['mɑːstəpiːs] *n* capolavoro *m*.

mat [mæt] *n (small rug)* tappetino *m*; *(on table)* sottopiatto *m*.

match [mætʃ] *n (for lighting)* fiammifero *m*; *(game)* partita *f*, incontro *m* ◆ *vt (in colour, design)* intonarsi a OR con; *(be as good as)* corrispondere a; *(be as good as)* uguagliare ◆ *vi (in colour, design)* intonarsi.

matchbox ['mætʃbɒks] *n* scatola *f* di fiammiferi.

matching ['mætʃɪŋ] *adj* intonato(-a).

mate [meɪt] *n (inf: friend)* amico *m* (-a *f*) ◆ *vi* accoppiarsi.

material [mə'tɪərɪəl] *n* materiale *m*; *(cloth)* stoffa *f* □ **materials** *npl (equipment)* occorrente *m*.

maternity leave [mə'tɜːnətɪ-] *n* congedo *m* di maternità.

maternity ward [mə'tɜːnətɪ-] *n* reparto *m* maternità.

math [mæθ] *(Am)* = **maths**.

mathematics [,mæθə'mætɪks] *n* matematica *f*.

maths [mæθs] *n (Br)* matematica *f*.

matinée ['mætɪneɪ] *n* matinée *f inv*.

matt [mæt] *adj* opaco(-a).

matter ['mætər] *n (issue, situation)* questione *f*; *(physical material)* materia *f* ◆ *vi* importare; **it doesn't ~ non importa; no ~ what happens** qualsiasi cosa accada; **there's something the ~ with my car** c'è qualcosa che non va con la mia macchina; **what's the ~?** che cosa c'è (che non va)?; **as a ~ of course** come è naturale; **as a ~ of fact** in realtà.

mattress ['mætrɪs] *n* materasso *m*.

mature [mə'tjʊər] *adj (person, behaviour)* maturo(-a); *(cheese, wine)* stagionato(-a).

mauve [məʊv] *adj (color)* malva *(inv)*.

max. [mæks] *(abbr of maximum)* max.

maximum [ˈmæksɪməm] *adj* massimo(-a) ♦ *n* massimo *m*.

may [meɪ] *aux vb* 1. (*expressing possibility*): it ~ be done as follows si può procedere come segue; it ~ rain può darsi che piova; they ~ have got lost può darsi che si siano persi.
2. (*expressing permission*): ~ I smoke? posso fumare?; you ~ sit, if you wish può sedersi, se vuole.
3. (*when conceding a point*): it ~ be a long walk, but it's worth it sarà anche lontano a piedi, ma ne vale la pena.

May [meɪ] *n* maggio *m*, → September.

maybe [ˈmeɪbiː] *adv* forse.

mayonnaise [ˌmeɪəˈneɪz] *n* maionese *f*.

mayor [meəʳ] *n* sindaco *m*.

mayoress [ˈmeərɪs] *n* sindaco *m* (donna).

maze [meɪz] *n* labirinto *m*.

me [miː] *pron* mi; (*after prep, stressed*) me; she knows ~ (lei) mi conosce; it's ~ sono io; send it to ~ mandalo a me; tell ~ dimmi; he's worse than ~ lui è peggio di me.

meadow [ˈmedəʊ] *n* prato *m*.

meal [miːl] *n* pasto *m*.

mealtime [ˈmiːltaɪm] *n* ora *f* di mangiare.

mean [miːn] (*pt & pp* meant) *adj* (*miserly*) avaro(-a), gretto(-a); (*unkind*) scortese, villano(-a) ♦ *vt* (*signify, matter*) significare, voler dire; (*intend, be serious about*) intendere; (*be a sign of*) significare; I didn't ~ it non dicevo sul serio; to ~ to do sthg avere l'intenzione di fare qc; the bus was meant to leave at 8.30 l'autobus sarebbe dovuto partire alle 8.30; it's meant to be good dovrebbe essere buono.

meaning [ˈmiːnɪŋ] *n* significato *m*, senso *m*.

meaningless [ˈmiːnɪŋlɪs] *adj* (*irrelevant*) insignificante.

means [miːnz] (*pl inv*) *n* (*method*) mezzo *m* ♦ *npl* (*money*) mezzi *mpl*; by all ~! ma certo!; by ~ of per mezzo di.

meant [ment] *pt & pp* → mean.

meantime [ˈmiːntaɪm]: in the meantime *adv* nel frattempo.

meanwhile [ˈmiːnwaɪl] *adv* nel frattempo.

measles [ˈmiːzlz] *n* morbillo *m*.

measure [ˈmeʒəʳ] *vt* misurare ♦ *n* (*step, action*) misura *f*, provvedimento *m*; (*of alcohol*) dose *f*; the room ~s 10 m² la stanza misura 10 m².

measurement [ˈmeʒəmənt] *n* misura *f*.

meat [miːt] *n* carne *f*; red ~ carne rossa; white ~ carne bianca.

meatball [ˈmiːtbɔːl] *n* polpetta *f* (di carne).

mechanic [mɪˈkænɪk] *n* meccanico *m*.

mechanical [mɪˈkænɪkl] *adj* (*device*) meccanico(-a).

mechanism [ˈmekənɪzm] *n* meccanismo *m*.

medal [ˈmedl] *n* medaglia *f*.

media [ˈmiːdjə] *n or npl*: the ~ i (mass) media.

medical [ˈmedɪkl] *adj* medico(-a) ♦ *n* visita *f* medica.

medication [ˌmedɪˈkeɪʃn] *n* medicine *fpl*.

medicine [ˈmedsɪn] *n* medicina f.

medicine cabinet n armadietto m dei medicinali.

medieval [,medr'i:vl] adj medievale.

mediocre [,mi:dr'əʊkə'] adj mediocre.

Mediterranean [,medɪtə'reɪnjən] n: **the ~** (region) la regione del Mediterraneo; **the ~ (Sea)** il (Mare) Mediterraneo.

medium ['mi:djəm] adj medio (-a); (sherry) semisecco(-a).

medium-dry adj semisecco(-a).

medium-sized [-saɪzd] adj di misura media.

medley ['medlɪ] n: **a ~ of cold meats** affettati mpl misti.

meet [mi:t] (pt & pp met) vt incontrare; (get to know) fare la conoscenza di, conoscere; (go to collect) andare a prendere; (need, requirement) soddisfare; (cost, expenses) far fronte a ♦ vi incontrarsi; (get to know each other) conoscersi ❑ **meet up** vi incontrarsi; **meet with** vt fus incontrare.

meeting ['mi:tɪŋ] n (for business) incontro m.

meeting point n (at airport, station) punto m d'incontro.

melody ['melədɪ] n melodia f.

melon ['melən] n melone m.

melt [melt] vi sciogliersi; (metal) fondersi.

member ['membə'] n membro m.

Member of Congress [-'kɒŋgres] n membro m del Congresso (Americano).

Member of Parliament n

= deputato m (-a f).

membership ['membəʃɪp] n (state of being a member) appartenenza f; (members) (numero dei) membri mpl.

memorial [mɪ'mɔ:rɪəl] n monumento m.

memorize ['meməraɪz] vt memorizzare.

memory ['memərɪ] n memoria f; (thing remembered) ricordo m.

men [men] pl → **man**.

menacing ['menəsɪŋ] adj minaccioso(-a).

mend [mend] vt accomodare, aggiustare; (clothes) rammendare.

menopause ['menəpɔ:z] n menopausa f.

men's room n (Am) gabinetto m degli uomini.

menstruate ['menstroeɪt] vi avere le mestruazioni.

menswear ['menzweə'] n abbigliamento m da uomo.

mental ['mentl] adj mentale.

mental hospital n ospedale m psichiatrico.

mentally   handicapped ['mentəlɪ-] adj mentalmente handicappato(-a) ♦ npl: **the ~** i portatori di handicap mentale.

mentally ill ['mentəlɪ-] adj malato(-a) di mente.

mention ['menʃn] vt accennare a; **don't ~ it!** non c'è di che!

menu ['menju:] n menu m inv; **children's ~** menu per bambini.

merchandise ['mɜ:tʃəndaɪz] n mercanzia f, merce f.

merchant marine [,mɜ:tʃənt-mə'ri:n] (Am) = **merchant navy**.

merchant navy [,mɜ:tʃənt-] n

(Br) marina *f* mercantile.

mercury ['mɜːkjʊrɪ] *n* mercurio *m*.

mercy ['mɜːsɪ] *n* pietà *f*.

mere [mɪə^r] *adj* semplice; **a ~ £5** solo 5 sterline.

merely ['mɪəlɪ] *adv* soltanto.

merge [mɜːdʒ] *vi (combine)* fondersi, unirsi; **'merge'** *(Am: AUT)* segnale che indica agli automobilisti che si immettono su un'autostrada di disporsi sulla corsia di destra.

merger ['mɜːdʒə^r] *n* fusione *f*.

meringue [mə'ræn] *n (egg white)* meringa *f*; *(cake)* meringa alla panna.

merit ['merɪt] *n* merito *m*.

merry ['merɪ] *adj* allegro(-a); **Merry Christmas!** Buon Natale!

merry-go-round *n* giostra *f*.

mess [mes] *n (untidiness)* disordine *m*, confusione *f*; *(difficult situation)* pasticcio *m*; **in a ~** *(untidy)* in disordine ❑ **mess about** *vi (inf) (have fun)* divertirsi; *(behave foolishly)* fare lo scemo; **to ~ about with sthg** *(interfere)* intromettersi in qc; **mess up** *vt sep (inf: ruin, spoil)* mandare a monte.

message ['mesɪdʒ] *n* messaggio *m*.

messenger ['mesɪndʒə^r] *n* messaggero *m (-a f)*.

messy ['mesɪ] *adj* disordinato(-a).

met [met] *pt & pp* → **meet**.

metal ['metl] *adj* metallico(-a), di metallo ♦ *n* metallo *m*.

metalwork ['metlwɜːk] *n (craft)* lavorazione *f* dei metalli.

meter ['miːtə^r] *n (device)* contatore *m*; *(Am)* = **metre**.

method ['meθəd] *n* metodo *m*.

methodical [mɪ'θɒdɪkl] *adj* metodico(-a).

meticulous [mɪ'tɪkjʊləs] *adj* meticoloso(-a).

metre ['miːtə^r] *n (Br)* metro *m*.

metric ['metrɪk] *adj* metrico(-a).

mews [mjuːz] *(pl inv) n (Br)* stradina o cortile di antiche scuderie trasformate in appartamenti.

Mexican ['meksɪkn] *adj* messicano(-a) ♦ *n* messicano *m (-a f)*.

Mexico ['meksɪkəʊ] *n* il Messico.

mg *(abbr of milligram)* mg.

miaow [miː'aʊ] *vi (Br)* miagolare.

mice [maɪs] *pl* → **mouse**.

microchip ['maɪkrəʊtʃɪp] *n* microcircuito *m* integrato, microchip *m inv*.

microphone ['maɪkrəfəʊn] *n* microfono *m*.

microscope ['maɪkrəskəʊp] *n* microscopio *m*.

microwave (oven) ['maɪkrəweɪv-] *n* forno *m* a microonde.

midday [,mɪd'deɪ] *n* mezzogiorno *m*.

middle ['mɪdl] *n* mezzo *m*, parte *f* centrale ♦ *adj (central)* di mezzo; **in the ~ of the road** in mezzo alla strada; **in the ~ of April** a metà aprile; **to be in the ~ of doing sthg** stare facendo qc.

middle-aged *adj* di mezza età.

middle-class *adj* borghese.

Middle East *n*: **the ~** il Medio Oriente.

middle name *n* secondo nome *m*.

middle school *n (in UK)* scuola *f* media *(per ragazzi dagli 8 ai 13 anni)*.

midge [mɪdʒ] *n* pappataci *m inv*.

midget ['mɪdʒɪt] n nano m (-a f).

Midlands ['mɪdləndz] npl: **the ~** le contee dell'Inghilterra centrale.

midnight ['mɪdnaɪt] n mezzanotte f.

midsummer ['mɪd'sʌmər] n piena estate f.

midway ['mɪd'weɪ] adv (in space) a metà strada; (in time) a metà.

midweek [adj 'mɪdwi:k, adv mɪd'wi:k] adj di metà settimana ♦ adv a metà settimana.

midwife ['mɪdwaɪf] (pl -wives [-waɪvz]) n levatrice f.

midwinter ['mɪd'wɪntər] n pieno inverno m.

might [maɪt] aux vb 1. (expressing possibility): **we ~ go to Wales this year** forse andremo in Galles quest'anno; **I suppose they ~ still come** può ancora darsi che arrivino; **they ~ have been killed** avrebbero potuto rimanere uccisi.
2. (fml: expressing permission): **~ I have a few words?** posso parlarle un attimo?
3. (when conceding a point): **it ~ be expensive, but it's good quality** sarà anche caro, ma è di buona qualità.
4. (would): **I'd hoped you ~ come too** speravo che venissi anche tu.
♦ n (physical strength) forza f.

migraine ['mi:greɪn, 'maɪgreɪn] n emicrania f.

Milan [mɪ'læn] n Milano f.

mild [maɪld] adj (cheese, person) dolce; (detergent, taste) delicato(-a); (effect, flu) leggero(-a); (weather, climate) mite; (curiosity, surprise) lieve ♦ n (Br: beer) birra f leggera.

mile [maɪl] n miglio m; **it's ~s away** è lontanissimo.

mileage ['maɪlɪdʒ] n distanza f in miglia, = chilometraggio m.

mileometer [maɪ'lɒmɪtər] n = contachilometri m inv.

military ['mɪlɪtrɪ] adj militare.

milk [mɪlk] n latte m ♦ vt (cow) mungere.

milk chocolate n cioccolato m al latte.

milkman ['mɪlkmən] (pl -men [-mən]) n lattaio m.

milk shake n frappé m inv.

milky ['mɪlkɪ] adj (drink) con tanto latte.

mill [mɪl] n (flour-mill) mulino m; (for pepper, coffee) macinino m; (factory) fabbrica f.

milligram ['mɪlɪgræm] n milligrammo m.

millilitre ['mɪlɪ,li:tər] n millilitro m.

millimetre ['mɪlɪ,mi:tər] n millimetro m.

million ['mɪljən] n milione m; **~s of** (fig) milioni di.

millionaire [,mɪljə'neər] n = miliardario m (-a f).

mime [maɪm] vi mimare.

min. [mɪn] (abbr of minute, minimum) min.

mince [mɪns] n (Br) carne f macinata.

mincemeat ['mɪnsmi:t] n (sweet filling) miscuglio a base di uvetta e spezie; (Am: mince) carne f macinata.

mince pie n pasticcino con ripieno a base di uvetta e spezie che si mangia durante il periodo natalizio.

mind [maɪnd] n mente f ♦ vt (be careful of) fare attenzione a; (look after) badare a ♦ vi: **I don't ~** non m'importa; **do you ~ if ...?** le dispiace se ...?; **never ~!** (don't worry) non preoccuparti!, non importa!; it slipped my ~ mi è sfuggito di mente; **to my ~** secondo me, a mio parere; **to bear sthg in ~** tenere presente qc; **to change one's ~** cambiare idea; **to have sthg in ~** avere in mente qc; **to have sthg on one's ~** essere preoccupato per qc; **to make one's ~ up** decidersi; **do you ~ the noise?** le dà fastidio il rumore?; **I wouldn't ~ a drink** non mi dispiacerebbe bere qualcosa; **'~ the gap!'** (on underground) annuncio che avverte i viaggiatori sulla metropolitana di fare attenzione alla buca tra le carrozze e il marciapiede.

mine[1] [maɪn] *pron* il mio (la mia), i miei (le mie) (*pl*); **a friend of ~** un mio amico.

mine[2] [maɪn] *n* (for coal etc) miniera *f*; (bomb) mina *f*.

miner ['maɪnəʳ] *n* minatore *m*.

mineral ['mɪnərəl] *n* minerale *m*.

mineral water *n* acqua *f* minerale.

minestrone [ˌmɪnɪ'strəʊnɪ] *n* minestrone *m*.

mingle ['mɪŋgl] *vi* mescolarsi.

miniature ['mɪnətʃəʳ] *adj* in miniatura ◆ *n* (bottle) bottiglia *f* mignon.

minibar ['mɪnɪbɑːʳ] *n* minibar *m* inv.

minibus ['mɪnɪbʌs] (*pl* -es) *n* minibus *m* inv.

minicab ['mɪnɪkæb] *n* (Br) radiotaxi *m* inv.

minimal ['mɪnɪml] *adj* minimo(-a).

minimum ['mɪnɪməm] *adj* minimo(-a) ◆ *n* minimo *m*.

miniskirt ['mɪnɪskɜːt] *n* minigonna *f*.

minister ['mɪnɪstəʳ] *n* (in government) ministro *m*; (in church) pastore *m*.

ministry ['mɪnɪstrɪ] *n* (of government) ministero *m*.

minor ['maɪnəʳ] *adj* minore, di secondaria importanza ◆ *n* (fml) minorenne *mf*.

minority [maɪ'nɒrətɪ] *n* minoranza *f*.

minor road *n* strada *f* secondaria.

mint [mɪnt] *n* (sweet) caramella *f* alla menta; (plant) menta *f*.

minus ['maɪnəs] *prep* (in subtraction) meno; **it's ~ 10** (degrees C) è meno 10 (gradi).

minuscule ['mɪnəskjuːl] *adj* minuscolo(-a).

minute[1] ['mɪnɪt] *n* minuto *m*; **any ~** da un momento all'altro; **just a ~!** (solo) un minuto!

minute[2] [maɪ'njuːt] *adj* minuscolo(-a).

minute steak [ˌmɪnɪt-] *n* fettina *f* (di carne).

miracle ['mɪrəkl] *n* miracolo *m*.

miraculous [mɪ'rækjʊləs] *adj* miracoloso(-a).

mirror ['mɪrəʳ] *n* specchio *m*; (on car) specchietto *m*.

misbehave [ˌmɪsbɪ'heɪv] *vi* comportarsi male.

miscarriage [ˌmɪs'kærɪdʒ] *n* aborto *m* spontaneo.

miscellaneous [ˌmɪsə'leɪnjəs] *adj* (things) vario(-a); (collection) misto(-a).

mischievous ['mɪstʃɪvəs] *adj* birichino(-a).

misconduct [ˌmɪs'kɒndʌkt] *n* condotta *f* scorretta.

miser ['maizə^r] n avaro m (-a f).

miserable ['mizrəbl] adj (unhappy) infelice; (place, news, weather) deprimente; (amount) misero(-a).

misery ['mizəri] n (unhappiness) tristezza f; (poor conditions) miseria f.

misfire [,mis'faiə^r] vi (car) perdere colpi.

misfortune [mis'fɔ:tʃu:n] n (bad luck) sfortuna f.

mishap ['mishæp] n disavventura f.

misjudge [,mis'dʒʌdʒ] vt giudicare male.

mislay [,mis'lei] (pt & pp -laid) vt smarrire.

mislead [,mis'li:d] (pt & pp -led) vt trarre in inganno.

miss [mis] vt perdere; (not notice) non vedere; (fail to hit) mancare ♦ vi sbagliare; **I ~ you** mi manchi ❑ **miss out** vt sep saltare, omettere ♦ vi: **to ~ out on sthg** perdersi qc.

Miss [mis] n Signorina f.

missile [Br 'misail, Am 'misl] n (weapon) missile m; (thing thrown) oggetto m (scagliato).

missing ['misiŋ] adj (lost) scomparso(-a); (after accident) disperso(-a); **to be ~** (not there) mancare.

missing person n persona f scomparsa.

mission ['miʃn] n missione f.

missionary ['miʃənri] n missionario m (-a f).

mist [mist] n foschia f.

mistake [mi'steik] (pt -took, pp -taken) n sbaglio m, errore m ♦ vt (misunderstand) fraintendere; **by ~** per sbaglio; **to make a ~** fare uno sbaglio; **to ~ sb/sthg for** scambiare qn/qc per.

Mister ['mistə^r] n Signor m.

mistook [mi'stuk] pt → **mistake**.

mistress ['mistris] n (lover) amante f; (Br: teacher) insegnante f.

mistrust [,mis'trʌst] vt diffidare di.

misty ['misti] adj nebbioso(-a).

misunderstanding [,misʌndə'stændiŋ] n malinteso m.

misuse [,mis'ju:s] n cattivo uso m.

mitten ['mitn] n muffola f, manopola f.

mix [miks] vt mescolare ♦ n (for cake, sauce) (miscuglio) preparato m ♦ vi (socially): **to ~ with people** veder gente; **to ~ sthg with sthg** mescolare qc a OR con qc ❑ **mix up** vt sep (confuse) confondere; (put into disorder) mescolare.

mixed [mikst] adj (school) misto(-a).

mixed grill n grigliata f mista.

mixed salad n insalata f mista.

mixed vegetables npl verdure fpl miste.

mixer ['miksə^r] n (for food) frullatore m; (drink) bevanda analcolica usata nella preparazione di cocktail.

mixture ['mikstʃə^r] n (combination) mescolanza f.

mix-up n (inf) confusione f.

ml (abbr of millilitre) ml.

mm (abbr of millimetre) mm.

moan [məun] vi (in pain, grief) gemere; (inf: complain) lamentarsi.

moat [məut] n fossato m.

mobile ['məubail] adj mobile.

mobile phone n telefono m cellulare, telefonino m.

mock [mɒk] adj finto(-a) ♦ vt deridere, prendersi gioco di ♦ n

(Br: exam) esercitazione *f* d'esame.

mode [məʊd] *n* modo *m*.

model ['mɒdl] *n* modello *m*; *(fashion model)* modello *m* (-a *f*).

moderate ['mɒdərət] *adj* moderato(-a).

modern ['mɒdən] *adj* moderno(-a).

modernized ['mɒdənaɪzd] *adj* rimodernato(-a).

modern languages *npl* lingue *fpl* moderne.

modest ['mɒdɪst] *adj* modesto(-a).

modify ['mɒdɪfaɪ] *vt* modificare.

mohair ['məʊheəʳ] *n* mohair *m*.

moist [mɔɪst] *adj* umido(-a).

moisture ['mɔɪstʃəʳ] *n* umidità *f*.

moisturizer ['mɔɪstʃəraɪzəʳ] *n* idratante *m*.

molar ['məʊləʳ] *n* molare *m*.

mold [məʊld] *(Am)* = **mould**.

mole [məʊl] *n* (*animal*) talpa *f*; *(spot)* neo *m*.

molest [mə'lest] *vt* molestare.

mom [mɒm] *n* (*Am: inf*) mamma *f*.

moment ['məʊmənt] *n* momento *m*; **at the ~** al momento; **for the ~** per il momento.

Mon. (*abbr of Monday*) lun.

monarchy ['mɒnəkɪ] *n*: **the ~** la monarchia.

monastery ['mɒnəstrɪ] *n* monastero *m*.

Monday ['mʌndɪ] *n* lunedì *m inv*, → **Saturday**.

money ['mʌnɪ] *n* denaro *m*, soldi *mpl*.

money belt *n* marsupio *m*.

money order *n* vaglia *m inv* (postale).

mongrel ['mʌngrəl] *n* cane *m* bastardo.

monitor ['mɒnɪtəʳ] *n* (*computer screen*) monitor *m inv* ◆ *vt* (*check, observe*) controllare.

monk [mʌŋk] *n* monaco *m*.

monkey ['mʌŋkɪ] (*pl* **monkeys**) *n* scimmia *f*.

monkfish ['mʌŋkfɪʃ] *n* bottatrice *f*.

monopoly [mə'nɒpəlɪ] *n* monopolio *m*.

monorail ['mɒnəʊreɪl] *n* monorotaia *f*.

monotonous [mə'nɒtənəs] *adj* monotono(-a).

monsoon [mɒn'suːn] *n* monsone *m*.

monster ['mɒnstəʳ] *n* mostro *m*.

month [mʌnθ] *n* mese *m*; **every ~** ogni mese; **in a ~'s time** fra un mese.

monthly ['mʌnθlɪ] *adj* mensile ◆ *adv* mensilmente, ogni mese.

monument ['mɒnjʊmənt] *n* monumento *m*.

mood [muːd] *n* umore *m*; **to be in a (bad) ~** essere di cattivo umore; **to be in a good ~** essere di buon umore.

moody ['muːdɪ] *adj* (*in a bad mood*) di malumore; (*changeable*) lunatico(-a), volubile.

moon [muːn] *n* luna *f*.

moonlight ['muːnlaɪt] *n* chiaro *m* di luna.

moor [mɔːʳ] *n* brughiera *f* ◆ *vt* ormeggiare.

moose [muːs] (*pl inv*) *n* alce *m*.

mop [mɒp] *n* (*for floor*) lavapavimenti *m inv* ◆ *vt* (*floor*) lavare con lo straccio ❑ **mop up** *vt sep* (*clean up*) asciugare con uno straccio.

moped ['məʊped] n ciclomotore m.

moral ['mɒrəl] adj morale ◆ n (lesson) morale f.

morality [mə'ræliti] n moralità f.

more [mɔːʳ] adj 1. (a larger amount of) più; **there are ~ tourists than usual** ci sono più turisti del solito. 2. (additional) altro(-a); **are there any ~ cakes?** ci sono altri OR ancora pasticcini?; **I'd like two ~ bottles** vorrei altre due bottiglie; **there's no ~ wine** non c'è più vino. 3. (in phrases): **~ and more** sempre più.
◆ adv 1. (in comparatives) più; **it's difficult than before** è più difficile di prima; **speak ~ clearly** parla più chiaramente. 2. (to a greater degree) di più; **we ought to go to the cinema ~** dovremmo andare più spesso al cinema. 3. (in phrases): **not ... any ~** non ... più; **I don't go there any more** non ci vado più; **once ~** ancora una volta, un'altra volta; **~ or less** più o meno; **we'd be ~ than happy to help** saremmo più che lieti di dare una mano.
◆ pron 1. (a larger amount) più; **I've got ~ than you** ne ho più di te; **~ than 20 types of pizza** oltre 20 tipi di pizza. 2. (an additional amount) ancora; **is there any ~?** ce n'è ancora?; **there's no ~** non ce n'è più.

moreover [mɔː'rəʊvəʳ] adv (fml) inoltre.

morning ['mɔːnɪŋ] n mattina f, mattino m; **two o'clock in the ~** le due di notte; **good ~!** buon giorno!; **in the ~** (early in the day) di mattina; (tomorrow morning) domattina.

morning-after pill n pillola f del giorno dopo.

morning sickness n nausea f mattutina.

Morocco [mə'rɒkəʊ] n il Marocco.

moron ['mɔːrɒn] n (inf) deficiente mf.

Morse (code) [mɔːs-] n alfabeto m Morse.

mortgage ['mɔːgɪdʒ] n mutuo m (ipotecario).

mosaic [mə'zeɪɪk] n mosaico m.

Moslem ['mɒzləm] = Muslim.

mosque [mɒsk] n moschea f.

mosquito [mə'skiːtəʊ] (pl -es) n zanzara f.

mosquito net n zanzariera f.

moss [mɒs] n muschio m.

most [məʊst] 1. adj (the majority of) la maggior parte di; **~ people agree** la maggior parte della gente è d'accordo. 2. (the largest amount of): **I drank (the) ~ beer** sono quello che ha bevuto più birra.
◆ adv 1. (in superlatives) più; **the ~ expensive hotel in town** l'albergo più caro della città. 2. (to the greatest degree) di più, maggiormente; **I like this one ~** questo è quello che mi piace di più. 3. (fml: very) molto, estremamente; **they were ~ welcoming** sono stati estremamente accoglienti.
◆ pron 1. (the majority) la maggior parte; **~ of the villages** la maggior parte dei paesi; **~ of the time** la maggior parte del tempo. 2. (the largest amount): **she earns (the) ~** è quella che guadagna

di più.

3. *(in phrases)*: **at ~** al massimo; **to make the ~ of sthg** sfruttare al massimo qc.

mostly ['məʊstlɪ] *adv* per lo più.

MOT *n (Br: test)* revisione annuale obbligatoria degli autoveicoli di più di tre anni.

motel [məʊ'tel] *n* motel *m inv*.

moth [mɒθ] *n* farfalla *f* notturna.

mother ['mʌðə*r*] *n* madre *f*.

mother-in-law *n* suocera *f*.

mother-of-pearl *n* madreperla *f*.

motif [məʊ'tiːf] *n* motivo *m*.

motion ['məʊʃn] *n (movement)* movimento *m*, moto *m* ♦ *vi*: **to ~ to sb** fare cenno a qn.

motionless ['məʊʃənlɪs] *adj* immobile.

motivate ['məʊtɪveɪt] *vt (encourage)* motivare, stimolare.

motive ['məʊtɪv] *n* motivo *m*.

motor ['məʊtə*r*] *n (engine)* motore *m*.

Motorail® ['məʊtəreɪl] *n* treno *m* auto-cuccette.

motorbike ['məʊtəbaɪk] *n* moto *f inv*.

motorboat ['məʊtəbəʊt] *n* motoscafo *m*.

motorcar ['məʊtəkɑː*r*] *n* automobile *f*.

motorcycle ['məʊtəˌsaɪkl] *n* motocicletta *f*.

motorcyclist ['məʊtəˌsaɪklɪst] *n* motociclista *mf*.

motorist ['məʊtərɪst] *n* automobilista *mf*.

motor racing *n* corse *fpl* automobilistiche.

motorway ['məʊtəweɪ] *n (Br)* autostrada *f*.

motto ['mɒtəʊ] *(pl -s)* *n* motto *m*.

mould [məʊld] *n (Br) (shape)* forma *f*, stampo *m*; *(substance)* muffa *f* ♦ *vt (Br)* formare, modellare.

mouldy ['məʊldɪ] *adj (Br)* ammuffito(-a).

mound [maʊnd] *n (hill)* monticello *m*, collinetta *f*; *(pile)* mucchio *m*.

mount [maʊnt] *n (for photo)* supporto *m*; *(mountain)* monte *m* ♦ *vt (horse)* montare a OR su; *(photo)* sistemare ♦ *vi (increase)* aumentare.

mountain ['maʊntɪn] *n* montagna *f*.

mountain bike *n* mountain bike *f inv*.

mountaineer [ˌmaʊntɪ'nɪə*r*] *n* alpinista *mf*.

mountaineering [ˌmaʊntɪ'nɪərɪŋ] *n*: **to go ~** fare alpinismo.

mountainous ['maʊntɪnəs] *adj* montagnoso(-a).

Mount Rushmore [-'rʌʃmɔː*r*] *n* il monte Rushmore.

---

i MOUNT RUSHMORE

I ritratti giganti dei presidenti degli Stati Uniti Washington, Jefferson, Lincoln e Theodore Roosevelt, scolpiti nella roccia granitica, hanno trasformato il monte Rushmore, nel Dakota del Sud, in monumento nazionale e grande centro di attrazione turistica.

---

mourning ['mɔːnɪŋ] *n*: **to be in ~** essere in lutto.

mouse [maʊs] *(pl* mice*)* *n (animal)* topo *m*; *(COMPUT)* mouse *m inv*.

moussaka [muːˈsɑːkə] *n* piatto

tipico della cucina greca e turca, composto da strati di carne macinata, melanzane e besciamella.

mousse [mu:s] n mousse f inv.

moustache [mə'sta:ʃ] n (Br) baffi mpl.

mouth [mauθ] n bocca f; (of cave, tunnel) entrata f, imboccatura f; (of river) foce f, bocca.

mouthful ['mauθful] n (of food) boccone m; (of drink) sorsata f.

mouthorgan ['mauθ,ɔ:gən] n armonica f (a bocca).

mouthpiece ['mauθpi:s] n (of telephone) microfono m; (of musical instrument) bocchino m.

mouthwash ['mauθwɒʃ] n collutorio m.

move [mu:v] n mossa f; (change of house) trasloco m ♦ vt (shift) muovere, spostare; (emotionally) commuovere ♦ vi (shift) muoversi, spostarsi; **to ~ (house)** cambiare casa, traslocare; **to make a ~ (leave)** andarsene ❑ **move along** vi circolare, andare avanti; **move in** vi (to house) andare/venire ad abitare; **move off** vi (train, car) partire; **move on** vi (after stopping) ripartire; **move out** vi (from house) sgombrare; **move over** vi spostarsi; **move up** vi (make room) spostarsi.

movement ['mu:vmənt] n movimento m.

movie ['mu:vɪ] n film m inv.

movie theater n (Am) cinema m inv.

moving ['mu:vɪŋ] adj (emotionally) commovente.

mow [məʊ] vt: **to ~ the lawn** tagliare l'erba (del prato).

mozzarella [,mɒtsə'relə] n moz-

zarella f.

MP n (abbr of Member of Parliament) = deputato m (-a f).

mph (abbr of miles per hour) miglia all'ora.

Mr ['mɪstər] abbr Sig.

Mrs ['mɪsɪz] abbr Sig.ra.

Ms [mɪz] abbr abbreviazione che comprende sia Mrs che Miss.

MSc n (abbr of Master of Science) (degree) master m inv in materie scientifiche.

much [mʌtʃ] (compar **more**, superl **most**) adj molto(-a); **I haven't got ~ money** non ho molti soldi; **as ~ food as you can eat** tanto cibo quanto ne riesci a mangiare; **how ~ time is left?** quanto tempo resta?; **they have so ~ money** hanno tanti di quei soldi; **we have too ~ work** abbiamo troppo lavoro.
♦ adv 1. (to a great extent) molto; **it's ~ better** è molto meglio; **I like it very ~** mi piace moltissimo; **it's not ~ good** (inf) non è un granché; **thank you very ~** grazie tante.
2. (often) spesso, molto; **we don't go there ~** non ci andiamo spesso.
♦ pron molto; **I haven't got ~** non ne ho molto; **as ~ as you like** quanto ne vuoi; **how ~ is it?** quant'è?, quanto costa?

muck [mʌk] n (dirt) sudiciume m ❑ **muck about** vi (Br) ((inf) (have fun) divertirsi; (waste time) gingillarsi; **muck up** vt sep (Br: inf) pasticciare.

mud [mʌd] n fango m.

muddle ['mʌdl] n: **to be in a ~** (confused) essere confuso; (in a mess) essere in disordine.

muddy ['mʌdɪ] adj fangoso(-a).

mudguard ['mʌdgɑ:d] n para-

myth

fango m.

muesli ['mju:zlɪ] n muesli m.

muffin ['mʌfɪn] n (roll) panino m soffice (mangiato caldo, con burro); (cake) pasticcino m soffice.

muffler ['mʌflər] n (Am: silencer) marmitta f.

mug [mʌg] n (cup) tazza f (cilindrica) ♦ vt aggredire e derubare.

mugging ['mʌgɪŋ] n aggressione f (a scopo di rapina).

muggy ['mʌgɪ] adj afoso(-a).

mule [mju:l] n mulo m.

multicoloured ['mʌltɪ,kʌləd] adj multicolore.

multiple ['mʌltɪpl] adj multiplo(-a).

multiplex cinema ['mʌltɪpleks-] n cinema m inv multisala.

multiplication [,mʌltɪplɪ'keɪʃn] n moltiplicazione f.

multiply ['mʌltɪplaɪ] vt moltiplicare ♦ vi moltiplicarsi.

multistorey (car park) [,mʌltɪ'stɔ:rɪ-] n parcheggio m multipiano.

mum [mʌm] n (Br: inf) mamma f.

mummy ['mʌmɪ] n (Br: inf: mother) mamma f.

mumps [mʌmps] n orecchioni mpl.

munch [mʌntʃ] vt sgranocchiare.

municipal [mju:'nɪsɪpl] adj municipale.

mural ['mjuərəl] n dipinto m murale.

murder ['mɜ:dər] n assassinio m, omicidio m ♦ vt assassinare.

murderer ['mɜ:dərər] n assassino m (-a f), omicida mf.

muscle ['mʌsl] n muscolo m.

museum [mju:'zi:əm] n museo m.

mushroom ['mʌʃrum] n fungo m.

music ['mju:zɪk] n musica f.

musical ['mju:zɪkl] adj musicale; (person) portato(-a) per la musica ♦ n musical m inv.

musical instrument n strumento m musicale.

musician [mju:'zɪʃn] n musicista mf.

Muslim ['muzlɪm] adj musulmano(-a) ♦ n musulmano m (-a f).

mussels ['mʌslz] npl cozze fpl.

must [mʌst] aux vb dovere ♦ n (inf): it's a ~ è d'obbligo; I ~ go devo andare; the room ~ be vacated by ten la camera deve essere lasciata entro le dieci; you ~ have seen it devi averlo visto; you ~ see that film devi vedere quel film; you ~ be joking! stai scherzando!.

mustache ['mʌstæʃ] (Am) = **moustache**.

mustard ['mʌstəd] n senape f, mostarda f.

mustn't ['mʌsənt] = **must not**.

mutter ['mʌtər] vt borbottare.

mutton ['mʌtn] n carne f di montone.

mutual ['mju:tʃʊəl] adj (feeling) reciproco(-a), mutuo(-a); (friend, interest) comune.

muzzle ['mʌzl] n (for dog) museruola f.

my [maɪ] adj il mio (la mia), i miei (le mie) (pl); ~ brother mio fratello.

myself [maɪ'self] pron (reflexive) mi; (after prep) me; I did it ~ l'ho fatto da solo.

mysterious [mɪ'stɪərɪəs] adj misterioso(-a).

mystery ['mɪstərɪ] n mistero m.

myth [mɪθ] n mito m.

N

N (abbr of North) N.

nag [næg] vt tormentare.

nail [neɪl] n (of finger, toe) unghia f; (metal) chiodo m ♦ vt (fasten) inchiodare.

nailbrush ['neɪlbrʌʃ] n spazzolino m da unghie.

nail file n limetta f per unghie.

nail scissors npl forbicine fpl da unghie.

nail varnish n smalto m per unghie.

nail varnish remover [-rə'muːvə'] n acetone m, solvente m per unghie.

naive [naɪ'iːv] adj ingenuo(-a).

naked ['neɪkɪd] adj (person) nudo(-a).

name [neɪm] n nome m ♦ vt (baby, animal) chiamare; (place) denominare; (identify) dire il nome di, nominare; (date, price) fissare; **first ~** nome di battesimo; **last ~** cognome m; **what's your ~?** come si chiama?; **my ~ is ...** mi chiamo ...

namely ['neɪmlɪ] adv cioè, vale a dire.

nan bread [næn-] n pane indiano schiacciato e soffice.

nanny ['nænɪ] n (childminder) bambinaia f; (inf: grandmother) nonna f.

nap [næp] n: **to have a ~** fare un pisolino.

napkin ['næpkɪn] n tovagliolo m.

Naples ['neɪplz] n Napoli f.

nappy ['næpɪ] n pannolino m.

nappy liner n pannolino m.

narcotic [naː'kɒtɪk] n narcotico m.

narrow ['nærəu] adj (road, gap) stretto(-a) ♦ vi (road, gap) restringersi.

narrow-minded [-'maɪndɪd] adj di idee ristrette.

nasty ['naːstɪ] adj (person, comment, taste) cattivo(-a); (accident, moment, feeling) brutto(-a).

nation ['neɪʃn] n nazione f.

national ['næʃənl] adj nazionale ♦ n cittadino m (-a f).

national anthem n inno m nazionale.

National Health Service n ≃ Servizio m Sanitario Nazionale.

National Insurance n (Br: contributions) ≃ Previdenza f Sociale.

nationality [,næʃə'nælətɪ] n nazionalità f inv.

national park n parco m nazionale.

---

[i] **NATIONAL PARK**

Come in Italia, anche in Gran Bretagna e negli Stati Uniti i parchi nazionali sono delle vaste zone protette per la loro bellezza naturale. Aperti al pubblico, sono sempre dotati di campeggi attrezzati. Fra i più famosi parchi della Gran Bretagna ricordiamo Snowdonia, il distretto dei Laghi e il Peak District, mentre Yellowstone e Yosemite sono fra i più famosi parchi nazionali americani.

---

nationwide ['neɪʃənwaɪd] adj su scala nazionale.

native ['neɪtɪv] *adj (customs, population)* indigeno(-a); *(country)* d'origine ◆ *n* nativo *m (-a f)*; **a ~ speaker of English** una persona di madrelingua inglese.

Native American *adj* indiano(-a) (d'America) ◆ *n* indiano *m (-a f)* (d'America).

NATO ['neɪtəʊ] *n* NATO *f*.

natural ['nætʃrəl] *adj (charm)* naturale; *(ability)* innato(-a); *(swimmer, actor)* nato(-a).

natural gas *n* metano *m*, gas *m* naturale.

naturally ['nætʃrəlɪ] *adv (of course)* naturalmente.

natural yoghurt *n* yogurt *m inv* naturale.

nature ['neɪtʃər] *n* natura *f*.

nature reserve *n* riserva *f* naturale.

naughty ['nɔːtɪ] *adj (child)* birichino(-a).

nausea ['nɔːzɪə] *n* nausea *f*.

navigate ['nævɪgeɪt] *vi (in boat, plane)* calcolare la rotta; *(in car)* fare da navigatore.

navy ['neɪvɪ] *n (ships)* marina *f* (militare) ◆ *adj*: **~ (blue)** blu scuro *(inv)*.

NB *(abbr of nota bene)* N.B.

near [nɪər] *adv* vicino ◆ *adj (place, object)* vicino; *(relation)* prossimo(-a) ◆ *prep*: **~ (to)** *(edge, object, place)* vicino a, presso; **in the ~ future** nel prossimo futuro.

nearby [nɪə'baɪ] *adv* vicino ◆ *adj* vicino(-a).

nearly ['nɪəlɪ] *adv* quasi.

near side *n (for right-hand drive)* destra *f*; *(for left-hand drive)* sinistra *f*.

neat [niːt] *adj (room)* ordinato(-a);

(writing) chiaro(-a); *(work)* preciso(-a); *(whisky, vodka etc)* liscio(-a).

neatly ['niːtlɪ] *adv (placed, arranged)* in modo ordinato; *(written)* in modo chiaro.

necessarily [ˌnesə'serɪlɪ, *Br* 'nesəsrəlɪ] *adv*: **not ~** non necessariamente.

necessary ['nesəsrɪ] *adj* necessario(-a); **it is ~ to do it** è necessario farlo.

necessity [nɪ'sesətɪ] *n* necessità *f inv* ❑ **necessities** *npl* necessità *fpl*.

neck [nek] *n* collo *m*.

necklace ['neklɪs] *n* collana *f*.

nectarine ['nektərɪn] *n* pescanoce *f*.

need [niːd] *n* bisogno *m* ◆ *vt* avere bisogno di; **to ~ to do sthg** dover fare qc; **you don't ~ to go** non c'è bisogno che tu ci vada.

needle ['niːdl] *n* ago *m*; *(for record player)* puntina *f*.

needlework ['niːdlwɜːk] *n (SCH)* cucito *m*.

needn't ['niːdənt] = **need not**.

needy ['niːdɪ] *adj* bisognoso(-a).

negative ['negətɪv] *adj* negativo(-a) ◆ *n (in photography)* negativo *m*; *(GRAMM)* negazione *f*.

neglect [nɪ'glekt] *vt* trascurare.

negligence ['neglɪdʒəns] *n* negligenza *f*.

negotiations [nɪˌgəʊʃɪ'eɪʃnz] *npl* negoziati *mpl*, trattative *fpl*.

negro ['niːgrəʊ] *(pl* **-es)** *n* negro *m (-a f)*.

neighbour ['neɪbər] *n* vicino *m (-a f)*.

neighbourhood ['neɪbəhʊd] *n* quartiere *m*, vicinato *m*.

neighbouring ['neɪbərɪŋ] *adj*

vicino(-a), confinante.

neither ['naɪðəʳ, ni:ðəʳ] *adj*: ~ **bag is big enough** nessuna delle due borse è abbastanza grande ♦ *pron*: ~ **of us** nessuno(-a) di noi (due) ♦ *conj*: ~ **do I** neanch'io, nemmeno io; ~ ... **nor** ... né ... né ...

neon light ['ni:ɒn] *n* luce *f* al neon.

nephew ['nefju:] *n* nipote *m*.

nerve [nɜːv] *n* (*in body*) nervo *m*; (*courage*) coraggio *m*; **what a ~!** che faccia tosta!

nervous ['nɜːvəs] *adj* nervoso(-a).

nervous breakdown *n* esaurimento *m* nervoso.

nest [nest] *n* nido *m*.

net [net] *n* rete *f* ♦ *adj* netto(-a).

netball ['netbɔːl] *n* specie di palla-canestro femminile.

Netherlands ['neðələndz] *npl*: **the ~** i Paesi Bassi.

nettle ['netl] *n* ortica *f*.

network ['netwɜːk] *n* rete *f*.

neurotic [ˌnjʊəˈrɒtɪk] *adj* nevrotico(-a).

neutral ['nju:trəl] *adj* (*country, person*) neutrale; (*in colour*) neutro(-a) ♦ *n* (*AUT*): **in ~** in folle.

never ['nevəʳ] *adv* (non ...) mai; **she's ~ late** non è mai in ritardo; **I ~ knew he was married** non sapevo che fosse sposato; **~ mind!** non preoccuparti!

nevertheless [ˌnevəðəˈles] *adv* tuttavia, ciononostante.

new [nju:] *adj* nuovo(-a).

newly ['nju:lɪ] *adv* di recente.

new potatoes *npl* patate *fpl* novelle.

news [nju:z] *n* (*information*) noti-zie *fpl*; (*on TV*) telegiornale *m*; (*on radio*) giornale *m* radio; **a piece of ~** una notizia.

newsagent ['nju:zeɪdʒənt] *n* (*shop*) giornalaio *m*.

newspaper ['nju:z,peɪpəʳ] *n* giornale *m*.

New Year *n* anno *m* nuovo.

ⓘ NEW YEAR

Anche in Gran Bretagna la notte di San Silvestro è celebrata con feste, in casa o fuori. Allo scoccare della mezzanotte, la fine dell'anno vecchio e l'arrivo di quello nuovo vengono tradizionalmente salutati cantando "Auld Lang Syne". La notte di fine anno riveste un'importanza del tutto particolare in Scozia, dove è nota come "Hogmanay". Così come in Italia, il giorno di Capodanno è un giorno festivo in tutta la Gran Bretagna.

New Year's Day *n* Capodanno.

New Year's Eve *n* l'ultimo *m* dell'anno, San Silvestro *m*.

New Zealand [-'zi:lənd] *n* la Nuova Zelanda.

next [nekst] *adj* prossimo(-a); (*room, house*) accanto ♦ *adv* (*afterwards*) dopo; (*on next occasion*) di nuovo; **when does the ~ bus leave?** quando parte il prossimo autobus?; ~ **to** (*by the side of*) accanto a; **the week after ~** la settimana dopo la prossima.

next door *adv* accanto.

next of kin [-kɪn] *n* parente *m* prossimo (parente prossima *f*).

NHS *n* (*abbr of National Health*

Service) = S.S.N. m.

nib [nɪb] n pennino m.

nibble ['nɪbl] vt (eat) mangiucchiare; (bite) mordicchiare.

nice [naɪs] adj (taste, meal) buono(-a); (day, clothes, house) bello(-a); (person, gesture) simpatico(-a), gentile; (feeling, job) piacevole; to have a ~ time divertirsi; ~ to see you! piacere di rivederti!

nickel ['nɪkl] n (metal) nichel m; (Am: coin) moneta da cinque centesimi di dollaro.

nickname ['nɪkneɪm] n soprannome m.

niece [niːs] n nipote f.

night [naɪt] n notte f; (evening) sera f; at ~ (not in daytime) di notte; (in evening) di sera; by ~ di notte; last ~ (yesterday evening) ieri sera; (very late) ieri notte.

nightclub ['naɪtklʌb] n locale m notturno.

nightdress ['naɪtdres] n camicia f da notte.

nightie ['naɪtɪ] n (inf) camicia f da notte.

nightlife ['naɪtlaɪf] n vita f notturna.

nightly ['naɪtlɪ] adv ogni notte; (every evening) ogni sera.

nightmare ['naɪtmeə] n incubo m.

night safe n cassa f continua.

night school n scuola f serale.

nightshift ['naɪtʃɪft] n turno m di notte.

nil [nɪl] n (SPORT) zero m.

Nile [naɪl] n: the ~ il Nilo.

nine [naɪn] num nove, → six.

nineteen [naɪn'tiːn] num diciannove; ~ ninety-five millenovecentonovantacinque, → six.

nineteenth [naɪn'tiːnθ] num diciannovesimo(-a), → sixth.

ninetieth ['naɪntɪθ] num novantesimo(-a), → sixth.

ninety ['naɪntɪ] num novanta, → six.

ninth [naɪnθ] num nono(-a), → sixth.

nip [nɪp] vt (pinch) pizzicare.

nipple ['nɪpl] n (of breast) capezzolo m; (of bottle) tettarella f.

nitrogen ['naɪtrədʒən] n azoto m.

no [nəʊ] adv no ♦ adj nessuno(-a) ♦ n no m inv: I've got ~ time non ho tempo; I've got ~ money left non ho più soldi.

noble ['nəʊbl] adj nobile.

nobody ['nəʊbədɪ] pron nessuno.

nod [nɒd] vi (in agreement) annuire.

noise [nɔɪz] n rumore m.

noisy ['nɔɪzɪ] adj rumoroso(-a).

nominate ['nɒmɪneɪt] vt (choose) nominare; (suggest) proporre come candidato.

non-alcoholic adj analcolico(-a).

none [nʌn] pron nessuno m (-a f); there's ~ left non ce n'è più.

nonetheless [ˌnʌnðə'les] adv tuttavia, nondimeno.

non-fiction n opere fpl non narrative (saggistica, ecc.).

non-iron adj: 'non-iron' 'lava e indossa', 'non stiro'.

nonsense ['nɒnsəns] n sciocchezze fpl, fesserie fpl.

non-smoker n non fumatore m (-trice f).

non-stick adj antiaderente.

non-stop adj (flight) diretto(-a); (talking, arguing) continuo(-a) ♦ adv (fly) senza scalo; (run, rain) ininterrottamente, senza sosta.

noodles ['nu:dlz] npl taglierini mpl.

noon [nu:n] n mezzogiorno m.

no-one = nobody.

nor [nɔ:ʳ] conj neanche, nemmeno; ~ **do I** neanch'io, nemmeno io, → neither.

normal ['nɔ:ml] adj normale.

normally ['nɔ:məlɪ] adv normalmente.

north [nɔ:θ] n nord m, settentrione m ♦ adj del nord ♦ adv (fly, walk) verso nord; (be situated) a nord; **in the ~ of England** nel nord dell'Inghilterra.

North America n l'America f del Nord.

northbound ['nɔ:θbaʊnd] adj diretto(-a) a nord.

northeast n nord-est m.

northern ['nɔ:ðən] adj settentrionale, del nord.

Northern Ireland n l'Irlanda f del Nord.

North Pole n Polo m Nord.

North Sea n Mare m del Nord.

northwards ['nɔ:θwədz] adv verso nord.

northwest n nord-ovest m.

Norway ['nɔ:weɪ] n la Norvegia.

Norwegian [nɔ:'wi:dʒən] adj norvegese ♦ n (person) norvegese mf; (language) norvegese m.

nose [nəʊz] n (of person) naso m; (of animal, plane) muso m; (of rocket) punta f.

nosebleed ['nəʊzbli:d] n emorragia f nasale.

no-smoking area n zona f non fumatori.

nostril ['nɒstrəl] n narice f.

nosy ['nəʊzɪ] adj curioso(-a).

not [nɒt] adv non; **she's ~ there** non c'è; ~ **yet** non ancora; ~ **at all** (pleased, interested) per niente; (in reply to thanks) di niente, prego.

notably ['nəʊtəblɪ] adv (in particular) in particolare.

note [nəʊt] n nota f; (message, bank note) biglietto m ♦ vt (notice) notare; (write down) annotare; **to take ~s** prendere appunti.

notebook ['nəʊtbʊk] n taccuino m.

noted ['nəʊtɪd] adj celebre.

notepaper ['nəʊtpeɪpəʳ] n carta f da lettere.

nothing ['nʌθɪŋ] pron niente, nulla; **he did ~** non ha fatto niente; ~ **new/interesting** niente di nuovo/interessante; **for ~** per niente.

notice ['nəʊtɪs] vt notare, accorgersi di ♦ n (written announcement) avviso m; (warning) preavviso m; **to take ~ of** fare caso a; **to hand in one's ~** dare il preavviso, licenziarsi.

noticeable ['nəʊtɪsəbl] adj evidente.

notice board n tabellone m per avvisi.

notion ['nəʊʃn] n idea f.

notorious [nəʊ'tɔ:rɪəs] adj famigerato(-a).

nougat ['nu:ga:] n torrone m.

nought [nɔ:t] n zero m.

noun [naʊn] n nome m, sostantivo m.

nourishment ['nʌrɪʃmənt] n nutrimento m.

Nov. (abbr of November) nov.

novel ['nɒvl] n romanzo m ♦ adj nuovo(-a).

novelist ['nɒvəlɪst] n romanziere m (-a f).

November [nə'vembər] n novembre m, → **September**.

now [naʊ] adv ora, adesso ♦ conj: ~ (that) adesso che, ora che; just ~ proprio ora; right ~ (at the moment) in questo momento; (immediately) subito; by ~ ormai; from ~ on d'ora in poi.

nowadays ['naʊədeɪz] adv oggigiorno.

nowhere ['nəʊwɛər] adv da nessuna parte, in nessun posto.

nozzle ['nɒzl] n boccaglio m.

nuclear ['nju:klɪər] adj nucleare.

nude [nju:d] adj nudo(-a).

nudge [nʌdʒ] vt dare un colpetto di gomito a.

nuisance ['nju:sns] n: it's a real ~! è una vera seccatura!; he's such a ~! è un tale scocciatore!

numb [nʌm] adj intorpidito(-a).

number ['nʌmbər] n numero m ♦ vt (give number to) numerare.

numberplate ['nʌmbəpleɪt] n targa f.

numeral ['nju:mərəl] n numero m, cifra f.

numerous ['nju:mərəs] adj numeroso(-a).

nun [nʌn] n suora f.

nurse [nɜ:s] n infermiera f ♦ vt (look after) avere cura di, curare; male ~ infermiere m.

nursery ['nɜ:sərɪ] n (in house) stanza f dei bambini; (for plants) vivaio m.

nursery (school) n scuola f materna.

nursery slope n pista f per sciatori principianti.

nursing ['nɜ:sɪŋ] n (profession) professione f d'infermiera.

nut [nʌt] n (to eat) frutta f secca (noci, nocciole, ecc.); (of metal) dado m.

nutcrackers ['nʌt,krækəz] npl schiaccianoci m inv.

nutmeg ['nʌtmeg] n noce f moscata.

nylon ['naɪlɒn] n nailon m ♦ adj di nailon.

o' [ə] abbr = of.

O n (zero) zero m.

oak [əʊk] n quercia f ♦ adj di quercia.

OAP abbr = old age pensioner.

oar [ɔ:r] n remo m.

oatcake ['əʊtkeɪk] n biscotto m di farina d'avena.

oath [əʊθ] n (promise) giuramento m.

oatmeal ['əʊtmi:l] n farina f d'avena.

oats [əʊts] npl avena f.

obedient [ə'bi:djənt] adj ubbidiente.

obey [ə'beɪ] vt (person, command) ubbidire a; (regulations) osservare.

object [n 'ɒbdʒɪkt, vb ɒb'dʒekt] n (thing) oggetto m; (purpose) scopo m; (GRAMM) complemento m oggetto ♦ vi: to ~ (to) (disapprove of) disapprovare; (oppose) opporsi (a), protestare (contro).

objection [əb'dʒekʃn] n obie-

zione f.
objective [əb'dʒektɪv] n obiettivo m.
obligation [ˌɒblɪ'geɪʃn] n obbligo m, dovere m.
obligatory [ə'blɪɡətrɪ] adj obbligatorio(-a).
oblige [ə'blaɪdʒ] vt: **to ~ sb to do sthg** obbligare qn a fare qc.
oblique [ə'bliːk] adj obliquo(-a).
oblong [ˈɒblɒŋ] adj oblungo(-a), rettangolare ♦ n rettangolo m.
obnoxious [əb'nɒkʃəs] adj odioso(-a).
oboe [ˈəʊbəʊ] n oboe m.
obscene [əb'siːn] adj osceno(-a).
obscure [əb'skjʊəʳ] adj oscuro(-a).
observant [əb'zɜːvnt] adj dotato(-a) di spirito d'osservazione.
observation [ˌɒbzə'veɪʃn] n osservazione f.
observatory [əb'zɜːvətrɪ] n osservatorio m.
observe [əb'zɜːv] vt (watch, see) osservare.
obsessed [əb'sest] adj ossessionato(-a).
obsession [əb'seʃn] n ossessione f.
obsolete [ˈɒbsəliːt] adj obsoleto(-a).
obstacle [ˈɒbstəkl] n ostacolo m.
obstinate [ˈɒbstənət] adj ostinato(-a).
obstruct [əb'strʌkt] vt (road, path) ostruire.
obstruction [əb'strʌkʃn] n (in road, path) ostruzione f.
obtain [əb'teɪn] vt ottenere.
obtainable [əb'teɪnəbl] adj ottenibile.

obvious [ˈɒbvɪəs] adj ovvio(-a), evidente.
obviously [ˈɒbvɪəslɪ] adv ovviamente.
occasion [ə'keɪʒn] n occasione f; (important event) avvenimento m.
occasional [ə'keɪʒənl] adj saltuario(-a), occasionale.
occasionally [ə'keɪʒnəlɪ] adv saltuariamente, di tanto in tanto.
occupant [ˈɒkjʊpənt] n occupante mf.
occupation [ˌɒkjʊ'peɪʃn] n lavoro m; (on form) occupazione f.
occupied [ˈɒkjʊpaɪd] adj (toilet) occupato(-a).
occupy [ˈɒkjʊpaɪ] vt occupare.
occur [ə'kɜːʳ] vi (happen) accadere, avvenire; (exist) trovarsi, essere presente.
occurrence [ə'kʌrəns] n (event) evento m, caso m.
ocean [ˈəʊʃn] n oceano m; **the ~** (Am: sea) il mare.
o'clock [ə'klɒk] adv: **it's one ~** è l'una; **it's seven ~** sono le sette; **at one ~** all'una; **at seven ~** alle sette.
Oct. (abbr of October) ott.
October [ɒk'təʊbəʳ] n ottobre m, → **September**.
octopus [ˈɒktəpəs] n polpo m, piovra f.
odd [ɒd] adj (strange) strano(-a); (number) dispari (inv); (not matching) spaiato(-a); (occasional) saltuario(-a), occasionale; **60 ~ miles** una sessantina di miglia; **some ~ bits of paper** vari pezzetti di carta; **~ jobs** lavori mpl occasionali.
odds [ɒdz] npl (in betting) quota f; (chances) probabilità fpl; **~ and ends** un po' di tutto.

.dor ['əʊdər] (Am) = **odour**.

.dour ['əʊdər] n (Br) odore m.

f [ʌv] prep 1. (gen) di; **the handle the door** la maniglia della porta; **~ group ~ schoolchildren** un gruppo di scolari; **a great love ~ art** un rande amore per l'arte.

(expressing amount) di; **a piece ~ ake** una fetta di torta; **a fall ~ 20%** n ribasso del 20%; **a town ~ ,0,000 people** una città di 50 000 bitanti.

(made from) di, in; **a house ~ one** una casa di pietra; **it's made wood** è di OR in legno.

(referring to time) di; **the summer 1969** l'estate del 1969; **the 26th August** il 26 agosto.

(indicating cause) di; **he died ~ ncer** è morto di cancro.

(on the part of) da parte di; **that as very kind ~ you** è stato molto ntile da parte tua.

(Am: in telling the time): **it's ten ~ ur** sono le quattro meno dieci.

f [ɒf] adv 1. (away): **to drive ~** artire; **to get ~ (from bus, train, ane, boat)** scendere; **we're ~ to ustria next week** partiamo per Austria la settimana prossima.

(expressing removal): **to cut sthg** tagliare qc; **to take sthg ~** togliere qc.

(so as to stop working): **to turn hg ~** (TV, radio, engine) spegnere ; (tap) chiudere qc.

(expressing distance or time away): **s 10 miles ~** è a 10 miglia (da ui); **it's two months ~** mancano ie mesi; **it's a long way ~** è lonta-

(not at work): **I'm ~ next Tuesday** artedì prossimo non lavoro; **I'm king a week ~** prendo una setti-

mana di ferie.

♦ prep 1. (away from) da; **to get ~ sthg** scendere da qc; **~ the coast** al largo della costa; **just ~ the main road** poco lontano dalla strada principale.

2. (indicating removal) da; **take the lid ~ the jar** togli il tappo dal barattolo; **they've taken £20 ~ the price** mi hanno fatto uno sconto di 20 sterline.

3. (absent from): **to be ~ work** essere assente dal lavoro.

4. (inf: from) da; **I bought it ~ her** l'ho comprato da lei.

5. (inf: no longer liking): **I'm ~ my food** non ho appetito, non mi va di mangiare.

♦ adj 1. (food) andato(-a) a male.

2. (TV, radio, engine) spento(-a); (tap) chiuso(-a).

3. (cancelled) annullato(-a).

4. (not available) esaurito(-a).

offence [ə'fens] n (Br) (minor crime) infrazione f; (serious crime) reato m; **to take ~ (at)** offendersi (per).

offend [ə'fend] vt (upset) offendere.

offender [ə'fendər] n (criminal) delinquente mf.

offense [ə'fens] (Am) = **offence**.

offensive [ə'fensɪv] adj (insulting) offensivo(-a).

offer ['ɒfər] n offerta f ♦ vt offrire; **on ~** (at reduced price) in offerta; **to ~ to do sthg** offrirsi di fare qc; **to ~ sb sthg** offrire qc a qn.

office ['ɒfɪs] n (room) ufficio m.

office block n palazzo m di uffici.

officer ['ɒfɪsər] n (MIL) ufficiale m; (policeman) agente m (di polizia).

official [əˈfɪʃl] *adj* ufficiale ♦ *n* funzionario *m* (-a *f*).

officially [əˈfɪʃəlɪ] *adv* ufficialmente.

off-licence *n* (Br) negozio *m* di bevande alcoliche.

off-peak *adj* (train) delle ore non di punta; (ticket) a tariffa ridotta.

off sales *npl* (Br) vendita *f* di bevande alcoliche da asporto.

off-season *n* bassa stagione *f*.

offshore [ˈɒfʃɔːr] *adj* (breeze) di terra.

off side *n* (for right-hand drive) lato *m* destro; (for left-hand drive) lato sinistro.

off-the-peg *adj* confezionato(-a).

often [ˈɒfn, ˈɒftn] *adv* spesso; **how ~ do the buses run?** ogni quanto passano gli autobus?; **every so ~** ogni tanto.

oh [əʊ] *excl* oh!

oil [ɔɪl] *n* olio *m*; (fuel) petrolio *m*.

oilcan [ˈɔɪlkæn] *n* oliatore *m*.

oil filter *n* filtro *m* dell'olio.

oil rig *n* piattaforma *f* petrolifera.

oily [ˈɔɪlɪ] *adj* unto(-a).

ointment [ˈɔɪntmənt] *n* unguento *m*, pomata *f*.

OK [ˌəʊˈkeɪ] *adv* (inf) (expressing agreement) va bene, d'accordo; (satisfactorily, well) bene ♦ *adj* (of average quality) non male; **is that ~?** va bene?; **are you ~?** tutto bene?

okay [ˌəʊˈkeɪ] = **OK**.

old [əʊld] *adj* vecchio(-a); (person) vecchio, anziano(-a); **how ~ are you?** quanti anni hai?; **I'm 36 years ~** ho 36 anni; **to get ~** invecchiare.

old age *n* vecchiaia *f*.

old age pensioner *n* pensionato *m* (-a *f*).

O-level *n* esame oggi sostituito da 'GCSE'.

olive [ˈɒlɪv] *n* oliva *f*.

olive oil *n* olio *m* d'oliva.

Olympic Games [əˈlɪmpɪk-] *npl* giochi *mpl* olimpici, Olimpiadi *fpl*

omelette [ˈɒmlɪt] *n* frittata *f*, omelette *f inv*; **mushroom ~** frittata ai funghi.

ominous [ˈɒmɪnəs] *adj* sinistro(-a).

omit [əˈmɪt] *vt* omettere.

on [ɒn] *prep* 1. (expressing position, location) su; **it's ~ the table** è su tavolo; **a picture ~ the wall** u quadro alla parete; **the exhaust ~ the car** il tubo di scappament dell'automobile; **~ my right** all. mia destra; **~ the right** a OR sull destra; **we stayed ~ a farm** c siamo fermati in una fattoria; **hotel ~ George Street** un alberg in George Street.

2. (with forms of transport): **~ th train/plane** in treno/aereo; **to get ~ a bus** salire su un autobus.

3. (expressing means, method): **~ foo** a piedi; **~ the radio** alla radio; **~ T** in TV, alla televisione; **~ the pian** al piano.

4. (using): **it runs ~ unleaded petro** va a benzina verde; **to be ~ medi cation** prendere medicine.

5. (about) su; **a book ~ Germany** u libro sulla Germania.

6. (expressing time): **~ arriva** all'arrivo; **~ Tuesday** martedì; **25th August** il 25 agosto.

7. (with regard to) su; **a tax ~ imports** una tassa sulle importa

zioni; **the effect ~ Britain** l'effetto sulla Gran Bretagna.

8. *(describing activity, state)* in; **~ holiday** in vacanza; **~ offer** in offerta; **~ sale** in vendita.

9. *(in phrases)*: **do you have any money ~ you?** *(inf)* hai un po' di soldi con te?; **the drinks are ~ me** offro io da bere.

♦ *adv* **1.** *(in place, covering)*: **to have sthg ~** *(clothes)* indossare qc; **put the lid ~** mettici il coperchio; **to put one's clothes ~** vestirsi.

2. *(film, play, programme)*: **the news is ~** c'è il telegiornale; **what's ~ at the cinema?** cosa danno al cinema?

3. *(with transport)*: **to get ~** salire.

4. *(functioning)*: **to turn sthg ~** *(TV, radio, engine)* accendere qc; *(tap)* aprire qc.

5. *(taking place)*: **how long is the festival ~?** quanto (tempo) dura il festival?

6. *(further forward)*: **to drive ~** continuare a guidare.

7. *(in phrases)*: **do you have anything ~ tonight?** fai qualcosa stasera?

♦ *adj (TV, engine, light)* acceso(-a); *(tap)* aperto(-a).

once [wʌns] *adv* una volta ♦ *conj* una volta che, non appena; *(immediately)* subito; *(at the same time)* insieme, contemporaneamente; **for ~** per una volta; **~ more** ancora una volta.

oncoming ['ɒn,kʌmɪŋ] *adj (traffic)* che procede in senso opposto.

one [wʌn] *num* uno(-a) ♦ *adj (only)* unico(-a) ♦ *pron* uno(-a); **thirty-~** trentuno; **~ fifth** un quinto; **that** ~ quello(-a); **which ~?** quale?; **this** ~ questo(-a); **I want ~** ne voglio uno; **the ~ I told you**

about quello di cui ti ho detto; **~ of my friends** uno dei miei amici; **~ day** un giorno.

one-piece (swimsuit) *n* costume *m* intero.

oneself [wʌn'self] *pron (reflexive)* si; *(after prep)* se stesso(-a), sé.

one-way *adj (street)* a senso unico; *(ticket)* di sola andata.

onion ['ʌnjən] *n* cipolla *f*.

onion bhaji [-'bɑːdʒɪ] *n polpetta a base di cipolla e spezie varie, fritta e servita come antipasto nella cucina indiana.*

onion rings *npl* rondelle *fpl* di cipolle fritte.

only ['əʊnlɪ] *adj* solo(-a), unico (-a) ♦ *adv* solo, soltanto; **he's an ~ child** è figlio unico; **I ~ want one** ne voglio solo uno; **we've ~ just arrived** siamo appena arrivati; **there's ~ just enough** ce n'è appena a sufficienza; **'members ~'** 'riservato ai soci'; **not ~** non solo.

onto ['ɒntuː] *prep (with verbs of movement)* su; **to get ~ sb** *(telephone)* chiamare qn.

onward ['ɒnwəd] *adv* = **onwards** ♦ *adj*: **the ~ journey** il proseguimento.

onwards ['ɒnwədz] *adv (forwards)* in avanti; **from now ~** da ora in poi; **from October ~** da ottobre in poi.

opal ['əʊpl] *n* opale *m* o *f*.

opaque [əʊ'peɪk] *adj (not transparent)* opaco(-a).

open ['əʊpn] *adj* aperto(-a) ♦ *vt* aprire ♦ *vi (door, lock, meeting)* aprirsi; *(shop, office, bank)* aprire; *(play, film)* cominciare; **are you ~ at the weekend?** siete aperti il fine settimana?; **wide ~** spalancato(-a);

in the ~ (air) all'aperto ❑ **open onto** vt fus dare su; **open up** vi aprire.

open-air adj all'aperto.

opening ['əʊpnɪŋ] n apertura f; (opportunity) opportunità f inv.

opening hours npl orario m di apertura.

open-minded [-'maɪndɪd] adj aperto(-a).

open-plan adj senza pareti divisorie.

open sandwich n tartina f.

opera ['ɒpərə] n opera f.

opera house n teatro m dell'opera.

operate ['ɒpəreɪt] vt (machine) azionare, far funzionare ◆ vi (work) funzionare, agire; **to ~ on sb** operare qn.

operating room ['ɒpəreɪtɪŋ-] n (Am) = **operating theatre**.

operating theatre ['ɒpəreɪtɪŋ-] n (Br) sala f operatoria.

operation [ˌɒpə'reɪʃn] n operazione f; **to be in ~** (law, system) essere in vigore; **to have an ~** operarsi.

operator ['ɒpəreɪtər] n (on phone) centralinista mf.

opinion [ə'pɪnjən] n opinione f, parere m; **in my ~** a mio parere, secondo me.

opponent [ə'pəʊnənt] n avversario m (-a f).

opportunity [ˌɒpə'tjuːnətɪ] n opportunità f inv, occasione f.

oppose [ə'pəʊz] vt opporsi a.

opposed [ə'pəʊzd] adj: **to be ~ to** essere contrario(-a) a.

opposite ['ɒpəzɪt] adj (facing) di fronte; (totally different) opposto

(-a), contrario(-a) ◆ prep di fronte a ◆ n: **the ~ (of)** il contrario (di).

opposition [ˌɒpə'zɪʃn] n opposizione f; (SPORT) avversari mpl.

opt [ɒpt] vt: **to ~ to do sthg** scegliere di fare qc.

optician's [ɒp'tɪʃns] n (shop) ottico m.

optimist ['ɒptɪmɪst] n ottimista mf.

optimistic [ˌɒptɪ'mɪstɪk] adj ottimistico(-a).

option ['ɒpʃn] n (alternative) scelta f, alternativa f; (optional extra) optional m inv.

optional ['ɒpʃənl] adj facoltativo(-a).

or [ɔːr] conj o, oppure; (otherwise) se no, altrimenti; (after negative): **I can't read ~ write** non so (né) leggere né scrivere.

oral ['ɔːrəl] adj orale ◆ n orale m.

orange ['ɒrɪndʒ] adj arancione ◆ n (fruit) arancia f; (colour) arancione m.

orange juice n succo m d'arancia.

orange squash n (Br) aranciata f non gassata.

orbit ['ɔːbɪt] n orbita f.

orbital (motorway) ['ɔːbɪtl-] n (Br) raccordo m anulare.

orchard ['ɔːtʃəd] n frutteto m.

orchestra ['ɔːkɪstrə] n orchestra f.

ordeal [ɔː'diːl] n (durissima) esperienza f, travaglio m.

order ['ɔːdər] n ordine m; (in restaurant, for goods) ordinazione f ◆ vt & vi ordinare; **in ~ to** allo scopo di, per; **out of ~** (not working) guasto; **in working ~** funzionante; **to ~ sb to do sthg** ordinare a qn di fare qc.

out

order form n modulo m d'ordinazione.

ordinary [ˈɔːdənrɪ] adj ordinario(-a), comune.

ore [ɔːʳ] n minerale m (grezzo).

oregano [ˌɒrɪˈɡɑːnəʊ] n origano m.

organ [ˈɔːɡən] n organo m.

organic [ɔːˈɡænɪk] adj (food) biologico(-a).

organization [ˌɔːɡənaɪˈzeɪʃn] n organizzazione f.

organize [ˈɔːɡənaɪz] vt organizzare.

organizer [ˈɔːɡənaɪzəʳ] n (person) organizzatore m (-trice f); (diary) agenda f.

oriental [ˌɔːrɪˈentl] adj orientale.

orientate [ˈɔːrɪenteɪt] vt: to ~ o.s. orientarsi.

origin [ˈɒrɪdʒɪn] n origine f.

original [əˈrɪdʒənl] adj (first) originario(-a); (novel) originale.

originally [əˈrɪdʒənəlɪ] adv (formerly) originariamente.

originate [əˈrɪdʒəneɪt] vi: to ~ (from) avere origine (da).

ornament [ˈɔːnəmənt] n (object) soprammobile m.

ornamental [ˌɔːnəˈmentl] adj ornamentale.

ornate [ɔːˈneɪt] adj molto ornato(-a).

orphan [ˈɔːfn] n orfano m (-a f).

orthodox [ˈɔːθədɒks] adj ortodosso(-a).

ostentatious [ˌɒstənˈteɪʃəs] adj pretenzioso(-a); (action, behaviour) ostentato(-a).

ostrich [ˈɒstrɪtʃ] n struzzo m.

other [ˈʌðəʳ] adj altro(-a) ◆ pron altro(-a) ◆ adv: ~ than a parte; the ~ (one) l'altro; the ~ day l'altro

giorno; one after the ~ uno dopo l'altro.

otherwise [ˈʌðəwaɪz] adv altrimenti.

otter [ˈɒtəʳ] n lontra f.

ought [ɔːt] aux vb dovere; **you ~ to have gone** avresti dovuto andarci; **you ~ to see a doctor** dovresti andare dal dottore; **the car ~ to be ready by Friday** la macchina dovrebbe essere pronta per venerdì.

ounce [aʊns] n (unit of measurement) = 28,35 g, oncia f.

our [ˈaʊəʳ] adj il nostro (la nostra), i nostri (le nostre) (pl); ~ **mother** nostra madre.

ours [ˈaʊəz] pron il nostro (la nostra), i nostri (le nostre) (pl); **a friend of ~** un nostro amico.

ourselves [aʊəˈselvz] pron (reflexive) ci; (after prep) noi stessi (-e), noi; **we did it ~** l'abbiamo fatto da soli.

out [aʊt] adj 1. (light, cigarette) spento(-a).
2. (wrong) inesatto(-a); **the bill's £10 ~** c'è un errore di 10 sterline nel conto.
◆ adv 1. (outside) fuori; **to get ~ (of)** (car) scendere (da); **to go ~ (of)** uscire (da); **it's cold ~** fa freddo fuori.
2. (not at home, work) fuori; **to go ~** uscire, andare fuori.
3. (so as to be extinguished): **to turn sthg ~** spegnere qc; **put your cigarette ~** spegni la sigaretta.
4. (expressing removal): **to pour sthg ~** versare qc; **to take sthg ~ (of)** tirar fuori qc (da); (from bank) ritirare qc (da).
5. (outwards): **to stick ~** sporgere.
6. (expressing distribution): **to hand sthg ~** distribuire qc.

7. (in phrases): **to stay ~ of the sun** evitare il sole; **made ~ of wood in** OR di legno; **five ~ of ten women** cinque donne su dieci; **I'm ~ of cigarettes** ho finito le sigarette.

outback ['autbæk] *n*: **the ~** l'outback *m*, l'entroterra *m* australiano.

outboard (motor) ['autbɔ:d-] *n* motore *m* fuoribordo.

outbreak ['autbreik] *n (of fighting)* scoppio *m*; *(of disease)* epidemia *f*.

outburst ['autbɜ:st] *n* scoppio *m*.

outcome ['autkʌm] *n* esito *m*, risultato *m*.

outcrop ['autkrɒp] *n* affioramento *m*.

outdated [,aut'deitid] *adj* antiquato(-a).

outdo [,aut'du:] (*pt* -**did**, *pp* -**done**) *vt* fare meglio di, superare.

outdoor ['autdɔ:ʳ] *adj* all'aperto.

outdoors [aut'dɔ:z] *adv* all'aperto, fuori.

outer ['autəʳ] *adj* esterno(-a).

outer space *n* spazio *m* cosmico.

outfit ['autfit] *n (clothes)* completo *m*.

outing ['autiŋ] *n* gita *f*.

outlet ['autlet] *n (pipe)* scarico *m*, sbocco *m*; **'no ~'** *(Am)* 'strada senza uscita'.

outline ['autlain] *n* profilo *m*.

outlook ['autluk] *n (for future)* prospettiva *f*; *(of weather)* previsioni *fpl*; *(attitude)* modo *m* di vedere.

out-of-date *adj (old-fashioned)* superato(-a); *(passport, licence)* scaduto(-a).

outpatients' (depart-

ment) ['aut,peiʃnts-] *n* reparto *m* pazienti esterni.

output ['autput] *n (of factory)* produzione *f*; *(COMPUT: printout)* output *m inv*, tabulato *m*.

outrage ['autreidʒ] *n (cruel act)* atrocità *f inv*.

outrageous [aut'reidʒəs] *adj (shocking)* scandaloso(-a).

outright [aut'rait] *adv (tell, deny)* apertamente; *(own)* completamente.

outside [*adv* ,aut'said, *adj, prep &* *n* 'autsaid] *adv* fuori, all'esterno ◆ *prep* fuori di ◆ *adj* esterno(-a) ◆ *n* **the ~** *(of building, car, container)* l'esterno *m*; *(AUT: in UK)* la destra; *(AUT: in Europe, US)* la sinistra; **an ~ line** una linea esterna; **~ of** *(Am)* *(on the outside of)* fuori di; *(apart from)* all'infuori di.

outside lane *n* corsia *f* di sorpasso.

outsize ['autsaiz] *adj (clothes)* di taglia forte.

outskirts ['autskɜ:ts] *npl* periferia *f*.

outstanding [aut'stændiŋ] *adj (remarkable)* eccellente; *(problem)* rilevante; *(debt)* da pagare, in sospeso.

outward ['autwəd] *adj (journey)* di andata; *(external)* esteriore.

outwards ['autwədz] *adv* verso l'esterno, in fuori.

oval ['əuvl] *adj* ovale.

ovation [əu'veiʃn] *n* ovazione *f*.

oven ['ʌvn] *n* forno *m*.

oven glove *n* guanto *m* da forno.

ovenproof ['ʌvnpru:f] *adj* da forno.

oven-ready *adj* pronto(-a) per

mettere in forno.

over ['əʊvə^r] *prep* 1. *(above)* sopra, su; **a bridge ~ the river** un ponte sul fiume.

2. *(across)* oltre, al di là di; **with a view ~ the park** con vista sul parco; **to walk ~ sthg** attraversare qc a piedi; **it's just ~ the road** è proprio qui di fronte.

3. *(covering)* su; **put a plaster ~ the wound** mettere un cerotto sulla ferita.

4. *(more than)* più di; **it cost ~ £1,000** è costato più di 1 000 sterline.

5. *(during)* durante; **~ the past two years** negli ultimi due anni.

6. *(with regard to)* su; **an argument ~ the price** una discussione sul prezzo.

7. *(in phrases)*: **all ~ the world/country** in tutto il mondo/paese.

♦ *adv* 1. *(downwards)*: **to fall ~** cadere; **to bend ~** piegarsi (in avanti).

2. *(referring to position, movement)*: **to fly ~ to Canada** andare in Canada in aereo; **~ here** qui; **~ there** là.

3. *(round to other side)*: **to turn sthg ~** rigirare qc.

4. *(more)*: **children aged 12 and ~** ragazzi dai 12 anni in su.

5. *(remaining)*: **to be (left) ~** restare.

6. *(to one's house)*: **to invite sb ~ for dinner** invitare qn a cena; **we have some friends coming ~** verranno a noi OR a trovarci degli amici.

♦ *adj (finished)*: **to be ~** essere finito(-a).

overall [*adv* l:r'əʊvɔːl, *n* 'əʊvɔːrl] ♦ *adv (in general)* complessivamente, nell'insieme ♦ *n (Br: coat)* grembiule *m*; *(Am: boiler suit)* tuta *f* (da lavoro); **how much does it cost ~?** quanto costa in tutto? ❑ **overalls** *npl (Br: boiler suit)* tuta *f* (da lavoro); *(Am: dungarees)* salopette *f inv*.

overboard ['əʊvəbɔːd] *adv (from ship)* in mare.

overbooked [ˌəʊvə'bʊkt] *adj*: **to be ~** avere più prenotazioni dei posti disponibili.

overcame [ˌəʊvə'keɪm] *pt* → overcome.

overcast [ˌəʊvə'kɑːst] *adj* coperto(-a).

overcharge [ˌəʊvə'tʃɑːdʒ] *vt* far pagare un prezzo eccessivo a.

overcoat ['əʊvəkəʊt] *n* cappotto *m*.

overcome [ˌəʊvə'kʌm] *(pt* **-came**, *pp* **-come)** *vt (defeat)* sopraffare; *(problem)* superare.

overcooked [ˌəʊvə'kʊkt] *adj* troppo cotto(-a).

overcrowded [ˌəʊvə'kraʊdɪd] *adj* sovraffollato(-a).

overdo [ˌəʊvə'duː] *(pt* **-did**, *pp* **-done)** *vt (exaggerate)* esagerare con; **to ~ it** esagerare.

overdone [ˌəʊvə'dʌn] *pp* → overdo ♦ *adj (food)* troppo cotto(-a).

overdose ['əʊvədəʊs] *n* overdose *f inv*.

overdraft ['əʊvədrɑːft] *n* scoperto *m (di conto)*.

overdue [ˌəʊvə'djuː] *adj (bus, flight)* in ritardo; *(rent, payment)* in arretrato.

over easy *adj (Am: egg)*: **eggs ~** uova al tegamino fritte da entrambe le parti.

overexposed [ˌəʊvərɪk'spəʊzd] *adj (photograph)* sovraesposto(-a).

overflow [*vb* ˌəʊvə'fləʊ, *n*

'ǝʊvǝ[ɡlǝʊ] vi (container, bath) trabocccare; (river) straripare ♦ n (pipe) troppopieno m.

overgrown [,ǝʊvǝ'ɡrǝʊn] adj (garden, path) ricoperto(-a) di erbacce.

overhaul [,ǝʊvǝ'hɔːl] n (of machine, car) revisione f.

overhead [adj 'ǝʊvǝhed, adv ,ǝʊvǝ'hed] adj aereo(-a) ♦ adv in alto, al di sopra.

overhead locker n (on plane) scomparto m in alto.

overhear [,ǝʊvǝ'hiǝʳ] (pt & pp -heard) vt sentire (per caso).

overheat [,ǝʊvǝ'hiːt] vi surriscaldarsi.

overland ['ǝʊvǝlænd] adv via terra.

overlap [,ǝʊvǝ'læp] vi sovrapporsi.

overleaf [,ǝʊvǝ'liːf] adv a tergo.

overload [,ǝʊvǝ'lǝʊd] vt sovraccaricare.

overlook [vb ,ǝʊvǝ'lʊk, n 'ǝʊvǝlʊk] vt (subj: building, room) dare su; (miss) lasciarsi sfuggire, trascurare ♦ n: (scenic) ~ (Am) punto m panoramico.

overnight [adv ,ǝʊvǝ'naɪt adj 'ǝʊvǝnaɪt] adv (during the night) durante la notte; (until next day) per la notte ♦ adj (train, journey) di notte.

overnight bag n piccola borsa f da viaggio.

overpass ['ǝʊvǝpɑːs] n cavalcavia m inv.

overpowering [,ǝʊvǝ'paʊǝrɪŋ] adj (heat, smell) opprimente, soffocante.

oversaw [,ǝʊvǝ'sɔː] pt → oversee.

overseas [adv ,ǝʊvǝ'siːz, adj 'ǝʊvǝsiːz] adv all'estero (oltremare) ♦ adj straniero(-a); (trade) estero(-a).

oversee [,ǝʊvǝ'siː] (pt -saw, pp -seen) vt sovrintendere a.

overshoot [,ǝʊvǝ'ʃuːt] (pt & pp -shot) vt (turning, motorway exit) oltrepassare.

oversight ['ǝʊvǝsaɪt] n svista f.

oversleep [,ǝʊvǝ'sliːp] (pt & pp -slept) vi non svegliarsi (all'ora prevista).

overtake [,ǝʊvǝ'teɪk] (pt -took, pp -taken) vt & vi sorpassare; 'no overtaking' 'divieto di sorpasso'.

overtime ['ǝʊvǝtaɪm] n straordinario m.

overtook [,ǝʊvǝ'tʊk] pt → overtake.

overture ['ǝʊvǝ,tjʊǝʳ] n (MUS) ouverture f inv.

overturn [,ǝʊvǝ'tɜːn] vi rovesciarsi.

overweight [,ǝʊvǝ'weɪt] adj sovrappeso (inv).

overwhelm [,ǝʊvǝ'welm] vt sopraffare.

owe [ǝʊ] vt dovere; **to ~ sb sthg** dovere qc a qn; **owing to** a causa di.

owl [aʊl] n gufo m.

own [ǝʊn] adj proprio(-a) ♦ vt possedere ♦ pron: **my ~** il mio (la mia), i miei (le mie) (pl); **a room of my ~** una stanza (solo) per me; **on my ~** da solo; **to get one's ~ back** prendersi la rivincita ❑ **own up** vi **to ~ up to sthg** ammettere qc.

owner ['ǝʊnǝʳ] n proprietario m (-a f).

ownership ['ǝʊnǝʃɪp] n proprietà f, possesso m.

ox [ɒks] (pl **oxen** ['ɒksən]) n bue m.

oxtail soup ['ɒksteɪl-] n minestra f di coda di bue.

oxygen ['ɒksɪdʒən] n ossigeno m.

oyster ['ɔɪstər] n ostrica f.

oz abbr = **ounce**.

ozone-friendly ['əʊzəʊn-] adj che non danneggia l'ozono.

P

p (abbr of page) p., pag. ◆ abbr = penny, pence.

pace [peɪs] n passo m.

pacemaker ['peɪs,meɪkər] n (for heart) pacemaker m inv.

Pacific [pə'sɪfɪk] n: the ~ (Ocean) il Pacifico, l'Oceano m Pacifico.

pacifier ['pæsɪfaɪər] n (Am: for baby) succhiotto m.

pacifist ['pæsɪfɪst] n pacifista mf.

pack [pæk] n (of washing powder) pacco m; (of cigarettes, crisps) pacchetto m; (Br: of cards) mazzo m; (rucksack) zaino m ◆ vt (suitcase, bag) preparare, fare; (clothes, camera etc) mettere in valigia; (to package) impacchettare, imballare ◆ vi (for journey) fare i bagagli OR le valigie; **a ~ of lies** un mucchio di bugie; **to ~ sthg into sthg** stipare qc in qc; **to ~ one's bags** fare i bagagli OR le valigie ❑ **pack up** vi (pack suitcase) fare la valigia; (tidy up) riordinare; (Br: inf: machine, car) guastarsi.

package ['pækɪdʒ] n pacchetto m ◆ vt imballare.

package holiday n vacanza f organizzata.

package tour n viaggio m organizzato.

packaging ['pækɪdʒɪŋ] n (material) imballaggio m, confezione f.

packed [pækt] adj (crowded) stipato(-a).

packed lunch n pranzo m al sacco.

packet ['pækɪt] n pacchetto m; **it cost a ~** (Br: inf) è costato un mucchio di soldi.

packing ['pækɪŋ] n (material) imballaggio m; **to do one's ~** fare i bagagli OR le valigie.

pad [pæd] n (of paper) blocco m; (of cloth, cotton wool) tampone m; (for protection) imbottitura f.

padded ['pædɪd] adj (jacket, seat) imbottito(-a).

padded envelope n busta f imbottita.

paddle ['pædl] n (pole) pagaia f ◆ vi (wade) sguazzare; (in canoe) remare (con la pagaia).

paddling pool ['pædlɪŋ-] n piscina f per bambini.

paddock ['pædək] n (at racecourse) paddock m inv.

padlock ['pædlɒk] n lucchetto m.

page [peɪdʒ] n (of book, newspaper) pagina f ◆ vt chiamare.

paid [peɪd] pt & pp → **pay** ◆ adj (holiday, work) pagato(-a).

pain [peɪn] n dolore m; **to be in ~** avere dolore, soffrire; **he's such a ~!** (inf) è un tale rompiscatole! ❑ **pains** npl (trouble) disturbo m.

painful ['peɪnfʊl] adj doloroso(-a).

painkiller ['peɪn,kɪlər] n analgesico m, antidolorifico m.

paint [peɪnt] n vernice f, colore m
♦ vt & vi dipingere; **to ~ one's nails**
dipingersi le unghie ❑ **paints** npl
(tubes, pots etc) colori mpl.

paintbrush ['peɪntbrʌʃ] n pennello m.

painter ['peɪntə'] n (artist) pittore
m (-trice f); (decorator) imbianchino m.

painting ['peɪntɪŋ] n (picture)
dipinto m, quadro m; (artistic activity) pittura f; (by decorator) tinteggiatura f.

pair [peə'] n (of two things) paio m;
in ~s a coppie, a due a due; **a ~ of
pliers** un paio di pinze; **a ~ of scissors** un paio di forbici; **a ~ of
shorts** un paio di calzoncini; **a ~ of
tights** un paio di collant; **a ~ of
trousers** un paio di pantaloni.

pajamas [pə'dʒɑːməz] (Am) =
pyjamas.

Pakistan [Br ˌpɑːkɪ'stɑːn, Am
ˌpækɪ'stæn] n il Pakistan.

Pakistani [Br ˌpɑːkɪ'stɑːnɪ, Am
ˌpækɪ'stænɪ] adj pakistano(-a) ♦ n
pakistano m (-a f).

pakora [pə'kɔːrə] npl frittelle piccanti a base di verdura e spezie varie
servite come antipasto nella cucina
indiana.

pal [pæl] n (inf) amico m (-a f).

palace ['pælɪs] n palazzo m.

palatable ['pælətəbl] adj (food,
drink) gustoso(-a).

palate ['pælət] n palato m.

pale [peɪl] adj pallido(-a).

pale ale n birra f chiara.

palm [pɑːm] n (of hand) palmo m;
~ (tree) palma f.

palpitations [ˌpælpɪ'teɪʃnz] npl
palpitazioni fpl.

pamphlet ['pæmflɪt] n opuscolo m.

pan [pæn] n (saucepan) pentola f;
(frying pan) padella f.

pancake ['pænkeɪk] n crêpe f inv.

pancake roll n involtino m
primavera.

panda ['pændə] n panda m inv.

panda car n (Br) auto f inv della
polizia.

pane [peɪn] n vetro m.

panel ['pænl] n (of wood) pannello
m; (group of experts) gruppo m di
esperti; (on TV, radio) giuria f.

paneling ['pænəlɪŋ] (Am) = **panelling**.

panelling ['pænəlɪŋ] n (Br) rivestimento m a pannelli.

panic ['pænɪk] (pt & pp -ked, cont
-king) n panico m ♦ vi farsi prendere dal panico.

panniers ['pænɪəz] npl (for bicycle) borse fpl da bicicletta.

panoramic [ˌpænə'ræmɪk] adj
panoramico(-a).

pant [pænt] vi ansare.

panties ['pæntɪz] npl (inf)
mutandine fpl.

pantomime ['pæntəmaɪm] n
(Br) spettacolo natalizio per bambini.

---

i | PANTOMIME

Spettacolo teatrale comico per
bambini, in cui si alternano parti
recitate a parti cantate, si ispira generalmente a favole famose e viene
rappresentato nel periodo natalizio.
Di solito il ruolo dell'eroe è interpretato da una giovane attrice, mentre
un attore comico interpreta la parte
della vecchia signora, la "dame".

pantry ['pæntrɪ] *n* dispensa *f*.

pants [pænts] *npl (Br: underwear)* mutande *fpl; (Am: trousers)* pantaloni *mpl*.

panty hose ['pæntɪ-] *npl (Am)* collant *m inv*.

papadum ['pæpədəm] = **poppa+dom**.

paper ['peɪpə'] *n (material)* carta *f; (newspaper)* giornale *m; (exam)* esame *m (scritto)* ◆ *adj* di carta ◆ *vt* tappezzare (con carta da parati); **a piece of ~** un pezzo di carta ▢ **papers** *npl (documents)* documenti *mpl*.

paperback ['peɪpəbæk] *n* libro *m* in brossura.

paper bag *n* sacchetto *m* di carta.

paperboy ['peɪpəbɔɪ] *n ragazzo che recapita i giornali a domicilio*.

paper clip *n* graffetta *f*.

papergirl ['peɪpəgɜːl] *n ragazza che recapita i giornali a domicilio*.

paper handkerchief *n* fazzoletto *m* di carta.

paper shop *n* giornalaio *m*.

paperweight ['peɪpəweɪt] *n* fermacarte *m inv*.

paprika ['pæprɪkə] *n* paprica *f*.

par [pɑː'] *n (in golf)* norma *f*.

paracetamol [.pærə'siːtəmɒl] *n* paracetamolo *m*.

parachute ['pærəʃuːt] *n* paracadute *m inv*.

parade [pə'reɪd] *n (procession)* parata *f; (of shops)* fila *f* di negozi.

paradise ['pærədaɪs] *n* paradiso *m*.

paraffin ['pærəfɪn] *n* cherosene *m*.

paragraph ['pærəgrɑːf] *n* paragrafo *m*.

parallel ['pærəlel] *adj*: **~ (to)** parallelo(-a) (a).

paralysed ['pærəlaɪzd] *adj (Br)* paralizzato(-a).

paralyzed ['pærəlaɪzd] *(Am)* = **paralysed**.

paramedic [.pærə'medɪk] *n* paramedico *m*.

paranoid ['pærənɔɪd] *adj* paranoico(-a).

parasite ['pærəsaɪt] *n* parassita *m*.

parasol ['pærəsɒl] *n* parasole *m inv*.

parcel ['pɑːsl] *n* pacco *m*, pacchetto *m*.

parcel post *n* servizio *m* pacchi postali.

pardon ['pɑːdn] *excl*: **~?** prego?; **~ (me)!** mi scusi!; **I beg your ~!** *(apologizing)* scusi!; **I beg your ~?** *(asking for repetition)* prego?

parent ['peərənt] *n* genitore *m*.

parish ['pærɪʃ] *n (of church)* parrocchia *f; (village area)* = comune *m*.

park [pɑːk] *n* parco *m* ◆ *vt & vi* parcheggiare.

park and ride *n* parcheggio decentrato presso una stazione di mezzi pubblici locali.

parking ['pɑːkɪŋ] *n* parcheggio *m*; **'no ~'** 'sosta vietata'.

parking brake *n (Am)* freno *m* a mano.

parking lot *n (Am)* parcheggio *m*, posteggio *m*.

parking meter *n* parchimetro *m*.

parking space *n* posto *m* per parcheggiare.

parking ticket *n* multa *f* per sosta vietata.

parkway ['pɑːkweɪ] *n (Am)* viale con alberi o piante nella banchina *spartitraffico.*

parliament ['pɑːləmənt] *n* parlamento *m*.

Parmesan (cheese) [pɑːmɪ'zæn-] *n* parmigiano *m*, grana *m*.

parrot ['pærət] *n* pappagallo *m*.

parsley ['pɑːslɪ] *n* prezzemolo *m*.

parsnip ['pɑːsnɪp] *n* pastinaca *f*.

parson ['pɑːsn] *n* curato *m*, parroco *m*.

part [pɑːt] *n* parte *f*; *(of machine, car)* pezzo *m*; *(of serial)* puntata *f*; *(Am: in hair)* scriminatura *f* ♦ *adv* in parte ♦ *vi (couple)* separarsi; **in this ~ of Italy** in questa zona dell'Italia; **to form ~ of** costituire parte di; **to play a ~ in** avere un ruolo in; **to take ~ in** prendere parte a; **for my ~** da parte mia; **for the most ~** per lo più, in generale; **in these ~s** da queste parti.

partial ['pɑːʃl] *adj (not whole)* parziale; **to be ~ to sthg** avere un debole per qc.

participant [pɑː'tɪsɪpənt] *n* partecipante *mf*.

participate [pɑː'tɪsɪpeɪt] *vi*: **to ~ (in)** partecipare (a).

particular [pə'tɪkjʊləʳ] *adj* particolare; *(fussy)* esigente; **in ~** in particolare, specialmente; **nothing in ~** niente di particolare □ **particulars** *npl (details)* particolari *mpl*.

particularly [pə'tɪkjʊləlɪ] *adv* particolarmente, soprattutto.

parting ['pɑːtɪŋ] *n (Br: in hair)* scriminatura *f*.

partition [pɑː'tɪʃn] *n (wall)* tramezzo *m*.

partly ['pɑːtlɪ] *adv* parzialmente, in parte.

partner ['pɑːtnəʳ] *n (husband)* marito *m*; *(wife)* moglie *f*; *(lover, in game, dance)* compagno *m* (-a *f*); *(COMM)* socio *m* (-a *f*).

partnership ['pɑːtnəʃɪp] *n* associazione *f*; *(COMM)* società *f* *inv*.

partridge ['pɑːtrɪdʒ] *n* pernice *f*.

part-time *adj & adv* part time.

party ['pɑːtɪ] *n (for fun)* festa *f*; *(POL)* partito *m*; *(group of people)* gruppo *m*; **to have a ~** fare una festa.

pass [pɑːs] *vt* passare; *(move past)* oltrepassare, passare davanti a; *(test, exam)* passare, superare; *(overtake)* sorpassare; *(law)* approvare ♦ *vi* passare ♦ *n (document)* lasciapassare *m inv*, permesso *m*; *(in mountain)* passo *m*; *(in exam)* sufficienza *f*; *(SPORT)* passaggio *m*; **to ~ sb sthg** passare qc a qn □ **pass by** *vt fus (building, window etc)* passare davanti a ♦ *vi* passare; **pass on** *vt sep (message)* passare; **pass out** *vi (faint)* svenire; **pass up** *vt sep (opportunity)* lasciarsi sfuggire.

passable ['pɑːsəbl] *adj (road)* transitabile; *(satisfactory)* passabile.

passage ['pæsɪdʒ] *n (corridor)* passaggio *m*, corridoio *m*; *(in book)* brano *m*, passo *m*; *(sea journey)* traversata *f*.

passageway ['pæsɪdʒweɪ] *n* corridoio *m*.

passenger ['pæsɪndʒəʳ] *n* passeggero *m* (-a *f*).

passerby [,pɑːsə'baɪ] *n* passante *mf*.

passing place ['pɑːsɪŋ-] *n (for cars)* piazzola *f*.

passion ['pæʃn] *n* passione *f*.

passionate ['pæʃənət] *adj (showing strong feeling)* appassionato(-a); *(sexually)* passionale.

passive ['pæsɪv] *n* passivo *m*.

passport ['pɑːspɔːt] *n* passaporto *m*.

passport control *n* controllo *m* passaporti.

passport photo *n* fototessera *f*.

password ['pɑːswɜːd] *n* (for computer) password *f inv*, parola *f* d'accesso.

past [pɑːst] *adj* passato(-a); (last) ultimo(-a); (former) ex (inv) ◆ *prep* (in times) dopo; (further than) oltre, al di là di; (in front of) davanti a ◆ *adv* oltre ◆ *n* (former time) passato *m*; ~ **(tense)** (GRAMM) passato *m*; **the ~ month** il mese scorso; **twenty ~ four** le quattro e venti; **to run ~** passare di corsa; **in the ~** in passato.

pasta ['pæstə] *n* pasta *f*.

paste [peɪst] *n* (spread) pasta *f*, crema *f* (da spalmare); (glue) colla *f*.

pastel ['pæstl] *n* (for drawing) pastello *m*; (colour) colore *m* pastello.

pasteurized ['pɑːstʃəraɪzd] *adj* pastorizzato(-a).

pastille ['pæstɪl] *n* pastiglia *f*.

pastime ['pɑːstaɪm] *n* passatempo *m*.

pastry ['peɪstrɪ] *n* pasta *f*.

pasture ['pɑːstʃəʳ] *n* pascolo *m*.

pasty ['pæstɪ] *n* (Br) pasticcio *m*.

pat [pæt] *vt* dare un colpetto (affettuoso) a.

patch [pætʃ] *n* (for clothes) toppa *f*; (of colour, cloud, damp) macchia *f*; (for skin) cerotto *m*; (for eye) benda *f*; **a bad ~** (fig) un brutto periodo.

pâté ['pæteɪ] *n* pâté *m inv*.

patent [Br 'peɪtənt, Am 'pætənt] *n* brevetto *m*.

path [pɑːθ] *n* (in park, country) sentiero *m*, viottolo *m*; (in garden) vialetto *m*.

pathetic [pəˈθetɪk] *adj* (pej: useless) penoso(-a).

patience ['peɪʃns] *n* (quality) pazienza *f*; (Br: card game) solitario *m*.

patient ['peɪʃnt] *adj* paziente ◆ *n* paziente *mf*, malato *m* (-a *f*).

patio ['pætɪəʊ] *n* terrazza *f*.

patriotic [Br ˌpætrɪˈɒtɪk, Am ˌpeɪtrɪˈɒtɪk] *adj* patriottico(-a).

patrol [pəˈtrəʊl] *vt* pattugliare ◆ *n* (group) pattuglia *f*.

patrol car *n* auto *f inv* di pattuglia.

patron ['peɪtrən] *n* (fml: customer) cliente *mf*; '**~s only**' 'riservato ai clienti'.

patronizing ['pætrənaɪzɪŋ] *adj* (person) che tratta con aria di superiorità.

pattern ['pætn] *n* (of shapes, colours) disegno *m*, motivo *m*; (for sewing) modello *m*.

patterned ['pætənd] *adj* fantasia (inv).

pause [pɔːz] *n* pausa *f* ◆ *vi* fare una pausa, soffermarsi.

pavement ['peɪvmənt] *n* (Br: beside road) marciapiede *m*; (Am: roadway) pavimentazione *f*.

pavilion [pəˈvɪljən] *n* edificio annesso a campo sportivo, adibito a spogliatoio.

paving stone ['peɪvɪŋ-] *n* lastra *f* di pietra.

pavlova *n* dolce composto da due strati di meringa farciti di panna montata e frutta.

paw [pɔː] *n* zampa *f*.

pawn [pɔːn] *vt* impegnare, dare

in pegno ♦ *n (in chess)* pedone *m*.
pay [peɪ] *(pt & pp* **paid)** *vt* pagare
♦ *vi (give money)* pagare; *(be profit-able)* rendere ♦ *n* paga *f*, stipendio
m; **to ~ sb for sthg** pagare qn per
qc; **to ~ money into an account**
versare dei soldi su un conto; **to ~
attention (to)** fare attenzione (a);
to ~ sb a visit fare visita a qn; **to ~
by credit card** pagare con la carta
di credito ❑ **pay back** *vt sep*
(money) restituire; *(person)* rimbor-sare; **pay for** *vt fus (purchase)* paga-re; **pay in** *vt sep (cheque, money)* ver-sare; **pay out** *vt sep (money)* sbor-sare; **pay up** *vi* saldare il debito.
payable ['peɪəbl] *adj (bill)* paga-bile; **~ to** *(cheque)* pagabile a,
intestato(-a) a.
payment ['peɪmənt] *n (of money,
bill)* pagamento *m*; *(amount)* paga-mento, versamento *m*.
payphone ['peɪfəʊn] *n* telefono
m pubblico.
PC *n (abbr of personal computer)* PC
m inv ♦ *abbr (Br)* = **police consta-ble**.
PE *abbr* = **physical education**.
pea [pi:] *n* pisello *m*.
peace [pi:s] *n* pace *f*; **to leave sb
in ~** lasciare qn in pace; **~ and
quiet** pace e tranquillità.
peaceful ['pi:sful] *adj (place, day,
feeling)* tranquillo(-a), calmo(-a);
(demonstration) pacifico(-a).
peach [pi:tʃ] *n* pesca *f*.
peach melba [-'melbə] *n* pe-sche *fpl* melba.
peacock ['pi:kɒk] *n* pavone *m*.
peak [pi:k] *n (of mountain)* cima *f*,
vetta *f*; *(of hat)* visiera *f*; *(fig: highest
point)* apice *m*, culmine *m*.
peak hours *npl* ore *fpl* di

punta.
peak rate *n* tariffa *f* ore di
punta.
peanut ['pi:nʌt] *n* arachide *f*,
nocciolina *f* americana.
peanut butter *n* burro *m* di
arachidi.
pear [peəʳ] *n* pera *f*.
pearl [pɜ:l] *n* perla *f*.
peasant ['peznt] *n* contadino *m*
(-a *f*).
pebble ['pebl] *n* ciottolo *m*.
pecan pie ['pi:kæn-] *n* torta di
noci pecan.
peck [pek] *vi (bird)* beccare.
peculiar [pɪ'kju:ljəʳ] *adj (strange)*
strano(-a), singolare; **to be ~ to**
(exclusive) essere peculiare di.
peculiarity [pɪˌkju:lɪ'ærətɪ] *n*
(special feature) particolarità *f inv*.
pedal ['pedl] *n* pedale *m* ♦ *vi*
pedalare.
pedal bin *n* pattumiera *f* a
pedale.
pedalo ['pedələʊ] *(pl* **-s)** *n* mo-scone *m* a pedali, pedalò® *m inv*.
pedestrian [pɪ'destrɪən] *n* pedo-ne *m* (-a *f*).
pedestrian crossing *n* pas-saggio *m* pedonale.
pedestrianized [pɪ'destrɪə-naɪzd] *adj* riservato(-a) ai pedoni.
pedestrian precinct *n (Br)*
zona *f* pedonale.
pedestrian zone *(Am)* =
pedestrian precinct.
pee [pi:] *vi (inf)* fare la pipì ♦ *n*: **to
have a ~** *(inf)* fare la pipì.
peel [pi:l] *n* buccia *f*; *(of orange,
lemon)* scorza *f* ♦ *vt (fruit, vegetables)*
sbucciare ♦ *vi (paint)* staccarsi;
(skin) spellarsi.

peep [pi:p] *n*: **to have a ~** dare una sbirciatina.

peer [pɪəʳ] *vi*: **to ~ at** fissare, scrutare.

peg [peg] *n* (*for tent*) picchetto *m*; (*hook*) attaccapanni *m inv*; (*for washing*) molletta *f*.

pelican crossing [ˈpelɪkən-] *n* (*Br*) passaggio pedonale con semaforo a comando manuale.

pelvis [ˈpelvɪs] *n* bacino *m*.

pen [pen] *n* (*for writing*) penna *f*; (*for animals*) recinto *m*.

penalty [ˈpenltɪ] *n* (*fine*) multa *f*, sanzione *f*; (*in football*) rigore *m*.

pence [pens] *npl* penny *m inv*; **it costs 20 ~** costa 20 penny.

pencil [ˈpensl] *n* matita *f*.

pencil case *n* portamatite *m inv*.

pencil sharpener *n* temperamatite *m inv*.

pendant [ˈpendənt] *n* pendente *m*, ciondolo *m*.

pending [ˈpendɪŋ] *prep* (*fml*) in attesa di.

penetrate [ˈpenɪtreɪt] *vt* penetrare.

penfriend [ˈpenfrend] *n* amico *m* (-a *f*) per corrispondenza.

penguin [ˈpeŋgwɪn] *n* pinguino *m*.

penicillin [ˌpenɪˈsɪlɪn] *n* penicillina *f*.

peninsula [pəˈnɪnsjʊlə] *n* penisola *f*.

penis [ˈpi:nɪs] *n* pene *m*.

penknife [ˈpennaɪf] (*pl* **-knives**) *n* temperino *m*.

penny [ˈpenɪ] (*pl* **pennies**) *n* (*in UK*) penny *m inv*; (*in US*) centesimo *m*.

pension [ˈpenʃn] *n* pensione *f*.

pensioner [ˈpenʃənəʳ] *n* pensionato *m* (-a *f*).

penthouse [ˈpenthaʊs, *pl* -haʊzɪz] *n* superattico *m*.

penultimate [peˈnʌltɪmət] *adj* penultimo(-a).

people [ˈpi:pl] *npl* (*persons*) persone *fpl*; (*in general*) gente *f* ◆ *n* (*nation*) popolo *m*; **the ~** (*citizens*) il popolo.

pepper [ˈpepəʳ] *n* (*spice*) pepe *m*; (*vegetable*) peperone *m*.

peppercorn [ˈpepəkɔ:n] *n* grano *m* di pepe.

peppermint [ˈpepəmɪnt] *adj* alla menta (piperita) ◆ *n* (*sweet*) caramella *f* di menta.

pepper pot *n* pepiera *f*.

pepper steak *n* bistecca *f* al pepe.

Pepsi® [ˈpepsɪ] *n* Pepsi® *f inv*.

per [pɜ:ʳ] *prep* per, a; **~ person** a persona; **~ week** alla settimana; **£20 ~ night** 20 sterline a notte.

perceive [pəˈsi:v] *vt* percepire.

per cent *adv* per cento.

percentage [pəˈsentɪdʒ] *n* percentuale *f*.

perch [pɜ:tʃ] *n* (*for bird*) posatoio *m*, asticella *f*.

percolator [ˈpɜːkəleɪtəʳ] *n* caffettiera *f* a filtro.

perfect [*adj & n* ˈpɜːfɪkt, *vb* pəˈfekt] *adj* perfetto(-a) ◆ *vt* perfezionare ◆ *n*: **the ~** (*tense*) il passato prossimo.

perfection [pəˈfekʃn] *n*: **to do sthg to ~** fare qc alla perfezione.

perfectly [ˈpɜːfɪktlɪ] *adv* (*very well*) perfettamente, alla perfezione.

perform [pəˈfɔ:m] *vt* (*task, opera-*

tion) eseguire, fare; *(play)* rappresentare; *(concert)* eseguire ♦ *vi (actor)* recitare; *(singer)* cantare.

performance [pə'fɔ:məns] *n (of play, concert, film)* spettacolo *m*; *(by actor)* interpretazione *f*; *(musician)* esecuzione *f*; *(of car)* prestazioni *fpl.*

performer [pə'fɔ:mə^r] *n* artista *mf.*

perfume [pɜ:fju:m] *n* profumo *m.*

perhaps [pə'hæps] *adv* forse.

perimeter [pərɪmɪtə^r] *n* perimetro *m.*

period ['pɪərɪəd] *n* periodo *m*; *(SCH)* lezione *f*; *(menstruation)* mestruazioni *fpl*; *(Am: full stop)* punto *m* ♦ *adj (costume, furniture)* d'epoca.

periodic [,pɪərɪ'ɒdɪk] *adj* periodico(-a).

period pains *npl* dolori *mpl* mestruali.

periphery [pə'nfərɪ] *n* periferia *f.*

perishable ['perɪʃəbl] *adj* deperibile.

perk [pɜ:k] *n* vantaggio *m.*

perm [pɜ:m] *n* permanente *f* ♦ *vt*: **to have one's hair ~ed** farsi la permanente.

permanent ['pɜ:mənənt] *adj* permanente.

permanent address *n* residenza *f.*

permanently ['pɜ:mənəntlɪ] *adv* permanentemente.

permissible [pə'mɪsəbl] *adj (fml)* permissibile, ammissibile.

permission [pə'mɪʃn] *n* permesso *m.*

permit [*vb* pə'mɪt, *n* 'pɜ:mɪt] *vt* permettere ♦ *n* permesso *m*; **to ~ sb to do sthg** permettere a qn di fare qc; '~ **holders only**' 'solo autorizzati'.

perpendicular [,pɜ:pən'dɪkjʊlə^r] *adj* perpendicolare.

persevere [,pɜ:sɪ'vɪə^r] *vi* perseverare.

persist [pə'sɪst] *vi* persistere; **to ~ in doing sthg** ostinarsi a fare qc.

persistent [pə'sɪstənt] *adj* persistente; *(person)* ostinato(-a).

person ['pɜ:sn] *(pl people)* *n* persona *f*; **in ~** di persona.

personal ['pɜ:sənl] *adj* personale.

personal assistant *n* segretario *m* (-a *f*) personale.

personal belongings *npl* effetti *mpl* personali.

personal computer *n* personal computer *m inv.*

personality [,pɜ:sə'nælətɪ] *n* personalità *f inv.*

personally ['pɜ:snəlɪ] *adv* personalmente.

personal property *n* beni *mpl* mobili.

personal stereo *n* walkman® *m inv.*

personnel [,pɜ:sə'nel] *npl* personale *m.*

perspective [pə'spektɪv] *n* prospettiva *f.*

Perspex® ['pɜ:speks] *n (Br)* = plexiglas® *m.*

perspiration [,pɜ:spə'reɪʃn] *n* traspirazione *f*, sudore *m.*

persuade [pə'sweɪd] *vt*: **to ~ sb (to do sthg)** persuadere qn (a fare qc); **to ~ sb that ...** persuadere qn che ...

persuasive [pə'sweɪsɪv] *adj* persuasivo(-a), convincente.

pervert ['pɜ:vɜ:t] *n* pervertito

m (-a *f*).

pessimist ['pesɪmɪst] *n* pessimista *mf*.

pessimistic [.pesɪ'mɪstɪk] *adj* pessimistico(-a).

pest [pest] *n (insect)* insetto *m* nocivo; *(animal)* animale *m* nocivo; *(inf: person)* peste *f*.

pester ['pestər] *vt* tormentare.

pesticide ['pestɪsaɪd] *n* pesticida *m*.

pet [pet] *n* animale *m* domestico; **the teacher's ~** il favorito dell'insegnante.

petal ['petl] *n* petalo *m*.

pet food *n* cibo *m* per animali (domestici).

petition [pɪ'tɪʃn] *n (letter)* petizione *f*.

petits pois *npl* pisellini *mpl*.

petrified ['petrɪfaɪd] *adj (frightened)* impietrito(-a) (dalla paura).

petrol ['petrəl] *n (Br)* benzina *f*.

petrol can *n (Br)* tanica *f* per la benzina.

petrol cap *n (Br)* tappo *m* del serbatoio.

petrol gauge *n (Br)* indicatore *m* di livello della benzina.

petrol pump *n (Br)* pompa *f* di benzina.

petrol station *n (Br)* stazione *f* di rifornimento.

petrol tank *n (Br)* serbatoio *m* della benzina.

pet shop *n* negozio *m* di animali.

petticoat ['petɪkəʊt] *n* sottoveste *f*.

petty ['petɪ] *adj (pej: person, rule)* meschino(-a).

petty cash *n* piccola cassa *f*.

pew [pju:] *n* panca *f* (di chiesa).

pewter ['pju:tər] *adj* di peltro.

PG *(abbr of parental guidance)* sigla che contraddistingue i film non vietati ai minori, per i quali è però consigliato l'accompagnamento dei genitori.

pharmacist ['fɑ:məsɪst] *n* farmacista *mf*.

pharmacy ['fɑ:məsɪ] *n (shop)* farmacia *f*.

phase [feɪz] *n* fase *f*.

PhD *n (degree)* = dottorato *m* di ricerca.

pheasant ['feznt] *n* fagiano *m*.

phenomena [fɪ'nɒmɪnə] *pl* → phenomenon.

phenomenal [fɪ'nɒmɪnl] *adj* fenomenale.

phenomenon [fɪ'nɒmɪnən] *(pl -mena)* *n* fenomeno *m*.

Philippines ['fɪlɪpi:nz] *npl:* **the ~** le Filippine.

philosophy [fɪ'lɒsəfɪ] *n* filosofia *f*.

phlegm [flem] *n (in throat)* catarro *m*.

phone [fəʊn] *n* telefono *m* ◆ *vt (Br)* telefonare a ◆ *vi (Br)* telefonare; **to be on the ~** *(talking)* essere al telefono; *(connected)* avere il telefono ▫ **phone up** *vt sep* telefonare a, chiamare ◆ *vi* telefonare.

phone book *n* elenco *m* telefonico.

phone booth *n* cabina *f* telefonica.

phone box *n (Br)* cabina *f* telefonica.

phone call *n* telefonata *f*.

phonecard ['fəʊnkɑ:d] *n* scheda *f* telefonica.

phone number *n* numero *m* di telefono.

photo ['fəʊtəʊ] *(pl -s)* *n* foto *f inv*;

to take a ~ of fare una foto a.

photo album n album m inv portafotografie.

photocopier [ˌfəʊtəʊˈkɒpɪəʳ] n fotocopiatrice f.

photocopy [ˈfəʊtəʊˌkɒpɪ] n fotocopia f ♦ vt fotocopiare.

photograph [ˈfəʊtəgrɑːf] n fotografia f ♦ vt fotografare.

photographer [fəˈtɒgrəfəʳ] n fotografo m (-a f).

photography [fəˈtɒgrəfɪ] n fotografia f.

phrase [freɪz] n espressione f.

phrasebook [ˈfreɪzbʊk] n vocabolarietto m con frasi tipiche.

physical [ˈfɪzɪkl] adj fisico(-a) ♦ n visita f medica.

physical education n educazione f fisica.

physically handicapped [ˈfɪzɪklɪ-] adj handicappato fisico (handicappata fisica).

physics [ˈfɪzɪks] n fisica f.

physiotherapy [ˌfɪzɪəʊˈθerəpɪ] n fisioterapia f.

pianist [ˈpɪənɪst] n pianista mf.

piano [pɪˈænəʊ] (pl -s) n pianoforte m.

pick [pɪk] vt (select) scegliere; (fruit, flowers) cogliere ♦ n (pickaxe) piccone m; to ~ a fight attaccar briga; to ~ one's nose mettersi le dita nel naso; to take one's ~ scegliere □ **pick on** vt fus prendersela con, prendere di mira; **pick out** vt sep (select) scegliere; (see) individuare, riconoscere; **pick up** vt sep (lift up) raccogliere; (collect) passare a prendere; (learn) imparare; (habit) prendere; (bargain) trovare; (hitchhiker) far salire; (inf: woman, man) rimorchiare ♦ vi (improve) ripren-

dersi; **to ~ up the phone** (answer) rispondere al telefono.

pickaxe [ˈpɪkæks] n piccone m.

pickle [ˈpɪkl] n (Br: food) sottaceti mpl; (Am: pickled cucumber) cetriolo m sottaceto.

pickled onion [ˈpɪkld-] n cipollina f sottaceto.

pickpocket [ˈpɪkˌpɒkɪt] n borsaiolo m.

pick-up (truck) n camioncino m.

picnic [ˈpɪknɪk] n picnic m inv.

picnic area n area per picnic.

picture [ˈpɪktʃəʳ] n (painting) quadro m; (drawing) disegno m; (photograph) fotografia f; (on TV) immagine f; (film) film m inv □ **pictures** npl: the ~s (Br) il cinema.

picture frame n cornice f.

picturesque [ˌpɪktʃəˈresk] adj pittoresco(-a).

pie [paɪ] n (savoury) pasticcio m; (sweet) torta f.

piece [piːs] n pezzo m; a 20p ~ un pezzo da 20 penny; a ~ of advice un consiglio; a ~ of clothing un capo di vestiario; a ~ of furniture un mobile; to fall to ~s andare in pezzi; in one ~ tutto intero.

pier [pɪəʳ] n molo m.

pierce [pɪəs] vt forare, perforare; to have one's ears ~d farsi i buchi alle orecchie.

pig [pɪg] n maiale m, porco m.

pigeon [ˈpɪdʒɪn] n piccione m.

pigeonhole [ˈpɪdʒɪnhəʊl] n casella f.

pigskin [ˈpɪgskɪn] adj di cinghiale.

pigtails [ˈpɪgteɪlz] npl trecce fpl.

pike [paɪk] n (fish) luccio m.

pilau rice ['pɪlaʊ-] n riso m pilaf.

pilchard ['pɪltʃəd] n sardina f.

pile [paɪl] n (heap) mucchio m; (neat stack) pila f ◆ vt ammucchiare; ~s of (inf: a lot) mucchi di □ **pile up** vt sep ammucchiare ◆ vi (accumulate) ammucchiarsi.

piles [paɪlz] npl (MED) emorroidi fpl.

pileup ['paɪlʌp] n tamponamento m a catena.

pill [pɪl] n pillola f.

pillar ['pɪlər] n colonna f.

pillar box n (Br) cassetta f delle lettere.

pillion ['pɪljən] n: **to ride ~** viaggiare sul sellino posteriore.

pillow ['pɪləʊ] n cuscino m.

pillowcase ['pɪləʊkeɪs] n federa f.

pilot ['paɪlət] n pilota mf.

pilot light n fiamma f pilota.

pimple ['pɪmpl] n foruncolo m.

pin [pɪn] n (for sewing, safety pin) spillo m; (drawing pin) puntina f; (Am: brooch, badge) spilla f ◆ vt (fasten) attaccare con uno spillo; a **two-~ plug** una spina bipolare; **~s and needles** formicolio m.

pinafore ['pɪnəfɔːr] n (apron) grembiule m; (Br: dress) scamiciato m.

pinball ['pɪnbɔːl] n flipper m inv.

pincers ['pɪnsəz] npl (tool) tenaglie fpl.

pinch [pɪntʃ] vt (squeeze) pizzicare, dare un pizzicotto a; (Br: inf: steal) fregare ◆ n (of salt) pizzico m.

pine [paɪn] n pino m ◆ adj di pino.

pineapple ['paɪnæpl] n ananas m inv.

pink [pɪŋk] adj rosa (inv) ◆ n (colour) rosa m inv.

pinkie ['pɪŋkɪ] n (Am) mignolo m.

PIN number n numero m di codice segreto.

pint [paɪnt] n (in UK) = 0,568 l, pinta f; (in US) = 0,473 l, pinta; **a ~ (of beer)** (Br) = una birra grande.

pip [pɪp] n (of fruit) seme m.

pipe [paɪp] n (for smoking) pipa f; (for gas, water) tubo m.

pipe cleaner n scovolino m.

pipeline ['paɪplaɪn] n conduttura f; (for oil) oleodotto m.

pipe tobacco n tabacco m da pipa.

pirate ['paɪrət] n pirata m.

Pisces ['paɪsiːz] n Pesci mpl.

piss [pɪs] vi (vulg) pisciare ◆ n: **to have a ~** (vulg) pisciare; **it's ~ing down** (vulg) piove a dirotto.

pissed [pɪst] adj (Br: vulg: drunk) sbronzo(-a); (Am: vulg: angry) incazzato(-a).

pissed off adj (vulg) incazzato(-a).

pistachio [pɪ'stɑːʃɪəʊ] (pl -s) n pistacchio m ◆ adj al pistacchio.

pistol ['pɪstl] n pistola f.

piston ['pɪstən] n pistone m.

pit [pɪt] n (hole) buca f, fossa f; (coalmine) miniera f (di carbone); (for orchestra) fossa dell'orchestra; (Am: in fruit) nocciolo m.

pitch [pɪtʃ] n (Br: SPORT) campo m ◆ vt (throw) lanciare; **to ~ a tent** piantare una tenda.

pitcher ['pɪtʃər] n brocca f.

pitfall ['pɪtfɔːl] n insidia f, pericolo m.

pith [pɪθ] n (of orange) parte f interna della scorza.

pitta (bread) ['pɪtə-] n tipo di schiacciatina di origine mediorientale.

pitted ['pɪtɪd] adj (olives) snoc-
ciolato(-a).

pity ['pɪtɪ] n (compassion) pietà f;
to have ~ on sb avere pietà di qn;
it's a ~ that ... è un peccato che
...; **what a ~!** che peccato!

pivot ['pɪvət] n perno m.

pizza ['pi:tsə] n pizza f.

pizzeria [,pi:tsə'ri:ə] n pizzeria f.

Pl. (abbr of Place) abbreviazione di
strada in alcuni indirizzi.

placard ['plæka:d] n cartello m.

place [pleɪs] n (location) posto m,
luogo m; (house, flat) casa f; (seat,
proper position, in race, list) posto ◆
vt (put) collocare, mettere; (an
order, bet) fare; **in the first ~** (firstly)
in primo luogo; **to take ~** avere
luogo, avvenire; **to take sb's ~**
(replace) prendere il posto di qn; **all
over the ~** dappertutto; **in ~ of** al
posto di.

place mat n (heat-resistant) sottopiatto m; (linen) tovaglietta f.

placement ['pleɪsmənt] n (work
experience) stage m inv.

place of birth n luogo m di
nascita.

plague [pleɪg] n peste f.

plaice [pleɪs] n (pl inv) platessa f.

plain [pleɪn] adj (simple) semplice; (in one colour) in tinta unita;
(clear) chiaro(-a); (paper) non riga-
to(-a); (pej: not attractive) scialbo(-a)
◆ n pianura f.

plain chocolate n cioccolato
m fondente.

plainly ['pleɪnlɪ] adv chiaramente.

plait [plæt] n treccia f ◆ vt intrecciare.

plan [plæn] n (scheme, project)

piano m, progetto m; (drawing)
pianta f ◆ vt (organize) programmare, progettare; **have you any ~s for
tonight?** hai qualche programma
per stasera?; **according to ~** secondo i piani; **to ~ to do sthg, to ~ on
doing sthg** progettare di fare qc.

plane [pleɪn] n (aeroplane) aereo
m; (tool) pialla f.

planet ['plænɪt] n pianeta m.

plank [plæŋk] n asse f, tavola f.

plant [plɑ:nt] n pianta f; (factory)
stabilimento m, fabbrica f ◆ vt
piantare; **'heavy ~ crossing'** 'uscita
mezzi pesanti'.

plantation [plæn'teɪʃn] n pian-
tagione f.

plaque [plɑ:k] n placca f.

plaster ['plɑ:stər] n (Br: for cut)
cerotto m; (for walls) intonaco m; **in
~** (arm, leg) ingessato.

plaster cast n (for broken bones)
ingessatura f.

plastic ['plæstɪk] n plastica f ◆
adj di plastica.

plastic bag n sacchetto m di
plastica.

Plasticine® ['plæstɪsi:n] n (Br)
plastilina® f.

plate [pleɪt] n (for food) piatto m;
(of metal, glass) piastra f.

plateau ['plætəʊ] n altopiano m.

plate-glass adj di vetro piano.

platform ['plætfɔ:m] n (at railway
station) marciapiede m (di binario);
(raised structure) piattaforma f;
(stage) palco m; **~ 12** binario 12.

platinum ['plætɪnəm] n platino m.

platter ['plætər] n (CULIN) piatto m
(di affettati, frutti di mare assortiti, ecc.)

play [pleɪ] vt (sport, game) giocare
a; (musical instrument, music) suona-

re; *(opponent)* giocare contro; *(CD, tape, record)* mettere (su); *(role, character)* interpretare ◆ *vi* giocare; *(musician)* suonare ◆ *n (in theatre, on TV)* dramma *m*, commedia *f*; *(button on CD, tape recorder)* play *m inv* ❑ **play back** *vt sep (tape)* riascoltare; *(video)* rivedere; **play up** *vi (machine, car)* fare i capricci.

player ['pleɪəʳ] *n (of sport, game)* giocatore *m* (-trice *f*); *(of musical instrument)* suonatore *m* (-trice *f*).

playful ['pleɪfʊl] *adj* scherzoso(-a), giocoso(-a).

playground ['pleɪgraʊnd] *n (in school)* cortile *m* per la ricreazione; *(in park etc)* parco *m* giochi.

playgroup ['pleɪgruːp] *n* asilo *m* infantile.

playing card ['pleɪɪŋ-] *n* carta *f* da gioco.

playing field ['pleɪɪŋ-] *n* campo *m* sportivo.

playroom ['pleɪrʊm] *n* stanza *f* dei giochi.

playschool ['pleɪskuːl] = **playgroup**.

playtime ['pleɪtaɪm] *n* ricreazione *f*.

playwright ['pleɪraɪt] *n* drammaturgo *m* (-a *f*).

plc *(Br: abbr of public limited company)* = S.r.l. *(quotata in borsa)*.

pleasant ['pleznt] *adj* piacevole, gradevole; *(person)* simpatico(-a).

please [pliːz] *adv* per favore, per piacere ◆ *vt* far piacere a; ~ **take a seat** prego, si sieda; **yes ~!** si, grazie!; **whatever you ~** quello che ti pare.

pleased [pliːzd] *adj* contento(-a); **to be ~ with** essere contento di; ~ **to meet you!** piacere!

pleasure ['pleʒəʳ] *n* piacere *m*; **with ~** con piacere; **it's a ~!** non c'è di che!, prego!

pleat [pliːt] *n* piega *f*.

pleated ['pliːtɪd] *adj* pieghettato(-a).

plentiful ['plentɪfʊl] *adj* abbondante.

plenty ['plentɪ] *pron:* **there's ~** ce n'è in abbondanza; ~ **of** un sacco di.

pliers ['plaɪəz] *npl* pinze *fpl*.

plimsoll ['plɪmsəl] *n (Br)* scarpa *f* da tennis.

plonk [plɒŋk] *n (Br: inf: wine)* vino *m* da poco.

plot [plɒt] *n (scheme)* complotto *m*; *(of story, film, play)* trama *f*; *(of land)* appezzamento *m*.

plough [plaʊ] *n (Br)* aratro *m* ◆ *vt (Br)* arare.

ploughman's (lunch) ['plaʊmənz-] *n (Br)* piatto a base di formaggi, sottaceti e pane, spesso servito nei pub.

plow [plaʊ] *(Am)* = **plough**.

ploy [plɔɪ] *n* tattica *f*.

pluck [plʌk] *vt (eyebrows)* depilare; *(chicken)* spennare.

plug [plʌg] *n (electrical)* spina *f*; *(for bath, sink)* tappo *m* ❑ **plug in** *vt sep* attaccare (a una presa).

plughole ['plʌghəʊl] *n* buco *m* (della vasca, ecc.).

plum [plʌm] *n* susina *f*, prugna *f*.

plumber ['plʌməʳ] *n* idraulico *m*.

plumbing ['plʌmɪŋ] *n (pipes)* tubature *fpl*.

plump [plʌmp] *adj* grassoccio(-a).

plunge [plʌndʒ] *vi (fall)* precipitare, cadere; *(dive)* tuffarsi; *(de-*

crease) precipitare.

plunge pool *n* piscina *f* piccola.

plunger ['plʌndʒəʳ] *n* (for unblocking pipe) sturalavandini *m inv*.

pluperfect (tense) [,plu:-'pɜːfɪkt-] *n*: **the ~** il piuccheperfetto.

plural ['plʊərəl] *n* plurale *m*; **in the ~** al plurale.

plus [plʌs] *prep* più ♦ *adj*: **30 ~** più di 30.

plush [plʌʃ] *adj* lussuoso(-a).

plywood ['plaɪwʊd] *n* compensato *m*.

p.m. *(abbr of post meridiem)*: **at 3 ~** alle 3 del pomeriggio; **at 10 ~** alle 10 di sera.

PMT *n* (abbr of premenstrual tension) sindrome *f* premestruale.

pneumatic drill [njuː'mætɪk-] *n* martello *m* pneumatico.

pneumonia [njuː'məʊnjə] *n* polmonite *f*.

poached egg [pəʊtʃt-] *n* uovo *m* in camicia.

poached salmon [pəʊtʃt-] *n* salmone *m* bollito.

poacher ['pəʊtʃəʳ] *n* bracconiere *m*.

PO Box *n* (abbr of Post Office Box) C.P.

pocket ['pɒkɪt] *n* tasca *f* ♦ *adj* tascabile.

pocketbook ['pɒkɪtbʊk] *n* (notebook) taccuino *m*; (Am: handbag) borsetta *f*.

pocket money *n* (Br) paghetta *f*, settimana *f*.

podiatrist [pə'daɪətrɪst] *n* (Am) pedicure *mf*, callista *mf*.

poem ['pəʊɪm] *n* poesia *f*.

poet ['pəʊɪt] *n* poeta *m* (-essa *f*).

poetry ['pəʊɪtrɪ] *n* poesia *f*.

point [pɔɪnt] *n* punto *m*; *(tip)* punta *f*; (Br: electric socket) presa *f* ♦ *vi*: **to ~ to** indicare; **five ~ seven** cinque virgola sette; **what's the ~?** a che serve?; **there's no ~** è inutile; **to be on the ~ of doing sthg** essere sul punto di fare qc ❑ **points** *npl* (Br: on railway) scambio *m*; **point out** *vt sep (object, person)* indicare; *(fact, mistake)* far notare.

pointed ['pɔɪntɪd] *adj (in shape)* appuntito(-a).

pointless ['pɔɪntlɪs] *adj* inutile.

point of view *n* punto *m* di vista.

poison ['pɔɪzn] *n* veleno *m* ♦ *vt* avvelenare.

poisoning ['pɔɪznɪŋ] *n* avvelenamento *m*, intossicazione *f*.

poisonous ['pɔɪznəs] *adj* velenoso(-a).

poke [pəʊk] *vt (with finger, stick, elbow)* dare un colpetto a.

poker ['pəʊkəʳ] *n* (card game) poker *m*.

Poland ['pəʊlənd] *n* la Polonia.

polar bear ['pəʊlə-] *n* orso *m* bianco.

Polaroid® ['pəʊlərɔɪd] *n* (photograph) foto *f inv* polaroid®; (camera) polaroid® *f inv*.

pole [pəʊl] *n* (of wood) palo *m*.

Pole [pəʊl] *n* (person) polacco *m* (-a *f*).

police [pə'liːs] *npl*: **the ~** la polizia.

police car *n* auto *f inv* della polizia.

police force *n* forze *fpl* di polizia OR dell'ordine.

policeman [pə'li:smən] (pl -men [-mən]) n poliziotto m.

police officer n agente m di polizia.

police station n posto m di polizia.

policewoman [pə'li:s,wumən] (pl -women [-,wimin]) n donna f poliziotto.

policy ['pɒləsɪ] n (approach, attitude) politica f; (for insurance) polizza f.

policy-holder n assicurato m (-a f).

polio ['pəulɪəu] n polio f.

polish ['pɒlɪʃ] n (for cleaning) lucido m, cera f ♦ vt lucidare.

Polish ['pəulɪʃ] adj polacco(-a) ♦ n (language) polacco m ♦ npl: **the** ~ i polacchi.

polite [pə'laɪt] adj cortese, gentile.

political [pə'lɪtɪkl] adj politico(-a).

politician [,pɒlɪ'tɪʃn] n politico m.

politics ['pɒlɪtɪks] n politica f.

poll [pəul] n (survey) sondaggio m (d'opinioni); **the** ~**s** (election) le elezioni.

pollen ['pɒlən] n polline m.

Poll Tax n (Br) tassa comunale pro capite.

pollute [pə'lu:t] vt inquinare.

pollution [pə'lu:ʃn] n inquinamento m.

polo neck ['pəuləu-] n (Br: jumper) maglione m a collo alto.

polyester [,pɒlɪ'estər] n poliestere m.

polystyrene [,pɒlɪ'staɪri:n] n polistirolo m.

polytechnic [,pɒlɪ'teknɪk] n =

politecnico m.

polythene bag ['pɒlɪθi:n-] n sacchetto m di plastica.

pomegranate ['pɒmɪ,grænɪt] n melagrana f.

pompous ['pɒmpəs] adj pomposo(-a).

pond [pɒnd] n stagno m.

pontoon [pɒn'tu:n] n (Br: card game) ventuno m.

pony ['pəunɪ] n pony m inv.

ponytail ['pəunɪteɪl] n coda f di cavallo.

pony-trekking [-,trekɪŋ] n (Br) escursione f a dorso di cavallo.

poodle ['pu:dl] n barboncino m.

pool [pu:l] n pozza f; (for swimming) piscina f; (game) biliardo m a buca ❑ **pools** npl (Br): **the** ~**s** = il totocalcio.

poor [pɔːr] adj povero(-a); (bad) mediocre, scadente ♦ npl: **the** ~ i poveri.

poorly ['pɔːlɪ] adv malamente, male ♦ adj (Br: ill): **to be** ~ stare poco bene.

pop [pɒp] n (music) musica f pop ♦ vt (inf: put) mettere ♦ vi (balloon) scoppiare; **my ears popped** mi si sono stappate le orecchie ❑ **pop in** vi (Br: visit) fare un salto.

popcorn ['pɒpkɔ:n] n popcorn m.

Pope [pəup] n: **the** ~ il papa.

pop group n gruppo m pop.

poplar (tree) ['pɒplər-] n pioppo m.

pop music n musica f pop.

poppadom ['pɒpədəm] n pane indiano molto sottile e croccante.

popper ['pɒpər] n (Br) bottone m a pressione.

poppy ['pɒpɪ] n papavero m.

Popsicle® ['pɒpsɪkl] *n (Am)* ghiacciolo *m*.

pop socks *npl* gambaletti *mpl*.

pop star *n* pop star *f inv*.

popular ['pɒpjʊlə^r] *adj* popolare; *(fashionable)* in voga.

popularity [,pɒpjʊ'lærətɪ] *n* popolarità *f*.

populated ['pɒpjʊleɪtɪd] *adj* popolato(-a).

population [,pɒpjʊ'leɪʃn] *n* popolazione *f*.

porcelain ['pɔːsəlɪn] *n* porcellana *f*.

porch [pɔːtʃ] *n (entrance)* portico *m*; *(Am: outside house)* veranda *f*.

pork [pɔːk] *n* carne *f* di maiale.

pork chop *n* braciola *f* OR costoletta *f* di maiale.

pork pie *n* pasticcio *m* di maiale.

pornographic [,pɔːnə'græfɪk] *adj* pornografico(-a).

porridge ['pɒrɪdʒ] *n* porridge *m*, farinata *f* d'avena.

port [pɔːt] *n* porto *m*.

portable ['pɔːtəbl] *adj* portatile.

porter ['pɔːtə^r] *n (at hotel, museum)* portiere *m*; *(at station, airport)* facchino *m*.

porthole ['pɔːthəʊl] *n* oblò *m inv*.

portion ['pɔːʃn] *n* porzione *f*.

portrait ['pɔːtreɪt] *n* ritratto *m*.

Portugal ['pɔːtʃʊgl] *n* il Portogallo.

Portuguese [,pɔːtʃʊ'giːz] *adj* portoghese ◆ *n (language)* portoghese *m* ◆ *npl*: **the ~** i portoghesi.

pose [pəʊz] *vt (problem, threat)* porre ◆ *vi (for photo)* posare.

posh [pɒʃ] *adj (inf) (person, accent)* snob *inv*, raffinato(-a); *(hotel, res-*

taurant) elegante, di lusso.

position [pə'zɪʃn] *n* posizione *f*; *(fml: job)* posto *m*; **'~ closed'** *(in bank, post office etc)* 'sportello chiuso'.

positive ['pɒzətɪv] *adj* positivo(-a); *(certain, sure)* sicuro(-a), certo(-a).

possess [pə'zes] *vt* possedere.

possession [pə'zeʃn] *n (thing owned)* bene *m*.

possessive [pə'zesɪv] *adj* possessivo(-a).

possibility [,pɒsə'bɪlətɪ] *n* possibilità *f inv*.

possible ['pɒsəbl] *adj* possibile; **it's ~ that we may be late** può darsi che facciamo tardi; **would it be ~ ...?** sarebbe possibile ...?; **as much as ~** il più possibile; **if ~** se possibile.

possibly ['pɒsəblɪ] *adv (perhaps)* forse.

post [pəʊst] *n (system, letters, delivery)* posta *f*; *(pole)* palo *m*; *(fml: job)* posto *m* ◆ *vt (letter, parcel)* spedire (per posta); **by ~** per posta.

postage ['pəʊstɪdʒ] *n* affrancatura *f*, spese *fpl* postali; **~ and packing** spese di spedizione (postale); **~ paid** franco di porto, affrancatura pagata.

postage stamp *n (fml)* francobollo *m*.

postal order ['pəʊstl-] *n* vaglia *m inv* postale.

postbox ['pəʊstbɒks] *n (Br)* cassetta *f* delle lettere.

postcard ['pəʊstkɑːd] *n* cartolina *f*.

postcode ['pəʊstkəʊd] *n (Br)* codice *m* (di avviamento) postale.

poster ['pəʊstə^r] *n* manifesto *m*,

poster m inv.

poste restante [,pəʊst-res'tɑ:nt] n (Br) fermo posta m.

post-free adv in franchigia postale, con affrancatura pagata.

postgraduate [,pəʊst-'grædʒʊət] n laureato(-a) che frequenta un corso di specializzazione.

postman ['pəʊstmən] (pl -men [-mən]) n postino m.

postmark ['pəʊstmɑ:k] n timbro m postale.

postmen pl → postman.

post office n (building) ufficio m postale; **the Post Office** = le Poste e Telecomunicazioni.

postpone [,pəʊst'pəʊn] vt rinviare, rimandare.

posture ['pɒstʃər] n postura f.

postwoman ['pəʊst,wʊmən] (pl -women [-,wɪmɪn]) n postina f.

pot [pɒt] n (for cooking) pentola f; (for jam, paint) vasetto m, barattolo m; (for coffee) caffettiera f; (for tea) teiera f; (inf: cannabis) erba f; **a ~ of tea** un tè (servito in una teiera).

potato [pə'teɪtəʊ] (pl -es) n patata f.

potato salad n patate fpl in insalata.

potential [pə'tenʃl] adj potenziale ◆ n potenziale m.

pothole ['pɒthəʊl] n (in road) buca f.

pot plant n pianta f da vaso.

pot scrubber [-'skrʌbər] n paglietta f.

potted ['pɒtɪd] adj (meat, fish) in vasetto, in scatola; (plant) in vaso.

pottery ['pɒtərɪ] n (clay objects) ceramiche fpl; (craft) ceramica f.

potty ['pɒtɪ] n (inf) vasino m.

pouch [paʊtʃ] n (for money, tobacco) borsellino f.

poultry ['pəʊltrɪ] n & npl pollame m.

pound [paʊnd] n (unit of money) sterlina f; (unit of weight) = 453,6 g, libbra f ◆ vi (heart) battere forte; (head) martellare.

pour [pɔːr] vt versare ◆ vi (flow) riversarsi; **it's ~ing (with rain)** sta piovendo a dirotto ❑ **pour out** vt sep (drink) versare.

poverty ['pɒvətɪ] n povertà f, miseria f.

powder ['paʊdər] n polvere f; (cosmetic) cipria f.

power ['paʊər] n (control, authority) potere m; (ability) capacità f inv; (strength, force) potenza f; (energy) energia f; (electricity) corrente f ◆ vt azionare; **to be in ~** essere al potere.

power cut n interruzione f di corrente.

power failure n interruzione f di corrente.

powerful ['paʊəfʊl] adj potente.

power point n (Br) presa f di corrente.

power station n centrale f elettrica.

power steering n servosterzo m.

practical ['præktɪkl] adj pratico(-a).

practically ['præktɪklɪ] adv (almost) praticamente.

practice ['præktɪs] n (training) pratica f; (training session) allenamento m, esercizio m; (of doctor, lawyer) studio m; (regular activity, custom) consuetudine f ◆ vt (Am) = **practise**; **out of ~** fuori allenamento.

practise ['præktɪs] *vt (sport, music, technique)* allenarsi a, esercitarsi a OR in ◆ *vi (train)* allenarsi, esercitarsi; *(doctor, lawyer)* esercitare ◆ *n (Am)* = **practice**.

praise [preɪz] *n* elogio *m*, lode *f* ◆ *vt* elogiare, lodare.

pram [præm] *n (Br)* carrozzina *f*.

prank [præŋk] *n* burla *f*.

prawn [prɔːn] *n* gamberetto *m*.

prawn cocktail *n* cocktail *m inv* di gamberetti.

prawn crackers *npl* nuvolette *fpl* di drago.

pray [preɪ] *vi* pregare; **to ~ for** sthg *(fig)* pregare per qc, invocare qc.

prayer [preəʳ] *n* preghiera *f*.

precarious [prɪ'keərɪəs] *adj* precario(-a).

precaution [prɪ'kɔːʃn] *n* precauzione *f*.

precede [prɪ'siːd] *vt (fml)* precedere.

preceding [prɪ'siːdɪŋ] *adj* precedente.

precinct ['priːsɪŋkt] *n (Br: for shopping)* centro *m* commerciale *(chiuso al traffico)*; *(Am: area of town)* circoscrizione *f*.

precious ['preʃəs] *adj* prezioso(-a).

precious stone *n* pietra *f* preziosa.

precipice ['presɪpɪs] *n* precipizio *m*.

precise [prɪ'saɪs] *adj* preciso(-a).

precisely [prɪ'saɪslɪ] *adv* precisamente.

predecessor ['priːdɪsesəʳ] *n* predecessore *m*.

predicament [prɪ'dɪkəmənt] *n* situazione *f* difficile.

predict [prɪ'dɪkt] *vt* predire.

predictable [prɪ'dɪktəbl] *adj* prevedibile.

prediction [prɪ'dɪkʃn] *n* predizione *f*.

preface ['prefɪs] *n* prefazione *f*.

prefect ['priːfekt] *n (Br: at school)* studente *m* (-essa *f*) con funzioni disciplinari.

prefer [prɪ'fɜːʳ] *vt*: **to ~** sthg **(to)** preferire qc (a); **to ~ to do** sthg preferire fare qc.

preferable ['prefrəbl] *adj* preferibile.

preferably ['prefrəblɪ] *adv* preferibilmente.

preference ['prefərəns] *n* preferenza *f*.

prefix ['priːfɪks] *n* prefisso *m*.

pregnancy ['pregnənsɪ] *n* gravidanza *f*.

pregnant ['pregnənt] *adj* incinta.

prejudice ['predʒudɪs] *n* pregiudizio *m*.

prejudiced ['predʒudɪst] *adj*: **~ (against)** prevenuto(-a) (contro); **~ (in favour of)** bendisposto(-a) (verso).

preliminary [prɪ'lɪmɪnərɪ] *adj* preliminare.

premature ['premə,tjuəʳ] *adj* prematuro(-a).

premier ['premjəʳ] *adj* primo(-a) ◆ *n* primo ministro *m*.

premiere ['premɪeəʳ] *n* prima *f*.

premises ['premɪsɪz] *npl* locali *mpl*; **on the ~** sul posto.

premium ['priːmjəm] *n (for insurance)* premio *m*.

premium-quality *adj (meat)*

di prima qualità.

preoccupied [pri:'ɒkjupaɪd] *adj* preoccupato(-a).

prepacked [ˌpri:'pækt] *adj* preconfezionato(-a).

prepaid ['pri:peɪd] *adj (envelope)* con affrancatura pagata.

preparation [ˌprepə'reɪʃn] *n* preparazione *f* □ **preparations** *npl (arrangements)* preparativi *mpl*.

preparatory school [prɪ'pærətrɪ-] *n (in UK)* scuola *f* elementare privata; *(in US)* scuola *f* secondaria privata *(che prepara agli studi universitari)*.

prepare [prɪ'peəʳ] *vt* preparare ◆ *vi* prepararsi.

prepared [prɪ'peəd] *adj (ready)* preparato(-a), pronto(-a); **to be ~ to do sthg** essere disposto(-a) a fare qc.

preposition [ˌprepə'zɪʃn] *n* preposizione *f*.

prep school [prep-] = **preparatory school**.

prescribe [prɪ'skraɪb] *vt* prescrivere.

prescription [prɪ'skrɪpʃn] *n (paper)* ricetta *f*; *(medicine)* medicine *fpl*.

presence ['prezns] *n* presenza *f*; **in sb's ~** in presenza di qn.

present [*adj & n* 'preznt, *vb* prɪ'zent] *adj (in attendance)* presente; *(current)* attuale ◆ *n (gift)* regalo *m* ◆ *vt* presentare; *(offer)* offrire; **the ~ (tense)** il (tempo) presente; **at ~** al momento, attualmente; **the ~** il presente; **to ~ sb to sb** presentare qn a qn.

presentable [prɪ'zentəbl] *adj* presentabile.

presentation [ˌprezn'teɪʃn] *n*

(way of presenting) presentazione *f*; *(ceremony)* consegna *f* (ufficiale).

presenter [prɪ'zentəʳ] *n (of TV, radio programme)* presentatore *m* (-trice *f*).

presently ['prezntlɪ] *adv (soon)* fra poco, a momenti; *(now)* attualmente.

preservation [ˌprezə'veɪʃn] *n* tutela *f*, protezione *f*.

preservative [prɪ'zɜ:vətɪv] *n* conservante *m*.

preserve [prɪ'zɜ:v] *n (jam)* marmellata *f* ◆ *vt (conserve)* mantenere; *(keep)* preservare, proteggere; *(food)* conservare.

president ['prezɪdənt] *n* presidente *mf*.

press [pres] *vt (push)* premere, pigiare; *(iron)* stirare ◆ *n*: **the ~** la stampa; **to ~ sb to do sthg** insistere perché qn faccia qc.

press conference *n* conferenza *f* stampa.

press-stud *n* bottone *m* a pressione, automatico *m*.

press-ups *npl* flessioni *fpl* (sulle braccia).

pressure ['preʃəʳ] *n* pressione *f*.

pressure cooker *n* pentola *f* a pressione.

prestigious [pre'stɪdʒəs] *adj* prestigioso(-a).

presumably [prɪ'zju:məblɪ] *adv* presumibilmente.

presume [prɪ'zju:m] *vt (assume)* presumere, supporre.

pretend [prɪ'tend] *vt*: **to ~ to do sthg** far finta di fare qc.

pretentious [prɪ'tenʃəs] *adj* pretenzioso(-a).

pretty ['prɪtɪ] *adj* grazioso(-a),

prevent 216

carino(-a) ◆ *adv (inf) (quite)* piuttosto, abbastanza; *(very)* assai.

prevent [prɪ'vent] *vt* evitare; **to ~ sb/sthg from doing sthg** impedire a qn/qc di fare qc.

prevention [prɪ'venʃn] *n* prevenzione *f*.

preview ['priːvjuː] *n* anteprima *f*.

previous ['priːvjəs] *adj* precedente.

previously ['priːvjəslɪ] *adv (formerly)* precedentemente, in precedenza; *(earlier, before)* prima.

price [praɪs] *n* prezzo *m* ◆ *vt* fissare il prezzo di.

priceless ['praɪslɪs] *adj* inestimabile, senza prezzo.

price list *n* listino *m* prezzi.

pricey ['praɪsɪ] *adj (inf)* costoso(-a).

prick [prɪk] *vt* pungere.

prickly ['prɪklɪ] *adj (plant, bush)* spinoso(-a).

prickly heat *n* sudamina *f*.

pride [praɪd] *n (satisfaction, self-respect)* orgoglio *m*; *(arrogance)* superbia *f* ◆ *vt*: **to ~ o.s. on sthg** vantarsi di qc.

priest [priːst] *n* prete *m*, sacerdote *m*.

primarily ['praɪmərɪlɪ] *adv* principalmente.

primary school ['praɪmən-] *n* scuola *f* elementare.

prime [praɪm] *adj (chief)* fondamentale; *(beef, cut)* di prima qualità.

prime minister *n* primo ministro *m*.

primitive ['prɪmɪtɪv] *adj* primitivo(-a).

primrose ['prɪmrəʊz] *n* primula *f*.

prince [prɪns] *n* principe *m*.

Prince of Wales *n* Principe *m* di Galles.

princess [prɪn'ses] *n* principessa *f*.

principal ['prɪnsəpl] *adj* principale ◆ *n (of school)* direttore *m* (-trice *f*); *(of university)* rettore *m* (-trice *f*).

principle ['prɪnsəpl] *n* principio *m*; **in ~** in linea di principio.

print [prɪnt] *n (words)* caratteri *mpl*; *(photo, of painting)* stampa *f*; *(mark)* impronta *f* ◆ *vt (book, newspaper, photo)* stampare; *(publish)* pubblicare; *(write)* scrivere a stampatello; **out of ~** esaurito ❑ **print out** *vt sep* stampare.

printed matter ['prɪntɪd-] *n* stampe *fpl*.

printer ['prɪntər] *n (machine)* stampante *f*; *(person)* tipografo *m* (-a *f*).

printout ['prɪntaʊt] *n* stampato *m*.

prior ['praɪər] *adj (previous)* precedente; **~ to** *(fml)* precedente.

priority [praɪ'ɒrɪtɪ] *n (important thing)* elemento *m* prioritario; **to have ~ over** avere la priorità rispetto a.

prison ['prɪzn] *n* prigione *f*.

prisoner ['prɪznər] *n* prigioniero *m* (-a *f*).

prisoner of war *n* prigioniero *m* (-a *f*) di guerra.

prison officer *n* guardia *f* carceraria.

privacy ['prɪvəsɪ] *n* privacy *f*.

private ['praɪvɪt] *adj* privato(-a); *(confidential)* confidenziale; *(place)* appartato(-a); *(bathroom)* in camera ◆ *n (MIL)* soldato *m* semplice; **in ~** in privato.

private health care *n* assistenza *f* medica privata.

private property *n* proprietà *f* privata.

private school *n* scuola *f* privata.

privilege ['prɪvɪlɪdʒ] *n* privilegio *m*; it's a ~! è un onore!

prize [praɪz] *n* premio *m*.

prize-giving [-gɪvɪŋ] *n* premiazione *f*.

pro [prəʊ] (*pl* **-s**) *n* (*inf: professional*) professionista *mf* ❑ **pros** *npl*: the ~s and cons i pro e i contro.

probability [ˌprɒbə'bɪlətɪ] *n* probabilità *f*.

probable ['prɒbəbl] *adj* probabile.

probably ['prɒbəblɪ] *adv* probabilmente.

probation officer [prə'beɪʃn-] *n* persona incaricata di seguire i criminali in libertà vigilata.

problem ['prɒbləm] *n* problema *m*; no ~! (*inf*) non c'è problema!

procedure [prə'si:dʒəʳ] *n* procedura *f*.

proceed [prə'si:d] *vi* (*fml*) procedere; '~ with caution' 'procedere con cautela'.

proceeds ['prəʊsi:dz] *npl* ricavato *m*.

process ['prəʊses] *n* processo *m*; to be in the ~ of doing sthg star facendo qc.

processed cheese ['prəʊsest-] *n* formaggio *m* fuso.

procession [prə'seʃn] *n* processione *f*.

prod [prɒd] *vt* (*poke*) pungolare.

produce [prə'dju:s] *vt* produrre; (*cause*) creare ◆ *n* prodotti *mpl*

agricoli.

producer [prə'dju:səʳ] *n* produttore *m* (-trice *f*).

product ['prɒdʌkt] *n* prodotto *m*.

production [prə'dʌkʃn] *n* produzione *f*.

productivity [ˌprɒdʌk'tɪvətɪ] *n* produttività *f*.

profession [prə'feʃn] *n* professione *f*.

professional [prə'feʃənl] *adj* (*relating to work*) professionale; (*not amateur*) professionista ◆ *n* professionista *mf*.

professor [prə'fesəʳ] *n* professore *m* (-essa *f*).

profile ['prəʊfaɪl] *n* profilo *m*.

profit ['prɒfɪt] *n* profitto *m* ◆ *vi*: to ~ (from) trarre profitto (da).

profitable ['prɒfɪtəbl] *adj* (*financially*) rimunerativo(-a); (*useful*) vantaggioso(-a).

profiteroles [prə'fɪtərəʊlz] *npl* profiterole *m inv*.

profound [prə'faʊnd] *adj* profondo(-a).

program ['prəʊgræm] *n* (COMPUT) programma *m*; (Am) = **programme** ◆ *vt* (COMPUT) programmare.

programme ['prəʊgræm] *n* (Br) programma *m*.

progress [*n* 'prəʊgres, *vb* prə'gres] *n* (*improvement*) progresso *m*; (*forward movement*) moto *m* ◆ *vi* (*work, talks, student*) progredire; (*day, meeting*) andare avanti; to make ~ (*improve*) fare progressi; (*in journey*) avanzare; in ~ in corso.

progressive [prə'gresɪv] *adj* (*forward-looking*) progressista.

prohibit [prə'hɪbɪt] *vt* proibire;

'smoking strictly ~ed' 'è severamente vietato fumare'.

project ['prɒdʒekt] n progetto m; *(at school)* ricerca f.

projector [prə'dʒektər] n proiettore m.

prolong [prə'lɒŋ] vt prolungare.

prom [prɒm] n *(Am: dance)* ballo m *(per studenti)*.

promenade [ˌprɒmə'nɑːd] n *(Br: by the sea)* lungomare m inv.

prominent ['prɒmɪnənt] adj *(person)* importante; *(noticeable)* evidente.

promise ['prɒmɪs] n promessa f ◆ vt & vi promettere; **to show ~** promettere (bene); **I ~!** te lo prometto; **I ~ (that) I'll come** prometto che verrò; **to ~ sb sthg** promettere qc a qn; **to ~ to do sthg** promettere di fare qc.

promising ['prɒmɪsɪŋ] adj promettente.

promote [prə'məʊt] vt *(in job)* promuovere.

promotion [prə'məʊʃn] n promozione f.

prompt [prɒmpt] adj *(quick)* pronto(-a) ◆ adv: **at six o'clock ~** alle sei in punto.

prone [prəʊn] adj: **to be ~ to sthg** essere incline a qc; **to be ~ to do sthg** essere incline a fare qc.

prong [prɒŋ] n *(of fork)* dente m.

pronoun ['prəʊnaʊn] n pronome m.

pronounce [prə'naʊns] vt *(word)* pronunciare.

pronunciation [prəˌnʌnsɪ'eɪʃn] n pronuncia f.

proof [pruːf] n *(evidence)* prova f; **to be 12% ~** *(alcohol)* avere 12 gradi.

prop [prɒp]: **prop up** vt sep *(support)* sostenere.

propeller [prə'pelər] n elica f.

proper ['prɒpər] adj *(suitable)* adatto(-a); *(correct)* giusto(-a); *(socially acceptable)* decoroso(-a).

properly ['prɒpəlɪ] adv *(suitably)* adeguatamente; *(correctly)* correttamente.

property ['prɒpətɪ] n proprietà f inv.

proportion [prə'pɔːʃn] n proporzione f; *(in art)* proporzioni fpl.

proposal [prə'pəʊzl] n *(suggestion)* proposta f.

propose [prə'pəʊz] vt *(suggest)* proporre ◆ vi: **to ~ (to sb)** fare una proposta di matrimonio (a qn).

proposition [ˌprɒpə'zɪʃn] n *(offer)* proposta f.

proprietor [prə'praɪətər] n *(fml)* proprietario m (-a f).

prose [prəʊz] n *(not poetry)* prosa f; *(SCH)* traduzione f *(dalla madrelingua)*.

prosecution [ˌprɒsɪ'kjuːʃn] n *(JUR: charge)* azione f giudiziaria.

prospect ['prɒspekt] n *(possibility)* prospettiva f; **I don't relish the ~** non mi attira la prospettiva ❑ **prospects** npl *(for the future)* prospettive fpl.

prospectus [prə'spektəs] *(pl -es)* n prospetto m.

prosperous ['prɒspərəs] adj prospero(-a).

prostitute ['prɒstɪtjuːt] n prostituta f.

protect [prə'tekt] vt proteggere; **to ~ sb/sthg from** proteggere qn/qc da; **to ~ sb/sthg against** proteggere qn/qc da.

protection [prəˈtekʃn] n prote-zione f.

protection factor n fattore m di protezione.

protective [prəˈtektɪv] adj (person) protettivo(-a); (clothes) di protezione.

protein [ˈprəutiːn] n proteina f.

protest [n ˈprəutest, vb prəˈtest] n protesta f ♦ vt (Am: protest against) protestare contro ♦ vi: to ~ (against) protestare (contro).

Protestant [ˈprɒtɪstənt] n protestante mf.

protester [prəˈtestəʳ] n dimostrante mf.

protractor [prəˈtræktəʳ] n goniometro m.

protrude [prəˈtruːd] vi sporgere.

proud [praud] adj (pleased) orglioso(-a); (pej: arrogant) superbo(-a); **to be ~ of** essere orglioso di.

prove [pruːv] (pp -d OR proven [ˈpruːvn]) vt (show to be true) dimostrare; (turn out to be) dimostrarsi.

proverb [ˈprɒvɜːb] n proverbio m.

provide [prəˈvaɪd] vt fornire; to ~ sb with sthg fornire qc a qn ❑ **provide for** vt fus (person) provvedere a.

provided (that) [prəˈvaɪdɪd-] conj purché.

providing (that) [prəˈvaɪdɪŋ-] = provided (that).

province [ˈprɒvɪns] n regione f.

provisional [prəˈvɪʒənl] adj provvisorio(-a).

provisions [prəˈvɪʒnz] npl provviste fpl.

provocative [prəˈvɒkətɪv] adj

provocatorio(-a).

provoke [prəˈvəuk] vt provocare.

prowl [praul] vi muoversi furtivamente.

prune [pruːn] n prugna f secca ♦ vt (tree, bush) potare.

PS (abbr of postscript) P.S.

psychiatrist [saɪˈkaɪətrɪst] n psichiatra mf.

psychic [ˈsaɪkɪk] adj dotato(-a) di poteri paranormali.

psychological [ˌsaɪkəˈlɒdʒɪkl] adj psicologico(-a).

psychologist [saɪˈkɒlədʒɪst] n psicologo m (-a f).

psychology [saɪˈkɒlədʒɪ] n psicologia f.

psychotherapist [ˌsaɪkəu-ˈθerəpɪst] n psicoterapeuta mf.

pt (abbr of pint) pt.

PTO (abbr of please turn over) v.r.

pub [pʌb] n pub m inv.

---

i PUB

Vera e propria istituzione, i pub sono al centro della vita sociale in Gran Bretagna. Soggetti fino a poco tempo fa a rigide restrizioni d'orario, oggi possono generalmente restare aperti dalle 11 alle 23 (e fino a più tardi in Scozia). Le restrizioni relative all'ingresso dei minori di sedici anni variano da regione a regione e da pub a pub mentre rimane il divieto di vendere alcolici ai minorenni. Oltre a una grande varietà di birre e altre bevande alcoliche e non, i pub offrono una discreta scelta di piatti tipici.

---

puberty [ˈpjuːbətɪ] n pubertà f.

public [ˈpʌblɪk] adj pubblico(-a)

◆ *n:* the ~ il pubblico; **in** ~ in pubblico.

publican ['pʌblɪkən] *n (Br)* gestore *m* (-trice *f*) di un pub.

publication [,pʌblɪ'keɪʃn] *n* pubblicazione *f.*

public bar *n (Br)* sala di un pub, in cui le bevande costano meno.

public convenience *n (Br)* gabinetti *mpl* pubblici.

public footpath *n (Br)* sentiero *m.*

public holiday *n* giorno *m* festivo.

public house *n (Br: fml)* pub *m inv.*

publicity [pʌb'lɪsɪtɪ] *n* pubblicità *f.*

public school *n (in UK)* scuola *f* privata; *(in US)* scuola statale.

public telephone *n* telefono *m* pubblico.

public transport *n* trasporti *mpl* pubblici.

publish ['pʌblɪʃ] *vt* pubblicare.

publisher ['pʌblɪʃər] *n (person)* editore *m* (-trice *f*); *(company)* casa *f* editrice.

publishing ['pʌblɪʃɪŋ] *n (industry)* editoria *f.*

pub lunch *n* pranzo semplice e a basso costo servito in un pub.

pudding ['pudɪŋ] *n (sweet dish)* budino *m;* *(Br: course)* dessert *m inv.*

puddle ['pʌdl] *n* pozzanghera *f.*

puff [pʌf] *vi (breathe heavily)* ansare ◆ *n (of air, smoke)* sbuffo *m;* **to ~ at** tirare una boccata di.

puff pastry *n* pasta *f* sfoglia.

pull [pul] *vt* tirare; *(trigger)* premere ◆ *vi* tirare ◆ *n:* **to give sthg a ~** dare una tirata a qc; **to ~ a face** fare una smorfia; **to ~ a muscle** farsi uno strappo muscolare; **'pull'** *(on door)* 'tirare' ☐ **pull apart** *vt sep (machine, book)* fare a pezzi; **pull down** *vt sep (lower)* abbassare; *(demolish)* demolire; **pull in** *vi (train)* arrivare; *(car)* accostare; **pull out** *vt sep (tooth, cork, plug)* estrarre ◆ *vi (train)* partire; *(car)* entrare in corsia; *(withdraw)* ritirarsi; **pull over** *vi (car)* accostare; **pull up** *vt sep (socks, trousers, sleeve)* tirare su ◆ *vi (stop)* fermarsi.

pulley ['pulɪ] *(pl* pulleys*)* *n* carrucola *f.*

pull-out *n (Am: beside road)* piazzola *f* (di sosta).

pullover ['pul,əuvər] *n* pullover *m inv.*

pulpit ['pulpɪt] *n* pulpito *m.*

pulse [pʌls] *n (MED)* polso *m.*

pump [pʌmp] *n* pompa *f* ☐ **pumps** *npl (sports shoes)* scarpe *fpl* da ginnastica; **pump up** *vt sep* gonfiare.

pumpkin ['pʌmpkɪn] *n* zucca *f.*

pun [pʌn] *n* gioco *m* di parole.

punch [pʌntʃ] *n (blow)* pugno *m;* *(drink)* punch *m inv* ◆ *vt (hit)* sferrare un pugno a; *(ticket)* forare.

Punch and Judy show [-'dʒuː-dɪ-] *n* spettacolo di burattini.

punctual ['pʌŋktʃuəl] *adj* puntuale.

punctuation [,pʌŋktʃu'eɪʃn] *n* punteggiatura *f.*

puncture ['pʌŋktʃər] *vt* forare ◆ *n:* **to get a ~** forare (una gomma).

punish ['pʌnɪʃ] *vt:* **to ~ sb (for sthg)** punire qn (per qc).

punishment ['pʌnɪʃmənt] *n* punizione *f.*

punk [pʌŋk] *n (person)* punk *mf inv;* *(music)* musica *f* punk.

punnet [ˈpʌnɪt] n (Br) cestino m.

pupil [ˈpjuːpl] n (student) alunno m (-a f); (of eye) pupilla f.

puppet [ˈpʌpɪt] n burattino m.

puppy [ˈpʌpɪ] n cucciolo m.

purchase [ˈpɜːtʃəs] vt (fml) acquistare ◆ n (fml) acquisto m.

pure [pjʊəʳ] adj puro(-a).

puree [ˈpjʊəreɪ] n purè m inv.

purely [ˈpjʊəlɪ] adv (only) soltanto.

purity [ˈpjʊərətɪ] n purezza f.

purple [ˈpɜːpl] adj viola (inv).

purpose [ˈpɜːpəs] n scopo m; **on ~** apposta.

purr [pɜːʳ] vi (cat) fare le fusa.

purse [pɜːs] n (Br: for money) portamonete m inv; (Am: handbag) borsa f.

pursue [pəˈsjuː] vt (follow) inseguire; (study) continuare; (matter, inquiry) approfondire.

pus [pʌs] n pus m.

push [pʊʃ] vt spingere; (button, doorbell) premere; (product) pubblicizzare ◆ vi spingere ◆ n: **to give sb/sthg a ~** dare una spinta a qn/qc; **to ~ sb into doing sthg** spingere qn a fare qc; 'push' (on door) 'spingere' ❑ **push in** vi (in queue) passare avanti; **push off** vi (inf: go away) andarsene.

push-button telephone n telefono m a tastiera.

pushchair [ˈpʊʃtʃeəʳ] n (Br) passeggino m.

pushed [pʊʃt] adj (inf): **to be ~** (for time) essere a corto di tempo.

push-ups npl flessioni fpl (sulle braccia).

put [pʊt] (pt & pp put) vt mettere; (responsibility) dare; (pressure) esercitare; (express) esprimere; (a question) porre; (estimate) stimare; **to ~ a child to bed** mettere a letto un bambino; **to ~ money into sthg** investire soldi in qc ❑ **put aside** vt sep (money) mettere da parte; **put away** vt sep (tidy up) mettere via; **put back** vt sep (replace) mettere a posto; (postpone) posporre; (clock, watch) mettere indietro; **put down** vt sep (on floor, table) posare; (passenger) far scendere; (Br: animal) abbattere; (deposit) mettere in acconto; **put forward** vt sep (clock, watch) mettere avanti; (suggest) suggerire; **put in** vt sep (insert) inserire; (install) installare; **put off** vt sep (postpone) rimandare; (distract) distrarre; (repel) disgustare; (passenger) far scendere; **put on** vt sep (clothes, glasses, make-up) mettersi; (weight) mettere su; (television, light, radio) accendere; (CD, tape, record) mettere; (play, show) mettere in scena; **put out** vt sep (cigarette, fire, light) spegnere; (publish) pubblicare; (hand, arm, leg) stendere; (inconvenience) disturbare; **to ~ one's back out** farsi male alla schiena; **put together** vt sep (assemble) montare; (combine) mettere insieme; **put up** vt sep (tent, statue, building) erigere; (umbrella) aprire; (a notice, sign) mettere; (price, rate) aumentare; (provide with accommodation) ospitare ◆ vi (Br: in hotel) alloggiare; **put up with** vt fus sopportare.

putter [ˈpʌtəʳ] n (club) putter m inv.

putting green [ˈpʌtɪŋ-] n campo m da minigolf.

putty [ˈpʌtɪ] n stucco m.

puzzle [ˈpʌzl] n (game) rompicapo *m*; *(jigsaw)* puzzle *m inv*; *(mystery)* enigma *m* ♦ *vt* confondere.

puzzling ['pʌzlɪŋ] *adj* sconcertante.

pyjamas [pə'dʒɑːməz] *npl* (Br) pigiama *m*.

pylon ['paɪlən] *n* traliccio *m*.

pyramid ['pɪrəmɪd] *n* piramide *f*.

Pyrenees [,pɪrə'niːz] *npl*: **the ~ i** Pirenei.

Pyrex® ['paɪreks] *n* pyrex® *m*.

quail [kweɪl] *n* quaglia *f*.

quail's eggs *npl* uova *fpl* di quaglia.

quaint [kweɪnt] *adj* pittoresco(-a).

qualification [,kwɒlɪfɪ'keɪʃn] *n* *(diploma)* qualifica *f*; *(ability)* qualità *f inv*.

qualified ['kwɒlɪfaɪd] *adj (having qualifications)* qualificato(-a).

qualify ['kwɒlɪfaɪ] *vi (for competition)* qualificarsi; *(pass exam)* abilitarsi.

quality ['kwɒlətɪ] *n* qualità *f inv* ♦ *adj* di qualità.

quarantine ['kwɒrəntiːn] *n* quarantena *f*.

quarrel ['kwɒrəl] *n* lite *f* ♦ *vi* litigare.

quarry ['kwɒrɪ] *n (for stone, sand)* cava *f*.

quart [kwɔːt] *n (in UK)* = 1,136 l, = litro *m*; *(in US)* = 0,946 l, =

litro.

quarter ['kwɔːtər] *n (fraction)* quarto *m*; *(Am: coin)* quarto di dollaro; *(4 ounces)* quarto di libbra; *(three months)* trimestre *m*; *(part of town)* quartiere *m*; **(a) ~ to five** (Br) le cinque meno un quarto; **(a) ~ of five** (Am) le cinque meno un quarto; **(a) ~ past five** (Br) le cinque e un quarto; **(a) ~ after five** (Am) le cinque e un quarto; **(a) ~ of an hour** un quarto d'ora.

quarterpounder [,kwɔːtə'paʊndər] *n* grosso hamburger *m inv*.

quartet [kwɔː'tet] *n* quartetto *m*.

quartz [kwɔːts] *adj (watch)* al quarzo.

quay [kiː] *n* banchina *f*.

queasy ['kwiːzɪ] *adj (inf)*: **to feel ~** avere la nausea.

queen [kwiːn] *n* regina *f*.

queer [kwɪər] *adj (strange)* strano(-a); *(inf: homosexual)* omosessuale; **to feel ~** *(ill)* sentirsi male.

quench [kwentʃ] *vt*: **to ~ one's thirst** dissetarsi.

query ['kwɪərɪ] *n* quesito *m*.

question ['kwestʃn] *n (query, in exam, on questionnaire)* domanda *f*; *(issue)* questione *f* ♦ *vt (person)* interrogare; **it's out of the ~** è fuori discussione.

question mark *n* punto *m* interrogativo.

questionnaire [,kwestʃə'neər] *n* questionario *m*.

queue [kjuː] *n (Br)* coda *f* ♦ *vi (Br)* fare la coda ❑ **queue up** *vi (Br)* fare la coda.

quiche [kiːʃ] *n* torta *f* salata.

quick [kwɪk] *adj* rapido(-a) ♦ *adv* rapidamente.

quickly ['kwɪklɪ] *adv* rapidamente.

quid [kwɪd] *(pl inv)* n *(Br: inf)* sterlina *f*.

quiet ['kwaɪət] *adj* silenzioso(-a); *(calm, peaceful)* tranquillo(-a) ◆ *n* quiete *f*; **in a ~ voice** a bassa voce; **keep ~!** silenzio!; **to keep ~** *(not say anything)* tacere; **to keep ~ about sthg** tenere segreto qc.

quieten ['kwaɪətn]: **quieten down** *vi* calmarsi.

quietly ['kwaɪətlɪ] *adv* silenziosamente; *(calmly)* tranquillamente.

quilt [kwɪlt] *n (duvet)* piumino *m*; *(eiderdown)* trapunta *f*.

quince [kwɪns] *n* mela *f* cotogna.

quirk [kwɜːk] *n* stranezza *f*.

quit [kwɪt] *(pt & pp quit)* vi *(resign)* dimettersi; *(give up)* smettere ◆ *vt (Am: school, job)* lasciare; **to ~ doing sthg** smettere di fare qc.

quite [kwaɪt] *adv (fairly)* abbastanza; *(completely)* proprio; **not ~** non proprio; **~ a lot (of)** un bel po' (di).

quiz [kwɪz] *(pl -zes)* n quiz *m inv*.

quota ['kwəʊtə] *n* quota *f*.

quotation [kwəʊ'teɪʃn] *n (phrase)* citazione *f*; *(estimate)* preventivo *m*.

quotation marks *npl* virgolette *fpl*.

quote [kwəʊt] *vt (phrase, writer)* citare ◆ *n (phrase)* citazione *f*; *(estimate)* preventivo *m*; **he ~d me a price of £50** mi ha dato un prezzo indicativo di 50 sterline.

R

rabbit ['ræbɪt] *n* coniglio *m*.

rabies ['reɪbiːz] *n* rabbia *f*.

RAC *n* = ACI *m*.

race [reɪs] *n (competition)* gara *f*; *(ethnic group)* razza *f* ◆ *vi (compete)* gareggiare; *(go fast)* correre; *(engine)* imballarsi ◆ *vt (compete against)* gareggiare con.

racecourse ['reɪskɔːs] *n* ippodromo *m*.

racehorse ['reɪshɔːs] *n* cavallo *m* da corsa.

racetrack ['reɪstræk] *n (for horses)* ippodromo *m*.

racial ['reɪʃl] *adj* razziale.

racing ['reɪsɪŋ] *n*: **(horse) ~** corse *fpl* (di cavalli).

racing car *n* automobile *f* da corsa.

racism ['reɪsɪzm] *n* razzismo *m*.

racist ['reɪsɪst] *n* razzista *mf*.

rack [ræk] *n (for coats)* attaccapanni *m inv*; *(for plates)* scolapiatti *m inv*; *(for bottles)* portabottiglie *m inv*; *(luggage)* ~ portabagagli *m inv*; **~ of lamb** carré *m inv* di agnello.

racket ['rækɪt] *n (for tennis, badminton, squash)* racchetta *f*; *(noise)* baccano *m*.

racquet ['rækɪt] *n* racchetta *f*.

radar ['reɪdɑː] *n* radar *m inv*.

radiation [ˌreɪdɪ'eɪʃn] *n (nuclear)* radiazione *f*.

radiator ['reɪdɪeɪtə] *n* radiatore *m*.

radical ['rædɪkl] *adj* radicale.

radii ['reɪdɪaɪ] *pl* → **radius**.

radio ['reɪdɪəʊ] (pl **-s**) n radio f inv
♦ vt (person) chiamare via radio; **on
the ~** alla radio.

radioactive [,reɪdɪəʊ'æktɪv] adj
radioattivo(-a).

radio alarm n radiosveglia f.

radish ['rædɪʃ] n ravanello m.

radius ['reɪdɪəs] (pl **radii**) n raggio m.

raffle ['ræfl] n lotteria f.

raft [rɑ:ft] n (of wood) zattera f;
(inflatable) materassino m (gonfiabile).

rafter ['rɑ:ftəʳ] n travicello m.

rag [ræg] n (old cloth) straccio m.

rage [reɪdʒ] n rabbia f.

raid [reɪd] n raid m inv; (robbery)
scorreria f ♦ vt (subj: police) fare
irruzione in; (subj: thieves) fare
razzia in.

rail [reɪl] n (bar) sbarra f; (for curtain) asta f; (on stairs) corrimano m
inv; (for train, tram) rotaia f ♦ adj
ferroviario(-a); **by ~** in treno.

railcard ['reɪlkɑ:d] n (Br) (for
young people) tessera per riduzione
ferroviaria; (for pensioners) = carta
d'argento.

railings ['reɪlɪŋz] npl ringhiera f.

railroad ['reɪlrəʊd] (Am) = **railway**.

railway ['reɪlweɪ] n ferrovia f.

railway line n (route) linea f ferroviaria; (track) binario m.

railway station n stazione f
ferroviaria.

rain [reɪn] n pioggia f ♦ v impers
piovere; **it's ~ing** sta piovendo.

rainbow ['reɪnbəʊ] n arcobaleno
m.

raincoat ['reɪnkəʊt] n impermeabile m.

raindrop ['reɪndrɒp] n goccia f

di pioggia.

rainfall ['reɪnfɔ:l] n precipitazione f.

rainy ['reɪnɪ] adj piovoso(-a).

raise [reɪz] vt sollevare; (increase)
aumentare; (money) raccogliere;
(child, animals) allevare ♦ n (Am:
pay increase) aumento m.

raisin ['reɪzn] n uva f passa.

rake [reɪk] n (gardening tool) rastrello m.

rally ['rælɪ] n (public meeting)
comizio m; (motor race) rally m inv;
(in tennis, badminton, squash) serie di
scambi della palla.

ram [ræm] n montone m ♦ vt
(bang into) speronare.

Ramadan [,ræmə'dæn] n
Ramadan m inv.

ramble ['ræmbl] n camminata f.

ramp [ræmp] n (slope) rampa f;
(in roadworks) dislivello m; (Am: to
freeway) rampa f d'accesso; **'ramp'**
(Br: bump) 'fondo dissestato'.

ramparts ['ræmpɑ:ts] npl ba-
stioni mpl.

ran [ræn] pt → **run**.

ranch [rɑ:ntʃ] n ranch m inv.

ranch dressing n (Am) maionese piuttosto liquida e piccante.

rancid ['rænsɪd] adj rancido(-a).

random ['rændəm] adj a caso ♦
n: **at ~** a caso.

rang [ræŋ] pt → **ring**.

range [reɪndʒ] n (of radio, telescope) portata f; (of aircraft) raggio
m; (for shooting) campo m di tiro; (of
prices, temperatures, goods) gamma f;
(of hills, mountains) catena f; (cooker)
cucina f economica ♦ vi (vary)
variare.

ranger ['reɪndʒəʳ] n (of park,

orest) guardia f forestale.

rank [ræŋk] n *(in armed forces, police)* rango m ◆ adj *(smell, taste)* rancido(-a).

ransom ['rænsəm] n riscatto m.

rap [ræp] n *(music)* rap m inv.

rape [reɪp] n stupro m ◆ vt stuprare.

rapid ['ræpɪd] adj rapido(-a) ❑

rapids npl rapide fpl.

rapidly ['ræpɪdlɪ] adv rapidamente.

rapist ['reɪpɪst] n stupratore m.

rare [reə'] adj *(not common)* raro(-a); *(meat)* al sangue.

rarely ['reəlɪ] adv raramente.

rash [ræʃ] n eruzione f cutanea ◆ adj impulsivo(-a).

rasher ['ræʃə'] n fettina f di pancetta.

raspberry ['rɑːzbən] n lampone m.

rat [ræt] n ratto m.

ratatouille [rætə'tuːɪ] n ratatouille f inv.

rate [reɪt] n *(level)* tasso m; *(charge)* tariffa f; *(speed)* ritmo m ◆ vt *(consider)* reputare; *(deserve)* meritare; ~ **of exchange** tasso di cambio; **at any** ~ in ogni caso; **at this** ~ di questo passo.

rather ['rɑːðə'] adv *(quite)* piuttosto; **I'd** ~ **not** preferirei di no; **would you** ~ ...? preferisci ...?; ~ **than** piuttosto che; ~ **a lot** molto.

ratio ['reɪʃɪəʊ] *(pl -s)* n rapporto m.

ration ['ræʃn] n *(share)* razione f ❑ **rations** npl *(food)* razioni fpl.

rational ['ræʃnl] adj razionale.

rattle ['rætl] n *(of baby)* sonaglio m ◆ vi sbatacchiare.

rave [reɪv] n *(party)* rave m inv.

raven ['reɪvn] n corvo m.

ravioli [,rævɪ'əʊlɪ] n ravioli mpl.

raw [rɔː] adj *(uncooked)* crudo(-a); *(unprocessed)* grezzo(-a).

raw material n materia f prima.

ray [reɪ] n raggio m.

razor ['reɪzə'] n rasoio m.

razor blade n lametta f (da barba).

Rd abbr = Road.

re [riː] prep in merito a.

RE n *(abbr of religious education)* religione f *(materia)* .

reach [riːtʃ] vt raggiungere ◆ n: **out of** ~ lontano; **within** ~ **of the beach** a poca distanza dalla spiaggia ❑ **reach out** vi: **to** ~ **out (for)** allungarsi (per raggiungere).

react [rɪ'ækt] vi reagire.

reaction [rɪ'ækʃn] n reazione f.

read [riːd] *(pt & pp read* [red]*)* vt leggere; *(subj: sign, note)* dire; *(subj: meter, gauge)* segnare ◆ vi leggere; **to** ~ **about** sthg leggere di qc ❑ **read out** vt sep leggere ad alta voce.

reader ['riːdə'] n *(of newspaper, book)* lettore m (-trice f).

readily ['redɪlɪ] adv *(willingly)* prontamente; *(easily)* facilmente.

reading ['riːdɪŋ] n *(of books, papers)* lettura f; *(of meter, gauge)* valore m indicato.

reading matter n qualcosa da leggere.

ready ['redɪ] adj pronto(-a); **to be** ~ **for** sthg *(prepared)* essere preparato(-a) per qc; **to be** ~ **to do** sthg *(willing)* essere pronto a fare qc; *(likely)* essere sul punto di fare qc; **to get** ~ prepararsi; **to get** sthg ~ preparare qc.

ready cash n contante m.

ready-cooked [-kʊkt] adj precotto(-a).

ready-to-wear adj confezionato(-a).

real ['rɪəl] adj vero(-a); (world) reale ♦ adv (Am) davvero.

real ale n (Br) birra rossa prodotta secondo metodi tradizionali.

real estate n proprietà fpl immobiliari.

realistic [,rɪə'lɪstɪk] adj realistico(-a).

reality [rɪ'ælətɪ] n realtà f inv; **in ~** in realtà.

realize ['rɪəlaɪz] vt rendersi conto di; (ambition, goal) realizzare; **to ~ (that)** ... rendersi conto che OR di ...

really ['rɪəlɪ] adv veramente; (in reality) realmente; **do you like it? - no, not ~** ti piace? - veramente no; **~?** (expressing surprise) davvero?

realtor ['rɪəltər] n (Am) agente mf immobiliare.

rear [rɪər] adj posteriore ♦ n (back) retro m inv.

rearrange [,rɪə'reɪndʒ] vt spostare.

rearview mirror ['rɪəvjuː-] n specchietto m retrovisore.

rear-wheel drive n trazione f posteriore.

reason ['riːzn] n motivo m; **for some ~** per qualche motivo.

reasonable ['riːznəbl] adj ragionevole; (quite big) buono(-a).

reasonably ['riːznəblɪ] adv (quite) piuttosto.

reasoning ['riːznɪŋ] n ragionamento m.

reassure [,rɪə'ʃɔːr] vt rassicurare.

reassuring [,rɪə'ʃɔːrɪŋ] adj rassicurante.

rebate ['riːbeɪt] n rimborso m.

rebel [rɪ'bel] n ribelle mf ♦ vi ribellarsi.

rebound [rɪ'baʊnd] vi (ball) rimbalzare.

rebuild [,riː'bɪld] (pt & pp rebuilt [,riː'bɪlt]) vt ricostruire.

rebuke [rɪ'bjuːk] vt rimproverare.

recall [rɪ'kɔːl] vt (remember) ricordare.

receipt [rɪ'siːt] n (for goods, money) ricevuta f; **on ~ of** al ricevimento di.

receive [rɪ'siːv] vt ricevere.

receiver [rɪ'siːvər] n (of phone) ricevitore m.

recent ['riːsnt] adj recente.

recently ['riːsntlɪ] adv recentemente.

receptacle [rɪ'septəkl] n (fml) ricettacolo m.

reception [rɪ'sepʃn] n (in hotel) reception f inv; (at hospital) accettazione f; (party) ricevimento m; (welcome) accoglienza f; (of TV, radio) ricezione f.

reception desk n banco m della reception.

receptionist [rɪ'sepʃənɪst] n receptionist mf inv.

recess ['riːses] n (in wall) nicchia f; (Am: SCH) intervallo m.

recession [rɪ'seʃn] n recessione f.

recipe ['resɪpɪ] n ricetta f.

recite [rɪ'saɪt] vt (poem) recitare; (list) elencare.

reckless ['reklɪs] adj avventato(-a).

reckon ['rekn] vt (inf: think) pensare □ **reckon on** *vt fus* aspettarsi; **reckon with** *vt fus* (*expect*) aspettarsi.

reclaim [rɪ'kleɪm] *vt* (*baggage*) ritirare.

reclining seat [rɪ'klaɪnɪŋ-] *n* sedile *m* reclinabile.

recognition [ˌrekəg'nɪʃn] *n* riconoscimento *m*.

recognize ['rekəgnaɪz] *vt* riconoscere.

recollect [ˌrekə'lekt] *vt* ricordare.

recommend [ˌrekə'mend] *vt* raccomandare; **to ~ sb to do sthg** consigliare a qn di fare qc.

recommendation [ˌrekəmen'deɪʃn] *n* (*suggestion*) indicazione *f*.

reconsider [ˌriːkən'sɪdər] *vt* riconsiderare.

reconstruct [ˌriːkən'strʌkt] *vt* ricostruire.

record [*n* 'rekɔːd, *vb* rɪ'kɔːd] *n* (*MUS*) disco *m*; (*best performance, highest level*) record *m inv*; (*account*) nota *f* ♦ *vt* (*keep account of*) annotare; (*on tape*) registrare.

recorded delivery [rɪ'kɔːdɪd-] *n* (*Br*) = raccomandata *f*.

recorder [rɪ'kɔːdər] *n* (*tape recorder*) registratore *m*; (*instrument*) flauto *m* diritto.

recording [rɪ'kɔːdɪŋ] *n* registrazione *f*.

record player *n* giradischi *m inv*.

record shop *n* negozio *m* di dischi.

recover [rɪ'kʌvər] *vt* (*stolen goods, lost property*) recuperare ♦ *vi* riprendersi.

recovery [rɪ'kʌvərɪ] *n* (*from illness*) guarigione *f*.

recovery vehicle *n* (*Br*) carro *m* attrezzi.

recreation [ˌrekrɪ'eɪʃn] *n* divertimento *m*.

recreation ground *n* parco *m* (giochi).

recruit [rɪ'kruːt] *n* recluta *mf* ♦ *vt* (*staff*) assumere.

rectangle ['rektæŋgl] *n* rettangolo *m*.

rectangular [rek'tæŋgjʊlər] *adj* rettangolare.

recycle [ˌriː'saɪkl] *vt* riciclare.

red [red] *adj* rosso(-a) ♦ *n* (*colour*) rosso *m*; **in the ~** in rosso.

red cabbage *n* cavolo *m* rosso.

Red Cross *n* Croce *f* Rossa.

redcurrant ['redkʌrənt] *n* ribes *m inv*.

redecorate [ˌriː'dekəreɪt] *vt* rimbiancare.

redhead ['redhed] *n* rosso *m* (-a *f*).

red-hot *adj* (*metal*) rovente.

redial [ˌriː'daɪəl] *vi* rifare il numero.

redirect [ˌriːdɪ'rekt] *vt* (*letter*) spedire a un nuovo indirizzo; (*traffic, plane*) dirottare.

red pepper *n* peperone *m* rosso.

reduce [rɪ'djuːs] *vt* ridurre ♦ *vi* (*Am: slim*) dimagrire.

reduced price [rɪ'djuːst-] *n* prezzo *m* ridotto.

reduction [rɪ'dʌkʃn] *n* riduzione *f*.

redundancy [rɪ'dʌndənsɪ] *n* (*Br*) licenziamento *m* (*per esubero*).

redundant [rɪ'dʌndənt] *adj* (*Br*): **to be made ~** essere licenziato(-a).

red wine *n* vino *m* rosso.

reed [riːd] *n* canna *f*.

reef [riːf] *n* scogliera *f*.

reek [riːk] *vi* puzzare.

reel [riːl] *n (of thread)* rocchetto *m*; *(on fishing rod)* mulinello *m*.

refectory [rɪˈfektərɪ] *n* refettorio *m*.

refer [rɪˈfɜː]: **refer to** *vt fus (speak about)* fare riferimento a; *(relate to)* riferirsi a; *(consult)* consultare.

referee [ˌrefəˈriː] *n (SPORT)* arbitro *m (-a f)*.

reference [ˈrefrəns] *n (mention)* riferimento *m*; *(letter for job)* lettera *f* di referenze ♦ *adj (book, library)* di consultazione; **with ~ to** con riferimento a.

referendum [ˌrefəˈrendəm] *n* referendum *m inv*.

refill [*n* ˈriːfɪl, *vb* ˌriːˈfɪl] *n (for pen)* ricambio *m*; *(inf: drink)* rifornimento *m* ♦ *vt* riempire.

refinery [rɪˈfaɪnərɪ] *n* raffineria *f*.

reflect [rɪˈflekt] *vt & vi* riflettere.

reflection [rɪˈflekʃn] *n (image)* riflesso *m*.

reflector [rɪˈflektəʳ] *n* catarifrangente *m*.

reflex [ˈriːfleks] *n* riflesso *m*.

reflexive [rɪˈfleksɪv] *adj* riflessivo(-a).

reform [rɪˈfɔːm] *n* riforma *f* ♦ *vt* riformare.

refresh [rɪˈfreʃ] *vt* rinfrescare.

refreshing [rɪˈfreʃɪŋ] *adj (drink, breeze, sleep)* rinfrescante; *(change)* piacevole.

refreshments [rɪˈfreʃmənts] *npl* rinfreschi *mpl*.

refrigerator [rɪˈfrɪdʒəreɪtəʳ] *n* frigorifero *m*.

refugee [ˌrefjʊˈdʒiː] *n* rifugiato *m (-a f)*.

refund [*n* ˈriːfʌnd, *vb* rɪˈfʌnd] *n* rimborso *m* ♦ *vt* rimborsare.

refundable [rɪˈfʌndəbl] *adj* rimborsabile.

refusal [rɪˈfjuːzl] *n* rifiuto *m*.

refuse¹ [rɪˈfjuːz] *vt (not accept)* rifiutare; *(not allow)* negare ♦ *vi* rifiutare; **to ~ to do sthg** rifiutare di fare qc.

refuse² [ˈrefjuːs] *n (fml)* rifiuti *mpl*.

refuse collection [ˈrefjuːs-] *n (fml)* raccolta *f* dei rifiuti.

regard [rɪˈgɑːd] *vt (consider)* considerare ♦ *n*: **with ~ to** riguardo a; **as ~s** per quanto riguarda ⧠ **regards** *npl (in greetings)* saluti *mpl*; **give them my ~s** li saluti da parte mia.

regarding [rɪˈgɑːdɪŋ] *prep* riguardo a.

regardless [rɪˈgɑːdlɪs] *adv* lo stesso; **~ of** senza tener conto di.

reggae [ˈregeɪ] *n* reggae *m inv*.

regiment [ˈredʒɪmənt] *n* reggimento *m*.

region [ˈriːdʒən] *n* regione *f*; **in the ~ of** circa.

regional [ˈriːdʒənl] *adj* regionale.

register [ˈredʒɪstəʳ] *n* registro *m* ♦ *vt* registrare; *(subj: machine, gauge)* segnare ♦ *vi (put one's name down)* iscriversi; *(at hotel)* firmare il registro.

registered [ˈredʒɪstəd] *adj (letter, parcel)* assicurato(-a).

registration [ˌredʒɪˈstreɪʃn] *n (for course, at conference)* iscrizione *f*

registration (number) *n (of car)* numero *m* di targa.

registry office [ˈredʒɪstrɪ-] *n* anagrafe *f*.

regret [rɪ'gret] n (thing regretted) impianto m ♦ vt rimpiangere; **I ~ telling her** mi dispiace (di) averglielo detto; **we ~ any inconvenience caused** ci scusiamo per il disagio causato.

regrettable [rɪ'gretəbl] adj spiacevole.

regular ['regjʊlər] adj regolare; (normal, in size) normale; (customer, reader) abituale ♦ n (customer) cliente mf abituale.

regularly ['regjʊləlɪ] adv regolarmente.

regulate ['regjʊleɪt] vt regolare.

regulation [ˌregjʊ'leɪʃn] n (rule) norma f.

rehearsal [rɪ'hɜːsl] n prova f.

rehearse [rɪ'hɜːs] vt provare.

reign [reɪn] n regno m ♦ vi regnare.

reimburse [ˌriːɪm'bɜːs] vt (fml) rimborsare.

reindeer ['reɪnˌdɪər] (pl inv) n renna f.

reinforce [ˌriːɪn'fɔːs] vt (wall, handle) rinforzare; (argument, opinion) rafforzare.

reinforcements [ˌriːɪn'fɔːsmənts] npl rinforzi mpl.

reins [reɪnz] npl briglie fpl.

reject [rɪ'dʒekt] vt (proposal, request, coin) respingere; (applicant, plan) scartare.

rejection [rɪ'dʒekʃn] n rifiuto m.

rejoin [ˌriː'dʒɔɪn] vt (motorway) riprendere.

relapse [rɪ'læps] n ricaduta f.

relate [rɪ'leɪt] vt (connect) collegare ♦ vi: **to ~ to** (be connected with) essere collegato a; (concern) riguardare.

related [rɪ'leɪtɪd] adj (of same family) imparentato(-a); (connected) collegato(-a).

relation [rɪ'leɪʃn] n (member of family) parente mf; (connection) rapporto m; **in ~ to** in rapporto a ❑ **relations** npl parenti mpl.

relationship [rɪ'leɪʃnʃɪp] n rapporto m, relazione f.

relative ['relətɪv] adj relativo(-a) ♦ n parente mf.

relatively ['relətɪvlɪ] adv relativamente.

relax [rɪ'læks] vi (person) rilassarsi.

relaxation [ˌriːlæk'seɪʃn] n (of person) relax m.

relaxed [rɪ'lækst] adj rilassato(-a).

relaxing [rɪ'læksɪŋ] adj rilassante.

relay ['riːleɪ] n (race) staffetta f.

release [rɪ'liːs] vt (set free) liberare; (let go of) mollare; (record, film) far uscire; (handbrake, catch) togliere ♦ n (record, film) uscita f.

relegate ['relɪɡeɪt] vt: **to be ~d** (SPORT) essere retrocesso.

relevant ['relɪvənt] adj (connected) pertinente; (important) importante; (appropriate) appropriato(-a).

reliable [rɪ'laɪəbl] adj (person, machine) affidabile.

relic ['relɪk] n (object) reperto m (archeologico).

relief [rɪ'liːf] n (gladness) sollievo m; (aid) aiuto m.

relief road n strada f di smaltimento.

relieve [rɪ'liːv] vt (pain, headache) alleviare.

relieved [rɪ'liːvd] adj sollevato(-a).

religion [rɪ'lɪdʒn] n religione f.

religious [rɪ'lɪdʒəs] adj religioso(-a).

relish ['relɪʃ] n (sauce) salsa f.

reluctant [rɪ'lʌktənt] adj riluttante.

rely [rɪ'laɪ] : rely on vt fus (trust) contare su; (depend on) dipendere da.

remain [rɪ'meɪn] vi rimanere □ remains npl resti mpl.

remainder [rɪ'meɪndəʳ] n resto m.

remaining [rɪ'meɪnɪŋ] adj restante.

remark [rɪ'mɑːk] n commento m ◆ vt commentare.

remarkable [rɪ'mɑːkəbl] adj notevole.

remedy ['remədɪ] n rimedio m.

remember [rɪ'membəʳ] vt (recall) ricordare; (not forget) ricordarsi (di) ◆ vi (recall) ricordarsi; to ~ doing sthg ricordarsi di aver fatto qc; to ~ to do sthg ricordarsi di fare qc.

remind [rɪ'maɪnd] vt: to ~ sb of sthg ricordare qc a qn; to ~ sb to do sthg ricordare a qn di fare qc.

reminder [rɪ'maɪndəʳ] n (for bill, library book) sollecito m.

remittance [rɪ'mɪtns] n rimessa f.

remnant ['remnənt] n resto m.

remote [rɪ'məʊt] adj remoto(-a).

remote control n telecomando m.

removal [rɪ'muːvl] n (taking away) rimozione f.

removal van n camion m inv dei traslochi.

remove [rɪ'muːv] vt togliere; (clothes) togliersi.

renew [rɪ'njuː] vt rinnovare.

renovate ['renəveɪt] vt rinnovare.

renowned [rɪ'naʊnd] adj rinomato(-a).

rent [rent] n affitto m ◆ vt (flat) affittare; (car, TV) noleggiare.

rental ['rentl] n (fee) affitto m.

repaid [riː'peɪd] pt & pp → repay.

repair [rɪ'peəʳ] vt riparare ◆ n: in good ~ in buone condizioni □ repairs npl riparazioni fpl.

repair kit n (for bicycle) borsetta f degli attrezzi.

repay [riː'peɪ] (pt & pp repaid) vt restituire.

repayment [riː'peɪmənt] n (of loan) rimborso m.

repeat [rɪ'piːt] vt ripetere; (gossip, news) riferire ◆ n (on TV, radio) replica f.

repetition [,repɪ'tɪʃn] n ripetizione f.

repetitive [rɪ'petɪtɪv] adj ripetitivo(-a).

replace [rɪ'pleɪs] vt rimpiazzare; (put back) mettere a posto.

replacement [rɪ'pleɪsmənt] n (substitute) sostituto m (-a f).

replay ['riː'pleɪ] n (rematch) partita f ripetuta; (on TV) replay m inv.

reply [rɪ'plaɪ] n risposta f ◆ vt & vi rispondere.

report [rɪ'pɔːt] n (account) relazione f; (in newspaper, on TV, radio) servizio m; (Br: SCH) = scheda f ◆ vt (announce) riportare; (theft, disappearance, person) denunciare ◆ vi (give account) riferire; (for newspaper, TV, radio) fare un servizio; to ~ te sb (go to) presentarsi a qn.

report card n = scheda f (sco-

lastica).

reporter [rɪ'pɔːtər] *n* reporter *mf inv.*

represent [ˌreprɪ'zent] *vt* rappresentare.

representative [ˌreprɪ'zentətɪv] *n* rappresentante *mf.*

repress [rɪ'pres] *vt (feelings)* reprimere; *(people)* opprimere.

reprieve [rɪ'priːv] *n (delay)* sospensione *f.*

reprimand ['reprɪmɑːnd] *vt* rimproverare.

reproach [rɪ'prəʊtʃ] *vt* rimproverare.

reproduction [ˌriːprə'dʌkʃn] *n* riproduzione *f.*

reptile ['reptaɪl] *n* rettile *m.*

republic [rɪ'pʌblɪk] *n* repubblica *f.*

Republican [rɪ'pʌblɪkən] *n* repubblicano *m* (-a *f*) ♦ *adj* repubblicano(-a).

repulsive [rɪ'pʌlsɪv] *adj* repellente.

reputable ['repjʊtəbl] *adj* di buona reputazione.

reputation [ˌrepjʊ'teɪʃn] *n* reputazione *f.*

reputedly [rɪ'pjuːtɪdlɪ] *adv* per quanto si dice.

request [rɪ'kwest] *n* richiesta *f* ♦ *vt* chiedere; **to ~ sb to do sthg** chiedere a qn di fare qc; **available on ~** (disponibile) su richiesta.

request stop *n (Br)* fermata *f* a richiesta.

require [rɪ'kwaɪər] *vt (subj: person)* avere bisogno di; *(subj: situation)* richiedere; **passengers are ~d to show their tickets** i passeggeri sono pregati di presentare i biglietti.

requirement [rɪ'kwaɪəmənt] *n (condition)* requisito *m; (need)* esigenza *f.*

resat [ˌriː'sæt] *pt & pp* → **resit.**

rescue ['reskjuː] *vt* salvare.

research [ˌrɪ'sɜːtʃ] *n* ricerca *f.*

resemblance [rɪ'zembləns] *n* somiglianza *f.*

resemble [rɪ'zembl] *vt* somigliare a.

resent [rɪ'zent] *vt* risentirsi per.

reservation [ˌrezə'veɪʃn] *n (booking)* prenotazione *f; (doubt)* riserva *f;* **to make a ~** fare una prenotazione.

reserve [rɪ'zɜːv] *n* riserva *f* ♦ *vt (book)* prenotare; *(save)* riservare.

reserved [rɪ'zɜːvd] *adj* riservato(-a).

reservoir ['rezəvwɑːr] *n* bacino *m* (idrico).

reset [ˌriː'set] *(pt & pp* reset) *vt (watch, device)* rimettere; *(meter)* azzerare.

reside [rɪ'zaɪd] *vi (fml)* risiedere.

residence ['rezɪdəns] *n (fml)* residenza *f;* **place of ~** *(fml)* luogo *m* di residenza.

residence permit *n* permesso *m* di soggiorno.

resident ['rezɪdənt] *n (of country)* residente *mf; (of hotel)* cliente *mf; (of area, house)* abitante *mf;* **'~s only'** *(for parking)* 'parcheggio riservato ai residenti'.

residential [ˌrezɪ'denʃl] *adj (area)* residenziale.

residue ['rezɪdjuː] *n* residuo *m.*

resign [rɪ'zaɪn] *vi* dare le dimissioni ♦ *vt:* **to ~ o.s. to sthg** rassegnarsi a qc.

resignation [ˌrezɪg'neɪʃn] *n (from*

job) dimissioni *fpl.*

resilient [rɪˈzɪlɪənt] *adj (person)* che ha buone capacità di ripresa.

resist [rɪˈzɪst] *vt (fight against)* opporre resistenza a; *(temptation)* resistere a; **I can't ~ chocolate** non so resistere al cioccolato; **to ~ doing sthg** trattenersi dal fare qc.

resistance [rɪˈzɪstəns] *n (refusal to accept)* opposizione *f;* *(fighting)* resistenza *f.*

resit [ˌriːˈsɪt] *(pt & pp resat) vt* ridare.

resolution [ˌrezəˈluːʃn] *n (promise)* proposito *m.*

resolve [rɪˈzɒlv] *vt (solve)* risolvere.

resort [rɪˈzɔːt] *n (for holidays)* luogo *m* di villeggiatura; **as a last ~** come ultima risorsa ❑ **resort to** *vt fus* ricorrere a; **to ~ to doing sthg** ricorrere a fare qc.

resource [rɪˈsɔːs] *n* risorsa *f.*

resourceful [rɪˈsɔːsful] *adj* pieno(-a) di risorse.

respect [rɪˈspekt] *n* rispetto *m* ♦ *vt* rispettare; **in some ~s** sotto certi aspetti; **with ~ to** per quanto riguarda.

respectable [rɪˈspektəbl] *adj (person, job etc)* rispettabile; *(acceptable)* decente.

respective [rɪˈspektɪv] *adj* rispettivo(-a).

respond [rɪˈspɒnd] *vi* rispondere.

response [rɪˈspɒns] *n* risposta *f.*

responsibility [rɪˌspɒnsəˈbɪlətɪ] *n* responsabilità *f inv.*

responsible [rɪˈspɒnsəbl] *adj* responsabile; **to be ~ (for)** *(accountable)* essere responsabile (di).

rest [rest] *n (relaxation)* riposo *m;* *(support)* sostegno *m* ♦ *vi (relax)* riposarsi; **the ~** *(remainder)* il resto; **to have a ~** riposarsi; **to ~ against** appoggiarsi contro.

restaurant [ˈrestərɒnt] *n* ristorante *m.*

restaurant car *n (Br)* carrozza *f* ristorante.

restful [ˈrestful] *adj* riposante.

restless [ˈrestlɪs] *adj (bored, impatient)* insofferente; *(fidgety)* agitato(-a).

restore [rɪˈstɔːr] *vt (building, painting)* restaurare; *(order)* ripristinare.

restrain [rɪˈstreɪn] *vt* controllare.

restrict [rɪˈstrɪkt] *vt* limitare.

restricted [rɪˈstrɪktɪd] *adj* limitato(-a).

restriction [rɪˈstrɪkʃn] *n* restrizione *f.*

rest room *n (Am)* toilette *f inv.*

result [rɪˈzʌlt] *n* risultato *m* ♦ *vi:* **to ~ in** avere come conseguenza; **as a ~ of** in seguito a.

resume [rɪˈzjuːm] *vi* riprendere.

résumé [ˈrezjuːmeɪ] *n (summary)* riassunto *m;* *(Am: curriculum vitae)* curriculum vitae *m inv.*

retail [ˈriːteɪl] *n* vendita *f* al dettaglio ♦ *vt (sell)* vendere al dettaglio ♦ *vi:* **to ~ at** essere venduto a.

retailer [ˈriːteɪlər] *n* dettagliante *mf.*

retail price *n* prezzo *m* al dettaglio.

retain [rɪˈteɪn] *vt (fml)* conservare.

retaliate [rɪˈtælɪeɪt] *vi* fare rappresaglie.

retire [rɪˈtaɪər] *vi (stop working)* andare in pensione.

retired [rɪˈtaɪəd] *adj* in pensione.

retirement [rɪˈtaɪəmənt] *n (leav-*

ing job) pensionamento *m; (period after retiring)* periodo *m* dopo il pensionamento.

retreat [rɪ'triːt] *vi (move away)* indietreggiare ♦ *n (place)* rifugio *m*.

retrieve [rɪ'triːv] *vt (get back)* recuperare.

return [rɪ'tɜːn] *n* ritorno *m; (Br: ticket)* biglietto *m* (di) andata e ritorno ♦ *vt (put back)* rimettere; *(give back)* restituire; *(ball, serve)* rimandare ♦ *vi* ritornare; *(happen again)* ricomparire ♦ *adj (journey)* di ritorno; **to ~ sthg (to sb)** *(give back)* restituire qc a qn; **by ~ of post** *(Br)* a giro di posta; **many happy ~s!** cento di questi giorni!; **in ~ (for)** in cambio (di).

return flight *n (journey back)* volo *m* di ritorno.

return ticket *n (Br)* biglietto *m* (di) andata e ritorno.

reunite [ˌriːjuː'naɪt] *vt* riunire.

reveal [rɪ'viːl] *vt* rivelare.

revelation [ˌrevə'leɪʃn] *n* rivelazione *f*.

revenge [rɪ'vendʒ] *n* vendetta *f*.

reverse [rɪ'vɜːs] *adj* inverso(-a) ♦ *n (AUT)* retromarcia *f; (of coin)* rovescio *m; (of document)* retro *m* ♦ *vt (decision)* ribaltare ♦ *vi (car, driver)* fare marcia indietro; **in ~** order in ordine inverso; **the ~** *(opposite)* l'inverso; **to ~ the car** fare marcia indietro; **to ~ the charges** *(Br)* fare una telefonata a carico del destinatario.

reverse-charge call *n (Br)* telefonata *f* a carico del destinatario.

review [rɪ'vjuː] *n (of book, record, film)* recensione *f; (examination)* esame ♦ *vt (Am: for exam)* ri-

passare.

revise [rɪ'vaɪz] *vt* rivedere ♦ *vi (Br: for exam)* ripassare.

revision [rɪ'vɪʒn] *n (Br: for exam)* ripasso *m*.

revive [rɪ'vaɪv] *vt (person)* rianimare; *(economy)* far riprendere; *(custom)* riportare in uso.

revolt [rɪ'vəʊlt] *n* rivolta *f*.

revolting [rɪ'vəʊltɪŋ] *adj* disgustoso(-a).

revolution [ˌrevə'luːʃn] *n* rivoluzione *f*.

revolutionary [ˌrevə'luːʃnərɪ] *adj* rivoluzionario(-a).

revolver [rɪ'vɒlvər] *n* revolver *m inv*.

revolving door [rɪ'vɒlvɪŋ-] *n* porta *f* girevole.

revue [rɪ'vjuː] *n* rivista *f (spettacolo)*.

reward [rɪ'wɔːd] *n* ricompensa *f* ♦ *vt* ricompensare.

rewind [ˌriː'waɪnd] *(pt & pp* re-wound [ˌriː'waʊnd]) *vt* riavvolgere.

rheumatism ['ruːmətɪzm] *n* reumatismo *m*.

rhinoceros [raɪ'nɒsərəs] *(pl inv* OR **-es)** *n* rinoceronte *m*.

rhubarb ['ruːbɑːb] *n* rabarbaro *m*.

rhyme [raɪm] *n (poem)* rima *f* ♦ *vi* fare rima.

rhythm ['rɪðm] *n* ritmo *m*.

rib [rɪb] *n (of body)* costola *f*.

ribbon ['rɪbən] *n* nastro *m*.

rice [raɪs] *n* riso *m*.

rice pudding *n* budino *m* di riso *(dolce)*.

rich [rɪtʃ] *adj* ricco(-a) ♦ *npl:* **the ~** i ricchi; **to be ~ in sthg** essere ricco di qc.

ricotta cheese [rɪ'kɒtə-] *n*

ricotta f.

rid [rɪd] vt: **to get ~ of** sbarazzarsi di.

ridden ['rɪdn] pp → ride.

riddle ['rɪdl] n indovinello m.

ride [raɪd] (pt **rode**, pp **ridden**) n (on horse) cavalcata f; (in vehicle, on bike) giro m ◆ vi (on horse) andare a cavallo; (on bike) andare in bicicletta; (in vehicle) viaggiare ◆ vt: **to ~ a horse** andare a cavallo; **to go for a ~** (in car) andare a fare un giro.

rider ['raɪdər] n (on horse) persona f a cavallo; (on bike) ciclista mf.

ridge [rɪdʒ] n (of mountain) cresta f; (raised surface) increspatura f.

ridiculous [rɪ'dɪkjʊləs] adj ridicolo(-a).

riding ['raɪdɪŋ] n equitazione f.

riding school n scuola f d'equitazione.

rifle ['raɪfl] n fucile m.

rig [rɪg] n (oilrig at sea) piattaforma f; (on land) pozzo m petrolifero ◆ vt (fix) manipolare.

right [raɪt] adj 1. (correct) giusto(-a), corretto(-a); **to be ~** (person) avere ragione; **to be ~ to do sthg** fare bene a fare qc; **have you got the ~ time?** ha l'ora esatta?; **that's ~!** esatto!; **is this the ~ way?** è la strada giusta?

2. (fair) giusto(-a); **that's not ~!** non è giusto!

3. (on the right) destro(-a); **the ~ side of the road** il lato destro della strada.

◆ n 1. (side): **the ~** la destra.

2. (entitlement) diritto m; **to have the ~ to do sthg** avere il diritto di fare qc.

◆ adv 1. (towards the right) a destra; **turn ~ at the post office** all'ufficio postale giri a destra.

2. (correctly) bene, correttamente; **am I pronouncing it ~?** lo pronuncio bene?

3. (for emphasis) proprio; **~ here** proprio qui; **I'll be ~ back** torno subito; **~ away** subito.

right angle n angolo m retto.

right-hand adj di destra.

right-hand drive n guida f a destra.

right-handed [-'hændɪd] adj (person) destrimano(-a); (implement) per destrimani.

rightly ['raɪtlɪ] adv (correctly) correttamente; (justly) giustamente.

right of way n (AUT) diritto m di precedenza; (path) sentiero m.

right-wing adj di destra.

rigid ['rɪdʒɪd] adj rigido(-a).

rim [rɪm] n (of cup) bordo m; (of glasses) montatura f; (of wheel) cerchione m.

rind [raɪnd] n (of fruit) buccia f; (of bacon) cotenna f; (of cheese) crosta f.

ring [rɪŋ] (pt **rang**, pp **rung**) n anello m; (of people) cerchio m; (sound) trillo m; (on cooker) fornello m; (for boxing) ring m inv; (in circus) pista f ◆ vt (Br: on phone) telefonare a; (bell) suonare ◆ vi (bell, telephone) suonare; (Br: make phone call) telefonare; **to give sb a ~** fare una telefonata a qn; **to ~ the bell** suonare il campanello ❑ **ring back** vt sep (Br) ritelefonare a ◆ vi (Br) ritelefonare; **ring off** vi (Br) mettere giù (il telefono); **ring up** vt sep (Br) telefonare a ◆ vi (Br) telefonare.

ringing tone ['rɪŋɪŋ-] n segnale m di libero.

ring road n circonvallazione f.

rink [rɪŋk] *n* pista *f* di pattinaggio.

rinse [rɪns] *vt* sciacquare ❑ **rinse out** *vt sep* sciacquare.

riot ['raɪət] *n* sommossa *f*.

rip [rɪp] *n* strappo *m* ◆ *vt* strappare ◆ *vi* strapparsi ❑ **rip up** *vt sep* strappare.

ripe [raɪp] *adj (fruit, vegetable)* maturo(-a); *(cheese)* stagionato(-a).

ripen ['raɪpn] *vi* maturare.

rip-off *n (inf)* fregatura *f*.

rise [raɪz] *(pt* rose, *pp* risen ['rɪzn]) *vi* alzarsi; *(sun, moon)* sorgere; *(increase)* aumentare ◆ *n* aumento *m*; *(slope)* salita *f*.

risk [rɪsk] *n* rischio *m* ◆ *vt* rischiare; **to take a ~** correre un rischio; **at your own ~** a suo rischio (e pericolo); **to ~ doing sthg** rischiare di fare qc; **to ~ it** arrischiarsi.

risky ['rɪskɪ] *adj* rischioso(-a).

risotto [rɪ'zɒtəʊ] *(pl* -s) *n* risotto *m*.

ritual ['rɪtʃʊəl] *n* rituale *m*.

rival ['raɪvl] *adj* rivale ◆ *n* rivale *mf*.

river ['rɪvər] *n* fiume *m*.

river bank *n* sponda *f* del fiume.

riverside ['rɪvəsaɪd] *n* riva *f* del fiume.

Riviera [,rɪvɪ'eərə] *n*: **the (Italian) ~** la riviera (ligure).

roach [rəʊtʃ] *n (Am: cockroach)* scarafaggio *m*.

road [rəʊd] *n* strada *f*; **by ~** in macchina.

road book *n* atlante *m* stradale.

road map *n* carta *f* stradale.

road safety *n* sicurezza *f* sulle strade.

roadside ['rəʊdsaɪd] *n*: **the ~** il bordo della strada.

road sign *n* segnale *m* stradale.

road tax *n* tassa *f* di circolazione.

roadway ['rəʊdweɪ] *n* carreggiata *f*.

road works *npl* lavori *mpl* stradali.

roam [rəʊm] *vi* vagabondare.

roar [rɔːr] *n (of crowd)* strepito *m*; *(of plane)* rombo *m* ◆ *vi (lion)* ruggire; *(crowd)* strepitare; *(traffic)* rombare.

roast [rəʊst] *n* arrosto *m* ◆ *vt* arrostire ◆ *adj* arrosto *(inv)*; **~ beef** roast beef *m*; **~ chicken** pollo *m* arrosto; **~ lamb** arrosto di agnello; **~ pork** arrosto di maiale; **~ potatoes** patate *fpl* arrosto.

rob [rɒb] *vt (house, bank)* svaligiare; *(person)* derubare; **to ~ sb of sthg** derubare qn di qc.

robber ['rɒbər] *n* rapinatore *m* (-trice *f*).

robbery ['rɒbərɪ] *n* rapina *f*.

robe [rəʊb] *n (Am: bathrobe)* accappatoio *m*.

robin ['rɒbɪn] *n* pettirosso *m*.

robot ['rəʊbɒt] *n* robot *m inv*.

rock [rɒk] *n* roccia *f*; *(Am: stone)* pietra *f*; *(music)* rock *m*; *(Br: sweet)* bastoncini *mpl* di zucchero ◆ *vt (baby)* cullare; *(boat)* far rollare; **on the ~s** *(drink)* con ghiaccio.

rock climbing *n* roccia *f* *(sport)*; **to go ~** fare scalate.

rocket ['rɒkɪt] *n (missile)* missile *m*; *(space rocket, firework)* razzo *m*.

rocking chair ['rɒkɪŋ-] *n* sedia *f* a dondolo.

rock 'n' roll [,rɒkən'rəʊl] *n* rock

and roll *m*.

rocky ['rɒkɪ] *adj* roccioso(-a).

rod [rɒd] *n* (pole) asta *f*; (for fishing) canna *f* (da pesca).

rode [rəʊd] *pt* → **ride**.

roe [rəʊ] *n* uova *fpl* di pesce.

role [rəʊl] *n* ruolo *m*.

roll [rəʊl] *n* (of bread) panino *m*; (of film) rullino *m*; (of paper) rotolo *m* ◆ *vi* (ball, rock) rotolare; (ship) rollare ◆ *vt* (ball, rock) far rotolare; (cigarette) arrotolare; (dice) tirare ❑ **roll over** *vi* (person, animal) rivoltarsi; (car) ribaltarsi; **roll up** *vt sep* arrotolare.

roller coaster ['rəʊlə,kəʊstə'] *n* otto *m* volante.

roller skate ['rəʊlə-] *n* pattino *m* a rotelle.

roller-skating ['rəʊlə-] *n* pattinaggio *m* a rotelle.

rolling pin ['rəʊlɪŋ-] *n* matterello *m*.

Roman ['rəʊmən] *adj* romano(-a) ◆ *n* romano *m* (-a *f*).

Roman Catholic *n* cattolico *m* romano (cattolica romana *f*).

romance [rəʊ'mæns] *n* (love) amore *m*; (love affair) avventura *f*; (novel) romanzo *m* sentimentale.

Romania [ru:'meɪnjə] *n* la Romania.

romantic [rəʊ'mæntɪk] *adj* romantico(-a).

Rome [rəʊm] *n* Roma *f*.

romper suit ['rɒmpə-] *n* pagliaccetto *m*.

roof [ru:f] *n* tetto *m*; (of cave) volta *f*.

roof rack *n* portapacchi *m inv*.

room [ru:m, rʊm] *n* stanza *f*, camera *f*; (space) spazio *m*.

room number *n* numero *m* di stanza.

room service *n* servizio *m* in camera.

room temperature *n* temperatura *f* ambiente.

roomy ['ru:mɪ] *adj* spazioso(-a).

root [ru:t] *n* radice *f*.

rope [rəʊp] *n* corda *f* ◆ *vt* legare.

rose [rəʊz] *pt* → **rise** ◆ *n* (flower) rosa *f*.

rosé ['rəʊzeɪ] *n* vino *m* rosé.

rosemary ['rəʊzmərɪ] *n* rosmarino *m*.

rot [rɒt] *vi* marcire.

rota ['rəʊtə] *n* turni *mpl*.

rotate [rəʊ'teɪt] *vi* ruotare.

rotten ['rɒtn] *adj* (food, wood) marcio(-a); (inf: not good) schifoso(-a); **I feel ~** (ill) mi sento uno schifo.

rouge [ru:ʒ] *n* fard *m inv*.

rough [rʌf] *adj* (surface, skin, cloth) ruvido(-a); (sea) burrascoso(-a); (person) rude; (approximate) approssimativo(-a); (conditions) disagiato(-a); (area, town) brutto(-a); (wine) scadente ◆ *n* (on golf course) rough *m*; **to have a ~ time** passarsela male.

roughly ['rʌflɪ] *adv* (approximately) approssimativamente; (push, handle) sgarbatamente.

roulade [ru:'lɑ:d] *n* rotolo *m*.

roulette [ru:'let] *n* roulette *f*.

round [raʊnd] *adj* rotondo(-a); (cheeks) paffuto(-a).

◆ *n* 1. (of drinks) giro *m*; **it's my ~** tocca a me offrire (questo giro).

2. (of sandwiches) tramezzini *mpl*.

3. (of toast) fetta *f*.

4. (of competition) turno *m*.

5. *(in golf)* partita f; *(in boxing)* round m inv, ripresa f.

6. *(of policeman, postman, milkman)* giro m.

♦ *adv* 1. *(in a circle)*: **to go ~** girare; **to spin ~** ruotare.

2. *(surrounding)*: **all (the way) ~** tutt'intorno.

3. *(near)*: **~ about** nei dintorni.

4. *(to one's house)*: **to ask some friends ~** invitare (a casa propria) degli amici; **we went ~ to her place** siamo andati da lei OR a casa sua.

5. *(continuously)*: **all year ~** tutto l'anno.

♦ *prep* 1. *(surrounding, circling)* intorno a; **to go ~ the corner** girare l'angolo; **we walked ~ the lake** abbiamo fatto il giro del lago a piedi.

2. *(visiting)*: **to go ~ a museum** visitare un museo; **to show sb ~ sthg** far fare il giro di qc a qn.

3. *(approximately)* circa, pressappoco; **~ (about) 100** circa 100; **~ ten o'clock** verso le dieci.

4. *(near)*: **~ here** da queste parti.

5. *(in phrases)*: **it's just ~ the corner** *(nearby)* è qui vicino; **~ the clock** 24 ore su 24.

❑ **round off** *vt sep (meal, day)* terminare.

roundabout ['raʊndəbaʊt] *n (Br) (in road)* isola f rotazionale; *(in playground, at fairground)* giostra f.

rounders ['raʊndəz] *n (Br)* gioco a squadre simile al baseball.

round trip *n* viaggio m di andata e ritorno.

route [ru:t] *n (way)* strada f; *(of bus, train)* percorso m; *(of plane)* rotta f ♦ *vt (change course of)* dirottare.

routine [ru:'ti:n] *n* routine f inv ♦ *adj* di routine.

row[1] [rəʊ] *n (line)* fila f ♦ *vt & vi* remare; **in a ~** *(in succession)* di fila.

row[2] [raʊ] *n (argument)* lite f; *(inf: noise)* baccano m; **to have a ~** litigare.

rowboat ['rəʊbəʊt] *(Am)* = **rowing boat**.

rowdy ['raʊdɪ] *adj* turbolento(-a).

rowing ['rəʊɪŋ] *n* canottaggio m.

rowing boat *n (Br)* barca f a remi.

royal ['rɔɪəl] *adj* reale.

royal family *n* famiglia f reale.

---

i ROYAL FAMILY

A capo della famiglia reale inglese è oggi la Regina Elisabetta. Altri membri di spicco della famiglia reale sono il principe consorte Filippo (Duca di Edimburgo), la Regina Madre, i figli Carlo (Principe di Galles), Andrea e Edoardo, e la figlia Anna. Quando uno o più membri della famiglia reale presenziano cerimonie ufficiali viene eseguito l'inno nazionale. La presenza della regina a palazzo è segnalata dalla Union Jack (la bandiera del Regno Unito).

---

royalty ['rɔɪəltɪ] *n (royal family)* reali mpl.

RRP *(abbr of recommended retail price)* prezzo m consigliato.

rub [rʌb] *vt & vi* strofinare; **to ~ sb's back** massaggiare la schiena a qn; **my shoes are rubbing** mi fanno male le scarpe ❑ **rub in** *vt sep (lotion, oil)* far penetrare sfregando; **rub out** *vt sep* cancellare.

rubber ['rʌbə'] *adj* di gomma ◆
n gomma *f*; *(Am: inf: condom)* preservativo *m*.

rubber band *n* elastico *m*.

rubber gloves *npl* guanti *mpl*
di gomma.

rubber ring *n* ciambella *f*.

rubbish ['rʌbɪʃ] *n* spazzatura *f*;
(inf: nonsense) cretinate *fpl*.

rubbish bin *n (Br)* pattumiera *f*.

rubbish dump *n (Br)* discarica *f*.

rubble ['rʌbl] *n* macerie *fpl*.

ruby ['ru:bɪ] *n* rubino *m*.

rucksack ['rʌksæk] *n* zaino *m*.

rudder ['rʌdə'] *n* timone *m*.

rude [ru:d] *adj (person)* sgarba-
to(-a); *(behaviour, joke, picture)* volgare.

rug [rʌg] *n (for floor)* tappeto *m*;
(Br: blanket) coperta *f*.

rugby ['rʌgbɪ] *n* rugby *m*.

ruin ['ru:ɪn] *vt* rovinare ❏ **ruins**
npl rovine *fpl*.

ruined ['ru:ɪnd] *adj (building)* in
rovina; *(clothes, meal, holiday)* rovi-
nato(-a).

rule [ru:l] *n (law)* regola *f* ◆ *vt
(country)* governare; **to be the** ~
(normal) essere la regola; **against
the** ~**s** contro le regole; **as a** ~ di
regola ❏ **rule out** *vt sep* escludere.

ruler ['ru:lə'] *n (of country)* capo *m*
di Stato; *(for measuring)* righello *m*.

rum [rʌm] *n* rum *m inv*.

rumor ['ru:mər] *(Am)* = **rumour**.

rumour ['ru:mə'] *n (Br)* voce *f*.

rump steak [,rʌmp-] *n* bistecca
f di girello.

run [rʌn] *(pt* **ran**, *pp* **run**) *vi* **1.** *(on
foot)* correre; **we had to** ~ **for the
bus** abbiamo dovuto fare una
corsa per prendere l'autobus.

2. *(train, bus)* fare servizio; **the bus
~s every hour** c'è un autobus ogni
ora; **the train is running an hour
late** il treno ha un'ora di ritardo.

3. *(operate)* funzionare; **to** ~ **on
sthg** andare a qc.

4. *(tears, liquid, river)* scorrere; **to** ~
through *(river, road)* passare per;
the path ~s along the coast il sentiero corre lungo la costa; **she left
the tap running** ha lasciato il rubinetto aperto.

5. *(play, event)* durare; **'now running
at the Palladium'** 'in cartellone al
Palladium'.

6. *(nose)* gocciolare, colare; *(eyes)*
lacrimare.

7. *(colour, dye, clothes)* stingere.
◆ *vt* **1.** *(on foot)* correre.

2. *(compete in):* **to** ~ **a race** partecipare a una corsa.

3. *(business, hotel)* dirigere.

4. *(bus, train):* **we're running a special bus to the airport** mettiamo a
disposizione una navetta per
andare all'aeroporto.

5. *(take in car)* dare un passaggio a;
I'll ~ **you home** ti do un passaggio
(fino) a casa.

6. *(water)* far correre.
◆ *n* **1.** *(on foot)* corsa *f*; **to go for a** ~
andare a fare una corsa.

2. *(in car)* giro *m*; **to go for a** ~ andare a fare un giro (in macchina).

3. *(for skiing)* pista *f*.

4. *(Am: in tights)* smagliatura *f*.

5. *(in phrases):* **in the long** ~ alla
lunga.

❏ **run away** *vi* scappare; **run
down** *vt sep (run over)* investire;
(criticize) criticare ◆ *vi (battery)* scaricarsi; **run into** *vt fus (meet)*
incontrare per caso; *(hit)* sbattere
contro; *(problem, difficulty)* incon-

trare; **run out** vi (be used up) esaurirsi; **run out of** vt fus finire, esaurire; **run over** vt sep (hit) investire.

runaway ['rʌnəwei] n fuggiasco m (-a f).

rung [rʌŋ] pp → **ring** ♦ n (of ladder) piolo m.

runner ['rʌnəʳ] n (person) corridore m; (for door, drawer) guida f; (for sledge) pattino m.

runner bean n fagiolo m rampicante.

runner-up (pl **runners-up**) n secondo m classificato (seconda classificata f).

running ['rʌnɪŋ] n (SPORT) corsa f; (management) amministrazione f ♦ adj: **three days** ~ tre giorni di fila; **to go** ~ andare a correre.

running water n acqua f corrente.

runny ['rʌnɪ] adj (sauce, egg, omelette) troppo liquido(-a); (nose) che cola; (eye) che lacrima.

runway ['rʌnwei] n pista f (di volo).

rural ['ruərəl] adj rurale.

rush [rʌʃ] n (hurry) fretta f; (of crowd) grosso afflusso m ♦ vi (move quickly) precipitarsi; (hurry) affrettarsi ♦ vt (work) fare in fretta; (food) mangiare in fretta; (transport quickly) portare d'urgenza; **to be in a** ~ avere fretta; **there's no** ~! non c'è fretta!; **don't** ~ **me!** non mettermi fretta!

rush hour n ora f di punta.

Russia ['rʌʃə] n la Russia.

Russian ['rʌʃn] adj russo(-a) ♦ n (person) russo m (-a f); (language) russo m.

rust [rʌst] n ruggine f ♦ vi arrugginirsi.

rustic ['rʌstɪk] adj rustico(-a).

rustle ['rʌsl] vi frusciare.

rustproof ['rʌstpruːf] adj inossidabile.

rusty ['rʌstɪ] adj arrugginito(-a).

RV n (Am: abbr of recreational vehicle) camper m inv.

rye [rai] n segale f.

rye bread n pane m di segale.

S

S (abbr of south, small) S.

saccharin ['sækərɪn] n saccarina f.

sachet ['sæʃei] n bustina f.

sack [sæk] n (bag) sacco m ♦ vt licenziare; **to get the** ~ essere licenziato.

sacrifice ['sækrɪfais] n (fig) sacrificio m.

sad [sæd] adj triste.

saddle ['sædl] n sella f.

saddlebag ['sædlbæg] n bisaccia f.

sadly ['sædlɪ] adv (unfortunately) sfortunatamente; (unhappily) tristemente.

sadness ['sædnɪs] n tristezza f.

s.a.e. n (Br: abbr of stamped addressed envelope) busta affrancata e completa d'indirizzo.

safari park [sə'fɑːrɪ-] n zoosafari m inv.

safe [seif] adj sicuro(-a); (out of harm) salvo(-a); (valuables) al sicuro ♦ n cassaforte f; **a** ~ **place** un posto sicuro; **(have a)** ~ **journey!** buon viaggio!; ~ **and sound** sano(-a) e salvo(-a).

safe-deposit box n cassetta f di sicurezza.

safely ['seɪflɪ] adv (not dangerously) senza pericolo; (arrive) senza problemi; (out of harm) al sicuro.

safety ['seɪftɪ] n sicurezza f.

safety belt n cintura f di sicurezza.

safety pin n spilla f da balia.

sag [sæg] vi avvallarsi.

sage [seɪdʒ] n (herb) salvia f.

Sagittarius [,sædʒɪ'teərɪəs] n Sagittario m.

said [sed] pt & pp → **say.**

sail [seɪl] n vela f ♦ vi (boat, ship) navigare; (person) andare in barca; (depart) salpare ♦ vt: **to ~ a boat** condurre una barca; **to set ~** salpare.

sailboat ['seɪlbəʊt] (Am) = **sailing boat.**

sailing ['seɪlɪŋ] n (activity) vela f; (departure) partenza f; **to go ~** fare della vela.

sailing boat n barca f a vela.

sailor ['seɪlə'] n marinaio m.

saint [seɪnt] n santo m (-a f).

sake [seɪk] n: **for my/their ~** per il mio/il loro bene; **for God's ~!** per l'amor di Dio!

salad ['sæləd] n insalata f.

salad bar n (Br: area in restaurant) tavolo m delle insalate; (restaurant) locale specializzato in insalate.

salad bowl n insalatiera f.

salad cream n (Br) salsa per l'insalata, simile alla maionese.

salad dressing n condimento m per l'insalata.

salami [sə'lɑːmɪ] n salame m.

salary ['sælərɪ] n stipendio m.

sale [seɪl] n (selling) vendita f; (at reduced prices) svendita f; **'for ~'** 'vendesi'; **on ~** in vendita ❑ **sales** npl (COMM) vendite fpl; **the ~s** (at reduced prices) i saldi.

sales assistant ['seɪlz-] n commesso m (-a f).

salesclerk ['seɪlzklɜːrk] (Am) = **sales assistant.**

salesman ['seɪlzmən] (pl **-men** [-mən]) n (in shop) commesso m; (rep) rappresentante m.

sales rep(resentative) n rappresentante mf.

saleswoman ['seɪlz,wʊmən] (pl **-women** [-,wɪmɪn]) n (in shop) commessa f.

saliva [sə'laɪvə] n saliva f.

salmon ['sæmən] (pl inv) n salmone m.

salon ['sælɒn] n (hairdresser's) salone m.

saloon [sə'luːn] n (Br: car) berlina f; (Am: bar) saloon m inv; **~ (bar)** (Br) sala f interna.

salopettes [,sælə'pets] npl salopette f inv.

salt [sɔːlt, sɒlt] n sale m.

saltcellar ['sɔːlt,selə'] n (Br) saliera f.

salted peanuts ['sɔːltɪd-] npl noccioline fpl salate.

salt shaker [-,ʃeɪkə'] (Am) = **saltcellar.**

salty ['sɔːltɪ] adj salato(-a).

salute [sə'luːt] n saluto m ♦ vi fare il saluto.

same [seɪm] adj stesso(-a) ♦ pron: **the ~** lo stesso (la stessa); **they look the ~** sembrano uguali; **I'll have the ~ as her** prendo lo stesso che ha preso lei; **you've got the ~**

book as me hai lo stesso libro che ho io; **it's all the ~** to me per me è tutto uguale.

samosa [sə'məʊsə] n fagottino fritto triangolare, ripieno di carne o verdure, tipico della cucina indiana.

sample ['sɑ:mpl] n campione m ◆ vt assaggiare.

sanctions ['sæŋkʃnz] npl sanzioni fpl.

sanctuary ['sæŋktʃʊərɪ] n (for birds, animals) riserva f.

sand [sænd] n sabbia f ◆ vt (wood) smerigliare ❑ **sands** npl spiaggia f.

sandal ['sændl] n sandalo m.

sandcastle ['sænd,kɑ:sl] n castello m di sabbia.

sandpaper ['sænd,peɪpəʳ] n carta f vetrata.

sandwich ['sænwɪdʒ] n tramezzino m.

sandwich bar n paninoteca f.

sandy ['sændɪ] adj (beach) sabbioso(-a); (hair) color sabbia (inv).

sang [sæŋ] pt → sing.

sanitary ['sænɪtrɪ] adj (conditions, measures) sanitario(-a); (hygienic) igienico(-a).

sanitary napkin (Am) = sanitary towel

sanitary towel n (Br) assorbente m igienico.

sank [sæŋk] pt → sink.

sapphire ['sæfaɪəʳ] n zaffiro m.

sarcastic [sɑ:'kæstɪk] adj sarcastico(-a).

sardine [sɑ:'di:n] n sardina f.

Sardinia [sɑ:'dɪnjə] n la Sardegna.

SASE n (Am: abbr of self-addressed stamped envelope) busta affrancata e completa del proprio indirizzo.

sat [sæt] pt & pp → sit.

Sat. (abbr of Saturday) sab.

satchel ['sætʃəl] n cartella f.

satellite ['sætəlaɪt] n (in space) satellite m; (at airport) zona f satellite.

satellite dish n antenna f parabolica.

satellite TV n televisione f via satellite.

satin ['sætɪn] n raso m.

satisfaction [,sætɪs'fækʃn] n soddisfazione f.

satisfactory [,sætɪs'fæktərɪ] adj soddisfacente.

satisfied ['sætɪsfaɪd] adj soddisfatto(-a).

satisfy ['sætɪsfaɪ] vt soddisfare.

satsuma [,sæt'su:mə] n (Br) mandarino m.

saturate ['sætʃəreɪt] vt (with liquid) impregnare.

Saturday ['sætədɪ] n sabato m; **it's ~** è sabato; **~ morning** sabato mattina; **on ~** sabato; **on ~s** OR di sabato; **last ~** sabato scorso; **this ~** questo sabato; **next ~** sabato prossimo; **~ week, a week on ~** sabato a otto.

sauce [sɔ:s] n salsa f.

saucepan ['sɔ:spən] n casseruola f.

saucer ['sɔ:səʳ] n piattino m.

Saudi Arabia [,saʊdɪ'reɪbjə] n l'Arabia f Saudita.

sauna ['sɔ:nə] n sauna f.

sausage ['sɒsɪdʒ] n salsiccia f.

sausage roll n rustico m con salsiccia.

sauté [Br 'səʊteɪ, Am səʊ'teɪ] adj saltato(-a).

savage ['sævɪdʒ] adj selvaggio(-a).

save [seɪv] vt (rescue, COMPUT) salvare; (money, time) risparmiare; (reserve) tenere; (SPORT) parare ◆ n parata f □ **save up** vi risparmiare; **to ~ up (for sth)** mettere da parte i soldi (per qc).

saver ['seɪvəʳ] n (Br: ticket) biglietto m ridotto.

savings ['seɪvɪŋz] npl risparmi mpl.

savings and loan association n (Am) = istituto m di credito fondiario.

savings bank n cassa f di risparmio.

savory ['seɪvəri] (Am) = savoury.

savoury ['seɪvəri] adj (Br: not sweet) salato(-a).

saw [sɔː] (Br pt -ed, pp sawn, Am pt & pp -ed) pt → see ◆ n (tool) sega f ◆ vt segare.

sawdust ['sɔːdʌst] n segatura f.

sawn [sɔːn] pp → saw.

saxophone ['sæksəfəun] n sassofono m.

say [seɪ] (pt & pp said) vt dire; (subj: clock, meter) segnare ◆ n: **to have a ~ in sth** avere voce in capitolo riguardo a qc; **could you ~ that again?** può ripetere, per favore?; **~ we met at nine?** diciamo che ci vediamo alle nove?; **what did you ~?** che cosa hai detto?

saying ['seɪɪŋ] n detto m.

scab [skæb] n (on skin) crosta f.

scaffolding ['skæfəldɪŋ] n impalcatura f.

scald [skɔːld] vt scottare.

scale [skeɪl] n scala f; (of fish, snake) squama f; (in kettle) incrostazione f □ **scales** npl (for weighing) bilancia f.

scallion ['skæljən] n (Am) cipollina f.

scallop ['skɒləp] n pettine m (mollusco).

scalp [skælp] n cuoio m capelluto.

scampi ['skæmpɪ] n gamberoni mpl impanati e fritti.

scan [skæn] vt (consult quickly) scorrere ◆ n (MED) esame m eseguito con scanner.

scandal ['skændl] n scandalo m.

Scandinavia [,skændɪ'neɪvjə] n la Scandinavia.

scar [skɑːʳ] n cicatrice f.

scarce ['skeəs] adj scarso(-a).

scarcely ['skeəslɪ] adv (hardly) a malapena.

scare [skeəʳ] vt spaventare.

scarecrow ['skeəkrəu] n spaventapasseri m inv.

scared ['skeəd] adj spaventato(-a).

scarf ['skɑːf] (pl scarves) n (woollen) sciarpa f; (for women) foulard m inv.

scarlet ['skɑːlət] adj scarlatto(-a).

scarves [skɑːvz] pl → scarf.

scary ['skeərɪ] adj (inf) terrificante.

scatter ['skætəʳ] vt spargere ◆ vi sparpagliarsi.

scene [siːn] n scena f; (view) vista f; **the music ~** il mondo della musica; **to make a ~** fare una scenata.

scenery ['siːnərɪ] n (countryside) paesaggio m; (in theatre) scenario m.

scenic ['siːnɪk] adj pittoresco(-a).

scent [sent] n odore m; (perfume) profumo m.

sceptical ['skeptɪkl] adj (Br) scettico(-a).

schedule [Br 'ʃedjuːl, Am

'skedʒul] n (of work, things to do) tabella f di marcia; (timetable) orario m; (list) tabella ♦ vt programmare; **according to** ~ secondo la tabella di marcia; **behind** ~ in ritardo sulla tabella di marcia; **on** ~ puntualmente.

scheduled flight [Br 'ʃedjuːld-, Am 'skedʒuld-] n volo m di linea.

scheme [skiːm] n (plan) piano m; (pej: dishonest plan) intrigo m.

scholarship ['skɒləʃɪp] n (award) borsa f di studio.

school [skuːl] n scuola f; (university department) facoltà f inv; (Am: university) università f inv ♦ adj scolastico(-a); **at** ~ a scuola.

schoolbag ['skuːlbæg] n cartella f.

schoolbook ['skuːlbʊk] n libro m di testo.

schoolboy ['skuːlbɔɪ] n scolaro m.

school bus n scuolabus m inv.

schoolchild ['skuːltʃaɪld] (pl -children [-tʃɪldrən]) n scolaro m (-a f).

schoolgirl ['skuːlgɜːl] n scolara f.

schoolmaster ['skuːlˌmɑːstər] n (Br) maestro m.

schoolmistress ['skuːlˌmɪstrɪs] n (Br) maestra f.

schoolteacher ['skuːlˌtiːtʃər] n insegnante mf.

school uniform n divisa f.

science ['saɪəns] n scienza f; (SCH) scienze fpl.

science fiction n fantascienza f.

scientific [ˌsaɪən'tɪfɪk] adj scientifico(-a).

scientist ['saɪəntɪst] n scienziato m (-a f).

scissors ['sɪzəz] npl: **(a pair of)** ~ (un paio di) forbici fpl.

scold [skəʊld] vt sgridare.

scone [skɒn] n pasta rotonda con uvette che si mangia con burro e marmellata durante il tè.

scoop [skuːp] n (for ice cream, flour) paletta f; (of ice cream) pallina f; (in media) scoop m inv.

scooter ['skuːtər] n (motor vehicle) scooter m inv.

scope [skəʊp] n (possibility) opportunità fpl; (range) portata f.

scorch [skɔːtʃ] vt bruciare.

score [skɔːʳ] n (total, final result) punteggio m; (current position) situazione f ♦ vt (SPORT) segnare; (in test) totalizzare ♦ vi (SPORT) segnare.

scorn [skɔːn] n disprezzo m.

Scorpio ['skɔːpɪəʊ] n Scorpione m.

scorpion ['skɔːpjən] n scorpione m.

Scot [skɒt] n scozzese mf.

scotch [skɒtʃ] n scotch m inv (whisky).

Scotch broth n minestra a base di brodo di carne, verdure e orzo perlato.

Scotch tape® n (Am) scotch® m.

Scotland ['skɒtlənd] n la Scozia.

Scotsman ['skɒtsmən] (pl -men [-mən]) n scozzese m.

Scotswoman ['skɒtswʊmən] (pl -women [-wɪmɪn]) n scozzese f.

Scottish ['skɒtɪʃ] adj scozzese.

scout [skaʊt] n (child) scout mf inv.

| i | SCOUTS |

Gli "scouts" sono membri della Scouting Association, fondata in Gran Bretagna nel 1908 da Lord Baden-Powell, allo scopo di promuovere lo spirito di avventura e il senso di responsabilità e disciplina fra i più giovani. I ragazzi fra gli 11 e i 16 anni sono organizzati in piccoli gruppi che, sotto la guida di un adulto, imparano tecniche di sopravvivenza all'aperto e di pronto soccorso. I ragazzi sotto gli 11 anni possono iscriversi ai "Cub Scouts" (Lupetti). Organizzazioni equivalenti per le ragazze sono le "Guides" e le "Brownies" (Coccinelle).

scowl [skaʊl] *vi* aggrottare le ciglia.

scrambled eggs [ˌskræmbld-] *npl* uova *fpl* strapazzate.

scrap [skræp] *n (of paper, cloth)* pezzo *m*; *(old metal)* rottami *mpl* (di metallo).

scrapbook ['skræpbʊk] *n* album *m inv*.

scrape [skreɪp] *vt (rub)* raschiare; *(scratch)* graffiare.

scrap paper *n (Br)* carta *f* da brutta copia.

scratch [skrætʃ] *n* graffio *m* ◆ *vt (cut, mark)* graffiare; *(rub)* grattare; **to be up to ~** essere all'altezza della situazione; **to start from ~** cominciare da zero.

scratch paper *(Am)* = **scrap paper**.

scream [skri:m] *n* strillo *m* ◆ *vi* strillare.

screen [skri:n] *n* schermo *m*; *(hall in cinema)* sala *f*; *(panel)* paravento *m* ◆ *vt (film)* proiettare; *(TV programme)* trasmettere.

screening ['skri:nɪŋ] *n (of film)* proiezione *f*.

screen wash *n* detergente *m* per il parabrezza.

screw [skru:] *n* vite *f* ◆ *vt (fasten)* avvitare; *(twist)* torcere.

screwdriver ['skru:ˌdraɪvər] *n* cacciavite *m inv*.

scribble ['skrɪbl] *vi* scarabocchiare.

script [skrɪpt] *n (of play, film)* copione *m*.

scrub [skrʌb] *vt* strofinare.

scruffy ['skrʌfɪ] *adj* trasandato(-a).

scrumpy ['skrʌmpɪ] *n* sidro ad alta gradazione alcolica tipico del sudovest dell'Inghilterra.

scuba diving ['sku:bə-] *n* immersioni *fpl* (con autorespiratore).

sculptor ['skʌlptər] *n* scultore *m*.

sculpture ['skʌlptʃər] *n* scultura *f*.

sea [si:] *n* mare *m*; **by ~** via mare; **by the ~** sul mare.

seafood ['si:fu:d] *n* frutti *mpl* di mare.

seafront ['si:frʌnt] *n* lungomare *m*.

seagull ['si:gʌl] *n* gabbiano *m*.

seal [si:l] *n (animal)* foca *f*; *(on bottle, container, official mark)* sigillo *m* ◆ *vt (envelope, container)* sigillare.

seam [si:m] *n (in clothes)* cucitura *f*.

search [sɜ:tʃ] *n* ricerca *f* ◆ *vt* perquisire ◆ *vi*: **to ~ for** cercare.

seashell ['si:ʃel] *n* conchiglia *f*.

seashore ['si:ʃɔ:r] *n* riva *f* del mare.

seasick ['si:sɪk] *adj*: **to be ~** avere il mal di mare.

seaside ['si:saɪd] *n*: **the ~** il mare.

seaside resort *n* località *f inv* balneare.

season ['si:zn] *n* stagione *f* ◆ *vt* condire; **in ~** *(fruit, vegetables)* di stagione; *(holiday)* in alta stagione;

out of ~ *(fruit, vegetables)* fuori stagione; *(holiday)* in bassa stagione.

seasoning ['siːznɪŋ] *n* condimento *m*.

season ticket *n* abbonamento *m*.

seat [siːt] *n (place, chair)* posto *m*; *(in parliament)* seggio *m* ♦ *vt:* **the minibus ~s 12** il minibus ha 12 posti a sedere; **'please wait to be ~ed'** cartello che avvisa i clienti di un ristorante di attendere il cameriere per essere condotti al tavolo.

seat belt *n* cintura *f* di sicurezza.

seaweed ['siːwiːd] *n* alghe *fpl*.

secluded [sɪ'kluːdɪd] *adj* appartato(-a).

second ['sekənd] *n* secondo *m* ♦ *num* secondo(-a); **~ gear** seconda *f* ❏ **seconds** *npl (goods)* merce *f* di seconda scelta; *(inf: of food)* bis *m inv*, → **sixth**.

secondary school ['sekəndrɪ-] *n* ≃ scuola *f* media inferiore e superiore.

second-class *adj (ticket)* di seconda classe; *(stamp)* per posta ordinaria sul territorio nazionale; *(inferior)* di seconda categoria.

second-hand *adj* di seconda mano.

Second World War *n:* **the ~** la seconda guerra mondiale.

secret ['siːkrɪt] *adj* segreto(-a) ♦ *n* segreto *m*.

secretary [Br 'sekrətrɪ, Am sekrə'teri] *n* segretario *m* (-a *f*).

Secretary of State *n (Am: foreign minister)* segretario *m* di Stato; ≃ ministro *m* degli Esteri; *(Br: government minister)* ministro.

section ['sekʃn] *n* sezione *f*.

sector ['sektə*r*] *n* settore *m*.

secure [sɪ'kjʊə*r*] *adj (safe, protected)* sicuro(-a); *(firmly fixed)* saldamente assicurato(-a); *(free from worry)* tranquillo(-a) ♦ *vt (fix)* assicurare; *(fml: obtain)* assicurarsi.

security [sɪ'kjʊərətɪ] *n (protection)* sicurezza *f*; *(freedom from worry)* tranquillità *f*.

security guard *n* guardia *f* giurata.

sedative ['sedətɪv] *n* sedativo *m*.

seduce [sɪ'djuːs] *vt* sedurre.

see [siː] *(pt* saw, *pp* seen) *vt* vedere; *(accompany)* accompagnare ♦ *vi* vedere; **I ~** *(understand)* capisco; **to ~ if one can do sthg** vedere se si può fare qc; **to ~ to sthg** *(deal with)* occuparsi di qc; *(repair)* riparare qc; **~ you!** arrivederci!; **~ you later!** a più tardi!; **~ you soon!** a presto!; **~ p 14** vedi pag. 14 ❏ **see off** *sep (say goodbye to)* (andare a) salutare.

seed [siːd] *n* seme *m*.

seedy ['siːdɪ] *adj* squallido(-a).

seeing (as) ['siːɪŋ-] *conj* visto che.

seek [siːk] *(pt & pp* sought) *vt (fml) (look for)* cercare; *(request)* chiedere.

seem [siːm] *vi* sembrare ♦ *v impers:* **it ~s (that)** ... sembra (che) ...

seen [siːn] *pp* → **see**.

seesaw ['siːsɔː] *n* altalena *f*.

segment ['segmənt] *n (of fruit)* spicchio *m*.

seize [siːz] *vt (grab)* afferrare; *(drugs, arms)* sequestrare ❏ **seize up** *vi* bloccarsi.

seldom ['seldəm] *adv* raramente.

select [sɪ'lekt] vt scegliere ♦ adj selezionato(-a).

selection [sɪ'lekʃn] n selezione f.

self-assured [,selfə'ʃʊəd] adj sicuro(-a) di sé.

self-catering [,self'keɪtərɪŋ] adj (flat) con uso di cucina.

self-confident [,self-] adj sicuro(-a) di sé.

self-conscious [,self-] adj timido(-a).

self-contained [,selfkən'teɪnd] adj (flat) autosufficiente.

self-defence [,self-] n autodifesa f.

self-employed [,self-] adj che lavora in proprio.

selfish [ˈselfɪʃ] adj egoista.

self-raising flour [,self'reɪzɪŋ-] n (Br) farina f con lievito.

self-rising flour [,self'raɪzɪŋ-] (Am) = self-raising flour.

self-service [,self-] adj self-service (inv).

sell [sel] (pt & pp sold) vt & vi vendere; **to ~ for** essere venduto per; **to ~ sb sthg** vendere qc a qn.

sell-by date n data f di scadenza.

seller [ˈselər] n (person) venditore m (-trice f).

Sellotape® [ˈseləteɪp] n (Br) nastro m adesivo.

semester [sɪ'mestər] n semestre m.

semicircle [ˈsemɪ,sɜːkl] n semicerchio m.

semicolon [,semɪ'kəʊlən] n punto m e virgola.

semidetached [,semɪdɪ'tætʃt] adj bifamiliare.

semifinal [,semɪ'faɪnl] n semifinale f.

seminar [ˈsemɪnɑːr] n seminario m.

semolina [,semə'liːnə] n semolino m.

send [send] (pt & pp sent) vt (letter, parcel, goods) spedire, mandare; (person) mandare; (TV or radio signal) trasmettere; **to ~ sthg to sb** mandare qc a qn ❑ **send back** vt sep (faulty goods) rimandare; **send off** vt sep (letter, parcel) spedire; (SPORT) espellere ♦ vi: **to ~ off (for sthg)** ordinare (qc) per corrispondenza.

sender [ˈsendər] n mittente mf.

senile [ˈsiːnaɪl] adj senile.

senior [ˈsiːnjər] adj di grado superiore ♦ n (Br: SCH) studente m più grande; (Am: SCH) studente dell'ultimo anno di scuola superiore o università.

senior citizen n anziano m (-a f).

sensation [sen'seɪʃn] n sensazione f; **to cause a ~** fare colpo.

sensational [sen'seɪʃənl] adj (very good) fantastico(-a).

sense [sens] n senso m; (common sense) buonsenso m; (of word, expression) senso, significato m ♦ vt sentire, percepire; **to make ~** avere senso; **~ of direction** senso dell'orientamento; **~ of humour** senso dell'umorismo.

sensible [ˈsensəbl] adj (person) ragionevole, assennato(-a); (clothes, shoes) pratico(-a).

sensitive [ˈsensɪtɪv] adj sensibile; (subject, issue) delicato(-a).

sent [sent] pt & pp → send.

sentence [ˈsentəns] n (GRAMM) proposizione f; (for crime) sentenza f, condanna f ♦ vt condannare.

sentimental [,sentɪ'mentl] adj

(pej) sentimentale.

Sep. *(abbr of September)* set.

separate [*adj* 'seprət, *vb* 'sepəreɪt] *adj* separato(-a); *(different)* diverso(-a) ♦ *vt* separare ♦ *vi* separarsi ❑ **separates** *npl (Br)* coordinati *mpl*.

separately ['seprətlɪ] *adv* separatamente.

separation [ˌsepə'reɪʃn] *n* separazione *f*.

September [sep'tembəʳ] *n* settembre *m*; **at the beginning of ~** all'inizio di settembre; **at the end of ~** alla fine di settembre; **during ~** durante il mese di settembre; **every ~** ogni anno a settembre; **in ~** a settembre; **last ~** lo scorso settembre; **next ~** il prossimo settembre; **this ~** a settembre (di quest'anno); **2 ~ 1995** *(in letters etc)* 2 settembre 1995.

septic ['septɪk] *adj* infetto(-a).

septic tank *n* fossa *f* settica.

sequel ['siːkwəl] *n (to book, film)* seguito *m*.

sequence ['siːkwəns] *n (series)* serie *f inv; (order)* ordine *m*.

sequin ['siːkwɪn] *n* lustrino *m*, paillette *f inv*.

sergeant ['sɑːdʒənt] *n (in police force)* ≈ brigadiere *m; (in army)* sergente *m*.

serial ['sɪərɪəl] *n (on TV, radio)* sceneggiato *m*, serial *m inv; (in magazine)* romanzo *m* a puntate.

series ['sɪərɪːz] *(pl inv) n* serie *f inv*.

serious ['sɪərɪəs] *adj* serio(-a); *(illness, problem)* grave, serio; **are you ~?** dici sul serio?

seriously ['sɪərɪəslɪ] *adv (really)* seriamente; *(badly)* gravemente.

sermon ['sɜːmən] *n* sermone *m*.

servant ['sɜːvənt] *n* domestico *m* (-a *f*).

serve [sɜːv] *vt* servire ♦ *vi (SPORT)* servire; *(work)* prestare servizio ♦ *n (SPORT)* servizio *m*; **to ~ as** *(be used for)* servire da; **the town is ~d by two airports** la città è servita da due aeroporti; **'~s two'** *(on packaging, menu)* 'per due persone'; **it ~s you right!** ben ti sta!

service ['sɜːvɪs] *n* servizio *m; (at church)* rito *m; (of car)* revisione *f* ♦ *vt (car)* revisionare; **'out of ~'** 'fuori servizio'; **'~ included'** 'servizio incluso'; **'~ not included'** 'servizio escluso'; **to be of ~ to sb** *(fml)* essere d'aiuto a qn ❑ **services** *npl (on motorway)* stazione *f* di servizio; *(of person)* servigi *mpl*.

service area *n* area *f* di servizio.

service charge *n* servizio *m*.

service department *n* servizio *m* clienti.

service station *n* stazione *f* di servizio.

serviette [ˌsɜːvɪ'et] *n* tovagliolo *m*.

serving ['sɜːvɪŋ] *n (helping)* porzione *f*.

serving spoon *n* cucchiaio *m* da portata.

sesame seeds ['sesəmɪ-] *npl* semi *mpl* di sesamo.

session ['seʃn] *n* seduta *f*; **a drinking ~** una bevuta.

set [set] *(pt & pp set) adj* **1.** *(price, time)* fisso(-a); **a ~ lunch** un menu fisso.

2. *(text, book)* assegnato(-a).

3. *(situated)* situato(-a).

♦ *n* **1.** *(of tools etc)* serie *f inv; (of cutlery, dishes)* servizio *m*; **chess ~**

gioco *m* degli scacchi.

2. *(TV):* **a (TV)** ~ un apparecchio televisivo, un televisore.

3. *(in tennis)* set *m inv.*

4. *(of play)* scenario *m.*

5. *(at hairdresser's):* **a shampoo and** ~ uno shampoo e messa in piega.

♦ *vt* **1.** *(put)* mettere, posare; **to ~ the table** apparecchiare.

2. *(cause to be):* **to ~ a machine going** avviare una macchina; **to ~ fire to sthg** dar fuoco a qc.

3. *(clock, alarm, controls)* regolare; ~ **the alarm for 7 a.m.** metti la sveglia alle 7.

4. *(price, time)* fissare.

5. *(a record)* stabilire.

6. *(homework, essay)* dare.

7. *(play, film, story):* **to be ~** essere ambientato(-a).

♦ *vi* **1.** *(sun)* tramontare.

2. *(glue)* fare presa; *(jelly)* rapprendersi.

❑ **set down** *vt sep (Br: passengers)* far scendere; **set off** *vt sep (alarm)* far scattare ♦ *vi (on journey)* mettersi in viaggio; **set out** *vt sep (arrange)* disporre ♦ *vi (on journey)* mettersi in viaggio; **set up** *vt sep (barrier)* erigere; *(equipment)* installare.

set meal *n* menu *m inv* fisso.

set menu *n* menu *m inv* fisso.

settee [se'ti:] *n* divano *m.*

setting ['setɪŋ] *n (on machine)* posizione *f; (physical surroundings)* scenario *m; (atmosphere)* ambiente *m.*

settle ['setl] *vt (argument)* sistemare, appianare; *(bill)* saldare, regolare; *(stomach, nerves)* calmare; *(arrange, decide on)* stabilire, decidere ♦ *vi (start to live)* stabilirsi; *(come to rest)* posarsi; *(sediment, dust)* depositarsi ❑ **settle down** *vi*

(calm down) calmarsi; *(sit comfortably)* accomodarsi; **settle up** *vi (pay bill)* saldare il conto.

settlement ['setlmənt] *n (agreement)* accordo *m; (place)* insediamento *m.*

seven ['sevn] *num* sette, → **six.**

seventeen [,sevn'ti:n] *num* diciassette, → **six.**

seventeenth [,sevn'ti:nθ] *num* diciassettesimo(-a), → **sixth.**

seventh ['sevnθ] *num* settimo(-a), → **sixth.**

seventieth ['sevntjəθ] *num* settantesimo(-a), → **sixth.**

seventy ['sevntɪ] *num* settanta, → **six.**

several ['sevrəl] *adj & pron* parecchi(-chie), diversi(-e).

severe [sɪ'vɪəʳ] *adj (conditions, damage, illness)* grave; *(criticism, person, punishment)* severo(-a); *(pain)* violento(-a), forte.

sew [səʊ] *(pp sewn) vt & vi* cucire.

sewage ['su:ɪdʒ] *n* acque *fpl* di scarico.

sewing ['səʊɪŋ] *n (activity)* cucito *m; (things sewn)* lavoro *m.*

sewing machine *n* macchina *f* da cucire.

sewn [səʊn] *pp* → **sew.**

sex [seks] *n (gender)* sesso *m; (sexual intercourse)* rapporto *m* sessuale; **to have ~ (with)** avere rapporti sessuali (con).

sexist ['seksɪst] *n* sessista *mf.*

sexual ['sekʃʊəl] *adj* sessuale.

sexy ['seksɪ] *adj* sexy *(inv).*

shabby ['ʃæbɪ] *adj* trasandato(-a).

shade [ʃeɪd] *n (shadow)* ombra *f; (lampshade)* paralume *m; (of colour)* sfumatura f, tonalità f inv ◆ vt (protect) fare ombra a ☐ **shades** npl (inf: sunglasses) occhiali mpl da sole.

shadow ['ʃædəʊ] n ombra f.

shady ['ʃeɪdɪ] adj (place) ombroso(-a); (inf: person, deal) losco(-a).

shaft [ʃɑ:ft] n (of machine) albero m; (of lift) pozzo m.

shake [ʃeɪk] (pt shook, pp shaken ['ʃeɪkn]) vt (tree, rug, person) scuotere; (bottle, dice) agitare; (shock) scuotere, turbare ◆ vi tremare; to ~ hands (with sb) dare OR stringere la mano (a qn); to ~ one's head (saying no) scuotere la testa.

shall [weak form ʃəl, strong form ʃæl] aux vb 1. (expressing future): I ~ be ready soon sarò pronto tra poco.
2. (in questions): ~ I buy some wine? devo comprare del vino?; ~ we listen to the radio? vogliamo ascoltare la radio?; where ~ we go? dove andiamo?, dove vogliamo andare?
3. (fml: expressing order): payment ~ be made within a week il pagamento dovrà essere effettuato entro una settimana.

shallot [ʃə'lɒt] n scalogno m.

shallow ['ʃæləʊ] adj poco profondo(-a).

shallow end n (of swimming pool) lato m meno profondo.

shambles ['ʃæmblz] n macello m, casino m.

shame [ʃeɪm] n vergogna f; it's a ~ è un peccato; what a ~! che peccato!

shampoo [ʃæm'pu:] (pl -s) n shampoo m inv.

shandy ['ʃændɪ] n bevanda a base di birra e limonata.

shape [ʃeɪp] n forma f; to be in good/bad ~ essere in/fuori forma.

share [ʃeəʳ] n (part) parte f; (in company) azione f ◆ vt dividere ☐ **share out** vt sep dividere.

shark [ʃɑ:k] n squalo m, pescecane m.

sharp [ʃɑ:p] adj (knife, razor) affilato(-a); (pin, nails) appuntito(-a); (teeth) aguzzo(-a); (clear) nitido(-a); (quick, intelligent) acuto(-a), scaltro(-a); (rise, change, bend) brusco(-a); (painful) acuto, lancinante; (food, taste) aspro(-a) ◆ adv (exactly) in punto.

sharpen ['ʃɑ:pn] vt (pencil) temperare; (knife) affilare.

shatter ['ʃætəʳ] vt (break) frantumare ◆ vi frantumarsi.

shattered ['ʃætəd] adj (Br: inf: tired) distrutto(-a).

shave [ʃeɪv] vt radere, rasare ◆ vi radersi, rasarsi ◆ n: to have a ~ farsi la barba.

shaver ['ʃeɪvəʳ] n rasoio m elettrico.

shaver point n presa f per rasoio elettrico.

shaving brush ['ʃeɪvɪŋ-] n pennello m da barba.

shaving cream ['ʃeɪvɪŋ-] n crema f da barba.

shaving foam ['ʃeɪvɪŋ-] n schiuma f da barba.

shawl [ʃɔ:l] n scialle m.

she [ʃi:] pron lei; ~'s tall è alta.

sheaf [ʃi:f] (pl sheaves) n (of paper, notes) fascio m.

shears [ʃɪəz] npl cesoie fpl.

sheaves [ʃi:vz] pl → sheaf.

shed [ʃed] (pt & pp shed) n capanno m ◆ vt (tears, blood) versare.

she'd [*weak form* ʃɪd, *strong form* ʃiːd] = she had, she would.

sheep [ʃiːp] (*pl inv*) *n* pecora *f*.

sheepdog ['ʃiːpdɒg] *n* cane *m* pastore.

sheepskin ['ʃiːpskɪn] *adj* di pelle di pecora.

sheer [ʃɪəʳ] *adj* (*pure, utter*) puro(-a); (*cliff*) a picco, a strapiombo; (*stockings*) velato(-a).

sheet [ʃiːt] *n* (*for bed*) lenzuolo *m*; (*of paper*) foglio *m*; (*of glass, metal*) lastra *f*; (*of wood*) pannello *m*.

shelf [ʃelf] (*pl* **shelves**) *n* scaffale *m*.

shell [ʃel] *n* (*of egg, nut, animal*) guscio *m*; (*on beach*) conchiglia *f*; (*bomb*) granata *f*.

she'll [ʃiːl] = she will, she shall.

shellfish ['ʃelfɪʃ] *n* (*food*) frutti *mpl* di mare.

shell suit *n* (*Br*) tuta *f* in acetato.

shelter ['ʃeltəʳ] *n* riparo *m*, rifugio *m*; (*at bus stop*) pensilina *f* ◆ *vt* (*protect*) proteggere, riparare ◆ *vi* proteggersi, ripararsi; **to take ~** mettersi al riparo.

sheltered ['ʃeltəd] *adj* (*place*) riparato(-a).

shelves [ʃelvz] *pl* → shelf.

shepherd ['ʃepəd] *n* pastore *m*.

shepherd's pie ['ʃepədz-] *n* tortino a base di carne macinata coperta da uno spesso strato di purè di patate.

sheriff ['ʃerɪf] *n* (*in US*) sceriffo *m*.

sherry ['ʃerɪ] *n* sherry *m inv*.

she's [ʃiːz] = she is, she has.

shield [ʃiːld] *n* scudo *m* ◆ *vt* proteggere.

shift [ʃɪft] *n* (*change*) cambiamento *m*; (*period of work*) turno *m* ◆ *vt* spostare ◆ *vi* (*move*) spostarsi;

(*change*) mutare, cambiare.

shin [ʃɪn] *n* stinco *m*.

shine [ʃaɪn] (*pt & pp* **shone**) *vi* brillare, splendere ◆ *vt* (*shoes*) lucidare, lustrare; (*torch*) puntare.

shiny ['ʃaɪnɪ] *adj* scintillante, lucido(-a).

ship [ʃɪp] *n* nave *f*; **by ~** (*travel*) con la nave; (*send, transport*) via mare.

shipwreck ['ʃɪprek] *n* (*accident*) naufragio *m*; (*wrecked ship*) relitto *m*.

shirt [ʃɜːt] *n* camicia *f*.

shit [ʃɪt] *n* (*vulg*) merda *f* ◆ *excl* (*vulg*) merda!

shiver ['ʃɪvəʳ] *vi* rabbrividire.

shock [ʃɒk] *n* (*surprise*) shock *m inv*; (*force*) urto *m*, scossa *f* ◆ *vt* (*surprise*) colpire, scioccare; (*horrify*) scioccare; **to be in ~** (*MED*) essere sotto shock.

shock absorber [-əb,zɔːbəʳ] *n* ammortizzatore *m*.

shocking ['ʃɒkɪŋ] *adj* (*very bad*) terribile.

shoe [ʃuː] *n* scarpa *f*.

shoelace ['ʃuːleɪs] *n* stringa *f*.

shoe polish *n* lucido *m* da scarpe.

shoe repairer's [-rɪ,peərəz] *n* calzolaio *m*.

shoe shop *n* negozio *m* di calzature.

shone [ʃɒn] *pt & pp* → shine.

shook [ʃʊk] *pt* → shake.

shoot [ʃuːt] (*pt & pp* **shot**) *vt* (*kill, injure*) sparare a; (*gun*) sparare; (*arrow*) tirare, scoccare; (*film*) girare ◆ *vi* (*with gun*) sparare; (*move quickly*) sfrecciare; (*SPORT*) tirare ◆ *n* (*of plant*) germoglio *m*.

shop [ʃɒp] *n* negozio *m* ◆ *vi* fare acquisti.

shop assistant *n* (Br) commesso *m* (-a *f*).

shop floor *n* (place) area di una fabbrica dove lavorano gli operai.

shopkeeper ['ʃɒp,ki:pə'] *n* negoziante *mf*.

shoplifter ['ʃɒp,lɪftə'] *n* taccheggiatore *m* (-trice *f*).

shopper ['ʃɒpə'] *n* cliente *mf*, acquirente *mf*.

shopping ['ʃɒpɪŋ] *n* spesa *f*; **to do the ~** fare la spesa; **to go ~** andare a fare spese.

shopping bag *n* borsa *f* per la spesa.

shopping basket *n* sporta *f* per la spesa.

shopping centre *n* centro *m* commerciale.

shopping list *n* lista *f* della spesa.

shopping mall *n* centro *m* commerciale.

shop steward *n* rappresentante *mf* sindacale.

shop window *n* vetrina *f*.

shore [ʃɔ:'] *n* riva *f*; **on ~** a terra.

short [ʃɔ:t] *adj* (not tall) basso(-a); (letter, speech) corto(-a), breve; (hair, skirt) corto; (in time, distance) breve ◆ *adv* (cut hair) corti ◆ *n* (Br: drink) bicchierino *m*; (film) cortometraggio *m*; **to be ~ of sthg** (time, money) essere a corto di qc; **to be ~ for sthg** (be abbreviation of) essere l'abbreviazione di qc; **to be ~ of breath** essere senza fiato; **in ~** in breve ☐ **shorts** *npl* (short trousers) calzoncini *mpl*, pantaloncini *mpl*; (Am: underpants) boxer *mpl*.

shortage ['ʃɔ:tɪdʒ] *n* carenza *f*.

shortbread ['ʃɔ:tbred] *n* biscotto *m* di pasta frolla.

short-circuit *vi* fare cortocircuito.

shortcrust pastry ['ʃɔ:tkrʌst-] *n* pasta *f* frolla.

short cut *n* scorciatoia *f*.

shorten ['ʃɔ:tn] *vt* accorciare.

shorthand ['ʃɔ:thænd] *n* stenografia *f*.

shortly ['ʃɔ:tlɪ] *adv* (soon) presto, fra poco; **~ before** poco prima di.

shortsighted [,ʃɔ:t'saɪtɪd] *adj* miope.

short-sleeved [-,sli:vd] *adj* a maniche corte.

short-stay car park *n* parcheggio *m* a tempo limitato.

short story *n* racconto *m*, novella *f*.

short wave *n* onde *fpl* corte.

shot [ʃɒt] *pt* & *pp* → **shoot** ◆ *n* (of gun) sparo *m*; (in football, tennis, golf etc) tiro *m*; (photo) foto *f inv*; (in film) ripresa *f*; (inf: attempt) prova *f*, tentativo *m*; (drink) bicchierino *m*.

shotgun ['ʃɒtgʌn] *n* fucile *m* da caccia.

should [ʃʊd] *aux vb* 1. (expressing desirability): **we ~ leave now** ora dovremmo OR sarebbe meglio andare.

2. (asking for advice): **~ I go too?** devo andarci anch'io?

3. (expressing probability): **she ~ be home soon** dovrebbe arrivare a momenti.

4. (ought to): **they ~ have won the match** avrebbero dovuto vincere la partita.

5. (fml: in conditionals): **~ you need anything, call reception** se dovesse aver bisogno di qualcosa, chiami

la reception.

6. (fml: expressing wish): **I ~ like to come with you** mi piacerebbe venire con voi.

shoulder ['ʃəʊldəʳ] n spalla f; (Am: of road) corsia f d'emergenza.

shoulder pad n spallina f.

shouldn't ['ʃʊdnt] = **should not**.

should've ['ʃʊdəv] = **should have**.

shout [ʃaʊt] n grido m, urlo m ♦ vt & vi gridare, urlare ❏ **shout out** vt sep gridare.

shove [ʃʌv] vt (push) spingere; (put carelessly) ficcare, cacciare.

shovel ['ʃʌvl] n pala f.

show [ʃəʊ] (pp -ed OR shown) n (at theatre, on TV) spettacolo m; (on radio) programma m; (exhibition) mostra f ♦ vt mostrare; (represent, depict) raffigurare; (accompany) accompagnare; (film, TV programme) dare ♦ vi (be visible) vedersi, essere visibile; (film) essere in programmazione; **to ~ sthg to sb** mostrare qc a qn; **to ~ sb how to do sthg** mostrare a qn come fare qc ❏ **show off** vi mettersi in mostra; **show up** vi (come along) farsi vivo, arrivare; (be visible) risaltare.

shower ['ʃaʊəʳ] n (for washing) doccia f; (of rain) acquazzone m ♦ vi fare la doccia; **to have a ~** fare la doccia.

shower gel n gel m inv per la doccia.

shower unit n blocco m doccia.

showing ['ʃəʊɪŋ] n (of film) proiezione f.

shown [ʃəʊn] pp → **show**.

showroom ['ʃəʊrʊm] n salone m d'esposizione.

shrank [ʃræŋk] pt → **shrink**.

shrimp [ʃrɪmp] n gamberetto m.

shrine [ʃraɪn] n santuario m.

shrink [ʃrɪŋk] (pt **shrank**, pp **shrunk**) n (inf: psychoanalyst) strizzacervelli mf inv ♦ vi (clothes) restringersi; (number, amount) ridursi, diminuire.

shrub [ʃrʌb] n arbusto m.

shrug [ʃrʌg] n scrollata f di spalle ♦ vi scrollare le spalle.

shrunk [ʃrʌŋk] pp → **shrink**.

shuffle ['ʃʌfl] vt (cards) mischiare ♦ vi (walk) camminare strascicando i piedi.

shut [ʃʌt] (pt & pp **shut**) adj chiuso(-a) ♦ vt chiudere ♦ vi (door, mouth, eyes) chiudersi; (shop, restaurant) chiudere ❏ **shut down** vt sep chiudere i battenti; **shut up** vi (inf: stop talking) tacere, stare zitto; **~ up!** chiudi il becco!

shutter ['ʃʌtəʳ] n (on window) imposta f; (on camera) otturatore m.

shuttle ['ʃʌtl] n (plane, bus etc) navetta f.

shuttlecock ['ʃʌtlkɒk] n volano m.

shy [ʃaɪ] adj timido(-a).

Sicily ['sɪsɪlɪ] n la Sicilia.

sick [sɪk] adj (ill) malato(-a); **to be ~** (vomit) vomitare; **to feel ~** (nauseous) avere la nausea; **to be ~ of** (fed up with) essere stufo(-a) di.

sick bag n sacchetto di emergenza per viaggiatori che soffrono di nausea e vomito.

sickness ['sɪknɪs] n (illness) malattia f.

sick pay n indennità f per malattia.

side [saɪd] n lato m; (of road, pitch)

margine m; (of river) sponda f; (team) squadra f; (in argument) parte f; (Br: TV channel) canale m ◆ adj (door, pocket) laterale; **at the ~ of a** fianco di; (road) al margine di; (river) sulla riva di; **on the other ~** dall'altra parte; **on this ~** da questo lato; **~ by ~** fianco a fianco.

sideboard ['saɪdbɔːd] n credenza f.

sidecar ['saɪdkɑːʳ] n sidecar m inv.

side dish n contorno m.

side effect n effetto m collaterale.

sidelight ['saɪdlaɪt] n (Br: of car) luce f di posizione.

side order n contorno m.

side salad n insalata f di contorno.

side street n traversa f.

sidewalk ['saɪdwɔːk] n (Am) marciapiede m.

sideways ['saɪdweɪz] adv (move) di lato, di fianco; (look) di traverso.

sieve [sɪv] n setaccio m.

sigh [saɪ] n sospiro m ◆ vi sospirare.

sight [saɪt] n (eyesight) vista f; (thing seen) spettacolo m; **at first ~** a prima vista; **to catch ~ of** intravedere; **in ~** in vista; **to lose ~ of** perdere di vista; **to be out of ~** non essere visibile ❑ **sights** npl (of city, country) luoghi mpl di maggiore interesse.

sightseeing ['saɪt,siːɪŋ] n: **to go ~** fare un giro turistico.

sign [saɪn] n (in shop, station) insegna f; (next to road) segnale m, cartello m; (symbol, indication) segno m; (signal) segnale ◆ vt & vi firmare; **there's no ~ of her** non c'è traccia di lei ❑ **sign in** vi (at hotel, club)

firmare il registro (all'arrivo).

signal ['sɪgnl] n segnale m; (Am: traffic lights) semaforo m ◆ vi (in car, on bike) segnalare.

signature ['sɪgnətʃəʳ] n firma f.

significant [sɪg'nɪfɪkənt] adj (large) considerevole; (important) importante.

signpost ['saɪnpəʊst] n cartello m stradale.

sikh [siːk] n Sikh mf inv.

silence ['saɪləns] n silenzio m.

silencer ['saɪlənsəʳ] n (Br: AUT) marmitta f.

silent ['saɪlənt] adj silenzioso(-a).

silk [sɪlk] n seta f.

sill [sɪl] n davanzale m.

silly ['sɪlɪ] adj sciocco(-a), stupido(-a).

silver ['sɪlvəʳ] n (substance) argento m; (coins) monete fpl d'argento ◆ adj d'argento.

silver foil n stagnola f, carta f argentata.

silver-plated [-'pleɪtɪd] adj placcato(-a) d'argento.

similar ['sɪmɪləʳ] adj simile; **to be ~ to** essere simile a.

similarity [,sɪmɪ'lærətɪ] n (resemblance) somiglianza f; (similar point) affinità f inv.

simmer ['sɪməʳ] vi cuocere a fuoco lento.

simple ['sɪmpl] adj semplice.

simplify ['sɪmplɪfaɪ] vt semplificare.

simply ['sɪmplɪ] adv semplicemente.

simulate ['sɪmjʊleɪt] vt simulare.

simultaneous [Br ,sɪməl'teɪnjəs, Am ,saɪməl'teɪnjəs] adj simultaneo(-a).

simultaneously [Br ˌsɪməl-'teɪnjəslɪ, Am ˌsaɪməl'teɪnjəslɪ] adv simultaneamente.

sin [sɪn] n peccato m ◆ vi peccare.

since [sɪns] adv da allora ◆ prep da ◆ conj (in time) da quando, da che; (as) dato che, poiché; **ever ~** prep fin da ◆ conj da che, fin da quando.

sincere [sɪn'sɪəʳ] adj sincero(-a).

sincerely [sɪn'sɪəlɪ] adv sincera-mente; **Yours ~** Distinti saluti.

sing [sɪŋ] (pt sang, pp sung) vt & vi cantare.

singer [ˈsɪŋəʳ] n cantante mf.

single [ˈsɪŋgl] adj solo(-a); (man) celibe; (woman) nubile ◆ n (Br: tick-et) biglietto m di sola andata; (record) 45 giri m inv; **every ~** ogni □ **singles** n (SPORT) singolo m ◆ adj (bar, club) per single.

single bed n letto m a una piaz-za.

single cream n (Br) panna f liquida.

single parent n genitore m single.

single room n camera f singo-la.

single track road n strada f a una carreggiata.

singular [ˈsɪŋgjʊləʳ] n singolare m; **in the ~** al singolare.

sinister [ˈsɪnɪstəʳ] adj sinistro(-a).

sink [sɪŋk] (pt sank, pp sunk) n lavandino m ◆ vi (in water, mud) affondare; (decrease) calare, dimi-nuire.

sink unit n blocco m lavello.

sinuses [ˈsaɪnəsɪz] npl seni mpl paranasali.

sip [sɪp] n sorso m ◆ vt sorseg-giare.

siphon [ˈsaɪfn] n sifone m ◆ v travasare.

sir [sɜːʳ] n signore m; **Dear Sir** Egregio Signore; **Sir Richard Blair** Sir Richard Blair.

siren [ˈsaɪərən] n sirena f.

sirloin steak [ˌsɜːlɔɪn-] n bistec-ca f di lombo.

sister [ˈsɪstəʳ] n sorella f; (Br: nurse) caposala f.

sister-in-law n cognata f.

sit [sɪt] (pt & pp sat) vi sedere; (be situated) trovarsi ◆ vt (to place) far sedere; (Br: exam) sostenere, dare; **to be sitting** essere seduto □ **sit down** vi sedersi; **to be sitting down** essere seduto; **sit up** vi (after lying down) tirarsi su a sedere; (stay up late) stare in piedi fino a tardi.

site [saɪt] n luogo m; (building site) cantiere m.

sitting room [ˈsɪtɪŋ-] n salotto m.

situated [ˈsɪtjʊeɪtɪd] adj: **to be ~** essere situato(-a).

situation [ˌsɪtjʊ'eɪʃn] n (state of affairs) situazione f; (fml: location) ubicazione f; **'~s vacant'** 'offerte di lavoro'.

six [sɪks] num adj & n sei; **to be ~ (years old)** avere sei anni; **it's ~** (o'clock) sono le sei; **a hundred and ~** centosei; **~ Hill Street** Hill Street (numero) sei; **it's minus ~ (degrees)** è meno sei.

sixteen [sɪks'tiːn] num sedici, → six.

sixteenth [sɪks'tiːnθ] num sedi-cesimo(-a), → sixth.

sixth [sɪksθ] num adj, adv & pron sesto(-a) ◆ num n sesto m; **the ~ (of September)** il sei (di settembre).

sixth form n (Br) ultimi due anni

facoltativi della scuola superiore.

sixth-form college *n (Br)* istituto *che prepara agli esami dell'ultimo anno di scuola superiore.*

sixtieth ['sɪkstɪəθ] *num* sessantesimo(-a), → **sixth**.

sixty ['sɪkstɪ] *num* sessanta, → **six**.

size [saɪz] *n* dimensioni *fpl*; *(of clothes, hats)* taglia *f*, misura *f*; *(of shoes)* numero *m*; **what ~ do you take?** che taglia porta?; **what ~ is this?** che taglia è?

sizeable ['saɪzəbl] *adj* notevole.

skate [skeɪt] *n (ice skate, roller skate)* pattino *m*; *(fish: pl inv)* razza *f* ♦ *vi* pattinare.

skateboard ['skeɪtbɔːd] *n* skateboard *m inv*.

skater ['skeɪtə'] *n* pattinatore *m* (-trice *f*).

skating ['skeɪtɪŋ] *n*: **to go ~** andare a pattinare.

skeleton ['skelɪtn] *n* scheletro *m*.

skeptical ['skeptɪkl] *(Am)* = **sceptical**.

sketch [sketʃ] *n (drawing)* schizzo *m*; *(humorous)* sketch *m inv*, scenetta *f* ♦ *vt* schizzare.

skewer ['skjʊə'] *n* spiedo *m*.

ski [skiː] *(pt & pp* **skied**, *cont* **skiing)** *n* sci *m inv* ♦ *vi* sciare.

ski boots *npl* scarponi *mpl* da sci.

skid [skɪd] *n* slittamento *m*, sbandamento *m* ♦ *vi* slittare, sbandare.

skier ['skiːə'] *n* sciatore *m* (-trice *f*).

skiing ['skiːɪŋ] *n* sci *m*; **to go ~** andare a sciare; **a ~ holiday** una vacanza sulla neve.

skilful ['skɪlfʊl] *adj (Br)* abile.

ski lift *n* sciovia *f*.

skill [skɪl] *n (ability)* abilità *f inv*; *(technique)* tecnica *f*.

skilled [skɪld] *adj (worker, job)* qualificato(-a); *(driver, chef)* provetto(-a).

skillful ['skɪlfʊl] *(Am)* = **skilful**.

skimmed milk ['skɪmd-] *n* latte *m* scremato.

skin [skɪn] *n* pelle *f*; *(on fruit, vegetable)* buccia *f*; *(on milk)* pellicola *f* tonico *m*.

skin freshener [-ˌfreʃnə'] *n* tonico *m*.

skinny ['skɪnɪ] *adj* magrissimo(-a).

skip [skɪp] *vi (with rope)* saltare la corda; *(jump)* saltellare ♦ *vt (omit)* saltare ♦ *n (container)* cassonetto *m*.

ski pants *npl* pantaloni *mpl* da sci.

ski pass *n* ski-pass *m inv*.

ski pole *n* racchetta *f* da sci.

skipping rope ['skɪpɪŋ-] *n* corda *f* per saltare.

skirt [skɜːt] *n* gonna *f*.

ski slope *n* pista *f* da sci.

ski tow *n* ski-lift *m inv*.

skittles ['skɪtlz] *n* birilli *mpl*.

skull [skʌl] *n* cranio *m*.

sky [skaɪ] *n* cielo *m*.

skylight ['skaɪlaɪt] *n* lucernario *m*.

skyscraper ['skaɪˌskreɪpə'] *n* grattacielo *m*.

slab [slæb] *n (of stone, concrete)* lastra *f*.

slack [slæk] *adj (rope)* non tirato(-a); *(careless)* negligente; *(not busy)* calmo(-a); *(period)* morto(-a).

slacks [slæks] *npl* pantaloni *mpl*.

slam [slæm] *vt & vi* sbattere.

slander ['slɑːndə'] *n* calunnia *f*; *(in law)* diffamazione *f*.

slang [slæŋ] n slang m, gergo m.

slant [slɑːnt] n (slope) pendenza f ♦ vi pendere.

slap [slæp] n (smack) schiaffo m ♦ vt schiaffeggiare.

slash [slæʃ] vt (cut) tagliare; (face) sfregiare; (fig: prices) ridurre ♦ n (written symbol) barra f.

slate [sleɪt] n (rock) ardesia f; (on roof) tegola f di ardesia.

slaughter ['slɔːtəʳ] vt (people, team) massacrare; (animal) macellare.

slave [sleɪv] n schiavo m (-a f).

sled [sled] = sledge.

sledge [sledʒ] n slitta f.

sleep [sliːp] (pt & pp slept) n sonno m ♦ vi dormire ♦ vt: the house ~s six la casa ha sei posti letto; did you ~ well? hai dormito bene?; I couldn't get to ~ non riuscivo a prender sonno; to go to ~ addormentarsi; to ~ with sb andare a letto con qn.

sleeper ['sliːpəʳ] n (train) treno m con vagoni letto; (sleeping car) vagone m letto; (Br: on railway track) traversina f; (Br: earring) campanella f.

sleeping bag ['sliːpɪŋ-] n sacco m a pelo.

sleeping car ['sliːpɪŋ-] n vagone m letto.

sleeping pill ['sliːpɪŋ-] n sonnifero m.

sleeping policeman ['sliːpɪŋ-] n (Br) piccolo dosso stradale che ha la funzione di rallentare il traffico.

sleepy ['sliːpɪ] adj insonnolito(-a); I'm ~ ho sonno.

sleet [sliːt] n nevischio m ♦ v impers: it's ~ing sta nevischiando.

sleeve [sliːv] n (of garment) manica f; (of record) copertina f.

sleeveless ['sliːvlɪs] adj senza maniche.

slept [slept] pt & pp → sleep.

slice [slaɪs] n fetta f ♦ vt affettare, tagliare a fette.

sliced bread [,slaɪst-] n pane m a cassetta.

slide [slaɪd] (pt & pp slid [slɪd]) n (in playground) scivolo m; (of photograph) diapositiva f; (Br: hair slide) fermacapelli m inv ♦ vi (slip) scivolare.

sliding door [,slaɪdɪŋ-] n porta f scorrevole.

slight [slaɪt] adj (minor) lieve; the ~est il minimo (la minima); not in the ~est niente affatto.

slightly ['slaɪtlɪ] adv (a bit) leggermente; I know him ~ lo conosco appena.

slim [slɪm] adj (person, waist) snello(-a) ♦ vi dimagrire.

slimming ['slɪmɪŋ] n dimagrimento m.

sling [slɪŋ] (pt & pp slung) vt (inf: throw) buttare ♦ n: to have one's arm in a ~ portare il braccio al collo.

slip [slɪp] vi scivolare ♦ n (mistake) errore m; (of paper) foglietto m; (petticoat) sottoveste f □ slip up vi (make a mistake) fare un errore.

slipper ['slɪpəʳ] n pantofola f.

slippery ['slɪpərɪ] adj scivoloso(-a).

slip road n (Br) raccordo m autostradale.

slit [slɪt] n fessura f.

slob [slɒb] n (inf) sciattone m (-a f).

slogan ['sləʊgən] n slogan m inv.

slope [sləʊp] n (incline) pendio m; (hill) fianco m; (for skiing) pista f da sci ◆ vi (hill, path) scendere; (floor, roof, shelf) essere inclinato.

sloping ['sləʊpɪŋ] adj (floor, roof, shelf) inclinato(-a); (hill) degradante.

slot [slɒt] n (for coin) fessura f; (groove) scanalatura f.

slot machine n (vending machine) distributore m automatico; (for gambling) slot-machine f inv.

Slovakia [sləˈvækɪə] n la Slovacchia.

slow [sləʊ] adj lento(-a); (business) fiacco(-a) ◆ adv lentamente; 'slow' (sign on road) 'rallentare'; a ~ train un accelerato; to be ~ (clock) essere indietro ❑ **slow down** vt sep & vi rallentare.

slowly ['sləʊlɪ] adv lentamente.

slug [slʌg] n (animal) lumaca f.

slum [slʌm] n (building) baracca f ❑ **slums** npl (district) bassifondi mpl.

slung [slʌŋ] pt & pp → **sling**.

slush [slʌʃ] n neve f in parte sciolta.

sly [slaɪ] adj (cunning) astuto(-a); (deceitful) scaltro(-a).

smack [smæk] n (slap) schiaffo m ◆ vt schiaffeggiare.

small [smɔːl] adj piccolo(-a); (in height) basso(-a).

small change n spiccioli mpl.

smallpox ['smɔːlpɒks] n vaiolo m.

smart [smɑːt] adj (elegant, posh) elegante; (clever) intelligente.

smart card n carta f intelligente.

smash [smæʃ] n (SPORT) smash m inv, schiacciata f; (inf: car crash) scontro m ◆ vt (plate, window) frantumare ◆ vi (plate, vase etc) frantumarsi.

smashing ['smæʃɪŋ] adj (Br: inf) fantastico(-a).

smear test ['smɪə-] n striscio m, pap-test m inv.

smell [smel] (pt & pp **-ed** OR **smelt**) n odore m; (bad odour) puzza f ◆ vt (sniff at) annusare; (detect) sentire odore di ◆ vi avere un odore; (have bad odour) puzzare; to ~ of sthg (pleasant) profumare di qc; (unpleasant) puzzare di qc.

smelly ['smelɪ] adj puzzolente.

smelt [smelt] pt & pp → **smell**.

smile [smaɪl] n sorriso m ◆ vi sorridere.

smoke [sməʊk] n fumo m ◆ vt & vi fumare; to have a ~ fumare una sigaretta.

smoked [sməʊkt] adj affumicato(-a).

smoked salmon n salmone m affumicato.

smoker ['sməʊkə[r]] n (person) fumatore m (-trice f).

smoking ['sməʊkɪŋ] n fumo m; 'no ~' 'vietato fumare'.

smoking area n area f per fumatori.

smoking compartment n scompartimento m per fumatori.

smoky ['sməʊkɪ] adj (room) fumoso(-a).

smooth [smuːð] adj (surface, skin, road) liscio(-a); (takeoff, landing) dolce, morbido(-a); (flight, journey, life) tranquillo(-a); (mixture, liquid) vellutato(-a), omogeneo(-a); (wine, beer) amabile; (pej: suave) mellifluo(-a) ❑ **smooth down** vt sep lisciare.

smother ['smʌðəʳ] vt (cover) coprire.

smudge [smʌdʒ] n sbavatura f.

smuggle ['smʌgl] vt contrabbandare.

snack [snæk] n spuntino m, snack m inv.

snack bar n snack-bar m inv, tavola f calda.

snail [sneɪl] n chiocciola f.

snake [sneɪk] n (animal) serpente m.

snap [snæp] vt (break) spezzare ◆ vi (break) spezzarsi ◆ n (inf: photo) foto f inv; (Br: card game) rubamazzo m.

snare [sneəʳ] n (trap) trappola f.

snatch [snætʃ] vt strappare.

sneakers ['sni:kəz] npl (Am) scarpe fpl da ginnastica.

sneeze [sni:z] n starnuto m ◆ vi starnutire.

sniff [snɪf] vi tirar su col naso ◆ vt (smell) annusare.

snip [snɪp] vt tagliare.

snob [snɒb] n snob mf inv.

snog [snɒg] vi (Br: inf) pomiciare.

snooker ['snu:kəʳ] n snooker m (specie di biliardo giocato con 22 palle).

snooze [snu:z] n pisolino m.

snore [snɔ:ʳ] vi russare.

snorkel ['snɔ:kl] n respiratore m (subacqueo).

snout [snaʊt] n muso m, grugno m.

snow [snəʊ] n neve f ◆ v impers: it's ~ing sta nevicando.

snowball ['snəʊbɔ:l] n palla f di neve.

snowdrift ['snəʊdrɪft] n cumulo m di neve.

snowflake ['snəʊfleɪk] n fiocco m di neve.

snowman ['snəʊmæn] (pl -men [-men]) n pupazzo m di neve.

snowplough ['snəʊplaʊ] n spazzaneve m inv.

snowstorm ['snəʊstɔ:m] n bufera f di neve.

snug [snʌg] adj (person) comodo(-a); (place) accogliente.

so [səʊ] adv 1. (emphasizing degree) così, talmente; it's ~ difficult (that ...) è così difficile (che ...). 2. (referring back): I don't think ~ credo di no; I'm afraid ~ temo proprio di sì; if ~ se è così, in tal caso. 3. (also): ~ do I anch'io. 4. (in this way) così, in questo modo. 5. (expressing agreement): ~ there is proprio così, già. 6. (in phrases): or ~ all'incirca; ~ as per, così da; ~ that affinché, perché.
◆ conj 1. (therefore) quindi, perciò; nobody answered ~ we went away non rispondeva nessuno perciò ce ne siamo andati. 2. (summarizing) allora; ~ what have you been up to? allora come vanno le cose? 3. (in phrases): ~ what? (inf) e allora?; ~ there! (inf) ecco!

soak [səʊk] vt (leave in water) mettere a bagno OR a mollo; (make very wet) impregnare, infradiciare ◆ vi: to ~ through sthg infiltrarsi in qc □ **soak up** vt sep assorbire.

soaked [səʊkt] adj fradicio(-a).

soaking ['səʊkɪŋ] adj fradicio(-a).

soap [səʊp] n sapone m.

soap opera n soap opera f inv,

telenovela f.

soap powder n detersivo m in polvere.

sob [sɒb] n singhiozzo m ♦ vi singhiozzare.

sober ['səubər] adj (not drunk) sobrio(-a).

soccer ['sɒkər] n calcio m.

sociable ['səuʃəbl] adj socievole.

social ['səuʃl] adj (problem, conditions, class) sociale.

social club n circolo m sociale.

socialist ['səuʃəlɪst] adj socialista ♦ n socialista mf.

social life n vita f sociale.

social security n previdenza f sociale.

social worker n assistente mf sociale.

society [sə'saɪətɪ] n società f inv; (organization, club) associazione f, società.

sociology [ˌsəusɪ'ɒlədʒɪ] n sociologia f.

sock [sɒk] n calzino m.

socket ['sɒkɪt] n (for plug) presa f; (for light bulb) portalampada m inv.

sod [sɒd] n (Br: vulg: nasty person) stronzo m (-a f).

soda ['səudə] n (soda water) seltz m inv; (Am: fizzy drink) spuma f.

soda water n acqua f di seltz.

sofa ['səufə] n divano m, sofà m inv.

sofa bed n divano m letto.

soft [sɒft] adj (bed, ground, skin) soffice, morbido(-a); (breeze, tap, sound) leggero(-a).

soft cheese n formaggio m molle.

soft drink n analcolico m.

software ['sɒftweər] n software m inv.

soil [sɔɪl] n (earth) suolo m.

solarium [sə'leərɪəm] n solarium m inv.

solar panel ['səulə-] n pannello m solare.

sold [səuld] pt & pp → sell.

soldier ['səuldʒər] n soldato m, militare m.

sold out adj esaurito(-a).

sole [səul] adj (only) solo(-a), unico(-a); (exclusive) esclusivo(-a) ♦ n (of shoe) suola f, (of foot) pianta f; (fish: pl inv) sogliola f.

solemn ['sɒləm] adj (person) serio(-a); (occasion) solenne.

solicitor [sə'lɪsɪtər] n (Br) = notaio m.

solid ['sɒlɪd] adj solido(-a); (not hollow) pieno(-a); (gold, silver, oak) massiccio(-a); (uninterrupted) ininterrotto(-a); **three hours ~** tre ore intere.

solo ['səuləu] (pl -s) n assolo m; '**~ m/cs**' (traffic sign) 'riservato ai motocicli'.

soluble ['sɒljubl] adj solubile.

solution [sə'luːʃn] n soluzione f.

solve [sɒlv] vt risolvere.

some [sʌm] adj 1. (certain amount of): ~ **meat** della carne; ~ **money** del denaro; **I had ~ difficulty getting here** ho avuto qualche difficoltà ad arrivare qui.

2. (certain number of): ~ **sweets** delle caramelle; ~ **boys** dei ragazzi; ~ **people** della gente; **I've known him for ~ years** lo conosco da anni.

3. (not all) certi(-e); ~ **jobs are better paid than others** certi lavori sono pagati meglio di altri.

4. (in imprecise statements): **she married ~ writer (or other)** ha sposato

un certo scrittore; **they're staying in ~ posh hotel** stanno in un albergo di lusso.
♦ *pron* 1. *(certain amount)* un po'; **can I have ~?** me ne dai un po'?; **~ of the money** una parte dei soldi. 2. *(certain number)* alcuni(-e), certi(-e); **can I have ~?** me ne dai qualcuno?; **~ (of them) left early** alcuni (di loro) sono andati via presto.
♦ *adv (approximately)* circa; **there were ~ 7,000 people** there c'erano circa 7 000 persone.

somebody ['sʌmbədɪ] = **someone**.

somehow ['sʌmhaʊ] *adv (some way or other)* in qualche modo, in un modo o nell'altro; *(for some reason)* per qualche motivo.

someone ['sʌmwʌn] *pron* qualcuno.

someplace ['sʌmpleɪs] *(Am)* = **somewhere**.

somersault ['sʌməsɔːlt] *n* capriola *f*, salto *m* mortale.

something ['sʌmθɪn] *pron* qualcosa; **it's really ~** è veramente eccezionale; **or ~** *(inf)* o qualcosa del genere; **~ like** all'incirca, pressappoco.

sometime ['sʌmtaɪm] *adv*: **~ in May** in maggio.

sometimes ['sʌmtaɪmz] *adv* a volte.

somewhere ['sʌmweəʳ] *adv (in or to unspecified place)* da qualche parte, in qualche posto; *(approximately)* all'incirca.

son [sʌn] *n* figlio *m*.

song [sɒn] *n* canzone *f*.

son-in-law *n* genero *m*.

soon [suːn] *adv* presto; **how ~ can**

you do it? fra quanto può farlo?; **~ as (non)** appena; **as ~ as possible** al più presto possibile; **~ after** poco dopo; **~er or later** prima o poi.

soot [sʊt] *n* fuliggine *f*.

soothe [suːð] *vt* calmare; *(pain)* alleviare.

sophisticated [sə'fɪstɪkeɪtɪd] *adj (refined, chic)* sofisticato(-a), raffinato(-a); *(complex)* sofisticato, complesso(-a).

sorbet ['sɔːbeɪ] *n* sorbetto *m*.

sore [sɔːʳ] *adj (painful)* dolorante; *(Am: inf: angry)* incavolato(-a) ♦ *n* piaga *f*; **to have a ~ throat** avere mal di gola.

sorry ['sɒrɪ] *adj*: **I'm ~!** scusa!; **I'm ~ I'm late** scusa il ritardo; **~?** *(asking for repetition)* scusa?; **to feel ~ for sb** dispiacersi per qn; **I'm ~ you can't come** mi dispiace che tu non venga; **I'm ~ about the mess** scusa il disordine.

sort [sɔːt] *n* tipo *m* ♦ *vt* ordinare; **~ of** *(more or less)* più o meno; **it's ~ of difficult** è piuttosto difficile □ **sort out** *vt sep (classify)* ordinare; *(resolve)* chiarire.

so-so *adj & adv (inf)* così così.

soufflé ['suːfleɪ] *n* soufflé *m inv*.

sought [sɔːt] *pt & pp* → **seek**.

soul [səʊl] *n (spirit)* anima *f*; *(soul music)* musica *f* soul.

sound [saʊnd] *n* suono *m*; *(noise)* rumore *m*; *(volume)* volume *m* ♦ *vt (horn, bell)* suonare ♦ *vi (alarm, bell, voice)* suonare; *(seem to be)* sembrare ♦ *adj (building, structure)* solido(-a); *(heart)* sano(-a); *(advice, idea)* valido(-a); **to ~ like** sembrare; *(seem to be)* sembrare, avere l'aria di.

soundproof ['saʊndpruːf] *adj*

insonorizzato(-a).

soup [su:p] *n* zuppa *f*, minestra *f*.

soup spoon *n* cucchiaio *m* da minestra.

sour ['savə^r] *adj (taste)* aspro(-a); *(milk)* acido(-a); **to go ~** inacidire.

source [sɔ:s] *n (supply, origin)* fonte *f*; *(cause)* causa *f*; *(of river)* sorgente *f*.

sour cream *n* panna *f* acida.

south [sauθ] *n* sud *m*, meridione *m* ◆ *adj* del sud ◆ *adv (fly, walk)* verso sud; *(be situated)* a sud; **in the ~ of England** nel sud dell'Inghilterra.

South Africa *n* il Sudafrica.

South America *n* l'America *f* del sud, il Sudamerica.

southbound ['sauθbaund] *adj* diretto(-a) a sud.

southeast [,sauθ'i:st] *n* sud-est *m*.

southern ['sʌðən] *adj* meridionale, del sud.

South Pole *n* Polo *m* Sud.

southwards ['sauθwədz] *adv* verso sud.

southwest [,sauθ'west] *n* sud-ovest *m*.

souvenir [,su:və'nıə^r] *n* souvenir *m inv*, ricordo *m*.

Soviet Union [,səuvıət-] *n*: **the ~** l'Unione *f* Sovietica.

sow[1] [sau] *(pp* **sown** [səun]) *vt (seeds)* seminare.

sow[2] [sau] *n (pig)* scrofa *f*.

soya ['sɔɪə] *n* soia *f*.

soya bean *n* seme *m* di soia.

soy sauce [,sɔɪ-] *n* salsa *f* di soia.

spa [spa:] *n* terme *fpl*.

space [speıs] *n* spazio *m*; *(empty place)* posto *m*; *(room)* spazio, posto; *(period)* periodo *m* ◆ *vt* distanziare.

spaceship ['speısʃıp] *n* astronave *f*.

space shuttle *n* shuttle *m inv*.

spacious ['speıʃəs] *adj* spazioso(-a).

spade [speıd] *n (tool)* vanga *f*, badile *m* ❑ **spades** *npl (in cards)* picche *fpl*.

spaghetti [spə'getı] *n* spaghetti *mpl*.

Spain [speın] *n* la Spagna.

span [spæn] *pt* → **spin** ◆ *n (of time)* periodo *m*, arco *m* di tempo.

Spaniard ['spænjəd] *n* spagnolo *m* (-a *f*).

spaniel ['spænjəl] *n* spaniel *m inv*.

Spanish ['spænıʃ] *adj* spagnolo(-a); *(language)* spagnolo *m*.

spank [spæŋk] *vt* sculacciare.

spanner ['spænə^r] *n* chiave *f (arnese)*.

spare [speə^r] *adj (kept in reserve)* di riserva; *(not in use)* in più ◆ *n (spare part)* ricambio *m*; *(spare wheel)* ruota *f* di scorta ◆ *vt*: **to ~ sb sthg** *(money)* dare qc a qn; **can you ~ me ten minutes?** hai dieci minuti?; **with ten minutes to ~** con dieci minuti di anticipo.

spare part *n* pezzo *m* di ricambio.

spare ribs *npl* costine *fpl* di maiale.

spare room *n* camera *f* degli ospiti.

spare time *n* tempo *m* libero.

spare wheel *n* ruota *f* di scorta.

spark [spa:k] *n* scintilla *f*.

sparkling ['spa:klıŋ-] *adj (mineral water, soft drink)* frizzante.

sparkling wine *n* vino *m* frizzante.

spark plug n candela f.

sparrow ['spærəʊ] n passero m.

spat [spæt] pt & pp → spit.

speak [spi:k] (pt **spoke**, pp **spoken**) vt (language) parlare; (say) dire ◆ vi parlare; **who's ~ing?** (on phone) chi parla?; **can I ~ to Sarah? - ~ing!** (on phone) posso parlare con Sarah? - sono io!; **to ~ to sb about sthg** parlare a qn di qc ❑ **speak up** vi (more loudly) parlare più forte.

speaker ['spi:kəʳ] n (at conference) oratore m (-trice f); (loudspeaker, of stereo) altoparlante m; **an English ~** una persona che parla inglese.

spear [spɪəʳ] n lancia f.

special ['speʃl] adj speciale ◆ n: **'today's ~'** 'piatto del giorno'.

special delivery n (Br) = espresso m.

special effects npl effetti mpl speciali.

specialist ['speʃəlɪst] n (doctor) specialista mf.

speciality [,speʃɪ'ælətɪ] n specialità f inv.

specialize ['speʃəlaɪz] vi: **to ~ (in)** specializzarsi (in).

specially ['speʃəlɪ] adv (specifically) specialmente; (on purpose) appositamente; (particularly) particolarmente.

special offer n offerta f speciale.

special school n (Br) = scuola f speciale.

specialty ['speʃltɪ] (Am) = **speciality**.

species ['spi:ʃi:z] n specie f inv.

specific [spə'sɪfɪk] adj (particular) specifico(-a).

specification [,spesɪfɪ'keɪʃn] n

(of machine, car) caratteristiche fpl tecniche.

specimen ['spesɪmən] n (MED) campione m; (example) esemplare m.

specs [speks] npl (inf) occhiali mpl.

spectacle ['spektəkl] n (sight) scena f.

spectacles ['spektəklz] npl occhiali mpl.

spectacular [spek'tækjʊləʳ] adj spettacolare.

spectator [spek'teɪtəʳ] n spettatore m (-trice f).

sped [sped] pt & pp → **speed**.

speech [spi:tʃ] n (ability to speak) parola f; (manner of speaking) modo m di parlare; (talk) discorso m.

speech impediment [-ɪm,pedɪmənt] n difetto m di pronuncia.

speed [spi:d] (pt & pp **-ed** OR **sped**) n velocità f inv; (fast rate) alta velocità; (of film) sensibilità f inv; (bicycle gear) marcia f ◆ vi (move quickly) andare velocemente; (drive too fast) andare a velocità eccessiva; **'reduce ~ now'** 'rallentare' ❑ **speed up** vi accelerare.

speedboat ['spi:dbəʊt] n fuoribordo m inv.

speeding ['spi:dɪŋ] n eccesso m di velocità.

speed limit n limite m di velocità.

speedometer [spɪ'dɒmɪtəʳ] n tachimetro m.

spell [spel] (Br pt & pp **-ed** OR **spelt**, Am pt & pp **-ed**) vt (word, name) scrivere; (subj: letters) formare la parola ◆ n (period) periodo m; (magic) incantesimo m.

spelling ['spelɪŋ] n (correct order) ortografia f.

spelt [spelt] *pt & pp (Br)* → **spell**.

spend [spend] (*pt & pp* **spent** [spent]) *vt (money)* spendere; *(time)* passare.

sphere [sfɪəʳ] *n* sfera *f*.

spice [spaɪs] *n* spezia *f* ♦ *vt* condire con delle spezie.

spicy [ˈspaɪsɪ] *adj* piccante.

spider [ˈspaɪdəʳ] *n* ragno *m*.

spider's web *n* ragnatela *f*.

spike [spaɪk] *n (metal)* punta *f*.

spill [spɪl] (*Br pt & pp* -ed OR **spilt**, *Am pt & pp* -ed) *vt* versare ♦ *vi* versarsi.

spin [spɪn] (*pt* span OR spun, *pp* spun) *vt (wheel)* far girare; *(washing)* centrifugare ♦ *n (on ball)* effetto *m*; **to go for a ~** *(inf)* andare a fare un giro in macchina.

spinach [ˈspɪnɪdʒ] *n* spinaci *mpl*.

spine [spaɪn] *n* spina *f* dorsale; *(of book)* costa *f*.

spinster [ˈspɪnstəʳ] *n* zitella *f*.

spiral [ˈspaɪərəl] *n* spirale *f*.

spiral staircase *n* scala *f* a chiocciola.

spire [spaɪəʳ] *n* guglia *f*.

spirit [ˈspɪrɪt] *n* spirito *m*; *(mood)* umore *m* ♦ **spirits** *npl (Br: alcohol)* superalcolici *mpl*.

spit [spɪt] (*Br pt & pp* spat, *Am pt & pp* spit) *vi (person)* sputare; *(fire, food)* scoppiettare ♦ *n (saliva)* saliva *f*; *(for cooking)* spiedo *m* ♦ *v impers*: **it's spitting** pioviggina.

spite [spaɪt] : **in spite of** *prep* nonostante.

spiteful [ˈspaɪtful] *adj* malevolo(-a).

splash [splæʃ] *n (sound)* tonfo *m* ♦ *vt* schizzare.

splendid [ˈsplendɪd] *adj* splen-

dido(-a).

splint [splɪnt] *n* stecca *f*.

splinter [ˈsplɪntəʳ] *n* scheggia *f*.

split [splɪt] (*pt & pp* split) *n (tear)* strappo *m*; *(crack, in skirt)* spacco *m* ♦ *vt (wood, stone)* spaccare; *(tear)* strappare; *(bill, cost, profits, work)* dividere ♦ *vi (wood, stone)* spaccarsi; *(tear)* strapparsi ◻ **split up** *vi (couple)* lasciarsi; *(group)* dividersi.

spoil [spɔɪl] (*pt & pp* -ed OR **spoilt**) *vt (ruin)* rovinare; *(child)* viziare.

spoke [spəʊk] *pt* → **speak** ♦ *n* raggio *m*.

spoken [ˈspəʊkn] *pp* → **speak**.

spokesman [ˈspəʊksmən] (*pl* -men [-mən]) *n* portavoce *m inv*.

spokeswoman [ˈspəʊks‚wʊmən] (*pl* -women [-‚wɪmɪn]) *n* portavoce *f inv*.

sponge [spʌndʒ] *n (for cleaning, washing)* spugna *f*.

sponge bag *n (Br)* nécessaire *m inv (da viaggio)*.

sponge cake *n* pan *m* di Spagna.

sponsor [ˈspɒnsəʳ] *n (of event, TV programme)* sponsor *m inv*.

sponsored walk [‚spɒnsəd-] *n* marcia *f* di beneficenza.

spontaneous [spɒnˈteɪnjəs] *adj* spontaneo(-a).

spoon [spuːn] *n* cucchiaio *m*.

spoonful [ˈspuːnful] *n* cucchiaiata *f*.

sport [spɔːt] *n* sport *m inv*.

sports car [spɔːts-] *n* automobile *f* sportiva.

sports centre [spɔːts-] *n* centro *m* sportivo.

sports jacket [spɔːts-] *n* giacca

f sportiva.

sportsman ['spɔːtsmən] (*pl* **-men** [-mən]) *n* sportivo *m*.

sports shop [spɔːts-] *n* negozio *m* di articoli sportivi.

sportswoman ['spɔːts,wumən] (*pl* **-women** [-,wimin]) *n* sportiva *f*.

spot [spɒt] *n (of paint, rain)* goccia *f; (on clothes)* macchia *f; (on skin)* brufolo *m; (place)* posto *m* ◆ *vt* notare; **on the ~** *(at once)* immediatamente; *(at the scene)* sul posto.

spotless ['spɒtlɪs] *adj* pulitissimo(-a).

spotlight ['spɒtlaɪt] *n* riflettore *m*.

spotty ['spɒtɪ] *adj* brufoloso(-a).

spouse [spaus] *n (fml)* coniuge *mf*.

spout [spaut] *n* beccuccio *m*.

sprain [spreɪn] *vt (ankle, wrist)* slogarsi.

sprang [spræŋ] *pt* → **spring**.

spray [spreɪ] *n (aerosol)* spray *m inv; (for perfume)* vaporizzatore *m; (droplets)* spruzzi *mpl* ◆ *vt* spruzzare.

spread [spred] *(pt & pp* **spread**) *vt (butter, jam, glue)* spalmare; *(map, tablecloth, blanket)* stendere; *(legs, fingers, arms)* distendere; *(disease, news, rumour)* diffondere ◆ *vi (disease, news, rumour)* diffondersi ◆ *n (food)* crema *f* da spalmare □ **spread out** *vi (disperse)* disperdersi.

spring [sprɪŋ] *(pt* **sprang**, *pp* **sprung**) *n (season)* primavera *f; (coil)* molla *f; (in ground)* sorgente *f* ◆ *vi (leap)* balzare; **in (the) ~** in primavera.

springboard ['sprɪŋbɔːd] *n* trampolino *m*.

spring-cleaning [-'kliːnɪŋ] *n* pulizie *fpl* di Pasqua.

spring onion *n* cipollina *f*.

spring roll *n* involtino *m* primavera.

sprinkle ['sprɪŋkl] *vt:* **to ~ sthg with sugar** spolverizzare qc di zucchero; **to ~ sthg with water** spruzzare dell'acqua su qc.

sprinkler ['sprɪŋklər] *n (for fire)* sprinkler *m inv; (for grass)* irrigatore *m*.

sprint [sprɪnt] *vi (run fast)* scattare ◆ *n (race):* **the 100-metres ~** i 100 metri piani. ’

Sprinter® ['sprɪntər] *n (Br: train)* treno usato su brevi distanze.

sprout [spraut] *n (vegetable)* cavoletto *m* di Bruxelles.

spruce [spruːs] *n* abete *m*.

sprung [sprʌŋ] *pp* → **spring** ◆ *adj (mattress)* a molle.

spud [spʌd] *n (inf)* patata *f*.

spun [spʌn] *pt & pp* → **spin**.

spur [spɜːr] *n (for horse rider)* sperone *m;* **on the ~ of the moment** d'impulso.

spurt [spɜːt] *vi* sprizzare.

spy [spaɪ] *n* spia *f*.

squall [skwɔːl] *n* burrasca *f*.

squalor ['skwɒlər] *n* squallore *m*.

square [skweər] *adj (in shape)* quadrato(-a) ◆ *n (shape)* quadrato *m; (in town)* piazza *f; (on chessboard)* scacco *m;* **2 ~ metres** 2 metri quadrati; **it's 2 metres ~** misura 2 metri per 2; **we're (all) ~ now** *(not owing money)* adesso siamo pari.

squash [skwɒʃ] *n (game)* squash *m; (Am: vegetable)* zucca *f; (Br: drink):* **orange/lemon ~** sciroppo *m* di arancia/limone ◆ *vt* schiacciare.

squat [skwɒt] *adj* tozzo(-a) ◆ *vi (crouch)* accovacciarsi.

squeak [skwiːk] *vi (door, wheel)*

cigolare; *(mouse)* squittire.

squeeze [skwi:z] *vt (tube, orange)* spremere; *(hand)* stringere ♦ *vi:* to ~ in infilarsi.

squid [skwɪd] *n* calamaro *m.*

squint [skwɪnt] *n* strabismo *m* ♦ *vi:* to ~ at guardare con gli occhi socchiusi.

squirrel [Br 'skwɪrəl, Am 'skwɜːrəl] *n* scoiattolo *m.*

squirt [skwɜːt] *vi* schizzare.

St *(abbr of Street)* V.; *(abbr of Saint)* S.

stab [stæb] *vt (with knife)* pugnalare.

stable ['steɪbl] *adj* stabile ♦ *n* stalla *f.*

stack [stæk] *n (pile)* pila *f;* ~s of *(inf: lots)* un mucchio di.

stadium ['steɪdjəm] *n* stadio *m.*

staff [stɑːf] *n (workers)* personale *m.*

stage [steɪdʒ] *n (phase)* stadio *m;* *(in theatre)* palcoscenico *m.*

stagger ['stægəʳ] *vt (arrange in stages)* scaglionare ♦ *vi* barcollare.

stagnant ['stægnənt] *adj* stagnante.

stain [steɪn] *n* macchia *f* ♦ *vt* macchiare.

stained glass [,steɪnd-] *n* vetro *m* colorato.

stainless steel ['steɪnlɪs-] *n* acciaio *m* inossidabile.

staircase ['steəkeɪs] *n* scala *f.*

stairs [steəz] *npl* scale *fpl.*

stairwell ['steəwel] *n* tromba *f* delle scale.

stake [steɪk] *n (share)* quota *f;* *(in gambling)* posta *f;* *(post)* palo *m;* at ~ in gioco.

stale [steɪl] *adj (food)* stantio(-a).

stalk [stɔːk] *n* gambo *m.*

stall [stɔːl] *n (in market, at exhibi-*

tion) banco *m* ♦ *vi (car, engine)* spegnersi ❑ **stalls** *npl (Br: in theatre)* platea *f.*

stamina ['stæmɪnə] *n* resistenza *f.*

stammer ['stæməʳ] *vi* balbettare.

stamp [stæmp] *n (for letter)* francobollo *m; (in passport, on document)* timbro *m* ♦ *vt (passport, document)* timbrare ♦ *vi:* to ~ on sthg pestare qc.

stamp-collecting [-kə,lektɪŋ] *n* filatelia *f.*

stamp machine *n* distributore *m* di francobolli.

stand [stænd] *(pt & pp stood)* *vi (be on feet)* stare in piedi; *(be situated)* trovarsi; *(get to one's feet)* alzarsi ♦ *vt (place)* mettere; *(bear)* sopportare; *(withstand)* tollerare ♦ *n (stall)* banco *m; (for umbrellas)* portaombrelli *m inv; (for coats)* attaccapanni *m inv; (on bike, motorbike)* cavalletto *m; (at sports stadium)* tribuna *f;* **newspaper ~** edicola *f;* to be ~ing stare in piedi; to ~ sb a drink offrire da bere a qn; 'no ~ing' *(Am: AUT)* 'divieto di sosta' ❑ **stand back** *vi* tirarsi indietro; **stand for** *vt fus (mean)* stare per; *(tolerate)* tollerare; **stand in** *vi:* to ~ in for sb sostituire qn; **stand out** *vi* spiccare; **stand up** *vi (be on feet)* stare in piedi; *(get to one's feet)* alzarsi ♦ *vt sep (inf: boyfriend, girlfriend etc)* tirare un bidone a; **stand up for** *vt fus* difendere.

standard ['stændəd] *adj (normal)* standard *(inv)* ♦ *n (level)* livello *m; (norm)* standard *m inv;* up to ~ *(di livello)* soddisfacente ❑ **standards** *npl (principles)* principi *mpl.*

standard-class *adj (Br: on train)* di seconda classe.

standby ['stændbaɪ] *adj (ticket)*

stand-by *(inv)*.

stank [stæŋk] *pt* → **stink**.

staple ['steɪpl] *n (for paper)* punto *m* metallico.

stapler ['steɪplə'] *n* cucitrice *f*.

star [stɑ:'] *n* stella *f* ♦ *vt (subj: film, play etc)* avere come protagonista ❑ **stars** *npl (horoscope)* oroscopo *m*.

starboard ['stɑːbəd] *adj* di tribordo.

starch ['stɑːtʃ] *n* amido *m*.

stare [steə'] *vi*: **to ~ at** fissare.

starfish ['stɑːfɪʃ] *(pl inv)* *n* stella *f* marina.

starling ['stɑːlɪŋ] *n* storno *m*.

Stars and Stripes *n*: **the ~** la bandiera a stelle e strisce.

STARS AND STRIPES

È uno dei tanti ·nomi con i quali viene comunemente indicata la bandiera americana, oltre a "Old Glory", "Star-Spangled Banner" e "Stars and Bars". Le 50 stelle ("stars") rappresentano i 50 stati che attualmente fanno parte degli Stati Uniti, mentre le 13 strisce ("stripes") rosse e bianche rappresentano i 13 stati che formavano originariamente l'Unione. Gli americani sono molto orgogliosi della loro bandiera e non è perciò raro vederla sventolare dalle case di molti privati cittadini.

---

start [stɑːt] *n (beginning)* inizio *m*; *(starting place)* partenza *f* ♦ *vt* cominciare, iniziare; *(car, engine)* mettere in moto; *(company, club)* fondare ♦ *vi* cominciare; *(car, engine, on journey)* partire; **prices ~ at** OR **from £5** i prezzi partono da 5

---

sterline; **to ~ doing sthg** OR **to do sthg** cominciare a fare qc; **to ~ with ...** per cominciare ... ❑ **start out** *vi (on journey)* partire; *(be originally)* cominciare; **start up** *vt sep (car, engine)* mettere in moto; *(business)* intraprendere; *(shop)* aprire.

starter ['stɑːtə'] *n (Br: of meal)* antipasto *m*; *(of car)* starter *m inv*; **for ~s** *(in meal)* per antipasto.

starter motor *n* motorino *m* di avviamento.

starting point ['stɑːtɪŋ-] *n* punto *m* di partenza.

startle ['stɑːtl] *vt* far trasalire.

starvation [stɑːˈveɪʃn] *n* fame *f*.

starve [stɑːv] *vi (have no food)* morire di fame; **I'm starving!** muoio di fame!

state [steɪt] *n* stato *m* ♦ *vt (declare)* dichiarare; *(specify)* specificare; **the State** lo Stato; **the States** gli Stati Uniti.

statement ['steɪtmənt] *n (declaration)* dichiarazione *f*; *(from bank)* estratto *m* conto.

state school *n* scuola *f* statale.

statesman ['steɪtsmən] *(pl* **-men** [-mən]*)* *n* statista *m*.

static ['stætɪk] *n (on radio, TV)* scarica *f* (elettrostatica).

station ['steɪʃn] *n* stazione *f*.

stationary ['steɪʃnərɪ] *adj* stazionario(-a).

stationer's ['steɪʃnəz] *n (shop)* cartoleria *f*.

stationery ['steɪʃnərɪ] *n* cancelleria *f*.

station wagon *n (Am)* station wagon *f inv*.

statistics [stəˈtɪstɪks] *npl (facts)* statistiche *fpl*.

statue ['stætʃuː] n statua f.
Statue of Liberty n: **the ~** la Statua della Libertà.

---

i STATUE OF LIBERTY

S u un'isoletta al largo del porto di New York si erge la Statua della Libertà, scultura gigante di una donna che regge nella mano destra una fiaccola. Fu donata agli Stati Uniti dalla Francia nel 1884 ed è aperta al pubblico.

---

status ['steɪtəs] n (legal position) stato m; (social position) condizione f sociale; (prestige) prestigio m.

stay [steɪ] n (time spent) soggiorno m ◆ vi (remain) rimanere; (as guest) alloggiare; (Scot: reside) abitare; **to ~ the night** passare la notte ❑ **stay away** vi: **to ~ away (from)** (not attend) non andare (a); (not go near) stare lontano (da); **stay in** vi rimanere a casa; **stay out** vi (from home) rimanere fuori; **stay up** vi rimanere alzato.

STD code n prefisso m.

steady ['stedɪ] adj (not shaking, firm) stabile; (gradual, stable) costante; (job) fisso(-a) ◆ vt (stop from shaking) tenere fermo.

steak [steɪk] n (type of meat) carne f di manzo; (piece of meat) bistecca f; (piece of fish) trancia f.

steak and kidney pie n pasticcio di carne di manzo e rognone.

steakhouse ['steɪkhaʊs,   pl -haʊzɪz] n ristorante m specializzato in bistecche.

steal [stiːl] (pt **stole**, pp **stolen**) vt rubare; **to ~ sthg from sb** rubare qc a qn.

steam [stiːm] n vapore m ◆ vt (food) cuocere a vapore.

steamboat ['stiːmbəʊt] n battello m a vapore.

steam engine n locomotiva f a vapore.

steam iron n ferro m a vapore.

steel [stiːl] n acciaio m ◆ adj di acciaio.

steep [stiːp] adj (hill, path) ripido(-a); (increase, drop) notevole.

steeple ['stiːpl] n campanile m.

steer ['stɪəʳ] vt (car, boat, plane) condurre.

steering ['stɪərɪŋ] n sterzo m.

steering wheel n volante m.

stem [stem] n stelo m.

step [step] n (stair) gradino m; (rung) piolo m; (pace) passo m; (measure) misura f; (stage) mossa f ◆ vi: **to ~ on sthg** calpestare qc; **'mind the ~'** 'attenti al gradino' ❑ **steps** npl (stairs) scala f; **step aside** vi (move aside) farsi da parte; **step back** vi (move back) tirarsi indietro.

step aerobics n step m.

stepbrother ['step,brʌðəʳ] n fratellastro m.

stepdaughter ['step,dɔːtəʳ] n figliastra f.

stepfather ['step,fɑːðəʳ] n patrigno m.

stepladder ['step,lædəʳ] n scala f (a pioli).

stepmother ['step,mʌðəʳ] n matrigna f.

stepsister ['step,sɪstəʳ] n sorellastra f.

stepson ['stepsʌn] n figliastro m.

stereo ['sterɪəʊ] (pl **-s**) adj stereofonico(-a) ◆ n (hi-fi) stereo m inv;

(stereo sound) stereofonia f.

sterile ['sterail] *adj* sterile.

sterilize ['sterəlaız] *vt* sterilizzare.

sterling ['stɜːlɪŋ] *adj (pound)* sterlina ♦ *n* sterlina f.

sterling silver *n* argento m di buona lega.

stern [stɜːn] *adj* severo(-a) ♦ *n* poppa f.

stew [stjuː] *n* stufato m.

steward ['stjuəd] *n (on plane, ship)* steward m *inv; (at public event)* membro m del servizio d'ordine.

stewardess ['stjuədɪs] *n* hostess f *inv.*

stewed [stjuːd] *adj (fruit)* cotto(-a).

stick [stɪk] *(pt & pp stuck) n (of wood)* bastone m; *(of chalk)* pezzetto m; *(of celery)* bastoncino m ♦ *vt (glue)* attaccare; *(push, insert)* ficcare; *(inf: put)* ficcare ♦ *vi (become attached)* attaccarsi; *(jam)* incastrarsi ❑ **stick out** *vi (protrude)* sporgere; *(be noticeable)* saltare agli occhi; **stick to** *vt fus (decision, promise)* mantenere; *(principles)* tener fede a; **stick up** *vt sep (poster, notice)* attaccare ♦ *vi* sporgere; **stick up for** *vt fus* difendere.

sticker ['stɪkəʳ] *n* adesivo m.

sticking plaster ['stɪkɪŋ-] *n* cerotto m.

stick shift *n (Am: car)* auto f con cambio manuale.

sticky ['stɪkɪ] *adj (substance, hands, weather)* appiccicoso(-a); *(label, tape)* adesivo(-a).

stiff [stɪf] *adj* duro(-a); *(back, neck, person)* rigido(-a) ♦ *adv*: **to be bored ~** *(inf)* essere annoiato a morte.

stile [staɪl] *n gradini per scavalcare un recinto.*

stiletto heels [stɪ'letəʊ-] *npl* tacchi *mpl* a spillo.

still [stɪl] *adv* ancora; *(despite that)* comunque ♦ *adj (motionless)* immobile; *(quiet, calm)* calmo(-a); *(not fizzy)* non gassato(-a); **we've ~ got ten minutes** abbiamo ancora dieci minuti; **~ more** ancora di più; **to stand ~** stare fermo.

Stilton ['stɪltn] *n* stilton m *(formaggio simile al gorgonzola).*

stimulate ['stɪmjʊleɪt] *vt (encourage)* stimolare.

sting [stɪŋ] *(pt & pp stung) vt* pungere ♦ *vi (skin, eyes)* pizzicare.

stingy ['stɪndʒɪ] *adj (inf)* tirchio(-a).

stink [stɪŋk] *(pt stank OR stunk, pp stunk) vi (smell bad)* puzzare.

stipulate ['stɪpjʊleɪt] *vt* stipulare.

stir [stɜːʳ] *vt* mescolare.

stir-fry *n* piatto m saltato ♦ *vt* saltare *(in padella).*

stirrup ['stɪrəp] *n* staffa f.

stitch [stɪtʃ] *n (in sewing, knitting)* punto m; **to have a ~** *(stomach pain)* avere una fitta ❑ **stitches** *npl (for wound)* punti *mpl.*

stock [stɒk] *n (of shop, business)* stock m *inv; (supply)* scorta f; *(FIN)* azioni *fpl; (in cooking)* brodo m ♦ *vt (have in stock)* avere in magazzino; **in ~** in magazzino; **out of ~** esaurito.

stock cube *n* dado m (per il brodo).

Stock Exchange *n* Borsa f valori.

stocking ['stɒkɪŋ] *n* calza f.

stock market *n* borsa *f* valori.

stodgy ['stɒdʒɪ] *adj (food)* pesante.

stole [stəʊl] *pt* → **steal**.

stolen ['stəʊln] *pp* → **steal**.

stomach ['stʌmək] *n (organ)* stomaco *m; (belly)* pancia *f.*

stomachache ['stʌməkeɪk] *n* mal *m* di stomaco.

stomach upset [-'ʌpset] *n* disturbo *m* di stomaco.

stone [stəʊn] *n (substance)* pietra *f; (in fruit)* nocciolo *m; (measurement: pl inv)* = 6,35 kg; *(gem)* pietra preziosa ◆ *adj* di pietra.

stonewashed ['stəʊnwɒʃt] *adj* délavé *(inv).*

stood [stʊd] *pt & pp* → **stand**.

stool [stuːl] *n (for sitting on)* sgabello *m.*

stop [stɒp] *n (for bus, train)* fermata *f* ◆ *vt (cause to cease)* porre fine a; *(car, machine)* fermare; *(prevent)* impedire ◆ *vi* fermarsi; **to ~ sb/sthg from doing sthg** impedire a qn/qc di fare qc; **to ~ doing sthg** smettere di fare qc; **to put a ~ to sthg** porre fine a qc; **'stop'** *(road sign)* 'stop'; **'stopping at ...'** *(train, bus)* 'ferma a ...'
❑ **stop off** *vi* fare una sosta.

stopover ['stɒpˌəʊvəʳ] *n* sosta *f.*

stopper ['stɒpəʳ] *n* tappo *m.*

stopwatch ['stɒpwɒtʃ] *n* cronografo *m.*

storage ['stɔːrɪdʒ] *n* immagazzinaggio *m.*

store [stɔːʳ] *n (shop)* negozio *m; (supply)* scorta *f* ◆ *vt* immagazzinare.

storehouse ['stɔːhaʊs, *pl* -haʊzɪz] *n* magazzino *m.*

storeroom ['stɔːrʊm] *n* stanzino *m.*

storey ['stɔːrɪ] *(pl* -s) *n (Br)* piano *m.*

stork [stɔːk] *n* cicogna *f.*

storm [stɔːm] *n* tempesta *f.*

stormy ['stɔːmɪ] *adj (weather)* burrascoso(-a).

story ['stɔːrɪ] *n (account, tale)* storia *f; (news item)* notizia *f; (Am)* = **storey**.

stout [staʊt] *adj (fat)* corpulento(-a) ◆ *n (drink)* birra *f* scura.

stove [stəʊv] *n (for cooking)* cucina *f; (for heating)* stufa *f.*

straight [streɪt] *adj (not curved)* diritto(-a); *(hair, drink)* liscio(-a); *(consecutive)* di seguito ◆ *adv (in a straight line)* dritto; *(upright)* in posizione eretta; *(directly, without delay)* direttamente; **~ ahead** sempre diritto; **~ away** subito.

straightforward [ˌstreɪt'fɔːwəd] *adj (easy)* semplice.

strain [streɪn] *n (force)* sforzo *m; (tension, nervous stress)* tensione *f; (injury)* distorsione *f* ◆ *vt (muscle, eyes)* sforzare; *(food)* scolare; *(tea)* filtrare.

strainer ['streɪnəʳ] *n* colino *m.*

strait [streɪt] *n* stretto *m.*

strange [streɪndʒ] *adj (unusual)* strano(-a); *(unfamiliar)* sconosciuto(-a).

stranger ['streɪndʒəʳ] *n (unfamiliar person)* sconosciuto *m* (-a *f); (person from different place)* forestiero *m* (-a *f).*

strangle ['stræŋgl] *vt* strangolare.

strap [stræp] *n (of bag, camera)* tracolla *f; (of watch, shoe)* cinturino *m; (of dress)* bretella *f.*

strapless ['stræplɪs] *adj* senza spalline.

strategy ['strætɪdʒɪ] *n (plan)* strategia *f*.

Stratford-upon-Avon [,strætfədəpɒn'eɪvn] *n* Stratford-upon-Avon.

---

i **STRATFORD-UPON-AVON**

Questa cittadina nella contea del Warwickshire è famosa per aver dato i natali al grande drammaturgo e poeta William Shakespeare (1564–1616). Oggi è un importante centro del teatro britannico e sede della Royal Shakespeare Company, che vi allestisce opere di Shakespeare e di altri drammaturghi.

---

straw [strɔː] *n* paglia *f*; *(for drinking)* cannuccia *f*.

strawberry ['strɔːbərɪ] *n* fragola *f*.

stray [streɪ] *adj (animal)* randagio(-a) ♦ *vi* vagare.

streak [striːk] *n (stripe, mark)* striscia *f*; *(period)* periodo *m*.

stream [striːm] *n (river)* ruscello *m*; *(of traffic, people, blood)* flusso *m*.

street [striːt] *n* via *f*, strada *f*.

streetcar ['striːtkɑːʳ] *n (Am)* tram *m inv*.

street light *n* lampione *m*.

street plan *n* piantina *f*.

strength [streŋθ] *n* forza *f*; *(of structure)* robustezza *f*; *(influence)* potere *m*; *(strong point)* punto *m* di forza; *(of feeling, smell)* intensità *f*; *(of drink)* gradazione *f* alcolica.

strengthen ['streŋθn] *vt (structure)* rafforzare.

stress [stres] *n (tension)* stress *m inv*; *(on word, syllable)* accento *m* ♦ *vt (emphasize)* sottolineare; *(word, syllable)* accentare.

stretch [stretʃ] *n (of land, water)* distesa *f*; *(of time)* periodo *m* ♦ *vt* tendere; *(body)* stirare ♦ *vi (land, sea)* estendersi; *(person, animal)* stirarsi; **to ~ one's legs** *(fig)* sgranchirsi le gambe ❑ **stretch out** *vt sep (hand)* tendere ♦ *vi (lie down)* distendersi.

stretcher ['stretʃəʳ] *n* barella *f*.

strict [strɪkt] *adj (person)* severo(-a); *(rule, instructions)* rigido(-a); *(exact)* stretto(-a).

strictly ['strɪktlɪ] *adv* strettamente; **~ speaking** per essere precisi.

stride [straɪd] *n* falcata *f*.

strike [straɪk] *(pt & pp* **struck)** *n (of employees)* sciopero *m* ♦ *vt (fml: hit)* colpire; *(fml: collide with)* urtare; *(a match)* accendere ♦ *vi (refuse to work)* scioperare; *(happen suddenly)* colpire; **the clock struck eight** l'orologio ha battuto le otto.

striking ['straɪkɪŋ] *adj (noticeable)* impressionante; *(attractive)* appariscente.

string [strɪŋ] *n* spago *m*; *(of pearls, beads)* filo *m*; *(of musical instrument, tennis racket)* corda *f*; *(series)* serie *f inv*; **a piece of ~** un pezzo di spago.

strip [strɪp] *n* striscia *f* ♦ *vt (paint, wallpaper)* togliere ♦ *vi (undress)* spogliarsi.

stripe [straɪp] *n* striscia *f*.

striped [straɪpt] *adj* a strisce.

strip-search *vt* perquisire (facendo spogliare).

strip show *n* spogliarello *m*.

stroke [strəʊk] *n (MED)* colpo *m*;

(in tennis) battuta f; *(in golf)* tiro m; *(swimming style)* stile m ◆ vt accarezzare; **a ~ of luck** un colpo di fortuna.

stroll [strəʊl] n passeggiata f.

stroller ['strəʊlər] n *(Am: pushchair)* passeggino m.

strong [strɒŋ] adj forte; *(structure, bridge, chair)* robusto(-a); *(feeling, smell)* intenso(-a).

struck [strʌk] pt & pp → **strike**.

structure ['strʌktʃər] n struttura f.

struggle ['strʌgl] n *(great effort)* sforzo m ◆ vi *(fight)* lottare; *(in order to get free)* divincolarsi; **to ~ to do sthg** sforzarsi di fare qc.

stub [stʌb] n *(of cigarette)* mozzicone m; *(of cheque, ticket)* matrice f.

stubble ['stʌbl] n *(on face)* barba f ispida.

stubborn ['stʌbən] adj *(person)* ostinato(-a).

stuck [stʌk] pt & pp → **stick** ◆ adj *(jammed)* incastrato(-a); *(unable to continue, stranded)* bloccato(-a).

stud [stʌd] n *(on boots)* borchia f; *(fastener)* bottone m automatico; *(earring)* miniorecchino m.

student ['stjuːdnt] n studente m (-essa f).

student card n carta f dello studente.

students' union [ˌstjuːdnts-] n *(place)* circolo m studentesco.

studio ['stjuːdɪəʊ] (pl **-s**) n studio m.

studio apartment (Am) = **studio flat**.

studio flat n (Br) miniappartamento m.

study ['stʌdɪ] n *(learning)* studio m ◆ vt & vi studiare.

stuff [stʌf] n *(inf)* roba f ◆ vt *(push roughly)* ficcare; *(fill)* riempire.

stuffed [stʌft] adj *(food)* ripieno(-a); *(inf: full up)* pieno(-a); *(dead animal)* imbalsamato(-a).

stuffing ['stʌfɪŋ] n *(food)* ripieno m; *(of pillow, cushion)* imbottitura f.

stuffy ['stʌfɪ] adj *(room, atmosphere)* che sa di chiuso.

stumble ['stʌmbl] vi *(when walking)* inciampare.

stump [stʌmp] n *(of tree)* ceppo m.

stun [stʌn] vt *(shock)* sbalordire.

stung [stʌŋ] pt & pp → **sting**.

stunk [stʌŋk] pt & pp → **stink**.

stunning ['stʌnɪŋ] adj *(very beautiful)* favoloso(-a); *(very surprising)* sbalorditivo(-a).

stupid ['stjuːpɪd] adj stupido(-a).

sturdy ['stɜːdɪ] adj robusto(-a).

stutter ['stʌtər] vi balbettare.

sty [staɪ] n *(pigsty)* porcile m; *(on eye)* orzaiolo m.

style [staɪl] n stile m ◆ vt *(hair)* acconciare.

stylish ['staɪlɪʃ] adj elegante.

stylist ['staɪlɪst] n *(hairdresser)* acconciatore m (-trice f).

sub [sʌb] n *(inf) (substitute)* riserva f; *(Br: subscription)* quota f (d'iscrizione).

subdued [səb'djuːd] adj *(person)* abbacchiato(-a); *(lighting, colour)* smorzato(-a).

subject [n 'sʌbdʒekt, vb səb'dʒekt] n *(topic)* argomento m; *(at school, university)* materia f; (GRAMM) soggetto m; *(fml: of country)* cittadino m (-a f) ◆ vt: **to ~ sb to sthg** sottoporre qn a qc; **'~ to availability'** 'fino ad esaurimento'; **they are ~ to an additional charge** sono suscettibili di soprapprezzo.

subjunctive [səb'dʒʌŋktɪv] *n* congiuntivo *m*.

submarine [ˌsʌbmə'riːn] *n* sottomarino *m*.

submit [səb'mɪt] *vt* presentare ◆ *vi* sottomettersi.

subordinate [sə'bɔːdɪnət] *adj* subordinato(-a).

subscribe [səb'skraɪb] *vi (to magazine, newspaper)* abbonarsi.

subscription [səb'skrɪpʃn] *n* abbonamento *m*.

subsequent [ˈsʌbsɪkwənt] *adj* successivo(-a).

subside [səb'saɪd] *vi (ground)* cedere; *(noise, feeling)* smorzarsi.

substance [ˈsʌbstəns] *n* sostanza *f*.

substantial [səb'stænʃl] *adj (large)* sostanziale.

substitute [ˈsʌbstɪtjuːt] *n (person)* sostituto *m* (-a *f*); *(thing)* surrogato *m*; *(SPORT)* riserva *f*.

subtitles [ˈsʌbˌtaɪtlz] *npl* sottotitoli *mpl*.

subtle [ˈsʌtl] *adj (difference, change)* sottile; *(person, plan)* astuto(-a).

subtract [səb'trækt] *vt* sottrarre.

subtraction [səb'trækʃn] *n* sottrazione *f*.

suburb [ˈsʌbɜːb] *n* sobborgo *m*; **the ~s** la periferia.

subway [ˈsʌbweɪ] *n (Br: for pedestrians)* sottopassaggio *m*; *(Am: underground railway)* metropolitana *f*.

succeed [sək'siːd] *vi (be successful)* avere successo ◆ *vt (fml: follow)* succedere a; **to ~ in doing sthg** riuscire a fare qc.

success [sək'ses] *n* successo *m*.

successful [sək'sesful] *adj (plan, attempt)* riuscito(-a); *(film, book, politician)* di successo; **to be ~** *(person)* riuscire.

succulent [ˈsʌkjʊlənt] *adj* succulento(-a).

such [sʌtʃ] *adj* tale ◆ *adv*: **~ a lot** così tanto; **it's ~ a lovely day** è una giornata così bella; **~ good luck** una tale fortuna; **~ a thing should never have happened** una cosa simile non sarebbe mai dovuta accadere; **~ as** come.

suck [sʌk] *vt* succhiare.

sudden [ˈsʌdn] *adj* improvviso(-a); **all of a ~** all'improvviso.

suddenly [ˈsʌdnlɪ] *adv* improvvisamente.

sue [suː] *vt* citare in giudizio.

suede [sweɪd] *n* pelle *f* scamosciata.

suffer [ˈsʌfər] *vt (defeat, injury)* subire ◆ *vi* soffrire; **to ~ from** *(illness)* soffrire di.

suffering [ˈsʌfrɪŋ] *n* sofferenza *f*.

sufficient [sə'fɪʃnt] *adj (fml)* sufficiente.

sufficiently [sə'fɪʃntlɪ] *adv (fml)* sufficientemente.

suffix [ˈsʌfɪks] *n* suffisso *m*.

suffocate [ˈsʌfəkeɪt] *vi* soffocare.

sugar [ˈʃʊgər] *n* zucchero *m*.

suggest [sə'dʒest] *vt* suggerire; **to ~ doing sthg** suggerire di fare qc.

suggestion [sə'dʒestʃn] *n (proposal)* suggerimento *m*; *(hint)* accenno *m*.

suicide [ˈsʊɪsaɪd] *n* suicidio *m*; **to commit ~** suicidarsi.

suit [suːt] *n (clothes)* completo *m*; *(in cards)* seme *m*; *(JUR)* causa *f* ◆ *vt* *(subj: clothes, colour, shoes)* star bene a; *(be convenient for)* andare bene a; *(be appropriate for)* addirsi a; **to be ~ed to** essere adatto a.

suitable ['su:təbl] *adj* adatto(-a); **to be ~ for** essere adatto a.

suitcase ['su:tkeɪs] *n* valigia *f*.

suite [swi:t] *n (set of rooms)* suite *f inv*; *(furniture):* **a three-piece ~** un divano e due poltrone (coordinati).

sulk [sʌlk] *vi* mettere il broncio.

sultana [səl'tɑ:nə] *n (Br)* uva *f* sultanina.

sultry ['sʌltrɪ] *adj (weather, climate)* caldo umido (caldo umida).

sum [sʌm] *n* somma *f* □ **sum up** *vt sep* riassumere.

summarize ['sʌməraɪz] *vt* riassumere.

summary ['sʌmərɪ] *n* riassunto *m*.

summer ['sʌmə^r] *n* estate *f*; **in (the) ~** d'estate; **~ holidays** vacanze *fpl* estive.

summertime ['sʌmətaɪm] *n* estate *f*.

summit ['sʌmɪt] *n (of mountain)* cima *f*; *(meeting)* summit *m inv*.

summon ['sʌmən] *vt (send for)* convocare; *(JUR)* citare.

sumptuous ['sʌmptʃʊəs] *adj* sontuoso(-a).

sun [sʌn] *n* sole *m* ◆ *vt*: **to ~ o.s.** prendere il sole; **to catch the ~** prendere il sole; **in the ~** al sole; **out of the ~** al riparo dal sole.

Sun. *(abbr of Sunday)* dom.

sunbathe ['sʌnbeɪð] *vi* prendere il sole.

sunbed ['sʌnbed] *n* lettino *m*.

sun block *n* crema *f* solare a protezione totale.

sunburn ['sʌnbɜ:n] *n* scottatura *f*.

sunburnt ['sʌnbɜ:nt] *adj* scottato(-a).

sundae ['sʌndeɪ] *n* gelato guarnito con frutta o cioccolato, nocciole e panna montata.

Sunday ['sʌndɪ] *n* domenica *f*, → **Saturday**.

Sunday school *n* ≃ scuola *f* di catechismo.

sundress ['sʌndres] *n* prendisole *m inv*.

sundries ['sʌndrɪz] *npl (on bill)* varie *fpl*.

sunflower ['sʌn,flaʊə^r] *n* girasole *m*.

sunflower oil *n* olio *m* di semi di girasole.

sung [sʌŋ] *pt* → **sing**.

sunglasses ['sʌn,glɑ:sɪz] *npl* occhiali *mpl* da sole.

sunhat ['sʌnhæt] *n* cappello *m (per il sole)*.

sunk [sʌŋk] *pp* → **sink**.

sunlight ['sʌnlaɪt] *n* luce *f* del sole.

sun lounger [-,laʊndʒə^r] *n (chair)* lettino *m*.

sunny ['sʌnɪ] *adj (day)* di sole; *(weather)* bello(-a); *(room, place)* soleggiato(-a); **it's ~** c'è il sole.

sunrise ['sʌnraɪz] *n* alba *f*.

sunroof ['sʌnru:f] *n* tettuccio *m* apribile.

sunset ['sʌnset] *n* tramonto *m*.

sunshine ['sʌnʃaɪn] *n* luce *f* del sole; **in the ~** al sole.

sunstroke ['sʌnstrəʊk] *n* insolazione *f*.

suntan ['sʌntæn] *n* abbronzatura *f*.

suntan cream *n* crema *f* abbronzante.

suntan lotion *n* lozione *f*

abbronzante.

super ['su:pə'] *adj* fantastico(-a)
♦ *n (petrol)* super *f inv*.

superb [su:'pɜ:b] *adj* splendi-
do(-a).

superficial [,su:pə'fɪʃl] *adj* superficiale.

superfluous [su:'pɜ:fluəs] *adj*
superfluo(-a).

Superglue® ['su:pəglu:] *n* colla *f*
a presa rapida.

superior [su:'pɪərɪə'] *adj* superiore ♦ *n* superiore *mf*.

supermarket ['su:pə,mɑ:kɪt] *n*
supermercato *m*.

supernatural [,su:pə'nætʃrəl]
adj soprannaturale.

Super Saver® *n (Br: rail ticket)*
biglietto ferroviario a tariffa ridotta,
con condizioni particolari.

superstitious [,su:pə'stɪʃəs] *adj*
superstizioso(-a).

superstore ['su:pəstɔ:'] *n* grande supermercato *m*.

supervise ['su:pəvaɪz] *vt* sorvegliare.

supervisor ['su:pəvaɪzə'] *n (of
workers)* sovrintendente *mf*.

supper ['sʌpə'] *n (evening meal)*
cena *f*; *(before bed)* spuntino *m*.

supple ['sʌpl] *adj* agile.

supplement [*n* 'sʌplɪmənt, *vb*
'sʌplɪment] *n* supplemento *m*; *(of
diet)* integratore *m* alimentare ♦ *vt*
integrare.

supplementary [,sʌplɪ'men-
tərɪ] *adj* supplementare.

supply [sə'plaɪ] *n (store)* scorta *f*;
(providing) approvvigionamento *m*;
(of electricity, gas etc) erogazione *f* ♦
vt fornire; **to ~ sb with sthg** fornire
qc a qn ❑ **supplies** *npl* scorte *fpl*.

support [sə'pɔ:t] *n (for cause*
candidate) appoggio *m*; *(object*
encouragement) sostegno *m* ♦ *v*
(cause, campaign, person) appoggiare; *(SPORT)* tifare per; *(hold up)* so
stenere; *(financially)* mantenere.

supporter [sə'pɔ:tə'] *n (SPORT*
tifoso *m* (-a *f)*; *(of cause, politica*
party) sostenitore *m* (-trice *f)*.

suppose [sə'pəʊz] *vt (assume*
immaginare; *(think)* credere ♦ *con*
= **supposing**; **I ~ so** penso di sì
you were ~d to be home at si
o'clock dovevate essere a casa all
sei; **it's ~d to be the best** è ritenu
to il migliore.

supposing [sə'pəʊzɪŋ] *conj* sup
ponendo che.

supreme [su'pri:m] *adj* eccezio
nale.

surcharge ['sɜ:tʃɑ:dʒ] *n* sovrap
prezzo *m*.

sure [ʃʊə'] *adj* sicuro(-a) ♦ *ad*
(inf: yes) certo!; *(Am: inf: certainly*
certamente; **to be ~ of o.s.** esser
sicuro di sé; **to make ~ that ..**
assicurarsi che ...; **for ~** di sicuro.

surely ['ʃʊəlɪ] *adv* sicuramente.

surf [sɜ:f] *n (foam)* spuma *f* ♦ *v*
fare surf.

surface ['sɜ:fɪs] *n* superficie *f*.

surface area *n* superficie
(esterna).

surface mail *n* posta *f* ordina
ria.

surfboard ['sɜ:fbɔ:d] *n* tavola
da surf.

surfing ['sɜ:fɪŋ] *n* surf *m*; **to go ~**
andare a fare surf.

surgeon ['sɜ:dʒən] *n* chirurgo *m*

surgery ['sɜ:dʒərɪ] *n (treatment*
chirurgia *f*; *(Br: building)* ambulato
rio *m*; *(Br: period)* orario *m* d'ambu

latorio.

surname ['sɜːneɪm] n cognome m.

surplus ['sɜːpləs] n eccedenza f.

surprise [sə'praɪz] n sorpresa f ◆ vt sorprendere.

surprised [sə'praɪzd] adj sorpreso(-a).

surprising [sə'praɪzɪŋ] adj sorprendente.

surrender [sə'rendə'] vi arrendersi ◆ vt (fml: hand over) consegnare.

surround [sə'raʊnd] vt circondare.

surrounding [sə'raʊndɪŋ] adj circostante ☐ **surroundings** npl dintorni mpl.

survey ['sɜːveɪ] n (investigation) studio m; (poll) sondaggio m; (of land) rilevamento m (topografico); (Br: of house) sopralluogo m.

surveyor [sə'veɪə'] n (Br: of houses) perito m; (of land) agrimensore m.

survival [sə'vaɪvl] n sopravvivenza f.

survive [sə'vaɪv] vi sopravvivere ◆ vt sopravvivere a.

survivor [sə'vaɪvə'] n sopravvissuto m (-a f).

suspect [vb sə'spekt, n & adj 'sʌspekt] vt sospettare ◆ n sospetto n ◆ adj sospetto(-a); **to ~ sb of** sthg sospettare qn di qc.

suspend [sə'spend] vt sospendere.

suspender belt [sə'spendə-] n reggicalza m inv.

suspenders [sə'spendəz] npl (Br: for stockings) giarrettiere fpl; (Am: for trousers) bretelle fpl.

suspense [sə'spens] n suspense f.

suspension [sə'spenʃn] n so-

spensione f.

suspicion [sə'spɪʃn] n (mistrust, idea) sospetto m; (trace) accenno m.

suspicious [sə'spɪʃəs] adj (behaviour, situation) sospetto(-a); **to be ~ of** (distrustful) sospettare di.

swallow ['swɒləʊ] n (bird) rondine f ◆ vt & vi ingoiare.

swam [swæm] pt → **swim**.

swamp [swɒmp] n palude f.

swan [swɒn] n cigno m.

swap [swɒp] vt (possessions, places) scambiare; (ideas, stories) scambiarsi; **to ~ sthg for sthg** scambiare qc con qc.

swarm [swɔːm] n (of bees) sciame m.

swear [sweə'] (pt **swore**, pp **sworn**) vi (use rude language) imprecare; (promise) giurare ◆ vt: **to ~ to do sthg** promettere di fare qc.

swearword ['sweəwɜːd] n parolaccia f.

sweat [swet] n sudore m ◆ vi sudare.

sweater ['swetə'] n maglione m.

sweatshirt ['swetʃɜːt] n felpa f.

swede [swiːd] n (Br) rapa f svedese.

Swede [swiːd] n svedese mf.

Sweden ['swiːdn] n la Svezia.

Swedish ['swiːdɪʃ] adj svedese ◆ n (language) svedese m ◆ npl: **the ~** gli svedesi.

sweep [swiːp] (pt & pp **swept**) vt (with brush, broom) scopare.

sweet [swiːt] adj dolce; (kind) gentile, carino(-a) ◆ n (Br) (candy) caramella f; (dessert) dolce m.

sweet-and-sour adj (pork) in agrodolce; (sauce) agrodolce.

sweet corn n granturco m.

sweetener ['swiːtnə'] n (for

drink) dolcificante *m*.

sweet potato *n* patata *f* americana.

sweet shop *n (Br)* negozio *m* di dolciumi.

swell [swel] *(pp* **swollen)** *vi (ankle, arm etc)* gonfiarsi.

swelling ['swelɪŋ] *n* gonfiore *m*.

swept [swept] *pt & pp* → **sweep**.

swerve [swɜːv] *vi (vehicle)* sterzare.

swig [swɪg] *n (inf)* sorsata *f*.

swim [swɪm] *(pt* **swam**, *pp* **swum)** *n* nuotata *f*, bagno *m* ♦ *vi (in water)* nuotare; **to go for a ~** andare a fare il bagno.

swimmer ['swɪmə'] *n* nuotatore *m* (-trice *f*).

swimming ['swɪmɪŋ] *n* nuoto *m*; **to go ~** andare in piscina.

swimming baths *npl (Br)* piscina *f* coperta.

swimming cap *n* cuffia *f*.

swimming costume *n (Br)* costume *m* da bagno.

swimming pool *n* piscina *f*.

swimming trunks *npl* costume *m* da bagno *(da uomo)*.

swimsuit ['swɪmsuːt] *n* costume *m* da bagno.

swindle ['swɪndl] *n* truffa *f*.

swing [swɪŋ] *(pt & pp* **swung)** *n (for children)* altalena *f* ♦ *vt & vi (from side to side)* dondolare.

swipe [swaɪp] *vt (credit card etc)* far passare nel lettore magnetico.

Swiss [swɪs] *adj* svizzero(-a) ♦ *n (person)* svizzero *m* (-a *f*) ♦ *npl:* **the ~** gli svizzeri.

Swiss cheese *n* formaggio *m* svizzero.

swiss roll *n* rotolo di pan di

Spagna farcito di marmellata.

switch [swɪtʃ] *n (for light, power, television set)* interruttore *m* ♦ *vt (change)* cambiare; *(exchange)* scambiare ♦ *vi* cambiare ❑ **switch off** *vt sep* spegnere; **switch on** *vt sep* accendere.

switchboard ['swɪtʃbɔːd] *n* centralino *m*.

Switzerland ['swɪtsələnd] *n* la Svizzera.

swivel ['swɪvl] *vi* girarsi.

swollen ['swəʊln] *pp* → **swell** ♦ *adj (ankle, arm etc)* gonfio(-a).

swop [swɒp] = **swap**.

sword [sɔːd] *n* spada *f*.

swordfish ['sɔːdfɪʃ] *(pl inv)* *n* pesce *m* spada.

swore [swɔː'] *pt* → **swear**.

sworn [swɔːn] *pp* → **swear**.

swum [swʌm] *pp* → **swim**.

swung [swʌŋ] *pt & pp* → **swing**.

syllable ['sɪləbl] *n* sillaba *f*.

syllabus ['sɪləbəs] *n* programma *m*.

symbol ['sɪmbl] *n* simbolo *m*.

sympathetic [,sɪmpə'θetɪk] *adj (understanding)* comprensivo(-a).

sympathize ['sɪmpəθaɪz] *vi:* **to ~ (with)** *(feel sorry)* provare compassione (per); *(understand)* capire.

sympathy ['sɪmpəθɪ] *n (understanding)* comprensione *f*.

symphony ['sɪmfənɪ] *n* sinfonia *f*.

symptom ['sɪmptəm] *n* sintomo *m*.

synagogue ['sɪnəgɒg] *n* sinagoga *f*.

synthesizer ['sɪnθəsaɪzə'] *n* sintetizzatore *m*.

synthetic [sɪn'θetɪk] *adj* sintetico(-a).

syringe [sɪ'rɪndʒ] *n* siringa *f*.

syrup ['sɪrəp] n (for fruit etc) sciroppo m.

system ['sɪstəm] n sistema m; (hi-fi, computer, for heating etc) impianto m.

T

ta [tɑː] excl (Br: inf) grazie!

tab [tæb] n (of cloth, paper etc) etichetta f; (bill) conto m; **put it on my ~** lo metta sul mio conto.

table ['teɪbl] n (piece of furniture) tavolo m; (of figures etc) tavola f.

tablecloth ['teɪblklɒθ] n tovaglia f.

tablemat ['teɪblmæt] n sottopiatto m.

tablespoon ['teɪblspuːn] n cucchiaio m da tavola.

tablet ['tæblɪt] n (pill) compressa f; (of chocolate) tavoletta f; **~ of soap** saponetta f.

table tennis n ping-pong® m.

table wine n vino m da tavola.

tabloid ['tæblɔɪd] n tabloid m inv.

tack [tæk] n (nail) puntina f.

tackle ['tækl] n (in football) tackle m; (in rugby) placcaggio m; (for fishing) attrezzatura f ♦ vt (in football) contrastare; (in rugby) placcare; (deal with) affrontare.

tacky ['tækɪ] adj (inf: jewellery, design etc) pacchiano(-a).

taco ['tækəʊ] n (pl -s) n taco m schiacciatina a base di farina di granurco farcita di carne o fagioli, tipica della cucina messicana).

tact [tækt] n tatto m.

tactful ['tæktfʊl] adj discreto(-a).

tactics ['tæktɪks] npl tattica f.

tag [tæg] n (label) etichetta f.

tagliatelle [,tæglɪə'telɪ] n tagliatelle fpl.

tail [teɪl] n coda f ❑ **tails** n (of coin) croce f ♦ npl (formal dress) frac m inv.

tailgate ['teɪlgeɪt] n (of car) portellone m.

tailor ['teɪlər] n sarto m.

Taiwan [,taɪ'wɑːn] n Taiwan f.

take [teɪk] (pt took, pp taken) vt 1. (gen) prendere.
2. (carry, drive) portare.
3. (do, make) fare; **to ~ a bath/shower** fare un bagno/una doccia; **to ~ an exam** OR **dare un esame**; **to ~ a decision** prendere una decisione.
4. (time, effort) volerci, richiedere; **how long will it ~?** quanto ci vorrà?; **it won't ~ long** non ci vorrà molto tempo.
5. (size in clothes, shoes) portare, avere; **what size do you ~?** (clothes) che taglia porta?; (shoes) che misura porta?
6. (subtract) sottrarre, togliere.
7. (accept) accettare; **do you ~ traveller's cheques?** accettate traveller's cheques?; **to ~ sb's advice** seguire il consiglio di qn.
8. (contain) contenere.
9. (control, power) assumere; **to ~ charge of** assumere la direzione di.
10. (tolerate) sopportare.
11. (assume): **I ~ it that ...** suppongo che ...
12. (rent) prendere in affitto. ❑ **take apart** vt sep (dismantle) smontare; **take away** vt sep (re-

move) portare via; *(subtract)* togliere; **take back** *vt sep (return)* riportare; *(statement)* ritrattare; **take down** *vt sep (picture, decorations)* togliere; **take in** *vt sep (include)* includere; *(understand)* capire; *(deceive)* abbindolare; *(clothes)* restringere; **take off** *vi (plane)* decollare ◆ *vt sep (remove)* togliere; *(as holiday):* **to ~ a week off** prendere una settimana di ferie; **take out** *vt sep (from container, pocket)* tirare fuori; *(loan, insurance policy)* ottenere; *(go out with)* portare fuori; **take over** *vi* assumere il comando; **to ~ over from sb** prendere le consegne da qn; **take up** *vt sep (begin)* dedicarsi a; *(use up)* prendere; *(trousers, dress)* accorciare.

takeaway ['teɪkə,weɪ] *n (Br) (shop)* locale che prepara piatti pronti da asporto; *(food)* cibo *m* da asporto.

taken ['teɪkn] *pp* → **take**.

takeoff ['teɪkɒf] *n (of plane)* decollo *m*.

takeout ['teɪkaʊt] *(Am)* = **takeaway**.

takings ['teɪkɪŋz] *npl* incasso *m*.

talcum powder ['tælkəm-] *n* borotalco® *m*.

tale [teɪl] *n (story)* storia *f*; *(account)* racconto *m*.

talent ['tælənt] *n* talento *m*.

talk [tɔːk] *n (conversation)* conversazione *f*; *(speech)* discorso *m* ◆ *vi* parlare; **to ~ to sb (about sthg)** parlare con qn (di qc); **to ~ with sb** parlare con qn ❑ **talks** *npl* negoziati *mpl*.

talkative ['tɔːkətɪv] *adj* loquace.

tall [tɔːl] *adj* alto(-a); **how ~ are you?** quanto sei alto?; **I'm five and a half feet ~** sono alto un

metro e 65.

tame [teɪm] *adj (animal)* addomesticato(-a).

tampon ['tæmpɒn] *n* tampone *m*

tan [tæn] *n (suntan)* abbronzatura *f* ◆ *vi* abbronzarsi ◆ *adj (colour)* marrone chiaro *(inv).*

tangerine [,tændʒə'riːn] *n (fruit)* mandarino *m*.

tank [tæŋk] *n (container)* serbatoio *m*; *(vehicle)* carro *m* armato.

tanker ['tæŋkər] *n (truck)* autocisterna *f*.

tanned [tænd] *adj (suntanned)* abbronzato(-a).

tap [tæp] *n (for water)* rubinetto *m* ◆ *vt (hit)* dare un colpetto a.

tape [teɪp] *n (cassette, video)* cassetta *f*; *(in cassette)* nastro *m*; *(adhesive material)* nastro *m* adesivo; *(strip of material)* fettuccia *f* ◆ *vt (record)* registrare; *(stick)* attaccare con nastro adesivo.

tape measure *n* metro *m*.

tape recorder *n* registratore *m*

tapestry ['tæpɪstrɪ] *n* arazzo *m*.

tap water *n* acqua *f* di rubinetto.

tar [taːr] *n (for roads)* catrame *m*; *(in cigarettes)* condensato *m*.

target ['taːgɪt] *n* bersaglio *m*.

tariff ['tærɪf] *n (price list)* tariffario *m*; *(Br: menu)* listino *m* prezzi; *(at customs)* tariffa *f* doganale.

tarmac ['taːmæk] *n (at airport)* pista *f* ❑ **Tarmac®** *n (on road)* asfalto *m*.

tarpaulin [taː'pɔːlɪn] *n* telone *m*

tart [taːt] *n (sweet)* crostata *f*.

tartan ['taːtn] *n (design)* scozzese *m*; *(cloth)* tartan *m*.

tartare sauce [,taːtə-] *n* salsa

tartara.

task [tɑ:sk] *n* compito *m*.

taste [teɪst] *n* gusto *m*; (*flavour*) gusto, sapore *m* ◆ *vt* (*sample*) assaggiare; (*detect*) sentire il gusto di ◆ *vi*: **to ~ of sthg** sapere di qc; **it ~s bad** ha un cattivo sapore; **it ~s good** ha un buon sapore; **to have a ~ of sthg** (*food, drink*) assaggiare qc; (*fig: experience*) provare qc; **bad ~** cattivo gusto; **good ~** buon gusto.

tasteful ['teɪstfʊl] *adj* di buon gusto.

tasteless ['teɪstlɪs] *adj* (*food*) insipido(-a); (*comment, decoration*) di cattivo gusto.

tasty ['teɪstɪ] *adj* gustoso(-a).

tattoo [tə'tu:] (*pl* **-s**) *n* (*on skin*) tatuaggio *m*; (*military display*) parata *f*.

taught [tɔ:t] *pt & pp* → **teach**.

Taurus ['tɔ:rəs] *n* Toro *m*.

taut [tɔ:t] *adj* teso(-a).

tax [tæks] *n* (*on income*) imposta *f*, tasse *fpl*; (*on import, goods*) tassa *f* ◆ *vt* (*goods, person*) tassare.

tax disc *n* (*Br*) ≃ bollo *m*.

tax-free *adj* esentasse (*inv*).

taxi ['tæksɪ] *n* taxi *m inv* ◆ *vi* (*plane*) rullare.

taxi driver *n* tassista *mf*.

taxi rank *n* (*Br*) posteggio *m* dei taxi.

taxi stand (*Am*) = **taxi rank**.

T-bone steak *n* costata *f* alla fiorentina.

tea [ti:] *n* tè *m inv*; (*evening meal*) cena *f*.

tea bag *n* bustina *f* di tè.

teacake ['ti:keɪk] *n* panino dolce all'uvetta.

teach [ti:tʃ] (*pt & pp* **taught**) *vt* (*subject*) insegnare; (*person*) insegnare a ◆ *vi* insegnare; **to ~ sb sthg, to ~ sthg to sb** insegnare qc a qn; **to ~ sb (how) to do sthg** insegnare a qn a fare qc.

teacher ['ti:tʃə'] *n* insegnante *mf*; (*in primary school*) maestro *m* (-a *f*); (*in secondary school*) professore *m* (-essa *f*).

teaching ['ti:tʃɪŋ] *n* insegnamento *m*.

tea cloth = **tea towel**.

teacup ['ti:kʌp] *n* tazza *f* da tè.

team [ti:m] *n* squadra *f*.

teapot ['ti:pɒt] *n* teiera *f*.

tear[1] [teə'] (*pt* **tore**, *pp* **torn**) *vt* (*rip*) strappare ◆ *vi* (*rip*) strapparsi; (*move quickly*) precipitarsi ◆ *n* (*rip*) strappo *m* ❑ **tear up** *vt sep* strappare.

tear[2] [tɪə'] *n* lacrima *f*.

tearoom ['ti:rʊm] *n* sala *f* da tè.

tease [ti:z] *vt* prendere in giro.

tea set *n* servizio *m* da tè.

teaspoon ['ti:spu:n] *n* cucchiaino *m*.

teaspoonful ['ti:spu:n,fʊl] *n* cucchiaino *m*.

teat [ti:t] *n* (*of animal*) capezzolo *m*; (*Br: of bottle*) tettarella *f*.

teatime ['ti:taɪm] *n* ora *f* del tè.

tea towel *n* strofinaccio *m*.

technical ['teknɪkl] *adj* tecnico(-a).

technical drawing *n* disegno *m* tecnico.

technicality [,teknɪ'kælətɪ] *n* (*detail*) dettaglio *m* tecnico.

technician [tek'nɪʃn] *n* tecnico *m* (-a *f*).

technique [tek'ni:k] *n* tecnica *f*.

technological [ˌteknəˈlɒdʒɪkl] *adj* tecnologico(-a).

technology [tekˈnɒlədʒɪ] *n* tecnologia *f*.

teddy (bear) [ˈtedɪ-] *n* orsacchiotto *m*.

tedious [ˈtiːdjəs] *adj* noioso(-a).

tee [tiː] *n* tee *m inv*.

teenager [ˈtiːnˌeɪdʒəʳ] *n* adolescente *mf*.

teeth [tiːθ] *pl* → **tooth**.

teethe [tiːð] *vi*: to be teething mettere i denti.

teetotal [tiːˈtəʊtl] *adj* astemio(-a).

telegram [ˈtelɪgræm] *n* telegramma *m*.

telegraph [ˈtelɪgrɑːf] *n* telegrafo *m* ♦ *vt* telegrafare.

telegraph pole *n* palo *m* del telegrafo.

telephone [ˈtelɪfəʊn] *n* telefono *m* ♦ *vt (person)* telefonare a ♦ *vi* telefonare; to be on the ~ *(talking)* essere al telefono; *(connected)* avere il telefono.

telephone booth *n* cabina *f* telefonica.

telephone box *n* cabina *f* telefonica.

telephone call *n* telefonata *f*.

telephone directory *n* elenco *m* telefonico.

telephone number *n* numero *m* di telefono.

telephonist [tɪˈlefənɪst] *n (Br)* centralinista *mf*.

telephoto lens [ˌtelɪˈfəʊtəʊ-] *n* teleobiettivo *m*.

telescope [ˈtelɪskəʊp] *n* telescopio *m*.

television [ˈtelɪˌvɪʒn] *n* televisione *f*; *(set)* televisore *m*; on (the) ~ *(broadcast)* alla televisione.

telex [ˈteleks] *n* telex *m inv*.

tell [tel] *(pt & pp* told) *vt* dire; *(story, joke)* raccontare; *(distinguish)* distinguere ♦ *vi*: I can ~ si vede; can you ~ me the time? sa dirmi l'ora?; to ~ sb sthg dire qc a qn; to ~ sb about sthg raccontare qc a qn; to ~ sb how to do sthg dire a qn come fare qc; to ~ sb to do sthg dire a qn di fare qc ❑ tell off *vt sep* rimproverare.

teller [ˈteləʳ] *n (in bank)* cassiere *m* (-a *f*).

telly [ˈtelɪ] *n (Br: inf)* tele *f*.

temp [temp] *n* impiegato *m* straordinario (impiegata *f* straordinaria) ♦ *vi* avere un impiego temporaneo.

temper [ˈtempəʳ] *n (character)* carattere *m*; to be in a ~ essere in collera; to lose one's ~ andare in collera.

temperature [ˈtemprətʃəʳ] *n* temperatura *f*; to have a ~ avere la febbre.

temple [ˈtempl] *n (building)* tempio *m*; *(of forehead)* tempia *f*.

temporary [ˈtempərərɪ] *adj* temporaneo(-a).

tempt [tempt] *vt* tentare; to be ~ed to do sthg essere tentato di fare qc.

temptation [tempˈteɪʃn] *n* tentazione *f*.

tempting [ˈtemptɪŋ] *adj* allettante.

ten [ten] *num* dieci, → **six**.

tenant [ˈtenənt] *n* inquilino *m* (-a *f*).

tend [tend] *vi*: to ~ to do sthg tendere a fare qc.

tendency ['tendənsı] n tendenza f.

tender ['tendə^r] adj tenero(-a); (sore) dolorante ◆ vt (fml: pay) presentare.

tendon ['tendən] n tendine m.

tenement ['tenəmənt] n caseggiato m.

tennis ['tenıs] n tennis m.

tennis ball n palla f da tennis.

tennis court n campo m da tennis.

tennis racket n racchetta f da tennis.

tenpin bowling ['tenpın-] n (Br) bowling m.

tenpins ['tenpınz] (Am) = **tenpin bowling**.

tense [tens] adj teso(-a) ◆ n (GRAMM) tempo m.

tension ['tenʃn] n tensione f.

tent [tent] n tenda f.

tenth [tenθ] num decimo(-a), → **sixth**.

tent peg n picchetto m da tenda.

tepid ['tepıd] adj (water) tiepido(-a).

tequila [tı'ki:lə] n tequila f.

term [tɜ:m] n (word, expression) termine m; (at school, university) trimestre m; **in the long ~** a lungo andare; **in the short ~** a breve scadenza; **in ~s of** per quanto riguarda; **in business ~s** dal punto di vista commerciale ❑ **terms** npl (price, of contract) condizioni fpl.

terminal ['tɜ:mınl] adj (illness) terminale ◆ n (for buses) capolinea m; (at airport) terminal m inv; (COMPUT) terminale m.

terminate ['tɜ:mıneıt] vi (train, bus) fare capolinea.

terminus ['tɜ:mınəs] n (of buses) capolinea m; (of trains) stazione f terminale.

terrace ['terəs] n (patio) terrazza f; **the ~s** (at football ground) le gradinate.

terraced house ['terəst-] n (Br) casa f a schiera.

terrible ['terəbl] adj terribile; (very ill): **to feel ~** stare malissimo.

terribly ['terəblı] adv (extremely) terribilmente; (very badly) malissimo.

terrier ['terıə^r] n terrier m inv.

terrific [tə'rıfık] adj (inf) fantastico(-a); (very great) grande.

terrified ['terıfaıd] adj terrorizzato(-a).

territory ['terətrı] n (political area) territorio m; (terrain) terreno m.

terror ['terə^r] n terrore m.

terrorism ['terərızm] n terrorismo m.

terrorist ['terərıst] n terrorista mf.

terrorize ['terəraız] vt terrorizzare.

test [test] n (at school) prova f; (check) controllo m; (MED) esame m ◆ vt (check) controllare; (give exam to) esaminare; (try) provare; **driving ~** esame di guida.

testicles ['testıklz] npl testicoli mpl.

tetanus ['tetənəs] n tetano m.

text [tekst] n testo m.

textbook ['tekstbuk] n libro m di testo.

textile ['tekstaıl] n tessuto m.

texture ['tekstʃə^r] n consistenza f; (of fabric) trama f.

Thai [taı] adj tailandese.

Thailand ['taɪlænd] *n* la Tai-
landia.

Thames [temz] *n*: **the** ~ il
Tamigi.

than [*weak form* ðən, *strong form*
ðæn] *prep* di ◆ *conj* che; **you're bet-**
ter ~ **me** sei più bravo di me; **I'd**
rather stay in ~ **go out** preferisco
restare a casa piuttosto che uscire;
more ~ **six** più di sei.

thank [θæŋk] *vt*: **to** ~ **sb (for**
sth) ringraziare qn (per qc) □
thanks *npl* ringraziamenti *mpl* ◆
excl grazie!; **~s to** grazie a; **many**
~s grazie infinite.

Thanksgiving ['θæŋks,gɪvɪn] *n*
festa *f* del Ringraziamento *(festa*
nazionale americana).

┌─┐
│*i*│ **THANKSGIVING**
└─┘

L e origini di questa festa nazionale, celebrata ogni anno negli
Stati Uniti il quarto giovedì di
novembre, risalgono al 1621, anno
in cui i Padri Pellegrini resero grazie
al Signore per il primo raccolto dal
loro arrivo dall'Inghilterra. Il tacchino arrosto e la torta di zucca sono i
due piatti tipici serviti durante il
pranzo della festa del Ringraziamento.

---

thank you *excl* grazie!; ~ **very**
much! tante OR mille grazie!; **no** ~!
no, grazie!

that [ðæt, *weak form of pron senses*
3, 4 & conj ðət] *(pl* **those**) *adj* **1.**
(referring to thing, person mentioned)
quel/quello (quella/quell', que-
gli/quei (quelle) *(pl)*; ~ **book** quel
libro; **who's** ~ **man?** chi è quell'uomo?; **those chocolates are delicious**

quei cioccolatini sono buonissimi.
2. *(referring to thing, person further*
away) quello(-a) là; **I prefer** ~ **book**
preferisco quel libro; **I'll have** ~
one prendo quello là.
◆ *pron* **1.** *(referring to thing mentioned)*
ciò; **what's** ~? che cos'è (quello)?; **I**
can't do ~ non posso farlo; **who's**
~? chi è quello?; **is** ~ **Lucy?** è Lucy?
2. *(referring to thing, person further*
away) quello(-a), quelli(-e) *(pl)*.
3. *(introducing relative clause)* che; **a**
shop ~ **sells antiques** un negozio
che vende oggetti d'antiquariato;
the film ~ **I saw** il film che ho
visto.
4. *(introducing relative clause: after*
prep) cui; **the person** ~ **I was telling**
you about la persona di cui ti stavo
parlando; **the place** ~ **I'm looking**
for il posto che sto cercando.
◆ *adv* tanto, così; **it wasn't** ~
bad/good non era così cattivo/
buono.
◆ *conj* che; **tell him** ~ **I'm going to**
be late digli che farò tardi.

thatched [θætʃt] *adj (roof)* di
paglia.

that's [ðæts] = **that is**.

thaw [θɔː] *vi (snow, ice)* sciogliersi
◆ *vt (frozen food)* scongelare.

the [*weak form* ðə, *before vowel* ðɪ,
strong form ðiː] *definite article* **1.** *(gen)*
il/lo (la), i/gli (le); ~ **book** il libro; ~
man l'uomo; ~ **mirror** lo specchio; ~
woman la donna; ~ **island** l'isola; ~
men gli uomini; ~ **girls** le ragazze; ~ **Wilsons** i Wilsons.
2. *(with an adjective to form a noun)*:
~ **British** i britannici; ~ **young** i
giovani.
3. *(in dates)*: **Friday** ~ **nineteenth of**
May venerdì diciannove maggio; ~
twelfth il dodici; ~ **forties** gli anni

quaranta.

4. *(in titles):* **Elizabeth ~ Second** Elisabetta Seconda.

theater ['θɪətəʳ] *n* (*Am*) (*for plays, drama*) = theatre; (*for films*) cinema *m inv.*

theatre ['θɪətəʳ] *n* (*Br*) (*for plays*) teatro *m.*

theft [θeft] *n* furto *m.*

their [ðeəʳ] *adj* il loro (la loro), i loro (le loro) (*pl*).

theirs [ðeəz] *pron* il loro (la loro), i loro (le loro) (*pl*); **a friend of ~** un loro amico.

them [*weak form* ðəm, *strong form* ðem] *pron* (*direct*) li (le); (*indirect*) gli; (*after prep with people*) loro; (*after prep with things*) essi(-e); **I know ~** li conosco; **it's ~** sono loro; **send it to ~** mandaglielo; **tell ~** diglielo; **he's worse than ~** è peggio di loro.

theme [θi:m] *n* tema *m.*

theme park *n* parco *m* di divertimenti.

themselves [ðəm'selvz] *pron* (*reflexive*) si; (*after prep*) se stessi (se stesse), sé; **they did it ~** l'hanno fatto da soli.

then [ðen] *adv* allora; (*next, afterwards*) dopo, poi; **from ~ on** da allora in poi; **until ~** fino ad allora.

theory ['θɪərɪ] *n* teoria *f*; **in ~** in teoria.

therapist ['θerəpɪst] *n* terapeuta *mf.*

therapy ['θerəpɪ] *n* terapia *f.*

there [ðeəʳ] *adv* (*at, in, to that place*) lì, là ♦ *pron:* **~ is** c'è; **~ are** ci sono; **is anyone ~?** c'è nessuno?; **is Bob ~, please?** (*on phone*) c'è Bob, per cortesia?; **we're going ~ tomorrow** ci andiamo domani; **over ~**

thereabouts [,ðeərə'baʊts] *adv:* **or ~** o giù di lì.

therefore ['ðeəfɔ:ʳ] *adv* perciò.

there's [ðeəz] = there is.

thermal underwear [,θɜ:ml-] *n* biancheria *f* termica.

thermometer [θə'mɒmɪtəʳ] *n* termometro *m.*

Thermos (flask)® ['θɜ:məs-] *n* thermos® *m inv.*

thermostat ['θɜ:məstæt] *n* termostato *m.*

these [ði:z] *pl* → this.

they [ðeɪ] *pron* essi (esse); (*referring to people*) loro; **~'re tall** sono alti.

thick [θɪk] *adj* (*in size*) spesso(-a); (*hair*) folto(-a); (*sauce, smoke*) denso(-a); (*fog*) fitto(-a); (*inf: stupid*) tonto(-a); **it's one metre ~** ha uno spessore di un metro.

thicken ['θɪkn] *vt* (*sauce, soup*) rendere più denso ♦ *vi* (*mist, fog*) infittirsi.

thickness ['θɪknɪs] *n* spessore *m.*

thief [θi:f] (*pl* **thieves** [θi:vz]) *n* ladro *m* (-a *f*).

thigh [θaɪ] *n* coscia *f.*

thimble ['θɪmbl] *n* ditale *m.*

thin [θɪn] *adj* sottile; (*person, animal*) magro(-a); (*soup, sauce*) liquido(-a).

thing [θɪŋ] *n* cosa *f*; **the ~** is il fatto è ❑ **things** *npl* (*clothes, possessions*) cose *fpl*; **how are ~s?** (*inf*) come vanno le cose?

thingummyjig ['θɪŋəmɪdʒɪg] *n* (*inf*) coso *m.*

think [θɪŋk] (*pt & pp* **thought**) *vt* pensare ♦ *vi* pensare; **to ~ that**

pensare che; **to ~ about** pensare a; **to ~ of** pensare a; **to ~ of doing** sthg pensare di fare qc; **I ~ so** penso di sì; **I don't ~ so** penso di no; **do you ~ you could ...?** potrebbe ...?; **I'll think about it** ci penserò; **I can't ~ of his address** non mi viene in mente il suo indirizzo; **to ~ highly of sb** avere una buona opinione di qn ❑ **think over** vt sep riflettere su; **think up** vt sep escogitare.

third [θɜːd] num terzo(-a), → **sixth**.

third party insurance n assicurazione f contro terzi.

Third World n: **the ~** il Terzo Mondo.

thirst [θɜːst] n sete f.

thirsty ['θɜːstɪ] adj: **to be ~** avere sete.

thirteen [ˌθɜː'tiːn] num tredici, → **six**.

thirteenth [ˌθɜː'tiːnθ] num tredicesimo(-a), → **sixth**.

thirtieth ['θɜːtɪəθ] num trentesimo(-a), → **sixth**.

thirty ['θɜːtɪ] num trenta, → **six**.

this [ðɪs] (pl **these**) adj **1.** (referring to thing, person mentioned) questo(-a); **these chocolates are delicious** questi cioccolatini sono buonissimi; **~ morning** stamattina; **~ week** questa settimana.
2. (referring to thing, person nearer) questo(-a); **I prefer ~ book** preferisco questo libro; **I'll have ~ one** prendo questo.
3. (inf: when telling a story): **there was ~ man ...** c'era un tizio ...
◆ pron **1.** (referring to thing, person mentioned) questo(-a); **~ is for you** questo è per te; **what are these?**

che cosa sono questi?; **~ is David Gregory** (introducing someone) questo è David Gregory; (on telephone) sono David Gregory.
2. (referring to thing, person nearer) questo(-a).
◆ adv: **it was ~ big** era grande così.

thistle ['θɪsl] n cardo m.

thorn [θɔːn] n spina f.

thorough ['θʌrə] adj (check, search) accurato(-a); (person) preciso(-a).

thoroughly ['θʌrəlɪ] adv (completely) a fondo.

those [ðəʊz] pl → **that**.

though [ðəʊ] conj benché, sebbene ◆ adv tuttavia; **even ~** anche se.

thought [θɔːt] pt & pp → **think**.
◆ n pensiero m; (idea) idea f.

thoughtful ['θɔːtfʊl] adj (quiet and serious) pensieroso(-a); (considerate) premuroso(-a).

thoughtless ['θɔːtlɪs] adj sconsiderato(-a).

thousand ['θaʊznd] num mille; **a** OR **one ~** mille; **~s of** migliaia di, → **six**.

thrash [θræʃ] vt (inf: defeat heavily) battere.

thread [θred] n (of cotton etc) filo m ◆ vt (needle) infilare.

threadbare ['θredbeəʳ] adj logoro(-a).

threat [θret] n minaccia f.

threaten ['θretn] vt minacciare; **to ~ to do sthg** minacciare di fare qc.

threatening ['θretnɪŋ] adj minaccioso(-a).

three [θriː] num tre, → **six**.

three-D n: **in ~** tridimensio-

...ale.

...hree-piece suite *n* divano
... e due poltrone coordinati.

...hree-quarters ['-kwɔːtəz] *n*
*...*re quarti *mpl*; **~ of an hour** tre
quarti d'ora.

...hreshold ['θreʃhəʊld] *n (fml)*
...oglia *f*.

...hrew [θruː] *pt* → **throw**.

...hrifty ['θrɪftɪ] *adj* parsimonio-
...o(-a).

...hrilled [θrɪld] *adj* contentissi-
...no(-a).

...hriller ['θrɪlər] *n* thriller *m inv*.

...hrive [θraɪv] *vi (plant, animal,
...erson)* crescere bene; *(business,
...urism, place)* prosperare.

...hroat [θrəʊt] *n* gola *f*.

...hrob [θrɒb] *vi (noise, engine)*
...ibrare; **my head is throbbing** ho
...n mal di testa lancinante.

...hrone [θrəʊn] *n* trono *m*.

...hrottle ['θrɒtl] *n (of motorbike)*
...alvola *f* a farfalla.

...hrough [θruː] *prep* attraverso;
...ecause of)* grazie a; *(from beginning
...o end of)* per tutta la durata di;
...cross all of)* per tutto(-a) ◆ *adv (to
...her side)* attraverso; *(from begin-
...ing to end)* dall'inizio alla fine ◆
...dj:* **to be ~ (with sthg)** *(finished)*
...vere finito (con qc); **you're ~** *(on
...hone)* è in linea; **Monday ~
...hursday** *(Am)* dal lunedì al giove-
...i; **to go ~** *(to somewhere else)* pas-
...are; **to let sb ~** far passare qn; **I
...ept ~ the entire film** ho dormito
...er tutto il film; **~ traffic** traffico *m*
...l attraversamento; **a ~ train** un
...reno diretto; **'no ~ road'** *(Br)* 'stra-
...a senza uscita'.

...hroughout [θruːˈaʊt] *prep
...day, morning, year)* per tutto(-a);

(place, country, building) in tutto(-a)
◆ *adv (all the time)* per tutto il
tempo; *(everywhere)* dappertutto.

throw [θrəʊ] *(pt* **threw**, *pp*
thrown [θrəʊn]) *vt* gettare; *(ball,
javelin)* lanciare; *(dice)* tirare; **to ~
sthg in the bin** gettare qc nel cestino ❑ **throw away** *vt sep (get rid of)*
buttare OR gettare via; **throw out**
vt sep (get rid of) buttare OR gettare
via; *(person)* buttare fuori; **throw
up** *vi (inf: vomit)* rimettere.

thru [θruː] *(Am)* = **through**.

thrush [θrʌʃ] *n (bird)* tordo *m*.

thud [θʌd] *n* tonfo *m*.

thug [θʌg] *n* delinquente *mf*.

thumb [θʌm] *n* pollice *m* ◆ *vt:* **to
~ a lift** fare l'autostop.

thumbtack ['θʌmtæk] *n (Am)*
puntina *f* da disegno.

thump [θʌmp] *n (punch)* pugno
m; (sound) tonfo *m* ◆ *vt* picchiare.

thunder ['θʌndər] *n* tuono *m*.

thunderstorm ['θʌndəstɔːm] *n*
temporale *m*.

Thurs. *(abbr of Thursday)* gio.

Thursday ['θɜːzdɪ] *n* giovedì *m
inv*, → **Saturday**.

thyme [taɪm] *n* timo *m*.

Tiber ['taɪbər] *n:* **the ~** il Tevere.

tick [tɪk] *n (written mark)* segno *m;
(insect)* zecca *f* ◆ *vt* spuntare ◆ *vi
(clock, watch)* fare tic tac ❑ **tick off**
vt sep (mark off) spuntare.

ticket ['tɪkɪt] *n (for travel, cinema,
theatre, match)* biglietto *m; (label)*
etichetta *f; (speeding ticket, parking
ticket)* multa *f*.

ticket collector *n* controllore *m*.

ticket inspector *n* controllore *m*.

ticket machine n distributore m automatico di biglietti.

ticket office n biglietteria f.

tickle ['tıkl] vt fare il solletico a.

ticklish ['tıklıʃ] adj: **to be** ~ soffrire il solletico.

tick-tack-toe n (Am) tris m (gioco).

tide [taıd] n (of sea) marea f.

tidy ['taıdı] adj (room, desk, person) ordinato(-a); (hair, clothes) in ordine ❑ **tidy up** vt sep riordinare, mettere in ordine.

tie [taı] (pt & pp **tied**, cont **tying**) n (around neck) cravatta f; (draw) pareggio m; (Am: on railway track) traversa f ◆ vt (fasten) legare; (laces) allacciare; (knot) fare ◆ vi (draw) pareggiare ❑ **tie up** vt sep (fasten) legare; (laces) annodare.

tied up ['taıd-] adj occupato(-a).

tiepin ['taıpın] n fermacravatta m inv.

tier [tıəʳ] n (of seats) fila f.

tiger ['taıgəʳ] n tigre f.

tight [taıt] adj stretto(-a); (rope) teso(-a); (chest) chiuso(-a); (inf: drunk) sbronzo(-a) ◆ adv (hold) stretto(-a).

tighten ['taıtn] vt stringere.

tightrope ['taıtrəup] n corda f (sulla quale si esibiscono i funamboli).

tights [taıts] npl collant m inv; a pair of ~ un paio di collant.

tile ['taıl] n (for roof) tegola f; (for floor, wall) mattonella f, piastrella f.

till [tıl] n (for money) cassa f ◆ prep fino a ◆ conj finché non.

tiller ['tıləʳ] n barra f del timone.

tilt [tılt] vt inclinare ◆ vi inclinarsi.

timber ['tımbəʳ] n (wood) legna-

me m; (of roof) trave f.

time [taım] n tempo m; (measure by clock) ora f; (of train, flight, bus) orario m; (moment) momento m; (occasion) volta f ◆ vt (measure) cronometrare; (arrange) programma re; **to** ~ **sthg well** fare qc al momento giusto; **I haven't got the** ~ non ho tempo; **it's** ~ **to go** è or di andare; **what's the** ~? che or sono?; **two** ~**s** **two** due per due two at a ~ due per volta; **five** ~**s** a much cinque volte tanto; **in** month's ~ fra un mese; **to have** good ~ divertirsi; **all the** ~ sempre every ~ ogni volta; **from** ~ **to** ~ c tanto in tanto; **for the** ~ **being** pe il momento; **in** ~ (arrive) in tempe **in good** ~ per tempo; **last** ~ l'ulti ma volta; **most of the** ~ la maggic parte del tempo; **on** ~ puntuale some of the ~ parte del tempo this ~ questa volta.

time difference n differenza di fuso orario.

time limit n termine m mass mo.

timer ['taıməʳ] n timer m inv.

time share n multiproprietà inv.

timetable ['taım,teıbl] n orari m; (of events) calendario m.

time zone n fuso m orario.

timid ['tımıd] adj (shy) timido(-a (easily frightened) pauroso(-a).

tin [tın] n (metal) stagno m; (con tainer) scatola f ◆ adj di latta.

tinfoil ['tınfɔıl] n stagnola f.

tinned food [tınd-] n (Br) cib m in scatola.

tin opener [-,əupnəʳ] n (Br) apr scatole m inv.

tinsel ['tınsl] n fili mpl argenta

per decorare l'albero di Natale).

tint [tɪnt] *n* tinta *f*.

tinted glass [ˌtɪntɪd-] *n* vetro *m* colorato.

tiny [ˈtaɪnɪ] *adj* molto piccolo(-a).

tip [tɪp] *n (point, end)* punta *f*; *(to waiter, taxi driver etc)* mancia *f*; *(piece of advice)* suggerimento *m*; *(rubbish dump)* discarica *f* ◆ *vt (waiter, taxi driver etc)* dare la mancia a; *(tilt)* inclinare; *(pour)* versare ❑ **tip over** *vt sep* rovesciare ◆ *vi* rovesciarsi.

tire [ˈtaɪə^r] *vi* stancarsi ◆ *n (Am)* = **tyre**.

tired [ˈtaɪəd] *adj* stanco(-a); **to be ~ of** *(fed up with)* essere stanco di.

tired out *adj* esausto(-a).

tiring [ˈtaɪərɪŋ] *adj* faticoso(-a).

tissue [ˈtɪʃuː] *n (handkerchief)* fazzolettino *m* di carta.

tissue paper *n* carta *f* velina.

tit [tɪt] *n (vulg: breast)* tetta *f*.

title [ˈtaɪtl] *n* titolo *m*.

T-junction *n* incrocio *m* a T.

to *[unstressed before consonant* tə, *unstressed before vowel* tʊ, *stressed* tuː] *prep* 1. *(indicating direction)* a; **to go ~ Milan** andare a Milano; **to go ~ France** andare in Francia; **to go ~ school** andare a scuola; **to go ~ the office** andare in ufficio.

2. *(indicating position)* a; **~ the left/right** a sinistra/destra.

3. *(expressing indirect object)* a; **to give sthg ~ sb** dare qc a qn; **to listen ~ the radio** ascoltare la radio.

4. *(indicating reaction, effect)* a; **to be favourable ~ sthg** essere favorevole a qc; **~ my surprise** con mia grande sorpresa.

5. *(until)* fino a; **to count ~ ten** contare fino a dieci; **we work from**

nine ~ five lavoriamo dalle nove alle cinque.

6. *(indicating change of state)*: **to turn ~ sthg** trasformarsi in qc; **it could lead ~ trouble** potrebbe causare problemi.

7. *(Br: in expressions of time)*: **it's ten ~ three** sono le tre meno dieci; **at quarter ~ seven** alle sette meno un quarto.

8. *(in ratios, rates)*: **40 miles ~ the gallon** ≃ 100 chilometri con 7 litri; **there are sixteen ounces ~ the pound** sedici once fanno una libbra.

9. *(of, for)*: **the keys ~ the car** le chiavi dell'automobile; **a letter ~ my daughter** una lettera a mia figlia.

10. *(indicating attitude)* con, verso; **to be rude ~ sb** essere scortese con qn.

◆ *with infinitive* 1. *(forming simple infinitive)*: **~ walk** camminare; **~ laugh** ridere.

2. *(following another verb)*: **to begin ~ do sthg** cominciare a fare qc; **to try ~ do sthg** cercare di fare qc.

3. *(following an adjective)*: **difficult ~ do** difficile da fare; **ready ~ go** pronto a partire.

4. *(indicating purpose)* per; **we came here ~ look at the castle** siamo venuti qui per visitare il castello.

toad [təʊd] *n* rospo *m*.

toadstool [ˈtəʊdstuːl] *n* fungo *m* velenoso.

toast [təʊst] *n (bread)* pane *m* tostato; *(when drinking)* brindisi *m inv* ◆ *vt (bread)* tostare; **a piece OR slice of ~** una fetta di pane tostato.

toasted sandwich [ˈtəʊstɪd-] *n* toast *m inv*.

toaster [ˈtəʊstə^r] *n* tostapane

m inv.

toastie ['təʊstɪ] = **toasted sand-wich.**

tobacco [tə'bækəʊ] *n* tabacco *m.*

tobacconist's [tə'bækənɪsts] *n (shop)* tabaccaio *m.*

toboggan [tə'bɒgən] *n* toboga *m inv.*

today [tə'deɪ] *n* oggi *m* ♦ *adv* oggi.

toddler ['tɒdlər] *n* bambino *m* (-a *f*) *(che muove i primi passi).*

toe [təʊ] *n (of person)* dito *m* del piede.

toe clip *n* puntapiedi *m inv.*

toenail ['təʊneɪl] *n* unghia *f* del piede.

toffee ['tɒfɪ] *n (sweet)* caramella *f* mou *(inv).*

together [tə'geðər] *adv* insieme; **~ with** insieme a.

toilet ['tɔɪlɪt] *n (room)* gabinetto *m; (bowl)* water *m inv;* **to go to the ~** andare al gabinetto; **where's the ~?** dov'è il gabinetto?

toilet bag *n* nécessaire *m inv* da toilette.

toilet paper *n* carta *f* igienica.

toiletries ['tɔɪlɪtrɪz] *npl* prodotti *mpl* cosmetici.

toilet roll *n* rotolo *m* di carta igienica.

toilet water *n* acqua *f* di colonia.

token ['təʊkn] *n (metal disc)* gettone *m.*

told [təʊld] *pt & pp* → **tell.**

tolerable ['tɒlərəbl] *adj (fairly good)* passabile; *(bearable)* sopportabile.

tolerant ['tɒlərənt] *adj* tollerante.

tolerate ['tɒləreɪt] *vt* tollerare.

toll [təʊl] *n (for road, bridge* pedaggio *m.*

tollbooth ['təʊlbu:θ] *n* casello *m*

toll-free *adj (Am):* **~ number =** numero *m* verde.

tomato [Br tə'mɑ:tau, Am t 'meɪtəʊ] *(pl* **-es)** *n* pomodoro *m.*

tomato juice *n* succo *m* pomodoro.

tomato ketchup *n* ketchup *m*

tomato puree *n* conserva *f* d pomodoro.

tomato sauce *n* sugo *m* d pomodoro.

tomb [tu:m] *n* tomba *f.*

tomorrow [tə'mɒrəʊ] *n* doman *m* ♦ *adv* domani; **the day after ~** dopodomani; **~ afternoon** doman pomeriggio; **~ morning** doman mattina; **~ night** domani sera.

ton [tʌn] *n (in Britain)* = 1016 kg *(in U.S.)* = 907 kg; *(metric tonne* tonnellata *f;* **~s of** *(inf)* un sacco *m*

tone [təʊn] *n (of voice)* tono *m; (* *phone)* segnale *m; (of colour)* tonali tà *f inv.*

tongs [tɒŋz] *npl (for hair)* arriccia capelli *m inv; (for sugar)* mollette *fp*

tongue [tʌŋ] *n* lingua *f.*

tonic ['tɒnɪk] *n (tonic water)* acqu *f* tonica; *(medicine)* ricostituente *m*

tonic water *n* acqua *f* tonica.

tonight [tə'naɪt] *n (night)* quest notte *f; (evening)* questa sera *f* ♦ *adv (night)* stanotte, questa notte *(evening)* stasera, questa sera.

tonne [tʌn] *n* tonnellata *f.*

tonsillitis [,tɒnsɪ'laɪtɪs] *n* ton sillite *f.*

too [tu:] *adv (excessively)* troppo *(also)* anche; **it's ~ late to go out**

troppo tardi per uscire; ~ **many** troppi(-e); ~ **much** troppo(-a).

took [tʊk] *pt* → **take**.

tool [tuːl] *n* attrezzo *m*.

tool kit *n* attrezzi *mpl*.

tooth [tuːθ] (*pl* **teeth**) *n* dente *m*.

toothache ['tuːθeɪk] *n* mal *m* di denti.

toothbrush ['tuːθbrʌʃ] *n* spazzolino *m* da denti.

toothpaste ['tuːθpeɪst] *n* dentifricio *m*.

toothpick ['tuːθpɪk] *n* stuzzicadenti *m*.

top [tɒp] *adj* (*highest*) più alto(-a); (*step, stair*) ultimo(-a); (*best*) migliore; (*most important*) più importante ◆ *n* (*of stairs, hill, page*) cima *f*; (*of table*) piano *m*; (*of class, league*) primo *m* (*-a f*); (*for bottle, tube, pen*) tappo *m*; (*for jar, box*) coperchio *m*; (*of pyjamas, bikini*) sopra *m inv*; (*blouse*) camicetta *f*; (*T-shirt*) maglietta *f*; **at the ~ (of)** (*stairs, list, mountain*) in cima (a); **on ~ of** (*table etc*) sopra, su; (*in addition to*) oltre a; **at ~ speed** a tutta velocità; ~ **gear** = quinta *f* ❑ **top up** *vt sep* (*glass, drink*) riempire ◆ *vi* (*with petrol*) fare il pieno.

top floor *n* ultimo piano *m*.

topic ['tɒpɪk] *n* argomento *m*.

topical ['tɒpɪkl] *adj* d'attualità.

topless ['tɒplɪs] *adj*: **to go ~** mettersi in topless.

topped [tɒpt] *adj*: ~ **with** (*cream etc*) ricoperto(-a) di.

topping ['tɒpɪŋ] *n* guarnizione *f* (*su pizza ecc.*).

torch [tɔːtʃ] *n* (*Br: electric light*) torcia *f* elettrica.

tore [tɔːʳ] *pt* → **tear**[1].

torment [tɔː'ment] *vt* (*annoy*) tormentare.

torn [tɔːn] *pp* → **tear**[1] ◆ *adj* (*ripped*) strappato(-a).

tornado [tɔː'neɪdəʊ] (*pl* **-es** OR **-s**) *n* tornado *m*.

torrential rain [tə,renʃl-] *n* pioggia *f* torrenziale.

tortoise ['tɔːtəs] *n* tartaruga *f*.

tortoiseshell ['tɔːtəʃel] *n* tartaruga *f*.

torture ['tɔːtʃəʳ] *n* tortura *f* ◆ *vt* torturare.

Tory ['tɔːrɪ] *n* membro del partito conservatore britannico.

toss [tɒs] *vt* (*throw*) lanciare; (*salad, vegetables*) mescolare; **to ~ a coin** fare testa o croce.

total ['təʊtl] *adj* totale ◆ *n* totale *m*; **in ~** in totale.

touch [tʌtʃ] *n* (*sense*) tatto *m*; (*small amount*) tantino *m*; (*detail*) tocco *m* ◆ *vt* toccare ◆ *vi* toccarsi; **to get in ~ (with sb)** mettersi in contatto (con qn); **to keep in ~ (with sb)** tenersi in contatto (con qn) ❑ **touch down** *vi* (*plane*) atterrare.

touching ['tʌtʃɪŋ] *adj* toccante.

tough [tʌf] *adj* duro(-a); (*resilient*) tenace; (*hard, strong*) resistente.

tour [tʊəʳ] *n* (*journey*) viaggio *m*; (*of city, castle etc*) visita *f*; (*of pop group, theatre company*) tournée *f inv* ◆ *vt* visitare; **on ~** in tournée.

tourism ['tʊərɪzm] *n* turismo *m*.

tourist ['tʊərɪst] *n* turista *mf*.

tourist class *n* classe *f* turistica.

tourist information office *n* ufficio *m* d'informazione turistica.

tournament ['tɔːnəmənt] n torneo m.

tour operator n operatore m turistico (operatrice turistica f).

tout [taut] n bagarino m.

tow [təʊ] vt rimorchiare.

toward [tə'wɔːd] (Am) = towards.

towards [tə'wɔːdz] prep (Br) verso; (with regard to) nei confronti di; (to help pay for) per.

towaway zone ['təʊəwei-] n (Am) zona f rimozione forzata.

towel ['tauəl] n asciugamano m.

toweling ['tauəlɪŋ] (Am) = towelling.

towelling ['tauəlɪŋ] n (Br) spugna f.

towel rail n portasciugamano m.

tower ['tauəʳ] n torre f.

tower block n (Br) grattacielo m.

Tower Bridge n Tower Bridge (famoso ponte levatoio di Londra).

TOWER BRIDGE

Costruito in stile gotico nel diciannovesimo secolo, questo ponte sul Tamigi è costituito da due caratteristici ponti levatoi gemelli che si alzano per permettere il passaggio delle navi più grandi.

Tower of London n: the ~ la Torre di Londra.

TOWER OF LONDON

Situata sulla riva nord del Tamigi, la Torre di Londra è una fortezza che risale all'undicesimo secolo e fu

residenza reale fino al diciassettesimo secolo. Oggi è un'attrazione turistica aperta al pubblico e ospita al suo interno un museo.

---

town [taun] n città f; (town centre, centro m (città).

town centre n centro m (città).

town hall n comune m.

towpath ['təʊpɑːθ, pl -pɑːðz] n alzaia f.

towrope ['təʊrəʊp] n cavo m d rimorchio.

tow truck n (Am) carro m at trezzi.

toxic ['tɒksɪk] adj tossico(-a).

toy [tɔɪ] n giocattolo m.

toy shop n negozio m di giocat toli.

trace [treɪs] n traccia f ♦ vt (fina rintracciare.

tracing paper ['treɪsɪŋ-] n cart f da ricalco.

track [træk] n (path) sentiero m (of railway) binario m, rotaie fp (SPORT) pista f; (song) pezzo m

track down vt sep trovare.

tracksuit ['træksuːt] n tuta f d ginnastica.

tractor ['træktəʳ] n trattore m.

trade [treɪd] n (COMM) commer cio m; (job) mestiere m ♦ vt scam biare ♦ vi commerciare.

trade-in n permuta f.

trademark ['treɪdmɑːk] n mai chio m di fabbrica.

trader ['treɪdəʳ] n commerciant mf.

tradesman ['treɪdzmən] (p -men [-mən]) n (deliveryman) adde to m alle consegne; (shopkeepe commerciante *mf*.

trade union *n* sindacato *m*.

tradition [trəˈdɪʃn] *n* tradizione *f*.

traditional [trəˈdɪʃənl] *adj* tradizionale.

traffic [ˈtræfɪk] (*pt* & *pp* **-ked**) *n* (*cars etc*) traffico *m* ♦ *vi*: **to ~ in** trafficare in.

traffic circle *n* (*Am*) rotatoria *f*.

traffic island *n* salvagente *m*.

traffic jam *n* ingorgo *m*.

traffic lights *npl* semaforo *m*.

traffic warden *n* (*Br*) = vigile *m* urbano (*addetto al controllo dei divieti e limiti di sosta*).

tragedy [ˈtrædʒədɪ] *n* tragedia *f*.

tragic [ˈtrædʒɪk] *adj* tragico(-a).

trail [treɪl] *n* (*path*) sentiero *m*; (*marks*) tracce *fpl* ♦ *vi* (*be losing*) essere in svantaggio.

trailer [ˈtreɪləʳ] *n* (*for boat, luggage*) rimorchio *m*; (*Am: caravan*) roulotte *f inv*; (*for film, programme*) trailer *m inv*.

train [treɪn] *n* (*on railway*) treno *m* ♦ *vt* (*teach*) formare; (*animal*) addestrare ♦ *vi* (*SPORT*) allenarsi; **by ~ in** treno.

train driver *n* macchinista *m*.

trainee [treɪˈniː] *n* (*for profession*) tirocinante *mf*; (*for trade*) apprendista *mf*.

trainer [ˈtreɪnəʳ] *n* (*of athlete etc*) allenatore *m* (-trice *f*) ❏ **trainers** *npl* (*Br: shoes*) scarpe *fpl* da ginnastica.

training [ˈtreɪnɪŋ] *n* (*instruction*) formazione *f*, addestramento *m*; (*exercises*) allenamento *m*.

training shoes *npl* (*Br*) scarpe *fpl* da ginnastica.

tram [træm] *n* (*Br*) tram *m inv*.

tramp [træmp] *n* vagabondo *m* (-a *f*).

trampoline [ˈtræmpəliːn] *n* trampolino *m*.

trance [trɑːns] *n* trance *f*.

tranquilizer [ˈtræŋkwɪlaɪzəʳ] (*Am*) = **tranquillizer**.

tranquillizer [ˈtræŋkwɪlaɪzəʳ] *n* (*Br*) tranquillante *m*.

transaction [trænˈzækʃn] *n* transazione *f*.

transatlantic [ˌtrænzətˈlæntɪk] *adj* transatlantico(-a).

transfer [*n* ˈtrænsfəːʳ, *vb* trænsˈfəːʳ] *n* trasferimento *m*; (*of power, property*) passaggio *m*; (*picture*) decalcomania *f*; (*Am: ticket*) biglietto che dà la possibilità di cambiare autobus, treno ecc. senza pagare alcun supplemento ♦ *vt* trasferire ♦ *vi* (*change bus, plane etc*) cambiare; '**~s**' (*in airport*) 'transiti'.

transfer desk *n* banco *m* transiti.

transform [trænsˈfɔːm] *vt* trasformare.

transfusion [trænsˈfjuːʒn] *n* trasfusione *f*.

transistor radio [trænˈzɪstəʳ-] *n* transistor *m inv*.

transit [ˈtrænzɪt] : **in transit** *adv* in transito.

transitive [ˈtrænzɪtɪv] *adj* transitivo(-a).

transit lounge *n* sala *f* transiti.

translate [trænsˈleɪt] *vt* tradurre.

translation [trænsˈleɪʃn] *n* traduzione *f*.

translator [trænsˈleɪtəʳ] *n* traduttore *m* (-trice *f*).

transmission [trænzˈmɪʃn] *n* trasmissione *f*.

transmit [trænz'mɪt] *vt* trasmettere.

transparent [træns'pærənt] *adj* trasparente.

transplant ['trænsplɑːnt] *n* trapianto *m*.

transport [*n* 'trænspɔːt, *vb* træn'spɔːt] *n (cars, trains, planes etc)* trasporti *mpl; (moving)* trasporto *m* ◆ *vt* trasportare.

transportation [ˌtrænspɔː'teɪʃn] *n (Am) (cars, trains, planes etc)* trasporti *mpl; (moving)* trasporto *m*.

trap [træp] *n* trappola *f* ◆ *vt*: **to be trapped** *(stuck)* essere intrappolato.

trapdoor [ˌtræp'dɔːʳ] *n* botola *f*.

trash [træʃ] *n (Am: waste material)* spazzatura *f*.

trashcan ['træʃkæn] *n (Am)* pattumiera *f*.

trauma ['trɔːmə] *n (bad experience)* trauma *m*.

traumatic [trɔː'mætɪk] *adj* traumatico(-a).

travel ['trævl] *n* viaggi *mpl* ◆ *vt (distance)* percorrere ◆ *vi* viaggiare.

travel agency *n* agenzia *f* di viaggi.

travel agent *n* agente *mf* di viaggi; **~'s** *(shop)* agenzia *f* di viaggi.

Travelcard ['trævlkɑːd] *n* biglietto che dà accesso ai mezzi pubblici di Londra per un'intera giornata.

travel centre *n (in railway, bus station)* ufficio informazioni e biglietteria.

traveler ['trævlər] *(Am)* = **traveller**.

travel insurance *n* assicurazione *f* viaggio.

traveller ['trævləʳ] *n (Br)* viag-

giatore *m* (-trice *f*).

traveller's cheque *n* traveller's cheque *m* inv.

travelsick ['trævlsɪk] *adj*: **to be ~** *(in car)* soffrire il mal d'auto; *(on boat)* soffrire il mal di mare; *(on plane)* soffrire il mal d'aria.

trawler ['trɔːləʳ] *n* peschereccio *m*.

tray [treɪ] *n* vassoio *m*.

treacherous ['tretʃərəs] *adj (person)* infido(-a); *(roads, conditions)* insidioso(-a).

treacle ['triːkl] *n (Br)* melassa *f*.

tread [tred] *(pt* **trod,** *pp* **trodden)** *n (of tyre)* battistrada *m inv* ◆ *vi*: **to ~ on sthg** calpestare qc.

treasure ['treʒəʳ] *n* tesoro *m*.

treat [triːt] *vt* trattare; *(patient, illness)* curare ◆ *n* regalo *m*; **to ~ sb to sthg** offrire qc a qn.

treatment ['triːtmənt] *n (MED)* cure *fpl; (of person)* trattamento *m; (of subject)* trattazione *f*.

treble ['trebl] *adj* triplo(-a).

tree [triː] *n* albero *m*.

trek [trek] *n* escursione *f*.

tremble ['trembl] *vi* tremare.

tremendous [trɪ'mendəs] *adj (very large)* enorme; *(inf: very good)* formidabile.

trench [trentʃ] *n* fosso *m*.

trend [trend] *n (tendency)* tendenza *f; (fashion)* moda *f*.

trendy ['trendɪ] *adj (inf)* alla moda.

trespasser ['trespəsəʳ] *n*: **'~s will be prosecuted'** 'vietato l'accesso; i trasgressori saranno puniti a termini di legge'.

trial ['traɪəl] *n (JUR)* processo *m; (test)* prova *f*; **a ~ period** un periodo di prova.

triangle ['traɪæŋgl] n triangolo m.

triangular [traɪˈæŋgjʊlər] adj triangolare.

tribe [traɪb] n tribù f inv.

tributary ['trɪbjʊtrɪ] n tributario m, affluente m.

trick [trɪk] n trucco m; (conjuring trick) gioco m di prestigio ♦ vt imbrogliare, ingannare; **to play a ~ on sb** giocare un brutto tiro a qn.

trickle ['trɪkl] vi (liquid) gocciolare, colare.

tricky ['trɪkɪ] adj difficile.

tricycle ['traɪsɪkl] n triciclo m.

trifle ['traɪfl] n (dessert) zuppa f inglese.

trigger ['trɪgər] n grilletto m.

trim [trɪm] n (haircut) spuntata f ♦ vt (hair, beard) spuntare; (hedge) regolare.

trinket ['trɪŋkɪt] n ciondolo m, gingillo m.

trio ['triːəʊ] (pl **-s**) n trio m.

trip [trɪp] n (journey) viaggio m; (short) gita f, escursione f ♦ vi inciampare ❑ **trip up** vi inciampare.

triple ['trɪpl] adj triplo(-a).

tripod ['traɪpɒd] n treppiedi m inv.

triumph ['traɪəmf] n trionfo m.

trivial ['trɪvɪəl] adj (pej) insignificante, banale.

trod [trɒd] pt → tread.

trodden ['trɒdn] pp → tread.

trolley ['trɒlɪ] (pl **-s**) n (Br: in supermarket, at airport, for food etc) carrello m; (Am: tram) tram m inv.

trombone [trɒmˈbəʊn] n trombone m.

troops [truːps] npl truppe fpl.

trophy ['trəʊfɪ] n trofeo m.

tropical ['trɒpɪkl] adj tropicale.

trot [trɒt] vi (horse) trottare ♦ n: **on the ~** (inf) di fila.

trouble ['trʌbl] n problemi mpl ♦ vt (worry) preoccupare; (bother) disturbare; **to be in ~** essere nei guai; **to get into ~** mettersi nei guai; **to take the ~ to do sthg** darsi la pena di fare qc; **it's no ~** non si preoccupi; (in reply to thanks) di niente.

trough [trɒf] n (for drinking) abbeveratoio m.

trouser press ['traʊzər-] n stiracalzoni m inv.

trousers ['traʊzəz] npl pantaloni mpl; **a pair of ~** un paio di pantaloni.

trout [traʊt] (pl inv) n trota f.

trowel ['traʊəl] n (for gardening) paletta f.

truant ['truːənt] n: **to play ~** marinare la scuola.

truce [truːs] n tregua f.

truck [trʌk] n (lorry) camion m inv, autocarro m.

true [truː] adj vero(-a).

truly ['truːlɪ] adv: **yours ~** distinti saluti.

trumpet ['trʌmpɪt] n tromba f.

trumps [trʌmps] npl atout m inv.

truncheon ['trʌntʃən] n sfollagente m inv.

trunk [trʌŋk] n (of tree) tronco m; (Am: of car) bagagliaio m; (case, box) baule m; (of elephant) proboscide f.

trunk call n (Br) interurbana f.

trunk road n (Br) strada f statale.

trunks [trʌŋks] npl costume m da bagno da uomo.

trust [trʌst] n (confidence) fiducia f ♦ vt (believe, have confidence in) fidarsi di, aver fiducia in; (fml: hope) sperare.

trustworthy ['trʌst,wɜːðɪ] adj degno(-a) di fiducia.

truth [truːθ] n (true facts) verità f; (quality of being true) veridicità f.

truthful ['truːθful] adj (statement, account) veritiero(-a); (person) sincero(-a).

try [traɪ] n (attempt) tentativo m, prova f ♦ vt provare; (JUR) giudicare ♦ vi provare; **to ~ to do sthg** provare a fare qc ❑ **try on** vt sep (clothes) provare, provarsi; **try out** vt sep provare.

T-shirt n maglietta f.

tub [tʌb] n (of margarine etc) vaschetta f; (inf: bath) vasca f (da bagno).

tube [tjuːb] n (container) tubetto m; (Br: inf: underground) metropolitana f; (pipe) tubo m; **by ~** in metropolitana.

tube station n (Br: inf) stazione f della metropolitana.

tuck [tʌk] : **tuck in** vt sep (shirt) mettersi dentro; (child, person) rimboccare le coperte a ♦ vi (inf) mangiare di buon appetito.

tuck shop n (Br) piccolo negozio di merendine, caramelle ecc., presso una scuola.

Tudor ['tjuːdər] adj Tudor (inv) (sedicesimo secolo).

Tues. (abbr of Tuesday) mar.

Tuesday ['tjuːzdɪ] n martedì m inv, → **Saturday**.

tuft [tʌft] n ciuffo m.

tug [tʌg] vt tirare ♦ n (boat) rimorchiatore m.

tuition [tjuːˈɪʃn] n lezioni fpl.

tulip ['tjuːlɪp] n tulipano m.

tumble-dryer ['tʌmbldraɪər] n asciugabiancheria m inv.

tumbler ['tʌmblər] n (glass) bicchiere m (senza stelo).

tummy ['tʌmɪ] n (inf) pancia f.

tummy upset n (inf) disturbi mpl di pancia.

tumor ['tuːmər] (Am) = **tumour**.

tumour ['tjuːmər] n (Br) tumore m.

tuna (fish) [Br 'tjuːnə, Am 'tuːnə] n (food) tonno m.

tuna melt n (Am) crostino di tonno e formaggio fuso.

tune [tjuːn] n (melody) melodia f ♦ vt (radio, TV) sintonizzare; (engine) mettere a punto; (instrument) accordare; **in ~** (person) intonato; (instrument) accordato; **out of ~** (person) stonato; (instrument) scordato.

tunic ['tjuːnɪk] n tunica f.

Tunisia [tjuːˈnɪzɪə] n la Tunisia.

tunnel ['tʌnl] n tunnel m inv, galleria f.

turban ['tɜːbən] n turbante m.

turbo ['tɜːbəʊ] (pl -s) n (car) turbo m inv.

turbulence ['tɜːbjʊləns] n (when flying) turbolenza f.

turf [tɜːf] n (grass) tappeto m erboso.

Turin [tjʊˈrɪn] n Torino f.

Turk [tɜːk] n turco m (-a f).

turkey ['tɜːkɪ] (pl -s) n tacchino m.

Turkey n la Turchia.

Turkish ['tɜːkɪʃ] adj turco(-a) ♦ n (language) turco m ♦ npl: **the ~** i turchi.

Turkish delight n dolciume fatto di gelatina e ricoperto di zucchero a velo.

turn [tɜːn] n (in road) curva f; (op

knob, key, switch) giro m; (go, chance) turno m ♦ vt girare; (a bend) prendere; (become) diventare; (cause to become) far diventare ♦ vi girare; (person) girarsi; (milk) andare a male; to ~ into sthg (become) diventare qc; to ~ sthg into sthg trasformare qc in qc; to ~ left/right girare a sinistra/a destra; it's your ~ tocca a te; at the ~ of the century all'inizio del secolo; to take it in ~s to do sthg fare qc a turno; to ~ sthg inside out rigirare qc □ **turn back** vt sep (person, car) mandare indietro ♦ vi tornare indietro; **turn down** vt sep (radio, volume, heating) abbassare; (offer, request) rifiutare; **turn off** vt sep (light, TV, engine) spegnere; (water, gas, tap) chiudere ♦ vi (leave road) girare, svoltare; **turn on** vt sep (light, TV, engine) accendere; (water, gas, tap) aprire; **turn out** vt fus (be in the end) rivelarsi ♦ vt sep (light, fire) spegnere ♦ vi (come, attend) affluire; to ~ out to be sthg risultare essere qc; **turn over** vi (in bed) girarsi, rigirarsi; (Br: change channels) cambiare canale ♦ vt sep girare; **turn round** vt sep (car, table etc) girare ♦ vi (person) girarsi, voltarsi; **turn up** vt sep (radio, volume, heating) alzare ♦ vi (come) venire.

turning ['tɜːnɪŋ] n (off road) svolta f.

turnip ['tɜːnɪp] n rapa f.

turn-up n (Br: on trousers) risvolto m.

turps [tɜːps] n (Br: inf) trementina f.

turquoise ['tɜːkwɔɪz] adj turchese.

turtle ['tɜːtl] n tartaruga f (acquatica).

turtleneck ['tɜːtlnek] n maglione m a collo alto.

Tuscany ['tʌskənɪ] n la Toscana.

tutor ['tjuːtəʳ] n (private teacher) insegnante m privato (insegnante f privata).

tuxedo [tʌkˈsiːdəʊ] (pl -s) n (Am) smoking m inv.

TV n tivù f inv, TV f inv; on ~ alla tivù.

tweed [twiːd] n tweed m.

tweezers ['twiːzəz] npl pinzette fpl.

twelfth [twelfθ] num dodicesimo(-a), → sixth.

twelve [twelv] num dodici, → six.

twentieth ['twentɪəθ] num ventesimo(-a); the ~ century il ventesimo secolo, → sixth.

twenty ['twentɪ] num venti, → six.

twice [twaɪs] adv due volte; it's ~ as good è due volte meglio; ~ as much il doppio.

twig [twɪg] n ramoscello m.

twilight ['twaɪlaɪt] n crepuscolo m.

twin [twɪn] n gemello m (-a f).

twin beds npl letti mpl gemelli.

twine [twaɪn] n spago m.

twin room n stanza f a due letti.

twist [twɪst] vt (wire) torcere, piegare; (rope, hair) attorcigliare; (bottle top, lid, knob) girare; to ~ one's ankle slogarsi la caviglia.

twisting ['twɪstɪŋ] adj (road, river) tortuoso(-a).

two [tuː] num due, → six.

two-piece adj (swimsuit, suit) a due pezzi (inv).

type [taɪp] n (kind) tipo m ♦ vt &

vi battere a macchina.

typewriter ['taɪp,raɪtə'] *n* macchina *f* da scrivere.

typhoid ['taɪfɔɪd] *n* tifoidea *f*.

typical ['tɪpɪkl] *adj* tipico(-a).

typist ['taɪpɪst] *n* dattilografo *m* (-a *f*).

tyre ['taɪə'] *n (Br)* gomma *f*, pneumatico *m*.

U *adj (Br: film)* per tutti.

UFO *n (abbr of unidentified flying object)* UFO *m inv*.

ugly ['ʌglɪ] *adj* brutto(-a).

UHT *adj (abbr of ultra heat treated)* UHT.

UK *n*: the ~ il Regno Unito.

ulcer ['ʌlsə'] *n* ulcera *f*.

Ulster ['ʌlstə'] *n* l'Ulster *m*.

ultimate ['ʌltɪmət] *adj (final)* finale; *(best, greatest)* ideale.

ultraviolet [,ʌltrə'vaɪələt] *adj* ultravioletto(-a).

umbrella [ʌm'brelə] *n* ombrello *m*.

umpire ['ʌmpaɪə'] *n* arbitro *m*.

UN *n (abbr of United Nations)*: the ~ l'ONU *f*.

unable [ʌn'eɪbl] *adj*: to be ~ to do sthg non poter fare qc.

unacceptable [,ʌnək'septəbl] *adj* inaccettabile.

unaccustomed [,ʌnə'kʌstəmd] *adj*: to be ~ to sthg non essere abituato(-a) a qc.

unanimous [ju:'nænɪməs] *adj* unanime.

unattended [,ʌnə'tendɪd] *adj (baggage)* incustodito(-a).

unattractive [,ʌnə'træktɪv] *adj (person, idea)* poco attraente; *(place)* privo(-a) di attrattiva.

unauthorized [ʌn'ɔ:θəraɪzd] *adj* non autorizzato(-a).

unavailable [,ʌnə'veɪləbl] *adj* non disponibile.

unavoidable [,ʌnə'vɔɪdəbl] *adj* inevitabile.

unaware [,ʌnə'weə'] *adj*: to be ~ of sthg/that ignorare qc/che.

unbearable [ʌn'beərəbl] *adj* insopportabile.

unbelievable [ʌnbɪ'li:vəbl] *adj* incredibile.

unbutton [ʌn'bʌtn] *vt* sbottonare.

uncertain [ʌn'sɜ:tn] *adj* incerto(-a).

uncertainty [ʌn'sɜ:tntɪ] *n* incertezza *f*.

uncle ['ʌŋkl] *n* zio *m*.

unclean [ʌn'kli:n] *adj* sporco(-a).

unclear [ʌn'klɪə'] *adj* non chiaro(-a).

uncomfortable [ʌn'kʌmftəbl] *adj (person, chair)* scomodo(-a); *(fig: awkward)* a disagio.

uncommon [ʌn'kɒmən] *adj (rare)* raro(-a).

unconscious [ʌn'kɒnʃəs] *adj (after accident)* privo(-a) di sensi; *(unaware)* inconsapevole.

unconvincing [,ʌnkən'vɪnsɪŋ] *adj* poco convincente.

uncooperative [,ʌnkəʊ'ɒpərətɪv] *adj* poco disposto(-a) a collaborare.

uncork [ʌn'kɔ:k] vt stappare.

uncouth [ʌn'ku:θ] adj villano(-a), grossolano(-a).

uncover [ʌn'kʌvər] vt scoprire.

under ['ʌndər] prep sotto; (less than) meno di, al di sotto di; (according to) secondo; **children ~ ten** bambini sotto i dieci anni; **~ the circumstances** date le circostanze; **to be ~ pressure** essere sotto pressione.

underage [ʌndər'eidʒ] adj minorenne.

undercarriage ['ʌndəˌkærɪdʒ] n carrello m.

underdone [ʌndə'dʌn] adj poco cotto(-a).

underestimate [ʌndər'estimeit] vt sottovalutare.

underexposed [ʌndərɪk'spəuzd] adj (photograph) sottoesposto(-a).

undergo [ʌndə'gəu] (pt **-went**, pp **-gone**) vt subire.

undergraduate [ʌndə'grædjuət] n studente m universitario (studentessa f universitaria).

underground ['ʌndəgraund] adj (below earth's surface) sotterraneo(-a); (secret) clandestino(-a) ♦ n (Br: railway) metropolitana f.

undergrowth ['ʌndəgrəuθ] n sottobosco m.

underline [ʌndə'lain] vt sottolineare.

underneath [ʌndə'ni:θ] prep & adv sotto ♦ n sotto m.

underpants ['ʌndəpænts] npl mutande fpl, slip m inv.

underpass ['ʌndəpɑ:s] n sottopassaggio m.

undershirt ['ʌndəʃɜ:t] n (Am)

maglietta f.

underskirt ['ʌndəskɜ:t] n sottoveste f.

understand [ʌndə'stænd] (pt & pp **-stood**) vt capire; (believe) credere ♦ vi capire; **I don't ~** non capisco; **to make o.s. understood** farsi capire.

understanding [ʌndə'stændɪŋ] adj comprensivo(-a) ♦ n (agreement) accordo m; (knowledge) conoscenza f; (interpretation) interpretazione f; (sympathy) comprensione f.

understatement [ʌndə'steitmənt] n: **that's an ~!** a dir poco!

understood [ʌndə'stud] pt & pp → **understand**.

undertake [ʌndə'teik] (pt **-took**, pp **-taken**) vt intraprendere; **to ~ to do sthg** impegnarsi a fare qc.

undertaker [ʌndəˌteikər] n impresario di pompe funebri.

undertaking [ʌndə'teikɪŋ] n (promise) promessa f; (task) impresa f.

undertook [ʌndə'tuk] pt → **undertake**.

underwater [ʌndə'wɔ:tər] adj subacqueo(-a) ♦ adv sott'acqua.

underwear ['ʌndəweər] n biancheria f intima.

underwent [ʌndə'went] pt → **undergo**.

undesirable [ʌndɪ'zaiərəbl] adj indesiderato(-a).

undo [ʌn'du:] (pt **-did**, pp **-done**) vt (coat, shirt) sbottonare; (shoelaces) slacciare; (tie) sciogliere il nodo di; (parcel) sfare.

undone [ʌn'dʌn] adj (coat, shirt) sbottonato(-a); (shoelaces) slacciato(-a).

undress [ʌn'dres] *vi* spogliarsi ◆ *vt* spogliare.

undressed [ʌn'drest] *adj* spogliato(-a); **to get ~** spogliarsi.

uneasy [ʌn'iːzɪ] *adj* a disagio.

uneducated [ʌn'edjʊkeɪtɪd] *adj* non istruito(-a).

unemployed [ʌnɪm'plɔɪd] *adj* disoccupato(-a) ◆ *npl*: **the ~** i disoccupati.

unemployment [ʌnɪm'plɔɪmənt] *n* disoccupazione *f*.

unemployment benefit *n* sussidio *m* di disoccupazione.

unequal [ʌn'iːkwəl] *adj (not the same)* disuguale; *(not fair)* iniquo(-a).

uneven [ʌn'iːvn] *adj (surface, speed, beat)* irregolare; *(share, distribution)* ineguale.

uneventful [ʌnɪ'ventfʊl] *adj* tranquillo(-a).

unexpected [ʌnɪk'spektɪd] *adj* inaspettato(-a).

unexpectedly [ʌnɪk'spektɪdlɪ] *adv* inaspettatamente.

unfair [ʌn'feər] *adj* ingiusto(-a).

unfairly [ʌn'feəlɪ] *adv* ingiustamente.

unfaithful [ʌn'feɪθfʊl] *adj* infedele.

unfamiliar [ʌnfə'mɪljər] *adj* sconosciuto(-a); **to be ~ with** non conoscere bene.

unfashionable [ʌn'fæʃnəbl] *adj* fuori moda.

unfasten [ʌn'fɑːsn] *vt (seatbelt, belt, laces)* slacciare; *(knot)* sfare, sciogliere.

unfavourable [ʌn'feɪvrəbl] *adj* sfavorevole.

unfinished [ʌn'fɪnɪʃt] *adj* incompiuto(-a).

unfit [ʌn'fɪt] *adj (not healthy)* non in forma; **to be ~ for sthg** *(not suitable)* essere inadatto(-a) a qc.

unfold [ʌn'fəʊld] *vt* spiegare *(tovaglia, cartina)*.

unforgettable [ʌnfə'getəbl] *adj* indimenticabile.

unforgivable [ʌnfə'gɪvəbl] *adj* imperdonabile.

unfortunate [ʌn'fɔːtʃnət] *adj (unlucky)* sfortunato(-a); *(regrettable)* infelice; **it is ~ that** è un peccato che.

unfortunately [ʌn'fɔːtʃnətlɪ] *adv* sfortunatamente.

unfriendly [ʌn'frendlɪ] *adj* poco amichevole.

unfurnished [ʌn'fɜːnɪʃt] *adj* non ammobiliato(-a).

ungrateful [ʌn'greɪtfʊl] *adj* ingrato(-a).

unhappy [ʌn'hæpɪ] *adj (sad)* infelice; *(not pleased)* insoddisfatto(-a); **to be ~ about sthg** essere insoddisfatto di qc.

unharmed [ʌn'hɑːmd] *adj* indenne.

unhealthy [ʌn'helθɪ] *adj (person)* malaticcio(-a); *(food, smoking)* dannoso(-a) per la salute; *(place)* malsano(-a).

unhelpful [ʌn'helpfʊl] *adj (person)* poco disponibile; *(advice, instructions)* inutile.

unhurt [ʌn'hɜːt] *adj* indenne.

unhygienic [ʌnhaɪ'dʒiːnɪk] *adj* non igienico(-a).

unification [juːnɪfɪ'keɪʃn] *n* unificazione *f*.

uniform ['juːnɪfɔːm] *n* uniforme *f*

unimportant [ˌʌnɪmˈpɔːtənt] adj senza importanza.

unintelligent [ˌʌnɪnˈtelɪdʒənt] adj poco intelligente.

unintentional [ˌʌnɪnˈtenʃənl] adj involontario(-a).

uninterested [ʌnˈɪntrəstɪd] adj indifferente.

uninteresting [ʌnˈɪntrestɪŋ] adj poco interessante, noioso(-a).

union [ˈjuːnjən] n (of workers) sindacato m.

Union Jack n: the ~ la bandiera nazionale del Regno Unito.

unique [juːˈniːk] adj unico(-a); to be ~ to essere proprio(-a) di.

unisex [ˈjuːnɪseks] adj unisex (inv).

unit [ˈjuːnɪt] n unità f inv; (department, building) reparto m; (piece of furniture) elemento m; (machine) apparecchio m.

unite [juːˈnaɪt] vt unire ♦ vi unirsi.

United Kingdom [juːˈnaɪtɪd-] n: the ~ il Regno Unito.

United Nations [juːˈnaɪtɪd-] npl: the ~ le Nazioni Unite.

United States (of America) [juːˈnaɪtɪd-] npl: the ~ gli Stati Uniti (d'America).

unity [ˈjuːnətɪ] n unità f.

universal [ˌjuːnɪˈvɜːsl] adj universale.

universe [ˈjuːnɪvɜːs] n universo m.

university [ˌjuːnɪˈvɜːsətɪ] n università f inv.

unjust [ʌnˈdʒʌst] adj ingiusto(-a).

unkind [ʌnˈkaɪnd] adj scortese.

unknown [ʌnˈnəʊn] adj sconosciuto(-a).

unleaded (petrol) [ʌnˈledɪd-] n benzina f senza piombo.

unless [ənˈles] conj a meno che non; ~ it rains a meno che non piova.

unlike [ʌnˈlaɪk] prep a differenza di; that's ~ her non è da lei.

unlikely [ʌnˈlaɪklɪ] adj improbabile; he is ~ to arrive before six è improbabile che arrivi prima delle sei.

unlimited [ʌnˈlɪmɪtɪd] adj illimitato(-a); ~ mileage = chilometraggio illimitato.

unlisted [ʌnˈlɪstɪd] adj (Am: phone number): to be ~ non essere sull'elenco telefonico.

unload [ˌʌnˈləʊd] vt scaricare.

unlock [ˌʌnˈlɒk] vt aprire.

unlucky [ʌnˈlʌkɪ] adj (unfortunate) sfortunato(-a); (bringing bad luck) che porta sfortuna.

unmarried [ʌnˈmærɪd] adj non sposato(-a).

unnatural [ʌnˈnætʃrəl] adj (unusual) inconsueto(-a); (behaviour, person) poco naturale.

unnecessary [ʌnˈnesəsərɪ] adj inutile.

unobtainable [ˌʌnəbˈteɪnəbl] adj (product) non disponibile; (phone number) non ottenibile.

unoccupied [ʌnˈɒkjʊpaɪd] adj (place, seat) libero(-a).

unofficial [ˌʌnəˈfɪʃl] adj non ufficiale; (strike) non autorizzato(-a).

unpack [ʌnˈpæk] vt (bags, suitcase) disfare ♦ vi disfare le valigie.

unpleasant [ʌnˈpleznt] adj (smell, weather, etc) sgradevole; (person) spiacevole, antipatico(-a).

unplug [ʌnˈplʌg] vt staccare.

unpopular [ʌnˈpɒpjʊləʳ] adj

impopolare.

unpredictable [ˌʌnprɪˈdɪktəbl] adj imprevedibile.

unprepared [ˌʌnprɪˈpɛəd] adj impreparato(-a).

unprotected [ˌʌnprəˈtektɪd] adj senza protezione.

unqualified [ˌʌnˈkwɒlɪfaɪd] adj (person) non qualificato(-a).

unreal [ˌʌnˈrɪəl] adj irreale.

unreasonable [ʌnˈriːznəbl] adj irragionevole.

unrecognizable [ˌʌnrekəgˈnaɪzəbl] adj irriconoscibile.

unreliable [ˌʌnrɪˈlaɪəbl] adj inaffidabile.

unrest [ʌnˈrest] n agitazione f.

unroll [ʌnˈrəʊl] vt srotolare.

unsafe [ʌnˈseɪf] adj (dangerous) pericoloso(-a); (in danger) in pericolo.

unsatisfactory [ˌʌnsætɪsˈfæktərɪ] adj insoddisfacente.

unscrew [ʌnˈskruː] vt (lid, top) svitare.

unsightly [ʌnˈsaɪtlɪ] adj brutto(-a).

unskilled [ʌnˈskɪld] adj (worker) non qualificato(-a).

unsociable [ʌnˈsəʊʃəbl] adj poco socievole.

unsound [ˌʌnˈsaʊnd] adj (building, structure) poco saldo(-a); (argument) che non regge.

unspoiled [ʌnˈspɔɪlt] adj (place, beach) incontaminato(-a).

unsteady [ʌnˈstedɪ] adj instabile; (hand) malfermo(-a).

unstuck [ʌnˈstʌk] adj: to come ~ (label, poster etc) staccarsi.

unsuccessful [ˌʌnsəkˈsesfʊl] adj che non ha successo.

unsuitable [ʌnˈsuːtəbl] adj inadatto(-a), inadeguato(-a); (moment) inopportuno(-a).

unsure [ʌnˈʃɔːʳ] adj: to be ~ (about) non essere sicuro(-a) (di).

unsweetened [ʌnˈswiːtnd] adj senza zucchero.

untidy [ʌnˈtaɪdɪ] adj (person) disordinato(-a); (room, desk) in disordine.

untie [ʌnˈtaɪ] (cont **untying** [ʌnˈtaɪɪŋ]) vt (person) slegare; (knot) sciogliere, sfare.

until [ənˈtɪl] prep fino a ♦ conj finché; (after negative, in past) prima che, prima di; **it won't be ready ~ Thursday** non sarà pronto prima di giovedì.

untrue [ˌʌnˈtruː] adj falso(-a).

untrustworthy [ʌnˈtrʌstˌwɜːðɪ] adj che non è degno(-a) di fiducia.

untying cont → untie.

unusual [ʌnˈjuːʒl] adj insolito(-a).

unusually [ʌnˈjuːʒəlɪ] adv (more than usual) insolitamente.

unwell [ʌnˈwel] adj indisposto(-a); to feel ~ non sentirsi bene.

unwilling [ʌnˈwɪlɪŋ] adj: to be ~ to do sth non voler fare qc.

unwind [ʌnˈwaɪnd] (pt & pp **unwound** [ʌnˈwaʊnd]) vt svolgere ♦ vi (relax) rilassarsi, distendersi.

unwrap [ʌnˈræp] vt aprire.

unzip [ʌnˈzɪp] vt aprire (la cerniera di).

up [ʌp] adv **1.** (towards higher position) su, in alto; to go ~ salire; **we walked ~ to the top** siamo saliti fino in cima; **to pick sth ~** raccogliere qc.
2. (in higher position) su, in alto;

she's ~ in her bedroom è su nella sua stanza; ~ there lassù.

3. *(into upright position)*: **to stand ~** alzarsi; **to sit ~** *(from lying position)* tirarsi su a sedere; *(sit straight)* stare seduto diritto.

4. *(to increased level)*: **prices are going ~** i prezzi stanno salendo.

5. *(northwards)*: **~ in Scotland** in Scozia.

6. *(in phrases)*: **to walk ~ and down** andare su e giù; **~ to ten people** fino a dieci persone; **are you ~ to travelling?** te la senti di viaggiare?; **what are you ~ to?** cosa stai combinando?; **it's ~ to you** sta a te decidere; **~ until ten o'clock** fino alle dieci.

♦ *prep* 1. *(towards higher position)*: **to walk ~ a hill** salire su per una collina; **I went ~ the stairs** sono salito per le scale.

2. *(in higher position)* in cima a; **~ a hill** in cima ad una collina; **~ a ladder** in cima ad una scala.

3. *(at end of)*: **they live ~ the road from us** abitano un po' più su di noi.

♦ *adj* 1. *(out of bed)* alzato(-a); **I was ~ at six today** mi sono alzato alle sei oggi.

2. *(at an end)*: **time's ~** tempo scaduto.

3. *(rising)*: **the ~ escalator** la scala mobile per salire.

♦ *n*: **~s and downs** alti e bassi *mpl*.

update [ˌʌp'deɪt] *vt* aggiornare.

uphill [ˌʌp'hɪl] *adv* in salita.

upholstery [ʌp'həʊlstərɪ] *n* tappezzeria *f*.

upkeep ['ʌpkiːp] *n* manutenzione *f*.

up-market *adj* rivolto(-a) alla fascia alta del mercato.

upon [ə'pɒn] *prep (fml: on)* su; **~ hearing the news ...** dopo aver appreso la notizia ...

upper ['ʌpə'] *adj* superiore ♦ *n* *(of shoe)* tomaia *f*.

upper class *n*: **the ~** i ceti alti.

uppermost ['ʌpəməʊst] *adj* *(highest)* il più alto (la più alta).

upper sixth *n (Br: SCH)* secondo anno del corso biennale che prepara agli 'A levels'.

upright ['ʌpraɪt] *adj (person)* diritto(-a); *(object)* verticale ♦ *adv* diritto.

upset [ʌp'set] *(pt & pp* upset*) adj (distressed)* addolorato(-a) ♦ *vt (distress)* addolorare, sconvolgere; *(cause to go wrong)* scombussolare; *(knock over)* rovesciare; **to have an ~ stomach** avere disturbi intestinali.

upside down [ˌʌpsaɪd-] *adj* capovolto(-a); *(person)* a testa in giù ♦ *adv* sottosopra.

upstairs [ʌp'steəz] *adj* di sopra ♦ *adv (on a higher floor)* di sopra, al piano superiore; **to go ~** andare di sopra.

up-to-date *adj (modern)* moderno(-a); *(well-informed)* aggiornato(-a).

upwards ['ʌpwədz] *adv (to a higher place)* verso l'alto, in su; *(to a higher level)* verso l'alto; **~ of 100 people** più di 100 persone.

urban ['ɜːbən] *adj* urbano(-a).

urban clearway [-'klɪəweɪ] *n (Br)* strada con divieto di sosta.

Urdu ['ʊəduː] *n* urdu *m*.

urge [ɜːdʒ] *vt*: **to ~ sb to do sthg** esortare qn a fare qc.

urgent ['ɜːdʒənt] *adj* urgente.

urgently ['ɜːdʒəntlɪ] *adv (immedia-*

tely) d'urgenza, urgentemente.

urinal [ˌjʊəˈraɪnl] *n (fml) (bowl)* orinale *m; (place)* vespasiano *m*.

urinate [ˈjʊərɪneɪt] *vi (fml)* urinare.

urine [ˈjʊərɪn] *n* urina *f*.

us [ʌs] *pron* ci; *(after prep)* noi; **they know ~** ci conosciamo; **it's ~** siamo noi; **send it to ~** mandacelo; **tell ~** dicci; **they're worse than ~** sono peggio di noi.

US *n (abbr of United States)*: **the ~** gli USA.

USA *n (abbr of United States of America)*: **the ~** gli USA.

usable [ˈjuːzəbl] *adj* utilizzabile.

use [*n* juːs, *vb* juːz] *n* uso *m* ◆ *vt* usare; *(run on)* andare a; **to be of ~** essere utile, servire; **to have the ~ of sthg** avere accesso a qc; **to make ~ of sthg** sfruttare qc; **'out of ~'** 'guasto'; **to be in ~** essere in uso; **it's no ~** non serve a niente; **what's the ~?** a che scopo?; **to ~ sthg as sthg** usare qc come qc; **'~ before ...'** *(food, drink)* 'da consumarsi preferibilmente entro ...' ❑ **use up** *vt sep* consumare.

used [*adj* juːzd, *aux vb* juːst] *adj (towel, glass etc)* sporco(-a); *(car)* usato(-a) ◆ *aux vb*: **I ~ to live near here** una volta abitavo qui vicino; **I ~ to go there every day** una volta ci andavo tutti i giorni; **to be ~ to sthg** essere abituato(-a) a qc; **to get ~ to sthg** abituarsi a qc.

useful [ˈjuːsfʊl] *adj* utile.

useless [ˈjuːslɪs] *adj* inutile; *(inf: very bad)*: **he's ~** non è buono a nulla.

user [ˈjuːzəʳ] *n* utente *mf*.

usher [ˈʌʃəʳ] *n (at cinema, theatre)* maschera *f*.

usherette [ˌʌʃəˈret] *n* maschera *f*.

USSR *n*: **the (former) ~** l'(ex) URSS *f*.

usual [ˈjuːʒəl] *adj* solito(-a); **as ~** *(in the normal way)* come al solito.

usually [ˈjuːʒəlɪ] *adv* di solito.

utensil [juːˈtensl] *n* utensile *m*.

utilize [ˈjuːtɪlaɪz] *vt (fml)* utilizzare.

utmost [ˈʌtməʊst] *adj* estremo(-a) ◆ *n*: **to do one's ~** fare tutto il possibile.

utter [ˈʌtəʳ] *adj* totale ◆ *vt (word)* proferire, pronunciare; *(cry)* emettere.

utterly [ˈʌtəlɪ] *adv* completamente, del tutto.

U-turn *n (in vehicle)* inversione *f* a U.

vacancy [ˈveɪkənsɪ] *n (job)* posto *m* vacante; **'vacancies'** 'si affittano camere'; **'no vacancies'** 'completo'.

vacant [ˈveɪkənt] *adj* libero(-a).

vacate [vəˈkeɪt] *vt (fml: room, house)* lasciare libero.

vacation [vəˈkeɪʃn] *n (Am) (period of time)* vacanze *fpl; (time off work)* ferie *fpl* ◆ *vi (Am)* passare le vacanze; **to go on ~** andare in vacanza.

vacationer [vəˈkeɪʃənər] *n (Am)* villeggiante *mf*.

vaccination [ˌvæksɪˈneɪʃn] *n* vaccinazione *f*.

vaccine [*Br* 'væksi:n, *Am* væk'si:n] *n* vaccino *m*.

vacuum ['vækjuəm] *vt* pulire con l'aspirapolvere.

vacuum cleaner *n* aspirapolvere *m inv*.

vague [veig] *adj* vago(-a); *(shape, outline)* indistinto(-a).

vain [vein] *adj* *(pej: conceited)* vanitoso(-a); **in ~** invano.

Valentine card ['væləntain-] *n* biglietto che si manda per San Valentino alla persona che si ama o di cui si è innamorati.

Valentine's Day ['væləntainz-] *n* San Valentino.

valet ['vælei, 'vælit] *n* (in hotel) chi si occupa del servizio lavanderia e stiratura.

valet service *n* (in hotel) servizio *m* di lavanderia; (for car) servizio di lavaggio.

valid ['vælid] *adj* (ticket, passport) valido(-a).

validate ['vælideit] *vt* (ticket) convalidare.

Valium® ['væliəm] *n* valium® *m*.

valley ['væli] *n* valle *f*.

valuable ['væljuəbl] *adj* (jewellery, object) di valore; (advice, help) prezioso(-a) ❑ **valuables** *npl* oggetti *mpl* di valore.

value ['vælju:] *n* (financial) valore *m*; (usefulness) utilità *f*; **a ~ pack** una confezione formato famiglia; **to be good ~** (for money) essere conveniente ❑ **values** *npl* (principles) valori *mpl*.

valve [vælv] *n* valvola *f*.

van [væn] *n* furgone *m*.

vandal ['vændl] *n* vandalo *m* (-a *f*).

vandalize ['vændəlaiz] *vt* vanda-

lizzare.

vanilla [və'nilə] *n* vaniglia *f*.

vanish ['væniʃ] *vi* svanire, scomparire.

vapor ['veipər] *(Am)* = **vapour**.

vapour ['veipər] *n* (Br) vapore *m*.

variable ['veəriəbl] *adj* variabile.

varicose veins ['værikəus-] *npl* vene *fpl* varicose.

varied ['veərid] *adj* vario(-a).

variety [və'raiəti] *n* varietà *f inv*.

various ['veəriəs] *adj* vari(-e).

varnish ['vɑ:niʃ] *n* vernice *f* ♦ *vt* verniciare.

vary ['veəri] *vi & vt* variare.

vase [*Br* vɑ:z, *Am* veiz] *n* vaso *m*.

Vaseline® ['væsəli:n] *n* vaselina *f*.

vast [vɑ:st] *adj* vasto(-a).

vat [væt] *n* tino *m*.

VAT [væt, vi:ei'ti:] *n* (abbr of value added tax) IVA *f*.

vault [vɔ:lt] *n* (in bank) camera *f* blindata; (in church) cripta *f*.

VCR *n* (abbr of video cassette recorder) videoregistratore *m*.

VDU *n* (abbr of visual display unit) monitor *m inv*.

veal [vi:l] *n* vitello *m*.

veg [vedʒ] *abbr* = **vegetable**.

vegan ['vi:gən] *adj* vegetaliano(-a) ♦ *n* vegetaliano *m* (-a *f*).

vegetable ['vedʒtəbl] *n* verdura *f*.

vegetable oil *n* olio *m* vegetale.

vegetarian [,vedʒi'teəriən] *adj* vegetariano(-a) ♦ *n* vegetariano *m* (-a *f*).

vegetation [,vedʒi'teiʃn] *n* vegetazione *f*.

vehicle ['vi:əkl] *n* veicolo *m*.

veil [veil] *n* velo *m*.

vein [vein] *n* vena *f*.

Velcro® ['velkrəʊ] n velcro® m.

velvet ['velvɪt] n velluto m.

vending machine ['vendɪŋ-] n distributore m automatico.

venetian blind [vɪˌniːʃn-] n veneziana f.

Venice ['venɪs] n Venezia f.

venison ['venɪzn] n carne m di cervo.

vent [vent] n (for air, smoke etc) presa f d'aria.

ventilation [ˌventɪ'leɪʃn] n ventilazione f.

ventilator ['ventɪleɪtər] n ventilatore m.

venture ['ventʃər] n impresa f ◆ vi (go) avventurarsi.

venue ['venjuː] n luogo m (di partita, concerto ecc.).

veranda [və'rændə] n veranda f.

verb [vɜːb] n verbo m.

verdict ['vɜːdɪkt] n verdetto m.

verge [vɜːdʒ] n (of road, lawn, path) bordo m; **'soft ~s'** 'banchina non transitabile'.

verify ['verɪfaɪ] vt verificare.

vermin ['vɜːmɪn] n roditori che portano malattie e distruggono raccolti.

vermouth ['vɜːməθ] n vermut m inv.

versa → **vice versa**.

versatile ['vɜːsətaɪl] adj versatile.

verse [vɜːs] n (of song, poem) strofa f; (poetry) versi mpl.

version ['vɜːʃn] n versione f.

versus ['vɜːsəs] prep contro.

vertical ['vɜːtɪkl] adj verticale.

vertigo ['vɜːtɪgəʊ] n: **to suffer from ~** soffrire di vertigini.

very ['verɪ] adv molto ◆ adj: at

the **~ bottom** proprio in fondo; **~ much** molto; **not ~ big** non molto grande; **my ~ own room** una stanza tutta per me; **~ rich** ricchissimo, molto ricco; **it's the ~ thing I need** è proprio quello di cui avevo bisogno.

vessel ['vesl] n (fml: ship) vascello m.

vest [vest] n (Br: underwear) maglietta f; (sleeveless) canottiera f; (Am: waistcoat) gilè m inv.

Vesuvius [vɪ'suːvjəs] n Vesuvio m.

vet [vet] n (Br) veterinario m (-a f).

veteran ['vetrən] n (of war) vecchio combattente m.

veterinarian [ˌvetərɪ'neərɪən] (Am) = **vet**.

veterinary surgeon ['vetərɪnrɪ-] (Br: fml) = **vet**.

VHF n (abbr of very high frequency) VHF f.

VHS n (abbr of video home system) VHS m.

via ['vaɪə] prep (place) via; (by means of) tramite.

viaduct ['vaɪədʌkt] n viadotto m.

vibrate [vaɪ'breɪt] vi vibrare.

vibration [vaɪ'breɪʃn] n vibrazione f.

vicar ['vɪkər] n pastore m.

vicarage ['vɪkərɪdʒ] n presbiterio m.

vice [vaɪs] n (moral fault) vizio m; (crime) crimine m; (Br: tool) morsa f.

vice-president n vice-presidente mf.

vice versa [ˌvaɪsɪ'vɜːsə] adv viceversa.

vicinity [vɪ'sɪnɪtɪ] n: **in the ~** nelle vicinanze.

vicious ['vɪʃəs] adj (attack) violento(-a); *(animal)* feroce; *(comment)* cattivo(-a), maligno(-a).

victim [ˈvɪktɪm] *n* vittima *f*.

Victorian [vɪkˈtɔːrɪən] *adj* vittoriano(-a).

victory [ˈvɪktərɪ] *n* vittoria *f*.

video [ˈvɪdɪəʊ] *(pl* -s*) n (video recording)* video *m inv; (videotape)* videocassetta *f; (video recorder)* videoregistratore *m* ♦ *vt (using video recorder)* videoregistrare; *(using camera)* filmare; **on ~** su videocassetta.

video camera *n* videocamera *f*.

video game *n* videogioco *m*.

video recorder *n* videoregistratore *m*.

video shop *n* videoteca *f*.

videotape [ˈvɪdɪəʊteɪp] *n* videocassetta *f*.

Vietnam [*Br* ˌvjetˈnæm, *Am* ˌvjetˈnɑːm] *n* il Vietnam.

view [vjuː] *n* vista *f; (opinion)* opinione *f* ♦ *vt (house)* vedere; *(situation)* considerare; **in my ~** secondo me; **in ~ of** *(considering)* considerato; **to come into ~** apparire.

viewer [ˈvjuːəʳ] *n (of TV)* telespettatore *m* (-trice *f*).

viewfinder [ˈvjuːˌfaɪndəʳ] *n* mirino *m*.

viewpoint [ˈvjuːpɔɪnt] *n (opinion)* punto *m* di vista; *(place)* punto d'osservazione.

vigilant [ˈvɪdʒɪlənt] *adj (fml)* vigile.

villa [ˈvɪlə] *n* villa *f*.

village [ˈvɪlɪdʒ] *n* paese *m*.

villager [ˈvɪlɪdʒəʳ] *n* abitante *mf* di paese.

villain [ˈvɪlən] *n (of book, film)* cattivo *m; (criminal)* malvivente *mf*.

vinaigrette [ˌvɪnɪˈgret] *n* condimento *per insalata a base di olio, aceto, sale, pepe ed erbe aromatiche.

vine [vaɪn] *n (grapevine)* vite *f; (climbing plant)* rampicante *m*.

vinegar [ˈvɪnɪgəʳ] *n* aceto *m*.

vineyard [ˈvɪnjəd] *n* vigna *f*.

vintage [ˈvɪntɪdʒ] *adj (wine)* d'annata ♦ *n (year)* annata *f*.

vinyl [ˈvaɪnɪl] *n* vinile *m*.

viola [vɪˈəʊlə] *n* viola *f*.

violence [ˈvaɪələns] *n* violenza *f*.

violent [ˈvaɪələnt] *adj* violento(-a).

violet [ˈvaɪələt] *adj* viola *(inv)* ♦ *n (flower)* viola *f*.

violin [ˌvaɪəˈlɪn] *n* violino *m*.

VIP *n (abbr of very important person)* vip *mf inv*.

virgin [ˈvɜːdʒɪn] *n* vergine *f*.

Virgo [ˈvɜːgəʊ] *(pl* -s*) n* Vergine *f*.

virtually [ˈvɜːtʃʊəlɪ] *adv* praticamente.

virtual reality [ˈvɜːtʃʊəl-] *n* realtà *f* virtuale.

virus [ˈvaɪrəs] *n* virus *m inv*.

visa [ˈviːzə] *n* visto *m*.

viscose [ˈvɪskəʊs] *n* viscosa *f*.

visibility [ˌvɪzɪˈbɪlətɪ] *n* visibilità *f*.

visible [ˈvɪzəbl] *adj* visibile.

visit [ˈvɪzɪt] *vt (person)* andare a trovare; *(place)* visitare ♦ *n* visita *f*.

visiting hours [ˈvɪzɪtɪŋ-] *npl* orario *m* delle visite.

visitor [ˈvɪzɪtəʳ] *n (to person)* visita *f; (to place)* visitatore *m* (-trice *f*).

visitor centre *n (at tourist attraction)* punto accoglienza per i visitatori di musei ecc.

visitors' book *n* registro *m*

dei visitatori.

visitor's passport *n* (*Br*) passaporto *m* provvisorio.

visor ['vaɪzə^r] *n* visiera *f*.

vital ['vaɪtl] *adj* vitale.

vitamin [*Br* 'vɪtəmɪn, *Am* 'vaɪtəmɪn] *n* vitamina *f*.

vivid ['vɪvɪd] *adj* vivido(-a).

V-neck *n* (*design*) scollo *m* a V.

vocabulary [və'kæbjʊlərɪ] *n* vocabolario *m*.

vodka ['vɒdkə] *n* vodka *f*.

voice [vɔɪs] *n* voce *f*.

volcano [vɒl'keɪnəʊ] (*pl* -es OR -s) *n* vulcano *m*.

volleyball ['vɒlɪbɔːl] *n* pallavolo *f*.

volt [vəʊlt] *n* volt *m inv*.

voltage ['vəʊltɪdʒ] *n* voltaggio *m*.

volume ['vɒljuːm] *n* volume *m*.

voluntary ['vɒləntrɪ] *adj* volontario(-a).

volunteer [,vɒlən'tɪə^r] *n* volontario *m* (-a *f*) ♦ *vt*: **to ~ to do sthg** offrirsi di fare qc.

vomit ['vɒmɪt] *n* vomito *m* ♦ *vi* vomitare.

vote [vəʊt] *n* voto *m*; (*number of votes*) voti *mpl* ♦ *vi*: **to ~ (for)** votare (per).

voter ['vəʊtə^r] *n* elettore *m* (-trice *f*).

voucher ['vaʊtʃə^r] *n* buono *m*.

vowel ['vaʊəl] *n* vocale *f*.

voyage ['vɔɪdʒ] *n* viaggio *m* (*per mare*).

vulgar ['vʌlgə^r] *adj* volgare.

vulture ['vʌltʃə^r] *n* avvoltoio *m*.

W (*abbr of west*) O.

wad [wɒd] *n* (*of paper, banknotes*) fascio *m*; (*of cotton*) batuffolo *m*.

waddle ['wɒdl] *vi* camminare come una papera.

wade [weɪd] *vi* camminare (*a fatica*).

wading pool ['weɪdɪŋ-] *n* (*Am*) piscina *f* per bambini.

wafer ['weɪfə^r] *n* (*biscuit*) cialda *f*.

waffle ['wɒfl] *n* (*pancake*) cialda dalla caratteristica superficie a quadretti che si mangia con sciroppo d'acero, panna o frutta ♦ *vi* (*inf*) parlare molto e dire poco.

wag [wæg] *vt* agitare.

wage [weɪdʒ] *n* salario *m* ❑ **wages** *npl* salario *m*.

wagon ['wægən] *n* (*vehicle*) carro *m*; (*Br: of train*) vagone *m*.

waist [weɪst] *n* vita *f*.

waistcoat ['weɪskəʊt] *n* gilè *m inv*.

wait [weɪt] *n* attesa *f* ♦ *vi* aspettare; **to ~ for sb to do sthg** aspettare che qn faccia qc; **I can't ~!** non vedo l'ora! ❑ **wait for** *vt fus* aspettare.

waiter ['weɪtə^r] *n* cameriere *m*.

waiting room ['weɪtɪŋ-] *n* sala *f* d'attesa OR d'aspetto.

waitress ['weɪtrɪs] *n* cameriera *f*.

wake [weɪk] (*pt* woke, *pp* woken) *vt* svegliare ♦ *vi* svegliarsi ❑ **wake up** *vt sep* svegliare ♦ *vi* svegliarsi.

Waldorf salad ['wɔːldɔːf-] *n*

insalata a base di mele, sedano e noci, condita con maionese.

Wales [weɪlz] *n* il Galles.

walk [wɔ:k] *n (journey, path)* passeggiata *f* ◆ *vi* camminare ◆ *vt (distance)* percorrere a piedi; *(dog)* portare a spasso; **to go for a ~** andare a fare una passeggiata; **it's a short ~** a piedi è vicino; **to take the dog for a ~** portare a spasso il cane; **'walk'** *(Am)* 'avanti'; **'don't ~'** *(Am)* 'alt' ❑ **walk away** *vi* andarsene; **walk in** *vi* entrare; **walk out** *vi (leave angrily)* andarsene.

walker [wɔ:kəʳ] *n* camminatore *m* (-trice *f*).

walking boots [wɔ:kɪŋ-] *npl* scarponcini *mpl*.

walking stick [wɔ:kɪŋ-] *n* bastone *m*.

Walkman® [wɔ:kmən] *n* walkman® *m inv*.

wall [wɔ:l] *n* muro *m; (internal)* parete *f*, muro.

wallet [wɒlɪt] *n (for money)* portafoglio *m*.

wallpaper [wɔ:l,peɪpəʳ] *n* carta *f* da parati.

wally [wɒlɪ] *n (Br: inf)* cretino *m* (-a *f*).

walnut [wɔ:lnʌt] *n (nut)* noce *f*.

waltz [wɔ:ls] *n* valzer *m inv*.

wander [wɒndəʳ] *vi* vagare.

want [wɒnt] *vt* volere; *(need)* aver bisogno di; **to ~ to do sthg** voler fare qc; **to ~ sb to do sthg** volere che qn faccia qc.

war [wɔ:ʳ] *n* guerra *f*.

ward [wɔ:d] *n (in hospital)* reparto *m*.

warden [wɔ:dn] *n (of park)* guardiano *m; (of youth hostel)* custode *mf*.

wardrobe [wɔ:drəʊb] *n (cupboard)* armadio *m; (clothes)* guardaroba *m inv*.

warehouse [weəhaʊs, *pl* -haʊzɪz] *n* magazzino *m*.

warm [wɔ:m] *adj* caldo(-a); *(person, smile)* cordiale; *(welcome)* caloroso(-a) ◆ *vt* scaldare, riscaldare; **to be ~** *(person)* avere caldo; **it's ~** *(weather)* è OR fa caldo ❑ **warm up** *vt sep* scaldare, riscaldare ◆ *vi (get warmer)* scaldarsi, riscaldarsi; *(do exercises)* riscaldarsi; *(machine, engine)* scaldare.

war memorial *n* monumento *m* ai caduti.

warmth [wɔ:mθ] *n* calore *m*.

warn [wɔ:n] *vt* avvertire, avvisare; **to ~ sb about sthg** avvisare qn di qc; **to ~ sb not to do sthg** avvertire qn di non fare qc.

warning [wɔ:nɪŋ] *n (of danger)* avvertimento *m; (advance notice)* preavviso *m*.

warranty [wɒrəntɪ] *n (fml)* garanzia *f*.

warship [wɔ:ʃɪp] *n* nave *f* da guerra.

wart [wɔ:t] *n* verruca *f*.

was [wɒz] *pt* → **be**.

wash [wɒʃ] *vt* lavare ◆ *vi* lavarsi ◆ *n:* **to give sthg a ~** dare una lavata a qc; **to have a ~** lavarsi; **to ~ one's hands/face** lavarsi le mani/il viso ❑ **wash up** *vi (Br: do washing-up)* lavare i piatti; *(Am: clean o.s.)* lavarsi.

washable [wɒʃəbl] *adj* lavabile.

washbasin [wɒʃ,beɪsn] *n* lavabo *m*.

washbowl [wɒʃbəʊl] *n (Am)* lavabo *m*.

washer [wɒʃəʳ] *n (ring)* rondella *f*.

washing ['wɒʃɪŋ] n bucato m.

washing line n corda f del bucato.

washing machine n lavatrice f.

washing powder n detersivo m in polvere.

washing-up n (Br): to do the ~ fare i piatti.

washing-up bowl n (Br) bacinella f.

washing-up liquid n (Br) detersivo m liquido per piatti.

washroom ['wɒʃrum] n (Am) bagno m, gabinetto m.

wasn't ['wɒznt] = was not.

wasp [wɒsp] n vespa f.

waste [weɪst] n (rubbish) rifiuti mpl ◆ vt sprecare; a ~ of money uno spreco di denaro; a ~ of time una perdita di tempo.

wastebin ['weɪstbɪn] n cestino m (dei rifiuti).

waste ground n terreno m abbandonato.

wastepaper basket [,weɪst-'peɪpəʳ-] n cestino m (per la carta straccia).

watch [wɒtʃ] n (wristwatch) orologio m ◆ vt (observe) guardare; (spy on) sorvegliare; (be careful with) fare attenzione a ❏ **watch out** vi (be careful) stare attento, fare attenzione; **to ~ out for** (look for) cercare.

watchstrap ['wɒtʃstræp] n cinturino m dell'orologio.

water ['wɔːtəʳ] n acqua f ◆ vt (plants, garden) annaffiare ◆ vi (eyes) lacrimare; **it makes my mouth ~** mi fa venire l'acquolina in bocca.

water bottle n borraccia f.

watercolour ['wɔːtə,kʌləʳ] n acquerello m.

watercress ['wɔːtəkres] n crescione m.

waterfall ['wɔːtəfɔːl] n cascata f.

watering can ['wɔːtərɪŋ-] n annaffiatoio m.

watermelon ['wɔːtə,melən] n cocomero m, anguria f.

waterproof ['wɔːtəpruːf] adj impermeabile.

water purification tablets [-pjʊərɪfɪ'keɪʃn-] npl compresse fpl per la disinfezione dell'acqua.

water skiing n sci m nautico.

watersports ['wɔːtəspɔːts] npl sport mpl acquatici.

water tank n cisterna f.

watertight ['wɔːtətaɪt] adj stagno(-a).

watt [wɒt] n watt m inv; **a 60-~ bulb** una lampadina da 60 watt.

wave [weɪv] n onda f; (of crime, violence) ondata f ◆ vt (hand) agitare; (flag) sventolare ◆ vi (to attract attention) fare un cenno (con la mano); (when greeting, saying goodbye) salutare con la mano.

wavelength ['weɪvleŋθ] n lunghezza f d'onda.

wavy ['weɪvɪ] adj (hair) ondulato(-a).

wax [wæks] n (for candles) cera f; (in ears) cerume m.

way [weɪ] n (manner, means) modo m; (route) strada f; (direction) parte f, direzione f; (distance travelled) tragitto m; **which ~ is the station?** da che parte è la stazione?; **the town is out of our ~** la città non è sulla nostra strada; **to be in the ~** essere d'intralcio; **to be on the ~** (person) stare arrivando; (meal) essere in arrivo; **to get out of sb's ~** lasciar passare qn; **to get under ~** cominciare; **a long ~ away** lontano; **to lose one's ~** smarrirsi; **on the ~ back** al ritorno; **on the ~ there** all'andata; **that ~** *(like that)* in quel modo; *(in that direction)* da quella parte; **this ~** *(like this)* in questo modo; *(in this direction)* da questa parte; **'give ~'** 'dare la precedenza'; **'~ in'** 'entrata'; **'~ out'** 'uscita'; **no ~!** *(inf)* neanche per sogno!

WC *n (abbr of water closet)* W.C. *m inv.*

we [wi:] *pron* noi; **~'re fine** stiamo bene.

weak [wi:k] *adj* debole; *(drink)* leggero(-a); *(soup)* liquido(-a).

weaken ['wi:kn] *vt* indebolire.

weakness ['wi:knıs] *n* debolezza *f.*

wealth [welθ] *n* ricchezza *f.*

wealthy ['welθı] *adj* ricco(-a).

weapon ['wepən] *n* arma *f.*

wear [weəʳ] *(pt* wore, *pp* worn) *vt* portare, indossare ♦ *n (clothes)* abbigliamento *m;* **~ and tear** usura *f* ❑ **wear off** *vi* passare; **wear out** *vi* consumarsi.

weary ['wıərı] *adj* stanco(-a).

weasel ['wi:zl] *n* donnola *f.*

weather ['weðəʳ] *n* tempo *m;* **what's the ~ like?** che tempo fa?; **to be under the ~** *(inf)* sentirsi poco bene.

weather forecast *n* previsioni *fpl* del tempo.

weather forecaster [-fɔ:-kɑ:stəʳ] *n* meteorologo *m* (-a *f*).

weather report *n* bollettino *m* meteorologico.

weather vane [-veın] *n* banderuola *f.*

weave [wi:v] *(pt* wove, *pp* woven) *vt* tessere.

web [web] *n (of spider)* ragnatela *f.*

Wed. *(abbr of Wednesday)* mer.

wedding ['wedıŋ] *n* matrimonio *m.*

wedding anniversary *n* anniversario *m* di matrimonio.

wedding dress *n* abito *m* da sposa.

wedding ring *n* fede *f.*

wedge [wedʒ] *n (of cake)* fetta *f; (of wood etc)* cuneo *m.*

Wednesday ['wenzdı] *n* mercoledì *m inv,* → **Saturday.**

wee [wi:] *adj (Scot)* piccolo(-a) ♦ *(inf)* pipì *f.*

weed [wi:d] *n* erbaccia *f.*

week [wi:k] *n* settimana *f;* **a ~ today** oggi a otto; **in a ~'s time** fra una settimana.

weekday ['wi:kdeı] *n* giorno *m* feriale.

weekend [,wi:k'end] *n* fine settimana *m inv.*

weekly ['wi:klı] *adj* settimanale ♦ *adv* ogni settimana ♦ *n* settimanale *m.*

weep [wi:p] *(pt & pp* wept) *vi* piangere.

weigh [weı] *vt* pesare; **how much does it ~?** quanto pesa?

weight [weıt] *n* peso *m;* **to lose ~** dimagrire; **to put on ~** ingrassare ❑ **weights** *npl (for weight training)* pesi *mpl.*

weightlifting ['weıt,lıftıŋ] *n* sollevamento *m* pesi.

weight training *n* allenamento *m* ai pesi.

weir [wıəʳ] *n* chiusa *f.*

weird [wıəd] *adj* strano(-a).

welcome ['welkəm] *adj (guest)* benvenuto(-a); *(appreciated)* gradito(-a) ♦ *n* accoglienza *f* ♦ *vt (greet)* dare il benvenuto a; *(be grateful for)* gradire ♦ *excl* benvenuto!; **you're ~ to help yourself** si serva pure; **to make sb feel ~** far sentire qn benaccetto; **you're ~!** prego!

weld [weld] *vt* saldare.

welfare ['welfeə^r] *n (happiness, comfort)* benessere *m*; *(Am: money)* sussidio *m*.

well [wel] *(compar* **better,** *superl* **best)** *adj* bene ♦ *adv* bene; *(a lot)* molto ♦ *n* pozzo *m*; **to get ~** guarire; **to go ~** andar bene; **~ done!** bravo!; **it may ~ happen** è assai probabile che accada; **it's ~ worth it** ne vale ben la pena; **as ~** *(in addition)* anche; **as ~ as** *(in addition to)* oltre a.

we'll [wi:l] = **we shall, we will.**

well-behaved [-br'hervd] *adj* educato(-a).

well-built *adj* aitante.

well-done *adj (meat)* ben cotto(-a).

well-dressed [-'drest] *adj* vestito(-a) bene.

wellington (boot) ['weliŋtən-] *n* stivale *m* di gomma.

well-known *adj* noto(-a).

well-off *adj (rich)* ricco(-a).

well-paid *adj* ben pagato(-a).

welly ['weli] *n (Br: inf)* stivale *m* di gomma.

Welsh [welʃ] *adj* gallese ♦ *n (language)* gallese *m* ♦ *npl:* **the ~** i gallesi.

Welshman ['welʃmən] *(pl* **-men** [-mən]) *n* gallese *m*.

Welsh rarebit [-'reəbɪt] *n* crostino *m* di formaggio fuso.

Welshwoman ['welʃˌwumən] *(pl* **-women** [-ˌwɪmɪn]) *n* gallese *f*.

went [went] *pt* → **go.**

wept [wept] *pt & pp* → **weep.**

were [wɜː^r] *pt* → **be.**

we're [wɪə^r] = **we are.**

weren't [wɜːnt] = **were not.**

west [west] *n* ovest *m*, occidente *m* ♦ *adj* dell'ovest ♦ *adv (fly, walk)* verso ovest; *(be situated)* a ovest; **in the ~ of England** nell'Inghilterra occidentale.

westbound ['westbaund] *adj* diretto(-a) a ovest.

West Country *n:* **the ~** l'Inghilterra *f* sud-occidentale.

West End *n:* **the ~** *(of London)* zona occidentale del centro di Londra, celebre per i suoi negozi, cinema e teatri.

western ['westən] *adj* occidentale ♦ *n (film)* western *m inv.*

West Indies [-'ɪndiːz] *npl* le Indie Occidentali.

Westminster ['westmɪnstə^r] *n* quartiere nel centro di Londra.

---

i **WESTMINSTER**

In questo quartiere di Londra, situato lungo il Tamigi, si trovano sia il Palazzo del Parlamento che l'Abbazia di Westminster. Il termine "Westminster" designa, per estensione, il Parlamento stesso.

Westminster Abbey *n* l'abbazia *f* di Westminster.

---

i **WESTMINSTER ABBEY**

Situata nel quartiere londinese di Westminster, questa è la chiesa dove ha luogo l'incoronazione dei sovrani britannici. Vi sono sepolti molti personaggi famosi e una parte della chiesa, il "Poet's Corner" ("l'angolo dei poeti"), ospita le tombe di poeti e scrittori di chiara fama, tra i quali Chaucer, Dickens e Hardy.

---

westwards ['westwədz] *adv* verso ovest.

wet [wet] (*pt & pp* **wet** OR **-ted**) *adj* (*soaked, damp*) bagnato(-a); (*rainy*) piovoso(-a) ◆ *vt* bagnare; **to get ~** bagnarsi; '~ **paint**' 'vernice fresca'.

wet suit *n* muta *f*.

we've [wi:v] = **we have**.

whale [weɪl] *n* balena *f*.

wharf [wɔ:f] (*pl* **-s** OR **wharves** [wɔ:vz]) *n* banchina *f*.

what [wɒt] *adj* 1. (*in questions*) che, quale; ~ **colour is it?** di che colore è?; **he asked me ~ colour it was** mi ha chiesto di che colore era. 2. (*in exclamations*): ~ **a surprise!** che sorpresa!; ~ **a beautiful day!** che bella giornata! ◆ *pron* 1. (*in direct questions*) (che) cosa; ~ **is going on?** (che) cosa succede?; ~ **are they doing?** (che) cosa fanno?; ~ **is that?** (che) cos'è?; ~ **is it called?** come si chiama?; ~ **are they talking about?** di (che) cosa parlano?; ~ **is it for?** a (che) cosa serve? 2. (*in indirect questions, relative clauses*) cosa; **she asked me ~ had happened** m'ha chiesto cos'era successo; **she asked me ~ I had seen** mi ha chiesto cosa avevo visto; **she asked me ~ I was thinking about** m'ha chiesto a cosa pensavo; ~ **worries me is …** ciò che OR quello che mi preoccupa …; **I did-**

n't see ~ **happened** non ho visto cos'è successo; **you can't have ~ you want** non puoi avere quello che vuoi. 3. (*in phrases*): ~ **for?** a che scopo?, perché?; ~ **about going out for a meal?** cosa ne diresti di mangiare fuori? ◆ *excl* come?

whatever [wɒt'evə^r] *pron*: **take ~ you want** prendi quello che vuoi; ~ **I do, I'll lose** qualsiasi cosa faccia, perderò; ~ **that may be** quale che sia.

wheat [wi:t] *n* grano *m*, frumento *m*.

wheel [wi:l] *n* ruota *f*; (*steering wheel*) volante *m*.

wheelbarrow ['wi:l,bærəu] *n* carriola *f*.

wheelchair ['wi:l,tʃeə^r] *n* sedia *f* a rotelle.

wheelclamp [,wi:l'klæmp] *n* bloccaruota *m inv*.

wheezy ['wi:zɪ] *adj* ansante.

when [wen] *adv* quando ◆ *conj* quando; (*although, seeing as*) sebbene, mentre; ~ **it's ready** quando è pronto; ~ **I've finished** quando avrò finito.

whenever [wen'evə^r] *conj* ogni volta che; ~ **you like** quando vuoi.

where [weə^r] *adv & conj* dove; **this is ~ you'll be sleeping** è qui che dormirai.

whereabouts ['weərəbauts] *adv* dove ◆ *npl*: **his ~ are unknown** nessuno sa dove si trovi.

whereas [weər'æz] *conj* mentre.

wherever [weər'evə^r] *conj* dovunque; ~ **you like** dove vuoi; ~ **that may be** dove che sia.

whether ['weðə^r] *conj* se; ~ **you**

like it or not ti piaccia o no.

which [wɪtʃ] *adj (in questions)*
quale; **~ room do you want?** quale
stanza vuole?; **~ one?** quale?; **she
asked me ~ room I wanted** mi ha
chiesto quale stanza volevo.
◆ *pron* 1. *(in questions)* quale; **~ is
the cheapest?** qual è il più economico?; **~ do you prefer?** quale preferisci?; **he asked me ~ was the
best** mi ha chiesto quale era il
migliore; **he asked me ~ I preferred**
mi ha chiesto quale preferivo.
2. *(introducing relative clause)* che;
the house ~ is on the corner la
casa che è all'angolo; **the television ~ I bought** il televisore che ho
comprato.
3. *(introducing relative clause: after
prep)* il quale (la quale); **the settee
on ~ I'm sitting** il divano su cui
siedo; **the book about ~ we were
talking** il libro di cui stavamo parlando.
4. *(referring back)* il che, cosa che;
he's late, ~ annoys me è in ritardo,
il che mi secca molto.

whichever [wɪtʃ'evəʳ] *pron* quel-
lo(-a), quelli(-e) *(pl)* che ◆ *adj*: **take
~ chocolate you like best** prendi il
cioccolatino che preferisci; **~ chocolate you take** qualsiasi cioccolatino tu prenda.

while [waɪl] *conj* mentre;
(although) sebbene ◆ *n*: **a ~** un po'
(di tempo); **for a ~** per un po'; **in a
~** fra un po'.

whim [wɪm] *n* capriccio *m*.

whine [waɪn] *vi* gemere; *(complain)* frignare.

whip [wɪp] *n* frusta *f* ◆ *vt (with
whip)* frustare.

whipped cream [wɪpt-] *n*
panna *f* montata.

whirlpool ['wɜːlpuːl] *n (Jacuzzi)*
vasca *f* per idromassaggi.

whisk [wɪsk] *n (utensil)* frusta *f*,
frullino *m* ◆ *vt (eggs, cream)* sbattere.

whiskers ['wɪskəz] *npl (of person)*
favoriti *m*; *(of animal)* baffi *m*.

whiskey ['wɪskɪ] *(pl -s) n* whisky
m inv (irlandese o americano).

whisky ['wɪskɪ] *n* whisky *m inv
(scozzese)*.

 WHISKY

L iquore scozzese ottenuto dal
malto d'orzo, il whisky viene
sempre invecchiato in botti di legno
e le sue diverse caratteristiche dipen-
dono dai metodi di produzione e dai
tipi di acqua usati. Il whisky di puro
malto ("single malt"), spesso prodotto in piccole distillerie regionali, è
comunemente considerato migliore
rispetto alle varietà miscelate
("blended"), di solito meno costose.

whisper ['wɪspəʳ] *vt & vi* sussurrare.

whistle ['wɪsl] *n (instrument)* fi-
schietto *m*; *(sound)* fischio *m* ◆ *vi*
fischiare.

white [waɪt] *adj* bianco(-a); *(tea)*
con latte ◆ *n* bianco *m*; *(person)*
bianco *m (-a f)*; **~ coffee** caffè *m inv*
con latte.

white bread *n* pane *m* bianco.

White House *n*: **the ~** la Casa
Bianca.

white sauce *n* besciamella *f*.

white spirit *n* acquaragia *f*.

whitewash ['waɪtwɒʃ] *vt* imbiancare.

white wine *n* vino *m* bianco.

whiting ['waɪtɪŋ] (pl inv) n merlango m.

Whitsun ['wɪtsn] n Pentecoste f.

who [hu:] pron (in questions) chi; (in relative clauses) che.

whoever [hu:'evə'] pron chiunque; ~ it is chiunque sia.

whole [həʊl] adj intero(-a) ◆ n: the ~ of the journey tutto il viaggio; **on the** ~ nel complesso; **the** ~ **time** tutto il tempo.

wholefoods ['həʊlfu:dz] npl prodotti mpl integrali.

wholemeal bread ['həʊlmi:l] n (Br) pane m integrale.

wholesale ['həʊlseɪl] adv (COMM) all'ingrosso.

wholewheat bread ['həʊl,wi:t] n (Am) = **wholemeal bread**.

whom [hu:m] pron (fml: in questions) chi; (in relative clauses) che; **to** ~? a chi?; **the person to** ~ **I wrote** la persona alla quale ho scritto.

whooping cough ['hu:pɪŋ] n pertosse f.

whose [hu:z] adj & pron: ~ **jumper is this?** di chi è questo maglione?; **she asked** ~ **jumper it was** ha chiesto di chi era il maglione; **this is the woman** ~ **son is a priest** questa è la donna il cui figlio è un prete; ~ **is this?** di chi è questo?

why [waɪ] adv & conj perché; ~ **not?** perché no?; ~ **not do it tomorrow?** perché non farlo domani?

wick [wɪk] n (of candle, lighter) stoppino m.

wicked ['wɪkɪd] adj (evil) malvagio(-a); (mischievous) malizioso(-a).

wicker ['wɪkə'] adj di vimini.

wide [waɪd] adj largo(-a); (opening) ampio(-a); (range, variety) vasto(-a); (difference, gap) grande ◆ adv: **to open sthg** ~ spalancare qc; **how** ~ **is the road?** quanto è larga la strada?; **it's 12 metres** ~ è largo 12 metri; ~ **open** spalancato.

widely ['waɪdlɪ] adv (known) generalmente; (travel) molto.

widen ['waɪdn] vt (make broader) allargare ◆ vi (gap, difference) aumentare.

widespread ['waɪdspred] adj molto diffuso(-a).

widow ['wɪdəʊ] n vedova f.

widower ['wɪdəʊə'] n vedovo m.

width [wɪdθ] n larghezza f.

wife [waɪf] (pl wives) n moglie f.

wig [wɪg] n parrucca f.

wild [waɪld] adj (animal, plant) selvatico(-a); (land, area) selvaggio(-a); (uncontrolled) sfrenato(-a); (crazy) folle; **to be** ~ **about** (inf) andare pazzo(-a) per.

wild flower n fiore m di campo.

wildlife ['waɪldlaɪf] n flora e fauna f.

will[1] [wɪl] aux vb 1. (expressing future tense): **I** ~ **see you next week** ci vediamo la settimana prossima; ~ **you be here next Friday?** sarai qui venerdì prossimo?; **yes I** ~ sì; **no I won't** no.
2. (expressing willingness): **I won't do it** mi rifiuto di farlo.
3. (expressing polite question): ~ **you have some more tea?** vuole ancora un po' di tè?
4. (in commands, requests): ~ **you please be quiet!** volete tacere!; **close that window,** ~ **you?** chiudi la finestra, per favore.

will[2] n (document) testamento m; **against one's** ~ contro la propria volontà.

willing ['wılıŋ] *adj*: **to be ~ to do sthg** essere disposto(-a) a fare qc.

willingly ['wılıŋlı] *adv* volentieri.

willow ['wıləʊ] *n* salice *m*.

win [wın] (*pt & pp* **won**) *n* vittoria *f* ◆ *vt* vincere; (*support, approval, friends*) guadagnarsi ◆ *vi* vincere.

wind[1] [wınd] *n* vento *m*; (*in stomach*) aria *f*.

wind[2] [waınd] (*pt & pp* **wound**) *vi* (*road, river*) snodarsi ◆ *vt*: **to ~ sthg round sthg** avvolgere qc intorno a qc ❑ **wind up** *vt sep* (*Br: inf: annoy*) dare sui nervi a; (*car window*) tirare su, chiudere; (*clock, watch*) caricare.

windbreak ['wındbreık] *n* frangivento *m*.

windmill ['wındmıl] *n* mulino *m* a vento.

window ['wındəʊ] *n* (*of house*) finestra *f*; (*of shop*) vetrina *f*; (*of car*) finestrino *m*.

window box *n* cassetta *f* per fiori.

window cleaner *n* lavavetri *mf*.

windowpane ['wındəʊpeın] *n* vetro *m*.

window seat *n* (*on plane*) posto *m* finestrino.

window-shopping *n*: **to go ~** andare a guardare le vetrine.

windowsill ['wındəʊsıl] *n* davanzale *m*.

windscreen ['wındskri:n] *n* (*Br*) parabrezza *m inv*.

windscreen wipers *npl* (*Br*) tergicristalli *mpl*.

windshield ['wındʃi:ld] *n* (*Am*) parabrezza *m inv*.

Windsor Castle ['wınzə-] *n* il

castello di Windsor.

 WINDSOR CASTLE

Situato nell'omonima cittadina della contea del Berkshire, questo castello risale all'undicesimo secolo, quando Guglielmo il Conquistatore ne iniziò la costruzione. È una delle residenze ufficiali del sovrano britannico ed è parzialmente aperto al pubblico.

windsurfing ['wınd,sɜ:fıŋ] *n* windsurf *m*; **to go ~** fare del windsurf.

windy ['wındı] *adj* ventoso(-a); **it's ~** c'è vento.

wine [waın] *n* vino *m*.

wine bar *n* (*Br*) ≃ enoteca *f*.

wineglass ['waıngla:s] *n* bicchiere *m* da vino.

wine list *n* lista *f* dei vini.

wine tasting [-'teıstıŋ] *n* degustazione *f* dei vini.

wine waiter *n* sommelier *mf inv*.

wing [wıŋ] *n* ala *f*; (*Br: of car*) fiancata *f* ❑ **wings** *npl*: **the ~s** (*in theatre*) le quinte.

wink [wıŋk] *vi* strizzare l'occhio.

winner ['wınə'] *n* vincitore *m* (-trice *f*).

winning ['wınıŋ] *adj* vincente.

winter ['wıntə'] *n* inverno; **in (the) ~** d'inverno.

wintertime ['wıntətaım] *n* inverno *m*.

wipe [waıp] *vt* pulire; **to ~ one's hands/feet** pulirsi le mani/le scarpe ❑ **wipe up** *vt sep* (*liquid*) asciugare; (*dirt*) pulire ◆ *vi* (*dry the dishes*) asciugare i piatti.

wiper ['waɪpə'] n (windscreen wiper) tergicristallo m.

wire ['waɪə'] n filo m di ferro; (electrical) filo (elettrico) ◆ vt (plug) collegare.

wireless ['waɪəlɪs] n radio f inv.

wiring ['waɪərɪŋ] n impianto m elettrico.

wisdom tooth ['wɪzdəm-] n dente m del giudizio.

wise [waɪz] adj saggio(-a).

wish [wɪʃ] n (desire) desiderio m ◆ vt (desire) desiderare; best ~es (for birthday, recovery) auguri; (in end of letter) cordiali saluti; I ~ you'd told me earlier! perché non me l'hai detto prima!; I ~ I was younger vorrei tanto essere più giovane; to ~ for sthg desiderare qc; to ~ to do sthg desiderare fare qc; to ~ sb luck/happy birthday augurare buona fortuna/buon compleanno a qn; if you ~ (fml) se vuole.

witch [wɪtʃ] n strega f.

with [wɪð] prep 1. (gen) con; come ~ me vieni con me; a man ~ a beard un uomo con la barba; a room ~ a bathroom una camera con bagno.
2. (at house of) da, a casa di; we stayed ~ friends siamo stati da amici.
3. (indicating emotion) di, per; to tremble ~ fear tremare di paura.
4. (indicating opposition): to argue ~ sb litigare con qn; to fight ~ sb combattere contro qn.
5. (indicating covering, contents) di; to fill sthg ~ sthg riempire qc di qc; topped ~ cream ricoperto di panna.

withdraw [wɪð'drɔː] (pt -drew, pp -drawn) vt (take out) ritirare;

(money) prelevare ◆ vi (from race, contest) ritirarsi.

withdrawal [wɪð'drɔːəl] n (from bank account) prelievo m.

withdrawn [wɪð'drɔːn] pp → withdraw.

withdrew [wɪð'druː] pt → withdraw.

wither ['wɪðə'] vi appassire.

within [wɪ'ðɪn] prep (inside) all'interno di; (not exceeding) entro ◆ adv all'interno, dentro; ~ walking distance raggiungibile a piedi; ~ 10 miles of ... a non più di 10 miglia da ...; it arrived ~ a week è arrivato nel giro di una settimana; ~ the next week entro la prossima settimana.

without [wɪð'aʊt] prep senza; ~ doing sthg senza fare qc.

withstand [wɪð'stænd] (pt & pp -stood) vt resistere a.

witness ['wɪtnɪs] n testimone mf ◆ vt (see) assistere a.

witty ['wɪtɪ] adj arguto(-a).

wives [waɪvz] pl → wife.

wobbly ['wɒblɪ] adj (table, chair) traballante.

wok [wɒk] n padella larga e profonda usata nella cucina cinese.

woke [wəʊk] pt → wake.

woken ['wəʊkn] pp → wake.

wolf [wʊlf] (pl wolves ['wʊlvz]) n lupo m.

woman ['wʊmən] (pl women) n donna f.

womb [wuːm] n utero m.

women ['wɪmɪn] pl → woman.

won [wʌn] pt & pp → win.

wonder ['wʌndə'] vi (ask o.s.) chiedersi, domandarsi ◆ n (amazement) meraviglia f; to ~ if domandarsi se; I ~ if I could ask you a favour? potrei chiederle un favore?

wonderful ['wʌndəful] *adj* meraviglioso(-a).

won't [wəunt] = **will not**.

wood [wud] *n (substance)* legno *m; (small forest)* bosco *m; (golf club)* mazza *f* di legno.

wooden ['wudn] *adj* di legno.

woodland ['wudlənd] *n* terreno *m* boschivo.

woodpecker ['wud,pekə'] *n* picchio *m*.

woodwork ['wudwɜːk] *n (SCH)* falegnameria *f*.

wool [wul] *n* lana *f*.

woolen ['wulən] *(Am)* = **woollen**.

woollen ['wulən] *adj (Br)* di lana.

woolly ['wuli] *adj* di lana.

wooly ['wuli] *(Am)* = **woolly**.

·Worcester sauce ['wustə'-] *n* salsa *f* Worcester.

word [wɜːd] *n* parola *f*; **in other ~s** in altre parole; **to have a ~ with sb** parlare con qn.

wording ['wɜːdɪŋ] *n* formulazione *f*.

word processing [-'prəusesɪŋ] *n* videoscrittura *f*.

word processor [-'prəusesə'] *n* sistema *m* di videoscrittura.

wore [wɔː'] *pt* → **wear**.

work [wɜːk] *n* lavoro *m; (painting, novel etc)* opera *f* ♦ *vi* lavorare; *(operate, have desired effect)* funzionare; *(take effect)* fare effetto ♦ *vt (machine, controls)* far funzionare; **out of ~** senza lavoro; **to be at ~** *(at workplace)* essere al lavoro; *(working)* lavorare; **to be off ~** *(on holiday)* essere in ferie; *(ill)* essere

in malattia; **the ~s** *(inf: everything)* tutto quanto; **how does it ~?** come funziona?; **it's not ~ing** non funziona ❑ **work out** *vt sep (price, total)* calcolare; *(understand)* capire; *(solution)* trovare; *(method, plan)* mettere a punto ♦ *vi (result, be successful)* funzionare; *(do exercise)* fare ginnastica; **it ~s out at £20 each** *(bill, total)* fa 20 sterline a testa.

worker ['wɜːkə'] *n* lavoratore *m* (-trice *f*).

working class ['wɜːkɪŋ-] *n*: **the ~** la classe operaia.

working hours ['wɜːkɪŋ-] *npl* orario *m* di lavoro.

workman ['wɜːkmən] *(pl* -men [-mən]*) n* operaio *m*.

work of art *n* opera *f* d'arte.

workout ['wɜːkaut] *n* allenamento *m*.

work permit *n* permesso *m* di lavoro.

workplace ['wɜːkpleɪs] *n* posto *m* di lavoro.

workshop ['wɜːkʃɒp] *n (for repairs)* officina *f*.

work surface *n* piano *m* di lavoro.

world [wɜːld] *n* mondo *m* ♦ *adj* mondiale; **the best in the ~** il migliore del mondo.

worldwide [,wɜːld'waɪd] *adv* in tutto il mondo.

worm [wɜːm] *n* verme *m*.

worn [wɔːn] *pp* → **wear** ♦ *adj (clothes, carpet)* consumato(-a).

worn-out *adj (clothes, shoes etc)* consumato(-a); *(tired)* esausto(-a).

worried ['wʌrɪd] *adj* preoccupato(-a).

worry ['wʌrɪ] *n* preoccupazione *f*

wring

♦ vt preoccupare ♦ vi: to ~ (about) preoccuparsi (per).

worrying ['wʌrɪɪŋ] adj preoccupante.

worse [wɜːs] adj peggiore ♦ adv peggio; **to get ~** peggiorare; **~ off** (in worse position) in una situazione peggiore; (poorer) più povero.

worsen ['wɜːsn] vi peggiorare.

worship ['wɜːʃɪp] n culto m ♦ vt adorare.

worst [wɜːst] adj peggiore ♦ adv peggio ♦ n: **the ~** il peggiore (la peggiore).

worth [wɜːθ] prep: **how much is it ~?** quanto vale?; **it's ~ £50** vale 50 sterline; **it's ~ seeing** vale la pena vederlo; **it's not ~ it** non ne vale la pena; **£50 ~ of traveller's cheques** traveller's cheques per un valore di 50 sterline.

worthless ['wɜːθlɪs] adj di nessun valore.

worthwhile [,wɜːθ'waɪl] adj: **to be ~** valere la pena.

worthy ['wɜːðɪ] adj (winner, cause) degno(-a); **to be ~ of sthg** essere degno di qc.

would [wʊd] aux vb **1.** (in reported speech): **she said she ~ come** ha detto che sarebbe venuta.

2. (indicating condition): **what ~ you do?** tu cosa faresti?; **what ~ you have done?** tu cosa avresti fatto?; **I ~ be most grateful** le sarei molto grato.

3. (indicating willingness): **she ~n't go** non ci è voluta andare; **he ~ do anything for her** farebbe qualsiasi cosa per lei.

4. (in polite questions): **~ you like a drink?** vuole qualcosa da bere?; **~ you mind closing the window?** le spiacerebbe chiudere la finestra?

5. (indicating inevitability): **he ~ say** that era ovvio che dicesse così.

6. (giving advice): **I ~ report it if I were you** se fossi in voi lo riferirei.

7. (expressing opinions): **I ~ prefer ...** preferirei ...; **I ~ have thought (that)** ... avrei pensato che ...

wound[1] [wuːnd] n ferita f ♦ vt ferire.

wound[2] [waʊnd] pt & pp → **wind**[2].

wove [wəʊv] pt → **weave**.

woven ['wəʊvn] pp → **weave**.

wrap [ræp] vt (package) incartare; **to ~ sthg round sthg** avvolgere qc intorno a qc ❑ **wrap up** vt sep (package) incartare ♦ vi (dress warmly) coprirsi bene.

wrapper ['ræpər] n (for sweets) carta f.

wrapping ['ræpɪŋ] n involucro m.

wrapping paper n (for present) carta f da regalo; (for parcel) carta da pacchi.

wreath [riːθ] n corona f.

wreck [rek] n (of plane, car) rottame m; (of ship) relitto m ♦ vt (destroy) distruggere; (spoil) rovinare; **to be ~ed** (ship) fare naufragio.

wreckage ['rekɪdʒ] n (of plane, car) rottami mpl; (of building) macerie fpl.

wrench [rentʃ] n (Br: monkey wrench) chiave f inglese; (Am: spanner) chiave.

wrestler ['reslər] n lottatore m (-trice f).

wrestling ['reslɪŋ] n lotta f libera.

wretched ['retʃɪd] adj (miserable) infelice; (very bad) orribile.

wring [rɪŋ] (pt & pp wrung) vt (clothes, cloth) strizzare.

wrinkle ['rɪŋkl] *n* ruga *f*.

wrist [rɪst] *n* polso *m*.

wristwatch ['rɪstwɒtʃ] *n* orologio *m* da polso.

write [raɪt] (*pt* wrote, *pp* written) *vt* scrivere; *(cheque, prescription)* fare; *(Am: send letter to)* scrivere a ◆ *vi* scrivere; **to ~ to sb** *(Br)* scrivere a qn □ **write back** *vi* rispondere; **write down** *vt sep* scrivere; **write off** *vt sep (Br: inf: car)* distruggere ◆ *vi*: **to ~ off for sthg** richiedere qc per posta; **write out** *vt sep (list, essay)* scrivere; *(cheque, receipt)* fare.

write-off *n (vehicle)* rottame *m*.

writer ['raɪtə^r] *n (author)* scrittore *m* (-trice *f*).

writing ['raɪtɪŋ] *n (handwriting)* scrittura *f*; *(written words)* scritto *m*; *(activity)* scrivere *m*.

writing desk *n* scrivania *f*.

writing pad *n* blocchetto *m* per appunti.

writing paper *n* carta *f* da lettere.

written ['rɪtn] *pp* → write ◆ *adj (exam, notice, confirmation)* scritto(-a).

wrong [rɒŋ] *adv* male ◆ *adj (incorrect, unsuitable)* sbagliato(-a); *(bad, immoral)*: **it's ~ to steal** non si deve rubare; **what's ~?** cosa c'è che non va?; **what's ~ with her?** cos'ha?; **something's ~ with the car** la macchina ha qualcosa che non va; **to be ~** *(person)* sbagliarsi; **to be in the ~** essere in torto; **to get sthg ~** sbagliare qc; **to go ~** *(machine)* non funzionare più; **'~ way'** *(Am)* cartello che segnala agli automobilisti il senso vietato.

wrongly ['rɒŋlɪ] *adv (accused)* ingiustamente; *(informed)* male.

wrong number *n*: **to get the ~** sbagliare numero.

wrote [rəʊt] *pt* → write.

wrought iron [rɔːt] *n* ferro *m* battuto.

wrung [rʌŋ] *pt & pp* → wring.

XYZ

xing *(Am: abbr of crossing)*: **'ped ~'** 'passaggio pedonale'.

XL *(abbr of extra-large)* XL.

Xmas ['eksməs] *n (inf)* Natale *m*.

X-ray *n (picture)* radiografia *f* ◆ *vt* fare una radiografia a; **to have an ~** farsi una radiografia.

yacht [jɒt] *n* yacht *m inv*.

yard [jɑːd] *n (unit of measurement)* = 91,44 cm, iarda *f*; *(enclosed area)* cortile *m*; *(Am: behind house)* giardino *m*.

yard sale *n (Am)* vendita di oggetti di seconda mano organizzata da un privato nel giardino di casa.

yarn [jɑːn] *n (thread)* filato *m*.

yawn [jɔːn] *vi (person)* sbadigliare.

yd *abbr* = yard.

yeah [jeə] *adv (inf)* sì.

year [jɪə^r] *n* anno *m*; **next ~** l'anno prossimo; **this ~** quest'anno; **I'm 15 ~s old** ho 15 anni; **I haven't seen her for ~s** *(inf)* sono anni che non la vedo.

yearly ['jɪəlɪ] *adj* annuale, annuo(-a).

yeast [jiːst] *n* lievito *m*.

yell [jel] *vi* urlare.

yellow ['jeləʊ] *adj* giallo(-a) ◆ *n* giallo *m*.

yellow lines *npl* strisce *fpl* gialle *(che regolano la sosta dei veicoli).*

---

i YELLOW LINES

In Gran Bretagna le linee gialle, singole o doppie, sul bordo della strada indicano restrizioni relative alla sosta dei veicoli. Un'unica linea gialla indica il divieto di sosta dalle ore 8 alle ore 18.30 dei giorni feriali, mentre una linea doppia indica il divieto di sosta permanente. La sosta è consentita quindi solo sulle linee gialle singole dopo le 18.30, oppure tutta la domenica.

Yellow Pages® *n*: **the** ~ le Pagine gialle.

yes [jes] *adv* sì; **to say** ~ dire di sì.

yesterday ['jestədɪ] *n* ieri *m* ◆ *adv* ieri; **the day before** ~ l'altro ieri; ~ **afternoon** ieri pomeriggio; ~ **morning** ieri mattina.

yet [jet] *adv* ancora ◆ *conj* ma; **have they arrived** ~? sono già arrivati?; **the best one** ~ il migliore fino a questo momento; **not** ~ non ancora; **I've** ~ **to do it** devo ancora farlo; ~ **again** ancora una volta; ~ **another delay** ancora un altro ritardo.

yew [ju:] *n* tasso *m (pianta).*

yield [ji:ld] *vt* dare, rendere ◆ *vi* (break, give way) cedere; **'yield'** (Am: AUT) 'dare la precedenza'.

YMCA *n* associazione cristiana dei giovani che offre alloggi a buon prezzo.

yob [jɒb] *n (Br: inf)* teppista *mf.*

yoga ['jəʊgə] *n* yoga *m.*

yoghurt ['jɒgət] *n* yogurt *m inv.*

yolk [jəʊk] *n* tuorlo *m*, rosso *m* d'uovo.

York Minster [jɔːk'mɪnstə^r] *n* la cattedrale di York.

---

i YORK MINSTER

Capolavoro dell'architettura gotica, nella città romana di York, nel nord dell'Inghilterra, questa cattedrale risale al dodicesimo secolo ed è famosa per le sue mura in pietra chiara e per il suo rosone. Danneggiata gravemente da un fulmine nel 1984, è stata parzialmente restaurata.

Yorkshire pudding ['jɔːkʃə] *n* focaccina soffice servita tradizionalmente con arrosti di manzo.

you [ju:] *pron* 1. (subject: singular) tu; (subject: polite form) lei; (subject: plural) voi; ~ **Italians** voi italiani. 2. (direct object: singular) ti; (direct object: polite form) la; (direct object: plural) vi; **I called** ~, **not him** ho chiamato te, non lui. 3. (indirect object: singular) ti; (indirect object: polite form) le; (indirect object: plural) vi. 4. (after prep: singular) te; (after prep: polite form) lei; (after prep: plural) voi; **I'm shorter than** ~ sono più basso di te/lei/voi. 5. (indefinite use) si; ~ **never know** non si sa mai; **swimming is good for** ~ nuotare fa bene.

young [jʌŋ] *adj* giovane ◆ *npl*: **the** ~ i giovani.

younger ['jʌŋgə^r] *adj* (brother, sister) minore, più giovane.

youngest ['jʌŋgəst] *adj* (brother,

sister) minore, più giovane.

youngster ['jʌŋstər] *n* giovane *mf.*

your [jɔːʳ] *adj* 1. *(singular subject)* il tuo (la tua), i tuoi (le tue) *(pl)*; *(singular subject: polite form)* il suo (la sua), i suoi (le sue) *(pl)*; *(plural subject)* il vostro (la vostra), i vostri (le vostre) *(pl)*; ~ **dog** il tuo/suo/vostro cane; ~ **house** la tua/sua/vostra casa; ~ **children** i tuoi/suoi/vostri bambini; ~ **mother** tua/sua/vostra madre.
2. *(indefinite subject)*: **it's good for ~ health** fa bene alla salute.

yours [jɔːz] *pron (referring to singular subject)* il tuo (la tua), i tuoi (le tue) *(pl)*; *(polite form)* il suo (la sua), i suoi (le sue) *(pl)*; *(referring to plural subject)* il vostro (la vostra), i vostri (le vostre) *(pl)*; **a friend of ~** un tuo/suo/vostro amico; **are these shoes ~?** queste scarpe sono tue/sue/vostre?

yourself [jɔː'self] *(pl* -selves) *pron*
1. *(reflexive: singular)* ti; *(reflexive: polite form)* si; *(reflexive: plural)* vi.
2. *(after prep: singular)* te; *(after prep: polite form)* sé; *(after prep: plural)* voi.
3. *(emphatic use: singular)* tu stesso(-a); *(emphatic use: polite form)* lei stesso(-a); *(emphatic use: plural)* voi stessi(-e); **did you do it ~?** *(singular)* l'hai fatto da solo?

youth [juːθ] *n (period of life)* gioventù *f*, *(quality)* giovinezza *f*; *(young man)* giovane *m.*

youth club *n* circolo *m* gio-

vanile.

youth hostel *n* ostello *m* della gioventù.

Yugoslavia [ˌjuːgə'slɑːvɪə] *n* la Jugoslavia.

yuppie ['jʌpɪ] *n* yuppie *mf inv.*

YWCA *n* associazione cristiana delle giovani che offre alloggi a buon prezzo.

zebra [Br 'zebrə, Am 'ziːbrə] *n* zebra *f.*

zebra crossing *n (Br)* strisce *fpl* pedonali.

zero ['zɪərəʊ] *(pl* -es) *n* zero *m*; **five degrees below ~** cinque gradi sotto zero.

zest [zest] *n (of lemon, orange)* scorza *f.*

zigzag ['zɪgzæg] *vi* procedere a zigzag.

zinc [zɪŋk] *n* zinco *m.*

zip [zɪp] *n (Br)* cerniera *f* OR chiusura *f* lampo *(inv)* ◆ *vt* chiudere la cerniera di ❑ **zip up** *vt sep* chiudere la cerniera di.

zip code *n (Am)* codice *m* di avviamento postale.

zipper ['zɪpəʳ] *n (Am)* cerniera *f* OR chiusura *f* lampo *(inv).*

zit [zɪt] *n (inf)* brufolo *m.*

zodiac ['zəʊdɪæk] *n* zodiaco *m.*

zone [zəʊn] *n* zona *f.*

zoo [zuː] *(pl* -s) *n* zoo *m inv.*

zoom (lens) [zuːm-] *n* zoom *m inv.*

zucchini [zuː'kiːnɪ] *(pl inv) n (Am)* zucchine *fpl.*